ENCYCLOPEDIA of
AFRICAN-AMERICAN
CULTURE and HISTORY

Editorial Board

second edition

THE BLACK EXPERIENCE
IN THE AMERICAS

ENCYCLOPEDIA *of*
AFRICAN~AMERICAN
CULTURE *and* HISTORY

published in association with
THE SCHOMBURG CENTER FOR RESEARCH IN BLACK CULTURE

COLIN A. PALMER
Editor in Chief

4 *M-P*
VOLUME

MACMILLAN REFERENCE USA
An imprint of Thomson Gale, a part of The Thomson Corporation

THOMSON
GALE

Detroit • New York • San Francisco • San Diego • New Haven, Conn. • Waterville, Maine • London • Munich

THOMSON
―――――★―――――™
GALE

Encyclopedia of African-American Culture and History, Second Edition

Colin A. Palmer, Editor in Chief

LIBRARY OF CONGRESS CATALOGING-IN-PUBLICATION DATA

Encyclopedia of African-American culture and history : the Black experience in the Americas / Colin A. Palmer, editor in chief.— 2nd ed.
   p. cm.
    Includes bibliographical references and index.
    ISBN 0-02-865816-7 (set hardcover : alk. paper) —
    ISBN 0-02-865817-5 (v. 1) — ISBN 0-02-865818-3 (v. 2) —
    ISBN 0-02-865819-1 (v. 3) — ISBN 0-02-865820-5 (v. 4) —
    ISBN 0-02-865821-3 (v. 5) — ISBN 0-02-865822-1 (v. 6)
    1. African Americans—Encyclopedias. 2. African Americans—History—Encyclopedias. 3. Blacks—America—Encyclopedias. 4. Blacks—America—History—Encyclopedias. I. Palmer, Colin A., 1942-

E185.E54 2005
973'.0496073'003—dc22

2005013029

This title is also available as an e-book.
ISBN 0-02-866071-4

Contact your Thomson Gale representative for ordering information.

Printed in the United States of America
10 9 8 7 6 5 4 3 2 1

Editorial *and* Production Staff

Contents

MABLEY, JACKIE "MOMS"

MARCH 19, 1897
MAY 23, 1975

The comedienne Jackie "Moms" Mabley was born Loretta Mary Aiken in Brevard, North Carolina; she was one of twelve children of mixed African-American, Cherokee, and Irish ancestry. During childhood and adolescence, she spent time in Anacostia (in Washington, D.C.) and Cleveland, Ohio. Mabley—who borrowed her name from Jack Mabley, an early boyfriend—began performing as a teenager, when she joined the black vaudeville circuit as a comedienne, singer, and dancer, appearing with such well-known performers as Dewey "Pigmeat" Markham, Cootie Williams, Peg Leg Bates, and Bill "Bojangles" Robinson. In the mid-1920s, she was brought to New York by the dance team of Butterbeans and Suzie. After making her debut at Connie's Inn, Mabley became a favorite at Harlem's Cotton Club and at the Club Harlem in Atlantic City, where she played with Louis Armstrong, Cab Calloway, Duke Ellington, and Count Basie, among others. It was during this time that she began cultivating the frumpily dressed, granny-like stage personality for which she be-

came famous. Trundling onto stage in a tacky housedress with a frilly nightcap, sagging stockings, and outsized shoes, "Moms"—as she was later known—would begin her ad-lib stand-up comedy routine, consisting of bawdy jokes ("The only thing an old man can do for me is bring a message from a young one") and songs, belted out in a gravelly "bullfrog" voice.

Mabley appeared in small parts in two motion pictures, *Jazz Heaven* (also distributed as *Boarding House Blues,* 1929) and *Emperor Jones* (1933), and collaborated with Zora Neale Hurston in the Broadway play *Fast and Furious: A Colored Revue in 37 Scenes* (1931) before she started performing regularly at the Apollo Theater in Harlem. By the time she made the film *Killer Diller* (1948), she had cultivated a considerable following among black audiences, as well as among fellow performers; it was not until 1960, however, when she cut her first album for Chess Records, that she became known to white audiences. *Moms Mabley at the U.N.,* which sold over a million copies, was followed by several others, including *Moms Mabley at the Geneva Conference, Moms Mabley—The Funniest Woman in the World, Moms Live at Sing Sing,* and *Now Hear This.* In 1962 Mabley performed at Carnegie Hall in a program featuring Cannonball Adderley and Nancy Wilson. She made her television debut five years later in an all-black comedy special, *A Time for Laughter,* produced by Harry

Belafonte. Throughout the late 1960s and early 1970s, she was featured in frequent guest spots on television comedy and variety shows hosted by Merv Griffin, the Smothers Brothers, Mike Douglas, Bill Cosby, Flip Wilson, and others. In 1974 Mabley played the leading role in the comedy *Amazing Grace*, a successful feature film about a black woman's efforts to reform a corrupt black politician. She died of a heart attack the following year.

See also Apollo Theater; Armstrong, Louis; Basie, William James "Count"; Belafonte, Harry; Calloway, Cab; Cosby, Bill; Cotton Club; Ellington, Edward Kennedy "Duke"; Hurston, Zora Neale; Robinson, Bill "Bojangles"

■ ■ *Bibliography*

Harris, Trudier. "Moms Mabley: A Study in Humor, Role Playing, and the Violation of Taboo." *Southern Review* 24, no. 4 (1988): 765–776.

"Jackie 'Moms' Mabley." *St. James Encyclopedia of Popular Culture*. Detroit: St. James Press, 1997.

Obituary. *New York Times*, May 24, 1975, p. 26.

Williams, Elsie A. *The Humor of Jackie Moms Mabley: An African American Comedic Tradition*. New York: Garland, 1995.

PAMELA WILKINSON (1996)
Updated bibliography

MACEO, ANTONIO

JUNE 14, 1845
DECEMBER 7, 1896

┫┣┫

The most celebrated leader of the Cuban Independence Wars of the late nineteenth century, Antonio Maceo—known as the "Bronze Titan"—is also the most recognizable Cuban of African descent of the period. His military exploits during the wars for independence against Spain (1868–1898) and his unyielding commitment to abolishing slavery and colonialism made him a national hero and a beloved international figure, particular among people of African descent.

Maceo was born free in Santiago de Cuba, the child of Marcos Maceo, a Venezuelan man of color, and Mariana Grajales, a free woman of color who was the daughter of Dominican immigrants. He was born during the height of plantation slavery in Cuba and raised in a colonial slave society, but he lived in the eastern part of the island, where slavery was less entrenched than in the more prosperous western provinces, where slave labor on sugar plantations produced enormous wealth for the local planter elite. Even though free people of color had more autonomy in the east, they still occupied a subordinate position. The slave plantation system helped maintain the Spanish colonial presence in Cuba long after the collapse of the Spanish empire in the mainland Americas.

On October 10, 1868, a group of Creole planters in the eastern part of the island staged an armed insurrection against Spanish colonial rule. The movement was led by Carlos Manuel de Céspedes, a disgruntled sugar planter and slave owner who was disenchanted with the Spanish colonial system. Céspedes freed his slaves on the condition that they fight for the insurgent forces. Maceo joined both slaves and free persons of color in answering the call. Maceo quickly distinguished himself as a skilled soldier. However, the presence of Maceo and other Afro-Cuban insurgents caused persistent anxiety within the nationalist ranks. The predominantly white leadership was constantly fearful that Maceo would lead a "race war" against the whites, a fear that the Spanish colonial government exploited to its full advantage. These tensions within the insurgent ranks continued to plague the Cuban separatist movement—as did the white separatists' refusal to invade the western region, which was heavily populated by slaves—and they contributed to the movement's destruction. Eventually the vast majority of insurgents surrendered to the Spanish commander Arsenio Martínez Campos and signed the Treaty of Zanjón in 1878.

It was at this moment that Antonio Maceo distinguished himself. On March 15, 1878, Maceo staged the dramatic Protest of Baraguá, in which he and a small group of separatists declared to Martínez Campos that they would continue to fight for independence because the two-fold objective, abolition and independence, had not been achieved. Maceo and his supporters continued the fighting sporadically over the next couple of weeks before he was forced to flee into exile.

After nearly two decades in exile, Maceo joined with José Martí and Máximo Gómez to lead another military struggle against Spain in February 1895. This time, the movement was more successful because the rebels took the war into the heart of Cuba's sugar zones, the western provinces, and it was Antonio Maceo who led the epic western invasion. Maceo's heroic battles against the Spanish forces helped attract thousands of Cubans of African descent into the insurgent ranks, turning the war into a potentially radical social revolution. However, in 1896 Maceo was killed in a Spanish ambush. Although the struggle for independence continued, Maceo's death was a major blow to the separatist cause, and particularly to Cubans of African descent.

Cuban 5-peso note, featuring an image of Antonio Maceo, a hero of the Cuban wars for independence against Spain (1868–1898). TNA ASSOCIATES

Maceo's fame grew in the years after his death. He became a symbol of black rebellion equal to the Haitian revolutionary leader Toussaint-Louverture. Like all icons, he is subject to multiple uses. In the years after the Cuban republic was established, Maceo became part of the nation's pantheon of founding fathers. Cuban politicians often used Maceo as a symbol of racial equality. In more recent years, the Cuban government headed by Fidel Castro has cited Maceo's Protest at Baraguá as a metaphor of Cuba's struggle for sovereignty in the face of hostility from the United States. To this day, he remains a source of inspiration.

See also Moncada, Guillermo

■ ■ *Bibliography*

Ferrer, Ada. *Insurgent Cuba: Race, Nation, and Revolution, 1868–1898.* Chapel Hill: University of North Carolina Press, 1999.

Foner, Philip, S. *Antonio Maceo: The "Bronze Titan" of Cuba's Struggle for Independence.* New York: Monthly Review Press, 1977.

Franco, José Luciano. *Antonio Maceo: Apuntes para una historia de su vida,* 3 vols. Havana: Editorial de Ciencias Sociales, 1975.

FRANK GURIDY (2005)

MACHADO DE ASSIS, JOAQUIM MARIA

JUNE 21, 1839
SEPTEMBER 29, 1908

■ ■ ■

The Brazilian writer Joaquim Maria Machado de Assis is considered by many to be the greatest Latin American literary figure of the nineteenth century. He was born on Quinta do Livramento, a semirural property in the environs of Rio de Janeiro. His paternal grandparents were freed slaves. His baptism certificate lists his mother as a Portuguese native from the Azores and his father as a *pardo* (a free man of dark skin). They were dependents of the Portuguese widow of a noted military figure and imperial senator, who is listed as Machado's godmother. They lived on the wealthy woman's estate under her protection, in exchange for their services. Machado's younger sister died at age four, and his mother passed away when he was nine years old. His father married a woman of mixed ancestry six years later. However, by his late teens Machado had also lost his father.

Machado de Assis had little formal education, but he was aggressively self-taught: he spoke French and studied German and Greek. His frequent allusions to biblical and classical literature and to the great writers of Europe illustrate an unusual breadth of reading. In his youth he took jobs in the printing trade and began to frequent the bookstores where Rio's most important intellectuals could be found. His first pieces of poetry were published in small local magazines when he was only fifteen. By the age of twenty-one he was making his living as a journalist. Thereafter, Machado's trajectory is one of unbroken ascendancy. He published in all the major genres, achieving particular distinction with the novel (he wrote nine in all) and the short story (more than 200, collected or uncollected). Perhaps the ultimate ratification of his prestige was his election as the first president of the Brazilian Academy of Letters in 1897.

Machado also held a series of bureaucratic appointments with the Brazilian government. These positions, normally rather undemanding of time and creativity, were intended as rewards and guarantees of financial stability for the country's most talented intellectuals. In 1869 Machado married a Portuguese woman, Carolina de Novais. This marriage has been celebrated for their devotion to each other, partly because of a now-famous sonnet Machado wrote after her death in 1904. The author struggled with epilepsy for most of his life, and contemporaries reported that he had a problem with stuttering. The fact that the marriage was childless may have been an additional disappointment.

Machado enjoyed an overwhelmingly positive critical reception; only after the proclamation of the republic of Brazil in 1889 does one begin to find notable detractors. Most of these critics attacked what they perceived as a lack of engagement with liberal causes. It is likely that Machado, while sympathetic to these causes, felt hampered by loyalty to the Emperor Dom Pedro II, whose government was his generous employer. Brazil's monarchy was closely tied to the proslavery landholding class, and Machado did not write overtly in favor of abolition. However, as a government official he fastidiously administered laws regarding freeborn children of slaves, usually acting against the interests of the landholders.

Machado de Assis's best work eschews the literary movements of his time. His most virtuosic novel, *Memórias póstumous de Brás Cubas* (*Posthumous Memoirs of Brás Cubas*), appeared in serial installments in 1880, and was published in book form in 1881. Essentially, it is the self-justifying autobiography of a man of privilege who wasted his life. Taking the form of a posthumously written memoir (rather than a posthumously published one), it defies realism in its very inception. His most profound novel is *Dom Casmurro* (the best translations preserve the original title, which approximately means "Lord Taciturn"), published in 1899. Here, with a tone that mixes nostalgia with bitterness, a highly problematic narrator tells why he thinks his wife (and former childhood sweet-

heart) betrayed him with his best friend. The novel is a monument of ambiguity, whose questions seem urgent but whose solutions are perhaps impossible.

Like many other mulatto writers in Brazil, Machado did not seem to identify himself as an Afro-Brazilian. There are, in fact, only a few moments in all of his writing when Machado deals directly with racial issues. A selection of these may illustrate the author's general practice of positing interesting problems, rather than engaging in facile judgments of characters or groups. *Memórias póstumas de Brás Cubas* presents a slave who suffers abuse from the protagonist. Later, after this slave has earned his freedom, he is found to have bought and abused his own slave. In the short story "O caso da vara" (translated as "The rod of justice"), an adolescent boy who is being forced to study for the priesthood escapes from the seminary to an influential woman's home, where he pleads for her to be his advocate. In order to gain her support, however, he must act as the woman's accomplice in beating a young black girl. "Pai contra mãe" (a short story translated as "Father versus mother") depicts a hunter of escaped slaves who captures a pregnant young woman and returns her to her master, despite her pleas for her freedom in the name of her unborn child. He must deliver her because he desperately needs the money to avoid giving his own newborn child up for adoption.

Nearly a century after his death, Machado de Assis attracts more critical attention than any other Brazilian writer, both in terms of sheer volume of scholarship and in terms of international impact. He has proved to be a writer's writer, judging by appreciative statements from the likes of Salman Rushdie, John Barth, Susan Sontag, and Carlos Fuentes. Outside of Brazil, his works have never sold as well as those of his compatriot, Jorge Amado, but they have remained in print through several editions. Two collections of short stories and all but one of his novels have been translated into English.

■■ *Bibliography*

Caldwell, Helen. *Machado de Assis: The Brazilian Master and His Novels.* Berkeley: University of California Press, 1970.

Fitz, Earl E. *Machado de Assis.* Boston: Twayne, 1989.

Machado de Assis. *The Psychiatrist and Other Stories.* Translated by William Grossman and Helen Caldwell. Berkeley: University of California Press, 1963.

Machado de Assis. *The Devil's Church and Other Stories.* Translated by Jack Schmitt and Lorie Ishimatsu. Austin: University of Texas Press, 1977.

Machado de Assis. *Posthumous Memoirs of Brás Cubas.* Translated by Gregory Rabassa. New York: Oxford University Press, 1997.

Machado de Assis. *Dom Casmurro*. Translated by John Gledson. New York: Oxford University Press, 1998.

Machado de Assis. *Quincas Borba*. Translated by Gregory Rabassa. New York: Oxford University Press, 1998.

Nunes, Maria Luisa. *The Craft of an Absolute Winner: Characterization and Narratology in the Novels of Machado de Assis*. Westport, Conn.: Greenwood, 1983.

PAUL B. DIXON (2005)

MACKEY, WILLIAM WELLINGTON

MAY 28, 1937

━ ■ ┃ ■ ━

Playwright William Wellington Mackey was born in Miami, Florida, and attended Southern University in Baton Rouge, Louisiana. After graduating in 1958, he returned to Miami, where he worked as a high school teacher. In 1964 he earned a master's degree in recreational and drama therapy from the University of Minnesota in Minneapolis. Shortly afterward, while working as a recreational therapist at Colorado State Hospital in Pueblo, he completed his first two plays, *Behold! Cometh the Vanderkellans* (1965) and *Requiem for Brother X* (1966). The first examines the effects of the rising black consciousness of the late 1950s on a privileged, upper-middle-class black family. The second explores how the lives of a black family living in the ghetto are shaped—and warped—by external factors. Mackey depicts the families of Brother X as trapped in the ghetto and conspicuously forgotten by affluent blacks. The use of the family play, a familiar American dramatic convention, to reveal and critique the aspirations, as well as the pretensions and hypocrisies of black family life, is characteristic of all Mackey's plays.

Shortly after his first two plays were produced in Denver, Mackey moved to Chicago and later to New York, where a number of his plays have been produced on Off-Broadway. Mackey's other plays include *Family Meeting* (1972), *Billy Noname* (1970, a musical), and *Love Me, Love Me Daddy, or I Swear I'm Gonna Kill You* (1982).

See also Drama

■ ■ *Bibliography*

Peterson, Bernard L., Jr. *Contemporary Black American Playwrights and Their Plays*. New York: Greenwood, 1988.

MICHAEL PALLER (1996)
Updated by publisher 2005

MADAME SATÃ (DOS SANTOS, JOÃO FRANCISCO)

FEBRUARY 25, 1900
APRIL 14, 1976

━ ■ ┃ ■ ━

João Francisco dos Santos, popularly known as Madame Satã (Madame Satan), was a streetwise rogue figure and longtime resident of Rio de Janeiro, Brazil. He projected the virile masculinity of a Brazilian *malandro* (bohemian, scoundrel, or hustler) and at the same time was a self-avowed homosexual. In the early 1970s Madame Satã became a symbol of a bygone era of bohemian Rio. He has been the subject of books and movies, including a feature-length, internationally released film, *Madame Satã* (2002), directed by Karim Aïnouz.

Santos was born in the town of Glória do Goitá in the hinterlands of the northeastern state of Pernambuco, Brazil, one of seventeen sisters and brothers. His mother, a descendent of slaves, came from a humble family. His father, the result of a sexual union between a former slave and a son of the local landed elite, died when he was seven. The next year, with seventeen mouths to feed, his mother swapped her young child to a horse trader in exchange for a mare. Within six months he had managed to escape from this harsh apprenticeship by running away with a woman who offered him work as a helper in a boardinghouse in Rio de Janeiro, at the time the nation's capital.

At age thirteen, Santos left the boardinghouse to live on the streets and sleep on the steps of the tenement houses in the Lapa neighborhood of downtown Rio de Janeiro, at the time the center of a bustling nightlife of clubs, prostitution, and gambling. For six years he worked at odd jobs in and around the neighborhood. In his memoirs Madame Satã remembered that he began sexual relations with other boys during this period. At age eighteen he was hired as a waiter at a brothel. Madames commonly employed young homosexuals as waiters, cooks, housekeepers, and even as part-time prostitutes if a client so desired.

During this period Santos assumed the public persona of a slick, well-dressed, and virile *malandro*. In 1928 he landed a small part in a musical review in which he sang and danced, wearing a red dress with his long hair falling down over his shoulders. His artistic career, however, was aborted when he was convicted of killing a security guard who had allegedly called him a faggot.

In 1938 some of his friends convinced him to enter a costume contest during a Carnival ball. Santos created a sequined-decorated outfit inspired after a bat from the northeast of Brazil, and won first prize. Several weeks later he was arrested with several other homosexuals while strolling through a park in downtown Rio de Janeiro. When the booking officer at the police station asked those detained to identify themselves, including their nicknames, Santos offered the appellation Madame Satã in reference to a recently released American film with the Brazilian title, *Madame Satã*. The name stuck.

Madame Satã projected multiple, apparently contradictory images. He identified himself as a *malandro* who was willing to fight and even kill to defend his honor. Yet in Brazil until the 1980s, popular notions associated homosexuality with effeminacy and passivity. Satã, therefore, became an anomaly. Satã was proud of his ability to wield a knife and win a fight, two marks of a *malandro*'s bravery and virility. Yet he openly admitted that he liked to be sexually penetrated, a desire that was socially stigmatized and the antithesis of the manliness of a piercing knife blade. While the popular respect usually afforded a *malandro* was linked to his potency, masculinity, and his willingness to die for his honor, Madame Satã simply contradicted the stereotype. He was aware of the anxiety his persona provoked, especially among the men who picked fights with him.

The myths surrounding Madame Satã's prowess and bravery grew with time and even followed him into prison, where he served multiple sentences for robbery, larceny, assault and battery, and murder. He retained widespread respect even though he was considered a "faggot." In the early 1970s he was rediscovered by journalists from the middle-class underground, and the satirical weekly *O Pasquim* ran a feature interview with him, depicting Madame Satã as the last surviving bohemian from the 1930s. He died a pauper in 1976 and was buried in the trademark attire of a *malandro*—a white suit, a stylish Panama hat, and a red rose.

See also Masculinity; Music, Religion and Crime in Early-Twentieth-Century Rio de Janeiro

■ ■ *Bibliography*

Aïnouz, Karim, dir. *Madame Satã* (film). Wellspring, 2002.

Green, James N. *Beyond Carnival: Male Homosexuality in Twentieth-Century Brazil*. Chicago: University of Chicago Press, 1999.

Green, James N. "Madame Satan, the Black 'Queen' of Brazilian Bohemia." In *The Human Tradition in Modern Brazil*, edited by Peter M. Beattie. Wilmington, Del.: Scholarly Resources, 2003.

JAMES N. GREEN (2005)

MADHUBUTI, HAKI R. (LEE, DON L.)

FEBRUARY 23, 1942

Born Don L. Lee in Little Rock, Arkansas, poet and essayist Haki Madhubuti was raised in Detroit, Michigan. His father deserted the family when Madhubuti was very young, and his mother died when he was sixteen. An unstable family life created hardship and forced Madhubuti to seek employment and overall self-reliance at an early age. Of the place of poetry in his childhood, Madhubuti commented that "poetry in my home was almost as strange as money."

In the late 1950s Madhubuti attended a vocational high school in Chicago. He joined the U.S. Army for three years beginning in 1960. From 1963 to 1967, while an apprentice curator at the DuSable Museum of African History, Madhubuti held jobs as a clerk in department stores and at the U.S. post office. During these years he also worked toward his associate degree at Chicago City College. Two decades later he received a master of fine arts from the University of Iowa.

With the publication of *Think Black!* (1967), *Black Pride* (1968), and *Don't Cry, Scream* (1969), Madhubuti quickly established himself as a leading poetic voice among his generation of black artists in America. His poetry generated critical acclaim, particularly among African-American commentators associated with the maturing Black Arts movement of the 1960s and early 1970s (the first major black artistic movement since the Harlem Renaissance).

His early literary criticism, including in *Dynamite Voices* (1971), was one of the first overviews of the new black poetry of the 1960s. In this volume Madhubuti insists on the essential connection between the African-American experience and black art and concludes with a call to black nation building. In his own poetry Madhubuti makes extensive use of black cultural forms, such as street talk and jazz music. His poetry also draws its inspiration from the work of Amiri Baraka (LeRoi Jones), the most influential black arts practitioner of the 1960s.

Judging simply by sales within the black community, no black poet in the black arts movement was more popular than Madhubuti. In the last few years of the 1960s, for instance, Madhubuti's slim paperbound books of poetry—each issued by the black publishing house Broadside Press—sold a remarkable one hundred thousand copies each without the benefit of a national distributor. His popularity and artistic promise made him a frequent writer-in-residence during this period at American universities such as Cornell and Howard.

In 1973 the poet rejected his "slave name" by changing it from Don L. Lee to the Swahili name Haki R. Madhubuti (which means "precise justice"). In the same year he published two collections, *From Plan to Planet* and *Book of Life*. These volumes of essays and poetry illustrate his commitment to black cultural nationalism, a philosophy that combines political activism with cultural preservation in the drive toward racial awareness and black unity.

Although his artistic production declined during the mid- to late 1970s, the publication of another volume of essays and poetry, *Earthquakes and Sun Rise Missions* (1984), renewed Madhubuti's advocacy of black nationalism. The poet's most recent collection, *Killing Memory, Seeking Ancestors* (1987), speaks to the reader who loves and understands black vernacular.

Like his literary compatriots in the black arts movement, Madhubuti attempts to create an artistic form and content that best represents the black community, speaks to their needs, and promotes cultural institutions that serve the coming of the black nation. He eschews Western notions of individualism in favor of collective self-sufficiency among blacks within the United States and throughout the world.

In 1978, when the author published *Enemies: The Clash of the Races*—a scathing critique of racism within white left as well as right political circles—Madhubuti was (what he calls) "whitelisted" and, as a result, lost anticipated income. Such experiences reinforced his commitment to black self-reliance. As founding editor of Third World Press and a founding member of the Organization of Black American Culture (OBAC) Writers Workshop (which includes black literary figures such as Gwendolyn Brooks and Carolyn Rodgers), Madhubuti continues to be active in Chicago-based organizations. He is also cofounder and director of the Institute of Positive Education in Chicago, an organization committed to black nation building through independent black institutions in areas such as education and publishing.

In 1990 Madhubuti published *Black Men: Obsolete, Single, Dangerous? The Afrikan American Family in Transition*, which addressed issues raised by the author's grassroots activism over the previous quarter century. Essays in this collection speak specifically to black men, offering analyses and guidance on topics ranging from fatherhood to AIDS. The first printing of the book (7,500 copies) sold out within a month and reconfirmed Madhubuti's popularity within a sizable portion of the black literary community in America and elsewhere.

Madhubuti teaches at Chicago State University. He published *Tough Notes: A Healing Call for Creating Exceptional Black Men* in 2002, and *Run Toward Fear* in 2004.

See also Baraka, Amiri (Jones, LeRoi); Black Arts Movement; Brooks, Gwendolyn Elizabeth; Literary Criticism, U.S.; Poetry, U.S.

■ ■ *Bibliography*

Giddings, Paula. "From a Black Perspective: The Poetry of Don L. Lee." In *Amistad 2*, edited by John A. Williams and Charles F. Harris, pp. 296–318. New York: Howard University Press, 1971.

"Haki R. Madhubuti (Don L. Lee)." In *The Black Aesthetic Movement*. Vol. 8 of the *Dictionary of Literary Biography Documentary Series*. Detroit: Gale, 1991, pp. 168–225.

Llorens, David. "Black Don Lee." *Ebony* (March 1969): 72–78, 80.

Melhem, D. H. "Interview with Haki R. Madhubuti." In *Heroism in the New Black Poetry*. Lexington: University Press of Kentucky, 1990, pp. 101–130.

Turner, Darwin T. Afterword to *Earthquakes and Sun Rise Missions*, by Haki R. Madhubuti. Chicago: Third World Press, 1984, pp. 181–189.

West, Hollie I. "The Poetry of Black Experience." *Washington Post*, April 1971, pp. H1, H6.

JEFFREY LOUIS DECKER (1996)
Updated by publisher 2005

MAIS, ROGER

AUGUST 11, 1905
JUNE 15, 1955

❚❚❚

One of seven children, Roger Mais was born in Kingston but grew up in the mountains of Jamaica on a coffee farm. Here he learned to love nature and the life of rural folk. His parents, Eustace and Anna Mais, occupied a clearly marked niche in Jamaican society of those times. Below the plantocracy in landed wealth, above many wealthier farmers by virtue of education and refinement, the light-skinned Maises—a druggist and schoolteacher respectively—brought up their children in devout knowledge of Christian liturgy and hymns, with the King James Bible as the basis of belief. At home and in school, Mais read the classics of English literature. Equally, Mais learned the Creole language, rituals, songs, tales, and proverbs of the Afro-Jamaican peasantry. In this isolated world, the two Jamaicas—African and British—coexisted naturally in the mind of a child such as Roger. Nothing in his life or work suggests that Mais ever saw himself as the "divided child" of Derek Walcott's colonial world. Division exists, but at the heart of his political doctrine lies a unifying mystical vision of the oneness of all humanity (D'Costa, 1978).

Mais's multi-faceted mind led him first through poetry, playwriting, and journalism into the political fray of the Caribbean nationalist politics of the 1930s and 1940s. His passion for social justice led him into the formation of Jamaica's political parties. A Fabian socialist, he joined the People's National Party under Norman W. Manley, and saw Alexander Bustamante, Manley's cousin and one-time ally, as a traitor to socialist ideals. One significant newspaper article stands out in this period: Mais's "Now We Know" (1944). This denunciation of Winston Churchill's vow to maintain colonial rule after the end of the war earned Mais a six-month prison sentence for sedition. When Mais mailed several copies of the article overseas to friends and foreign newspapers, the letters fell into the hands of the postal censors and formed the grounds for his arrest and imprisonment.

From these experiences came material that fired his landmark novels, *The Hills Were Joyful Together* (1953), and *Brother Man* (1954). These depictions of Jamaica's urban poor broke like thunder on the educated classes. While earlier writers had depicted the lives of Jamaica's poor, no one had ever used the novel so ruthlessly to exhibit and analyze the emotional and social pathologies of the urban underclass. No novel had chosen its central, Christlike martyr hero from the despised Rastafarians. In Mais's third and last novel, *Black Lightning* (1955), he takes the reader on a tragic journey into the center of a Jamaican artist's sensibility. Mais's significance as writer and activist are well presented in Daphne Morris's 1986 study of his work.

Written in the last eight years of Mais's life, his three novels represent his most creative period. At this time his friendships with other rising Jamaican and Caribbean writers flourished: he spent two years (1952–1954) in England and France with novelist John Hearne, returning to Jamaica only when his health became seriously impaired.

Fifty years after his death, Roger Mais challenges the postcolonial world to examine progress toward social justice. Mais's passion for national self-determination upheld the rights of all individuals and groups to discover their true natures, exploring their roles in history while creating a social contract open and beneficial to all. His journalism, playwriting, poetry, painting, and even his ventures into farming burn with a single purpose: to urge the dysfunctional colonial world of his lifetime to look at itself, unsparingly, and to use this examination as a first step toward social and political health.

See also Literature of the English-Speaking Caribbean; Manley, Norman; People's National Party

■ ■ *Bibliography*

D'Costa, Jean. *Roger Mais.* London: Longman, 1978.

Mais, Roger. "Now We Know." *Public Opinion* (July 11, 1944): 1.

Morris, Daphne. "Roger Mais." In *Fifty Caribbean Writers,* edited by Daryl Cumber Dance. Westport, Conn.: Greenwood Press, 1986.

JEAN D'COSTA (2005)

MAKANDAL, FRANÇOIS

C. 1715?
JANUARY 17, 1758

After being captured and convicted of leading a small group of notorious poisoners, François Makandal was publicly executed by burning on January 17, 1758, in Cap Français, Saint Domingue (modern Haiti). There is no consensus as to the exact nature of his activities, but a majority of scholars regard Makandal as the leader of a large Maroon, or fugitive slave, conspiracy who conducted a lengthy, but ultimately unsuccessful, poisoning campaign to overthrow the French planters in the North province of the colony. Others—notably David Geggus and Pierre Pluchon—argue that the contemporary records indicate Makandal's role was significantly different in breadth and scope than is commonly believed. They contend that there was neither a large conspiracy nor an overall political element to the poisonings, but rather a concerted effort that reflected personal motivations. Both interpretations are plausible, but there is certainly much that will remain conjectural due to the limitations and discrepancies of the source material.

Born in Africa—most likely the West Central region of Kongo-Angola—François Makandal is thought to have been enslaved and brought to Saint Domingue as a youth, but relatively little is known about his early years. He was a slave on the LeNormand de Mézy plantation near Limbé, close to present-day Cap Haïtien, Haiti. While the exact details of his escape are not known, his motivations for *maronnage* have variously been attributed to either a work accident or a dispute with his master over a beautiful female slave. In the former, his hand was apparently crushed in the machinery of a cane mill—necessitating amputation—after which he was put in charge of tending livestock, a situation he easily escaped from. In the latter scenario, rather than submit to the whip, he chose to defy his master and flee the plantation. Subsequently, he became a Maroon, a status he maintained for somewhere between ten and eighteen years.

He has variously been portrayed as a Muslim fluent in Arabic, or as being a Vodou high priest—otherwise known as a *houngan*. But perhaps he would be more appropriately described as a *bókó*, or sorcerer. He has been celebrated for his intelligence, rhetorical ability, sexual prowess, and organizational skill, as well as his stature as a religious cult leader. But, as Geggus has argued, he was not referred to as a Maroon leader until twenty years after his death.

There is little doubt that the scale of the poisonings prior to his execution—perhaps as many as six-thousand fatalities—inspired fear and terror, not only in the white population but also among the slaves and free people of color. But the fact that the largest number of victims came from the ranks of the slaves and free blacks has led some scholars to categorize this poisoning campaign separately from other instances of Maroon resistance.

The source of his knowledge with herbal poisons is not clear, though the sheer length of his time as a maroon may be sufficient to explain it; that he possessed great skill as a poisoner is certain. He is also said to have maintained an "open school" for those wishing to learn his techniques. Before his capture he likely had three or four close associates with whom he created and distributed the poison. They were thought to be in the process of planning to poison the water source for Cap Français, when Makandal was captured—allegedly after being betrayed by a fellow slave.

His public execution galvanized an already fearsome reputation and contributed to his legendary status. While being burnt at the stake he is said to have broken free and fallen out of the fire. Although quickly retied and put back in the blaze to expire, Makandal's adherents saw the event as proof of his supernatural powers. In the popular imagination he is understood to have transformed himself into a mosquito—sometimes reported as a fly—thus fulfilling his own prophecy that he could not be killed.

Makandal's position in the national pantheon of Haitian heroes would seem to be secure, particularly since he is so often portrayed as the revolutionary forerunner to Boukman Dutty, a leader in the first weeks of the 1791 slave insurrection. Within the modern lexicon of the Haitian language, the word *makandal* retains a number of significant meanings relating to magic, secret societies, and amulets. While it is believed that his execution resulted in this cultural-linguistic legacy, there seems to be compelling evidence that the word—most likely Kikongo—predates him and was already a part of the vernacular. Regardless, his name was—and still is—associated with poison, Vodou, slave resistance, and *marronage*.

See also Haitian Revolution; Runaway Slaves in Latin America and the Caribbean; Voodoo

■ ■ *Bibliography*

Fick, Carolyn. *The Making of Haiti: The Saint Domingue Revolution from Below.* Knoxville: University of Tennessee Press, 1990.

Geggus, David P. *Haitian Revolutionary Studies.* Bloomington: Indiana University Press, 2002.

Pluchon, Pierre. *Vaudou, sorciers, empoisonneurs: de Saint-Domingue á Haïti.* Paris: Karthala, 1987.

THORALD M. BURNHAM (2005)

MALCOLM X

MAY 19, 1925
FEBRUARY 21, 1965

Nationalist leader Malcolm X, born Malcolm Little and also known by his religious name, El-Hajj Malik El-Shabbazz, was the national representative of Elijah Muhammad's Nation of Islam, a prominent black nationalist, and the founder of the Organization of Afro-American Unity. He was born in Omaha, Nebraska. His father, J. Early Little, was a Georgia-born Baptist preacher and an organizer for Marcus Garvey's Universal Negro Improvement Association. His mother, M. Louise Norton, also a Garveyite, was from Grenada. After J. Early Little was murdered, Malcolm's mother broke under the emotional and economic strain, and the children became wards of the state. Malcolm's delinquent behavior landed him in a detention home in Mason, Michigan.

Malcolm journeyed to Boston and then to New York, where, as "Detroit Red," he became involved in a life of crime—numbers, peddling dope, con games of many kinds, and thievery of all sorts, including armed robbery. A few months before his twenty-first birthday, Malcolm was sentenced to a Massachusetts prison for burglary. While he was in prison, his life was transformed when he discovered, through the influence of an inmate, the liberating value of education and, through his family, the empowering religious/cultural message of Elijah Muhammad's Nation of Islam. Both gave him what he did not have: self-respect as a black person.

Malcolm X addressing the crowd at a rally, 1963. A fiery orator and controversial black nationalist, Malcolm X was assassinated in 1965. In the decades since, many commentators have begun to reevaluate the extent of his vast influence on the political and social thinking of African Americans. UPI/CORBIS-BETTMANN. REPRODUCED BY PERMISSION.

Malcolm was released from prison in 1952, but not before he had honed his reading and debating skills. He soon became a minister in the Nation of Islam and its most effective recruiter and apologist, speaking against black self-hate and on behalf of black self-esteem. In June 1954 Elijah Muhammad appointed him minister of Temple Number 7 in Harlem. In the temple and from the platform on street corner rallies, Malcolm told Harlemites, "We are black first and everything else second." Initially his black nationalist message was unpopular in the African-American community. The media, both white and black, portrayed him as a teacher of hate and a promoter of violence. It was an age of integration, and love and nonviolence were advocated as the only way to achieve it.

Malcolm did not share the optimism of the civil rights movement and found himself speaking to unsympathetic audiences. "If you are afraid to tell truth," he told his audience, "why, you don't deserve freedom." Malcolm relished the odds against him; he saw his task as waking up "dead Negroes" by revealing the truth about America and about themselves.

The enormity of this challenge motivated Malcolm to attack the philosophy of the Rev. Dr. Martin Luther King Jr. and the civil rights movement head-on. He rejected integration: "An integrated cup of coffee is insufficient pay for 400 years of slave labor." He denounced nonviolence as "the philosophy of a fool": "There is no philosophy more befitting to the white man's tactics for keeping his foot on the black man's neck." He ridiculed King's 1963 "I Have a Dream" speech: "While King was having a dream, the rest of us Negroes are having a nightmare." He also rejected King's command to love the enemy: "It is not possible to love a man whose chief purpose in life is to humiliate you and still be considered a normal human being." To blacks who accused Malcolm of teaching hate, he retorted: "It is the man who has made a slave out of you who is teaching hate."

As long as Malcolm stayed in the Black Muslim movement, he was not free to speak his own mind. He had to represent the "Messenger," Elijah Muhammad, who was the sole and absolute authority in the Nation of Islam. When Malcolm disobeyed Muhammad in December 1963 and described President John F. Kennedy's assassination as an instance of "chickens coming home to roost," Muhammad rebuked him and used the incident as an opportunity to silence his star pupil. Malcolm realized that more was involved in his silence than what he had said about the assassination. Jealousy and envy in Muhammad's family circle were the primary reasons for his silence and why it would never be lifted.

Malcolm reluctantly declared his independence in March 1964. His break with the Black Muslims represented another important turning point in his life. No longer bound by Muhammad's religious strictures, he was free to develop his own philosophy of the black freedom struggle.

Malcolm had already begun to show independent thinking in his "Message to the Grass Roots" speech, given in Detroit three weeks before his silence. In that speech he endorsed black nationalism as his political philosophy, thereby separating himself not only from the civil rights movement but, more importantly, from Muhammad, who had defined the Nation as strictly religious and apolitical. Malcolm contrasted "the black revolution" with "the Negro revolution." The black revolution, he said, is international in scope, and it is "bloody" and "hostile" and "knows no compromise." But the so-called "Negro revolution," the civil rights movement, was not even a revolution, according to Malcolm, who mocked it: "The only revolution in which the goal is loving your enemy is the Negro revolution. It's the only revolution in which the goal is a desegregated lunch counter, a desegregated theater, a desegregated public park, a desegregated public toilet; you can sit down next to white folks on the toilet."

After his break Malcolm developed his cultural and political philosophy of black nationalism in "The Ballot or the Bullet." Before audiences in New York, Cleveland, and Detroit, he urged blacks to acquire their constitutional right to vote and move toward King and the civil rights movement. Later he became more explicit: "Dr. King wants the same thing I want—freedom." Malcolm went to Selma, Alabama, while King was in jail in support of King's efforts to secure voting rights. Malcolm wanted to join the civil rights movement in order to expand it into a human rights movement, thereby internationalizing the black freedom struggle, making it more radical and more militant.

During his period of independence, which lasted for approximately one year before he was assassinated, nothing influenced Malcolm more than his travel abroad. His pilgrimage to Mecca transformed his theology. Malcolm became a Sunni Muslim, acquired the religious name El-Hajj Malik El-Shabbazz, and concluded that "Orthodox Islam" was incompatible with the racist teachings of Elijah

Malcolm X (1925–1965). AP/WIDE WORLD PHOTOS. REPRODUCED BY PERMISSION.

Malcolm X

"Freedom is essential to life itself. Freedom is essential to the development of the human being. If we don't have freedom we can never expect justice and equality."

MUHAMMAD SPEAKS, SEPTEMBER 1960

Muhammad. The sight of "people of all races, colors, from all over the world coming together as one" had a profound effect upon him. "Brotherhood," and not racism, was seen as the essence of Islam.

Malcolm's experiences in Africa also transformed his political philosophy. He discovered the limitations of skin-nationalism, since he met whites who were creative participants in liberation struggles in African countries. In his travels abroad he focused on explaining the black struggle for justice in the United States and linking it with other liberation struggles throughout the world. "Our problem is your problem," he told African heads of state: "It is not a Negro problem, nor an American problem. This is a world problem; a problem of humanity. It is not a problem of civil rights but a problem of human rights."

When Malcolm returned to the United States, he told blacks: "You can't understand what is going on in Mississippi, if you don't know what is going on in the Congo. They are both the same. The same interests are at stake." He founded the Organization of Afro-American Unity, patterned after the Organization of African Unity, to implement his ideas. He was hopeful of influencing African leaders "to recommend an immediate investigation into our problem by the United Nations Commission on Human Rights."

Malcolm X was not successful. On February 21, 1965, he was shot down by assassins as he spoke at the Audubon Ballroom in Harlem. He was thirty-nine years old.

No one made a greater impact upon the cultural consciousness of the African-American community during the second half of the twentieth century than Malcolm X. More than anyone else, he revolutionized the black mind, transforming some self-effacing colored people into proud blacks and self-confident African Americans. In the wake of the civil rights movement, and to some extent as a consequence of Malcolm X's appeal, some preachers and religious scholars created a black theology and proclaimed God as liberator and Jesus Christ as black. College students demanded and got courses and departments in black studies. Artists created a new black aesthetic and proclaimed, "Black is beautiful."

No area of the African-American community escaped Malcolm's influence. Some mainstream black leaders who first dismissed him as a rabble-rouser embraced his cultural philosophy following his death. Malcolm's most far-reaching influence, however, was among the masses of African Americans in the ghettos of American cities. Malcolm loved black people deeply and taught them much about themselves. Before Malcolm, many blacks did not want to have anything to do with Africa. But he reminded them that "you can't hate the roots of the tree and not hate the tree; you can't hate your origin and not end up hating yourself; you can't hate Africa and not hate yourself."

Malcolm X was a cultural revolutionary. Poet Maya Angelou called him a "charismatic speaker who could play an audience as great musicians play instruments." Disciple Peter Bailey said he was a "master teacher." Writer Alfred Duckett called him "our sage and our saint." In his eulogy, actor Ossie Davis bestowed upon Malcolm the title "our shining black prince." Malcolm can be best understood as a cultural prophet of blackness. African Americans who are proud to be black should thank Malcolm X. Few have played as central a role as he in making it possible for African Americans to claim their African heritage.

The meaning of Malcolm X grows deeper as people of color continue to study his life and thought. The recent "gift" of a trove of his speeches, photographs, letters, and journals to the New York Public Library's Schomburg Center for Research in Black Culture in Harlem (2002) promises to yield new insights into his growth and development as a thinker and leader. These important documents will eventually be made available for scholarly assessment.

Earlier in 1999, a previously unknown collection of Malcolm X's letters, school notebooks, and photographs was deposited at Emory University's Woodruff Library in Atlanta, Georgia. They date from 1941 to 1955. They show Malcolm as an articulate and eloquent writer, even as a teenager, and seriously interested in writing a book. This contrasts sharply with his portrayal of himself as ignorant in his *Autobiography*.

With the passage of time, Malcolm's image has soared. In 1965 he was widely rejected as a fiery demagogue, but today his image adorns a U.S. postage stamp. Indeed, he is regarded by many as an important African-American leader alongside of Martin Luther King Jr.

See also Civil Rights Movement, U.S.; Garvey, Marcus; Muhammad, Elijah; Nation of Islam; Universal Negro Improvement Association

■■ *Bibliography*

Breitman, George. *By Any Means Necessary*. New York: Pathfinder Press, 1970.

Breitman, George, ed. *Malcolm X Speaks*. New York: Grove Press, 1965.

Cone, James H. *Martin & Malcolm & America: A Dream or a Nightmare*. Maryknoll, N.Y.: Orbis Books, 1991.

Goldman, Peter. *The Death and Life of Malcolm X,* 2nd ed. Urbana: University of Illinois Press, 1979.

Malcolm X, with Alex Haley. *Autobiography of Malcolm X*. New York: Ballantine, 1965.

Malcolm X Papers, New York Public Library's Schomburg Center for Research in Black Culture, Harlem, NY.

Malcolm X Collection, 1941–1955, Robert W. Woodruff Library, Emory University, Atlanta, Georgia.

JAMES H. CONE (1996)
Updated by author 2005

MALÊ REBELLION

On the night of January 24 to 25, 1835, African-born slaves and freedpeople in the northeastern Brazilian city of Salvador da Bahia carried out a rebellion intended to liberate themselves from slavery and create an Islamic homeland. The revolt of the Malês, a nineteenth-century Brazilian term for Muslims, involved an estimated six hundred Yoruba and Hausa from present-day Nigeria. After hours of armed battle for control of the city, military and police forces defeated the rebels and left some seventy Africans dead. Though short-lived, the 1835 rebellion stands as one of the most significant urban slave revolts in the Americas.

BACKGROUND

The Malê Rebellion was one of a series of slave uprisings between 1807 and 1835 in the province of Bahia. Historians attribute this insurrectionist wave to an influx in slave imports from the Bight of Benin that brought a heavy concentration of Hausa and Yoruba, also known as Nagô, to Bahia within a few decades. Foes in Africa, the two groups overcame religious and ethnic differences to form alliances that would ultimately prove dangerous for masters. Most of these rebellions erupted in the Recôncavo, the fertile sugar area surrounding the Bay of All Saints and home to Brazil's wealthiest slave owners. The 1835 revolt differed from previous uprisings in that rebels from both the city and countryside worked to coordinate their resistance.

The structure of Brazil's urban slave system provided opportunities for conspirators to plan their attack. For urban slavery to function, slaves required a degree of autonomy to move through city streets. Many Hausa and Yoruba worked as *ganhadores*, slaves-for-hire who sold their labor on the streets of Salvador. Some maintained their own residences and saw their masters only weekly, while others turned over their wages each evening. *Ganhadores* hauled goods to and from the port or carried sedan chairs that Bahians hailed like cabs. Others worked as tailors, masons, or carpenters. The Hausa freedman Caetano Ribeiro traveled to the city to sell tobacco and other goods he purchased in the Recôncavo. Trial records indicate that female street vendors also took part in the conspiracy. The Muslim cleric Dandará, who earned his living trading tobacco at the local market, was one of several holy men involved in the movement. Through instruction in the Qur'an, clerics won converts to Islam and persuaded followers to join the movement. Slaves and freedpeople thus planned their movement in the midst of Bahia's thriving urban slave system.

THE UPRISING

The Muslim conspirators planned their attack to coordinate with the celebration of Our Lady of Bonfim, a Catho-lic holiday commemorated at a church located eight miles from the city center. The rebellion also corresponded with the end of the Muslim holiday Ramadan. The rebellion was set to begin on January 25 at 5:00AM, an hour when Africans fetched water at public fountains. Their plans, however, were betrayed. Two African freedwomen, Guilhermina Rosa de Souza and Sabina da Cruz, wife of a Nagô leader, pieced together details of the conspiracy. On the night of January 24 Guilhermina told a white neighbor about the rebels' plans. Upon learning of the plot, Provincial President Francisco de Souza Martins ordered police forces to search the homes of Africans whom Sabina da Cruz had identified as central to the conspiracy. Within two hours, forces led by police chief Francisco Gonçalves Martins entered into battle with African rebels in the streets of the upper city, amid the government buildings, theater, and churches frequented by the white slaveholding elite. For several hours the Muslim rebels engaged in armed resistance in a determined effort to overturn Bahia's white slaveholding society and replace it with an Islamic homeland. At approximately 3:00AM on January 25, Gonçalves Martins's forces met the African rebels in what would be the final battle of the uprising—in Agua de Meninos, located north of Salvador's central port along the Bay of All Saints. Some two hundred Africans fought in this last battle for control of the city, but it was Bahia's police forces that emerged victorious after killing nineteen Africans and wounding another thirteen. During the entire revolt, over seventy Africans lost their lives.

REPRESSION

The Malê insurgents killed nine white and mixed-race Bahians, but the panic that gripped the city far exceeded those casualties. Rumors of continued insurrection circulated for weeks. Terrified, some white families left their homes to sleep offshore in canoes. Provincial President Martins dispatched military and police authorities to route out possible conspirators. In the two days following the insurrection, police arrested at least forty-five slaves and fifty freedpeople. Raids continued for months; hundreds of Africans eventually found themselves in police custody. Trials resulted in harsh punishment: death, imprisonment, flogging, and deportation. The sentences handed down conformed to masters' property interests. Slaves did not face prison terms but were instead subjected to forced labor and flogging, ensuring that owners did not lose the monetary value slave labor provided. Freedmen, on the other hand, found themselves sentenced to prison terms and, more commonly, deportation to the African coast. Floggings ranged from fifty to twelve hundred lashes. The court sentenced Pácifico Lucitan to one thousand lashes, despite the fact he had been in jail when the rebellion began. Among those sentenced to death were Belchoir and Gaspar da Silva Cunha, who had hosted meetings where conspirators planned their attack.

In the months following the trials, many masters sold Nagô slaves out of the province—even if there was no evidence they had been involved in the conspiracy—rather than run the risk of future violence. National lawmakers responded to the Malês' revolt by passing an exceptional death penalty law that mandated death without ordinary recourse to appeal for any slave who killed or seriously injured his master, the overseer, or a member of either's family. Widespread repression of African cultural and religious expression and tightened restrictions on urban slaves ensured that the 1835 rebellion would be Bahia's last major slave insurrection.

See also Muslims in the Americas; Palmares

■ ■ *Bibliography*

Goody, Jack. "Writing, Religion, and Revolt in Bahia." *Visible Language* 20 (1986): 318–343.

Lovejoy, Paul. "Background to Rebellion: The Origins of Muslim Slaves in Bahia." *Slavery and Abolition* 15 (1994): 151–180.

Reis, João José. *Slave Rebellion in Brazil: The Muslim Uprising of 1935.* Baltimore, Md.: Johns Hopkins University Press, 1993.

ALEXANDRA K. BROWN (2005)

MANLEY, EDNA

MARCH 1, 1900
1987

■ ■ ■

Edna Manley was born to Harvey Swithenbank and Martha Elliot Shearer. Her father, a Wesleyan priest from Yorkshire in England, met Martha, who was a Jamaican of mixed descent, while he was on a tour of duty in Jamaica. They were married in Jamaica in 1895. Edna, the fifth of nine children, was born in England, where the family had moved after the birth of the first two children.

After leaving high school, Edna studied art at a number of English art institutions, including the prestigious St. Martin's School of Art in London. She also studied privately with Maurice Harding, the animal sculptor. In 1921 she married her cousin, Norman Manley, a Jamaican of mixed parentage and a Rhodes scholar studying law at Ox-

ford University. After the birth of their first child, Douglas, they returned in 1922 to Jamaica, where a second son, Michael, was born in 1924.

Initially, Manley exhibited her London-made sculptures, but her work quickly evolved into personal observations of Jamaican life. Despite her European training and background, she immediately identified with the Jamaican environment and made conscious efforts to incorporate Negro-influenced forms into her work. Her first Jamaican masterpiece, *The Beadseller,* was produced in 1922. When she began making such sculptures as *Negro Aroused* (1935), *Market Woman* (1936), and *Young Negro* (1936) and exhibiting them locally, she created her own brand of European modernism, a brand of vorticism, but she infused it with a definite Caribbean take and subject matter. Vorticism was a branch futurism, headlined by British artist Wyndham Lewis, a movement that incorporated dynamism and significant form in the art of sculpture. By the 1930s Manley was concentrating on exhibiting and devoting her energies fully to Jamaica, although she still maintained connections with the London group, some of whom were members of the Bloomsbury Group.

Until the 1930s there had been little interest in contemporary art in Jamaica. Manley belonged to a group of middle-class revolutionaries who openly criticized the policies and practices of the Institute of Jamaica. Founded in 1879, the institute was mandated to "encourage the pursuit of literature, science and art in Jamaica." Despite the zeal of its librarian/curator Frank Cundall and board chair in H. G. De Lisser, the institute promoted the culture of Jamaica, thought to have no culture of its own, as part of the British Empire, privileging works by famous British artists, photographers, and printmakers. Manley and the group of middle-class revolutionaries, including Basil Parkes, S. R. Braithewaite, Douglas Judah, N. N. Nethersole, W. E. Foster-Davies, and Norman Manley, forced a resolution in 1936 to create changes in the institute's programs, among these the Junior Centre catering to the artistic needs of Jamaica's youth and the establishment of the Jamaica School of Art and Craft.

By 1940 the School of Visual Arts began as a workshop and ran for ten years, offering free art classes at the Junior Centre of the Institute of Jamaica. Jamaican youth aged eight to eighteen, such as Ralph Campbell, Albert Huie, David Pottinger, Henry Daley, Lloyd Van Patterson, and Vernal Reuben, began receiving their earliest instruction there. Petrine Archer Straw commented that there was a sympathy of vision and shared interest between tutors in painting Jamaican folk and lifestyles. Manley encouraged a movement away from the "anaemic and imitative" earlier work and introduced postimpressionism.

In the present postcolonial discourses, Edna Manley's artistic legacy in Jamaica is being recast, contextualizing her origins and class position. Because of her efforts, however, a contemporary Jamaican art movement provides a dialogue with itself, a history of artistic production, and an institution that she helped to build, using the influence of her position as the prime minister's wife. In 1995 the Cultural Training Centre of Jamaica was renamed the Edna Manley College for the Visual and Performing Arts. Her sculptural pieces, such as *Prophet* (1935), *Diggers* (1936), *Pocomania* (1936), and *Prayer* (1937), are treasured as Jamaican classics in its National Gallery and other collections. *Angel* (1970), in the Kingston Parish Church, is one of the best known of her later works.

After Norman Manley died in 1969, Edna Manley continued her prolific production of sculpture, modeled works in other media, and painting, leaving other insightful observations on her experience of Jamaica, including *Ghetto Mother* (1981) and *Birth* (1986). She died early in 1987. Her life with Norman, spiritual father of Jamaica's national movement toward independence, was mirrored in her role as image maker demonstrating Jamaica's independence struggle and unique voice.

See also Art in the Anglophone Caribbean; Manley, Norman

■ ■ *Bibliography*

Boxer, David. *Edna Manley: The Seventies* (exhibition catalog). Kingston, Jamaica: The Gallery, 1980.

Boxer, David. *Edna Manley, Sculptor.* Kingston, Jamaica: Edna Manley Foundation and National Gallery of Jamaica, 1990.

Boxer, David, and Veerle Poupeye. *Modern Jamaican Art.* Mona, Jamaica: Ian Randle Press, University of the West Indies Development and Endowment Fund, 1998.

Brown, Wayne. *Edna Manley: The Private Years, 1900–1938.* London: Andre Deutsch, 1975.

Manley, Rachel, ed. *Edna Manley: The Diaries.* Kingston: Heinemann (Caribbean), 1989.

Paul, Annie. "Legislating Taste: The Curator's Palette." *Small Axe: A Journal of Caribbean Criticism* 4 (September 1998): 65–85.

PATRICIA MOHAMMED (2005)

MANLEY, MICHAEL

DECEMBER 10, 1924
MARCH 6, 1997

┫╋┣

Michael Norman Manley was born in suburban Kingston, Jamaica, the son of very accomplished parents. His father,

Former Jamaican prime minister Michael Manley (left) with former U.S. president George H. W. Bush in Washington, D.C., 1990. Manley, son of People's National Party founder Norman Manley, became Jamaica's fourth prime minister in 1972. He served the nation in that capacity until 1980 and again from 1989 until his retirement in 1992. AFP/GETTY IMAGES

Norman Washington Manley (1893–1969), was a brilliant lawyer, Rhodes scholar, phenomenal all-round schoolboy athlete, and decorated World War I veteran who later founded a national social welfare commission, led the successful campaigns for universal suffrage and independence, and was posthumously declared a National Hero of Jamaica. His mother, Edna Manley, née Swithenbank (1900–1987), was an outstanding sculptor and a facilitator and patron of Jamaican arts. Their son grew up under his mother's wings in the enriching environment and milieu of Drumblair, his parents' suburban manor, a Mecca for aspiring young writers and painters, as well as for the legal luminaries, trade unionists, and fledgling politicians who benefited from his father's counsel.

EDUCATION

Michael Manley was the first school captain of his preparatory school, and he received his secondary education at the prestigious Jamaica College, where he captained the swimming team to victory in the annual schools championships in 1942. From an early age, Manley took a keen interest in Jamaica's nascent political movement as the democratic socialist People's National Party (PNP), then the only broad-based political organization in Jamaica, was launched in 1938, with his father presiding over the drafting of its constitution and being elected its first president.

While awaiting external examination results at Jamaica College, Michael Manley became involved in a bitter conflict over students' rights with two young Englishmen, one a teacher and the other the headmaster. Refusing to apologize for his utterances, Manley, then a boarding student, packed his bags and left, thereby unwittingly precipitating a two-week students' strike.

Enrolled at McGill University in Montreal, Canada, in 1943, he joined the Royal Canadian Air Force during World War II, attaining the rank of pilot officer. After the war, he entered the London School of Economics, where he was tutored by the distinguished democratic socialist theoretician Professor Harold Laski. Manley earned a bachelor's degree in economics and government. He also completed a year's postgraduate study on contemporary political developments in the Caribbean.

Manley was a founding executive of the West Indian Students' Union. He was always in the vanguard of the union's negotiations with the British Colonial Office. He was one of the principal organizers of a strike against the living conditions endured by many Caribbean students in London. He also became a member of the Caribbean Labour Congress. Manley campaigned against racial discrimination in London and supported the movement for a West Indies Federation and political independence for the Anglophone Caribbean.

Manley worked for a year (1950–1951) as a journalist with the British Broadcasting Corporation (BBC), then returned to Jamaica in December 1951 as associate editor of the socialist weekly newspaper *Public Opinion*. He was elected to the National Executive Council of the PNP in September 1952. Several powerful members of the PNP were expelled on the grounds that they were more Marxist than democratic socialist, and the leftist-controlled Trade Union Congress was disaffiliated from the party. To fill the void, the PNP leadership swiftly established a more compatible trade union, the National Workers Union (NWU), in 1953.

TRADE UNION CAREER

Manley became the sugar supervisor of the new National Workers Union in 1953. In 1955 he was elected island supervisor and first vice president of the NWU. He founded the Caribbean Mine and Metal Workers Federation in 1961 and served as its president for thirteen years.

A legendary trade unionist who brought unprecedented creativity and energy to his work, Manley earned great benefits for NWU-member workers and won acceptance for fundamental principles affecting employer-employee relationships. In 1953 the NWU won recognition of the principle that wages in the bauxite/alumina industry should be based on the companies' ability to pay rather than on parity with other wages. The result was a 300-percent increase in bauxite/alumina workers' wages. In 1962 Manley proved that Jamaica's sugar industry had made $4 million in unreported profits, and he forced a $2.5 million wage increase.

In 1964 Manley led one of the longest strikes in Jamaica's history, following the dismissal of two journalists at the state-owned Jamaica Broadcasting Corporation. Contending that the dismissals were arbitrary and unjust, Manley, a handsome six-footer, fearless warrior, and spellbinding orator, now enjoying the status of senator, led a civil-disobedience campaign that resonated throughout Jamaica. When he lay down on Kingston's streets to paralyze peak-hour traffic, he was joined by masses of Jamaicans of all classes, including some of his critics and supporters of the government who were perceived as the instigators of the dismissals. The authorities teargassed demonstrators and refused to negotiate. Manley called a nationwide strike. The government promptly established a Commission of Inquiry, which subsequently ruled in Manley's favor.

ENTRY INTO POLITICS

Manley entered representational politics in the 1967 general election, winning the Central Kingston constituency. After his father's retirement, he comfortably won the contest for party leadership. He was consequently appointed opposition leader in the Jamaica Parliament.

Manley zeroed in on the failings of the Jamaica Labour Party (JLP) administration, which had held the reins since independence in 1962. He inveighed against social injustice and inequality, which, he claimed, pervaded Jamaica. While acknowledging significant economic growth in the decade under the JLP government (1962–1972), Manley contended that the benefits were restricted to a small minority. Too many in the society faced "the blank wall of poverty," he asserted, and he attacked the human-rights record of the administration. Manley advocated a deepening of democracy, donned casual bush-jacket suits, and mobilized reggae artists to write and perform songs that carried his message—Power for the People. Manley's populism and charisma yielded thirty-seven of the fifty-three seats in the House of Representatives in the election held on leap-year day 1972. He was sworn in two days later as Jamaica's fourth prime minister.

PRIME MINISTER MANLEY

Michael Manley and his government embarked on the most profound and wide-ranging program of social and economic reform in Jamaica's history. Among other legislative measures, they established a national minimum wage, maternity leave with pay, gender equity in pay scales, the right of workers to join trade unions, a land-reform program, a national literacy program, free education to the tertiary level, a law that ended discrimination against children born out of wedlock, and a National Housing Trust that received funds from universal payroll deductions and dispensed benefits by lottery to contributors in need of housing. An inequitable Masters and Servants Act was repealed, as were laws permitting arbitrary arrest and detention of persons on flimsy grounds of suspicion. The government vigorously promoted education, cooperative development, child welfare, community health, women's rights, worker participation, and self-reliance at national and community levels. In promoting self-reliance, Manley often led communities in manual work to provide themselves with social facilities and amenities.

Following the breakdown of negotiations with U.S. multinational corporations for a more equitable share of the proceeds of Jamaican bauxite (aluminum ore), the Manley government imposed a bauxite production levy, which set alarm bells ringing not only among overseas investors but also within the Jamaican business sector.

There was apprehension too when the PNP in November 1974 reaffirmed its democratic socialist philosophy, first adopted in 1940. Although the blueprint included a mixed economy, with a clearly defined role for the private sector, some feared that the government's stated intention to control public utilities and other strategically sensitive entities signaled an encroachment of state capitalism into what was previously regarded as private-sector territory.

Despite a concerted attempt at public education to promote the democratic socialist model nationwide, within Manley's party itself there was a broad spectrum of political ideology ranging from slightly left of center to near-Marxist. Jamaican and foreign investors were rattled by the rhetoric of some of the more radical socialists. Manley's democratic instincts and reflexes would not allow him to silence his left-wingers as some critics urged, which was itself regarded as further evidence of impending communism.

WORLD STATESMAN

Confusion multiplied as Manley made his mark internationally. Attending the Conference of the Non-Aligned Movement in Algiers in September 1973, Manley accepted a ride in neighbor Fidel Castro's aircraft. At the conference, he repeated a truism that Che Guevara brought to attention at a Food and Agriculture Organization (FAO) conference in Rome in 1964—that the terms of trade were hopelessly skewed against primary-producing third-world countries of the south and in favor of the industrialized countries of the north, and that it required more and more sugar exports to finance the purchase of a single imported tractor. Manley often repeated this theme and called for a New International Economic Order (NIEO) in which, among other things, prices of primary products and manufactured goods would be indexed against each other. His was a highly respected voice, especially in such bodies as the Commonwealth of Nations, the Non-Aligned Movement, the Group of 77, the Socialist International, and the African, Caribbean, and Pacific (ACP) countries. In addition, Manley was a vice president and later honorary president (1992–1997) of the Socialist International and also chair of its Economic Committee.

Manley developed a close bond with the social democrats of northern Europe—especially Swedish Prime Minister Olof Palme and Norwegian Prime Minister Odvar Nordli—whose brand of socialism was in line with the PNP's. Manley had no difficulty, however, finding common cause with more radical socialists like Cuba's Fidel Castro, whose intellect, humanity, and principled activism he admired. Manley and Castro shared the view that justice must be universal, whether in terms of domestic or international economic relations or the power equations between races.

When in December 1975 U.S. Secretary of State Henry Kissinger warned Manley not to support Cuba's presence in Angola to defend that country against apartheid South Africa's incursion, Manley declined to commit Jamaica to opposing Cuba's defense of Angola or to neutrality, despite hints that noncompliance would jeopardize urgently needed financial aid. Jamaica, in concert with all of Africa, voted at the United Nations in favor of the Cuban presence in Angola. As a result, the proposed U.S. financial assistance did not materialize, and the number of operatives of the U.S. Central Intelligence Agency (CIA) in Kingston was promptly doubled.

Manley achieved considerable success in international politics, notably in negotiations leading to Zimbabwe's independence and in bringing pressure on the apartheid system through the isolation of South Africa. However, the domestic and foreign coalition against his government was overwhelming. Investment dried up. Bauxite production declined. Hotels in the vital tourism sector closed their doors. To keep the economy and vital industries alive, Jamaica's cash-strapped government bought hotels and other businesses, further fuelling fears of a communist design. The government, finding the conditionalities of the

International Monetary Fund (IMF) more and more unacceptable, decided to end its borrowing relationship with the fund and seek an alternative path. Manley turned to the oil-producing Middle Eastern states, whose mobilization of the Organization of Petroleum Exporting Countries (OPEC) had enriched them, partly at the expense of non-oil-producing countries like Jamaica. However, the Middle Eastern countries were more interested in investing in the developed North.

Manley's call for an NIEO was tempered by his belief in self-reliance. He became an apostle of "south-south cooperation," citing as an example the possibilities of establishing aluminum smelters and extrusion industries by marrying Jamaican bauxite with the energy derived from oil or natural gas produced by another third-world nation.

Manley was one of six hemispheric heads of government who advised Panamanian President Omar Torrijos in his successful negotiation with the United States of a new treaty to govern the ownership and use of the Panama Canal. He was a principal proponent of a Law of the Sea to provide that the world's ocean resources are harnessed as the common heritage of all humankind. His efforts contributed to the adoption of the Law of the Sea Convention and the location of the International Seabed Authority in Kingston, Jamaica.

With the flight of capital and curtailment of investment, economic conditions in Jamaica deteriorated in the 1970s. Amid accusations of destabilization by the CIA, the IMF, foreign investors, the U.S. media, and elements of the domestic business sector and the opposition JLP, politically motivated violence escalated, exacerbating an already problematic situation. Violent crimes became rampant. In June 1976 Manley declared a state of emergency during which there was some curtailment of civil liberties, including the detention of scores of alleged troublemakers. Relative calm returned during the state of emergency. Manley called a general election in December 1976 in which the PNP won forty-seven seats in the sixty-member House of Representatives. Manley's detractors subsequently contended that the state of emergency, which lasted for a year, was designed to entrench his government.

ELECTORAL DEFEAT AND RETURN TO POWER

Economic conditions continued worsening after the 1976 general election. So also did politically motivated violence. Manley called a general election in October 1980, at which his party was routed, winning only nine of the sixty seats in the House of Representatives.

Within two years, the impeccably accurate Carl Stone polling organization showed Manley's PNP with a com-

fortable lead over the JLP. However, the assassination in 1983 of Maurice Bishop, Grenada's revolutionary prime minister, and the subsequent involvement of the Jamaican army in the United States–led invasion of Grenada, was followed by a dramatic reversal in the opinion polls. Jamaica's JLP prime minister, Edward Seaga, called a snap general election for October 1983. Claiming that voter registration was overdue and that a high proportion of voters would be disfranchised, Manley led a PNP boycott of the election. The JLP won all sixty seats in the House of Representatives. The PNP waged its opposition through "people's forums" all over Jamaica.

In February 1989 Manley was swept back into power by forty-five seats to the JLP's fifteen. However, there was a sea change in his economic policy. Manley admitted that his government of the 1970s had moved too fast in attempting to cure Jamaica's social ills, and that despite a number of effective programs aimed at social and human development, the economy had contracted, resulting in hardship for many Jamaicans. Manley also admitted to the failure of his 1970s government's attempt to unite third-world countries into what he referred to as a trade union of the poor of the world. Manley acknowledged that first-world countries followed their own agenda in the face of new technologies that led to the increasing globalization of the world economy. His prescription for dealing with this new reality was liberalization of the economy and privatization of government assets. Manley argued that new-style democratic socialism would build participatory democracy on the foundation of social justice and broad ownership of the means of production. He believed that socialism had to adapt to changing times but must maintain its commitment to empowerment. After putting the new policy into effect, Manley retired in March 1992 due to ill health.

Manley subsequently worked as a consultant, journalist, coffee farmer, award-winning horticulturist, and distinguished visiting professor at six universities. He died of prostate cancer on March 6, 1997, and was buried in Jamaica's National Heroes Park in Kingston. He was survived by his wife, Glynne, whom he married in 1992, and five children by previous marriages—Rachel, Joseph, Sarah, Natasha, and David.

Michael Manley received numerous international honors and awards, mainly for his contributions toward the struggle against South African apartheid, the advocacy of the NIEO, and the deepening of democracy in Jamaica and the Caribbean. Among his honors was a United Nations gold medal and the World Peace Council's Joliot Curie Peace Award. He was the author of seven books on politics, economics, international relations, and the sport of cricket.

See also Manley, Norman; People's National Party

▪ ▪ *Bibliography*

Brandt, Willy, and Michael Manley. *Global Challenge, from Crisis to Cooperation: Breaking the North-South Stalemate.* London: Pan Books, 1985.

Brown, Wayne. *Edna Manley: The Private Years, 1900–1938.* London: Deutsch, 1975.

Kaufman, Michael. *Jamaica under Manley: Dilemmas of Socialism and Democracy.* London: Zed Books, 1985.

Manley, Michael. *The Politics of Change: A Jamaican Testament.* London: Deutsch, 1974.

Manley, Michael. *A Voice at the Workplace: Reflections on Colonialism and the Jamaican Worker.* London: Deutsch, 1975.

Manley, Michael. *Up the Down Escalator: Development and the International Economy, a Jamaican Case Study.* Washington, D.C.: Howard University Press, 1987.

Manley, Michael. *The Poverty of Nations: Reflections on Underdevelopment and the World Economy.* London: Pluto, 1991.

Manley, Rachel. *Drumblair: Memories of a Jamaican Childhood.* Toronto: Knopf, 1996.

Manley, Rachel. *Slipstream: A Daughter Remembers.* Kingston, Jamaica: Ian Randle, 2000.

Panton, David. *Jamaica's Michael Manley: The Great Transformation (1972–92).* Kingston, Jamaica: LMH Books, 1994.

LOUIS MARRIOTT (2005)

MANLEY, NORMAN

JULY 4, 1893
SEPTEMBER 2, 1969

▪▪▪

Norman Washington Manley stood in the forefront of modern Jamaican public life from the late 1930s until his death in the late 1960s. He advocated the cause of workers, founded the People's National Party (PNP), and planned and guided the transfer of power from colonial rule. He prepared his compatriots for independence, which came in 1962, and left a legacy of faith and confidence that allowed the people of Jamaica to be the architects of their destiny. After almost five centuries of colonial rule, three of these under slavery, this was no small accomplishment.

Manley laid foundations for Jamaica's two-party system, and with it an enduring form of democratic governance. He taught the Jamaican people the sanctity of the rule of law and imbued them with a will to freedom via self-government and nationhood. In addition, he left them with an understanding of the interdependence of politics and labor, of immigration and race, and taught the signifi-

Norman Manley, prime minister of Jamaica, pictured at the Jamaica High Commission in London, 1960. A former Rhodes Scholar who studied law at Oxford University, Manley founded the People's National Party in Jamaica, helping to lay the foundation for a democratic two-party political system in that nation. VAL WILMER/GETTY IMAGES

cance of intellect and imagination, of formal knowledge and artistic culture, to the shaping of a people emerging out of slavery and still struggling against colonialism. In his final public address, in 1969, he charged his Jamaicans to meet the challenge of "reconstructing the social and economic life of Jamaica," a charge that was to take on enduring relevance in the decades that followed, particularly with the hegemonic presence of the World Bank, the International Monetary Fund (IMF), the World Trade Organization (WTO), and globalization.

Manley was born in rural Jamaica, the son of a produce dealer who was "the illegitimate son of a woman of the people" and a mother who was a postmistress (postal clerk) and an "almost pure white woman" (a "quadroon" in the color-coded hierarchy of postslavery Jamaican society). He had two sisters and a brother. During his primary and secondary schooling he developed into a brilliant, hardworking, argumentative, articulate, and intellectually curious young man, with (in his own words) "an unquenchable belief in excellence." He was "almost wholly unconscious of my country and its problems. . . . colour meant little to me. I did not, could not, allow it to be an obsession since I was totally without any idea of 'white superiority.' It was not so much arrogance but a highly developed critical faculty. The only superiority I accepted was the superiority of excellence and I suppose I knew what I was good at but found it easy to recognise and respect quality even when I knew I could not equal it."

This spirit and intelligence, as well as his prowess as a schoolboy athlete, helped to earn him a Rhodes Scholarship in 1914 to study law at Oxford. This was to lead to an illustrious legal career in his native Jamaica, as well as in the British West Indies, where his peers soon recognized in him "a lawyer learned in the law, a man honest in his presentation of a case and an effective but eminently courteous cross-examiner." His learning and versatility were epitomized in the 1951 Vicks trademark case, when the British Lord Chancellor described his submissions as "the best argument I have ever heard in a trade mark case."

In 1914, before joining his two sisters and brother in London, where they were already studying, Manley went to visit with a maternal aunt in Penzance. She had been married to a Methodist parson from Yorkshire, who had spent almost five years in Jamaica but had since died, leaving her with nine children. There he met Edna Swithenbank, his cousin and future wife. He described her as "a little girl of 14, a strange, shy and highly individualistic person, quite unlike the rest of her family and unlike anybody I had ever known."

His studies at Jesus College, Oxford, were interrupted by war service from 1915 until 1919. He enlisted as a private in the Royal Field Artillery, refusing to be made an officer and fighting instead with the rank and file of "cockneys with a view of life all their own." To these men, he was to become something of a referee and sage. Three years of active service on the Western Front (including the battles of Somme and Ypres) brought him both sorrow (his brother was killed in action) and glory (he was decorated with a Military Medal for bravery in action).

Manley resumed studies at Oxford in 1919, and he was called to the bar on April 20, 1921. That same year he married Edna, who was to become a well-known sculptor. He then spent some time in the London chambers of S. C. N. Goodman, followed a number of famous advocates "all over the Court," and "learnt not only technique but style; and I learnt that to watch a man in action—good, bad, or indifferent—was the quickest and surest way to learn what to do and what not to do and how to do it." He returned to Jamaica in August 1922, "with a clear sum of £50, a wife, a baby and a profession." He was to develop a legendary expertise in the practice of his profession, rising to prominence as an advocate and acknowledged leader of the bar in Jamaica and the British West Indies. Manley's legal career was, however, to be subordinated, at great personal sacrifice (according to his colleague Vivian Blake), "to the major effort of his life, securing the independence of Jamaica and earning for him[self] the popular title *Father of the Nation*." Indeed, Norman Washington Manley is clearly the foremost architect of modern Jamaica.

None of his accomplishments, as Norman Manley so well knew, were achievable without the establishment of appropriate and serviceable institutional frameworks to facilitate and foster the growth and development of individuals in communities. Such communities, he felt, had to be informed by a civic responsibility that would render citizens proud to be citizens, so that they would be imbued with the knowledge and understanding not only of the rights of individuals, but also of their obligations as part of a community, society, or nation.

As is evident in his numerous speeches and informal utterances, Manley possessed a deep understanding of the need to shape institutions that could cradle, nurture, and finally develop a vision of freedom, self-reliance, self-worth, and opportunity for all Jamaicans. It is no surprise, then, that he provided a transformational leadership (which included the enduring idea of being part of a wider Caribbean) that put into place the relevant institutions that could serve as an infrastructure for shaping a new society. That society, he believed, would in time liberate itself from what he said was the sort of "dependency which allowed no definite economy of our own, with no control over our own markets, no representatives of an authoritative character that can speak for ourselves and our own interest in the councils and debates that will take place" in the world at large.

Between 1955 and 1962, when the People's National Party held power, Manley (first as chief minister and then as premier), gave priority to agriculture, education, and industrialization. Thousand of small farmers received subsidies, and new markets were opened. The democratization of the once elitist system of secondary education was begun, along with an increase in scholarships. Primary schools were built; public library facilities were extended to all parishes; and the Jamaica Broadcasting Corporation was established. A stadium was built to help foster sports, and the Scientific Research Council was established.

Manley was also the first political leader in the English-speaking Caribbean to give arts and culture a portfolio. He wanted to reverse the systemic denigration of African culture and the force of the Eurocentrism that had frustrated native expressions and threatened the quest for cultural certitude among the majority. As far back as 1939, Manley is recorded as saying "The immediate past has attempted to destroy the influence of the glory that is Africa, it has attempted to make us condemn and mistrust the vitality, vigour, the rhythmic emotionalism that we get from our African ancestors. It has flung us into conflict with the

English traditions of the public schools and even worse it has imposed on us the Greek ideal of balanced beauty." Interestingly, this speech came in the wake of his wife's prophetic and iconic piece of sculpture titled *Negro Aroused*.

Other transformational institutions were also established. The Agricultural Development Corporation and the Industrial Development Corporation were a part of Manley's vision, and they survive in one form or another to this day. So were the financial institutions, including the Bank of Jamaica, which were conceived by Noel Nethersole, Norman Manley's trusted chief lieutenant. A legislative program produced the Beach Control Act, the Facilities for Titles Act, the Land Bonds Act, the Land Development Duty Act, the Jamaica Standards Act, and the Watersheds Protection Act. Manley's empowerment of Parliament as the forum of the people's accredited representatives and as a major instrument of democratic discourse and of intellectual vigor was one of his great achievements. The Farm Development Program and the Jamaica Youth Corps, which both addressed the needs of rural and urban youth, made it possible for unemployed young men and women to realize their potential and become active citizens of their country.

Manley's institutional devising went beyond the outward signs of formal physical structures into the inward grace of human development. The neglect of this aspect of good governance since his death has presented a challenge as his successors to return to the blueprint he prepared for a self-respecting nation and a regenerative society, which he envisaged his country had to become in order to cope with the turbulent changes of an unpredictable world.

Manley's vision can be seen in Jamaica Welfare Limited, a community development modality for social and individual human development, established in 1937. The people, "the mass of the population," were a priority for Manley, and all institutional frameworks were intended to foster their retreat from the marginalization of the colonial era. Jamaica Welfare was to be nonpartisan, people-centered, and national. Unfortunately, Manley felt he had to resign his chairmanship of this institution when the People's National Party—itself transformed by the early 1940s from a movement into a full-blown political party—demanded his full attention. He was therefore disappointed greatly when, after 1962, Jamaica Welfare was replaced by a new community development program named the "Hundred Village Scheme," which he felt betrayed the principles on which the institution was founded.

If Jamaica Welfare Limited (later the Social Welfare Commission, and still later the Social Development Com-

mission) demonstrated an institutional breakthrough towards the creative shaping of a new Jamaica, so did the founding and development of the People's National Party (PNP). Envisioned as an instrument of organized politics, political continuity, and democratic governance, this institution has stayed its course, if only because it was firmly rooted in some of the finest attributes the Jamaican people have shown themselves to possess. The PNP was a genuinely new beginning for Jamaica, and it has served as a model for similar political organizations, both at home and in the wider Caribbean. The party itself, thanks to its articulated mission statements, the vision of its founding leader, and the rationality of its internal organization, has survived the vicissitudes of being both in power and out of power (as the "Opposition").

The remarkable thing about the institutions Norman Manley helped to found was that they were neither monuments to self nor cold edifices of steel and mortar parading in high-rise splendor. Rather, they were created on the organic idea of the ultimate "independence of a self-governing Jamaica, which to him meant the liberation of the Jamaican people from centuries of psychological and structural bondage, the non-negotiable claim to human dignity and self-respect, self-definition as (full-fledged) members of the human race, and the attainment of power which comes to a people only on the conviction that they are the creators of their own destiny."

Paradoxically, Manley's efforts to have the British West Indies integrate into a federation failed after a short trial run from 1958 to 1961, when he was forced to call a referendum that resulted in the rejection of the short-lived West Indies Federation. "The people have spoken" was his immediate response of respectful concurrence, as it always was on his losing subsequent national elections. Nonetheless, Jamaica achieved independence in 1962, ending 307 years of British colonial rule. And Manley's vision of an integrated region, with a common history and contemporary problems, was to find a continuing manifestation in what is now the Caribbean Community and Common Market (CARICOM).

Manley gave to Jamaica and the wider Caribbean (itself a part of the African diaspora), the full power and force of a giant intellect and the sense and sensibility of a fertile creative imagination. His personal courage and profound decency transcended narrow partisan politics, though he admitted to having a quick "flaming temper" which took him "half a lifetime to learn to control . . . with its place . . . taken by a sort of arrogant indifference which was constantly mistaken for the real me." He nonetheless remains a role model for all leaders of African ancestry in the Americas, if only because of his single-mindedness and dedication, his financial disinterestedness in the pursuit of public duties, and his personal integrity. His remarkable intellectual powers and gift of advocacy underlay his total commitment to the betterment of the material and spiritual welfare of the people of Jamaica. It is small wonder, then, that the government and people of his country bestowed on him the rare honor of "National Hero" soon after his death.

See also Manley, Michael; People's National Party

■ ■ *Bibliography*

Brown, Wayne. *Edna Manley: The Private Years 1900–1938.* London: Andre Deutsch, 1975.

Eisner, Gisela. *Jamaica, 1830–1930: A Study in Economic Growth.* Manchester, U.K.: Manchester University Press, 1961.

Jamaica Journal 25, no. 1 (October 1993—special issue to mark Norman Manley Centenary).

Manley, Rachel. *Drumblair: Memories of a Jamaican Childhood.* Kingston, Jamaica: Ian Randle, 1966.

Manley, Rachel, ed. *Edna Manley: The Diaries.* Kingston, Jamaica: West Indies Publishing, 1989.

Nettleford, Rex M., ed. *Manley and the New Jamaica: Selected Speeches and Writings 1938–1968.* Kingston, Jamaica: Longman Caribbean, 1971.

Ranston, Jackie. *Lawyer Manley: First Time Up.* Barbados: University Press of the West Indies, 1998.

Reid, Vic. *The Horses of the Morning.* Kingston, Jamaica: Caribbean Authors Publishing Company, 1985.

Sherlock, Philip M. *Norman Manley: A Biography.* London: Macmillan, 1980.

REX M. NETTLEFORD (2005)

MANNING, PATRICK

AUGUST 17, 1946

Patrick Mervyn Augustus Manning, the third child and only son of Elaine and Arnold Manning, was born in Trinidad. His father, an early member of the Peoples National Movement (PNM), worked diligently for the party in the San Fernando East Constituency, and his home virtually became its office. Consequently, from his early childhood Patrick became acquainted with many politicians, such as Nicholas Simonette, C. L. R. James, De Wilton Rogers, and Andrew Carr, who visited his parents' home to discuss party matters.

Patrick attended the San Fernando government primary school, from which he won a scholarship to Presentation College in San Fernando. There, he earned a Cambridge School Certificate, Grade 1. He went on to study for the Higher School Certificate examination, gaining passes in pure mathematics, applied mathematics, and physics. His ambition was to study engineering in the United States. This goal was dashed when he failed to win a scholarship from an American university. He received one from Texaco Trinidad Inc., however, to study geology at the University of the West Indies in Mona, Jamaica. On campus, Manning met other Caribbean leaders, including Percival J. Patterson, future Jamaican prime minister, and Edwin Carrington, who would become the secretary of the Caribbean Community Market (CARICOM). The first indication that he had political aspirations was his decision to contest the election for the chairmanship of his undergraduate residence hall. His slogan was "PUT A MANNING." His colleagues did not. After graduation Manning returned to Trinidad to work for the Texaco Oil Company as a geologist.

The rise of the Black Power movement at the end of the 1960s forced the PNM to make adjustments to its representation in the House of Representatives. The PNM accepted the resignation of Gerard Montano, a white man, founding member of the party, and the representative for San Fernando East since 1956. After several interviews Manning was selected as the new candidate for the constituency. The opposition did not contest the elections in 1970 because of its "no-vote campaign." Thus, the thirty-five PNM candidates, including Manning, were elected by acclaim. Since then, Manning has had an uninterrupted career in national politics in Trinidad and Tobago. He held several ministerial positions during the Eric Williams years. He was parliamentary secretary in the Ministry of Works, Transport, and Communications (1976–1978), minister for the public service in the Ministry of Finance, and minister of information in the Office of the Prime Minister. Manning also acted as minister of labor, social security, and cooperatives; external affairs; national security; and agriculture, lands, and fisheries. His most prestigious duty during his apprenticeship was representing the prime minister at the Zimbabwean independence celebrations in 1980.

One of Manning's most delicate assignments came when he was appointed as the minister in charge of Tobago affairs in the Prime Minister's Office when the Ministry of Tobago Affairs was disbanded in 1976. Tobagonians voted the PNM members out of office in the 1976 elections. In spite of his long career as a representative during Williams's tenure in office, Manning was never a member of the cabinet (his earlier positions were not cabinet-level ones). His first full ministerial office was his appointment to the Energy and Natural Resources portfolio during George Chambers's government (1981–1986). Manning served in this capacity until 1986, when the PNM was soundly defeated thirty-three to three by the National Alliance for Reconstruction (NAR), led by A. N. R. Robinson. Manning was one of the three PNM incumbents who held their seats. President Ellis Clarke then appointed him leader of the opposition. He held this office until 1990, when Basdeo Panday formed the United National Congress (UNC) and was appointed opposition leader.

Manning led the PNM's return to power in 1991, becoming the fourth prime minister of Trinidad and Tobago. He continued in this position until he called a hasty election in 1995 and lost the government to Panday's UNC. Both parties won seventeen seats, and President A.N.R. Robinson reportedly swung the two NAR seats in Tobago to the UNC. Manning remained in opposition until 2001, when another deadlocked result created a constitutional crisis. President Robinson appointed Manning prime minister, and in the following year he won the 2002 election, thus remaining the prime minister of Trinidad and Tobago. In the 2003 county council elections, Manning scored his most impressive political victory over the UNC. This achievement indicated that he had made inroads, even if only temporarily, into UNC strongholds.

See also Black Power Movement; Chambers, George; Clarke, Ellis; Peoples National Movement; Politics and Politicians in the Caribbean; Robinson, A. N. R.; Williams, Eric

■ ■ *Bibliography*

Beach, Silene. "The Political Life of Patrick Manning Since 1971." UC 300 Project, 1994.

Ryan, Selwyn. *Revolution and Reaction: A Study of Party Politics in Trinidad and Tobago 1970–1981*. St. Augustine, Trinidad: University of the West Indies, Institute of Social and Economic Research, 1982.

SELWYN H. H. CARRINGTON (2005)

MANUMISSION SOCIETIES

The manumission societies of the first half of the century after American independence were eventually eclipsed by the more radical antislavery organizations of the 1830s,

1840s, and 1850s. While the manumission societies looked to a day when the slave system would be uprooted and destroyed, they, unlike the "immediatists" in the camp of William Lloyd Garrison, were prepared to see emancipation proceed gradually. The rhetoric was also strikingly different. The later generation of abolitionists would denounce slave owners as "man-stealers" and "woman-whippers," while the earlier generation saw them not as moral degenerates but as misguided individuals who needed to be shown the error of their ways.

There was also the issue of who should participate in the work of emancipation. The manumission societies were exclusively male and exclusively white. There was none of the involvement of white women and African Americans that would characterize Garrisonian abolition and outrage its opponents. And yet, despite the differences, the older organizations prepared the way for their more outspoken successors, while the "gradualist" impulse was not entirely absent from the later phase of the antislavery struggle.

The Pennsylvania Abolition Society was a Quaker monopoly when it was established in 1775. It initially focused on rescuing free people unlawfully held as slaves. Moribund during the Revolutionary War, it was revived in 1784 by individuals from various religious denominations. In the interval Pennsylvania had enacted a gradual-abolition law, and monitoring its enforcement became a major part of the society's work. Other states and cities followed the lead of Pennsylvania. From 1784 to 1791 manumission societies were established in every state except the Carolinas and Georgia, and by 1814 societies could be found as far west as Tennessee and Kentucky.

The socioeconomic status of the abolitionists varied from region to region. In the North, Benjamin Franklin, John Jay, Alexander Hamilton, and Benjamin Rush joined the antislavery ranks. In contrast, the Kentucky Abolition Society was composed of men in "low or . . . middling circumstances" (Berlin, p. 28). The Maryland Abolition Society was made up of local merchants and skilled craftsmen—those least likely to use slaves or to lose money and prestige if slavery were abolished.

Policy on admitting slaveholders to membership varied. The Pennsylvania and Providence, Rhode Island, societies excluded them altogether. The Maryland society made them eligible for some offices. The Alexandria, Virginia, society admitted them, as did the New York Manumission Society. Indeed, as Shane White (1991) points out, some New Yorkers acquired slaves after joining. White contends that for some years the emphasis of the New Yorkers was not so much on challenging slavery as on removing the worst abuses in the slave system. They saw themselves as humane masters who were reacting against what they regarded as appalling acts of cruelty perpetrated by southern and Caribbean slave owners, and occasionally by those in their own state.

As the character of the membership varied, so did the goals of the individual societies. On some things they were agreed. The foreign slave trade must be outlawed; abusive treatment of slaves should be punished; where they had been enacted, manumission laws should be enforced. In New York, New Jersey, and the upper South, where gradual-emancipation laws had not been passed, the societies attempted to exert pressure on lawmakers. There were some notable successes, although it is debatable how much was due to the humanitarian impulse. In the upper South, economic dislocation after the Revolutionary War had brought changes in labor requirements and patterns of agricultural production. In 1782 Virginia legislators repealed the ban on private manumissions, and Maryland and Delaware quickly followed suit.

The manumission societies made efforts to address the plight of free people of color, since there was general agreement that their freedom must be safeguarded. Free blacks were offered advice about their conduct and encouraged to use their influence with slave kinfolk and friends to urge them to endure patiently. There was also practical assistance. The Pennsylvania and New York societies sponsored schools that trained a generation of African-American community leaders. The Pennsylvanians in particular developed a number of economic initiatives: would-be entrepreneurs received assistance, employment offices were established, and prosperous African Americans and sympathetic whites were encouraged to hire black indentured servants.

In 1791 there was a concerted effort by nine manumission societies to petition Congress to limit the foreign slave trade. When that effort failed, the New York society proposed the formation of a national convention to coordinate future action. In 1794 a convention was held in Philadelphia to organize the American Convention for Promoting the Abolition of Slavery and Improving the Condition of the African Race.

Conventions were annual until 1806, after which they became less frequent. At each meeting, member societies presented reports on their progress. Representatives from more distant societies were often unable to attend, but they submitted reports. There were contacts with foreign organizations, such as the London-based African Institution and Les Amis des Noirs in Paris. Delegates occasionally heard from influential African Americans, such as James Forten. As for policy decisions, in 1818 Forten denounced the work of the American Colonization Society (ACS) in an address to the convention. In 1821 the convention expressed its disapproval of the Liberian scheme, but in 1829, after many individual societies had already endorsed the ACS, the convention announced its approval of voluntary emigration.

Gradually the power and influence of the manumission societies declined. For more than two decades, the abolitionist impulse remained strong in the upper South. In 1827, for instance, the American Convention reported that while the free states had twenty-four societies, the slave states had 130. Many factors led to the demise of abolition societies in the region, including slave rebellions and the spread of the plantation economy south and west, which meant a lively market for "surplus" slaves.

In the North the crisis surrounding the Missouri Compromise took a toll. The Pennsylvania Abolition Society, for instance, suffered a wave of resignations in the early 1820s. As for the American Convention, it met for the last time in 1832 and was formally dissolved in 1838, by which time it had been supplanted by a new and, in many respects, more radical antislavery movement.

See also Abolition; Slavery

▪ ▪ *Bibliography*

Berlin, Ira. *Slaves without Masters: The Free Negro in the Antebellum South.* New York: Pantheon, 1974.

Fogel, Robert. *Without Consent or Contract.* New York: Norton, 1989.

Litwack, Leon. *North of Slavery: The Negro in the Free States, 1790–1860.* Chicago: University of Chicago Press, 1961.

Newman, Richard S. *The Transformation of American Abolitionism: Fighting Slavery in the Early Republic.* Chapel Hill: University of North Carolina Press, 2002.

Quarles, Benjamin. *Black Abolitionists.* New York: Oxford University Press, 1969.

White, Shane. *Somewhat More Independent: The End of Slavery in New York City, 1770–1810.* Athens: University of Georgia Press, 1991.

Zilversmit, Arthur. *The First Emancipation: The Abolition of Slavery in the North.* Chicago: University of Chicago Press, 1967.

JULIE WINCH (1996)
Updated by author 2005

MANZANO, JUAN FRANCISCO

C. 1797
1853

▌▐▐ ————————————————————

Born during a sugar boom that was transforming Cuba into the world's most valuable slave-based colony, Juan Francisco Manzano became not only a celebrated poet but also the author of the only autobiography ever written by a Latin American slave that was published before Emancipation. He learned to read and write while serving as a domestic slave in the urban households of the island's titled nobility. He published his first verses, *Poesías líricas,* in 1821. His talents attracted the attention of Domingo del Monte, the island's most influential intellectual, and in 1836, after hearing Manzano recite "Mis treinta años," a touching personal sonnet, del Monte and members of his literary circle raised a sum equivalent to $800 to purchase Manzano's freedom from María de la Luz de Zayas.

Encouraged by del Monte, Manzano had begun writing his autobiography the previous year. Only the first of two parts of the completed manuscript has survived. In 1839 del Monte handed an edited, fifty-two-page Spanish version of part one to Richard Robert Madden, a visiting British official and abolitionist, who seized on Manzano's words to promote the international antislavery crusade. In Britain, Madden translated the manuscript along with samples of Manzano's poetry for publication. He introduced Manzano's story in 1840 as "the most perfect picture of Cuban slavery that ever has been given to the world." Madden depicted a humble, unambiguous slave suffering unremitting humiliation and debasement by whites, although, in truth, he simplified Manzano's more complicated portrayal of himself and his insular world by omitting and reordering passages in the Spanish manuscript. Not until 1937, after Cuba's national library purchased a manuscript copy of part one of the autobiography once owned by del Monte, was a Spanish edition of the manuscript published for the first time.

Manzano speaks of the "vicissitudes" of life, as his fortunes swing between masters and mistresses of different temperament. The Marquesa de Jústiz de Santa Ana (Beatriz de Jústiz y Zayas) doted on Manzano in his early youth as if he were her own child. His subsequent mistress, the Marquesa de Prado-Ameno (María de la Concepción Aparicio del Manzano y Jústiz), capriciously brutalized him. For various missteps, Manzano suffered lashings, beatings, head shavings, imprisonment in stocks or makeshift jails, and transportation to the countryside for a stretch of hard time on a sugar plantation. He expressed ambivalent feelings for those above and below him in Cuba's graduated color hierarchy. He practiced Catholicism, and although he tended to identify with white culture, he remained lovingly attached to his mixed-race family members, from whom he was often distanced. While receiving punishment in the countryside, Manzano felt abandoned, like "a mulatto among blacks." He married twice, first to a woman of darker skin (Marcelina Campos). His second marriage in 1835 to a free woman of color (María del Rosario) provoked dissent from her kin who complained that Manzano's slave status and darker phenotype made him unworthy.

Anticipating that one day he would obtain his "natural right" to freedom, Manzano consciously developed the skills of an artist, tailor, chef, and artisan. Creating poetry helped ease the burdens of a delicate, intellectual man, and in his artistic endeavors, he acquired a substantial measure of self-redemption from the social death of slavery. Indeed, he ends part one of the manuscript in rebellion against his abusive treatment, fleeing to Havana on a stolen mount. In 1844 Spanish officials arrested Manzano along with thousands of other persons of color on suspicion of involvement in the alleged revolutionary Conspiracy of La Escalera. He remained in jail for about a year, a repressive experience that appears to have silenced his creative voice.

See also Autobiography, U.S.; Literature

▪ ▪ *Bibliography*

Manzano, Juan Francisco. *The Autobiography of a Slave; Autogiografía de un esclavo: A Bilingual Edition.* Translated by Evelyn Picon Garfield. Detroit: Wayne State University Press, 1996.

Mullen, Edward J. *The Life and Poems of a Cuban Slave: Juan Francisco Manzano, 1797–1854* [sic]. Hamden, Conn.: Archon Books, 1981.

ROBERT L. PAQUETTE (2005)

MARLEY, BOB

FEBRUARY 6, 1945
MAY 11, 1981

▌▐▐ ————————————————————

Robert (Bob) Nesta Marley was born under British colonialism in the parish of St. Ann's. In the 1950s he moved to the capital city of Kingston, where he resided in the working-class community of Trench Town, a cauldron of black redemptive ideas and practices, and the home of extraordinarily talented musicians. Marley and the musicians Neville O'Riley Livingston (Bunny Wailer), Peter McIntosh (Peter Tosh), and Junior Braithwaite, along with two female singers (Beverley Kelso and Cherry Smith) formed The Wailing Rudeboys, the forerunner of Bob Marley and the Wailers. Marley was particularly influenced by African-American rhythm and blues (R&B) vocal groups and by the culturally transgressive behavior of the Jamaican urban "Rudebwoys." By the 1960s in Jamaican popular musical culture, African-American R&B began to give way to ska, a musical form composed of jazz references and R&B lead singers' riffs, though the driving beat was faster and drew from the indigenous Jamaican mento musical tradition.

Marley's early musical and cultural influences were many. In the American state of Delaware, where he briefly lived, the civil rights movement and the musical talents of Curtis Mayfield and the Impression influenced him. In 1966, when he returned to Trench Town, Marley developed a relationship with a central figure of the Rastafari movement, Mortimer Planno. By then Rastafari had become the most important intellectual and musical influence on popular Jamaican music, and ska had changed into reggae. Marley's music represented one of reggae's most subtle and radical voices. For Marley, reggae was "the people's music . . . it was music about ourselves and history . . . things that they would never teach you in school" (Marr, 2000). In Jamaica, Marley became an important voice, and he deployed music as a form of social commentary and criticism against Jamaican postcolonial society. Using the philosophy of Rastafari, Marley composed music that carved out his place as a major figure in international black popular culture, and in world culture in general. He regarded himself as a revolutionary who used music as a weapon: "mi is a revolutionary that tek no bribe and fight single hand with music" (Marr, 2000).

Although credited with placing reggae as a distinct international musical form in twentieth-century popular culture, Marley's genius was that of a songwriter. Using the musical vocabulary of reggae, Marley's lyrics were derived from three sources: Jamaican proverbs, Rastafari philosophy, and an interpretation of the Bible. In black popular and intellectual traditions, he stands as a prophetic figure writing and singing about the experiences of black modernity—especially slavery, displacement, exile, colonialism, the meaning of Africa to the New World black population, and redemption. His enduring popularity resides in the fact that his musical vision represents a search for the meaning of freedom. As he sang in "Redemption Song": "Won't you help to sing these songs of freedom." Bob Marley died from cancer on May 11, 1981.

See also Rastafarianism; Reggae

■ ■ *Bibliography*

Bogues, Anthony. *Black Heretics, Black Prophets: Radical Political Intellectuals.* New York: Routledge, 2003.

Cooper, Carolyn. *Noises in the Blood: Orality, Gender, and the "Vulgar" Body of Jamaican Popular Culture.* Durham, N.C.: Duke University Press, 1995.

Davis, Stephen. *Bob Marley.* Rev. ed. Rochester, Vt.: Schenkman, 1990.

Dawes, Kwame. *Bob Marley: Lyrical Genius.* London: Sanctuary, 2003.

Marr, Jeremy, dir. and prod. *Rebel Music: The Bob Marley Story.* Antelope Productions, 2000.

DISCOGRAPHY (ALBUMS)

The Best of the Wailers. Kingston, Jamaica: Beverley's, 1971.

Catch a Fire. London: Island, 1973.

Burning. London: Island, 1973.

Natty Dread. London: Island, 1974.

Soul Rebels. Kingston, Jamaica: Lee Perry, 1975.

Soul Revolution. Kingston, Jamaica: Lee Perry, 1976.

RastaMan Vibration. London: Island, 1976.

Exodus. London: Island, 1977.

Kaya. London: Island, 1978.

Survival. London: Island, 1979.

Uprising. London: Island, 1980.

Confrontation. London: Island, 1983.

Songs of Freedom. London, Island, 1992

ANTHONY BOGUES (2005)

MAROON ARTS

❙❙❙

Throughout the Americas, from Brazil to the United States, there were Africans who escaped from slavery, banded together, and forged a new life beyond the reach of their former "masters." These people, and their present-day descendants, are known as Maroons. In many instances their communities were destroyed by colonial armies, but in others their long wars of liberation were finally successful, and they won their freedom (and territorial integrity) well before the general emancipation of slaves.

Among the numerous societies that have survived and retained a distinctive identity as Maroons (e.g., in Jamaica, Colombia, Brazil, Belize, Mexico, and the United States), those that were formed in the Dutch colony of Suriname, on the northeast shoulder of South America, have long been recognized as the largest and most culturally distinctive. Their population today is roughly 120,000. The six groups of Suriname Maroons (one of which crossed into neighboring French Guiana at the end of the eighteenth century), each with its own political leadership, share their history of rebellion and the main lines of their way of life in villages along the rivers of the rain forest, though they also differ culturally in many ways. The Saramaka and Matawai people of central Suriname speak variants of a language known to linguists as Saramaccan, while the Ndyuka, Paramaka, and Aluku people of eastern Suriname and western French Guiana speak a different language known as Ndyuka (closely related to the language of the smallest Suriname Maroon group, the Kwinti, the farthest to the west). The staple food of the eastern Maroons is cassava, and that of the central Maroons is rice. Musical forms, tale-telling genres, religious cults, patterns of wage labor, the division of labor by gender, and other aspects of life also vary significantly, especially between the central and eastern groups.

These Maroons (once known as "Bush Negroes") have a long-standing reputation as accomplished artists. Until recently this meant woodcarving, which is done by men, but the women's arts of patchwork, embroidery, and calabash carving are now recognized as well. As with other aspects of their cultures, the arts of the Maroons of central Suriname and those to the east display marked differences.

WOODCARVING

Maroon men have always carved a variety of objects needed for life in the rain forest, many of which they embellish and present as gifts to wives and lovers. The list is long: houses, canoes and paddles, stools, storage cabinets, trays, peanut-grinding boards, kitchen utensils, laundry beaters, combs, mortars and pestles, drums, and more. In the past they also created ingenious African-style door locks; today, the repertoire continues to expand—in the form of elaborately carved planks used for the back seats of motorcycles, for example. Central Maroons often embellish their carvings with decorative tacks, inlays of different woods, and *pyrogravure*. Eastern Maroons have developed a very different style that combines woodcarving with colorful designs executed with commercial paints.

In addition to producing carvings for use in the villages of the interior, some men (mainly Saramakas) have, since at least the early twentieth century, been making objects for tourists, selling them at roadside stands or, through middlemen, to souvenir stores in the coastal cities. Today, as Maroons adopt an increasingly Westernized

Saramaka openwork door, carved about 1930 by Heintje Schmidt. From Sally Price and Richard Price, Maroon Arts: Cultural Vitality in the African Diaspora, *Beacon Press, 1999.* COPYRIGHT © 1999 BY SALLY PRICE AND RICHARD PRICE

lifestyle, a few young artists (especially Alukus and Ndyukas in French Guiana) are becoming full-time professionals— painting on canvas, exhibiting their work in museums, and selling to an international market. These artists have endorsed a long-standing staple of received wisdom about Maroon art: the idea that it centers on "readable" motifs with symbolic meanings, thus turning a Western stereotype of "primitive art" into a lucrative interpretive discourse.

Early writing on Maroon woodcarving described it as an original African art form, and visitors to Maroon villages were quick to imagine direct formal continuities with the arts of Africa. Today, however, it is known that African influences in Maroon art are subtle underpinnings to a dynamic and constantly evolving art history; specific forms and decorative styles are more marked by change and innovation than by rigid fidelity to an African past. Long-term research by the French geographer Jean Hurault has documented four distinct styles of woodcarving through time among the Aluku Maroons, and parallel work among the Saramaka has also produced a definitive sequence of styles. In both cases, the earliest evidence of a woodcarving tradition among Maroons dates back only to about the mid-nineteenth century, when the relatively crude beginnings were made with tools that are still in use: knives, chisels, and compasses.

A quick summary of Saramaka woodcarving styles will illustrate the nature of change, conceptualized by Maroon woodcarvers as a march of progress—something along the lines of (as one elderly man explained it) the changes between automobiles of the 1920s and those of the late twentieth century. Carving during the second half of the nineteenth century, generally known to Saramakas as "owls' eyes" and "jaguars' eyes," consisted of crudely pierced circular and semicircular holes, crescent-shaped incisions, a small number of motifs in bas-relief, and limited use of decorative texturing. The next style—"monkey-tail" carving, which came into vogue in the early twentieth century—represented considerable technical refinement, with scrolls and spirals dominating the complex designs and the use of decorative tacks (purchased in coastal towns) expanding significantly. A third style—"wood-within-wood"—centered on sinuous patterns of interwoven bas-relief bands, combined with greater amounts of textural detail and a gradually diminishing use of tacks. Men carved wood-within-wood designs for much of the twentieth century, and they are still producing them, sometimes in conscious imitation of earlier designs, which they carefully copy from illustrations in books on Maroon art. Around the 1960s a fourth style, more angular than sinuous, was developed, as carvers began downplaying the prominence of bas-relief, increasing the role of incised lines (either running along the center of interwoven bands or creating nestled forms of concentric shapes), and allowing crosshatching and other texturing patterns to overtake piercing and tacks in importance.

Textile Arts

Maroon clothing has, from the first, been sewn from commercial-trade cotton rather than locally woven fabric. The cloth was first obtained via raids on the plantations during the wars of liberation. Following the eighteenth-century peace treaties, it was received as part of the tribute paid to the Maroons by the colonists. After the general emancipation of slaves in the colony, when Maroon men began conducting wage-labor trips to the coast, often for several years at a stretch, their earnings provided the cash to stock up on cloth, tools, kitchenware, kerosene, salt, and a variety of manufactured necessities (which today include outboard motors, tape recorders, and chain saws) for life back in the villages.

A Saramaka comb, collected in the late 1920s. COPYRIGHT © 1999 BY SALLY PRICE AND RICHARD PRICE. REPRODUCED BY PERMISSION OF THE AMERICAN MUSEUM OF NATURAL HISTORY.

In Maroon villages, the basic items of dress are breech cloths for men and boys, wrap-skirts for women, and pubic aprons for teenage girls, supplemented by varying amounts of ritual jewelry, such as protective armbands and necklaces. In the early years, clothing for the upper body was minimal, but, over time, shoulder capes became more and more standard for men. Women used some of the imported cotton for their own wrap-skirts, which they simply hemmed on the edges and secured at the waist with a sash or kerchief. During the second half of the nineteenth century, they began to embellish the men's monochrome or subtly striped capes with curvilinear embroidery designs, sometimes supplemented with patchwork or appliqué. The contours were first sketched out with a piece of charcoal, and then executed in thread that had been laboriously extracted from lengths of cloth. The dominant colors were red, white, and black.

With the passage of time, patchwork and appliqué spread onto the whole garment, and in the early twentieth century capes were being sewn in vibrant compositions made up of monochrome fabric (still predominately in red, white, and black) cut into small rectangles and triangles and sewn into strips, which were then joined together to form the whole. Later, when coastal stores began stocking colorfully striped cloth, women used it for their own unembellished skirts, turning the leftover edge trimmings into a new art of narrow-strip patchwork, mainly for men's capes; this style has reminded many observers of West African kente cloth, even though it was invented many generations after the Maroons' last contact with Africa.

Cross-stitch embroidery, introduced by missionaries, was the rage for much of the second half of the twentieth century, but it in no way signaled the end of internal change in Maroon textile arts. New forms, such as elaborate yarn crochet-work and sinuous designs in reverse-appliqué, marked the 1990s, and a decade later men's capes were being made with an innovative double-layer technique never seen before.

Calabash Carving

The Maroon art of carving bowls from the fruit of the calabash tree has, over time, moved from men's hands to those of women, and from the exterior surface of the fruit to the interior surface of the shell that remains once the fruit's pulp has been removed. Nineteenth-century calabashes were often made into covered containers for storing rice and other foodstuffs, and these *apaki*, which displayed geometric designs incised and textured with men's wood-carving tools such as compasses and chisels, continued to be made throughout the twentieth century. Fairly early on,

however, women began experimenting with the unused interiors of the bowls, making crude scratchings on them with pieces of broken glass. Their technical mastery of this recycled tool quickly evolved, producing a new, aesthetically organic art totally unlike the men's rigidly geometric style. The designs of Eastern Maroon women center on convex forms defined by scraped-away borders, and those of central Maroon women on concave shapes defined by internal scraping. Some calabash carvings can be read in terms of either their convex or their concave forms, suggesting the possibility of a common beginning for the art of the two regions, followed by a gradual divergence in the definition of figure and ground. Calabashes carved by women provide a range of objects, from spoons and ladles to bowls for rinsing rice and drinking water. The most elegantly carved are served to groups of men who eat together, providing both drinking cups and bowls for washing hands at the end of the meal.

Performance Arts

Maroons' appreciation of novelty and innovative ideas, which runs through the entire history of their visual arts, characterizes the verbal and performative arts as well. Speech itself is a creative domain, as cohorts of young men communicate among themselves in play languages they have invented, as older folks hone the fine art of speaking in esoteric proverbs, as women assign fanciful names to new cloth patterns from the coast, and as everyone enjoys mimicry, ellipsis, and witty manipulations of normal speech. Popular songs (whether, for example, in the form of Saramaka *seketi*, Aluku *awawa*, or Ndyuka *aleke)* are created spontaneously, and change as rapidly as popular music in the United States.

Large-scale communal events, especially certain stages of the long and complex process that ushers a deceased person into the realm of the ancestors, provide an occasion for the performance of secular song and dance, a range of drumming traditions (including appropriate phrases on the *apinti,* or "talking drum"), and tales that weave back and forth from teller and listeners, with the narration punctuated by song and dance. Different classes of deities (warrior gods, forest spirits, snake-gods, and more) also participate, manifesting themselves through spirit possession. Special ritual singing is performed, and the ancestors are addressed through prayer. Culinary delicacies are provided for the whole crowd, and apart from close family members, who wear the drab garments of mourning, participants dress in the latest fashions. Romantic encounters are an expected part of the festivities. A large, joyful multimedia celebration stands as the community's ultimate honor to a departed brother or sister.

A Saramaka round-top stool, carved 1997 by Menie Betian. From *Sally Price and Richard Price,* Maroon Arts: Cultural Vitality in the African Diaspora, *Beacon Press, 1999.* COPYRIGHT © 1999 BY SALLY PRICE AND RICHARD PRICE

LIFE BEYOND THE RAIN FOREST

During the final decades of the twentieth century, political events in Suriname and French Guiana brought dramatic changes to the Maroons. Suriname moved away from its ties to Europe by becoming an independent republic, and French Guiana moved closer to Europe through rapid development in connection with the establishment of the Guiana Space Center, from which the European Space Agency launches satellites, in 1968. A six-year civil war in Suriname, and the consequent exodus of thousands of Maroons to French Guiana, produced further upheavals. The territorial sovereignty, political independence, cultural integrity, and economic opportunities of Maroons, not to mention basic issues of health and personal dignity, have fallen victim to these developments.

Adaptations in the artistic life of Maroons have been just one aspect of the larger adjustments being made. Woodcarving has taken a turn toward commercialization, and the previously unchallenged assumption that every man would be able to carve everything from combs to canoes is on the way out. Women have, by force of necessity,

become increasingly independent, supporting themselves in coastal settings through the sale of their art or through jobs as domestics. More generally, the market in Maroon art, formerly a male domain, has come to include women's work as well, with the formation of cooperatives promoting the sale of embroidered hammocks, appliquéd beach-chair seats, carved calabashes, and more. And significant numbers of Maroons now live in Europe (especially the Netherlands), where they hold jobs, for example as school-teachers or nurses.

Does this mean that aesthetic creativity, verbal play, richly elaborated oratory, the role of the ancestors, and a sense of community are things of a traditional past? No, at least not for a long time to come. The cultural life of Maroons has always displayed (indeed, thrived on) resilience and adaptability. From apartment blocks in Rotterdam to thatch-roofed houses on the upper Suriname River, Maroons are confronting the ever-increasing threats to their cultural life with the same strong sense of identity that allowed their early ancestors to carve out their independence against overwhelming odds.

See also Art; Healing and the Arts in Afro-Caribbean Cultures; Maroon Wars; Performance Art; Runaway Slaves in Latin America and the Caribbean

■ ■ *Bibliography*

Bilby, Kenneth. "Introducing the Popular Music of Suriname." In *Caribbean Currents: Caribbean Music from Rumba to Reggae,* edited by Peter Manuel, Kenneth Bilby, and Michael Largey. Philadelphia: Temple University Press. 1995.

Bilby, Kenneth. "'Roots Explosion': Indigenization and Cosmopolitanism in Contemporary Surinamese Popular Music." *Ethnomusicology* 43 (1999): 256–296.

"Maroons in the Americas." *Cultural Survival Quarterly,* special winter issue (2002).

Herskovits, Melville J., and Frances S. Herskovits. *Rebel Destiny: Among the Bush Negroes of Dutch Guiana.* New York: McGraw-Hill, 1934.

Hurault, Jean. *Africains de Guyane: la vie matérielle des Noirs réfugiés de Guyane.* Paris-La Haye: Mouton, 1970.

Price, Richard. *Alabi's World.* Baltimore, Md.: Johns Hopkins University Press, 1990.

Price, Richard. *First-Time: The Historical Vision of an African American People,* 2d ed. Chicago: University of Chicago Press, 2002.

Price, Richard, ed. *Maroon Societies: Rebel Slave Communities in the Americas,* 3d ed. Baltimore, Md.: Johns Hopkins University Press, 1996.

Price, Richard, and Sally Price. *Two Evenings in Saramaka.* Chicago: University of Chicago Press, 1991.

Price, Richard, and Sally Price. *Enigma Variations.* Cambridge, Mass.: Harvard University Press, 1995.

Price, Richard, and Sally Price. *The Root of Roots: Or, How Afro-American Anthropology Got Its Start.* Chicago: Prickly Paradigm Press, 2003.

Price, Richard, and Sally Price, eds. *Stedman's Surinam: Life in an Eighteenth-Century Slave Society.* Baltimore, Md.: Johns Hopkins University Press, 1992.

Price, Sally. *Co-Wives and Calabashes,* 2d ed. Ann Arbor: University of Michigan Press, 1993.

Price, Sally, and Richard Price. *Maroon Arts: Cultural Vitality in the African Diaspora.* Boston: Beacon Press, 1999.

Thoden van Velzen, H. U. E., and W. van Wetering. *The Great Father and the Danger: Religious Cults, Material Forces, and Collective Fantasies in the World of the Surinamese Maroons.* Dordrecht, the Netherlands: Foris, 1988.

SALLY PRICE (2005)

MAROON SOCIETIES IN THE CARIBBEAN

The term *marronage*—derived from the Spanish word *cimarron,* originally applied to escaped cattle living in the wild—came to refer exclusively to the phenomenon of persons running away to escape from the bonds of enslavement, which was almost universal wherever plantation slavery existed in the Americas. From the early days of slavery, French commentators distinguished between *petit marronage,* a short-term and temporary running away of small numbers of slaves, and the far more serious *grand marronage,* involving large, self-sustaining, and often long-lasting African-American communities that were adept in guerrilla tactics of self-defense and even threatened the safety of the colonial plantation regimes.

MAROON SOCIETIES

It was almost axiomatic that *grand marronage* occurred whenever and wherever there was a sufficient number of willing and capable escapees and suitable refuges, and it succeeded for long periods when such persons and locations fulfilled certain basic criteria. Runaway communities established themselves in areas of forest, swamp, or mountains, which provided ample concealment and were easily defended in guerrilla warfare. These locales also provided adequate sustenance, in the way of wild fauna and flora, the running of semi-wild stock, and forms of shifting (though far from casual) cultivation. Generically referred to as Maroon settlements in the anglophone literature, such communities were variously known in different parts of Latin America as *palenques, quilombos, cumbes, mocambos, mambises* or *ladeiras.* All, however, exhibited essential similarities.

Leadership, community organization, and demographic factors were as vital as ingenuity, determination, and hardihood in keeping these settlements going. In the earliest years, and in areas where Amerindians were leading the struggle against European colonial incursions, African runaways often pooled resources and skills with the pre-Columbian natives, gradually miscegenating, and even becoming dominant, among such obdurate and effective resisters as the "Black Caribs" (Garifuna) of Dominica, St. Vincent, and Honduras; the Afro-Indians of the "Miskito Shore" of Central America; and the Seminoles of early-nineteenth-century Florida. Just as often, though, Amerindians did not mix with African-American Maroons, and at times they even allied themselves with the colonial regimes as runaway slave catchers. Accordingly, the majority of successful Maroon communities (most famously, the long-lived *quilombo* of Palmares in Portuguese Brazil and the Djuka and Saramaka of Dutch Suriname) as far as possible retained the lineaments of a transplanted African culture, including their language, customs, beliefs, material crafts, and foodways, as well as fighting modes and, where and when it was preferable, opportunistic diplomacy.

Given the calculated policy of the colonial regimes to mix African slaves as far as possible, the Africanness of Maroon communities was more generic than specific to any one area of origin. Large concerted groups of runaways were rarely of the same African ethnicity, and they were in the process of forging an Afro-Creole identity that, especially as time went on, owed as much to the plantations from which they had escaped and the American mainland or Caribbean environment in which they now lived. For example, they usually employed a creolized version of the language of the dominant colonial power as a *lingua franca,* and they showed great flexibility in adapting to American cultivation methods and cultigens. However, the leadership of runaways, warriors, and nascent Maroon polities did tend to devolve on to individuals who came from, or borrowed the characteristics of, the most stalwart and obdurate of African peoples. Most notable of these were the Akan speakers of the Ashanti region of modern Ghana—usually called Coromantees—who had a long and distinguished reputation as warriors, were adept at subsistence in the forest, and had legendary skills in the arts of guerrilla warfare, including concealment, camouflage, rapid movement, long-distance communication (by drum, conch shell, and the cowhorn *abeng*), and the expert use of firearms.

No such community, however, could sustain itself in a posture of perpetual war, and the relationship between all Maroon groups and the dominant plantation regimes

Fugitive slaves, known as maroons, gather around a campfire by a river bank. *The image is from* Harper's Weekly, *c. 1860.* PHOTOGRAPHS AND PRINTS DIVISION, SCHOMBURG CENTER FOR RESEARCH IN BLACK CULTURE, THE NEW YORK PUBLIC LIBRARY, ASTOR, LENOX AND TILDEN FOUNDATIONS.

was necessarily closer and more symbiotic than some commentators have been willing to acknowledge. Few, if any, Maroon communities were totally sundered from the colonial plantation economy and society. Though slave families often ran away together, the majority of slave runaways were mature males. To sustain Maroon communities over a long period, it was, of course, vital to achieve a viable demographic balance, and slave plantations were a necessary source of nubile females and children, as well as mature male warrior recruits.

Plantations and colonial towns were also the necessary sources of those commodities which the Maroons could not, easily or at all, produce or manufacture for themselves, such as stock animals and other foodstuffs, salt, cloth, needles, tools, metals and (most vital and dangerous of all) firearms and gunpowder. These were often captured, looted, or rustled, but to a remarkable degree they were also obtained through trade. In any case, quite

apart from the geographical limits imposed on Maroon communities situated on islands, it was inevitable that the majority of Maroon and colonial communities were located within easy reach of each other, with plantation provision grounds on the margins of estates and the market-places of colonial seaside towns becoming complex meeting grounds and crossing points—constituting what has been termed a "semi-permeable membrane" in the structure of colonial slave societies. In the Caribbean, a remarkable number of disaffected slaves "ran away" by sea, and Maroon communities often demonstrated great ingenuity and skill in moving and communicating between islands and the mainland by canoe—making a hitherto under-studied category of "maritime Maroons."

Even more complicating were the formal or informal diplomatic arrangements that Maroons and colonists forged, either from necessity or through mutual convenience. Colonial regimes attempted to extirpate Maroons wherever they could, and Maroon communities were often prepared to fight to the death rather than surrender. But in cases so numerous as almost to constitute a rule, the sides were persuaded by stalemated or unsustainable fighting to negotiate treaties of accommodation. Typically, Maroon communities that were already recognized polities under acknowledged leaders were granted lands, limited rights of self-government, minimal oversight, and permission to trade—in return for promises of peace and help in the return of further runaways, and in the event of foreign attacks.

Such treaties, however superficially generous their wording, were predictably slanted in favor of the imperial regimes that wrote them, and they were notoriously reversible once the balance of power shifted once again. The Maroon communities—like those of Jamaica, which retained their political and cultural (if not economic) autonomy through the prolonged turmoil of the Age of Revolution, slave emancipation, and plantation decline into the era of political independence—are therefore magnificent manifestations of the will and ability of oppressed peoples to resist the dominant tides of history, to make a life of their own, and to endure.

THE JAMAICAN MAROONS

Of the dozens of Maroon communities, containing thousands of individuals and lasting hundreds of years (notably in Brazil, Colombia, Venezuela, Ecuador, the Guianas, and the islands of the Greater Antilles), and the almost innumerable lesser examples of *grand marronage* occurring on the margins of plantation economies throughout colonial America, those of Jamaica are probably the best known and the most quintessential. They exhibit and illustrate virtually all the general features and phases of Maroon history and society already mentioned, and they extend over the five hundred years from the coming of the first European colonists up to modern times, long after colonial independence.

Jamaica is not a huge island (some 140 miles east to west and 45 miles at most from north to south) but its topography and climate made it almost ideal as a Maroon habitat. Though its well-watered plains and interior valleys are extremely fertile and suitable for plantations, especially those growing sugar, its predominantly limestone geology provided rocky and forested refuges on the very margins of the cultivable land. Even more important than this general feature, Jamaica also possessed two major areas of awesome impenetrability; the vertiginous Blue Mountains (peaking at 7,400 feet) in the windward Northeast, and the 500 square miles of confusingly jumbled "Cockpit Country," stretching over much of the central and northwestern

sections of the island. Though the one was as isolated and easily defensible as the other, it was not just the differences in these two habitats, but the difficulties of access to and communication between them, that made for subtle variations between the Jamaican Windward and Leeward Maroons, as well as the small but significant differences in their histories.

The history of Jamaican Maroons dates back to the takeover and minimal exploitation of the island by the Spaniards in the early sixteenth century, but it was substantially shaped by the English conquest of Jamaica in 1655 and the subsequent development of slave plantations. There were troublesome *palenques* in the Jamaican backwoods throughout the Spanish period, and the last settlements of the Amerindian aboriginals probably survived in the Blue Mountains at least until 1600. In 1655 the Spanish authorities positively encouraged their black slaves and mulatto freedmen to take to the woods to share the resistance to the English invasion. But the most notable *palenquero*, Juan de Bolas (alias Juan Lubolo), whose "polink" was on the southern slope of Lluidas Vale in the center of the island, set a local precedent by siding with the invaders in return for a title for himself and virtual autonomy for his followers. De Bolas assisted in the final defeat and expulsion of the Spaniards in 1660, but was himself ambushed and killed by the unyielding "Varmahaly Negroes" led by his rival Juan de Serras in 1663.

Because of de Bolas's evident affinity for Jamaica and his accommodationist tactics the novelist Victor Stafford Reid characterized him as the first authentic Jamaican in 1976. However, de Bolas has, perhaps understandably, never been accorded the official modern title of Jamaican Hero. More fortunate have been the less equivocal leaders of the subsequent resistance to the spread of the colonial slave plantation economy—the Coromantees Nanny, Cuffee (Kofi) and Quao (Kwahu) of the Windward Maroons, and Cudjoe (Kojo) and his brothers Accompong and Johnny of the Leeward Maroons—Of these, the almost legendary Nanny is the sole woman elected to the official pantheon of Jamaican National Heroes.

The spread of the Jamaican plantation economy was slowed both by the topography and the difficulties of preventing the necessary slave laborers from escaping and defending themselves in the interior fastnesses. Over more than a half century, the Jamaican Maroons were steadily reinforced by runaways, including some entire plantation slave populations rebelling and fleeing together, such as those of Lobby's Estate (1673), Guanaboa Vale (1685), Sutton's (1690) and Down's Estate (1725). By the 1720s the Maroons came to be numbered in their thousands rather than hundreds. In the East, a fairly loose confederacy of Maroon bands entrenched themselves on the almost unassailable northern slopes of the Blue Mountains, centered on the fortified "town" named for Nanny (alias Grandy Nanni), to whom tradition accords the combined roles of a Coromantee warrior queen and priestess. Even more formidable was the force of Ashanti-style warriors forged by the autocratic Cudjoe (son of the leader of the Sutton's revolt of 1690), whose two townships on the western edge of the Cockpit Country (named for Cudjoe and his brother Accompong) were backed by the secret recesses of Petty River Bottom deep in the Cockpits themselves.

During the lull in international fighting sometimes called the era of Walpole's Peace, the British plantocratic regime and imperial authorities determined in the 1730s to implement the forward policy against the Jamaican Maroons that constituted the First Maroon War. Nanny Town was captured with great difficulty and destroyed in 1734, but its inhabitants simply dispersed, while the resistance led by Quao and Cudjoe proved even more stubborn and successful. So effective were Maroon tactics and marksmanship (along with the other hazards of fighting in the bush) that it was said that the casualties among the white regular soldiers and militiamen outnumbered those of the Maroons by ten to one, with an almost unimaginable ratio of five soldiers killed for every one wounded.

By 1739, both sides had had enough of the fighting. Urged on by the imperial authorities, the colonial government sued for peace, though craftily skewing the written terms to their longer-term advantage. On March 1, 1739, in one of the most momentous if controversial episodes in Jamaican history, after ten days of polite but cautious negotiations, "Captain" Cudjoe signed a fifteen-clause treaty with the representatives of the colonial regime. A general amnesty was declared, even for those who had fled to Cudjoe in the previous two years, and, with some exaggeration, Cudjoe's community was promised a state of "perfect liberty and freedom." Cudjoe's followers were granted the freehold of 1,500 acres surrounding their main settlement (renamed Trelawny Town after the colonial governor), with the right to run stock and grow all but plantation crops and trade them in the colonial markets. To facilitate communications, the Maroons agreed to cut and maintain roadways into their territory. Cudjoe and his successors were accorded the status of magistrate (to judge all but capital cases), but they were to be monitored by two white superintendants, one resident in Trelawny Town, the other in Accompong Town. Most important of all, Cudjoe's people pledged not to harbor, and to return, all future runaways, to serve on the colonial side in the event of any slave insurrection or foreign invasion, and to parade once a year before the colonial governor.

Though Cudjoe's Treaty established a pattern based on the colonial regime's principle of dividing the opposition, it specifically applied only to Cudjoe's people, rather than to the Jamaican Maroons as a whole. Four months later, a similar (though slightly tougher) treaty was signed with Quao. No formal treaty was made with Nanny and her faithful adherents. Instead, in 1740 Nanny and her immediate followers were given a freehold grant of 500 acres at New Nanny Town (later renamed Moore Town after another governor), worded exactly as if Nanny had been a normal colonial immigrant with her household—with the sole exception of a rider that Nanny, her people, and heirs "shall upon any insurrection mutiny rebellion or invasion which may happen in our island during her residence on the same be ready to serve us . . . in arms upon Command of our Governor or Commander in Chief" (Jamaica Archives, Patents 1741, quoted in Craton, p. 94). Not surprisingly, this arrangement has been open to countervailing interpretations; on the one side it has been seen as a recognition of success and a charter of independence, and on the other as a signal of willing integration into the colonial system. The truth surely lies somewhere in the middle: a mutual agreement to seek peaceful coexistence and even cooperation in an area of Jamaica more suited to a peasant lifestyle than to slave plantations.

Despite plantocratic unease at times of internal and external threat, the Jamaican Maroons remained remarkably faithful to the terms of their treaties. Cudjoe proved a particularly trustworthy (and picturesque) character in western Jamaica, promoted to the title of colonel for his contribution to the suppression of the Coromantee uprising of 1742 and providing invaluable help in defeating the widespread rebellion led by Tacky in 1760. Edward Long gave a famous account of the annual display of acrobatic martial tactics and marksmanship by the Maroons before Governor Lyttelton in Spanish Town in 1764, though it may have seemed as much a warning as a reassurance to some spectators. As late as the Morant Bay Rebellion of 1865, the descendants of Nanny called the Hayfield Maroons disappointed the rebels and sided with the authorities, actually tracking down the rebel leader Paul Bogle and handing him over to the regime for execution.

However, the Jamaican authorities demonstrated much less fidelity to the letter and spirit of the Maroon treaties than did the Maroons, most notoriously provoking the limited conflict in western Jamaica in 1795-1796 referred to as the Second Maroon War. The general cause was the competition between the western planters and the expanding population of Maroons unrealistically constrained by the original grant of 1,500 acres of indifferent land. But the situation was exacerbated by the plantocratic regime's paranoid response to the threat of revolutionary infection from the events in the Americas, Haiti, and France, and by its determination to take advantage of the division and perceived weakness of the Leeward Maroons following the death of Cudjoe and his brothers.

A first crisis occurred in 1776, when almost all the slaves in Hanover parish plotted to rebel, seizing the opportunity of the military distractions in North America, and it was rumored (by rebels and regime alike) that they were to be aided by the Trelawny Town Maroons. This panic passed and the plot was savagely repressed. However, mutual distrust and tension gradually increased over the following two decades. This reached a critical level early in 1795, when several Maroons were imprisoned and flogged (ignominiously by slaves) on the orders of the civil authorities in Montego Bay and a newly appointed superintendent—replacing one more popular and diplomatic—was driven by force from Trelawny Town. This occurred at the same time that the government was receiving word that French agents were infiltrating Jamaica to stir up a Maroon revolution in conjunction with the Haitian slaves. The choleric and militaristic Governor Lord Balcarres decided on a draconian policy, declaring martial law, recalling troops from Haiti, and clapping in irons six Leeward Maroon leaders on their way to Spanish Town to lodge complaints.

The Trelawny Maroons, chiefly under the resolute leadership of Leonard Parkinson, demonstrated that they had not lost all of their traditional guerrilla skills. They might well have prevailed had they been able to raise up the rest of the Maroons (even those of Accompong Town sided with the government), and had the regime not brought in expert slave-hunters and a hundred fierce hunting dogs from Cuba. Even then, the military commander in the field, Major General George Walpole, was so impressed by Maroon successes that he was prepared to offer terms similar to those negotiated with Cudjoe in 1739. Balcarres and the Jamaican legislators, however, decided otherwise. Parkinson and more than 500 Trelawny Maroons, over Walpole's disgusted objections, were tricked into deportation, first to Nova Scotia and then, four years later, to Sierra Leone—where, along with shiploads of "black loyalists" from the American War of Independence, they formed part of Sierra Leone's ultimately ill-starred "Creole" elite. Thus ended the armed resistance of the Jamaican Maroons to British imperialism, but not the proud, if controversial, history of the distinctive Jamaican Maroon communities.

JAMAICAN MAROONS TODAY

Those regarding themselves as true Maroons living in Jamaica at the beginning of the twenty-first century are said to total 5,000, (out of a resident Jamaican population of some 2.5 million), with perhaps twice as many relatives and descendants widely dispersed abroad, mainly in the United States, Canada, and the United Kingdom. Those Maroons still living in Jamaica remain concentrated in four scattered small villages: the Windward descendants of Nanny and Quao live mainly in three of these villages, in Moore Town and Charles Town in Portland parish and Scott's Hall in St. Mary's; while the genetic and spiritual descendants of Cudjoe and his brothers live at Accompong, in the parish of St. Elizabeth (Trelawny Town having been destroyed during the Second Maroon War). Each settlement claims a large degree of autonomy from the rest of Jamaica, including their own distinctive flag, the custom of electing their own "Colonel" and council for five year terms, the right to legislate and police themselves, and freedom from most forms of Jamaican taxation.

But the status of the Maroon villages as political and cultural enclaves within Jamaica faces ever increasing obstacles, the chief of which are the difficulties of sustaining economic self-sufficiency and an acceptable level of material well-being in a country that, though poor and overcrowded, has aspirations towards modernization. Maroons, whose settlements are at least as materially deprived as the majority of Jamaican interior villages, are attracted by the marginally better facilities and opportunities available in Jamaican towns and cities, and by the even greater promise of life in developed economies abroad.

The Jamaican Maroons have always expressed a fierce pride in having escaped from the bonds of slavery, in never having been defeated in warfare against the forces of imperialism, and in retaining strong (if creolized) vestiges of their original Afro-Caribbean culture. However, the long-term survival of Jamaican Maroon identity is seemingly more assured by at least three more or less extraneous factors. The first is the perhaps surprising, though convenient, tendency of Jamaicans as a whole (overwhelmingly the descendants of slaves) to forget that Maroon survival and autonomy were largely bought at the price of cooperation with and accommodation to the colonial regime, and to co-opt the Maroons' history as a symbol of a more general drive towards political and spiritual independence by Jamaica and Jamaicans at large. Added to this are the ever widening interest of outsiders in the Maroons and their traditional lifeways as cultural phenomena, as well as the exploitation of this heritage by the Jamaican government through tourism.

All in all, there has been a steadily escalating interest in the Jamaican Maroons among foreign visitors, as well as other Jamaicans, since the 1960s. Put most broadly, this has resulted from the confluence of a novel academic concern for the history and anthropology of resistance, and from a hunger on the part of people emerging from colonialism to recover (even to reinvent) the lives, lifestyles, and achievements of the pioneers in the struggle to avoid cultural submergence, to win freedom, and to help shape an authentic national identity. One early manifestation of this trend was the establishment of the permanent Sam Streete Maroon Museum at Moore Town in the 1960s; another is the collections of audio and visual material begun by Kenneth M. Bilby in the late 1970s. Even more important have been the comparative studies, symposia and displays sponsored by the Smithsonian Museum, the Library of Congress, and UNESCO, with the eager cooperation of the Institute of Jamaica and the Jamaican Ministries of Education and Tourism. An outstanding example of this development was the publication in July 2004 by the Smithsonian of a fascinating audiovisual presentation, hosted by the Institute of Jamaica under the title "The Musical Heritage of the Moore Town Maroons: An International Masterpiece."

Most dynamic of all, however, has been the hugely expanding popularity of the annual Cudjoe Day (or Treaty Day) celebrations held at Accompong on the weekend nearest to January 6, and the parallel but distinct Quao Day (or Kwahu Day) celebrations hosted by the Windward Maroons each year around June 23. In January 2003, no less than 25,000 persons (the great majority of them Jamaicans) were said to have ventured to remote Accompong Village (population 500) for the annual weekend celebrations. In June of the same year, the Quao Day festivities at Charles Town (more accessible than either Moore Town or Accompong to the Jamaican capital) were distinguished by the participation of thirty delegates from the Kwahu-Ashanti region of Ghana, along with a number of visitors from the Ghanaian community in the United States.

As described by its promoters in their publicity for the event, the 2003 Charles Town occasion was planned to include an interesting cultural melange of generically Afro-Jamaican as well as purely Maroon elements: "The Quao Day celebrations this year will begin at sundown on Friday, June 20 and culminate at midnight on June 23, Quao Day. . . . The festivities will involve drumming, dancing, arts and crafts, culinary exhibitions (featuring Jamaican culinary queen Ma Mable from the Charles Town Maroons), story telling, symposiums on Maroon medicine and use of herbs, sports, nature tours, and the display of rituals and artifacts from the Maroon communities of Charles Town, Moore Town and Scotts Hall and the smaller Maroon communities in Portland, St. Mary, St. Catherine and St. Thomas. The Saturday night will feature a live concert with invited performers Michael Rose, former lead singer of Black Uhuru, Abijah, Sister Carol, Carl Dawkins, the Mystic Revelation of Rastafari and L'cadco Dance Company" (none of the latter specifically Maroons).

At the equally successful Charles Town festivities in June 2004—which included presentations by Carey and Beverly Robinson, two of the leading popular historians of the Maroons; Barry Chevannes, head of the Department of Social Studies at the University of the West Indies; the Rastafarian poet Mutubaru; and Ted Emmanuel, "a well known herbalist"—the Jamaican prime minister P.J. Patterson gave a careful and politic summary of the way that the Maroon experience had been incorporated into (not to say appropriated by) the history and culture of Jamaica as a whole. "The history of the Maroons in Jamaica is a significant feature of our heritage and the spirit of these ancestors is evident in many aspects of our daily lives," he declared. "It is fitting therefore that we recognize their contribution to the early development of Jamaica and shows evidence for the rich legacy that they bequeathed to us in dance, music, cuisine, craft and many other areas of natural life."

See also Emancipation in Latin America and the Caribbean; Maroon Arts; Nanny of the Maroons; Palenque San Basilio; Palmares; Runaway Slaves in Latin America and the Caribbean; San Lorenzo de los Negros

■ ■ *Bibliography*

Agorsah, E. Kofi, ed. *Maroon Heritage: Archaeological, Ethnographic, and Historical Perspectives.* Kingston, Jamaica: Canoe Press, 1994.

Aptheker, Herbert. "Maroons within the Present Limits of the United States." *Journal of Negro History,* 24 (1939): 167–184.

Brathwaite, Edward K. *Wars of Respect: Nanny, Sam Sharpe, and the Struggle for People's Liberation.* Kingston, Jamaica: Agency for Public Information, 1977.

Campbell, Mavis C. *The Maroons of Jamaica, 1655–1796: A History of Resistance, Collaboration, and Betrayal.* Granby, Mass.: Bergin & Garvey, 1988.

Craton, Michael. *Testing the Chains: Resistance to Slavery in the British West Indies.* Ithaca, N.Y.: Cornell University Press, 1982.

Hall, Neville A.T. "Maritime Maroons: Grand Marronage from the Danish West Indies." *William and Mary Quarterly* 42 (1985) 476–498.

Kopytoff, Barbara K. "Jamaican Maroon Political Organization: The Effects of the Treaties." *Social and Economic Studies* 25, no. 2 (1976): 87–105.

Price, Richard. *Maroon Societies: Rebel Slave Communities in the Americas*, 3d ed. Baltimore, Md.: Johns Hopkins University Press, 1996.

Robinson, Carey. *The Iron Thorn: The Defeat of the British by the Jamaican Maroons.* Kingston, Jamaica: Kingston Publishers Ltd., 1993.

Schwartz, Stuart B. "Resistance and Accommodation in Eighteenth-Century Brazil." *Hispanic American Historical Review* 57 (1977): 69–81.

Walker, James W. St. G. *The Black Loyalists: The Search for a Promised Land in Nova Scotia and Sierra Leone.* 1783–1870. New York: Africana Publishers, 1976. Reprint, Toronto: University of Toronto Press, 1992.

MICHAEL CRATON (2005)

MARRANT, JOHN

JUNE 15?, 1755
C. 1791

❚❚❚

What little is known about the writer John Marrant's life comes mainly from his publications. Born to free black parents in New York, he was four years old when his father died. His mother moved with her four children to the South. There they lived in Saint Augustine, Florida; Georgia; and Charleston, South Carolina, where Marrant went to school. He became interested in music and was influenced by Rev. George Whitefield, the English preacher of the Great Awakening. For some time Marrant lived among the Cherokee Indians, and he learned their language and converted some to Christianity. During the Revolutionary War, he served in the British Royal Navy, spending almost seven years at sea.

After his discharge, Marrant resided for a while in London, sponsored by the Countess of Huntington. She persuaded him to go as a Methodist missionary to Nova Scotia, where he preached in and around Halifax for nearly four years. In 1784 he joined the Masons under Prince Hall and by 1789 had become chaplain of the African Lodge in Boston. Marrant's *A Narrative of the Lord's Wonderful Dealings with John Marrant, A Black, (Now going to Preach the Gospel in Nova-Scotia) Born in New-York, in North-America. Taken down from his own Relation, Arranged, Corrected, and Published, by the Rev. Mr. Aldridge* (London, 1785) is one of the earliest African-American narratives, and one of the most popular of the eighteenth century. Editor-librarian Dorothy Porter lists nineteen different printed versions of the *Narrative*, the latest published in 1835.

Marrant's *A Journal of the Rev. Marrant, from August the 18th, 1785, to the 16th of March 1790. To which are added Two Sermons* (London, 1790) is a reflection of his preaching and missionary experiences in Nova Scotia. A third publication, *A Sermon Preached on the 24th Day of June 1789. Being the Festival of St. John the Baptist, At the Request of the Right Worshipful the Grand Master Prince Hall and the Rest of the Brethren of the African Lodge of the Honorable Society of Free and Accepted Masons in Boston* (Boston, 1789), is significant because of Marrant's interpretation of the Bible and his short note indicating that both speaker and audience were black. Arthur A. Schomburg, who reprinted the Masonic sermon, considered Marrant among the first African-American ministers in North America as well as among the first to bring the Christian religion to the Native Americans.

See also Slave Narratives

■ ■ *Bibliography*

Logan, Rayford, and Michael R. Winston, eds. *Dictionary of American Negro Biography.* New York: Norton, 1982.

DORIS DZIWAS (1996)

MARSALIS, WYNTON

OCTOBER 18, 1961

❚❚❚

Born in New Orleans, Louisiana, jazz trumpeter and composer Wynton Marsalis grew up in a musical family. His father, Ellis (pianist), and brothers, Branford (tenor and soprano saxophonist), Delfeayo (trombonist), and Jason (drummer), are themselves well-known jazz artists. From an early age he studied privately and played in a children's marching band directed by the eminent New Orleans musician/scholar Danny Barker. As a youngster Marsalis made notable contributions in both classical and jazz genres. He performed at the New Orleans Jazz and Heritage Festival, and at the age of fourteen he performed Haydn's Trumpet Concerto in E-flat with the New Orleans Philharmonic Orchestra. He attended the Berkshire Music Center at Tanglewood and enrolled at Juilliard in 1980. While a student at Juilliard, he joined Art Blakey's Jazz Messengers (1980) and toured in a quartet with former Miles Davis personnel Herbie Hancock, Ron Carter, and Tony Williams. He recorded his first album as a leader, *Wynton Marsalis*, in 1981.

After leaving Blakey in 1982, Marsalis formed his first group, a quintet that included several young and extremely talented musicians—his brother Branford (tenor saxophone), Kenny Kirkland (piano), Charles Fambrough (bass), and Jeff Watts (drums). In addition to performing with his own group, Marsalis replaced Freddie Hubbard for the V.S.O.P. II tour (1983). In 1984 he became the first musician to win Grammy Awards for both jazz (*Think of One*, 1982) and classical (Haydn, Hummel, and Leopold Mozart trumpet concertos, 1984) recordings. Since the late 1980s, Marsalis has concentrated on jazz performance with a group consisting of Wes Anderson and Todd Williams (saxophones), Reginald Veal (bass), Wycliffe Gordon (trombone), Herlin Riley (drums), and Eric Reed (piano). Marsalis has won critical acclaim for his virtuosic technique, musical sensitivity, and gift for improvisation. He has become an articulate spokesperson for the preservation of "mainstream" jazz (a style rooted in bop and hard bop) through his performances and writings, and, beginning in 1991, as artistic director of the classical jazz program at Lincoln Center in New York.

During the 1990s Marsalis built the jazz program into the most prestigious center for jazz in the United States, although he faced frequent complaints that he concentrated on playing the music of a small canon of jazz greats and ignored the contributions of white jazz musicians. Marsalis also composed several pieces, including *In My Father's House* (1995) and *Blood on the Fields* (1996), for which he was awarded the Pulitzer Prize in 1997, as well as several adaptations of the music of his hero Duke Ellington, including *Harlem* (1999). In 2001 the secretary-general of the United Nations named Marsalis one of nine peace messengers who would publicize the work of the United Nations at performances and public appearances. In 2003 he was named musician of the year by the Musical America International Directory of the Performing Arts.

See also Blakey, Art (Buhaina, Abdullah Ibn); Davis, Miles; Hancock, Herbie; Jazz

■ ■ *Bibliography*

Crouch, Stanley. "Wynton Marsalis: 1987." *Downbeat* 54, no. 11 (1987): 17–19.

Giddins, Gary. "Wynton Marsalis and Other Neoclassical Lions." In *Rhythm-a-ning: Jazz Tradition and Innovation in the '80s*, edited by Gary Giddens. New York: Oxford University Press, 1985, pp. 156–161.

EDDIE S. MEADOWS (1996)
Updated by publisher 2005

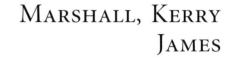

MARSHALL, KERRY JAMES

OCTOBER 17, 1955

Kerry James Marshall is an African-American artist who utilizes established compositional devises to explore the differing cultural perceptions of race and aesthetics. Marshall was born in Birmingham, Alabama, during the civil rights movement, and he was raised in Los Angeles during the subsequent Black Power movement. At that time, artistic collaboratives, such as the Chicago-based AfriCobra (African Commune of Bad Relevant Artists), encouraged artists of African decent, including Marshall, to thwart negative stereotypes and caricatures of African-Americans by producing more radically conscious and affirmative race-centered art forms.

After completing his studies with the artist Charles White at Otis Art Institute in 1978, Marshall briefly gave up drawing and painting to begin work on a series of collages. In these, for the first time, he used black backgrounds as a way to resist narrative imagery, endeavoring to produce sharp contrasts between various foreground and background elements. From this point on the color black would become a major symbolic and compositional element in his work.

In 1980 Marshall once again took up figurative painting. In the painting *A Portrait of the Artist as a Shadow of Himself* (1980), the artist reintroduced the idea of narration into his compositions while continuing to make use of the color black as a defining figurative element and a predominant motif for his subjects. During the following decade, Marshall began to see black as not only serving a race-affirming function, but a rhetorical one as well; the color was at the center of a conceptual strategy that signified the affirming beauty of both the color and, by extension, the people too often associated with the derogatory connotations of darkness. As the artist has stated, "the reason why I painted them as black as they are was so that they would operate [as] rhetorical figures. They are literally and rhetorically black in the same way that we describe ourselves as black people in America; we use that extreme position to designate ourselves in contrast to a white power structure of the country or the white mainstream" (Rowell, p. 265).

Marshall's large allegorical paintings address the complexity of African-American life with an authority grounded in the artist's mastery of the medium. He is especially concerned with the knowledge of how representation is essentially linked to specific cultural, social, and historical

Many Mansions (Kerry James Marshall, 1994). REPRODUCTION, THE ART INSTITUTE OF CHICAGO. COURTESY OF JACK SHAINMAN GALLERY, NEW YORK.

experiences. Thus, Marshall's paintings employ an ever-widening range of historical references from the Western art canon, as well as those particular to African-American culture. The artist's complex conceptual and contextual trajectories, therefore, tend toward the necessarily unpredictable, layering diverse meanings as a way to expose important implications for the historical moments he links together and consequently redefines for his audience.

Marshall is equally concerned with the intersections between tradition, influence, and individuality, as well as the strategic use of culture- and class-specific symbolism therein. For example, in the *Garden Project* (1994–1995) and *Souvenir* series (1997–1998), Marshall pays homage to both the pictorial innovations occurring during the history of modern painting as well as the stayed perseverance

and diversity within African-American communities. For his efforts, Marshall received a prestigious MacArthur Fellowship in 1997. In other projects such as *Laid to Rest* (1998), *RYTHM MASTR* (1999), and the exhibition *One True Thing: Meditations on Black Aesthetics* (2003), Marshall's artistic scope has continued to broaden, encompassing painting as well as photography, video, illustration, and sculpture.

See also Painting and Sculpture

■ ■ *Bibliography*

Marshall, Kerry James. *Kerry James Marshall*. New York: Harry N. Abrams, 2000.

Marshall, Kerry James. *One True Thing: Meditations on Black Aesthetics*. Chicago: Museum of Contemporary Art, 2003.

Rowell, Charles H. "An Interview with Kerry James Marshall." *Callaloo* 21, no. 1 (1998): 265.

LERONN BROOKS (2005)

MARSHALL, PAULE

APRIL 9, 1929

Novelist Paule Marshall was born Valenza Pauline Burke in Brooklyn, New York, the daughter of Samuel and Ada (Clement) Burke, who had emigrated from Barbados shortly after World War I. Marshall lived in a richly ethnic "Bajan" neighborhood in Brooklyn and visited Barbados for the first time when she was nine years old. At twenty-one she married Kenneth Marshall, whom she divorced in 1963. She graduated from Brooklyn College, *cum laude* and Phi Beta Kappa, in 1953. While attending New York's Hunter College in the mid-1950s, she began her first novel, *Brown Girl, Brownstones*. Its publication in 1959 was followed by a Guggenheim Fellowship (1960). Later awards include the Rosenthal Award of the National Institute for Arts and Letters (1962) for *Soul Clap Hands and Sing*, a Ford Foundation grant (1964–1965), a National Endowment for the Arts grant (1967–1968), the American Book Award of the Before Columbus Foundation for *Praisesong for the Widow* (1984), and a MacArthur Foundation Award (1992).

During the 1950s Marshall was a staff writer for a small magazine, *Our World*, which sent her on assignments to Brazil and the Caribbean. Since the publication of *Brown Girl, Brownstones*, she has been a full-time writer and a part-time teacher. She has taught African-American literature and creative writing at Yale, Columbia, Iowa, and Virginia Commonwealth universities. Since 1996 she has held the Helen Gould Sheppard Chair of Literature and Culture at New York University.

Marshall's writing explores the interaction between the materialist and individualist values of white America and the spiritual and communal values of the African diaspora. With the exception of *Soul Clap Hands and Sing* (1961), a collection of four long stories about aging men, Marshall's work is focused on African-American and Caribbean women. Each of her novels presents a black woman in search of an identity that is threatened or compromised by modern society. Marshall's narratives locate that search within black communities that are still connected to ancient spiritual traditions, sharpening the contrast between Americanized Africans and various diasporic modes of Africanizing the New World.

In her essays and interviews Marshall explained the influence of the Bajan community of her childhood on her work. Listening to the "poets in the kitchen," as she called her mother's women friends and neighbors in a 1983 *New York Times Book Review* essay, she learned the basic skills that characterize her writing—trenchant imagery and idiom, relentless character analysis, and a strong sense of ritual. Her development of her poetic relationship to the community of storytelling Bajan women has made her an intensely ethnic writer, one whose themes and manner measure the difference between the homeland of the West Indies and Africa and the new land of the United States.

Marshall's fiction explores the divided immigrant or colonized self. In *Brown Girl, Brownstones*, the protagonist Selina Boyce is an adolescent girl torn between the assimilationist materialism of her mother, Silla, and the dreamy resistance to Americanization of her father, Deighton. As she matures Selina learns from both the Bajan community and the world at large how to be her own woman. Each of the four stories in *Soul Clap Hands and Sing* explores a man in old age who reaches out toward a woman in the hope of transforming a failed and empty life. The stories contrast men defeated by materialism, colonialism, and internal compromise with young women full of vitality and hope. Like the men in numerous stories by Henry James, Marshall's old men cannot connect, and the young women serve as the painful instruments of their self-realization.

Marshall's second novel, *The Chosen Place, The Timeless People* (1969), is her largest literary conception. The central figure is Merle Kinbona, a middle-aged West Indian woman educated in Britain and psychologically divided in a number of ways. The struggle to resolve the divided self is fully elaborated, here again seen as inextricably related to a community and its history. The rituals of recovery are more broadly drawn here, for they are more self-consciously communal in nature. Merle wants to be a leader in the development of her community, but she is almost literally catatonic with impotence until she comes to terms with her personal past and its relationship to the colonial order that is her communal past. As Merle is both the product and emblem of her divided community, her self-healing and newly found clarity of purpose prefigure the possibilities for the community as well.

Marshall's third novel, *Praisesong for the Widow* (1983), presents a middle-class black American woman who, like the old men of the four long stories, realizes the depth of her spiritual emptiness. Unlike the old men, Avatara is able, through dream and ritual, to recover her spiritual past. *Daughters* (1991) is the complex story of how Ursa McKenzie, the only child of a Caribbean politician father and an African-American mother, comes to grips with her ambivalent feelings about her father's emotional domination. Ursa's liberation involves every aspect of her life—her past in her island homeland, her professional life in New York City, her love life and friendships, and her understanding of political and economic relations between the United States and the island nations of the Caribbean.

After the broad canvas of *Daughters*, in *The Fisher King* (2000) Marshall produced a novel as compressed as a short story. The narrative focuses on Sonny, the Paris-born eight-year-old grandson of a famous African-American jazz pianist, who is brought home to Brooklyn by Hattie, his dead grandfather's childhood friend, manager, and lover, to visit his two great-grandmothers, one as yet unreconciled to the elder Sonny's choice of jazz over European classical music and the other still furious at his decision to flee to Europe with her daughter, young Sonny's grandmother. The boy's visits with his aged grandmothers and his great uncle and his family in the Brooklyn community of African Americans and West Indian immigrants subtly suggest movement from wounded anger and alienation toward reconciliation.

In all her works Marshall develops a rich psychological analysis, making use of powerful scenes of confrontation, revelation, and self-realization. Her style, while essentially realistic, is always capable of expressionist and surrealist scenes and descriptions, which are seamlessly integrated in the fabric of the narrative. Marshall's originality—her prototypical black feminism, her exploration of "the international theme" arising from the African diaspora, and her control of a wide range of narrative techniques—places her in the first rank of twentieth- and twenty-first-century African-American writers.

See also Literature of the United States

■■ *Bibliography*

Christian, Barbara. "Paule Marshall: A Literary Biography." In *Black Feminist Criticism: Perspectives on Black Women Writers*. New York: Pergamon, 1985.

Collier, Eugenia. "The Closing of the Circle: Movement from Division to Wholeness in Paule Marshall's Fiction." In *Black Women Writers (1950–1980): A Critical Evaluation*, edited by Mari Evans. New York: Anchor, 1984.

Marshall, Paule. "Shaping the World of My Art." *New Letters* 40 (1973): 97–112.

Marshall, Paule. "The Making of a Writer: From the Poets in the Kitchen." *The New York Times Book Review* (January 9, 1983): 3, 34–35.

McCluskey, John, Jr. "'And Called Every Generation Blessed': Theme, Setting and Ritual in the Works of Paule Marshall." In *Black Women Writers (1950–1980): A Critical Evaluation*, edited by Mari Evans. New York: Anchor, 1984.

Pettis, Joyce. *Toward Wholeness in Paule Marshall's Fiction*. Charlottesville: University of Virginia Press, 1995.

JOSEPH T. SKERRETT JR. (1996)
Updated by author 2005

MARSHALL, THURGOOD

JULY 2, 1908
JANUARY 24, 1993

Thurgood Marshall, a civil rights lawyer and associate justice of U. S. Supreme Court, distinguished himself as a jurist in a wide array of settings. As the leading attorney for the National Association for the Advancement of Colored People (NAACP) from 1938 to 1961, he pioneered the role of professional civil rights advocate. As the principal architect of the legal attack against de jure racial segregation, Marshall oversaw the most successful campaign of social reform litigation in American history. As a judge on the United States Court of Appeals, solicitor general of the United States, and associate justice of the Supreme Court, he amassed a remarkable record as a public servant. Given the influence of his achievements over a long span of time, one can reasonably argue that Thurgood Marshall may have been the outstanding attorney of twentieth-century America.

Marshall was born in Baltimore, Maryland, where his father was a steward at an exclusive all-white boat club, and his mother was an elementary school teacher. He attended public schools in Baltimore before proceeding to Lincoln University in Pennsylvania, where he shared classes with, among others, Cabell "Cab" Calloway, the entertainer; Kwame Nkrumah, who became president of Ghana; and Nnamdi Azikiwe, who became president of Nigeria. After graduating, he was excluded from the University of Maryland School of Law because of racial segregation. Marshall attended the Howard University School of Law, where he fell under the tutelage of Charles Hamilton Houston. Houston elevated academic standards at Howard, turning it into a veritable hothouse of legal education and training many of those who would later play important roles in the campaign against racial discrimination. Marshall graduated in 1933, first in his class.

After engaging in a general law practice briefly, Marshall was persuaded by Houston to pursue a career working as an attorney on behalf of the NAACP. Initially he worked as Houston's deputy, but in 1939 he took over from his mentor as the NAACP's special counsel. In that position Marshall confronted an extraordinary array of legal problems that took him from local courthouses, where he served as a trial attorney, to the Supreme Court of the United States, where he developed his skills as an appellate advocate. Over a span of two decades, he argued thirty-two cases before the Supreme Court, winning twenty-nine of them. He convinced the Court to invalidate practices that excluded blacks from primary elections (*Smith v. Allwright*, 1944), to prohibit segregation in interstate transportation (*Morgan v. Virginia*, 1946), to nullify convictions obtained from juries from which African Americans had been barred on the basis of their race (*Patton v. Mississippi*, 1947), and to prohibit state courts from enforcing racially restrictive real estate covenants (*Shelley v. Kraemer*, 1948).

Marshall's greatest triumphs arose, however, in the context of struggles against racial discrimination in public education. In 1950, in *Sweatt v. Painter*, he successfully argued that a state could not fulfill its federal constitutional obligation by hurriedly constructing a "Negro" law school that was inferior in tangible and intangible ways to the state's "white" law school. That same year he successfully argued in *McLaurin v. Oklahoma State Regents* that a state university violated the federal constitution by admitting an African-American student and then confining that student, on the basis of his race, to a specified seat in classrooms and a specified table in the school cafeteria. In 1954, in *Brown v. Board of Education*, Marshall culminated his campaign by convincing the Court to rule that racial segregation is invidious racial discrimination and thus invalid under the Fourteenth Amendment to the federal Constitution.

In 1961, over the objections of white supremacist southern politicians, President John F. Kennedy nominated Marshall to a seat on the U.S. Court of Appeals for the Second Circuit in New York. Later, President Lyndon B. Johnson appointed Marshall to two positions that had never previously been occupied by an African American. In 1965 President Johnson appointed Marshall as solicitor general, and in 1967 he nominated him to a seat on the Supreme Court.

Throughout his twenty-four years on the Court, Marshall was the most insistently liberal of the justices, a stance that often drove him into dissent. His judgments gave broad scope to individual liberties (except in cases involving asserted claims to rights of property). Typically he supported claims of freedom of expression over competing concerns and scrutinized skeptically the claims of law enforcement officers in cases implicating federal constitu-

tional provisions that limit the police powers of government. In the context of civil liberties, the most controversial positions that Marshall took involved rights over reproductive capacities and the death penalty. He viewed as unconstitutional laws that prohibit women from exercising considerable discretion over the choice to continue a pregnancy or to terminate it through abortion. Marshall also viewed as unconstitutional all laws permitting the imposition of capital punishment.

The other side of Marshall's jurisprudential liberalism was manifested by an approach to statutory and constitutional interpretation that generally advanced egalitarian policies. His judgments displayed an unstinting solicitude for the rights of labor, the interests of women, the struggles of oppressed minorities, and the condition of the poor. One particularly memorable expression of Marshall's empathy for the indigent is his dissent in *United States v. Kras* (1973), a case in which the Court held that a federal statute did not violate the Constitution by requiring a $50 fee of persons seeking the protection of bankruptcy. Objecting to the Court's assumption that, with a little self-discipline, the petitioner could readily accumulate the required fee, Marshall wrote that

> It may be easy for some people to think that weekly savings of less than $2 are no burden. But no one who has had close contact with poor people can fail to understand how close to the margin of survival many of them are. . . . It is perfectly proper for judges to disagree about what the Constitution requires. But it is disgraceful for an interpretation of the Constitution to be premised upon unfounded assumptions about how people live.

Marshall retired from the Court in 1991, precipitating the most contentious confirmation battle in the nation's history when President George Bush nominated as Marshall's successor Clarence Thomas, an ultraconservative African-American jurist.

After his death, Marshall's extraordinary contributions to American life were memorialized in an outpouring of popular grief and adulation greater than that expressed for any previous justice. Marshall has been the object of some controversy since his death. Immediately after his death, a public debate opened over Marshall's instructions regarding his confidential Supreme Court papers. Ultimately, the Library of Congress opened them to public access without restriction. In 1996 newly uncovered documents demonstrated that Marshall had passed secret information to FBI director J. Edgar Hoover during his years at the National Association for the Advancement of

Colored People. These developments have not detracted from Marshall's heroic position in American history, in tribute to which he was honored by the erection of a statue in his native Baltimore in 1995.

See also *Brown v. Board of Education of Topeka, Kansas;* Civil Rights Movement, U.S.; Fourteenth Amendment; National Association for the Advancement of Colored People (NAACP); *Sweatt v. Painter*

■ ■ *Bibliography*

Bland, Randall W. *Private Pressure on Public Law: The Legal Career of Justice Thurgood Marshall.* Port Washington, N.Y.: Kennikat Press, 1973.

Kluger, Richard. *Simple Justice: The History of Brown v. Board of Education and Black America's Struggle for Equality.* New York: Vintage, 1977.

Rowan, Carl. *Dream Makers, Dream Breakers: The World of Justice Thurgood Marshall.* Boston: Little, Brown, 1993.

Williams, Juan. *Thurgood Marshall: American Revolutionary.* New York: Random House, 2001.

RANDALL KENNEDY (1996)
Updated bibliography

MARSON, UNA

FEBRUARY 6, 1905
MAY 6, 1965

The Afro-Jamaican woman Una Marson was born in 1905 to a Baptist minister and his wife in rural Jamaica. She was one of the most important contributors to Anglophone Caribbean literature in the first half of the twentieth century. Her literary output includes four books of poetry and at least three plays, including *At What a Price?* (1932), the first play with a black cast and director produced in London's West End, and her last play, *Pocomania,* which was heralded by Joan Grant as the "birth of Jamaican national drama" in 1938. Marson played a decisive role in the establishment of Jamaican national literature. As the editor of *Cosmopolitan* from 1928 to 1931 she promoted local writers such as Archie Lindo, and she led various organizations to promote Jamaican literature, including the Readers and Writers Club (1937) and the Pioneer Press (1949). During the Second World War, Marson helped institutionalize Caribbean culture and literature through the BBC program *Caribbean Voices* (1943–1958). This program may have been Marson's most significant contribution as it provided a broad range of writers—including the

West Indian novelist George Lamming (b. 1927) and the Trinidadian writer V. S. Naipaul ((b. 1932)—their first large audience and financial support.

Marson saw establishing a Jamaican national literature as part of a larger political goal to promote the status of the people of Africa and its diaspora. She began her career in social and political work with the Jamaican Salvation Army and YMCA after graduating from Hampton High School in 1922. She was one of the founding members of the Jamaica Stenographers Association in 1928 and editor of its monthly journal, *The Cosmopolitan.* She also founded the Jamaican Save the Children Fund (1938). Marson continued her political and social activism in London, where she lived from 1932 to 1936 and from 1938 to 1946. In 1933 and 1934, she worked for the League of Coloured Peoples, and in 1935 and 1936 she served as secretary for the Abyssinian Minister in London and for Haile Selassie when he Addressed the League of Nations. Marson also became a prominent speaker for women's organizations in England, focusing on the need to improve the economic and social status of women in the Caribbean and Africa. She continued her social and political work until her death in 1965.

Despite her importance to the development of Anglophone Caribbean literature, Marson's contribution has only come to light since the mid-1980s, when feminist scholars began to study her life and work. Her writings remain largely out of print and inaccessible. Her obscurity results in part from the incompatibility of Marson's feminism with the male-dominated discourses of Pan-Africanism and Jamaican nationalism. Marson's obscurity may also be a result of her historical position as a transitional figure. Her political and aesthetic vision emerged in the 1920s, a time when leading intellectuals believed that Jamaica would progress to modernity through respectability and loyalty to the British Empire. She matured during the 1930s and 1940s, when labor rebellions and political nationalism transformed the Anglophone Caribbean, leading to the anticolonial politics and literature of the 1950s.

Feminist scholars have sought to reestablish Marson's critical reputation by emphasizing her critique of Jamaica's middle-class patriarchy. For example, her parodic poems in *Tropic Reveries* (1930) question the necessity of marriage, while *At What a Price?* employs a marriage plot to assert women's right to sexual experience and social standing. Her later work combines her feminist concerns with her growing investment in Pan-African politics and African diaspora aesthetics. Marson's third collection of poetry, *The Moth and the Star* (1937), echoes the work of the Harlem Renaissance poet Langston Hughes in its use of vernacular language and working-class personae, foreshadowing much Caribbean writing of the 1950s. However, unlike many writers of the 1950s, Marson focused on the implications of nationalism for women. In so doing, she revealed that Jamaican nationalism excluded both the working classes and middle-class women from the freedom and status it promised.

See also Literature of the English-Speaking Caribbean

■ ■ *Bibliography*

French, Joan, and Honor Ford-Smith. *Women, Work and Organization in Jamaica, 1900–1944.* Kingston, Jamaica: Sistren Research, 1986. A book-length manuscript held at the University of West Indies Library, Mona, Jamaica.

Grant, Joan. *The Daily Gleaner* (January 6, 1938): 5.

Jarrett-Macaulay, Delia. *The Life of Una Marson, 1905–1965.* Manchester, UK: Manchester University Press, 1998.

Smilowitz, Erika. "Marson, Rhys, and Mansfield." Ph.D. diss., University of New Mexico, 1984.

LEAH READE ROSENBERG (2005)

MARTIN, JOHN SELLA

SEPTEMBER 1832
AUGUST 1876

The minister and lecturer John Sella Martin was born a slave in Charlotte, North Carolina, in 1832. The child of a mulatto slave and her owner's nephew, he was sold with his mother to people in Columbia, Georgia, and he remained a slave until his escape on a Mississippi riverboat in December 1855.

In January 1856, Martin arrived in Chicago where he associated with abolitionists and began his long career of oratory. His friend Frederick Douglass (1818–1895), in particular, was known to have admired his oratorical skills. In the latter part of 1856, he moved to Detroit, where he studied for the Baptist ministry. In 1857 he was ordained to preach and received the pastorate at Michigan Street Baptist Church in Buffalo, New York. In 1859 he moved to Boston and substituted for the vacationing preacher of Tremont Temple, drawing large, approving crowds. He then spent eight months as pastor of the Baptist Church in Lawrence, Massachusetts, which had a large white congregation, before accepting the pulpit of the Joy Street Church, one of the oldest black Baptist churches in Boston. During this same year, Martin published a poem, "The Sentinel of Freedom," in *Anglo-African Magazine.*

In August 1861, Martin made the first of several trips to England on a speaking tour sponsored by Massachusetts governor John Andrew to gain support for the Union during the Civil War. He returned to the United States in February 1862. On the occasion of Abraham Lincoln's signing of the Emancipation Proclamation on January 1, 1863, he addressed a famous meeting at Tremont Temple, as did Frederick Douglass. Later that month, Martin returned to Europe to preach in London at the behest of the industrialist Harper Twelvetrees. In April 1864, having journeyed back from England, he began to preach at Shiloh Presbyterian Church in New York. The following April he returned to Great Britain in a fund-raising capacity for the American Missionary Association (AMA). As a delegate of the AMA, he delivered an address to the Paris Anti-Slavery Conference on August 27, 1867.

One year later, Martin accepted the pastorate of the Fifteenth Street Presbyterian Church in Washington, D.C. He attended the formation meeting of the Colored National Labor Union (CNLU) in Washington, D.C., in December 1869, was appointed to its executive board, and was named editor of the CNLU's short-lived official organ, *The New Era.* When the publication foundered shortly afterward, he moved to New Orleans, where he was involved in local politics and earned his living as a lecturer. In 1875 he was a founding member and president of the New Orleans Atheneum Club and a member of the Louisiana Progressive Club. He died in Louisiana in 1876.

See also Abolition; Baptists; Douglass, Frederick; Emancipation in the United States

■ ■ *Bibliography*

Blackett, R. J. M. *Beating Against the Barriers: Biographical Essays in Nineteenth-Century Afro-American History.* Baton Rouge: Louisiana State University Press, 1986.

LYDIA MCNEILL (1996)

MASCULINITY

Any discussion of African-descended men as a group must first acknowledge their multifarious differences rooted in particular histories, nationalities, religions, languages, cultures, sexualities, and socioeconomic classes. Nonetheless, due to a larger shared history entangled in European imperial conquest, chattel enslavement, and colonialism, diasporan men can instructively be understood as possessing, if not an identical, at least a similar relation to maleness.

SLAVERY, INSURGENCY, AND THE ORIGINS OF BLACK MALE SUBJECTIVITY

The origins of the notion that some men are naturally superior to others remain obscure, but it probably can be traced to the earliest hunter-gatherer societies. Even though many ancient practices of masculine aggression and domination arose from and contributed to tribal, clan, and ethnic rivalries, they were not structured on modern notions of racial difference. In Europe during the Middle Ages, the devil, demons, and saints' executioners were sometimes imaged as dark-faced men. Highly allegorical and fantastic in nature, these emblems conflated the color black—symbolizing melancholy, death, sin, and the unknown—with a general notion of ethnic difference, as the executioners of Christ were sometimes represented as monstrous dark men or black Jews. At the same time, the other most prominent artistic image of black maleness in the medieval era was a redemptive figure, the black Magi, one of the three Wise Men who brought gifts to the Christ child. Clearly, the concept of black maleness was a malleable abstraction based in religious allegory, limited geographic knowledge (terra incognita), and ethnocentric fears and fantasies. By the twelfth century, Europeans had already begun to establish rudimentary notions of ethnicized manhood in terms of what Felipe Fernández-Armesto calls "Europe's 'internal' primitives: the peripheral, pastoral, bog or mountain folk, like the Basques, Welsh, Irish, Slavs and pagan Scandinavians" (1987, p. 225).

Although the interaction and intermixing between Europeans and Africans is a long, complicated affair dating to prehistory, the racial construct of masculinity emerges most markedly in response to European exploration, the succeeding colonization of native peoples, and particularly the rise of the transatlantic African slave trade. European literature of this era of exploration and colonization provides evidence of how the discourse on darker-skinned men as a "race" apart was still unsettled, if formative. The most celebrated representation of such a figure, William Shakespeare's tragic eponymous hero of *Othello* (1604), images the Moor not only as a great military leader but also as a gentleman of the highest character. While Othello seems to belong to the noble "race" of aristocrats born to rule, some characters use color epithets to attack him, and the play flirts with references to his African features marking him as racially alien, ignoble, inferior, and bestial. Eighty years later, in *Oroonoko, or the Royal Slave, a True History* (1688), Aphra Behn absorbed, and helped to disseminate, a racial ideology that gendered black male identity as a Noble Savage. Behn constructed Oroonoko from a combination of long-established Oriental myth

"Am I not a Man and a Brother?" The most prolific image of black maleness in the late eighteenth and early nineteenth centuries, the medallion pictured here served usefully in the abolitionist cause, but did nothing to enhance the image of black masculinity. PHOTOGRAPH BY KARI SHUDA. AP/WIDE WORLD PHOTOS. REPRODUCED BY PERMISSION.

and newly emerging racial consensus about African-descended men, whose increasing association with the debased condition of chattel signals their deficit as both less than human and also less than manly. Othello and Oroonoko embody the binaristic representation of black manliness that dominated the discourse for centuries: on the one hand, the black man represents a naturally virile, seductively commanding, savage presence eliciting desire and fear; on the other, he is projected as a servile, childlike, desexualized presence eliciting pity and contempt.

From the sixteenth through the eighteenth centuries, visual representations of dark-skinned men in European art turned repeatedly to the image of a boyish page standing at service to Europeans. As we can see in William Hogarth's satire on English gluttony and excess, the dark skin of this figure betokens his servile nature, which in turn confirms the white patriarch's civilized refinement, mercantile accumulation, and natural right to rule—all lampooned by Hogarth. The most prolific image of black maleness in the late eighteenth and early nineteenth century also used a servile pose ironically to proselytize on behalf of slave abolition. Entitled "Am I Not a Man and a Brother?" this medallion figures the black male slave manacled and kneeling in a pleading position. Despite the beneficent abolitionist intention, the emblems of this medallion partake in a global visual grammar of black male dependence, implying that only Europeans, particularly white men, can answer the question of the Negro's relation to the brotherhood of man, for only they have the power to bring an end to slavery.

During the Enlightenment, the racial concept of masculinity intensified with the development of scientific classification systems in natural history. Paradoxically, the same men who articulated the Enlightenment principles of natural rights, individual worth, universal reason, and manhood equality simultaneously erected a rationale for racial difference based in gender disparity. Enlightenment thinkers like Charles de Secondat-Baron de Montesquieu, John Locke, Thomas Jefferson, and Georg Wilhelm Friedrich Hegel theorized the natural right to property, progeny, and shared political power as the foundation of white male freedom and subjectivity. In his 1830s lectures on history, Hegel makes this logic absolute by suggesting that Africans exist totally outside of world history, and thus outside of the natural progress toward self-conscious human (i.e., masculine) mastery, subjectivity, and freedom brought about by world-historical great (white) men.

Against the dominant image of natural slavishness, black men—captive and free—were storming the world stage performing virile feats from which these Enlightenment thinkers wanted to exclude them—perhaps out of a subliminal reaction to the rising tide of African men boldly displaying their mettle in Europe and America. They manned the ships that bridged the Atlantic, fought alongside European men in international wars, led slave insurrections that rattled the white masters with constant fright, and governed free Maroon societies in open defiance of armed militias across the Americas. They also infiltrated European societies through public enactments of critical self-reflection, literary and artistic accomplishment, political protest, and sometimes interracial marriage.

As black men began to tell their stories in slave narratives, they sometimes pleaded for mercy, but they also more assertively demanded their right to ownership of their own persons, manhood emancipation, and political equality. Some, like the autobiographer Olaudah Equiano (1750–1797), used the tactic of adopting—almost mimetically—the clothes, manners, poses, habits, and values of European gentlemen as a way of exposing the arbitrary logic of racial classification and the hypocrisy of Christian morals, universal reason, and equal rights. Through his famous *Interesting Narrative*, and the portrait that fronts it, he presents the image of a regular gentleman, educated, worldly, Christianized, disciplined, and enterprising. Other Negro men followed his example, using literacy, free African heritage, or a public display of their own manly bodies and alert minds to carve out spaces of manly subjectivity in an environment hostile to their humanity

and, particularly, their assertion of being free men. Among the most notable of these men were Francis Williams of Jamaica, Frederick Douglass of the United States, Juan Francisco Manzano of Cuba, and Ottobah Cugoano of Grenada.

Rebellious slaves and freed men constantly troubled the profit-making engines of slave ships, plantations, and great houses. Kidnapped Africans sometimes fought back under alien conditions that cut them off from the resources of their native lands, as in the celebrated case of Sengbe (or Cinque), who in 1839 led a rebellion aboard a slave ship. When Nathaniel Jocelyn painted his portrait for posterity, the artist imagined him in the Oroonoko tradition of the Noble Savage. At other times, New World Africans were motivated to insurgency by a combination of factors related to masculine enactments of belligerent self-defense, religious prophecy, and revolutionary consciousness, partly inspired by the American and French Revolutions.

After the success of the Haitian Revolution, led by Toussaint-Louverture, revolutionary violence was buttressed by a vision of black republican nationalism. As Toussaint was lauded by European intellectuals and artists as a sort of black George Washington, black revolutionaries took him as a model of violently sacrificial determination, an image enhanced by his martyrdom in a French prison. In the United States, organizers of slave rebellions and conspiracies, such as Denmark Vesey, Gabriel Prosser, and Nat Turner, rallied their troops using the Haitian example. Abolitionist propagandists like David Walker and Martin Robison Delany forged a Pan-African-American consciousness in which colored men, aided by women, would rise to arms in a systematic revolution across the Americas. As men of African descent revised, subverted, and rejected the dominant discourse of black male savagery, servility, and commodification in multiple ways, they staked their claim to manhood emancipation, as well as to the "free" subjectivity endowed by this masculine claim.

RACE MEN, NEW NEGROES, AND EMANCIPATED CITIZENRY

From England in 1772 to Brazil in 1888, nations gradually outlawed slavery. If, on the one hand, emancipation meant freedom from forced labor for males and females, for men of color it also possessed a double connotation, suggesting the ongoing struggle for those rights and privileges granted to white men upon reaching the age of adult emancipation. Although frequently working with women of color to extend political, property, and civil rights to all humans, many black men also concentrated on forging a culture of emancipated manliness. They formed fraternal lodges, se-

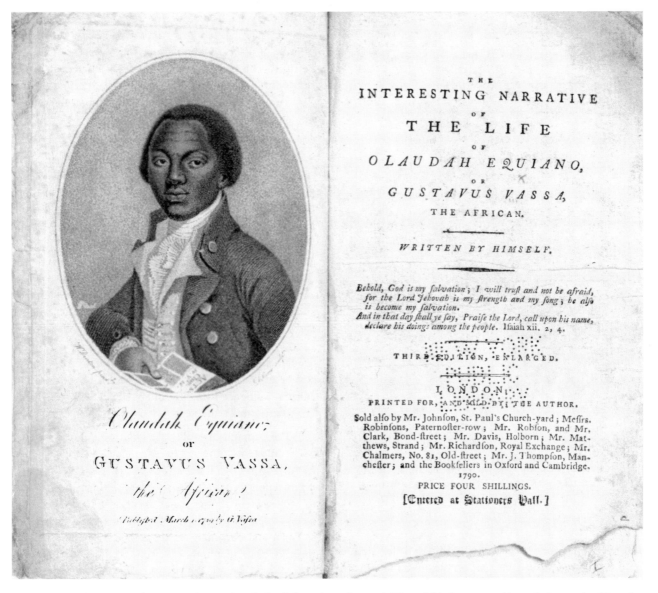

Title page and frontispiece for the autobiography of Olaudah Equiano (b. 1745). Through his famous autobiography Interesting Narrative *and the portrait that accompanied it, the former slave Equiano presented himself as a regular gentleman, educated, worldly, Christianized, disciplined, and enterprising.* MANUSCRIPTS, ARCHIVES AND RARE BOOKS DIVISION, SCHOMBURG CENTER FOR RESEARCH IN BLACK CULTURE, THE NEW YORK PUBLIC LIBRARY, ASTOR, LENOX AND TILDEN FOUNDATIONS.

cret societies, and other organizations devoted to tutoring men for civic responsibility. They forged political organizations and movements to agitate for full citizenship or national independence. They formed labor unions, self-help enterprises, business cooperatives, and other agencies devoted to industrial and economic uplift. And with interested whites and black women, they formed religious, cultural, and educational institutions, most frequently headed by males. Out of this maelstrom of masculine tutelage, they shaped notions of the "manhood of the race"—the idea that black men had an obligation to head the racial family, to defend women and children, to modernize

themselves in industry and commerce, and to lead the struggle for full inclusion in the patrimony of their respective nations (Carby, 1998; Wallace, 2002; Ross, 2004).

In the late nineteenth and early twentieth centuries, the question arose of how to fit colored men, whether former slave or colonial subject, for a useful position in the industrial economy—that is, how to train them for industry while forestalling their demands for political equality, economic parity, and national independence. Booker T. Washington promulgated the notion of the "accommodating" Negro leader. Honing his public image with careful detail, as in the photograph of him surveying the Tus-

Joseph Cinque. *Nathaniel Jocelyn's portrait of Cinque depicts the leader of the 1839 revolt aboard the slave ship* Amistad *in the guise of the "Noble Savage."* FROM AN ILLUSTRATION IN "THE AMISTAD SLAVE REVOLT AND AMERICAN ABOLITION," BY KAREN ZEINERT. LINNET BOOKS, 1997. REPRODUCED BY PERMISSION OF THE NEW HAVEN COLONY HISTORICAL SOCIETY.

kegee grounds on his horse, Washington fostered a political and media machine that, on the one hand, calmed fears of black unrest, migration, and insurgency, while, on the other, popularized the notion that a black man could legitimately lead the Negro race by emulating the self-made myth of white male mentors. Washington's model of industrial education and accommodating black male leadership spread to the West Indies, Latin America, Africa, and Asia.

The reaction to Washington was intensely ambivalent, frequently colored by the idea that he was unmanning the race and stalling its progress. Conflicting strategies for racial modernization and renewal were brought to the fore through a figure often labeled the "New Negro." One of Washington's most influential foes, W. E. B. Du Bois, for instance, charged in his early writings that Negroes would remain a "bastard" race until exceptional, confident, uncompromising black men trained themselves to join with the best men of the white race to lift up the masses. Inspired by Washington's notion of economic

self-help, the Jamaican Marcus Garvey developed an international male-headed organization focused on the display of militant blackness, military order, and pride in African heritage. The gallant uniformed black horsemen of the cavalry unit of Garvey's Universal African Legions powerfully communicated the heroic nature of their nationalizing endeavor.

Other New Negro agendas encouraged the cultivation of "race men" in diverse ways. Leading race men often concentrated their efforts on molding an urbane, cosmopolitan race consciousness, one that wavered between political agitation and avant-garde aestheticism, between European mastery and Pan-African separatism, and between elite literariness and black folk identity. This versatile program of race renewal, called the New Negro Renaissance, or *Négritude* among Francophone-African and Caribbean advocates, positioned men like James Weldon Johnson and Alain Locke of the United States, Arturo Schomburg and Jesús Colón of Puerto Rico, Eric Williams and George Padmore of Trinidad, Claude McKay of Jamaica, Léopold Sédar Senghor of Senegal, Aimé Césaire of Martinique, and Léon Damas of Guiana in highly visible positions of cultural influence in metropolitan capitals like New York City, Paris, and London.

The demand for political rights and cultural renewal was intimately connected to black men's struggle for economic autonomy in labor systems that prevented the traditional role of family provider and head of house. Due to the legacy of chattel enslavement, a general perception of black male workers tended to view them as lagging in agrarian and personal service sectors. In his pivotal portrayal of black manhood cast from Freudian, sociological, and Marxist theory, Richard Wright constructs the mentality of *Native Son*'s Bigger Thomas by playing on this perception of black men's working-class unconsciousness. In other works, Wright and other black male writers spotlighted the revolutionary potential of the emerging black working class. Similarly, the psychiatrist and cultural theorist Frantz Fanon used his own experience of anticolonial struggle in Martinique, France, and Algeria to develop complex psychoanalytic theories of racialized gender dynamics, suggesting the need to overcome a black male mentality deformed and paralyzed by racial-colonial oppression through the process of psychologically transformative revolutionary action. As blacks became increasingly attracted to political radicalism and the labor movement, particularly in the 1930s, the radical black laborer and union man became an explosive figure of social change. Black men flocked to new unions, many organized by a new generation of working-class-identified black male leaders, such as Tubal Uriah Butler in Trinidad, Nor-

Booker T. Washington at the Tuskegee Institute. *Washington established a carefully honed image of accommodating black male leadership, urging industrial education and promoting the idea of the "self-made man" in an effort to calm fears of black unrest.* THE LIBRARY OF CONGRESS.

man Manley and William Alexander Bustamante in Jamaica, and A. Phillip Randolph and Angelo Herndon in the United States. Labor organizing set the stage for mass anticolonial and other forms of political protest in unprecedented numbers.

In the middle years of the twentieth century, black men argued the benefits of a militantly violent masculine upheaval versus a more pacific tactic of manhood reform through peaceful mass resistance. After Mahatma Gandhi used nonviolent resistance to wrest India from the British Empire, black men were attracted to the image of the singular colored man of great moral courage leading (literally or symbolically) a disciplined phalanx of followers against the mighty armed empire. Revising this strategy to combat white supremacy in the United States, the mass movements identified with Martin Luther King Jr. constructed a black male leadership with arms linked in the front line of progress but taking the high moral ground through disciplined nonviolence. As famous photographs from the Memphis sanitation workers' strike indicate, this stance was intended to communicate not only the arrival of full citizenship but also the claim of uncompromising manhood identity. Answering across the ages the abolitionist "Am I Not a Man and a Brother?" medallion, each of the demonstrators carried a sign with the simple slogan, "I Am a Man"—as if the assertion of manhood itself could alter the oppressive reality of economic deprivation and social marginality.

Civil rights marchers wear "I am a Man" placards, flanked by National Guardsmen brandishing bayonets on one side and by tanks on the other, Memphis, Tennessee, 1968. Occasioned by a sanitation workers strike, the group's march through downtown Memphis was its third in as many days. Answering the question posed on the famous abolitionist medallion ("Am I not a man and a brother?"), the demonstrator's asserted their manhood with the simple slogan pictured here. © BETTMANN/CORBIS

All across Africa, the West Indies, and North America, a more belligerent face was also being placed on the anticolonial movements for national independence. Black nationalist ideology appealed directly to the fierce black man as guerilla warrior, committed to the blood brotherhood of violent self-defense. Eschewing Gandhi and King, many black male youths adopted as their heroes such national liberation fighters as the Mau Mau (the secret brotherhood of armed resistance initiated by the Gikuyu in Kenya), Patrice Lumumba of the Congo, and Fidel Castro of Cuba. Malcolm X, the Black Panthers, and other black nationalists and liberationists in the United States figured the imperialist West as a white man mired in the decadence of an overly affluent consumer civilization. This was an effeminate figure, and thus vulnerable to a robust vanguard of black male liberators.

BLACK MANHOOD IN CRISIS?

In the late twentieth and the early twenty-first centuries, the faces and bodies of black men proliferated in a mass media driven by the consumption of the new, the shocking, and the taboo. On the one hand, the media offered up myriad model black men, a revision of Washington's good clean Negro. At first, this concentrated on men who broke color barriers in sports, the military, politics, literature, popular music, and entertainment. As long as the black men breaking these barriers were represented as Good Negroes who dutifully demonstrated their competence in an alliance with white society, the threat of new interracial interactions could be minimized. Along with King, Sidney Poitier best embodied this impulse, as he rose to global celebrity through movies that repeatedly plotted the theme of an incorruptible black manhood eager to aid and save whiteness from itself. From Joe Louis to Lenox Lewis in boxing, from Goose Tatum to Michael Jordan in basketball, from Garry Sobers to Brian Lara in cricket, and countless others in various sports, the black male athlete became so visible as to cause some white men to rehash the mythology of black biological difference, this time as natural physical superiority, a notion already embedded in the slave owners' argument that only Africans could withstand hard labor in the tropics.

The black superstar's hypervisibility in mass media seemed to contradict a growing sense of alarm over the future of ordinary black men. A common worry at the turn of the twenty-first century focused on the concept of black male crisis in various guises. In the United States, persistently low educational levels, high unemployment, high incarceration rates, female-headed families, drug addiction, gang crime and homicide, suicide, AIDS, and other social problems caused some to declare black men an "endangered species." Similarly, in the Caribbean and Africa, where the AIDS epidemic was devastating populations, black men were often scapegoated as promiscuous carriers whose traditional sexual customs threatened to depopulate whole nations—a literalization of the backward African. The media focused attention on corrupt, murderous African and Caribbean heads of state—constantly raising the specter of a black manhood incapable of managing its national household after winning emancipation.

If the quotidian experience of black male identity remained largely inaudible and off-screen, scandalous controversies over black men's integrity, sexuality, and criminality were spotlighted in a variety of venues, giving rise to a whole subfield of sociological discourse trained on understanding black male deviance. The public image of black men, however, was not only proliferating, it was also splintering in response to larger social and sexual movements. As black gay men took a page from black feminists, they began to demand a visible place in black communities—challenging black homophobia and coaxing an enlarged sense of brotherly bonding across sexual orientation (Beam, 1986; Hemphill, 1991).

Ironically, the postmodern culture of hip-hop often turned these anxieties over black male identity into profitable commodities. Hyping the world's fascination with black male danger and trouble, many hip-hop artists exorcised these demons by performing them on stage and screen, and they sometimes converted the performance of menacing danger into an actual living out of it. Intensifying the phenomenon of hypervisibility, hip-hoppers like Tupac Shakur bared their hardened bodies to a seduced public, who in turn consumed those bodies as an authentic embodiment of black male jeopardy—a belated histori-

Tupac Shakur. PHOTOGRAPH BY RAYMOND BOYD. © RAYMOND BOYD/MICHAEL OCHS ARCHIVES/VENICE, CA. REPRODUCED BY PERMISSION.

cal repetition of those former slaves who bared their striped backs as proof of the horrors of slavery. Covered with hip-hop hieroglyphics and haunted by the specter of a predictable early death by homicide, Tupac, inverting the formula of the Good Negro, marked his own price into his flesh: the deadly cost of becoming a black man.

See also African Diaspora; Black Power Movement; Civil Rights Movement, U.S.; Feminist Theory and Criticism; Identity and Race in the United States

■ ■ *Bibliography*

Awkward, Michael. *Negotiating Difference: Race, Gender, and the Politics of Positionality.* Chicago: University of Chicago Press, 1995.

Beam, Joseph, ed. *In the Life: A Black Gay Anthology.* Boston: Alyson, 1986.

Carby, Hazel V. *Race Men.* Cambridge, Mass.: Harvard University Press, 1998.

Equiano, Olaudah. *The Interesting Narrative of the Life of Olaudah Equiano, or Gustavus Vassa, the African, Written by Himself* (1789). Reprint, New York: Penguin Books, 1995.

Fernández-Armesto, Felipe. *Before Columbus: Exploration and Colonization from the Mediterranean to the Atlantic, 1229–1492.* Philadelphia: University of Pennsylvania Press, 1987.

Harper, Phillip Brian. *Are We Not Men? Masculine Anxiety and the Problem of African-American Identity.* New York: Oxford University Press, 1996.

Hemphill, Essex, ed. *Brother to Brother: New Writings by Black Gay Men.* Boston: Alyson, 1991.

Lemelle, Anthony J. *Black Male Deviance.* Westport, Conn.: Praeger, 1995.

Mercer, Kobena. *Welcome to the Jungle: New Positions in Black Cultural Studies.* New York: Routledge, 1994.

Ross, Marlon B. *Manning the Race: Reforming Black Men in the Jim Crow Era.* New York: New York University Press, 2004.

Staples, Robert. *Black Masculinity: The Black Male's Role in American Society.* San Francisco: Black Scholar Press. 1982.

Wallace, Maurice O. *Constructing the Black Masculine: Identity and Ideality in African American Men's Literature and Culture, 1775–1995.* Durham: Duke University Press, 2002.

MARLON B. ROSS (2005)

MATHEMATICIANS

Mathematics was the first scientific field in which African Americans made significant contributions. In the late eighteenth century, Benjamin Banneker applied his knowledge of mathematics in the fields of surveying, clock-making, and astronomy. His calculations of the positions of celestial bodies, published in a series of almanacs between 1792 and 1797, were noted for their accuracy. A free black, Banneker was a counterexample to the widely held belief that blacks lacked reasoning and other intellectual abilities. Although many slaves used such skills as part of their daily routine, their work generally went unrecognized.

Mathematics provided a basis for the work of Edward Bouchet, the first black to be awarded a Ph.D. at an American university. Bouchet earned a doctorate in physics at Yale University in 1876 with a dissertation entitled "Measuring Refractive Indices." The first African American to earn a Ph.D. in pure mathematics was Elbert Frank Cox, at Cornell University in 1925. Cox's work on polynomial solutions, differential equations, and interpolation theory was highly regarded. He taught at Shaw University, West Virginia State College, and Howard University.

Before World War II, at least five other African Americans earned Ph.D.'s in mathematics. Dudley Weldon Woodard took his degree at the University of Pennsylvania in 1928; William Waldron Schieffelin Claytor, University of Pennsylvania, 1933; Walter Richard Talbot, University of Pittsburgh, 1934; Reuben Roosevelt McDaniel, Cornell University, 1938; and Joseph Alphonso Pierce, University of Michigan, 1938. Like Cox, they taught principally at black colleges and universities. In 1949 Evelyn Boyd (she later took the married names Granville and Collins) and Marjorie Lee Browne became the first African-American women to earn doctorates in mathematics, from Yale University and the University of Michigan, respectively. Browne taught at North Carolina Central University. In addition to teaching, Boyd's career included a period (1963–1967) as research specialist in celestial mechanics and orbit computation with the Apollo Project. J. Ernest Wilkins, Jr., worked on the Manhattan Project (1944–1946) after earning a Ph.D. in mathematics at the University of Chicago in 1942. David Harold Blackwell, who was awarded a Ph.D. at the University of Illinois in 1941, became internationally known for his work in statistics and was elected to the National Academy of Sciences in 1965.

Although few in number, black mathematicians were in the vanguard of the struggle against racial discrimination in science. Their efforts to participate in the field—at meetings of professional associations, for example—prompted changes in institutional policy and shifts in attitude and outlook within the scientific community during the 1950s. While some associations had admitted members regardless of race prior to that period, meetings were still convened in cities where African Americans experienced difficulty with accommodations and access to social events. In 1951 Evelyn Boyd and other members of the mathematics department at Fisk University helped motivate the American Mathematical Society and the Mathematical Association of America to adopt guidelines prohibiting the use of segregated sites and facilities for meetings.

With the passage of the Civil Rights Bill in 1964, graduate departments in mathematics at white universities became more open to admitting African Americans. The numbers, however, have remained small. During the 1980s and 1990s less than 2 percent of all Ph.D.'s in mathematics were awarded to African Americans. By 2003 that number had risen to just over 3 percent. In the 1990s William Massey of Bell Laboratories (now Lucent Technologies) took the first steps toward the formation of the Conference for African-American Researchers in the Mathematical Sciences (CAARMS), which holds annual meetings at major universities.

See also Banneker, Benjamin

Bibliography

Dean, Nathaniel, Cassandra M. McZeal, and Pamela J. Williams, eds. *African-Americans in Mathematics II: Fourth Conference for African-American Researchers in the Mathematical Sciences, June 16–19, 1998, Rice University, Houston, Texas.* Providence, R.I.: American Mathematical Society, 1999.

Newell, Virginia K., Joella H. Gipson, L. Waldo Rich, and Beauregard Stubblefield, eds. *Black Mathematicians and Their Works.* Ardmore, Penn.: Dorrance, 1980.

Pearson, Willie, Jr., and H. Kenneth Bechtel, eds. *Blacks, Science, and American Education.* New Brunswick, N.J.: Rutgers University Press, 1989.

Van Sertima, Ivan, ed. *Blacks in Science: Ancient and Modern.* New Brunswick, N.J.: Transaction Books, 1983.

KENNETH R. MANNING (1996)
JESSICA HORNIK-EVANS (2005)

MATHIAS, JOHN ROYCE

See Mathis, Johnny (Mathias, John Royce)

MATHIS, JOHNNY (MATHIAS, JOHN ROYCE)

SEPTEMBER 30, 1935

❚❚❚

Born John Royce Mathias in San Francisco in 1935, singer Johnny Mathis took an early interest in sports, and it was as an outstanding high jumper that he gained recognition at San Francisco State College. During that time he also began singing in a jazz sextet. In 1955 he sang in nightclubs in San Francisco and New York, where his smooth, mellow ballad style led to his first recording, "Wonderful, Wonderful" (1956), which was a huge hit. In 1957 he recorded two more million-selling records, "Chances Are" and "It's Not for Me to Say," as well as the popular "Twelfth of Never." In 1958 his album *Johnny Mathis's Greatest Hits* sold more than two million copies and remained on the charts for almost ten years. During this time, Mathis also appeared in two films, *Lizzie* (1957) and *A Certain Smile* (1958).

With a style derived more from popular crooning traditions than jazz or blues, Mathis was one of the great crossover singers of the 1950s and 1960s, extremely popular with both white and black audiences. In the 1960s and 1970s he toured widely and recorded prolifically ("Too

Much, Too Little, Too Late," with Deniece Williams, 1978; "Friends in Love," with Dionne Warwick, 1982). Mathis has maintained his popularity with numerous successful recordings, concert tours, and radio and television appearances. In 1993 he released a compilation album, *A Personal Collection,* featuring a duet with Barbra Streisand, and made a triumphant appearance at Carnegie Hall. In 1998 he appeared on the A&E cable network's *Live by Request.* In 2005 Columbia Records released *Isn't It Romantic: The Standards Album,* a new album of Mathis standards produced from recording sessions directed by Grammy winner Jorge Calandrelli.

See also Music in the United States

Bibliography

"In Step with Johnny Mathis." *Washington Post,* November 15, 1992.

LaBlanc, Michael, ed. *Contemporary Musicians: Profiles of the People in Music.* Vol. 2. Detroit, Mich.: Gale, 1990.

JAMES E. MUMFORD (1996)
Updated by publisher 2005

MAYFIELD, JULIAN

JUNE 6, 1928
OCTOBER 20, 1984

❚❚❚

Actor, writer, and activist Julian Hudson Mayfield was born in Greer, South Carolina, and grew up in Washington, D.C. After graduating from Dunbar High School, he entered the army and served briefly in the Pacific theater before receiving a medical discharge. Mayfield then enrolled at Lincoln University in Pennsylvania but gave up his studies to move to New York City in 1949.

In New York Mayfield held many jobs to make ends meet—from washing dishes to writing for the leftist black newspaper *Freedom.* At the newspaper he met Paul Robeson, Lorraine Hansberry, Langston Hughes, and other black leftists—meetings that deeply influenced his intellectual formation. Mayfield soon became an actor, debuting on Broadway as Absalom, the juvenile lead in *Lost in the Stars* (1949), Kurt Weill's adaptation of Alan Paton's novel *Cry, the Beloved Country* (1948). In 1952 Mayfield coproduced Ossie Davis's first play, *Alice in Wonder.* While in New York he became a member of the Harlem Writers Guild, a cooperative enterprise in which members critiqued each other's work.

In 1954 Mayfield married Ana Livia Cordero, and the couple moved to Puerto Rico. Mayfield helped establish the first English-language radio station on the island and, in 1956, founded the *Puerto Rico World Journal,* a magazine about international affairs. While in Puerto Rico he wrote his first novel, *The Hit* (1957), based on *417,* a one-act play he had written earlier about the numbers game in Harlem. *The Long Night* (1958) also centered on the numbers game but presented a much bleaker, less romantic view of Harlem than its predecessor.

By the time his third novel, *The Grand Parade* (1961), was published, Mayfield—who had met Malcolm X and W. E. B. Du Bois—had become a radical black nationalist. This was reflected in the novel, which focused on efforts to integrate a school in a "nowhere" city situated between the northern and southern United States. The novel's vision was deeply pessimistic and expressed his advocacy of "Blackist Marxism."

In 1960 Mayfield visited Cuba after Fidel Castro's revolution in the company of Le Roi Jones, Robert Williams, and others. In this period, he published many magazine articles on African-American affairs and was active in black nationalist circles. In 1961, after Williams was accused of kidnapping a white couple, Mayfield, who was with Williams at the time, was wanted for questioning by the FBI. Mayfield fled to Canada, then England, before arriving in Ghana in 1962.

In Ghana Mayfield served as a speechwriter and aide to President Kwame Nkrumah and founded and edited *African Review.* In keeping with his internationalism, Mayfield edited *The World Without the Bomb* (1963), the report of a conference on disarmament held in Ghana and attended mostly by third-world scientists. He was in Spain in 1966 when Nkrumah was overthrown in a coup. Mayfield moved to England for a while, then returned to the United States in 1968.

In 1968 Mayfield was given a fellowship at New York University. Two years later he became the first Distinguished W. E. B. Du Bois Fellow at Cornell University. That same year he edited *Ten Times Black,* a collection of stories by younger African-American authors. During this time he cowrote the screenplay for *Uptight* (1968), about life inside a black nationalist organization, in which he played the lead; this was his much acclaimed film debut. Mayfield also wrote the screenplays for *The Hitch* (1969), *Children of Anger* (1971), and, with Woodie King, *The Long Night* (1976).

In 1971 Mayfield moved to Guyana in South America as an adviser to the minister of information and later functioned as an assistant to Prime Minister Forbes Burnham. Mayfield returned to the United States in 1974 and taught

for two years at the University of Maryland in College Park. He later served as a senior Fulbright-Hays Fellow, teaching in Europe and Tunisia. In 1977 he relocated to the University of Maryland, and the next year he accepted an appointment as writer-in-residence at Howard University, a position he maintained until his death of a heart ailment in Takoma Park, Maryland, in 1984.

See also Baraka, Amiri (Jones, LeRoi); Burnham, Forbes; Caribbean/North American Writers (Contemporary); Harlem Writers Guild

■ ■ *Bibliography*

Davis, Arthur P. *From the Dark Tower: Afro-American Writers.* Washington, D.C.: Howard University Press, 1981.

Forman, Robert. *The Making of Black Revolutionaries.* New York: Macmillan, 1972.

Mayfield, Julian. "Into the Mainstream and Oblivion." In *The American Negro Writer and His Roots.* New York: American Society of African Culture, 1960.

Richards, Phillip M. Foreword to *The Hit and the Long Night.* Boston: Northeastern University, 1989.

Williams, Robert. *Negroes with Guns.* New York: Marzani and Munsell, 1962.

PETER SCHILLING (1996)

MAYORS

The area in which African Americans made the greatest political gains during the late twentieth century was in city government. By 1990 most of the large cities in the United States, including four of the top five, had elected African-American mayors. This political shift took place with astounding swiftness. Although a few black mayors were elected in small southern towns during Reconstruction, and numerous all-black towns during the Jim Crow era had black chief executives, the first African-American mayors of large cities were elected only in 1967, with the elections of Carl Stokes in Cleveland, Ohio, and Richard Hatcher in Gary, Indiana. That same year, Walter Washington was appointed mayor of Washington, D.C., although he was not elected to that office until 1974.

The institution of black political control in the urban areas of the United States at the end of the twentieth and into the beginning of the twenty-first centuries was the product of several factors, including the shifting racial demography of cities. As the industrial sector of the American economy declined, unemployment as well as taxes increased while city services declined. As a result, many affluent city residents, overwhelmingly white, moved from cities to adjacent suburbs, and black-majority or near-majority populations were created within city limits.

The other important factors were the civil rights and Black Power movements of the 1960s. The effects were most evident in the South, where movement efforts inspired passage of the Voting Rights Act of 1965 and other measures that ensured full political participation and provided federal protection to blacks attempting to exercise their right to vote. However, even in the areas of the country where blacks were able to vote throughout the twentieth century, the civil rights movement provided an inspiring ideology and model for black political action. Many of the black activists who went south returned as cadres and organizers responsible for voter registration and the formation of alliances. The Black Power movement, with its emphasis on black control of black areas, also proved influential. The urban riots and rebellions of the 1960s, which publicized black powerlessness and at the same time hastened white outmigration, accelerated the election of African-American mayors.

Another factor that shaped the early black urban governments was the federal government. Federal civil rights legislation and affirmative-action programs improved the political and economic status of black communities. In addition, Great Society antipoverty programs provided black communities with sources of organization and patronage outside the control of white-dominated urban political machines and stimulated black interest in electoral politics.

African-American mayors can be divided into two main types: those from black-majority or near-majority cities (including virtually all southern cities with black mayors) and those with predominantly white electorates. The first wave of mayors, with the exception of Carl Stokes, came from black-majority industrial cities in the North and Midwest that had previously been the site of riots and other racial tensions. Elected with the help of black communities and movement organizations, they generally had little or no white voting support. Richard Hatcher (1933–), the first of these mayors, was elected mayor in the declining steel town of Gary, Indiana, where blacks represented just over 50 percent of the population. Another notable figure, Coleman Young (1918–1997), of Detroit, a former United Auto Workers activist, was elected in 1973.

One model of this type of mayor is Kenneth Gibson (1932–) of Newark, New Jersey, who was elected in 1970. Newark's industrial core and population had declined through the postwar period and by the late 1960s had a

Coleman A. Young. *Young was Detroit's first black mayor and the city's longest-serving chief executive, holding the office from 1974 to 1994.* AP/WIDE WORLD PHOTOS. REPRODUCED BY PERMISSION.

black-majority population. The city's notoriously corrupt machine-dominated government had traditionally excluded blacks. In 1967, one year after Gibson, a city councilman, ran unsuccessfully for mayor, a major racial uprising in the city occurred. In 1969 Newark's mayor, Hugh Addonizio, was convicted on federal corruption charges and removed from office. Meanwhile, black militants led by writer Amiri Baraka organized a coalition of African-American and Puerto Rican voters and selected Gibson as a consensus candidate. In 1970, with the help of heavy black voter-registration efforts and bloc voting, Gibson was narrowly elected. Once in office, Gibson reached out to the white business community to counteract economic decline and attempted to assure a black majority on the city school board. He drew heavy criticism from black radicals over his perceived inattention to black community problems and from whites over municipal corruption, but he remained a popular figure and was reelected for several terms before being defeated by another African American.

Gibson's experience in office typifies the problems of mayors of black-majority cities. Black mayors come to office amid high expectations of policy reforms in the police department, school board, and welfare agency. However, administrative change is difficult and hard to finance, particularly in declining "rust belt" cities with straitened budgets. Mayoral power over city agencies is often limited, and the health of city economies depends on relations among mayors, white-dominated business interests, and state and federal government officials. However, despite some disappointments, African-American mayors of black cities tend to be reelected for several terms, and then are usually followed by other African Americans.

African-American mayors of southern cities—such as Willie Herenton of Memphis, elected in 1992; Bernard Kincaid of Birmingham, elected in 1999; and C. Ray Nagin of New Orleans, elected in 2002—have also come from black-majority or near-majority cities. Little Rock, Arkansas, was the only predominantly white southern city of any size to elect black mayors during the 1970s and 1980s. However, they have differed in a few respects from their northern counterparts. First, not surprisingly, given the electoral history of the South, these candidates had little or no prior experience in electoral politics. Also, while some came from declining "New South" industrial cities, the southern mayors tended to inherit more viable city economies. Thus, although these mayors were elected by a united black vote, they have often run as moderates, hoping to cement links with white business interests. Also, southern black mayors, particularly in Atlanta, have developed affirmative-action programs and provided assistance that has helped expand and solidify the black middle class in their cities.

The other major type of black mayor has been the "crossover" mayor: chief executives elected with significant white support, usually in cities without dominant black populations. The best-known members of this group include Carl Stokes of Cleveland, elected in 1967; Tom Bradley of Los Angeles, elected in 1973; Wilson Goode of Philadelphia, elected in 1983; Harold Washington of Chicago, elected in 1983; David Dinkins of New York City, elected in 1989; and John Street of Philadelphia, elected in 1999. To this list might be added Sidney Barthelemy of New Orleans, who, in 1986, was elected mayor of a black-majority city over another African-American candidate. While Barthelemy's opponent gained a majority of the black vote, Barthelemy won with a small black vote and a solid white vote.

The "crossover" mayors form a diverse group. Many of these mayors, of whom Dinkins is the most celebrated example, came to office in cities torn by racial tension, campaigned as peacemakers, and convinced white voters that a black mayor could more effectively "control" crime and urban rebellions. Through personal charisma and skill in reaching out to diverse minority and interest groups (Latinos, Jews, gays and lesbians, labor unions, women's groups, etc.), these candidates were able to forge successful coalitions.

Tom Bradley, former mayor of Los Angeles. *Bradley was the first African American mayor of Los Angeles, where he served an unprecedented five terms in a city where African Americans constituted only a minority of the electorate.* PHOTOGRAPHS AND PRINTS DIVISION, SCHOMBURG CENTER FOR RESEARCH IN BLACK CULTURE, THE NEW YORK PUBLIC LIBRARY, ASTOR, LENOX AND TILDEN FOUNDATIONS.

By the early 1990s black mayoral politics had entered a new stage of development. Black mayors were being elected to office in greater numbers of cities. Among them were several black women, representing both major cities (Sharon Sayles Belton of Minneapolis, elected in 1994; Sharon Pratt Dixon of Washington, D.C., elected in 1990; and Shirley Franklin of Atlanta, elected in 2002) and smaller cities (Carrie Perry of Hartford, Connecticut, elected in 1987; Jessie Rattley of Newport News, Virginia, elected in 1986; Lottie Shackleford of Little Rock, Arkansas, elected in 1987; and Brenda Lawrence, of Southfield, Michigan, elected in 2001).

Furthermore, in the 1990s greater numbers of African Americans were coming to office in cities in which African Americans represented only a small percentage of the population. For example, Norman Rice of Seattle, elected in 1990, and Sharon Sayles Belton of Minneapolis presided in cities where blacks were, respectively, some 10 percent and 13 percent of the population. In 2000 Michael B. Coleman was elected mayor of Columbus, Ohio, where blacks are about a quarter of the population. Previously (with the exception of Tom Bradley of Los Angeles), only a few cities without significant black populations, such as Boulder, Colorado; Spokane, Washingon; and Santa Monica, California—university towns and other areas that tend to vote liberal—had had black mayors.

In some cases black mayors in nonblack-majority cities were succeeded by other African Americans, but in many cities black electoral power was not fully expressed until the late twentieth or early twenty-first century. For example, it was not until 1999 that Macon, Georgia, elected its first black mayor. Jackson, Mississippi, and Savannah, Georgia, despite their black majorities, did not have black chief executives until 1997 and 2003, respectively. Moreover, most black mayors in racially mixed cities were elected by very narrow margins; their victories consisted of overwhelming percentages of the black vote along with a split white vote. For example, in his successful mayoral bid in 1983, Harold Washington won 51 percent of the vote, gaining 99 percent of the black vote, 60 percent of the Hispanic vote, and 19 percent of the white vote. Similarly, David Dinkins won the 1989 election by 47,080 votes, the closest election in city history, with 92 percent of the black vote, 65 percent of the Hispanic vote, and 27 percent of the white vote. Their electoral majorities remained vulnerable, and many of these mayors were defeated following small shifts in voter support in subsequent elections, while increasing racial polarization in large nonblack-majority cities made the election of future black mayors extremely difficult. By 1993 white mayors had succeeded blacks in the nation's four largest cities—New York City, Los Angeles, Chicago, and Philadelphia. That year, following a shift of fewer than 100,000 votes, New York Mayor David Dinkins lost a close mayoral race, becoming the first big-city black mayor to fail to be reelected. The negative trend continued in the mid-1990s.

Although in 1995 Lee Brown became the first black mayor of Houston, and Ron Kirk became Dallas's first African-American mayor, the heavily black city of Gary, Indiana, elected a white mayor that year, and white mayors took power following the departure of black mayors in Seattle in 1998 and Oakland in 1999. In 1999 Philadelphia again elected a black mayor, John Street; in 2005 Street was the nation's only black mayor of a city with a population of more than a million. Despite setbacks, the office of mayor continues to be a main focus of black political aspiration, and African Americans have established themselves as solid, responsible chief executives in cities in every part of the country.

See also Bradley, Tom; Dinkins, David; Hatcher, Richard Gordon; Politics in the United States; Stokes, Carl Burton; Voting Rights Act of 1965; Washington, Harold; Young, Coleman

▨ ▨ *Bibliography*

Browning, Rufus, Dale Rogers Marshall, and David H. Tabb, eds. *Racial Politics in American Cities,* 3rd ed. New York: Longman, 2003.

Colburn, David R., and Jeffrey S. Adler, eds. *African-American Mayors: Race, Politics, and the American City.* Urbana: University of Illinois Press, 2001.

Greer, Edward. *Big Steel: Black Politics and Corporate Power in Gary, Indiana.* New York: Monthly Review Press, 1979.

Karnig, Albert, and Susan Welch. *Black Representation and Urban Policy.* Chicago: University of Chicago Press, 1980.

Thompson, J. Phillip, III. *Double Trouble: Black Mayors, Black Communities, and the Call for a Deep Democracy.* New York: Oxford University Press, 2005.

GREG ROBINSON (1996)
JESSICA HORNIK-EVANS (2005)

MAYS, BENJAMIN E.

AUGUST 1, 1894
MARCH 28, 1984

┣┃┃━━━━━━━

The educator and clergyman Benjamin Elijah Mays was born in Ninety-Six, South Carolina, the eighth and youngest child of Hezekiah and Louvenia Carter Mays. His father supported the family as a sharecropper. A year at Virginia Union University in Richmond preceded Mays's matriculation at Bates College in Maine, from which he graduated with honors in 1920. At the divinity school of the University of Chicago, he earned an M.A. degree in 1925. Ten years later, while engaged in teaching, social work, and educational administration, Mays received a Ph.D. from the same divinity school.

Mays lived in Tampa, Florida, in the early 1920s, where he was active in social work in the Tampa Urban League, exposing police brutality and attacking discrimination in public places. However, higher education soon became his principal vocation. Teaching stints at Morehouse College in Atlanta and South Carolina State College in Orangeburg between 1921 and 1926 put Mays in the classroom as an instructor in mathematics, psychology, religious education, and English.

In 1934, with his Ph.D. nearly finished, Mays went to Howard University in Washington, D.C., as dean of the school of religion. He served for six years, and during that time graduate enrollment increased, the quality of the faculty improved, and the school's library was substantially augmented. During his tenure the seminary gained accreditation from the American Association of Theological Schools.

Mays's administrative successes at Howard University convinced the trustees of Morehouse College to elect him as the new president of their institution in 1940. He served until 1967. During his tenure, the percentage of faculty with Ph.D.s increased from 8.7 percent to 54 percent, and the physical plant and campus underwent numerous improvements. One of Mays's protégés at Morehouse was Martin Luther King Jr., who attended the college from 1944—when he entered as a fifteen-year-old—through 1948. Mays, both by example and personal influence, helped persuade the young King to seek a career in the ministry. Mays remained a friend of King's throughout his career, urging him to persevere in the Montgomery bus boycott. In 1965 Mays was instrumental in King's election to the Morehouse board of trustees.

In addition to his activities in higher education, Mays remained involved in religious affairs. Although he was active as a pastor for only a few years in the early 1920s, he became a familiar presence in the affairs of the National Baptist Convention and in several ecumenical organizations. In 1944 he became vice president of the Federal Council of Churches of Christ, a national organization of mainline Protestant denominations. In 1948 Mays helped organize the World Council of Churches (WCC) in Amsterdam, Holland, where he successfully pushed for a resolution to acknowledge racism as a divisive force among Christians. When a delegate from the Dutch Reformed Church proposed that an all-white delegation from the WCC investigate apartheid in South Africa, Mays argued convincingly for an interracial team.

Mays was a distinguished scholar of the black church and black religion. In 1930 the Institute of Social and Religious Research in New York City asked Mays and Joseph W. Nicholson, a minister in the Colored Methodist Episcopal Church, to survey black churches in twelve cities and four rural areas. In their study, *The Negro's Church* (1933), they argued that black churches represented "the failure of American Christianity." They found that there was an oversupply of black churches, that too many churches had untrained clergy, and that they carried too much indebtedness. These shortcomings deprived the members and the communities they served of adequate programs to deal with the broad range of social and economic ills they faced. Nonetheless, Mays and Nicholson praised the autonomy of black churches and their promotion of educa-

tion, economic development, and leadership opportunities for African Americans.

In 1938 Mays produced a second important volume, *The Negro's God as Reflected in His Literature,* a study of how blacks conceptualized God and related the deity to their temporal circumstances. Mays argued that many blacks believed God to be intimately involved in and mindful of their condition as an oppressed group. Even those who doubted or rejected either the notion of God or the social dimension of the deity, Mays argued, were still influenced by their understanding of the social purpose of God. In later years Mays wrote an autobiography, *Born to Rebel* (1971), which was published in an abridged version in 1981 as *Lord, the People Have Driven Me On.*

After his retirement in 1967, Mays won election to the Atlanta Board of Education in 1969. He became president of that body in 1970.

Mays married twice. His first wife, Ellen Harvin Mays, died in 1923. His second wife, whom he married in 1926, was Sadie Gray Mays. She died on October 11, 1969. In 1982 Mays was awarded the National Association for the Advancement of Colored People (NAACP)'s Spingarn Medal. Mays died in Atlanta, Georgia, in 1984.

See also Howard University; Montgomery, Ala., Bus Boycott; Morehouse College; National Baptist Convention, U.S.A., Inc.; National Urban League; Spingarn Medal

▪ ▪ *Bibliography*

Carson, Clayborne, Ralph E. Luker, and Penny A. Russell, eds. *The Papers of Martin Luther King, Jr.,* vol. 1, *January 1929-June 1951.* Berkeley: University of California Press, 1992.

Carter, Lawrence Edward, Sr., ed. *Walking Integrity: Benjamin Elijah Mays, Mentor to Martin Luther King, Jr.* Macon, Ga.: Mercer University Press, 1998.

Bennett, Lerone. "Benjamin E. Mays: Last of the Great Schoolmasters." *Ebony* (October 1994). Reprint, *Ebony* 59, no. 11 (September 2004): 172–175.

Mays, Benjamin E. *Born to Rebel.* New York, 1971, rev. ed. Athens: University of Georgia Press, 2002.

Mays, Benjamin E. *Lord, the People Have Driven Me On.* New York: Vantage, 1981.

Mays, Benjamin E. *The Negro's God as Reflected in His Literature.* Boston: Chapman and Grimes, 1938.

Mays, Benjamin E. and Joseph W. Nicholson. *The Negro's Church.* New York: Institute of Social and Religious Research, 1933.

DENNIS C. DICKERSON (1996)
Updated bibliography

MAYS, WILLIE

MAY 6, 1931

The son of steel-mill worker Willie Howard Mays and Ann Mays, baseball player Willie Howard Mays Jr. was born in Westfield, Alabama. After his parents divorced soon after his birth, Mays was raised by an aunt in Fairfield, Alabama. At Fairfield Industrial High School he starred in basketball, football, and baseball.

At the age of seventeen Mays began his professional career, joining the Birmingham Black Barons of the Negro National League. During three seasons with the Black Barons, he played 130 games in the outfield and compiled a batting average of .263. In 1950 he started the season with the Black Barons, but he was soon signed by the New York Giants. He played on the Giants' minor league teams until early in the 1951 season, when he joined the major league club. Mays was voted the National League Rookie of the Year and acquired the nickname "the 'Say Hey' kid" when he forgot a teammate's name in 1951 and used the phrase.

In 1952 and 1953 Mays served in the U. S. Army, but he returned to baseball in 1954 to play one of his best seasons ever. He led the National League with a .345 batting average and had 41 home runs and 110 runs batted in, leading the Giants to the 1954 National League pennant and world championship. In the first game of the World Series with the Cleveland Indians at the Polo Grounds in New York City, Mays made one of the most famous catches in baseball history: With his back to home plate, he ran down Vic Wertz's 440-foot drive to center field, wheeled around, and fired a perfect throw to the infield, thus preventing the Indians from scoring. Mays was named the National League's Most Valuable Player for 1954. He won the award a second time in 1965.

Mays is often considered the most complete ballplayer of the postwar era, if not of all time. He excelled in every aspect of the game. He hit over .300 in ten seasons, and totaled 660 home runs. He was one of the game's great base runners and a superlative fielder. (His fielding earned him twelve consecutive Gold Gloves from 1957 to 1968.) Mays played in every All-Star game from 1954 to 1973 and in four World Series (in 1951 and 1954 with the New York Giants; in 1962 with the San Francisco Giants; and in 1973 with the New York Mets).

Because of his formidable abilities, and because of racism, Mays was also the target of an inordinate number of "bean balls"—pitches thrown at the batter's head. However, Mays was one of the first black superstars to receive widespread adulation from white fans. In the 1960s he was among the many black athletes who were criticized for not publicly supporting the civil rights movement. As on most controversial issues, Mays projected a naive innocence when confronted about his political silence. "I don't picket in the streets of Birmingham," he said. "I'm not mad at the people who do. Maybe they shouldn't be mad at the people who don't."

Mays played with the Giants (the team moved to San Francisco in 1958) until 1972, when he was traded to the New York Mets. The following year he retired as a player but was retained by the Mets as a part-time coach. He was inducted into the National Baseball Hall of Fame in 1979. Three months later, he was ordered by Major League Baseball commissioner Bowie Kuhn to choose between his job with the Mets and fulfilling a public relations contract with the Bally's Casino Hotel. Mays, along with Mickey Mantle, chose the latter and was banned from any affiliation with professional baseball. In 1985 the new commissioner, Peter Ueberroth, lifted the ban.

In 2000 a statue of Mays was unveiled at Pacific Bell Park, the new home of the San Francisco Giants.

See also Baseball

■ ■ *Bibliography*

Mays, Willie, and Charles Einstein. *Willie Mays: My Life In and Out of Baseball.* New York: Dutton, 1972.

Mays, Willie, and Lou Sahadi. *Say Hey: The Autobiography of Willie Mays.* New York: Simon and Schuster, 1988.

Reilly, Rick. "Say Hey Again." *Sports Illustrated* 99 (September 15, 2003): 100.

THADDEUS RUSSELL (1996)
Updated by publisher 2005

MCBURNIE, BERYL

NOVEMBER 2, 1913
MARCH 30, 2000

Beryl Eugenia McBurnie, a pioneer of Trinidad and Tobago's folk dance scene, was born in Trinidad. A child with a natural aptitude for dance who converted her parents' backyard into a theater, McBurnie resented the British colonial school system that promoted "foreign" culture, as opposed to her indigenous heritage. Native mores and influences were deemed substandard at best, and were scorned at worst.

In the early 1940s, during a stint at New York's Columbia University studying cultural anthropology with

Melville Herskovitz, McBurnie refined her dance techniques with Martha Graham, all the while continuing to build a name for herself in her native country. She collaborated with several ardent Pan-Caribbeanists there. Eric Williams, a scholar and the first prime minister of Trinidad and Tobago, and C. L. R. James, a noted Marxist intellectual, persuaded her to apply her talent to the cause of West Indian unity and independence. Local folklorists Carlton Comma and Andrew Carr saw in her career the artistic expression of the political and social upheavals that followed the nation's demand for self-determination, as well as the intellectual research ability that characterized her efforts to broaden the scope of Trinidad and Tobago's cultural life.

Encouraged to study Caribbean folk heritage and influences, McBurnie visited South America in the mid-1940s and it was in Cayenne that she discovered the model for the theater she subsequently established in Trinidad and Tobago. The 1948 opening of the Little Carib Theatre was a triumph. Paul Robeson, the American baritone and Pan-Africanist, attended, as did Eric Williams, who said that the Little Carib is, in the broadest sense a political event, in that it is West Indian and rooted in the West Indian people and environment. "I never felt as proud of the West Indies or as optimistic of their future as I did last night" (Williams, 1948).

At various times in the 1950 to 1952 period, McBurnie toured England, Europe, and North Africa herself, seeking cultural ties with the West Indies and the necessary funding for her brainchild, which never received the requisite governmental support. Yet her troupe did not lack acclaim—in Puerto Rico in August 1952, in Jamaica at the country's tercentenary celebrations in 1955, and in Canada at the 1958 Stratford Shakespeare Festival. The troupe later performed for Britain's Queen Elizabeth II in 1966.

Beryl McBurnie single-handedly bucked the colonial artistic system. Through meticulous research, she rescued Trinidad and Tobago's rich and forgotten heritage, recalling its French, African, and Venezuelan roots in both music and dance, yet always portraying that which was common to her country. For her efforts, she was awarded the Order of the British Empire in 1959, Trinidad and Tobago's Humming Bird Gold Medal in 1969, and her country's highest honor, The Trinity Cross, in 1989. Through her art, Beryl McBurnie raised the political consciousness of a people. A precursor of the freedom of spirit that crystallized in Trinidad and Tobago's independence from Britain in 1962, she gave meaning to the preservationist's mantra: if we fail to pay attention to the roadmarks of the past, the present begins to lose its points of reference.

See also Dance, Diasporic; James, C. L. R.; Williams, Eric

■ ■ *Bibliography*

Ahye, Molly. *Cradle of Caribbean Dance*. Petit Valley, Trinidad and Tobago: Heritage Cultures, 1983.

Anthony, Michael. *Historical Dictionary of Trinidad and Tobago*. Lanham, Md.: Scarecrow Press, 1997.

Anthony, Michael. "People of the Century," Part 1. *Trinidad Express*, sec. 2, pp. 20–21. April 12, 2000.

Williams, Eric. Letter to Beryl McBurnie marking the opening night of the Little Carib Theatre, November 26, 1948. Eric Williams Memorial Collection, University of the West Indies, Trinidad and Tobago.

ERICA WILLIAMS CONNELL (2005)

McDaniel, Hattie

June 10, 1895
October 26, 1952

Singer and actress Hattie McDaniel was born in Wichita, Kansas. Her father, Henry McDaniel, was a Baptist preacher and an entertainer, and her mother, Susan (Holbert) McDaniel, was a choir singer. McDaniel was one of thirteen children. Soon after her birth the family moved to Colorado, and in 1901 they settled in Denver. In 1910, at the age of fifteen, she was awarded a gold medal by the Women's Christian Temperance Union for excellence in "the dramatic art" for her recital of "Convict Joe," which reportedly "moved the house to tears." On the strength of this success, McDaniel persuaded her family to allow her to leave school and join her brothers in her father's newly formed traveling company, the Henry McDaniel Minstrel Show. Over the next decade she traveled and performed on the West Coast, mostly with her father's company, and she began at this time to develop her abilities as a songwriter and singer.

Around 1920 McDaniel came to the notice of George Morrison, one of Denver's notable popular musicians. Taken on as a singer with Morrison's orchestra, McDaniel became increasingly well known throughout the West Coast vaudeville circuit. She also appeared with the orchestra on Denver radio during this time, and she is reputed to be the first black woman soloist to sing on the radio. In 1929 she secured a place with a traveling production of *Show Boat*, but the stock market crash of October 1929 eliminated the show's financing.

After the crash, McDaniel moved to Milwaukee, where she worked in the coatroom of the Club Madrid and eventually got an opportunity to perform. Encouraged by her success, she moved to Hollywood in 1931 and soon began working regularly in radio and film. Over the next two decades she appeared in more than three hundred films, though mostly in minor, uncredited roles. Her debut was in *The Golden West* (1932). The first film for which she received screen credit was *Blonde Venus* (1932), in which she played the affectionate, loyal, but willful domestic, a type character that was virtually the only role available at the time to large black women in Hollywood. Over the course of the next two decades McDaniel successfully established herself in this role, gaining substantial, credited parts in over fifty films, including *Alice Adams* (1935), *The Mad Miss Manton* (1935), *Show Boat* (1936, with Paul Robeson), *Affectionately Yours* (1941), *Since You Went Away* (1944), and Walt Disney's animated *Song of the South* (1946).

McDaniel's career reached its high point in 1939 when she won an Academy Award, the first ever given to a black performer, for her portrayal of Mammy in *Gone with the Wind*. Praised by some and maligned by others for the image she portrayed, McDaniel in her Oscar acceptance speech (said to have been written by her studio) announced that she hoped always to be a credit to her race and to her industry. Despite Hollywood's evident self-satisfaction with this award, it is important to note that McDaniel (along with the other black cast members) had been excluded from the Atlanta premiere of the film and that her portrait was removed from the promotional programs that the studio distributed in the South.

McDaniel continued to play similar roles throughout the 1940s despite increased criticism from the NAACP, which felt that McDaniel and the other black actors who played servile stereotypes were helping to perpetuate them. In 1947, after the controversy with the NAACP had passed, McDaniel signed her first contract for the radio show *Beulah*, in which she once again played a southern maid. In the contract McDaniel insisted that she would not use dialect, and she demanded the right to alter any script that did not meet her approval. Both of her demands were met.

McDaniel died in Los Angeles in 1952 after completing the first six episodes of the television version of *Beulah*.

See also Film in the United States

■ ■ *Bibliography*

Jackson, Carlton. *Hattie: The Life of Hattie McDaniel*. Lanham, Md.: Madison Books, 1990.

MATTHEW BUCKLEY (1996)

McDaniel, Otha Elias

See Diddley, Bo (McDaniel, Otha Elias)

McHenry, Donald F.
October 13, 1936

■ ■ ■

Born in St. Louis, United Nations (UN) ambassador Donald F. McHenry grew up in an impoverished neighborhood in East St. Louis, Illinois, and graduated from Illinois State University in 1957. He received his master's degree from Southern Illinois University in 1959 and then became an English instructor at Howard University. After studying international relations at Georgetown University, he joined the Department of State as a foreign affairs officer in the Dependent Areas Section, Office of UN Political Affairs (1963–1966). He briefly served as assistant to the secretary of state, and from 1968 to 1969 he acted as special assistant to the counselor of the Department of State.

The Brookings Institute invited McHenry to be guest scholar (1971–1973), during which time he also was a lecturer at Georgetown University. He then was director of humanitarian policy studies at the Carnegie Endowment for International Peace (1973–1977) and lectured at American University in 1975.

President Jimmy Carter named McHenry deputy representative in the UN Security Council. He and his friend, UN Ambassador Andrew Young, established a good relationship and complemented each other at the UN. From 1978 to 1979 McHenry worked with Angola to strengthen its relationship with the United States and brought an end to negotiations on a UN plan for Namibia independence. McHenry was chief U.S. negotiator for other UN plans involving South Africa.

After Young resigned under pressure on August 15, 1979, McHenry was sworn in the following month as U.S. permanent representative to the UN and ambassador and U.S. deputy representative to the UN Security Council, remaining in that office until January 20, 1981. Since that time, McHenry has served on the board of directors of several prominent corporations, including Coca-Cola, AT&T, International Paper, and Fleet National Bank, and has held a number of board and trustee positions in nonprofit organizations and foundations. He is a Distinguished Professor in the Practice of Diplomacy at the School of Foreign Service at Georgetown University, and principal owner and president of the IRC Group, an international consulting firm based in Washington, D.C.

See also Politics in the United States

■ ■ *Bibliography*

Current Biography Yearbook. New York: Wilson, 1980.

JESSIE CARNEY SMITH (1996)
Updated by publisher 2005

MCINTOSH, GEORGE

MARCH 6, 1886
NOVEMBER 1, 1963

George Augustus McIntosh can arguably be described as the most outstanding political leader in St. Vincent and the Grenadines in the first fifty years of the twentieth century. Born in 1886, he was the son of a Scottish father, Donald McIntosh, and a Vincentian mother who worked as a cook. His was a pharmacist by profession, beginning at the age of seventeen as a trainee at the Kingstown General Hospital. McIntosh is best known, however, as a political and labor leader.

George McIntosh, or "Dada," as he was called, first entered the political arena when he became one of the founders of the St. Vincent Representative Government Association, an organization that struggled for the reintroduction of elected representation in the legislature and politics of the country. As a pharmacist, he was consulted on a regular basis by the poorer classes of the community. His establishment of a pharmacy near the Kingstown market meant that on Saturdays, after selling their goods at the market, the peasantry and working people would patronize his store, which was not limited to pharmaceutical products. It was this relationship that brought him into prominence at the time of the riots in 1935, when he was arrested on the belief that he was the mastermind behind the riots.

Because of his relationship with the country's working people, they consulted him at the time of the riots and sought his help in intervening with the governor to plead for improvements in their dire social and economic situation. After his case was dismissed at the preliminary trial, McIntosh sought to capture the energies and hopes of the working people through the formation of the St. Vincent Workingmen's Cooperative Association, a movement that was part union and part political party.

Despite the fact that the majority of his supporters could not meet the franchise requirements, McIntosh's association held the majority of seats in parliament in 1937 and did so until the introduction of universal adult suffrage in 1951. McIntosh took issues related to the working people to parliament at a time when even as leader of his party he had virtually no power under the crown colony system of government. He was, however, able to highlight their problems and had their support as an extraparliamentary force. McIntosh stressed issues centered on land settlement for the working people and was instrumental in forcing the government to extend land settlement through the 1945 Land Settlement Scheme. He also took up the struggle of the Spiritual Baptists, then called Shakers, a religion that was banned in 1912. He constantly raised the issue in parliament and set the stage for the eventual repeal of the law in 1965. McIntosh also served in the Kingstown Town Board from 1924 to the time of his death, acting as chair on numerous occasions. He was in the forefront of efforts to form a political union of English-speaking Caribbean colonies and of the integration of the regional labor movement.

McIntosh kept a portrait of Soviet leader Joseph Stalin in his shop, wore a red tie, and held—on at least one occasion—a dinner in honor of the Russian Revolution. He was in the forefront of radical and progressive politics but was "no Leninist insurrectionist" according to Gordon Lewis. McIntosh died in 1963, still holding a seat on the Kingstown Town Board.

■ ■ *Bibliography*

Fraser, Adrian. "Peasants and Agricultural Labourers in St. Vincent and the Grenadines 1899–1951." Ph.D. diss., University of Western Ontario, London, Ontario, 1986.

Gonsalves, Ralph E. *The Trial of George McIntosh: The McIntosh Trial and the October 1935 Uprising in St. Vincent and the Grenadines, West Indies.* New York: Caribbean Diaspora Press, 1996.

John, Kenneth. "The Political Life and Times of George McIntosh." Paper presented at the St. Vincent and the Grenadines Country Conference, May 22–24, 2003. Available from <http://www.uwichill.edu.bb/bnccde/svg/conference/papers/john.html>.

John, Rupert. *Pioneers in Nation Building in a Caribbean Mini-State.* New York: Unitar, 1979.

Lewis, Gordon K. *The Growth of the Modern West Indies.* New York: Modern Reader, 1968.

ADRIAN FRASER (2005)

McKay, Claude

September 15, 1889
May 22, 1948

‖‖‖ ─────────────────────

The poet and novelist Festus Claudius "Claude" McKay was the child of independent small farmers. In 1912 he published two volumes of Jamaican dialect poetry, *Songs of Jamaica* and *Constab Ballads*. They reflect the British imperial influences of his youth and reveal that the rebellion that characterized McKay's American poetry lay in both his Jamaican experience and his later experience of white racism in the United States. His Jamaican poetry also contains early versions of his pastoral longing for childhood innocence and his primal faith in the self-sufficiency and enduring virtues of the rural black community of his childhood and youth.

McKay left Jamaica in 1912 to study agriculture at Tuskegee Institute and Kansas State University, but in 1914 he moved to New York City, where he began again to write poetry. In 1919, he became a regular contributor to the revolutionary literary monthly the *Liberator,* and he achieved fame among black Americans for his sonnet "If We Must Die," which exhorted African Americans to fight bravely against the violence directed against them in the reactionary aftermath of World War I. Although expressed in traditional sonnet form, McKay's post–World War I poetry heralded modern black expressions of anger, alienation, and rebellion, and he quickly became a disturbing, seminal voice in the Harlem Renaissance of the 1920s. His collected American poetry includes *Spring in New Hampshire and Other Poems* (1920) and *Harlem Shadows* (1922).

The years between 1919 and 1922 marked the height of McKay's political radicalism. In 1922 he journeyed to Moscow, where he attended the Fourth Congress of the Third Communist International, but his independence and his criticisms of American and British Communists led to his abandonment of communism. In the 1930s he became a vocal critic of international communism because of its antidemocratic dominance by the Soviet Union.

From 1923 until 1934, McKay lived in western Europe and Tangiers. While abroad, he published three novels—*Home to Harlem* (1928), *Banjo* (1929), and *Banana Bottom* (1933)—plus one collection of short stories, *Gingertown* (1932). In his novels, McKay rebelled against the genteel traditions of older black writers, and he offended leaders of black protest by writing, in *Home to Harlem* and *Banjo,* of essentially leaderless rural black migrants and their predicaments in the modern, mechanistic, urban West. Both are picaresque novels that celebrate the natural resilience and ingenuity of "primitive" black heroes. To McKay's critics, his characters were irresponsible degenerates, not exemplary models of racial wisdom, and he was accused of pandering to the worst white stereotypes of African Americans.

In *Gingertown* and *Banana Bottom,* McKay retreated to the Jamaica of his childhood to recapture a lost pastoral world of blacks governed by their own rural community values. Although critics still debate the merits of McKay's fiction, it provided encouragement to younger black writers. *Banjo,* in particular, by stressing that blacks should build upon their own cultural values, influenced the founding generation of the Francophone *Négritude* movement.

In 1934, the Great Depression forced McKay back to the United States, and for the rest of his life he wrote primarily as a journalist critical of international communism, middle-class black integrationism, and white American racial and political hypocrisy. In his essays he continued to champion working-class African Americans, whom he believed understood better than their leaders the necessity of community development. He published a memoir, *A Long Way from Home* (1937), and a collection of essays, *Harlem, Negro Metropolis* (1940), based largely on materials about Harlem folk life he collected as a member of New York City's Federal Writers Project. In 1944—ill, broke, and intellectually isolated—he joined the Roman Catholic Church, and he spent the last years of his life in Chicago working for the Catholic Youth Organization.

Although he is best known as a poet and novelist of the Harlem Renaissance, McKay's social criticism in the 1930s and 1940s was not negligible, though it was controversial, and it has since remained hard to grasp because he was neither a black nationalist, an internationalist, nor a traditional integrationist. He instead believed deeply that blacks, in their various American ethnicities, had much to contribute as ethnic groups and as a race to the collective American life, and that in the future a recognition, acceptance, and celebration of differences between peoples—and not simply individual integration—would best strengthen and bring together the American populace.

See also *Liberator, The*; Harlem Renaissance; Poetry, U.S.; Négritude

■ ■ *Bibliography*

Cooper, Wayne F., ed. *Claude McKay: Rebel Sojourner in the Harlem Renaissance: A Biography.* Baton Rouge: Louisiana State University Press, 1987.

Giles, James R. *Claude McKay.* Boston: Twayne, 1976.

McKay, Claude. *The Passion of Claude McKay: Selected Poetry and Prose, 1912–1948,* edited by Wayne F. Cooper. New York: Schocken, 1973.

Tillery, Tyrone. *Claude McKay: A Black Poet's Struggle for Identity.* Amherst: University of Massachusetts Press, 1992.

WAYNE F. COOPER (1996)

MCKINNEY, CYNTHIA ANN

MARCH 15, 1955

U.S. Congresswoman Cynthia Ann McKinney was born in Atlanta, Georgia. She was educated at the University of Southern California, where she earned a bachelor's degree in 1978, and at the Fletcher School of Law and Diplomacy of Tufts University.

Following graduation from college, McKinney was exposed to the painful sting of racism. On a trip with her father to Alabama to protest the conviction of Tommy Lee Hines, a retarded black man accused of a sexual attack on a white woman, Ku Klux Klan members threatened her. The National Guard settled the disturbance at the event. She decided then that she would enter politics.

McKinney was a fellow (studying diplomacy) at Spelman College in 1984. From 1988 to 1992 she taught at Clark Atlanta University and Agnes Scott College. Her career in politics began in 1988, when she was elected as an at-large member to the Georgia State House of Representatives. Her father, Billy McKinney, was already a member of the legislature and the two became the only father-daughter team in a state legislature. McKinney was elected to the U.S. Congress in 1992 where she quickly made a reputation as an outspoken, liberal crusader for the poor and rural citizens of her state. She gained notoriety with vehement arguments against Republicans on such issues as abortion.

McKinney's congressional district was redrawn prior to the 1996 election after being ruled unconstitutional, eliminating the black voter majority McKinney had enjoyed in her previous election wins. An overwhelmingly negative campaign between McKinney and her white Republican opponent followed, but McKinney won reelection for a third term, proving that a black liberal candidate could win in a white majority district.

In 2002 Democrat Denise Majette beat McKinney in her bid for reelection. McKinney had angered many with her comments that President George W. Bush knew beforehand about the terrorist attacks of September 11, 2001, and profited from them. In 2004 McKinney ran for her old seat in Congress and won handily over her Republican opponent.

See also Politics in the United States

■ ■ *Bibliography*

"Cynthia Ann McKinney." *Notable Black American Women,* Vol. 3. Detroit, Mich.: Gale, 2002.

RAYMOND WINBUSH (1996)
Updated by publisher 2005

MCKISSICK, FLOYD B.

MARCH 9, 1922
APRIL 28, 1991

Civil rights activist Floyd McKissick was born in Asheville, North Carolina. His father, Ernest Boyce McKissick, worked as a bellhop and was committed to providing his son with educational opportunities to ensure him a better economic future. After serving in the army during World War II, McKissick attended Morehouse College and graduated from North Carolina College (now North Carolina Central University) with a bachelor of arts degree in 1951. He became the first African-American student to attend the University of North Carolina Law School at Chapel Hill after NAACP lawyer Thurgood Marshall successfully filed suit on his behalf. Subsequently, McKissick challenged segregation laws by filing suits to gain admission for his five children into all-white schools.

McKissick had taken part in civil rights activism that was spreading throughout the South as early as 1947 when he challenged segregated interstate travel laws by participating in the Journey of Reconciliation sponsored by the Fellowship of Reconciliation (FOR), a pacifist organization committed to integration. In 1960 McKissick established a legal practice in Durham, North Carolina, and became a key legal adviser for the Congress of Racial Equality (CORE)—an interracial civil rights organization that grew out of FOR. McKissick served as legal adviser for CORE and often defended CORE activists who had been arrested for civil disobedience. He played a central role in organizing the Durham chapter of CORE and was appointed head of the chapter in 1962.

As time progressed, McKissick and other black activists in CORE, who had faced unyielding southern white violence and become increasingly disillusioned with white liberalism, began to question the integrationist goals of the movement. McKissick's disillusionment was fueled by the harassment that his children had faced in the "integrated" school setting that he had fought so hard to place them in. Influenced by the rising tide of black nationalism that characterized the Black Power movement, he led the call for black economic empowerment and black control over black institutions within CORE. By 1966, when he replaced James Farmer as national director, McKissick had become a militant advocate of Black Power and steered CORE toward black economic development and a repudiation of interracialism. Two years later, he was replaced as national director by Roy Innis.

After leaving CORE, McKissick established his own consulting firm, Floyd B. McKissick Enterprises, to promote his philosophy of black capitalism. In 1969 he authored *Three-Fifths of a Man*, a book that suggested a combination of nationalist strategies and government assistance for African Americans economically. He led a Ford Foundation project to help African Americans attain positions of responsibility in the cities where they were approaching a majority of the population. In culmination of these efforts, McKissick founded the "Soul City" Corporation in Warren County, North Carolina (an area just south of the Virginia border), in 1974. His aim was to create a community in which African Americans would have political and economic control that could serve as a prototype for the creation of other black-controlled cities and, eventually, states. However, outside funding was cut and the city was not able to attract enough business to become self-sufficient. By June 1980 all of the corporation's property and assets—except eighty-eight acres of the project that contained the headquarters—were taken over by the federal government.

McKissick remained active in public life. He began a successful law firm, McKissick and McKissick (with his son Floyd McKissick Jr.) in Durham, served as pastor of Soul City's First Baptist Church, and in 1990 was appointed district court judge for North Carolina's ninth district by Governor Jim Martin. The following year, McKissick, who had been suffering from lung cancer, died in his Soul City home.

See also Black Power Movement; Civil Rights Movement, U.S.; Congress of Racial Equality (CORE); Farmer, James; Marshall, Thurgood; Morehouse College

■ ■ *Bibliography*

Meier, August, and Elliot Rudwick. *CORE: A Study in the Civil Rights Movement, 1942–1968*. New York: Oxford University Press, 1973.

Van Deburg, William. *A New Day in Babylon: The Black Power Movement and American Culture, 1965–1975*. Chicago: University of Chicago Press, 1992.

ROBYN SPENCER (1996)

MCMILLAN, TERRY

OCTOBER 18, 1951

❙❙❙

The eldest of five children, novelist and short story writer Terry McMillan was born in Point Huron, Michigan, where she spent much of her adolescence in a household headed by her mother. At seventeen, she left Point Huron for Los Angeles, and in 1978 received a bachelor's degree in journalism from the University of California at Berkeley. While she was at Berkeley, author and teacher Ishmael Reed persuaded her to pursue a career in writing. She left California to pursue a master's degree in film at Columbia University, but she left there in 1979, still several credits short of the degree, to join the Harlem Writers Guild.

The first story McMillan read aloud to the guild became the opening chapter of her first novel, *Mama* (1987), which thrust her into prominence. A semi-autobiographical work, *Mama* earned critical praise for its depiction of one woman's struggle to provide for her family during the 1960s and 1970s. The success of the novel is largely due to its realistic, gritty portrayal of Mildred's attempts to cope with the care of five children single-handedly at the age of twenty-seven. McMillan established her reputation further in the genre of the popular novel through her second novel, *Disappearing Acts* (1989). In *Disappearing Acts*, McMillan continues to present strong African-American characters in a New York City setting. The work is a love story that manages to address numerous issues facing many urban African-American communities. The love story of Zora and Franklin becomes a vehicle for an exploration of the complex issues of class and culture that affect relationships between black professionals and working-class partners.

McMillan's third novel, *Waiting to Exhale* (1992), became a best seller within the first week of its release. Although this novel deals with many African-American themes, McMillan's treatment of male-female relationships in a gripping narrative ensures a wide readership. The novel centers on the friendships among four African-American women in Phoenix, Arizona, and how each of them looks for and hides from love. McMillan's tough, sexy style clearly has a wide appeal; the paperback rights for *Waiting to Exhale* were auctioned in the sixth week of its hardcover publication for $2.64 million.

McMillan's next book, *How Stella Got Her Groove Back* (1996) also quickly became a best seller. The work deals with the revitalization of a black woman through her affair with a young West Indian man she meets while on vacation. During the 1990s both *Waiting to Exhale* and *How Stella Got Her Groove Back* were turned into hit movies, whose success at the box office demonstrated both strong appeal to black (especially female) viewers and a sizable crossover to white audiences. The acclaim received by these film adaptations not only fueled McMillan's sales and popularity but also provided vital employment opportunities for African-American casts and directors.

Nevertheless, the commercial success of *Waiting to Exhale* and *How Stella Got Her Groove Back* confirmed for some critics the belief that McMillan is more a writer of potboilers than she is a serious novelist. But McMillan hoped her success would open doors for other African-American writers. To that end, in 1991 she also edited *Breaking Ice: An Anthology of Contemporary African-American Fiction,* which includes short stories and book excerpts by fifty-seven African-American writers, ranging from well-known to new voices.

A Day Late and a Dollar Short, another best seller from McMillan that published in 2001, employs six first-person voices to explore the dynamics of one family as the beloved matriarch lies dying in the hospital. McMillan did not shy away from portraying the most devastating aspects of modern life in the novel, tackling infidelity, drug and alcohol abuse, sexual abuse, and sibling rivalry, while allowing her characters to defend—and condemn—themselves through their own commentary. The characteristic emphasis on relationships in the novel underscores a recurring theme of the author's work.

See also Caribbean/North American Writers (Contemporary); Harlem Writers Guild; Reed, Ishmael

■ ■ *Bibliography*

Awkward, Michael. "Chronicling Everyday Travails and Triumphs." *Callaloo* 2, no. 3 (summer 1988): 649–650.

Edwards, Audrey. "Terry McMillan: Waiting to Inhale." *Essence* (October 1992): 77–78, 82, 118.

Richards, Paulette. *Terry McMillan: A Critical Companion.* Westport, Conn.: Greenwood Press, 1999.

Wilkinson, Brenda. *African American Women Writers.* New York: Wiley, 2000.

AMRITJIT SINGH (1996)
Updated by publisher 2005

McRae, Carmen

April 8, 1922
November 10, 1994

■■■

Born in New York City, jazz singer Carmen McRae studied piano as a child and won an Apollo Theater amateur night contest as a pianist-singer. She began her singing career with Benny Carter's orchestra in 1944. In 1948 she began performing regularly in Chicago, where she lived for nearly four years before returning to New York. By 1952 she was the intermission pianist at Minton's in Harlem, a birthplace of bebop. Married briefly to bop drummer Kenny Clarke, she made her first records under the name Carmen Clarke. Influenced by both Billie Holiday (1915–1959) and Sarah Vaughan (1924–1990), she was named Best New Female Singer by *Down Beat* magazine in 1954, after which she signed a recording contract with Decca Records, for whom she recorded until 1959. Following a move to Los Angeles in the 1960s, McRae made recordings for a number of different labels, including Columbia, Mainstream, Atlantic, Concord, and Novus.

McRae also had an active presence on the international jazz scene, appearing regularly at clubs and festivals until May 1991, when she withdrew from public performance because of failing health. She is one of the important singers who integrated bebop into her vocal style, combining bop phrasing and inflection with sensitivity for the lyrics and dynamics of her material. Among her notable recordings are collections of songs associated with other jazz greats, including Billie Holiday (released in 1962), Nat "King" Cole (1984), Thelonious Monk (1991), and Sarah Vaughan (1991). She died at her home in Beverly Hills California, after suffering a stroke.

See also Holiday, Billie; Jazz Singers; Vaughan, Sarah

■ ■ *Bibliography*

Giddins, Gary. *Rhythm-a-ning: Jazz Tradition and Innovation in the 80s.* New York: Oxford University Press, 1985. Reprint, New York: Da Capo Press, 2000.

Gourse, Leslie. *Carmen McRae: Miss Jazz.* New York: Billboard Books, 2001.

BUD KLIMENT (1996)
Updated bibliography

Media and Identity in the Caribbean

■■■

On any given day in every Caribbean country, with the exception of Cuba, the majority of citizens get their news and information about what is happening in the world from one of six primary sources: CNN, ABC, CBS, Fox News, NBC, or BBC. However, this plurality does not represent an equal diversity of views. Operating as businesses that provide eyes and ears to global advertisers, these six news organizations offer essentially two perspectives to viewers: a British and an American, and "embedded" perspectives in the case of war reporting from Iraq. And what regularly constitutes newsworthy information and makes the headlines depends, for example, on whether or not a famous entertainer is on trial for child molestation or the life support system is withdrawn from a fifteen yearlong comatose individual.

This one-dimensional and lowest-common-denominator perspective on news—dubbed infotainment—is bred by the dominance of entertainment as the ubiquitous form of information globally. In style and format, if not in content, local Caribbean television news replicates the American model. The assumption is that audiences have limited appetites and equally limited attention spans for any information that may force them to think. One result is that local news, especially in the broadcast media, thrives on the violent and the bizarre, paying very little attention to matters of greater relevance and significance to the people of the region. A cursory reading of select regional newspapers in early 2005, for example, showed that coverage of the Caribbean Single Market and Economy (CSME) was virtually nonexistent even though the CSME has widespread economic, political, and social implications for the region's people.

Over ninety percent of all non-news content originates from U.S. distributors and is relayed via local cable operators. Throughout the Caribbean, popular channels include HBO, TNT, TBS, Cinemax, ESPN, the Disney Channel, Nickelodeon, Showtime, MTV, Fox Sports, A&E, Lifetime, and BET. As a result, even though it is played in few Caribbean countries (notably Cuba, the Dominican Republic, and Puerto Rico), baseball may be as popular in the region as cricket, which, for historical reasons, is considered the regional sport of the English-speaking Caribbean. And basketball is more popular than baseball across the region.

Operating on significantly lower budgets and with far smaller audiences, local program producers also tend to mimic the styles and formats of their U.S counterparts. Soap operas in Trinidad and Tobago and Jamaica, for example, are patterned on such shows as *The Bold and the Beautiful* and *The Young and the Restless,* both of which have had their loyal viewers across the region. However, the high production costs of such local programs for regional and extraregional consumption make them economically uncompetitive and hence, rare.

GLOBALIZATION BY HAPPENSTANCE?

When in the late 1970s U.S. domestic satellites were first used to distribute television programs across the continental United States, the signal overspill from these satellites was easily accessed in the region via parabolic dish receivers. Among other things, this led to the emergence of unregulated cable television services in most Caribbean countries provided by local entrepreneurs who saw an opportunity to satisfy the demand for multiple channels by those who could not afford to own their own dish receivers. The launch in 1986 by Westar of its V1-S C-band satellite covered the entire Caribbean and Central America, including as well Venezuela, Colombia, Guyana, and Suriname on the South American mainland. Suddenly, television viewers in the entire region had access to multiple broadcast channels where before, especially in the English-speaking Caribbean, they were limited to programs usually provided by a single government-owned channel. Free access to a cornucopia of television images in color by audiences then became the norm throughout the region.

This was to change with the introduction of the Caribbean Basin Recovery Act (The Caribbean Basin Initiative, or CBI) in 1983 by the Reagan administration. The emerging contours of the nascent global media industry dominated by a handful of largely North American media conglomerates had become evident. So too had the convergence of computer, satellite, and audiovisual technologies made possible by the digitalization of information. The resulting commodification of information led to creation of a hospitable market environment for the new global media industry in the interests of content creators and distributors. The CBI therefore mandated that beneficiary countries of the region meet certain conditions. One of these was structural adjustment of their economies, which, among other things, required them to divest and privatize government-owned enterprises, liberalize and deregulate their economies, and conform to the rules and regulations of the General Agreement on Tariffs and Trade and subsequently the World Trade Organization. Significantly, the CBI bill singled out broadcasting for special treatment, explicitly stating that "the President shall not designate a country a beneficiary country if a government-owned entity in such a country engages in the broadcast of copyrighted material, including films or television material belonging to the United States copyright owners without their express consent."

Full liberalization of the regional media soon followed, with all governments granting multiple broadcast licenses to commercial operators. As a result, with the sole exception of Cuba, all countries of the Caribbean are now served by a multiplicity of predominantly privately owned commercial media including radio, television, and cable services. In this constellation Barbados is an unusual case because the government broadcaster also has a monopoly on cable television. At the other extreme, the governments of Jamaica and Belize divested and privatized their national broadcast services—in the case of the Jamaica Broadcasting Corporation, after thirty-seven years of broadcasting. Public service broadcasting patterned on the BBC model that had been accepted as the norm from the inception of broadcasting in the Anglophone Caribbean from the mid-1930s up until the early 1980s is today nonexistent in these two countries. Where government broadcasters still exist elsewhere, they operate on the margins of the media marketplace as conduits for government information.

In short, the worldwide ascendancy of neoliberal political ideology and technological convergence have resulted in the global media industry being dominated by an oligopoly of vertically and horizontally integrated media conglomerates including TimeWarner, Disney, Bertelsmann, News Corporation, Samsung, and Sony. These global media giants are the primary content providers for the Caribbean's television and cable industries with local video productions operating on the fringes of the industry. Proximity to North America, a shared common language, and heavy reliance on tourism as a major foreign exchange earner make the Anglophone Caribbean countries virtual appendages of the United States.

RADIO BROADCASTING

For the majority of Caribbean citizens, radio remains the most accessible and ubiquitous medium. Its mobility, immediacy, low cost, and the fact that it does not require literacy in a region where literacy levels remain relatively low are its inherent strengths. It is not surprising, then, that in the Caribbean, radio is the medium through which popular culture is given greatest exposure and that media liberalization policies have led to market segmentation by owners seeking niches and greater market share, resulting in a wider choice of content for listeners.

In keeping with global trends, the pattern of media conglomeration is also discernible in the region. In Jamaica the RJR Group owns four radio stations, one television station, and a jointly owned London-based weekly newspaper. Starcom Network in Barbados owns four radio channels, and in Trinidad and Tobago CCN owns a major national daily newspaper and a national television channel.

The diversity of programming on radio, though predominantly music oriented, provides exposure for local musicians in a variety of genres. Predictably, in Jamaica,

where radio helped to foster the emergence of reggae—the national music—there is an all-reggae station, and most of the other fourteen stations also playing some reggae; in Trinidad and Tobago, where fifty percent of the population is of (East) Indian heritage, there are stations specializing in all-Indian music as well as stations specializing in indigenous calypso and soca music. Sports programming also has widespread popularity on regional radio stations, with international cricket being broadcast regularly across the region.

Talk radio, hugely popular in Jamaica since the mid-1970s, remains a staple of programming in that country, with even greater audience participation in light of the prevalence of cellular telephones. The Ministry of Industry and Commerce in Jamaica estimates ownership at two million mobile phones in a population of 2.6 million. Elsewhere there is at least one popular talk radio program in virtually every English-speaking country. Given the mountainous topography of most Caribbean countries, prior to the advent of mobile phones, access to call-in radio programs was primarily limited to urbanites. Although there remain pockets of exclusion in some countries, contemporary technologies have made for greater accessibility and inclusiveness with much wider national participation across the region. Streaming of programming on the Internet by some of the larger radio stations also makes local programs accessible to the Caribbean diaspora globally, and it is not unusual to have Caribbean citizens in New York City, London, and Toronto participating in local discussion and call-in programs via the Internet.

The relative diversity of radio programs notwithstanding, market and business considerations limit the production of local/national and regional news to a handful of larger radio stations in the Caribbean. The main source of regional news from a Caribbean perspective is the Caribbean Media Corporation (CMC)—an alliance of the defunct Caribbean News Agency and the Caribbean Broadcasting Union (CBU), which supplies news to subscriber newspapers and to radio and television stations regionally. However, the perceived high cost of CMC news limits carriage to the larger and better-endowed broadcasters. That these also happen to be the more popular local stations, however, mitigates the relative paucity of regionally generated broadcast news in domestic markets. The BBC, employing Caribbean personnel, also provides a free daily half hour Caribbean news and sports magazine program that is carried by many radio stations. In Jamaica, Radio Mona, owned by the University of the West Indies, provides Jamaican listeners with news from a variety of perspectives by carrying the weekday services of U.S. National Public Radio (NPR), Radio France International, the BBC, as well as Radio Canada International.

THE PRESS AND PRESS FREEDOM

Freedom of the press is highly valued, if not always practiced, in all Caribbean countries and is enshrined in the constitutions of some. However, readers have access to daily newspapers only in the Dominican Republic, Puerto Rico, Jamaica, Trinidad and Tobago, Barbados, Guyana, and the Bahamas. Everywhere, though, weekly and community papers catering to special and parochial interests are widely available.

The *Daily Gleaner* of Jamaica, founded in 1834 and continuously published since, is the oldest English-language paper in the Western Hemisphere, with an international reputation as a newspaper of record. Like its daily counterparts elsewhere, with the exception of Guyana, it is privately owned and considered to be mildly conservative editorially. Favoring the business class and business interests, national dailies nevertheless have a reputation for providing wide coverage of national issues and providing a broad spectrum of political views from columnists of varying ideological hues. Heavy reliance is placed on both the Associated Press and Reuters news agencies as sources of international news, with some regional news provided by the CMC. The major dailies also have online editions that are available globally.

CONCLUSION

Since the mid-1980s, the Caribbean has been exposed to the full range of visual media content emanating from the United States via satellite. Its media-rich environment—television, cable, radio, the press, and more recently the Internet—is supported by neoliberal government media policies that extol the virtues of the free market. In this environment citizens have differential access to a variety of media depending on their levels of income and literacy as well as their interests. While virtually all international news via television is provided by and from the perspective of American and British networks, radio, which is accessible to all, provides culturally relevant programming to the region's citizens. Radio is inclusive and acts as a conduit for the expression of popular culture.

See also Filmmakers in the Caribbean

■ ■ *Bibliography*

Brown, Aggrey. "New Communication Technologies and Communication Policies in the Caribbean." In *Democratizing Communication: Comparative Perspectives on Information and Power,* edited by Mashoed Baille and Dwayne Winseck, pp. 159–171. Cresskill, N.J.: Hampton Press, 1997.

Brown, Aggrey, and Roderick Sanatan. *Talking with Whom? A Report on the State of the Media in the Caribbean.* Kingston: CARIMAC, 1987.

Demac, Donna, and Aggrey Brown. "Caribbean Telecommunications: The Satellite Option." In *Satellites International,* edited by J. Pelton and J. Howkins, pp. 79–83. London: Macmillan, 1988.

Gordon, Ken. *Getting It Write: Winning Caribbean Press Freedom.* Kingston: Ian Randle Publishers, 1999.

Ramcharitar, Raymond. *Breaking the News: Media and Culture in Trinidad.* San Juan, Trinidad: Lexicon Trinidad Ltd, 2005.

Regis, Humphrey A. *Culture and Mass Communication in the Caribbean.* Gainesville: University Press of Florida, 2001.

Surlin, Stewart, and Walter Soderlund, eds. *Mass Media and the Caribbean.* Philadelphia: Gordon and Breach, 1990.

AGGREY BROWN (2005)

MEDICAL ASSOCIATIONS

■■■

Professional organizations of physicians—whose goals are to promote the science and art of medicine and to improve the public health—serve as major components of the health-care infrastructure in the United States. Medical associations have as their mission the establishment and maintenance of a scientifically rigorous, occupationally specific, professional educational training and standards; defining medical ethical codes of practice and behavior; and establishing internal mechanisms for evaluating, disciplining, and sanctioning physicians on technical and ethical grounds. This professional authority is grounded in a culture-based belief in science and medicine and the general acceptance of medical progress as a perceived public good. In the United States the influence of the medical association grew tremendously after the nineteenth century. Organized medicine gained the authority to write most of the nation's public-health and medical-licensing laws; to control its medical-education system; to guide its local, regional, and national health policy; and to influence public attitudes about health.

The country's health system is burdened with a history of racial and medical-social problems. Examples include an increasing health-system apartheid based on race and class and the unequal state of the nation's medical associations. The American Medical Association (AMA) is the better-known medical professional association. It is influential, wealthy, and largely white and represents the country's traditional health interests. Since its founding in 1847, it has become the anchor and focal point of American organized medicine. African-American physicians and patients, and other medically poor and disadvantaged groups, are represented by the lesser-known, largely minority National Medical Association (NMA), which was founded in 1895. These two medical associations' policies, ideologies, and perspectives are startlingly different.

The Western medical profession originated from Egyptian, Sub-Saharan African, and Mesopotamian roots. Early unsuccessful attempts to establish medicine as a profession were based on an increasingly specialized body of knowledge, spiritual authority related to medicine's early ties with religious and priestly functions, and the taking of an oath. During the Renaissance the European medical profession became a highly prestigious, university-affiliated "calling," which gained formal professional recognition by the sixteenth century. The first professional associations began in Italy in the Middle Ages, and memberships were built around the faculties of early medical schools. As this practice spread northward, the English physician Thomas Linacre obtained what may have been the first official charter for a medical association. At his request King Henry VIII of England granted a charter for the College of Physicians in 1518. Other European nations followed this precedent.

In comparison, American medicine gained professional status, authority, and prestige only in the nineteenth century. The low status of the medical professional was demonstrated by the late formation of stable, functional professional associations and the absence of medical-licensing laws until the late nineteenth century. Despite the emergence of a few well-trained black physicians before the Civil War, such as James McCune Smith, John Sweat Rock, and Martin Robison Delany, the professional exclusion of African Americans was a routine aspect of American medical subculture.

After the institutionalization of the Atlantic slave trade in the fifteenth and sixteenth centuries, the participation of blacks as health caregivers in Western-oriented slave-based cultures was restricted to the functions of traditional healers, root doctors, and granny midwives. They worked in an inferior, slave-based health subsystem that matured in the New World. African-American attainment of formal Western medical education in this era was virtually unknown. After the Civil War, the country's medical profession helped strengthen a dual and unequal health system. The inferior lower tier was reserved for blacks and the poor; the compelling health needs of the newly freed slaves, and their already poor and deteriorating health status, were virtually ignored by the profession. White medi-

cal associations and their infrastructure continued to exclude African Americans from training and participation in the medical profession. These policies generated an African-American health crisis after the Civil War. The alarming black death rates and the health outcomes that resulted led to emergency passage of legislation enacting the Freedmen's Bureau health programs and the opening of race-, gender-, and class-neutral medical schools. The first of the sixteen multiracial medical schools in America was at Howard University in Washington, D.C. (founded in 1868), and the second was Meharry Medical College of Nashville, Tennessee (founded in 1876). The subsequent development of a cadre of black health professionals, including physicians, dentists, nurses, pharmacists, and allied health professionals, had salutary effects on the health status of African Americans and increased their access to high-quality health and hospital care. The African-American health professionals produced by the black schools functioned as the sole professionally trained advocates for black health progress; started sorely needed black hospital, clinic, and health-professional-training movements; organized medical associations; and offered the African-American community access to the most up-to-date medical care.

Beginning in the 1870s black physicians began efforts to correct the AMA's exclusionary and discriminatory racial policies. Howard University's racially integrated medical school faculty struggled unsuccessfully to desegregate the AMA at local levels, through litigation and pressure from the U.S. Congress, in a campaign lasting several years. These actions pressured white organized medicine to declare racial segregation as its official national policy by 1872. In frustration, black physicians, dentists, and pharmacists established more than fifty local, state, and regional black medical associations organized around the NMA by the 1920s. The NMA is now a multicomponent national organization representing approximately fifteen thousand physicians. The earliest desegregated medical professional associations were the National Medical Society of the District of Columbia (1870), the Academy of Medicine (1872), and the State Colored Medical Association in Nashville, Tennessee (1880). African-American health-professions associations became permanent fixtures with the founding of the Medical Chirurgical Society of the District of Columbia in 1884, the Lone Star State Medical Association in Galveston, Texas, in 1886, and the NMA in Atlanta, on November 18, 1895.

The Civil War dramatically exposed the inadequacies of America's medical-education system. Therefore, a great deal of pressure was generated within the white medical profession and by the AMA for medical-education reform.

This reform era, lasting from the late nineteenth century through the 1920s, focused on rigorous scientific standards and technology, bedside clinical training, higher entry requirements, and the limitation of physician supply.

The AMA and the corporate-based educational infrastructure closed six of the eight extant black health-professions schools between 1910 and 1923 and underfunded the remainder. This resulted from an educational reform movement led by Abraham Flexner, an educational consultant hired by the Carnegie Foundation and the AMA to coordinate an upgrading of the nation's medical schools, based on European models. Throughout the "Flexner era," the NMA fought vigorously, but unsuccessfully, to improve and maintain existing entry points for African Americans into the health professions. Flexner reform adversely impacted black health status and outcomes, cut African-American access to basic services, and decreased black representation in the health professions. Though Meharry and Howard were forced to serve as virtually the sole sources of black health-care personnel from 1910 to 1970 on shoestring financing, they were also excluded from the stewardship white medical schools were obtaining over America's government and city hospitals and clinics. Control of these institutions provided clinical training bases critical to the new accreditation processes and requirements. Yet the racially segregated health system supported the survival of the remaining black health-professions schools. The NMA was crucial in maintaining the accreditation and financing of these schools and allied hospitals and health facilities. Despite vigorous campaigns by the NMA, black representation in the medical profession in America has remained tenuous, ranging between 2 percent and 3 percent of physicians since the turn of the twentieth century.

From its beginnings the NMA was forced to function as a civil rights organization. It has worked in concert with the NAACP, the National Urban League, and many other black civil rights and service organizations to further the cause of African-American health concerns. This was a natural development, since African Americans are the only racial or ethnic group forced to view health care as a civil rights issue. On several levels the NMA's policies represent a positive response to the AMA's traditional policies of racial segregation, massively funded campaigns against progressive health-care legislation, health discrimination based on race and class, and insensitivity to the health status, needs, and concerns of the nation's African-American, poor, and other underserved patient populations. The NMA has been singular at both the community and national levels in supporting progressive health-care legisla-

tion—from before the Wagner Plan in the 1930s through Medicare and Medicaid in 1965 to a fair national health plan in the 1990s. The NMA continues its history-based struggle to end race and class discrimination in the health system, to form a socially responsible covenant between the medical profession and American society, and to obtain justice and equity in health care for African Americans.

See also Professional Organizations

▪ ▪ *Bibliography*

Bullough, Vern L. *The Development of Medicine as a Profession: The Contribution of the Medieval University to Modern Medicine.* New York: Hafner, 1966.

Byrd, W. Michael. "Race, Biology, and Health Care: Reassessing a Relationship." *Journal of Health Care for the Poor and Underserved* 1 (1990): 278–296.

Byrd, W. Michael. *A Black Health Trilogy* [videotape and learning package]. Nashville, Tenn., 1991.

Byrd, W. Michael, and Linda A. Clayton. "The 'Slave Health Deficit': Racism and Health Outcomes." *Health/PAC Bulletin* 21 (1991): 25–28.

Cash, P. "Pride, Prejudice, and Politics." *Harvard Medical Alumni Bulletin* 54 (1980): 20–25.

Cobb, W. Montague. "The Black American in Medicine." *Journal of the National Medical Association* 73 (1981, Supplement 1): 1183–1244.

Greenberg, Daniel S. "Black Health: Grim Statistics." *Lancet* 355 (1990): 780–781.

Health Policy Advisory Center. "The Emerging Health Apartheid in the United States." *Health PAC Bulletin* 21 (1991): 3–4.

Konold, Donald E. *A History of American Medical Ethics, 1847–1912.* Madison: University of Wisconsin, 1962.

Lundberg, George D. "National Health Care Reform: An Aura of Inevitability Is Upon Us." *Journal of the American Medical Association* 265 (1991): 2566–2567.

Morais, Herbert M. *The History of the Negro in Medicine.* New York: Publishers Co., 1967.

MICHAEL BYRD (1996)

Meek, Carrie

April 29, 1926

▪ ▪ ▪

The granddaughter of a slave and the daughter of a sharecropper and a domestic, educator and U.S. Congresswoman Carrie Pittman Meek was born in Tallahassee, Florida. She graduated from Florida A & M University with a B.S. degree in 1946. In 1948 she received her M.S. degree from the University of Michigan and later studied at Florida Atlantic University.

Meek began a teaching career at Bethune-Cookman College from 1949 to 1958. She moved to Florida A & M University for the next three years (1958–1961). She was women's basketball coach at both institutions. After teaching at Miami-Dade Community College from 1961 to 1968, she moved into administrative posts as associate to the president (1968–1979) and as special assistant to the vice president beginning in 1982.

In the 1960s and 1970s Meek became acquainted with the inequity in federally funded programs for blacks in Dade County and concluded that only the government could correct the problem. In 1979, she ran in a special election to fill the former seat of Dade County's state representative Gwen Cherry, killed in an automobile accident. Meek won, and was reelected to the Florida House of Representatives in 1980. Meek was so popular in her senatorial district that she decided to run for Congress in 1992, representing the 17th District, and won by a staggering margin. A sixty-seven-year-old grandmother, she became the first African-American woman since Reconstruction to be elected to Congress from Florida. Her record in Congress was impressive; she served on the House Appropriations Committee, drafted a bill to ease restrictions on Haitian refugees, and advised President Bill Clinton as he worked to reduce the budget deficit without cutting social welfare programs.

Meek retired in 2002 after a ten-year career in Congress. Her son, Kendrick, was elected to take her place.

See also Politics in the United States

■ ■ *Bibliography*

Bigelow, Barbara Carlisle, ed. *Contemporary Black Biography.* Detroit, Mich.: Gale, 1992.

Davies, Frank. "Charm Made Carrie Meek Effective Even When Outnumbered." *Knight Ridder/Tribune News Service* (December 11, 2002).

Smith, Jessie Carney, ed. *Notable Black American Women.* Detroit, Mich.: Gale, 1996.

RAYMOND WINBUSH (1996)
Updated by publisher 2005

MEREDITH, JAMES H.

JUNE 25, 1933

━ ■ ■ ■ ━━━━━━━━━━━━━━━━━━━

Born in Kosciusko, Mississippi, civil rights activist James Howard Meredith became the central figure in two major events of the civil rights movement. He had studied at Jackson State University in Jackson, Mississippi, when in September 1962 he sought to enroll in the University of Mississippi to complete his bachelor's degree. The state university system was segregated, and although a court order confirmed Meredith's right to enter the school, Mississippi governor Ross Barnett led the opposition and personally stood in the doorway of the registrar's office to block Meredith's enrollment. In response, the Kennedy administration dispatched federal marshals to escort Meredith to classes. To quell the subsequent rioting, U.S. troops policed the campus, where they remained until Meredith graduated in 1963.

During the next year, Meredith studied at Ibadan University in Nigeria, and on his return to the United States he began taking courses for a law degree at Columbia University. In the summer of 1966 Meredith announced he would set out on a sixteen-day "walk against fear," which would take him from Memphis to the Mississippi state capital in Jackson. He sought both to spur African-American voter registration for the upcoming primary election and to show that blacks could overcome the white violence that had so long stifled aspirations.

On the second day of the hike, an assailant shot Meredith with two shotgun blasts. His wounds were not serious, but the attack sparked great outrage, and the major civil rights organizations carried on a march to Jackson from the place where Meredith had been shot. This procession was marked by Stokely Carmichael's call for black power and a resulting rift between the moderate and militant wings of the movement. Meredith left the hospital after several days and was able to join the marchers before they reached Jackson.

Later in 1966 Meredith published *Three Years in Mississippi* and lectured on racial justice. Returning to law school, Meredith received his degree from Columbia University in 1968. That same year he ran unsuccessfully for Adam Clayton Powell Jr.'s Harlem seat in the U.S. House of Representatives, then returned to Mississippi, where he became involved in several business ventures. In 1984 and 1985 he taught a course on blacks and the law at the University of Mississippi. From 1989 to 1991 Meredith worked for North Carolina senator Jesse Helms, an arch-conservative, as domestic policy adviser.

In 1995 Meredith published *Mississippi: A Volume of Eleven Books.* Meredith's papers are collected at the University of Mississippi.

See also Carmichael, Stokely; Civil Rights Movement, U.S.; Voting Rights Act of 1965

■ ■ *Bibliography*

Garrow, David J. *Bearing the Cross: Martin Luther King Jr., and the Southern Christian Leadership Conference.* New York: Morrow, 1986.

Peake, Thomas R. *Keeping the Dream Alive: A History of the Nineteen-Eighties.* New York: P. Lang, 1987.

STEVEN J. LESLIE (1996)
Updated by publisher 2005

MESSENGER, THE

The Messenger was founded by A. Philip Randolph and Chandler Owen, both active in New York City's radical and socialist circles. Hired in 1917 to edit the *Hotel Messenger* for the Headwaiters and Sidewaiters Society of Greater New York, the pair was fired after eight months on the job for exposing exploitative treatment of common waiters and pantry workers by the more established union members themselves. With initial support from the Socialist Party and Socialist-led unions, they launched the independent *Messenger*.

The Messenger alarmed the white and black establishments by both advocating socialism and heralding the advent of the "New Crowd Negro," who promised an aggressive challenge both to post-Reconstruction "reactionaries" such as Booker T. Washington and to mainstream civil rights leaders such as W. E. B. Du Bois. The self-styled "Only Radical Negro Magazine in America" opposed World War I, championed the Russian Revolution of 1917, hailed the radical interracial organizing of the Industrial Workers of the World (IWW), and advocated armed self-defense by black people against racist attacks.

In 1919, during the rising wave of racial disturbances and labor unrest, *The Messenger* was caught in the sweep of federal repression that followed. Of all the black publications investigated by the Justice Department for "radicalism and sedition," it was *The Messenger* that Attorney General A. Mitchell Palmer termed "the most able and the most dangerous." Its second-class mailing permit, revoked by the U.S. Post Office in 1918 after publication of an article entitled "Pro Germanism Among Negroes," was not restored until 1921.

With the weakening of both the socialist movement and the IWW in the early 1920s, the word "Radical" disappeared from *The Messenger*'s masthead. The magazine sought to preserve its influence in the black community by campaigning actively against Marcus Garvey and promoting the independent organization of black workers. Owen left the magazine in 1923, and Randolph, though technically still at the helm, turned his attention to the Brotherhood of Sleeping Car Porters (BSCP), which he hoped to affiliate with the American Federation of Labor.

With Owen's departure and Randolph's union activities, effective editorial control was shifted to George Schuyler and Theophilis Lewis. Under their tutelage, *The Messenger*'s political and economic radicalism gave way to celebrations of black entrepreneurs and appeals to the mainstream (and racially exclusionary) labor movement. In addition to a "Business and Industry" page, the magazine began to feature society items, sports news, and articles directed at women and children. In 1925, when *The Messenger* became the official organ of the Brotherhood, it also began to carry union-related news and commentary.

Schuyler and Lewis left another indelible mark on the magazine. While *The Messenger* had published socialist-oriented literary contributions in the past by figures such as Claude McKay, it had not explicitly allied itself with the Harlem Renaissance. Now, it became more directly concerned with black arts and culture, including theater, and solicited the work of leading luminaries, among them Langston Hughes and Georgia Douglas Johnson. This approach gained even greater currency when Wallace Thurman filled in briefly for Schuyler in 1926. By late 1927 *The Messenger*'s motto had become "The New Opinion of the New Negro."

Still, *The Messenger,* as a union publication, continued to reach an audience comprising largely black trade unionists. It folded in 1928 when Randolph determined the BSCP could no longer afford the drain on its limited resources.

See also Brotherhood of Sleeping Car Porters; Du Bois, W.E.B.; Garvey, Marcus; Labor and Labor Unions; McKay, Claude; Owen, Chandler; Randolph, Asa Philip; Schuyler, George S.; Thurman, Wallace; Washington, Booker T.

■ ■ *Bibliography*

Johnson, Abby Arthur, and Ronald Maberry Johnson. *Propaganda and Aesthetics: The Literary Politics of African-American Magazines in the Twentieth Century.* Amherst, Mass.: University of Massachusetts Press, 1979.

Kornweibel, Theodore, Jr. *No Crystal Stair: Black Life and the Messenger, 1917–1928.* Westport, Conn.: Greenwood, 1975.

Vincent, Theodore G., ed. *Voices of a Black Nation: Political Journalism in the Harlem Renaissance.* San Francisco: Ramparts Press, 1973.

Wolseley, Roland E. *The Black Press, U.S.A.*, 2d ed. Ames, Iowa: University of Iowa Press, 1990.

RENEE TURSI (1996)
TAMI J. FRIEDMAN (1996)

METCALFE, RALPH

MAY 30, 1910
OCTOBER 10, 1978

The athlete and congressman Ralph Horace Metcalfe was born in Atlanta, Georgia, but moved to Chicago at an early age. While an undergraduate at Marquette University in Milwaukee, Metcalfe was the National Collegiate Athletic Association (NCAA) champion in the 100 yards and 220 yards three years in a row (1932–1934). During the same period, he won the Amateur Athletic Union (AAU) championship in the 100 meters (1932–1934) and 200 meters (1932–1936). He also won the silver medal in the 100 meters at the 1932 Olympics in Los Angeles, running in the same official time (10.3) as the winner (officials declared Metcalfe second after a lengthy study of a film showing the finish), and the bronze medal in the 200 meters. Although he was the dominant sprinter in the world during the early 1930s and set or tied the world records in the 40 yards, 60 yards, 60 meters, 100 yards, 100 meters, 220 yards, and the 200 meters, he again finished second in the 100 meters at the 1936 Olympics in Berlin, this time behind Jesse Owens. Metcalfe won an Olympic gold medal as a member of the 1936 U.S. 4- by 100-meter relay team.

In 1936 Metcalfe retired from sprinting and graduated from Marquette. While teaching political science and coaching the track team at Xavier University in New Orleans from 1936 to 1942, he also completed work for an M.A. in political science from the University of Southern California (1939). He joined the army in 1942, and after the war returned to Chicago to become the director of the Department of Civil Rights for the Chicago Commission on Human Rights (1945). From 1949 to 1952 he was the Illinois athletic commissioner, the first African American to hold this position. He became active in Democratic politics in Chicago and was the Democratic Party committeeman for the 3rd Ward of Chicago (1952–1972), and later alderman (1955–1969). In 1970 he was elected to the U.S. House of Representatives. As a congressman, Metcalfe worked to make more home and business loans available to minority communities. He served on the Interstate and Foreign Commerce Committee as well as the Committee on Merchant Marine and Fisheries, where as chair of the Subcommittee on the Panama Canal he supported the 1978 treaty turning control of the canal over to Panama.

During his long political career in Chicago, Metcalfe became a political insider and a part of Mayor Richard Daley's political machine. But in 1972 he broke with Daley, challenging him on the issue of police brutality toward blacks. Daley ran a candidate against Metcalfe in the Democratic primary, but with the assistance of the Congressional Black Caucus Metcalfe defeated Daley's candidate. He was in his fourth term as a congressman and was running unopposed for a fifth when he died of a heart attack in 1978.

See also Congressional Black Caucus; Politics in the United States; Sports

■ ■ *Bibliography*

Ashe, Arthur R., Jr. *A Hard Road to Glory: A History of the African-American Athlete, 1919–1945.* New York: Warner, 1988.

Obituary. *New York Times*, November 6, 1978.

Ragsdale, Bruce A., and Joel D. Treece. *Black Americans in Congress, 1870–1989.* Washington, D.C.: U.S. Government Printing Office, 1990.

PETER SCHILLING (1996)

MFUME, KWEISI

OCTOBER 24, 1948

Civil rights leader, president of the National Association for the Advancement of Colored People (NAACP), and former U.S. congressman Kweisi Mfume was born Frizzell Gray in Maryland, the eldest of four children, and grew up in a poor community just outside of Baltimore. His mother, Mary Willis, worked on an assembly line for an airplane parts manufacturer. His stepfather, Clifton Gray, abandoned the family when Mfume was twelve years old. Four years later, his mother was diagnosed with cancer. Devastated by his mother's death, Mfume dropped out of high school and began working odd jobs to make ends meet while he and his three sisters lived with relatives. Mfume found that he could make much more money hustling on the streets than working for wages shining shoes or pushing bread through a slicer.

By the age of twenty-two, Mfume's life seemed to have completely spun out of control; he had five children with four different women, gang life was becoming deadly, and a number of his closest friends had been killed in Viet-

Kweisi Mfume. AP/WIDE WORLD PHOTOS. REPRODUCED BY PERMISSION.

nam. Mfume resolved to turn his life around. He began taking night GED courses for his high school equivalency degree and then enrolled at Baltimore Community College. Mfume developed a keen interest in politics in the early 1970s while working as a disc jockey at local radio stations. During this time, he changed his name from Frizzell "Pee Wee" Gray to Kweisi Mfume (a West African Igbo name roughly translating as "conquering son of kings").

In 1976 Mfume graduated magna cum laude with a degree in urban planning from Morgan State University. Two years later, he parlayed his growing fame as a talk-radio provocateur to win a seat as a maverick Democratic Party member on the Baltimore City Council. Mfume served two terms on the city council and then went on to graduate school at Johns Hopkins University, where he received an M.A. in political science. In 1986 he won the seat of the Seventh Congressional District vacated by his political mentor, Parren J. Mitchell. Mfume went on to serve five terms in U.S. Congress, rising to the position of chair of the Congressional Black Caucus.

Mfume's campaign to end apartheid in South Africa earned him the friendship of Nelson Mandela in the early 1990s. However, while he supported democracy abroad, Mfume remained more committed to the preservation of the Democratic Party than the expansion of independent electoral options for African Americans. During the 1990s he joined other black elected officials in limiting the growth of a multiracial political movement that attempted to challenge the control of the electoral process by both major parties. In 1996 Mfume left Congress to lead the NAACP, where he pursued corporate donations to retire the organization's debt. Mfume resigned from his post as president of the NAACP in 2004.

The recipient of seven honorary doctoral degrees, Mfume serves on the board of trustees at Johns Hopkins University and the Enterprise Foundation. His autobiography, *No Free Ride: From The Mean Streets to the Mainstream,* details his life.

See also Civil Rights Movement, U.S.; Congressional Black Caucus; National Association for the Advancement of Colored People (NAACP); Politics in the United States

■ ■ *Bibliography*

Mfume, Kweisi. *No Free Ride: From The Mean Streets to the Mainstream.* New York: One World, 1996.

Robinson, Alonford James, Jr. *Africana: The Encyclopedia of the African American Experience.* Edited by Kwame Anthony Appiah and Henry Louis Gates Jr. Oxford: Perseus, 1999.

OMAR H. ALI (1996)
Updated by author 2005

MICHAUX, ELDER

NOVEMBER 7, 1884
OCTOBER 2, 1968

The religious leader and radio evangelist Elder Lightfoot Solomon Michaux was born in Newport News, Virginia, one of thirteen children. During his youth he worked in the family seafood business, peddling fish to soldiers on the wharves. It was there he learned, as he would later say, "the power of persuasion."

As a young adult, Michaux maintained a successful wholesale food business and remained uninterested in a religious career until 1917, when his wife, a devout Baptist, convinced him to finance the building of a branch of the Church of Christ (Holiness) in Hopewell, Virginia. Soon Michaux was called to the pulpit by his wife and friends, who were impressed with his rhetorical skills, and he became the church's permanent pastor. When the end of World War I depopulated Hopewell, Michaux's fledgling church was forced to close, and in late 1919 he moved back to Newport News to organize a church under his own denomination, the Church of God.

Michaux's services were notable for being attended by significant numbers of white people. In 1924 Michaux even traveled to Baltimore to preach to an all-white congregation dominated by members of the Ku Klux Klan. He was arrested in 1926 after he held racially integrated services to challenge Virginia's laws banning interracial religious gatherings. Michaux appeared in court as his own counsel. Citing the Bible as his defense, he declared, "the sacred word of the Supreme Being makes no reference to class, division or race." He was fined but continued to hold integrated services despite repeated harassment by the police and townspeople.

In 1928 Michaux moved to Washington, D.C., "to save souls on a larger scale." There he established a branch of the Church of God and in 1929 began his first radio broadcasts from local station WJSV. By 1933 Michaux was broadcast nationally by CBS. Known as the "Happy Am I" evangelist, Michaux used his radio pulpit to support numerous causes, among them President Franklin D. Roosevelt and the New Deal. Along with his political pronouncements, Michaux developed a social dimension to his ministry and, through the Church of God, provided shelter and food to destitute persons in Washington during the Great Depression.

In the 1930s Michaux also gained fame by holding mass baptisms, first in the Potomac River and after 1938 at Griffith Stadium. In the ballpark, home to the Washington Senators baseball team, Michaux baptized hundreds at a time in a large tank filled with water allegedly drawn from the river Jordan. The mass baptisms were accompanied by fireworks and colorful pageantry, including floats, marching bands, and elaborate enactments of the second coming of Christ. Michaux's mass baptisms continued into the 1960s, when they were moved to other large outdoor venues. A reporter for the *Washington Post* noted, "Michaux made headlines for many feats, but the 'Happy Am I' preacher probably will be remembered longest for his ball park meetings, religious extravaganzas that qualify him as a great showman."

In addition to his religious and political work, Michaux developed Mayfair Mansions, one of the largest privately owned housing projects for African Americans, which opened in Washington, D.C., in 1946. In the 1950s Michaux's popularity among African Americans waned when he broke with the Democratic Party to endorse President Dwight D. Eisenhower. At the end of his career

Michaux became embroiled in controversies over his and the church's finances, which were both heavily invested in real estate. Many members of his congregation accused Michaux of hiding church financial information and of secretly transferring assets to his personal accounts. Despite the dark clouds over his final years, Michaux's Church of God has remained after his death as a monument to his successful and flamboyant career.

See also Great Depression and the New Deal; Holiness Movement; Protestantism in the Americas

■ ■ *Bibliography*

Logan, Rayford W., and Michael R. Winston, eds. *Dictionary of American Negro Biography.* New York: Norton, 1982.

Webb, Lillian Ashcraft. *About My Father's Business: The Life of Elder Michaux.* Westport, Conn.: Greenwood, 1981.

THADDEUS RUSSELL (1996)

MICHEAUX, OSCAR
JANUARY 2, 1884
MARCH 25, 1951

The novelist and filmmaker Oscar Micheaux was born in Metropolis, Illinois, one of thirteen children of former slaves Swan and Bell Micheaux. The early events of his life are not clear and must be gleaned from several fictionalized versions he published. He evidently worked as a Pullman porter, acquiring enough capital to buy two 160-acre tracts of land in South Dakota, where he homesteaded. Micheaux's homesteading experiences were the basis of his first novel, *The Conquest: The Story of a Negro Pioneer* (1913). In order to publicize the book, Micheaux established the Western Book Supply Company and toured the Midwest. He sold most of the books, and stock in his first company, to white farmers, although his later ventures were financed by African-American entrepreneurs. From his bookselling experiences, he wrote a second novel, *The Forged Note: A Romance of the Darker Races* (1915). Micheaux's third novel, *The Homesteader* (1917), attracted the attention of George P. Johnson, who, with his Hollywood actor brother Noble, owned the Lincoln Film Company, with offices in Los Angeles and Omaha. The Johnson brothers were part of the first wave of African-American independent filmmakers to take up the challenge to D. W. Griffith's white supremacist version of American History, *The Birth of a Nation* (1915), and produce their own stories of African-American life. Fascinated by the new medium, Micheaux offered to sell the Johnson Brothers film rights to his novel, on the condition that he direct the motion picture version. When they refused, Micheaux decided to produce and direct the film himself, financing it through what became the Micheaux Book and Film Company, with offices located in New York, Chicago, and Sioux City, Iowa.

The film version of Micheaux's third novel, *The Homesteader* (released in 1918), was the first of about fifty films he directed. He distributed the films himself, carrying the prints from town to town, often for one-night stands. His films played mostly in white-owned (but often black-managed) black theaters both in the North and the South. He even had some luck convincing southern white cinema owners to let him show his films at all-black matinees and interracial midnight shows in white theaters. While the black press at the time sometimes criticized Micheaux for projecting a rich black fantasy world and ignoring ghetto problems, he dealt frankly with such social themes as interracial relationships, "passing," intraracial as well as interracial prejudice, and the intimidation of African Americans by the Ku Klux Klan.

Micheaux's second film, *Within Our Gates* (1919), contains a disturbing sequence representing a white lynch mob hanging an innocent black man and his wife. When Micheaux tried to exhibit the film in Chicago, less than a year after a major race riot in that city, both black and white groups urged city authorities to ban the film. Micheaux's response to such censorship was to cut and re-edit his films as he traveled from town to town. Showman and entrepreneur that he was, he would promote a film that had been banned in one town by indicating in the next town that it contained "censored" footage. Produced on a shoestring, his films earned him just enough money to continue his filmmaking.

Some twelve of Micheaux's films are extant, and they give an idea, though incomplete, of his style. His interior scenes are often dimly lit, but his location scenes of urban streets are usually crisp and clear, providing a documentary-like glimpse of the period. He seldom had money for more than one take, with the result that the actors' mistakes sometimes became part of the final film. However, Micheaux had a genius for negotiating around tight budgets, improvising with limited resources, and synchronizing production with distribution. In the early 1920s, in order to purchase the rights to African-American author Charles Waddell Chesnutt's *The House Behind the Cedars* (1900), he offered the author shares in his film company.

To create appeal for his films, Micheaux features some of the most talented African-American actors of his time, including Andrew Bishop, Lawrence-Chenault, A. B. Comithiere, Lawrence Criner, Shingzie Howard, and Evelyn Preer, many of whom were associated with the Lafayette Players stock company. The actor and singer Paul Robeson (1898–1976) made his first motion picture appearance in Micheaux's *Body and Soul* (1924), in a dual role as both a venal preacher and his virtuous brother. Micheaux returned often to the theme of the hypocritical preacher, a portrait inspired by the betrayal of his father-in-law, a Chicago minister. Of the actors whom Micheaux made celebrities in the black community, the most notable was Lorenzo Tucker, a handsome, light-skinned actor dubbed "the colored Valentino." Micheaux's films also featured cabaret scenes, chorus line dancers, and, after the coming of sound, jazz musicians and comedians.

Although his company went bankrupt in 1928, Micheaux managed to survive the early years of the Depression, continuing to produce silent films. Although *Daughter of the Congo* (1930) featured some songs and a musical score, *The Exile* (1931) was thought to be the first African-American-produced all-talking picture. Micheaux went on to make a number of sound films, but many moments in these films were technically compromised because his technicians could not surmount the challenges produced by the new sound-recording technology. In the late 1930s, after the brief notoriety of *God's Stepchildren* (1937), Micheaux's film activities began to wind down and he returned to writing novels. He published *The Wind from Nowhere* (1941), a reworking of *The Homesteader,* and three other novels during the next five years. In 1948 he produced a large-budget version of *The Wind from Nowhere,* titled *The Betrayal* and billed as the first African-American motion picture to play in major white theaters. However, the film received unfavorable reviews in the press, including the *New York Times*. At a time of his decline in popularity as both novelist and filmmaker, Micheaux died during a promotional tour in 1951 in Charlotte, North Carolina.

Micheaux's work was first rediscovered by film scholars in the early 1970s. However, these critics still disdained the wooden acting and unmatched shots in his films, and they decried what they thought to be the escapist nature of his stories. More recent critics, however, have hailed Micheaux as a maverick stylist who understood, but was not bound by, classical Hollywood cutting style; who used precious footage economically; who was adept in his use of the flashback device; and whose "rough draft" films were vaguely avant-garde. However, Micheaux is not recognized for his "protest" films and his use of social types to oppose caricature rather than to reinforce stereotype.

Thus, though largely ignored during his lifetime, Micheaux began to receive recognition in the later twentieth century. The Black Filmmakers Hall of Fame inaugurated an annual Oscar Micheaux Award in 1974. In 1985, the Directors' Guild posthumously presented Micheaux with a special Golden Jubilee Award, and in 1987 he received a star on the Hollywood Walk of Fame. The recent discovery of prints of two silent Micheaux films, *Within Our Gates* (1919) and *Symbol of the Unconquered* (1920), in archives in Spain and Belgium, respectively, has increased the interest in his work.

See also Chesnutt, Charles W.; Film; Robeson, Paul

■ ■ *Bibliography*

Bowser, Pearl, Jane Gaines, Charles Musser, eds. *Oscar Micheaux and His Circle: African-American Filmmaking and Race Cinema of the Silent Era.* Bloomington: Indiana University Press, 2001.

Cripps, Thomas. *Slow Fade to Black: The Negro in American Film, 1900-1942,* 2nd ed. New York: Oxford University Press, 1989.

Gaines, Jane M. "Fire and Desire: Race, Melodrama, and Oscar Micheaux." In *Black American Cinema: History, Theory, Criticism,* edited by Manthia Diawara. New York: Routledge, 1993.

Green, Ron. "Oscar Micheaux's Production Values." In *Black American Cinema: History, Theory, Criticism,* edited by Manthia Diawara. New York: Routledge, 1993.

Peterson, Bernard L., Jr. "A Filmography of Oscar Micheaux: America's Legendary Black Filmmaker." In *Celluloid Power,* edited by David Platt. Metuchen, N.J.: Scarecrow Press, 1992.

Regester, Charlene. "Lynched, Assaulted, and Intimidated: Oscar Micheaux's Most Controversial Films." *Popular Culture Review* 5, no. 1 (February 1994): 47–55.

JANE GAINES (1996)
CHARLENE REGESTER (1996)
Updated bibliography

MIDWIFERY

┣━┫━┫

The evocation of the word *midwifery* calls up two images. The first is a medically trained nurse who specializes in obstetrics and gynecology and is licensed to attend childbirths in the hospital and, less frequently, in freestanding birthing centers or the homes of clients. The second and older image is the tradition of social childbirth, in which women gave birth at home in the presence of other women and with the guidance of a skilled folk practitioner. Due to a number of economic, cultural, and political factors, social childbirth declined in significance for native-born northern white women relatively early. By the

late 1760s, they had already begun to rely on male physicians to deliver their children. Traditional midwifery, however, continued to flourish among European immigrants who settled in the cities along the northeastern seaboard from the late nineteenth through the early twentieth century.

In the South, the midwifery tradition has been for the most part an African-American one, with the midwife mediating the reproductive experiences of both black and white women, especially in the region's rural communities, from the early seventeenth to the closing decades of the twentieth century. By the 1940s, social childbirth had been largely replaced by scientific childbirth in the hospital, but a few surviving traditional African-American midwives continued to offer their services in the late 1980s, as reported by Debra Susie (1988) in Florida and by Linda Holmes (1986) and Annie Logan (1989) in Alabama.

Throughout the slaveholding South, African-American midwives had the responsibility for managing pregnancy and childbirth. Often, these women were slaves practicing not only on the plantations where they resided, but also attending births on neighboring plantations, for which their owners collected a fee. In the rural areas of the South, slave midwives also delivered the children of white women. Powerful in their knowledge of the physiological, medicinal, and spiritual aspects of childbirth, slave midwives inhabited an intensely ambiguous role. They wielded an expertise that allowed them to compete successfully with "scientifically" trained white male physicians of the period while they remained classified as property, rarely receiving remuneration, and subject to sanctions should the infant or mother die. Given the close association of childbirth with other aspects of bodily functioning, slave midwives were also generally recognized as healers, and they attended the sick as part of their practice. The medical historian Todd Savitt notes that free black women also marketed their skills as birth attendants to a white clientele, while at the same time offering their services to neighbors and kin in their own communities (Savitt, 1978, p. 182).

In the African-American community, across historical periods, women who became midwives did so either through apprenticeship to another midwife (often a family member), or through the experience of having given birth themselves. Whatever the practical route of transmission, the emphasis in the articulation of an identity as a midwife was on the spiritual nature of the practice. Women were said to be "called" to become midwives in the same manner that a person is called to religious ministry; the decision was not under the control of the individual practitioner. So too were prayer and divine guidance crucial to the midwife's success in delivering babies and nurturing the mother back to health.

Childbirth, in this framework, did not end with the physical emergence of the infant. The midwife was also responsible for postpartum care, ensuring that both mother and child—spiritually as well as physically vulnerable—were protected from harm. Though the length of time varied, new mothers were expected to refrain from normal activities, avoid eating certain foods, and keep close to home for up to a month after birth, under the guidance of their midwives.

The dual nature of midwifery as skilled craft and as spiritual service to others was intrinsic to its emergence during the slave period, and it continued as an essential feature through the end of the twentieth century. It is important to recognize, then, that African-American midwives historically viewed themselves as socially embedded in the cultural and religious belief systems of their own communities, as well as having control of a set of skills that allowed them a measure of independence and authority in the broader society.

See also Nursing

■ ■ *Bibliography*

Holmes, Linda J. "African-American Midwives in the South." In *The American Way of Birth*, edited by Pamela S. Eakins. Philadelphia: Temple University Press, 1986, pp. 273–291.

Logan, Annie Lee, as told to Katherine Clark. *Motherwit: An Alabama Midwife's Story*. New York: Dutton, 1989.

Savitt, Todd. *Medicine and Slavery: The Diseases and Health Care of Blacks in Antebellum Virginia*. Urbana: University of Illinois Press, 1978.

Susie, Debra A. *In the Way of Our Grandmothers: A Cultural View of Twentieth-Century Midwifery in Florida*. Athens: University of Georgia Press, 1988.

GERTRUDE J. FRASER (1996)

MIGRATION
┿━┿━┿

This entry consists of two distinct articles with differing geographic domains.

MIGRATION IN THE AFRICAN DIASPORA
Michael A. Gomez

U.S. MIGRATION/POPULATION
Joe W. Trotter, Jr.

MIGRATION IN THE AFRICAN DIASPORA

Migration, both voluntary and involuntary, is clearly the means through which people of African descent have been dispersed throughout the world. In addition to developments outside of the continent, there have been major redistributions of populations within Africa itself. To briefly consider the latter, the idea of African communities in physical transition runs contrary to popular notions of a continent in which human habitation has been static and uninterrupted for millennia. However, the African landscape has witnessed tremendous change over long periods of time.

MIGRATION IN ANTIQUITY

A brief consideration of ancient Africa reminds one that the African diaspora did not begin with the transatlantic slave trade. Rather, the dissemination of African ideas and persons began long before, when ideas were arguably more significant than the number of people dispersed. For example, Egypt was a major civilization between 3100 and 332 BCE. Its relations with Nubia (or Kush) to the south (what is now southern Egypt and northern Sudan) were important, as Nubia was a source of gold and other precious materials, as well as soldiers and laborers, and was a political force alternating as enemy and ally. This was an important disapora of Africans into an African land that was the center of the Near Eastern world, at a time of African preeminence rather than weakness.

Africans also moved outside of the continent during antiquity. The Mediterranean world came to know Africans from a number of locations, especially Egypt and Nubia, and in varying capacities. But they also came from North Africa (from what is now Libya, west to Morocco), the southern fringes of the Sahara desert, and West Africa proper. Nubians were a part of the Egyptian occupation of Cyprus under Amasis (570–526 BCE), and a large number of Nubians fought under Xerxes of Persia in 480 to 479 BCE. Carthage, founded no earlier than 750 BCE, was served by a number of sub-Saharan Africans in the military. The Punic Wars (264–241, 218–201, 149–146 BCE) also saw Africans employed in the invasion of Italy.

Africans enslaved in the Greco-Roman world were but a small fraction of the total number of slaves in these territories and only a portion of the overall African population in southern Europe. Africans in Rome worked as musicians, actors, jugglers, gladiators, wrestlers, boxers, religious specialists, and day laborers. Some became famous, such as the black athlete Olympius. Africans also served in the Roman armies, as was the case with the elite Moorish cavalry from northwest Africa. Black soldiers even served in the Roman army as far north as Britain.

AFRICANS IN ISLAMIC LANDS AND INDIA

The slave trades were a major form of migration for Africans, the consideration of which begins with the Islamic lands. While many sub-Saharan Africans would convert to Islam and live as free persons in Islamic lands, many others entered as slaves. Muslim societies used slaves from all over the reachable world—Europeans were just as eligible as Africans, and Slavic and Caucasian populations were the largest source of slaves for the Islamic world well into the eighteenth century, especially in the Ottoman Empire.

Regarding Africa, tentative estimates for the trans-Saharan, Red Sea, and Indian Ocean slave trades are in the range of twelve million individuals from 650 CE to the end of the sixteenth century, and another four million from the seventeenth through the nineteenth centuries. In other words, as many or more captive Africans may have been exported through these trades as were shipped across the Atlantic, although the latter took place within a much more compressed period (the fifteenth through the nineteenth centuries). Such estimates are imprecise, but the number of enslaved Africans in the Islamic world was clearly significant.

The trans-Saharan, Red Sea, and Indian Ocean slave trades were primarily transactions in females and children. Young girls and women were used as domestics and concubines, and often as both, as the male slaveholder enjoyed the right of sexual access. In contrast to the Americas, the children of a slaveholder and a concubine were granted the status of the father and became free. Enslaved Africans were also used in the military, and slave armies were in a number of places in the Islamic world by the ninth century, although most military slaves were non-African. African boys were used as eunuchs, and males were also employed as laborers in large agricultural ventures and mining operations.

In addition to the central Islamic lands, Africans also migrated and made contributions to Iberia (Spain and Portugal), the site of a remarkable Muslim civilization from 711 to 1492. When Muslim forces crossed Gibraltar into Iberia in 711, it was a combined army of Berbers, sub-Saharan Africans, and Arabs. The Almoravids, mostly Berbers with some West African soldiers (slave and free), seized control of al-Andalus (Iberia) by the end of the eleventh century. A single African power would control much of North Africa and Iberia for the next three hundred years.

Africans also went to India. Research on this migration is in its infancy, complicated by an ancient society in which the four major castes (Brahman, Kshatriya, Vaishya, and Sudra) are hierarchically arranged in a manner corresponding with color (varna). The lowest, servile caste, the Sudra, is characterized in the ancient Vedic literature as "black" and "dark-complexioned," but as there are many dark-skinned populations throughout the world, locating Sudra origins in Africa is difficult.

Africans traveled to India prior to the rise of Islam in the seventh century, but their presence is better documented with that religion's movement into the subcontinent (as early as 711). Free Africans (as well as non-Africans) operated in Muslim-ruled India as merchants, seafarers, clerics, bodyguards, and even bureaucrats, and enslaved African women and men served as concubines and soldiers. Called *Habshis* and *Sidis*, Africans settled in a variety of locales. Enclaves of Sidis can presently be found in such places as Gujarat (western India), Habshiguda in Hyderabad (central India) and Janjira Island (south of Bombay). There were also a number of African Muslim rulers during the time of the Mughals (1526–1739), and there were at least several Habshi rulers in the breakaway province of Bengal (eastern India) and in the Deccan.

The fate of all these African slaves in the Islamic world is by no means obvious, especially since descent through the free male line obscures, if not erases, African maternal ancestry. In Morocco the plight of sub-Saharan blacks is clearer, as the descendants of slaves, the *ḥaraṭīn* (called *bella* further east), were in servile subjection to Arabic- and Berber-speaking masters. The free descendants of the *ḥaraṭīn* were also second-class citizens through the nineteenth and into the twentieth centuries. They were heavily dependent upon patron families. One famous community of blacks in Morocco is the Gnawa, noted for their distinct musical traditions. In Morocco, Tunisia, and Algeria, the descendants of sub-Saharan and North Africans practice Islam along with *bori*, a mix of spirits—infants, nature gods, spirits of deceased Muslim leaders, Muslim *jinn* (spirits), and so on—who cause illness and are appeased through offerings, sacrifice, and dance possession.

In India and Pakistan, the descendants of the Habshis and Sidis no longer speak African languages, but their worship, music, and dance are suffused with African content. In addition to those of clear African descent, there are vast millions descended from intermarriages between Africans and Dalits (formerly called "untouchables") or Sudras.

THE TRANSATLANTIC MIGRATION IN CHAINS

The use of African slaves to cultivate sugarcane did not begin in the Americas, but in the Mediterranean and on such West African coastal islands as Madeira, São Tomé, and Principe, beginning in the early fifteenth century. Columbus's 1492 voyage to the "Indies," therefore, set into motion a process that, among other things, transferred a system of slavery from the Old World to the New World. The introduction of diseases (e.g., smallpox, measles, influenza, diphtheria, whooping cough, chicken pox, typhoid, trichinosis) previously unknown in the Americas further stimulated the trafficking in Africans, as it resulted in the "Great Dying" of indigenous peoples who had no immunity to these diseases. Not all Africans entering the New World in the sixteenth century were enslaved, however, and some free Africans took part in the military conquest alongside white conquistadors.

But slavery accounts for the overwhelming majority of those Africans making the involuntary transatlantic migration. The export figure remains a matter of debate, but it would appear that approximately 11.9 million Africans were exported from Africa, out of which 9.6 to 10.8 million arrived alive, translating into a loss during the Middle Passage of about 10 to 20 percent. Some 64.9 percent of the total were males, and 27.9 percent were children. The transatlantic slave trade spanned four hundred years, from the fifteenth through the nineteenth centuries. The apex of the trade, between 1700 and 1810, saw approximately 6.5 million Africans shipped out of the continent. Some 60 percent of all Africans imported into the Americas made the fateful voyage between 1721 and 1820, while 80 percent were transported between 1701 and 1850. In comparison with the trade in Africans through the Sahara, the Red Sea, and the Indian Ocean, the bulk of the Atlantic trade took less than one-tenth of the time.

Many European nations were involved in the slave trade, and of all the voyages for which there is data between 1662 and 1867, nearly 90 percent of captive Africans wound up in Brazil and the Caribbean; indeed, Brazil alone imported 40 percent of the total trade. That part of the Caribbean in which the English and French languages became dominant received 37 percent of the trade, in more or less equal proportions. Spanish-claimed islands accounted for 10 percent of the Africans, after which North America took in 7 percent or less.

Nearly 85 percent of those exported through the transatlantic trade came from one of only four regions in Africa: West Central Africa (36.5%), the Bight of Benin (20%), the Bight of Biafra (16.6%), and the Gold Coast (11%). Slavers (slave ships) often took on their full complement of captives in single regions of supply, and Africans emanating from the same regions tended to be transported to the same New World destinations. Captives from West Central Africa made up the majority of those who came to Saint Domingue (present-day Haiti) and South America, accounting for an astounding 73 percent of the Africans imported into Brazil. The Bight of Benin, in turn, contributed disproportionately to Bahia (northeastern Brazil) and the Francophone Caribbean outside of Saint Domingue; six out of every ten from the Bight of Benin went to Bahia, while two out of every ten arrived in francophone areas. The Bight of Biafra constituted the major source for the British Leeward Islands and Jamaica, while the Gold Coast supplied 37 percent of those who landed in Jamaica, and this area was clearly the leading supplier to Barbados, the Guyanas, and Suriname. Sierra Leone (a region that includes the Windward Coast) provided 6.53 percent of the total export figure, followed by Southeast Africa and Senegambia at 5.14 percent and 4.3 percent, respectively. In addition, transshipments between New World destinations could be substantial.

The transatlantic slave trade qualifies as a quintessential moment of transfiguration. With millions forcibly removed from family and friends and deposited in lands both foreign and hostile, it cannot be compared with the millions of Europeans who voluntarily crossed the Atlantic, a journey that, for all of their troubles, was their collective choice.

MIGRATIONS UNDER SLAVERY

During slavery, movement of Africans and their descendants between territories in the Americas was common and significant. Small parcels of enslaved persons were regularly brought from the English-speaking Caribbean to such northern mainland ports as New York City throughout the eighteenth century (especially the first half of the century). The Haitian Revolution of 1791 to 1804 saw planters flee the island with their slaves in every direction, including to Cuba, Louisiana, South Carolina, and Trinidad. Within territories, economic developments often led to the expansion of slavery. In Brazil, for example, the majority of Africans were brought to such northeastern captaincies (provinces) as Bahia and Pernambuco from the sixteenth century through the seventeenth. From the late seventeenth century through the mid-eighteenth century, however, gold and diamond mining redirected as many as two-thirds of all Africans to Minas Gerais, Mato Grosso, and Goiás. Cotton and coffee became significant crops in the nineteenth century, resulting in the growth of African slavery in central and southern Brazil, particularly Rio de Janeiro, Minas Gerais, and São Paulo. Similarly, slavery's expansion in what became the United States saw black migration from the Upper to the Lower South, coupled with a steady encroachment westward to and beyond the Mississippi Valley.

There were also migrations back to Africa during slavery. Beginning in 1787, Jamaican Maroons (escaped slaves) and blacks who had fought for the British during the American War of Independence embarked from Canada, where they had taken refuge, for the British settlement of Sierra Leone. These initial groups would be later joined by captives taken from slavers bound for the Americas, the result of the British effort to interdict the transatlantic trade. Sierra Leone would receive thousands of such recaptives, reaching a peak in the 1840s. In the United States, repatriation became an organized, state-sanctioned enterprise beginning in 1817 with the founding of the American Colonization Society, which in turn began a colony in 1822 in what would become Monrovia, Liberia. All told, not more than 15,000 blacks participated in the return, a number augmented by the resettlement of recaptives similarly liberated from slavers by the American navy.

In contrast to state-supported efforts, some Africans and their descendants financed their own repatriation. In North America, the African-American merchant Paul Cuffe (1757–1817), the son of a former slave, personally carried thirty-eight individuals back to Africa in 1815. Fraternal organizations in Cuba and Brazil pooled their resources and helped support the return of many of their members. The returnees would be called *amaros* and *saros* in Nigeria and Sierra Leone, respectively.

The United States's prohibition of the transatlantic slave trade would take effect in 1808, but it took the whole of the nineteenth century for slavery itself to be outlawed throughout the Americas.

LATE NINETEENTH- AND EARLY TWENTIETH-CENTURY DEVELOPMENTS

Tremendous disappointment followed the end of slavery throughout the Americas. The realities of debt peonage, rural wage labor, peasant impoverishment, and either wide-ranging, systematic, state-backed terrorism or a heavy-handed colonialism meant that, whether on an island or the mainland, most people were trapped in economic and political oppression.

Changes in the international economy and two world wars created cracks in this prisonlike environment through the demand for labor. Conditions were so desperate that many left family and friends. The Caribbean emerged as the quintessential region of migratory activity. Divided into several phases, the first of the region's major redistributions took place between 1835 and 1885, when activity centered on the islands themselves. Persons from economically depressed areas, such as Barbados, sought opportunities elsewhere, especially in Trinidad and Tobago and British Guyana. About 19,000 left the eastern Caribbean for Trinidad and British Guyana between 1835 and 1846; from 1850 to 1921, some 50,000 emigrated to Trinidad, Tobago, and British Guyana from Barbados alone. Destinations during this initial phase were not limited to the islands, as 7,000 from Dominica, for example, left for the goldfields of Venezuela.

Such a considerable flight of labor caused concern within the sugar industry, resulting in government recruitment of workers from outside the Caribbean. In response, labor was drawn from two sources. The first were "post-emancipation Africans," persons seized from slave ships and taken to Sierra Leona and Saint Helena in West Africa. Some 36,120 were subsequently spread throughout the British-held Caribbean between 1839 and 1867, where their arrival also reinvigorated cultural ties to Africa. The second source was Asia, principally the Indian subcontinent (but also China). Between 1838 and 1917, approximately 500,000 indentured laborers were imported from Asia to such places as Jamaica, Trinidad, Grenada, Martinique, Saint Lucia, and Saint Vincent.

A second migratory phase originating within the Caribbean between the 1880s and the 1920s was both intra-Caribbean as well as an out-migration. Destinations included Panama, Cuba, the Dominican Republic, Costa Rica, and the United States, as well as other Central American sites. It was construction of the Panama Canal that laid the foundation for this important phase.

By the time the canal was completed in 1914, thousands of workers from the Caribbean, many from Barbados, had labored on the canal. The United Fruit Company then transported thousands of the laborers to its banana and sugar plantations and railroads in Costa Rica, Honduras, Cuba, and the Dominican Republic. Cuba alone took in 400,000 Jamaicans and Haitians between 1913 and 1928, and, as is true of Panama, a significant community of their descendants remain in Cuba.

The United States became a destination for others. By 1930, over 130,000 had arrived in U.S. urban areas, including Miami and other Floridian cities, but their major port of call was New York City, where some 40,000 took up residence in Harlem between 1900 and 1930, providing a substantial proportion of the professional and entrepreneurial classes. Most were from the English-speaking islands, but they also came from Cuba, Puerto Rico, and the Dominican Republic.

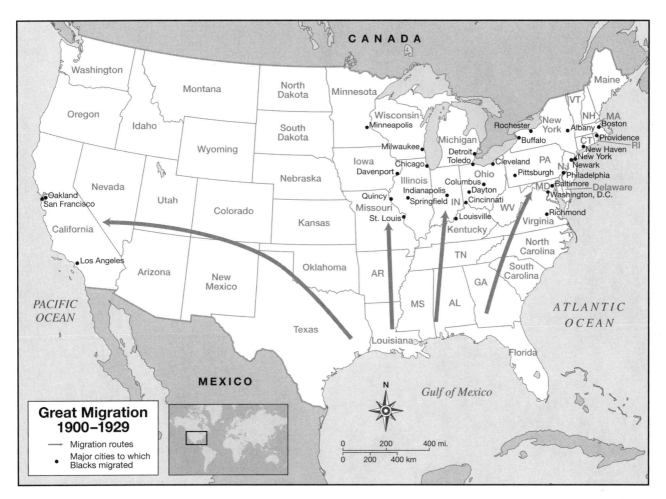

Map of the United States, showing primary migration routes and the major northern and western cities to which African Americans moved during the first three decades of the twentieth century. From the southeast, the majority of departing blacks traveled to cities like New York, Boston, Philadelphia, and Washington, DC. From the middle south, blacks departed for midwestern cities like Chicago and Cincinnati. From the southwest, most journeyed to the Pacific Coast, especially Los Angeles. More than one million blacks left the South during these years. MAP BY XNR PRODUCTIONS. THE GALE GROUP.

Postwar Developments

Emigration from the Caribbean, where the rise of agribusiness resulted in the collapse of plantation agriculture and rising unemployment, continued after World War II. Haitians went to the sugar fields of the Dominican Republic; both Haitians and Dominicans came to Florida along with others from the Caribbean and Central America; and Puerto Ricans and Dominicans undertook major migrations to New York City. Those from the English- and French-speaking islands also relocated to the cities of Britain and France, and they would find their way to Canada in a movement that became much more significant in the 1950s and 1960s.

In North America, the Great Migration between 1916 and 1930 witnessed more than one million blacks leave the South for the North, with over 400,000 boarding trains between 1916 and 1918. This was an intense period of reloca-

tion, propelled by such factors as economic despair (related to the ravages of the boll weevil) and white racism in the South. The latter element had become particularly pernicious, as more than 3,600 people were lynched between 1884 and 1914, with the vast majority of victims being black southerners. Those moving north were also motivated by the high demand for labor in the North, occasioned by global war and the precipitous decline in foreign immigration from Europe (from 1.2 million in 1914 to 110,000 by 1918). World War II had a similar effect, and in the 1940s an additional 1.6 million black southerners are estimated to have left for the North and the West, especially the Los Angeles and San Francisco-Oakland areas), a figure that does not include movement to the South Atlantic region and the Gulf Coast, where many found jobs in defense-related industries. Such migratory activity continued in the 1950s and 1960s, when 2.9 million are estimated

The Great Migration. *A Negro Family arrives in Chicago from the rural South. The image is from* The Negro in Chicago: A Study of Race Relations and a Race Riot *(1922).* PHOTOGRAPHS AND PRINTS DIVISION, SCHOMBURG CENTER FOR RESEARCH IN BLACK CULTURE, THE NEW YORK PUBLIC LIBRARY, ASTOR, LENOX AND TILDEN FOUNDATIONS.

to have left the South. The movement north would transform the majority of African Americans into urban dwellers, and by 1950 some 52 percent of African Americans were living in cities and large towns (a figure that would increase to 81 percent by 1980).

Paralleling the economic experiences of those in North America and the Caribbean were people of African descent in Brazil. In the sugar-producing northeast, black Brazilians remained as wage laborers and tenants on the plantations, but in the coffee region of the southeast there was considerable migration to the rapidly developing cities of São Paulo and Rio de Janeiro. There, they ran into the issue of *embranquecimento,* or "whitening," an effort to increase European immigration and thereby achieve "civilized" status as a nation. In response to this policy, some

90,000 Europeans immigrants, called *colonos,* arrived in Brazil between 1886 and 1889.

From the mid-1960s onward, many of the Caribbean colonies achieved independent status, paralleling events in Africa and Asia, but agribusiness maintained pressure on the unemployed to emigrate. In addition to New York, Toronto, Paris, and London, such emigrants journeyed to rural areas as well. Haitians and Dominicans followed the earlier pattern of migrating to the United States and Canada, where they were joined by American southerners and Central Americans in picking fruit and vegetable harvests and working as domestics. Migrant workers often did not come to stay, but rather to save enough money to create better conditions for themselves and their families back home. Whether temporary or permanent, some 300,000 people per year were leaving the Caribbean by the early 1960s.

As for Europe, two principal sites for the African diaspora have been Britain and France. Enslaved Africans arrived in England in the sixteenth century, and by the late eighteenth century there were as many as ten thousand enslaved blacks in the country, mostly in London, Bristol, and Liverpool, a major port in the slave trade. Black seamen had also become fixtures in the various ports, where they played leading roles in labor struggles. Early twentieth-century England boasted a small black community numbering in the thousands, but subsequent immigration of colonial subjects from Asia, Africa, and the Caribbean in response to the labor and soldiering needs of two world wars significantly augmented their numbers. Caribbean labor continued to arrive in the 1950s to assist in the rebuilding of Britain's postwar economy, but a growing black presence had the effect of increasing white resentment, xenophobia, and violence.

Developments in France were analogous. The conflict with Algeria has profoundly impacted race relations in France, and the experience of the North African immigrant, originally recruited to fill labor needs, has been the most critical of all. Anti–North African sentiment in France was inflamed not only by the end of the Second World War and the reclamation of jobs by white Frenchmen, but by the Algerian Revolution. Islam is an important dynamic, as North Africans are highly integrated into the Muslim world. North and West Africans are the principal targets of France's xenophobia.

Since the Second World War, African and African-descended populations have achieved appreciable numerical levels throughout Europe. Italy, Portugal, Spain, the Netherlands, and Germany (via American troops) all have recognizable populations of African descendants. Even Russia has a black history—Soviet Russia was a magnet for African university students and visiting black intellectuals. Since the 1980s, efforts to enter Europe have included illegal immigration from sub-Saharan Africa (an often perilous and deadly undertaking). Exploitation of young girls and women via prostitution has also been part of the phenomenon. In all cases, immigrants and their descendants wrestle with the meaning of their identities, maintaining, in many instances, ties to Africa or the Caribbean, while agitating for full acceptance and equal citizenship in their adopted European homes.

See also African Diaspora; Economic Condition, U.S.; Slave Trade; Slavery

■ ■ *Bibliography*

Abun-Nasr, Jamil M. *A History of the Maghrib in the Islamic Period.* Cambridge, UK: Cambridge University Press, 1987.

Austen, Ralph. *African Economic History: Internal Development and External Dependency.* London: Heinemann, 1987.

Baptiste, Fitzroy A. "The African Presence in India." *Africa Quarterly* 38 (1998): 92–126.

Blakely, Allison. *Russia and the Negro: Blacks in Russian History and Thought.* Washington, D.C.: Howard University Press, 1986.

Butler, Kim D. *Freedoms Given, Freedoms Won: Afro-Brazilians in Post-Abolition São Paulo and Salvador.* New Brunswick, N.J.: Rutgers University Press, 1998.

Donadoni, Sergio, ed. *The Egyptians.* Translated by Robert Bianchi, et al. Chicago: University of Chicago Press, 1997.

Eltis, David, Stephen D. Behrendt, David Richardson, and Herbert Klein. *The Trans-Atlantic Slave Trade: A Database on CD-ROM.* Cambridge, UK: Cambridge University Press, 1999.

Ennaji, Mohammed. *Serving the Master: Slavery and Society in Nineteenth-Century Morocco.* Translated by Seth Graebner. New York: St. Martin's Press, 1999.

Franklin, John Hope, and Alfred A. Moss Jr. *From Slavery to Freedom: A History of African Americans,* 8th ed. New York: McGraw Hill, 2000.

Gomez, Michael A. *Exchanging Our Country Marks: The Transformation of African Identities in the Colonial and Antebellum South.* Chapel Hill: University of North Carolina Press, 1998.

Higman, B. W. *Slave Populations of the British Caribbean, 1807–1834.* Baltimore, Md.: Johns Hopkins University Press, 1984.

Hunwick, John O. "African Slaves in the Mediterranean World: A Neglected Aspect of the African Diaspora." In *Global Dimensions of the African Diaspora,* edited by Joseph E. Harris. Washington, D.C.: Howard University Press, 1993.

Inikori, Joseph E. *Forced Migration: The Impact of the Export Slave Trade on African Societies.* New York: Africana, 1982.

James, Winston. *Holding Aloft the Banner of Ethiopia: Caribbean Radicalism in Early Twentieth-Century America.* London and New York: Verso, 1998.

James, Winston and Clive Harris, eds. *Inside Babylon: The Caribbean Diaspora in Britain.* London: Verso, 1993.

Jelloun, Tahar Ben. *French Hospitality: Racism and North African Immigrants.* Translated by Barbara Bray. New York: Columbia University Press, 1999.

Linebaugh, Peter and Marcus Rediker. *The Many-Headed Hydra: Sailors, Slaves, Commoners, and the Hidden History of the Revolutionary Atlantic.* Boston: Beacon, 2000.

Lovejoy, Paul E. *Transformations in Slavery: A History of Slavery in Africa.* Cambridge, UK: Cambridge University Press, 1983.

Manning, Patrick. *Slavery and African Life: Occidental, Oriental, and African Slave Trades.* Cambridge, UK: Cambridge University Press, 1990.

Northrup, David. *Africa's Discovery of Europe: 1450–1850.* New York: Oxford University Press, 2002.

Palmer, Colin. *Slaves of the White God: Blacks in Mexico, 1570–1650.* Cambridge, Mass.: Harvard University Press, 1976.

Schuler, Monica. *"Alas, Alas Kongo": A Social History of Indentured African Immigration into Jamaica, 1841–1865.* Baltimore, Md.: Johns Hopkins University Press, 1980.

Shepherd, Verene, and Hilary McD. Beckles. *Caribbean Slavery in the Atlantic World: A Student Reader*. Princeton, N.J.: Markus Weiner, 2000.

Snowden, Frank M., Jr. *Blacks in Antiquity: Ethiopians in the Greco-Roman Experience*. Cambridge, Mass.: Belknap Press, 1970.

Trotter, Joe William, Jr., ed. *The Great Migration in Historical Perspective: New Dimensions of Race, Class, and Gender*. Bloomington: Indiana University Press, 1991.

Verger, Pierre. *Trade Relations between the Bight of Benin and Bahia from the 17th to 19th Century*. Translated by Evelyn Crawford. Ibadan, Nigeria: Ibadan University Press, 1976.

Walvin, James. *Making the Black Atlantic: Britain and the African Diaspora*. London and New York: Cassell, 2000.

Watkins-Owens, Irma. *Blood Relations: Caribbean Immigrants and the Harlem Community, 1900–1930*. Bloomington: Indiana University Press, 1996.

MICHAEL A. GOMEZ (2005)

U.S. Migration/ Population

Migration has been a persistent theme throughout African-American history. Africans entered the New World as slaves, unlike European immigrants and their Asian counterparts. With the advent of the Civil War and Emancipation, black population movement took on a voluntary character and slowly converged with that of other groups. Nonetheless, only with the coming of World War I and its aftermath did blacks make a fundamental break with the land and move into cities in growing numbers. The Great Migration of the early twentieth century foreshadowed the transformation of African Americans from a predominantly rural to a predominantly urban population. It reflected their quest for freedom, jobs, and social justice; the rise of new classes and social relations within the African-American community; and the emergence of new patterns of race, class, and ethnic relations in American society as a whole.

From the colonial period through the antebellum era, Africans and their American descendants experienced forced migration from one agricultural region to another. One and a half million blacks reached the United States via the international slave trade, primarily from the west coast of Africa. Through natural increase, their numbers rose to an estimated four million by 1860. By 1750, there were more than 144,000 blacks in the tobacco-growing states of Maryland and Virginia, representing the highest concentration of slaves in the country. In the wake of the American Revolution, however, slaves experienced a dramatic relocation from the tobacco region of the Upper South to the emerging cotton-growing areas of the Deep South. The tobacco country slowly declined in fertility during the late eighteenth century, and planters first transported or sold their slaves to the neighboring states of Kentucky and Tennessee. After the close of the international slave trade to the United States in 1808, this movement accelerated. Between 1810 and 1820, an estimated 137,000 slaves left the Chesapeake Bay region and North Carolina for the cotton-growing states of the Deep South, particularly Alabama and Mississippi.

Some slaves entered the Deep South with their masters, but growing numbers came via the domestic slave trade. Whether they traveled by water or by land, they moved to their new homes in handcuffs and chains. As one ex-slave recalled, "We were handcuffed in pairs, with iron staples and bolts, with a short chain about a foot long uniting the handcuffs and their wearers." Contemporary travelers frequently commented on the sight of migrating slaves. In 1834, for example, an English traveler reported on his trip from Virginia to Alabama: "In the early grey of the morning, we came up with a singular spectacle, the most striking one of the kind I have ever witnessed. It was a camp of Negro slave-drivers, just packing up to start; they had about three hundred slaves with them, who had bivouacked the preceding night in chains in the woods; these they were conducting to Natchez, upon the Mississippi River."

Although Africans, and increasingly African Americans, were the victims of coerced migrations during this period, they were by no means passive. Slaves acted in their own behalf by running away, planning rebellions, and deepening their efforts to build a viable slave community. According to one historian, the transition from an African to a predominantly American-born slave-labor force facilitated the emergence of new forms of rebellion and demands for liberation in the new republic. As slaves learned the language, gained familiarity with the terrain, and built linkages to slaves on other plantations, they increased their efforts to resist bondage. Newspaper advertisements for runaways increased as planters and slave traders mediated the transfer of slaves from the tobacco-growing regions to the "cotton kingdom." Advertisements for runaways not only reflected the slaves' resistance, but also the harsh conditions they faced: "Bill is a large fellow, very black, shows the whites of his eyes more than usual, has a scar on his right cheek bone, several on his breast, one on his arm, occasioned by the bite of a dog, his back very badly scarred with the whip."

The Civil War and Reconstruction radically transformed the context of black migration. Black population movement accelerated, spurred by the presence of federal troops, the ending of chattel slavery, the enactment of full

Distribution of African Americans. *A map from* The Great South *(1874), by Edward King, shows that the distribution of the black population had not changed dramatically by 1874, even though free blacks and runaways from the South created small black communities in northern cities like New York, Boston, Philadelphia, and Cincinnati.* GENERAL RESEARCH AND REFERENCE DIVISION, SCHOMBURG CENTER FOR RESEARCH IN BLACK CULTURE, THE NEW YORK PUBLIC LIBRARY, ASTOR, LENOX AND TILDEN FOUNDATIONS.

citizenship legislation, and rising white hostility. In the first years following Emancipation, one Florida planter informed his cousin in North Carolina, "The negroes don't seem to feel free unless they leave their old homes . . . just to make it sure they can go when and where they choose." A South Carolina family offered to pay its cook double the amount that she would receive in another village, but the woman insisted, "No, Miss, I must go. . . . If I stay here I'll never know I am free."

When the promise of freedom faded during the late 1870s, the Exodus of 1879 symbolized the new mobility of the black population. Within a few months, some six thousand blacks left their homes in Louisiana, Mississippi, and Texas for a new life in Kansas. As one black contemporary stated, "There are no words which can fully express or explain the real condition of my people throughout the south, nor how deeply and keenly they feel the necessity of fleeing from the wrath and long pent-up hatred of their old masters which they feel assured will ere long burst loose like the pent-up-fires of a volcano and crush them if they remain here many years longer." Still, the Exodus was a rural-to-rural migration, with blacks moving to

Kansas when an earlier Tennessee option proved fruitless. African Americans expected to resettle on available farmland and continue their familiar, but hopefully freer, rural way of life.

Despite the predominance of rural-to-rural migration, the migration of blacks to American cities had deep antebellum roots. Boston launched its career as a slave-holding city as early as 1638, when the Salem ship *Desire* returned from the West Indies with a cargo of "salt, cotton, tobacco, and Negroes." Slavery in New York City, beginning under Dutch control in 1626, entered an era of unprecedented growth under the British in 1664. In Philadelphia in 1684, within three years after the first Quakers settled in Pennsylvania, the first fifty Africans arrived. The number of slaves in the seaports of the Northeast rose from negligible numbers during the seventeenth century to sizable proportions by the mid-eighteenth century, when there were over 1,500 in Boston, over 1,400 in Philadelphia, and over 2,000 in New York. Southern cities such as New Orleans, Mobile, Charleston, Baltimore, Louisville, Savannah, and Richmond also had sizable antebellum black populations.

Black migration to American cities escalated during the late eighteenth and early nineteenth centuries. Moreover, in the aftermath of the Civil War and Reconstruction, blacks increasingly moved into rural industrial settings such as the coalfields of Alabama, Tennessee, Kentucky, and West Virginia. Others gained increasing access to nonagricultural jobs as lumber and railroad hands in the expanding industrial order. Still, as late as 1910, nearly 90 percent of the nation's black population lived in the South, and fewer than 22 percent of southern blacks lived in cities.

After World War I, blacks made a fundamental break with their southern rural heritage and moved into cities in growing numbers. An estimated 700,000 to one million blacks left the South between 1917 and 1920. Another 800,000 to one million left during the 1920s. Whereas the prewar migrants moved to southern cities such as Norfolk, Louisville, Birmingham, and Atlanta (and to a few northern cities such as Chicago, Philadelphia, and New York), blacks now moved throughout the urban North and West. Beginning with relatively small numbers on the eve of World War I, the black urban population in the Midwest and Great Lakes region increased even more dramatically than that of the Northeast. Detroit's black population increased by 611 percent during the war years and by nearly 200 percent during the 1920s, rising from fewer than 6,000 to over 120,000. Cleveland's black population rose from fewer than 8,500 to nearly 72,000. In St. Louis, the increase was from under 45,000 in 1910 to nearly 94,000 in 1930.

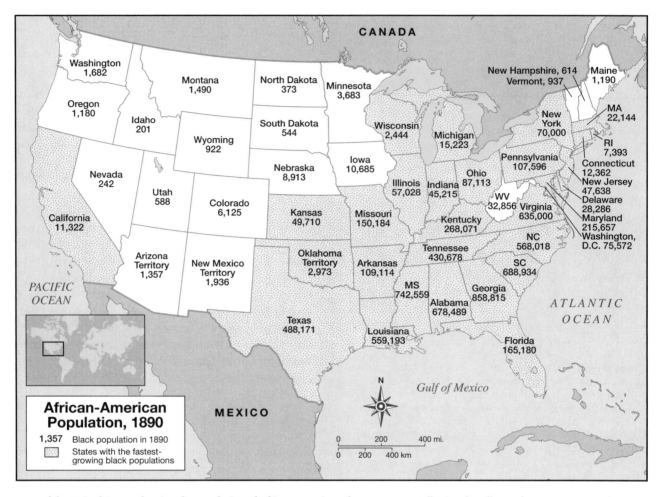

CANADA

Washington
1,682

Oregon
1,180

Idaho
201

Montana
1,490

Wyoming
922

North Dakota
373

Minnesota
3,683

South Dakota
544

New Hampshire, 614
Vermont, 937

Maine
1,190

Nevada
242

Utah
588

Colorado
6,125

Nebraska
8,913

Iowa
10,685

Wisconsin
2,444

Michigan
15,223

New
York
70,000

MA
22,144

RI
7,393

Connecticut
12,362

New Jersey
47,638

Delaware
28,286

Maryland
215,657

Washington,
D.C. 75,572

California
11,322

Arizona
Territory
1,357

New Mexico
Territory
1,936

Kansas
49,710

Missouri
150,184

Illinois
57,028

Indiana
45,215

Ohio
87,113

WV
32,856

Pennsylvania
107,596

Virginia
635,000

Kentucky
268,071

NC
568,018

PACIFIC
OCEAN

Oklahoma
Territory
2,973

Arkansas
109,114

Tennessee
430,678

SC
688,934

MS
742,559

Georgia
858,815

Alabama
678,489

ATLANTIC
OCEAN

Texas
488,171

Louisiana
559,193

Florida
165,180

MEXICO

Gulf of Mexico

N

African-American Population, 1890

1,357   Black population in 1890

   States with the fastest-
   growing black populations

0   200   400 mi.
0   200   400 km

Map of the United States, showing the population of African Americans by state, 1890. Following the collapse of Reconstruction in the 1870s, many blacks began leaving the South for western states and northern and midwestern cities, increasing the African American population in these areas dramatically by the turn of the century. MAP BY XNR PRODUCTIONS. THE GALE GROUP.

In the urban West, the black population increased most dramatically in Los Angeles, growing from 7,600 in 1910 to nearly 40,000 in 1930. Nonetheless, as in the prewar era, New York City, Chicago, and Philadelphia continued to absorb disproportionately large numbers of black new-comers. Between 1910 and 1930, Chicago's black popula-tion increased more than fivefold, from 44,000 to 234,000; New York's more than tripled, from about 100,000 to 328,000; and Philadelphia's grew from 84,500 to an esti-mated 220,600.

Upper South and border states remained important sources of black migrants during World War I and the 1920s, but Deep South states increased their importance. Blacks born in Mississippi, Alabama, Georgia, South Car-olina, and Louisiana now dominated the migration stream to Illinois and Chicago, for example, making up over 60 percent of the black population increase in that area be-tween 1910 and 1920. African Americans from the Upper South predominated in New York City more so than in

Chicago, but blacks from South Carolina, Georgia, and Florida came in growing numbers. In the rapidly industri-alizing cities of Cleveland and Detroit, the ratio of black men to black women escalated from just a few more men than women in 1910 to between 120 and 140 men to every 100 women during the war years. In Milwaukee, where the ratio of men to women was 95 to 100 in 1910, the ratio reversed itself, and the number of men versus women in-creased between 1910 and 1920. Finally, in the northeast-ern cities of New York and Philadelphia, where women significantly outnumbered men before the war, the ratio evened out.

A variety of factors underlay black population move-ment. African Americans sought an alternative to sha-recropping, disfranchisement, and racial injustice in the South. In 1917 the *AME Review* articulated the forces that propelled blacks outward from the South: "Neither char-acter, the accumulation of property, the fostering of the Church, the schools and a better and higher standard of

An alley on the Lower West Side of New York City. The photograph, from The Negro in the Cities of New York *(1905), gives a hint of the crowded conditions in which many poor migrants lived in American's northern cities of the early twentieth century.* GENERAL RESEARCH AND REFERENCE DIVISION, SCHOMBURG CENTER FOR RESEARCH IN BLACK CULTURE, THE NEW YORK PUBLIC LIBRARY, ASTOR, LENOX AND TILDEN FOUNDATIONS.

the home" had made a difference in the status of black Southerners. "Confidence in the sense of justice, humanity and fair play of the white South is gone," the paper concluded. One migrant articulated the same mood in verse: "An' let one race have all de South—Where color lines are drawn—For 'Hagar's child' done [stem] de tide—Farewell—we're good and gone."

African Americans were also attracted by the lure of opportunities in the North. The labor demands of northern industries, immigration-restriction legislation, and greater access to the rights of citizens (including the franchise) all encouraged the movement of blacks into northern cities. Wages in northern industries usually ranged from $3 to $5 per eight-hour day, compared with as little as 75 cents to $1 per day in southern agriculture and with

no more than $2.50 for a nine-hour day in southern industries. Moreover, between 1915 and 1925, the average wages of domestics in some northern cities doubled. Northern cities also promised access to better health care. The nonwhite infant-mortality rate dropped in New York City from 176 deaths per 1,000 live births in 1917 to 105 in 1930; in Boston, from 167 to 90; and in Philadelphia, from 193 to 100. Between 1911 and 1926, according to the Metropolitan Life Insurance Company, the incidence of tuberculosis among the nation's blacks declined by 44 percent for black males and 43 percent for black females. New York, Philadelphia, and Chicago showed similar patterns of decline.

With better social conditions, higher wages, and the franchise, it is no wonder that African Americans viewed the Great Migration to northern cities in glowing terms, with references to "the Promised Land," the "flight out of Egypt," and "going into Canaan." One black man wrote back to his southern home, "The (Col.) men are making good. [The job] never pays less than $3.00 per day for (10) hours." In her letter home, a black woman related, "I am well and thankful to say I am doing well . . . I work in Swifts Packing Company." "Up here," another migrant said, "our people are in a different light." Over and over again, African Americans confirmed that: "Up here, a man can be a man." As one southern black man wrote home from the North, "I should have been here twenty years ago . . . I just begin to feel like a man . . . My children are going to the same school with the whites and I don't have to humble to no one. I have registered. Will vote in the next election and there isn't any yes Sir or no Sir. It's all yes and no, Sam and Bill."

The Great Migration was by no means a simple move from southern agriculture to northern cities. It had specific regional and subregional components. More blacks migrated to southern cities between 1900 and 1920 than to northern ones. Moreover, African Americans frequently made up from 25 percent to 50 percent of the total population in southern cities, compared with little more than 10 percent in northern cities. Before moving to Philadelphia, Boston, or New York, for example, rural migrants first moved to cities such as New Orleans, Jacksonville, Savannah, Memphis, Charleston, and Birmingham. The Jefferson County cities of Birmingham and Bessemer, with extensive rail connections, served as the major distribution points for blacks going north from Alabama. The Southern, the Louisville and Nashville, the Chicago, St. Louis, and San Francisco, and the Illinois Central railroads all traveled northward from Birmingham and Bessemer. In Georgia, cities such as Columbus, Americus, and Albany served as distribution points for blacks leaving from western Georgia and eastern Alabama, while Valdosta, Waycross, Brunswick, and Savannah were distribution centers for those leaving the depressed agricultural counties of southern and southeastern Georgia. To blacks moving north from Mississippi, Arkansas, Alabama, Louisiana, and Texas, Chicago was the logical destination, whereas cities in Pennsylvania, New Jersey, New York, and New England attracted blacks from Florida, South Carolina, Virginia, and Georgia.

Upon the arrival of blacks in northern cities, their population movement usually developed secondary streams. As one contemporary observer noted, "All of the arrivals here [Chicago] did not stay. . . . They were only temporary guests awaiting the opportunity to proceed further and settle in surrounding cities and towns. With Chicago as a center there are within a radius of from one hundred to one hundred and fifty miles a number of smaller industrial centers. . . . A great many of the migrants who came to Chicago found employment in these satellite places." In Philadelphia, black migration also "broke bulk" and radiated outward to Lancaster, York, Altoona, and Harrisburg in central Pennsylvania, as well as to Wilmington, Delaware.

Southern blacks helped to organize their own movement into the urban North. They developed an extensive communications network, which included railroad employees, who traveled back and forth between northern and southern cities; northern black weeklies such as the *Chicago Defender* and the *Pittsburgh Courier;* and an expanding chain of kin and friends. Using their networks of families and friends, African Americans learned about transportation, jobs, and housing in an area before going there. As one contemporary observer noted, "The chief stimuli was discussion. . . . The talk in the barber shops and grocery stores . . . soon began to take the form of reasons for leaving." Also fueling the migration process were the letters, money, and testimonies of migrants who returned to visit. One South Carolina migrant to Pittsburgh recalled, "I was plowing in the field and it was real hot. And I stayed with some of the boys who would leave home and [come] back . . . and would have money, and they had clothes. I didn't have that. We all grew up together. And I said, 'Well, as long as I stay here I'm going to get nowhere.' And I tied that mule to a tree and caught a train."

Other migrants formed migration clubs, pooled their resources, and moved in groups. Black women, deeply enmeshed in black kin and friendship networks, played a conspicuous role in helping to organize the black migration. As recent scholarship suggests, women were the "primary kinkeepers." Moreover, they often had their own gender-specific reasons for leaving the rural South. Afri-

can-American women resented stereotyped images of the black mammy, who presumably placed loyalty to white families above attachment to her own. Black women's migration reinforced the notion that lifting the race and improving the image of black women were compatible goals.

Black migration was fundamentally a movement of workers, and as blacks moved into northern cities in growing numbers, a black industrial working class emerged. Southern black sharecroppers, farm laborers, sawmill hands, dock workers, and railroad hands all moved into new positions in the urban economy. Labor agents helped to recruit black workers for jobs in meatpacking, auto, steel, and other mass-production industries. As suggested above, however, these labor agents were soon supplanted by the expansion of black familial and communal networks. Employers attested: "After the initial group movement by agents, Negroes kept going by twos and threes. These were drawn by letters, and by actual advances of money, from Negroes who had already settled in the North." Further, "Every Negro that makes good in the North and writes back to his friends starts off a new group."

Wartime labor demands undermined the color barrier in basic industries. In Cleveland, Pittsburgh, Detroit, and Milwaukee, the percentage of black men employed in industrial jobs increased from an estimated 10 to 20 percent of the black labor force in 1910 to about 60 or 70 percent in 1920 and 1930. An official of Cleveland's National Malleable Casting Company exclaimed: "We have [black] molders, core makers, chippers, fitters, locomotive crane operators, melting furnace operators, general foremen, foremen, assistant foremen, clerks, timekeepers[;] in fact, there is no work in our shop that they cannot do and do well, if properly supervised." In the Pittsburgh district, the number of black steelworkers rose from less than 800 on the eve of World War I to nearly 17,000 by 1923. In Detroit, the Ford Motor Company outdistanced other automakers in the employment of African Americans, with the number of black employees rising from fewer than 100 in 1916 to nearly 10,000 in 1926. Black women also entered industrial jobs, although their gains were far less than those of black men. In Chicago the number of black women in manufacturing trades increased from fewer than 1,000 in 1910 to over 3,000 in 1920. Industrial jobs now employed 15 percent of the black female labor force, compared with less than 7 percent in 1910. Buffalo and Pittsburgh offered neither black nor white women substantial industrial opportunities, but the war nonetheless increased their numbers in manufacturing. In Harlem, black women gained increasing employment in the garment industry and in commercial laundries. Still, few

A large and well-dressed crowd of travelers, mostly African Americans, c. 1910. Of the period known as the Great Migration, James Weldon Johnson wrote: "Migrants came north in thousands, tens of thousands, hundreds of thousands—from the docks of Norfolk, Savannah, Jacksonville, Tampa, Mobile, New Orleans, and Galveston: from the cotton fields of Mississippi, and the coal mines and steel mills of Alabama and Tennessee; from workshops and wash-tubs and brickyards and kitchens they came." PHOTOGRAPHS AND PRINTS DIVISION, SCHOMBURG CENTER FOR RESEARCH IN BLACK CULTURE, THE NEW YORK PUBLIC LIBRARY, ASTOR, LENOX AND TILDEN FOUNDATIONS.

black women entered the major factories of the industrial North. Moreover, despite black men's increasing participation in the new industrial sectors, most moved into jobs at the bottom rung of the industrial ladder.

If African Americans helped to shape their own movement into cities, they also played a role in shaping their experiences within the labor force. In order to change the terms on which they labored, they frequently moved from job to job seeking higher wages and better working conditions. In Milwaukee, at one very disagreeable tannery plant, a black worker related, "I worked there one night and I quit." During the war years, the steel mills of western Pennsylvania frequently experienced a 300 percent turnover rate among black workers. In 1923, for instance, the A. M. Byers iron mill in Pittsburgh employed 1,408 African Americans in order to maintain a work force of 228. At the same time, some African Americans served

as strikebreakers; they expressed bitter resentment over the discriminatory practices of white workers, who frequently referred to blacks as a "scab race" and justified their exclusionary policies. Black workers also organized independent all-black unions such as the Brotherhood of Sleeping Car Porters. When whites occasionally lowered racial barriers, others joined white unions such as the Amalgamated Meat Cutters and Butcher Workmen. During the 1930s, the Congress of Industrial Organizations built upon these traditions of collective action among black workers.

Closely intertwined with the increasing urbanization of the black population was the rise of the ghetto. As the black urban population increased, residential segregation increased in all major cities. The index of dissimilarity (a statistical device for measuring the extent of residential segregation) rose from 66.8 to 85.2 percent in Chicago;

A group of migrants journeying from Florida to New Jersey. *Thousands of African Americans left the South during the decade of the Great Depression.* COURTESY OF THE FDR LIBRARY

60.6 to 85.0 percent in Cleveland; 64.1 to 77.9 percent in Boston; and 46.0 to 63.0 percent in Philadelphia. The increasing segregation of blacks in the city not only reflected their precarious position in the urban economy, but also the intensification of racial restrictions in the urban housing market. In cities with large black populations, like New York and Chicago, the World War I migration intensified a process that was already well under way. Harlem—planned as an exclusive, stable, upper- and upper-middle-class white community—represented a desirable location to the city's expanding black population.

Although an economic depression undercut the flow of whites into Harlem, white residents resisted black occupancy. Between 1910 and 1915, the Harlem Property Owners' Improvement Corporation waged a vigorous fight to keep blacks out. It launched a restrictive covenant campaign and informed black realtors that houses in the area were not available to black buyers. Although the

movement failed to keep Harlem white, discriminatory prices, along with the dearth of necessary repairs, undermined housing quality during the 1920s.

In Chicago and elsewhere, both North and South, blacks faced similar restrictions in the housing market. When legal tactics failed, whites resorted to violence. Race violence erupted in Chicago, East St. Louis, Pittsburgh, and Philadelphia during the era of the Great Migration. Race riots not only helped to reinforce residential segregation in northern cities, they highlighted the growing nationalization of the "race question" in American society.

African Americans developed cross-class alliances and fought racial discrimination in the housing, institutional, and political life of the cities. The black migration reinforced a long tradition of black urban institution-building activities. As early as the 1790s, blacks launched the African Methodist Episcopal (AME) Church in Philadelphia, followed closely by the African Methodist Episcopal Zion

(AMEZ) Church in New York, and the Baptist Church in both cities. In 1886, African Americans formed the National Baptist Convention and spearheaded the formation of new churches.

Along with churches, blacks soon formed a variety of mutual aid societies and fraternal orders, including the Masons, Odd Fellows, and Independent Order of St. Luke. The National Association of Colored Women, formed in 1895, emphasized service to the community. Mobilizing under its credo "Lifting as We Climb," the association organized, administered, and supported a variety of social-welfare activities, including homes for the aged, young women, and children; relief funds for the unemployed; and legal aid to combat injustice before the law. Under the impact of World War I and its aftermath, new expressions of black consciousness (as reflected in the emergence of the Harlem Renaissance) and the growing participation of blacks in northern politics demonstrated solidarity across class and status lines.

The alliance between black workers and black elites was by no means unproblematic. As the new black middle class expanded during the 1920s, for example, it slowly moved into better housing vacated by whites, leaving the black poor concentrated in certain sections. In his studies of Chicago and New York, the sociologist E. Franklin Frazier demonstrated the increasing division of the black urban community along socioeconomic lines. While each city contained significant areas of interclass mixing, poverty increasingly characterized specific sections of the ghetto.

Moreover, the rise of working-class-oriented organizations such as the Universal Negro Improvement Association created substantial conflicts between black workers and established middle-class leadership. Emphasizing "race first," black pride, and solidarity with Africa, the Garvey movement struck a responsive chord among large numbers of black workers. Its Jamaican-born leader, Marcus Garvey (1887–1940), frequently exclaimed, "The Universal Negro Improvement Association . . . believes that the Negro race is as good as any other race, and therefore should be as proud of itself as others are. . . . It believes in the spiritual Fatherhood of God and the Brotherhood of Man." As one migrant stated, "We will make a great mistake if we step out of the path of the Universal Negro Improvement Association." While race-conscious black business and professional people endorsed aspects of Garvey's ideas, they feared his growing appeal and often complained that his message appealed primarily to the "ignorant class" of newcomers from the South.

Despite conflicts between black workers and middle-class black leaders, African Americans continued to forge cross-class alliances. In 1914 Oscar DePriest defeated his white opponents to become Chicago's first black alderman. In 1928 DePriest also symbolized the growing shift of black electoral power from the South to northern urban centers when he gained the Republican Party's endorsement and won a seat in the U.S. Congress, serving the First Congressional District of Illinois. When blacks sought a similar goal in New York, they failed because skillful gerrymandering had split the black vote between the Nineteenth and Twenty-First Assembly districts. In 1944, when the boundaries were redrawn, blacks elected the black minister Adam Clayton Powell, Jr., to the House of Representatives. Harlem thus became the second northern congressional district to send a black to Congress. By then, African Americans had realigned their party affiliation from Republican to Democrat and had become an indispensable element in the New Deal coalition.

Although black electoral politics reflected the growing segregation of the urban environment, black elites retained a core of white allies. African Americans had cultivated a small number of white friends and launched the interracial National Urban League in 1911 and the National Association for the Advancement of Colored People (NAACP) in 1909. During the 1930s and 1940s, this inter- and intraracial unity gained even greater expression with the rise of the Congress of Industrial Organizations, New Deal social-welfare programs, and the March on Washington movement. When President Franklin D. Roosevelt issued Executive Order 8802 in 1941, calling for an end to racial barriers in defense industries, African Americans achieved a major victory against racial exploitation.

As the nation entered the years after World War II, a variety of forces again transformed the context of black migration. The technological revolution in southern agriculture, the emergence of the welfare state, and the militant civil rights and Black Power movements all helped to complete the long-run transformation of blacks from a predominantly rural to a predominantly urban people. The African-American population increased from thirteen million in 1940 to over twenty-two million in 1970. The proportion of blacks living in cities rose to over 80 percent, 10 percent higher than the population at large. Beginning as the most rural of Americans, blacks had become the most urbanized.

The Great Migration helped to transform both black and white America. It elevated the issues of race and southern black culture from regional to national phenomena. It was often a volatile process, involving both intra- and interracial conflicts. Distributed almost equally among regions, by the late 1970s the black urban migration had run its familiar twentieth-century course. Increases in black urban population were now primarily the

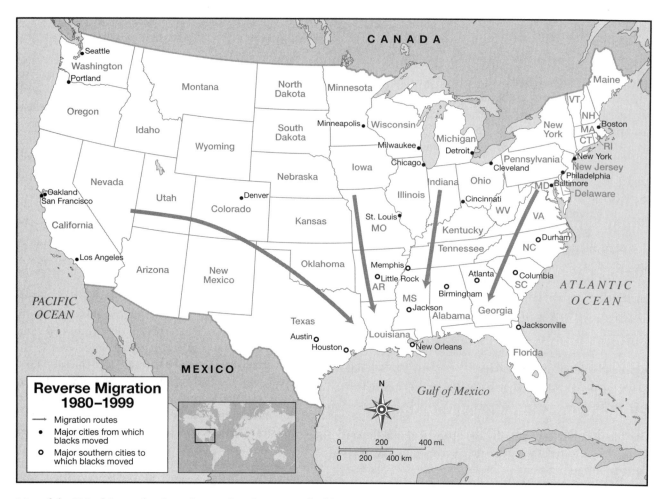

CANADA

Seattle
Washington
Portland

Oregon

Montana

Idaho

Wyoming

North
Dakota

South
Dakota

Minnesota

Minneapolis

Wisconsin

Milwaukee

Michigan

Detroit

Maine

VT

NH

Boston

New
York

MA

CT

RI

New York

Nevada

Utah

Colorado

Denver

Nebraska

Iowa

Chicago

Illinois

Indiana

Ohio

Cleveland

Cincinnati

WV

Pennsylvania

New Jersey

Philadelphia

MD

Baltimore

Delaware

Oakland
San Francisco

California

Los Angeles

Arizona

New
Mexico

Kansas

Oklahoma

St. Louis
MO

Kentucky

Tennessee

Memphis
Little Rock
AR

MS

Jackson

Birmingham

Alabama

VA

NC

Durham

Columbia
SC

Atlanta

Georgia

ATLANTIC
OCEAN

PACIFIC
OCEAN

Texas

Austin

Houston

Louisiana

New Orleans

Jacksonville

Florida

MEXICO

**Reverse Migration
1980–1999**

— Migration routes
● Major cities from which
   blacks moved
○ Major southern cities to
   which blacks moved

N

Gulf of Mexico

0   200   400 mi.
0 200 400 km

Map of the United States showing primary migration routes of African Americans moving from the North and West to the South, and the major southern cities to which many blacks relocated during the last two decades of the twentieth century. MAP BY XNR PRODUCTIONS. THE GALE GROUP.

product of births over deaths rather than interregional movements. Moreover, southern-born blacks from the North and West returned home in rising numbers. During the 1980s, the proportion of African Americans living in the South increased, after declining for more than a century. At the same time, black migration to American suburbs escalated. While the outcome of this new migration is yet to be determined, the suburban migrants are faring better than their inner-city counterparts. The returning migrants are also much better off than those who left, and they envision a "New South," one that is much different from the one their forebears abandoned.

See also *Chicago Defender*; Brotherhood of Sleeping Car Porters; Civil War, U.S.; DePriest, Oscar Stanton; Emancipation in the United States; Garvey, Marcus; Harlem, New York; National Urban League; Universal Negro Improvement Association

■ ■ *Bibliography*

Adero, Malaika, ed. *Up South: Stories, Studies and Letters of African American Migrations.* New York: New Press, 1993.

Berlin, Ira, and Ronald Hoffman, eds. *Slavery and Freedom in the Age of the American Revolution.* Charlottesville: University Press of Virginia, 1983.

Griffin, Farah Jasmine. *"Who Set You Flowin'?": The African-American Migration Narrative.* New York: Oxford University Press, 1995.

Grossman, James R. *Land of Hope: Chicago, Black Southerners, and the Great Migration.* Chicago: University of Chicago Press, 1989.

Harris, Robert L., Jr. "Coming of Age: The Transformation of Afro-American Historiography." *Journal of Negro History* 57, no. 2 (1982): 107–121.

Harrison, Alferdteen, ed. *Black Exodus: The Great Migration from the American South.* Jackson: University Press of Mississippi, 1991.

Hine, Darlene Clark, ed. *The State of Afro-American History: Past, Present and Future.* Baton Rouge: Louisiana State University Press, 1986.

Lemann, Nicholas. *The Promised Land: The Great Black Migration and How It Changed America*. New York: Knopf, 1991.

Lewis, Earl. *In Their Own Interests: Race, Class, and Power in Twentieth-Century Norfolk, Virginia*. Berkeley: University of California Press, 1991.

Marks, Carole. *Farewell—We're Good and Gone: The Great Migration*. Bloomington: Indiana University Press, 1989.

Meier, August, and Elliot Rudwick. *Black History and the Historical Profession, 1915–1980*. Urbana: University of Illinois Press, 1986.

Nash, Gary. *Forging Freedom: The Formation of Philadelphia's Black Community, 1720–1840*. Cambridge, Mass.: Harvard University Press, 1988.

Painter, Nell Irvin. *Exodusters: Black Migration to Kansas after Reconstruction*. New York: Knopf, 1976. Reprint. Lawrence: University Press of Kansas, 1986.

Phillips, Kimberly. *Alabama North: African-American Migrants, Community, and Working-Class Activism in Cleveland, 1915–45*. University of Illinois Press, 1999.

Stack, Carole. *Call to Home: African-Americans Reclaim the Rural South*. New York: Basic Books, 1996.

Trotter, Joe W., Jr. "Afro-American Urban History: A Critique of the Literature." In *Black Milwaukee: The Making of an Industrial Proletariat, 1915–45*. Urbana: University of Illinois Press, 1985.

Trotter, Joe W., Jr., ed. *The Great Migration in Historical Perspective: New Dimensions of Race, Class, and Gender*. Bloomington: Indiana University Press, 1991.

Wilson, William J. *The Truly Disadvantaged: The Inner City, the Underclass, and Public Policy*. Chicago: University of Chicago Press, 1987.

JOE W. TROTTER, JR. (1996)
Updated bibliography

MILITARY EXPERIENCE, AFRICAN-AMERICAN

African-American military history is inextricably linked with the struggle of black people for social and political equality in the United States. Since the Civil War, African Americans have seen participation in the armed forces as a vehicle for the establishment of true democracy. America's legacy of racial discrimination has likewise shaped the nature of black military service and the opportunities afforded to African Americans to fight on the nation's behalf. Black soldiers have thus symbolized both the denial and promise of equal citizenship in the United States.

In 1866, the U.S. Congress reduced the size of the regular army and reorganized the approximately 12,500 African-American soldiers of the former Union army into the 9th and 10th Cavalry and 38th, 39th, 40th, and 41st Infantry regiments. The four infantry regiments were later combined to form the 24th and 25th Infantries. Throughout the late 1870s and the 1880s, black soldiers of the regular army were stationed in the American West and served in the Dakota, Platte, and Missouri military departments. Labeled "buffalo soldiers" by the Plains Indians, black soldiers fought in the so-called Indian Wars to make the frontier secure for continued settlement.

The Spanish-American War coincided with the erosion of African-American citizenship rights. The explosion of the battleship USS *Maine* in Havana Harbor on February 15, 1898, with twenty-six African Americans among the casualties, created an opportunity for African Americans to determine if patriotic service would transform white racial attitudes and loosen the grip of systemic discrimination and violence. While questioning the imperialist aims of the United States, African Americans identified racially with the Cubans, who were struggling for independence from Spain, and supported the use of black soldiers in the war. African Americans responded to the call for volunteers by President McKinley by forming National Guard militias in Illinois, Ohio, Massachusetts, Kansas, Indiana, North Carolina, and Virginia, although the short duration of the war prevented their incorporation into the regular army. The War Department ordered the 28,000 black soldiers to Florida for embarkation, where they endured virulent racial abuse from southern whites. The black army regiments, in only three days of fighting at El Caney, Las Guásimas, and San Juan Hill, performed extremely well. On June 23, the 10th Cavalry rescued Theodore Roosevelt's famed "Rough Riders" 1st Volunteer Cavalry Regiment from severe casualties at Las Guásimas, the first battle of the war. Black soldiers later fought in the Philippines to quell the anti-American insurgency led by Emilio Aguinaldo (1869–1964). The guerilla warfare here was much more vicious than the fighting in Cuba had been, as was American racism. The United States racialized Filipinos in their efforts to undermine the insurgency and in the process tested the loyalties of black soldiers.

Following the Spanish-American War the black army regiments were transferred to duty in Texas along the United States–Mexico border. Racial tensions with white Texans ran high, culminating in an incident at Brownsville, Texas. After shots rang out on the night of August 13, 1906, local whites accused black soldiers of the 25th Infantry's 1st Battalion of killing one man and wounding several others. Although they steadfastly denied involvement in the shooting, President Theodore Roosevelt gave dishonorable discharges to 167 soldiers without a public hearing. Brownsville further fueled the perception among whites, particularly in the South, of black soldiers as a source of violent racial unrest.

African American soldiers of the Army's 368th infantry, c. 1910. *Prior to World War I, African Americans were joining the military in increasing numbers. By the start of that war, there were 23,000 black soldiers serving in the various branches of the military; by the end, more than 400,000 had served in the military in some capacity.* CORBIS

When the United States entered World War I in April 1917, Woodrow Wilson's pronouncement that the United States would fight to make the world "safe for democracy" spurred African-American hopes that the conflict would lead to a social and political transformation of American society on a par with Reconstruction following the Civil War. African Americans quickly appropriated Wilson's rhetoric of freedom and democracy to connect military service to demands for civil rights. However, instead of offering hope, the war exacerbated social relations and heightened racial tensions. The prospect of black soldiers stationed in the South aroused opposition and anxiety about their potential negative influence. White fears came to fruition in Houston, Texas, where the 3rd Battalion of the 24th Infantry was stationed at nearby Camp Logan. On the night of August 23, 1917, after enduring persistent racial abuse and fueled by rumors that Houston police had killed Corporal Charles Baltimore, over one hundred armed soldiers marched to the city and killed fifteen whites, including five policemen. Following a summary

court-martial, the military hastily executed thirteen soldiers without due process, while forty-one others received sentences of life imprisonment.

The events in Houston served as an omen of the broader treatment of black soldiers in the United States military, which replicated the racial customs of civilian life in the wartime army. The War Department, in response to pressure from the National Association for the Advancement of Colored People (NAACP), created a segregated training camp for black officer candidates at Des Moines, Iowa. Of the initial 1,250 candidates, 639 received officer commissions, although none higher than the rank of captain. The military made a concerted effort to undermine the opportunities for black officers to excel, most notably evidenced in the forced retirement of Colonel Charles Young (1864–1922), at the time the highest-ranking African American in uniform. Approximately 387,000 African Americans served in the United States army during the war. The majority of black soldiers toiled in stevedore and other service units both in France and the United States. Of the 200,000 black soldiers who served overseas, approximately 40,000 were combat soldiers in the 92nd and 93rd Divisions. Soldiers in the 92nd Division, which comprised drafted black men, waged a constant battle against the racism of white officers throughout the duration of their service, and military effectiveness suffered as a result. The 93rd Division, comprising mostly national guardsmen, served with the French military. They received more equitable treatment from the French and fought with distinction. The 369th Infantry from New York performed exceptionally well and earned international acclaim for its regimental band, led by Lieutenant James Reese Europe (1881–1919).

World War II yet again tested the loyalties and patriotism of African Americans. African Americans were less idealistic than previously, however, as the United States readied itself for war. The unfulfilled hopes of World War I caused black social leaders to accompany support for the war with explicit demands for African-American civil rights, as captured in the "Double V" slogan popularized by the *Pittsburgh Courier* and symbolizing the dual defeat of fascism and American racism. Asa Phillip Randolph (1889–1979), head of the Brotherhood of Sleeping Car Porters, organized the March on Washington movement, intended to pressure President Franklin Roosevelt to end discrimination in wartime contracting. On June 25, 1941, one week before the march, Roosevelt issued Executive Order 8802, banning racial discrimination in defense industries, and created the Fair Employment Practices Commission. The order was largely symbolic, however, as little enforcement occurred.

Roughly one million African Americans served in the various branches of the armed forces during World War II, nearly half engaged in overseas duty. Many facets of the military did not change from World War I. African Americans represented only five of the military's five thousand officers at the beginning of the war. Benjamin O. Davis Sr. (1877–1970) was the only black general. Although the Selective Service Act of 1940 forbade racial discrimination, local draft boards initially turned away African-American volunteers and later routinely denied exemption claims when manpower was needed. African Americans continued to serve in segregated units, as military officials continued to question the fighting capabilities of black soldiers. The War Department reactivated the all-black 92nd and 93rd Divisions established during the First World War and combined the 9th and 10th Cavalry to form the 2nd Cavalry Division. The 93rd Division served in the Pacific theater, along with the 24th and 25th Infantries, but saw little combat. The 2nd Cavalry Division served in North

A 1943 poster for war bonds, featuring one of the Tuskegee Airmen. *The success of the Tuskegee Airmen of the 99th Pursuit Squadron dispelled the myth that African Americans could not become effective aviators.* NATIONAL ARCHIVES AND RECORDS ADMINISTRATION

Africa. The 92nd Division served in the Italian campaign, but, after performing poorly in their first combat action, racist military officials derided the division for the remainder of the war. On the home front, black soldiers were subjected to dangerous work conditions. In July 1944, 258 black sailors stationed at Port Chicago refused to work following two explosions. Forty-four men who refused to return to work were court-martialed and received sentences of eight to fifteen years hard labor and dishonorable discharges.

Military necessity ushered in new opportunities for African Americans during the war. These opportunities tested traditional institutional prejudices. Officer training camps allowed African-Americans to enlist and by the end of the war over seven thousand black men received commissions. African Americans distinguished themselves in various combat units, most notably the 761st Tank Battalion. The War Department authorized the creation of the 99th Pursuit Squadron of the United States Air Force, stationed at Tuskegee, Alabama. The "Tuskegee Airmen" of the 99th, which later became part of the 332nd Fighter Group, dispelled the myth that African Americans could not become effective aviators. On April 7, 1942 the U.S. Navy announced that African Americans could enlist in positions other than mess attendants. Although the navy's legacy of racial discrimination deterred enlistment, by the end of the war 150,000 African Americans served. One ship, the *Mason*, had a majority black crew. The war also created increased opportunities for African-American women, who served in the Women's Army Corps (WACs) and as WAVES (Women Appointed for Volunteer Emergency Service) in the Navy.

Despite these gains, southern whites greeted returning black soldiers with violence reminiscent of the First World War. The federal government, however, took decisive action to institutionalize the racial progress made within the military during the war. On July 26, 1948, President Truman issued Executive Order 9981, which immediately outlawed racial segregation in the United States armed forces. The executive order was seen as a turning point in the fight for African-American racial equality and equal citizenship.

Against the backdrop of Cold War politics, Korea represented the first test of the United States military's commitment to racial desegregation. In 1950, American military forces were hastily assembled to stop the North Korean advance into South Korea, and, as a result, integration was far from complete. The 24th Infantry, stationed in Japan prior to deployment to Korea, remained completely segregated and suffered from a lack of preparation and poor leadership. In addition, resistance by General Douglas MacArthur and other white officers slowed the pace of integration. Nevertheless, several regiments began to integrate their ranks based on manpower necessity and reported improved military effectiveness. MacArthur's predecessor, General Matthew Ridgeway, actively enforced Truman's executive order, resulting in 90 percent of the black soldiers in Korea serving in integrated units by the time of the cease-fire of July 27, 1953. By the end of the war, 220,000 black soldiers served in the army, 13 percent of total American forces.

The modern civil rights movement spurred the Eisenhower and Kennedy administrations' commitment to enforcing integration of the armed forces. At the beginning of American involvement in Vietnam, the army touted itself as the most racially democratic institution in the United States. Military service in Vietnam initially went hand in hand with the expansion of African-American civil rights, for the armed forces provided opportunities unavailable to African Americans in civilian life. Many black men volunteered for combat units, and blacks reenlisted at a higher rate than whites. However, as the war dragged on and black casualties mounted, African Americans became increasingly critical of the war and their participation in it. By 1968 the war had reshaped the tenor of the civil rights movement, as Black Power coincided with the antiwar movement to fuel increased pessimism regarding the high cost of American citizenship.

Approximately 275,000 African Americans served in Vietnam, and race remained a persistent feature of the military experience of black soldiers, just as it did in civilian life. The racial composition of the military reflected the social and economic disparities African Americans faced in civilian life. The draft targeted poor and working-class Americans—groups in which black people were heavily represented—while upper- and middle-class whites obtained deferments or served in National Guard units. Sixty-four percent of eligible African Americans were drafted in 1967, as opposed to 31 percent of whites. In 1966, faced with troops shortages, the War Department established Project 100,000, which enlisted men previously declared ineligible because of low intelligence scores. Project 100,000 indirectly targeted African Americans, and between October 1966 and June 1969, 40 percent of the 246,000 men inducted through the program were black. Higher numbers of African Americans on the front lines led to disproportionate casualty rates. Between 1965 and 1967, African Americans represented 20 percent of battlefield casualties, though pressure to remove black soldiers from the front lines resulted in their casualty rate dropping to 13 percent for the entire war. Despite racial inequities, African Americans served valiantly, receiving 20 of the 237 Congressional Medals of Honor awarded during the war.

In the years following Vietnam, the military transformed itself into an exclusively volunteer army in order to avoid the problem of low morale associated with conscription. During the late 1970s and 1980s, the armed forces continued to offer African Americans employment, educational opportunities, and an escape from the postindustrial ravages of inner-city life. Thus, by the time of the 1991 Gulf War, the face of the military had become increasingly black. African Americans made up nearly 25 percent of the army during Operation Desert Storm, and General Colin Powell, an African-American and chair of the Joint-Chiefs of Staff, was arguably the most recognizable face of the war. Concerns regarding the overrepresentation of African Americans in the armed forces have persisted into the twenty-first century. In January 2003, as the United States again prepared for war against Iraq, Congressman Charles Rangel of New York introduced legislation to reinstitute the draft in order to rectify racial and class inequities within the military. Thus, African-American military service remains tied to the dilemma of true racial equality.

See also Civil War, U.S.; Davis, Benjamin O., Jr.; Europe, James Reese; Randolph, Asa Philip

■ ■ *Bibliography*

Astor, Gerald. *The Right to Fight: A History of African Americans in the Military.* Novato, Calif: Presidio, 1998.

Barbeau, Arthur E., and Florette Henri. *The Unknown Soldiers: Black American Troops in World War I.* Philadelphia: Temple University Press, 1974. Reprinted as *The Unknown Soldiers: African-American Troops in World War I.* New York: Da Capo, 1996.

Bowers, William T., et al. *Black Soldier, White Army: The 24th Infantry Regiment in Korea.* Washington, D.C.: Center of Military History, U. S. Army, 1996.

Brandt, Nat. *Harlem at War: The Black Experience in WW II.* Syracuse, N.Y.: Syracuse University Press, 1996.

Buckley, Gail. *American Patriots: The Story of Blacks in the Military from the Revolution to Desert Storm.* New York: Random House, 2001.

Bussey, Charles M. *Firefight at Yechon: Courage and Racism in the Korean War.* Washington, D.C.: Brassey's, 1991. Reprint, Lincoln: University of Nebraska Press, 2002.

Christian, Garna L. *Black Soldiers in Jim Crow Texas, 1899–1917.* College Station: Texas A&M University Press, 1995.

Dobak, William A., and Thomas D. Phillips. *The Black Regulars, 1866–1898.* Norman: University of Oklahoma Press, 2001.

Donaldson, Gary. *The History of African-Americans in the Military: Double V.* Malabar, Fla.: Krieger, 1991.

Edgerton, Robert B. *Hidden Heroism: Black Soldiers in America's Wars.* Boulder, Colo.: Westview Press, 2001.

Earley, Charity Adams. *One Woman's Army: A Black Officer Remembers the WAC.* College Station: Texas A&M University Press, 1989.

Gatewood, Willard B., Jr. *"Smoked Yankees" and the Struggle for Empire: Letters from Negro Soldiers, 1898-1902.* Urbana: University of Illinois Press, 1971. Reprint, Fayetteville: University of Arkansas Press, 1987.

Goff, Stanley, and Sanders Robert. *Brothers: Black Soldiers in the Nam.* Novato, Calif.: Presidio Press, 1982.

Hargrove, Hondon B. *Buffalo Soldiers in Italy: Black Americans in World War II.* Jefferson, N.C.: McFarland, 1985.

Leiker, James N. *Racial Borders: Black Soldiers along the Rio Grande.* College Station: Texas A&M University Press, 2002.

Motley, Mary Penick, ed. *The Invisible Soldier: The Experience of the Black Soldier, World War II.* Detroit, Mich.: Wayne State University Press, 1975. Reprint, 1987.

Nalty, Bernard C. *Strength for the Fight: A History of Black Americans in the Military.* New York: Free Press, 1986.

Powell, Colin. *My American Journey.* New York: Random House, 1995.

Putney, Martha S. *When the Nation Was in Need: Blacks in the Women's Army Corps during World War II.* Metuchen, N.J.: Scarecrow, 1992.

Terry, Wallace. *Bloods: An Oral History of the Vietnam War by Black Veterans.* New York: Random House, 1984.

Westheider, James E. *Fighting on Two Fronts: African Americans and the Vietnam War.* New York: New York University Press, 1997.

Wynn, Neil A. *The Afro-American and the Second World War.* New York: Holmes and Meier, 1975.

CHAD WILLIAMS (2005)

MILLION MAN MARCH
⊢■■■⊣

In early 1995 Minister Louis Farrakhan of the Nation of Islam proposed a Million Man March on Washington, D.C., for that fall. The organizers described the march as an opportunity for black men to take responsibility for their lives and communities, and to demonstrate repentance for their mistreatment of black women. In addition, the march was designed to unite blacks and point up the lack of national action against racial inequality.

Even as march organizers, most notably ousted National Association for the Advancement of Colored People (NAACP) head Rev. Benjamin F. Chavis Muhammad, began an extensive publicity campaign, many whites and African Americans spoke out against the march. The feminist scholar Angela Davis and the black leader Amiri Baraka led the criticism of the exclusion of black women, and journalist Carl Rowan and scholar Roger Wilkins denounced the whole idea as racially discriminatory. Many blacks who supported the idealistic goals of the march refused to participate because of its association with Farrakhan and his nationalist, anti-Semitic message, although many blacks who disagreed with Farrakhan's views nonetheless participated in the gathering.

On October 16, 1995, the march gathered at the Lincoln Memorial, site of the 1963 March on Washington. Organizers claimed a million blacks participated, although the Park Service counted 400,000. Numerous speakers, including Dorothy Height and the Rev. Jesse Jackson, addressed the crowd. Farrakhan delivered the climactic address, reminding the marchers, "We are in progress toward a more perfect union." The march stimulated black voter registration and political activism, but its long-term impact is unclear.

See also Baraka, Amiri (Jones, LeRoi); Chavis, Benjamin Franklin, Jr.; Davis, Angela; Farrakhan, Louis; Height,

The Million Man March, October 16, 1995. *Louis Farrakhan, leader of the Nation of Islam, conceived this "day of atonement and reconciliation" for African-American men.* © JAMES LEYNSE/CORBIS

Dorothy; Jackson, Jesse; Nation of Islam; Rowan, Carl T.

■ ■ *Bibliography*

Madhubuti, Haki R., and Maulana Karenga. *Million Man March/Day of Absence: A Commemorative Anthology.* Chicago: Third World, 1996.

GREG ROBINSON (1996)
Updated bibliography

MINGUS, CHARLES

APRIL 22, 1922
JANUARY 5, 1979

Born in Nogales, Arizona, jazz musicians Charles Mingus straddled the bebop and free jazz eras. Although he became a virtuoso bassist early in his career, his main contri-
bution to jazz was as a composer and bandleader. For over thirty years Mingus created a body of compositions matched in quality and variety only by Duke Ellington and Thelonious Monk, and ranging from somber but gritty tributes to Lester Young, Charlie Parker, and Eric Dolphy to roaring evocations of African-American gospel prayer meetings. Taking a cue from Ellington, Mingus generally wrote music for particular individuals in his superb ensembles, and such compositions were developed or "workshopped" through in-concert rehearsals rather than from fixed and polished scores prior to performance and recording. Mingus's mercurial personality thrived in these improvisational settings, but this process often made for chaos and disaster as well. He was notorious for berating audiences and musicians from the bandstand, even firing and rehiring band members during the course of performances. However, the workshops also achieved a spontaneity and musical passion unmatched in the history of jazz, as Mingus conducted and shouted instructions and comments from the piano or bass, at times in a wheelchair at the end of his life, even improvising speeches on civil rights.

Charles Mingus Jr. grew up in the Watts section of Los Angeles, and in his youth studied trombone and cello before switching at age sixteen to the bass. He studied with Britt Woodman, Red Callender, Lloyd Reese, and Herman Rheinschagen, and began performing professionally while still a teenager. He played in the rhythm sections of the bands of Lee Young (1940), Louis Armstrong (1941–1943), Barney Bigard (1942), and Lionel Hampton (1947–1948). He made his first recordings with Hampton in 1947, a session that included Mingus's first recorded composition, "Mingus Fingers." Mingus played in Red Norvo's trio from 1950 to 1951, quitting in anger after Mingus, who was not a member of the local musicians' union, was replaced by a white bassist for a television performance. Mingus settled in New York in 1951 and played stints with Duke Ellington, Billy Taylor, Stan Getz, and Art Tatum. His most important work in his early period was a single concert he organized and recorded for his own record label, Debut Records, at Toronto's Massey Hall in May 1953, featuring pianist Bud Powell, drummer Max Roach, and the reunited team of Charlie Parker and Dizzy Gillespie—the definitive bebop quintet.

Mingus formed his own music workshop in 1955 in order to develop compositions for a core of performers, and it is from this point that his mature style dates. He had played in the cooperative Jazz Composers' Workshop from 1953 to 1955, but it was as the tempestuous leader of his own group that he created his most famous works, which in concerts often became long, brooding performances, building to aggressive, even savage climaxes. His compositions used folk elements such as blues shouts, field hollers, call and response, and gospel-style improvised accompanying riffs. In this middle period, which lasted from 1955 to 1966, Mingus employed a number of notable musicians, including saxophonists Eric Dolphy, Rahsaan Roland Kirk, Jackie McLean, Booker Ervin, John Handy, Clifford Jordan, and Charles McPherson; drummer Dannie Richmond; pianists Mal Waldron and Jaki Byard; trombonist Jimmy Knepper; and trumpeter Ted Curson. He produced numerous albums that are considered classics, including *Tijuana Moods* (1957), *Mingus Ah-Um* (1959), the orchestral *Pre-Bird* (1960), *Mingus Oh Yeah* (1961), *Town Hall Concerts* (1962, 1964), and *Mingus Mingus Mingus* (1963), and notable compositions such as "Love Chant" (1955), "Foggy Day" (1955), "Percussion Discussion" (1955), "Pithecanthropus Erectus" (1956), "Reincarnation of a Lovebird" (1957), "Haitian Fight Song" (1957), and "The Black Saint and the Sinner Lady" (1963).

Politics also began to enter Mingus's music in the 1950s, and the two eventually became inseparable, with Mingus issuing explicit musical attacks against segregation and racism. "Meditations on Integration" (1964) was written in response to the segregation and mistreatment of black prisoners in the American South and recorded live at the Monterey Jazz Festival, while "Fables of Faubus" (1959) protested Orval Faubus, the segregationist governor of Arkansas. Mingus's activism also extended to attempts at having jazz musicians wrest control of their careers out of the hands of club owners and recording executives. He twice organized his own record companies, Debut Records in 1952 and Charles Mingus Records in 1963. In 1960 he helped lead a musical revolt against the staid Newport Jazz Festival, and along with Ornette Coleman, Coleman Hawkins, and Max Roach, he formed a group known as the Newport Rebels, which held a counterfestival.

In his peak years Mingus often performed in settings outside the workshops. In 1958 he led a quintet accompanying Langston Hughes reciting his poetry on *The Weary Blues of Langston Hughes*. Further, though he gained fame early as a bassist in the tradition of Jimmy Blanton and Oscar Pettiford, he also on occasion hired a bassist and performed at the piano, and he released *Mingus Plays Piano* in 1963. In 1962 he recorded *Money Jungle*, a trio album with Duke Ellington and Max Roach.

In 1966 Mingus stopped performing, largely as a result of the psychological problems that had always plagued him. In 1969 financial problems forced him out of retirement, and despite his deteriorating physical condition due to amyotrophic lateral sclerosis, a progressive degenerative disease of the nervous system (also known as Lou Gehrig's disease), he experienced a new burst of creativity in the 1970s. He published his picaresque, fictionalized autobiography, *Beneath the Underdog*, and was awarded a Guggenheim Fellowship in 1971. He thereafter worked regularly, recording *Mingus Moves* (1973), until 1977, when he fell ill after recording *Three or Four Shades of Blue*. He released his last albums, *Me, Myself an Eye* and *Something like a Bird*, in 1978. His last appearance on record was on *Mingus*, an album by the singer Joni Mitchell, in 1978. He died in Cuernavaca, Mexico.

See also Armstrong, Louis; Coleman, Ornette; Ellington, Duke; Gillespie, Dizzy; Jazz; Monk, Thelonious Sphere; Parker, Charlie

■ ■ *Bibliography*

Berendt, Joachim. "Mingus and the Shadow of Duke Ellington." *Jazz* 4, no. 4 (1965): 17–25.

Coleman, Janet, and Al Young. *Mingus/Mingus: Two Memoirs.* New York: Limelight, 1991.

Jost, Ekkehart. "Charles Mingus." In *Free Jazz*. Graz, Austria: Universal Edition, 1974, pp. 35–44.

Mingus, Charles. *Beneath the Underdog*. New York: Random House, 1971.

Priestley, Brian. *Mingus: A Critical Biography*. New York: Perseus Books, 1983.

EDDIE S. MEADOWS (1996)

MINSTRELS/
MINSTRELSY

▮▮▮

The minstrel show was the first uniquely American form of stage entertainment. Begun by white performers using black makeup and dialect to portray African Americans, the minstrel show was a popular sensation in the 1840s. It dominated American show business until the 1890s, and had profound and enduring impacts on show business, racial stereotypes, and African Americans in the performing arts.

White men in blackface had portrayed black people almost since the first contact of the races. But in the 1820s—when American show business was in its infancy, and audiences demanded stage shows about American, not European, characters and themes—some white performers began to specialize in blackfaced acts they called "Ethiopian Delineation." In 1828 in Louisville, Kentucky, one of these "Delineators," Thomas D. Rice, saw a crippled African-American stablehand named Jim Crow doing an unusual song and dance. Rice bought the man's clothes, learned the routine, and became a stage star with his "Jump Jim Crow" act. After that, blackfaced whites became more and more popular on America's stages.

In 1843 in New York City, four of these blackfaced entertainers, calling themselves the Virginia Minstrels, staged the first full evening of what they billed as "the oddities, peculiarities, eccentricities, and comicalities of that Sable Genus of Humanity." The Virginia Minstrels were a great hit. Within a year, the minstrel show became a separate entertainment form that audiences loved. Although it was centered in the big cities of the North, it was performed almost everywhere, from frontier camps to the White House. In fact, when Commodore Perry's fleet entered Japan in 1853-1854, the sailors put on a blackfaced minstrel show for the Japanese. Minstrel shows had three distinct parts. The first opened with a rousing group song and dance. Then the minstrels sat in a semicircle facing the audience. The dignified man in the middle, the interlocutor, used a commanding voice and precise, pompous language as the master of ceremonies. Flanking him, holding instruments such as banjos and fiddles, were entertainers who performed the musical numbers, most notably the songs of Stephen Foster. In his string of minstrel hits, including "Old Folks at Home," "Oh Susanna," "My Old Kentucky Home," and "Old Black Joe," Foster was a pioneer of a new eclectic American popular music, blending European parlor music he heard at home, frontier music he heard in Cincinnati theaters, and African-American music he heard in a servant's church. On the ends of the semicircle sat the most popular minstrels, the comedians, "Mr. Tambo" and "Mr. Bones," who were named after their instruments, the tambourine and the rhythm clacker bones (various performers assumed these two roles). Wearing flashy clothes and exaggerated black makeup, and speaking in heavy dialects laden with humorous malapropisms, the endmen traded puns, riddles, and jokes with the interlocutor (sitting between them). This new fast-paced verbal humor later matured in vaudeville and radio. The first part ended with an upbeat song and dance.

The second part, the olio, was essentially a variety show with performers coming on stage one at a time to do their specialties, everything from acrobatics to animal acts. Again, this was a forerunner of vaudeville—and of radio and television variety shows.

The third part, a one-act production with costumes, props, and a set, was at times a parody of a popular play or a current event. But in the early years, it was usually a happy plantation scene with dances, banjo playing, sentimentalism, slapstick, and songs such as "Dixie," a minstrel hit first introduced in New York City. These productions, mixing music, comedy, and dance, provided the seeds for the later development of the musical comedy.

Minstrelsy was not just precedent-setting entertainment. It was entertainment in blackface. It was about race and slavery, and it was born when those issues threatened to plunge America into civil war. During that period of rising tensions, northern whites, with little knowledge of African Americans, packed into theaters to watch white men in blackface act out images of slavery and black people that the white public wanted to see. From its inception, in every part of the show, minstrelsy used makeup, props, gestures, and descriptions to create grotesque physical caricatures of African Americans—including big mouths and lips, pop eyes, huge feet, woolly hair, and literally black skin. Minstrels also evolved sharp contrasts between African Americans in the North and in the South. In the show's first part, some of the olio, and the nonplantation farces, northern minstrel blacks were either lazy, ignorant good-for-nothings or flashy, preening dandies. Southern minstrel blacks, in first-part songs and plantation finales,

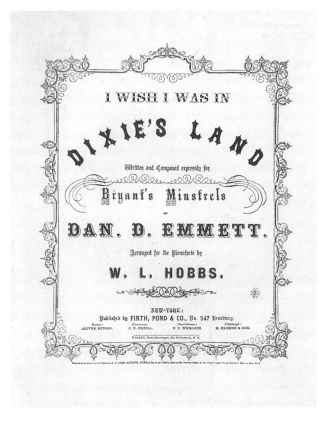

Sheet music for "I Wish I Was in Dixie's Land" (1859), by Daniel Decatur Emmett. The song, an immediate hit, premiered on Broadway in 1859 at a performance of Bryant's Minstrels, for whom Emmett played violin.

were happy, frolicking "darkies" or nostalgic "old uncles" and loving "mammies" devoted to their kind, doting masters and mistresses. In the 1850s, as political conflicts grew, minstrelsy often portrayed unhappy plantation runaways who longed to be back in the land of cotton. It even converted the powerful antislavery messages of *Uncle Tom's Cabin* into closing plantation farces of "Happy Uncle Tom."

Minstrelsy never pretended to be anything but escapist entertainment, but its racial caricatures and stereotypes allowed its huge northern white audiences to believe that African Americans were inferior people who did not belong in the North and were happy and secure only on southern plantations. So there was no need for a civil war over slavery or for acceptance of African Americans as equals. Even after the Civil War and the abolition of slavery, minstrelsy continued these stereotypes, as if to support the racial caste system that replaced slavery and kept African Americans "in their place" in the South.

After the Civil War, for the first time, a large number of African Americans themselves became minstrels. Realizing that the popularity of blackfaced whites gave them

a unique wedge into show business, early African-American minstrels emphasized their race. They billed themselves as "genuine," "bona fide" "colored" people who were untrained ex-slaves recreating their lives on the plantation. Except for the endmen, they rarely wore blackface. Northern white audiences were astonished by the variety of African Americans' skin colors and delighted by their shows. Although African-American minstrels did modify and diversify their material in subtle ways, the bulk of their shows reproduced and, in effect, added credibility to ingrained minstrel stereotypes. African-American minstrel troupes were so popular that they performed all over the United States, in Europe, and in the South Pacific, and they forced white minstrels to cut back their plantation material to avoid the new competition. One "Minstrel Wanted" ad in 1883 even warned, "Non-colored performers need not apply."

By the 1880s, as a result of minstrelsy, African Americans were established in all phases of show business as performers, composers, managers, and owners, though the most successful troupes were owned by whites. But the successes of African-American minstrels came at great expense. Personally, they faced discrimination daily. Professionally, they did not get the credit they deserved as performing artists because of their image as untrained, natural entertainers. Creatively, they had to stay within restrictive roles. Racially, they appeared to confirm negative stereotypes of African Americans. But, for decades, there were no other real choices for blacks in show business. For instance, Sam Lucas, a top minstrel composer and star by 1873, repeatedly tried to break free of minstrelsy. In 1875 he costarred in *Out of Bondage,* a serious musical drama about blacks' progress from slavery to the "attainment of education and refinement," and in 1878, he was the first of his race to star in a serious production of *Uncle Tom's Cabin,* a role long considered too difficult for an African American. But each time, he had to return to minstrelsy to make a living. Still, he and the other pioneers laid the foundation for future generations.

Although minstrelsy as an entertainment institution was originally created and shaped by white performers playing to white audiences, African-American culture was part of its appeal from the beginning. Some blackfaced stars, like Thomas D. Rice, admitted copying their acts directly from individual African Americans. More often, touring white minstrels bragged in general of learning new material and performance styles from black people, and there is considerable evidence in early minstrelsy that they did. Commentator Hans Nathan has identified African-derived syncopated rhythms in early banjo tunes that were the forerunners of ragtime and jazz. Robert C. Toll has

Poster for a minstrel show, c. 1900. The first uniquely American form of stage entertainment, minstrelsy dominated show business in the United States during the nineteenth century. CORBIS. REPRODUCED BY PERMISSION.

found characteristically African-American folklore and humor in the early shows. But minstrelsy's biggest debts to African-American culture were in dance. In fact, the only African-American star in early minstrelsy was the dancer William Henry "Juba" Lane. Before emigrating to England in 1848, he repeatedly outdanced whites with "the manner in which he beats time with his feet." Virtually the father of American tap dance, Lane was, according to dance historian Marian Hannah Winter, the "most influential single performer of nineteenth century American dance." Most African-American influence on minstrel dance was less direct but no less real, as Marshall Stearns and Jean Stearns have demonstrated, with everything from the "buck and wing" to the "soft shoe."

When a number of black people became minstrels, they brought a new infusion of African-American culture. For the first time, spirituals were part of minstrelsy. Black composers drew on traditional culture, as black dancers did with African-American steps and styles. Comedians,

such as Billy Kersands, used the double-edged wit and guile of black folk to get the African Americans seated in segregated sections to laugh with them at the same time that whites laughed at them.

Since these examples have to be gleaned from the few studies of sparse nineteenth-century sources, they are probably the tip of the iceberg. Still, they do indicate that minstrelsy was the first example of the enormous influence that African-American culture would have on the performing arts in America. It was also the first example of white Americans exploiting and profiting from the creativity of African Americans.

By the 1890s, as public interest shifted from plantations and ex-slaves to big cities and new European immigrants, minstrelsy's national popularity faded, though it survived in some areas for a long time. For white minstrels, the blackface that was once such an asset became a handicap, limiting their ability to compete with vaudeville — which could make race just one part of its shows — and with nonracial musicals. Ultimately, the blackfaced dialect act moved into vaudeville, musicals, movies, and radio. For African Americans, though minstrelsy remained a limited possibility, more promising opportunities opened up in musicals, popular music, and vaudeville. But the struggles against bias, restrictions, and discrimination had only begun. Long after minstrelsy was gone, its negative stereotypes and caricatures of African Americans remained deeply embedded in American show business and popular culture.

See also Jim Crow; Musical Theater; Walker, George; Williams, Bert

■ ■ *Bibliography*

Bean, Annemarie, James V. Hatch, and Brooks McNamara, eds. *Inside the Minstrel Mask: Readings in Nineteenth-Century Blackface Minstrelsy.* Hanover, N.H.: Wesleyan University Press, 1996.

Cockrell, Dale. *Demons of Disorder: Early Blackface Minstrels and Their World.* Cambridge, UK: Cambridge University Press, 1997.

Fletcher, Tom. *One Hundred Years of the Negro in Show Business.* New York, 1954. Reprint, New York: Da Capo Press, 1984.

Lhamon, W. T., Jr. *Jump Jim Crow: Lost Plays, Lyrics, and Street Prose of the First Atlantic Popular Culture.* Cambridge, Mass.: Harvard University Press, 2003.

Lott, Eric. *Love and Theft: Blackface Minstrelsy and the American Working Class.* New York: Oxford University Press, 1995.

Nathan, Hans. *Dan Emmett and the Rise of Early Negro Minstrelsy.* Norman: University of Oklahoma Press, 1962.

Simond, Ike. *Old Slack's Reminiscences and Pocket History of the Colored Profession from 1865 to 1891.* Edited by Robert C.

Toll and Francis Lee Utley. 1891. Reprint, Bowling Green, Ohio: Popular Press, 1974.

Stearns, Marshall, and Jean Stearns. *Jazz Dance: The Story of American Vernacular Dance.* New York: Macmillan, 1968. Updated edition, New York: Da Capo Press, 1994.

Toll, Robert C. "From Folktype to Stereotype: Images of Slaves in Antebellum Minstrelsy." *Journal of the Folklore Institute* 8 (June 1971): 38–47.

Toll, Robert C. *Blacking Up: The Minstrel Show in Nineteenth Century America.* New York: Oxford University Press, 1974.

Toll, Robert C. "Showbiz in Blackface: The Evolution of the Minstrel Show as a Theatrical Form." In *American Popular Entertainment: Papers and Proceedings of the Conference on the History of American Popular Entertainment,* edited by Myron Matlaw. Westport, Conn.: Greenwood Press, 1979.

Winter, Marian Hannah. "Juba and American Minstrelsy." *Dance Index* 6 (February 1947): 2847.

Wittke, Carl. *Tambo and Bones: A* History of the American Minstrel Stage. Durham, N.C.: Duke University Press, 1930. Reprint, New York, Greenwood Press, 1968.

ROBERT C. TOLL (1996)

MISSIONARY MOVEMENTS

Missionary movements among African-American Christians in the United States can be characterized in a number of ways. First, the distinction should be made between domestic or home missions and overseas or foreign missions. Second, the missionary efforts of African Americans may be categorized based upon the activities of historically black denominations and agencies, or those of predominantly white groups, or some means of cooperation or joint endeavors between the two.

Third, mission movements are characterized by two dimensions, spiritual and temporal. The spiritual dimension refers to the efforts of Christians to convert others to the faith: preaching, religious instruction, and the construction of houses of worship. The temporal includes the educational, medical, and other humanitarian interests that cover the concerns of the body and not simply the soul. On a practical level it is often impossible to distinguish neatly between the domestic and the overseas, the various means of evangelizing, and the spiritual and the temporal. They are all often intimately related and interwoven, both organizationally and theologically.

The black missionary tradition derives from eighteenth-century evangelicalism. It was the evangelical type of Christianity that appealed to most blacks, whites, and Native Americans in the United States in that period. At the core of this religious approach was the conviction that God deals directly with the individual and that it was the sacred duty of every faithful Christian to share the faith with others. For black Christians and those whites committed to black and African evangelization, a scripture verse, Psalm 68:31, applied specifically to racial evangelization and uplift. According to the King James translation, princes were to come from Egypt, and Ethiopia was to extend hands to God. Egypt and Ethiopia together represented the totality of the African race, and this verse was understood to predict that the black race should and must be evangelized, as a result of which temporal progress would occur.

As the United States moved further from its Revolutionary era, the early antislavery ardor of many evangelical churches among Methodists, Baptists, Presbyterians, and others declined. This reduction of active religious opposition to slavery was also occasioned in part by the fact that white evangelicals in the South increasingly became slaveholders and slave traders. In addition, the 1780s and 1790s witnessed a greater willingness on the part of white Christians to apply even stricter discriminatory measures against their black counterparts within the churches.

On the one hand, these antiblack developments led to the rise of independent black congregations and denominations. On the other hand, the rise in proslavery and discriminatory attitudes led some whites and blacks to conclude that African-American Christians would fare better on the mother continent, where they could, more successfully than whites, effect spiritual and temporal progress among their African kinfolk.

When black Christians began to secede from white-controlled congregations and denominations in the latter part of the 1700s, they sought greater freedom in worship and church leadership. They wanted to influence in a more organized manner the lives of fellow blacks, whom they considered to have been overlooked by white-controlled Christian bodies. Richard Allen, one of the founders of the African Methodist Episcopal (AME) denomination, cited the need at an early point in his ministry for more evangelical attention to African Americans.

During the Second Great Awakening (1790–1825), many black congregations saw the same need. Thus, one of the first steps these new congregations and denominations took was the organization of outreach agencies for domestic and foreign missions. Through their church disciplines, religious publications, active involvement in antislavery activities, and establishment of schools and institutes, these black Christians often made it clear that they associated spiritual salvation with temporal betterment and physical freedom.

"Black Harry" Hosier. A powerful nineteenth century preacher, Hosier was also a frequent evangelistic companion of the famous white Methodist preacher and bishop Francis Asbury. DREW UNIVERSITY. REPRODUCED BY PERMISSION.

It would be a mistake, however, to view black evangelistic enterprises as confined solely to ministry within the race. It is true that Christianity in the United States spread more intraracially than interracially, but the latter was quite substantial and commonplace. Henry Evans, an eighteenth-century black Methodist minister, established the Methodist Episcopal Church in the Fayetteville, North Carolina, area with his influential preaching and pastoral efforts. At one point his church's black members were crowded out by whites, who, after initial opposition, responded in great numbers to his ministry. "Black Harry" Hosier, esteemed for his powerful preaching, was a frequent evangelistic companion of the famous white Methodist preacher and bishop Francis Asbury. He was highly regarded by Asbury, Freeborn Garrettson, Thomas Coke, and other eminent American Methodists.

The missionary labors of John Stewart indicate the profound impact that individual black Christians had upon white-controlled denominational and missionary endeavors. Stewart's missionary activities to the Wyandotte Indians in Ohio demonstrated not only the biracial but the multiracial character of American religious history. In addition, the racially mixed, but white-controlled, Methodist Episcopal General Conference of 1820, inspired by the work of Stewart, for the first time set up a separate denominational agency for missions. Blacks of other de-

nominations also participated in ministry on an interracial or multiracial basis, including the Baptists William Lemon, Josiah Bishop, and "Uncle Jack."

In addition to denominational and local outreach efforts, Christianity spread during the eighteenth and nineteenth centuries through "camp meeting" revivalistic gatherings, to which people came from miles around to hear the preaching and exhortations of ministers of various denominations and races and both genders. The autobiographical accounts of nineteenth-century black female ministers such as Zilpha Elaw and Jarena Lee demonstrate the interracial character of many of these camp meetings, the powerful roles often played by women and blacks in them, and the crucial significance of itinerant preaching by black men and women.

By and large, the independent black denominations and associations were confined to northern, free states and territories prior to the 1860s because of the antipathy of the southern slave system to independent black enterprises. With the advent of the Civil War, this situation changed profoundly. Many northern missionaries went south to do missionary work among the freedpeople. These missionaries included both clergy and laypeople, blacks and whites, males and females, and individuals and agencies representing practically all of the major denominations, black and white.

Included among these northern missionaries and church organizers were black Christians such as Rev. James Walker Hood of the African Methodist Episcopal Zion Church (AMEZ), who organized and built a host of churches in Virginia, North Carolina, and South Carolina during and following the Civil War. Charlotte L. Forten, a prominent laywoman in the African Methodist Episcopal Church, left a moving and insightful account of her life, *The Journal of Charlotte L. Forten*, which includes descriptions of her years of missionary service and teaching during the Civil War among freedpeople of the Port Royal, South Carolina, area.

It would be misleading, however, to leave the impression that all missionary work among freedpeople was conducted by northern Christians. Though pre–Civil War enslaved black Christians did not enjoy the advantages of independent organized groups, they nevertheless played the greatest roles in spreading the faith within their own communities. By and large, blacks who were enslaved received religious teaching from other blacks, clergy and laity—not from white plantation preachers, as is often assumed. Similarly, southern black Christians, such as Rev. Joseph C. Price, who founded Livingstone College in Salisbury, North Carolina, continued to play a major role in missionary outreach after the Civil War. These activities during the nineteenth and twentieth centuries established or helped establish a host of churches, schools and colleges, hospitals and medical clinics, banks and insurance companies, farm cooperatives, newspapers, and social agencies dedicated to the uplift of the disadvantaged.

In foreign missions the greatest expenditures of time, resources, and personnel of the black churches were in Canada, the Caribbean, and Africa. During the eighteenth and nineteenth centuries, a number of blacks fleeing southern slavery and northern discrimination migrated to Canada. They sometimes took their churches with them, and sometimes they were followed by churches of various denominations, especially Baptists and Methodists. There was also a conscious expansion of Christianity by black North Americans into the Caribbean and South America during the nineteenth century, especially prior to the Civil War. Sometimes this extension was carried on by black denominations and associations. At other times, black missionaries representing predominantly white denominations, such as the Episcopalian James Theodore Holly, ventured to countries such as Haiti to establish Protestantism there.

The loyalties of some black Christians and/or their slaveholders to the British during the Revolutionary War had forced some of them to retire or be transported to either the British-controlled Caribbean or portions of Canada. George Liele, a Georgia Baptist, ventured to Jamaica and there established the first Baptist church on the island. David George, another Georgia Baptist, traveled to Nova Scotia, ministered there for a number of years, and then journeyed with a group of Afro-Canadians to the British colony for repatriated enslaved persons in West Africa, Sierra Leone. There he helped found the first Baptist church on the continent. Black Baptist denominational historians have traditionally accorded these persons the distinction of being the first two black American missionaries.

In many ways the African missions movement represented the most dramatic and sustained efforts of black Americans to evangelize other lands. All major denominations of black Christians—Baptists, Methodists, and Pentecostalists—participated in missionizing the continent, especially in its western and southern regions. The Presbyterian William Henry Sheppard, a missionary to the Congo in the late nineteenth and early twentieth centuries, however, represented two other types of black missionaries: those who ventured to other portions of Africa and those supported by predominantly white denominations. African missions among black Christians may be divided into three major periods: the colonization phase, from the latter part of the eighteenth century to the American Civil War; the independent organizational phase, from the Civil War to World War I; and the phase since World War I.

Prior to the Civil War a great deal of African missionary outreach by black Christians was carried out in conjunction with movements to establish free blacks on the continent of Africa; thus, most of the evangelization efforts were concentrated in Liberia or nearby regions. Shortly after the formation of the predominantly white General Missionary Convention of the Baptist Denomination of the United States for Foreign Missions (or Triennial Convention) in 1814, a white Baptist deacon in Richmond, Virginia, William Crane, along with two black ministers, Lott Carey and Collin Teague, established the Richmond African Baptist Missionary Society for the express purpose of sending the gospel to Africa. The efforts of the society coincided with the foreign-missions interest of the Triennial Convention and the rising colonization movement to repatriate free blacks to Africa. This was symbolized and represented by the founding of the American Colonization Society in 1816–1817. William W. Colley, Teague, and their families relocated in Liberia as a result of their own fund-raising activities and in cooperation with the Triennial Convention and the American Colonization Society. A similar scenario occurred with Rev. Daniel Coker of the AME Church. He ventured to Sierra Leone in 1820 as a colonist supported by the American Colonization Society. But while there he also received support from the AME Church in the United States and established mission stations on behalf of the denomination.

With the conclusion of the Civil War, black Christians were free (and usually encouraged by many of their white counterparts) to pursue independent ecclesiastical arrangements. Interwoven with this ecclesiastical independence was the continuing conviction that American black Christians had a providential role to lift Africa from religious "paganism" and cultural "barbarism." Thus, state, regional, and national black Baptist groups and the two major black Methodist groups began to establish institutional apparatuses that would be devoted wholly to, or focused heavily upon, African missions (e.g., Virginia Baptist State Convention, Baptist Foreign Mission Convention, Women's Home and Foreign Mission Society of the AMEZ Church). This second phase of African missions was sometimes related to, but usually not as directly dependent upon, the principle of black migration or colonization as the first period. William W. Colley, John and Lucy Coles, Emma B. DeLaney, and most other missionaries did not venture to Africa with the intention of renouncing American citizenship or encouraging others to do so. They were more strictly missionaries, not colonists.

In addition, African missions geographically broadened during this period. The first phase tended to focus upon West Africa, especially Liberia. The independent organizational phase continued that focus but also expanded to central and southern Africa. Though Henry McNeal Turner, an AME bishop, at the turn of the century renounced his American citizenship and called for some form of limited emigration to Africa, his focus on missionary work in southern Africa transcended his politics and helped to commit the denomination to intense involvement in that region. Emma B. DeLaney, a Florida Baptist, was a missionary in both southern and western Africa during the first two decades of the twentieth century. Her missionary activities indicate the presence of women on the mission fields, sometimes as partners with their husbands and sometimes, as with Delaney, as unmarried missionaries and evangelistic pioneers.

The Azusa Street Revival (1906–1909), which originated among black worshipers in Los Angeles, California, was the major impetus for the rise of most modern denominations of Pentecostalism. Blacks, whites, and others came from throughout the United States, around the world, and all walks of life to receive Pentecostal blessings in a crusade led by the black preacher William J. Seymour. Both in the domestic sphere and overseas, the Pentecostal movement gave rise to a host of missionary endeavors. The revival, therefore, played a great role in extending Christianity to Africa as well as other lands. It was the activities of this second period that most clearly established the foundation of African missions for black Christians.

The third phase, from the time of World War I, has been characterized by an expansion upon the earlier foundation, continued interaction between many black and continental African Christians, and a slow but steady recognition of greater participation of Africans in the denominational apparatuses of the American-based churches. The urgency for evangelism and sense of racial solidarity and commitment that characterized the former periods have significantly subsided from the African-American churches' missions programs, especially since World War II. To the extent that this is the case, it is partly related to the greater role continental Africans have played in both politics and religion, and increased opportunities for black American involvement in domestic matters.

See also African Methodist Episcopal Zion Church; Baptists; Carey, Lott; Christian Denominations, Independent; Liele, George; National Black Evangelical Association; Religion

■■ *Bibliography*

Coker, Daniel. *Journal of Daniel Coker*. Baltimore, Md., 1820.

Drake, St. Clair. *The Redemption of Africa and Black Religion.* Chicago: Third World Press, 1977.

Jacobs, Sylvia M., ed. *Black Americans and the Missionary Movement in Africa*. Westport, Conn.: Greenwood Press, 1982.

Martin, Sandy D. *Black Baptists and African Missions: The Origins of a Movement, 1880–1915*. Macon, Ga.: Mercer, 1989.

Sernett, Milton C. *Black Religion and American Evangelicalism: White Protestants, Plantation Missions, and the Flowering of Negro Christianity, 1787–1865*. Metuchen, N.J.: Scarecrow Press, 1975.

Walker, James W. St. G. *The Black Loyalists: The Search for a Promised Land in Nova Scotia and Sierra Leone, 1783–1870*. New York: Africana, 1976.

Williams, Walter L. *Black Americans and the Evangelization of Africa, 1877–1900*. Madison: University of Wisconsin Press, 1982.

Wills, David W., and Richard Newman, eds. *Black Apostles at Home and Abroad: Afro-Americans and the Christian Mission from the Revolution to Reconstruction*. New York: Macmillan, 1982.

SANDY DWAYNE MARTIN (1996)

MISSISSIPPI FREEDOM DEMOCRATIC PARTY

■ ■ ■

The Mississippi Freedom Democratic Party (MFDP), a predominantly African-American party that existed from 1964 through the early 1970s, was one of America's most significant third political parties. The Student Nonviolent Coordinating Committee (SNCC) did not establish the MFDP to permanently replace the regular Mississippi Democratic Party. On the contrary, SNCC intended the MFDP to be an alternative that would allow black and white Mississippians to be in a party that shared the same views as the national organization.

The MFDP contested the right of the regular Mississippi Democratic Party to represent the state's black voting-age population at the 1964 and 1968 conventions of the Democratic National Committee (DNC). They did this because the state Democratic Party and state election officials had deprived most blacks of the opportunity to take part in state politics, and because the regular Mississippi Democratic Party opposed the civil rights positions of the national party. At the state Democratic Convention of July 1964, delegates passed a resolution calling for the immediate repeal of the recently passed Civil Rights Act of 1964. Furthermore, the party repudiated the Democratic presidential and vice presidential candidates, Lyndon Johnson and Hubert Humphrey, urging white citizens of the state to vote for the Republican candidate, Barry Goldwater. The MFDP supported the national Democratic Party's positions and nominee.

Aaron Henry, leader of the Mississippi Freedom Democratic Party (MFDP), 1964. Henry argues for seats at the Democratic National Convention for his delegation from Mississippi at a meeting of the credentials committee in Atlantic City, New Jersey. The MFDP contested the right of the state's regular Democratic Party to represent its black voting-age population at the 1964 and 1968 conventions, because the state's regular Democratic party opposed the civil rights positions of the national party. AP/WIDE WORLD PHOTOS. REPRODUCED BY PERMISSION.

Initially, black Mississippians organized the MFDP in part to take the place of the regular state party at the 1964 Democratic National Convention if the state party walked out over the issue of civil rights. But, in addition to being a party waiting in the wings, the MFDP registered black voters by the tens of thousands. Thus, it succeeded in empowering blacks in Mississippi politics for the first time since the end of the nineteenth century, despite white harassment. It emphasized political education to help black Mississippians learn about the political process, so as to make informed choices once they exercised their right of franchise in earnest.

The idea for the formation of the MFDP developed shortly after the end of SNCC's "Freedom Vote" campaign to protest the 1963 Mississippi gubernatorial election. Responding to the success of that campaign, Robert Moses of SNCC proposed that blacks participate in mock state elections to vote for "Freedom candidates." To create na-

tional attention, the Freedom Summer campaign used white northern college students to help SNCC conduct a mock protest vote by registering thousands of blacks to express their outrage with the wholesale disfranchisement of blacks in Mississippi. Realizing the futility of registering thousands of blacks without challenging the discriminatory practices of the state Democratic Party, in April 1964 SNCC founded the MFDP to run candidates in Mississippi and to contest the loyalty of the Mississippi Democrats to the national party. SNCC took these measures to expose the fact that few blacks could take part in precinct meetings of the regular state party. In the few cases where party officials permitted blacks access to meetings, they denied blacks the right to speak or vote. After experiencing similar treatment at county conventions and the state convention, MFDP members conducted their own precinct meetings and held their own state convention in June 1964 to select delegates to the DNC Convention in Atlantic City who would support the national ticket.

Members of the MFDP went to Atlantic City believing that their planned contest of the seats assigned to the state party had a reasonable chance of success. In reality, the MFDP leadership received an education on how politics at the national level operated. While a number of MFDP delegates sincerely believed that moral persuasion would lead the DNC to refuse the regular state party the state's allotment of seats, President Johnson had his own agenda. Johnson, running without opposition for the nomination for president, wanted a smooth convention. He feared a southern walkout if the DNC seated the MFDP. Johnson ordered the FBI to wiretap the MFDP office, as well as the hotel rooms of the Reverend Dr. Martin Luther King Jr. and Bayard Rustin. Johnson knew the positions of civil rights groups and key leaders throughout the convention. He also threatened the patronage of those who might have been inclined to support the MFDP. In addition, he coerced Walter Reuther, the head of the United Auto Workers union, to threaten to cut off financial support to SNCC and the MFDP in Mississippi if the challenge was not withdrawn.

This threat did not alter the determination of the protestors. Before a televised hearing of the Credentials Committee, the deeply affecting testimony of Fannie Lou Hamer led Johnson to stage a news conference in an effort to stop public opinion from mounting to the point that he had to give seats to the MFDP. Johnson forced Hubert Humphrey to try to convince the challengers not to go forward. This was a test of Humphrey's personal loyalty, and Johnson told him the vice presidential position on the ticket depended on how he handled the controversy. Humphrey offered the MFDP two seats representing the state of Mississippi, and the rest of the MFDP delegation were to be "honored guests" at the convention. The MFDP refused this offer, demanding at least the seats proportionate to the state's blacks of voting age. Unwilling to compromise, the challengers got no seats, but they did manage to obtain the credentials of sympathetic delegates from states that disapproved of the regular Mississippi delegation. Several members of the MFDP staged a sit-in demonstration on the convention floor, but security guards quickly removed the protestors.

MFDP members left the convention embittered by their experience. Feeling betrayed by the actions of northern liberals and civil rights moderates such as King and Rustin who had supported the compromise option proposed by Humphrey, the MFDP and SNCC became more militant after the convention. The DNC did unseat the regular Mississippi Democrats in 1968 (as promised at the 1964 convention) when the state party persisted in denying access to blacks. As a consequence of this action, the Mississippi Democratic Party ended the discriminatory practices and customs it had used to exclude blacks from meaningful participation in party affairs.

See also Freedom Summer; Hamer, Fannie Lou (Townsend, Fannie Lou); Moses, Robert Parris; Student Nonviolent Coordinating Committee (SNCC)

■ ■ *Bibliography*

Andrews, Kenneth T. *Freedom Is a Constant Struggle: The Mississippi Civil Rights Movement and Its Legacy.* Chicago: University of Chicago Press, 2004.

Erenrich, Susan. *Freedom is a Constant Struggle: An Anthology of the Mississippi Civil Rights Movement.* Montgomery, Ala.: Black Belt Press, 1999.

McLemore, Leslie B. *The Mississippi Freedom Democratic Party: A Case Study of Grass Roots Politics.* Ph.D. diss., University of Massachusetts, 1971.

Payne, Charles M. *I've Got the Light of Freedom: The Organizing Tradition and the Mississippi Freedom Struggle.* Berkeley: University of California Press, 1995.

MICHAEL A. COOKE (1996)
Updated bibliography

MITCHELL, ARTHUR

MARCH 27, 1934

■┃■┃■

Born in New York City, the oldest son of five children, dancer and choreographer Arthur Adams Mitchell Jr. began tap-dance lessons at the age of ten, sang in the Police Athletic League Glee Club, and attended the High School of Performing Arts, where he progressed quickly through a modern dance major. He began his professional career while still a senior in high school when he appeared in the 1952 Paris revival of Virgil Thomson and Gertrude Stein's opera *Four Saints in Three Acts.* Upon graduation from high school he was the first male to receive the school's prestigious Dance Award.

Mitchell was accepted as a scholarship student at the School of American Ballet in 1952. Determined to overcome a late start in classical ballet technique, he also studied with ballet master Karel Shook at the Studio of Dance Arts in New York. His vibrant, agile performance style made him highly sought by contemporary modern dance choreographers; and during this period he performed with the Donald McKayle Company, Sophie Maslow and the New Dance Group, Louis Johnson, and Anna Sokolow. In 1955, after only three years of concentrated ballet study,

Mitchell joined the John Butler Company for a brief European tour. He returned to New York to join the New York City Ballet (NYCB) in November 1955.

Within his first week with NYCB, Mitchell danced a featured role in George Balanchine's *Western Symphony*. He became the first African-American principal dancer permanently associated with that company but asked that there be no publicity about breaking a color barrier. In 1957 Balanchine created the centerpiece pas de deux of *Agon* for Mitchell and ballerina Diana Adams. Performances of this technically demanding, modernist work gained Mitchell international recognition as a principal dancer imbued with supple control and precise partnering skills. Mitchell stayed with the NYCB for fifteen years, dancing a range of leading roles that included spare, sensual works (Jerome Robbins's *Afternoon of a Faun*), neo-classic works (Balanchine's *Four Temperaments*), and pure classical ballets (Balanchine's *Allegro Brillante*). In 1962 Mitchell created the role of Puck in Balanchine's version of *A Midsummer Night's Dream,* winning critical and audience praise for his dramatic abilities and charismatic warmth.

Mitchell also performed in the Broadway productions of *House of Flowers* (1954), *Shinbone Alley* (1957), and Noel Coward's *Sweet Potato* (1968). He choreographed for Eartha Kitt at the Newport Jazz Festival in 1957 and appeared at the 1960 and 1961 Festival of Two Worlds in Spoleto, Italy. He danced as a guest artist with the Metropolitan Opera (1962), the Munich Ballet Festival (1963), the Stuttgart Opera Ballet (1963), and the National Ballet of Canada (1964). In 1967, at the invitation of the U.S. government, he helped organize the National Ballet Company of Brazil.

Well aware of his role as a trailblazer, Mitchell encouraged others to follow his example of excellence in classical ballet. He taught at the Katherine Dunham School, the Karel Shook Studio, and the Harlem School of the Arts, as well as the Jones-Hayward School in Washington, D.C. In 1968 Mitchell and Shook reacted to the assassination of Rev. Dr. Martin Luther King Jr., by forming the school that became the Dance Theatre of Harlem (DTH), although Mitchell "never actually started out to have a company. I wanted to start a school to get kids off the streets. But I couldn't tell the young people in the school to be the best they could when they had no place to go." DTH was cofounded in February 1969 by Mitchell and Shook to "prove that there is no difference, except color, between a black ballet dancer and a white ballet dancer."

Mitchell has received numerous honors and awards, including the 1975 Capezio Dance Award, the New York

Public Library "Lion of the Performing Arts" Award for outstanding contributions to the performing arts, the NAACP's Image Award of Fame, and numerous honorary doctorates, including ones from Harvard, Princeton, and Williams College. In 1993 he was honored by David Dinkins, mayor of New York City, with a Handel Medallion Award and by President Bill Clinton at the Kennedy Center Honors for lifetime contribution to American culture. In June 1994 he was awarded a MacArthur Fellowship. In 1998 Mitchell choreographed *South African Suite* in collaboration with two South African dancers. In 1999 he was inducted into the Hall of Fame at the National Museum of Dance in Saratoga Springs, New York.

See also Ballet; Dance Theater of Harlem; Dinkins, David; Kitt, Eartha Mae

■ ■ *Bibliography*

"Arthur Mitchell." In *Current Biography Yearbook*. New York: H. W. Wilson, 1966, pp. 278–280.

Goodman, Saul. "Brief Biographies: Arthur Mitchell." *Dance Magazine* (December 1957): 47.

Gruen, John. *People Who Dance: Twenty-two Dancers Tell Their Own Stories*. Princeton, N.J.: Princeton Book Company, 1988.

Latham, Jacqueline Quinn. "A Biographical Study of the Lives and Contributions of Two Selected Contemporary Black Male Dance Artists—Arthur Mitchell and Alvin Ailey—in the Idioms of Ballet and Modern Dance, Respectively." Ph.D. diss., Texas Woman's University, Denton, Texas, 1973.

Maynard, Olga. "Arthur Mitchell and the Dance Theater of Harlem." *Dance Magazine* (March 1970): 52–62.

THOMAS F. DEFRANTZ (1996)
Updated by author 2005

MITCHELL, ARTHUR WERGS

DECEMBER 22, 1883
MAY 9, 1968

■■■

The politician Arthur Wergs Mitchell was born in Chambers County, Alabama. He left home at age fourteen and walked to Tuskegee Institute, where he obtained work as an office assistant for Booker T. Washington (1856–1915). He eventually entered Tuskegee as a student.

Mitchell taught in rural schools in Georgia and Alabama, and he founded the Armstrong Agricultural School in West Butler, Alabama, where he served as president for ten years. Mitchell continued his education at Columbia University and Harvard University School of Law, but he never completed the requirements for a law degree. However, he was able to earn admission to the Washington, D.C., bar in 1927, and he subsequently began to purchase tracts of real estate in the nation's capital. In 1928 Mitchell moved to Chicago, opened a law practice, and became involved with local Republican Party politics.

Mitchell changed his political affiliation to the Democratic Party when, in the wake of the Great Depression, the Democrats adopted a more activist position toward aiding the unemployed than did the Republicans. In 1934 Mitchell ran for the Democratic nomination for Congress from the First District of Chicago. He lost the nomination contest to Harry Baker, but when Baker died before the general election, Mitchell was selected to run for the seat in his stead. Identifying his candidacy with the New Deal, Mitchell defeated the black Republican Oscar DePriest (1871–1951) in the 1934 general election and, in doing so, became the first black Democrat elected to the House of Representatives. Mitchell began the first of his four terms in the House of Representatives in January 1935.

As a congressman, Mitchell supported President Franklin Roosevelt's New Deal and sided with the president during such controversial administration battles as the 1937 "court-packing plan" debate. Mitchell, by inclination something of a temporizer, was perhaps ill suited for his role as the sole African-American congressman, and he was often criticized for being insufficiently stalwart in his commitment to civil rights. Mitchell introduced an antilynching bill in Congress in 1935 that was attacked by Walter White of the National Association for the Advancement of Colored People (NAACP) for being toothless. Mitchell garnered similar criticism when he was slow to condemn Italy's invasion of Ethiopia, and for his support for the U.S. Supreme Court nomination of Alabama senator Hugo L. Black, a former member of the Ku Klux Klan. (Despite the misgivings of many African-American leaders, Black was confirmed and proved to be a strong supporter of civil rights decisions during more than thirty years on the Court.)

Perhaps Mitchell's most significant civil rights battle occurred outside of the halls of Congress. In 1937, while riding on the Chicago and Rock Island Railroad in a first-class carriage, Mitchell was obliged to leave the first-class car when the train reached Arkansas. Mitchell filed suit against the railroad with the Interstate Commerce Commission, which dismissed the complaint. Mitchell then brought a civil suit against the railroad, which eventually reached the U.S. Supreme Court—with Mitchell himself

arguing his case before the high court. In 1941, the Supreme Court ruled in *Mitchell v. United States* that segregated coach laws for interstate travel were illegal. The decision, however, was largely ignored.

Mitchell left Congress after his fourth term and moved to Pittsburgh, Virginia. For the next twenty-five years, he lived as a farmer and real-estate investor. He occasionally served as an unofficial adviser to the War and Defense departments and became involved in local political campaigns. Mitchell was also active in the Southern Regional Council, a moderate interracial organization that was dedicated to reform of discriminatory racial legislation. Mitchell died in his Pittsburgh, Virginia, home on May 9, 1968.

See also DePriest, Oscar Stanton; Politics in the United States; Washington, Booker T.

■ ■ *Bibliography*

Christopher, Maurine. *Black Americans in Congress*. New York: T. Y. Crowell, 1976.

Clay, William L. *Just Permanent Interests: Black Americans in Congress, 1870-1992*. New York: Amistad Press, 1992.

Nordin. Dennis S. *The New Deal's Black Congressman: A Life of Arthur Wergs Mitchell*. Columbia: University of Missouri Press, 1997.

KAREN E. REARDON (1996)
DURAHN TAYLOR (1996)
Updated bibliography

MITCHELL, CLARENCE, JR.

MARCH 8, 1911
MARCH 18, 1984

The lawyer and lobbyist Clarence Maurice Mitchell Jr. was born in Baltimore, Maryland, the son of Clarence Maurice Mitchell Sr., a chef in a fancy Annapolis restaurant, and Elsie Davis Mitchell. He attended Lincoln University in Pennsylvania, where he received an A.B. degree in 1932. The following year he joined the *Baltimore Afro-American* as a reporter and columnist, covering the trials of the Scottsboro Boys and reporting on racial violence in Princess Anne County, Maryland. In 1934 he ran unsuccessfully for the Maryland House of Delegates on the Socialist Party ticket. In 1937 he spent a year doing graduate work at the Atlanta School of Social Work, briefly became Maryland

Clarence Mitchell. *The chief lobbyist for the NAACP and president of the Leadership Conference on Civil Rights, Mitchell played a key role in the passage of civil rights legislation from the 1950s through the 1970s.* AP/WIDE WORLD PHOTOS. REPRODUCED BY PERMISSION.

state director of the Negro National Youth Administration, and married activist Juanita Jackson. The couple had four children, two of whom were later elected to local office in Baltimore.

In 1938 Mitchell was named executive secretary of the National Urban League branch in Saint Paul, Minnesota, where he established his expertise in labor questions. In 1942 he became assistant director of Negro Manpower Service in the War Manpower Commission, and at the same time served on the Fair Employment Practices Committee (FEPC). The next year, he joined the FEPC full time and became associate director of its Division of Field Operation. He supervised antidiscrimination efforts until the committee was disbanded in 1946.

In 1946 Mitchell joined the National Association for the Advancement of Colored People (NAACP) as labor secretary in the organization's Washington bureau, where he cemented ties with organized labor and lobbied for civil

rights legislation. Mitchell organized the National Council for a Permanent FEPC and pushed for enforcement of executive orders banning discrimination. In 1949 he blocked the United Nations Food and Agricultural Organization from locating at the University of Maryland because of the university's discriminatory practices. The following year he became head of the Washington bureau of the NAACP.

In November 1949 Mitchell called a National Emergency Civil Rights Mobilization Conference in order to form a broad-based interracial pressure group for equality that would be built on the nucleus of the National Council for a Permanent FEPC. In January 1950 delegates from sixty organizations met and formed a steering committee, the Leadership Conference on Civil Rights. Mitchell was appointed legislative chairman and served in that role for the next twenty-eight years. As the chief civil rights lobbyist on Capitol Hill, Mitchell was such a ubiquitous figure in Congress that he was often known as the hundred-and-first senator. A courteous, gentle man, he formed alliances with both Democrats (notably Senator and later President Lyndon B. Johnson) and Republicans (such as Senator Everett Dirksen). In 1957 Mitchell marshaled support for a civil rights bill, the first since Reconstruction. He aided the passage of the Civil Rights Acts in 1960, 1964, and 1968, as well as the 1965 Voting Rights Act and its extension in 1975.

Mitchell was known for his devotion to legal processes. He once explained that "when you have a law, you have an instrument that will work for you permanently," whereas private agreements were more ephemeral. He was also willing to protest personally against discrimination. In 1956 he became nationally known when he was arrested in Florence, Alabama, for using a whites-only door to the railroad station, an incident that became a cause célèbre. In 1958 he entered the University of Maryland's evening law school, obtaining his law degree in 1962. In 1968 Mitchell opposed the efforts of civil rights supporters to procure an executive order banning housing discrimination and pushed President Lyndon Johnson to recommend congressional legislation. For his success in bringing about the Civil Rights Act of 1968, which provided legal protection against discrimination in rental housing, the NAACP awarded him the Spingarn Medal in 1969.

In 1975 Mitchell was named a member of the United States delegation at the United Nations by President Gerald Ford. After his retirement in 1978 Mitchell served as a consultant and operated a law practice. In 1980 President Jimmy Carter awarded him the Presidential Medal of Freedom. He died in Washington, D.C., in 1984. The following year the Baltimore city courthouse was named in his honor.

See also Baltimore Afro-American; National Association for the Advancement of Colored People (NAACP); National Urban League; Spingarn Medal; Voting Rights Act of 1965

■ ■ *Bibliography*

Watson, Denton L. *Lion in the Lobby: Clarence Mitchell, Jr.'s, Struggle for the Passage of Civil Rights Laws.* New York: Morrow, 1990.

Whalen, Charles, and Barbara Whalen. *The Longest Debate: A Legislative History of the 1964 Civil Rights Act.* Washington, D.C.: Seven Locks, 1985.

GREG ROBINSON (1996)

See also Politics in the United States

■ ■ *Bibliography*

Clay, William L. *Just Permanent Interests: Black Americans in Congress, 1870–1991.* New York: Amistad, 1992.

Gross, Delphine Ave. "Parren J. Mitchell." In *Notable Black American Men,* edited by Jessie Carney Smith. Detroit, Mich.: Gale, 1999.

"Parren J. Mitchell." In *Contemporary Black Biography,* Vol. 42. Detroit, Mich.: Gale, 2004.

ROBERT L. JOHNS (1996)
Update bibliography

MITCHELL, PARREN J.

APRIL 29, 1922

━ ■ ■ ━

Parren James Mitchell was born in Baltimore, Maryland, and became a member of Congress in 1970. From 1942 to 1946 he served as an army infantry officer and in 1950 he earned a bachelor's degree from Morgan State College. After suing the University of Maryland for admission to their school of graduate studies, he became the first black student to complete the program, earning a master's degree in sociology in 1952. After teaching for two years at Morgan State College, he worked for local government and community programs in such positions as probation officer, executive secretary to a commission overseeing enforcement of the new state law on public accommodations, and executive secretary of an antipoverty program. In 1968 he returned to teach at Morgan State.

Mitchell ran unsuccessfully in the Democratic primary for the Seventh Congressional District seat in 1968, but in 1970 he secured the nomination and won the election, becoming Maryland's first African-American congressman and the first elected since 1895 south of the Mason-Dixon line. He served in Congress until he retired in 1987.

In Congress, Mitchell was chair of the Small Business Committee and also held other committee assignments; he was whip-at-large and chair of the Congressional Black Caucus. He was much concerned about empowering minority businesses. In 1976, for example, he secured a 10 percent set-aside in federal grants to local governing bodies for minority contractors. He also won an increase in the 1978 Small Business Administration budget. His interest in supporting minority economic development led him to found the Minority Business Enterprise Legal Defense and Education Fund (MBELDEF) after he left Congress.

MODERN JAZZ QUARTET

━ ■ ■ ━

Comprising vibraharpist Milt Jackson, pianist-composer John Lewis, bassist Percy Heath, and drummer Connie Kay, the Modern Jazz Quartet (MJQ) epitomizes the style that came to be known as "cool jazz." Although grounded in the fiery bebop style of the late 1940s, its repertory is characterized by elegant ensemble precision, a restrained emotional atmosphere (aided by the relatively cool timbres of the vibraharp and piano), and a self-conscious attempt to bring compositional techniques derived from European art music into a working relationship with jazz improvisation.

Jackson and Lewis were originally members of Dizzy Gillespie's big band and occasionally performed as a quartet in the late 1940s with Kenny Clarke on drums and Ray Brown on bass. The Modern Jazz Quartet proper made its recording debut in 1952 for the Prestige label. Wearing tuxedos on stage, members of the MJQ brought jazz to audiences accustomed to European chamber music. Such early Lewis compositions as "Vendome" (1952) and "Concorde" (1955) attracted attention for their use of fugal textures, while later projects such as *The Comedy* (1962) made more ambitious use of a modern compositional idiom derived in part from contemporary European "classical" music and were associated with the Third Stream movement.

The music of the MJQ has nevertheless remained firmly rooted in African-American culture, through the soulful improvising of Jackson and a continuous exploration of the blues—for example, the album *Blues at Carnegie Hall,* 1966. In 1974 the group disbanded, only to reform for tours and recordings in 1981.

See also Gillespie, Dizzy; Jazz; Lewis, John

■ ■ *Bibliography*

Williams, Martin. "John Lewis and the Modern Jazz Quartet: Modern Conservative." In *The Jazz Tradition*, rev. ed. New York and Oxford: Oxford University Press, 1983, pp. 172–182.

SCOTT DEVEAUX (1996)

MONCADA, GUILLERMO

JUNE 25, 1840
APRIL 1895

Guillermo Moncada, also known as Guillermón, was a high-ranking black officer in the revolutionary forces during Cuba's three wars of independence against Spain (1868–1878, 1879–1880, 1895–1898), struggles in which the issues of slavery and racial equality figured prominently. He was born in the city of Santiago de Cuba to a free woman of color, and as a youth he trained as a carpenter. Oral tradition holds that even before the start of the struggle for independence, Moncada had made manifest his antipathy to colonial rule during the city's annual carnival festivities, as he belonged to a carnival group that celebrated the efforts of Maroons to free plantation slaves in the area.

Moncada joined the armed independence movement in November 1868, approximately one month after the start of the conflict. By January 1870 he held the rank of captain. When a majority of Cuban insurgents accepted the Treaty of Zanjón in 1878, Moncada was among a dissident group of rebels, led by the mulatto general Antonio Maceo (1845–1896), who repudiated the treaty, arguing that they would not surrender until the rebel demands for the abolition of slavery and the independence of the island were met. The colonial state, however, granted only moderate political reforms and enacted only a limited abolition, freeing only those slaves who had served in either the rebel or colonial army during the conflict.

During the second war of independence—the *Guerra Chiquita*, or Little War—Moncada came to hold one of the highest-ranking positions among the rebel forces active on the island. However, the previous ten years of war and Spain's concession of political reforms led many Cubans to reject this second call to arms. In addition, important white leaders of the first insurgency were still in exile as part of the settlement from the first war. But if white support seemed weaker than in the Ten Years' War, this new effort was immediately embraced by slaves, who had seen their companions who had fled to join the first insurgency freed, and by free people of color. The high proportion of black supporters led colonial officials and their Cuban allies to denounce the movement as a race war aimed at establishing a black republic. As one of the principle leaders of the military effort, Moncada became a target of racist rumor and denunciation. He was accused of violating white women and holding them in harems; and he was said to have proclaimed himself emperor. Moncada himself denied the rumors, countering that the war was a struggle "for liberty, our rights, and, in a word, for the independence of our beloved country." He was among the last rebel leaders to surrender in June 1880, when he headed a force of 370 followers, the vast majority of whom were people of color, including 168 runaway slaves.

In the long interregnum between the end of hostilities in 1880 and the start of the third full-fledged rebellion against Spain in 1895, Moncada spent some time in prison, where he contracted tuberculosis. When the war began in February 1895, he took the rank of major general as head of the army in southern Oriente. However, he died of tuberculosis while leading his troops in April 1895.

To this day, Moncada is considered a major military figure in the struggle for Cuban independence. In 1953, when Fidel Castro launched his offensive against Fulgencio Batista, he did so by attacking the Cuban army at the largest military installation outside Havana, the Moncada Barracks in Santiago de Cuba, named in honor of the black general.

See also Maceo, Antonio

■ ■ *Bibliography*

Diccionario enciclopédico de historia militar de Cuba, volume 1, *Biografías*. Havana: Ediciones Verde Olivo, 2001.

Ferrer, Ada. *Insurgent Cuba: Race, Nation, and Revolution, 1868–1898*. Chapel Hill: University of North Carolina Press, 1999.

Helg, Aline. *Our Rightful Share: The Afro-Cuban Struggle for Equality, 1886–1912*. Chapel Hill: University of North Carolina Press, 1995.

ADA FERRER (2005)

Thelonious Monk. Pictured here during a performance at the Newport Jazz Festival, wearing his trademark hat, Monk was one of the twentieth century's most accomplished jazz composers and improvisers. © TED WILLIAMS/CORBIS

MONK, THELONIOUS SPHERE

OCTOBER 10, 1917
FEBRUARY 17, 1982

▮▮▮

Jazz pianist and composer Thelonious Monk was born in Rocky Mount, North Carolina, but moved with his family to New York at age four and grew up in the San Juan Hill district of Manhattan. He began a career as a professional pianist in the mid-1930s, playing at house rent parties and touring for two years as the accompanist to a female evangelist. By 1940 he was a member of the house rhythm section at Minton's Playhouse, a nightclub in Harlem well known among musicians for its nightly jam sessions. Surviving live recordings from this period document a piano style firmly rooted in the stride-piano tradition, as well as a penchant for unusual reharmonizations of standard songs.

Monk had already written several of his best-known compositions by this period: "Epistrophy" and " 'Round Midnight" were performed and recorded by the Cootie Williams big band as early as 1944, while "Hackensack" (under the name "Rifftide") was recorded in Monk's professional recording debut with the Coleman Hawkins Quartet in the same year. With their astringent and highly original approach to harmony, these compositions attracted the attention of the most adventurous jazz musicians and placed Monk at the center of the emergent bebop movement during World War II.

Although well known within the inner circle of bebop musicians, Monk did not come to more general attention until later in the 1940s. Beginning in 1947 he made a series of recordings for the Blue Note label, documenting a wide range of his compositions. These recordings, which include "Criss Cross," "Ruby, My Dear," and "Straight, No Chaser," feature him as both improviser and composer.

While Monk was admired as a composer, his unusual approach to the piano keyboard, lacking the overt virtuosity of such bebop pianists as Bud Powell and bristling with dissonant combinations that could easily be misinterpreted as "wrong notes," led many to dismiss him initially as a pianist. An incident in 1951 in which he was accused of drug possession led to the loss of his cabaret card, precluding further performances in New York City until 1957. But he continued to record for the Prestige label, including the famous "Bags Groove" session with Miles Davis in 1954, and he began making a series of recordings for Riverside, including *Brilliant Corners* (1956).

An extended residency at the Five Spot, a New York nightclub, in the summer of 1957 with John Coltrane finally drew attention to Monk as one of the most important figures in modern jazz. From the late 1950s through the 1960s, Monk worked primarily with his quartet, featuring tenor saxophonist Charlie Rouse, touring both in this country and abroad and recording prolifically for Columbia. Increasingly, he turned to the solo piano, recording idiosyncratic performances not only of his own compositions but also of such decades-old popular songs as "Just a Gigolo." The feature-length film *Straight, No Chaser* (1988; directed by Charlotte Zwerin) documents Monk's music and life in the late 1960s. After 1971 he virtually retired from public life. But his reputation continued to grow as a younger generation of musicians discovered his compositions and responded to the challenge of improvising within their distinctive melodic and harmonic framework.

See also Coltrane, John; Jazz

■■ *Bibliography*

Blake, Ran. "Round About Monk: The Music." *Wire* 10 (1984): 23–33.

Van Der Bliek, Rob, ed. *The Thelonious Monk Reader.* New York: Oxford University Press, 2001.

Williams, Martin. "Thelonious Monk: Modern Jazz in Search of Maturity." In *The Jazz Tradition,* rev. ed. New York: Oxford University Press, 1983, pp. 154–171.

SCOTT DEVEAUX (1996)
Updated bibliography

MONTEJO, ESTEBAN

DECEMBER 26, 1860
FEBRUARY 10, 1973

■■■

Esteban Montejo was born into slavery on a plantation in the Las Villas region of Cuba (now the province of Sancti Spíritus). Montejo quickly realized the limitations of his status and opted for the perilous existence of a *cimarrón,* or runaway slave. Nearly a century later, in 1963, at the age of 103, Montejo narrated his life story to Cuban anthropologist Miguel Barnet. Barnet published the interview in 1966 as *Biografía de un cimarrón (Biography of a Runaway Slave).* Ever since, Montejo's account has served as one of the few narratives of nineteenth-century Cuba told from the perspective of a former slave. Montejo describes a salient moment in Cuban history, the transition from slavery to wage labor. His story also illustrates the complexities and nuances of a young Afro-Cuban coming of age during Cuba's wars for independence. At the start of the first revolutionary war, in 1868, Montejo was eight. Consequently, the thirty years of fighting, which finally ended with independence from Spain in 1898, shaped and influenced how Montejo envisioned both the Cuban nation and himself.

Slavery separated Montejo from his biological parents at an early age, and he was left to grow up without any immediate family on the Flor de Sagua plantation. His first job was as a mule driver; he began working in the cooling room of a sugar mill when he was about ten. Within a couple of years, he attempted to escape but was captured and forced to wear shackles on his feet as punishment. Montejo's desire for freedom outgrew his fears of being caught, however, and he ran away again a few years later. He succeeded in remaining free, albeit in hiding, until Spain abolished slavery in 1886. Emancipation allowed Montejo to renounce his life as a *cimarrón,* yet he quickly learned that little had changed. As a cane cutter on various sugar plantations after emancipation, Montejo experienced the limited options available to newly freed people of African descent. Trained for little more than harvesting cane, many former slaves continued to live and labor under the same harsh conditions as they had before abolition.

Montejo served in the revolutionary forces during the Cuban wars for independence. He enlisted with a regiment in the eastern region of the island in 1895, at the age of thirty-five. He fought under the leadership of two prominent Afro-Cuban generals, Antonio Maceo and Quintín Banderas, in the battle of Mal Tiempo, and noted the large number of blacks involved in the rebellion. For Montejo, Afro-Cuban participation in the war demonstrated a sincere investment in the nation and justified Afro-Cubans' demands for equal rights. However, when Montejo arrived in Havana shortly after the fighting ended, he discovered that some white Cubans wanted to deny the role blacks had played on the battlefield in order to limit Afro-Cuban influence in the new government. Disappointed with the outcome of the war and with only one peso in his pocket, Montejo returned to Las Villas. For the remainder of his life, he supported himself by working as a wage laborer at various odd jobs, including positions at a sugar mill, as an auctioneer, and as a night watchman. When Barnet interviewed Montejo in 1963, he lived in a nursing home, where he died in 1973 at the age of 113.

See also Afrocubanismo; Maceo, Antonio

■■ *Bibliography*

Barnet, Miguel. *Biography of a Runaway Slave.* Translated by W. Nick Hill. Willimantic, Conn: Curbstone, 1994.

DEVYN M. SPENCE (2005)

MONTGOMERY, ALA., BUS BOYCOTT

■■■

The Montgomery Bus Boycott began on December 5, 1955, as an effort by black residents to protest the trial that day in the Montgomery Recorder's Court of Rosa McCauley Parks. She had been arrested on December 1 for violating the city's ordinance requiring racial segregation of seating on buses. The boycott had initially been intended to last only for the single day of the trial, but local black support of the strike proved so great that, at a meeting that afternoon, black community leaders decided to continue the boycott until city and bus company authorities met black demands for (1) the adoption by the bus company

Rosa Parks with Rev. E. D. Nixon (to her left), March 1956.
© BETTMANN/CORBIS

in Montgomery of the pattern of seating segregation used by the same company in Mobile; (2) the hiring of black bus drivers on predominantly black routes; and (3) greater courtesy by drivers toward passengers. The leaders formed the Montgomery Improvement Association (MIA) to run the extended boycott. At a mass meeting that evening, several thousand blacks ratified these decisions.

The Mobile plan sought by the boycott differed from the Montgomery pattern in that passengers, once seated, could not be unseated by drivers. In Mobile, blacks seated from the back and whites from the front, but after the bus was full, the racial division could be adjusted only when riders disembarked. On Montgomery's buses, the front ten seats were irrevocably reserved for whites, whether or not there were any whites aboard, and the rear ten seats were in theory similarly reserved for blacks. The racial designation of the middle sixteen seats, however, was adjusted by the drivers to accord with the changing racial composition of the ridership as the bus proceeded along its route. In Rosa Parks's case, when she had taken her seat, it had been in the black section of the bus. Two blocks farther on, all the white seats and the white standing room were taken, but some standing room remained in the rear. The bus driver, J. Fred Blake, then ordered the row of seats in which Parks was sitting cleared to make room for boarding whites. Three blacks complied, but Mrs. Parks refused and was arrested. She was fined fourteen dollars.

Black Montgomerians had long been dissatisfied with the form of bus segregation used in their city. It had originally been adopted for streetcars in August 1900, and had provoked a boycott that had lasted for almost two years. In October 1952 a delegation from the black Women's Po-

litical Council had urged the city commission to permit the use of the Mobile seating plan. In a special election in the fall of 1953, a racial liberal with strong black support, Dave Birmingham, was elected to the three-member city commission. Following his inauguration, blacks again pressed the seating proposal at meetings in December 1953 and March 1954, though to no avail. In May 1954, the president of the Women's Political Council, Jo Ann G. Robinson, a professor of English at Alabama State College for Negroes, wrote to the mayor to warn that blacks might launch a boycott if white authorities continued to be adamant. During the municipal election in the spring of 1955, black leaders held a candidates' forum at which they posed questions about issues of interest to the black community. At the head of the list was the adoption of the Mobile seating pattern.

On March 2, only weeks before the election, a black teenager, Claudette Colvin, was arrested for violation of the bus segregation ordinance. Following this incident, representatives of the city and the bus company promised black negotiators that a seating policy more favorable to African Americans would be adopted. However, Dave Birmingham, the racially liberal city commissioner elected in 1953, had integrated the city police force in 1954. As a result of hostility to this action and other similar ones, he was defeated for reelection in 1955 by an outspoken segregationist, Clyde Sellers. The other commissioners at once became less accommodating. By the time that Rosa Parks was arrested in December, the discussions had come to a standstill. Mrs. Parks, the secretary of the Montgomery branch of the National Association for the Advancement of Colored People (NAACP), shared with other black leaders the frustration that grew out of the negotiations with municipal authorities. This frustration produced her refusal to vacate her seat.

From the city jail, Parks telephoned Edgar D. Nixon, a Pullman porter who was a former president of the Montgomery NAACP branch. After Nixon had posted bail for Parks, he called other prominent blacks to propose the one-day boycott. The response was generally positive. At Jo Ann Robinson's suggestion, the Women's Political Council immediately began distributing leaflets urging the action. It was then endorsed by the city's black ministers and other leaders at a meeting at the Dexter Avenue Baptist Church. The result was almost universal black participation.

At the December 5 meeting, when it was decided to continue the boycott and to form the Montgomery Improvement Association (MIA), the Reverend Dr. Martin Luther King Jr. was chosen as the MIA's president, principally because, as a young man who had lived in the city only fifteen months, he was not as yet involved in the bitter rivalry for leadership of the black community between Nixon and Rufus A. Lewis, a funeral director. Nixon was elected the MIA's treasurer, and Lewis was appointed to organize car pools to transport blacks to their jobs without having to use buses. The Reverend Ralph D. Abernathy was named to head the committee designated to reopen negotiations with the city and the bus company.

Initially, the renewed negotiations seemed promising. Mayor William A. Gayle asked a committee of white community leaders to meet with the MIA's delegates. But by January 1956, these discussions had reached a stalemate. The MIA's attorney, Fred D. Gray, urged that the MIA abandon its request for the Mobile plan in favor of filing a federal court lawsuit seeking to declare unconstitutional all forms of seating segregation. The MIA's executive board resisted this proposal until January 30, when Martin Luther King's home was bombed. On the next day, the executive board voted to authorize the suit, which was filed as *Browder v. Gayle* on February 1.

Meanwhile, similar strains were at work in the white community. A group of moderate businessmen, the Men of Montgomery, was attempting to mediate between the MIA and the city commission. But segregationists were pressing authorities to seek the indictment of the boycott's leaders in state court for violating the Alabama Anti-Boycott Act of 1921, which made it a misdemeanor to conspire to hinder any person from carrying on a lawful business. On February 20, an MIA mass meeting rejected the compromise proposals of the Men of Montgomery, and on February 21, the county grand jury returned indictments of eighty-nine blacks, twenty-four of whom were ministers, under the Anti-Boycott Act.

Martin Luther King, the first to be brought to trial, was convicted by Judge Eugene Carter at the end of March and was fined $500. King appealed, and the remainder of the prosecutions were suspended while the appellate courts considered his case. On May 11, a three-judge federal court heard *Browder v. Gayle* and on June 5, in an opinion by Circuit Judge Richard Rives, it ruled two to one that any law requiring racially segregated seating on buses violated the equal protection clause of the Constitution's Fourteenth Amendment. The city appealed to the U.S. Supreme Court. Both segregation and the boycott continued while the appeal was pending.

Throughout the thirteen months of negotiations and legal maneuvers, the boycott was sustained by mass meetings and its car-pool operation. The weekly mass meetings, rotated among the city's black churches, continually reinforced the high level of emotional commitment to the movement among the black population. The car pool,

modeled on one used during a brief bus boycott in Baton Rouge in 1953, initially consisted of private cars whose owners volunteered to participate. But as contributions flowed in from sympathetic northerners, the MIA eventually purchased a fleet of station wagons, assigned ownership of them to the various black churches, hired drivers, and established regular routes. Rufus Lewis administered the car pool until May 1956, when he was succeeded by the Rev. B. J. Simms.

White authorities eventually realized that the MIA's ability to perpetuate the boycott depended on its successful organization of the car pool. In November the city sued in state court for an injunction to forbid the car-pool operation on the ground that it was infringing on the bus company's exclusive franchise. On November 13, Judge Eugene Carter granted the injunction, and the car pool ceased operation the next day. But on that same day, the U.S. Supreme Court summarily affirmed the previous ruling of the lower federal court that bus segregation was unconstitutional. The city petitioned the Supreme Court for rehearing, and a final order was delayed until December 20. On December 21, 1956, the buses were integrated and the boycott ended.

The city was at once plunged into violence. Snipers fired into the buses, with one of the shots shattering the leg of a pregnant black passenger, Rosa Jordan. The city commission ordered the suspension of night bus service. On January 10, 1957, four black churches and the homes of the Reverend Ralph Abernathy and of the MIA's only white board member, the Reverend Robert Graetz, were bombed and heavily damaged. All bus service was then suspended. On January 27, a home near that of Martin Luther King was bombed and destroyed, and a bomb at King's own home was defused. On January 30, Montgomery police arrested seven bombers, all of whom were members of the Ku Klux Klan.

The arrests ended the violence, and in March full bus service resumed. However, the first two of the bombers to come to trial were acquitted in May 1957, despite their confessions and the irrefutable evidence against them. Meanwhile, in April, the Alabama Court of Appeals had affirmed on technical grounds King's conviction under the Anti-Boycott Act. Because it was now clear that the other bombing prosecutions would be unsuccessful, and because the boycott had ended in any case, prosecutors in November agreed to dismiss all the remaining bombing and anti-boycott-law indictments in return for King's payment of his $500 fine.

The Montgomery Bus Boycott marked the beginning of the civil rights movement's direct action phase, and it made Martin Luther King Jr. a national figure. Although the integration of the buses was actually produced by the federal court injunction rather than by the boycott, it was the boycott that began the process of moving the civil rights movement out of the courtroom by demonstrating that ordinary African Americans possessed the power to control their own destiny.

See also Abernathy, Ralph David; Jim Crow; King, Martin Luther, Jr.; Montgomery Improvement Association; National Association for the Advancement of Colored People (NAACP); Nixon, Edgar Daniel; Parks, Rosa; Southern Christian Leadership Conference

■ ■ *Bibliography*

Burns, Stewart. *Daybreak of Freedom: The Montgomery Bus Boycott.* Chapel Hill: University of North Carolina Press, 1997.

Garrow, David J., ed. *The Walking City: The Montgomery Bus Boycott, 1955–1956.* Brooklyn, N.Y.: Carlson, 1989.

Graetz, Robert S. *Montgomery: A White Preacher's Memoir.* Minneapolis: Fortress Press, 1991.

Gray, Fred. *Bus Ride to Justice: Changing the System by the System.* Montgomery, Ala.: Black Belt Press, 1995.

King, Martin Luther, Jr. *Stride Toward Freedom: The Montgomery Story.* New York: Harper, 1958.

Robinson, JoAnn Gibson. *The Montgomery Bus Boycott and the Women Who Started It: The Memoir of Jo Ann Gibson Robinson,* edited by David J. Garrow. Knoxville: University of Tennessee Press, 1987.

Thornton, J. Mills, III. "Challenge and Response in the Montgomery Bus Boycott of 1955–1956." *Alabama Review* 33 (1980): 163–235.

Yeakey, Lamont H. *The Montgomery, Alabama, Bus Boycott, 1955–1956.* Ph.D. diss., Columbia University, 1979.

J. MILLS THORNTON III (1996)
Updated bibliography

MONTGOMERY IMPROVEMENT ASSOCIATION

▪▪▪

The Montgomery Improvement Association (MIA) was formed in Montgomery, Alabama, on December 5, 1955, to direct the black boycott of the city's bus system. Black leaders had called a one-day boycott for December 5, to protest the trial of Mrs. Rosa L. Parks, who had been arrested for violating the city ordinance requiring buses to maintain racially segregated seating. This boycott had proven so successful that on the afternoon of December

5, at a meeting of the community's black leaders at the Mount Zion African Methodist Episcopal Zion Church, those present decided to extend the boycott until the city and the bus company agreed to adopt the bus segregation pattern used in Mobile, Alabama, which did not require the unseating of passengers who were already seated. The leaders decided to create a new organization to run the boycott, and at the suggestion of the Reverend Ralph D. Abernathy (1926–1990), they named it the Montgomery Improvement Association. Rufus A. Lewis, a local funeral director, then nominated his pastor, the Reverend Dr. Martin Luther King Jr., as the association's president. The twenty-six-year-old King was taken by surprise at this unexpected designation, but he accepted it. That night, at a mass meeting at the Holt Street Baptist Church attended by some five thousand people, black Montgomerians ratified these actions.

Perhaps the MIA's most important achievement during the course of the boycott was the organization of an efficient car-pool operation to replace the buses. Without this operation to get the mass of black participants to and from work, the boycott would soon have begun to weaken, and it was the ability of blacks to create and administer such an operation that most confounded the expectations of their white segregationist opponents. Rufus Lewis ran the car pool during the first six months of the boycott, and he was succeeded in May 1956 by the Reverend B. J. Simms. Almost equally as important as the car pool were the MIA's weekly mass meetings. These meetings, held in rotation at each of the city's principal black churches, were an effective means of maintaining the enthusiasm and commitment of the boycott's participants.

The MIA was governed by a self-constituted board of directors, consisting primarily of the leaders who had attended the December 5 organizational meeting. When a vacancy occurred, the remaining members selected a person to fill it. The only white member was the Reverend Robert Graetz, a Lutheran pastor of an all-black congregation. The board proved extremely reluctant to move beyond the initial black demand for a more acceptable pattern of seating segregation. Throughout the boycott's first two months, board members refused to permit the association's attorney, Fred D. Gray, to file suit in federal court seeking a declaration that seating segregation ordinances were unconstitutional. Only when the Martin Luther King's home was bombed on January 30, 1956, was the board pushed into authorizing the suit. The resultant case, *Browder v. Gayle,* produced the U.S. Supreme Court's holding that bus segregation laws violated the Constitution's Fourteenth Amendment, and thus led to a successful conclusion of the boycott on December 21, 1956.

The association continued to exist after the boycott. It became one of the founding organizations of the Southern Christian Leadership Conference in 1957, conducted a largely ineffective voter registration drive in Montgomery, sought unsuccessfully to create a credit union for blacks, and in 1958 sponsored the filing of a suit to integrate the city's parks and playgrounds, a suit that only resulted in the city's closure of all of them. The MIA threatened a suit to integrate Montgomery's schools, but the suit was never filed. King moved to Atlanta in 1960, and Abernathy followed him there in 1961. After this, the association became less and less active. Its last important achievement came in the spring of 1962, when, under the leadership of the Reverend Solomon S. Seay Sr., it managed to persuade the bus company to hire blacks as bus drivers, an action that had been one of the original demands of the boycott. Seay was succeeded by the Reverend Jesse Douglas, and Douglas by Mrs. Johnnie Carr. By the last decades of the twentieth century, however, the MIA had ceased to play any active role in the life of the community.

See also Abernathy, Ralph David; King, Martin Luther, Jr.; Montgomery, Ala., Bus Boycott; Parks, Rosa; Southern Christian Leadership Conference

■ ■ *Bibliography*

Garrow, David J. *Bearing the Cross: Martin Luther King, Jr., and the Southern Christian Leadership Conference.* New York: William Morrow, 1986.

King, Martin Luther, Jr. *Stride Toward Freedom: The Montgomery Story.* New York: Harper, 1958.

Thornton, J. Mills, III. "Challenge and Response in the Montgomery Bus Boycott of 1955–1956." *Alabama Review* 33 (1989): 163–235.

J. MILLS THORNTON III (1996)

MOODY, ANNE

SEPTEMBER 15, 1940

Born near Centreville, Mississippi, to poor sharecroppers, civil rights activist and writer Anne Moody attended segregated schools in the area and worked as a domestic and at other jobs. She went to Natchez Junior College on a basketball scholarship in 1959 and to Tougaloo College in Jackson, receiving her B.S. in 1964.

While in college, Moody became involved in the civil rights movement and was jailed several times. In 1963 she

and two other blacks were among the first sit-in demonstrators at a Woolworth's lunch counter in Jackson, Mississippi. Moody was a Congress of Racial Equality (CORE) organizer from 1961 to 1963 and a fund-raiser in 1964. From 1964 to 1965 she served as the civil rights project coordinator for Cornell University. Complaining that the civil rights campaign had become "narrowly nationalistic," she shortly thereafter left it, moved to New York, and began to pursue a writing career.

Moody's best known work is her autobiography, *Coming of Age in Mississippi* (1968). It chronicles her growing up in poverty, her struggles to get an education, southern white racism, and the early battles of the civil rights movement. This compelling and moving book is among the best accounts of the southern black experience; it received many prizes, including the Best Book of the Year Award (1969) from the National Library Association.

In 1975 Moody published *Mr. Death,* four somber short stories for children that had been completed in 1972. She continued to write but has published little after that.

See also Civil Rights Movement, U.S.; Congress of Racial Equality (CORE)

■ ■ *Bibliography*

Moody, Anne. *Coming of Age in Mississippi.* New York: Dial Press, 1968. Reprint, New York: Delta Trade Paperbacks, 2004.

Sewell, George, and Margaret Dwight, eds. *Mississippi Black History Makers.* Jackson: University Press of Mississippi, 1984.

Stone, Albert E. "After Black Boy and Dusk of Dawn: Patterns in Recent Black Autobiography." *Phylon* 9, no. 1 (1978): 18–34.

QADRI ISMAIL (1996)
Updated bibliography

MOODY, HAROLD ARUNDEL

OCTOBER 8, 1882
APRIL 24, 1947

Dr. Harold Arundel Moody was born in Kingston, Jamaica, but he lived most of his adult life in England, involved in the struggle for the rights of people of color around the world. His early life was centered in Kingston, where his father was a retail chemist. Moody worked in his father's pharmaceutical business while still a student at Wolmer's School, where he obtained his secondary education with a distinction in mathematics. After graduating, Moody opened a short-lived private school and also taught at his alma mater. In 1904 he had accumulated enough money to pursue medical studies in England, at King's College, University of London.

At King's College Hospital, Moody earned several academic honors and awards, and by 1910 he had become a member of the Royal College of Surgeons and the London Royal College of Physicians. In 1919 he received his Doctor of Medicine degree. He also pursued postgraduate work in ophthalmic medicine at the Royal Eye Hospital, London. However, although he was a qualified and distinguished medical school graduate, he encountered blatant racism in his attempt to obtain an appointment.

First, his own college hospital refused him a position. An appointment at another London hospital was withdrawn because the matron of the institution would not allow "a coloured doctor" to work there. However, Moody found employment as a medical superintendent at the Marylebone Medical Mission. On May 10, 1913, he married Olive Mabel Tranter, a nurse. The union resulted in six children, two of whom, Christina and Harold Jr., also became medical practitioners. The senior Moody established a private medical practice in Peckham, southeast London, in 1913, and he continued in that location for thirty-five years.

While in Jamaica, Moody was a Congregationalist and continued as a member of that denomination in the United Kingdom. He also forged close ties with the Church Missionary Society (CMS), becoming a board member in 1912 and its chair in 1921. He was a member of the Christian Endeavour Union and became its president by 1931, and in 1943 he was named chair of the London Missionary Society (LMS), with which he had had a long association. His ecumenical connections afforded him lifelong support in his quest to improve the lives of people of African ancestry.

Moody's ties with these organizations also provided him with a platform from which to argue for the rights of people of color. His residence in Peckham soon became a well-known place for recently arrived West Indian students and others in England to visit and seek guidance and assistance. He soon envisioned an organization that would represent the interest of colored people in the United Kingdom.

The help to launch such an organization materialized in March, 1931, when Dr. Charles Wesley, the chair of the history department at Howard University in Washington, D.C., arrived in England. Using the YMCA at Tottenham Court Road, London, as a forum, Wesley and Moody held meetings and organized the League of Coloured Peoples (LCP), following the structure of the National Association for the Advancement of Colored People (NAACP), of which Wesley was a member. The LCP would provide Moody with a venue "to promote and protect the social, educational, economical, and political interests of its members . . . and the welfare of coloured people" worldwide.

At first, the LCP's membership consisted mainly of students of color from the British colonies, especially the Caribbean and East and West Africa. Whites who were attached to religious institutions and retired colonial civil servants, as well as persons from India and Ceylon (Sri Lanka), also participated in the activities of the LCP. In fact, the LCP was a multiracial organization led by people of color. Other African Americans involved with the LCP included St. Clair Drake, Paul Robeson, and W. E. B. Du Bois. Other members of the LCP include C. L. R. James, the noted author from Trinidad and Tobago; Sir Learie Constantine, the famous Trinidadian cricketer and jurist; the Grenadian Sir David Pitt; and Sir Arthur Lewis, a Nobel Laureate from Saint Lucian.

The *Keys*, the journal of the organization, began publication in 1933, the same year the first annual conference of the LCP was held. Branches of the LCP were organized in areas of the British Empire, such as Sierra Leone. In British Guiana (later known as Guyana), a branch was formed by Dulcina Ross-Armstrong, who had worked with Dr. Moody in London.

As president of the LCP, Moody engaged in a number of racially and politically sensitive matters, not only in the United Kingdom but also abroad. He used various protest methods and sent deputations to the governments of the countries concerned. Among the issues he was concerned with were the trial of the "Scottsboro Boys" in the United States and the plan to incorporate Bechuanaland, Basutoland, and Swaziland into South Africa. (This latter plan did not occur, and the three countries remained under British control). Although Moody returned to Jamaica on only three occasions—in 1912, 1919, and during 1946 and 1947—he took active interests in Caribbean affairs. In 1937, economic, social, and political unrest swept through the entire Caribbean region, and several West Indian leaders were incarcerated by the colonial authorities. Moody and the LCP sent deputations to the Colonial Office, a move that led to the Moyne Royal Commission. Eventually, the Colonial Development and Welfare Act of 1940 was passed, providing financial resources for social and economic changes in the Caribbean.

Italy's invasion of Abyssinia in 1935 and the issue of classifying colonial seamen as aliens to preclude them from employment in Cardiff, Wales, engaged his attention. Moody lobbied the Unemployment Branch of the Board of Trade and the National Seamen's Union to intervene on the seamen's behalf. He also solicited the help of the member of parliament for Cardiff South and the home secretary to get the Aliens Registration Act rescinded. In other issues concerning racial discrimination, Moody contacted a wide range of entities, including government, private, commercial, and other businesses, as well as hotel and boarding house proprietors on behalf of people of African descent.

In the 1940s Moody and the LCP played a significant role in the Colonial Office's efforts to open hostels in the United Kingdom for use by residents of the British Empire. In addition to his contributions in helping to counter racial prejudice against people of color he also promoted matters in their interests. By March 1944, he envisioned the establishment of a LCP Cultural Center aimed at providing accommodation and assistance for new arrivals from British colonies, "to adjust . . . to a new environment by means of social and cultural amenities . . . and to make known the achievements of coloured peoples in the fields of science, art, music, and letters." Moody embarked on fund-raising efforts to establish the center. He visited the Caribbean and the United States during 1946 and 1947, but ill health thwarted his efforts. Dr. Moody died on April 24, 1947, soon after returning to Great Britain.

Bibliography

Adi, Hakim. *West Africans in Britain, 1900-1960: Nationalism, Pan-Africanism, and Communism.* London: Lawrence and Wishart, 1998.

Adi, Hakim, and Marika Sherwood. *Pan-African History: Political Figures from Africa and the Diaspora.* London: Routledge, 2003.

"Dr. Harold Moody." In *A History of the Black Presence in London.* London: The Greater London County Council, 1986.

Killingray, David. "To Do Something for the Race: Harold Moody and the League of Coloured Peoples." In *West Indian Intellectuals in Britain,* edited by Bill Schwartz. Manchester, U.K.: Manchester University Press, 2003.

Roderick Macdonald, ed. *The Keys: The Official Organ of the League of Colored Peoples.* Millwood, N.Y.: Kraus-Thompson, 1976.

BARBARA P. JOSIAH (2005)

MOORE, ARCHIE
DECEMBER 13, 1913 (OR 1916)
DECEMBER 9, 1998

The boxing champion Archibald Lee "Archie" Moore, nicknamed "The Mongoose," was one of America's greatest and most colorful fighters. The year and place of his birth are uncertain. He was born Archibald Lee Wright on either December 13, 1913, in Benoit, Mississippi, or on that same date in 1916 in Collinsville, Illinois. Moore's father, Tommy Wright, was a day laborer, and his mother, Lorena Wright, was a housewife. Following his parents separation, Moore was raised by an uncle and aunt, Cleveland and Willie Moore, in St. Louis, Missouri.

Moore's early years were difficult ones. He never liked school and sometimes found himself in trouble. He spent twenty-two months in Missouri's Booneville Reformatory for stealing coins from a streetcar motorman. Fortunately, Moore eventually channeled his aggression into the ring, carving out a boxing career that would last thirty years. He made his professional debut in 1935, knocking out Piano Man Jones in a bout organized by Moore's fellow Civilian Conservation Corps workers from St. Louis. Following his bout against Jones, Moore spent years traveling the country fighting anyone who would enter the ring with him. He had a terribly difficult time, however, in securing a championship fight. The ineptitude of his managers, combined with racial discrimination and the refusal of the best boxers to fight him, forced Moore to wait a long time before engaging in a title bout. Finally, in 1952, he got his chance, and he took advantage of it by beating Joey Maxim for the light heavyweight championship. He successfully defended the championship against Harold Johnson in 1954 and Bobo Olson in 1955. In that same year, Moore fought for the heavyweight championship against Rocky Marciano. Although performing admirably, Moore lost to Marciano, the great undefeated heavyweight champion putting him to the canvas four times before knocking him out in the ninth round.

In 1956 Moore fought again for the heavyweight championship against Floyd Patterson. At Chicago Stadium, Moore was knocked out by the much younger Patterson in the fifth round. Moore never fought again for the heavyweight championship, but he did capture four more light heavyweight titles. He defeated Tony Anthony in 1957, the French-Canadian Yvon "The Fighting Fisherman" Durelle in 1958 and 1959, and Italy's Giulio Rinaldi in 1961. Perhaps the most memorable of these four title fights was Moore's bout against Durelle in 1958. He was knocked down three times in the first round and once in the fifth round by Durelle, but somehow managed to recover and knocked out the very tough French-Canadian fighter in the eleventh round. As a result, he was named Fighter of the Year by *Ring* magazine.

In 1962 Moore was stripped of his light heavyweight championship because of his refusal to engage in more title defenses. But he did continue to fight. Not long after being stripped of his light heavyweight championship, Moore fought the young Cassius Clay in Los Angeles. Either in his late forties or early fifties at the time of the fight, Moore lost to the future heavyweight champion in a fourth round knockout. In 1963 Moore defeated Mike DiBiase before retiring from the ring. His final career numbers included 228 bouts, a record 140 knockouts, 53 wins by decisions, and 24 losses. Following his retirement, Moore pursued a career in show business, served as a trainer and boxing manager, and worked with inner-city youth through his ABC ("Any Boy Can") program. Among his many honors was election to *Ring* magazine's Boxing Hall of Fame in 1966 and the International Boxing Hall of Fame in 1990. He died at a hospice in San Diego following a long illness.

See also Boxing

■ ■ *Bibliography*

Ashe, Arthur R., Jr. *A Hard Road To Glory: A History of the African-American Athlete.* New York: Warner, 1988.

Moore, Archie, and Leonard B. Pearl. *Any Boy Can: The Archie Moore Story.* Englewood Cliffs, N.J.: Prentice-Hall, 1971.

DAVID K. WIGGINS (2005)

MOORE, AUDLEY "QUEEN MOTHER"

JULY 27, 1898
MAY 7, 1997

▬▬▬

Queen Mother Moore's long career in service to African Americans provides an example of a consummate community organizer and activist. Born and raised in Louisiana, Moore became a member of the Universal Negro Improvement Association and a follower of Marcus Garvey in 1919. Through Garvey she was first exposed to African history. Moore and her family moved to Harlem along with the flood of southern migrants during the 1920s. Here she founded the Harriet Tubman Association to assist black women workers. Moore also used the Communist Party as a vehicle for achieving her aims. Impressed with its work on the Scottsboro case, she used the information and skills she acquired through the party to address the needs of the Harlem community by organizing rent strikes, fighting evictions, and taking other actions. Eventually, the racism she encountered in the party moved Moore to resign.

The major theme of Moore's career was developing a Pan-African consciousness. From Garvey through involvement with the National Council of Negro Women to Malcolm X's Organization of Afro-American Unity, Moore emphasized a knowledge of and pride in African history and its African-American connections. She brought this to the fore in her campaign for reparations, begun in 1955, as she did in founding other institutions in the black community. Among these were the World Federation of African People and a tribute to her sister in the Eloise Moore College of African Studies in Mount Addis Ababa, New York. She was also one of the founders of the Ethiopian Orthodox Church of North and South America, of which she was an archabbess. Moore received the title Queen Mother of the Ashanti people when in Ghana on one of her many trips to Africa.

See also Garvey, Marcus; Malcolm X; National Council of Negro Women; Reparations; Universal Negro Improvement Association

■ ■ *Bibliography*

Hill, Ruth Edmonds, ed. *The Black Women Oral History Project.* 10 vols. Westport, Conn.: Meckler, 1991.

"Interview: Queen Mother Moore." *Black Scholar* 4 (March–April 1973): 47–55.

Lanker, Brian. *I Dream a World: Portraits of Black Women Who Changed the World.* New York: Stewart, Tabori & Chang, 1989.

JUDITH WEISENFELD (1996)

MOORE, RICHARD BENJAMIN

AUGUST 9, 1893
AUGUST 18, 1978

▬▬▬

The civil rights activist Richard Benjamin Moore was born in Hastings, Christ Church, Barbados. He left school at the age of eleven to work as a clerk in a department store. He emigrated to New York on July 4, 1909, and worked as an office boy and elevator operator, and then at a silk manufacturing firm, where he received regular promotions until he became head of the stock department. The racism he encountered in the United States prompted Moore to a life of activism. In 1911 he served as president of the Ideal Tennis Club, which built Harlem's first tennis courts. In 1915 he founded and was treasurer of the Pioneer Cooperative Society, a grocery store featuring southern and West Indian products. A self-educated bibliophile, he began to amass an impressive book collection and formed the People's Educational Forum (later the Harlem Educational Forum), where he organized debates and lectures.

In 1918 Moore became a member of 21st Assembly District Branch of the Socialist Party. Around this time he also joined the American Blood Brotherhood (ABB), a secret organization formed in response to race riots for the purpose of the "liberation of people of African descent all over the world." In 1920 Moore was cofounder and contributing editor of *The Emancipator,* of which ten issues were produced.

In 1921 Moore left the Socialist Party, disenchanted with its lack of concern for African Americans, and subsequently joined the Communist Party (the actual date of membership is uncertain). Moore was elected to the general executive board and council of directors of the American Negro Labor Congress (ANLC) at its founding meeting on October 25–31, 1925, and he was a contributing editor to the ANLC's *The Negro Champion.* When Moore was fired from the silk manufacturing firm in 1926, he was put on the ANLC payroll as a paid organizer. In 1927, representing the ANLC at the International Congress Against Colonial Oppression and Imperialism and for National Independence in Brussels, Belgium, he drafted the *Common Resolution on the Negro Question,* which was unanimously adopted. In August of that year he attended the Fourth Pan-African Congress held in New York. In January 1928, as an employee of the ANLC, he organized and was president of The Harlem Tenants League. By 1931 Moore was vice president of the International Labor Defense (ILD), where he struggled during the 1930s on behalf of the Scottsboro Boys, organizing mass demonstrations, preparing press releases, and making use of his brilliant gift for oratory in speeches delivered across the nation.

In February 1940, Moore founded the Pathway Press and the Frederick Douglass Historical and Cultural League, and he republished *The Life and Times of Frederick Douglass* (1892), which had been out of print for forty years. Moore had been motivated by his reading of this work during his early years in New York. In 1942 he opened the Frederick Douglass Book Center at 141 West 125th Street, a bookshop and meeting place specializing in African, Afro-American, and Caribbean history and literature. The center remained a Harlem landmark until it was razed in 1968.

After his expulsion from the Communist Party in 1942, Moore shifted his attention to agitating for Caribbean independence. June 1940 marked the foundation of the West Indies National Emergency Committee (later the West Indies National Council [WINC]) of which he was vice president. He drafted "The Declaration of the Rights of the Caribbean Peoples to Self-Determination and Self-Government," which he submitted to the Pan-American Foreign Ministers' Conference held at Havana, Cuba, in July 1940. In 1945 Moore was a delegate of the West Indies National Council to the United Nations conference in San Francisco. He was, at the time, secretary of the United Caribbean American Council, founded in 1949.

In the 1960s Moore founded the Committee to Present the Truth About the Name Negro. In 1960 he published *The Name "Negro"—Its Origin and Evil Use* as a part of his campaign to promote the adoption of "Afro-American" as the preferred designation of black people. He was instrumental in convincing the Association for the Study of Negro Life and History to change its name to the Association for the Study of Afro-American Life and History in 1972 (the organization is now called the Association for the Study of African American Life and History).

In 1966 Moore was invited by the government of Barbados to witness the Barbadian independence celebration. Although he continued to have his primary residence in the New York City area, he spent increasing amounts of time in the land of his birth. Moore died in Barbados in 1978; his extensive book collection is housed there at the University of the West Indies.

See also Association for the Study of African American Life and History; Communist Party of the United States; Douglass, Frederick; Pan-Africanism; Scottsboro Case

▪ ▪ *Bibliography*

Rose, Peter I., ed. *Americans from Africa: Old Memories, New Moods,* vol. 2. New York: Atherton, 1970.

Turner, W. Burghardt, and Joyce Moore Turner. *Richard B. Moore, Caribbean Militant in Harlem: Collected Writings, 1920–1972.* Bloomington: Indiana University Press, 1988.

LYDIA MCNEILL (1996)

George W. Gordon, c. 1860s. *A Jamaican national hero, Gordon's expulsion from the local vestry played a role in the Morant Bay Rebellion of 1865.* PHOTOGRAPHS AND PRINTS DIVISION, SCHOMBURG CENTER FOR RESEARCH IN BLACK CULTURE, THE NEW YORK PUBLIC LIBRARY, ASTOR, LENOX AND TILDEN FOUNDATIONS

MORANT BAY REBELLION

The Morant Bay Rebellion broke out in southeastern Jamaica on October 11, 1865, when several hundred black people marched into the town of Morant Bay, the capital of the predominantly sugar-growing parish of St. Thomas in the East. They raided the police station and stole the weapons stored there, and then confronted the volunteer militia that had been called up to protect the meeting of the vestry, the political body that administered the parish. Fighting soon broke out, and by the end of the day the crowd had killed eighteen people and wounded thirty-one others. In addition, seven members of the crowd died. In the days following the outbreak, bands of people in different parts of the parish killed two planters and threatened the lives of many others. The disturbances spread across the parish of St. Thomas in the East, from its western border with St. David to its northern boundary with Portland.

The response of the Jamaican authorities was swift and brutal. Making use of British troops, Jamaican forces, and a group of Maroons (runaway slaves) who had been formed into an irregular but effective army of the colony, the government forcefully put down the rebellion. In the process, nearly five hundred people were killed and hundreds of others seriously wounded. The nature of the suppression led to demands in England for an official inquiry, and a royal commission subsequently took evidence in Jamaica on the disturbances. Its conclusions were critical of the governor, Edward John Eyre, and of the severe repression in the wake of the rebellion. As a result, the governor was dismissed, the political constitution of the colony was transformed, and its two-hundred-year-old assembly was abolished. Direct rule from London—known as Crown Colony government—was established in its place.

In the months following the outbreak, and in the period since, there has been considerable debate about the origin and nature of the disturbances. The governor and nearly all the whites and browns (or coloreds, meaning those of mixed racial ancestry) in the colony believed that the island was faced with a rebellion at the time. They saw it as part of an island-wide conspiracy to put blacks in power. This was not a surprising view in light of the Haitian revolution at the end of the eighteenth century and the massive 1831 slave revolt in Jamaica. Equally important, Jamaican society was demographically skewed: the overwhelming proportion of the population was black, while whites and people of mixed race formed only a small segment of the population. For the whites and browns of Jamaica, the governor's actions in putting down the rebellion had saved the colony for Britain and preserved them from annihilation.

At the same time, there was a different perspective of the outbreak, especially in Britain. The outbreak was perceived by some as a spontaneous disturbance, a riot that did not warrant the repression that followed in its wake. John Stuart Mill (one of the leading liberal philosophers of the nineteenth century) and others formed the Jamaica Committee, hoping to bring the governor to trial in England and thereby establish the limits of imperial authority.

The evidence suggests that the outbreak was indeed a rebellion, since it was characterized by advance planning and by a degree of organization. The leader of the rebellion was Paul Bogle, a small landowner living in Stony Gut, a mountainous village about four miles inland from Morant Bay. Bogle, along with other associates, organized secret meetings in advance of the outbreak. At these meetings, oaths were taken and volunteers enlisted in expectation of a violent confrontation at Morant Bay. The meetings were often held in native Baptist chapels or meeting houses; this was important because the native Baptists provided a religious and political counterweight to the prevailing white norms of the colonial society.

Bogle was careful to take into account the forces that would be arrayed against him, and he attempted to win over the Jamaican Maroons. Moreover, Bogle's men were carefully drilled—when they marched into the town of Morant Bay to confront the vestry, their first target was the police station and the weaponry stored there.

It is significant that the rebellion took place in St. Thomas in the East. One of the parish's representatives to the House of Assembly was George William Gordon (1820–1865), a colored man who had clashed with the local vestry and was ultimately ejected from it in 1864. Gordon had also grown increasingly close to the native Baptists in St. Thomas in the East and to Paul Bogle, a deacon of the church. In fact, Bogle served as Gordon's political agent in St. Thomas in the East. This identification with the native Baptists marked Gordon as a religious and political radical, but he was also a very popular figure in the parish. His expulsion from the vestry led to a bitter court case, which was scheduled for a further hearing when the Morant Bay Rebellion broke out.

This was not the only grievance of the people in St. Thomas in the East. Their stipendiary magistrate, T. Witter Jackson, was also a highly respected figure. As a neutral magistrate appointed by the Crown, Jackson, who was colored, was perceived as an impartial magistrate and very different from the planter-dominated magistracy. Yet a month before the outbreak of the rebellion, parish officials engineered Jackson's transfer out of St. Thomas in the East.

There were also other problems which created bitter feelings among the populace of the parish. Many people in the parish believed that it was impossible to obtain justice in the local courts. Since almost the entire magistracy was dominated by planters, it was often the case that employers were judging the cases of their employees. High court fees also made it very difficult for laborers and small settlers to pursue cases in court. One of the grievances of the crowd at Morant Bay, and in the rebellion generally, was the lack of justice in the parish. For example, when asked the reason for the rebellion the day after the events at Morant Bay, one of the members of the crowd at Bath claimed it had broken out "because the poor black had no justice in St. Thomas in the East . . . there was no other way to get satisfaction in St. Thomas in the East, only what they had done" (Heuman, p. 268).

For the blacks in the parish, there was at least one other alternative that some of them had tried. In several parts of the parish, blacks had organized their own courts. These "people's courts" were held in districts not far from Morant Bay, and offenses were punished by fines and by flogging. Such alternative courts seem to have existed in other parts of the island as well, providing further evidence of the dissatisfaction of the people with the administration of justice.

Another source of difficulty for the people of St. Thomas in the East was the issue of wages, particularly the low wages provided on the sugar estates of the parish. There were also serious complaints about the irregularity of payment for work on the estates. A missionary reported that his parishioners believed that they were "not paid regularly on some of the estates, that their money was docked, [and] their tasks were heavy" (Heuman, p. 268). Two of the prominent figures killed at Morant Bay, Custos Ketelhodt and Rev. Herschell, had experienced problems with their laborers over this issue. At Ketelhodt's estate in the parish, there were complaints about low pay for the workers. Many of the people who worked on the estate came from Stony Gut and the surrounding villages. Given the lack of redress in the courts, the concern about wages figured prominently among the grievances of the crowd at Morant Bay.

In addition to these issues, there was also the problem of land. More specifically, there was a belief that the provision grounds away from the estates (the land that peasants and laborers used to grow their own crops) belonged to the people and not to the estates. The people's view was that they should have this land without paying rent. It is likely that Augustus Hire, one of the planters killed in the days following the outbreak at Morant Bay, was a target of the crowd because of his stance on this issue.

These problems over land, justice, and wages need to be seen in light of the wider problems affecting Jamaica as a whole, as well as the specific history of the colony. A significant aspect of Jamaica's history has been the large number of rebellions and conspiracies, especially during the slave period. The most important of these occurred in 1831 and was instrumental in the emancipation of the slaves. Slaves in the 1831 rebellion made use of the structure of the missionary churches and chapels to organize the outbreak.

After the abolition of slavery, the tradition of protest persisted. Riots continued in the post-emancipation period (including in 1848, for example) because of a rumor that slavery was to be reimposed. The Morant Bay Rebellion can therefore be seen in the context of a long history of protest in Jamaica.

The economic problems that afflicted Jamaica during this period, especially in the 1860s, also contributed to the rebellion. Sugar was the economic mainstay of the island's economy, but it underwent a steep decline in the decades after emancipation. Partly because of the loss of a protected market in Britain in the 1840s, and partly because of the relatively high cost of producing sugar in Jamaica, many estates failed. By 1865, at least half of the sugar plantations that had operated in the 1830s no longer existed.

In the 1860s, Jamaica's economic situation worsened considerably. The American Civil War had the effect of dramatically increasing prices for imported goods, including foodstuffs, and a series of prolonged droughts devastated the peasants' provision grounds, further adding to the cost of food. The output of sugar was also reduced, and work on the dwindling number of estates became harder to find.

Jamaica's problems in 1865 were highlighted by a letter from Edward Underhill, the secretary of the Baptist Missionary Society in England, to the British Secretary of State for the Colonies. In the letter, Underhill complained about the dire situation in Jamaica, pointing especially to the starving condition of the peasantry. For Underhill, there was no doubt about "the extreme poverty of the people," which was evidenced "by the ragged and even naked condition of vast numbers of them." The Colonial Office forwarded Underhill's letter to Jamaica, where it was widely circulated, and meetings were held all over the island in the spring and summer of 1865 to discuss the letter. These meetings were heavily attended by blacks, and therefore often dominated by members of the opposition to the local administration. Dissidents such as George William Gordon traveled from parish to parish, speaking at these gatherings and highlighting the oppression of the population. Some of the language he was reported to have used worried the authorities. In one parish, Gordon was alleged to have encouraged the people to follow the example of Haiti—in effect, to institute their own Haitian Revolution.

In St. Thomas in the East, Paul Bogle and other leaders of the rebellion were organizing meetings at which people expressed their grievances, especially over the issues of land, justice, and wages. At these meetings, oaths were administered to willing adherents. Those who refused to swear the oath were not allowed into the meetings. These oaths were similar to the cries of the mob at Morant Bay and elsewhere: "Color for color; skin for skin; cleave to the black." There was a clear antiwhite and antibrown feeling among the crowd at Morant Bay, although the people agreed to save any black or brown person who joined them. There were also many subsequent reports of men engaging in military drills and preparing for "war."

Faced with an unyielding government and ruling class, Bogle and his allies saw no solution to their grievances. They were concerned about the lack of justice in the parish and the problem of access to land and to work. They were supported by an African-oriented religion, and

they believed they had allies in Britain and in Kingston, and the atmosphere was rife with arguments about white oppression of the blacks. Fearful that they might even be re-enslaved, the people marched into Morant Bay.

See also Bogle, Paul; Gordon, George William; Haitian Revolution; Maroon Wars

■ ■ *Bibliography*

Bakan, Abigail. *Ideology and Class Conflict in Jamaica: The Politics of Rebellion.* Montreal and Kingston, Jamaica: McGill-Queen's University Press, 1990.

Curtin, Philip D. *Two Jamaicas: The Role of Ideas in a Tropical Colony, 1830-1865.* Cambridge, Mass: Harvard University Press, 1955.

Heuman, Gad. *The Killing Time: The Morant Bay Rebellion in Jamaica.* Knoxville: University of Tennessee Press, 1994.

Heuman, Gad. "Post-Emancipation Protest in Jamaica: The Morant Bay Rebellion, 1865." In *From Chattel Slaves to Wage Slaves: The Dynamics of Labour Bargaining in the Americas,* edited by Mary Turner. Kingston, Jamaica: Ian Randle, 1995.

Holt, Thomas C. *The Problem of Freedom: Race, Labor, and Politics in Jamaica and Britain, 1832-1938.* Baltimore, Md.: Johns Hopkins University Press, 1992.

GAD HEUMAN (2005)

MORAVIAN CHURCH
▬ ▬ ▬

The Moravian Church was one of the first churches in America to admit African Americans—both slave and free—to membership. Originally part of the Protestant Reformation, the church became increasingly active as a missionary church among non-Christians outside Europe, and its members arrived among West Indian slaves early in the 1730s. Moravians came to America in 1735 to escape persecution and to work among Native Americans and African-American slaves. After settling briefly in Georgia, they moved to Pennsylvania, establishing the community of Bethlehem in 1741. In 1753 they settled in central North Carolina, near what later became Salem and then Winston-Salem. Although nineteenth-century congregations emerged in the Ohio Valley, the upper Midwest, and the Southeast, Bethlehem and Winston-Salem still contain the largest Moravian communities in the United States.

Eighteenth-century Moravians counted all races among "the Children of God," but they also practiced chattel slavery. Moravian missionaries welcomed slaves as potential converts while reminding them to accept their divinely ordained servitude. The church also bought slaves to profit from their labor while bringing them the gospel. Conversion was difficult for blacks, though, because they had to adopt the same dress, behavior, music, and family patterns as whites. A handful of slaves living in or near Bethlehem or Salem did join the church, however, in the decades before the American Revolution. These early converts still suffered some cruelties of slavery, fear of sale and the absence of surnames, for example, but they also enjoyed some aspects of racial equality. Black Moravians often worked and lived in the same quarters and conditions as white Moravians. Blacks sat with whites in the meeting house, participated in church synods, were buried in racially integrated cemeteries, and even participated in ceremonies such as foot-washing and the kiss of peace that involved direct physical contact with white members.

After the American Revolution, Pennsylvania enacted a gradual emancipation law in 1780, and the black population of Bethlehem decreased. In North Carolina, at the same time, slavery continued to expand, and in and around Salem, the number of black Moravians continued to rise. But white Moravians in North Carolina grew more restrictive toward slaves and free blacks. Also, younger Moravians began to demand that the church separate black and white members, excluding blacks from foot-washing, from the kiss of peace, from the cemetery, and finally from the meeting house itself. In 1822 a segregated Moravian Church established a separate congregation, with a white minister, for its black members.

In the years between their expulsion from white services and their emancipation from slavery, black Moravians maintained their own religious community around Salem. They had a separate meeting house, cemetery, and, briefly, a school. It was hardly an independent community, though; the minister and teachers were white, and both services and lessons followed white models and emphasized white values. As a result, many slaves and free blacks around Salem ignored it, preferring instead to attend Methodist services or sermons preached by nondenominational black preachers. This trend continued after Emancipation.

Yet the black Moravian community survived. Early in the twentieth century it finally gained a formal designation, Saint Philip's Moravian Church, and in 1966 it received its first black minister. In 2000 Saint Philip's was one of the South's oldest black churches in continuous operation and served a small but proud congregation.

See also Christian Denominations, Independent; Protestantism in the Americas

■ ■ *Bibliography*

Sensbach, Jon. F. *A Separate Canaan: The Making of an Afro-Moravian World in North Carolina, 1763–1840.* Chapel Hill: University of North Carolina Press, 1998.

Thorp, Daniel B. "Chattel with a Soul: The Autobiography of a Moravian Slave." *Pennsylvania Magazine of History and Biography* 112 (1988): 433–451.

Thorp, Daniel B. "New Wine in Old Bottles: Cultural Persistence Among Non-White Converts to the Moravian Church." *Transactions of the Moravian Historical Society* 30 (1998): 1–8.

DANIEL B. THORP (1996)
Updated bibliography

MOREHOUSE COLLEGE

In 1867 the Augusta Baptist Seminary was established in Augusta, Georgia, with the aid of the Washington, D.C.–based National Theological Institute. The seminary soon became affiliated with the American Baptist Home Mission Society (ABHMS), which provided financial and moral support to the fledgling venture. The first class of thirty-seven men and women took courses in the Springfield Baptist Church; the class had three female missionary teachers.

In 1871 Joseph T. Robert became the first president of the institution. After seven years of pressure to move the seminary to Atlanta, the ABHMS purchased land, and the seminary moved in 1879. It was rechristened the Atlanta Baptist Seminary. Accompanying the move was an increased determination to improve the quality of education at the seminary. Within three years, the all-male institution opened a collegiate department; students could enroll in either a four-year scientific course or a six-year classical course.

By the end of the nineteenth century, school officials sought to amend the charter, changing the name of the school to Atlanta Baptist College in 1897. Nine years later, John Hope became the first African-American president; he would lead the college until 1931. Hope oversaw the rapid expansion of the institution and was largely responsible for its excellent reputation both in the region and the country. In 1913 the name of the college was again changed to honor longtime ABHMS stalwart Henry Lyman Morehouse. The newly renamed Morehouse College had about sixty students in the collegiate program in 1915.

Morehouse offered an education weighted heavily toward both spiritual and academic advancement. Teachers such as Morehouse alumnus Benjamin Brawley, who taught there in 1902–1910 and 1912–1920, provided intellectual stimulation and served as role models for the student body. During John Hope's tenure, the "Morehouse man" began to symbolize an honest, intelligent African-American male who could succeed at anything. Partially as a result of the spread of this image, the school was criticized for catering primarily to the black elite and restricting its educational efforts to the Talented Tenth.

Morehouse College, Spelman College, and Atlanta University merged some of their operations in 1929 to streamline administrative functions and pacify philanthropists who believed the merger would simplify donations to any of the participants. Academic resources were pooled. Atlanta became solely a university for graduate study; Spelman catered to undergraduate women, and Morehouse to undergraduate men. Students could take courses at the affiliated schools. Classroom space and some faculty responsibilities were also shared.

While the affiliation maintained each school's financial and administrative autonomy, the Great Depression caused Morehouse significant difficulty. John Hope's successor, Samuel Archer, turned over much of Morehouse's financial and budgetary control to Atlanta University, leaving Morehouse with almost no decision-making power.

Students and faculty at Morehouse chafed under the new arrangements. When Benjamin Elijah Mays became president of Morehouse in 1940, he made the reempowerment of Morehouse a priority. Mays was responsible for drastically increasing the college's endowment, wresting financial control from Atlanta University, and instituting an aggressive program of construction and expansion. He was also leading Morehouse when the 1957 creation of Atlanta University Center further consolidated operations between the original three participants and the new additions of Morris Brown College, Gammon Theological Seminary, and Clark University.

Morehouse was ahead of some of its contemporaries by instituting a non-Western studies program in the early 1960s. Students at Morehouse were also active participants in the civil rights movement. The most notable Morehouse alumnus undoubtedly was the Rev. Dr. Martin Luther King Jr., a 1948 graduate. Julian Bond, a student at Morehouse in the early 1960s, left school to be a full-time activist with the Student Nonviolent Coordinating Committee (SNCC).

Mays retired in 1967, passing the torch to Hugh Gloster, who led Morehouse for the next twenty years. Gloster attempted to expand the endowment, which was always a critical issue at Morehouse. The late 1970s saw the establishment of the Morehouse School of Medicine (1978), originally a two-year institution providing a grounding in primary-care and preventive medicine to students who would then continue at four-year institutions. In 1981 the medical school, which remained autonomous from the college, switched to a four-year curriculum; its finances were bolstered by millions of dollars in donations from governmental and private donations.

Leroy Keith Jr. became president of Morehouse in 1987. He faced many of the same problems as his predecessors had. Budget difficulties, the endowment, and other issues remained pressing crises. Other events, like fatalities caused by fraternity hazing, brought unwanted attention to the college and threatened to tarnish the image of the three thousand "Morehouse men" enrolled there. In September 1994 Keith resigned under pressure after a financial audit revealed that he might have received more than $200,000 in unapproved benefits. Despite these setbacks, Morehouse remained one of the most prestigious of historically black colleges, committed to academic excellence and the distinctive educational needs of African Americans.

In June 1995 Dr. Walter Massey became the president of Morehouse. During his tenure the college has worked to improve its infrastructure and academic programs. The following year the college inaugurated a capital campaign, The Campaign for a New Century, to raise more than $100 million. As of 2004, Morehouse had raised more than $80 million toward that goal. That same year, Oprah Winfrey announced a second gift of $5 million to the college, bringing to $12 million the total amount of money pledged by her to Morehouse over time.

See also Brawley, Benjamin Griffith; Civil Rights Movement, U.S.; Great Depression and the New Deal; Hope, John; Mays, Benjamin E.; Student Nonviolent Coordinating Committee (SNCC)

▪▪ *Bibliography*

Brawley, Benjamin G. *History of Morehouse College.* 1917. Reprint, College Park, Md.: McGrath, 1970.

Butler, Addie Louis Joyner, ed. *The Distinctive Black College: Talladega, Tuskegee, and Morehouse.* Metuchen, N.J.: Scarecrow Press, 1977.

Jones, Edward Allen. *A Candle in the Dark: A History of Morehouse College.* Valley Forge, Pa.: Judson Press, 1967.

JOHN C. STONER (1996)
Updated by author 2005

MOREJÓN, NANCY

1944

Afro-Cuban poet Nancy Morejón belongs to the second generation of writers who emerged after the 1959 Cuban Revolution. Her poetry, which was mainly apolitical in the 1960s, began to address social and political issues more formally in the 1970s and early 1980s, as the Cuban Revolution and its official ideology made their imprint on her representation of the Cuban experience. Criticism of local reality, which is the hallmark of much Caribbean and Latin American literature, is noticeably absent in Morejón's work. This is a reflection of the officially promoted view of the Revolution as the solution for social ills. Race and gender are also treated in a manner that is consistent with the Revolution's concept of a united Cuban nation and in particular with the socialist view of the ideal society as one in which distinctions of race, class, and gender disappear. While Morejón's treatment of racial issues in general may be described as indirect, a distinct race consciousness is nevertheless evident in poems that memorialize black family members or are dedicated to other individuals of African descent. Morejón also weaves African motifs subtly into her poetic discourse, through symbolic use of figures in the pantheon of African deities and the incorporation of Afro-Cuban folk beliefs.

Among her best-known poems are those that are feminist in orientation, featuring real-life black women in diverse private and public roles. These include her mother, aunt, and grandmother and symbolic female subjects such as the Afro-Cuban protagonist of "Mujer negra" (Black Woman) and the black slave woman of "Amo a mi amo" (I love my master). Although feminism, like black consciousness, does not control her poetic voice, Morejón's feminist sensitivity is expressed in oblique ways, for example, in her creation of female figures as agents and makers of history and not as victims.

Every area of experience—from family life to historical moments in national life, as well as international events—is the subject matter of her poetry. The patriotism evident in her celebration of love for Havana in her early poetry widens into a nationalism expressed in direct and indirect ways in her later works. She finds poetic inspiration as easily in the historical achievements of the Revolution as in popular Cuban dance music. Events in contemporary Caribbean history, such as the 1983 invasion of Grenada by the United States and slavery as lived experience, also form part of Morejón's thematic repertoire. Like many postcolonial writers, her poetry is impelled by the desire to subvert or rewrite the dominant versions of his-

tory. Morejón's singular accomplishment is her creation of a body of poetry through which she speaks for the Cuban Revolution without falling into naked propagandizing. Her desire to speak with a communal voice has not caused a silencing of her personal voice. A lyrical current flows through much of her work, linking successive collections in which ideologically charged poems often appear side by side with poems that evoke sentimental moments from her personal life or reflect her deep engagement with others.

See also Women Writers of the Caribbean

■ ■ *Bibliography*

Afro-Hispanic Review 16, no. 1 (1996). Entire issue.

DeCosta-Willis, Miriam, ed. *Singular Like a Bird: The Art of Nancy Morejón.* Washington, D.C.: Howard University Press, 1999.

CLAUDETTE WILLIAMS (2005)

MORGANFIELD, McKINLEY

See Muddy Waters (Morganfield, McKinley)

MORRIS, STEVLAND

See Wonder, Stevie (Morris, Stevland)

MORRIS KNIBB, MARY

1886
1964

Mary Lenora Morris Knibb was one of the pioneering and vocal women of pre-independent Jamaica who challenged the race and gender status quo. She was in the forefront of social and political activism in the 1930s and the 1940s and the first woman to contest electoral politics in Jamaica.

Born in Newmarket, St. Elizabeth, she married Zechariah Knibb, a sanitary foreman. She was a Moravian, and her commitment to the church was evident to the time of her death, when she left her legacy to the church. As a Moravian she was well placed to the education she needed to qualify her for entry into Shortwood Teachers College. She was already a teacher at the age of twenty-one years. She taught at Saint Georges School from 1907 to 1917 and at the Wesley School from 1917 to 1928. Her pioneering spirit led her in 1928 to establish her own school, the Morris-Knibb Preparatory School, which she operated out of her own home in Woodford Park, St Andrew.

As a social and political activist in Jamaica, Morris Knibb organized, with Amy Bailey, the Women's Liberal Club in 1936 with the aim of training young women. The Women's Liberal Club was only one of the social and charitable organizations with which she was associated. She founded the Shortwood Old Girls' Association, was a member of the Women Teachers' Association, and served as vice president of the Jamaica Federation of Women. She was also associated with the Jamaica Save the Children Fund.

Much of Morris Knibb's work was devoted to the elevation of women and their children. The Women's Liberal Club provided the support she need to successfully agitate for women's entry into the public arena. Through the Women's Liberal Club, she sought to change the condition of lower-class young women by offering training in homemaking skills. She looked after the interest of middle-class women by encouraging the Women Teachers' Federation within the Jamaica Union of Teachers (JUT).

Because of her work among middle- and lower-class women and her association with other women in other service organizations, Knibb was aware of the class and race differences among women in Jamaica, and this awareness sometimes brought her in conflict with middle-class women over their attitude to black women. She was especially prepared, therefore, to give informed testimony to the Moyne Commission of 1938–1939. Her social awareness, interest in the well-being of women, and social activism qualified her for entry into the political arena. In 1939 she was elected to the Kingston and St. Andrew Corporation (KSAC), and by 1944 she had graduated to being the representative for East St. Andrew in the Jamaica Legislative Council. She ran as an independent candidate who was nominated by the club she had helped to form.

See also Education; Politics

■ ■ *Bibliography*

Levy, Owen L., and D. G. Wood, eds. *Personalities in the* Caribbean. Kingston, Jamaica: Personalities Ltd, 1962.

Shepherd, Verene A. ed. *Women in Caribbean History*. Kingston, Jamaica: Ian Randle Publishers, 1999.

Vassell, Linette. *Voices of Women in Jamaica, 1898–1939*. Kingston, Jamaica: Department of History, University of West Indies, 1993.

ALERIC J. JOSEPHS (2005)

MORRISON, TONI

FEBRUARY 18, 1931

By the 1980s Toni Morrison was considered by the literary world to be a major American novelist. In 1992—five years after she received the Pulitzer Prize for *Beloved* and the year of publication both for her sixth novel, *Jazz,* and for a series of lectures on American literature, *Playing in the Dark*—Morrison was being referred to internationally as one of the greatest American writers of all time. In 1993 she became the first black woman in history to be awarded the Nobel Prize for Literature.

The road to prominence began with Morrison's birth into a family she describes as a group of storytellers. Born Chloe Anthony Wofford in Lorain, Ohio, she was the second of four children of George Wofford (a steel-mill welder, car washer, and construction and shipyard worker) and Ramah Willis Wofford (who worked at home and sang in church).

Her grandparents came to the North from Alabama to escape poverty and racism. Her father's and mother's experiences with and responses to racial violence and economic inequality, as well as what Morrison learned about living in an economically cooperative neighborhood, influenced the political edge of her art. Her early understanding of the "recognized and verifiable principles of Black art," principles she heard demonstrated in her family's stories and saw demonstrated in the art and play of black people around her, also had its effect. Morrison's ability to manipulate the linguistic qualities of both black art and conventional literary form manifests itself in a prose that some critics have described as lyrical and vernacular at the same time.

After earning a B.A. from Howard University in 1953, Morrison moved to Cornell University for graduate work in English and received an M.A. in 1955. She taught at Texas Southern University from 1955 to 1957 and then at Howard University until 1964, where she met and married Harold Morrison, a Jamaican architect, and gave birth to two sons. Those were years that Morrison described as a period of almost complete powerlessness, when she wrote quietly and participated in a writers' workshop, creating the story that would become *The Bluest Eye.*

Toni Morrison. *Considered one of America's best novelists, Morrison received the Pulitzer Prize in 1988 for her fifth novel,* Beloved. © KATE KUNZ

In 1964 Morrison divorced her husband and moved to Syracuse, New York, where she began work for Random House. She later moved to a senior editor's position at the Random House headquarters in New York City—continuing to teach, along the way, at various universities. Since 1988 she has been Robert F. Goheen Professor of the Humanities at Princeton University.

Morrison's first novel, *The Bluest Eye* (1970), is a text that combines formal "play" between literary aesthetics and pastoral imagery with criticism of the effects of racialized personal aesthetics. *Sula* (1973) takes the pattern of the heroic quest and the artist-outsider theme and disrupts both in a novel that juxtaposes those figurations with societal gender restrictions amid the historical constraint of racism. *Song of Solomon* (1977), *Tar Baby* (1981), and *Beloved* (1987) are engagements with the relation to history of culturally specific political dynamics, aesthetics, and ritualized cultural practices.

Song of Solomon sets group history within the parameters of a family romance; *Tar Baby* interweaves the effects of colonialism and multiple family interrelationships that are stand-ins for history with surreal descriptions of landscape; and *Beloved* negotiates narrative battles over story and history produced as a result of the imagination's inability to make sense of slavery. In *Jazz,* Morrison continued her engagement with the problems and productiveness of individual storytelling's relation to larger, public history.

The lectures published as *Playing in the Dark* continue Morrison's interest in history and narrative. The collection abstracts her ongoing dialogue with literary criticism and history around manifestations of race and racism as narrative forms themselves produced by (and producers of) the social effects of racism in the larger public imagination.

Morrison's work sets its own unique imprimatur on that public imagination as much as it does on the literary world. A consensus has emerged that articulates the importance of Morrison to the world of letters and demonstrates the permeability of the boundary between specific cultural production—the cultural production that comes out of living as part of the African-American group—and the realm of cultural production that critics perceive as having crossed boundaries between groups and nation-states.

Morrison's ability to cross the boundaries as cultural commentator is reflected in *Race-ing Justice and Engendering Power: Essays on Anita Hill, Clarence Thomas, and the Construction of Social Reality,* a collection of essays about the nomination of Supreme Court Justice Clarence Thomas and the accusations of sexual harassment brought against him by law professor Anita Hill. The essays in the collection were written by scholars from various fields, then edited and introduced by Morrison. At the same time, she wrote poetry and lyrics for the song cycles "Dare Degga" and "Honey and Rue."

Morrison's reputation was confirmed in 1998 by the critical success of her novel *Paradise.* That year, with aid from entertainer Oprah Winfrey, her work also reached a new, wider public. After an endorsement from Winfrey's "Oprah's Book Club," sales of *Paradise* climbed into bestseller range. The same year, Winfrey produced and starred in a film adaptation of Morrison's novel *Beloved.*

Morrison's eighth novel, *Love,* was published in 2003 to high praise from critics. The following year, she also released a book for young people telling the story of school integration.

See also Literary Criticism, U.S.; Literature

■ ■ *Bibliography*

Campbell, W. John. *Toni Morrison: Her Life and Works.* New York: SparkNotes, 2003.

Lubiano, Wahneema. "Toni Morrison." In *African American Writers,* edited by Lea Baechler and A. Walton Litz. New York: Scribner's, 1991.

Middleton, David L. *Toni Morrison: An Annotated Bibliography.* New York: Taylor & Francis, 1987.

Morrison, Toni. "Memory, Creation, and Writing." *Thought* 59 (December 1984): 385–390.

WAHNEEMA LUBIANO (1996)
Updated by publisher 2005

MORTALITY AND MORBIDITY

▌ ▐ ▌ ──────────

This entry consists of two distinct articles examining mortality and morbidity among African Americans from differing geographic perspectives.

MORTALITY AND MORBIDITY IN LATIN
AMERICA AND THE CARIBBEAN
Carolina Giraldo
Keith Wailoo

MORTALITY AND MORBIDITY IN THE UNITED
STATES
Willie J. Pearson, Jr.
Norris White Gunby, Jr.

MORTALITY AND MORBIDITY IN LATIN AMERICA AND THE CARIBBEAN

Over the past five centuries, mortality and morbidity changes among the people of Afro-Latin America have been closely related to living conditions during the enslavement of Afro-Latin populations, and to their evolving socioeconomic situations after emancipation. High mortality during the slave period was related to many factors, including the length of time of the transatlantic journey and the diseases encountered during the journey; grueling labor conditions; poor housing and nutrition; and waves of epidemic disease that compromised people's health throughout the region. Of the estimated twelve million Africans transported by slave ships to the Americas between the sixteenth and the nineteenth centuries, an estimated 1.5 million died in transit (approximately 12.5 percent per

journey, although the mortality rate decreased from 40 percent in the sixteenth century to 5 to 10 percent in the nineteenth century). Transit within the colonies and into new disease environments brought further health risks.

Many enslaved Afro-Latin Americans came to reside in the tropical lowlands of Central and South America and on Caribbean islands. They labored on plantations, in ports, and along rivers where mosquito-related diseases, such as malaria and yellow fever, were prominent. It is frequently argued that Africans were more resistant to smallpox and malaria than Native Americans and Spaniards, but these and other infectious diseases were nonetheless among the leading causes of death among Afro-Latin Americans from the sixteenth century through the nineteenth and into the twentieth century. Afro-Latin Americans also died from yellow fever, typhoid, syphilis, measles, tuberculosis, and pneumonia. Throughout the colonial period, such epidemic outbreaks were frequent although localized; they could occasionally lead to the virtual extinction of entire communities.

Child mortality in such diverse contexts remained severe, particularly for populations of African descent. In the early nineteenth century, for example, Trinidad's slave infant mortality rate was 365 for every 1,000 live births. While it is certain that malnutrition accounted for heavy infant mortality, the exact toll on slave children remains uncertain. In some haciendas in Peru, for example, as many as 45 percent of black children never reached the age of twenty-two. Life expectancy at birth for enslaved peoples in Brazil was twenty-seven years in 1872.

Throughout the nineteenth century, a variety of factors—intense military conflicts and regional wars, trends in urbanization—altered mortality and morbidity patterns for Afro-Latin Americans. The promise of manumission brought many Afro-Latin Americans into the ranks of the patriot and royalist armies in the Spanish American wars, where soldiers fought under poor hygienic conditions, in inhospitable terrain, and where death tolls were high. With nineteenth-century urbanization, new epidemic diseases (cholera and tuberculosis most notoriously) emerged in high-poverty urban areas, resulting in disproportionately heavy mortality among enslaved and freed people who migrated to the cities. In Havana, Cuba, for example, a cholera epidemic in 1835 took the lives of 18,500 black men and women (a death rate 3.5 times higher than whites).

Despite the mortality threats posed by slavery, labor, urbanization, and epidemic disease, between 1700 and the mid-nineteenth century, Afro-Latin Americans witnessed a constant decrease in mortality. Whether the abolition of slavery had any large impact on morbidity and mortality trends remains a topic of debate.

In the twentieth century, high mortality rates associated with epidemics and endemic diseases persisted. The industrial nations of Europe and North America witnessed an "epidemiological transition" from the late nineteenth to the early- to mid-twentieth centuries—a decreasing death toll due to infectious disease and a rising toll due to degenerative and chronic diseases. Such a transition did not define the Central and South American disease experience, however. Where people in the industrial world experienced sharp declines in infant mortality and significant extensions in life expectancy, throughout Latin America this transition began to occur only after World War II. These trends were advanced, in no small part, by the spread of modern health institutions, by improvements in sanitation and hygiene, and by better access to health care for the general population.

Since the mid-twentieth century, Afro-Latin American morbidity and mortality have been linked to differential access to health care, the availability of proper nutrition, and poor hygienic conditions. These factors continue to put the Afro-Latin American populations (from Colombia to the Caribbean, from Haiti to Brazil) at a disadvantage when compared to the nonblack populations in these countries. Although there are differences between nations, the historical pattern of health inequality persists. In Brazil, for example, between 1960 and 1980 Afro-Brazilians could expect to live (on average) seven fewer years than the white population. In the Pacific region of Colombia the infant mortality rate was 191 per 1,000 births in 1993, a rate that surpassed the national average for every year since the 1960s.

Historically and in recent years, Afro-Latin American's mortality and morbidity experience has varied according to the wealth of the country. At one end of the spectrum today, Afro-Uruguayans (a group with good access to health services and making up 6 percent of the nation's population) experience respiratory diseases, asthma, high blood pressure, and diabetes (among the elderly) as their most prominent health problems. At the other end of the spectrum is Haiti, a country experiencing extreme poverty (and where 95 percent of the population claims African descent), which has one of the highest infant mortality rates in the world (95.23 deaths per 1,000 live births in 2001). Haiti's maternal mortality also remains remarkably high at 523 deaths per 100,000 live births. In 2000, life expectancy was forty-two years for Haitian women and forty-three for Haitian men.

The cases of Uruguay and Haiti exemplify the diverse epidemiological challenges faced by Afro-Latin Americans at the turn of the twenty-first century. Many nations of the region today, however, echo both situations. In Honduras,

72 percent of children show signs of malnutrition. In Ecuador, according to UNICEF, the predominant diseases among the black population of the Esmeraldas region are a combination of infectious diseases and chronic degenerative maladies, including malaria, uterine cancer, hypertension, vertigo, sexually transmitted diseases, respiratory problems (from pollution), malnutrition, anemia, cholera, dengue, and typhoid. Throughout the region, the socioeconomic situation of the Afro-Latino populations make them vulnerable to new infectious diseases such as HIV/AIDS and to sexually transmitted diseases. In Brazil and other nations of the region, the incidence of HIV has increased dramatically since the mid-1990s, especially among women. In Haiti, AIDS has become the leading cause of death, followed by tuberculosis, typhoid fever, malaria, and diarrhea.

See also AIDS in the Americas; Race and Science

■ ■ *Bibliography*

Barrett, Ronald, Christopher W. Kuzawa, Thomas McDade, and George J. Armelagos. "Emerging and Re-emerging Infectious Diseases: The Third Epidemiological Transition" *Annual Review of Anthropology* 27 (1998): 247–271.

Curtin, Philip D. "Epidemiology and the Slave Trade." *Political Science Quarterly* 83, no. 2 (1968): 190–216.

Cushner, Nicholas. "Slave Mortality and Reproduction on Jesuit Haciendas in Colonial Peru" *The Hispanic American Historical Review* 55, no. 2 (1975): 177–199.

Farmer, Paul. *AIDS and Accusation: Haiti and the Geography of Blame.* Berkeley: University of California Press, 1992.

Farmer, Paul. *Infections and Inequalities: The Modern Plagues.* Berkeley: University of California Press, 1999.

John, A. Meredith. *The Plantation Slaves of Trinidad, 1783–1816: A Mathematical and Demographic Enquiry.* New York: Cambridge University Press, 1988.

Karasch, Mary C. *Slave Life in Rio de Janeiro, 1808–1850.* Princeton, N.J.: Princeton University Press, 1987.

Kiple, Kenneth F. "Cholera and Race in the Caribbean." *Journal of Latin American Studies* 17, no. 1 (1985): 157–177.

Klein, Herbert S. *The Middle Passage: Comparative Studies in the Atlantic Slave Trade.* Princeton, N.J.: Princeton University Press, 1978.

Klein, Herbert S. *African Slavery in Latin America and the Caribbean.* New York: Oxford University Press, 1986.

Leff, Nathaniel H. "Long-Term Viability of Slavery in a Backward Closed Economy." *Journal of Interdisciplinary History* 5, no. 1 (1974): 103–108.

Manning, Patrick. "Migrations of Africans to the Americas: The Impact on Africans, Africa, and the New World." *The History Teacher* 26, no. 3 (1993): 279–296.

Morner, Magnus. "Recent Research on Negro Slavery and Abolition in Latin America." *Latin American Research Review* 13, no. 2 (1978): 265–289.

Sánchez, Margarita, Michael Franklin, and Cowater International Inc. *Poverty Alleviation Program for Minority Communities in Latin America: Communities of African Ancestry in Latin America—History, Population, Contributions, and Social Attitudes, Social and Economic Conditions* (Preliminary Version). Washington, D.C.: Inter-American Development Bank, 1996.

Scheper-Hughes, Nancy. *Death Without Weeping: The Violence of Everyday Life in Brazil.* Berkeley: University of California Press, 1992.

Wailoo, Keith. *Dying in the City of the Blues: Sickle Cell Anemia and the Politics of Race and Health.* Chapel Hill: University of North Carolina Press, 2001.

Wailoo, Keith. *Drawing Blood: Technology and Disease Identity in Twentieth-century America.* Baltimore: Johns Hopkins University Press, 1997.

Wood, Charles H., and José Alberto Magno de Carvalho. *The Demography of Inequality in Brazil.* New York: Cambridge University Press, 1988.

CAROLINA GIRALDO (2005)
KEITH WAILOO (2005)

MORTALITY AND MORBIDITY IN THE UNITED STATES

In the United States, African Americans, in comparison with whites, suffer enormous disadvantages in health status. In general, African Americans are at greater health risks throughout their life span. Because of this inequality, they do not live as long as whites.

INFANT MORTALITY

Over the past decades, infant mortality declined rapidly in the United States. Despite these declines, the United States still ranks twentieth worldwide in infant mortality. The rate varies considerably by race in the United States. For example, despite the improvements that have been made, in 2002 an African-American child was about 2.5 times as likely as a white child to die within the first year of life. Between 1960 and 2002 the infant-mortality rate for whites declined from 22.9 per 1,000 live births to 5.8 per 1,000 live births, whereas the African-American infant-mortality rate dropped from 44.3 per 1,000 to 14.4 per 1,000 live births. In some cities with large African-American populations, such as Washington, D.C., and Detroit, the infant-mortality rate of African-American babies exceeds that of some developing countries of Central America. In 2002, if the African-American and white infant mortality rates were equal, approximately 5,100 additional African-American babies would have survived.

In the United States the two leading causes of infant mortality are birth defects (19.2 percent) and length of gestation/low birth weight/fetal malnutrition (16.8 percent). While birth defects are the leading cause, it is developmental disabilities that result from low birth weights that appear to differentiate more greatly along racial lines. For example, African-American infants are 1.95 times as likely as white infants to be low weight (5.5 pounds or less). To a large extent these racial disparities may be explained by the vestiges of poverty, including poor or no prenatal care, poor nutrition, and lack of information about health care during pregnancy.

Typically, maternal mortality is defined as the number of deaths to women per 100,000 live births due to complications of pregnancy or childbirth or within ninety days postpartum. The disparities between African-American and white maternal-mortality rates actually exceed the infant-mortality rate differences. Despite overall reductions in maternal-mortality rates for both races, African-American mothers continue to experience a mortality rate that is greater than five times that of whites. In 2002, for example, the maternal-mortality rate for African Americans was 24.9, compared with only 4.8 for whites. There is considerable evidence that many of these deaths could have been prevented through early and adequate prenatal care.

LIFE EXPECTANCY

In 1960 white Americans could expect to live about 69.1 years, while African Americans and other races could expect to live roughly 8.3 years less. By 2002 the life expectancy of white and African Americans had climbed to 77.7 and 72.3 years, respectively, a difference of 5.4 years. Throughout this forty-two-year period, the gap between white and African-American life expectancy continued to decline, yet the persistence of this difference is still disturbing to health officials. Much of the variability in life expectancy is due to the continuing and alarmingly high death rates of young African-American males. In 2002 the life expectancy of African-American males was 6.8 years less than that of African-American females, and where the cause of death was homicide, the rate for African-American males was 38.4 per 100,000 while it was only 6.1 for everyone else. The death rate for African-American females aged fifteen to twenty-four is 54.4 per 100,000, while the rate for African-American males is 172.6; black males in this age cohort are three times more likely to die due to preventable risk factors.

LEADING CAUSES OF DEATH

Heart disease and stroke account for 35.5 percent of all excess deaths for African Americans under age seventy. (*Excess deaths* refers to the differential between the actual deaths and the number that would have occurred had African Americans and whites had the same death rates for each cohort and both sexes.) In 2002 there was a higher prevalence among African Americans than whites for cancer of the esophagus, larynx, lung, stomach, cervix, and pancreas. Generally, African-American women are 28 percent less likely than white women, and African-American men are 20 percent more likely than white men, to have cancer.

African Americans have lower five-year survival rates for all of the major cancer categories tracked by the National Cancer Institute, with the highest differentials in survival in uterine, bladder, and malignant neoplasms of the larynx.

OTHER DISEASES

The rate of blindness and visual impairment among African Americans is nearly twice that of whites. Among white and African Americans between the ages of forty and seventy-nine, African Americans have a higher rate of visual impairment. While African Americans represent approximately 12 percent of the population, they are overrepresented with 18 percent of the cases of blindness and visual impairment.

A goal of the U.S. Department of Health and Human Services is to eliminate childhood lead poisoning in the country by 2010. The percentage of persons with elevated blood lead levels is 5.3 for African Americans and only 1.5 for white Americans. This disparity represents a 350 percent higher rate of lead poisoning in African Americans. Lead poisoning has been associated with a number of social problems, including higher school dropout rates, higher incidence of reading disabilities, and lower performance and achievement in school.

In 2002 African Americans were diagnosed with end stage renal disease (ESRD) at a rate 3.9 times that of white Americans, and approximately 33 percent of the kidney failure incidence among African Americans can be attributed to hypertension. Additionally, African Americans were four times more likely to have ESRD as a result of diabetes than white Americans. Of the Americans in dialysis, 19.9 percent are African American. However, for those who receive transplants within three years of their initial diagnosis, the percentage for white Americans is 26.2 percent and only 11.6 percent for African Americans. These disparities could be greatly reduced by eliminating existing cultural barriers in organ donations and by aggressive action to find suitable matches between donors and recipients.

In 1981 acquired immune deficiency syndrome (AIDS) first received national media attention. The disease was widely regarded to be a gay disease, mostly affecting white males. During much of the 1980s the African-American community was reluctant to acknowledge the problem among its citizens. Some scholars attributed this denial to the strong cultural taboo against homosexuality. As the disease spread to other segments of the population, African Americans could no longer deny the problem. According to reports published in 1989 by the Federal Centers for Disease Control, African Americans were twice as likely as whites to contract AIDS. The reports concluded that more than half of all women afflicted with the disease in this country are African Americans; about 70 percent of babies born with the AIDS virus are African Americans, as are nearly one-fourth of all males with the disease. Unfortunately, these statistics have gotten progressively worse. In 2003 the AIDS rate for every 100,000 African-American males was eight times that of white males; for African-American females, the rate was twenty-two times that of white females. This differential rate in females also translates into a fifteen-fold difference in AIDS in African-American children compared to white children. The incidence of AIDS in the African-American community is attributable, in large measure, to the higher rate of intravenous drug use, in which drug users frequently exchange dirty needles. This practice of sharing needles is further complicated when the intravenous drug users engage in sexual practices that put themselves, their partners, and unborn children at risk.

See also AIDS in the Americas; Race and Science

■■ *Bibliography*

Blackwell, James E. *The Black Community: Diversity and Unity*, 3rd ed. New York: HarperCollins, 1991.

Health, United States, 2004 with Chartbook on Trends in the Health of Americans. Hyattsville, Md.: National Center for Health Statistics, National Vital Statistics System, 2004.

Jaynes, Gerald D., and Robin M. Williams, Jr., eds. *A Common Destiny: Blacks and American Society.* Washington, D.C.: National Academy Press, 1989.

McCord, C., and H. P. Freeman. "Excess Mortality in Harlem." *New England Journal of Medicine* 322 (1990): 173–177.

National Center for Health Statistics. *Health, United States, 2000.* Hyattsville, Md.: Public Health Service, 2000.

National Health and Nutrition Examination Surveys (NHANES), United States, 1991–1994 and 1999–2002.

Ries, L. A. G., et al., eds. *SEER Cancer Statistics Review, 1975–2002*, National Cancer Institute, Bethesda, Md. Available from <http://seer.cancer.gov/csr/1975_2002>, based on November 2004 SEER data submission, posted to the SEER Web site 2005.

United States Census Bureau, International Database. Available from <http://www.census.gov/ipc/www/idbprint.html>.

WILLIE J. PEARSON, JR. (1996)
NORRIS WHITE GUNBY, JR. (2005)

MOSELEY-BRAUN, CAROL

AUGUST 16, 1947

Carol Moseley, a U.S. Senator, was born and raised in Chicago, the daughter of a Chicago police officer. She was educated at public schools in Chicago and the University of Illinois at Chicago, and received a law degree from the University of Chicago in 1972. Although now divorced, she has used her married name throughout her public career but hyphenated it after joining the Senate.

Moseley-Braun worked for three years as a prosecutor in the U.S. Attorney's office in Chicago. For her work there she won the U.S. Attorney General's Special Achievement Award. She began her career in politics in 1978, when she successfully campaigned for a seat in the Illinois House of Representatives. While in the Illinois House she was an advocate for public education funding, particularly for schools in Chicago. She also sponsored a number of bills banning discrimination in housing and private clubs. After two terms Moseley-Braun became the first woman and first African American to be elected assistant majority leader in the Illinois legislature.

In 1987 Moseley-Braun again set a precedent by becoming the first woman and first African American to hold executive office in Cook County government when she was elected to the office of Cook County Recorder of Deeds. She held the office through 1992, when she waged a campaign for the U.S. Senate. When she defeated two-term incumbent Alan Dixon and wealthy Chicago attorney Al Hofeld in the Democratic primary, Moseley-Braun became the first black woman nominated for the Senate by a major party in American history. She then went on to defeat Republican nominee Rich Williamson in a close general election, becoming the first black woman to hold a seat in the U.S. Senate.

During her first year in the Senate Moseley-Braun sponsored several pieces of civil rights legislation, including the Gender Equity in Education Act and the 1993 Violence Against Women Act, and reintroduced the Equal Rights Amendment. She became unpopular following revelations of her personal use of campaign funds and as a result of her public support for Sami Abocha's dictatorial regime in Nigeria, where she visited in 1996. Following an acrimonious campaign, she was narrowly defeated for reelection in 1998.

Moseley-Braun accepted an appointment by the Clinton administration to become an ambassador to New Zealand and Samoa in 1999. She returned to the United States in 2001 and accepted a position as a visiting distinguished professor and scholar in residence at Morris Brown College. After a year there, she moved on to teach business law at DePaul University's College of Commerce. In 2003 Moseley-Braun added her name to the list of Democratic challengers for the party's 2004 presidential nomination. After a poor showing, she dropped out of the race in January 2004 and supported the candidacy of Vermont governor Howard Dean.

See also Politics and Political Parties, U.S.

▓ Bibliography

Hine, Darlene Clark, ed. *Black Women in America: An Historical Encyclopedia.* New York: Carlson, 1993.

Shalit, Ruth. "A Star Is Born." *New Republic* 209 (November 15, 1993): 18–25.

THADDEUS RUSSELL (1996)
Updated by publisher 2005

MOSES, ROBERT PARRIS

JANUARY 23, 1935

Civil rights activist and educator Bob Moses was born in New York City and raised in Harlem. He graduated from Hamilton College in 1956 and began graduate work in philosophy at Harvard University, receiving his master's degree one year later. Forced by his mother's death to leave school, Moses taught mathematics at a private school in New York City. He became active in the civil rights movement in 1959, when he worked with Bayard Rustin, a prominent Southern Christian Leadership Conference activist, on organizing a youth march for integrated schools. A meeting with civil rights activist Ella Baker inspired Moses to immerse himself in the civil rights movement that was sweeping the South. In 1960 he joined the Student Nonviolent Coordinating Committee (SNCC) and became the fledgling organization's first full-time voter registration worker in the Deep South.

Robert Parris Moses. Through his work with the Student Nonviolent Coordinating Committee (SNCC), Moses helped to elevate the struggle for civil rights in 1960s Mississippi from lunch-counter sit-ins to aggressive campaigns to educate and register black voters. PHOTOGRAPH BY RON CEASAR. REPRODUCED BY PERMISSION.

Moses, who often worked alone and faced many dangerous situations, was arrested and jailed numerous times. In McComb, Mississippi, he spearheaded black voter registration drives and organized Freedom Schools. He grew to play a more central role in SNCC, and in 1962 he became the strategic coordinator and project director of the Congress of Federated Organizations (COFO), a statewide coalition of the Congress of Racial Equality (CORE), SNCC, and the National Association for the Advancement of Colored People (NAACP). In 1963, COFO, with Moses as its guiding force, launched a successful mock gubernatorial election campaign, called the Freedom Ballot, in which black voters were allowed to vote for candidates of their choosing for the first time. Its success led Moses to champion an entire summer of voter registration and educational activities to challenge racism and segregation in 1964, called Freedom Summer, to capture national attention and force federal intervention in Mississippi.

During Freedom Summer, Moses played an integral role in organizing and advising the Mississippi Freedom Democratic Party, an alternative third party challenging the legitimacy of Mississippi's all-white Democratic Party delegation at the Democratic national convention in At-lantic City. After the 1964 summer project came to an end, SNCC erupted in factionalism. Moses's staunch belief in the Christian idea of a beloved community, nonhierarchical leadership, grassroots struggle, local initiative, and pacifism made him the leading ideologue in the early years of SNCC. Finding himself unwillingly drawn into the factional struggle, Moses left the organization and ended all involvement in civil rights activities. Later that year he adopted Parris—his middle name—as his new last name, to elude his growing celebrity.

A conscientious objector to the Vietnam War, Moses fled to Canada to avoid the draft in 1966. Two years later he traveled with his family to Tanzania, where he taught mathematics. In 1976 Moses returned to the United States and resumed his graduate studies at Harvard University. Supplementing his children's math education at home, however, led him away from the pursuit of a doctorate and back into the classroom. In 1980 he founded the Algebra Project, using money received from a MacArthur Foundation Genius Award, to help underprivileged children get an early grounding in mathematics to better their job opportunities in the future.

Moses viewed the Algebra Project—whose classes were directly modeled on Freedom Schools and citizenship schools of the early 1960s—as a continuation of his civil rights work. He oversaw all teacher training to ensure that they emphasized student empowerment, rather than dependence on the teachers. Creating a five-step process to help children translate their concrete experiences into complex mathematical concepts, Moses pioneered innovative methods designed to help children become independent thinkers. After demonstrating success by raising students' standardized test scores in Massachusetts public schools, the project branched out to schools in Chicago, Milwaukee, Oakland, and Los Angeles, and Moses was once again propelled into the public eye. In 1992, in what he saw as a spiritual homecoming, Moses returned to the same areas of Mississippi where he had registered African-American voters three decades earlier, and launched the Delta Algebra Project to help ensure a brighter future for children of that impoverished region.

Moses has been the recipient of numerous awards, including a 1997 Essence Award, a 1997 Peace Award from the War Resisters League, and a 1999 Heinz Award in the Human Condition.

See also Baker, Ella J.; Congress of Racial Equality (CORE); Freedom Summer; Mississippi Freedom Democratic Party; National Association for the Advancement of Colored People (NAACP); Rustin, Bayard; Southern Christian Leadership Conference (SCLC); Student Nonviolent Coordinating Committee (SNCC)

■ ■ *Bibliography*

Carson, Clayborne. *In Struggle: SNCC and the Black Awakening of the 1960s.* Cambridge, Mass.: Harvard University Press, 1981.

Jetter, Alexis. "Mississippi Learning." *New York Times Magazine* (February 21, 1993): 28.

McAdam, Doug. *Freedom Summer.* New York: Oxford University Press, 1988.

MARSHALL HYATT (1996)
Updated by publisher 2005

MOTLEY, ARCHIBALD JOHN, JR.

1891
JANUARY 19, 1991

■ ■ ■

The painter Archibald John Motley Jr. was born in New Orleans. In 1894, he and his family, who were Roman Catholic and of Creole ancestry, settled on Chicago's South Side. Motley graduated from Englewood High School in 1914, receiving his initial art training there, and then began four years of study at the School of the Art Institute of Chicago, from which he graduated in 1918.

During his study at the School of the Art Institute, Motley executed highly accomplished figure studies. In their subdued coloring, careful attention to modeling, and slightly broken brushwork, these works reflect the academic nature of the training he received at that institution. In the late 1910s and 1920s, as racial barriers thwarted his ambition to be a professional portraitist, Motley hired models and asked family members to pose for him. His sensitive, highly naturalistic portraits show his strong feeling for composition and color.

The young painter was honored in a commercially successful one-man exhibition of his work at New York City's New Gallery in 1928, and he spent the following year in Paris on a Guggenheim Fellowship. For this show Motley painted several imaginative depictions of African ethnic myths. Following the exhibition, he visited family members in rural Arkansas, where he created portraits and genre scenes, as well as landscapes of the region.

During his stay in Paris in 1929–1930, Motley portrayed the streets and cabarets of the French capital. In *Blues*, perhaps his best-known painting, he captured the vibrant and energetic mood of nightlife among Paris's African community.

After finding little outlet for his ambitions as a portraitist, Motley turned his talents to the subject of everyday life in Chicago's Black Belt. Deeply influenced by the syncopated rhythms, vibrant colors, and dissonant and melodic harmonies of jazz, his paintings evoke the streets, bars, dance halls, and outdoor gathering spots of Chicago's Bronzeville during its heyday of the 1920s and 1930s. He treated these subjects in a broad, simplified abstract style distinct from that of his portraits. Motley's Bronzeville views are informed by a modernist aesthetic.

A figure in Chicago's creative renaissance known as the New Negro movement and a participant in such mainstream artistic endeavors as the WPA Federal Arts Project, Motley applied a modernist sense of color and composition to images whose subjects and spirit drew on his ethnic roots. Between 1938 and 1941, he joined numerous other Illinois artists as an employee of the federally sponsored arts projects of the Depression era. For institutions in Chicago and other parts of the state he painted easel pictures and murals, the latter often on historical or allegorical themes.

Motley visited Mexico several times in the 1950s, where he joined his nephew, the writer Willard Motley, and a host of expatriate artists. His Mexican work ranges from brightly colored, small-scale landscapes to large, mural-like works that were influenced in style and subject by the social realism of modern Mexican art.

At the end of his career, Motley experimented in several new directions. In his long lifetime he produced a relatively small number of works, of which the most important, *The First One Hundred Years,* is his only painting with an overt political message. Today Motley is recognized as one of the founding figures of twentieth-century African-American art.

See also Art in the United States, Contemporary

■ ■ *Bibliography*

"Archibald Motley, Jr." *Contemporary Black Biography,* vol. 30. Detroit, Mich.: Gale, 2001.

Robinson, Jontyle Theresa. "Archibald John Motley, Jr.: Pioneer Artist of the Urban Scene." In *American Visions: Afro-American Art-1986,* edited by Carroll Greene Jr. Washington, D.C.: Visions Foundation, 1987.

Powell, Richard J. and David A. Bailey, eds. *Rhapsodies in Black: Art of the Harlem Renaissance.* Exhibition catalogue. Berkeley: University of California Press, 1997.

Robinson, Jontyle Theresa. "The Art of Archibald John Motley, Jr.: A Notable Anniversary for a Pioneer." In *Three Masters: Eldzier Cortor, Hughie Lee-Smith, Archibald John Motley, Jr.* Exhibition catalogue. New York: Kenkeleba Gallery, 1988.

Robinson, Jontyle Theresa, and Wendy Greenhouse. *The Art of Archibald J. Motley, Jr.* Chicago: Chicago Historical Society, 1991.

JONTYLE THERESA ROBINSON (1996)
Updated bibliography

MOTLEY, CONSTANCE BAKER

SEPTEMBER 14, 1921

Constance Baker Motley was the first African-American woman to be elected to the New York State Senate, the first woman to be elected Manhattan borough president, and the first black woman to be appointed a federal judge. She was born in New Haven, Connecticut, to immigrants from the Caribbean island of Nevis. She graduated from high school with honors in 1939 but could not afford college. Impressed by her participation in a public discussion and by her high school record, Clarence Blakeslee, a local white businessman, offered to pay her college expenses.

Motley enrolled at Fisk University in February 1941, transferred to New York University, and received a bachelor's degree in economics in October 1943. She enrolled at Columbia Law School in February 1944 and graduated in 1946. In 1945, during her final year at Columbia, she began to work part-time as a law clerk for Thurgood Marshall at the National Association for the Advancement of Colored People's (NAACP) Legal Defense and Educational Fund and continued there full-time after graduation, eventually becoming one of its associate counsels. Because Marshall's staff was small and there was little work being done in civil rights, Motley had the unusual opportunity to try major cases before circuit courts of appeal and the United States Supreme Court. From 1949 to 1964, she tried cases, primarily involving desegregation, in eleven southern states and the District of Columbia, including cases that desegregated the University of Mississippi (*Meredith v. Fair*, 1962) and the University of Georgia (*Homes v. Danner*, 1961). She helped write the briefs for the landmark desegregation case *Brown v. Board of Education* (1954) and won nine of the ten cases she argued before the Supreme Court.

She left the NAACP in 1964 to run for the New York State Senate, to which she was elected in February 1964, becoming only the second woman elected to that body. She left the Senate in February 1965, when she was elected Manhattan borough president, becoming only the third black to hold this office. On January 25, 1966, President Lyndon B. Johnson (1908–1973; served 1963–69) appointed her to the bench of the United States District Court for the Southern District of New York. She was confirmed in August 1966, becoming both the first black and the first woman to be a federal judge in that district. On June 1, 1982, she became the chief judge of her court, serving in this position until October 1, 1986, when she became a senior judge. Her memoir, *Equal Justice Under Law: An Autobiography,* was published in 1998. Five years later, Motley was inducted into the National Women's Hall of Fame. At the beginning of the twenty-first century, she was an active member of the Just The Beginning Foundation, an organization that commemorates and documents African-American lawyers and judges.

See also *Brown v. Board of Education of Topeka, Kansas*; Marshall, Thurgood; Politics and Political Parties, U.S.

■ ■ *Bibliography*

Lanker, Brian. *I Dream a World.* New York: Harry N. Abrams, 1989.

Motley, Constance Baker. "Some Reflections on My Career." *Law and Inequality* 6 (May 1988): 35–40.

Motley, Constance Baker. *Equal Justice Under Law: An Autobiography.* New York: Farrar, Straus, and Giroux, 1998.

SIRAJ AHMED (1996)
Updated by publisher 2005

MOTON, ROBERT RUSSA

AUGUST 26, 1867
MAY 31, 1940

Born in Amelia County, Virginia, and raised in Prince Edward County, Virginia, Robert Russa Moton, an educator, was educated by the daughter of his parents' plantation master. He entered Hampton Institute in Hampton, Virginia, in 1885, but three years later he interrupted his work to study law and teach. Moton received a license to practice law in 1888, then returned to Hampton. He studied and drilled in the student cadet corps, reaching the rank of assistant commandant. After graduation in 1890 he was named commandant of the corps and given the rank of "major," the title he would use for the rest of his life. He was the school disciplinarian, assigned to check on students' rooms and work. He had faculty and administrative responsibilities and was a liaison between the white faculty and the black student body.

During his later years at Hampton Moton also became a protégé and lieutenant of Booker T. Washington, president of Tuskegee Institute in Tuskegee, Alabama. He became active in Washington's National Negro Business League and accompanied Washington on speaking and fund-raising tours. Moton echoed Washington's views, emphasizing the need for self-improvement, thrift, and industrial education. In 1909 he helped the Tuskegee leader preview and comment on a draft of President Taft's inaugural address. In the early 1910s, after the creation of the NAACP, he tried to restrain its members from attacking accommodationist ideas. In 1915 he founded the Virginia Cooperative Association, a farmer's aid organization, which he hoped would be the basis of a nationwide movement.

In 1915, following the death of Booker T. Washington, Moton was chosen to succeed him as principal of Tuskegee Institute. Moton was never the charismatic figure Washington was, and he let Washington's political machine dissolve, but he continued Washington's work and racial leadership role. He lectured and wrote pieces extolling the Tuskegee philosophy and became chair of the National Negro Business League in 1919. He also became active in forming government commissions, which he thought a better avenue than civil rights legislation for resolving racial conflict. During World War I, Moton spoke at Liberty Bond rallies and tried to drum up support for the war effort. In 1918, after a spate of lynchings in the South, he helped form the Commission on Interracial Cooperation, which thereafter annually published lynching statistics. Moton retained a measure of Washington's control over federal political patronage to African Americans and advised government on racial policies. In 1918, after he privately warned President Woodrow Wilson of the growth of black unrest in America, Wilson sent him to France in order to speak to black soldiers and make a report on their treatment. He reported on his experiences in his autobiography, *Finding a Way Out* (1920).

During the 1920s Moton restructured Tuskegee, adding an accredited junior college program and planning a four-year curriculum. The school offered its first B.S. degree program in 1926. A skilled fund-raiser, Moton tripled Tuskegee's endowment. His concern for white donors' sensibilities caused him to crack down on black self-assertion and dissent at Tuskegee. However, he was willing to defend what he considered African Americans' best interests. He lobbied successfully for the creation of a black Veterans Administration hospital at Tuskegee Institute, to be staffed by African-American doctors and nurses. The Ku Klux Klan threatened violence unless he installed white medical staff, and a hundred Klansmen marched on Tus-

kegee. Moton barricaded the campus and called on alumni to help defend the institute. His actions won him widespread applause among blacks, including W. E. B. Du Bois, a frequent ideological adversary. Moton's general philosophy was expressed in his book *What the Negro Thinks* (1929). Moton forthrightly demanded an end to legislated racial inequality. However, he accepted segregation and called for compromise and black patience and work rather than activism to achieve civil rights aims.

Throughout the 1920s and 1930s Moton undertook public duties. He devised and lobbied for government assistance with National Negro Health Week. He succeeded Booker T. Washington on the board of trustees for Fisk University. In 1924 he founded and became president of the National Negro Finance Corporation in Durham, North Carolina. In 1927 he headed a committee of African Americans involved with the Hoover presidential commission on the Mississippi Flood Disaster. He served on President Herbert Hoover's National Advisory Committee on Education and recommended federal funding to reduce racial inequality in education. He also served on a commission on education in Liberia and wrote a strong report on educational inequities in Haiti. For his work Moton received the Harmon Award in Race Relations in 1930 and the NAACP's Spingarn Medal in 1932. Moton retired from Tuskegee in 1935 and died five years later at his home in Capahosic, Virginia, where the Robert R. Moton Foundation was later established in his memory to aid black scholars.

See also Du Bois, W. E. B.; Hampton Institute; Lynching; Spingarn Medal; Tuskegee University

■ ■ *Bibliography*

Anderson, James D. *The Education of Blacks in the South, 1860–1935.* Chapel Hill: University of North Carolina Press, 1988.

Bennett, Lerone Jr. "Chronicles of Black Courage: Robert R. Moton risked life in fight for Black doctors at Tuskegee Veterans Hospital." *Ebony* 57, no. 9 (July 2002): 158–160.

Butler, Addie Louise Joyner. *The Distinctive Black College: Talladega, Tuskegee, and Morehouse.* Metuchen, N.J.: Scarecrow Press, 1977.

Harlan, Louis, and Raymond W. Smock, eds. *The Booker T. Washington Papers,* vols. 3, 10–13. Urbana: University of Illinois Press, 1972–1989.

GREG ROBINSON (1996)
Updated bibliography

MOUND BAYOU, MISSISSIPPI

Considered by many to be the first all-African-American town in the South, Mound Bayou, Mississippi, was founded in 1888 by Isaiah T. Montgomery and Benjamin Green. The two cousins created what they believed to be a haven for African Americans who sought self-determination; the community also served as a capital venture intended to improve the fortunes of the Montgomery family.

The idea for Mound Bayou was conceived in the 1880s after the Louisville, New Orleans, and Texas Railroad (L.N.O. & T.) began developing a railroad line stretching from Memphis, Tennessee, to Vicksburg, Mississippi. Railroad officials believed that few whites would settle along the swampy land where the potential for disease was high; they thought, however, that African Americans were racially suited to the climate and could flourish under such conditions. As a result, the company set aside tracts of wilderness along the route for sale. Mound Bayou was forged from an 840-acre section of wetland, including two merging bayous and a number of Native American burial mounds, which lay on both sides of the tracks that ran through Bolivar County, Mississippi.

The first settlers cleared land, planted crops, and opened their own businesses. Through mass advertising campaigns, which encouraged black settlers to form an all-black community, and with the support of national figures such as Booker T. Washington, Mound Bayou thrived and grew to become one of the Mississippi Delta's most successful towns. It also had the distinction of being the largest African-American city in the nation. At its peak in 1907, Mound Bayou was home to more than eight hundred families, with a total of approximately four thousand residents.

In an era of sharecropping and peonage for much of Mississippi's black population, inhabitants of Mound Bayou—mostly doctors, lawyers, and small farmers—had a standard of living that exceeded most black, and some white, communities. It was a close-knit town that brought local issues before town meetings and sought the approval of its citizens before embarking upon new projects. Residents, citing a negligible crime rate, boasted of having torn down the local jail. They attributed this fortune to community spirit.

Community spirit aside, much of Mound Bayou's good fortune came from outside sources. Booker T. Washington was a vocal supporter of Mound Bayou in the early twentieth century; through Washington's intercession with financiers around the country, Charles Banks (1873–1923), a leading developer in Mound Bayou at the time, was able to float several ambitious projects, including a cottonseed oil mill and the Bank of Mound Bayou. The oil mill, whose stock was bolstered by contributions from such outside investors as white philanthropist Julius Rosenwald, was initially capitalized at $100,000; it promised to be the industrial centerpiece of the small town.

By 1914, however, economic problems plagued Mound Bayou. The falling price of cotton and a lack of capital forced many residents to depend upon credit extended by white merchants from other communities. As economic conditions worsened, it became more and more difficult for local farmers to get the credit they needed for planting. The much heralded oil mill, opened in dramatic fashion by Booker T. Washington in November 1912, never actually went into production under the supervision of African Americans; its owners and shareholders were forced to cede control of the mill to B. B. Harvey of Memphis, an unscrupulous white businessman, while the bank failed in the fall of 1914 amid allegations of mismanagement. As the price of cotton rose during World War I, the corresponding drop in prices after the war brought little relief to the residents. Hundreds fled north as part of the first great migration during the war in search of better economic opportunities. Fewer than nine hundred residents remained by 1930.

Mound Bayou remained troubled during the 1930s and 1940s. A fire decimated most of the business district in 1941. In the same year, one observer noted that Mound Bayou was "mostly a town of old folks an' folks getting old." By World War II prosperity and pride had been replaced by poverty and disillusionment.

After World War II general prosperity nationwide brought a limited degree of revitalization to Mound Bayou. In the 1960s some black nationalists brought Mound Bayou back to the spotlight by endorsing the desirability of all-black towns. In 1966 the Tufts University Department of Community Medicine, funded by a grant from the federal Office of Economic Opportunity, established an outpatient health center in Mound Bayou. Although there was some population increase, the number of inhabitants never again reached its 1907 peak. The 1970 census showed a population of slightly more than two thousand.

The 1970s witnessed an economic upsurge. Under the administration of Mayor Earl Lucas, who was elected in 1969, Mound Bayou attracted outside support for various projects. Tufts University continued to channel funds from the federal government into the local clinic and hospital. Although the funds were now granted by the Depart-

Booker T. Washington speaks to a crowd at the dedication of a cotton seed mill in Mound Bayou, Mississippi, c. 1912. With the support of national figures like Washington, Mound Bayou grew to a city of some four thousand residents early in the twentieth century, becoming the largest African-American city in the U.S. during that period. © CORBIS

ment of Health and Human Services (HHS), Tufts was charged with the administration of the clinic, which served the four surrounding counties. The clinic merged with the Mound Bayou Community Hospital in 1978. The two facilities were responsible for 450 jobs and served as the bulwark of the local economy. In 1977 Mound Bayou also received $4.9 million in public works funds from the U.S. Economic Development Agency; the grant was almost half of the $10 million appropriation for the entire state. In the same year, civil rights activist Fannie Lou Hamer, who spent her last years in Mound Bayou, died at the local hospital.

Unfortunately, by the beginning of the 1980s, the town had once again fallen on hard times. Economic cutbacks under the Reagan administration eliminated the jobs of some townspeople; at one point more than half of the residents of the town relied on either federal or state assistance for support. In 1982 a Memphis radio station raised $120,000 from the black community in one week to help diminish Mound Bayou's $209,000 debt. While this measure showed the overall support for the town, the 1990 census only registered 2,200 residents; more than one quarter of the town's population left Mound Bayou during the 1980s.

In the 1990s various other crises affected Mound Bayou. While Mayor Earl Lucas had been partly responsible for attracting funding for the hospital and federal grants, his administration left office after twenty-four years in 1993 with a municipal debt of more than $500,000. Although Lucas had been defeated in a 1989 election, due to a lawsuit alleging election improprieties in 1989, no new mayor was allowed to take office in Mound Bayou until Nerissa Norman became its first female mayor in a court-ordered special election in June 1993. Norman pledged to try to curtail municipal spending and attempted to reduce some of the small town's debt.

See also Black Towns; Migration

Bibliography

Chambers, Caneidra. "Mound Bayou: Jewel of the Delta." Available from <http://ocean.st.usm.edu/~aloung/mbayou.htm>.

Crockett, Norman L. *The Black Towns.* Lawrence: Regents Press of Kansas, 1979.

Hermann, Janet Sharp. *The Pursuit of a Dream.* New York: Oxford University Press, 1981.

Mound Bayou, Mississippi Centennial Celebration: July 6–12, 1987. Mound Bayou, Miss., 1987.

JOEL N. ROSEN (1996)
Updated bibliography

MOVIMENTO NEGRO UNIFICADO

The Movimento Negro Unificado (MNU, or Unified Black Movement), widely considered the most influential black organization in Brazil in the second half of the twentieth century, was founded in São Paulo in 1978 as the Movimento Unificado Contra Discriminacao Racial (United Movement Against Racial Discrimination, or MUCDR). It arose from a collection of black organizations that had been meeting for two years with similar groups from Rio de Janeiro, with the intention of forming a national black movement. Two events in São Paulo acted as catalysts: the killing of a black worker, Robson Silveira de Luz, by the police; and the race-based expulsion of four black boys from a volleyball team.

The new organization was founded on June 18, 1978, to protest those acts and to start a national black movement. Its first act was a demonstration on the steps of the Municipal Theater in São Paulo on July 7th, 1978. At the time, Brazil was under a military dictatorship. However, while Brazil's vast African-descended population was virtually excluded from any arena of leadership and was mired in poverty and illiteracy, the regime portrayed the country as a racial democracy. The impetus for starting a black movement came from intellectuals, students, and trade union members intent on correcting this distortion of reality.

Approximately 2,000 people attended the July 7 demonstration, an unprecedented occurrence during the dictatorship. On July 23, the organization changed its name to the Movimento Negro Unificado Contra Discriminacao Racial (United Black Movement Against Racial Discrimination, or MNUCRD). At the first National Congress in Rio de Janeiro, in December 1979, the name was shortened to the Movimento Negro Unificado (Unified Black Movement). The organization adopted two national campaigns: one named Jobs for Blacks, and one calling for an end to police violence.

Because race is ambiguous in Brazil (with Brazilians generally focusing on color, rather than race), a chief responsibility of the MNU was to develop and popularize a useful definition of blackness. The standard chosen was appearance: namely, skin color, facial appearance, and hair. At the end of the congress, the MNU stopped being a national black movement and became the only national black organization. It established structures, procedures, officers, and membership categories. Despite its name, the MNU was not all-encompassing. It did not unite black organizations, nor was it a movement. It was, explicitly, an organization *within* a movement.

The MNU adopted ambitious national and international agendas. Domestically, within four years the organization established chapters in nine states. The MNU worked with other black and progressive organizations, attacking the myth of racial democracy and calling for the establishment of a true racial democracy. A black vision of politics for Brazil was thus established. The MNU castigated police violence, the oppression of black women, and the marginalization of gays. The organization proposed November 20 as the National Day of Black Consciousness, in memory of Zumbi, the legendary leader of the *quilombo* (Maroon society), Palmares. The MNU also supported the ancestral rights of contemporary *quilombo* residents. A quarterly newspaper was established, at first entitled *Nego*, and after 1989 called the *MNU Jornal.*

Internationally, MNU members participated in progressive conferences on apartheid, women's rights, and black rights. They presented research papers on Afro-Brazilians at academic conferences, trying to set the record straight about race in Brazil. Through the mid-1990s, the MNU set the tone for Brazilian militant black organizations. While recognizing the importance of culture, it stressed the significance of politics, for its strength was political education. Publications and numerous activities, such as demonstrations, lobbying, public forums, public celebrations, electoral politics, and legal action, were used to inform the population. The MNU endorsed political candidates and sponsored its own. MNU members have been elected to the National Congress, state legislatures, and city councils. Most MNU members elected to office have been members of the Workers' Party, though the MNU has no affiliation with any political party and its members belong to many parties.

In 1995 the MNU was the primary organizer of the March for Zumbi, a protest against Brazilian racism and a celebration of the 300-year anniversary of Zumbi's death. At least 40,000 activists arrived in the nation's capital of Brasília for the march on November 20. It was the largest national black demonstration ever held in Brazil.

The MNU fell on hard times during the late 1990s, mainly due to Brazil's financial troubles; internal disputes; and the development of other black organizations, notably domestic nongovernmental organizations (NGOs). National congresses became infrequent, and the *MNU Journal* was published irregularly. Although the MNU continued, it lacked its earlier vigor. In 2000 the MNU, along with the whole Brazilian Black Movement, was reinvigorated by prospects for the third United Nations World Conference against Racism, scheduled to be held in Durban, South Africa, during August and September of 2001. The MNU adopted an aggressive organizing strategy, joined other black organizations to develop a national black agenda, and sent a substantial delegation to Durban. By the time of the 2002 World Social Forum, held in Porto Alegre, Brazil, the MNU was the principal black organizational participant. Internally, it had adopted the practice of democratic centralism, a program calling for reparations for African-descended peoples globally, and the goal of a socialist Brazil.

The MNU has been an articulate voice in the struggle to destroy prevailing Brazilian racial myths and to create new understandings. The organization has never achieved a mass base, however, but has always been comprised primarily of students, intellectuals, trade union members, and other activists. Nonetheless, it was the most consistent, and perhaps the most effective, voice in changing Brazil's public discourse on race during the last quarter of the twentieth century, and it has continued its work at the beginning of the twenty-first century.

See also Frente Negra Brasileira

■■ *Bibliography*

Covin, David. "Afrocentricity in *O Movimento Negro Unificado.*" *Journal of Black Studies* 21, no. 2 (December, 1990): 126–144.

Covin, David. *Axe', The Unified Movement in Brazil and the Search for Black Political Power (1978–2002).* Jefferson, N.C.: McFarland & Co., Inc., 2005.

Gonzalez, Lelia. "The Unified Black Movement: A New Stage in Black Political Mobilization." In *Race, Class, and Power in Brazil,* edited by Pierre-Michele Fontaine. Los Angeles: Center for Afro-American Studies, UCLA, 1985.

Hanchard, Michael. *Orpheus and Power: the Movimento Negro of Rio de Janeiro and São Paulo Brazil, 1945–1988.* Princeton, N.J.: Princeton University Press, 1994.

Hanchard, Michael, ed. *Racial Politics in Contemporary Brazil.* Durham, N.C.: Duke University Press, 1999.

DAVID L. COVIN (2005)

MOYNE COMMISSION

■■■

By the time of the Great Depression, which was particularly devastating for the plantation/mineral economies of the British Caribbean, the British government had established a tradition of appointing special committees or commissions to investigate the causes of crises that periodically occurred in different parts of the British Empire. Such crises were generally economic or political, and depending on the perceived gravity of the situation, the investigating team would carry the special seal of British authority by being designated a Royal Commission.

Such was the situation in the British Caribbean in the 1930s, which led to the appointment in late 1938 of a ten-member Royal Commission of Enquiry chaired by Lord Moyne. Moyne was the former Walter Guinness, who had had a distinguished record as a British member of Parliament from 1907 to 1931 and subsequently served as chairman of a number of committees or commissions appointed by the British government. The other members of the Royal Commission were each chosen for his or her expertise, deemed relevant to the commission's investigation, in such fields as tropical disease, social work, trade union activity, colonial administration, economics, tropical agriculture, banking, and politics.

LABOR UNREST

At the time of the commission's appointment, the British Caribbean from Belize to Barbados was being overtaken by a wave of labor unrest, beginning as "hunger marches" of the unemployed in the early 1930s and then developing in the later 1930s into strikes on plantations and mineral zones, accompanied by some violence and fatalities. The most threatening of these strikes were those that developed in the oilfields of Trinidad in June 1937 and spread quickly to sugar and cocoa plantations. In the same year, the normally tranquil Barbados experienced labor unrest on its sugar plantations, and the following year the strike movement spread to Jamaica. Such labor unrest was not confined to the British Caribbean colonies in the 1930s but engulfed American-administered Puerto Rico as well as politically independent Mexico and Venezuela. This was clear evidence that the root causes of the unrest were systemic, that is, a product of the crisis in the global capitalist system. This system was even more severe on the colonial and neocolonial economies of the Caribbean, which remained dependent on a very narrow base of raw material exports to meet the requirements of growing populations for the basic necessities of life, not to mention an improved standard of living.

The commission was given the broad mandate to "investigate social and economic conditions in Barbados, British Guiana, British Honduras, Jamaica, the Leeward Islands, Trinidad and Tobago, and the Windward Islands, and matters connected therewith, and to make recommendations" (Cmd 6607, p. xiii). It was understood that the commission's mandate included the consideration of constitutional problems insofar as they might be relevant to social and economic problems.

MOYNE COMMISSION'S RECOMMENDATIONS

Appointed by royal warrant on August 5, 1938, the commission arrived on November 1, 1938, in the Caribbean, where it spent approximately five months, with some members even visiting Puerto Rico and the French islands, presumably with a view to comparing general conditions there with those in the British Caribbean.

By the time the commission's report was submitted on December 21, 1939, the European phase of World War II had broken out. The British government decided to release only a summary of the commission's recommendations during the war, the full report being officially withheld until July 1945. Among the recommendations was the establishment of an imperial financial grant, known as the West Indian Welfare Fund, amounting to one million pounds sterling per annum over a twenty-year period to assist in development and social welfare programs. This was a relatively paltry sum for the whole of the British West Indies. Nevertheless, the publication of this recommendation was intended to have propaganda value by convincing the British Caribbean peoples that even though it was engaged in war, the British government was taking its responsibility as trustee for its Caribbean colonies seriously and it expected His Majesty's Caribbean subjects to remain loyal to Great Britain in its hour of need. Even so, popular Caribbean opinion was not impressed. Most trenchant perhaps was the comment of the Trinidad labor leader and lawyer Adrian Cola Rienzi, who pointedly observed that Great Britain was spending six million pounds sterling per day on war but "could only afford one million pounds sterling a year for twenty years to remedy the disgraceful and shocking conditions which exist in the colonies and for which she, as Trustee, must be held accountable" (Singh, 1994, p. 190).

The full report of the commission, when it was eventually released in 1945, was quite comprehensive, covering almost every aspect of the economic, social, and political conditions in the British Caribbean. Yet, as the report itself confessed, most of these conditions had been known and deplored for many years, being the subject of numerous inquiries, both local and imperial. Nor did the report go much beyond what previous reports had recommended, except in the proposal for the West Indian Welfare Fund, to be administered by a new brace of colonial officials. The commission, like its predecessors, saw little economic prospect for most of the islands except as plantation colonies, with a greater degree of peasant agriculture and, where possible, some agroprocessing industries. Politically, it was prepared to concede constitutional reform but not political independence for the islands either as individual units or collectively as a federation. Indeed, it argued that "the claim for independence is irreconcilable with that control which, though not necessarily in its present form, must continue to be exercised, in the interests of the home taxpayer, over the finances of the colonies receiving substantial financial assistance from funds provided by Parliament" (Cmd 6607, p. 374). The commission was, therefore, not prepared to dispense with executive control by colonial governors over local legislative councils. Even though it was receptive to the popular Caribbean demand for a widening of the elective franchise, it looked forward to co-opting leading elected members of reformed legislative councils into the governor's executive council and select committees. In short, political change would be more in form than in substance.

It is hardly any wonder that once the recommendations became known, political and labor leaders in the British Caribbean became more convinced than ever that only political independence would enable their countries to achieve significant economic and social change.

See also International Relations in the Anglophone Caribbean; Urban Poverty in the Caribbean

■■ *Bibliography*

Bolland, O. Nigel. *On the March: Labour Rebellions in the British Caribbean, 1934–1939*. Kingston, Jamaica: Ian Randle, 1975.

Cartwright, Timothy J. *Royal Commissions and Departmental Committees in Britain*. London: Hodder and Stoughton, 1975.

Cmd 6607: West Indian Royal Commission (Moyne) Report. London: His Majesty's Stationery Office, 1945.

Johnson, Howard. "The Political Uses of Commissions of Enquiry: The Foster and Moyne Commissions." In *The Trinidad Labour Riots of 1937: Perspectives 50 Years Later*, edited by Roy Thomas. St. Augustine, Trinidad: Extra-Mural Studies Unit, University of the West Indies, 1985.

Singh, Kelvin. *Race and Class Struggles in a Colonial State: Trinidad 1917–1945*. Calgary, Alberta: University of Calgary Press; Mona, Jamaica: The Press–University of the West Indies, 1994.

KELVIN SINGH (2005)

MUDDY WATERS (MORGANFIELD, MCKINLEY)

APRIL 4, 1915
APRIL 30, 1983

▪▪▪

The blues singer and guitarist McKinley Morganfield, commonly known as Muddy Waters, grew up in Clarksdale, Mississippi, and took up the harmonica at age seven. He switched to the guitar at seventeen and soon began playing at local gatherings. He recorded both as a soloist and with a string band in 1941-1942 for a Library of Congress field-recording project. After moving to Chicago in 1943, he began playing the electric guitar, and by 1947 he was recording for the Aristocrat label (later Chess Records) under the name Muddy Waters. He began performing with a band that featured the harmonica player Little Walter; their recording "Louisiana Blues," made late in 1950, became a nationwide hit, entering the rhythm-and-blues Top Ten. The band, which also included Otis Spencer (pianist) and Jimmy Rogers (guitar), had many Top Ten hits in the 1950s, including "I'm Your Hoochie Coochie Man" (1953) and "I'm Ready" (1954). Muddy Waters continued to tour throughout the United States and Europe in the 1960s and received much acclaim as a primary influence on many "British Invasion" musicians. He remained active as a performer for the rest of his life, winning Grammy awards for several later recordings. He was inducted posthumously into the Rock and Roll Hall of Fame in 1987.

Muddy Waters retained a style that evoked the sound of the Delta blues. His Library of Congress recordings illustrate the influence of Son House through their searing slide guitar playing, which he maintained throughout his band recordings in the 1950s. In contrast to the smoother Chicago blues of Big Bill Broonzy (1893–1958), Muddy Waters brought a tough, aggressive edge to the urban blues, making him a seminal figure in the development of the style and establishing him among the most important post–World War II blues singers.

See also Blues, The

▪▪ *Bibliography*

Gordon, Robert. *Can't Be Satisfied: The Life and Times of Muddy Waters.* Boston: Little, Brown, 2002.

Obrecht, Jas. "Biography of a Bluesman." *Guitar Player* 17, no. 8 (August 1983): 48–57.

Oliver, Paul. *Muddy Waters.* Bexhill-on-Sea, England, 1964.

Tooze, Sandra B. *Muddy Waters: The Mojo Man.* Toronto: ECW Press, 1997.

Waters, Muddy. *Muddy Waters: The Anthology, 1947–1972.* Compact disc. MCA Records, 2000.

DANIEL THOM (1996)
Updated bibliography

MUHAMMAD, ELIJAH

OCTOBER 10, 1897
FEBRUARY 25, 1975

▪▪▪

The religious leader Elijah Muhammad was born Robert Elijah Poole in Sandersville, Georgia. He was one of thirteen children of an itinerant Baptist preacher and sharecropper. In 1919 he married Clara Evans and they joined the black migration to Detroit, where he worked in the auto plants. In 1931 he met Master Wallace Fard (or Wali Farad), founder of the Nation of Islam, who eventually chose this devoted disciple as his chief aide. Fard named him "Minister of Islam," dropped his slave name, Poole, and restored his true Muslim name, Muhammad. As the movement grew, a Temple of Islam was established in a Detroit storefront. It is estimated that Fard had close to 8,000 members in the Nation of Islam, consisting of poor black migrants and some former members from Marcus Garvey's Universal Negro Improvement Association and Noble Drew Ali's Moorish Science Temple.

After Fard mysteriously disappeared in 1934, the Nation of Islam was divided by internal schisms. Elijah Muhammad led a major faction to Chicago, where he established Temple of Islam No. 2 as the main headquarters for the Nation. He also instituted the worship of Master Fard as Allah and himself as the Messenger of Allah and head of the Nation of Islam, always addressed with the title "the Honourable." Muhammad built on the teachings of Fard and combined aspects of Islam and Christianity with the black nationalism of Marcus Garvey into a "proto-Islam," an unorthodox Islam with a strong racial slant. The Honorable Elijah Muhammad's message of racial separation focused on the recognition of true black identity and stressed economic independence. "Knowledge of self" and "do for self" were the rallying cries. The economic ethic of the Black Muslims has been described as a kind of black puritanism, consisting of hard work, frugality, the avoidance of debt, self-improvement, and a conservative lifestyle. Muhammad's followers sold the Nation's newspaper, *Muhammad Speaks,* and established their own educational system of Clara Muhammad schools and small businesses such as bakeries, grocery stores, and outlets selling fish and bean pies. More than one hundred temples were founded. The disciples also followed strict dietary rules outlined in Muhammad's book *How to Eat to Live,* which enjoined one meal per day and complete abstention from pork, drugs, tobacco, and alcohol. The Nation itself owned farms in several states, a bank, trailer trucks for its fish and grocery businesses, an ultramodern printing press, and other assets.

Muhammad's ministers of Islam found the prisons and the streets of the ghetto a fertile recruiting ground. His message of self-reclamation and black manifest destiny struck a responsive chord in the thousands of black men and women whose hope and self-respect had been all but defeated by racial abuse and denigration. As a consequence of where they recruited and the militancy of their beliefs, the Black Muslims have attracted many more young black males than any other black movement.

Muhammad had an uncanny sense of the vulnerabilities of the black psyche during the social transitions brought on by two world wars; his *Message to the Black Man in America* diagnosed the problem as a confusion of identity and self-hatred caused by white racism. The cure he prescribed was radical surgery through the formation of a separate black nation. Muhammad's 120 "degrees," or lessons, and the major doctrines and beliefs of the Nation of Islam all elaborated on aspects of this central message. The white man is a "devil by nature," absolutely unredeemable and incapable of caring about or respecting anyone who is not white. He is the historic, persistent source of harm and injury to black people. The Nation of Islam's central theological myth tells of Yakub, a black mad scientist who rebelled against Allah by creating the white race, a weak, hybrid people who were permitted temporary dominance of the world. Whites achieved their power and position through devious means and "tricknology." But, according to the Black Muslim apocalyptic view, there will come a time in the not-too-distant future when the forces of good and the forces of evil—that is to say, blacks versus whites—will clash in a "Battle of Armageddon," and the blacks will emerge victorious to recreate their original hegemony under Allah throughout the world.

After spending four years in a federal prison for encouraging draft refusal during World War II, Elijah Muhammad was assisted by his chief protégé, Minister Malcolm X, in building the movement and encouraging its rapid spread in the 1950s and 1960s. During its peak years, the Nation of Islam had more than half a million devoted followers (while influencing millions more) and accumulated an economic empire worth an estimated $80 million. Besides his residence in Chicago, Muhammad also lived in a mansion outside of Phoenix, Arizona, since the climate helped to reduce his respiratory problems. He had eight children with his wife, Sister Clara Muhammad, but also fathered a number of illegitimate children with his secretaries, a circumstance that was one of the reasons for Malcolm X's final break with the Nation of Islam in 1964.

With only a third-grade education, Elijah Muhammad was the leader of the most enduring black militant movement in the United States. He died in Chicago and was succeeded by one of his six sons, Wallace Deen Muhammad. After his death, Muhammad's estate and the property of the Nation were involved in several lawsuits over the question of support for his illegitimate children.

See also Garvey, Marcus; Malcolm X; Nation of Islam; Noble Drew Ali; Universal Negro Improvement Association

▪ ▪ *Bibliography*

Lincoln, C. Eric. *The Black Muslims in America.* 3d ed. Grand Rapids, Mich.: W. B. Eerdsmans, 1993.

Muhammad, Elijah. *How to Eat to Live.* Chicago: Muhammad Mosque of Islam No. 2, 1972.

Muhammad, Elijah. *Message to the Blackman in America.* Chicago: Muhammad Mosque of Islam No. 2, 1965; reprint, Newport News, Va.: United Brothers, 1992.

LAWRENCE H. MAMIYA (1996)

MULZAC, HUGH
MARCH 26, 1886
JANUARY 31, 1971

◼▌◼

Hugh Mulzac, a seaman, was born on March 26, 1886, on Union Island, one of the small islands of the multistate of St. Vincent and the Grenadines. After completing secondary education in the capital town, Kingstown, he was lured to the sea. This was not surprising since in the small islands of the Grenadines the sea was always a central part of one's childhood consciousness. Moreover his father had moved from cotton planting to a preoccupation with the shipbuilding and whaling business. He began by sailing the islands of the eastern Caribbean in a ship captained by his brother before deciding to volunteer as a seaman on a ship commanded by a Norwegian, the son of a missionary.

Thus began a career that found him working on a variety of ships in England and Europe before moving to

America in 1911. He worked his way through the ranks while at the same time educating himself at the Swansea Nautical School in Wales, and later obtained a master's license in the United States with a perfect score. Mulzac held two diplomas and master's papers for some twenty years before he was given his own ship and gained the distinction of being the first black person to command an American merchant ship. That ship was the *Booker T. Washington,* named after the famous black American who founded the Tuskegee Institute. The launching of the *Booker T.* was a much celebrated occasion that highlighted a performance by the famous black contralto, Marion Anderson.

Mulzac's achievement came after a long struggle against racial discrimination. Despite his qualifications and experience, for a long period of time he was only able to receive work as a steward and chief cook. When given command of the *Booker T. Washington* in 1942, the intention was to put him in charge of what would have been a Jim Crow ship. He refused and demanded an integrated crew, which he finally got. Under Mulzac the *Booker T. Washington* became a model ship with union meetings, educational activities, and fund-raising for a variety of causes being held on board.

Despite his war service, Mulzac was blacklisted during the McCarthy era for his membership in a number of organizations, among them the Council for West Indian Federation. He was called before a House Committee and questioned about his political beliefs and associations. He had been involved with Marcus Garvey's Universal Negro Improvement Association and actually commanded the *Yarmouth,* one of the ships in Garvey's Black Star Line until the collapse of that enterprise. He involved himself in other Pan-African movements and tried unsuccessfully for political office at the borough level as a member of the American Labour Party.

After retirement from active service in the Merchant Marine and still subjected to racism, he returned to St. Vincent. He died during a brief visit to the United States at age eighty-four. Hugh Mulzac is one of a select group slated for National Hero status in the country of his birth. He has so far had one of the country's Coast Guard ships, the *Hugh Mulzac,* named after him.

See also Pan-Africanism; Universal Negro Improvement Association

■ ■ *Bibliography*

Islander (December–February, 1973).

Mulzac, Hugh. *A Star to Steer By.* New York: International Publishers, 1963.

New York Times (February 1, 1971).
Times Newspaper (June 17, 1919).
Vincentian (February 6, 1971).

ADRIAN FRASER (2005)

MUM BETT, MUMBET

See Freeman, Elizabeth (Mum Bett, Mumbet)

MURALISTS

■ ■ ■

A culturally hybrid art form, the African-American mural is deeply rooted in ancient and modern African cultures; it also draws from both traditional and modernist Euro-American aesthetic and sociopolitical values. Inspired as much by social and economic conditions as by artistic vision, the African-American mural has reflected historical developments in American life and also helped effect social change. In black communities and on historically black college campuses across the United States, the African-American mural is an ongoing source of cultural pride. Because murals have been among the works most often selected by textbook editors to illustrate African-American achievement in the visual arts, murals by such artists as Aaron Douglas, Hale Woodruff, and Charles White are among the most widely reproduced and readily recognized examples of African-American art.

While confronting the artist with numerous technical challenges, the mural form nonetheless enables him or her to reach countless individuals who may not visit museums or galleries. As a large-scale work of public art, the mural addresses great numbers of viewers from all walks of life. Its large size and usual placement in public spaces make it an especially forceful and effective communication medium. This essential democratic nature makes the mural ideal for celebrating the historical, mythic, and symbolic aspects of African-American life and culture.

Broadly speaking, a mural is a large-scale work of art specifically designed to fill and complement an interior or exterior architectural space—a wall, ceiling, or floor. Not all murals are painted; bas- (low) relief murals may be carved from a flat wood or stone surface, creating a design that is raised in low relief from the background. Other materials may also be used. Glazed tiles, enameled steel panels, terrazzo, and other durable materials can make even exterior murals relatively permanent.

The mural's flat surface and spatial amplitude are especially well suited to telling a story, recounting a historic event, or celebrating the heroism and achievements of historical figures. Because its story or message is expressed through visual images rather than words, the mural enables an artist to communicate with viewers regardless of their language or literacy. A relatively permanent, site-specific work, a mural seldom changes owners and frequently remains in perpetuity under the custodianship of a public institution where it is preserved and presented as a cultural treasure.

THE AFRICAN-AMERICAN MURALIST

African-American muralists are neither an identifiable group nor a school of artists; their common features include only their ethnicity and their occasional production of murals. All have worked primarily in other media. Because they have pursued different visions and styles in different eras and at different stages of their careers, they cannot easily be categorized or characterized. While many have worked primarily with black subjects and themes and addressed their work primarily to minority audiences, others have chosen to work with cross-cultural subjects and themes, creating works for broader audiences. Some identify themselves as "black artists," others as "artists who happen also to be black." Recognizing this multiplicity of aims, audiences, and self-identifications is central to understanding and appreciating African-American artists, for no single characterization adequately encompasses the rich diversity of subjects, themes, and styles with which they have worked.

Because the mural gives powerful voice to an artist's narrative, historical, and sometimes propagandistic or didactic impulses, artists sometimes choose this form when they wish to make an especially important and lasting statement. Socially conscious artists sometimes employ the mural to offer both aesthetic and intellectual nourishment to ordinary citizens who often assume that art is inaccessible or irrelevant to their lives.

FROM AFRICA TO THE AMERICAS

Since the dawn of civilization in the great river valleys of Africa, visual artists have recorded, recounted, celebrated, and preserved human history, achievements, and cultural values by decorating their homes, tombs, and public buildings with figurative and symbolic representations of heroic events and everyday life. Throughout Africa, ancient and modern peoples have created murals using whatever materials were available to them. Ancient Egyptian artisans painted elaborate scenes on plastered or stuccoed interior walls and carved detailed bas-relief scenes on stone panels to decorate exterior walls. Today, women of

the Bantu-speaking peoples of southern Africa continue ancient traditions, covering the mud plaster exterior walls of their homes with painted, incised, and inlaid designs combining centuries-old patterns and symbols with images drawn from modern life. Whether the sophisticated products of highly skilled artists or the humble, individual expressions of housewives preserving the vernacular ancestral arts, African murals demonstrate a timeless impulse to decorate architectural surfaces with scenes, images, and symbols depicting a people's history, values, and aesthetic visions.

In Europe the mural experienced its apex with the fresco painting of the Italian Renaissance. Although mural painting never died out completely in the West, it fell generally out of favor until Diego Rivera (1886–1957), José Clemente Orozco (1883–1949), and David Alfaro Siqueiros (1896–1974) revived the mural form in Mexico during the late 1920s and 1930s. A flurry of mural painting in the United States soon followed. The Mexican muralists' methods and motives proved a pivotal influence on African-American artists during the 1930s. Observing how these masters of politically and socially charged public art effectively employed the mural form to educate and raise the nationalistic consciousness of a largely illiterate and disunited people in Mexico, leading black American artists recognized the mural's great potential for raising racial consciousness and validating racial identity among black Americans. The influence of the Mexican muralists is readily evident in the murals of Charles Alston, Aaron Douglas, Vertis Hayes, Charles White, Hale Woodruff, and many others.

MATERIALS AND METHODS

African-American muralists work with both traditional and new materials and methods. Murals painted on plaster are called frescoes. To paint a fresco, artists first render the design in a small-scale drawing called a cartoon. Then they enlarge the design and transfers its basic outlines to the prepared surface. The painting may be done with the help of one or more skilled assistants. In the case of a buon (true) fresco, a smooth final layer of lime plaster (the intonaco) must be applied to the surface a small section at a time to ensure that it is still wet when painted. The artist must work quickly and cannot go back and make revisions. Fresco secco is more commonly used today. Less difficult but also less permanent, it is made by applying water-based paint to dry plaster.

Many murals today are painted in an artist's studio on large canvas panels, tailored to the exact dimensions and shapes of the architectural spaces they are to occupy. When completed, the canvas panels are assembled and in-

Landscape Mural, Robert S. Duncanson, oil on plaster, 1850–1852. *Duncanson, a traditionalist painter best known for his classical-romantic landscape studies, painted a series of eight landscape frescoes for the foyer of a former Cincinnati mansion, now the Taft Museum.* BEQUEST OF CHARLES PHELPS AND ANNA SINTON TAFT, TAFT MUSEUM OF ART, CINCINNATI, OHIO.

stalled under the artist's supervision in the spaces for which they were created, perhaps under the arc formed by a vaulted ceiling or on the wall of a multiple-storied atrium or stairwell.

HISTORY OF THE AFRICAN-AMERICAN MURAL

The history of the African-American mural reflects the rough outlines of the development of African-American art. Its story is largely confined to the twentieth century and rooted in the institutions of the black community. The wide diversity among the murals black American artists have created over more than a century's time reflects broad developments in African-American art as well as the individual visions of the artists.

THE TRADITIONALISTS. Because opportunities for training and patronage were limited for African-American artists prior to the 1930s, few are known to have created murals before the revival brought on by the Mexican muralists. The finest example from the nineteenth century

is Robert Scott Duncanson. Duncanson was a traditionalist painter best known for his classical-romantic landscape studies. From 1848 to 1850 he painted a series of eight landscape frescoes for the foyer of a former Cincinnati mansion, now the Taft Museum.

Although William Édouard Scott's career bridged the romantic and modern eras, he remained a traditionalist painter long after his younger colleagues had embraced African art, European modernism, and New Negro themes. In 1913 Scott painted two murals for public schools in Indianapolis, each depicting childhood themes and featuring black subjects. In 1933 he completed two murals for the Harlem YMCA in New York City.

THE NEW NEGRO RENAISSANCE. The New Negro Renaissance of the late 1920s and 1930s was a watershed for African-American visual arts. Modernist aesthetic theories and styles joined forces with the ideas of the New Negro Movement, creating a fresh and vital artistic vision. By nurturing a community of race-conscious black artists and intellectuals, by providing new sources of training and patronage, and by establishing alternative means for validating the achievements of black artists within the institutions of the African-American community, the Harlem Renaissance set the intellectual and aesthetic stage for the flurry of mural painting activity in the 1930s.

Pioneering black modernist and New Negro artist Aaron Douglas was the first African-American artist successfully to combine African imagery and sensibilities with European modernist styles, creating a culturally hybrid African-American art. He was also the most prolific African-American muralist. Early in his career, Douglas painted murals for Harlem cabarets. *Club Ebony* (1927) and *Club Harlem* (1928) are long gone; with them disappeared Douglas's exotic Africanesque scenes fusing jungle drums, rhythms, and dances with the music and dance of Jazz Age Harlem.

As the cultural renaissance of the 1920s flowed seamlessly into the 1930s, Douglas undertook a number of important mural projects, perfecting his original and distinctive style. In these monumental works he documented with heroic grandeur and mystical wonder his people's journey from ancient Africa to modern urban America, celebrating their aspirations and achievements. Douglas's mural style is distinguished by hard-edge, larger-than-life figures dominating flat, geometrically segmented grounds. His most significant murals include an extensive series of frescoes for Fisk University's Cravath Library (1930), nightclub murals for Chicago's Sherman Hotel (1930), a panel commemorating Harriet Tubman for Bennett College in Greensboro, North Carolina (1931), a fresco for

Aaron Douglas (1899–1979). *One of the most significant African-American muralists of the twentieth century, Douglas began his career as an illustrator in Harlem, providing sketches and other images for the journals* Crisis *and* Opportunity *during the 1920s and 1930s.* GIBBS MUSEUM OF ART/CAA. REPRODUCED BY PERMISSION.

Harlem's 135th Street YMCA (1933), a series of four canvas panels for the 135th Street Branch of the New York Public Library (1934), and a series of four murals for the Texas Centennial Exposition (1936).

Although they did not turn to mural painting until well into the 1930s, several other important artists are also identified with this earliest generation of race-conscious black American artists. Although only a few years older than their students, this so-called "Harlem Renaissance generation" mentored younger artists whose careers began in the 1930s. Both generations were prolific producers of murals during the latter part of that decade.

Hale Woodruff's powerful 1939 series of three mural panels commemorating the centennial of the Amistad slave mutiny and trial stands among the finest examples of the African-American mural. It is owned by Talladega College in Talladega, Alabama. Charles Alston's interest in the healing arts of ancient magic and modern medicine resulted in an important and compelling pair of canvas panels for Harlem Hospital (1936–1937). In 1938 sculptor Richmond Barthé created a monumental pair of bas-relief marble panels for the exterior facade of the Harlem River Housing Project in New York City. Archibald Motley was the premiere black Chicago painter of his era. He created

a number of murals for schools and public buildings, including *United States Mail* (1937), a vivid stagecoach scene for the Wood River, Illinois, Post Office. On the West Coast, sculptor Sargent Johnson also produced several murals during the 1930s.

THE 1930S. New Negro artists' thinking about art and society was further refined by the new ideas of a new decade. The strong leftist sympathies that swept through American artistic and intellectual circles in the 1930s joined forces with the "cultural democracy" aims of New Deal art programs, creating a compelling ideological base for a socially conscious, nonelitist "people's art." Many black muralists joined the radical left. For radicalized New Negro artists, cultural democracy meant employing their art to engender racial unity and pride. By using public art to teach the black masses about their rich history and cultural heritage, artists helped to raise black consciousness, setting the stage for the civil rights movement a generation later.

Increased patronage in the late 1930s further stimulated mural production among African-American artists. New Deal art programs provided unprecedented government patronage. The U.S. Treasury Department's Public Works of Art Project (PWAP) (1933–1934), Section of Painting and Sculpture (1934–1942), and Treasury Relief Art Project (TRAP) (1935–1936); the Federal Emergency Relief Act (FERA) programs administered through the states (1933–1935); and the Federal Arts Project (FAP) of the Works Progress Administration (WPA) (1935–1942) hired artists to decorate public buildings across America. Although these programs professed a commitment to nondiscrimination, they hired few black artists until after the Harlem Artists Guild began lobbying federal agency officials for more jobs. Guild members included Charles Alston, Selma Day (active 1933–1951), Aaron Douglas, Vertis Hayes (1911–), Elba Lightfoot (1910–), Sara Murrell (active 1936–1939), and Georgette Seabrooke Powell, all of whom secured employment on federal mural projects. The guild's efforts significantly increased the number of black artists hired by New Deal agencies nationwide and helped to place a few black artists in supervisory positions. More than a hundred African-American artists were employed on New York City's WPA/FAP. Although black women artists benefited in significant numbers, sexism usually relegated them to jobs teaching art rather than producing it. This may in part explain the relative dearth of black women muralists, for many of their male counterparts were initiated into the mural medium through their work on New Deal mural projects.

THE INTERIM YEARS. While the period spanning the first great black cultural awakening of the 1920s and 1930s and the black arts movement of the late 1960s and 1970s saw significantly less activity in African-American mural production, it nonetheless yielded some outstanding murals by well-established black artists. The loss of federal patronage was a significant factor in the decline in the number of mural commissions.

During these relatively lean years for black artists, much of their patronage came from within the black community. Blacks commissioned murals for their homes, businesses, and community gathering places. Aaron Douglas painted murals for two private residences in Wilmington, Delaware. Charles Alston and Hale Woodruff were commissioned in 1948 by the Golden State Mutual Life Insurance Company to paint a pair of mural panels documenting the contributions of black people in settling and building the state of California. In 1953 a Houston minister commissioned John T. Biggers to paint *The Contribution of Negro Women to American Life and Education* for the Blue Triangle Branch of the Houston YWCA.

America's historically black colleges and universities played a central and ongoing patronage role during these years. In 1943 Charles White completed Hampton University's *The Contribution of the Negro to American Democracy,* a kaleidoscopic "visual textbook" surveying the faces and figures of more than twenty great African-American men and women. His mentorship had a lasting effect on Hampton undergraduates who watched him as he painted; Persis Jennings (active c. 1942–1944) subsequently painted murals at Fort Eustis, Virginia (1942) and the East End Baptist Church in Suffolk, Virginia (c. 1942–1944). Hale Woodruff's *Art of the Negro,* a series of six panels completed in 1950 for the Arnett Library at Atlanta University, is an outstanding example from this period.

For decades, white philanthropies—whose patronage and interest had been carefully cultivated in the 1920s and 1930s by intermediary patrons like W. E. B. Du Bois and Charles S. Johnson—continued to award fellowships to black artists. Yet their support dwindled after the 1930s. The Julius Rosenwald Fund of Chicago and the Carnegie Foundation of New York provided a good deal of support for black artists but funded very few mural projects after their interests shifted to the education and training of artists.

THE BLACK ARTS MOVEMENT. The black arts movement of the late 1960s and 1970s marked the second major cultural awakening in black America. Led by young artists radicalized by the Black Power movement, the black arts movement earned the support of some elder black artists but created sharp tensions among others. It helped to revitalize a languishing African-American art and stimulated a resurgent interest in mural painting.

The African-American mural moved out of doors and into the streets of America's urban ghettoes in the late 1960s, when radicalized artists recognized and seized upon the public mural's communication potential. In cities across the country, militant black artists organized massive-scale, collaborative mural projects in an effort to create a "people's art." Submerging the artists' individual identities and voices in a collective, revolutionary chorus, they brought art into neighborhoods where social and economic conditions attested to the oppression and exploitation these artists reviled. Covering entire exterior walls of inner-city buildings with boldly colorful, naive images of black pride, black power, African heritage, and African-American heroes and heroines, they raised race consciousness and fostered pride and dignity among America's dispossessed minorities.

Best known of these outdoor murals is Chicago's *Wall of Respect* (1967). Created by AfriCobra (African Commune of Bad Relevant Artists) leader and Howard University art professor Jeff Donaldson (1932–) and other members of the Organization of Black American Culture (OBAC), this work spawned hundreds of similar outdoor murals in cities all across the United States. Conceived and executed as vehicles for community involvement, these projects brought skilled, socially committed artists together with young people who learned to reclaim their cultural heritage as they painted its imagery on neighborhood walls.

Even after the black arts movement declined, the painting of murals on neighborhood walls continued. In the 1990s inner-city walls were dotted with portraits of black heroes, tributes to slain rap singers, and slogans. This rich vernacular tradition in turn influenced artistic professionals. A notable example was Jean-Michael Basquiat, the wunderkind of the 1980s, who used a colorful palette and action-packed composition in a notable mural on New York's East Village.

THE RECENT PAST. The mural is not a static art form; its evolution in black America reflects a changing American society over time, as well as the artists' changing relationship with that society. In recent decades established and respected African-American artists have won prestigious mural commissions both in and outside the black community. Two of the most prominent artists are Romare Bearden and Jacob Lawrence. Both only undertook mural commissions in their mature years after establishing their reputations in other media.

The pioneering and best-known collagist of his time, Bearden was nearly sixty when he created *The Block* (1971), a six-panel collage depicting life in the buildings of a block-long stretch of a busy Harlem street. A tape recording of street sounds is part of the mural's installation. His 1983 mosaic, *Baltimore Uproar,* marks the subway station near Billie Holiday's birthplace in Baltimore. In 1984 Bearden completed *Pittsburgh Recollections,* a ceramic tile mosaic mural depicting that city's black history and installed in an underground subway station.

Jacob Lawrence, who for decades had expressed his narrative impulses through extensive series of small images collectively recounting long, heroic stories drawn from dramatic episodes in African-American history, was in his sixties before he began combining multiple images into murals. In 1979, he completed *Games,* a ten-panel sports mural for Seattle's Kingdome Stadium. In 1985 Lawrence completed *Theater* for the University of Washington.

Contemporary ideas, materials, and styles have continued to keep African-American murals vital, fresh, and dynamic. Lawrence's *Exploration* (1980) is a thematically and visually connected series of twelve enamels on steel panels. A fresh and vital exploration of the interrelationships among the academic disciplines, the mural was installed in Howard University's Blackburn University Center in 1980. In *Origins* Lawrence used the same materials for a visual exploration of Harlem history and life. This work was installed near *Exploration* in 1984.

One of the most unusual and moving murals of recent years is Houston Conwill's 1990 floor mural, *Rivers,* inspired by Langston Hughes's poem "The Negro Speaks of Rivers." Installed in the lobby outside the Langston Hughes Auditorium at the Schomburg Center for Research in Black History of the New York Public Library, Conwill's terrazzo "cosmogram" celebrates the spread of African culture throughout the world. The mural also covers the tomb in which the poet's ashes were interred in 1990.

One of the students who had watched Charles White paint his fresco at Hampton in 1942 and 1943 was John T. Biggers. Nearly four decades later, Biggers returned to his alma mater to paint two panels flanking the five-story atrium of the university's new Harvey Library. *House of the Turtle* and *Tree House* were completed in 1992. Their mystical, mythic figures, symbolic images, and repetitive geometric patterns express a cosmology that spiritually and functionally interconnects their human figures, the natural world, and the built environment.

See also *Amistad* Mutiny; Bearden, Romare; Black Arts Movement; Douglas, Aaron; Du Bois, W. E. B.; Harlem Renaissance; Holiday, Billie; Johnson, Charles Spurgeon; Lawrence, Jacob; New Negro; Painting and Sculpture; Tubman, Harriet; Woodruff, Hale

■■ *Bibliography*

Campbell, Mary Schmidt, et al. *Harlem Renaissance: Art of Black America.* New York: Abrams, 1987.

Changuion, Paul, Annice Changuion, and Tom Matthews. *The African Mural.* London: New Holland, 1989.

Cockcroft, Eva, et al. *Toward a People's Art: The Contemporary Mural Movement.* New York: Dutton, 1977.

Dover, Cedric. *American Negro Art.* Greenwich, Conn.: Greenwood Press, 1960.

Driskell, David C. *Two Centuries of Black American Art.* New York: Knopf, 1976.

Fine, Elsa Honig. *The Afro-American Artist: A Search for Identity.* New York: Holt, Rinehart & Winston, 1973.

McKinzie, Richard D. *The New Deal for Artists.* Princeton, N.J.: Princeton University Press, 1975.

Mecklenburg, Virginia. *The Public as Patron: A History of the Treasury Department Mural Program.* College Park: University of Maryland, 1979.

O'Connor, Francis V., ed. *Art for the Millions: Essays from the 1930s by Artists and Administrators of the WPA Federal Art Project.* Boston, Mass.: New York Graphic Society, 1973.

Porter, James A. *Modern Negro Art.* New York: Dryden Press, 1943.

LINDA NIEMAN (1996)

MURPHY, EDDIE

APRIL 3, 1961

❚❚❚

Actor and comedian Eddie Murphy was born in Brooklyn, New York. His father was a New York policeman and amateur comedian, and his mother a phone operator. Murphy's father was killed on duty when his son was three years old; his mother remarried, and the family moved from Brooklyn, when Murphy was nine, to the Long Island, New York, town of Roosevelt.

Murphy's talent at "ranking," a version of the "dozens" (a traditional street pastime of trading witty insults), earned him a position as a host of an after-school talent show at a local hangout, the Roosevelt Youth Center. After the favorable response he received from his Al Green impression, Murphy became a stand-up comedian, and soon was making $25 and $50 a week performing at Long Island nightclubs. In 1979, when he was just out of high school, he appeared at the Comic Strip in Manhattan, which led to a successful audition for the television show *Saturday Night Live.*

Murphy emerged as a success on *Saturday Night Live* through his satirical impressions of such well-known African Americans as Bill Cosby, Stevie Wonder, and Muhammad Ali. Among his most famous characters were "Mister

Robinson," a mean-spirited inner-city version of the children's television host Mister Rogers; a grown-up "Buckwheat" from "The Little Rascals"; "Velvet Jones," a book-writing, irreverent pimp; and "Tyrone Green," an illiterate convict poet.

In 1982 Murphy recorded an album of live stand-up material, earning him a gold record and a Grammy nomination. In the same year he costarred in his first motion picture, the highly successful *48 Hours,* playing a fast-talking convict who is released for two days to help track down a criminal. Murphy reached the height of his popularity in the 1980s with the films *Trading Places* (1983), *Beverly Hills Cop* (1985), *The Golden Child* (1986), *Beverly Hills Cop II* (1987), and *Raw* (1987), a highly successful though controversial, full-length concert film. In 1988 he played multiple roles in *Coming to America,* and in 1989 he wrote, directed, and starred in *Harlem Nights*; he also made his recording debut with the album *So Happy.* In 1992 Murphy starred in two more films, *Boomerang* and *The Distinguished Gentleman,* though their box office success was only moderate.

Following a stream of largely unsuccessful films, including *Vampire in Brooklyn* (1995), Murphy's career was revitalized in 1996 by *The Nutty Professor,* a remake of the Jerry Lewis classic that was successful enough to prompt a sequel, *Nutty Professor II: The Klumps* (2000), also starring Murphy. In 1998 the actor starred in another popular remake, *Dr. Dolittle,* which was also followed by a sequel, and in the same year his voice was featured in the animated film *Mulan.* In another animated offering, Murphy was heard in the voice of a donkey in the hit movie *Shrek (2001),* a popular and critical success that led to the sequel *Shrek 2* in 2004. In 2003 Murphy starred in the Walt Disney film *The Haunted Mansion.*

Murphy started his own company, Eddie Murphy Enterprises, Ltd., in 1986, which, in a special agreement with CBS, has produced series, pilots, and specials for network television.

See also Ali, Muhammad; Comedians; Cosby, Bill; Wonder, Stevie (Morris, Stevland)

■ ■ *Bibliography*

"Ebony Interview with Eddie Murphy." *Ebony* (July 1985): 40–48.

Sanello, Frank. *Eddie Murphy: The Life and Times of a Comic on the Edge.* New York: Carol Publishing, 1997.

Wilburn, Deborah A. *Eddie Murphy.* New York: Chelsea House, 1993.

SUSAN MCINTOSH (1996)
Updated by publisher 2005

Pauli Murray (1910–1985). *A lifelong civil rights advocate, Murray served as a lawyer, educator, deputy attorney general, and ordained minister. Often the first African-American woman to fill the many positions she occupied, Murray worked tirelessly to destroy the legal and political obstacles created by racism and racial discrimination and fought the stereotypes that limited the lives of women—especially African-American women—in equally damaging ways.* AP/WIDE WORLD PHOTOS. REPRODUCED BY PERMISSION.

MURRAY, PAULI

NOVEMBER 20, 1910
JULY 1, 1985

During the course of a remarkably diverse life, lawyer, poet, and minister Pauli Murray was a pioneer among African Americans and women in a number of fields. She was born in Baltimore, Maryland. Her postsecondary education spanned six decades, beginning at Hunter College (B.A., 1933); continuing at Howard University Law School (LL.B., 1944); the University of California, Berkeley (LL.M., 1945), and Yale Law School, where in 1965 she became the first African American to receive the degree of doctor of juridical science. Her education culminated in 1976 at General Theological Seminary in New York, where, as the only African-American female enrolled, she received the master of divinity degree.

When not pursuing her studies, Murray maintained several distinct careers. She served as deputy attorney general of California, becoming, in January 1946, the first African American to hold that position. During the 1967–1968 school year, she was vice president of Benedict College. From 1968 to 1973 she was professor of American studies at Brandeis University; in 1972 she was named Louis Stulberg Professor of Law and Politics at Brandeis. From 1977 until her retirement from public life in 1984, she was an Episcopal priest in Washington, D.C., and Baltimore.

Murray's published writings include *States' Laws on Race and Color* (1951), which Supreme Court Justice Thurgood Marshall (1908–1993) referred to as the bible for lawyers fighting segregation laws; *Dark Testament and Other Poems* (1970), a collection of poetry; and her autobiography, *Song in a Weary Throat: An American Pilgrimage* (published posthumously in 1987, it received both the Robert F. Kennedy Book Award and the Christopher Award).

Murray's achievements and honors also included being named Woman of the Year in 1946 by the National Council of Negro Women and in 1947 by *Mademoiselle* magazine; serving as one of the thirty-two founders of the National Organization for Women in 1966; receiving the Eleanor Roosevelt Award from the Professional Women's Caucus in 1971; and, on January 8, 1977, becoming the first African-American woman ordained as a priest in the Episcopal church. On July 1, 1985, Pauli Murray died of cancer in Pittsburgh, Pennsylvania.

See also Marshall, Thurgood

■ ■ *Bibliography*

Murray, Pauli. *Song in a Weary Throat: An American Pilgrimage.* New York: Harpercollins, 1987.

Murray, Pauli. *Pauli Murray: The Autobiography of a Black Activist, Feminist, Lawyer, Priest, and Poet.* Knoxville: University of Tennessee Press, 1989.

O'Dell, Darlene. *Sites of Southern Memory: The Autobiographies of Katharine Du Pre Lumpkin, Lillian Smith, and Pauli Murray.* Charlottesville: University of Virginia Press, 2001.

SIRAJ AHMED (1996)
Updated bibliography

MUSEUMS

The spirit of innovation, survival, and black creative expression has been preserved for more than a century through a range of research libraries, archives, and museums. Devoted to the black experience in the Americas and throughout the globe, these institutions document the history of struggle and achievement that are the hallmarks of African-American life and culture. Since the founding of the College Museum at Hampton Institute in Hampton, Virginia, in 1868, material culture—household artifacts, photographs, diaries and letters, and other memorabilia, as well as sculpture, paintings, and more contemporary media such as films and videos—has been vigorously collected and interpreted to enhance public awareness and appreciation. Today, this tradition of cultural presentation is maintained by nearly 140 institutions and galleries throughout the United States.

Hampton's College Museum (now Hampton University Museum) was truly a pioneer in this effort. Established to enrich vocational and academic instruction and to provide the broader community with otherwise unavailable cultural experiences, the museum was the brainchild of Colonel Samuel Chapman Armstrong. Today, the Hampton University Museum is noted for its important collection of African artworks, acquired by a black nineteenth-century missionary to Africa. Its holdings also include significant works of African-American and Native American artists (the latter group a reflection of the student body at the time of the museum's establishment) and a major bequest from the Harmon Foundation, which sponsored a prestigious national competition for African-American artists from 1926 until 1933.

Black cultural preservation was also advanced through the formation of literary societies and church archives. Beginning with the Bethel Literary and Historical Association (founded circa 1880) and the Negro Historical Society (1887), and, following the turn of the century, the Negro Society for Historical Research, these organizations were, in many ways, precursors to African-American museums.

Early research collections were often formed from materials lovingly accumulated by race-conscious bibliographies and lay historians. Such was the case for Howard University's Library of Negro Life in Washington, D.C., which received a 1,600-volume library from former abolitionist Lewis Tappan in 1873 and a gift of 3,000 books and historical ephemera from Reverend Jesse Moorland in 1914. The collection was augmented in 1946 by a donation of the considerable library of famed civil rights attorney Arthur Spingarn, becoming in the process the Moorland-Spingarn Library (now the Moorland-Spingarn Research Center). In New York, Arthur Alfonso Schomburg, a black Puerto Rican immigrant, responded to a teacher's comment that "the Negro has no history" by exhaustively seeking information on Africans and their descendants throughout the world. He began seriously collecting in 1910 and rapidly developed diverse holdings of manuscripts, rare books, pamphlets, sheet music, and artworks.

By 1926, the magnitude of the Schomburg Collection led to its purchase by the Carnegie Foundation for the Harlem branch of the New York Public Library. Today, the Schomburg Center for Research in Black Culture is considered the foremost research facility of its kind in the world, with holdings in excess of five million items detailing the histories of blacks in Africa, the Americas, and elsewhere.

With the racial pride and interest in Africa that emerged in the 1920s, the campuses of historically black colleges and universities aimed to enhance teaching generally for the black academic community and to make works of art available to the general public. Howard University began the trend in 1928, soon followed by Fisk (Nashville), Lincoln (Pennsylvania), Tuskegee (Alabama), Morgan State (Baltimore), and Talladega (Florida) universities, among others. The galleries at these schools provided one of the few sources for exhibition and criticism for a generation of black artists and performed a major service to contemporary African-American art history by preserving a body of artwork and related historical documents that might otherwise have been dispersed, lost, or destroyed. The significant outpouring of black creative expression that resulted from the Harlem Renaissance, and, later, the large number of works commissioned through the Federal Arts Project of the Works Project Administration (WPA) during the Depression era, make up the primary holdings of many of these institutions.

Assisted by the WPA in the 1940s, organizations such as the Uptown Art Center in New York (founded in sculptor Augusta Savage's garage studio), Cleveland's Karamu House, and Chicago's South Side Community Art Center provided free art instruction for local residents and aspiring artists and in many ways performed museum-like functions. Major artists, including Charles White, Archibald Motley, Romare Bearden, and Jacob Lawrence, received early training through these centers. In a similar fashion, the Barnett-Aden Gallery in Washington, D.C., which opened in 1940, provided a focal point for artistic activity in that city by mounting numerous exhibitions of black artists of the late nineteenth and early twentieth centuries, in addition to hosting public lectures and gallery talks.

The civil rights movement of the 1950s and 1960s created a new black cultural renaissance. The museums established during this period moved awareness of African-American history to a new plateau. In their expression of a black perspective and through their efforts to preserve black history, these institutions sought to use their collections to motivate African Americans to "define themselves, their future and their understanding of their past"

(Harding, 1967, p. 40). This came at a time when information about black achievements was generally excluded from common history texts and from other museums. Black history was seen, says Vincent Harding, "as a weapon for the Civil Rights Movement." Responding to the void of available information, the San Francisco African American Historical and Cultural Society was founded in 1955, soon followed by the DuSable Museum of African American History (originally the Ebony Museum) in 1961 in Chicago and the Afro-American Museum of Detroit in 1965.

During this period, a unique effort involving students, scouts, local scholars, and government agencies in an urban-archaeology project in Brooklyn, New York, uncovered a black settlement dating back to the nineteenth century, which led to the formation of the Society for the Preservation of Historic Weeksville. Today it continues its archaeological research on a forgotten early black community. The efforts of the Museum of Afro-American History in Boston during this period were instrumental in the preservation of the oldest existing black church building, the African Meeting House. The restored building serves as the centerpiece of the fourteen-site Black Heritage Trail, which explores Boston's rich nineteenth-century African-American community. Also in Boston, the Museum of the National Center of Afro-American Artists was created to provide a leading showcase for artists of the African diaspora.

The Smithsonian Institution created the Anacostia Neighborhood Museum (now the Anacostia Museum and Center for African American History and Culture) in 1967 in Washington, D.C., as a "storefront" model for museum outreach. Its goal was to "enliven the community and enlighten the people it serves" (American Association of Museums, 1972, p. 6). Such an outreach was invaluable in the wake of the civil unrest that followed the Rev. Dr. Martin Luther King Jr.'s April 1968 assassination. Although the Smithsonian Institution provided funding support and technical expertise, exhibition planning, public programs, and overall administration were determined by the surrounding community. As a result, exhibition themes addressed community issues and urban problems as much as historical events. Other mainstream museums, often in response to confrontations with angry artists, were forced to reevaluate their relationships with urban communities and initiated outreach programs. Thus, the Junior Council of the Museum of Modern Art in New York played an important role in the creation of the Studio Museum of Harlem (1968), now the nation's foremost showcase for African-American artists. The Brooklyn Museum replicated the Smithsonian's effort by establishing an outreach center known as the New Muse.

The most noteworthy points of contention between mainstream museums and African-American artists and museum professionals regarded the exclusion of African-American artists in museum exhibitions. Two exhibitions in New York forced the issue of institutional discrimination: the Whitney Museum of American Art's "The 1930's: Painting and Sculpture in America" (1968) and the Metropolitan Museum of Art's "Harlem on My Mind: Cultural Capital of Black America, 1900–1968" (1969).

With the Black Power movement of the 1960s and 1970s, African-American museums were founded with increasing frequency with the view that such institutions fostered "a way of empowerment" and a method of moving black history to a new plateau of public awareness. To provide space for these expressions and to serve greatly heightened interest, museums were formed throughout the country. The Afro-American Historical Society in New Haven, Connecticut, was founded as a research library with an estimated 250,000 volumes; and in Providence, the Rhode Island Black Heritage Society instituted pioneering techniques to involve black audiences in the actual collection and cataloging of artifacts. The Black Archives of Mid-America, based in both Kansas and Missouri, collects black cultural information from the midwestern region. To preserve the experience of blacks in the West, the Black America West Museum and Heritage Center in Denver was established. The United States bicentennial led to the creation of Philadelphia's Afro-American Historical and Cultural Museum and led the way for tapping municipal, state, and federal support for African-American museums.

Between 1975 and 1990, black museums were formed in California, Texas, South Carolina, Oklahoma, Colorado, Florida, Tennessee, Georgia, and Virginia, including new institutions devoted to the civil rights movement. In 1991 the National Civil Rights Museum opened in Memphis at the site of the Lorraine Motel where Dr. Martin Luther King Jr. was assassinated in 1968. In addition, nearly twenty museums dedicated to exploring the history of African Americans and the African diaspora were founded in the 1990s in such states as Iowa, Louisiana, California, Washington, Florida, Maryland, and Indiana. Struggling with limited economic and human resources, these institutions nonetheless serve the broadest possible mandate—cultural, educative, political, social, and civic. Their tradition of service forges a vital historical link between past and future.

In 2003 President George W. Bush signed legislation to establish the National Museum of African American History and Culture. Slated to open in 2012, this museum will gain national prominence on the mall in Washington, D.C., as part of the Smithsonian Institution. The symbolism of the prestigious location has already fulfilled the dreams of many African Americans who have sought the national recognition of African-American contributions through an institution in the nation's capital.

See also Archival Collections; Art Collections; Historians/Historiography; Music Museums and Historical Sites; Schomburg, Arthur

■ ■ *Bibliography*

American Association of Museums. *Museums: Their New Audience.* Washington, D.C.: Author, 1972.

Austin, Joy Ford. "Their Face to the Rising Sun: Trends in the Development of African American Museums." *Museum News* 6 (1986): 30–32.

Collier-Thomas, Bettye. "An Historical Overview of Black Museums and Institutions with Museums' Functions: 1800–1980." *Negro History Bulletin* 44, no. 3 (1981): 56–58.

Dickerson, Amina. "Afro-American Museums: A Future Full of Promise." *Roundtable Reports* 9, nos. 2 and 3 (1984): 14–18.

Harding, Vincent. "Power from Our People: The Source of the Modern Revival of Black History." *Black Scholar* 18 (1967): 40.

Horton, James Oliver, and Spencer R. Crew. "Afro-Americans and Museums: Towards a Policy of Inclusion." In *History Museums in the United States: A Critical Assessment,* edited by Warren Leon and Roy Rosenzweig. Urbana and Chicago: University of Illinois Press, 1989.

Reynolds, Gary A. and Beryl J. Wright. *Against the Odds: African-American Artists and the Harmon Foundation.* Newark, N.J.: The Newark Museum, 1989.

Roach, Ronald. "One Step Closer." *Black Issues in Higher Education* 21, no. 26 (2005). Available from <http://www.blackissues.com/Archives.asp>.

Trescott, Jacqueline. "Museums on the Move." *American Visions* 1, no. 2 (1986): 24–34.

AMINA DICKERSON (1996)
BRIDGET R. COOKS (2005)

MUSIC

This entry consists of three distinct articles examining music in African-American culture in Latin America, in the United States, and an essay on the intersection of music, religion, and crime in early-twentieth-century Brazil, with a specific concentration on Rio de Janeiro.

MUSIC IN LATIN AMERICA
James Peterson
Marcela Poveda

MUSIC IN THE UNITED STATES
Portia K. Maultsby

MUSIC, RELIGION, AND PERCEPTIONS OF
CRIME IN EARLY TWENTIETH-CENTURY RIO
DE JANEIRO
Marc Adam Hertzman

MUSIC IN LATIN AMERICA

Nicolas Slonimsky, the author of *Music of Latin America* (1945), the first comprehensive account of Latin American music published in the United States, divides the developments of the music in this region (Latin America) into four periods: (1) Pre-Columbian, (2) Early Centuries of the Conquest, (3) Formation of National Cultures, and (4) Modern. The Pre-Columbian Cultures period includes all of the musical cultures that existed prior to Columbus's forays into the "New World." This period features "primitive musical instincts expressed in singing and rhythmic stamping" (Slonimsky, p. 71) and a variety of *sui generis* musical instruments—such as drums made from hollow tree trunks and animal skins, and gourds fashioned into shakers by placing dried seeds inside. The Early Centuries of the Conquest period covers the years from 1492 to 1750. It is marked by the influx of nonaboriginal cultures and music to the region, including the church music of Jesuits and the "infusion of African rhythms consequent upon the importation of Negro slaves" (Slonimsky, p. 71). The Formation of National Cultures period (1750–1900) is marked by the region's sense of nationalism, especially as it is manifest in the creation of national anthems following the wars of independence. Finally, what Slonimsky calls the Modern Era of Latin American Music (1900–1950) includes two signal paradigmatic shifts in the musical cultures of Latin America. The first of these was the "[e]mergence of native creative composers who combine-[d] in their music a deep racial and national consciousness with modern technique" (Slonimsky, p. 72). The second shift reflected European and North American acceptance of Latin America "into the commonwealth of universal musical culture on equal terms with the great schools of composition" (Slonimsky, p. 72).

Slonimksy's work clearly reflects certain racial and cultural biases inherent in music scholarship. The purpose of this essay, however, is not to produce a critical analysis of the historiography of Latin American musical scholarship; nor is it to rehearse the comprehensive work of scholars such as Nicolas Slonimsky (1945), Gerard Behague (1979) and John Schechter (1999). Instead, the models established by these scholars will be used to focus on the historical contributions and influences of African peoples on the music of Latin America. The most significant contributions relate to African continuity and influences on the music, and the postmodern contribution to the development of hip-hop culture in particular Latin American countries. This hip-hop era in Latin American music began in the 1980s.

Latin America consists of more than twenty republics, not all of which contain significant African populations. These twenty republics are: Argentina, Bolivia, Brazil, Chile, Colombia, Costa Rica, Cuba, Dominican Republic, Ecuador, Guatemala, Haiti, Honduras, Mexico, Nicaragua, Panama, Paraguay, Peru, El Salvador, Uruguay, and Venezuela. However, only the following countries warrant consideration for the African influences on their respective music and cultures: Argentina, Brazil, Colombia, Cuba, Dominican Republic, Mexico, Panama, Uruguay, and Venezuela. Because of their cultural and geographic relation to the Atlantic Ocean and the African slave trade, these nations have engendered more pronounced musical influences from various African cultures. For an important theoretical reference, consider the impressive cultural studies work of sociologist Paul Gilroy in his seminal text *The Black Atlantic* (1993), in which he employs the symbols of slave ships crossing the Atlantic as key cultural indicators of the reciprocal influences of African cultures on the new world, and vice-versa.

For example, Argentina does not boast a large population of African descendants. However "African rhythms have profoundly affected Argentine popular music" (Slonimsky, p. 77). This influence is most evident in the milonga tango, which features a swing-oriented rhythm that derives from African percussive expressions. In fact, the most popular folk music, driven by the figure of the *gaucho*, a minstrel figure who traveled and performed songs of the poor folk, was crystallized through its thematic connection to the plight of African slaves. These subtle influences derive from the eastern seaboard of the country, and even now they cannot be pinpointed beyond the very general assessment made here. The foremost scholar on these matters, John Charles Chasteen, has conducted extensive research into the African origins of the tango. Through various articles and books, Chasteen has explored the origins of tango in Afro-Argentinean communities, concluding that most of the tango's aboriginal developments are lost in its more current identification with upper-class ballroom dancing in Argentina and abroad. In terms of musical prominence, Argentina is most widely known for the tango, which is only occasionally connected to the African rhythms referenced by Slonimsky.

There are, however, demonstrable themes that manifest themselves in most, if not all Latin American music. These thematic consistencies include and incorporate the African cultural presence in Latin American music. According to John Schechter, a music scholar at the University of California, Santa Cruz, there are four of these themes: nostalgia, descriptive balladry, commentary on current events, and communication with the supernatural. Nostalgic themes focus on migration, notions of the Latin American homeland, pastoral reflections on nature and Latin American landscapes, and various other regional contemplations—including the attributes and characteristics of women in particular locales, as well as the specific musical instruments that derive form regional developments in the musical cultures. Themes centered on descriptive balladry tend toward narratives that detail the experiences of local figures, historical events, and cultural myths, including the oral transmission of indigenous Native American histories. Romantic and Christian themes find their expressions in this thematic musical form as well. Commentary on current events is as pervasive a theme in Latin American music as any of the other three. These "musical-political expressions" address the myriad instances of colonialism, cultural hegemony, and post-colonial residue, especially in those Latin American regions plagued most by sociopolitical oppression. It should come as little surprise that many of these oppressed regions (ghettos, barrios, etc.) are also populated by Latin Americans of African descent. Finally, themes of supernatural communication are present in Latin American music as well. These communicative themes should not be readily considered religious, however, since they encompass all manner of engagement with the dead, spirits, ancestors, and divine entities. In these thematic musical expressions reside the artistic outlets of shaman, ancestral conduits, and those who are periodically possessed by spirits.

The simplest way, then, to proceed is through brief explications of African-influenced musical traditions in each of the Latin American countries. Nearly all Latin American countries bear some cultural connection to the content of Africa. Those highlighted here reflect the most significant connections through traditions, religions, populations, and common experiences.

BRAZIL

Brazil is the largest country in Latin America. It borders all South American countries except for Chile and Ecuador, has the largest population, and also has the largest population of African-descended peoples: Brazilians of African descent make up approximately half of the country's population. These factors make Brazil an important indi-

A woman dances Candombé during the Llamadas Parade in Montevideo, Uruguay, 2004. © ANDRES STAPFF/REUTERS/CORBIS

cator for the developments and influences of African culture in Latin American music. Since Brazil was the forced destination of the largest percentage of African slaves, African influences are prevalent in religion, food, and, of course, music.

For all of the African cultural influences in Brazil, notions of race and identifications with blackness are complex and rare. Census data from 1991 suggests that only about 5 percent of the Brazilian population identify themselves as being black (Neate, p. 207). This suggests that the majority population of Brazil is white, with mulattos being a close second. However, the concept of blackness represents an extremely negative ethnic identification in Brazil, and the racial culture there is based upon class, nuanced color consciousness, and the inevitability of a racially intermixed population.

That being said, there are many manifestations of Afro-Brazilian attributes in Brazilian music. In the state of Bahia, the city of Salvador is the center of the rich religious traditions of Candomblé. Directly descended from the West African Yoruba religion, the various groups of people who practice Candomblé engage in various African beliefs and rituals, particularly through music and spirit possession. These rituals are driven and enacted through Candomblé drum ensembles. The ensembles have a musico-spiritual leader, the álabe, whose knowledge of musical rifts and percussive patterns is extensive. Additional drummers follow his lead on various-sized atabaque drums. "The music of candomblé, especially the drumming, serves not only as a crucial element of the candomble rituals themselves, but is also important symbolically as a cultural focus of African values" (Crook, p. 223).

As socioeconomic conditions for black Brazilians deteriorated in urban enclaves such as Rio de Janeiro and

São Paulo during the twentieth century, ideological battles developed over music, especially forms like samba that represented Eurocentric colonization of Afro-Brazilian forms. This is ironic, since samba "can be considered as the first decisive step toward musical nationalism in Brazil" in the nineteenth century (Behague, p. 32). But in its developments over time, samba came to be associated with Eurocentric cultural appropriation (as did tango and even American jazz). In attempts to reclaim or re-establish the music, "Afro-Bloc" organizations became prominent in the 1970s during Carnival celebrations. These Afro Blocs celebrated the African roots of Brazilian culture and, in response to white domination, eventually turned to African-American musical forms (first funk and soul, and more recently, hip-hop) for cultural redemption.

COLOMBIA

The music of Colombia exemplifies a mixture of African, native, and European (especially Spanish) influences. Cumbia, Colombia's national musical form, originally arose on the Atlantic coast and is a mixture of African music (brought by slaves) and Spanish influences. After slavery was abolished in the nineteenth century, Africans, Indians, and other ethnic groups mixed more frequently, helping cumbia to evolve into more intricate styles like bambuco, vallenato, and porro. While early cumbia bands used only percussion and vocals, more modern forms include trumpets, saxophones, keyboards, and trombones.

African influences are also significantly apparent in cumbia dancing. Some believe it is a direct export from Guinea, which has a popular "cumbe" dance. Others claim the dance tells the story of an African man courting a native woman, even acknowledging that the shuffling footwork may be a depiction of African slaves trying to dance while bound by iron chains around their ankles.

It is important to note that some Colombian cities—such as Cartagena, which has a large seaport on the north coast, and Providencia Island—have large African communities descended from slaves, and cultural mixing is not frequent in these areas. As a result, the music of these areas has changed little since being imported from various cultures of Africa, particularly West Africa. Cartagena, for example, is well known for its champeta music, which has very strong soukous influences. Soukous came from Zaire and the Congo in the early twentieth century, and like cumbia it was originally performed with strings and a percussive instrument (i.e., a guitar and bottle).

Today, champeta is an Afro-Colombian musical style also known as champeta criolla (or creole); it is a hybrid of Colombian rhythms like soukous, juju, and rumba and Caribbean rhythms such as soca, calypso, reggae and com-

pás. Modern influences on the evolvement of champeta can be traced back to Caribbean music festivals of the past and to the manual distribution of soukous albums from sailors coming in to Cartagena from Africa in the 1960s. Recordings by Nigeria's Prince Nico Mbarga and the Oriental Brothers infiltrated the Colombian coast, and local Colombian DJs played original African hits and combined them with champetas at parties. Radio stations also picked up the trend.

During the Colombian hippie movement of the 1970s, champeta artists were becoming well known for their unique style. Examples include Wganda Kenya and La Verdad Orchestra. Despite the spread of champeta as a musical phenomenon, it was not accepted by the social elite of Cartagena until much later. In fact, the origins of the word champeta can be traced to critics of the movement connecting it to its lower-class origins and reasoning that the name derived from brawls that were started in parties with knives known as "champetas." A more accurate, interpretation is that it derives from a creole language in which champeteaux means something characteristic of the people, making champeta "a music of the people."

CUBA

Throughout history, the music of Cuba has had such an impact on various countries and cultures that the task of trying to summarize even its African-influenced elements in this tiny space is difficult. Cuban music contributed to the developments of salsa, tango (of Argentina), West African Afrobeat, and jazz in the United States. Like the Brazilian developments detailed above, the Yoruba religion Santería, and all of its attendant musical traditions, infiltrated Cuban culture, including its music. Considering the fact that mambo, rumba, and the conga all developed out of Afro-Cuban musical traditions, Cuba is a veritable mecca of African-influenced musical culture in Latin America. Cuban musical innovations originated in the sociological interplay between African slaves and Spanish people who worked on sugar plantations and smaller tobacco farms. Like most African-influenced aspects of Latin American music, percussive elements formulate the foundation of the musical innovations. Thus, the clave, bongos, congas, and the bata drums are each central components to particular forms of Afro-Cuban music. In Cuba, slaves preserved various elements of their African heritage in cabildos (venues where Africans fellowshipped and socialized). Through these insulated social experiences, various forms of Afro-Cuban music developed.

One of the oldest and maybe the most important of these developments was that of *son* music. *Son* music is defined by its anticipated bass lines and its canny synthesis of African rhythms and Spanish guitar rifts. *Son* developed in the latter half of the nineteenth century and influenced most forms of Cuban music that developed after it. Although *son* music's content originally centered on romance and nationalism, it eventually began to take more sociopolitical issues as its theme.

Two of the more popular cabildos, Lucumi and Kongo, were responsible for music developments that led directly to the advent of rumba. The Lucumi cabildo became widely known for its use of bata drums, while the Kongo engendered similar notoriety for its use of yuka drums. Yuka drum music developed into rumba. Rumba bands traditionally used claves, palitos and one of the most ubiquitous elements of African influences on world culture: the call and response vocals. Despite mainstream perceptions of rumba as static ballroom music, its origins are improvisational and generally less formal. Still, it is internationally popular.

Through the 1920s and 1930s, rumba and son music enjoyed international popularity. Unfortunately, commercial success tended to dilute the cultural traditions of the music. In the 1940s one of the most revered and well-known soneros in Cuba, Arsenio Rodriquez, helped to recalibrate son music with its African rhythmic roots. Cuban music of the 1960s and 1970s, much like its United States musical counterparts, tended toward the intermingling of genres. This musical sense of the intermezzo facilitated the further popularization of Cuban music and contributed to the cultural space where modern salsa was born out of Arsenio Rodriguez's revitalized son style and various other Latin musical forms (the mambo and rumba). At the end of the twentieth century, timba—a lively, postmodern, dance-oriented music—and reggaeton—a mixture of hip-hop and reggae—captured the attention of Cuban youth along with other Latin musical strains.

Mexico

Mexican music is a hybrid of influences from African, European, Spanish, indigenous, and other Latin American musical forms. Considering three centuries of Spanish rule—and about 300,000 African slaves inhabiting various Mexican states—these influences were inevitable. Despite being separated geographically from Mexico by Central America, Colombia has also had a great influence on Mexican music. Colombian cumbia, with its complex rhythms and African influence became immensely popular in Mexico during the 1980s, becoming the dominant genre of that decade until the emergence of banda in the 1990s.

Mexico is mostly known, however, for its mariachi music which originated in the state of Jalisco as early as 1852. The musical form continued to evolve into the end of the nineteenth century, becoming a mixture of Spanish, European, and indigenous influence. African influences can be seen in the rhythmic pattern and syncopated styling known as *son*. Variations of the *son* (related to but not to be confused with Afro-Cuban *son* music) developed in other areas of Mexico, such as Veracruz (on the Gulf of Mexico), and is called *son jarocho* or *son veracruzano*. The music is characterized by the use of a harp instead of guitars as the primary instrument.

Venezuela

Though Venezuela is largely known for its salsa and merengue, African influences exist in Venezuelan folk music, which includes African-derived percussion with multiple rhythms like sangeo, fulia, and parranda. The Spanish contribution can be seen in the gaita rhythm. Gaita is the Spanish and Portuguese name for a bagpipe used in Galicia, Asturias, and northern Portugal.

Uruguay

As with all countries in Latin America, Uruguayan music has various influences. While there are Spanish influences in Uruguay's milonga, a Spanish guitar and song form, African influence can be seen in the Afro-Uruguayan percussion-based form of candombe, which is based on Bantu African drumming with some European and tango influences. It is also related to other musical forms of African origin, such as the Cuban son and tumba and the maracatu of Brazil. While candombe was used during ceremonial processions for the kings of Congo, it was also used during the time of African slavery in South America, when it was seen as a threat to the elites, who sought to ban the music and its dance in the beginning of the nineteenth century. This proved slightly difficult due to its mass appeal and the nature of how it is performed and danced. Typically, candombe is performed by a cuerda, or a group of fifty to one hundred drummers who use a variety of barrel-shaped drums called tambores, which vary according to their size and function. Tambores are made of wood and animal skin and are played with one stick and one hand, with the aide of a shoulder strap called a tali.

Today, candombe is still very much present in Uruguay, with about ninety cuerdas (candombe performance groups) in existence. Some groups perform regularly on Sunday nights in the streets of Montevideo, while a number of groups perform en masse during holidays, including January 6, December 25, and January 1. All cuerdas perform and compete annually during Uruguay's Carnival parade, called "llamadas" (calls), which takes place during the Carnival season.

PANAMA

Panama's national identity has evolved immensely since gaining its independence from Colombia in 1903. Though it is mostly inhabited by mestizos, or people of mixed African, European, and indigenous descent, a small minority of Africans remain in the Azuero region, located in the west of Panama.

Afro-Latin songs accompanied by dance and story-telling continue to exist in Panama. A dance called the tamborito, derived from the tambora drum, is danced by groups of men and women who sing, clap their hands, and stomp their feet. The women play "hard to get" and playfully whirl away when the men attempt to face them directly. The congo, a similar dance performed by the black communities of the eastern coast of Panama, uses upright drums. The instruments used in Panamanian music include drums of various sizes, a heavy brass bowl that gives a sharp metallic ring when struck, a five-stringed guitar, and a three-stringed violin. Typically, guitar derivatives are examples of Spanish influence, while drums are examples of African influence.

Due to major Colombian historical influence, the musical forms of salsa and cumbia top the charts more frequently than Panama's own popular music. Known for its distinctive vocal style, Panama's pop music is believed to have derived from Sevillians (people from the southern Spanish city of Sevilla) of African descent that arrived in the sixteenth century.

DOMINICAN REPUBLIC

The Dominican Republic is mostly known for its merengue music, though bachata is also popular. Both forms were initially associated with lower social classes, but they are now enjoyed by people from all classes and backgrounds. Bachata, meaning "a rowdy or lower-class party," is derived from bolero, a Cuban genre, and is largely recognized by its guitar-based ensembles. Some experts have theorized that the dance form of bachata also resembles slaves attempting to dance while shackled to one another.

Although the word *merengue* literally means "whipped egg whites and sugar," it also is used to describe the music and dance form that has become an integral part of Dominican culture. Typically, it is a combination of guiro or maracas percussion sections, the guyano or tambora drum (also used in Panama), wild accordions or saxophones, as well as a box bass. The guiro and the tambora drum were brought to the island by West African slaves.

The exact origins of merengue are still disputed today, though influences are apparent and obvious. Geographi-

Dancing to merengue in Las Terrenas, Dominican Republic. Featuring a combination of guiro or maracas percussion sections, the guyano or tambora drum, wild accordions or saxophones as well as a box base, merengue is a form of music and dance that has become an integral part of Dominican culture. © CATHERINE KARNOW/CORBIS

cally, many have pointed to its neighbor Haiti as influencing the creation of merengue. As the only two countries on the island of Hispaniola, perpetually intertwined cultures and various influences are only natural. Some say merengue may be related to the Hatian *mereng*, which is similar in sound but dominated by guitars rather than accordions. Others claim it is a mixture of the Spanish *decimal* and African *plena* music, whose beats and rhythms are derived from the African conga drum. Historically, plena also evolved into a traditional form of Puerto Rican music with African, indigenous (Taino), and Spanish influences. "Dominican social dance as a whole, past and present, integrates European-derived fashion, introduced through the social clubs of the urban elite, with African-influenced music and dance, of rural origin" (Davis, 1996).

Some Dominican dances have strong Haitian and Caribbean influences, while some evolved from foreign military occupation forces. The "pambiche" form of merengue, for example, is supposedly an imitation of American soldiers attempting to dance the merengue during the U.S. occupation in the Dominican Republic from 1916 to 1922. Afro-Caribbean urban dances of the nineteenth century also popular in the Dominican Republic included the Cuba's danzon son and bolero, as well as the Puerto Rican danza. Lastly, strong African influences can be seen in other traditions, such as salve, a type of singing used in ceremonies, parties, and pilgrimages dedicated to saints. Salve singing is a call-and-response form and is accompanied by African instruments such as panderos and atabales. Call and response (between musical instruments) is a West African tradition that involves the succession of two distinct phrases played by two different musicians.

The pattern has evolved over the centuries into various forms of cultural expression, including public gatherings, religious ceremonies, children's rhymes, and African-American music such as gospel, the blues, rhythm-and-blues, jazz, and, more recently, hip-hop.

Hip-Hop Culture in Latin America

As in the United States, hip-hop in Latin America originated as a form of expression for youth who wished to speak out against historical oppressions that took place in their native country and communities.

COLOMBIA. While showing a Colombian influence musically—with smooth blends of Latin melodies and salsa cadences mixed into hip-hop breaks—lyrically, the songs deal with issues of social injustices and reflect on Colombia's five hundred years of imperialism, in which its people have been massacred, enslaved, forced to migrate, and during which the country itself was robbed of its natural resources. Resistance to these injustices began centuries ago, with African natives creating "palenques," or free and independent towns, in order to defend their territories. Insurgent movements, social uprisings, and coup d'etats continued to plague Colombia, resulting in today's war between Colombia's government and armed antigovernment groups such as the Revolutionary Armed Forces of Colombia (FARC).

Colombian rap groups such as Cescru Enlace, Zona Marginal, and La Etnia frequently cover political issues such as Colombia's drug-fueled guerilla war, which continues to claim the lives of innocent victims, and the fleeing of Colombian refugees who fear for their lives in the midst of their country's civil conflicts.

Though rap is not considered part of the mainstream music scene in Colombia, it has grown immensely among Colombian youth in major cities like Bogotá and Cali, as well as in areas like Aguablanca (located on the outskirts of Cali). Typically, Colombian hip-hop artists make their own CD's and sell them in local record stores or in the streets. This "underground movement" has spread quickly and acquired enough popularity to gain the interest of larger record labels, who are becoming more interested in making hip-hop a part of the larger music establishment. There are, however, concerns regarding the political and controversial issues covered in a large portion of these records, making it more difficult to push Colombian hip-hop above its underground status.

Others who see the need to spread consciousness about these issues however, find ways to give Colombian hip-hop the exposure they feel it deserves. In Colombia's capital, Bogotá, a rap festival was organized by local groups, while a hip-hop cultural center was created by a group of rappers in Bogotá's colonial center, offering classes in graffiti art, break dancing, and music mixing.

ARGENTINA. Hip-hop in Argentina has existed since the 1980s in certain areas of Buenos Aires, where artists like Frost, Mike Dee, and Jazzy Mel were popular. Much like historical trading and influential migrations of the past, hip-hop songs infiltrated into Argentine culture through cassettes brought into the country by tourists, while hip-hop videos ultimately gained copious rotations on television and radio. By the mid-1990s a group called the "Argentine Union of Hip-Hop" (known today as "The Union.") was created, and artists and groups like Tombs, $$uper-a, AMC, and Race became popular.

MEXICO. Mexican rap can be traced to the early 1990s and a dance-pop act named Calo, which was made up of one MC (master of ceremonies) and four dancers. Their music was composed of singing over popular synthesized dance music and initiated an underground movement that spread throughout Mexico. Some of the influences on Mexican rap include Kid Frost from East Los Angeles, California; The Mexakinz from Long Beach, California; Cypress Hill from South Central, Los Angeles; and Delinquent Habits from Los Angeles. Groups like Control Machete and Molotov emerged in the mid 1990s as a result of these American-based groups. Though they achieved commercial success by blending their rap style with Mexican country music and traditional Latin riffs, hip-hop in Mexico remains undiscovered by the mainstream. Radio exposure is limited, and it is an underground movement in working-class neighborhoods, or "barrios," where artists burn their own CDs and have small labels reproduce them for sale to a loyal audience. As in the early years of hip-hop in the United States and Colombia, Mexican rappers focus on the inequalities that plague their country, including seventy years with the same political party in power (until the 2000 elections) and the Spanish conquests that historically enhanced racial conflicts. More modern problems include drug-trafficking gangs, poverty, and police corruption. Unknown artists have even renamed their Mexican rap "rapza," which is a combination of the words *rap* and *raza*, meaning "race" in Spanish.

CUBA. The history of hip-hop in Cuba is similar to the history of hip-hop in other countries. Its evolution, however, has been vastly different. Cuban audiences first heard and saw hip-hop in the 1980s through radio and television broadcasts from Miami, Florida. Though originally audiences focused on break dancing, the collapse of the Soviet Union, which had been a huge supporter of the Cuban economy, brought about a period of frustration in which Cuban youth were looking for ways to express themselves. Due to the sensitive relations between the United States and Cuba, hip-hop was initially seen as a vulgar, explicit, violent, and improper cultural invasion from the United States. With the help of a progressive hip-hop movement begun by Nehanda Abiodun, a U.S. Black Liberation Army activist in political exile in Cuba, Cuban hip-hop began to evolve into a personal art about Cuba and its unique culture, government, and way of life.

Since then, hip-hop has been embraced in Cuba, and there is an annual hip-hop festival in the Havana district of Alamar. According to Ariel Fernández of Asociacion Hermanos Saíz (AHS), one of the cosponsoring organizations for the festival, Cuban hip-hop is a revolution within a revolution. Musically, Cuban rap incorporates instruments like batas (tall drums), the guitar bass, live drums and congas. With an estimated two hundred hip-hop groups in Havana, and about three hundred throughout the island (as of 2002), Cuban hip-hop shows no signs of slowing down. Groups like "Amenaza" (the Threat) and "Primera Base" (First Base) formed in the mid-1990s, followed by "Instinto" (Instinct), Cuba's first female rap group, and more modern groups like "Anonimo Consejo" (Anonymous Advice), "Bajo Mundo" (Under World), and "Freehole Negro" (Freehole Black).

Cuban rap is a complicated phenomenon, however, as it is accepted under Fidel Castro's maxim "within the revolution, everything," and it is not seen as a threat as long as it is not viewed to be counter-revolutionary. Inevitably, this is difficult to guarantee, considering the opinionated nature of hip-hop in general and the tendency for rappers to speak out against the norm, whatever it may be. Though Fidel Castro himself is reportedly impressed by hip-hop, the boundaries of acceptable hip-hop in Cuba are still sensitive and subject to various opinions and definitions.

BRAZIL. Hip-hop was introduced in Brazil in the 1980's, and it has developed into what is now called "Hippy Hoppy." Brazil has managed to embrace and develop all elements of hip-hop in its own way, having representation in international DJ and break-dancing competitions, as well as hosting the first world show of graffiti in the city of Santo Andre during the Summer of 2003. In fact, rap in Brazil has developed to the point of having seven different styles, including gospel, gangster, futuristic, underground, and rock fusion. Some even claim American rap is hardly listened to anymore.

The origins of hip-hop in Brazil, however, are similar to those in the United States, Colombia, and Mexico. Marginalized youth with limited access to employment and education used, and continue to use, hip-hop as an outlet and a way to criticize the social and economic injustices around them, such as the drug-infested Brazilian shantytowns, or favelas, which are poverty-stricken ghettos with high levels of crime and violence.

Hip-hop has also been used in Brazil to educate its population regarding the ideas of revolution, democracy and the country's history, including various Afro-Brazilian leaders and Brazil's struggle to end its military dictatorship. Today, many have continued the sociopolitical progression of Brazilian hip-hop and the construction of a new Brazil, with hip-hop–focused community projects and centers that are dedicated to educating and helping local Brazilian youth.

Musically, Brazilian hip-hop is as diverse as its culture, combining hip-hop beats and samba rhythms with instruments like the bossa nova guitar. Older rap groups and artists like MVBill (Mensagerio de Verdad) and Racionais (the Rationals) publicly and aggressively address social injustices using Brazilian percussion and hip-hop beats, while more modern groups like Somos Nós A Justica use funky piano riffs and a care-free style of experimentation.

See also Candomblé; Dance, Diasporic; Folk Music; Hip-Hop; Music; Rap; Slavery

■ ■ *Bibliography*

Behague, Gerard. *Music in Latin America: An Introduction.* Englewood Cliffs, N.J.: Prentice Hall, 1979.

Beezley, William H., and Linda A. Curcio-Nagy, eds. *Latin American Popular Culture: An Introduction.* Wilmington, Del.: Scholarly Resources, 2000.

Chasteen, John C. "Black Kings, Blackface Carnival, and Nineteenth-Century Origins of the Tango." In *Latin American Popular Culture*, edited by W. H. Beezly and L. A. Cuicio-Nagy, pp. 43–45. Wilmington, Del.: Scholarly Resources Inc., 2000.

Chasteen, John C. *Born in Blood and Fire: A Concise History of Latin America.* New York: Norton, 2001.

Crook, Larry. "Northeastern Brazil." In *Music in Latin American Culture: Regional Traditions*, edited by John M. Schechter. New York: Schirmer, 1999.

Davis, Ellen Martha. "Dominican Republic: A Creole Culture." *New Routes: Traditional Music and Dance in America*, May, 22, 1996.

Forero, Juan. "For Colombia's Angry Youth, Hip-Hop Helps Keep it Real." *New York Times,* April 16, 2004.

Marshall, Jesse. "Hip-Hop in Brazil." *People's Weekly World Newspaper* (July 2003).

Neate, Patrick. *Where You're At: Notes from the Frontline of a Hip Hop Planet.* New York: Riverhead Books, 2003.

O'Neil, Tim. "The Rough Guide to Brazilian Hip-Hop" (Review). Available from <http://www.popmatters.com/music/reviews/various/various-roughguidebrazilianhiphop.shtml>.

Pratt, Timothy. "The Rap Cartel and Other Tales from Colombia." *The Courier,* July, 2000.

Schechter, John M., ed. *Music in Latin American Culture: Regional Traditions.* New York: Schirmer, 1999.

Slonimsky, Nicolas. *Music of Latin America.* New York: Thomas Y. Cromwell, 1945.

Sublette, Ned. *Cuba and Its Music: From the First Drums to the Mambo.* Chicago: A Cappella, 2004.

Umlauf, Simon. "Cuban Hip-Hop: The Rebellion within the Revolution." CNN.com (November 25, 2002).

JAMES PETERSON (2005)
MARCELA POVEDA (2005)

MUSIC IN THE UNITED STATES

The African-American music tradition comprises many different genres and forms, including spirituals, work songs, blues, gospel music, jazz, and popular music. Each genre includes a complex of subdivisions and is associated with a specific cultural function, social context, and historical period. Despite these distinguishing factors, the various genres exist as part of a musical continuum of African origin. The secular and sacred forms share musical features, demonstrating that the two spheres are complementary rather than oppositional.

The web of African-American musical genres is a product of interactions between people of African descent and various environmental forces in North America. The African-American music tradition documents the ways African Americans reconciled their dual national identity and forged a meaningful life in a foreign environment, first as slaves and later as second-class citizens.

AFRICAN CULTURE IN AMERICA

When Africans arrived as slaves in America, they brought a culture endowed with many traditions foreign to their European captors. Their rituals for worshiping African gods and celebrating ancestors, death, and holidays, for example, displayed features uncommon to Western culture. Most noticeable among African practices was the prominent tie of music and movement. The description of a ritual for a dying woman, recorded by the daughter of a Virginia planter in her *Plantation Reminiscences* (n.d.), illustrates the centrality of these cultural expressions and the preservation of African traditions in slave culture:

Several days before her death . . . [h]er room was crowded with Negroes who had come to perform their religious rites around the death bed. Joining hands they performed a savage dance, shouting wildly around her bed. Although [Aunt Fanny was] an intelligent woman, she seemed to cling to the superstitions of her race.

After the savage dance and rites were over . . . I went, and said to her: ". . . we are afraid the noise [singing] and dancing have made you worse."

Speaking feebly, she replied: "Honey, that kind of religion suits us black folks better than your kind. What suits Mars Charles' mind, don't suit mine." (Epstein 1977, p. 130)

Slaveholders and missionaries assumed that exposure to Euro-American cultural traditions would encourage slaves to abandon their African way of life. For some slaves, particularly those who were in constant contact with whites through work and leisure activities, such was the case. The majority of slaves, however, systematically resisted cultural imprisonment by reinterpreting European traditions through an African lens. A description of the slaves' celebration of Pinkster Day, a holiday of Dutch origin, illustrates how the event was transformed into an African-style festival characterized by dancing, drumming, and singing. Dr. James Eights, an observer of this celebration in the late 1700s, noted that the principal instrument accompanying the dancing was an eel-pot drum. This kettle-shaped drum consisted of a wide, single head covered with sheepskin. Over the rhythms the drummer repeated "hi-a-bomba, bomba, bomba."

These vocal sounds were readily taken up and as oft repeated by the female portion of the spectators not otherwise engaged in the exercises of the scene, accompanied by the beating of time with their ungloved hands, in strict accordance with the eel-pot melody.

Merrily now the dance moved on, and briskly twirled the lads and lasses over the well trampled green sward; loud and more quickly swelled the sounds of music to the ear, as the excited movements increased in energy and action. (Eights [1867], reprinted in Southern 1983, pp. 45–46)

The physical detachment of African Americans from Africa and the widespread disappearance of many original African musical artifacts did not prevent Africans and their descendants from creating, interpreting, and experiencing music from an African perspective. Relegated to the status of slaves in America, Africans continued to perform songs of the past. They also created new musical forms and reinterpreted those of European cultures using the vocabulary, idiom, and aesthetic principles of African traditions. The earliest indigenous musical form created within the American context was known as the *Negro spiritual*.

THE EVOLUTION OF NEGRO SPIRITUALS

The original form of the Negro spiritual emerged at the turn of the nineteenth century. Later known as the *folk spiritual*, it was a form of expression that arose within a religious context and through black people's resistance to cultural subjugation by the larger society. When missionaries introduced blacks to Christianity in systematic fashion (c. 1740s), slaves brought relevance to the instruction by reinterpreting Protestant ideals through an African prism. Negro spirituals, therefore, symbolize a unique religious expression, a black cultural identity and worldview that is illustrated in the religious and secular meanings that spirituals often held—a feature often referred to as *double entendre*.

Many texts found in Negro spirituals compare the slave's worldly oppression to the persecution and suffering of Jesus Christ. Others protest their bondage, as in the familiar lines "Befor' I'd be a slave, I'd be buried in my grave, and go home to my Lord and be free." A large body of spiritual texts is laced with coded language that can be interpreted accurately only through an evaluation of the performance context. For example, a spiritual such as the one cited below could have been sung by slaves to organize clandestine meetings and plan escapes:

If you want to find Jesus, go in the wilderness,
   Mournin' brudder,
You want to find Jesus, go into the wilderness,
I wait upon de Lord, I wait upon de Lord,
I wait upon de Lord, my God, Who take away de sin of
   de world.

The text of this song provided instructions for slaves to escape from bondage: "Jesus" was the word for "freedom"; "wilderness" identified the meeting place; "de Lord" referred to the person who would lead slaves through the Underground Railroad or a secret route into the North (the land of freedom). This and other coded texts were incomprehensible to missionaries, planters, and other whites, who interpreted them as "meaningless and disjointed affirmations."

The folk spiritual tradition draws from two basic sources: African-derived songs and the Protestant repertory of psalms, hymns, and spiritual songs. Missionaries introduced blacks to Protestant traditions through Christian instruction, anticipating that these songs would replace those of African origin, which they referred to as "extravagant and nonsensical chants, and catches" (Epstein 1977, pp. 61–98). When slaves and free blacks worshiped with whites, they were expected to adhere to prescribed Euro-American norms. Therefore, blacks did not develop a distinct body of religious music until they gained religious autonomy.

When blacks were permitted to lead their own religious services, many transformed the worship into an African-inspired ritual of which singing was an integral part. The Reverend Robert Mallard described the character of this ritual, which he observed in Chattanooga, Tennessee, in 1859:

> I stood at the door and looked in—and such confusion of sights and sounds! . . . Some were standing, others sitting, others moving from one seat to another, several exhorting along the aisles. The whole congregation kept up one monotonous strain, interrupted by various sounds: groans and screams and clapping of hands. One woman especially under the influence of the excitement went across the church in a quick succession of leaps: now [on] her knees . . . then up again; now with her arms about some brother or sister, and again tossing them wildly in the air and clapping her hands together and accompanying the whole by a series of short, sharp shrieks. (Myers 1972, pp. 482–483)

During these rituals slaves not only sang their own African-derived songs but reinterpreted European psalms and hymns as well.

An English musician, whose tour of the United States from 1833 to 1841 included a visit to a black church in Vicksburg, Virginia, described how slaves altered the original character of a psalm:

> When the minister gave out his own version of the Psalm, the choir commenced singing so rapidly that the original tune absolutely ceased to exist—in fact, the fine old psalm tune became thoroughly transformed into a kind of negro melody; and so sudden was the transformation, by accelerating the time. (Russell 1895, pp. 84–85)

In 1853 the landscape architect Frederick Law Olmsted encountered a similar situation, witnessing a hymn change into a "confused wild kind of chant" (Olmsted 1904). The original tunes became unrecognizable because blacks altered the structure, melody, rhythm, and tempo in accordance with African aesthetic principles.

The clergy objected not only to such altered renditions of Protestant songs but also to songs created independently. John Watson, a white Methodist minister, referred to the latter as "short scraps of disjointed affirmations, pledges or prayers, lengthened out with long repetitive choruses." The rhythmic bodily movements that accompanied the singing caused even more concern among the clergy:

> With every word so sung, they have a sinking of one or other leg of the body alternately, producing an audible sound of the feet at every step. . . .If some in the meantime sit, they strike the sounds alternately on each thigh. What in the name of religion, can countenance or tolerate such gross perversions of true religion! (Watson [1819] in Southern 1983, p. 63)

As they had long done in African traditions, audible physical gestures provided the rhythmic foundation for singing.

The slaves' interpretation of standard Christian doctrine and musical practice demonstrated their refusal to abandon their cultural values for those of their masters and the missionaries. Undergirding the slaves' independent worship services were African values that emphasized group participation and free expression. These principles govern the features of the folk spiritual tradition: (1) communal composition; (2) call-response; (3) repetitive choruses; (4) improvised melodies and texts; (5) extensive melodic ornamentation (slurs, bends, shouts, moans, groans, cries); (6) heterophonic (individually varied) group singing; (7) complex rhythmic structures; and (8) the integration of song and bodily movement.

The call-response structure promotes both individual expression and group participation. The soloist, who presents the call, is free to improvise on the melody and text; the congregation provides a fixed response. Repetitive chorus lines also encourage group participation. Melodic ornamentation enables singers to embellish and thus intensify performances. Clapped and stamped rhythmic patterns create layered metrical structures as a foundation for gestures and dance movements.

Folk spirituals were also commonplace among many free blacks who attended independent African-American churches in the eighteenth and nineteenth centuries. These blacks expressed their racial pride by consciously rejecting control and cultural domination by the affiliated white church. Richard Allen, founder of Bethel African Methodist Episcopal (AME) Church in Philadelphia in 1794, was the first African-American minister of an independent black church to alter the cultural style of Protestant worship so that it would have greater appeal for his black congregation.

Recognizing the importance of music, Allen chose to compile his own hymnal rather than use the standard one for Methodist worship (which contained no music). The second edition of this hymnal, *A Collection of Spiritual Songs and Hymns Selected from Various Authors, by Richard Allen, Minister of the African Methodist Episcopal Church* (1801), contains some of Allen's original song texts, as well as other hymns favored by his congregation. To some of these hymns Allen added refrain lines and choruses to the typical stanza or verse form to ensure full congregational participation in the singing. Allen's congregation performed these songs in the style of folk spirituals, which generated much criticism from white Methodist ministers. Despite such objections, other AME churches adopted the musical practices established at Bethel.

In the 1840s, Daniel A. Payne, an AME minister who later became a bishop, campaigned to change the church's folk-style character. A former Presbyterian pastor educated in a white Lutheran seminary, Payne subscribed to the Euro-American view of the "right, fit, and proper way of serving God" (Payne [1888] in Southern 1983, p. 69). Therefore, he restructured the AME service to conform to the doctrines, literature, and musical practices of white elite churches. Payne introduced Western choral literature performed by a trained choir and instrumental music played by an organist. These forms replaced the congregational singing of folk spirituals, which Payne labeled "cornfield ditties." While some independent urban black churches adopted Payne's initiatives, discontented members left to join other churches or establish their own. However, the majority of the AME churches, especially those in the South, denounced Payne's "improvements" and continued their folk-style worship.

Payne and his black counterparts affiliated with other AME and with Episcopalian, Lutheran, and Presbyterian churches, represented an emerging black educated elite that demonstrated little if any tolerance for religious practices contrary to Euro-American Christian ideals of "reverence" and "refinement." Their training in white seminaries shaped their perspective on an "appropriate" style of worship. In the Protestant Episcopal Church, for example, a southern white member noted that these black leaders "were accustomed to use no other worship than the regular course prescribed in the *Book of Common Prayer*, for the day. Hymns, or Psalms out of the same book were sung, and printed sermon read. . . . No extemporary address, exhortation, or prayer, was permitted, or used" (Epstein 1977, p. 196). Seminary-trained black ministers rejected traditional practices of black folk churches because they did not conform to aesthetic principles associated with written traditions. Sermons read from the written script, musical performances that strictly adhered to the printed score, and the notion of reserved behavior marked those religious practices considered most characteristic and appropriate within Euro-American liturgical worship.

In contrast, practices associated with the black folk church epitomize an oral tradition. Improvised sermons, prayers, testimonies, and singing, together with demonstrative behavior, preserve the African values of spontaneity and communal interaction.

SECULAR MUSIC IN THE SLAVE COMMUNITY

The core secular genres among African-American slaves were work songs, field calls and street cries, social and game songs, and dance music. Work songs accompanied all forms of labor, providing encouragement and strength and relieving boredom. The texts, improvised by field workers, stevedores, dockworkers, weavers, boat rowers, and others, frequently reflected the type of work performed. In sociopolitical terms, work songs provided an outlet for protest and criticism while the song rhythms coordinated the efforts of workers and regulated the rate of labor. Performances of work songs exhibit call-response and repetitive chorus structures; melodic, textual, and timbral variation; heterophonic vocal textures; and percussive delivery.

Field calls (rural) and street cries (urban) were used by workers for personal communication. Field calls enabled workers to maintain contact with one another from a distance, make their presence known (e.g., the water boy), attract attention, or communicate a mood. Street vendors used special cries to advertise their products. Both field calls and street cries consisted of short, improvised phrases performed in a free and highly individual style. These features contrast with the call-response and the repetitive choruses that characterize work songs.

Game songs accompanied children's activities, facilitating play and the development of motor and social skills. Song texts provided instructions for playing games, as well as a vehicle for the expression of children's fantasies and worldview. Game songs embody all of the aesthetic features associated with folk spirituals, including group interaction, clapping, and stamping.

Slaves spent much of their leisure time singing and dancing. Accounts of these activities and holiday celebrations from the seventeenth and eighteenth centuries indicate that a variety of African instruments—drums, xylophones, calabashes, horns, banjos, musical bows, tambourines, triangles, and jawbones—were played in a distinctly African style and accompanied dancing.

Beginning in the 1740s, however, as a consequence of slave revolts, many colonies passed legislation that prohibited the playing of African drums and horns. Such legislation did not restrict the musical and dance activities of slaves. Over time, as traditional African instruments disappeared, blacks found functional substitutes for some of these instruments and constructed modified versions of others. Wooden boxes, stamping, and clapping replaced drums; spoons, washboards, and washtubs substituted for rattles, scrapers, and other percussion instruments; panpipes, fifes, and jugs substituted for flutes and other wind instruments; and the diddly bow and washtub bass were adapted versions of the musical bow. Using these instruments, slaves created new forms of dance accompaniment that later became a part of the blues tradition.

Slaves also adopted European instruments, which they learned to play as early as the 1690s. The fiddle and fife were popular among slaves, and they played them in conjunction with African instruments. By the nineteenth century, the fiddle and banjo (a derivation from the African lute) had become the most common instruments to accompany dancing. Combining African-derived instruments with European instruments, African Americans created an original form of improvised and rhythmically complex dance music that would give birth to ragtime and jazz in the late nineteenth and twentieth centuries, respectively.

THE RECONSTRUCTION ERA

The end of the Civil War in 1865 symbolically marked the freedom of slaves. The social upheaval and political maneuvering that followed the war, however, restricted the freedmen's integration into mainstream society. While some ex-slaves had access to the new educational institutions established for blacks, the vast majority had few if any options for social advancement and economic stability.

In the Reconstruction South, many African-Americans remained effectively enslaved because of an emergent system called *sharecropping*. This system, defined by an inequitable economic arrangement between landlords (former slaveholders) and sharecroppers (freed blacks), kept blacks in debt and subjugated them to southern whites. Most sharecroppers lived in the same shacks on the same farms and plantations that they had as slaves. For nearly a century this arrangement isolated most African Americans from mainstream society, restricted their mobility, and limited their economic empowerment. African Americans survived this oppressive environment by preserving fundamental values of the past, as they had

University Singers of New Orleans, c. 1880. PHOTOGRAPHS AND PRINTS DIVISION, SCHOMBURG CENTER FOR RESEARCH IN BLACK CULTURE, THE NEW YORK PUBLIC LIBRARY, ASTOR, LENOX AND TILDEN FOUNDATIONS.

done as slaves. These values manifested themselves in new forms of musical expression.

ARRANGED SPIRITUALS

The evolution of new and diverse musical forms during the post–Civil War years paralleled the divergent lifestyles among African Americans. While the social and economic conditions of many ex-slaves remained virtually unchanged, the establishment of black colleges that had begun in 1856 (Wilberforce University in Wilberforce, Ohio) provided some with opportunities for social and economic advancement. Within this context, black students adopted various Euro-American cultural models dictated by the established Eurocentric college curricula.

At Fisk University, founded in 1866 in Nashville, Tennessee, the white treasurer, George White, organized the Fisk Jubilee Singers to raise money for the school. The Jubilee Singers initially performed both the standard European repertory and arranged Negro spirituals. Responding to the preferences of white audiences, White centered the group's performances around spirituals. The Fisk Jubilee

Singers were the first to popularize the choral arrangement of spirituals. Their successful concerts, presented throughout the nation and world beginning in 1871, inspired the subsequent formation of similar groups at Hampton Institute in Virginia and at other black colleges.

George White, influenced by his musical background, arranged the folk spiritual in a European concert form and insisted on a performance style that appealed to the aesthetics and preferences of white audiences. In doing so, according to John Work, he "eliminated every element that detracted from the pure emotion of the song. . . .Finish, precision and sincerity were demanded by this leader. Mr. White strove for an art presentation" (Work 1940, p. 15).

White's "art presentation" of spirituals required strict conformity to the written tradition. In his arrangements, four-part harmony replaced heterophonic singing, and strict adherence to the printed score eliminated melodic and textual improvisation and the clapping and stamping accompaniment. Despite the removal of elements associated with the oral tradition, evidence of the folk spiritual tradition remained in call-response, syncopation, polyrhythms, melodic and textual repetition, and linguistic dialect.

The legacy of the Fisk Jubilee Singers continued in the 1920s when Hall Johnson and Eva Jessye formed professional choirs specializing in this idiom. Both choirs gave concerts in major halls and on radio, and appeared in theatrical and film productions.

During the second decade of the twentieth century, another concert version of the folk spiritual appeared. This form transformed the folk spiritual into an art song for solo voice. Conservatory-trained singer-composer Harry T. Burleigh provided the model, arranging "Deep River" (1916) for voice and piano. Burleigh's arrangement brought publication to this musical form, which eventually became a standard part of the repertory of African-American concert singers. Influenced by Burleigh, performers such as Roland Hayes, Marian Anderson, Paul Robeson, and Dorothy Maynor concluded their solo concerts with arranged solo spirituals, as black college choirs continue to do even today. William Warfield, McHenry Boatwright, Camilla Williams, Willis Patterson, Rawn Spearman, Jessye Norman, Leontyne Price, Grace Bumbry, Shirley Verrett, George Shirley, Simon Estes, Martina Arroyo, and Kathleen Battle are among those who followed this tradition in the post–World War II years.

THE USE OF FOLK IDIOMS IN CONCERT MUSIC OF AFRICAN-AMERICAN COMPOSERS

During the first decade of the twentieth century, a core group of black composers sought to create a school of composition using African and African-derived vernacular forms. Harry T. Burleigh, Samuel Coleridge-Taylor, Will Marion Cook, R. Nathaniel Dett, Clarence Cameron White, and the brothers John Rosamond Johnson and James Weldon Johnson were among the first composers to arrange and/or write choral and small instrumental works inspired by folk spirituals, blues, ragtime, and other vernacular forms for the concert stage. They pioneered a nationalist school of composition that preserved the spirit and musical features of black folk idioms. In *Six Plantation Melodies for Violin and Piano* (1901) and *Jubilee Songs of the United States of America* (1916, a collection of spirituals arranged for solo voice and piano accompaniment), for example, Burleigh sought to maintain the racial flavor of the original folk melody. To achieve this, Eileen Southern noted, Burleigh's piano accompaniments "rarely overpower the simple melodies but rather set and sustain a dominant emotional mood throughout the song" (Southern 1983, p. 268).

Samuel Coleridge-Taylor (born in England of African and British ancestry) also made every effort to preserve the integrity of original folk melodies in his compositions. Inspired by the appearance of the Fisk Jubilee Singers in London, Coleridge-Taylor arranged traditional African and African-American folk melodies in a piece for piano, *Twenty-four Negro Melodies*, Op. 59 (1904). Coleridge-Taylor's notes on this work emphasized that he employed original melodies without the "idea of 'improving' the original material any more than Brahms' Variations on the Haydn Theme 'improved' that" (reprint of liner notes to *Twenty-four Negro Melodies*, recorded by Francis Walker).

Sharing Coleridge-Taylor's perspective, other nationalist composers used vernacular materials with the intent of maintaining their original character. Dett's *In the Bottoms* (1913), a suite for piano, employs various dance rhythms associated with African-American folk culture. Its opening "Prelude" mimics the texture and rhythms of a syncopated banjo, and the last piece, "Dance (Juba)," captures the complex rhythms of *pattin' juba*. Pattin' juba was a popular self-accompanying dance common among slaves that involved singing and stamping while alternately clapping the hands and striking each shoulder and thigh.

Dett's use of black folk rhythms, melodies, textures, and timbres demonstrates one way in which nationalist composers preserved the integrity of the folk idiom. Their efforts to create a distinct racial artistic identity using European models were advanced by African-American creative artists and intellectuals of the 1920s and 1930s in what became known as the Harlem Renaissance.

Throughout the Harlem Renaissance, African-American intellectuals and university-trained writers, musicians, and visual artists discussed ways to liberate themselves from the restrictions of European cultural expression. As a group they pioneered the concept of the New Negro—one who claimed an identity founded on self-respect, self-dependence, racial pride, and racial solidarity. The New Negro's ultimate concern, according to William Grant Still, was "the development of our racial culture and . . . its integration into American culture" (Still [n.d.] in Haas 1972, p. 129). Both intellectuals and creative artists agreed that this goal could be achieved by incorporating African-American folk materials into European concert and literary forms. They disagreed, however, on the appropriate presentation of these materials.

Whereas the pioneer nationalists shared the belief that the original character of folk idioms should be preserved, the Harlem Renaissance group expressed the need to adapt or "elevate" these idioms to the level of "high art" (Locke 1925, p. 28; Locke 1936, pp. 21–23; Still [n.d.] in Haas 1972, p. 134). The issues appear to have concerned

A postcard celebrates the Washington Trio as "Masters of Melody." *Originally published in* Progress and Achievements of the Colored People *(1917), by Joseph R. Gay and Kelly Miller.* GENERAL RESEARCH AND REFERENCE DIVISION, SCHOMBURG CENTER FOR RESEARCH IN BLACK CULTURE, THE NEW YORK PUBLIC LIBRARY, ASTOR, LENOX AND TILDEN FOUNDATIONS.

the degree to which the folk idiom could be altered through thematic development without losing its authentic character, the use of arrangements that supported rather than diluted the spirit of the folk form, and the preservation of the folk quality without restricting the creative impulses of composers (Burleigh [1924], quoted in Southern 1983, p. 268; Locke 1925, pp. 207–208). Composers of the Harlem Renaissance, including William Grant Still, William Dawson, and Howard Swanson, employed various approaches in establishing racial identity in their music. Some utilized authentic folk melodies; others composed thematic material in the spirit and with the flavor of vernacular idioms; and still others worked to capture the ambience of the folk environment.

William Grant Still, known as the dean of African-American composers, wrote many works using a broad range of African, American-African, and Caribbean folk material. In the first movement of his well-known *Afro-American Symphony* (1930), for example, Still juxtaposes original blues and spiritual melodies; in the third movement he introduces the banjo, the most familiar of all Afri-

can instruments in the New World. In *Levee Land* (1925), a work for orchestra and soloist, he experiments with jazz elements. *Sahdji* (1930), a ballet for orchestra and chorus, and *Mota* (1951), an opera, dramatize African life. The opera *Troubled Island* (1941) captures the spirit of Haitian culture.

William Dawson, using a slightly different approach, juxtaposed existing folk and folk-inspired themes in his *Negro Folk Symphony* (1934). The Harlem Renaissance composers also established racial identities in their vocal and choral works by employing texts by such African-American writers as Langston Hughes, Countee Cullen, Paul Laurence Dunbar, and Arna Bontemps. Hughes, for example, wrote the poems for Howard Swanson's "The Negro Speaks of Rivers" (1942) and "Lady's Boogie" (1947) and the libretto for Still's *Troubled Island.*

Despite the efforts of these conservatory-trained musicians to preserve the integrity of folk expressions, their music had limited appeal outside middle-class audiences. Even within this group, some expressed concern about over-elaboration and the tendency to place too much emphasis on formal European conventions. Anthropologist-folklorist Zora Neale Hurston vehemently objected to concert presentations of Negro spirituals. She argued that the aesthetic ideas of oral traditions that allow for spontaneous, improvisatory, and interactive expression could not be captured in the written score or reproduced by trained musicians (Hurston 1976, pp. 344–345).

The wider African-American folk community shared Hurston's views, objecting that the new modes of presentation were too "pretty" (Work 1949, pp. 136–137). The community simply did not share the aesthetic ideals of the black elite. Even though many composers attempted to preserve vocabulary, form, structure, rhythms, textures, tonal qualities, and aesthetic devices of folk forms, the printed score changed the character of the original style. Because of this, most of the African-American folk community was unable to relate to the aesthetic qualities associated with concert presentations of folk idioms.

RAGTIME

Ragtime refers to both a style of performance and a musical genre characterized by a syncopated, or "ragged," melody played over a quarter- or eighth-note bass pattern. The ragtime style evolved out of syncopated banjo melodies in the 1880s and was popularized in African-American communities by itinerant pianists and brass bands. The pianists, who played in honky-tonks, saloons, and brothels, improvised on folk and popular tunes, transforming them into contemporary African-American dance music. In a similar fashion, black brass bands "ragged" the melodies of traditional marches, hymns, spirituals, and folk and popular songs during funeral processions, parades, and other celebrations, changing the character of these melodies.

By the late 1890s, ragtime had come to identify a body of composed syncopated piano and vocal music published for mass consumption. As such, its improvisatory character and syncopated embellishments became formalized and simplified in written form. The availability of ragtime as sheet music resulted in the ragtime explosion of the first two decades of the twentieth century. Ragtime's syncopated rhythms quickly became popular among amateur and professional pianists. Responding to the demand for this music, publishers flooded the market with ragtime arrangements of popular and folk tunes, marches, and European classical songs for dance orchestras and marching and concert bands and vocal versions for singers. African-American ragtime composers include Thomas Turpin, Scott Joplin, Jelly Roll Morton, Eubie Blake, and Artie Matthews.

The vocal counterparts of instrumental ragtime were labeled *coon songs*. Popularized by minstrel performers in the late 1800s, coon songs became mainstays in vaudeville and Broadway productions in the 1900s. Coon songs are distinguished from other vocal genres of twentieth-century popular music by the use of black dialect and often denigrating lyrics. Between 1900 and 1920, vocal and instrumental ragtime dominated musical performances in theaters, saloons, ballrooms, and the homes of the white middle class, giving a degree of respectability to a form once associated with brothels and minstrel shows.

BLUES

The blues evolved from work songs and field calls during the 1880s in response to the inhumane treatment and second-class citizenship that had defined black life in America for seven decades. The blues share the aesthetic qualities of folk spirituals, and like spirituals they attempt to make sense of and give meaning to life. Two historic rulings by the U.S. Supreme Court, in 1883 and 1896, created the social and political environment from which the blues sprang. The first declared the 1875 Civil Rights Act unconstitutional, and the second upheld the "separate but equal" policy related to the *Plessy v. Ferguson* (1896) court case, which sanctioned segregation or Jim Crow as the law of the land. These decisions resulted in discriminatory state laws, violent activities of the Ku Klux Klan, unfair treatment by landlords and employers, and political powerlessness. In effect, the Supreme Court rulings eliminated any hope for social equality and community empowerment and forced African Americans to struggle just to survive. Music, especially the blues, proved to be an important tool for enduring an oppressive existence.

Blues performers, like black preachers, served as spokespersons and community counselors; their messages addressed the social realities of daily life. As entertainers, blues musicians provided a temporary escape from daily oppression by performing for barbecues, house parties, social clubs, and informal gatherings in juke joints and bars.

The blues became a way of life, as illustrated by the various blues styles—rural (folk), vaudeville (classic), urban, and boogie-woogie (instrumental). The earliest blues form, known as *rural* or *folk blues*, is the product of the segregated rural South. Performed primarily by men, the texts address economic hardships, sharecropping experiences, unjust imprisonment, broken relationships, travels, and opposition to the Jim Crow system. Folk blues is performed as vocal and instrumental music and consists of a series of verses that vary in structure (usually eight to sixteen bars and two to five lines of text) and length.

Chord structures often center around the tonic and sometimes the subdominant or dominant chords. Acoustic instruments, including the guitar, harmonica, banjo, mandolin, fiddle, diddly bow, kazoo, jug, fife and drum, washboard, and washtub bass, provide the accompaniment. The instruments, functioning as accompaniment and as a substitute for singers, often double and respond to the vocal melody. Prominent rural blues musicians include Robert Johnson, Charley Patton, Son House, Blind Lemon Jefferson, Blind Boy Fuller, Sonny Terry, Brownie McGhee, Blind Blake, and Gus Cannon.

BOOGIE-WOOGIE. Boogie-woogie is a piano form of the blues that evolved between the late 1890s and the early 1900s in barrelhouses (also known as juke joints) in logging, sawmill, turpentine, levee, and railroad camps throughout the South. Barrelhouses, which served as social centers for migrant workers living in these camps, consisted of a room with a piano, dance area, and bar. Itinerant boogie-woogie pianists traveled the barrelhouse circuit providing the entertainment—music for dancing.

Early boogie-woogie styles incorporated the chord structures, bass patterns, form, and tonality of the folk blues and the melodic and rhythmic properties of ragtime. Boogie-woogie pianists adapted these elements to reflect the dance function of the music, as well as their own percussive and regional improvisatory style. The various regional styles emphasized a heavy and rhythmic eight-note triadic bass line (1-3-5-6-1 or flatted 7) over which flowed syncopated melodic phrases.

Boogie-woogie pianists were among the southern migrants who moved to Chicago after World War I. High rents and low wages forced Chicago's South Side residents to raise money to pay rent. To do so, they hosted rent parties that featured boogie-woogie pianists. This music was so popular among Chicago's southern migrants that it also provided the entertainment on excursion trains that transported blacks to the South on holidays. The trains, called honky-tonks, were converted baggage cars that contained a bar and a dance floor. Boogie-woogie remained the music associated with the lower social strata of black society until the 1930s, when the style entered the repertory of jazz bands and was featured in a concert at New York's Carnegie Hall. By the 1940s, boogie-woogie had become the new craze in American jazz and popular music, which brought respectability to the form. Pioneering boogie-woogie pianists include Charles "Cow Cow" Davenport, Clarence "Pine Top" Smith, Little Brother Montgomery, Clarence Lofton, Roosevelt Sykes, Jimmy Blythe, Jimmy Yancey, Meade "Lux" Lewis, and Albert Ammons.

VAUDEVILLE BLUES. At the turn of the century, a new blues style, which provided the transition from a folk to a commercial style, evolved within the context of traveling minstrel, carnival, and vaudeville shows. Known as vaudeville or classic blues, it showcased black female singers. Most of these women had grown up in the South, and they escaped their impoverished environments by becoming professional entertainers. Relocating in cities, they created widespread awareness of the blues tradition, appearing in cabarets, dance halls, off-Broadway productions, and on records.

Vaudeville blues was the first black music style recorded by a black performer and accompanied by black musicians. The popularity of the song "Crazy Blues," composed by the professional songwriter Perry Bradford and sung by Mamie Smith in 1920, resulted in the recording of many types of black music written and performed by black musicians.

The vaudeville blues tradition is distinguished from rural blues by instrumentation, musical form, harmonic structure, and performance style. Vaudeville singers were accompanied by blues-ragtime-jazz pianists or a New Orleans–style jazz band. As a commercial form the blues structure became standardized through the use of a twelve-bar, three-line (AAB) verse or stanza structure, the tonic-subdominant-dominant harmonic progression, and the blues tonality of the flatted third and seventh degrees.

As in rural blues, textual themes varied and included economic hardship, relationships, imprisonment, travels, urban experiences, and southern nostalgia. Many singers, including Ma Rainey, Ida Cox, Victoria Spivey, Alberta Hunter, and Bessie Smith, wrote their own blues songs, bringing a feminist perspective to many topics common to the blues tradition. Other songs were drawn from the folk blues and composed by professional black male songwriters.

The Great Depression led to a decline in the recording of black music during the 1930s. The demand for the blues, nevertheless, continued to grow. The World War II migration of rural southern blacks to urban centers engendered a consumer market for black music that surpassed the previous decades. Urban blues was one of the most popular black music forms to emerge during the 1940s.

URBAN BLUES. Urban blues shares the musical features (form, structure, tonality, and textual themes) of vaudeville blues. Musically it is more akin to the rural tradition, from which it is distinguished by a more developed instrumental style and influences from jazz and popular music.

Urban blues evolved in cities where southern black migrants struggled to cope with daily life. City life proved harsher than anticipated; the expectation of social and racial equality quickly abated in the face of covert discriminatory practices. Yet blacks adjusted by adapting southern traditions to the demands of city living. The blues played a pivotal role in this process.

In bars, lounges, and clubs where African Americans gathered to socialize, rural blues performers Muddy Waters, Howlin' Wolf, Sonny Boy Williamson, and Sam "Lightnin'" Hopkins, among others, provided the entertainment. The noise level of these venues, combined with surrounding street and factory sounds, forced these musicians to amplify their voices and instruments. The density and intensity of these gatherings soon demanded that blues musicians expand their instrumentation to include a drummer and electric bass guitar and, in some cases, horns. Over these amplified instruments, blues singers shouted and moaned about city life—the good times, the bad times, and the lonely times. Performers who brought inspiration to inner-city dwellers included T-Bone Walker, B. B. King, Bobby "Blue" Bland, Elmore James, Homesick James, Junior Wells, Buddy Guy, Otis Span, Willie Dixon, and Ko Ko Taylor.

JAZZ

Jazz, an ensemble-based instrumental music, is a twentieth-century form. Like the blues, it comprises many styles, each one associated with a specific historical period, social context, and cultural function. While the various styles may be distinguished by certain musical features and instrumentation, they share certain African-American aesthetic properties, which link them as a whole and to the larger body of African-American music.

Early jazz styles evolved around the turn of the century out of the syncopated brass-band tradition. Brass bands borrowed ragtime's syncopated rhythmic style to create an ensemble-based dance music employing conventions of the oral tradition. The bands led by Joe "King" Oliver, Louis Armstrong, Kid Ory, and Bunk Johnson popularized this tradition, providing collectively improvised versions of marches, hymns, folk tunes, popular melodies, and original compositions. They performed in black entertainment venues throughout the urban South, at funerals, and at community social gatherings. Later known as New Orleans jazz, this style featured a small ensemble consisting of cornet, trombone, clarinet, banjo, tuba, and drums.

Many New Orleans musicians and those from other areas migrated to Chicago, Kansas City, or New York during the World War I era. In these cities social dancing had become popular, and the number of nightclubs, cabarets, and ballrooms increased dramatically. In this context and by the 1930s, a distinctive style of instrumental dance music labeled *jazz* had evolved out of the New Orleans tradition. This new jazz style, in which improvisation remained a salient feature, differed from the New Orleans tradition in composition, instrumentation, repertory, and musical structure. The number of musicians increased from six or seven to twelve to sixteen; the instrumentation consisted of trumpets, trombones, saxophones, piano, string bass, and drums; the repertory included complex rhythmic arrangements of popular songs, blues, and original compositions; and the musical structure, which featured soloists, took on a more formal yet flexible quality. Prominent bands of this era (labeled *big bands* in the late 1920s and *swing bands* in the mid-1930s) included those of Bennie Moten, Count Basie, Fletcher Henderson, Jimmie Lunceford, Duke Ellington, Andy Kirk, Chick Webb, Cab Calloway, Coleman Hawkins, Earl "Fatha" Hines, and Lionel Hampton.

The World War II era engendered yet another change in the jazz tradition. During the war years, the musical tastes and social patterns of many Americans began to change. After the war, small clubs replaced ballrooms as centers for musical activity, and experimental jazz combos (rhythm section, trumpet, saxophone, and trombone) came into vogue. Over the next six decades, these combos created new and diverse styles of improvised music that were known as bebop, hard bop, cool jazz, soul jazz, jazz fusion, modern jazz, and new jazz swing. Each of these styles introduced new musical concepts to the jazz tradition.

Bebop (1940s), hard bop (1950s), cool jazz (1950s), and modern jazz (1960s) musicians experimented with timbre and texture and expanded harmonic language, melodic and rhythmic structures, and tempos beyond the parameters associated with big bands. Musicians of these styles altered and extended traditional chord structures, introduced unconventional chord sequences, and employed abstract, nonvocal melodies and unpredictable rhythmic patterns. In the process, they transformed jazz from dance music to music for listening. Bebop's major innovators were Charlie Parker, Dizzy Gillespie, Thelonius Monk, Kenny Clarke, and Max Roach. Hard bop's pioneers included Clifford Brown, Lee Morgan, Sonny Rollins, John Coltrane, J. J. Johnson, Horace Silver, Cannonball Adderley, Wes Montgomery, and Kenny Burrell. Cool jazz is associated with Miles Davis and the Modern Jazz Quartet, among others. Modern jazz (also known as avant-garde or free jazz) innovators include Ornette Coleman, Cecil Taylor, Archie Shepp, Sun Ra, and the Art Ensemble of Chicago.

Some musicians rooted in the bebop or hard bop style experimented with various non-Western musical traditions. John Coltrane, Alice Coltrane, McCoy Tyner, and Ralph MacDonald, for example, drew inspiration from the music of India, Japan, Africa, the Caribbean, and Latin America. Some performers even employed instruments from these countries. While many musicians expanded on bebop's musical foundation during the 1950s and 1960s, others evolved jazz styles that differed conceptually from this tradition.

Retaining the sensibilities and improvisatory style of the jazz tradition, soul jazz (1960s), jazz fusion (1970s), and new jazz swing (1990s) musicians turned to popular idioms (soul music, funk, and rap) for creative inspiration. Fusing the musical language, stylings, rhythms, and synthesized instruments of various popular forms with the harmonic vocabulary of jazz, they not only brought a new sound to the jazz tradition but recaptured jazz's original dance function as well.

Ramsey Lewis, Les McCann, Cannonball Adderley, Jimmy Smith, and Richard "Groove" Holmes are among musicians who popularized the soul jazz style; Herbie Hancock (who introduced the synthesizer to jazz), George Duke, George Benson, Noel Pointer, and Hubert Laws forged the jazz fusion concept.

In the 1990s such jazz musicians as Greg Osby, Miles Davis, Roy Ayers, Donald Byrd, Lonnie Liston Smith, Courtney Pine, and Branford Marsalis teamed up with rap (also known as hip-hop) artists to produce a new sound called *new jazz swing*. This style fuses rap's lyrics, hip-hop rhythms, scratching (sounds produced with the needle by rotating a record backward and forward), rhythm-and-blues and funk samples (phrases extracted from prerecorded songs), and multilayered textures with the improvisational character and vocabulary of jazz. The musical borrowings across genres gave birth not only to new jazz forms but also to a new body of religious music labeled *gospel*.

Gospel

Gospel is a twentieth-century form of sacred music developed by African-Americans within an urban context. As described by ethnomusicologist Mellonee Burnim, gospel functions multidimensionally, holding historical, religious, cultural, and social significance among African Americans (Burnim 1988, pp. 112–120). As an urban response to the sociocultural climate that supported racial oppression, gospel provides a spiritual perspective on the secular events that negatively impacted the lives of African Americans. As such, it expresses the changing ideas and ideals held by blacks in their attempt to establish a meaningful life in an urban environment.

The gospel tradition relies on three primary sources for its repertory: (1) spontaneous creations by church congregations in the oral tradition; (2) original composition by individuals; and (3) rearrangements of hymns, spirituals, blues, and popular idioms. Given these distinct musical sources, gospel music utilizes many structural forms, including call-response, verse-chorus, blues, and theme and variation. Gospel performances, which are highly improvisatory, are accompanied by a variety of instruments, particularly piano, Hammond organ, bass, tambourine, and drums.

GOSPEL AS ORAL COMPOSITION. Gospel music, as an oral form of religious expression, has its roots in Pentecostalism, established in the late 1800s. The Pentecostal church, a by-product of the post–Civil War Holiness movement, became a refuge for many African Americans from lower socioeconomic strata who sought spiritual uplift and deliverance from hardship and struggle. The worship style of the Pentecostal church appealed to these and other African Americans because it retained the improvisatory preaching style, spontaneous testimonies, prayer, and music traditions of the past. Pentecostal congregations brought an urban flavor to these expressions, especially the folk spiritual tradition, which they transformed into an urban folk gospel style.

The feature that distinguishes folk gospel from folk spirituals is the addition of accompanying instruments, including tambourines, washboards, triangles, guitars, pianos, horns, and drums. Pentecostal ministers sanctioned the use of these instruments, citing *Psalm* 150, which encouraged the use of trumpets, harps, lyres, tambourines, strings, flutes, and cymbals to praise the Lord. Blues, ragtime, and jazz performers were among those who responded to this invitation, bringing their instruments and secular style of performance into the Pentecostal church.

Congregational singing accompanied by instruments increased the intensity and spontaneity of urban black folk services. The bluesy guitar lines, ragtime and boogie-woogie rhythms, horn riffs, and polyrhythmic drum patterns brought a contemporary sound to old traditions.

GOSPEL AS WRITTEN COMPOSITION. Gospel music as written composition emerged as a distinct genre in independent black churches in the 1930s. The prototype, known as a *gospel hymn*, was developed during the first two decades of the twentieth century by the Philadelphia Methodist minister Charles A. Tindley. Tindley grew up in rural Maryland, where he attended a folk-style rural church. Influenced by this experience, his ministry catered to the spiritual, cultural, and social needs of black people.

Tindley gave special attention to the poor, who flocked to his church in large numbers, as did people of all classes and races. His socioeconomically and culturally diverse congregation responded positively to his style of worship, which intertwined the liturgical and cultural practices of the Pentecostal, Baptist, and Methodist churches. These services "embraced both the order and selections of well-loved 'high' church literature and the practice, richness, intensity, and spontaneity found in the most traditionally based Black form of worship. These were hymns, anthems, prayers, and creeds. There were 'amens' and hand-claps and shouts of 'Thank you Jesus' and a spirit that ran throughout the service" (Reagon 1992, p. 39).

The music, woven into every component of worship, was as diverse as the liturgy. The choir performed George Frideric Handel's *Messiah* (1742) at Christmas and the music of other Western classical composers and the African-American tradition during Sunday morning service. At evening testimonials the congregation sang spirituals, lined hymns, and other songs from the oral tradition.

The church's musical repertory also included Tindley's original compositions, which he wrote specifically for his congregation and as an extension of his sermons. His song texts related the scriptures to everyday life experiences. A recurring theme in Tindley's songs and sermons, according to cultural historian Bernice Johnson Reagon, "is the belief that true change or release from worldly bondage can be attained only through struggle" (1992, p. 45).

The theme of deliverance through struggle is one feature that distinguishes Tindley's gospel hymns from the hymns of white songwriters, whose texts focus on conversion, salvation, and heaven. Other distinguishing elements are the construction of melodies in a fashion that allows for improvisation and interpolation and the use of melodic, harmonic, and rhythmic components of the black folk tradition. Among Tindley's well-known songs are "Some Day," published in 1901, and "Stand By Me," "The Storm Is Passing Over, Hallelujah," and "By and By," all published in 1905. These and other compositions, which are included in hymnbooks of all denominations, have become part of the black oral tradition. They are sung in a variety of styles by congregations, gospel soloists, duos, quartets, and numerous traditional and contemporary ensembles and choirs.

Tindley's compositions had a profound impact on Thomas A. Dorsey, a Baptist, who evolved Tindley's gospel-hymn model into an original gospel song. Dorsey, a former blues and ragtime performer, brought a different kind of song structure, melody, harmony, rhythm, and energy to the black sacred tradition. Dorsey was known as the "Father of Gospel," and his compositions fuse blues-style melodies with blues and ragtime rhythms. His texts are testimonies about the power of Jesus Christ, which provides spiritually inspired yet earthly solutions to daily struggles. Among Dorsey's well-known compositions are "Take My Hand, Precious Lord" (1932), "There'll Be Peace in the Valley for Me" (1938), "Hide Me in Thy Bosom" (1939), "God is Good to Me" (1943), and "Old Ship of Zion" (1950).

Despite the "good news" about Jesus Christ of which gospel music speaks, most ministers of independent black churches rejected Dorsey's songs because of their "secular" beat and musical style and because they did not conform to the established religious musical conventions. He therefore used unorthodox strategies to introduce them to church congregations. Throughout the 1930s Dorsey, along with Sallie Martin, Mahalia Jackson, and Willie Mae Ford Smith, sang his songs on the sidewalks outside churches, at church conventions, and at the gospel music convention, the National Convention of Choirs and Choruses, that Dorsey founded with Sallie Martin, Willie Mae Ford Smith, Theodore Fry, and Magnolia Lewis Butts in 1932.

Also during the 1930s, many established jubilee quartets added Dorsey's songs and those of such composers as Lucie Campbell, William Herbert Brewster, Roberta Martin, and Kenneth Morris, among others, to their traditional repertory of Negro spirituals. By the 1940s, several newly formed semiprofessional and professional gospel quartets, female and mixed groups, and local choirs specialized in gospel music. In the 1950s, as a result of the proliferation of gospel church choirs, gospel music became the standard repertory in many independent black church choirs.

Performers that brought widespread public notice to the gospel-music tradition of Dorsey and his contemporaries include the gospel quartets Fairfield Four, Famous Blue Jay Singers, Golden Gate Quartet, Soul Stirrers, Highway Q.C.'s, Dixie Hummingbirds, Swan Silvertones, and the Blind Boys; the gospel groups of Roberta Martin, Sally Ward, Clara Ward, and the Barrett Sisters; and the soloists Mahalia Jackson, Sallie Martin, Willie Mae Ford Smith, Marion Williams, Bessie Griffin, Albertina Walker, Alex Bradford, James Cleveland, and Shirley Caesar. Gospel quartets performed a cappella or with guitar accompaniment, and gospel groups and soloists performed with piano and Hammond organ.

The gospel songs of Dorsey and other songwriters were disseminated in printed form. The musical score, however, provides only the text and a skeletal outline of the basic melody and harmonies. Vocalists and instrumentalists bring their own interpretations to these songs, employing the aesthetic conventions of the oral tradition. Thus, gospel music represents both a style of performance and a body of original composition. This style of performance is manifested in the gospel arrangement of the white hymn "Oh, Happy Day," which transformed the traditional style of Thomas Dorsey into a contemporary sound.

CONTEMPORARY GOSPEL. When Edwin Hawkins, a Pentecostal, recorded his version of the hymn "Oh, Happy Day" in 1969, he ushered in a new era of gospel music—an era that coincided with the changed social climate engendered by the civil rights movement. Hawkins and his contemporaries evolved the gospel sound by blending traditional elements with those of contemporary popular, jazz, blues, folk, and classical music. "Oh, Happy Day," for example, is laced with elements of soul music, particularly its danceable beat. This song attracted the attention of top-forty and soul-music programmers, who added it to their play list. The popularity of "Oh, Happy Day" within and outside the religious community inspired other gospel performers to exploit Hawkins's model. Since the recording of "Oh, Happy Day," the musical boundaries have expanded and this song now falls under the category of traditional gospel.

In the 1970s Andrae Crouch experimented with every black secular form, employing melodies, harmonies, rhythms, and instrumentation from ragtime, jazz, blues, and funk; Rance Allen borrowed rhythms and instrumentation from the rhythm-and-blues and soul-music traditions; and Vernard Johnson elevated the saxophone to the status of a solo gospel instrument. Contemporary gospel songwriters-performers also introduced new textual themes to the tradition. While retaining the established theme of salvation in some compositions, they do not mention God or Jesus directly in others. Instead, themes of peace, compassion, and universal love inspired by the civil rights movement and the spiritually based teachings of Martin Luther King Jr. prevail. These themes and the musical innovations, which demonstrate the affinity between gospel and popular forms, led to debates regarding appropriate sacred musical expression.

Perhaps the most controversial practice of the 1970s and 1980s was the recording of popular songs as gospel. James Cleveland, for example, recorded a gospel version of George Benson's "Everything Must Change"; the Twenty-First Century Singers presented a rendition of Melba Moore's "Lean on Me" as "Lean on Him"; and Shirley Caesar and the Thompson Community Singers recorded Curtis Mayfield's "People Get Ready," a song inspired by Mayfield's religious beliefs. The only significant change made to the original songs was the substitution of "Jesus" for "baby," "my woman," and "my man."

In the 1980s gospel and classical performers joined forces to record a historic album, *Edwin Hawkins Live* (1981), with the Oakland Symphony Orchestra. The fusion of classical elements with gospel has its origins in the style of the Roberta Martin Singers. During the 1940s, Roberta Martin, a songwriter and classically trained pianist, incorporated scales and arpeggios in the piano accompaniment and operatic vocal stylings from the classical tradition in the group's performances. During the 1970s and 1980s, Pearl Williams-Jones and Richard Smallwood, who also were trained classical pianists, maintained Martin's tradition of fusing classical with gospel piano techniques in gospel music.

Throughout the 1980s and into the 1990s, gospel performers continued to borrow the language, instrumentation, and technology (synthesizers, drum machines, and sound effects) of popular idioms. At the same time, performers of popular music turned to the gospel tradition for inspiration, as they had done for the previous four decades, employing gospel vocal stylings, harmonies, and rhythms and recording gospel songs under the label of soul. The Clark Sisters, Vanessa Bell Armstrong, Tramaine Hawkins, Walter Hawkins, Commissioned, Bebe and CeCe Winans, Take 6, Nu Colors, Sounds of Blackness, Daryl Coley, Keith Pringle, John P. Kee, Little Saints in Praise, Kinnection, and Kirk Franklin (gospel rap) are among those performers who created new gospel styles by stretching traditional musical parameters.

CIVIL RIGHTS FREEDOM SONGS

Civil rights freedom songs are the products of the 1950s and 1960s civil rights and Black Power movements, respectively. In the mid-1950s, African Americans from the South mounted a series of grassroots activities to protest their social status as second-class citizens. These activities, which gained widespread momentum and attracted national attention in the 1960s, evolved into the civil rights and Black Power movements. Music was integral to both and served a multitude of functions. It galvanized African Americans into political action; provided them with strength and courage; united protesters as a cohesive group; and supplied a creative medium for mass communication.

Freedom songs draw from many sources and traditions, including folk and arranged spirituals; unaccompanied congregational hymn singing; folk ballads; gospel quartets, groups, and choirs; rhythm and blues and soul music; and original creations. Protesters reinterpreted the musical repertory of African Americans, communicating their determination to effect social and political change. The singing captured the energy and spirit of the movement. The power of the songs, according to Bernice Johnson Reagon, "came from the linking of traditional oral expression to the everyday experiences of the movement" (1987 p. 106). Well-known freedom songs include "We Shall Overcome," "Come Bah Yah," "Ain't Gonna Let Nobody Turn Me Around," "99½ Won't Do," and "Get Your Rights, Jack."

RHYTHM AND BLUES

During the World War II era, urban areas throughout the country became centers for the evolution of a distinct body of African-American popular music. Labeled *rhythm and blues*, this music consisted of many regional styles, reflecting the migration patterns of African Americans and the musical background of performers. In Los Angeles, for example, former swing band and blues musicians formed five- to eight-member combos (bass and rhythm guitar, drums, piano, saxophone, trumpet, and trombone) and created a distinctive rhythm-and-blues style. A hybrid dance style, it fused the twelve-bar blues and boogie-woogie bass line with the repetitive melodic riffs and drum patterns of the swing bands of the Southwest and the West (specifically Kansas City). This tradition also featured instrumental saxophone solos and the vocals of "moaning" and "shouting" blues singers. This style is illustrated in the recordings of Louis Jordan, Joe Liggins, Roy Milton, Johnny Otis, and Big Jay McNeely, among others. The West Coast sound also resonated in the instrumentals of musicians recording in the Midwest and on the East Coast, including Wild Bill Moore, Harold Singer, Sonny Thompson, and Paul Williams.

Paralleling the emergence of rhythm-and-blues combos in Los Angeles in the 1940s was a style known as *club blues* and *cocktail music* in African-American and white clubs, respectively. Associated with the King Cole Trio, this music was performed primarily in lounges and small, intimate clubs as background or listening music. It featured a self-accompanying jazz or blues-oriented pianist-vocalist augmented by guitar and bass performing in a subdued or tempered style, in contrast to the high-energy sounds of the rhythm-and-blues dance combos. Popularizers of club blues include Cecil Gant, Charles Brown and the Three Blazers, Roy Brown, Amos Milburn, and Ray Charles.

In New Orleans, a younger generation of performers such as Fats Domino, Little Richard, Lloyd Price, and Shirley & Lee evolved the 1940s rhythm-and-blues combo style into a contemporary youthful expression. This form of musical expression fuses elements from gospel music with the blues, Latin traditions, and the innovations of musicians, which are summarized as gospel-derived vocal stylings, repeated triplet and rolling-octave piano blues figures, a Cuban-derived rumba bass pattern, and an underlying fast sixteenth-note cymbal pattern accented on beats two and four on the snare drum. Little Richard created this drum pattern, which became known as the *rock 'n' roll* beat. By the mid-1950s, New Orleans rhythm and blues had inspired related yet personalized combo styles, including the Atlantic Sound (Atlantic Records), popularized by Ruth Brown and La Vern Baker, the rock 'n' roll style of guitarists Chuck Berry and Bo Diddley, and the up-tempo vocal group styles of the Cadillacs, El Dorados, Flamingos, and Coasters.

The vocal harmony group tradition was the most popular rhythm-and-blues form among teenagers, especially those living in urban centers. In the densely populated cities on the East Coast, in Chicago, and in Detroit, teenagers formed a cappella groups, performing for school dances and other social activities. Rehearsing on street corners, apartment stoops, and in school yards, parks, and subway trains, they evolved a type of group harmony that echoed the harmonies of jubilee and gospel quartets and gospel groups. Among the first groups of this tradition in the early 1950s were the Orioles, Spaniels, and the Five Keys, who specialized in ballads that appealed to the romantic fantasies of teenagers.

By the mid-1950s, vocal harmony groups had transformed the smooth and romantic delivery of ballads into a rhythmic performance style labeled *doo-wop*. This concept featured a rhythmic deliverance of the phrase "doo-doo-doo-wop" or "doo-doo-doo-doo" sung by bass singers, which provided movement for a cappella vocal groups. First popularized by the Spaniels in the early 1950s, the rhythmic doo-wop phrases eventually replaced the sustained "oohs and ahs" background vocals of the early vocal harmony groups. This vocal group style is associated with the Moonglows, Monotones, Frankie Lymon and the Teenagers, Five Satins, Channels, Charts, Heartbeats, Chantels, and Crests, among others.

Overlapping the doo-wop vocal group style was a pop-oriented sound that featured orchestral arrangements, gospel-pop-flavored vocal stylings, sing-along (as opposed to call-response) phrases known as *hook lines*, and Latin-derived rhythms. This style, associated with the Platters and the post-1956 Drifters, provided the framework for musical arrangements and hook lines that undergird the mid- to late 1960s vocal group sound of Smokey Robinson and the Miracles, the Supremes, Four Tops, Temptations, Dells, and Impressions.

By the late 1960s, the rhythm-and-blues tradition had begun exhibiting new sounds that reflected the discontentment of many African Americans engaged in the struggle for social and racial equality. The pop-oriented vocal stylings of the Drifters, the cha-cha beat of some rhythm-and-blues singers, and the youthful sound and teen lyrics of Motown's groups gave way to a more spirited type of music labeled *soul*.

SOUL MUSIC. Soul, distinguished by its roots in black gospel music and socially conscious messages, is associated with the 1960s era of Black Power—a movement led by college-age students who rejected the integrationist philosophy of the 1950s civil rights leaders. The ideology of Black Power promoted nationalist concepts of racial pride, racial unity, self-empowerment, self-control, and self-identification. As a concept, soul became associated with an attitude, a behavior, symbols, institutions, and cultural products that were distinctively black and reflected the values and worldview of people of African descent.

Many black musicians supported the Black Power movement, promoting the nationalist ideology and galvanizing African Americans into social and political action. They identified with their African heritage, wearing African-derived fashions and hairstyles; their song lyrics advocated national black unity, activism, and self-pride; and their musical style captured the energy, convictions, and optimism of African Americans during a period of social change.

Soul music embodies the vocal and piano stylings, call-response, polyrhythmic structures, and aesthetic conventions of gospel music. This style is represented in the recordings "Soul Finger" (1967) by the Bar-Kays; "Soul Man" (1967) by Sam and Dave; "Respect" (1967) by Aretha Franklin; "We're a Winner" (1967) and "This Is My Country" (1968) by the Impressions; "Say It Loud, I'm Black and Proud" (1968) and "I Don't Want Nobody to Give Me Nothing" (1969) by James Brown; "Freedom" (1970) by the Isley Brothers; "Respect Yourself" (1971) by the Staple Singers; "Give More Power to the People" (1971) by the Chi-Lites; and "Back Stabbers" (1972) by the O'Jays, among others.

The optimism that had prevailed during the 1960s began to fade among a large segment of the African-American community in the early 1970s. New opportunities for social and economic advancement engendered by the pressures of the civil rights and Black Power movements resulted in opposition from mainstream society. Resistance to affirmative-action programs, school desegregation, busing, open housing, and other federal policies designed to integrate African Americans fully into the mainstream hindered their progress toward social, economic, and racial equality. The lyrics of Marvin Gaye's "What's Going On" (1971) and "Inner City Blues" (1971); James Brown's "Down and Out in New York City" (1973) and "Funky President" (1974); and the O'Jays' "Survival" (1975) express mixed feelings about social change. Reflecting the disappointments and the continued struggle toward racial equality, new forms of popular expressions labeled *funk*, *disco*, and *rap* evolved out of the soul style in the 1970s.

FUNK MUSIC. Funk describes a form of dance music rooted in the rhythm-and-blues and soul music traditions of James Brown and Sly Stone. Funk is characterized by group singing, complex polyrhythmic structures, percussive instrumental and vocal timbres, a riffing horn section, and lyrics that encourage "partying" or "having a good time." The primary function of funk was to provide temporary respite from the uncertainties and pressures of daily life. In live performances and on studio recordings, funk musicians created an ambience, a party atmosphere, that encouraged black people to express themselves freely and without the restrictions or cultural compromises often experienced in integrated settings.

The therapeutic potential of funk is reflected in key recurring phrases: "have a good time," "let yourself go," "give up the funk," and "it ain't nothing but a party." Among the pioneering funk performers were Sly and the Family Stone, Kool and the Gang, Ohio Players, Graham Central Station, Bar-Kays, and Parliament/Funkadelic.

George Clinton, founder of Parliament, Funkadelic, and other funk groups extended the definition of *funk* beyond a musical style to embrace a philosophy, attitude, and culture. Known as *P-funk* (pure funk), this philosophy is manifested in the creation of an imaginary planet— the planet of funk. On this planet blacks acquire new values, a worldview, and a lifestyle free of earthly social and cultural restrictions. Clinton's P-funk songs combined the party theme with social commentary in a comic style. This theme and the philosophy of P-funk prevail in Parliament's "Chocolate City" (1975); "P. Funk (Wants to Get Funked Up)" (1975); "Prelude" (1976); "Dr. Funkenstein" (1976); "Bop Gun (Endangered Species)" (1977); and "Funkentelechy" (1977). Musically, the P-funk style advances the concepts of Sly Stone, who achieved mood and textural variety through the use of electronic distorting devices and synthesizers.

By the late 1970s, advancements in musical technology and the emergence of disco as a distinct electro-pop style influenced the reconfiguration and shifts in the musical direction of many funk bands. To remain competitive against the disco craze, some funk bands, such as Heatwave and Con Funk Shun, incorporated disco elements in their music, replacing horn players with synthesizers and juxtaposing disco rhythms in the funk groove. Others, including the Bar-Kays, Lakeside, Gap Band, Cameo, Rick James, and Instant Funk, combined synthesizers with the traditional funk instrumentation in ways that preserved the aesthetic of the earlier funk styles. Taking a different approach, Zapp and Roger from Dayton, Ohio, used advanced technologies to create an electro-based Dayton funk sound centering on the vocoder (an electronic and distorting talk box); a heavy, synthesized bottom; and distorted instrumental timbres.

At the same time, rap music deejay Afrika Bambaataa and the Soul Sonic Force developed their own brand of electro-funk based on the innovations of European proto-techno group Kraftwerk. Borrowing and reworking a musical phrase from Kraftwerk's "Planet Rock" (1982), Bambaataa used programmable synthesizers, drum machines, and other electronic equipment to produced a danceable space-oriented techno-funk style characterized by a series of varying sound effects. Other groups such as the Planet Patrol ("Play at Your Own Risk," 1982), and the Jonzun Crew ("Space Is the Place," 1982) popularized this style.

GO-GO. Go-go, a derivative funk style, evolved in Washington, D.C.'s inner-city neighborhoods during the mid-1970s. It is distinguished from traditional funk styles in that it is a performance-oriented music and not easily replicated in the studio. Live and continuous audience participation is essential to go-go performances. The audience and performers spontaneously create and exchange phrases in an antiphonal style. Songs are extended and different songs are connected through the use of percussion instruments, resulting into a twenty- to ninety-minute performance. Go-go pioneer Chuck Brown popularized this style, which highlights horns and percussion, in his hits "Bustin' Loose" (1978) and "We Need Some Money" (1985). Film director Spike Lee brought national notoriety to the idiom when he featured E.U. (Experience Unlimited) performing "Da' Butt" in his film *School Daze* (1988). Other go-go groups include Trouble Funk, Rare Essence, Little Benny and the Masters, Slim, and Redds and the Boys.

Disco

Disco is a term first used to identify dance music played in discotheques during the 1970s. The majority of these recordings were black music, as evidenced by the first "Top 50 Disco Hits" chart that appeared in 1974 in *Billboard* (a music industry publication). With few exceptions, the songs that comprise this chart were soul, Latin soul, funk, and the new sounds from Philadelphia International Records (known as the "Sound of Philadelphia" or the "Philly Sound," the latter created by the songwriter-producers Kenny Gamble, Leon Huff, and songwriter-arranger-producer Thom Bell).

By the late 1970s, *disco* referred to a new body of extended-play dance music (i.e., remixes of songs that exceeded the standard three-minute recording) distinguished by orchestral-styled arrangements and synthesized sound effects anchored around a distinctive drum pattern known as the *disco beat*. This style, defined as the "Philly Sound," has its origins in the drum beats and arrangements that combine melodic strings with percussively played horn lines over a four-to-the-bar bass drum pattern subdivided by beats of the high-hat cymbal (and variations of this pattern). The groups MFSB ("TSOP," 1973; "Love Is the Message," 1974) and Harold Melvin and the Blue Notes ("Bad Luck," 1975) and the singer Thelma Houston ("Don't Leave Me This Way," 1976) propelled this sound into the mainstream, and disco became a worldwide musical phenomenon.

Both American and European disco producers appropriated the Philly Sound, especially the drum pattern, to create various disco styles. These include the orchestral-style arrangements of Gloria Gaynor ("Never Can Say Good-bye," 1974; "I Will Survive," 1978) and Salsoul Orchestra ("Tangerine," 1975); the Euro-disco styles of the Ritchie Family ("Brazil," 1975; "The Best Disco in Town," 1976), Donna Summer ("Love to Love You, Baby," 1975), the Trammps ("That's Where the Happy People Go," 1976), and the Village People ("San Francisco," 1977; "Macho Man," 1978); the Latin-soul styles of Carl Douglas ("Doctor's Orders," 1974), and Van McCoy ("The Hustle," 1974; "The Disco Kid," 1975); and the funk-based disco of Silver Convention ("Fly, Robin, Fly," 1975), B. T. Express ("B. T. Express," 1974), Taste of Honey ("Boogie Oogie Oogie," 1978), and Chic ("Good Times," 1979).

After the release of the disco film *Saturday Night Fever* (1977), disco crossed over from a primarily black and gay audience into the mainstream. The popularity of the film's sound track resulted in the disco craze. Record companies flooded the market with recordings that reduced earlier innovative disco sounds to a formula—the disco beat, synthesized sound effects, and repetitive vocal refrain lines. By the early 1980s, disco had lost its originality and soon faded from the musical landscape.

Filling the void for original dance music, black deejay Frankie Knuckles evolved a disco-derivative style known as *house music* in the mid-1980s in Chicago. His creations incorporated gospel-style vocals over a repetitive bass line and drum pattern programmed on synthesizers and drum machines. Similar to disco and funk, the lyrics of house encourage dancers to have a good time. House performers include Marshall Jefferson ("Move Your Body [The House Music Anthem]," 1986), Exit ("Let's Work It Out," 1987), Fast Eddie ("Yo Yo Get Funky," 1988), Inner City ("Big Fun," 1988), and Technotronic ("Pump Up the Jam," 1989; "Move This," 1989).

RAP AND HIP-HOP MUSIC

Rap music has its origins in hip-hop culture, which emerged in African-American, Afro-Caribbean, and Latino communities of the Bronx and spread to other sections of New York City in the early 1970s. Encompassing four performance expressions—graffiti or aerosol art, b-boying/girling (break dancing), DJ-ing, and MC-ing (rapping)—hip-hop became popular throughout the city through its association with gang culture. The rise in unemployment, the lack of educational opportunities, and the decline of federally funded job training and social programs contributed to increased poverty, community decay, and the proliferation of drugs during the years following the civil rights protest activities of the 1960s. Between the late 1960s and the early 1970s, gang violence escalated to new levels throughout New York City. Searching for alternative and nonviolent forms of competitive gang warfare, ex-gang members turned to hip-hop culture. Beginning in 1974, hip-hop became the vehicle through which gang members elevated their social status and developed a sense of pride, displaying their verbal, dance, and technological skills. By the mid-1970s, hip-hop culture had begun to dominate the expressions of all inner-city youth, and in 1979 the first commercial recordings of rap music appeared on vinyl. Since the 1990s, the term hop-hop is often synonymous with rap music or rhythm-and-blues–rap fusion. This reference to hip-hop places less emphasis on the original four cultural components—graffiti, b-boying/girling, DJ-ing, and MC-ing.

Rap/hip-hop music can be defined as rhymed poetry recited in rhythm over musical tracks. It draws from the cultural and verbal traditions of the African diaspora. The verbal component is rooted in the African-derived oral traditions of storytelling, toasting (narrative poems that sometimes bestow praises), boasting (self-aggrandizement), and signifying or "playing the dozens" (the competitive exchange of insults). The performance style of rappers employs rhymes, rhythmic speech patterns, and the rhetorical approach of the 1950s African-American deejays who talked, or "rapped," over music. These deejays inspired the sound and verbal innovations of Jamaican mobile disk jockeys, whose large and powerful sound systems (consisting of turntables, speakers, amplifiers, and a microphone) were central to the development of rap as a musical genre. As performers for outdoor parties (known as blues dances) in Jamaica, deejays competed for audiences through their display of skills in sequencing records (including rhythm and blues), manipulating volume, and complimenting the dancers through their toasts. To focus more on the technical aspects of the performance, these deejays hired assistants to verbally interact with the crowd. These assistants later became known as MCs (from "master of ceremonies"). After deejays from the Caribbean migrated to the Bronx, they eventually joined forces with African-American rappers, and collectively they created rap music as a distinctive genre.

Rap (or hip-hop) music consists of several subgenres and stylistic subcategories, including party rap, hardcore rap (conscious, nationalist, message, or Afro-centric rap; gangsta or reality rap; and X-rated rap), pop rap (novelty or humorous rap), and commercial rap (rap ballad and rhythm-and-blues rap). The first commercial rap recording, "Rapper's Delight" by the Sugarhill Gang, released in 1979, established party rap as the model for early rap recordings. This rap style exploited the art of boasting and often featured a group of rappers (known as a posse or crew). While bragging about their verbal facility and ability to "rock the house," they identified their physical attributes, material possessions, and other personal characteristics. Rappers competed with each other within and across individual groups. Popularizers of the party-rap style include Sequence ("Funk You Up," 1979), Curtis Blow ("The Breaks," 1980), Grandmaster Flash and the Furious Five ("Freedom," 1980; "Birthday Party," 1981), Funky Four Plus One ("Rapping and Rocking the House," 1980), Lady B. ("To the Beat [Y'all]," 1980), Grandmaster Flash and the Furious Five and Furious Five Meets the Sugarhill Gang ("Showdown," 1981).

In the mid-1980s a new generation of rappers from the inner cities and suburbs broadened the scope of rap. While "rockin' the house," boasting, and signifyin', these rappers introduced new lyric themes and musical styles to the tradition. Some told humorous stories and tall tales, and others recounted adolescent pranks, fantasies, and romantic encounters. In 1984 UTFO ("Roxanne Roxanne"), Roxanne Shante ("Roxanne's Revenge"), and the Real Roxanne ("The Real Roxanne") popularized verbal dueling, or "signifyin'," between genders. In "La Di Da Di" (1985), Doug E. Fresh incorporated rhythmic vocal effects in a concept known as the human beat box, which became the trademark of the comic group the Fat Boys ("Jail House Rap," 1984; "The Fat Boys Are Back," 1985). The humorous style of the Fat Boys established the model for what became known as *pop rap*. DJ Jazzy Jeff and the Fresh Prince brought notoriety to this style through their parodies of the suburban black middle class as illustrated in "Girls Ain't Nothing but Trouble" (1986) and "Parents Just Don't Understand" (1988), as did De La Soul in "Potholes in My Lawn" (1989), "Plug Tunin'" (1989), and "Me Myself and I" (1989). LL Cool J introduced the rap ballad in "I Need Love" (1987), which brought a softer edge and a romantic dimension to hip-hip music. MC Hammer brought a rhythm-and-blues flavor to rap by borrowing songs from the rhythm-and-blues tradition as his soundtrack (*Please Hammer, Don't Hurt 'Em,* 1990). Queen Latifah, the Real Roxanne, and Positive K introduced a feminist perspective in "Ladies First" (1989), "Respect" (1988), and "I Got a Man" (1992), respectively.

In the late 1980s rap became a public forum for social and political commentary as well as the expression of inner-city rage and X-rated behavior. Throughout this decade, inner-city communities continued to deteriorate. A recession (1980–1982), ongoing fiscal conservatism, the continuing rise in unemployment due to deindustrialization, and the absence of a black middle class resulted in the expansion of the "urban underclass" and the relocation of wealthier African-Americans to the suburbs. These changing economic and social conditions led to a proliferation of drugs and related violence and chaos in inner-city communities. Such conditions inspired a new rap form characterized by an aggressive tone and graphic descriptions of the social ills and harshness of inner-city life. Labeled *hardcore*, this rap form constitutes three stylistic categories: conscious, nationalist, or message rap; gangsta or reality rap; and X-rated rap.

The first hip-hop recordings that exposed the economic woes, social ills, and deteriorating conditions of inner cities were by East Coast rappers, including Curtis Blow's "Hard Times" (1980), Grandmaster Flash and the Furious Five's "The Message" (1982) and "New York, New York" (1983), and Grandmaster Flash and Melle Mel's "White Lines (Don't Do It)" (1983). In the late 1980s, politically oriented rappers began expounding on these themes, condemning social injustices, drugs, police brutality, violence, and black-on-black crime. As a solution to these social ills, they promoted the 1960s Black Nationalist agenda advanced by the Nation of Islam and the Five Percent Nation, who advocated political confrontation and identification with an African heritage. Innovators and popularizers of conscious rap include Public Enemy ("It Takes a Nation of Millions to Hold Us Back," 1988; "Fear of a Black Planet," 1989–1990); Jungle Brothers ("Straight Out of the Jungle," 1988; "Done by the Forces of Nature," 1989); Boogie Down Productions ("By All Means Neces-

sary," 1988; "Ghetto Music: The Blueprint of Hip Hop," 1989); Paris ("The Devil Made Me Do It," 1989–1990); X-Clan ("To the East, Blackwards," 1990); Brand Nubian ("One for All," 1990; "In God We Trust," 1992), and Sister Souljah ("360 Degrees of Power," 1992).

The political voices of nationalist rappers overlapped with the harsh and violent messages and aggressive style of another group of hardcore rappers primarily from the West Coast. Labeled *gangsta rap* (by the media) and *reality rap* (by the rappers themselves), performers of this rap style described the chaos and the rough and seedy side of inner-city life using graphic language laced with expletives. Although their tales of violence and sexual exploits exposed aspects of life in inner-city communities, they often exploited and dramatized these experiences by glorifying drugs, violence, criminal acts, and misogynistic behavior. Such rappers include N.W.A. ("Straight Outta Compton," 1988; "Niggaz 4 Life," 1991); Eazy-E ("Eazy-Duz-It," 1988); Ice Cube ("Amerikkka's Most Wanted," 1990); Dr. Dre ("The Chronic," 1992); and Snoop Doggy Dogg ("Doggystyle," 1993). Early representation of this subgenre can also be found on the East Coast (Slick Rick, "Children's Story," 1988), in the South (2 Live Crew, "As Nasty As They Wanna Be," 1989), and in the Southwest (Geto Boys, "The Geto Boys," 1989; "Uncut Dope," 1992).

In the early 1990s the gangsta style of West Coast rappers (Los Angeles, Oakland, Compton, and Long Beach) had begun supplanting the nationalist message of East Coast rappers (New York, New Jersey, and Philadelphia) in national popularity and in record sales. This shift in the regional preference for rap music fuelled verbal battles that came to be known as the East Coast–West Coast feud. The East Coast rappers publicly condemned the West Coast rappers as being fake and "studio gangsters" (i.e., creating a fictional gangster lifestyle). In response, West Coast rappers vilified their East Coast counterparts, accusing them of being "soft" and disrespecting the West Coast contributions to hip-hop. These differences in perspectives and the "authentic" representation of black people in hip-hop underscore the issues that fueled the East-West feud. Public Enemy's "I Don't Wanna Be Called Yo Nigga" (1991), for example, confronts the disrespectful overuse of the term *nigga* in "Niggas 4 Life" (1991) by N.W.A. (for Niggas With Attitude). In response, in "Endangered Species (Tales from the Darkside)" (1990), N.W.A.'s Ice Cube accused Public Enemy and other conscious rappers of focusing too much on Africa and nationalist issues rather than the struggles of the black poor in America. This feud moved to personal levels with the release of "Fuck Compton" (1991) by the Bronx rapper Tim Dog, to which Compton rapper Snoop Doggy Dogg responded on Dr.

Dre's single "Fuck Wit Dre Day (and Everybody's Celebratin')" (1992), which implied that Tim Dog engaged in homosexual acts—a major insult in hip-hop culture.

By the mid-1990s, the earlier preference for message-oriented hardcore rap on the East Coast gave way to the gangsta style and the notoriety of rappers Wu-Tang Clan from Staten Island, Junior M.A.F.I.A. from Brooklyn, and Notorious B.I.G. (a.k.a. Biggie Smalls) from Brooklyn, among others. The level of competition escalated the East/West rivalry to new heights (spurred on by the hip-hop media) and culminated in the deaths of Oakland rapper Tupac Shakur in 1996 and Notorious B.I.G. in 1997. While leaving a New York City recording studio in 1994, Shakur was shot five times, and he publicly blamed Notorious B.I.G. and producer Sean "Puffy" Combs of arranging his attempted murder. After a year of verbal exchanges via the media and public events, Shakur insulted Notorious B.I.G. in the song "Hit 'Em Up" (1995) by bragging about a supposed sexual encounter between Shakur and Smalls's wife, vocalist Faith Evans. Smalls responded on Jay-Z's "Brooklyn's Finest" (1996), with threats to engage in violent mob-style retaliation.

Despite the messages of violence and the tendency of some gangsta rappers to devalue human life, many expressed their commitment to improving the conditions of inner-city communities, and they frequently denounced behavior that had a negative impact on African Americans. Ice T ("I'm Your Pusher" and "High Rollers," 1988), for example, condemned drugs and criminal activity. N.W.A. ("F___ Tha Police," 1988) and Ice T ("Cop Killer," 1992) spoke out against police brutality. Other rappers addressed a broader array of social issues, ranging from the plight of unwed mothers to that of the homeless and those on welfare. Such socially conscious performers included Tupac Shakur ("Keep Ya Head Up," 1993), Arrested Development ("Mama's Always on Stage" and "Mr. Wendall," 1992), Queen Latifah ("The Evil That Men Do," 1989), Common ("Book of Life," 1994), Roots ("What They Do," 1996), and Kanye West ("All Falls Down," 2004).

Hardcore hip-hop is distinguished from the other styles by an aggressive, polytextured, and polysonic aesthetic produced electronically and digitally. Often referred to as *noise*, this aesthetic draws, combines, and remixes samples from many sound sources—street noises (sirens, gunshots, babies crying, screams, etc.), political speeches of African-American leaders, TV commercials, and so on—into a sound collage. This collage captures the ethos, chaos, tensions, anger, despair, and the sometimes violent nature of inner-city life, thus supporting the harsh lyrics and assertive delivery style of hardcore rappers. Hardcore

hip-hop contrasts the less dense and more melodic rhythm-and-blues/funk-derived aesthetic associated with the 1970s party-style music produced by live studio musicians. Grandmaster Flash and the Furious Five and Afrika Bambaata and the Soul Sonic Force provide the sonic transition from the party to the hardcore hip-hop aesthetic. In "The Adventures of Grandmaster Flash on the Wheels of Steel" (1981) and "The Message" (1982), deejay Grandmaster Flash incorporates the street-styled production techniques of hip-hop deejays in studio recordings. Drawing and reassembling (remixing) short excerpts from several recordings (rather than different sections of the same record) to which he added scratching sounds, Grandmaster Flash created a new musical track best described as a sound collage. Further experimentations of Grandmaster Flash resulted in the use of programmed electronic instruments (synthesizers and the beat box) in conjunction with live musicians.

Deejay Afrika Bambaata in "Planet Rock" (1982) further facilitated the transition from live musical production to music generated by electronic and digital instruments, a feature that distinguishes party from hardcore rap. "Planet Rock," based on a short melodic phrase from "Trans-Europe Express" by the proto-techno group Kraftwerk, was produced electronically, with programmed percussion and keyboard instruments. Afrika Bambaata's next recording, "Looking for the Perfect Beat" (1983), featured samples as substitutes for programmed synthesizers. A year later, Run-D.M.C. fused rock with rap in "Rock Box" (1984), a technique the group used again in "King of Rock" (1985) and "Walk This Way" (1986). Run-D.M.C.'s collaboration with rock guitarist Eddie Martinez and the rock group Aerosmith gave a hard, raw edge to the hip-hop aesthetic. Public Enemy added multiple layers of sampled raw sounds and textures to this aesthetic framework, which become the group's signature sound as well as the reference for defining hardcore hip-hop.

Since the mid-1990s, innovative hip-hop productions have moved beyond the East Coast and West Coast to what became known as the "The Dirty South." Representative performers included OutKast and Goodie MoB from Atlanta, Master P. from New Orleans, and Geto Boys and Scarface from Houston. Innovative hip-hop was also being produced in the Midwest by Bone Thugs-N-Harmony from Cleveland, Common from Chicago, Eminem and Royce the 5'9" from Detroit, and Nelly from Saint Louis. Although these performers have unique local identities, they cross stylistic boundaries, fusing and reformulating concepts from earlier hip-hop traditions.

New Jack Swing

By the late 1980s, new black popular styles were being created by independent producers, including Teddy Riley, Dallas Austin, and the teams of James "Jimmy Jam" Harris and Terry Lewis and Antonio "L. A." Reid and Kenneth "Babyface" Edmonds. One style that evolved from the innovations of these producers, and was imitated by others, was labeled *new jack swing*. The style, pioneered by Teddy Riley, represents postmodern soul; it is defined by its sparse instrumentation and a marked underlying drum pattern blended with or sometimes above the tempered vocals. Variations of this pattern incorporate a snare drum emphasis on the second and fourth beats, giving the sound a 1970s syncopated swing associated with James Brown and Earth, Wind, and Fire. The rhythms and production techniques of new jack swing became the beat and mix of the late 1980s and 1990s. It can be heard in Guy's "Groove Me" (1988), "You Can Call Me Crazy" (1988), and "Don't Clap . . . Just Dance" (1988); Heavy D. and The Boyz' "We Got Our Own Thang" (1989); Keith Sweat's "Make You Sweat" (1990); Hi Five's "I Just Can't Handle It" (1990); the gospel group Winans' "A Friend" (1990); and Michael Jackson's "Remember the Time" (1992), among others.

Future trends in black popular music will be pioneered by individuals and groups who continue to cross traditional genres and borrow from existing styles to create music that expresses the changing ideas and ideals of the African-American community.

See also Ballet; Blues, The; Dorsey, Thomas A.; Fisk Jubilee Singers; Gospel Music; Hip-Hop; Jazz; Music Collections, Black; Ragtime; Rap; Rhythm and Blues; Spirituals; Still, William Grant

■ ■ *Bibliography*

Barlow, William. *Looking Up at Down: The Emergence of Blues Culture.* Philadelphia: Temple University Press, 1989.

Bebey, Francis. *African Music: A People's Art.* Translated by Josephine Bennett. New York: L. Hill, 1974.

Berlin, Edward A. *Ragtime: A Musical and Cultural History.* Berkeley: University of California Press, 1980.

Brown, James. *I Feel Good: A Memoir of a Life of Soul.* New York: New American Library, 2005.

Burnim, Mellonee. "Functional Dimensions of Gospel Music Performance." *Western Journal of Black Studies* 12 (1988): 112–120.

Burnim, Mellonee V., and Portia K. Maultsby, eds. *African American Music: An Introduction.* New York: Routledge, 2005.

Chang, Jeff. *Can't Stop Won't Stop: A History of the Hip-Hop Generation.* New York: St. Martin's Press, 2005.

Charters, Samuel B., and Leonard Kunstadt. *Jazz: A History of the New York Scene.* Garden City, N.Y.: Doubleday, 1962. Reprint, New York: Da Capo, 1981.

Cone, James H. *The Spirituals and the Blues: An Interpretation.* New York: Seabury, 1972.

Courlander, Harold. *Negro Folk Music U.S.A.* New York: Columbia University Press, 1963. Reprint, New York: Dover, 1992.

De Lerma, Dominique-René. *Black Music in Our Culture: Curricular Ideas on the Subjects, Materials, and Problems.* Kent, Ohio: Kent State University Press, 1970.

Du Bois, W. E. B. *The Souls of Black Folk: Essays and Sketches.* Chicago: McClurg, 1903.

Epstein, Dena. *Sinful Tunes and Spirituals: Black Folk Music to the Civil War.* Urbana: University of Illinois Press, 1977.

Fletcher, Tom. *One Hundred Years of the Negro in Show Business* (1954). New York: Da Capo, 1984.

Floyd, Samuel, Jr., ed. *Black Music in the Harlem Renaissance: A Collection of Essays.* New York: Greenwood, 1990.

Forman, Murray, and Mark Anthony Neal, eds. *That's the Joint! The Hip-Hop Studies Reader.* New York: Routledge, 2004.

Franklin, Kirk, with Jim Nelson Black. *Church Boy: My Music and My Life.* Nashville, 1998.

Fricke, Jim, and Charlie Ahearn. *Yes Yes Y'all: The Experience Music Project Oral History of Hip-Hop's First Decade.* Cambridge, Mass.: Da Capo, 2002.

Garland, Phyl. *The Sound of Soul.* Chicago: Regnery, 1969.

Garofalo, Reebee. *Rockin' Out: Popular Music in the USA,* 3d ed. Upper Saddle River, N.J.: Prentice Hall, 2005.

George, Nelson. *The Death of Rhythm & Blues.* New York: Pantheon, 1988.

Haas, Robert Bartlett, ed. *William Grant Still and the Fusion of Cultures in American Music,* 2d ed. Los Angeles: Black Sparrow Press, 1972. 3d ed., Flagstaff, Ariz.: Master-Player Library, 1995.

Harris, Michael W. *The Rise of Gospel Blues: The Music of Thomas Andrew Dorsey in the Urban Church.* New York: Oxford University Press, 1992.

Harrison, Daphne Duval. *Black Pearls: Blues Queens of the 1920s.* New Brunswick, N.J.: Rutgers University Press, 1988.

Hinson, Glenn. *Fire in My Bones: Transcendence and the Holy Spirit in African American Gospel.* Philadelphia: University of Pennsylvania Press, 2000.

Hurston, Zora Neale. "Spirituals and Neo-Spirituals." In *Voices from the Harlem Renaissance,* edited by Nathan Irvin Huggins. New York: Oxford University Press, 1976.

Keil, Charles. *Urban Blues.* Chicago: University of Chicago Press, 1966. Reprint, 1991.

Keyes, Cheryl. *Rap Music and Street Consciousness.* Urbana: University of Illinois Press, 2002.

Kilham, Elizabeth. "Sketches in Color: IV." In *The Negro and His Folklore in Nineteenth-Century Periodicals,* edited by Bruce Jackson. Austin: University of Texas Press, 1967.

Leigh, James Wentworth. *Other Days.* London: Unwin, 1921.

Levine, Lawrence. *Black Culture and Black Consciousness: Afro-American Folk Thought from Slavery to Freedom.* New York: Oxford University Press, 1977.

Locke, Alain. "The Negro Spirituals." In *The New Negro: An Interpretation* (1925), edited by Alain Locke. New York: Arno, 1969.

Locke, Alain. *The Negro and His Music* (1936). New York: Arno, 1969.

Lornell, Kip, and Charles C. Stephenson Jr. *The Beat: Go-Go's Fusion of Funk and Hip-Hop.* New York: Billboard, 2001.

Maultsby, Portia K. "Africanisms in African-American Music." In *Africanisms in American Culture,* edited by Joseph E. Holloway. Bloomington: Indiana University Press, 1990.

Myers, Robert Manson, ed. *The Children of Pride: A True Story of Georgia and the Civil War.* New Haven, Conn.: Yale University Press, 1972.

Neal, Anthony Mark. *What the Music Said: Black Popular Music and Black Culture.* New York: Routledge, 1999.

Neal, Anthony Mark. *Soul Babies: Black Popular Culture and the Post-Soul Aesthetic.* New York: Routledge, 2002.

Nketia, Kwabena J. H. *The Music of Africa.* New York: Norton, 1974.

Nketia, Kwabena J. H. "African Roots of Music in the Americas: An African View." In *Report of the Twelfth Congress, Berkeley, 1977* (International Musicological Society), edited by Daniel Heartz and Bonnie Wade. Philadelphia: American Musicological Society, 1981.

Olmsted, Frederick Law. *A Journey in the Seaboard Slave States in the Years, 1853–1854, with Remarks on their Economy* (1856). New York: Putnam, 1904.

Pearson, Nathan W., Jr. *Goin' to Kansas City.* Urbana: University of Illinois Press, 1987.

Peretti, Burton W. *The Creation of Jazz: Music, Race, and Culture in Urban America.* Urbana: University of Illinois Press, 1992.

Pough, Gwendolyn D. *Check It While I Wreck It: Black Womanhood, Hip-Hop Culture, and the Public Sphere.* Boston: Northeastern University Press, 2004.

Ramsey, Guthrie P., Jr. *Race Music: Black Cultures from Bebop to Hip-Hop.* Berkeley: University of California Press, 2003.

Reagon, Bernice Johnson. "Let the Church Sing 'Freedom'" *Black Music Research Journal* 7 (1987): 105–118.

Reagon, Bernice Johnson. *We'll Understand It Better By and By: Pioneering African American Gospel Composers.* Washington, D.C.: Smithsonian Institution Press, 1992.

Rose, Trisa. *Black Noise: Rap Music and Black Culture in Contemporary America.* Hanover, N.H.: University Press of New England, 1994.

Russell, Henry. *Cheer! Boys, Cheer! Memories of Men and Music.* London: J. McQueen, 1895.

Schafer, William J. *Brass Bands and New Orleans Jazz.* Baton Rouge: Louisiana State University Press, 1977.

Shipton, Alyn. *A New History of Jazz,* rev. ed. London: Continuum, 2004.

Silvester, Peter J. *A Left Hand like God: A History of Boogie-Woogie Piano.* New York, 1989.

Southern, Eileen, ed. *Readings in Black American Music,* 2d ed. New York: Norton, 1983.

Southern, Eileen. *The Music of Black Americans: A History,* 3d ed. New York: Norton, 1997.

Still, William Grant. "A Composer's Viewpoint." In *Black Music in Our Culture: Curricular Ideas on the Subjects, Materials, and Problems,* edited by Dominique-René de Lerma. Kent, Ohio: Kent State University Press, 1970.

Toll, Robert C. *Blacking Up: The Minstrel Show in Nineteenth-Century America.* New York: Oxford University Press, 1977.

Toop, David. *The Rap Attack 3: African Rap to Global Hip Hop,* 3d ed. London: Serpent's Tail, 2000.

Werner, Craig. *A Change Is Gonna Come: Music, Race, and the Soul of America.* New York: Plume, 1999.

Werner, Craig. *Higher Ground: Stevie Wonder, Aretha Franklin, Curtis Mayfield, and the Rise and Fall of American Soul.* New York: Crown, 2004.

Wesley. Fred, Jr. *Hit Me, Fred: Recollections of a Sideman.* Durham, N.C.: Duke University Press, 2002.

Work, John W. *American Negro Songs and Spirituals.* New York: Bonanza, 1940.

Work, John W. "Changing Patterns in Negro Folk Songs." *Journal of American Folklore* 62 (1949): 136–144.

PORTIA K. MAULTSBY (1996)
Updated by author 2005

MUSIC, RELIGION, AND PERCEPTIONS OF CRIME IN EARLY TWENTIETH-CENTURY RIO DE JANEIRO

In 1908 the well-known senator Pinheiro Machado held a party at his house in Rio de Janeiro. For musical entertainment, he contracted several musicians, among them the young João Guedes, better known as João da Baiana. Guedes did not arrive at the party, and when Pinheiro Machado inquired of his whereabouts, he was informed that days earlier the police had stopped Guedes, harassed him, and confiscated his tambourine. With no musical instrument, Guedes had little reason to show up at the party and thus stayed away. Angered by the story, Machado took matters into his own hands, asking Guedes to meet him at the Senate. When Guedes arrived, he found an order for a new tambourine to be made bearing an inscription of admiration signed by the famous senator. This encounter was probably not the only one between João da Baiana and Machado. In interviews decades later, João da Baiana would recall the presence of Machado and other well-known public figures at the musical gatherings organized by his mother, Tia Perciliana. Rumors about politicians and public figures attending *batuques* (drum parties), *samba* circles, and religious gatherings organized by blacks circulated widely in early twentieth-century Rio, but such meetings were also subject to police repression. The story of João da Baiana and Pinheiro Machado, and the larger trends of society elites attending the same gatherings that also suffered police attacks, demonstrate the often contradictory reactions to African-influenced music and religious practices in late nineteenth- and early twentieth-century Rio de Janeiro. This entry explores those reactions first with a brief historical overview of racial ideology and police postures toward music and popular celebrations, and then by focusing on the following contexts and figures: dance and Carnival clubs, *capoeira*, the popular Festa da Penha celebration, and *samba* music's iconic *malandro* figures.

HISTORICAL OVERVIEW

The era in which the João da Baiana–Pinheiro Machado encounter took place was one of great transition in Brazil. As the nation felt its way through dramatic institutional change, African-descendent Brazilians forged new spaces in society, while also encountering new obstacles. The abolition of slavery (1888) and the transfer from monarchical to republican government (1889) created new opportunities, as well as new challenges. This was the same period in which neighboring Latin American countries were developing racial philosophies that trumpeted unique *mestizaje* races, those derived through mixture but dominated by purportedly white and European characteristics at the expense of supposedly weaker and dying or extinct indigenous and African elements. But in Brazil, where nonwhite peoples represented approximately 60 percent of the population from the 1870s to the 1890s, forgetting or hiding those peoples was not a viable option. Instead, elites imagined a process of gradual whitening, or *embranquecimento*, while also recognizing and sometimes embracing African influences.

For musicians, this recognition meant growing acceptance tempered by marginalization and sometimes repression. As the story of João da Baiana and Pinheiro Machado suggests, popular musicians were invited into the homes of elites and also harassed on the street. On the one hand, musicians saw their music celebrated as "pure" and "authentic" representations of their nation and its African heritage. On the other hand, they suffered repression and faced moralists who looked down on their music. There still exists little research about the extent and nature of that repression, and it is possible that some stories about police attacking musicians have been exaggerated over the years. However, there exists enough evidence in oral traditions and in studies about the police to show that musicians did in fact suffer at the hands of authorities.

After gaining independence from Portugal in 1822—a process that produced not a republican state but instead a politically autonomous, Brazilian-run monarchy—authorities in Rio retained some of the same characteristics of their predecessors, including a concern for public order and the regulation and registration of public festivals and celebrations. The postindependence police force was intent on transforming Rio into an internationally respected and European-style capital, and as part of that project, the police cast a vigilant eye on slave and free-black gatherings. Police prohibited processions by religious slave brotherhoods and often broke up *batuques* and other popular musical gatherings frequented by slaves. Viewed by authorities to be as low as crustaceans, those attending *batuques* suffered cruelly, and police raids came to be known infamously as "shrimp dinners" for the brutal beatings leveled by the police, which often produced flayed pink flesh.

The police mission was a general attempt to maintain order and prevent the noise, consumption of alcohol, general disorder, and danger that officials considered part and parcel of public gatherings. That mission also had clear designs on maintaining both race- and class-based hierarchies. While the control of public celebrations and the often harsh treatment of *batuques* and other musical gatherings can be understood as parts of larger projects to maintain order and control the general population, those larger projects cannot be divorced from the desire and intention to whiten, "civilize," and Europeanize Brazil. Targeting black gatherings continued after slavery ended. Fears of paganism, disorder, and social and racial "degeneration" often marked public discussions of African-Brazilian religions and popular music, even as both also became part of movements to recognize and valorize black Brazil. The 1890 Penal Code made no explicit reference to music, but that did not stop police from harassing musicians, nor did it prevent certain sectors of society from associating popular music with criminal behavior. The code was more explicit about religion, criminalizing spirit possession, magic, and herbal healing. Among other things, those laws resulted in debates about which kind of African-influenced religious practices were acceptable. While the Penal Code left unanswered questions about the legality of certain practices, society's perceptions could be just as ambiguous, as popular gatherings and African-Brazilian music and religion were seen by some as representations of a deep and unique past and by others as examples of savagery.

CLUBS, *CAPOEIRISTAS*, AND THE FESTA DA PENHA

The tension between repressing and valorizing African-Brazilian culture is evident in the policing of dance and Carnival clubs during the early twentieth century. These clubs and societies—which varied in size as well as in the social composition of their membership—offered members a place to dance and socialize, as well as the opportunity to parade and party during Carnival. They also often served as a lightning rod for critiques about the immorality and even danger of popular dancing and music. Required to register with the police both to parade during Carnival and to function during the year, the clubs provided an opportunity for the police to control, or at least keep an eye on, popular gatherings. The press often replicated the police's association of music and dancing with disorder. Stories about fights and trouble at the clubs frequently appeared in newspapers. But neither the police nor journalists viewed all associations as the same. While clubs existed throughout the city and included members of varying socioeconomic backgrounds, it was Rio's *suburbios* and *morros* ("outskirts" and "hills," respectively, both known as homes to poor, predominately black communities) that were most often associated with crime and disorder.

Music, crime, and religion converged in *capoeira*, a practice that was part martial art, part dance, developed in Africa as well as by slaves in Brazil. Fixtures at public celebrations throughout the nineteenth century, groups and gangs of *capoeiristas* were remembered by end-of-the-century writers both for the fear they inspired with knives and aggressive behavior and for the music and noise they created with drums, tambourines, and song. While often associated with violence, disorder, and music, *capoeiristas* shared a somewhat paradoxical relationship with city authorities. Though they often clashed with police, on other occasions *capoeiristas* were hired by politicians to intimidate and control voters. *Capoeiristas* also found spaces for demonstrating their abilities in public, performing at religious celebrations or parading at the front of military processions to the delight and fascination of onlookers.

While *capoeira* inspired curiosity as well as fear, it was the latter that dominated most interactions with the police. The 1890 Penal Code outlawed the practice, though most crackdowns took place before a law was on the books. During the nineteenth century, those crackdowns often occurred during Rio de Janeiro's most popular festivals, especially those around Christmas and Carnival. The high incidence of *capoeira* arrests during such festivals; the popular association made between *capoeiristas*, disorder, and music; and *capoeira*'s African and slavery roots indicate how crime, religion, and music often intersected in popular perceptions of Rio de Janeiro's African-descendant residents. That *capoeiristas* were also hired by politicians and found acceptable spaces in public celebrations indicates the tension that marked many of those perceptions.

Like *capoeira*, popular religious festivals themselves were subject to repression while also providing unique spaces of acceptance for otherwise stigmatized practices. One such festival was the Festa da Penha, an annual celebration held at the famous Santuário de Nossa Senhora da Penha, which sits atop a well-known elevated rock point in Rio de Janeiro. While diverse groups frequented Penha, the African-Brazilian presence was especially influential. *Capoeiristas* circulated and performed, and visitors enjoyed African-influenced foods, prepared by *tias*, female African-Brazilian community and spiritual leaders who exercised important roles in the festival's organization and execution. (Such *tias* as João da Baiana's mother Perciliana also hosted private get-togethers like those that Pinheiro Machado attended and that proved crucial to the development of Brazilian popular music.)

The Festa da Penha also served as a place for musicians to play and publicize their work, and friends and families gathered in *samba* and *batuque* circles to enjoy early forms of music that would rise to national prominence in the 1920s and 1930s. During the first two decades of the twentieth century, just before *samba* became a unified and widely popular genre, and before the music market exploded in Brazil, the Festa da Penha served as an informal but crucial launching pad for musicians. Falling four to five months before the start of pre-Lenten festivities, Penha served as an unofficial commencement to the lucrative Carnival season. Musicians would often debut their songs at Penha, seizing the opportunity to make their work known and to position themselves for popularity and success during Carnival.

At Penha celebrations, the lines between sacred and profane, black and white, rich and poor, and order and disorder often blurred. During the late nineteenth and early twentieth centuries, crowds often included black, white, and mixed-race revelers, coming from varying socioeconomic backgrounds. Well-to-do families, along with those from Rio de Janeiro's lower class *suburbios*, enjoyed picnics, food and drink stands, and the music that marked the festivities.

Heterogeneity and mixture, however, did not mean an absence of attempts to isolate and reprimand unwanted groups and behaviors. On various occasions tambourines and guitars were prohibited from the festival, robbing musicians of their valuable stage and denying partygoers a main attraction. Indeed, João da Baiana was purportedly on his way to a Penha celebration when the police grabbed his instrument. Local newspapers often commented on the police's ability to control the festivities, sometimes critiquing authorities for not doing enough, other times applauding forceful police actions.

MALANDROS

Crime and music merged in the *malandro*, flashy street hustlers, similar in appearance to early twentieth-century zoot-suiters in the United States. As in the cases of dance and Carnival clubs, *capoeiristas*, and Festa da Penha revelers, society both shunned and embraced *malandros*. Though research tracing the origins of the *malandro* is scarce, most observers agree that the figure became a popular icon in the 1920s and 1930s, largely as a result of Brazil's increasing interest in *samba* music. Glorified for their success with women, for resisting authority, and for their ability to make money without working, *malandros* walked the thin lines between the acceptable flaunting of legal and moral codes and the ire of authorities and social commentators who guarded those lines. As such, Brazilian society and its burgeoning music market offered both lucrative opportunities and restrictive limits to musicians who presented themselves as *malandros* or otherwise celebrated *malandragem* (the many *malandro* traits and activities, such as womanizing and trickery). Censorship of *malandro* images and references during the early 1940s was sandwiched between periods in which such musicians as Wilson Batista, Moreira da Silva, and Geraldo Pereira gained fame and money as *malandro sambistas*. Some musicians were arrested for petty crime or involvement with illegal gambling, or under vaguely defined antivagrancy codes. Descriptions of run-ins with the authorities often made their way into song lyrics, and *malandragem* became synonymous not just with womanizing, cleverness, and irreverence but also criminality. The *malandro* also found a religious manifestation in the divine being Zé Pelintra, an *exu* responsible for communications between humans and *orixás* (African-Brazilian deities). Visual depictions of Zé Pelintra represent a composite image of snappily dressed *malandros* from the early twentieth century, complete with white linen suit, white shoes, red tie, matching handkerchief, and Panama hat. To this day, one can find cigarettes, roses, liquor, and even cooked steaks on street corners in Rio, left by those asking Zé Pelintra for help and protection.

CONCLUSION

African-influenced cultural practices met with contradictory responses in late nineteenth- and early twentieth-century Rio de Janeiro. On the one hand, African-Brazilian music and religion found new spaces and new levels of acceptance in society. On the other hand, police maintained vigilant watch over those who danced at clubs or in the streets during Carnival or who gathered at religious festivals like the Festa da Penha. *Capoeiristas* drew the ire of authorities, but also led processions and influenced elections. *Malandros* alternately cashed in on and were reprimanded for extolling the virtues of womanizing, resisting authority, and avoiding work. In each case, it is possible to glimpse the larger tensions felt in Brazil during the late nineteenth and early twentieth centuries between embracing and rejecting African influences.

See also Capoeira; Madame Satã (dos Santos, João Francisco); Music; Samba; Tia Ciata

■ ■ *Bibliography*

Abreu, Martha. *O Imp rio do divino: Festas religiosas e cultura popular no Rio de Janeiro, 1830–1900*. Rio de Janeiro, Brazil: Editora Nova Fronteira, 1999.

As vozes desassombradas do museu. Rio de Janeiro, Brazil: MIS, 1970.

Borges, Dain. "Healing and Mischief in Brazilian Law and Literature, 1890–1922." In *Crime and Punishment in Latin America: Law and Society since Late Colonial Times*, edited by R. Salvatore, C. Aguirre, and G. Joseph. Durham, N.C.: Duke University Press, 2001.

Holloway, Thomas H. *Policing Rio de Janeiro: Repression and Resistance in a Nineteenth-Century City*. Stanford, Calif.: Stanford University Press, 1993.

Karasch, Mary C. *Slave Life in Rio de Janeiro, 1808–1850*. Princeton, N.J.: Princeton University Press, 1987.

Líbano Soares, Carlos Eugênio. "Festa e violência: Os capoeiras e as festas populares na corte do Rio de Janeiro (1809–1890)." In *Carnavais e outras f(r)estas: Ensaios de história social da cultura*, edited by M. C. Pereira Cunha. Campinas, Brazil: CECULT, 2002.

Moura, Roberto. *Tia ciata e a pequena África no Rio de Janeiro*. Rio de Janeiro, Brazil: FUNARTE, 1983.

Pereira, Leonardo Affonso de Miranda. "E o Rio Dan ou: Identidades e rensões nos clubes recreativos cariocas (1912–1922)." In *Carnavais e outras f(r)estas: Ensaios de história social da cultura*, edited by M. C. Pereira Cunha. Campinas, Brazil: CECULT, 2002.

Skidmore, Thomas E. *Brazil: Five Centuries of Change*. New York: Oxford University Press, 1999.

Soihet, Rachel. "Festa da Penha: Resistência e iterpenetração cultural (1890–1920)." In *Carnavais e outras f(r)estas: Ensaios de história social da cultura*, edited by M. C. Pereira Cunha. Campinas, Brazil: CECULT, 2002.

MARC ADAM HERTZMAN (2005)

MUSICAL INSTRUMENTS

Many of the most popular musical instruments in American music derive from African Americans, who used traditional African instruments and developed new ones ac-

A jug band performs during a wedding in Palm Beach, Florida, 1948. *The washtub bass, likely originating from an African instrument called the earthbow or mosquito drum, played a central role in folk blues and jug bands. The instrument was created by stringing a rope from the bottom of an inverted metal washtub to the end of a stick.* © BETTMANN/CORBIS

cording not only to musical needs, but to the natural and manufactured materials at hand and the legal restrictions placed on them by slave owners regarding the making of music. The prominence of stringed instruments in early African-American music was no doubt due to plantation prohibitions on drum and wind instruments, which slave-masters believed would be used for long-distance and mass communication among slaves.

STRINGED INSTRUMENTS

Although the banjo, the earliest and most important African-American instrument, is today used almost exclusively in white music, the instrument derives from the West African "banja," or "banza," which was brought to the New World by slaves. References to a gourd covered with sheepskin and strung with four strings along an attached stick occur in accounts of the Americas as early as 1678.

Both fretless and fretted banjos were used by African-American musicians, and open tunings were common. Slaves also pioneered most of the techniques that became standard on the modern instrument, including the various kinds of strumming and plucking heard in twentieth-century bluegrass and country music. Although informal banjo playing was a central feature of African-American domestic life in the eighteenth century, it was through nineteenth-century minstrel shows that the instrument was first widely noticed among whites. The banjo was used by white musicians before the Civil War and was being commercially produced using a wood frame (Contrary to some accounts, the now-standard fifth string was a feature of the banjo before the white minstrel musician Joel Walker Sweeney [1810–1860] helped popularize the instrument). Soon, the banjo was considered as much a parlor instrument among white families as a staple of rural black music. Among the best early recordings of black banjo music are "Long Gone Lost John" (1928) by Papa Charlie Jackson (1890–1950), and "Money Never Runs Out" (1930) by Gus Cannon (1883–1979), who recorded under the name Banjo Joe. Early jazz bands also used the banjo extensively, most notably Johnny St. Cyr (1890–1966), a sideman with Louis Armstrong and Jelly Roll Morton in the 1920s. After the late 1920s, however, the guitar supplanted the banjo as a rhythm instrument. After that time the banjo became the almost exclusive province of white country, bluegrass, and folk music, although some black folk musicians, including Elizabeth Cotten (1895–1987), continued to play the banjo.

African Americans also developed many types of single-string instruments. The diddley bow was a type of simple guitar popular among black musicians in the South well into the twentieth century. Elias McDaniel's prowess on the instrument as a child was so great that he was known by the name Bo Diddley (1928–1955) well before he gained fame as a blues musician in the 1950s. The blues guitarist and singer Elmore James (1918–1963) learned music on a jitterbug, a variant of the diddley bow that is strung between two nails along a wall. The washtub bass, or gutbucket, played a central role in folk blues and jug bands (the word "gutbucket" has also come to mean a crude, raucous, earthy style of jazz or blues). This instrument was created by stringing a rope from the bottom of an inverted metal washtub to the end of a stick, the other end of which stands on the tub. Plucked much in the manner of the modern jazz bass, the washtub bass is still in use today in informal street ensembles. It probably originated from an African instrument called the earthbow, or mosquito drum, in which resonating material was stretched over a hole in the ground. The practice of using a hard object to create glissandos on the guitar is of unclear origin—certainly the "Hawaiian" style of picking with the right hand while using a slide with the left, introduced in the late nineteenth century, was influential—but African-American musicians were the first to master the use of broken-off bottlenecks, knives, and medicine bottles for this purpose, now typical of blues guitar playing.

WIND INSTRUMENTS

Numerous types of flutes, pipes, and fifes were brought by African slaves to the New World, and despite being outlawed in slave states, these wind instruments played a central part in the development of African-American music. Wooden or metal fifes, similar to European transverse flutes, were used in ubiquitous fife and drum bands as early as the eighteenth century. The kazoo, a small cylinder with a resonating membrane set into motion by humming or singing, was also probably of African-American ori-

gin—although it bears similarities to European musical devices—and became a popular folk instrument among whites and blacks after being manufactured commercially starting around 1850.

Perhaps the most distinctive African-American wind instrument is the quills. These pan pipes were traditionally made from cane, reed, or willow stalks cut from riverbanks, but their name suggests that at one time they may have been made with feathers. After being cut down to a length of approximately one foot, a hole was bored through the center, and finger and mouth holes were also created. Among the earliest and most representative of the quill recordings are "Arkansas" (1927) by Henry Thomas (1874–1930), and "Quill Blues" (1927) by Big Boy Clarence.

The domestic earthen jug, which produces a sound when blown across its mouth, was another wind instrument popular among African Americans, and it gave its name to an independent genre of music in the late nineteenth century. Throughout the South, and well into the twentieth century, jug bands—consisting of a jug, fiddle and bass, kazoo or harmonica, and often a washboard scraped and played as a percussion instrument—performed folk-blues music often suited for dancing. Early examples of jug bands include the Memphis Jug Band, the Dixieland Jug Blowers, who recorded "Skip Skat Doodle Do" in 1926, and Gus Cannon's Jug Stompers, who recorded "K.C. Moan" in 1929.

PERCUSSION INSTRUMENTS

Many African-American percussion instruments were developed from common household or agricultural materials that lent themselves to use as knockers, rattles, and scrapers. Clapping together small sections of dried bone or wood was a long-standing feature of European folk music by the time the slave trade began, but playing "the bones" was elevated to a virtuosic state by black minstrels in nineteenth-century America. In fact, the player of the bones was such an important part of African-American culture that the role was immortalized alongside the tambourine player in minstrel shows as the characters of Tambo and Bones. The practice of striking and shaking the weathered jawbone of a donkey or horse probably derives from African slaves—although visual images and literary references to jawbone percussion are also found in medieval and Renaissance Europe—and was a conspicuous aspect of both white and black minstrel shows early in the nineteenth century.

Although the playing of drums was proscribed on most plantations, the striking of skin stretched on a sturdy frame remained a part of black musical life. The marching bands that were so popular in the nineteenth century, at both parades and military functions, were driven by drummers using a variety of instruments, from huge bass drums to smaller snare drums.

Although the origin of the snare drum is not clear, the use of bamboo or feathers stretched across a drumhead to give an impure, buzzing tone is a characteristic of many African instruments. The tuned or talking drums of Africa also had their counterparts in America, as African-American musicians played peg drums, which used posts on the side of the frames to tighten or loosen the skin head, and therefore raise or lower the pitch of the drum.

The decline of marching music in favor of the dance music played at nightclubs where musicians remained stationary made possible the trap drum set, whose combination of bass drum, snare, tom-tom, and cymbals was developed by popular dance drummers and early jazz musicians such as Baby Dodds (1898–1959) and Zutty Singleton (1898–1975). In the 1940s, Cuban musicians such as Chano Pozo (1915–1948) brought Latin-style drums and drumming to jazz. The Afro-Cuban tradition, which used congas and bongos played with the hands, as opposed to drumsticks, was directly linked to West African religious practices that had been carried over and sustained in Cuba.

The marimba is sometimes called an Amerindian creation, but some scholars believe that this melodic percussion instrument, with its parallel wooden blocks gathered together and struck with a mallet, was brought to the Americas by African slaves. Its use is documented in Virginia as early as 1775.

EUROPEAN INSTRUMENTS

In addition to using instruments of African origin, or creating ones, African Americans have also approached traditional European instruments from such a new perspective that instruments such as the saxophone, violin, harmonica, and piano were transformed into virtually new instruments. Perhaps the best such example is the double bass, which in the European tradition was almost always bowed, forming the harmonic underpinning of the orchestra. In the 1920s, African Americans began to use the bass as a timekeeper, making the pizzicato, or plucked technique, its main feature in jazz and jug bands. Among the finest early recorded example of jazz bass playing is the performance by John Lindsay (1894–1950) on Jelly Roll Morton's "Black Bottom Stomp" (1926). A slightly different example of the metamorphosis of a purely European instrument is the plunger-muted trumpet. In the European tradition, trumpeters used mutes to muffle their sounds. In the 1920s, African-American jazz trumpeters such as

Joe "King" Oliver (1885–1938), Bubber Miley (1903–1932), and, later, Cootie Williams (1910–1985), adapted rubber toilet plungers as mutes that, when manipulated in front of the bell of the horn, could create a whole new range of growls and speech-like sounds, a practice that was also extended to the trombone in the playing of Joe "Tricky Sam" Nanton (1904–1946).

NEWER INSTRUMENTS

The development of African-American instruments has continued into the twenty-first century. The Chicago musicians' collective known as the Association for the Advancement of Creative Musicians (AACM) integrated the use of unusual tools and household items into its percussion array. One AACM member, Henry Threadgill (b. 1944), invented a percussion instrument made of automobile hubcaps. In more recent years, African-American disc jockeys have developed the technique of "scratching"—manually moving records backwards and forwards on turntables to create melodic rhythms. Digital electronics have allowed African-American musicians to develop "sampling," in which fragments of older recordings by various musicians are integrated into new musical works. These modern techniques demonstrate how the response by African Americans to both musical and material imperatives continues to inspire the development of new African-American musical instruments.

See also Armstrong, Louis; Association for the Advancement of Creative Musicians; Diddley, Bo (McDaniel, Otha Elias); Minstrels/Minstrelsy

■ ■ *Bibliography*

Evans, David. "Afro-American One-Stringed Instruments." In *Afro-American Folk Art and Crafts*, edited by William Ferris, pp. 181–198. Boston: G. K. Hall, 1983.

Evans, David. "Black Fife and Drum Music in Mississippi." In *Afro-American Folk Art and Crafts*, pp. 163–172. Boston: G. K. Hall, 1983.

MacLeod, Bruce. "The Musical Instruments of North American Slaves." *Mississippi Folklore Register* 11 (1977): 34–49.

MacLeod, Bruce. "Quills, Fifes, and Flutes before the Civil War." *Southern Folklore Quarterly* 42 (1978): 201–208.

Webb, Robert Lloyd. *Ring the Banjar: The Banjo from Folklore to Factory*. Cambridge, Mass.: MIT Museum, 1984.

JONATHAN GILL (1996)

MUSICAL THEATER

Musical theater—formal, staged entertainments combining songs, skits, instrumental interludes, and dances—was relatively uncommon in America before the middle of the eighteenth century. It is very likely that slave musicians occasionally took part in the earliest colonial-period musical theatricals, called *ballad operas*, at least in the orchestra pit, because many slaves were known to be musically accomplished. Less than fully developed theatrical shows that involved satirical skits by slaves about white masters are recorded in the late eighteenth century. These skits, related to African storytelling traditions, were the seeds from which black American theatricality sprang. "Negro songs" or "Negro jigs" are also recorded in the shows of this period, suggesting the impact of an unnotated tradition of black music-making on the musical theater song repertory.

UP TO THE CIVIL WAR

The 1821 opening of the African Grove theater near lower Broadway in New York inaugurated the staging of plays with music "agreeable to Ladies and Gentlemen of Colour" (Southern, 1983, p. 119). Led by playwright Henry Brown, the African Grove players produced Shakespeare's *Hamlet, Othello,* and *Richard III* (including inserted songs), popular potpourris such as *Tom and Jerry; or Life in London,* and the pantomime *Obi; or, Three Finger'd Jack.* James Hewlett was the company's principal singer and actor. Ira Aldridge, who later made his career in Europe, sang at the Grove. Despite the theater's popularity, it was plagued by hooligans and closed in 1829.

Various musical shows were produced with black performers periodically in Philadelphia and New Orleans, although very little information survives about these shows. New Orleans could command orchestral forces (as opposed to the modest pit band of violin, clarinet, and double bass at the African Grove) for theatricals, and it engaged black players in the 1840s. In the 1850s and 1860s, African-American actors became traveling entertainers or joined minstrel shows.

THE LATE NINETEENTH CENTURY

The Hyers Sisters touring company, founded in 1876, became the first established African-American musical comedy troupe. Managed by Sam Hyers, the company featured his two daughters, Emma Louise and Anna Madah, and a string of male comedy singer/actors: Fred Lyon, Sam Lucas, Billy Kersands, Wallace King, and John and Alexander Luca. The Hyers began as a concert-giving group but moved on to fully staged musical plays that often dealt with racial themes: *Out of Bondage* (1876); *Urlina, or The African Princess* (1879); *Peculiar Sam; or, The Underground Railroad* (1879); and *Plum Pudding* (1887). The music they presented included jubilee songs, spirituals, operatic excerpts, and new popular songs and dances.

By the 1890s, a few specific plays regularly toured and featured parts for black singers, usually in the guise of plantation slaves. Bucolic scenes or other scenarios in the cotton field, on the levee, or in a camp meeting were meant to evoke an idyllic antebellum South. Turner Dazey's *In Old Kentucky* (1892) and *The South Before the War* (1893) included black singers and dancers, as did the most famous of all shows of this type, *Uncle Tom's Cabin* (based on Harriet Beecher Stowe's 1852 novel). The huge number and variety of staged versions of this powerful work made it a unique dramatic vehicle in American culture. Many African-American jubilee singing groups, typically male quartets, took part in the play, although early performances rarely used black actors. It served the careers of solo banjo virtuoso Horace Weston in 1877 and vaudevillian Sam Lucas, who played the role of Uncle Tom in the 1880s.

At least half a dozen all-black companies, as well as some integrated ones, appeared before the end of the century. Black choral singers and supernumeraries, including children, brought literally hundreds of people to the stage in productions in the 1880s and 1890s. Other festivals featuring black vaudeville acts, musical specialties, and historical tableaux, with titles like *Black America* (1895) and *Darkest America* (1897), were well-attended showcases but did not present complete plays.

The most widely acclaimed operatic singer of the period to become involved with traveling musical theatrical companies was Sissieretta Jones, known as the Black Patti (after the renowned soprano Adelina Patti). In 1896 she formed the Black Patti Troubadours and remained an important presence on the road for two decades, eventually mounting full-fledged musical comedies.

White burlesque entrepreneur Sam T. Jack formed the Creole Company in 1890 to do the skit *The Beauty of the Nile; or, Doomed by Fire,* using the novelty of black women in a minstrel line that emphasized glittery, revealing costumes and diverse musical acts. John Isham, Jack's advance man, developed his own potpourri shows presented by mixed male and female companies known as the Octoroons (1895), one of which toured in Europe. All of Isham's shows exploited the popularity of exotic costumes, operatic excerpts, musical specialties, spectacular scenery, and attractive women, while avoiding farcical minstrel show caricatures.

THE FIRST BLACK MUSICALS AND THE GROWTH OF BLACK VAUDEVILLE, 1897–1920

Within this world of extravagant eclecticism, full-length musical comedies—plays in which songs were frequent and newly composed, if not integral—became more and more common. The first musical written by and for African Americans, Bob Cole and Billy Johnson's *A Trip to Coontown* (1897), was built up from Cole's songs and vaudeville turns with the Black Patti Troubadours (Cole had also managed her show in its first season) and other elements: a trio from Verdi's opera *Attila*, Sousa's new march "The Stars and Stripes Forever," a tune by Cole that was later adapted to become Yale University's fight song "Boola Boola," energetic dancing, topical humor, and social commentary. The show eschewed the Old South nostalgia typical of the earlier touring shows. Minstrel tunes were replaced by snappy up-tempo, occasionally syncopated songs written by various composers.

At the same time, cakewalk dancers/comedians Bert Williams and George Walker, in the course of several productions from 1898 to 1908, expanded their routines to even more ambitious dimensions, with elaborate plots and often African settings: *The Policy Players* (1899); *The Sons of Ham* (1900); *In Dahomey* (1902); *Abyssinia* (1905); and *Bandanna Land* (1907). Will Marion Cook, classical violinist and European-trained composer, wrote most of the music for these landmark shows in a unique syncopated style. Cook's sensational Broadway debut—his musical skit "Clorindy" was produced at the Casino Theatre Roof Garden in 1898—established him as a leading figure, along with its dancing star, Ernest Hogan.

In 1899 Bob Cole formed a partnership with the brothers J. Rosamond Johnson and James Weldon Johnson. This young trio wrote songs for many shows and performers, black and white, to great success, and later composed comic operettas for all-black casts entitled *The Shoo-Fly Regiment* (1906) and *The Red Moon* (1908); they also starred in the shows themselves. Black, white, and mixed audiences found these many early twentieth-century efforts attractive, but any hope for sustained development was dashed by the premature deaths of the leaders, Ernest Hogan, George Walker, and Bob Cole, around 1910 and the unremitting financial burden of mounting and touring with a large cast. Racism and professional jealousies among competing companies also limited the success of these shows.

Black-owned theaters rapidly increased in number in the early twentieth century, providing sites for a wide variety of musical-theater activities. Following the opening of the Pekin Theatre in Chicago in 1905, many black-owned

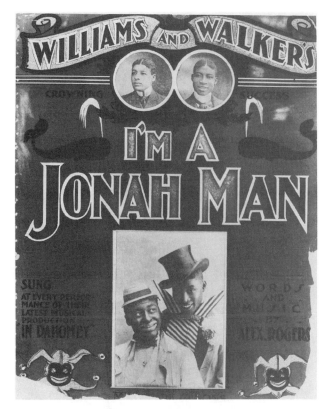

***Sheet music for Bert Williams's theme song for the Williams and Walker musical* In Dahomey.** *The musical enjoyed a command performance at Buckingham Palace after a successful turn-of-the-century run in New York.* MANUSCRIPTS, ARCHIVES AND RARE BOOKS DIVISION, SCHOMBURG CENTER FOR RESEARCH IN BLACK CULTURE, THE NEW YORK PUBLIC LIBRARY, ASTOR, LENOX AND TILDEN FOUNDATIONS.

or black-managed houses were built. By 1920 some 300 theaters around the country were serving black patrons (approximately one-third of these were black-run). This in turn led to the formation of resident stock companies that provided a regular menu of musical plays and developed loyal audiences. Many short-lived shows of the 1920s and 1930s filled the Lafayette, Lincoln, and Alhambra theaters in Harlem, the Howard in Washington, D.C., the Regal in Baltimore, Maryland, the Monogram in Chicago, the 81 in Atlanta, Georgia, and the Booker T. Washington in Saint Louis, Missouri, among others.

A few large companies continued to tour—J. Leubrie Hill's Darktown Follies (from 1911 to 1916) and the various Smart Set shows run by S. H. Dudley, H. Tutt, and S. T. Whitney—but many acts appeared in vaudeville as well. By 1920 the Theatre Owners' Booking Association (TOBA) was formed to facilitate the booking of black acts into theaters that served black audiences exclusively. The TOBA circuit of theaters eventually embraced houses all over the South and survived until the Great Depression.

J. Rosamond Johnson. *In the first decade of the twentieth century, Johnson joined forces with his brother James Weldon Johnson and Bob Cole to create all-black comic operettas.* PHOTOGRAPHS AND PRINTS DIVISION, SCHOMBURG CENTER FOR RESEARCH IN BLACK CULTURE, THE NEW YORK PUBLIC LIBRARY, ASTOR, LENOX AND TILDEN FOUNDATIONS.

Vaudeville acts and musicals of the first decades of the twentieth century served as apprenticeships for many young ragtime pianists and composers who wanted to break into the business. J. Tim Brymn, James Vaughan, Charles "Luckey" Roberts, James Price Johnson, and Will Vodery played, wrote songs for, and directed forgotten shows with titles like *George Washington Bullion Abroad* (1915) and *Baby Blues* (1919) before going on to arrange, perform, and write for military bands, Broadway shows, and films.

SHUFFLE ALONG AND ITS SUCCESSORS, 1921–1939

Eubie Blake and Noble Sissle's 1921 *Shuffle Along* kicked off a major revival of black musical comedies in New York. Light, fast-moving, and filled with catchy melodies, it captured crowds for over 500 Broadway performances and spent two years on the road. Its lead comedians, still in blackface, were Aubrey Lyles and Flournoy Miller, who

wrote the book, developing material they had been using for years. Many cast members later found individual stardom: Florence Mills, Josephine Baker, Adelaide Hall, Hall Johnson, Paul Robeson, William Grant Still, Ethel Waters, and Caterina Yarboro.

The upsurge in black shows in the wake of *Shuffle Along* has not been equaled since. Their number paralleled the high-water mark of new productions of all kinds on Broadway in the late 1920s. Many were close imitations of *Shuffle Along,* but a few broke new ground with respect to both characters and music: *Put and Take* (1921); *Liza* (1922); *Strut Miss Lizzie* (1922); *Plantation Days* (1923); *Runnin' Wild* (1923); *Bottomland* (1927); *Africana* (1927); *Rang Tang* (1927); and five shows produced by Lew Leslie called *Blackbirds* (*of 1926, 1928, 1930, 1933,* and *1939*).

Hot Chocolates (1929), by Andy Razaf and Fats Waller, epitomized the successful post–*Shuffle Along* show of the late 1920s: a revue (i.e., a string of topical acts and songs rather than a plotted story show) filled with new dance steps—the Black Bottom, the Lindy, the Shimmy, and the Charleston all appeared in these shows—with an attractive chorus line, blues songs, and repartee closer to the real speech of Harlem than to either the pseudo-dialect of minstrelsy or the clean, cute shows of white Broadway. James P. Johnson, Tom Lemonier, Donald Heyward, Maceo Pinkard, Joe Jordan, Henry Creamer, Ford Dabney, and Perry Bradford emerged as songwriters with these shows.

The spirituals arranged by Hall Johnson and sung by his choir helped to make *The Green Pastures* the hit play of 1930. Weaving humor and gentleness together to create a naive picture of a black heaven, the superb cast was well received. Ironically, its very success led to bookings in exclusionary theaters where no blacks were admitted to the auditorium. Both this show and its successor, *Run Little Chillun* (1933), helped to ensure the continued employment of black players and singers during the general decline of the 1930s.

The Works Progress Administration (WPA) Negro Theatre Project (1935–1939) brought African Americans into all aspects of theater production, and a few musicals were performed: *Did Adam Sin?* (1936), using African-American folklore themes and music; *Theodore Brown's Natural Man* (1937), a retelling of the John Henry legend; *Swing It* (1937), by Cecil Mack (a.k.a. R. Cecil McPherson); and *Swing Mikado* (1939), a jazz transformation of Gilbert and Sullivan.

DEVELOPMENTS SINCE WORLD WAR II

The only major shows featuring black stars in the 1940s were *Cabin in the Sky* (1940) with Ethel Waters and *St.*

Louis Woman (1946) with Pearl Bailey and the Nicolas Brothers. Otherwise, opportunities for blacks in the New York musical theater scene through the 1940s, 1950s, and 1960s were few. A desire to eliminate stereotyped roles for black actors and the problem of dealing with serious race-related social issues in the normally lighthearted style of musicals resulted in the temporary elimination of nearly all black participation. No all-black-cast shows were staged in the early 1950s, nor were more than a handful of African Americans employed on- or offstage during this period. A small group of shows with integrated casts or a single black star did well at the box office, notably *Jamaica* (1957) with Lena Horne and *Golden Boy* (1964) with Sammy Davis Jr.

In the wake of the civil rights movement, African Americans returned to Broadway and touring companies via the revival of older black musical styles and the folk songs that had always found an audience. The plays of Langston Hughes with various musical collaborators, *Simply Heavenly* (1957), *Black Nativity* (1961), *Tambourines to Glory* (1963), and *The Prodigal Son* (1965), embraced black culture and ignored the politics of integration. Vinnette Carroll adapted James Weldon Johnson's verse sermons for *Trumpets of the Lord* (1963). Gospel songs, spirituals, and folk songs also infused *A Hand Is at the Gate* (1966), *Don't Bother Me, I Can't Cope* (1972), and *Your Arms Too Short to Box with God* (1976).

More direct social criticism was offered in the calypso musical *Ballad for Bimshire* (1963) and in Melvin Van Peebles's angry and challenging plays *Ain't Supposed to Die a Natural Death* (1971) and *Don't Play Us Cheap* (1972). Blues, jazz, and the special styles of famous artists in earlier eras of black music added a nostalgic aura to the shows of the rest of the 1970s and 1980s: *Me and Bessie* (1975), *One Mo' Time* (1979), *Eubie* (1979), *Sophisticated Ladies* (1981), *Blues in the Night* (1982), *Dreamgirls* (1982), *Williams and Walker* (1986), and *Black and Blue* (1989).

The same decades saw the successful conversion of straight plays by black playwrights (Ossie Davis, Lorraine Hansberry, and James Baldwin) into musicals: *Purlie* (1970), *Raisin* (1973), *The Amen Corner* (1983), as well as the improbable remake of *Sophocles* into the fervid gospel-music show *The Gospel at Colonus* (1988). A uniquely whimsical and tuneful adaptation of L. Frank Baum's *Wizard of Oz,* with music by Charles Smalls, became *The Wiz* (1975, revived in 1984), and black-cast versions of the white shows *Hello Dolly* (1963 and 1975) and *Guys and Dolls* (1976) and self-conscious historical song summaries like *Bubbling Brown Sugar* (1976) and *Black Broadway* (1980) also appeared. As in the 1930s, the revue format succeeded best with audiences and critics. *Ain't Misbe-*

Gregory (r) and Maurice Hines dance in the Broadway musical **Sophisticated Ladies,** *1982.* © BETTMAN/CORBIS

havin', using the tunes of Fats Waller, won the Tony Award for Best Musical in 1978.

APPROACHING THE MILLENNIUM: 1980–2000

American musical theater was transformed fundamentally in the wake of the civil rights and women's movements and the decline in government arts funding between 1975 and 2000. Racial, ethnic, and gender images onstage came under closer scrutiny, and producers began to recognize that casting practices should more fully reflect America's diverse social fabric. It was not lost on administrators and marketing directors that increased inclusiveness helped attract a larger paying audience.

As nondiscriminatory hiring and color-blind casting became fashionable in mainline white theaters, black directors, such as Idris Ackamoor, Rhodessa Jones and her brother Bill T. Jones, George C. Wolf (*Bring in da Noise, Bring in da Funk,* 1995), and Donald Byrd, found opportunities to advance new theatrical concepts of dance, dialogue, and song that challenged basic genre boundaries and mooted to some degree issues of racial integration within older forms.

Major shifts in taste shaped the kind of productions that arose. Caribbean- and African-inspired themes found audiences. Lynn Ahrens and Stephen Flaherty created *Once on This Island* (1990) with Trinidadian motifs. *Sarafina!* (1987), *Song of Jacob Zulu* (1993), *Umbatha: The Zulu Macbeth* (1997), and *Kat and the Kings* (1999) all took South Africa during the apartheid era for their setting. The standard musical fare changed also as Tin Pan Alley's popular songs were replaced by gospel tunes, rap, and digitally

Actors Gregory Hines, Tonya Pilkins, and Keith David are pictured at the 1992 opening night party for the Broadway musical Jelly's Last Jam, *based on the life of the pianist and composer Jelly Roll Morton.* TIME LIFE PICTURES/GETTY IMAGES

generated dance music. Old-style musical comedies, revues, and operettas virtually disappeared, to be replaced by solo performance pieces, historical medleys, experimental plays with incidental music, song-and-dance shows, and revivals of old hits. Earthy, assertive rappers and break dancers emerged from the South Bronx and spread across the country in this period to challenge and rejuvenate basic components within musical theater.

Shows high on energy, retrospection, and creative movement, but less apt to be driven by a powerful book, remained the norm. *Jelly's Last Jam* (1992), featuring dancing sensation Gregory Hines, and the one-man show created by Vernel Bagneris, *Jelly Roll!* (1994), both treated the near-legendary figure of jazz history, Jelly Roll Morton. The former was hailed by *Variety* as "original, outrageous, and exuberant" and received eleven Tony Award nominations.

Individual African-American stars shone in a variety of productions: Brian Stokes Mitchell in the musical version of Doctorow's novel *Ragtime* (1997); Audra McDonald also in *Ragtime* and as the central figure in *Marie Christine* (1999), a remarkable representation of the Medea myth set in New Orleans in 1894; and soprano Heather Headley in the Elton John/Tim Rice recreation of *Aida* (2000).

By 2000, Broadway itself had become only one of many places in which to find validation for original productions. The steady decline of New York City as an affordable workshop site for new ideas combined with steep cutbacks in federal and state patronage of the performing arts to affect developments everywhere. Other media, such as MTV and the movies, opened remunerative pathways for emerging artists, and live theater found increasingly that it needed to market itself through videos and CDs.

See also Lincoln Theatre; Minstrels/Minstrelsy; Opera; Ragtime; Spirituals; Theatrical Dance

■ ■ *Bibliography*

Bean, Annemarie, James V. Hatch, and Brooks McNamara, eds., with a foreword by Mel Watkins. *Inside the Minstrel Mask: Readings in Nineteenth-Century Black Minstrelsy.* Hanover, N.H.: Wesleyan University Press, 1996.

Charters, Ann. *Nobody: The Story of Bert Williams.* New York: Macmillan, 1970.

Cook, Will Marion. "Clorindy; or, The Origin of the Cakewalk." In *Readings in Black American Music,* edited by Eileen Southern. New York: W. W. Norton, 1983.

Flanagan, Hallie. *Arena: The History of the Federal Theatre* (1940). New York: Arno, 1990.

Fletcher, Tom. *100 Years of the Negro in Show Business: The Tom Fletcher Story.* New York: Burdge, 1954. Reprint, New York: Da Capo, 1984.

Graziano, John. "Black Musical Theatre and the Harlem Renaissance Movement." In *Black Music in the Harlem Renaissance: A Collection of Essays,* edited by Samuel A. Floyd Jr. Westport, Conn.: Greenwood, 1990.

Hatch, James V. *Black Image on the American Stage: A Bibliography of Plays and Musicals, 1770–1970.* New York: DBS, 1970.

Hatch, James V., and Ted Shine, eds. *Black Theater, U.S.A.: Plays by Black Americans 1847 to Today.* New York: Free Press, 1996.

Hill, Errol G., and James V. Hatch. *A History of African American Theatre.* Cambridge, UK: Cambridge University Press, 2003.

Hughes, Langston, and Milton Meltzer. *Black Magic: A Pictorial History of the Negro in American Entertainment.* Englewood Cliffs, N.J.: Prentice-Hall, 1967.

Johnson, James Weldon. *Black Manhattan.* New York: Knopf, 1930.

Kimball, Robert, and William Bolcom. *Reminiscing with Sissle and Blake.* New York: Viking, 1973.

Riis, Thomas L. *Just Before Jazz: Black Musical Theater in New York, 1890 to 1915.* Washington, D.C.: Smithsonian Institution Press, 1989.

Sampson, Henry. *Blacks in Blackface: A Sourcebook on Early Black Musical Shows.* New York: Scarecrow, 1980.

Southern, Eileen. *The Music of Black Americans: A History.* New York: Norton, 1983.

Stearns, Marshall, and Jean Stearns. *Jazz Dance: The Story of American Vernacular Dance.* New York: Macmillan, 1968.

Woll, Allen. *Black Musical Theatre: From Coontown to Dreamgirls.* Baton Rouge: Louisiana State University Press, 1989.

THOMAS L. RIIS (1996)
Updated by author 2005

MUSIC COLLECTIONS, BLACK

Black music—that is, music composed or performed by people of African descent—is basic to the study of African-American history and culture, and to an understanding of American culture in general. Libraries collect it in all formats and genres, from scores and sheet music of classical compositions for study and performance to recordings of the latest popular music. Black music collections are found in institutions of all sorts, including major research collections, nationally recognized collections devoted to black culture, special-collections departments of college and university libraries, historical societies and museums, music libraries, and public library collections. All have a role in the documentation and study of black music.

Specialized collections exist to preserve the various black music styles, including popular music, blues, and jazz, and to collect the works of black composers. Library collections also document the contributions of African-American performers in broader genres, such as opera and musical theater, and the work of African-American music educators and organizations. Black music collections can be used by researchers not only to study and perform the music itself, but to gain insight into historical and social processes, and to document the broader cultural contributions of African Americans.

Serious documentation of blacks in musical culture began early in the twentieth century with the establishment of library collections devoted to black history. Important special collections have been maintained by the historically black educational institutions, with the holdings of the Moorland-Spingarn Research Center at Howard University, in Washington, D.C., founded in 1914, particularly outstanding. The Schomburg Center for Black

History and Culture of the New York Public Library, containing one of the largest black collections, was established in 1926. Another respected research collection, the Amistad Research Center, established at Fisk University in Nashville in 1966, is now located at Tulane University in New Orleans. These three repositories, which cover the broad spectrum of black history and culture, have devoted serious efforts to collecting music materials.

The first publicly accessible collection devoted exclusively to black music and blacks in the performing arts was the E. Azalia Hackley Collection of the Detroit Public Library, founded in 1943. Collections focusing on jazz include the Institute of Jazz Studies at Rutgers University in New Brunswick, New Jersey, founded in 1952, and the William Ransom Hogan Jazz Archive at Tulane University, founded in 1958. A serious effort to collect and preserve scores by black composers began at the Music Library of Indiana University at Bloomington in 1970. The Center for Black Music Research at Columbia College in Chicago, founded in 1983, opened its Library and Archives in 1992.

National agencies, such as the Library of Congress and the Smithsonian Institution in Washington, D.C., are also important resources, as are general performing-arts collections, such as the New York Public Library for the Performing Arts at Lincoln Center. Popular-music collections such as those at the University of California at Los Angeles (UCLA), Bowling Green State University in Ohio, and Middle Tennessee State University in Murfreesboro are general in scope but do justice to the importance of black popular styles. Specialist repositories, such as the University of Mississippi Blues Archive, the Archive of African American Music and Culture at Indiana University, and various ethnomusicology archives, devote themselves to preserving oral and recorded traditions. The collections of these repositories will be discussed later in greater detail.

Any attempt to describe black music collections in the United States is obsolete almost before it is completed, because collections are constantly growing and backlogs being cataloged, bringing newly processed materials to the attention of scholars. Many libraries now catalog their holdings on national library databases, such as the Online Computer Library Center (OCLC) and the Research Libraries Information Network (RLIN), making information available to any researcher who has access to these networks.

Repositories often make their catalogs and finding aids accessible through the Internet as well. The catalogs of some of the major libraries, including the Schomburg and Moorland-Spingarn collections, were published in book form before the library community came to rely on the national online networks. A catalog of the Hackley Collection was published in 1979, and guides to other individual collections have also been published.

Archives often supplement their standard cataloging with online databases. For example, the CBMR Library Database at the Center for Black Music Research in Chicago indexes music, books, dissertations, and vertical-file materials in the CBMR Library and Archives. The Center for Popular Music at Middle Tennessee State University has an online database that allows searching of its archival collections, sheet music, song books, and trade catalogs.

Black music is a broad field encompassing many material types, genres, and possible research approaches. In addition to art music in many compositional styles, there are the various genres in the vernacular tradition, including spirituals, jazz, blues, rhythm and blues, gospel, and a number of current popular styles. Music collections tend to concentrate on sheet music and scores, and on recordings in numerous formats, but they also collect ephemera, photographs, periodicals, and other unique documents, including letters, diaries, and music manuscripts, when they exist. Such written documents may be scarce, partly because musicians are often too busy to keep them, and sometimes because the musicians find written means of expression uncongenial. In some cases, especially when the music is itself orally transmitted (blues) or dependent on improvisation for musical effect (jazz, some forms of gospel), libraries may turn to oral history, which ensures the survival of important information while freeing informants from the necessity of creating a written document.

Knowledge of black music is absolutely essential to the study of American popular music. Many general popular-music collections therefore collect black music as part of their larger holdings. Sheet music was the only format for music, popular or otherwise, before the advent of recording technology in the late nineteenth century, and collections of early sheet music tend to make few distinctions between popular and art genres. Such collections include the J. Francis Driscoll Collection at the Newberry Library in Chicago, the Corning Sheet Music Collection of the William L. Clements Library at the University of Michigan in Ann Arbor, and the Lester S. Levy Collection at the Milton S. Eisenhower Library at John Hopkins University. All have substantial holdings of minstrel songs and of nineteenth-century music by black composers or on black topics.

The Sam De Vincent Collection of Illustrated Sheet Music at the Archives Center of the Smithsonian Institution has a large component of black music. There are also sizable collections of popular sheet music at the Archive of Popular American Music at UCLA, and at the Center for Popular Music at Middle Tennessee State University. Sheet music of minstrel songs, ragtime, and similar music, including songs by black composers, is highly collectible, and in recent years collectors have donated or sold their holdings to libraries in increasing numbers. Libraries now possessing such collections include the Special Collections Division of the Michigan State University Libraries in East Lansing and the music libraries of the University of Michigan and the University of Illinois at Urbana-Champaign. The American Music Collection of the New York Public Library for the Performing Arts has an extensive collection of piano ragtime compositions, and the Buffalo and Erie County Public Library has a collection of minstrel songs and songsters (collections of song lyrics). The Music Division of the Library of Congress retains sheet music deposited for copyright registration.

In addition to the collections named above, two major research repositories, the Schomburg Center for Research in Black Culture and the Moorland-Spingarn Research Center, have comprehensive collections of sheet music, popular and otherwise, by black composers. Many items in their collections are extremely rare. The Gershwin Memorial Collection at Fisk University contains photographs and other materials about black composers, as well as music. The Hackley Collection at the Detroit Public Library has an impressive sheet-music component. The NCNB Black Musical Heritage Collection in the Special Collections Department of the University of South Florida Library in Tampa contains five thousand pieces of sheet music, much of it popular.

Some repositories have scanned sheet music collections and made them available online. Such collections include Duke University's Historic American Sheet Music website (http://odyssey.lib.duke.edu/sheetmusic/), "Music For the Nation," a part of the American Memory project of the Library of Congress (http://memory.loc.gov/ammem/smhtml) and the African American Sheet Music collection of the John Hay Library at Brown University (http://memory.loc.gov/ammem/award97/rpbhtml/). Not only do online collections make the music instantly available for study and performance, they also provide images of sheet music covers, which are an excellent resource for social historians.

RECORDINGS

Recordings are the primary source for the study of popular music during the twentieth century. One of the premier collections of popular-music recordings in the United States is in the Music Library and Sound Archives at Bowling Green State University in Bowling Green, Ohio. A collection of sound recordings numbering nearly six hundred thousand is supported by a research collection of printed materials, periodicals, and ephemera. The Center for Popular Music at Middle Tennessee State and the Archive of Popular American Music at UCLA both have extensive collections of sound recordings. Finally, the Library of Congress has a department devoted to recordings as part of its Motion Picture, Broadcasting and Recorded Sound Division. Again, these collections are general in scope but contain numerous recordings of black music and black performers. The Center for Black Music Research has collections of commercial recordings covering various genres. Especially important is the Fred Crane Collection, composed of cylinders and discs of black performers and their imitators who recorded before 1920.

POPULAR MUSIC

Libraries have only begun to collect documentary materials relating to contemporary popular musicians. Indiana University's Archives of African American Music and Culture is a major repository. Collections donated by publicist Karen Shearer and author Phyl Garland contain files on numerous popular musicians, and collections of research materials from Charles Sykes and Nelson George document Motown. Interviews received from author Michael Lydon concern the life and music of soul musician Ray Charles. Oral history interviews with musicians and record producers film *Record Row: Cradle of Rhythm & Blues* are also in the collection. Collections on black radio, from the likes of Jack "The Rapper" Gibson and bandleader Johnny Otis are a major strength of the archives. The Amistad Research Center has a small collection relating to the rhythm-and-blues singer James Brown (b. 1933), and the Western Historical Manuscript Collection at the University of Missouri–St. Louis has a similar one devoted to the rock-and-roll pioneer Chuck Berry (b. 1926). A collection received from Sue Cassidy Clark at the Center for Black Music Research contains photographs, research files, and recorded interviews with musicians from the early 1970s. The music library at Bowling Green State University collects popular fan magazines and ephemeral publications. The Chicago Public Library's Music Information Center and the Center for Black Music Research keep vertical files on contemporary performers.

FOLK MUSIC

Ethnomusicology collections can be useful to researchers in African-American music, because these sources include noncommercial field recordings of traditional music from America and other parts of the world. Study of recordings of African, Afro-Caribbean, and South American music can provide insights into the development of African-American musical forms. African-American folk music, work songs, ballads, dance music, games, and sermons, along with well-known forms such as spirituals and folk blues, must be studied to obtain insights into both popular and classical compositions.

An extensive collection of field recordings of traditional African-American performers can be found at the Archive of Folk Culture at the American Folklife Center of the Library of Congress. Since its founding in 1928, a succession of folklorists—including Robert Winslow Gordon, John and Alan Lomax, Herbert Halpert, Zora Neale Hurston, and Laura Bolton—working directly for the archive or for other government agencies have recorded and documented American folk music and culture. Numerous other scholars have contributed additional collections. Among the many African-American musicians who are represented in the collections are Jelly Roll Morton, James P. Johnson, Albert Ammons, Meade "Lux" Lewis and Pete Johnson, Leadbelly (Huddie Ledbetter), and bluesmen Son House, John Hurt, and Muddy Waters. In addition to field recordings, the Archive of Folk Culture collects books, published sound recordings, manuscripts, photographs, and moving-image materials. It publishes an excellent series of commercial recordings based on its holdings, as well as a useful series of bibliographies and finding aids.

The Archives of Traditional Music at Indiana University in Bloomington has field collections of traditional music, spirituals, blues, gospel music, and sermons and tales collected by Natalie Curtis Burlin, Harold Courlander, Richard Dorson, John Hasse, Guy B. Johnson, and John, Alan, and Elizabeth Lomax, among others. It also holds numerous African collections and about forty thousand commercial recordings of blues, jazz, and other musical styles. Two other archives with holdings of commercial as well as field recordings are the Ethnomusicology Archive at UCLA and the Ethnomusicology Archives at the University of Washington, in Seattle, which has few American collections but over fifty collections of field recordings from sub-Saharan Africa. The archive of Folkways Records, a company that specializes in commercially issued field recordings, many of them African-American, is at the Smithsonian Institution.

Ethnographic films are another important source of information on traditional music. The Motion Picture Division of the Library of Congress and the Human Studies Film Archives at the Smithsonian Institution have African-American materials, both commercial films and field recordings. The Center for Southern Folklore in Memphis distributes several films on southern folk music and blues, and also holds the Gail Mooney collection of photographs and footage of Delta Bluesmen, and the Rev. W. O. Taylor collection of photographs and film footage of religious events, including one hundred 78-rpm acetate recordings of religious music.

Repositories that specialize in traditional music may concentrate on a specific region. The Avery Research Center for African American History and Culture in Charleston, South Carolina, focuses on the Gullah culture of the Sea Islands. In its holdings are field recordings made in the Sea Islands by Lorenzo Dow Turner and recordings of the Moving Star Hall Singers. The Southern Folklife Collection at the University of North Carolina at Chapel Hill holds both commercial and field recordings of black music in a general collection devoted to southern traditional music. For example, the field recordings of the activist folk musicians Guy and Candie Carawan include recordings of religious music from the Sea Islands, music of the civil rights movement, and gospel music performances. The collection is particularly strong in early blues and gospel and in string-band music, a still-neglected area of study. An interesting component is a group of forty-six wax cylinders recorded on South Carolina's Saint Helena Island in 1928 by folklorist Guy B. Johnson.

BLUES COLLECTIONS

Blues is the popular-music form closest to traditional music. The University of Mississippi Blues Archive has not only over twenty thousand sound recordings of blues and related genres, but also the files of *Living Blues* magazine, the business papers of Trumpet Records, and jazz and gospel session books of Savoy Records, plus collections relating to performers as diverse as B. B. King (b. 1925) and Gertrude "Ma" Rainey (1886–1939). Two major blues collectors have donated collections: Sheldon Harris donated the research files from his book *The Blues Who's Who* along with periodicals and other historical materials. Gayle Dean Wardlow's collection includes oral histories conducted in the 1960s with several traditional musicians. Other oral-history holdings include interviews made for *Living Blues,* collections contributed by several blues journalists, and the archive's own oral-history project, carried out with north Mississippi musicians. The Victoria Spivey (1906–1976) papers at the Robert W. Woodruff Library, Emory University document her career as head of her own blues record company. The Chicago Blues Archives at the Music Information Center of the Chicago Public Library has recordings and files on blues musicians, a collection concerning Delmark Records, and a collection of recordings and papers devoted to the annual Chicago Blues Festi-

val, at which many contemporary musicians have performed.

Blues oral-history projects of note include the Bull City Blues oral histories and performances at the North Carolina Division of Archives and History in Raleigh, North Carolina, and the Robert Neff and Anthony Connor Blues Collection of interviews with blues musicians, housed at the Yale University School of Music's Oral History, American Music Project. The History of the Oakland Blues, an ongoing project initiated at the Regional Oral History Office of the Bancroft Library at the University of California, Berkeley, aims at documenting the blues in Oakland, California.

GOSPEL MUSIC COLLECTIONS

There are no repositories devoted exclusively to traditional black religious music or gospel music. The archives of the black colleges that first brought spirituals to a broader public after the Civil War have documented their performing groups: Fisk University has collections relating to the Fisk Jubilee Singers, and the Hampton University Archives has papers of the Hampton Singers, plus field recordings and papers of folklorist Natalie Curtis Burlin. The Adam Knight Spence and John Wesley Work (1873–1925) collection at the Auburn Avenue Research Library on African American Culture and History of the Atlanta-Fulton Public Library also contains information about the Fisk Jubilee Singers. A collection devoted to the Wings Over Jordan Choir, including the personal papers of the choir's founder, Rev. Glynn T. Settle, can be found at the National Afro-American Museum and Cultural Center in Wilberforce, Ohio.

The Southern Folklife Collection at the University of North Carolina, Chapel Hill, has papers, recordings, and sheet music from the Gospel Light Music Store of Philadelphia. Included are original acetate recordings of local gospel groups from the 1950s. The Vivian G. Harsh Collection of the Chicago Public Library has the papers of the Chicago gospel pioneer Lucy Smith, including a sizable collection of gospel sheet music. A small but significant collection concerning the recording career of gospel pioneer Arizona Dranes is at Indiana University's Archives of African American Music and Culture, which also has a collection relating to television producer Bobby Jones and a collection of commercial gospel videos from producer Debbie May, while ethnomusicologist Mellonee Burnim has donated audio and video field recordings of concerts, worship services and interviews documenting gospel music. A research collection an African American religious music compiled by the scholar and performer Bernice

Johnson Reagon is in the Archives Center at the Smithsonian.

Gospel sheet music can be found in the holdings of the Schomburg Center, the Center for Black Music Research, and the Library of Congress. Over fifteen hundred pieces of gospel music published by the Martin and Morris Publishing Company of Chicago are in the Chicago Public Library's Music Information Center, while the business records of Martin and Morris, plus sheet music as well, are in the Archives Center at the Smithsonian. The Center for Popular Music at Middle Tennessee State University collects gospel songbooks and commercial and field recordings, with a specialty in black shape-note singing and gospel quartets, notably the Fairfield Four and the Four Eagles. The Music Information Center of the Chicago Public Library has videotapes of one hundred programs of the television series *Jubilee Showcase* (1963–1984), on which most major gospel artists performed. Despite efforts in the last few years, gospel music remains the most undergocumented genre of black music. Major collections are held by private collectors, or by the musicians themselves and their families; very few are accessible in libraries.

Jazz

The situation is much different with jazz. Not only do several specialist repositories and collections exist, but major figures have archives devoted solely to them. For example, papers, business records, photographs, manuscripts, and recordings of Duke Ellington are in the Duke Ellington Collection, housed in the Archives Center of the Smithsonian Institution. Queens College, in New York, holds the Louis Armstrong Archive. Such collections give important figures the emphasis they deserve.

The Institute of Jazz Studies at Rutgers University collects jazz materials in all formats comprehensively. The institute holds the world's most extensive collection of jazz periodicals and maintains a Jazz Oral History Project and a collection of transcriptions of big-band arrangements. Important individuals whose papers are in the Institute's collections include musicians Mary Lou Williams (1910–1981) and James P. Johnson (1894–1955), and jazz historian Leonard Feather.

The William Ransom Hogan Jazz Archive at Tulane University focuses on New Orleans jazz, with fifty thousand recordings, sheet music, vertical files, and manuscripts. Other New Orleans collections include the New Orleans Jazz Club Collection at the Louisiana State Museum, comprising recordings, sheet music, photographs, and ephemera; and the New Orleans Jazz and Heritage Foundation Oral History Project, which is housed at the Amistad Research Center and includes interviews with forty-nine New Orleans musicians. The Historic New Orleans Collection houses the collection of the jazz collector and historian William Russell, which includes interviews, photographs, and research materials.

Other cities important in the development of jazz have collections devoted to them. The Jazzmen Project at the Western Historical Manuscript Collection consists of recorded interviews and performances of Saint Louis musicians. Microfilmed scrapbooks of riverboat musicians Eddie Johnson and Elijah Shaw are also available. The Marr Sound Archives of the Miller Nichols Library at the University of Missouri–Kansas City documents Kansas City jazz, and also houses the more general Frank Driggs Jazz Oral History Collection. The Jazz Institute of Chicago has placed its collection at the Chicago Jazz Archive at the University of Chicago. It contains recordings, oral histories, and collections devoted to Chicago musicians. The Chicago Jazz Archive also houses the collection of the jazz collector, producer, and scholar, John Steiner, which includes the business records of Paramount Records. Jazz in New York City is documented in the Otto Hess collection of photographs of jazz events from the 1940s and 1950s (held by the American Music Collection of the New York Public Library for the Performing Arts), and by the papers of the New York Jazz Museum at the Schomburg Center. On the West Coast, the Central Avenue Sounds Oral History Project of the UCLA Oral History Program documents Los Angeles's Central Avenue from the 1920s through the 1950s. Notable informants include Art Farmer, Frank Morgan, Buddy Collette, and Melba Liston.

The Amistad Research Center also has papers of the jazz arranger Fletcher Henderson (1897–1952). Henderson's arrangements for Benny Goodman can be found in the American Music Collection of the New York Public Library for the Performing Arts, which also houses scores of the arranger Sy Oliver (1910–1988). Scores and lead sheets of the trombonist, composer, and arranger, Melba Liston (1926–1999) are at the Center for Black Music Research.

Jazz recordings can also be found in the Maxwell O. Reade Collection in the African-American Music Collection at the University of Michigan, and at the Center for Black Music Research. The Valburn Ellington Collection at the Library of Congress contains ten thousand Duke Ellington recordings, including nearly every commercial recording and hundreds of noncommercial recordings. Another major collection of the recordings of Duke Ellington, numbering over eight hundred commercial recordings and eighty-eight tape recordings (some of them unique), is held by the University of North Texas Music Library.

The Boston University's Mugar Memorial Library specializes in collecting the papers of popular performers.

Its jazz-related holdings include collections devoted to Cab Calloway and Ella Fitzgerald. The papers of W. C. Handy, Don Redman, Ronald L. Carter, and Mabel Mercer are at the Schomburg Center. The W. C. Handy Museum in Handy's hometown of Florence, Alabama, also has archival materials.

ORAL-HISTORY INTERVIEWS

A relatively new development is the videotaped oral-history interview. The Nathaniel C. Standifer Video Archive of Oral History in the African-American Music Collection at the University of Michigan has over one hundred interviews with major figures, including a number of jazz musicians and classical performers and composers. The Schomburg Center also has a videotaping program aimed at recording musical events and interviews with individuals.

MUSICAL THEATER

Library collections pertaining to classically trained African-American composers and performers are diverse and sometimes scattered. Before the mid-twentieth century, racial discrimination shunted aspiring black performers and composers into vaudeville and musical theater. As in the case of popular music, materials from the early years of black theater can be found in general theater collections, including the Harvard Theatre Collection, the Theatre Arts Library at the University of Texas at Austin, and the New York Public Library for the Performing Arts at Lincoln Center. The Channing Pollock Theater Collection at Howard University and the Countee Cullen Memorial Collection at Atlanta University Center's Robert W. Woodruff Library specialize in African-American contributions in theater and the performing arts.

Other theater-oriented collections include the *Porgy and Bess* collection at the African American Music Collection, University of Michigan, which includes files on the original production. Materials on other productions of *Porgy and Bess* are in the Robert E. Lee Theatre Research Institute at Ohio State University in Columbus. The Schomburg Center has the papers of theatrical composer Luther Henderson (1919–2003) and actor-songwriter Emmett "Babe" Wallace. The George Peabody Collection at Hampton University consists of four scrapbooks on black music and musicians dating from 1824 to 1921. Scrapbooks of vocalist Sissieretta Jones (1968–1933) are at the Moorland-Spingarn Research Center. The Maryland Historical Society in Baltimore has an archive devoted to composer and performer Eubie Blake (1883–1983).

EDUCATORS AND ORGANIZATIONS

The papers of educators and organizations are of great importance, especially for the time when discrimination prohibited black performers and composers from full participation in mainstream organizations. The papers of George Washington Glover (1873–1986) at the Schomburg Center contain extensive information on the National Association of Negro Musicians (NANM). The Amistad Research Center has the records of two branches of NANM, the Chicago Music Association and the B-Sharp Music Club of New Orleans. Records of NANM and of the Chicago Music Association are also included in the Theodore Charles Stone papers at the Center for Black Music Research, which also houses a separate NANM collection and records of the R. Nathaniel Dett Club, another Chicago-based NANM branch. The Schomburg Center has papers of the educator and composer Blanche K. Thomas and the educator Isabelle Taliaferro Spiller (1888–1974). Additional Spiller materials are at the Moorland-Spingarn Research Center, which also has papers of Gregoria Fraser Goins (1883–1964), prominent in several musical organizations in Washington, D.C., and records of the Washington Conservatory of Music. The papers of the National Opera Association are at the Library of Congress, and the papers of Opera/South, an African-American opera company that premiered eight operas by black composers, including William Grant Still and Ulysses Kay, are in the Henry T. Sampson Library at Jackson State University, Jackson, Mississippi. The Center for Black Music Research has the records of the Society of Black Composers, a group active in New York in the the early 1970s.

CLASSICAL MUSIC

When it comes to archival collections of classical composers and performers, the major research collections have extensive holdings. The Music Division of the Library of Congress has correspondence and manuscripts of several black composers and performers. Outstanding examples include two manuscripts of William Grant Still's (1895–1978) *Afro-American Symphony* (1930) and manuscripts of several early works by Ulysses Kay (1917–1995). An in-house card file compiled by Walter E. Whittlesey, a library staff member, covers from around 1900 through the 1930s and serves as an adjunct to the library's catalogs and copyright records. Researchers have found it extremely useful as a guide to information about otherwise obscure individuals.

The Schomburg Center has the records of the Symphony of the New World, and of Mary Cardwell Dawson (1894–1962), founder of the National Negro Opera Company (1941), plus the papers of the composers Edward Boatner (1898–1981) and Clarence Cameron White (1880–1960). Classical performers documented at the Schomburg Center include Marion Cumbo, Lawrence Brown, Melville Charlton, and Philippa Duke Schuyler.

The Amistad Research Center has also documented African-American performers and composers. The papers of the composer Howard Swanson (1907–1978) are primarily music manuscripts; there are also collections relating to the composers Roger Dickerson (b. 1934) and Hale Smith (b. 1925). Collections pertaining to performers include papers of Carol Brice, Camilla Williams, Mattiwilda Dobbs, William Warfield, and Jessie Covington Dent.

Collections dealing with individual performers are also scattered in other repositories. At least three have collections on the actor and singer Paul Robeson (1898–1976): The Moorland-Spingarn Research Center has the bulk of Robeson's papers, but there are also collections of Robeson materials at the Schomburg Center and at the Charles L. Blockson Collection at Temple University in Philadelphia. The Hackley Collection received the papers of the tenor Roland Hayes (1887–1977) in 1989. The Marian Anderson (1897–1993) papers are in the Annenberg Rare Book and Manuscript Library at the University of Pennsylvania in Philadelphia. The Center for Black Music Research has a collection on the operatic baritone Ben Holt (1955–1990), and the Wendell G. Wright Collection, which includes recordings of a long-running concert series that featured many prominent performers. Hampton University Archives has a collection relating to the soprano Dorothy Maynor (1910–1996). Scrapbooks and papers of the singer Todd Duncan (1903–1998) are in the African American Music Collection at the University of Michigan. The papers of the pianist and author Maude Cuney Hare (1874–1936) are at the Atlanta University Center's Robert W. Woodruff Library. They also contain biographical information on other African-American composers and musicians.

Documenting the early years of African-American composition can be problematic, because so few materials have survived the passage of time. Fortunately, some manuscript materials from the nineteenth century have survived. These include a manuscript music book and sheet music of black bandleader and composer Francis Johnson (1792–1844), at the Library Company of Philadelphia, and a Johnson holograph manuscript at the Library of Congress.

Ragtime collections appear to consist mainly of sheet music and recordings, including piano rolls made by the composers. James Scott (1885–1938), Scott Joplin (1868–1917), and John William "Blind" Boone (1864–1927) are documented in the ragtime collection at State Fair Community College in Sedalia, Missouri. The State Historical Society of Missouri also has collections relating to Boone and Joplin. A Joplin collection at Fisk University contains correspondence about the composer by his wife and others. The Scott Joplin House State Historic Site in St. Louis has piano rolls that were recorded by Joplin.

Papers and manuscripts of individual composers are to be found in numerous repositories. Papers of H. T. Burleigh (1866–1949) can be found at the Erie County Historical Society in Erie, Pennsylvania, and at the Pennsylvania Historical and Museum Commission in Harrisburg. Three repositories have papers of R. Nathaniel Dett (1882–1943), including the Archives at Hampton University, with which he was associated for many years; the University Archives and Historical Collections at Michigan State University; and the Local History Department of the Niagara Falls Public Library, in Niagara Falls, New York. Papers and manuscripts of John Wesley Work III (1901–1967) are at Fisk University, which also has papers of composers Julia Perry (1924–1979) and Arthur Cunningham (1928–1997). The papers of J. Rosamond Johnson (1873–1954) are in the Music Library at Yale University in New Haven, Connecticut. Manuscripts and published arrangements by N. Clark Smith (1877–1935) are in the Miller Nichols Library of the University of Missouri in Kansas City. Papers and scores of William Levi Dawson are in Special Collections and Archives at the Robert W. Woodruff Library, Emory University, and music manuscripts of the singer and composer Julius (Jules) Bledsoe (1898–1943) are in the Texas Collection at Baylor University. The music manuscripts of Edmund Thornton Jenkins (1894–1926), unlocated for years, are now at the Center for Black Music Research.

The Special Collections Department of the University of Arkansas Libraries has the papers of two major twentieth-century composers, Florence Price (1887–1953) and William Grant Still (1895–1978). Still materials can also be found in the Special Collections Library at Duke University. The Center for Black Music Research has papers of the composers James Furman (1937–1989), Lee V. Cloud (1950–1995), Talib Rasul Hakim (1940–1988), Irene Britton Smith (1907–1999), Richard C. Moffat (1927–1983), William Banfield (b. 1961), and Leslie Adams (b. 1932). Composers represented in the Center's extensive collections of scores include David Baker, Ed Bland, Glenn Burleigh, Wallace Cheatham, Mark Fax, Wendell Logan, Joyce Solomon Moorman, Jeffrey Mumford, Robert Owens, Coleridge-Taylor Perkinson, Daniel Roumain, Gregory Walker, and Michael Woods. The Eva Jessye Collection is a major component of the African-American Music Collection at the University of Michigan, and Jessye (1895–1992) materials can also be found at the Amistad Research Center of Tulane University. The Special Collections Department at Pittsburg State University in Pittsburg, Kansas, has a sizable amount of Jessye's correspondence and manuscripts, as well as photographs, interviews, and recordings of her folk oratorio *Paradise Lost and Regained*.

Mention should also be made of other personal collections of great research value. The James Weldon Johnson Collection in the Beinecke Rare Book and Manuscript Library at Yale covers black music extensively, and it contains holograph scores by several African-American composers. The American Music Research Center at the University of Colorado, Boulder, has music by black women composers collected and donated by Helen Walker-Hill, a prominent scholar and bibliographer in the field. Walker-Hill's research papers on black women composers, along with duplicate scores, are at the Center for Black Music Research. The Center also has the papers and research materials of three pioneering scholars of black music: Dena J. Epstein (b. 1916), Dominique-René de Lerma (b. 1928) and Eileen Southern (1920–2002).

Archival collections documenting composers perform two functions: They provide materials for the study of an individual's life and times, as well as for the study of his or her music, including analysis of the compositional process. They point to obstacles and triumphs, and to the uniqueness of the African-American contribution to American music. The names of many libraries and of many individuals have been mentioned above, attesting to the preservation of African-American music materials in publicly accessible repositories. The tragedy—for the study of black music and American music, and for recognition of the importance of the African-American heritage—is in the names that are missing: names of important composers whose works are scattered or destroyed, or are still inaccessible in private hands; and names of performers who never made recordings or whose scrapbooks and letters are missing or destroyed, whose contributions therefore will never be completely recognized.

See also Archival Collections; Blues, The; Fisk University; Folk Music; Gospel Music; Howard University; Jazz; Music in the United States; Music Museums and Historical Sites; National Association of Negro Musicians; Opera; Schomburg, Arthur

■ ■ *Bibliography*

"Afrocentric Voices in 'Classical' Music." Available from <http://www.afrovoices.com>.

Ash, Lee, and William G. Miller. *Subject Collections: A Guide to Special Book Collections and Subject Emphases as Reported by University, College, Public, and Special Libraries and Museums in the United States and Canada.* 6th ed. New York: R. R. Bowker Co., 1985.

Floyd, Samuel A., Jr., and Marsha J. Reisser. *Black Music in the United States: An Annotated Bibliography of Selected Reference and Research Materials.* Millwood, N.Y.: Kraus International Publications, 1983.

Floyd, Samuel A., Jr., ed. *International Dictionary of Black Composers.* Chicago; London: Fitzroy Dearborn, 1999.

Geist, Christopher D., Ray B. Browne, Michael T. Marsden, and Carol E. Palmer. *Directory of Popular Culture Collections.* Phoenix, Ariz.: Oryx Press, 1989.

Ham, Debra Newman. *The African-American Mosaic: A Library of Congress Resource Guide for the Study of Black History and Culture.* Washington: Library of Congress, 1993.

Krummel, D. W., Jean Geil, Doris J. Dyen, and Dean L. Root. *Resources of American Music History: A Directory of Source Materials from Colonial Times to World War II.* Urbana: University of Illinois Press, 1981.

Southern, Eileen. *The Music of Black Americans: A History.* 3d ed. New York: Norton, 1997.

SUZANNE FLANDREAU (1996)
Updated bibliography

MUSLIMS IN THE AMERICAS

■■■

Approximately twenty percent of Africans brought to the Americas between the 1500s and 1900 CE were Muslims. By the fifteenth century, Muslims, almost constantly at war with Christians across the Mediterranean Sea since Islam had begun to spread across North Africa around 660 CE, had traveled to well below the Sahara Desert. Arabs and Berbers came first as commercial and religious agents, mixed with locals in the eleventh century, and by the late eighteenth century their black progeny and followers had become jihadists and nation builders. Since then, Muslim spheres of influence, control, and struggle have enlarged to cover much of West Africa. Their extensive trading and educational networks, demonstrating and teaching Muslim principles and practices—incorporating some indigenous ways—necessarily adjusted to or conflicted with local non-Muslim powers such as the Bambara, Ashanti, Dahomeyans, and Yorubans. These conflicts involved slave trading of one another and people caught in the middle. Multi-ethnic Muslim-led nations, opposed to slavery of their own people, including self-asserting theocracies, rose and fell as they worked out their changing political, economic, and religious relations with rival Muslims as well as non-Muslim peoples. These struggles led to four centuries of the capture and sale of non-Muslims by Muslims, and more to the point, of enemy Muslims by Muslims and of Muslims by non-Muslims to European and American purchasers in trading posts along the Atlantic Coast and along the banks of a few rivers.

Like many non-Muslim captives who were not peasant Africans but from wealthy, powerful trading or ruling families and potent age-group brotherhoods accustomed to being leaders in social, political, religious, military, or agricultural matters, many Muslims embodied senses of spiritual selves, dignity, and pride that gave problems to their purchasers. Unlike non-Muslims, however, Muslims stood out because of their insistence on covering their bodies, on avoiding alcohol and pork, on praying to one god, on appearing to look down on both white and black non-Muslims—and when discovered—on writing and reading Arabic. Such attributes inspired both respect and apprehension and some exploration and exploitation of their grave, even haughty manners, mix of acceptance of their fate and demands on their purchasers, antipathy to field labor, recognizable management skills, and aptness as personal servants. The extent of their influence is only recently being calculated, but to those who recorded contacts with them in the era of the Atlantic slave trade, many African Muslims were impressive people.

African Muslims came from below the Sahara Desert between Lake Chad and the continent's closest point to the New World. They were Kanuri, Hausa, Songhai, Kassonke, Manding, Serahules, Fulas, Wolofs; few were Moors or Arabs. At least two hundred are known by references, names, short notices, longer accounts by others, or from their own writings. Some thirty manuscripts in Arabic written in the Americas and at least as many translations or as-told-to stories in European languages provide even more information. Many are assertions of the writer's faith, of recognition of African teachers and texts in Arabic or local languages using phonetic Arabic letters, or letters urging fellow Muslims to uphold or to fight for their faith.

A few of these documents written in North America (elaborated on below) tell about lives and educations in Africa, about capture, marches to the sea, the bitter Middle Passage, and adjustments to and by purchasers, missionaries, and amanuenses. Many are informative and corrective relative to the careless ignorance of nearly all non-Africans about their homelands and histories. These are often the only firsthand accounts by African-born individuals on relevant transatlantic conditions, events, and attitudes upon which historians and litterateurs—until very recently—have provided only surmises and generalizations. Lamine Kebe, freed after thirty years of slavery in

Georgia, put this succinctly in 1835: "There are good men in America, but all are ignorant of Africa" (Dwight, 1864). The most important accounts are by Job Ben Solomon from Senegal (1734), Ibrahima Abd al-Rahman from Guinea (1828), Umar ibn Said from Senegal (1831), Abu Bakr es-Siddiq from Ghana (1835), Salih Bilali from Mali (1843), Mahommah Baquaqua from Benin (1854), and Mohammed or Nicholas Said from Chad (1867, 1882).

Further individualizing and authentication may be found in nine surviving portraits: two of Job Ben Solomon, enslaved in Maryland and freed in 1733; two (including a marvelous 1819 painting by Charles Willson Peale) of Yarrow Mamout, probably also from Senegal, slave and self-purchased freeman in the District of Columbia; two engravings of Mahommah Baquaqua, enslaved in Brazil, freed and educated in New York, part author of his *Biography;* an 1856 drawing of Osman, a Maroon in North Carolina; an 1828 etching from a Henry Inman crayon portrait of Abd al-Rahman, enslaved for forty years in Mississippi before being freed at the age of sixty-five and undertaking a partially successful campaign extending from Natchez to Boston to buy his children before his return to Africa; a daguerreotype of Umar ibn Said, taken shortly before his death in 1864 to accompany his several manuscripts in Arabic produced in North Carolina; and an 1863 ambrotype *carte de visite* of Nicholas Said in the Union Army uniform of the 55th Massachusetts Colored Regiment.

Though uniquely legislated against in Spanish regulations, and despite leading the first slave revolt (Hispaniola in 1522) and numerous others in the Americas, Muslims accompanied the first discoverers and conquistadores from Columbus on. Some were apparently selected, probably after a pretense of conversion, for various purposes, including personal servanthood in the New World. Hundreds, perhaps only recently Islamized, and thousands of their children fit into the new scheme, but there were those who resisted Christian slavery in various ways. There were antislavery and anti-Catholic/anti-Christian renegades and preachers, some of whom, called "Mandingas" were suspected of being "sorcerers" who made and sold Muslim amulets or gris-gris across Latin America. Theirs was a popular but clandestine operation in the punishing mining and agricultural slave regime imposed by Christians. Some preaching came with the amulets, but this had to be carefully done. Lope de la Pena was imprisoned in Peru for preaching Islam in 1560. Similar punishments were imposed everywhere in following years.

Many ran away; some formed their own self-reliant, self-help communities in the hinterlands. In the 1750s Haitian Maroons under Macandal (after whom illness-preventing and death-defying amulets were named), a Muslim who offered a remarkably extensive revolutionary plan, preceded several other Muslim-influenced revolts, including those that militarily ousted the French in 1804. Early in the 1800s Muslims revolted in Brazil; their most widespread and well-thought-out slave revolt, involving at least a thousand Muslims and allies in Bahia, occurred in 1835 (see Reis, *Slave Rebellion in Brazil*, 1993). After it was put down, many Muslims were executed, but others were exported or paid their own way back to African ports between the Gold Coast and Nigeria. This repatriation continued until late in the nineteenth century. Many of these returnees founded trade relations across the Atlantic Ocean extending familiar African commercial routes intercontinentally to before unimagined and only recently investigated lengths. Latin American Catholicism, and African syncretic religions surviving today such as Candomblé, vodou, and Santería, display Muslim elements. Indeed, Fredrika Bremer, a respected Swedish journalist, thought in the early 1850s that Muslims were the main teachers and preachers outside Havana in Cuba. Gilberto Freyre wrote that Brazilians had insufficiently noted the influence of African Muslims in their national dress, language, religion, diet, sexual mores, self-help organizations, rebellious ways, and continued relations with Africa (Freyre, 1956). The same could be said for many of the surrounding South American and Caribbean countries.

Outlines of some of these individual African Muslims more particularly illustrate what may be learned from them about their homelands and lives. Macandal, Job, Mohammad Kaba from Guinea, Muhammad (Jonas) Bath, probably from Guinea, Anna Moosa from Mali, Abu Bakr es Siddiq from Ghana, Abd al-Rahman, Umar ibn Said, Kebe from Guinea, Bilali Muhammad from Guinea, Mahommah Baquaqua from Benin, and Nicholas Said from Chad were from prominent clerical, mercantile, military, or educational families. Job was a trader and religious leader, Al-Rahman a cavalry officer, Kebe and Umar teachers. All were husbands and fathers before their capture. Job, Macandal, al-Rahman, Kebe, Bilali, Charno, Umar, Abu Bakr es Siddiq, "William Rainsford," "Charles Larten," a "Moorish" slave on the Mississippi River, "Capt. Anderson's slave," Salih Bilali, and others noticed above learned to read in Arabic in Africa. All but the last wrote Arabic—and often their own languages using Arabic characters. Manuscripts from Job, Muhammad Kaba, Capt. Anderson's slave, al-Rahmann, rebels in Brazil, Bath, Abu Bakr, Bilali, Charno, Umar, and Sana Sy in Panama are extant. Many others are reported. London used phonetic Arabic characters to write black English in antebellum Florida. Abu Bakr kept Jamaican plantation records in similar style. Job, Umar, Mahommah, Salih Bilali,

Abu Bakr, Anna Moosa, and a Muslim from Charles Ball's slave narrative told of captures in Africa. Abd al-Rahman, Umar, and Kebe were taken in battle, the others kidnapped. Job, Abd al-Rahman, Mahommah, and Kebe told their stories to amanuenses. Abu Bakr followed his own autobiography in Arabic with an extended travelogue describing his family's trading posts from the Atlantic Ocean on the Gambia River to Katsina in northern Nigeria and from Timbuktu to the Gulf of Guinea (1835). They wrote of marches to the sea and of their sea voyages.

Job, Abd al-Rahman, and Umar ran away from their first masters, as did others, but the majority had no place or allies to go to. Sambo and Osman in North Carolina were more successful in swamplands. Job and Jay were returned to Africa after fewer than five years of slavery because Job impressed the gentlemen and intelligentsia of 1730s England with his dignity, intelligence, and spirituality. Abd al-Rahman and Kebe were returned after thirty-some years of slavery in Mississippi and Georgia, respectively. Mohammed from Antigua was freed because of his evident religiosity, and Abu Bakr was freed because of his exemplary service. The latter became a guide for an unsuccessful English exploratory expedition toward Timbuktu. But Bath, imam of the Mandingo Society of Trinidad, was not able via prayers and petitions to the king of England to gain African repatriation. Muhammad Kaba's letters on maintaining the faith while under great pressure to convert in Jamaica have only recently come to light (Addoun and Lovejoy, 2004).

Abd al-Rahman, Bilali, and Salih Bilali took American wives and became parents here; Yarrow Mamout, Kebe, and Umar apparently chose not to do so. Abd al-Rahman, Abu Bakr, S'Quash, King, Bilali, and Salih Bilali became trusted slave managers.

All of those named above remained true to their Muslim faith, with the possible exceptions of London, Umar, and Mahommah. London transcribed the Gospel of John; Umar was regularly mentioned in North Carolina papers because he was willingly baptized and wrote the Lord's Prayer and Christian avowals in Arabic. None of his available eleven manuscripts, however, are without Quranic elements, including the *Bismillah,* which precedes all Muslim endeavors. His last pastor, probably correctly, expressed some doubt on the totality of his conversion. Mahommah proposed a return to Africa to preach Christianity, but his 1854 biography-autobiography emphasizes his desire to go home. Abd al-Rahman and Kebe made similar promises but both reverted upon their landing in Africa. Abd al-Rahman declared that Christianity was a "good law" but not followed in America. Once a captive joined the religion of his master in Africa, he was freed.

That had not happened to him under Christians. The "Moor" on the Mississippi was even more critical as he proudly claimed that Americans were not as polite, hospitable, comfortable, or learned as his people.

More impressively, Jonas Bath helped create a Muslim society in Trinidad; Brazilian Muslims had their own organizations, and Bilali and Salih Bilali each created Muslim communities on Sapelo and St. Simon's Islands in Georgia. The last two leaders, their praying on beads and rugs, their relatives with Muslim names and practices, were recalled as late as the 1940s. Bilali's thirteen-page "book" in Arabic attempted to codify basic requirements for Muslims. The church on Sapelo retains important Muslim aspects today (Bailey, 2000). Toni Morrison's *Song of Solomon* and Julie Dash's *Daughters of the Dust* both refer to Bilali.

Sources of information had been widely scattered. Mentions of African Muslims in Latin America were scarce, as were mentions of Muslims in Iberian history until very recently. Inclusions in North American histories have been only slightly better. The most often noticed were Job, who was treated so well by the British; Abd al-Rahman, because he was thought to be a prince; and Umar, the devoutly wished-for (by Christians) convert. Often they were called Moors, de-Africanized, despite contrary portraits and descriptions. In the U.S. antebellum era, only one New York ethnologist (Theodore Dwight Jr.) sought to collect Arabic manuscripts and paid serious attention to Kebe's knowledge of education in Africa. Only one geographer, Frenchman George Renouard, drew from an African (Abu Bakr) in the New World information about a wide sphere of West Africa largely unknown elsewhere. Only one southern linguist, William B. Hodgson, attempted to gather African Arabic writings. Only one abolitionist, Irishman Richard R. Madden, became sincerely involved in finding out what he could about African Muslims in Jamaica. Only one southern newspaperman, Cyrus Griffin, and later, a few missionaries and Colonization Society people made notes about Abd al-Rahman's Africa, hoping to convert him into a Moor and a Christian. No westerners asked them to tell about their experiences in slavery in the New World.

Literary references are also rare. Herman Melville stripped Islam from the historical black rebels he fictionalized in *Benito Cereno*. Harriet Beecher Stowe made her hero in *Dred* a Mandingo but not a Muslim. Joel Chandler Harris made his hero Aaron, based upon white and black Christian-denouncing Bilali, into an Arab who denigrated black people. Mark Twain opined in his sketch of Abd al-Rahman that his subject was a cannibal. It was not until 1976, with Alex Haley's novel *Roots*, that African Muslims began to be fairly included in the New World's story.

See also Islam

■ ■ *Bibliography*

Addoun, Yacine Daddi and Paul E. Lovejoy. "Muhammad Kaba Saghanughu and the Muslim Community of Jamaica." In *Slavery on the Frontiers of Islam,* edited by Paul E. Lovejoy. Princeton, N.J.: Markus Wiener Publishers, 2004.

Austin, Allan D., ed. *African Muslims in Antebellum America: A Sourcebook.* New York: Garland, 1984.

Austin, Allan D. *African Muslims in Antebellum America: Transatlantic Stories and Spiritual Struggles.* New York: Routledge, 1997.

Bailey, Cornelia W., with Christena Bledsoe. *God, Dr. Buzzard, and the Bolito Man: A Saltwater Geechee Talks about Life on Sapelo Island.* New York: Anchor, 2000.

Diouf, Sylviane A. *Servants of Allah: African Muslims Enslaved in the Americas.* New York: New York University Press, 1998.

Dwight, Theodore, Jr. "Condition and Character of Negroes in Africa," *Methodist Quarterly Review* (January 1864).

Freyre, Gilberto. *Masters and Slaves.* New York: Knopf, 1956.

Law, Robin, and Paul E. Lovejoy, eds. *The Biography of Mahommah Gardo Baquaqua.* Princeton, N.J.: Markus Wiener Publishers, 2001.

Reis, Joao Jose. *Slave Rebellion in Brazil: The Muslim Uprising of 1835 in Bahia.* Baltimore, Md.: Johns Hopkins University Press, 1993.

ALLAN D. AUSTIN (1996)
Updated by author 2005

MUTUAL AID SOCIETIES

"Badly off, and in want, indeed!" exclaims the black Philadelphian Charles Ellis in Frank J. Webb's 1857 novel *The Garies and Their Friends*. "We not only support our own poor, but assist the whites to support theirs!" Such a sentiment was echoed in the nineteenth-century black press, which repeatedly cited statistics demonstrating that taxes paid by African Americans consistently exceeded public assistance awarded "their" poor. Because popular representation often figured freed blacks as an indigent burden on the government, black communities took great pride in their self-reliance. By 1857, this had been primarily accomplished through the establishment of mutual aid societies, which organized the free black populations in cities from Newport, Rhode Island, to New Orleans, Louisiana. Such groups promoted African-American political interests by supporting each other financially while constructing a sense of kinship. Through monthly membership dues, mutual aid societies dispensed sick benefits and funeral benefits while also serving as a network for jobs; because the earliest groups were organized by men, most also provided support for the widows and orphans of their members. However, women soon established both auxiliaries to existing societies and societies of their own, and by the twentieth century women surpassed men in membership.

It has generally been accepted that the first of these societies was the Free African Society of Philadelphia. Originally envisioned as a religious society by the ex-slaves Richard Allen and Absalom Jones, the Free African Society quickly developed into a nondenominational organization that provided sick benefits to its members, maintained marriage records, and established the first African-American cemetery. After the withdrawal of Allen, the group also established the first African-American church in Philadelphia. Despite the significance of the Free African Society, its founding date is debated. Though an article in *The Colored American* on August 19, 1837, reports that "fifty-five" mutual aid societies had incorporated in Philadelphia by that year, most official documentation has yet to be uncovered and what scholars do know has primarily been gleaned from references to such groups in the press. Thus, while many date the formation of the Free African Society at 1787, others, such as Leonard P. Curry, place its establishment in 1778, a date confirmed by an article in the *Christian Recorder* from April 3, 1884. Similarly, though it has been suggested that such associations had been instituted in Newport as early as 1770, documentation of that city's Free African Union Society is scarce until 1780.

The inspiration for such societies has also been debated. While some believe that black mutual aid societies were modeled on white benevolent societies, others argue that they find their roots in the West African concept of Sou-Sou. Taken from the Yoruba word *esusu*, the Sou-Sou is a cooperative arrangement that, in addition to providing for sick members, often served as a bank (banks modeled on the Sou-Sou, such as the Woman's Responsive Sou-Sou Bank of Trinidad, still exist in Africa and the Caribbean today). An Afro-Cuban mutual aid society, the still-extant Martí-Maceo Society of Florida, may provide a clue in this debate. In nineteenth-century Cuba, free blacks established *cabildos*, or mutual aid societies that prioritized traditional African religious customs. These groups eventually evolved into *sociedades mutuo socorro y recreo* (society of mutual help and recreation), which focused more on economic independence and education as Afro-Cubans sought equality within the larger Cuban society. This evolution led to the formation of the Martí-Maceo

Society in the United States in 1900; similar processes of cultural negotiation probably prompted the first African-American mutual aid societies as well.

While mutual aid societies were the result of material necessity, they also responded to a desire to shape a distinctly African-American identity. The Free African Society was established as a reaction to what its founders called "the irreligious and uncivilized state" in which their neighbors lived. Well into the twentieth century, mutual aid societies stressed the virtue and the civic duty of their members. If these societies scrutinized the behavior of their members, it was due to an awareness of being scrutinized from without. Thus, mutual aid societies became an exercise in self-representation. During Philadelphia's yellow fever epidemic in 1793, for example, Jones and Allen proposed that serving as nurses and gravediggers would demonstrate black moral superiority, while other mutual aid societies argued that education would prove black equality, and they organized schools to this end. The seeming ubiquity with which such groups paraded through the streets suggests that members believed their visibility would counter negative characterizations; this was self-conscious self-representation at its most literal. Noticed they were, though not always positively, as an article from *The Colored American* from April 29, 1837, revealed when it charged the *New York Times* with willfully misrepresenting an anniversary celebration of the Clarkson Benevolent Society as a mob protesting the trial of a fugitive slave.

But the white press was not the only opponent of mutual aid societies. Fearing the interaction between slaves and free blacks, Maryland passed a law in 1842 that charged membership in mutual aid societies as a felony, and Charleston's Free Dark Men of Color were shut down by whites fearful of slave insurrections in the 1820s. It is no surprise that antebellum whites found black mutual aid societies threatening, as many societies were active in abolition efforts. As the nineteenth century progressed into the twentieth, mutual aid societies broadened their political scope. The Colored Knights of Pythias were some of the most ardent members of the Florida movement to regain blacks' right to vote after World War I. Female mutual aid societies fought for women's rights and suffrage. Others lobbied for antilynching legislation. With increased membership, mutual aid societies could also fund larger ventures. The United Order of True Reformers encouraged black entrepreneurship through the institution of the True Reformers' Savings Bank of Richmond, Virginia, while also establishing a hotel, newspaper, and home for the elderly. Other mutual aid societies funded hospitals. And the death benefits so important to early groups eventually grew into life insurance companies, such as the Atlanta Life Insurance Company, which still exists today.

Despite the fact that mutual aid societies played a significant role in African-American life for well over 150 years, few organizations still exist today. Some scholars claim that new forms of entertainment diminished the demand for such organizations, while others point to commercial insurance companies. The Great Depression irreparably weakened mutual aid societies, as it left many members unable to pay dues. Historian David Beito locates the demise of these societies in the modern welfare state, claiming that government-sponsored worker's compensation and widow's benefits left mutual aid societies obsolete. "Universal" as Beito claims these benefits were, however, the Social Security Act Amendment of 1935 effectively excluded many African Americans by denying coverage to personal servants, domestics, and casual and agricultural workers.

Regardless, such legislation did anticipate the eventual dissolution of mutual aid societies. Their legacy, however, can be found in the civil rights movement and even in organizations that exist in the twenty-first century, from 100 Black Men of America, which seeks to dispel negative representations of the black man in society through community service, to the Cultural Wellness Center of Minneapolis, which provides culturally sensitive medical care to African-American patients. The history of African-American mutual aid societies should serve as a source of empowerment and pride. Yet one need be cautious in wishing for their return, as they represent the dire necessity left by a state that refused to fulfill its responsibilities toward all of its citizens equally, a process still evolving today.

See also Christian Denominations, Independent; Fraternal Orders; Fraternities, U.S.; Sororities, U.S.

■ ■ *Bibliography*

Beito, David. *From Mutual Aid to the Welfare State: Fraternal Societies and Social Services, 1890–1967.* Chapel Hill: University of North Carolina Press, 2000.

Curry, Leonard P. *The Free Black in Urban America, 1800–1850: The Shadow of the Dream.* Chicago: University of Chicago Press, 1981.

Nash, Gary B. *Forging Freedom: The Formation of Philadelphia's Black Community, 1720–1840.* Cambridge, Mass.: Harvard University Press, 1988.

Ortiz, Paul. *Emancipation Betrayed: The Hidden History of Black Organizing and White Violence in Florida from Reconstruction to the Bloody Election of 1920.* Berkeley: University of California Press, 2005.

ROBINA KHALID (2005)

MYAL

Myal was an African-Jamaican form of divination and a ritual dance by which spirit mediums drew on the power of ancestors to heal and to alleviate misfortune ascribed to the jealousy, greed, and enmity of others. Obeah, another type of divination, inspired terror during periods of insecurity when people believed that evil Obeah specialists endangered them. To counteract the danger, they called on Myal mediums.

Even before leaving Africa as slaves, Africans associated malevolent sorcery with enslavement, devising fantastic symbolic tales and rumors about slave trafficking and slavery that acted as a critique of African and European slavers and slave owners. These tales described slave dealers and owners as cannibals or vampires who consumed African flesh and blood and processed them into a variety of European or American goods—cheeses, red wines, and gunpowder—desired by continental Africans. Slaves took these beliefs to Jamaica.

In the 1760s, a time of slave revolts, Jamaican planter Edward Long described the founding of a new society, open to all, that he called Myal. Its initiation ritual, the drinking of water mixed with calalu, preceded energetic dancing that produced a condition resembling death. Another mixture revived the subject. Myal initiation supposedly made slaves invulnerable to death from white men's bullets. Creole slaves, who feared African sorcery more than European bullets, pinned their hopes on Christian baptism's power of protection. Baptism by immersion as practiced by John the Baptist infused a new spirit, the Holy Spirit, in the baptized and eventually became the initiation rite of choice for many. Both ceremonies, however, were rituals of death and rebirth.

The Myal Society described by Long appears to have been the progenitor of sugar estate–based Myal bands whose activities gained notoriety after slave emancipation (1838). By then, they combined African problem-solving with Jamaican Native Baptist practices; their ranks included archangels, angels, and ministering angelics who recruited converts, excavated buried charms, and caught stolen shadows or second souls.

In 1841 Myal spirit mediums began a revitalization movement catalyzed by unexplained deaths and job competition. They responded to invitations to expose plantation residents suspected of selfish behavior, using physical force to compel public confessions. Myal members stopped working and would not resume, saying they had to clear the land for Jesus, who was returning soon to set the world right. In a show of independence they denounced the authorities, seized missionary meeting-houses, condemned missionaries for incorrect baptizing, and issued new revelations.

By November 1842 official suppression drove the movement underground. A larger revival occurred in 1860, conferring the name *Revivalist* on religious sects that now proliferated and in which the Myal spirit persisted as the Holy Spirit. Jamaican conceptions of evil, its sources in black and white cupidity, and how it may be overcome flow through Myal, Native Baptist, Revivalist, Rastafarian, and even Marcus Garvey's discourse. In the twentieth century Myal practices survived with a few Christian accretions in St. Elizabeth and Manchester parishes, where the Myal dance was known as *gombay* (drum) play. An elaboration, known as *Jonkonnu*, led by a Myal man wearing a large house headdress representing the plantation great house, was held at Christmastime. In Portland and St. Thomas parishes, Maroons and Central African descendants were familiar with gombay play and intense Myal possession. "When we got myal," a Central African Kumina queen told Monica Schuler in 1971, "we can find a thing bury [that is, an Obeah charm] but when we normal, we can't do these things" (Schuler, 1980).

See also Central African Religions and Culture in the Americas; Divination and Spirit Possession in the Americas; Obeah; Yoruba Religion and Culture in the Americas

■ ■ *Bibliography*

Beckwith, Martha W. *Black Roadways: A Study of Jamaican Folk Life.* Chapel Hill: University of North Carolina Press, 1929. Reprint, New York: Negro Universities Press, 1969.

Bilby, Kenneth. "The Strange Career of 'Obeah': Defining Magical Power in the West Indies." Institute for Global Studies in Culture, Power, and History; Johns Hopkins University, General Seminar, Fall 1993.

Bilby, Kenneth. "Gumbay, Myal, and the Great House: New Evidence on the Religious Background of Jonkonnu in Jamaica." *ACIJ Research Review* 4 (1999): 47–70.

Brodber, Erna. *Myal.* London: New Beacon, 1988.

Chevannes, Barry. *Rastafari Roots and Ideology.* Syracuse, N.Y.: Syracuse University Press, 1994.

Schuler, Monica. "Myalism and the African Religious Tradition." In *Africa and the Caribbean: The Legacies of A Link,* edited by Margaret E. Crahan and Franklin W. Knight. Baltimore: Johns Hopkins University Press, 1980.

Stewart, Robert J. *Religion and Society in Post-Emancipation Jamaica.* Knoxville: University of Tennessee Press, 1992.

MONICA SCHULER (2005)

MYERS, ISAAC
JANUARY 13, 1835
JANUARY 26, 1891

Born free in Baltimore, labor leader Isaac Myers was the son of poor workers. He attended Rev. John Fortie's day school and at sixteen was apprenticed to James Jackson, a well-known African-American caulker in Baltimore's shipyards. By the time the Civil War broke out, Myers had become an independent caulker.

In October 1865 white caulkers angered by black competition went on strike, demanding that black workers be excluded from waterfront work. Police joined in, and African Americans were driven from the shipyards. The unemployed black caulkers and waterfront men held a meeting. Myers suggested they form their own union, buy up a shipyard and railway line, and run their own business cooperatively. Baltimore blacks responded to Myers's pleas for help by investing $10,000. Myers borrowed an additional $30,000 from a ship captain and set up a shipyard and railway. The cooperative, called the Chesapeake Marine Railway and Dry Dock, opened in February 1866 and paid its three hundred workers an average of three dollars per day. Myers also organized the Colored Caulkers' Trades Union and was named its first president. He expanded his union role to political activism, calling for civil rights and black suffrage.

The shipyard was successful almost immediately, and Myers and his partners were able to pay off their original debts within five years. The cooperative's influence and example assured that white Baltimore workers did not exclude blacks from other fields. Soon it began hiring white workers, and Myers worked closely with the white caulkers' union. From his collaboration he dreamed of interracial activism on a large scale. In 1868 he was one of nine blacks invited to attend the convention of the National Labor Union (NLU), the largest white labor organization, in Philadelphia. Myers underlined the importance of interracial collaboration and asserted that blacks would be happy to work with whites for common goals. His efforts met with white indifference, but he invited white delegates to a National Labor Convention that December in Washington, D.C. At the convention, the (black) National Labor Union was born. Myers helped write the union's constitution and served as its president. He spent the next several months on a speaking tour, attempting unsuccessfully to draw support for the union. Myers reminded his audiences that labor could succeed only if both races united. That August he attended another NLU convention, but white and black delegates divided over blacks' support of the Republican Party. The black NLU remained small and financially strapped. It dissolved before the end of 1871, and Myers left the labor movement.

In later life Myers became a detective in the Post Office Department, opened an unsuccessful coal yard, and became a U.S. tax collector. He headed several black business organizations in Baltimore and was active in the African Methodist Episcopal (AME) Church, spending fifteen years as superintendent of Baltimore's Bethel AME School and writing an unpublished sacred drama. A grand master of Maryland's black Masons, he edited an issue of *Mason's Digest*. He died in Baltimore in 1891 after a paralytic stroke.

See also Civil War, U.S.; Free Blacks, 1619–1860

■ ■ *Bibliography*

Foner, Philip S. *History of the Labor Movement in the United States*. Vol. 1. New York: International Publishers, 1947.

GREG ROBINSON (1996)

NAACP

See National Association for the Advancement of Colored People (NAACP)

NAACP Legal Defense and Educational Fund

Created by the National Association for the Advancement of Colored People (NAACP) in 1940 as a tax-exempt fund for litigation and education, the NAACP Legal Defense and Educational Fund (LDF), based in New York, has been the central organization for African-American civil rights advances through the legal system. While the LDF, popularly known as the "Inc. Fund," had from the beginning a board of directors and a separate fund-raising apparatus from those of the NAACP, it was planned as an integrated component of the larger organization, designed to carry out Charles H. Houston's plan for a legal assault on segregation in public education. The LDF's leadership was represented on the NAACP board and helped design orga-

nizational strategy. The LDF was set up with a loose administrative structure, with a director-counsel as the chief officer. The first LDF director-counsel, former NAACP counsel Thurgood Marshall, hired a staff of five lawyers.

During the 1940s and 1950s such lawyers as Robert Carter, Franklin Williams, and Constance Baker Motley joined the staff. Marshall made the LDF the main locus of civil rights law, and the LDF litigated a variety of landmark civil rights cases before the Supreme Court. In 1944 the LDF successfully argued in *Smith v. Allwright* that primaries that legally excluded blacks were unconstitutional. In 1946 *Morgan v. The Commonwealth of Virginia* outlawed segregation on interstate bus lines. In 1948 the LDF brought *Shelley v. Kramer* to the U.S. Supreme Court. The Court ruled that racially restrictive housing covenants that prohibited sales of homes to blacks were unenforceable.

However, much of the LDF's work was done not at the Supreme Court but in small southern towns, fighting lawsuits or defending arrested blacks under adverse and dangerous conditions. LDF lawyers, forced to work on a shoestring budget, received death threats and ran from lynch mobs. While they frequently lost cases, their presence helped assure fair trials. In 1950 the Supreme Court ruling in *Shepard and Irvin v. Florida* helped establish the now-familiar doctrine that defendants must be tried in a venue free of prejudice against them.

Education cases were the centerpiece of LDF legal efforts. Following the NAACP's successful strategy in *Mississippi ex rel. Gaines v. Canada* (1938), the LDF attacked discrimination in graduate education. Beginning in 1946 the LDF brought a series of cases before the Supreme Court, culminating in *Sipuel v. Board of Regents of the University of Oklahoma* (1948), *McLaurin v. Oklahoma State Regents* (1950), and *Sweatt v. Painter* (1950). In the latter, the Court ruled that segregated facilities led to discrimination, though the case did not directly challenge the principle of "separate but equal" in primary education. LDF lawyers also brought suit to eliminate pay differentials between white and black teachers, in part to demonstrate the enormous expense of a dual school system. By 1951 the LDF, preparing for a direct challenge to segregation, was working on twenty elementary and high school cases and a dozen higher-education cases. The LDF's efforts were crowned with success in 1954 with the decision in *Brown v. Board of Education of Topeka, Kansas,* argued by Thurgood Marshall.

By 1954, however, personal differences among staff members and disagreements over organizational mission led to a total split with the NAACP. The NAACP considered the LDF a vehicle for arguing civil rights cases. LDF leaders considered achieving educational equality their prime responsibility. The LDF and the NAACP formally parted in 1956, establishing separate boards of directors.

After the implementation ruling in *Brown v. Board of Education,* which ordered desegregation "with all deliberate speed," was announced in 1955, the LDF began designing desegregation plans and fighting court cases to force compliance, notably *Cooper v. Aaron* (1958), in which the Court mandated the integration of Arkansas's Little Rock Central High School. LDF lawyers continued to work to combat segregation in other fields. In 1956 the LDF began a central involvement in the civil rights movement when it won *Gayle v. Browder,* the case of the Montgomery bus boycott led by the Rev. Dr. Martin Luther King Jr.

At the same time, southerners determined to keep the LDF from operating. Legislatures charged that the LDF created cases in which it had no legitimate interest or standing. The Supreme Court finally ruled in 1963 that LDF litigation was constitutionally protected. By 1965 LDF lawyers had taken school cases as they had arisen in every southern state. Eventually, in *Griffin v. County School Board of Prince Edward County* (1964), the Court renounced "all deliberate speed," and in *Green v. County School Board of New Kent County* (1968) ordered immediate and total desegregation.

In 1961 Thurgood Marshall was appointed a federal judge by President John F. Kennedy and left the LDF. Jack Greenberg, his white assistant, who had come to the LDF in 1949, succeeded him as the new director-counsel, a position he would hold for the next twenty-three years. During the 1960s the LDF continued as an active force in the civil rights movement, defending sit-in protesters in cases such as *Boynton v. Virginia* (1961) and *Shuttlesworth v. Alabama* (1964), as well as defending Freedom Riders and providing bail funds for the many activists who were arrested during the struggle.

The Black Power movement of the late 1960s and early 1970s brought about tensions within the LDF over its white leadership and its refusal to defend black radicals except in those few cases where civil rights issues were involved, such as exorbitant bail fees for incarcerated Black Panther Party members. In 1970 several LDF lawyers pressed the organization to take up the defense of black radical Angela Davis after she was implicated in a courthouse shootout, but the LDF board of directors and Director-Counsel Greenberg vetoed the idea. The same year, when Julian Bond was refused his seat in the Georgia legislature because he opposed the Vietnam War, the LDF refused his case on the grounds that a white antiwar legislator would have suffered the same fate.

In recent decades the LDF has concentrated on other pressing civil rights areas. In *Griggs v. Duke Power* (1971), the LDF persuaded the Supreme Court to strike down discriminatory educational or testing requirements irrelevant to job performance. The LDF then argued numerous affirmative action cases based on *Griggs* in the following years. The most important of these was *Regents of the University of California v. Bakke* (1979), in which the LDF worked largely successfully in opposing Allan Bakke's "reverse discrimination" suit.

Capital punishment was a particular focus of LDF's efforts. In preparation for the Supreme Court case *Maxwell v. Bishop* (1970), which involved an Arkansas African American convicted of the rape of a white woman, the LDF organized a study that showed that 89 percent of defendants around the country given the death penalty for rape between 1930 and 1962 were black, and demonstrated patterns of racial discrimination in death sentences given for rape in Arkansas between 1945 and 1965. While the Court declined to rule on the LDF's statistics, Jack Greenberg continued to lead the campaign against the death penalty, which achieved temporary victory in *Furman v. Georgia* (1972). Capital punishment was reinstated in 1976, but the death penalty in cases of rape, a special concern of blacks, was declared unconstitutional in *Coker v. Georgia* (1977). The LDF continued to appeal death penalty sentences for African Americans. In the early 1980s it commissioned the so-called Baldus Study, a mam-

Roy Wilkins (l) and Thurgood Marshall, director and special counsel for the NAACP's Legal Defense and Education Fund, flank Autherine Lucy at a press conference at NAACP headquarters in New York City, March 2, 1956. After months of litigation, Lucy became the first African-American admitted to the University of Alabama. She was soon suspended from classes, however, when officials claimed they could not ensure her safety. THE LIBRARY OF CONGRESS

moth study of the influence of race on death penalty sentencing, following which lawyers argued *McCleskey v. Kemp* (1987). However, the Supreme Court refused to rule solely on the basis of this statistical evidence that the death penalty was arbitrary or racially discriminatory.

In 1984 Julius LeVonne Chambers took over as director-counsel and continued to concentrate on litigation in the areas of poverty law, education, fair housing, capital punishment, fair employment, environmental justice, and voting rights. A housing discrimination suit the LDF brought in the San Fernando Valley in 1992 was settled for $300,000, one of the largest awards ever granted victims of racial bias in housing.

In 1992 Chambers resigned and was replaced by Elaine Ruth Jones. Jones had previously been head of the LDF's regional office in Washington, D.C., where she had helped draft and implement civil rights legislation, notably the Civil Rights Restoration Act (1988), the 1988 Fair

Housing Act, and the Civil Rights Act of 1991. Jones redirected LDF's focus toward cases of environmental and health care discrimination. Environmental activism covers suits to ensure equal treatment of blacks victimized by toxic wastes and cases enforcing federal laws mandating free lead-poisoning exams for poor children. Examples of health care cases include a suit filed in Contra Costa, California, charging with violation of civil rights statutes officials who built a county hospital largely inaccessible to the district's African-American population.

At the beginning of the twenty-first century, the LDF continued its involvement in poverty law, voting rights, criminal justice, and education, which remained an especially active arena centering on widely contested issues including public school vouchers, federal funding, and affirmative action. In 2005, LDF Director-Counsel and President Theodore M. Shaw sent a letter to the U.S. Commission on Civil Rights criticizing the Commission's proposal for a comprehensive review of public primary and secondary school desegregation decrees and court orders, noting that such a review would not help to reverse the perception of a trend toward racial resegregation in the United States.

Since 1964, the LDF has also provided scholarship programs to aid African-American law students.

See also Black Panther Party for Self-Defense; *Brown v. Board of Education of Topeka, Kansas*; Bond, Julian; Civil Rights Movement, U.S.; Houston, Charles Hamilton; Marshall, Thurgood; Montgomery, Ala., Bus Boycott; Motley, Constance Baker; National Association for the Advancement of Colored People (NAACP); *Sweatt v. Painter*

■ ■ *Bibliography*

Baldus, David, George Woodworth, and Charles A. Pulaski Jr. *Equal Justice and the Death Penalty: Legal and Empirical Analysis*. Boston: Northeastern University Press, 1990.

Hall, Kermit, ed. *The Oxford Companion to the Supreme Court*. New York: Oxford University Press, 1992.

Kluger, Richard. *Simple Justice*. New York: Knopf, 1975.

Rowan, Carl. *Dream Makers, Dream Breakers: The World of Justice Thurgood Marshall*. Boston: Little, Brown, 1992.

Tushnet, Mark. *The NAACP's Legal Strategy Against Segregation, 1925–1950*. Chapel Hill: University of North Carolina Press, 1987.

GREG ROBINSON (1996)
Updated by publisher 2005

NABRIT, JAMES MADISON

SEPTEMBER 4, 1900
DECEMBER 27, 1997

■■■

Born in Atlanta, Georgia, lawyer and educator James Madison Nabrit was the son of the Rev. J. M. and Gertrude Nabrit. In 1919 he received his high school diploma from Morehouse College, and four years later graduated from Morehouse with a B.A. degree. Although he left school in 1925 to teach political science and coach football at Leland College, Nabrit received a J.D. degree from Northwestern University Law School in 1927. While at Northwestern, he was an honor student and was elected to the Order of the Coif, the highest legal scholarship fraternity. After law school, he served as a dean at Arkansas State College for two years.

In 1930 Nabrit moved to Houston, Texas, where he practiced law. In his six years in Houston, he became involved in civil rights law. He participated in over twenty-five such cases, most of which were concerned with voting rights. In 1936 he began his twenty-four-year career at Howard University as an associate professor of law. While at Howard, he developed a syllabus that collected more than two thousand civil rights cases. He organized the first course in civil rights taught at a law school in the United States. In 1954 Nabrit served as the legal adviser to the governor of the Virgin Islands. He joined in the NAACP's legal assault on segregation, and he wrote one of the briefs opposing Jim Crow schools in the cases that led to the Supreme Court's landmark *Brown v. Board of Education* desegregation decision in 1954. In 1960 Nabrit was named President of Howard University, where he served for nine stormy years. Ironically, given his longtime fight for civil rights, he was assailed by militant students in the late 1960s as an Uncle Tom. In 1981 he received an honorary degree from Howard University.

See also *Brown v. Board of Education of Topeka, Kansas*; Civil Rights Movement, U.S.

■ ■ *Bibliography*

"James Madison Nabrit." *Negro History Bulletin* 24, no. 4 (January 1961): 75–76.

Logan, Rayford. *Howard University: The First Hundred Years*. New York: New York University Press, 1969.

SASHA THOMAS (1996)

NAMES AND NAMING, AFRICAN

■■■

Africans arriving in the American colonies and later the United States continued to give their children African names well into the nineteenth century. In the seventeenth and eighteenth centuries African-American slaves retained Africanisms in their naming practices. The highest percentage of African names was found among male slaves in the eighteenth century, when the majority of the black population was still unacculturated. During the colonial period the practice of naming children after the days of the week, the months, and the seasons was retained. Such names as January, April, May, June, September, November, March, August, Christmas, and Midday were popular. Numerous examples exist of Akan day names (sometimes modified or anglicized): Cudjoe (Monday), Cubbenah (Tuesday), Quao (Wednesday), Quaco (Thursday), Cuffe (Friday), Quamin (Saturday), and Quashee (Sunday). Many took on varied forms. Quao became Quaro and later Jacco, Jack, and Jackson. Other African names common in the eighteenth century were Sambo, Mongo, and Juba.

NAME CHANGES

In western and central Africa names are given at stages in an individual's life, and—as happens among all people for whom magic is important—the identification of a name with the personality of its bearer is held to be so complete that the person's real name (usually the one given at birth) must be kept secret lest it be used by someone working magic against the person. That is why among Africans a person's name may change with time, a new designation being assumed on the occasion of some striking occurrence in life. When one of the rites marking a new stage in the person's development occurs, a name change also occurs to note the event.

Likewise, African Americans changed their names to correspond to major life changes. Take the case of Frederick Douglass, for example. His original last name, Bailey, had an African origin. He was descended from Belali Mohomet, a Mande-speaking slave from Timbo, Futa Jallon. (Bailey is a common African-American surname along the Atlantic coast. In Talbot County, Maryland, the records list no white Baileys from whom the slave name Bailey could have been taken.) Belali was owned by Richard Skinner, a wealthy tobacco planter near the Miles River. Belali's granddaughter Betsy belonged to Skinner's granddaughter Ann Catherine. Frederick Bailey was born in 1817.

Soon after escaping slavery, Bailey changed his name to Douglass. In similar fashion, Sojourner Truth was known as Isabella Baumfree until she had a dream that told her about her new name and mission. Malcolm Little, at different stages of his life, was variously known as Malcolm X, Homeboy, Detroit Red, Big Red, Satan, and el-Hajj Malik el-Shabazz.

MULTIPLE NAMES

Almost every black person is known by two names: a given name and a name used only within the family circle. Lorenzo Dow Turner (1895–1972), a leading scholar of African retentions in American English, found a dual naming system among the Gullahs in the Sea Islands of South Carolina. This system (which still exists) involves an English (American) name given at birth and a more intimate name—sometimes called a "basket name" or a "day name"—used exclusively by the family and community. Slaveholders recognized this dual naming practice among enslaved Africans in the eighteenth century. In advertisements of runaways, owners always included "proper" (given) names and "country" names, which were the African names.

Among enslaved Africans the use of nicknames was also widespread. Pie Ya, Puddin'-tame, Frog, Tennie C., Monkey, Mush, Cooter, John de Baptist, Fat-Man, Preacher, Jack Rabbit, Sixty, Pop Corn, Old Gold, Dootes, Angle-Eye, Bad Luck, Sky-up-de-Greek, Cracker, Jabbo, Cat-Fish, Bear, Tip, Odessa, Pig Lasses, Rattler, Pearly, Luck, Buffalo, Old Blue, Red Fox, and Coon are some of the most common.

GULLAH NAMES

A few examples of Gullah basket names that are unchanged from their African roots are Ndomba, Mviluki, Sungila, Kamba, Anyika, and Sebe. Ndomba is the name given to a breech-delivered Gullah child whose hand protrudes first at birth. It means "I am begging (with outstretched hand)." Mviluki means "a penitent." Its Luba source word is *mvuluki,* "one who doesn't forget his sins." The basket name Sungila means "to save, help, deliver," while Kamba, a very common Luba name, comes from *munkamba,* meaning "ancestor." Anyika, a Gullah name meaning "she is beautiful," is related to a Luba word meaning "to praise the beauty of." Sebe, a Gullah name meaning "a leather ornament," comes from the Luba word for hide or leather, *tshisebe.* Others—Tulu ("sleep"), Tuma ("send"), Pita ("pass by"), Mesu ("eyes"), Kudima ("to work or hoe"), and Kudiya ("to eat")—are all Gullah day names, exactly the same in Gullah and Luba.

In the Sea Islands children sometimes have not only given names and basket names but also community names. The community gives the child a name that characterizes the individual, such as Smart Child or Shanty ("showoff"). This practice parallels Bantu naming practices in Zaire. The name of Georgetown University's former basketball center Dikambe Mutombo (he is from Zaire) illustrates this point. His full name is Dikamba Mutombo Mpolondo Munkamba Diken Jean-Jean Jacque wa Mutombo. In order, these names are his uncle's name, his family surname, his grandfather's name, his village nickname, his name given at birth, and his hometown village, wa Mutombo (which means "from the village of Mutombo").

Other creolized Gullah nicknames typical of Bantu naming practices are names of animals or fish: De Dog, Doggie, Kitty, Fish, Yellowtail Croker, Frog, Spider, Boy,

Gal, Jumper, Tooti, Crocki, Don, Cuffy, Akebee, Dr. Buzzer, and Dr. Eagle.

In Gullah naming practices, as in African naming practices, children are named after parents because it is believed that the parent spirit resides in the children. The same name might appear in several generations of a family. In the Sea Islands the name Litia appeared in four generations of female children.

AFRICAN REVIVAL

By the time of the Civil War and the emancipation of four million African-American slaves, African personal names had almost completely disappeared. It was not until the 1920s, when the early black Islamic revivalist Noble Drew Ali began to use Arabic and Islamic names, that the practice was revived. These practices were followed by Elijah Muhammad and the Nation of Islam. They used African and Arabic words and names to instill in their followers a sense of racial pride.

By the 1960s and 1970s African names had gained respectability in the wake of the civil rights, African independence, and Black Power movements. Movements such as Kawaida of Maulana Karenga stressed the use of Swahili and Yoruba names. African names such as Dashanaba, Tameka, Kwame, and Maat again became common.

African names have come full circle. Their use reflects many changes in attitude, from strong African identification to nationalism, from integration and assimilation back to cultural identification.

See also Africanisms; Black Power Movement; Civil Rights Movement, U.S.; Douglass, Frederick; Gullah; Karenga, Maulana; Kawaida; Malcolm X; Truth, Sojourner; Turner, Lorenzo Dow

■ ■ *Bibliography*

Dillard, J. L. *All-American English.* New York: Random House, 1975.

Dillard, J. L. *Black English: Its History and Usage in the United States.* New York: Random House, 1975.

Dillard, J. L. *Black Names.* The Hague, Netherlands: Mouton, 1976.

Dillard, J. L. *Lexicon of Black English.* New York: Seabury, 1977.

Haley, Alex. *The Autobiography of Malcolm X.* New York: Grove, 1965.

Holloway, Joseph E. *Africanisms in American English.* Bloomington: Indiana University Press, 1990.

Holloway, Joseph E. *The African Heritage of American English.* Bloomington: Indiana University Press, 1993.

McFeely, William S. *Frederick Douglass.* New York: Norton, 1991.

Mencken, H. L. *The American Language: An Inquiry into the Development of English in the United States.* New York: Knopf, 1936.

JOSEPH E. HOLLOWAY (1996)

NAMES CONTROVERSY

Naming has played an important role in developing a sense of group identity among African Americans. Black leaders have frequently argued that the names borne by African Americans influence their self-esteem and help determine their place in American life. The black journalist T. Thomas Fortune counseled in 1906 that "until we get this racial designation properly fixed in the language and literature of the country we shall be kicked and cuffed and sneered at" (Berry and Blassingame, 1982, p. 389). But what African Americans should collectively be called has often engendered controversy among the race's foremost voices.

Africans brought to the North American continent as slaves during the seventeenth and eighteenth centuries belonged to particular nations or ethnic groups (e.g., Ibo, Yoruba, Mandingo, Bakongo). But such diverse allegiances were difficult to maintain in the complex world of plantation slavery, and a new "African" identity emerged. Blacks consistently referred to themselves as Africans throughout the colonial period, and as communities of free blacks emerged in the decades following the American Revolution, they placed the prefix "African" before the names of nearly all of their churches, schools, lodges, and social organizations.

Only in a few cities such as Charleston, South Carolina, and New Orleans did free men and women of mixed African and European (and sometimes Native American) ancestry reject identification with their darker brothers and sisters and encourage the development of a tripartite racial system. They often preferred to be called "brown" or "creole."

After 1816, the rise of a white-led colonization movement bent on carrying African Americans back to the African continent caused a major shift in how free blacks referred to the race. Fearful that continuing to call themselves "African" would merely encourage the colonizationists, growing numbers of blacks avoided the term. Most opted for the safer appellation "colored." A few ultra-integrationists, such as Philadelphian William Whipper, urged that all racial designations be abandoned. He convinced the 1835 black national convention to pass a resolution exhorting African Americans to abandon the word "colored" and to remove "African" from the names of their institutions. Yet by the 1830s, "colored" was widely used throughout the North, a fact symbolized by the title of the leading black journal of the era, the *Colored American*. Between 1827 and 1899, 34 percent of all black newspapers and magazines containing a racial designation in their title bore the name "colored."

"Negro," a term derived from the Portuguese word for black, vied for primacy with "colored" after the Civil War. Blacks increasingly viewed the latter name as offensive, even though many whites continued to use it as a racial designation. After 1900, "Negro" gained broad acceptance among both races. As more and more blacks adopted the term, black leaders began to attack whites for spelling the word with a diminutive "n." Contending that whites spelled all other proper nouns with capital letters, they charged that their failure to capitalize "Negro" was a deliberate effort to label blacks as inferior. With the support of Booker T. Washington, W. E. B. Du Bois, and a majority of black leaders, the capital "N" campaign convinced the federal government and most editors, even in the southern press, to adhere to the rule by 1950.

"Negro" was never a term of universal approbation. The Reverend J. C. Embry of Philadelphia argued in 1892 that slaveholders had invented the word to stigmatize blacks. Observing that "Negro" lacked a geographic locus and failed to recognize blacks' African past, Embry and Fortune led a campaign to adopt the name "Afro-American." From the late 1880s through the first decade of the twentieth century, "Afro-American" competed with "Negro" as a popular racial designation.

Some ordinary blacks simply opposed the term "Negro" because it was easily corrupted into derisive expressions such as "nigger" and "nigra." There was a steady increase in opposition to the name after 1920. One of the most intense and influential attacks came from the pen of Richard B. Moore, an African-American activist of West Indian descent. His pamphlet "The Name 'Negro': Its Origin and Evil Use" (1960) summarized objections to the term and contended that the term itself—"because of its slave origin, its consequent degradation, and its still prevalent connection in the minds of people generally with prejudice, vileness, inferiority, and hostility"—was a major factor in keeping the race in a subordinate state.

In the midst of the turbulent battles of the Civil Rights movement of the 1960s, many African Americans abandoned the term "Negro"—what Moore called "the oppressors' vicious smear name." The Nation of Islam (especially Malcolm X), Black Power advocates, and other black cultural nationalists renewed the assault on the term, linking it almost irrevocably in the minds of many young blacks with slavery and Uncle Tomism. "Black" quickly became the most popular racial identifier, in large part because it stood in symbolic opposition to white dominance—the enemy of Black Power. African Americans spoke proudly of being "black" and infused the term into their rhetoric, writing, and organizational names. Convinced anew of the value of recognizing their African heritage, black cultural nationalists also revived use of the term "Afro-American".

In 1988 the civil rights leader Jesse Jackson reopened the debate over racial nomenclature when he announced that blacks should begin to refer to themselves as "African Americans." Criticizing the term "black" for its singular reference to skin color, he maintained that the name offered African Americans no connection to their land of origin or their cultural heritage. During a conference after a gathering of African-American leaders in December 1988, Jackson said, "Just as we were called colored, but were not that, and then Negro, but not that, to be called black is just as baseless. . . . To be called African Americans has cultural integrity. It puts us in our proper historical context." The new terminology achieved rapid acceptance, first among activists and academics, then within the broader black population. By the late 1990s it had become the preferred self-designation for one out of three Americans of African descent.

The names controversy has been a source of continuing conflict among black leaders since the early nineteenth century. Yet in each era, a few have questioned the value of this debate to the advancement of the race. Some have labeled it a distraction and a waste of time, energy, and resources. Others have viewed it as a reflection of African-American powerlessness. Writing in *The Content of Our Character* (1990), Shelby Steele observed that "this self-conscious reaching for pride through nomenclature suggests nothing so much as a despair over the possibility of gaining the less conspicuous pride that follows real advancement" (p. 47).

See also Black Power Movement; Du Bois, W. E. B.; Fortune, T. Thomas; Identity and Race in the Americas; Malcolm X; Moore, Richard Benjamin; Nation of Islam; Washington, Booker T.

■ ■ *Bibliography*

Berry, Mary Frances, and John W. Blassingame. "Black Nationalism." In *Long Memory: The Black Experience in America*, pp. 388–428. New York: Oxford University Press, 1982.

Philogene, Gina. *From Black to African American: A New Social Representation*. Westport, Conn.: Praeger, 1999.

Smith, Tom W. "Changing Racial Labels: From 'Colored' to 'Negro' to 'Black' to 'African American'." *Public Opinion Quarterly* 56 (1992): 496–514.

Stuckey, Sterling. "Identity and Ideology: The Names Controversy." In *Slave Culture: Nationalist Theory and the Foundations of Black America*, pp. 193–244. New York: Oxford University Press, 1987.

ROY E. FINKENBINE (1996)
Updated by author 2005

NANNY OF THE MAROONS

C. 1700

C. 1750

∎ ∎ ∎

Nanny, a national heroine of Jamaica, was the leader of the Windward Maroons, ex-slaves living in interior communities in the eastern or windward area of Jamaica during colonial times. As such, her history is integrated with that of the Maroons, warriors fundamental to the history of resistance in the Caribbean. Next to the Guianas, Jamaica had the largest Maroon community in the British-colonized Caribbean, with Portland, St. Thomas-in-the-East, St. Mary, Trelawny, and St. Elizabeth being the parishes with the largest centers of Maroon settlement. *Marronage*, derived from *Maroons*, signifies flight to the forest or mountains (or by sea to other territories) and the formation of Maroon communities. The height of marronage activity came after 1655, when the English captured Jamaica from the Spaniards. Between 1655 and 1739, when the first Maroon War ended, Maroon Towns had been established firmly at Accompong (St. Elizabeth), Trelawny Town (the Leeward Maroons in the Cockpit country), Scott's Hall (St. Mary), and at Crawford Town, Nanny Town, and Moore Town in the Blue Mountain range of eastern Jamaica (the Windward Maroons).

Nanny has emerged as the most important female figure in the history of the liberation struggles in Jamaica. Her name (properly *Nanani*) was derived from the Akan (Ghanaian) word meaning "ancestress" and "mother," and this establishes her ethnic origin. It is widely believed that she was born in Africa in the late seventeenth century and was transported to Jamaica with captives via the transatlantic trade. There are differing views about whether or not she arrived in Jamaica as an enslaved woman or as a free black woman with enslaved people of her own. Some say she was married to Cudjoe, a Maroon leader, others to a man named Adou. Nanny's exploits in eastern Jamaica in the eighteenth century are both real and legendary, although, as a historical figure, she has more visibility than the majority of black women in pre-emancipation Jamaica. For some, she exists as a shadowy, mythical figure with supernatural powers; an Obeah woman (meaning she would have been a practitioner of the religious belief of African origin involving folk magic practiced in some parts of the Caribbean) whose pumpkin seeds, after only a few days of being planted, sprouted miraculously to feed her starving people, and whom bullets from British muskets could not harm, for she had the power to catch them in a certain part of her anatomy (following that genre of writing that represents female resisters as unsexed amazons).

But Maroon historiography details her real existence and contribution to Jamaican resistance history. She is credited, both in the oral and written history, with employing guerilla tactics—especially between 1724 and 1739—to help her people to defeat the British, uniting the Maroon communities in Jamaica, and negotiating land for her people as part of the 1739 treaty with the British. Her original base, Nanny Town, was destroyed by the British in 1734. Moore Town (or New Nanny Town) then became the primary town of the Windward Maroons. As a military leader, her historical presence predictably diminished in the post-treaty period. She is believed to have died around 1750.

See also Folklore: Latin American and Caribbean Culture Heroes and Characters; Maroon Wars; Runaway Slaves in Latin America and the Caribbean; Women and Politics in Latin America and the Caribbean

■ ■ *Bibliography*

Brathwaite, Kamau. *Wars of Respect: Nanny, Sam Sharpe, and the Struggle for People's Liberation*. Kingston, Jamaica: Agency for Public Information, 1977.

Carey, Beverley. *Maroon Story: The Authentic and Original History of the Maroons in the History of Jamaica, 1490–1880*. Gordon Town, Jamaica: Agouti Press, 1997.

Gottlieb, Karla. *The Mother of Us All: A History of Queen Nanny, Leader of the Windward Jamaican Maroons*. London: Africa World Press, 2000.

Mathurin Mair, Lucille. *The Rebel Woman in the British West Indies during Slavery*. Kingston, Jamaica: Institute of Jamaica, 1975.

Sharpe, Jenny. *Ghosts of Slavery: A Literary Archaeology of Black Women's Lives* Minneapolis: University of Minnesota Press, 2003.

VERENE A. SHEPHERD (2005)

NARRATIVES, SLAVE

See Slave Narratives

NASCIMENTO, ABDIAS DO

MARCH 14, 1914

▪▪▪

Abdias do Nascimento, who celebrated his ninetieth birthday on March 14, 2004, is considered one of the most important activists in the fight against racism in Brazil and in the Americas. Born in the city of Franca, in the interior of the state of São Paulo, he migrated to the city of São Paulo at the beginning of the 1930s and immediately began to participate in events organized by the Frente Negra Brasileira (Brazilian Black Front), an activist group founded in 1931. In the same decade, he became an activist in the Integralist Party (a nationalist party accused of fascism, but which attracted thousands of black people and maintained an ideological dispute with the Communist Party). In his role as an Integralist, he worked together with Sebastião Rodrigues Alves, another black activist. At the beginning of the 1940s, after a long journey to the interior of Brazil and to part of Latin America, Nascimento created the Teatro Experimental do Negro (Experimental Black Theater) in 1944. An artistic, political, and cultural movement, the theater brought together important intellectuals and black artists on the Afro-Brazilian scene, people like Agnaldo Camargo, Edison Carneiro, Ironides Rodrigues, Ruth de Souza, Léa Garcia, and the sociologist Alberto Guerreiro Ramos. The artistic and political articulation of Nascimento's performances constantly denounced racism while offering debates and solutions.

During this period, Nascimento organized, with various other leaders, the Convenção Nacional do Negro (National Negro Convention), which took place in São Paulo in 1945, and in Rio de Janeiro the following year. He also played an important role in the work of the Brazilian Constituent Assembly of 1946, offering critiques and proposing methods to eradicate racism. In 1950 he convened the Congresso do Negro Brasileiro (Black Brazilian Congress) in the city of Rio de Janeiro.

Persecuted by the military dictatorship that began in 1964, Nascimento decided to leave Brazil in 1968, a move that began his long history of international activity. Beyond participating in important congresses and meetings with black leaders in the Americas and Africa, he was active in various universities. He was the founding chair in African Culture in the New World at the Puerto Rican Studies and Research Center, State University of New York at Buffalo, where he worked as a lecturer at this university until 1981. He also lectured in the School of Dramatic Arts at Yale University and as a visiting professor at Temple University and at the University of Ifé, in Nigeria.

Since the 1940s, Nascimento has published various works (some of them translated), some of which he re-edited for the collection *O Brasil na mira do Pan-Africanismo* (2002). In addition to being an author, poet, and playwright, Nascimento developed an international career as a plastic artist.

Nascimento participated in the Sixth Pan-African Congress held in Dar es Salaam, Tanzania, in 1974. He participated in and helped organize the first Congress of Black Culture in the Americas, which took place in 1977 in Columbia, as well as the two succeeding congresses, the second in 1980 in Panama and the third in 1982 in Brazil.

After returning to Brazil in the 1980s, Nascimento resumed his political activism, serving as a federal deputy (1983–1986) and senator (1991, 1997–1999). In his parliamentary role, he emphasized legal projects for affirmative action and the fight against racial discrimination. Moreover, in 1992 he directed the office of the Secretary for the Defense and Promotion of Afro-Brazilian Populations, and in 1999 he directed the office of the Secretary of Human Rights and Citizenship, both in the government of the state of Rio de Janeiro.

Nascimento received the title of Doutor Honoris Causa from the State University of Rio de Janeiro (1990) and from the Federal University of Bahia (2000). In 2004 he was awarded the UNESCO Toussaint Louverture Prize for his work against racism.

See also Frente Negra Brasileira; Politics; Racial Democracy in Brazil

▪▪ *Bibliography*

Andrews, George Reid. *Blacks and Whites in São Paulo, Brazil, 1888–1988*. Madison: University of Wisconsin Press, 1991.

Barcelos, Luiz Cláudio. "Mobilização racial no Brasil: uma revisão crítica." *Afro-Ásia* 17 (1996): 187–212.

Butler, Kim. *Freedoms Given, Freedoms Won: Afro-Brazilians in Post-Abolition São Paulo and Salvador*. New Brunswick, N.J.: Rutgers University Press, 1998.

Cunha, Olívia Maria Gomes da. "Black Movements and Identity Politics in Brazil." In *Culture of Politics/Politics of Cultures: Re-Visioning Latin-American Social Movements*, edited by A. Escobar, E. Danigno, and S. Alvarez. Boulder, Colo.: Westview, 1998.

Hanchard, Michael. *Orpheus and Power: The Movimento Negro of Rio de Janeiro and São Paulo, Brazil, 1945–1988*. Princeton, N.J.: Princeton University Press, 1994.

Hanchard, Michael. *Racial Politics in Contemporary Brazil*. Duke University Press, 1999.

Leite, José Correia. *E disse o velho militante José Correia Leite*. São Paulo: Secretaria Municipal de Cultura, 1992.

Moura, Clóvis. "Organizações Negras." In *São Paulo: o povo em movimento,* edited by Paul Singer. Petrópolis, Brazil: Editora Vozes, 1980.

Nascimento, Abdias do. *O Genocídio do negro Brasileiro.* Rio de Janeiro: Paz e Terra, 1978.

Nascimento, Abdias do. *O negro revoltado.* Rio de Janeiro: Editora Vozes, 1982.

Nascimento, Abdias do. *O Brasil na mira do Pan-Africanismo.* (Segunda edição das obras "O Genocídio do Negro Brasileiro e Sitiado em Lagos".) Salvador: EDUFBA/CEAO, 2002.

FLÁVIO GOMES (2005)

NASCIMENTO, EDSON ARANTES DO

See Pelé (Nascimento, Edson Arantes do)

NASH, DIANE

MAY 15, 1938

▮▮▮————————————————————

Civil rights activist Diane Bevel Nash was born in Chicago. She was raised in a middle-class Roman Catholic household and attended Howard University in Washington, D.C. In 1959 she transferred to Fisk University in Nashville, Tennessee, majoring in English. In Nashville she was confronted by rigid racial segregation for the first time in her life, and later that year she joined with other students from local colleges to organize protests against racism and segregation. She also began to attend nonviolence workshops led by James Lawson, a student of Mahatma Gandhi's theories of nonviolent resistance. Skeptical at first, Nash found the concept of moral resistance highly compatible with her strong religious beliefs and came to embrace nonviolence as a way of life.

Nash was elected chairperson of the Student Central Committee and was one of the key participants in sit-ins in local department stores in Nashville that began in February 1960. Nash's picture was printed in the local newspaper and she was often quoted as the spokesperson for the emerging student movement. She gained more celebrity when she confronted Nashville's mayor, Ben West, during a protest demonstration and forced him to admit that he felt local lunch counters should be desegregated.

In April 1960 Nash was one of the founding members of the Student Nonviolent Coordinating Committee (SNCC) in Raleigh, North Carolina. In February 1961 she and a group of ten other students were arrested in Rock Hill, South Carolina, for civil rights activities and refused the opportunity for bail. Their actions dramatized racial injustice, popularized the plight of African Americans in the South, and set a precedent of "jail, no bail" that was followed by many other activists during the civil rights movement.

In May 1961 SNCC activists recommenced Freedom Rides, after the violent southern white response to the initial Freedom Rides led the Congress of Racial Equality (CORE) to discontinue them. Leaving Fisk to devote herself full-time to the movement, Nash played a pivotal role as coordinator of the SNCC Freedom Rides, serving as liaison with governmental officials and the press. Later that year she was appointed head of direct action in SNCC, married James Bevel, a fellow civil rights activist, and moved to Jackson, Mississippi, where she continued her commitment to social activism. (She adopted her husband's last name as her middle name.) In August 1962 Nash and Bevel moved to Georgia and both became involved in the Southern Christian Leadership Conference (SCLC).

The couple proved to be a highly effective organizing team and played an integral role in organizing many SCLC campaigns including the 1964–1965 Selma voting rights campaign. In 1965 they were awarded the Rosa Parks Award from SCLC for their commitment to achieving social justice through nonviolent direct action.

Diane Nash's prominent role in the student sit-in movement made her one of the few well-known female activists of the civil rights movement. She has maintained an unwavering commitment to black empowerment and over the years has broadened the scope of her activism to include antiwar protest and issues of economic injustice. Now divorced, Nash has remained politically active in the 1980s and 1990s, living and teaching in Chicago, doing tenant organizing and advocating housing reform. In 2004 she and other sit-in leaders were invited back to Nashville for the dedication of the Civil Rights Room at the new Nashville Public Library.

See also Congress of Racial Equality (CORE); Southern Christian Leadership Conference (SCLC); Student Nonviolent Coordinating Committee (SNCC)

■■ *Bibliography*

Branch, Taylor. *Parting the Waters: America in the King Years, 1954–63.* New York: Simon and Schuster, 1988.

Clayborne, Carson. *In Struggle: SNCC and the Black Awakening of the 1960s.* Cambridge, Mass.: Harvard University Press, 1981.

Powledge, Fred. *Free At Last?: The Civil Rights Movement and the People Who Made It.* Boston: Little, Brown, 1991.

LYDIA MCNEILL (1996)
ROBYN SPENCER (1996)
Updated by publisher 2005

NASH, WILLIAM BEVERLY

C. 1822
JANUARY 19, 1888

▌▐▌

Virginia-born slave and later politician William Nash, commonly known as Beverly, was brought at age thirteen to Columbia, South Carolina. Little is known of his early life except that before the Civil War he worked at Hunt's Hotel in Columbia and apparently held many jobs there, including work as a bootblack, porter, and waiter. At the hotel he learned to read; through his master, local politician W. C. Preston, and the clientele of the hotel, he was exposed to politics. In addition, it is possible that Nash may have been able to earn enough from tips or from doing extra work for money to buy his freedom. In his hotel work Nash acquired a veneer of gentility and social grace that would be advantageous in his political career.

During Reconstruction Nash was a grocer and became active in the Republican Party. In 1865 he represented Columbia in the South Carolina all-black convention convened to overturn the repressive black codes. He gained statewide prominence in 1866 when he criticized the Freedmen's Bureau's policy toward inland South Carolina and its alleged favoritism of the coastal regions. In 1867 he gained his first official political appointment when he was named a magistrate for Columbia. Nash was also a delegate to the National Freedmen's Convention in 1867 in Washington, D.C., where he campaigned for a universal male suffrage plan without property or literacy qualifications. In 1868 he was elected to the state senate. To achieve a more equitable land distribution, he proposed that large plantations be taxed heavily, which would force landowners to sell property in parcels, thereby creating small farms that blacks and poor whites could afford. He also favored a law mandating schooling for all children. Essentially moderate in his policies, Nash opposed confiscation of the land of former Confederates, arguing that that power did not belong to the state.

Even though he was a Republican, Nash socialized and conducted business deals with prominent South Car-

olinians, many of them white Democrats. He made wide use of his contacts both in honorable and questionable transactions. In 1869 he and an associate bribed the land commissioner to resign so that an African American could take his post. Three years later, when railroad barons proposed that the state purchase a half-completed railroad, Nash accepted a $5,000 bribe in return for an affirmative vote in the South Carolina Senate. The following year, Nash and two friends bought a brickyard and Nash persuaded the state senate to buy bricks from the yard for a new penitentiary. In 1877, as Reconstruction was ending and southern blacks were forced from positions of power, insurgent white Democrats threatened to expose his role in government graft. Nash resigned his position, paying back the money he had misappropriated. He continued his business, particularly real estate, but never again held public office. He died in Columbia in 1888.

See also Bureau of Refugees, Freedmen, and Abandoned Lands; Politics in the United States

■ ■ *Bibliography*

Foner, Eric. *Freedom's Lawmakers: A Directory of Black Office-holders During Reconstruction.* New York: Oxford University Press, 1993.

Williamson, Joel. *After Slavery: The Negro in South Carolina During Reconstruction, 1861–1877.* Chapel Hill: University of North Carolina Press, 1965.

ALANA J. ERICKSON (1996)

NATIONAL AFRO-AMERICAN LEAGUE/ AFRO-AMERICAN COUNCIL

▌▐▌

In 1887 *New York Age* editor T. Thomas Fortune wrote editorials calling for the formation of a National Afro-American League. He planned for the league to seek the elimination of disfranchisement, lynching, segregation on railroads and in public accommodations, and abuse of black prisoners. Although Fortune aimed most of his attacks at the segregated South, he also addressed discrimination in the North. He helped establish local league branches in New England, New York, Pennsylvania, and California.

The first convention of the league as a national organization, consisting of local branches from the South as well as the North, took place in Chicago in 1890. The convention, which consisted entirely of African-American delegates, adopted a constitution pledging to fight racial injustice by influencing popular opinion through the press and by obtaining favorable decisions from the courts. Although Fortune was temporary chairman of the convention, the delegates did not elect him president, in part because Fortune's distrust of political activity angered some delegates to the convention. Instead, the delegates chose North Carolina educator and clergyman Joseph C. Price as president and made Fortune the league's secretary.

The league was short-lived, however, because of the inability of local branches to support themselves financially. The second convention in Knoxville in 1891 attracted far fewer delegates than the first. Although this convention elevated Fortune to the presidency, he did not have the funds to pursue a test case against railroad segregation as he had planned. By 1893 Fortune was forced to admit the bankruptcy and imminent dissolution of the league.

Yet the persistence of lynching and disenfranchisement throughout the late 1890s gave impetus to a drive to restore the league. Fortune and Bishop Alexander Walters of the African Methodist Episcopal Zion Church revived the organization as the Afro-American Council on September 15, 1898, in Rochester, New York. At the time of its founding the council was the largest organization of national African-American leaders in the nation. At the council's second meeting in December 1898, Bishop Walters became the council's first president, Fortune the first chairman. Walters attacked Booker T. Washington's accommodationist approach to race relations, while Fortune attacked President William McKinley for failing to publicly oppose racial violence. Despite Walters's attacks, Washington, who was extremely influential in the council, was able to have most of the important positions filled with his loyal followers. Fortune depended on Washington for political favors and the financing of the *New York Age*.

Washington did not openly oppose the council when it condemned segregation and lynching, and he joined the council in supporting President Theodore Roosevelt for being receptive to African-American concerns. Yet Washington did oppose other council proposals made under Walters's leadership; among these was an 1898 council motion that called for states that disfranchised blacks to have their congressional representation curtailed. Washington made efforts to have Walters replaced by Fortune as council president, and achieved this in 1902.

Fortune resigned from the council in 1904 in order to give more time and financial support to the *New York Age*. The council declined briefly as a result of Fortune's departure, but the next year Bishop Walters, with some

support from Washington, revitalized the council as its new president. However, by 1907 Walters began to associate with members of W. E. B. Du Bois's Niagara Movement, and Washington withdrew his influence and support from the council. In 1908 Walters officially joined the Niagara Movement, and in 1909 he joined the fledgling National Association for the Advancement of Colored People (NAACP). With Washington's abandonment of the council, the nervous collapse of Fortune in 1907, and the emerging alliance of Walters with Du Bois, the council became moribund by 1908.

See also Fortune, T. Thomas; National Association for the Advancement of Colored People (NAACP); Niagara Movement; Washington, Booker T.

■ ■ *Bibliography*

Harlan, Louis R. *Booker T. Washington: The Wizard of Tuskegee, 1901–1915.* New York: Oxford University Press, 1983.

Thornbrough, Emma Lou. "The National Afro-American League, 1887–1908." *Journal of Southern History* 37 (November 1961): 494–512.

Thornbrough, Emma Lou. *T. Thomas Fortune, Militant Journalist.* Chicago: University of Chicago Press, 1972.

DURAHN TAYLOR (1996)

NATIONAL ASSOCIATION FOR THE ADVANCEMENT OF COLORED PEOPLE (NAACP)

❚❚❚

Since its organization in 1909, the National Association for the Advancement of Colored People (NAACP) has been the premier civil rights organization in the United States. It has been in the forefront of numerous successful campaigns on behalf of African-American rights, from the effort to suppress lynching to the long struggle to overturn legal segregation and the still-ongoing effort to secure the implementation of racial justice. The growth and evolution of the NAACP mirrors the growth of African-American political power and the vigorous debates this process engendered.

FOUNDING AND EARLY DAYS

The NAACP owes its origins to the coalescence of two political movements of the early twentieth century. The early years of the century saw the emergence of a group of black intellectuals opposed to the accommodationism of Booker T. Washington. While William Monroe Trotter was the first important figure to break with Washington, he was temperamentally unsuited to the uniting of political forces, and it was W. E. B. Du Bois who soon came to be the most prominent black figure among the anti-Bookerites, as Washington's opponents were called. At the same time there was a revival of political agitation by a small group of white "neo-abolitionists," many of them descended from those who had led the antebellum fight against slavery and who were increasingly distressed by the deterioration in the legal rights and social status of African Americans.

The Niagara Movement, formed by Du Bois, Trotter, and twenty-eight other African-American men at a conference on the Canadian side of Niagara Falls in August 1905, was the organized expression of anti-Bookerite sentiment. The movement was forthright in its opposition to Washingtonian accommodationism and in its commitment to civil equality. At a 1906 meeting of the organization at Harpers Ferry, West Virginia, the site of John Brown's Raid, the organization declared:

> We shall not be satisfied with less than full manhood rights . . . We claim for ourselves every right that belongs to a free-born American — political, civil, and social — and until we get these rights, we shall never cease to protest and assail the ears of America with the story of its shameful deeds toward us.

Despite its oratory, the Niagara Movement was loosely organized and poorly funded and was largely ineffective as a national civil rights organization during its brief history. Weakened by internal controversy and hounded by members of Washington's extensive and effective network in the black community (the "Tuskegee Machine"), the Niagara Movement's existence was tentative and brief. After its dissolution, many of its active members joined the NAACP.

The catalyst for the founding of the NAACP was a violent race riot in 1908 in Springfield, Illinois, Abraham Lincoln's hometown. William English Walling (1877–1936), a white socialist and labor activist, graphically described the violence he had witnessed in an article in *The Independent*. Walling invoked the spirit of Lincoln and the abolitionist Elijah Lovejoy in a call for citizens to come to the assistance of blacks and to fight for racial equality.

Walling's article was read by Mary White Ovington (1865–1951), a white journalist and social worker from a well-to-do abolitionist family who worked and lived in a black tenement in New York, doing research for her landmark sociological work *Half a Man: The Status of the Negro in New York* (1911). She responded to his plea and invited Dr. Henry Moskowitz (1879-1936), a labor reformer and social worker among New York immigrants, to join her in meeting with Walling in his New York apartment to discuss the "Negro Question." The three were the principal founders of the NAACP. Two other members of the core group were Charles Edward Russell (1860-1941), another socialist whose father had been the abolitionist editor of a small newspaper in Iowa, and Oswald Garrison Villard (1872–1949), grandson of the abolitionist William Lloyd Garrison and publisher of the liberal *New York Evening Post* journal and later the *Nation*.

Ovington also invited two prominent black New York clergymen, Bishop Alexander Walters of the African Methodist Episcopal Zion Church, a former president of the National Afro-American Council, and the Rev. William Henry Brooks, minister of Mark's Methodist Episcopal Church, to join the continuing discussions. The expanded group agreed to issue a call on February 12, 1909, for a conference in New York.

Written by Villard, the call reflected the Niagara Movement's platform and emphasized protection of the civil and political rights of African Americans guaranteed under the Fourteenth and Fifteenth Amendments. Of the sixty people signing the call, seven were black: Professor William L. Bulkley, a New York school principal; Du Bois; the Rev. Francis J. Grimké of Washington, D.C.; Mary Church Terrell of Washington, D.C.; Dr. J. Milton Waldron of Washington, D.C.; Bishop Walters; and Ida B. Wells-Barnett.

The founders' overriding concern was guaranteeing true equality to all citizens. They demanded all rights "which underlie our American institutions and are guaranteed by our Constitution"—legal, educational, and political—as well as an end to all forms of segregation and intimidation. The organization was founded as a small elite group that would rely primarily on agitation and legal battles rather than mass action against racial discrimination.

As a result of the call, the National Negro Conference met at the Charity Organization Hall in New York City on May 31 and June 1, 1909. The conference created the National Negro Committee (also known as the Committee of Forty on Permanent Organization and initially known as the National Committee for the Advancement of the Negro) to develop plans for an effective organization. The committee's plans were implemented a year later at a second meeting in New York, when the organization's permanent name was adopted. The organization chose to include the phrase "colored people" in its title to emphasize the broad and anti-imperialist concerns of its founders, and not to limit the scope of the organization to the United States. The NAACP's structure and mission inspired the formation of several other civil rights groups, such as South Africa's African National Congress, formed in 1912.

The NAACP's organizers created a formal institutional structure headed by an executive committee composed largely of members of the Committee of Forty. While Du Bois and a handful of other black men, largely moderates, were included, black women—notably Ida B. Wells-Barnett—were excluded from the committee. Kathryn Johnson served as field secretary from 1910 through 1916 (on a volunteer basis for the first four years), becoming the first of many black women to serve in that position; but black women were not offered leadership roles in the NAACP for several decades. Moorfield Storey (1845–1929), a former secretary to antislavery senator Charles Sumner, and one of the country's foremost constitutional lawyers, was named the organization's president. In addition to Storey and Du Bois, the only black and only salaried staffer, its first officers were Walling, chairman; John E. Milholland, treasurer; Villard, assistant treasurer; and Ovington, secretary. In addition to their official positions, Villard and Ovington were the principal organizers, providing direction and ideas. Francis Blascoer served as national secretary (becoming the second salaried staffer) from February 1910 to March 1911, when Ovington resumed the position pro bono for a year. May Childs Nerney took over the position in 1912.

Soon after the 1910 conference, the NAACP established an office at 20 Vesey St. in New York City (it moved to its longtime home of 70 Fifth Ave. a few years later). In its first year, it launched programs to increase job opportunities for blacks, and to obtain greater protection for them in the South by crusading against lynching and other forms of violence.

The organization's most important act that year was hiring Du Bois as director of publications and research. Du Bois's visionary ideas and militant program were his primary contributions to the NAACP. His hiring signaled the final demise of the Niagara Movement; while Du Bois brought its central vision to the new organization, the NAACP had better funding and a much more well-defined structure and program than the Niagara Movement.

In November 1910, Du Bois launched *The Crisis* as the NAACP's official organ. *The Crisis* soon became the principal philosophical instrument of the black freedom struggle. From an initial publication of 1,000 copies in November 1910, the magazine's circulation increased to 100,000 a month in 1918. In its pages, Du Bois exposed and protested the scourge of racial oppression in order to educate both his black and white audiences on the nature of the struggle and to instill pride in his people. *The Crisis* was not only known for political articles; in its pages Du Bois introduced works by African-American writers, poets, and artists.

Following the report of a Committee on Program headed by Villard, the NAACP was incorporated in New York on June 20, 1911. The organizers invested overall control in a board of directors, which replaced the executive committee. Moorfield Storey remained as president, while Villard succeeded Walling as chairman of the board of directors. The chairman of the board, rather than the president, was designated the most powerful officer in the organization, because Storey had a highly successful practice in Boston and was unable to devote much attention to the NAACP.

The executive committee centralized control of the organization in a national body, to which memberships belonged; it decentralized other significant aspects of the organization's work through local groups called vigilance committees, which became its branches. To ensure that the movement spread as quickly as possible, the committee authorized mass meetings in Chicago, Cleveland, and Buffalo.

The first local NAACP branch was organized in New York in January 1911. Joel E. Spingarn, former chair of the department of comparative literature at Columbia University, became the branch's first president. His brother Arthur, a lawyer, also became active in the branch. The following year, branches were created in Boston, Baltimore, Detroit, Indianapolis, St. Louis, and Quincy, Illinois. In 1913, other branch offices were created in Chicago, Kansas City, Tacoma, Washington, and Washington, D.C. Membership in the organization was contingent upon acceptance of NAACP philosophy and programs.

While the local branches were largely staffed by African Americans, the national NAACP was a largely white group during its early days. Whites had the financial resources to devote themselves to NAACP work; throughout the NAACP's early days, all of the board members contributed a considerable amount of time to the organization. Arthur Spingarn, for example, estimated that he devoted "half and probably more" of his time to the NAACP. Also, whites had the education, the administrative experience, and the access to money that were required to build the organization. For example, Villard initially provided office space for the NAACP in his *New York Post* building. He also gave his personal funds to save the infant organization from imminent collapse. Joel Spingarn paid for his own travel from city to city, soliciting memberships and funds during what were called the New Abolition tours. While he did not make sizable personal contributions to the organization until 1919, Spingarn's knowledge of the management of stocks and bonds also enabled him to direct the organization's financial policies. Furthermore, he donated funds to establish the annual Spingarn Medal, first awarded in 1915, which rapidly became the most prestigious African-American award.

Despite essential contributions of white activists, blacks were increasingly uneasy about white control of an organization that was meant for African Americans. Those differences had surfaced at the founding conference, when Ida B. Wells-Barnett openly expressed concern over the leading roles that whites were playing in the movement. She and William Monroe Trotter shied away from involvement in the new organization because of its domination by whites. Black resentment about white control was manifested in the frequent clashes between Du Bois and Villard, two prickly and irreconcilable personalities.

Du Bois especially resented the intrusion of whites into the editorial affairs of *The Crisis*, which he maintained as an independent, self-supporting magazine. While it remained part of the NAACP, it had its own staff of eight to ten people (led by business manager Augustus Dill, one of the NAACP's few black staff members). Many whites, including Villard, felt that *The Crisis* did not report NAACP news sufficiently. They maintained that Du Bois's often acerbic denunciations of whites were inflammatory and said his editorial style was propagandistic and unbalanced, since he refused to cover negative topics, such as black crime.

In 1914, following clashes with Du Bois, Villard resigned as chairman of the board, and Joel Spingarn succeeded him. Even after Villard's departure, the issue of white control continued, and it caused considerable conflict between Du Bois and Spingarn, his long-time friend. Though, as Du Bois admitted, his haughty personality contributed to the problem, he also interpreted his role within a racial context and felt that he could not accept even the appearance of inferiority or subservience to whites without betraying the race ideals for which he stood. Spingarn felt strongly that Du Bois devoted too much time to lecturing and writing at the expense of association work, but he and Ovington sided with Du Bois in board matters. After Ovington, a long-time ally and supporter, became NAACP chair in 1919, she too became a severe critic of Du Bois's refusal to follow board policy, though she accepted his independence in management of *The Crisis*.

The problem of white domination led to frank discussion about whether whites should continue in top-level positions in the NAACP. While Du Bois challenged any sign of black subordination, he feared that whites would refuse to aid a black-dominated organization and that it would compromise the NAACP's integrationist program. Spingarn and Ovington both acknowledged the difficulties inherent in white leadership, but felt it was a necessary evil until blacks had sufficient resources to run organizations without assistance.

In 1916 Mae Nerney resigned her post as secretary. She recommended that the board choose a black person to succeed her, but the board chose a white man, Roy Nash. It could not, however, escape the pressure to hire another black executive, so it chose James Weldon Johnson, a writer for the *New York Age* and a highly respected man of letters, as field secretary later that year.

Several events in the NAACP's first years combined to define and unite the fledgling organization. The first was the NAACP's ten-year protest campaign for the withdrawal of the film *The Birth of a Nation*, beginning in 1915. The film, directed by D. W. Griffith, featured racist portrayals of blacks. The NAACP charged that the film "assassinated" the character of black Americans and undermined the very basis of the struggle for racial equality. The organization arranged pickets of movie theaters and lobbied local governments to ban showings of the film. The NAACP branches succeeded in leading thousands of blacks in protests and forced the withdrawal of the film from several cities and states. The struggle provided important evidence that African Americans would display opposition to racist images and actions.

Upon the death of Booker T. Washington in 1915, the NAACP reached another turning point. With the end of effective opposition by those who preferred accommodation with the South's Jim Crow policies, *The Crisis*, under Du Bois's leadership, became the leading principal instrument of black opinion. As leadership passed from Washington to the militant "race men" of the North, the NAACP fully established itself as the primary black organization. Consolidating the NAACP's power, in 1916 Du Bois initiated a conference of black leaders, including Washington's men, and their friends. This was the first Amenia conference, which was held at Joel Spingarn's Troutbeck estate at Amenia, north of New York City. The fifty or so participants adopted resolutions that were aimed at breaching the division between the Washington group and the NAACP. The conference participants endorsed all forms of education for African Americans — not just the type of industrial schooling that Washington had advocated; recognized complete political freedom as essential for the development of blacks; agreed that organization and a practical working understanding among race leaders was necessary for development; urged that old controversies, suspicions, and factional alignments be eliminated; and suggested that there was a special need for understanding between leaders in the South and in the North. Du Bois reiterated the African-American demand for full equality and political power.

World War I and related events combined to set the NAACP on its primary mission, a two-pronged legal and political course against racial violence. During the war, Du Bois instituted a controversial policy of black support for American military efforts, with the goal of greater recognition for civil rights afterward. However, the migration of southern blacks to northern urban areas during and after the war led to racial tension, and the clash between increasingly assertive blacks, and whites who refused to countenance changes in the racial status quo, led to violent riots, particularly during the postwar Red Summer of 1919.

Security of person was the most pressing problem that blacks faced, since the taking of a person's life by mob action violated the most basic constitutional right. At first, the NAACP's primary strategy against lynching involved a publicity campaign backed by pamphlets, in-depth studies, and other educational activities to mobilize public support for ending the crime. From its earliest years, the NAACP devoted most of its resources to seeking an end to lynchings and other forms of mob violence; the organization's protest campaign after a lynching in Coatesville, Pennsylvania, in 1911 resulted in its first substantial publicity. In 1917 it led the celebrated silent protest parade of 15,000 people through Harlem with muffled drums to protest the violent riots that year against blacks in East St. Louis, Illinois, and discrimination in general.

The strengthening of the branch structure heightened NAACP influence. As field secretary, James Weldon Johnson was charged with organizing branches, which carried out most of the organization's protest activity. Johnson's most immediate challenge was to increase significantly the number of NAACP branches in the South, a mission that exposed him to the dangers of Jim Crow in the region. Johnson began by organizing a branch in Richmond, Virginia, in 1917. Initially, his progress was slow, but by the end of 1919, the NAACP had 310 branches, including 31 in the South. The Atlanta branch, founded in late 1916, had become one of the organization's strongest, with a membership of more than 1,000. The NAACP's total membership jumped from 9,282 in 1917 to 91,203 in 1919.

In 1921 Johnson became NAACP secretary, establishing the permanent line of blacks to hold the position.

Johnson's assumption of this power reflected the clearer administrative lines that were developing within the NAACP, and signaled the rising influence of paid African-American staff members within the organization. Johnson's predecessor, John Shillady, hired in 1918, had served as the first professional secretary. Shillady assumed responsibility for fund-raising, coordinating the branches, and developing the strategy for implementing the organization's programs. Johnson worked even harder to further the organization's goals. The NAACP strengthened its executive staff in 1922 when it hired Herbert J. Seligman as its first full-time director of publicity. Johnson was succeeded as field secretary by Dr. William A. Pickens, who later served as director of branches until 1942.

THE "NEW NEGRO" ERA

Despite its promising beginnings, by 1919 it was clear that the NAACP's reliance on agitation and education had proved largely ineffective against racial violence. The most promising avenue of redress was by political challenge. Walter White, a young insurance salesman from Atlanta whom Johnson met during an organizing trip, and who joined the national staff in 1918, was named assistant secretary with responsibility for investigating lynchings. White's effectiveness with this mission—in part because as a very light-skinned African American he could blend into white mobs—won him national respect.

In 1919, the NAACP published its report *Thirty Years of Lynching in the United States, 1889-1918*. The book provided documentation for the campaign against the crime that White was leading. A resurgence of violence helped the NAACP to get the Republican party during the 1920 campaign to urge Congress "to consider the most effective means to end lynching." Two years later, through Johnson's extraordinary effort, the House passed an antilynching bill introduced by Congressman L. C. Dyer of Missouri, but Southerners in the Senate killed the Dyer Bill with a filibuster.

Even though Congress failed to pass antilynching legislation during the Coolidge and Hoover administrations, the Republican party's repeated pledge in 1924 to seek such a law was a strong indication that the NAACP's political emphasis held considerable promise. During the administration of Franklin D. Roosevelt the NAACP continued pressing for the passage of antilynching laws in Congress. Two more bills were introduced in this period, but one died in the House of Representatives and the other in the Senate. Congress never passed an antilynching law, but the NAACP eventually helped end the crime through publicity.

Led by Du Bois, the NAACP continued to extend its influence abroad. In 1919, with NAACP support, Du Bois organized the first of a series of Pan-African Congresses in Paris, as the most effective means for demanding the removal of colonial shackles in Africa, India, the West Indies, and all other such territories. The following year, the NAACP expanded its international program by sending Johnson to Haiti to investigate the U.S. occupation of the country. After spending six weeks there, Johnson conducted an extensive campaign in the United States to get both the president and Congress to take action to protect the sovereignty of Haiti and the rights of its citizens. Although his effort was not immediately fruitful, Johnson brought to national attention the occupation and the discriminatory treatment of persons of African descent by American troops in Haiti.

Despite its preeminent position in the black community, the NAACP was not without its critics during the 1920s. Proponents of radical protest, such as A. Philip Randolph and Chandler Owen of the journal *The Messenger* criticized the NAACP for excessive emphasis on legalism, claiming the organization should support self-defense efforts against racial violence. Furthermore, the NAACP engaged in a strong rivalry with Marcus Garvey and his Universal Negro Improvement Association. Garvey scorned the NAACP's interracial, integrationist philosophy and its predominantly light-skinned, middle-class black leadership. The NAACP, meanwhile, opposed Garvey's Back-to-Africa movement as chauvinist and overly visionary and because it rejected integration and espoused separatism. Du Bois called Garvey "the most dangerous man in America," while Robert Bagnall, the NAACP's director of branches, said that Garvey was "insane" and collaborated with United States government officials in their successful attempt to deport Garvey.

Under James Weldon Johnson's leadership, the NAACP became a recognized power in the United States during the 1920s. In 1930 Johnson, who had taken a year's leave of absence to devote his time to creative writing, retired from the NAACP, and Walter White was appointed secretary. White, in turn, hired Roy Wilkins, a former managing editor of the *Kansas City Call*, as his assistant.

The NAACP began the 1930s with 325 branches, which were located in every state of the Union except Maine, New Hampshire, Vermont, Idaho, and North Dakota. The association's branch work was now directed by two field secretaries, Dr. William Pickens and Daisy E. Lampkin. The branches served as information bureaus for the national office and stimulated the cultural life of African Americans. In addition to the field staff, the national officers visited them regularly, led conferences, did intense organizational work, and solicited financial support as well as regular and life memberships. The broad organizational independence of the branches enabled them to put together actions, such as mass demonstrations, that differed strongly from national office policy.

The NAACP's influence was demonstrated by Walter White's successful campaign in 1930 to defeat President Herbert Hoover's nomination of Judge John J. Parker to the U.S. Supreme Court. Parker was from North Carolina and had previously, as a gubernatorial candidate, spoken against black suffrage. While he had opposition from labor unions and other groups, the NAACP was effective in forming coalitions and lobbying senators against Parker's confirmation. Parker's defeat, after a close vote, was a dramatic accomplishment for the NAACP, and widespread denunciation of the organization by white Southerners after the battle reinforced its stature as a formidable political force.

THE NAACP LEGAL CAMPAIGN

Well before it had launched its political efforts, the NAACP had begun using the courts to improve the status of blacks. The scarcity of good black lawyers during the organization's early years made it crucial for whites to dedicate their services to the organization. The NAACP engaged lawyers to conduct its legal work as the need arose and when funds permitted. Because of this inability to fund a legal program, Arthur Spingarn and his law partner Charles H. Studin, along with Moorfield Storey, volunteered their legal services. Arthur Spingarn assumed leadership of this program in 1929.

The NAACP's first significant court action was the legal struggle to save the life of Pink Franklin, an illiterate farmhand in South Carolina, which led the NAACP to establish a legal redress department in 1910. Franklin had been sentenced to death for killing a law officer attempting to arrest him for leaving his employer after he had received advances on his wages. This case was noteworthy because it forced the U.S. Supreme Court, which for some time had been evading all questions relating to the citizenship rights of African Americans, to rule on whether serfdom could be legally established in the country. While the Court affirmed the decision of the lower courts, the NAACP got the South Carolina governor to commute Franklin's sentence to life imprisonment.

An important victory came in 1915, when Storey wrote an amicus curiae brief of the NAACP in *Guinn v. United States*, challenging the constitutionality of the Oklahoma "grandfather clause." The U.S. Supreme Court ruled that the clause violated the Fifteenth Amendment, giving the NAACP its first legal victory and incentive to seek further redress of civil rights cases.

Through the early part of the century, the NAACP won other significant cases. In 1917 the NAACP struck a strong, though not final, blow against residential segregation when the U.S. Supreme Court ruled in *Buchanan v. Warley* that the Louisville, Kentucky, residential segregation ordinance was unconstitutional. The case resulted in the striking down of mandatory housing segregation in Norfolk, Baltimore, St. Louis, and other cities. In 1919, the NAACP conducted an investigation of the convictions of twelve black Elaine, Arkansas, farmers arrested during a riot in 1919 and sentenced to death, and took their case to the U.S. Supreme Court. The Court threw out the convictions in *Moore v. Dempsey* (1923), ruling that the trial had been dominated by a mob atmosphere. In 1935, in the Court's ruling in *Hollins v. Oklahoma*, the NAACP won the reversal of two death penalty convictions due to racial discrimination in jury selection.

Aside from opposition to lynching, the NAACP's primary fight in the 1920s continued to be against racial injustices in the courts, and it handled hundreds of civil rights cases. It considered its task of educating the public, both white and black, about racial wrongs to be an even greater challenge than resolving specific problems. Thus, it had two criteria for accepting a case: first, whether it involved discrimination and injustice based on race or color; second, whether it would establish a precedent for protecting the rights of African Americans as a group. The case of Dr. Ossian Sweet of Detroit met those criteria. In 1925, Sweet moved his family into a house he had purchased in a middle-class white neighborhood. The house was surrounded by a white mob. Sweet shot at the mob in self-defense, and killed one of its members. The NAACP hired Clarence Darrow, the greatest trial lawyer of the day, and he successfully defended Sweet.

One notable area of NAACP interest was the "White Primary," which effectively disfranchised southern blacks. In 1927, the Supreme Court declared in a unanimous decision in *Nixon v. Herndon* that a Texas state primary law that excluded blacks from voting was unconstitutional. Soon afterward, a special session of the Texas legislature passed a new statute authorizing the Democratic state committee to make its own decisions on the eligibility of voters in party primaries. The NAACP appealed, and in 1932 the Supreme Court ruled in *Nixon v. Condon* that the Fourteenth Amendment forbade such distinctions. (Despite NAACP efforts, however, in 1935, the U.S. Supreme Court ruled in *Grovey v. Townshend* that a party was a private body and could exclude blacks from primary elections; the white primary was finally struck down in 1944.)

Such victories led the NAACP to declare after 1932 that "for the present, the avenue of affirmation and defense of the Negro's fundamental rights in America lies through the courts." Those, of course, were the Supreme Court and the lower federal courts, which the NAACP regarded as bulwarks in this struggle, because at that level "the atmosphere of sectional prejudice is notably absent." Its legal victories, it concluded, were "clear-cut" and "matters of prominent record."

In 1929, Arthur Spingarn organized the NAACP legal committee, and served as its chair until 1939, when he succeeded his deceased brother Joel as president of the NAACP. The first members of the legal committee included the distinguished labor lawyer Clarence Darrow, Harvard law professor and future U.S. Supreme Court justice Felix Frankfurter; liberal Michigan governor and future U.S. Supreme Court justice Frank Murphy; and American Civil Liberties Union lawyer Arthur Garfield Hays.

Darrow and Hays represented the NAACP in the Sweet case, as well as the Scottsboro case, which involved nine young black men who were convicted of raping two white women on a train passing through Scottsboro, Alabama, in 1931. Eight of the Scottsboro defendants were sentenced to death. The NAACP, which lacked a regular legal department, was unable to move quickly into action, and the International Labor Defense, closely allied with the Communist Party, took control of the case. In 1933 the NAACP, spurred by black community criticism of its inaction on the famous case, formed the Scottsboro Defense Committee in an uneasy alliance with the International Labor Defense. After a series of protracted legal battles, the defendants' lives were saved. (The ILD abandoned the case after it lost publicity value. On November 29, 1976, the NAACP finally won freedom for Clarence Norris, the last of the Scottsboro nine, when the Alabama Board for Pardons and Paroles pardoned him.)

THE NAACP IN THE DEPRESSION

The frustrations of the Scottsboro case were the beginning of a contentious and difficult period for the NAACP. The collapse of the national economy in 1929 brought disproportionate hardship to African Americans. Many blacks hailed the New Deal's programs for economic recovery in the hope that minimum wage, maximum working hours, and other such reforms would benefit blacks. However, early New Deal programs were unable to alter the low social and economic status of the African-American masses; in some cases these worsened their situation. Bitterly disappointed, many intellectuals were attracted by Marxism and other radical philosophies. The communist party and allied groups such as the League of Struggle for Negro

Rights presented themselves in black areas as rivals to the NAACP, whose reformist stance they sought to discredit as inadequate for addressing the economic injustice African Americans were suffering.

Similarly, the Great Depression brought sharp criticisms of the NAACP by a generation of younger intellectuals, and pressure on the organization to make radical shifts in its strategies and programs to meet the needs of impoverished blacks. One of the severest critics was Ralph Bunche, a political scientist at Howard University. Bunche maintained that the NAACP's program of political and civil liberties was doomed to failure unless there was an improvement in the economic condition of the black masses. Bunche was also uncomfortable with having whites in policy-making positions in the NAACP, maintaining that its interracial structure was "an undoubted source of organizational weakness." He felt that the "white sympathizers were in the main either cautious liberals or mawkish, missionary-minded sentimentalists on the race question."

Another important critic was Dr. Abram L. Harris, a Howard University economics professor and member of the NAACP board of directors. Harris insisted that the NAACP launch a more vigorous attack on fundamental economic problems and that the masses of African Americans organized in the local branches play a more significant role in the organization's work. He and Bunche advocated efforts by the NAACP to reach out to white labor unions and secure greater union affiliation for black workers.

The organization did respond to economic discrimination during the early 1930s. For example, in 1931, Helen Boardman, a white NAACP investigator, reported that the 30,000 blacks on the War Department's Mississippi Flood Control project were receiving 10 cents an hour for an 84-hour week. In 1933, Roy Wilkins and George S. Schuyler, a former Socialist and writer for the *Messenger*, disguised themselves as laborers in order to investigate the deplorable, peonage-like conditions under which blacks on the project were working. White officials discovered their identities, and both men barely escaped with their lives. The Wilkins and Schuyler investigations enabled the NAACP to get the Secretary of War to quadruple the hourly pay for unskilled laborers and shorten their work week to thirty hours.

Nevertheless, while the NAACP leaders did not share Bunche's view of the futility of legal efforts, some staffers, notably Du Bois, felt that the NAACP lacked a clear sense of direction. The criticisms convinced younger staffers such as Wilkins that "among the liberals and radicals, both Negro and white, the impression prevails that the Associa-

tion is weak because it has no economic program and no economic philosophy."

In the face of the criticisms, in August 1933 the NAACP held a Second Amenia Conference. This time whites were barred from the assemblage on Joel Spingarn's estate. Among the delegates were several young leaders who would later achieve distinction. Notable were Bunche and Harris; sociologists E. Franklin Frazier and Ira De A. Reid; attorney Louis Redding; Sterling A. Brown, a literary critic and poet; and Juanita Jackson, who with her mother Lillie Mae Jackson in 1935 would begin leading the NAACP struggle to desegregate their home state of Maryland. The major emphasis at the conference was on economics and the need for power among blacks that could make the government more responsive to the demands of their community. The participants were upset by the national NAACP's reluctance to launch a mass movement, in contrast to the efforts of branches such as Baltimore.

There was general agreement on the need for the NAACP to develop the type of comprehensive economic program that the Amenia Conference delegates demanded. Not everyone within the organization, however, subscribed to the young activists' focus on race pride; neither did they initially support their call for greater solidarity between the black and white working class. Walter White, for one, had grave reservations about moving toward a more "mass-oriented" program and felt that many of his colleagues were being "stampeded by temporary or emotional situations and conditions." Nevertheless, in the aftermath of the conference and significant prodding by Joel Spingarn, the NAACP created a Committee on Future Plan and Program in 1935 to consider the concerns raised by the Amenia Conference. The members of the committee were Harris, chairman; Rachel Davis Du Bois; Dr. Louis T. Wright; James Weldon Johnson; Sterling Brown; and Mary White Ovington, who had resigned from the board in 1931 following disagreements with White. The committee reinforced the priority of economic concerns and urged solidarity between black and white workers. It forced the organization to declare that its interests were "inextricably intertwined with those of white workers." The importance of this emphasis was realized with the subsequent creation of the Congress of Industrial Organizations (CIO) which, unlike the American Federation of Labor (AFL), opened its ranks to black workers, and which was closely allied with the NAACP.

White made some modifications in the NAACP's programs to accommodate the economic concerns and activism of the young militants in the late 1930s. For example, the NAACP was one of the twenty-four civil rights and religious organizations supporting the Joint Committee on

National Recovery, a Washington-based economic lobbying and information group founded by Robert C. Weaver and John P. Davis in 1935. Also, the NAACP negotiated with leaders of the CIO on behalf of black automobile workers in Detroit. However, White redoubled the organization's efforts in its traditional areas of education, agitation, and court litigation. More than ever, court action defined the NAACP's identity, while direct action was left to small groups such as the National Negro Congress and the Congress of Racial Equality (CORE), founded in 1942.

As disquieting as most of the criticisms from young radicals were for White, none created anything as near a schism as those offered by Du Bois. He too had grown impatient with the pace of the NAACP's achievements. Openly challenging White and the NAACP, he shifted from his long-held position of urging integration, because that was not achieving racial equality fast enough, and promoted independent black economic development. (One possible factor in Du Bois's 180-degree shift in position from emphasis on integration to tactical segregation was his deep, personal differences with White). Du Bois's stand made his departure from *The Crisis* and the NAACP board inevitable, and he resigned in 1934. Wilkins, in addition to being in charge of the organization's administration, succeeded him as editor of *The Crisis*.

Another significant development was the revamping of the NAACP hierarchy. More and more, the paid staff exercised control of the organization. In effect, White made the executive secretary the association's chief executive officer as well as its chief spokesperson. White was able to effect such changes because the bulk of the organization's strength and finances now came from its vastly expanded branch structure. Despite the severe hardships of the Depression, the branches in 1936 contributed $26,288 toward the total income of $47,724. Most of the remaining income came from contributions, as well as a life membership program that was created in 1927. This pattern of support had been established from around 1920. Between that year and 1931, the NAACP raised $545,407 in general funds, of which $374,896 came from the branches.

The board, as a result, underwent a shift in direction. In 1934, Dr. Louis T. Wright, a physician and Fellow in the American College of Surgeons, was elected as the first in the permanent line of blacks to be chair of the NAACP board. As Charles Hamilton Houston, who was chair of the board revision committee explained, among other things, the changes made the board more representative of the organization's membership. Previously, he said, board meetings were "in substance executive committee meetings." He added, "I favor calling a spade by its name. The board meetings would deal with policies rather than details." While whites remained on the board in diminishing numbers, by mid-1936 the NAACP's organizational revolution was so stark that the NAACP no longer depended on whites for administrative expertise or for the bulk of its fiscal support. Mary White Ovington complained that the board of directors had adopted "the rubber stamp attitude" in sanctioning the staff's actions. She was especially unhappy with Walter White, whom she lamented was virtually "the dictator" of the organization. She complained that the board's discussions had little effect on its actual programs and policies.

Throughout the late 1930s, much of the NAACP's activism was organized by individual branches. For example, in Baltimore, Boston, and elsewhere, NAACP Youth Council leaders formed "don't-buy-where-you-can't-work" boycotts and pickets to protest job discrimination in stores located in black communities. In New Orleans, the NAACP paid residents' poll taxes to fight voting restrictions. In Kansas City, an NAACP-led protest campaign desegregated municipal golf courses. In New York, NAACP officials joined a committee to improve conditions in Harlem after a riot broke out in 1935.

The national NAACP also engaged in several campaigns during the 1930s, lobbying Congress for antilynching legislation and struggling against discrimination in New Deal programs. One important NAACP action was its protest against the Italian invasion of Ethiopia. The organization collected donations for war relief, sent official protests to the League of Nations and U.S. State Department, and lobbied against pro-Italian amendments in the 1935 Neutrality Act. Another important struggle dealt with media stereotypes. NAACP representatives met with newspaper editors to persuade them to offer positive coverage of African Americans and to cease the practice of discussing the race of alleged criminals. The NAACP also launched a campaign to end stereotypes in Hollywood films and radio programs, notably the popular radio series *Amos 'n' Andy*, which the organization claimed presented demeaning stereotypes of blacks. NAACP lobbying helped secure the signing of black performers such as Lena Horne to film studio contracts.

THE LEGAL ASSAULT ON SEGREGATION

To end its dependence on volunteer lawyers, which had proved a large handicap in the Scottsboro case, as well as to wage an all-out fight against segregation, the NAACP in 1935 created its legal department. The creation of the NAACP legal department resulted from a comprehensive study of the association's legal program that Nathan Ross Margold, a white public service lawyer in New York, conducted in 1930 under a grant from the American Fund for

Paul Robeson joins NAACP picket line, Baltimore, Maryland. Acclaimed actor and singer Robeson participates in an NAACP protest in front of Ford's Theatre, objecting to the theatre's policy of racial segregation. Pictured (left to right) are: Ada Jenkins, Paul Robeson, Earl Robinson (Robeson's accompanist), Dr. J. E. T. Camper, Paul Kaufman, Rhoda Peasom, and Dan Atwood. PHOTOGRAPHS AND PRINTS DIVISION, SCHOMBURG CENTER FOR RESEARCH IN BLACK CULTURE, THE NEW YORK PUBLIC LIBRARY, ASTOR, LENOX AND TILDEN FOUNDATIONS.

Public Service (later the Garland Fund). Margold suggested that the NAACP "strike directly at the most prolific sources of discrimination" by boldly challenging "the constitutional validity of segregation if and when accompanied irremediably by discrimination." He recommended, furthermore, that the NAACP focus on the glaring disparities between white and black schools.

The NAACP hired Charles H. Houston, the highly respected dean of Howard University School of Law, as its first special counsel. Walter White was responsible for bringing Houston into the NAACP. White had become very impressed with Houston's brilliant defense in 1932 of George Crawford, an African American who was ac-

cused of murdering two white women in Virginia. Although a jury convicted Crawford and he was sentenced to life in prison, Houston saved him from the death penalty.

Houston diverged from the Margold report by attacking the unequal financial support of black schools in the South. His strategy was to force the states either to strengthen black institutions or to abandon them because it was too expensive to maintain the avowed "separate but equal" practice. In order to accumulate evidence of unequal funding, Houston and his protegé, Thurgood Marshall, toured the South, investigating conditions. Houston also laid the foundations of the NAACP's successful strategy of sociological jurisprudence in the subsequent direct attack on segregation.

Houston's first line of attack was graduate and professional schools. He successfully tested this strategy in the Maryland Supreme Court case *Murray v. Maryland* in 1935, the first of a series of challenges that would lead to the U.S. Supreme Court's landmark *Brown v. Board of Education* decision in 1954. Houston left the NAACP in 1938 to return to private law practice in Washington, and was succeeded by Marshall, a graduate of Howard University Law School who had been working with the Baltimore NAACP branch.

Continuing to attack racial inequalities in education, the NAACP filed its first teacher's discrimination pay case in behalf of William Gibbs against the Montgomery County Board of Education in Maryland. The county was paying Gibbs $612 a year, whereas a white school principal with comparable qualifications was receiving $1,475. In 1938 the court ordered the county to equalize teachers' salaries, setting a precedent for similar NAACP challenges in other parts of the country. The same year, the NAACP won in *Missouri ex rel. Gaines v. Canada*. Chief Justice Charles Evans Hughes said in the Supreme Court's majority opinion that Missouri's offer of tuition aid to Lloyd Gaines to attend an out-of-state university law school did not constitute equal treatment under the Constitution. In 1939, William H. Hastie, a black scholar and federal judge, succeeded Arthur Spingarn as chair of the NAACP Legal Committee. Soon after, the NAACP Legal Defense and Educational Fund was incorporated to receive tax deductible contributions for those areas of the NAACP's work that met the Internal Revenue Service's guidelines. The LDF, dubbed the "Inc. Fund" and headed by Thurgood Marshall, was tied to the parent NAACP by interlocking boards.

As in the earlier years, the NAACP's cases covered four major areas: disfranchisement, segregation ordinances, restrictive covenants and due process, and equal protection for blacks accused of crimes. Among the fundamental victories won before the Supreme Court were *Smith v. Allwright* (1944), in which the all-white Texas Democratic primary was declared unconstitutional; *Morgan v. Virginia* (1946), in which it was declared that state laws requiring segregated travel could not be enforced in interstate travel; and *Shelley v. Kraemer* and *McGhee v. Sipes* (1948), in which it was declared that restrictive housing covenants could not be legally enforced. (Two other cases, *Hurd v. Hodge* and *Urciolo v. Hodge*, were argued with the Kraemer and McGhee cases.)

WORLD WAR II AND POSTWAR PERIODS

The NAACP's legal campaign during the 1940s was reinforced by its efforts at education and lobbying. During World War II, the NAACP made an enormous effort to secure equal treatment for blacks in the military and in war industries. For example, NAACP officials lobbied successfully for a Navy officer training program for African Americans, and investigated reports of discrimination against black GIs; Walter White personally conducted investigations of discrimination complaints in the European and Pacific theaters. White also championed A. Philip Randolph's 1941 March on Washington movement and was an adviser in the creation of the Fair Employment Practices Committee (FEPC). In 1942, NAACP investigators reported on living and working conditions in overcrowded cities, although they were largely ignored. After rioting broke out in Detroit and New York's Harlem in 1943, the NAACP backed interracial committee efforts. In 1944, the NAACP organized a Wartime Conference, in which it recorded its "special stake in the abolition of imperialism," due to the preponderance of people of color in colonized nations. With the aid of such staffers as Ella Baker, director of branches from 1943 through 1946, the NAACP grew from 355 branches and 50,556 members in 1940 to 1,073 branches and some 450,000 members by 1946.

After the end of the war, the NAACP redoubled its efforts to pass antilynching legislation. In the face of rising racial violence, such as an antiblack riot in Columbia, Tennessee, the NAACP called for federal civil rights protection. In 1946, Walter White organized a National Emergency Committee against Mob Violence, and met with President Harry Truman to demand action. In 1947, the NAACP provided financial and logistical support for CORE's Journey of Reconciliation, a series of interracial bus rides to challenge discrimination in interstate travel. Clarence Mitchell Jr., director of the NAACP's Washington Bureau, led the fight for a permanent FEPC, which was realized in the Equal Employment Opportunity Commission, created by the 1964 Civil Rights Act.

An important factor in NAACP progress was the unprecedented support for civil rights shown by President Harry Truman. In fall 1946, in response to demands from the NAACP for presidential leadership on civil rights, Truman appointed the President's Committee on Civil Rights and made Walter White a key adviser to it. The committee's 1947 Report To Secure These Rights further sharpened the focus of the struggle to destroy segregation and grant full equality to African Americans. It closely followed NAACP recommendations for government action against segregation. In 1947 Truman became the first president to attend an NAACP convention when he addressed the organization's thirty-eighth annual convention in Washington.

In 1948, following NAACP pressure, President Truman issued an executive order barring segregation in the armed forces. The NAACP fought over the next years to implement the mandate. This fight was led by Thurgood Marshall, who conducted studies on the progress of military integration during the Korean War; and by Clarence Mitchell, who led the struggle in Washington to get President Eisenhower and the Defense Department to end all forms of segregation at military establishments in the United States and elsewhere.

During the late 1940s, the NAACP considerably strengthened its antidiscrimination programs and strategies. But with the rise of the Cold War and concerns over communism, the NAACP feared that it, too, would become a target for red baiting. To preserve its integrity, the NAACP adopted a strict anticommunist membership policy and avoided any association with the Communist Party. The NAACP, furthermore, strongly opposed loyalty probes among government workers, fully realized that such investigations would make African Americans scapegoats purely on the basis of race. The organization scored a significant victory in this struggle when Frank Barnes, president of the NAACP's Santa Monica branch, was reinstated in his post office job as a result of the NAACP's intensive campaign to clear his name of charges of disloyalty to the United States.

At the same time, the NAACP directed worldwide attention to the problem of colonialism by sending Walter White and W. E. B. Du Bois as its representatives in 1945 to the founding United Nations Conference on International Organization in San Francisco. In 1947 Du Bois dramatically reinforced the NAACP's anticolonial program by presenting to the UN "An Appeal to the World," a 155-page petition composed of five chapters that linked the plight of Africans and other subjects of colonial imperialism with that of African Americans in the United States. The drafting committee of the UN Human Rights Commission debated the petition for two days at a meeting in Geneva.

In 1948 the NAACP continued to express its views on human rights, genocide, and colonialism at the Paris session of the UN General Assembly. That year, the NAACP welcomed the General Assembly's adoption of a Declaration of Human Rights and a Genocide Convention, and regretted that the colonial issue was not promptly settled. The NAACP won considerable support from other nongovernmental agencies for its demand that all colonial territories be placed under UN trusteeship and administered

in a manner that would encourage development of indigenous populations. It strongly opposed attempts to return Somaliland and Eritrea, former colonies in Africa, to Italy or to turn them over to any other nation for administration.

Despite Du Bois's continuing contributions to the NAACP in raising world concern over the plight of the darker races in Africa, Asia, and the Caribbean, strong differences in 1948, caused by his inability to work with Walter White and resulting refusal to follow the organization's administrative procedures, led the NAACP board of directors to refuse to renew his contract. Thus, even though upon Du Bois's return in 1944 as director of special research he remained the symbol of NAACP history, he again left the organization in 1948.

In 1949, Roy Wilkins wrote an editorial in *The Crisis* strongly attacking black activist Paul Robeson, who was accused of pro-Soviet sentiments. In 1950, the NAACP organized a National Emergency Civil Rights Mobilization in Washington to demand passage of civil rights laws. Led by Roy Wilkins, a group of 4,000 delegates representing 100 organizations met with Truman to enlist his support for the struggle in Congress. The mobilization, culminating a decade of NAACP efforts to get Congress to pass fair employment practice and other civil rights laws, signaled the birth of the Leadership Conference on Civil Rights (LCCR).

The core of the NAACP's struggle for the passage of antiviolence and other civil rights laws was waged through its Washington bureau, which was created in 1942, as well as its branches. In addition to being executive secretary, Walter White served as the bureau's first director from its creation until 1950, when he relinquished the position to Clarence Mitchell, who also served as legislative chair of the LCCR. Mitchell's function in developing the organization's political strategy and legislative program was similar to Thurgood Marshall's in the legal area. Both men served in positions that were a notch under the executive secretary.

The most important element in the civil rights struggle, nevertheless, was the NAACP's branches, which provided essential grassroots support and lobbying clout. In 1951, the association had 1,253 branches, youth councils, and college chapters, and a membership of 210,000 which for the first time since 1947 represented an encouraging increase. An indication of the NAACP's strength was that in 1950, for the first time in its history, it held its annual conference in the Deep South in Atlanta. There, 7,500 blacks and whites packed the municipal auditorium to hear Nobel Peace Prize laureate Ralph Bunche, the NAACP's onetime critic. Bunche, by then an NAACP

NAACP headquarters, Detroit, Michigan, c. 1950s. © CORBIS

board member, assailed the "tyranny of the segregation laws of the South" and the failure of Congress to pass civil rights legislation.

Since Southerners in Congress continued to block passage of civil rights laws, the best promise of success lay with the courts, as the NAACP had determined earlier. In 1950, the Supreme Court took decisive steps in two cases brought by the NAACP toward ending the "separate but equal" doctrine. In the first case, *Sweatt v. Painter*, the Court ruled that the separate black law school the state of Texas had established to accommodate Heman Sweatt was not and could not be equal to that provided for white students at the University of Texas. In the second case, *McLaurin v. Oklahoma*, the Supreme Court ruled unanimously that the University of Oklahoma could not segregate G. W. McLaurin within its graduate school once he had been admitted.

Encouraged by the decisions in *Sweatt v. Painter* and *McLaurin v. Oklahoma*, the NAACP in 1951 launched a well-planned "Equality Under Law" campaign to overturn racial separation at its roots — in elementary and secondary schools. This drive was launched with the filing of lawsuits against school districts in Atlanta; Clarendon County, South Carolina; Topeka, Kansas; and Wilmington, Delaware.

In 1953, Dr. Channing H. Tobias, the newly elected chair of the NAACP board of directors, launched a "Fight for Freedom Fund" campaign and a goal of "Free by '63." This slogan was designed to mobilize all of the organization's resources for what the NAACP saw as the final phase of the struggle to eliminate all state-imposed discrimination in celebration of the centennial of Lincoln's Emancipation Proclamation. Reinforcing the climate of great anticipation within the civil rights community, President Eisenhower on May 10 addressed the NAACP's "Freedom

Fulfillment" conference in Washington. He pledged that wherever the federal authority extended he would do his utmost to bring about racial equality. With help from the fund-raising campaign, the NAACP's membership grew to 240,000 by 1954.

On May 17, 1954, the Supreme Court handed down its landmark ruling in the four school desegregation cases that the NAACP had initiated, plus another case challenging segregation in the District of Columbia. Reasserting the full meaning of the Fourteenth Amendment, the court declared in *Brown v. Board of Education* that "in the field of public education the doctrine of 'separate but equal' has no place. Separate educational facilities are inherently unequal." Shortly thereafter, the NAACP won another historic victory, when the Department of Defense reported that as of August 31, 1954, there were "no longer any all-Negro units in the services."

IMPLEMENTING *BROWN*

Less than a year after he had led the celebrations of the school desegregation case victory, Walter White died. He had developed the organization that James Weldon Johnson had passed on to him into the most powerful vehicle of its kind for achieving racial equality. *Brown v. Board of Education* was his crowning achievement as much as it was Thurgood Marshall's. However, in his last years, White was an increasingly embattled figure. His flamboyant style and overinvolvement in outside activities had made him many enemies on the NAACP board, and many African Americans angrily criticized his marriage to a white woman in 1949. That year White took a leave of absence and, upon his return in 1950, the board sharply restricted his policy-making power.

White left a staff of experienced professionals in their prime of productivity; in addition to Wilkins, White had hired Clarence Mitchell as labor secretary, Gloster B. Current as director of branches in 1946, and Henry Lee Moon, a former newspaper reporter, as director of public relations in 1948.

Roy Wilkins, who was elected in April 1955 to succeed White as NAACP executive director, faced enormous challenges. Wilkins's first problem was pressing for the enforcement of the *Brown* decision and for passage of FEPC and other civil rights laws. NAACP lawyers participated in the formation of desegregation plans and monitored compliance with *Brown*. In 1956, under NAACP sponsorship, Autherine Lucy, an African American, won a court ruling admitting her to the University of Alabama. University officials expelled her, however, on the pretext of preventing violence. The NAACP also made its struggle for passage of civil rights laws in Congress a top priority.

At the same time, the organization was forced to expend effort combatting the onslaught that the South had unleashed on the organization. The NAACP's trail-blazing victories in the courts, especially the *Brown* decision, made it a main target of the South's campaign of "massive resistance."

The resurgent Ku Klux Klan figured strongly in the backlash of white violence, but it was not the only threat the NAACP faced from the South. Less than two months after the *Brown* decision was handed down, political leaders, businessmen, and the professional elite organized the White Citizens' Council in Mississippi. Overnight, councils sprang up in other states. Regarded as "manicured kluxism," the White Citizens' Councils used economic and political pressure to prevent implementation of the *Brown* decision. In March 1956, nearly all of the southerners in Congress showed their defiance of *Brown* by signing the "Southern Manifesto," which called the Supreme Court decision "illegal."

Prior to this period, Southerners had targeted individual blacks through lynchings and other forms of violence in their campaign of terror. Now the NAACP was attacked by these groups. On Christmas night of 1951, the home of Harry T. Moore, the NAACP's field secretary in Mims, Florida, was bombed. Moore died in the blast and his wife died a few days later from injuries she received that night. In 1955, NAACP officials the Rev. George W. Lee and Lamar Smith of Belzoni, Mississippi were shot to death, and Gus Courts, president of the Belzoni NAACP branch, was shot, wounded, and later forced to abandon his store and flee to Chicago.

The NAACP charged that racial violence was a manifestation of the broader pattern of opposition to civil rights and demanded that the Justice Department protect blacks in the state and elsewhere in the South. The Justice Department, however, responded that it lacked authority to prosecute suspected murderers and civil rights violaters in what it claimed were state jurisdictions.

Despite the violence, the NAACP continued to grow. The number of branches in Mississippi increased from ten to twenty-one during 1955, while membership jumped 100 percent. The NAACP took several steps to aid local blacks. In December, the NAACP board of directors voted to deposit $20,000 in the Tri-State Bank in Memphis in order to increase the bank's reserves and enable it to make more loans to embattled blacks. The board called for an investigation of the operation in Mississippi of the federal "surplus commodities" program, which provided food to the destitute, to see if it discriminated against blacks. National NAACP officials also pushed for a meeting with the Mississippi Power and Light Company to inquire about cutoffs of power to businessmen active with the NAACP and overcharges for restoration.

In 1956, Louisiana led the South in a more deliberate assault on the NAACP when its attorney general demanded that the association's branches file their membership lists with the state. Because the NAACP refused to do so, the attorney general obtained an injunction barring the organization from operating in Louisiana. Alabama, Texas, and Georgia followed with similar punitive actions. In 1958, the Supreme Court (in *National Association for the Advancement of Colored People v. Alabama ex rel. Patterson*) overturned Alabama's fine of $100,000 against the NAACP because it refused to disclose the names and addresses of its members. But the Court then did not lift the injunction that barred the NAACP from operating in Alabama. Furthermore, the supreme courts in Arkansas and Florida held that the High Court's ruling did not affect those states. Not until June 1, 1964, after four appeals, would the U.S. Supreme Court rule unanimously that the NAACP had a right to register in Alabama as a foreign corporation. The ruling, in effect, overturned similar bans against the NAACP in other southern states and paved the way for it to resume operations in Alabama on October 29.

On January 14, 1963, for the Supreme Court in another significant case (*National Association for the Advancement of Colored People v. Button*) also overturned Virginia's antibarratry law, which was enacted in 1956, prohibiting the NAACP from sponsoring, financing, or providing legal counsel in suits challenging the validity of the state's segregation and other anti-civil rights laws.

One consequence of the southern crusade against the NAACP following the *Brown* decision was the splitting off of the NAACP Legal Defense and Educational Fund, a process that began in 1956 and ended in 1961. The split was caused by threats from the Southerners to rescind the LDF's tax-exempt status, and by personal differences within the NAACP. The LDF made the battle in the courts for school desegregation its main project, while the parent NAACP continued its strategy of legal and political action in numerous forms. Robert Carter, who was on the LDF's staff, was chosen as the NAACP's general counsel and he began setting up a new legal department. Carter led the NAACP's battle against the state injunctions.

The South's response to desegregation made the NAACP intensify its call for President Eisenhower to enforce *Brown*, and to provide the leadership which it regarded as essential for defeating the South's steadfast resistance to the passage of civil rights laws in Congress. NAACP leaders argued that the President's prestige could overwhelm the Southerners' use of committee chairmanships and the filibuster rule in the Senate to bottle up civil rights legislation. Eisenhower, a state's rights advocate, nevertheless supported the NAACP's demand that there should be no discrimination in federally funded programs and in the armed forces; but he was opposed to federal action to enforce *Brown*.

In 1956, responding to the NAACP's demands, election-year domestic considerations, and international pressure, Eisenhower called for civil rights legislation in his State of the Union address. The administration's package became the basis of debate in the bill H.R. 627. Senate Majority Leader Lyndon Baines Johnson of Texas, who believed that passage of some civil rights legislation was inevitable, began maneuvering to shape a compromise on the bill that would blunt its strongest provisions and break the southern filibuster. The civil rights forces were therefore left with what was essentially a weak voting rights law. Still, the 1957 Civil Rights Act created a division of civil rights in the Justice Department and a bipartisan Civil Rights Commission. Furthermore, the Civil Rights Act of 1957, the first such bill passed by Congress in eighty-two years, broke the psychological barrier to civil rights measures, making it easier for future efforts to succeed.

The encouraging breakthrough of the passage of the Civil Rights Act was somewhat overshadowed that September by the Little Rock crisis, in which Governor Orval Faubus used the Arkansas National Guard to block implementation of a federal court desegregation order at Central High School. To uphold the Constitution and end rioting, President Eisenhower federalized the Arkansas National Guard and ordered 1,000 members of the 101st Airborne Division into Little Rock. His action enabled nine black children (the "Little Rock Nine") to attend the school.

THE CIVIL RIGHTS MOVEMENT

The NAACP launched its "Golden Anniversary" celebrations on February 12, 1959, with services at the Community Church of New York City. One of the most promising indications of the organization's future strength was the presence of 624 youths among the 2,000 delegates who packed the New York Coliseum during the annual convention, which concluded with a rally at the Polo Grounds. In December, the NAACP held its third annual Freedom Fund dinner in New York, where it honored Marian Anderson, the celebrated concert singer, and Gardner Cowles, publisher of *Look* magazine. The celebrations revealed the broad acceptance of the NAACP as an institution. However, its mastery was to be challenged in the 1960s by a new generation of more militant activists.

The first sign of the tensions the NAACP would face came in 1955 and 1956, when blacks in Alabama, led by the Rev. Dr. Martin Luther King Jr., organized the Montgomery Improvement Association (MIA) to lead the boycott against segregated city buses. Although the movement was sparked by NAACP legal victories against segregation and the principal leaders of the boycott were also local NAACP leaders, the strategy of nonviolent demonstrations that they adopted was a substantial departure from the association's well-defined legal and political program. Similarly, while NAACP lawyers successfully argued the U.S. Supreme Court case *Gayle v. Browder* (1956), which handed victory to the boycotters, the MIA displayed impatience with the NAACP's carefully structured programs and centralized direction.

Inspired by the tactics of nonviolent protest, NAACP Youth Council chapters in Wichita, Kansas, and Oklahoma City further successfully tested a new confrontation strategy in 1958 by staging "sit-downs" at lunch counters to protest segregation. The protests led to the desegregation of 60 or more lunch counters. In 1959, the NAACP chapter at Washington University in St. Louis conducted sit-ins to end segregation at local lunch counters. The same year, the NAACP hired former CORE activist James Farmer as program director, but he was unable to move the association toward support for mass demonstrations, and he returned to CORE as executive director after less than two years.

As important as the Youth Council demonstrations were, however, they did not capture national media attention because they were not conducted in parts of the United States where racial tensions were highest. On February 1, 1960, four students from North Carolina Agricultural and Technical College sat at a segregated store lunch counter in Greensboro and refused to leave until they were served. Two of the students, Ezell Blair and Joseph McNeil, were former officers of the NAACP's college chapter. The NAACP was heavily involved — the sit-in was conducted in consultation with Dr. George Simpkins, president of the Greensboro NAACP branch, and Ralph Jones, president of the branch's executive committee. The Greensboro actions set the stage for the sit-in movement, which spread like brush fire through the South.

The NAACP declared that it was proud that many of its youth members, from Virginia to Texas, were participating in the sit-ins. NAACP branch officials, notably Mississippi field secretary Medgar Evers, coordinated protest campaigns. Nevertheless, the students' confrontations with Jim Crow was an expression of impatience with the NAACP's carefully executed legal and political programs. There was a dramatic clash of strategies, with the NAACP

adhering firmly to its philosophy of change through court action and legislation, while King and the students marched under the banner of nonviolent direct action and local change. (The problems of strategy and organizational discipline merged as early as 1959, when Roy Wilkins suspended Robert Williams, president of the NAACP's Monroe, North Carolina, branch, for advocating that the NAACP meet "violence with violence.") Despite the ideological clash and the intense competition for financial contributions, media attention, and historical recognition, the young activists' strategy complemented the NAACP's. The NAACP provided large sums for bail money and legal support for the demonstrators and joined more militant movement groups in local alliances, such as the Council of Federated Organizations (COFO), which sponsored voter registration and other activities in Mississippi.

Despite the media attention that the demonstrations in the South drew, by 1962 the NAACP's 388,347 members in 46 states and the District of Columbia helped it to remain the leader in civil rights. That growth was especially significant, given that repeated court injunctions, state administrative regulations, punitive legislation, and other intimidating actions prevented many people from working with the NAACP in the South. The restrictions on the NAACP opened a window of opportunity for action by groups such as the Southern Christian Leadership Conference (SCLC) and the Student Nonviolent Coordinating Committee (SNCC; organized with the aid of NAACP veteran Ella Baker), as well as NAACP spinoffs such as the Alabama Christian Movement for Human Rights.

Meanwhile, the NAACP's board was undergoing a change. Robert C. Weaver, an economist and national housing expert, was elected chair in 1960. Weaver resigned in 1961 when President John F. Kennedy appointed him administrator of the Federal Housing and Home Financing Administration. He was succeeded by Bishop Stephen Gil Spottswood of the African Methodist Episcopal Zion Church.

The NAACP's most outstanding contribution to the civil rights movement continued to be its legal and lobbying efforts. In 1958, the NAACP forced the University of Florida to desegregate. A similar lawsuit was pending against the University of Georgia when it desegregated in 1961. In 1962, the NAACP led the battle to desegregate the University of Mississippi. The effort was directed by Constance Baker Motley of the LDF staff. Nevertheless, the fact that the parent NAACP featured the struggle in its 1962 annual report showed the extent to which the battle to enroll James H. Meredith in the university was also its own. After Mississippi governor Ross Barnett defied a federal court order, President Kennedy was forced to send in federal troops to quell a riot and assure Meredith's admittance.

The NAACP used the President's pleas for compliance, as well as the South's brutal opposition to the nonviolent demonstrations, to reinforce its struggle in Washington for passage of a meaningful civil rights law. Following the breakthrough in 1957, the NAACP had gotten Congress to pass the 1960 Civil Rights Act. That, however, was only a weak voting rights amendment to the 1957 act. Kennedy, insisting that comprehensive civil rights legislation would not pass, refused to send any to Congress. In February 1963, Kennedy submitted a weak civil rights bill. Mobilizing a historic coalition through the LCCR, the NAACP began an all-out struggle for passage of the bill as well as the strengthening of its provisions. NAACP pickets in Lawrence, Kansas, New York City, Newark, and Philadelphia helped highlight the struggle for such provisions as a national fair employment practice law.

Events in 1963 reshaped the civil rights bill and the struggle. The demonstrations in Birmingham that King led during the spring provoked national outrage. On June 11th, in response to the demonstrations, President Kennedy delivered a televised civil rights address. The following night, Medgar Evers was assassinated in Jackson, Mississippi. On June 19, the day Evers was buried at Arlington Cemetery, Kennedy sent Congress a revised civil rights bill that was much stronger than the one he had submitted in February.

The climactic event of 1963 was the March On Washington for Jobs and Freedom (MOW). A. Philip Randolph had initiated the call for a march in January. The NAACP, nevertheless, led in organizing it and saw to it that the march, held on August 28 at the Lincoln Memorial, broadened its focus to include the legislative struggle. From a strategic point of view, Clarence Mitchell and the NAACP Washington bureau regarded the legislative conference it held with NAACP branch leaders earlier in August as more meaningful to the struggle in Congress than the MOW had been. Both, nevertheless, served the intended purpose.

Following the assassination of President Kennedy in November 1963, Lyndon Johnson vowed to ensure passage of his predecessor's civil rights bill and provided the leadership that the NAACP had demanded from the executive branch. In the final, crucial phase of the struggle in the Senate, Johnson orchestrated the coordinated leadership of Majority Leader Sen. Mike Mansfield (D-Mont.) and Minority Leader Sen. Everett Dirksen (R-Ill.). Debate on the 1964 civil rights bill, H.R. 7152, began in earnest on March 10 and lasted until June 10, when the civil rights forces were finally able to break the filibuster.

The Civil Rights Act of 1964 was an immense victory for the NAACP. Following its passage, the NAACP began work on legislation to protect the right to vote. Following the Selma-to-Montgomery march, led by King, to protest the continuing disfranchisement of blacks in the South, the national climate was favorable to such a bill, and the NAACP was again left to direct the struggle in Congress for passage of the Voting Rights Act of 1965. This struggle was much less dramatic than that of 1964, perhaps because many expected its passage. Even so, as in 1957, the NAACP was hard-pressed to ward off attempts to weaken the bill. Its success in this battle was evident by the strong law that Congress passed.

Following passage of the civil rights laws, the NAACP switched its attention to enforcement, particularly in the areas of public school desegregation, employment, and housing. It also sought and won passage of strengthening provisions, such as amendments to the equal employment opportunity title of the 1964 Civil Rights Act. It won the first extension of the 1965 Voting Rights Act in 1970 with a provision extending protection for the right to vote, as well as subsequent ones. The programs remained centered in large part on the activities of the branches and its labor, education, and housing departments.

Despite the NAACP's crucial contribution to legislation which ended state-sponsored racial discrimination, the organization, with its interracial structure and integrationist philosophy, was scorned by increasing numbers of young blacks during the late 1960s as old-fashioned and overly cautious. The cycle of urban racial violence during the 1960s displayed the limits of the NAACP's program in appealing to frustrated urban blacks. President Johnson appointed Roy Wilkins a member of the National Advisory Commission on Civil Disorders, and the commission's well-known 1968 report reflected fully the NAACP's concerns.

Despite the radical criticism of the NAACP's program, the vitality of the organization's legal strategy was manifest by its success in passing legislation despite the embittered climate for black rights. While the NAACP shared credit with the other civil rights organizations for passage of the 1964 Civil Rights Act and the Voting Rights Act, there can be no doubt about its central role in 1968, when the Fair Housing Act was passed. Fearing the failure of a legislative struggle for fair housing legislation, many black leaders asked President Johnson to issue instead a comprehensive executive order barring discrimination in government-sponsored housing programs and federally insured mortgages. Johnson, however, did not want to deal with the problem piecemeal, and the NAACP supported him. The wisdom of that decision was evident on April 11, when President Johnson signed the 1968 Fair Housing Act, although its final version was somewhat weaker than the NAACP had originally intended. The final days of this struggle were overshadowed by the assassination of Dr. King in Memphis on April 4. The following day, at a meeting of civil rights leaders at the White House, the NAACP agreed to a suggestion that Congress be urged to pass the fair housing bill as a tribute to the slain leader.

During the late 1960s and early 1970s, the NAACP faced new and sometimes more difficult challenges than in the past. These problems now resulted from systemic or endemic discrimination, which were more difficult to identify than state-imposed segregation and required the development of new strategies to correct. One of the organization's most important functions became the designing and implementing of affirmative action and minority hiring programs with government and private business. This struggle was led by Nathaniel R. Jones, who replaced Robert Carter as the NAACP's general counsel in 1969. (Jones served in this position for ten years, before leaving to become a judge on the United States Court of Appeals, Second Circuit, in Cincinnati.) The NAACP brought suits or sent amicus curiae briefs in many notable affirmative action cases during the 1960s and 1970s. For example, in 1969 the NAACP brought *Head v. Timken Roller Bearing Co., of Columbus, Ohio*, a landmark antidiscrimination lawsuit. In 1976, it won a consent decree, with a settlement by which twenty-five black workers were awarded back pay and won expanded promotional opportunities into previously all-white craft jobs. As a result of another lawsuit, filed against the Indiana State Police Department, twenty black troopers were hired, bringing the number on the thousand-man force to twenty-three.

Another aspect of the NAACP's legal struggle was the campaign against the death penalty. This struggle was led primarily by the NAACP Legal Defense and Educational Fund, which monitored death penalty cases and compiled statistics demonstrating racial disproportions in death penalty sentencing outcomes. As a result, in *Furman v. Georgia* (1972), the U.S. Supreme Court temporarily struck down the death penalty.

Among the NAACP's other achievements was a continuation of the thirty-eight-year-old struggle to defeat unfavorable nominees to the Supreme Court. The NAACP scored a double victory against the nomination in 1969 of Judge Clement F. Haynsworth of South Carolina and in 1970 of Judge G. Harrold Carswell of Florida as Supreme Court justices. The NAACP opposed them because of their records on racial issues. The NAACP would continue to be influential in the confirmation process — for example, in 1987 the organization led the successful opposition to the Supreme Court appointment of Robert Bork and in 1990 helped defeat the confirmation of William Lucas, an

African-American conservative, as assistant attorney for civil rights.

Still another focus of NAACP efforts was its ongoing campaign against media stereotypes. NAACP pressure had succeeded in removing *Amos 'n' Andy* from network first-run television in the early 1950s; in the 1960s, NAACP pressure was partly responsible for the creation of the TV series *Julia*, the first series with a positive African-American leading character. In the 1980s, the NAACP organized protests of Steven Spielberg's film *The Color Purple* owing to its white director and negative portrayal of black men.

THE SEARCH FOR NEW DIRECTION

By the mid-1970s, the NAACP once again was forced into a period of transition. Henry Lee Moon retired in 1974. In 1976 Roy Wilkins retired as NAACP executive director. He had devoted forty-five years to the struggle and fulfilled most of his goals. In 1978 Clarence Mitchell also retired. Meanwhile, as a sign of the growing influence of women in the organization and the civil rights movement, in 1975 Margaret Bush Wilson, a St. Louis lawyer, was elected to chair the NAACP board of directors. Twenty years later, Myrlie Evers, the widow of Medgar Evers, was elected as its chair, and Hazel Dukes was named president of the powerful New York state chapter.

Along with the problems connected with the change in administration, the NAACP faced grave financial problems and some opposition to its program among blacks, who continued to criticize the NAACP as irrelevant to black needs. This opposition was an important challenge facing Benjamin L. Hooks, a minister, lawyer, and member of the Federal Communications Commission, when he became executive director of the association in January 1977. Hooks assumed command of the NAACP at a time when it was not only struggling to devise an effective strategy for new civil rights challenges but battling for its very existence.

In 1976, two adverse judgments in lawsuits against the NAACP in Mississippi had presented it with the worst crisis in its lifetime: A court awarded Robert Moody, a state highway patrolman, $250,000 as a result of a lawsuit charging libel and slander that he had filed against the NAACP. Local NAACP officials and its state field director had charged Moody with police brutality because he had allegedly beaten a black man while arresting him on a reckless driving charge. To protect its assets, the NAACP had to borrow money to post the required $262,000 bond, though it eventually won reversal of the judgment in appeals.

Then, the Hinds County chancery court in Jackson, Mississippi, handed down a $1.25 million judgment against the NAACP as a result of a lawsuit that local businessmen had filed against the organization following a boycott of their stores. Under Mississippi law, in order to forestall the seizure of its assets pending an appeal, the NAACP had to post a cash bond amounting to 125 percent of the judgment, which was $1,563,374. The U.S. Supreme Court reversed the judgment in 1982. However, the experience was sobering.

The NAACP was disconcerted by the Supreme Court ruling in *Regents of the University of California v. Bakke* in 1978. The Court ruled five to four that Title VI of the 1964 Civil Rights Act barred a university medical school's special admissions program for blacks and ordered a white applicant's admission. Although another bare majority ruled that race was a constitutionally valid criterion for admission programs, the Court had increased the difficulty of developing specific programs to meet constitutional tests.

The election of Ronald Reagan as president in 1980, at a time when the NAACP was still groping for effective programs to meet new challenges, was an even more ominous development. The Reagan administration all but destroyed the effectiveness of the U.S. Civil Rights Commission, the Civil Rights Division of the Justice Department, and the Equal Employment Commission. In 1984, Benjamin Hooks led a 125,000-person March on Washington to protest the "legal lynching" of civil rights by the Reagan administration.

Questions concerning Hooks's leadership gained national attention in 1983 when Board Chair Margaret Wilson unilaterally suspended him. Outraged that Wilson had reprimanded Hooks without its approval, the board replaced her with Kelly Alexander Sr., a North Carolina mortician. Following Alexander's death in 1986, the board elected Dr. William F. Gibson, a South Carolina dentist, as chairman. In order to oust Gibson, who was bitterly criticized for his leadership of the NAACP, Myrlie Evers led one of the fiercest internal battles in the organization's history.

Despite those setbacks, Hooks led the NAACP in winning several promising agreements from corporations, such as $1 billion from the American Gas Association, to provide jobs and other economic opportunities for blacks under a fair share program he inaugurated. In 1986, Hooks relocated the NAACP's national headquarters to Baltimore. Among his other accomplishments was the ACT-SO (Afro-Academic Cultural Technological Scientific Olympics) program he created to promote academic experience among minority youth through local, regional, and national competition. His goal was to seek proficiency in all academic areas, but with a special emphasis in the arts and humanities and the applied, technical, and social sciences. Hooks also continued the NAACP's political action programs with a special emphasis on voter registration.

In April 1993, Hooks retired as NAACP executive director. The board of directors had considerable difficulty deciding on a successor. Candidates included the Rev. Jesse Jackson. The board finally selected the Rev. Benjamin F. Chavis, Jr., an official of the United Church of Christ in Cleveland, who had once served more than four years in prison after being wrongly convicted on charges of conspiracy and arson for setting fire to a grocery store in Wilmington, North Carolina, in 1972. Chavis, much younger than his predecessor, was chosen in an attempt to revitalize the NAACP by attracting new sources of funding and reaching out to young African Americans. Chavis also called for the NAACP to expand its efforts to serve other minority interests.

Chavis's short tenure proved extremely controversial. In accord with his policy of attracting young African Americans, he shifted NAACP policy in a nationalistic direction and embraced black separatists, whom the NAACP had previously denounced. Chavis succeeded in increasing youth interest in the NAACP and was praised for his meetings with gang leaders, but he was widely criticized for inviting black radicals such as Nation of Islam chair Louis Farrakhan to a black leadership conference, and for refusing to disassociate himself from the Nation's anti-Semitic policies. The NAACP's membership dropped significantly as a result.

Chavis also met with opposition to his administrative policies. NAACP board members were angered by his unauthorized policy statements, such as his approval of the North American Free Trade Agreement. Furthermore, Chavis was blamed for running up the organization's deficit, already swelled by declining memberships, to $1.2 million through staff salary increases. When in the summer of 1994 it was disclosed that Chavis had used organization money in an out-of-court settlement of a sexual harassment suit filed by a female staffer, there began to be calls for his resignation. On August 20, 1994, in a meeting of the board of directors, Chavis was removed as executive director.

The schism over Chavis's policies provided a forum for fundamental disagreements between blacks over the role of civil rights organizations. With full legal equality substantially achieved, the NAACP continued to face questions regarding the best use of its leadership and the appropriate strategy to employ in attacking the problems of African Americans.

NAACP Chairman Julian Bond (l) and CEO Kweisi Mfume, 2002.
© REUTERS/CORBIS

The NAACP spent most of the following years attempting to assess its role. In February 1995, NAACP Board Chair William Gibson was forced to resign, and Myrlie Evers-Williams, widow of slain civil rights leader Medgar Evers, was named to the position. Under Evers-Williams's supervision, the organization restructured its finances and reaffirmed its intergrationist mission. In December 1995, Representative Kweisi Mfume announced that he would leave Congress to take over the daily operation of the NAACP. Under Mfume's leadership, the organization erased its fiscal deficit and renewed its activism on many fronts, including human rights, environmental racism, and justice for African Americans. In February 1998, Evers-Williams resigned and civil rights veteran Julian Bond became chair of the board. Bond spoke forcefully of the need for the NAACP to renew its focus on encouraging blacks to gain power through voting, and the NAACP took credit for the increase in the black vote in the 1998 congressional elections.

Bond has continued as chair of the NAACP into the twenty-first century, although the organization has once again come under attack, this time for remarks made by Bond during his keynote address at the NAACP's July 11, 2004 convention in Philadelphia in which he criticized both political parties and also challenged President George W. Bush's policies on the war in Iraq, civil liberties, the economy, and education. This has led to an investigation by the IRS into a possible violation of the NAACP's tax-exempt status, which bars nonpartisan, nonprofit groups from improper political bias and campaign intervention. If the government rules that the NAACP is too partisan to be considered a legitimate nonprofit, the IRS could then revoke the group's tax-exempt status.

The NAACP underwent another change in leadership with the resignation of President and CEO Kweisi Mfume in January 2005. Mfume cited a desire to spend more time with his family as his reason for stepping down. He later announced his intention to run for the U.S. Senate (for Maryland) in 2006. During his nine-year tenure, Mfume succeeded in retiring the organization's debt and put a focus on increasing the participation of a younger generation of African Americans, including increasing the number of NAACP college campus branches to more than 140. However, his detractors point out that he did little to draw attention to health, education, and criminal justice issues in the black community. Membership is also stagnant at an estimated 500,000, although the NAACP is working to increase its overall membership by 20 percent in the coming years. Dennis Courtland Hayes served as General Counsel in charge of the NAACP's legal program to eliminate racial discrimination and was the interim President and CEO until June 2005. While the NAACP's focus remains on civil rights enforcement, voter and economic empowerment, educational excellence, and youth recruitment, members also hope that new leadership with come up with a clear and inclusive message for the black community and promote grassroot efforts that will connect both locally and nationally. In June 2005 Bruce S. Gordon was named as the new president and CEO of the NAACP.

See also Bagnall, Robert; Bunche, Ralph; Civil Rights Movement, U.S.; Congress of Racial Equality (CORE); *Crisis, The*; Du Bois, W. E. B.; Garvey, Marcus; Great Depression and the New Deal; Johnson, James Weldon; Lynching; *Messenger, The*; National Negro Congress; Niagara Movement; Politics in the United States; Randolph, Asa Philip; Riots and Popular Protests; Scottsboro Case; Socialism; Spingarn Medal; Trotter, William Monroe; Universal Negro Improvement Association; Washington, Booker T.; White, Walter Francis; Wells-Barnett, Ida B.

■ ■ *Bibliography*

Archer, Leonard Courtney. *Black Images in the American Theatre: NAACP Protest Campaigns — Stage, Screen, Radio & Television*. Brooklyn, N.Y.: Pageant-Poseidon, 1973.

Ballard, Scotty. "Civil rights groups: why they're essential today." *Jet*. (January 31, 2005): 4.

Cortner, Richard C. *A Mob Intent on Death: The NAACP and the Arkansas Riot Cases*. Middletown, Conn.: Wesleyan University Press, 1988.

Crockett, Roger O. "How the NAACP Could Get Its Clout Back." *Business Week*. (February 21, 2005): 73.

Dalfiume, Richard M. "The Forgotten Years of the Negro Revolution," *Journal of American History* 55 (June 1968): 105-106.

Davis, Kimberly. "The New NAACP Turns Up the Heat." *Ebony* (April, 2000): 102.

Downey, Dennis, and Raymond M. Hyster. *No Crooked Death: Coatesville, Pennsylvania, and the Lynching of Zachariah Walker*. Urbana: University of Illinois Press, 1991.

Eichel, Larry. "NAACP urged into new role." *Knight-Ridder/Tribune News Service*. (January 3, 2005): K5511,

Finch, Minnie. *The NAACP, Its Fight for Justice*. Metuchen, N.J.: Scarecrow Press, 1981.

Fox, Stephen R. *The Guardian of Boston: William Monroe Trotter*. New York: Atheneum, 1970.

Goings, Kenneth W. *The NAACP Comes of Age: The Defeat of Judge John J. Parker*. Bloomington: Indiana University Press, 1990.

Greenberg, Jack. *Crusaders in the Courts: How a Dedicated Bunch of Lawyers Fought For the Civil Rights Revolution*. New York: Basic Books, 1994.

Hamilton, Anita and Peter Bailey. "Recharging the Mission." *Time*. (January 17, 2005): 50.

Harlan, Louis R. *Booker T. Washington: The Wizard of Tuskegee, 1901-1915*. New York: Oxford University Press, 1983.

Haywood, Richette. "Can Kweisi Mfume turn the NAACP around?" *Ebony* (January, 1977): 94.

Horne, Gerald. *Black and Red: W. E. B. Du Bois and the Afro-American Response to the Cold War*. Albany: State University of New York Press, 1986.

Hughes, Langston. *Fight for Freedom: The Story of the NAACP*. New York: Berkley Pub. Corp., 1962.

Janken, Kenneth Robert. *White: The Biography of Walter White, Mr. NAACP*. New York: New Press, 2003.

Jones, Gilbert. *Sword: The NAACP and the Struggle Against Racism in America, 1909–1969*. New York: Routledge, 2004.

Kellogg, Charles Flint. *NAACP: A History of the National Association for the Advancement of Colored People*, vol. 1: 1909-1920. Baltimore, M.D.: Johns Hopkins Press, 1967.

Kellogg, Peter J. "Civil Rights Consciousness in the 1940s." *The Historian* 42, no. 1 (November 1979): 18-41.

Kinnon, Joy Bennett. "What's behind the biggest upheaval ever in Black Leadership?" *Ebony*. (April 2005): 162.

Kluger, Richard. *Simple Justice: The History of Brown v. Board of Education and Black America's Struggle for Equality*. New York: Knopf, 1976.

Lawrence, Charles Radford. *Negro Organizations in Crisis: Depression, New Deal, World War II*. Ph.D. diss., Columbia University, 1953.

Lewis, David Levering. *W. E. B. Du Bois: Biography of a Race, 1868-1919*. New York: H. Holt, 1993.

McNeil, Genna Rae. *Groundwork, Charles Hamilton Houston and the Struggle for Civil Rights*. Philadelphia: University of Pennsylvania Press, 1983.

McPherson, James. *The Abolitionist Legacy*. Princeton, N.J.: Princeton University Press, 1975.

Mfume, Kweisi. *No Free Ride: From the Mean Streets to the Mainstream*. New York: One World, 1996.

Muse, Edward B. *Paying For Freedom: History of the NAACP and the Life Membership Program, 1909-1987*. Baltimore, M.D.: National Association for the Advancement of Colored People, 1987.

National Negro Conference. *Proceedings of the National Negro Conference*. New York, 1909.

Ovington, Mary White. "How the National Association for the Advancement of Colored People Began." *The Crisis* 8 (August 1914): 184-188.

Ovington, Mary White. *The Walls Came Tumbling Down*. 1947. Reprint. New York: Schocken Books, 1970.

Record, Wilson. *Race and Radicalism: The NAACP and the Communist Party in Conflict*. Ithaca, N.Y.: Cornell University Press, 1964.

Reed, K. Terrell. "NAACP's Mfume Steps Down; Nation's Oldest Civil Rights Group May Face Internal Turmoil." *Black Enterprise* (February, 2005): 31.

Ross, D. Joyce. *J. E. Spingarn and the Rise of the NAACP*. New York: Atheneum, 1972.

Rowan, Carl. *Dream Makers, Dream Breakers: The World of Justice Thurgood Marshall*. Boston: Little, Brown & Co., 1992.

Rudwick, Elliott, and August Meier. "The Rise of the Black Secretariat in the NAACP, 1909-1935." In *Along the Color Line: Explorations in the Black Experience*. Urbana: University of Illinois Press, 1976.

Sitkoff, Harvard. *A New Deal for Blacks, The Emergence of Civil Rights as a National Issue: The Depression Decade*. New York: Oxford University Press, 1978.

St. James, Warren D. *NAACP: Triumphs of a Pressure Group, 1909-1980*. Smithtown, N.Y.: Exposition Press, 1980.

Tillman, Jr., Nathaniel Patrick. *Walter Francis White: A Study in Interest Group Leadership*. Ph.D. diss., University of Wisconsin, 1961.

Tushnet, Mark. *The NAACP's Legal Strategy Against Segregation, 1925-1950*. Chapel Hill: University of North Carolina Press, 1987.

Vose, Clement E. *Caucasians Only: The Supreme Court, the NAACP, and the Restrictive Covenant Cases*. Berkeley: University of California Press, 1959.

Watson, Denton L. *Lion in the Lobby, Clarence Mitchell, Jr.'s Struggle for the Passage of Civil Rights Laws*. New York: Morrow, 1990.

Watson, Denton L. "The NAACP at the Crossroads—Organization No Longer Effective in Addressing Discrimination." *The Humanist*. (Jan-Feb., 1998): 28.

White, Walter. *A Man Called White*. New York: Viking Press, 1948.

Wilkins, Roy. "The Negro Wants Full Equality." In Rayford W. Logan, ed. *What the Negro Wants*. Chapel Hill: University of North Carolina Press, 1944.

Wilkins, Roy, with Tom Matthews. *Standing Fast, the Autobiography of Roy Wilkins*. New York: Viking Press, 1982.

Wolters, Raymond. *Negroes in the Great Depression*. Westport, Conn.: Greenwood Pub. Corp., 1970.

Zangrando, Robert L. *The NAACP Crusade Against Lynching, 1909-1950*. Philadelphia: Temple University Press, 1980.

DENTON L. WATSON (1996)
CHRISTINE TOMASSINI (2005)

NATIONAL ASSOCIATION OF COLORED WOMEN

Predating the National Association for the Advancement of Colored People and the National Urban League, the National Association of Colored Women (NACW) was the first national black organization in the United States and has proved to be one of the longest lasting. Founded in 1896, NACW's roots lay in decades of local political activity by African-American women. This activity often took the form of women's clubs and was the result of heightened racism, a need for social services within the black community, and the exclusionary policies of many white-run organizations.

The local clubs and reform efforts of black women in churches, mutual aid societies, and literary clubs were part of a larger reform effort during the late nineteenth century. Little state assistance was available for the needy. Clubwomen provided aid to the aged, young, and other dependents, strengthened racial solidarity, and developed leadership. These local efforts, which were usually short-lived and unconnected, became the basis of a national coalition.

A series of events facilitated the emergence of the National Association of Colored Women. In 1895 a national convention of black women was called to respond to a racist letter sent by James Jacks, a southern journalist, to a British reformer. Jacks wrote that blacks lacked morality and that black women were prostitutes, natural liars, and thieves. Because of the local clubs and women's magazines that were in existence, in particular *The Woman's Era,* a national black women's journal, African-American women were able to respond quickly and effectively to the slanderous letter.

The 1895 convention led to the formation of the National Federation of Afro-American Women. Shortly thereafter the National League of Colored Women broke from the federation because of differences about how to deal with segregation at the Atlanta Exposition. But because of concerns about the lack of unity, the two organizations merged in 1896 to form the National Association of Colored Women. Committed to social reform and racial betterment, the NACW achieved its greatest growth from the 1890s to the 1920s. Shortly after it was founded, the NACW had five thousand members. Twenty years later, it had fifty thousand members in twenty-eight federations and over a thousand clubs. By 1924 it had reached 100,000 members.

The NACW was involved in a variety of projects to address problems of health, housing, education, and working conditions and to create a social space for black women. It was the primary organization through which African-American women channeled their reform efforts. Embodied in their slogan "Lifting as we Climb" was a commitment not only to improve their own situation but to aid the less fortunate. They built schools, ran orphanages, founded homes for the aged, set up kindergarten programs, and formed agencies in New York and Philadelphia to help female migrants from the South find jobs and affordable housing. Black women who formed the backbone of the NACW were primarily middle class and often professional women involved in teaching or other social service occupations. Their local activities were the seeds for multiservice centers that combined the many goals of the NACW reform efforts. They provided material assistance through day care, health services, and job training to help women secure jobs.

While the movement comprised many local groups with differing philosophies, the national agenda was dominated by women less interested in confrontation than in accommodation. In the early years the NACW journal, *National Notes,* was printed at Tuskegee Institute under the direction of Margaret Murray Washington. The first president of the NACW, Mary Church Terrell, was also a supporter of Booker T. Washington and accommodationist policies. At the request of organizers in Chicago, Terrell chose not to invite outspoken anti-accommodationist Ida B. Wells-Barnett to the first NACW meeting.

The political orientation of women in the NACW was also evident in the programs and policies of the organization. Black clubwomen adhered to middle-class values of self-improvement and moral purity. As Terrell expressed in 1902, "Self-preservation demands that [black women] go among the lowly, illiterate, and even vicious, to whom they are bound by ties of race and sex . . . to reclaim them." They taught thrift through penny-saving societies and supported the temperance movement. Some of their old-age homes accepted only the respectable poor and elderly, not those who were indigent because of what the NACW considered laziness or immorality. They conducted classes in domestic service and child rearing to teach the poor proper health and hygiene, how to maintain a household, and techniques to raise their children. They maintained that women could play an important role in reforming society by using their virtuous qualities and superior moral sensibilities to create a safe and comfortable home. Women in the NACW wanted to instill racial pride in African Americans and counter negative images of black women. They believed their commitment to racial solidar-

First Congress of Negro Women, 1895. *The convention pictured here led to the formation of the National Federation of Afro-American Women and a splinter group, the National League of Colored Women. The two organizations merged in 1896 to form the National Association of Colored Women.* PHOTOGRAPHS AND PRINTS DIVISION, SCHOMBURG CENTER FOR RESEARCH IN BLACK CULTURE, THE NEW YORK PUBLIC LIBRARY, ASTOR, LENOX AND TILDEN FOUNDATIONS.

ity and helping the poorest African Americans would improve the position of the entire race.

Although immersed in social reform and racial uplift efforts, the NACW also took strong stands against the roots of racial injustice. In the early years black clubwomen opposed segregation and the brutal convict-lease system. *National Notes* became a tool to discuss ideas and disseminate information. By 1910 they had expanded their goals to include the women's suffrage amendment and the federal antilynching bill and had also come to believe that to effect change, more than simply exposure of the brutalities that African Americans faced was necessary. After the Red Summer of 1919, the NACW, under the leadership of Mary Talbert, joined the crusade against lynching and mobilized black women, raised money, and educated the public. While never a militant organization, the NACW made verbal protests against racial injustice and advocated boycotts of segregated facilities. It was successful in creating a national political voice for African-American women. As the organization expanded its agenda, its overwhelming influence by northeastern urban women was tempered by greater involvement of women from the South.

During the Great Depression, the stature and importance of the NACW began to decline, and for a time the organization met only periodically. Many of the welfare and social services NACW provided were available through better-funded local, state, and private agencies created expressly for this purpose. In addition, obvious dire need for direct material assistance during the 1930s made the self-help and moral uplift ideology of the NACW somewhat anachronistic. These issues, coupled with a declining membership and financial insecurity, made the NACW a less effective organization.

In 1935 Mary McLeod Bethune, who served as president of NACW from 1924 to 1928, formed the National Council of Negro Women, which acted as an umbrella for black women's organizations. This led to a redefinition of NACW, which was no longer the only national black women's organization. In 1957 NACW changed its name to the National Association of Colored Women's Clubs (NACWC). In the early 1990s the NACWC had close to forty thousand members in fifteen hundred local clubs. Today it is primarily involved in educational, social service, and fund-raising activities. The NACWC sponsors forums on HIV infection, provides college scholarships for young black women, and raises money for children's hospitals. Despite the ebbs and flows in its work, the NACWC has admirably endured over a century of service and commitment to African-American women.

See also Bethune, Mary McLeod; National Association for the Advancement of Colored People (NAACP); National Council of Negro Women; Red Summer; Terrell, Mary Eliza Church; Wells-Barnett, Ida B.

■ ■ *Bibliography*

Giddings, Paula. *When and Where I Enter: The Impact of Black Women on Race and Sex in America.* New York: Bantam Books, 1984.

Salem, Dorothy. *To Better Our World: Black Women in Organized Reform, 1890–1920.* Brooklyn, N.Y.: Carlson, 1990.

Wesley, Charles H. *The History of the National Association of Colored Women's Clubs: A Legacy of Service.* Washington, D.C.: The Association, 1984.

PREMILLA NADASEN (1996)

NATIONAL ASSOCIATION OF NEGRO MUSICIANS

❙❙❙

The National Association of Negro Musicians (NANM) was established in Chicago on July 29, 1919. The foundation was laid for this event nearly three months earlier in Washington, D.C., at a meeting inspired by an idea first voiced in 1906 by Harriet G. Marshall, founder of the Washington Conservatory of Music and School of Expression. Designated as the Temporary Organization of Musicians and Artists, the Washington meeting was held under the leadership of public school teacher Henry L. Grant. Officers were elected and a July meeting in Chicago with other interested musicians was planned. These officers—Henry L. Grant (Washington, D.C.), president; Nora D. Holt (Chicago), vice president; Alice Carter Simmons (Tuskegee, Alabama), secretary; Fred ("Deacon") Johnson (New York)—were installed at the Chicago meeting, which was the first NANM convention.

Parallel efforts by other nationally recognized musicians were associated with NANM's founding, including attempts by composers Clarence Cameron White in 1916 and R. Nathaniel Dett in 1918, to initiate a national meeting and vigorous promotion of the idea by music critic Holt in *Chicago Defender* newspaper columns.

NANM's purpose as stated by Holt (1974, pp. 234–235) was that of "furthering and coordinating the musical forces of the Negro race for the promotion of economic, educational, and fraternal betterment." To that end NANM sponsored young music students in recital, gave scholarships, attempted to gather information regarding the employment status of the black music teacher, encouraged performance of works by black composers, and promoted concerts by its members. The membership, composed mainly of public-school and private-studio music teachers, representatives from conservatories, concert artists, and students, participated in the local branches of their home cities and also enjoyed much-needed opportunities for fellowship in the annual conventions held in a different city each year.

The annual conventions offered an abundance of music, including performances by eminent musicians, workshops, lectures, and clinics as well as unusual events, such as the presentation of *Aida* by the National Negro Opera Company in 1941 at Pittsburgh in a fully staged production prior to the official opening of the company, and the presentation of Scott Joplin's opera *Treemonisha* in 1979 at St. Louis under the direction of Kenneth Billups, choral director and college and public-school music teacher.

Scholarship winners frequently achieved national and international prominence as did Marian Anderson, the first scholarship recipient (1921), composer and pianist Margaret Bonds, composer Julia Perry, mezzo-soprano Grace Bumbry, conductor James Frazier, and concert pianists Leon Bates and Awadagin Pratt.

While NANM at first promoted classical music and musicians almost exclusively, the focus broadened around 1940 to include gospel, jazz, and the blues. NANM honored established musicians in various areas of performance such as Harriet Gibbs Marshall, R. Augustus Lawson (pianist), Lulu V. Childers (founder, School of Music at Howard University), Thomas Dorsey (gospel music composer and performer), Duke Ellington (jazz musician), and Jessye Norman (soprano). The organization was the first of its kind in the United States and continues to function in the twenty-first century.

See also Joplin, Scott; Music in the United States; Professional Organizations

■ ■ *Bibliography*

Allen, Clarence G. "Negro Musicians Urge Against Perversion of Their Songs, at Second Convention." *Musical America* (August 7, 1920): 4.

Holt, Nora. "The Chronological History of the NANM." *Music and Poetry* (July 1921); reprinted in *Black Perspective in Music* 2, no. 1 (fall 1974): 234–235.

McGinty, Doris Evans, ed. *A Documentary History of the National Association of Negro Musicians.* Chicago: Center for Black Music Research, 2004.

DORIS EVANS MCGINTY (1996)
Updated bibliography

NATIONAL BANKERS ASSOCIATION

▪▪▪

The National Bankers Association (NBA) was created in 1927 in response to discriminatory practices of the American Bankers Association (ABA), which would not accept African Americans into membership. In 1926 R. R. Wright of Citizens Bank and Trust Company of Philadelphia and C. C. Spaulding of Mechanics and Farmers Bank of Durham, North Carolina, met with representatives of nineteen black-owned and -operated banks and savings-and-loan institutions. The group met at Pythias Hall in Philadelphia and discussed the need to form an organization to serve the common needs of black bankers.

In 1927 the group met in Durham to form the National Negro Bankers Association. The principal purposes of the NBA were to develop programs designed to strengthen the existing member banks, increase their number, and increase their economic impact on their communities. Over the years, the NBA has become more aligned with the "mainstream" banking system, including the change to its current name in 1948. Beginning in the 1960s NBA member banks were encouraged to become ABA members as well.

During this period the NBA also began to consult with various local, state, and federal officials. They sought financial assistance because of their relatively weak position in the banking world, and in 1968 the NBA was awarded a grant from the Economic Development Administration. Despite its financial difficulties, the NBA has continued to survive and to maintain its commitment to aid in the expansion of capital and management resources in the African-American community, as well as to provide assistance to other minority and women-owned financial institutions.

■ ■ *Bibliography*

"The National Bankers Association: What's It All About?" *Black Business Digest* 2, no. 2 (December 1971): 31–32.

SASHA THOMAS (1996)

NATIONAL BAPTIST CONVENTION, U.S.A., INC.

▪▪▪

The National Baptist Convention, U.S.A., Inc., founded on September 24, 1895, constitutes the largest body of organized African-American Christians in the world. With over 7.5 million members, this influential body's roots go deep into the early religious and cooperative efforts of free blacks and slaves in antebellum America.

As early as 1834, African Americans in Ohio organized the Providence Baptist Association to strengthen the work of local Baptist churches. The formation of this association established a trend for other local churches, resulting in the organization of other associations, state conventions, regional conventions, and national bodies. The first significant trend toward a national body was the organization in 1894 of the Tripartite Union, consisting of the New England Baptist Foreign Missionary Convention, the African Foreign Mission Convention, and the Foreign Mission Convention of America. Although this Tripartite Union attempt failed by 1895, the spirit of national cooperation eventually prevailed.

In 1895, Reverends S. E. Griggs, L. M. Luke, and A. W. Pegues, former leaders of the Tripartite Union movement, led another attempt at national unity among African-American Baptists. They successfully encouraged the Foreign Mission Convention, the National Baptist Educational Convention, and the American National Baptist Convention to merge into the National Baptist Convention, U.S.A.

The purpose of the newly formed national convention was multipartite. The former work of the National Baptist Educational Convention was increased through the new convention's aggressive involvement in the education of the race. Local churches were encouraged to increase their support of secondary schools and colleges throughout the southern region of the United States. Internationally, the National Baptist Convention, U.S.A. advanced foreign missionary projects in Africa, Central America, and the West Indies. Schools, churches, and medical institutions were expanded in various mission stations on these foreign fields. A large number of the leaders among Africans on the developing continent, as well as Africans of the diaspora, were trained by these institutions.

In order to facilitate practical operations in the National Baptist Convention, U.S.A., the leadership was careful to develop comprehensive plans for a viable structure. The basic strategy was to organize the work of the convention through specialized boards. The leadership organized a Foreign Mission Board, Home Mission Board, Educational Board, Baptist Young People's Union, and Publishing Board. These were designed to carry out the mandates of the convention as articulated by Reverend Elias Camp Morris, the organization's first president. The pattern of specialized boards was continued by the subsequent leadership of the convention, but it proved problematic in practice.

Problem areas developed within two of the strongest boards, Foreign Mission and Publishing. By 1897 there was enough internal disturbance in the convention to threaten the unity of the denomination. When the annual session was convened at Ebenezer Baptist Church in Boston, a group of ministers of national prominence led a debate over several key emotion-laden issues, namely: (1) the advisability of moving the Foreign Mission Board from Richmond to Louisville; (2) the use of American Baptist literature and cooperation with white Baptists in general; and (3) a greater emphasis on foreign missions as a primary policy of the convention. The leadership was not able to resolve these points, especially the last. Consequently, several clergymen from Virginia and North Carolina who were in favor of stronger foreign missions issued a call to like-minded ministers to meet at Shiloh Baptist Church in Washington, D.C., on December 11, 1897, for the purpose of developing a new convention strategy. Out of this movement emerged the Lott Carey Baptist Home and Foreign Mission Convention, specializing in foreign missions.

The second problem area was the Publishing Board. The National Baptist Publishing Board, under the leadership of Reverends Henry Allen Boyd and C. H. Clark, was given the exclusive right to publish all church and Sunday-school literature for local Baptist churches. With a significant increase in its financial holdings, the National Baptist Publishing Board tended to act independently of the general leadership of the convention. This resulted in a split within the leadership and the formation of the National Baptist Convention of America in 1915.

The National Baptist Convention, U.S.A., Inc., emerged from these splits, however, as the majority convention among African-American Baptists. Its scheme of organizational structure through major boards remained intact. Morris, the national president, was careful to require responsibility and accountability from the specialized boards' leadership. This policy facilitated unity within the convention until the middle of the twentieth century.

In 1956, a serious debate erupted over the question of tenure. Reverend Joseph H. Jackson, president of the convention, had risen to a position of such power and prestige that a majority of the convention's leaders and delegates desired the continuation of his leadership beyond the tenure limits of the constitution. Tensions increased, resulting in a strong challenge to Jackson's leadership by a group favoring the election of Reverend Gardner C. Taylor of Brooklyn to the presidency. The 1961 presidential election became a crisis that resulted in a civil court battle between Jackson and "the Taylor team." Jackson's position was confirmed by the court.

The Jackson victory did not calm the troubled waters, however. On September 11, 1961, a national call was issued for the organization of the Progressive National Baptist Convention. The rationale for creating a new convention was a protest against Jackson's policy of "gradualism" in civil rights issues, as well as a demonstration of support for Taylor's election bid for the presidency. Moreover, the new convention rallied to give stronger support to the civil rights movement under the leadership of the Reverend Dr. Martin Luther King Jr.

The National Baptist Convention remained the largest convention of African-American Baptists. But the advance of the civil rights movement and the growth in power and influence of Martin Luther King Jr. seriously challenged the moral and racial leadership of the majority convention. This trend continued until King's assassination and the rise of the Reverend T. J. Jemison to the presidency of the convention. The new president, a veteran civil rights leader, made efforts to restore the convention to its previous leadership role.

In 1994, Dr. Henry Lyons was elected president of the convention. In 1999, however, Lyons was convicted of racketeering and stealing more than $4 million from the convention. In September of that year, the Reverend William Shaw succeeded Lyons as president.

See also Baptists; Griggs, Sutton Elbert; Jackson, Joseph Harrison; King, Martin Luther, Jr.; Primitive Baptists

■ ■ *Bibliography*

Fitts, Leroy. *A History of Black Baptists*. Nashville, Tenn.: Broadman and Holman, 1985.

Gilbreath, Edward. "Redeeming Fire." *Christianity Today* 43 (December 1999): 38.

Washington, James M. *Frustrated Fellowship: The Black Baptist Quest for Social Power*. Macon, Ga.: Mercer University Press, 1986.

LEROY FITTS (1996)
Updated by publisher 2005

NATIONAL BLACK EVANGELICAL ASSOCIATION

▪▪▪

Founded in 1963 as the National Negro Evangelical Association, the National Black Evangelical Association (NBEA) functions as an umbrella association of individuals, organizations, and churches. A theologically conservative organization, the NBEA is of the same theological genus as the larger, modern, white American fundamentalist movement. This modern American fundamentalist movement had its beginning in the late nineteenth and early twentieth centuries with the fundamentalist-versus-modernist religious controversy. The National Association of Evangelicals (NAE), founded in 1942 as an outgrowth of this controversy, brought together evangelicals from a variety of theological positions, including fundamentalist, dispensational, Calvinist, Reformed, covenantal, Pentecostal, and charismatic. These all hold in common the belief in the historic "fundamentals" of the Protestant tradition: the Reformation and Arminian doctrine of complete reliability and final authority of the Bible in matters of faith and practice; the real, historical character of God's saving work recorded in Scripture; personal eternal salvation only through belief in Jesus Christ; evidence of a spiritually transformed life; and the importance of sharing this belief and experience with others through evangelism and mission works.

In the early twentieth century, a distinct group of Christians within the African-American community aligned themselves with the fundamentalist movement and developed separately from traditional African-American churches. Traditional African-American churches, some of whose history dated back to the seventeenth century, emphasized moral and social reform in the areas of personal piety, slavery, and discrimination. They generally saw themselves as "Bible believers." Black fundamentalists, on the other hand, placed more emphasis on conservative, propositional, and doctrinal aspects of faith. The black fundamentalists charged that African-American churches were one of two types: poor congregations, who were "otherworldly" and emotionally focused in worship; or middle-class congregations, who were theological liberals and embraced modern science. This history caused some strains between these two movements. Some black evangelicals characterized the historic black church as "apostate and un-Biblical," and some in mainline black churches labeled black evangelicals as doctrinaire and schismatic "fanatics." This history led to the presence of African Americans in white fundamentalist and evangelical bible schools and seminaries in the late 1940s and 1950s. Black alumni from these institutions helped to develop the NBEA.

At the time of its founding, the NBEA did not view itself as racially separatist but as an association focused on developing African-American leadership to minister with clear evangelical emphasis to the black community. During this early stage many black evangelicals were also frustrated with the white evangelical movement. This tension focused on what blacks perceived as white evangelicals' indifference to and lack of sympathy for the evangelistic needs of the African-American community. This frustration eventually led some black evangelicals to charge their white counterparts with a spiritual "benign neglect." Eventually the charge of neglect evolved into a stronger allegation of racism. From the beginning its social-action commission raised social issues within the NBEA, yet major social concerns were not in the forefront of its work. Instead the NBEA concentrated on strategies for effectively communicating its particular brand of evangelicalism within the African-American community.

Like all social movements, black evangelicalism has not always been unified in its efforts. The movement could not avoid confronting the civil rights and Black Power movements and their attendant black theology movements of the late 1960s and early 1970s. The challenges of these new movements, with their emphasis on social justice and self-determination, created anxiety, ambivalence, and dissension within the black evangelical movement. These rifts became evident in several of the annual NBEA conventions.

The civil rights movement forced black evangelicals, in several NBEA conferences between 1968 and 1970, to look at the issues of social justice and racial discrimination and their relationship to presenting the gospel. The conservatives in the movement felt that their first priority was the promulgation of personal salvation rather than attacking social injustice. If society were to be changed, it would be through the changing of human hearts rather than through altering the individual person's social condition. The activists within the black evangelical movement argued that social action and the verbal proclamation of the gospel were equal tasks in evangelical missions. The whole truth of the gospel could be received only when the social concerns of the individual were met.

The Black Power movement challenged the black evangelical movement with issues of self-determination. This was reflected in several NBEA conferences from 1970 through 1975. Activist black evangelicals, drawing from Black Power advocates, believed that white evangelicals were too paternalistic in their support and that blacks were too dependent upon whites. The activists argued that African Americans should develop institutions and support within their own communities. They were not completely opposed to white support, however. Whites could contribute to the cause but without any conditions attached. The conservative wing countered that this stance smacked of divisiveness within the body of Christ. They argued for a more conciliatory role with their white evangelical counterparts, emphasizing Christian reconciliation. This debate forced the movement to look anew at its historical links to the black church as a source of strength and self-determination. These discussions led to another major debate within the black evangelical movement revolving around the role of black theology and African-American culture in the movement as interpretative tools.

Black theology as a movement and the challenge of African-American history and culture were the catalysts of a major debate within the black evangelical movement. This rift surfaced in several of the NBEA conferences in the late 1970s. Some within the black evangelical movement, such as William Bentley and Columbus Salley, closely followed the writings of black theologians. They disagreed with some black theologians' liberal assumptions regarding biblical authority. Yet these activist black evangelicals agreed with black theologians' interpretative critique of both the liberal and conservative European and white American theologians' claim of universality and, therefore, repudiated the appropriateness and normativeness of white theology in all situations. To these black critics, all theology was culturally bound and, therefore, culturally specific. Theology, then, had to be culturally relevant, and this was especially so for the African-American community. The conservatives countered that what was at stake in the activists' critique of conservative white theology was the very essence of the theological foundation of this movement. They felt that the use of black theology, with its liberal theological foundation, compromised too much. It contradicted the very basis of their faith. The conservatives also feared that the activists placed too much emphasis on the importance of black culture at the expense of the gospel message.

These issues drove the NBEA to examine the historic role of the black church as an institution and its relationship to social issues. This was evident in the 1990 convention in which the delegates discussed the viability of dropping the term *evangelical* because it conjured images of political conservatism, which, some felt, further alienated the movement from the historic African-American church.

The NBEA's numerical strength is unknown, but its leadership estimates its mailing list at five thousand, with a larger black-evangelical constituency of between thirty thousand and forty thousand. Its annual convention draws several hundred participants, and smaller numbers participate in the meetings sponsored by local chapters. The NBEA has been an arena in which the differing factions of the black evangelical movement have been able to dialog, to discuss disagreements, and to reach compromise. It has been a delicate balancing act over the years. It remains to be seen whether the movement, and especially the NBEA as an organization, can continue to hold its various camps under its umbrella and simultaneously continue to stretch the canvas to include and win favor with the historic black church community as well.

See also Theology, Black

■ ■ *Bibliography*

Bentley, William H. "Bible Believers in the Black Community." In *The Evangelicals: What They Believe, Who They Are, Where They Are Changing,* edited by David F. Wells and John D. Woodbridge, pp. 108–121. Nashville, Tenn.: Abingdon Press, 1975.

Bentley, William H. *The National Black Evangelical Association: Evolution of a Concept of Ministry.* Chicago, 1979.

Bentley, William H. *The National Black Evangelical Association: Bellwether of a Movement.* Chicago, 1988.

Marsden, George, ed. *Evangelicalism and Modern America.* Grand Rapids, Mich.: W. B. Eerdmans, 1984.

Pannell, William. *My Friend, the Enemy.* Waco, Tex.: Word Books, 1968.

Pannell, William. "The Religious Heritage of Blacks." In *The Evangelicals: What They Believe, Who They Are, Where They Are Changing,* edited by David F. Wells and John D. Woodbridge, pp. 96–107. Nashville, Tenn.: Abingdon Press, 1975.

Quebedeaux, Richard. *The Young Evangelicals: Revolution in Orthodoxy.* New York: Harper & Row, 1974.

Salley, Columbus, and Ronald Behm. *What Color Is Your God? Black Consciousness and the Christian Faith.* Rev. ed., Downers Grove, Ill.: InterVarsity Press, 1981.

ALBERT G. MILLER (1996)

NATIONAL BLACK POLITICAL CONVENTION OF 1972

See Gary Convention

NATIONAL COUNCIL OF NEGRO WOMEN

▮▮▮

The National Council of Negro Women (NCNW) has been among the most influential African-American women's organizations of the twentieth century, particularly under the guidance of its founder, Mary McLeod Bethune, and its later president Dorothy Height. Bethune seized on the idea of an umbrella organization to bring together the skills and experience of black women in a variety of organizations. This national council would provide leadership and guidance to make African-American women's voices heard in every arena of social and political life. When Bethune began to pursue this goal in 1929, she met with some resistance from the leadership of other national organizations, particularly the National Association of Colored Women. But she was successful in convincing the skeptics that a National Council of Negro Women would respect the achievements and strengths of other groups and streamline the cooperative operations of black women's organizations rather than supersede existing groups.

The NCNW was founded in New York City on December 5, 1935, after five years of planning. The true signs of Bethune's diplomatic ability were the presence at the founding meeting of representatives of twenty-nine organizations and the election of such important figures as Mary Church Terrell and Charlotte Hawkins Brown to leadership positions. Bethune was elected president by a unanimous vote. The effectiveness of the council and its leadership was immediately apparent. One of its areas of greatest success was labor issues. With Bethune's influence in the federal government, the NCNW, in conjunction with other organizations, pressed for federal jobs for African Americans and was one of the forces behind the founding of the Fair Employment Practices Committee. Under Bethune's leadership the NCNW also established an important journal, the *Aframerican Woman's Journal,* which in 1949 became *Women United.* The council expressed an interest in international affairs, supporting the founding of the United Nations. From its founding, the United Nations has had an NCNW official observer at its proceedings.

Bethune retired from the presidency of the NCNW in 1949 and was succeeded by Dorothy Boulding Ferebee, the grandniece of Josephine St. Pierre Ruffin and former NCNW treasurer. During Ferebee's tenure, the council continued to press the issues with which it had always been concerned—civil rights, education, jobs, and health care, among others. However, the organization experienced a crisis as it moved beyond merely defining goals and issues toward providing more tangible services to its constituency. This issue carried over to the term of its third president, Vivian Carter Mason, elected in 1953. During her four years in office, Mason employed administrative skills to improve the operation of the national headquarters and to forge closer ties between the local and national councils. Under Mason the NCNW continued to develop as a force in the struggle for civil rights. Just as Bethune led the organization to fight for the integration of the military, Mason fought for swift implementation of school desegregation.

In 1957 the NCNW elected Dorothy I. Height to be the organization's fourth president. Height came to her work at the council with experience on the national board of the Young Women's Christian Association, eight years as president of Delta Sigma Theta, and involvement in a host of organizations and institutions. Height set out to place the NCNW on firm financial ground through gaining tax-exempt status (accomplished in 1966) and through grants from foundations. She was successful in garnering support from the Ford Foundation and the U.S. Department of Health, Education, and Welfare to expand the scope of the NCNW's work.

Among Height's other major accomplishments as president was the construction of the Bethune Memorial Statue, unveiled in Lincoln Park, Washington, D.C., in 1974. The memorial pays tribute to the contributions of an extraordinary woman. The NCNW continued its commitment to preserve the history of black women through the founding of the National Archives for Black Women's History. Although the council desired such an institution from its founding, the archives did not become a reality until 1979. This collection preserves the papers of the NCNW, the National Committee on Household Employment, and the National Association of Fashion and Accessory Designers. The personal papers of a number of women are also housed there. Through this collection and through conferences sponsored by the archives, the NCNW has become an important force in preserving the records and achievements of black women in the twentieth century.

The list of organizations affiliated with the National Council of Negro Women is long and varied, reflecting the council's commitment to building bridges to create a united voice for black women. Affiliated groups include ten national sororities, the National Association of Negro Business and Professional Women's Clubs, Inc., the Auxiliary of the National Medical Association, women's missionary societies of the National Baptist Convention and the African Methodist Episcopal Church, and Trade

Union Women of African Heritage. The NCNW has also developed an international component to its work. In addition to maintaining a presence at the United Nations, it has worked with women in Africa (in Togo and Senegal, for example) and other areas of the diaspora, such as Cuba.

The NCNW has been successful in creating a national organization through which African-American women can address the issues facing them and their families. It has enabled black women from a variety of backgrounds to design and implement programs and develop themselves as community leaders. The longevity and effectiveness of the council are the result of the willingness of its leadership to change and to shape programs and methods to the emerging needs of African-American communities.

See also Brown, Charlotte Hawkins; National Association of Colored Women; Terrell, Mary Eliza Church

■ ■ *Bibliography*

Collier-Thomas, Bettye. *N.C.N.W., 1935–1980.* Washington, D.C., 1981.

Giddings, Paula. *When and Where I Enter: The Impact of Black Women on Race and Sex in America.* New York: William Morrow, 1984.

JUDITH WEISENFELD (1996)

NATIONAL FEDERATION OF AFRO-AMERICAN WOMEN

Established in 1895 in Boston, the National Federation of Afro-American Women (NFAAW) was one of the first organizations created to represent African-American women on a national scale. Founded during the First National Conference of Colored Women of America, its mandate was to improve the image of black women by uplifting the race through middle-class domestic values. During its one year of existence, the federation included 104 delegates representing fifty-four women's clubs from fourteen states.

Several events crystallized the need for black women's groups to join together as a national entity in the early 1890s. The Women's Pavilion at the Columbian Exposition (1893) denied the participation of black women's organizations. The incident galvanized black women's groups in Washington D.C., New York, Boston, and Chicago and showed them they could no longer afford to limit their activism to the local arena.

The final catalyst toward unification was a letter written by James Jacks, president of the Missouri Press Association, to Florence Balgarnie, secretary of England's Anti-Lynching Society, in which Jacks attacked black women, claiming they were immoral, sexually promiscuous, and likely to be liars and thieves. Balgarnie sent the letter to Joseph Ruffin, founder of Boston's Women's Era Club, and Ruffin had it published in their journal, *Women's Era*. Women from all over the country met at the First National Conference of Colored Women of America in Boston (1895) to discuss the letter and other issues facing women, such as education, employment, and child rearing. While they stressed that white women could join their organization, they were less eager to admit lower-class blacks and centered their agenda around middle-class concerns.

At the close of the conference, the women voted to create a new, permanent national organization called the National Federation of Afro-American Women, which would try to change the image of the black woman, raise the moral standard of the lower class, and cultivate black middle-class women's domestic skills.

The National Federation of Afro-American Women coexisted with another organization, the National League of Colored Women, but both groups became convinced that to be effective they needed to come together in one organization. In 1896 the National Association of Colored Women was organized in an attempt to overcome the factionalism that had limited black women's political effectiveness throughout the 1890s. The merger spelled the dissolution of the National Federation of Afro-American Women after one year of existence.

See also Black Women's Club Movement

■ ■ *Bibliography*

Harley, Sharon, and Rosalyn Terborg-Penn, eds. *The Afro-American Woman: Struggles and Images.* Port Washington, N.Y.: Kennikat Press, 1978.

Salem, Dorothy. "Foundations for Organized Reform." In *To Better Our World: Black Women in Organized Reform, 1890–1920*, vol. 14 of *Black Women in U.S. History*, edited by Darlene Clark Hine. New York: Carlson, 1990.

MARIAN AGUIAR (1996)

NATIONAL HOSPITAL ASSOCIATION

The National Hospital Association (NHA) was established in August 1923 by the National Medical Association at its annual meeting in St. Louis. The parent body founded this new auxiliary organization to coordinate and guide its efforts in African-American hospital reform. The NHA's specific goals included the standardization of black hospitals and of the curricula at black nurse-training schools, the establishment of additional black hospitals, and the provision of more internships for black physicians.

African-American medical leaders' concerns that the growing importance of hospital standardization and accreditation would lead to the elimination of black hospitals prompted their establishment of the NHA. They recognized that many black hospitals were inferior institutions that were ineligible for approval by certifying agencies. But these facilities were critical to the careers of African-American physicians and, in many locations, to the lives of black patients. The NHA sought to improve black hospitals by attempting to ensure proper standards of education and efficiency in them. Therefore, one of its first actions was to issue in 1925 a set of minimum standards for its member hospitals. These standards included criteria on hospital supervision, record keeping, and the operation of nurse-training schools. Compared to the guidelines of the larger and more influential American College of Surgeons, these were rudimentary. Nonetheless, the NHA hoped that its efforts would forestall the closure of African-American hospitals and demonstrate to white physicians that their black colleagues could keep abreast of changes in medical and hospital practice.

Other activities of the NHA included the provision of technical assistance to hospitals, the sponsorship of professional conferences, and the publication of literature promoting proper hospital administration. The association also lobbied major health-care organizations such as the American Medical Association, the American College of Surgeons, and the American Hospital Association, urging them to take on a role in the improvement of black hospitals.

The NHA was a short-lived organization with limited effectiveness. It never had a full-time administrator or a permanent office. During its first ten years Knoxville physician H. M. Green served as its president while maintaining a busy medical practice. The NHA ran entirely on modest membership fees and often operated at a deficit. It never received financial or programmatic support from foundations or other health-care organizations. It lacked the financial and political muscle to implement and enforce its policies and failed to convince many black physicians of the importance of its goals. By the early 1940s the NHA had disbanded.

Despite these limitations the NHA played a significant role in African-American medical history. It provided black physicians and nurses with opportunities to learn about and discuss trends in hospital care. And it helped the National Medical Association to publicize and articulate the plight of black physicians, their patients, and their hospitals at a time when few outlets for voicing such concerns existed.

See also Nursing

■ ■ *Bibliography*

Gamble, Vanessa Northington. "The Negro Hospital Renaissance: The Black Hospital Movement." In *The American General Hospital: Communities and Social Contexts,* edited by Diana E. Long and Janet Golden, pp. 182–205. Ithaca, N.Y.: Cornell University Press, 1989.

Green, H. M. "Some Observations on and Lessons from the Experience of the Past Ten Years." *Journal of the National Medical Association* 26 (1934): 21–24.

VANESSA NORTHINGTON GAMBLE (1996)

NATIONALISM IN THE UNITED STATES IN THE NINETEENTH CENTURY

There have been numerous efforts to define *black nationalism,* a term that suggests some form of militancy that is somehow different from sit-ins or marches. Some associate the phrase with violence, while others equate black nationalism with some form of separatism, or simply as a counter to integration. One need only take a quick glance at a few anthologies about black nationalism to notice that a number of political projects and personalities with varying aims and ends are described as examples of black nationalism. But how does one go about identifying these as nationalistic? On what basis can one single out the essential features that specify black nationalism?

One possible point of departure can be found in Jeffrey Stout's claim that black nationalism "put the discourses of race and nation together, by projecting an imagined community—a people—for whom blackness serves as emblem" (Stout, 2002. p. 242). This view assumes there is something all black people share as black people—and that is readily recognizable by others. But there are any number of ways to think about this basic assumption.

Black nationalism, for example, is sometimes taken to mean a biological basis of national belonging. Here, the word *nation* points to a common biological or ontological essence among black people. Often drawing an analogy with a biological organism, this view sees *nation* as the essential unit in which the black individual's nature is fully realized. Another view holds that the character of a nation is environmentally determined: that there is something about one's place of origin that determines the essential features of the nation. Still, others invoke the phrase to talk of a community of shared ends or aspirations. These ends may vary. Some may seek recognition as a sovereign political unit among the community of nations. Others may simply hold self-determination as the desired end and expect to control the resources of their community or, perhaps, to return to a place of origin. Any number of these views overlap. They range from a kind of piety—a recognition of the sources upon which the existence of black people depends—to a way of imagining a future, something towards which black people aspire. And any of these views of black nationalism can be thought of in economic, political, or cultural terms.

The endless variations on the basic themes of black nationalism make it difficult, if not impossible, to say exactly what black nationalism is, though this is not necessarily a bad thing. Too often, scholarly efforts to use a set criterion to distinguish black nationalism from other political ideologies fall into rather ahistorical accounts of messy politics. If the term is to be helpful at all, one must go instead to the thicket of historical description; and the criterion is whether or not the term *black nationalism* "aids us in finding our way around the discursive terrain we occupy, which is partly a matter of knowing how to cope with the ambiguities one is likely to encounter there" (Stout, 2002. p. 242). In other words, one can always set aside the question of whether black nationalism has been correctly defined, and ask instead whether the varied practices singled out by the term are worth debate and investigation.

The practices singled out by nineteenth-century variants of black nationalism are, for the most part, rooted in a profound skepticism about the possibility of blacks flourishing in the United States. Already the victims of brutal social dislocation because of the transatlantic slave trade, African Americans, slave and free, witnessed the founding of a nation based on democratic principles and undemocratic practices, on an idea of freedom and the reality of a lack of freedom. John Adams's remarks during the struggle for independence best captures this basic contradiction at the heart of America's beginnings. "We won't be their [Britain's] negroes. Providence never designed us for negroes. I know, if it had it would have given us black hides and thick lips . . . which it hasn't done, and therefore never intended us for slaves" (Roediger, 1991, p. 28). Adams's understanding of freedom and his articulation of it as a basis for rebellion was predicated on an intimate knowledge of the lack of freedom represented by colonial slavery. For him and many others, African Americans were radically different, and the egalitarian principles of the American Revolution could not wipe those differences away. Alexis de Tocqueville recognized this as well. He wrote in *Democracy in America (1835-1840)*:

> The modern slave differs from his master not only in lacking freedom but also in his origins. You can make the Negro free, but you cannot prevent him facing the European as a stranger. That is not all; this man born in degradation, this stranger brought by slavery into our midst, is hardly recognized as sharing the common features of humanity. His face appears to us hideous, his intelligence limited, and his tastes low; we almost take him for something being intermediate between beast and man. (Tocqueville, 1969, pp. 341–342)

Tocqueville believed that slavery was the most formidable evil threatening the nation's future. And, in the end, doubting that black folk could ever experience the equality so critical to American democracy (they were unassimilable), he concluded that violent conflict between American blacks and whites in the South was "more or less distant but inevitable." The contradiction at the heart of this fragile experiment in democracy, as well as the persistent threat of arbitrary racial violence, led many African Americans to believe that America could never truly be home. Indeed, the precariousness of their conditions of living and the discourses of white supremacy that justified those conditions warranted a preoccupation with protection from racial violence, a demand for the recognition of African-American humanity, and a practical need for association among similarly situated selves.

PROTECTION, RECOGNITION, AND ASSOCIATION

A preoccupation with protection, recognition, and association constituted the basis of the rudimentary commitments informing many of the practices labeled as black nationalism in the nineteenth century. Collective humiliation, which the philosopher Isaiah Berlin clearly saw as the constitutive element of nationalisms generally, was the main impetus for African-American uses of the language of nationhood in the nineteenth century. This humiliation yielded a response—like the bent twig of the poet Friedrich von Schiller's (1759–1805) theory—of lashing back and a refusal to accept such conditions of living. As the fiery antebellum minister David Walker (c. 1785–1830) wrote in his *Appeal to the Coloured Citizens of the World* (1829): "There is an unconquerable disposition in the breasts of the blacks which, when it is fully awakened and put in motion will be subdued, only with the destruction of the animal existence. Get the blacks started, and if you do not have a gang of tigers and lions to deal with, I am a deceiver of the blacks and of the whites." This response involved solidaristic efforts among African Americans—that is, forms of active association predicated on common suffering and aimed at alleviating an oppressive situation. Of course, racial solidarity was thought of in a number of ways during the nineteenth century, ranging from a sense of collective purpose derived from the context of slavery and the reality of racial violence to claims of an essential racial self based in biology. In any case, the point to be made is that a concept of nation or peoplehood (conceived of in a number of different ways) informed much of African-American politics throughout the nineteenth century.

Invocations of peoplehood during this period involved varied appeals to solidarity based in what can be called a Black Christian imagination (i.e., a set of religious meanings specific to African-American life emerging out of the slave quarters and the condition of second-class citizenship). These appeals, often involving claims about civilization and moral respectability, ranged from calls for emigration from individuals, such as the shipowner Paul Cuffe (1759–1817) and the sail manufacturer James Forten (1766–1842), who advocated a back-to-Africa movement, to the formation of independent black churches by figures such as Richard Allen (1760–1831), the first bishop of the African Methodist Episcopal Church, and James Varick (1750–1827) and Abraham Thompson, founders of the African Methodist Episcopal Zion Church. To be sure, many African Americans found in the Christian gospel not only resources to imagine themselves as individually saved, but also ways to imagine themselves as collectively saved. African Americans often read the story of Hebrew bondage in Egypt and God's eventual deliverance of his chosen people as if they were the main characters: America was Egypt; they were the Israelites. In addition, many invoked *Psalms* 68:31—"Princes shall come out of Egypt, Ethiopia shall soon stretch forth her hands unto God"—as evidence of the inevitable liberation and flourishing of African-descended peoples. Such uses signaled a conception

of African-American collective identity. By appropriating the Bible, African-American Christians gave voice to their own sense of peoplehood and secured for themselves a common destiny and history as they elevated their experiences to biblical drama. This black Christian imagination influenced much of African-American life in the nineteenth century and produced manifold meanings about the conditions of African-American living, which became paradigmatic for the construction of black identity and politics.

African-American politics have seemingly been forever stamped with this Christian imprimatur, and black religious vocabularies informed black nationalism throughout the nineteenth century. However, what was distinctive about its use during the early nineteenth century was that racial solidarity and ideas of racial obligation were not based on some specious notion of race. That is to say, figures like David Walker, the enigmatic Robert Young (author of *The Ethiopian Manifesto* [1829]), the newspaper editor Samuel Cornish (1795–1858), and Bishop Richard Allen did not invoke a form of racial solidarity based in what the historian Wilson Moses describes as "a belief in consanguinity, a commitment to the conservation of racial or genetic purity, a myth of commonality and purity of blood" (Moses, 1996, pp. 4–5). Nor did these figures, and many like them, invoke the idea of solidarity in the name of forming a distinctive territorial unit based on such notions. Instead, the battle was engaged on the basis of common suffering and involved a set of responses on the part of a people acting for themselves to alleviate their condition.

Certainly, the period between the Fugitive Slave Act of 1850 and the end of the nineteenth century involved competing conceptions of racial solidarity and nation. The convulsions of the nineteenth century fundamentally transformed how individuals and groups understood themselves. The rising influence of science and the new technologies it created, the impact of large-scale industry, the rise of new states, and the waning authority of Christianity all contributed to a different sort of preoccupation with the search for origins. The meanings of words like *race* and *nation* shifted, and those shifts settled into common sense. Supported by the rising authority of science, race came to signify not only a common descent but also a way of marking, in nature, radical Otherness. Uses of *nation* assumed the importance of language, ethnicity, and territory in defining the boundaries of "the people" to extend beyond earlier uses. The focus was now on a set of common interests rather than a set of opposing interests.

African Americans were certainly not exempt from all of this. To be sure, the context of African-American living remained precarious. The Fugitive Slave Act, the failed promises of Reconstruction, and the sedimentation of Jim Crow reinforced the belief among many African Americans that America was not home and that liberty was the sole possession of white individuals. The desire for protection, recognition, and association remained and grew stronger in light of the repressive realities of the period. But the articulation of solidaristic efforts to resist such conditions drew on conceptions of race and nation that reflected the shifts mentioned earlier. Figures like Martin Delaney, Edward Blyden, Alexander Crummell, Bishop Henry McNeil Turner, W. E. B. Du Bois, and, eventually, Marcus Garvey sought to create political units reflective of a people bound to one another not only because of their common condition but also because of their race. Biology now mattered.

This is not to suggest that the older forms of thinking about racial solidarity fell away. Those ideas stood alongside the new ones and often commingled with them in what sometimes seemed a muddled and confused politics. Perhaps this is the source of much of the conceptual confusion in the study of nineteenth-century black nationalism. However, by turning one's attention to the actual practices singled out by the phrase, one sees African Americans groping for protection from arbitrary racial violence, demanding recognition of their humanity in the face of state-sanctioned apartheid, and finding comfort and solace among those similarly situated. All in the search, perhaps, for a place they could truly call home.

See also Afrocentrism; Allen, Richard; Black Power Movement; Blyden, Edward Wilmot; Civil Rights Movement, U.S.; Cornish, Samuel E.; Crummell, Alexander; Cuffe, Paul; Delany, Martin R.; Du Bois, W. E. B.; Forten, James; Garvey, Marcus; Labor and Labor Unions; Turner, Henry McNeal; Varick, James; Walker, David

■ ■ ■ *Bibliography*

Bracey, John, Jr., August Meier, and Elliot Rudwick, eds. *Black Nationalism in America*. Indianapolis, Ind.: Bobbs-Merrill, 1970.

Glaude, Eddie, Jr. *Exodus! Religion, Race, and Nation in Early Nineteenth-Century Black America*. Chicago: University of Chicago Press, 2000.

Glaude, Eddie, Jr., ed. *Is it Nation Time? Contemporary Essays on Black Power and Black Nationalism*. Chicago: University of Chicago Press, 2002.

Hobsbawm, E. J. *Nations and Nationalism Since 1780: Programme, Myth, Reality*. Cambridge, UK: Cambridge University Press, 1990.

Moses, Wilson. *The Golden Age of Black Nationalism, 1850–1925*. Hamden, Conn.: Archon Books, 1978.

Moses, Wilson, ed. *Classical Black Nationalism: From the American Revolution to Marcus Garvey*. New York: New York University Press, 1996.

Roediger, David. *The Wages of Whiteness: Race and the Making of the American Working Class*. London: Verso, 1991.

Stout, Jeffrey. "Theses on Black Nationalism." In *Is It Nation Time? Contemporary Essays on Black Power and Black Nationalism*, edited by Eddie S. Glaude Jr. Chicago: University of Chicago Press, 2002.

Tocqueville, Alexis de. *Democracy in America* (1835–1840). Translated by George Lawrence. Garden City, N.Y.: Doubleday, 1969.

Van DeBurg, William, ed. *Modern Black Nationalism: From Marcus Garvey to Louis Farrakhan*. New York: New York University Press, 1997.

West, Cornel. *Beyond Eurocentrism and Multiculturalism,* vol 2: *Prophetic Reflections: Notes on Race and Power in America*. Monroe, Me: Common Courage Press, 1993.

EDDIE S. GLAUDE JR. (2005)

NATIONAL LEAGUE FOR THE PROTECTION OF COLORED WOMEN

Founded by Frances Kellor and S. W. Layten in 1906, the National League for the Protection of Colored Women concerned itself with the predicament of women in domestic labor in northern cities. Job opportunities for African-American women in the cities were severely restricted; nearly 90 percent were employed in households as domestic servants. Wages were low and unregulated, and the hours were extremely long for women who worked as live-in domestics. Layten, a black Baptist activist, and Kellor, a white reformer, joined black and white women in New York to study these conditions and to try to change them. In addition to its base in New York, chapters of the league were active in Philadelphia, Baltimore, Washington, D.C., and Chicago.

A major focus of the league's work was the migration of southern African Americans to northern cities in search of a better life. Whereas the numbers migrating at the turn of the century were fewer than would come later, the predicament of young women was a matter of great concern for workers in the league. Many women arrived knowing no one, with little money, and with no arrangements for lodging. The league feared that these women might fall into dangerous situations, especially associations with houses of prostitution. Additional difficulties were presented by labor agents working in the South to encourage migration. Often, anxious migrants were tricked into signing contracts that left them little of their wages at the end of the month.

In order to deal with these issues, the league distributed information among southern black women about the realities of life in the North and warning of unscrupulous labor agents. In addition, it sent out its own people to meet new arrivals at train stations and ports to guide them to safe places to lodge. The league worked in conjunction with existing black women's shelters and created an effective network to deal with these problems. In 1911 the league became one of the founding organizations under the umbrella of the National Urban League.

See also National Urban League

■ ■ *Bibliography*

Kellor, Frances A. *Out of Work: A Study in Unemployment.* New York: G. P. Putnam's Sons, 1915. Reprint, New York, 1974.

Layten, S. W. "The Servant Problem." *Colored American* 12 (January 1907): 13–17.

Weiss, Nancy J. *The National Urban League, 1910–1940.* New York: Oxford University Press, 1974.

JUDITH WEISENFELD (1996)

NATIONAL NEGRO CONGRESS

The National Negro Congress (NNC) emerged from the Howard University Conference on the status of the Negro held in May 1935 in Washington, D.C. The organization formally got under way in 1936, held meetings at irregular intervals, and was composed predominantly of organizations and individuals active in the African-American community. For Ralph Bunche and others, the National Negro Congress held the promise of an interclass alliance including labor, clerics, entrepreneurs, elected officials, and others. The NNC's mission included protest against Jim Crow and organizing for the social, political, and economic advancement of African Americans.

Sponsors of the NNC included Charles H. Houston of the National Association for the Advancement of Colored People (NAACP), Alain Locke and Ralph Bunche of Howard University, Lester Granger of the National Urban League, John P. Davis of the Joint Committee on National Recovery, A. Philip Randolph of the Brotherhood of Sleeping Car Porters (who served as the organization's first president), and James Ford of the Communist Party.

The participation of the Communist Party caused controversy. From the beginning, the party played a prominent role within the NNC and grew after the 1937 convention. Its point of view was that the NNC was a united front of African Americans, meaning that despite class and ideological differences blacks should unite for common goals. However, by 1938 some noncommunists, such as Bunche, were troubled by the Communist Party's influence and left the NNC.

Critics of the NNC, ultimately including Randolph, were of the opinion that the organization was a front for the party and that it refused to take positions at variance with those of the Communists. These criticisms became sharper after the Nazi-Soviet Pact was concluded in August 1939, which led to the German invasion of Poland and the onset of World War II.

Many Communists were hesitant to criticize the pact, and NNC critics (for example, Randolph) began to drift away from the organization. Those who refused to leave the NNC felt that disputes over the pact were examples of the kind of ideological differences that should be submerged in the interest of a united front for the betterment of African Americans.

Despite these internecine conflicts, during its brief history the NNC rivaled the NAACP as a tribune for African Americans. It had fifty branch councils in nineteen states, published a number of communications organs, and sponsored numerous conferences.

In Harlem, where the NNC was particularly strong, it enjoyed the participation of the Rev. Adam Clayton Powell Jr. and the Harvard-educated Communist lawyer Benjamin J. Davis, and it spearheaded campaigns to secure jobs for blacks in mass transit. Across the nation the NNC could be found boycotting department stores that engaged in racial discrimination, protesting police brutality, and demanding federal antilynching legislation and investigation of the Ku Klux Klan and Black Legion. The NNC vigorously protested the Italian invasion of Ethiopia and they perceived as laggard the policies of the U.S. State Department in opposing this action.

In a number of communities, the NNC worked closely with NAACP branches, affiliates of the Congress of Industrial Organizations (CIO), the Southern Conference for Human Welfare, and the American Committee for the Protection of the Foreign Born. After the United States entered World War II in 1941, this kind of collaboration increased. Since the United States was allied with the Soviet Union from 1941 to 1945, the role of Communists within the NNC was not seen by many noncommunists as a bar to cooperation and the NNC experienced some growth during this period after the difficulties of 1939.

Between 1942 and 1945 the NNC played a leading role in the formation of the Negro Labor Victory Committee (NLVC), which in Harlem and elsewhere mobilized African Americans against fascism abroad and Jim Crow at home.

Nevertheless, neither the NNC nor the NLVC was able to survive the end of the war and the onset of the Cold War and Red Scare. By 1946 it was common for the NNC to be referred to as a communist front and a tool of Moscow. The transformation of the Soviet Union from an ally to an enemy of the United States was a leading factor in this changed perception, and in the NNC's eventual demise. Between 1946 and 1947 the NNC was subsumed by the Civil Rights Congress, another organization closely related to the Communist Party but one whose mission, fighting political and racist repression, was broader and less exclusively focused on African-American affairs.

See also Brotherhood of Sleeping Car Porters; Bunche, Ralph; Civil Rights Congress; Communist Party of the United States; Ford, James W.; Jim Crow; Locke, Alain Leroy; National Association for the Advancement of Colored People (NAACP); National Urban League; Randolph, Asa Philip

■■ *Bibliography*

Horne, Gerald. *Communist Front? The Civil Rights Congress, 1946–1956.* Rutherford, N.J.: Fairleigh Dickinson University Press, 1988.

Hughes, Cicero Alvin. "Toward a Black United Front: The National Negro Congress Movement." Ph.D. diss., Ohio University, 1982.

Streater, John Baxter. "The National Negro Congress, 1936–1947." Ph.D. diss., University of Cincinnati, 1981.

GERALD HORNE (1996)

NATIONAL NEGRO LABOR COUNCIL

❙❙❙

The National Negro Labor Council (NNLC) was established in 1951 to promote the cause of African-American workers. Although beleaguered and ultimately extinguished by the repressive political environment of the 1950s, the organization contested economic discrimination in a variety of settings and thus helped to keep alive the battle for civil rights in the realm of labor.

During the New Deal and World War II, the Congress of Industrial Organizations (CIO), along with such allies as the National Negro Congress, the March on Washington Movement, and at times, the National Association for the Advancement of Colored People, had done much to transform organized labor from a bastion of Jim Crow into a leading agent of civil rights struggle. Mass campaigns for racial equality at work and in unions, together with the wartime mobilization, advanced the position of African Americans in the workplace and spawned a new generation of black union leadership. After the war, however, the outlook for black workers turned increasingly dismal. Peacetime reconversion, spreading mechanization, and a hardening of workplace discrimination conspired to squeeze large numbers of African Americans out of industry, even as thousands of displaced black farmers were moving from the rural South into the industrial North. Meanwhile, the conservative climate of the emerging cold war era dampened the CIO's commitment to civil rights organizing; indeed, the expulsion from its ranks of communist-oriented unions in the late 1940s banished significant strongholds of black membership, along with many of the CIO's most energetic exponents of racial justice.

In June 1950 over nine hundred labor activists, predominantly black, gathered in Chicago at a National Labor Conference for Negro Rights. During the following year twenty-three Negro Labor Councils (NLCs) were established in key industrial centers around the country. In October 1951 representatives from these councils met in Cincinnati to form the National Negro Labor Council. In a founding Statement of Principles, the NNLC pledged to "work unitedly with the trade unions to bring about greater cooperation between all sections of the Negro people and the trade union movement." While it focused on equal economic opportunity, the NNLC advocated all measures essential to "full citizenship," including an end to police brutality and mob violence, the right to vote and hold public office, and the abolition of segregation in housing and in other public facilities.

The NNLC drew much of its leadership and active followers either from the unions recently expelled from the CIO—including the United Electrical, Radio, and Machine Workers; the International Mine, Mill, and Smelter Workers; the Food, Tobacco, Agricultural and Allied Workers; the National Union of Marine Cooks and Stewards; the International Fur and Leather Workers; and the International Longshoremen's and Warehousemen's Union—or from the left-wing bastions of mainstream unions, such as the United Packinghouse Workers, the Amalgamated Clothing Workers, and the United Auto Workers. (Detroit's vast UAW Local 600, a center of militant black leadership, made up a particularly vital base of

Delegates to the Third Annual Convention of the National Negro Labor Council, Chicago, Illinois, 1953. *Detroit's vast UAW Local 600, a center of militant black leadership, made up a particularly vital base of support, with William R. Hood, recording secretary for Local 600, serving as president of the national organization, and Coleman A. Young, organizer for Amalgamated Clothing Workers in Detroit, serving as executive secretary.* PHOTOGRAPHS AND PRINTS DIVISION, SCHOMBURG CENTER FOR RESEARCH IN BLACK CULTURE, THE NEW YORK PUBLIC LIBRARY, ASTOR, LENOX AND TILDEN FOUNDATIONS.

the support). In cities such as San Francisco, Detroit, Washington, D.C., Chicago, Cleveland, New York, and Louisville, NLCs cultivated allies within the African-American community, as well as among sympathetic whites. William R. Hood, recording secretary of UAW Local 600, served as president of the national organization. Coleman A. Young, then organizer for the Amalgamated Clothing Workers in Detroit, served as executive secretary. World-renowned singer, actor, and civil rights leader Paul Robeson was an active supporter.

Over the first half of the 1950s, the NNLC initiated or rallied behind a series of public campaigns around the country. Local NLCs confronted racial barriers to hiring or advancement at a number of enterprises, including the Ford Motor Company, the Statler and Sherry Netherland

hotels (New York), Sears-Roebuck (Cleveland, San Francisco), General Electric (Louisville), the U.S. Bureau of Engraving (Washington, D.C.), the Detroit Tigers, Drexel National Bank (Chicago), and American Airlines. Through petitions and write-in drives, picket lines and local publications, visiting committees and job-training programs, the NNLC helped to open up employment for African-American men and women as streetcar motormen and conductors, hotel workers, truck drivers, clerks and salespeople, and bank officials, and in previously unobtainable levels of skilled industrial work. The NNLC called on unions to demand the inclusion of a model "Fair Employment Practices" clause in labor contracts and to bring African Americans into leadership positions. The NNLC also mobilized support for strikes in which black workers figured prominently, including those at International Harvester in Chicago (1952) and among sugarcane workers in Louisiana (1953).

The NNLC encountered a formidable array of obstacles. Employers remained widely resistant to the call for nonracial hiring; the airline industry, for example, continued to deny blacks access to skilled jobs, as did virtually all employers around the South targeted by the NNLC. Most of the labor establishment, for its part, turned a cold shoulder to the NNLC. CIO leaders such as Walter Reuther and James B. Carey regularly condemned it as an agent of communism, while many AFL unions remained openly opposed to organizing black workers on an equal basis, if at all. Much of the African-American community remained aloof from the NNLC, or openly condemned it, because of its "communist" associations. The NAACP and the National Urban League were particularly vocal in their denunciations. Finally, government repression took its toll. The NNLC was called before the House Committee on Un-American Activities and Subversive Activities Control Board to answer charges that it was a "Communist-Front organization." In 1956, faced with insurmountable legal expenses, the NNLC leadership voted to disband the organization.

Historical assessments of the NNLC have diverged sharply, reflecting, often extending, the heated debates of contemporaries. Anticommunist scholars have tended flatly to characterize it as a "front" organization, a creation of the Communist Party lacking authentic roots in the black community (Record, 1964). Historians sympathetic to the Communist Party, on the other hand, have stressed the self-directed enterprise of black labor activists as the driving force behind the NNLC and de-emphasized the role of the party (Foner, 1974). In the 1980s and early 1990s historians began to paint a more nuanced and varied picture of the relationship between African-American workers and the Communist Party (Korstad and Lichtenstein, 1988; Kelley, 1990). But many of the campaigns in which the NNLC played a role still await in-depth scholarly attention. Such research is likely to bring to light an organization closely linked but not reducible to the Communist Party—an expression at once of the party's rhetorical and tactical approach and of the genuine initiative of black workers, both in and out of the party.

However portrayed, the NNLC left a mixed legacy. Its influence and impact, although in some instances dramatic, were ultimately limited, and racial discrimination at the workplace and in unions remained pervasive at the time of its demise. A new civil rights movement was then in the making, but its center of gravity would materialize in the black church and independent protest organizations.

See also Labor and Labor Unions

■ ■ *Bibliography*

Foner, Philip S. "The National Negro Labor Council, 1951–1955." In *Organized Labor and the Black Worker, 1619–1973.* New York: Praeger, 1974, pp. 293–311.

Kelley, Robin D. G. *Hammer and Hoe: Alabama Communists During the Great Depression.* Chapel Hill: University of North Carolina Press, 1990.

Korstad, Robert, and Nelson Lichtenstein. "Opportunities Found and Lost: Labor, Radicals, and the Early Civil Rights Movement." *Journal of American History* 75 (1988): 786–811.

Record, Wilson. "Since 1950." In *Race and Radicalism: The NAACP and the Communist Party in Conflict.* Ithaca, N.Y.: Cornell University Press, 1964, pp. 169–221.

Thomas, Richard. "Blacks and the CIO." In *Working for Democracy: American Workers from the Revolution to the Present*, edited by Paul Buhle and Alan Dawley, pp. 93–100. Urbana: University of Illinois Press, 1985.

Thompson, Mindy. *The National Negro Labor Council: A History.* New York: AIMS Press, 1978.

DANIEL LETWIN (1996)

NATIONAL URBAN LEAGUE

■ ■ ■

Founded in New York City in 1911 through the consolidation of the Committee for Improving the Industrial Condition of Negroes in New York (1906), the National League for the Protection of Colored Women (1906), and the Committee on Urban Conditions Among Negroes (1910), the National Urban League quickly established itself as the principal organization then dealing with the economic and social problems of blacks in American cities.

The league divided with its contemporary, the National Association for the Advancement of Colored People, the work of the emerging struggle for racial advancement. Securing the legal rights of black Americans was the principal business of the NAACP; promoting economic opportunity and social welfare was the responsibility of the Urban League.

Committed to improving employment opportunities for blacks, the Urban League placed workers in the private sector, attacked the color line in organized labor, and sponsored programs of vocational guidance and job training. While it first concentrated on changing discriminatory employment practices in the private sector, it became involved increasingly over time in trying to influence the development of public policy. During the Great Depression, it lobbied for the inclusion of blacks in federal relief and recovery programs; in the 1940s, it pressed for an end to discrimination in defense industries and for the desegregation of the armed forces.

In the 1950s the league still measured its accomplishments in terms of pilot placements of blacks in jobs previously closed to them because of race. In the 1960s, with the passage of civil rights legislation and the pressures of urban violence, the climate changed. Now the league reported tens of thousands of placements annually in new or upgraded jobs. It sponsored an array of new projects to improve employment opportunities: a national skills bank, for example, which matched blacks who had marketable skills with positions that utilized their talents, and an on-the-job-training program that placed unskilled workers in training slots in private industry. In the 1970s and 1980s, the league pioneered a range of other employment programs providing skills training, apprenticeships, and job placements.

The league grounded its work in social welfare in scientific investigations of conditions among urban blacks that provided the basis for practical reform. Its studies—some published independently, some reported in the league's magazine, *Opportunity: Journal of Negro Life* (1923–1949)—contributed importantly to the development of a body of reliable literature on aspects of black urban life and helped to shape public and private policy with respect to race.

The Urban League pioneered professional social service training for blacks. The agency encouraged black colleges to incorporate instruction in economics, sociology, and urban problems in their curricula, and it cooperated in establishing the first training center for black social workers. An Urban League fellowship program enabled promising blacks to pursue advanced studies at designated schools of social work while gaining some practical experience at the Urban League or similar agencies. The result was a corps of professional black social workers, whom the league placed in a wide range of social service agencies.

The Urban League adapted for blacks the welfare services already offered to whites by settlement houses, charitable agencies, and immigrant aid societies. Working principally through a network of local affiliates, the league counseled blacks new to the cities on behavior, dress, sanitation, health, and homemaking, and sponsored community centers, clinics, kindergartens and day nurseries, and summer camps. League staff members engaged in casework to deal with individual problems, including juvenile delinquency, truancy, and marital adjustment.

In the 1960s the Urban League supplemented its traditional social service approach with a more activist commitment to civil rights. It embraced direct action and community organization, sponsored leadership development and voter education and registration projects, helped organize the March on Washington of 1963 and the Poor People's Washington Campaign of 1968, called for a domestic Marshall Plan, and began to concentrate on building economic and political power in inner cities. The agency's services reflected a combination of new activism and the traditional Urban League concerns: assistance to black veterans, campaigns for open housing, consumer protection, efforts to find adoptive families for hard-to-place black children, as well as tutoring programs for ghetto youngsters, and street academies to prepare high school dropouts to go to college.

In the 1970s the league became a major subcontractor for government employment and social welfare programs and worked increasingly closely with Congress, the executive departments, and the regulatory agencies as an advocate of the interests of black Americans. It significantly expanded its research capacity, with a range of new monographs and special studies, a policy research journal, *The Urban League Review* (1975–), and a widely publicized annual report, *The State of Black America* (1976–). In the 1980s, as federal social programs were cut back, the organization looked increasingly to black self-help, seeking to mobilize the institutions of the black community to address some of the most persistent problems of the ghetto—the crisis in the public schools and the high incidence of teenage pregnancy, single female-headed households, and crime.

Guided in its earliest years by George Edmund Haynes, a sociologist who was the first black to earn a Ph.D. from Columbia University, in 1917 the National Urban League came under the direction of his assistant, Eugene Kinckle Jones, a former high school teacher who also held an advanced degree in sociology. Jones was succeeded as executive secretary in 1941 by Lester B. Granger, a social worker who had been secretary of the league's Workers' Bureau. Granger stepped down in 1961, turning the league's leadership over to Whitney M. Young Jr., dean of the Atlanta School of Social Work, who served until his death in 1971. Vernon E. Jordan, a lawyer then serving as executive director of the United Negro College Fund, was named president of the National Urban League in 1972. Jordan was succeeded in 1982 by John E. Jacob, also a social worker, who had spent his professional career in a number of Urban League posts, including that of executive vice president of the national organization.

During the 1990s, under the administration of Hugh Price, the league regained some of its former importance, and became a leading clearinghouse and lobbying group in the struggle to reduce racial disparities in education. Price's principal goals were to strengthen the organization's commitment to education and youth development, individual and community-wide economic empowerment, affirmative action, and inclusiveness. Before the end of his tenure in 2003, he established the league's Institute of Opportunity and Equality and the Campaign for African American Achievement. Price's successor, former New Orleans mayor Marc H. Morial, in his first year as president of the Urban League secured over ten million dollars in funding to support affiliate programs and created the Legislative Policy Conference, called "NUL on the Hill," referring to Capitol Hill in Washington, D.C. Morial also created a multimillion-dollar equity fund for new minority-owned businesses through a tax-credit program.

See also *Opportunity: Journal of Negro Life*; Civil Rights Movement, U.S.; National Association for the Advancement of Colored People (NAACP); United Negro College Fund

■ ■ *Bibliography*

Allman, Christian. "Marc Morial: Keeping Economic Empowerment for African Americans Front and Center." *Black Collegian* (October 1, 2003): pp. 106 ff.

Moore, Jesse Thomas, Jr. *A Search for Equality: The National Urban League, 1910–1961*. University Park: Pennsylvania State University Press, 1981.

National Urban League. *Eightieth Anniversary, 1910–1990*. New York: National Urban League, 1990.

Parris, Guichard, and Lester Brooks. *Blacks in the City: A History of the National Urban League*. Boston: Little, Brown, 1971.

Weiss, Nancy J. *The National Urban League, 1910–1940*. New York: Oxford University Press, 1974.

Weiss, Nancy J. *Whitney M. Young, Jr., and the Struggle for Civil Rights*. Princeton, N.J.: Princeton University Press, 1989.

NANCY J. WEISS (1996)
Updated by publisher 2005

NATIONAL WELFARE RIGHTS ORGANIZATION

The National Welfare Rights Organization (NWRO) was a militant organization of poor women on welfare that mobilized in the 1960s and early 1970s to lobby for changes in welfare policy, press for increased aid to recipients, and demand more humane treatment by government caseworkers. It was founded in spring 1966 by middle-class activists and women on welfare who had been organizing since the early 1960s. The organization was overwhelmingly African American, and membership was limited to welfare recipients, most of whom received Aid to Families with Dependent Children (AFDC). The NWRO grew rapidly, more than doubling from 10,000 in 1968 to 22,000 in 1969. Actual participation in the movement was much higher, perhaps reaching 100,000 at its peak in 1969. The NWRO supported, coordinated, and directed efforts of local groups in places such as Los Angeles, Newark, Boston, Philadelphia, Baltimore, and Des Moines, with the largest chapter in New York City.

The welfare rights movement was an important example of the changing nature of political struggle in the 1960s. After years of intense protest around desegregation and voting rights, many civil rights leaders became disillusioned with a strategy that did not address the immediate needs of most members of the African-American community. They increasingly came to the conclusion that civil rights without economic justice was a hollow victory. In its early years the NWRO got widespread support from liberal churches, civil rights organizations, and government antipoverty programs that were part of President Lyndon Johnson's Great Society program.

Welfare leaders of the NWRO sought to address problems of urban poverty by targeting the welfare system. They fought to get an adequate monthly grant, decent day care, and practical job-training programs. They believed the state had a responsibility to provide for all of its citizens in need. One of their central demands was a guaranteed annual income, which they believed the federal government should provide for every American. They opposed "morality" investigations by government caseworkers, which they found degrading, and affirmed the legitimacy of female-headed households. The NWRO believed that AFDC recipients should have access to decent-paying jobs but also supported the right of these mothers to stay home and care for their children.

The primary strategy for the welfare rights movement was to apply for "special grants" for clothing and household items to which welfare recipients were entitled. Anywhere from thirty to three hundred women would go to a welfare office together and demand money immediately for such things as school clothing and new furniture. If welfare officials refused their request, they would hold a sit-in or another form of protest until their demands were met. By inundating welfare offices with such requests, activists hoped to put pressure on the system and effect more fundamental changes to improve the lives of recipients. In the early years this strategy was very successful and was the key way in which leaders built up the membership of their organization. The NWRO also developed alliances with other political groups, publicized their grievances, and held mass rallies and marches.

For the women on welfare, their goals became two-fold: to pose direct and militant challenges to the state and to create an organization of poor women that was truly led by poor women. Women organizers on welfare, such as Johnnie Tillmon in Watts, Los Angeles, and Beulah Sanders in New York City, made up the National Coordinating Committee and were invested with formal decision-making authority. However, much of the day-to-day running of the organization was in the hands of the executive director and the mostly white, male, middle-class staff. George Wiley, an African-American chemistry professor and former associate director of the Congress of Racial Equality (CORE), was elected executive director of NWRO in 1966 and remained in that position until 1973. Wiley and his staff raised money, planned conferences and meetings, and set short-term goals. However, tension developed within the NWRO as the women struggled to define their goals, outline their strategy, and assert their autonomy.

By the early 1970s the NWRO was in trouble. As the demands for special grants led to fewer material gains because of changes in state and city policy, membership began to decline. In addition, mainstream and liberal support waned as an antiwelfare backlash swept the nation and popular support for sweeping reforms diminished. This contributed to the decline of the NWRO. In 1972 the NWRO was $150,000 in debt. The following year the resignation of the organization's primary fund-raiser, George Wiley, did little to resolve the financial difficulties of the organization. In 1975 NWRO was forced to file for bankruptcy, and it ceased operations shortly thereafter.

Although often defined as a movement of poor people, the welfare rights movement was also a movement of black women. They saw their struggle as one in which race, class, and gender were inextricably tied together. They fought for the right of economic security, challenged the popular assumption that families headed by black women were dysfunctional, and identified their movement as part of the larger struggle for black liberation. In so doing, they laid the groundwork for future grassroots struggles by poor black women.

See also Congress of Racial Equality (CORE)

■ ■ *Bibliography*

Piven, Frances Fox, and Richard Sloward. *Poor People's Movements: How They Succeed, Why They Fail.* New York: Vintage Books, 1979.

Pope, Jacqueline. *Biting the Hand That Feeds Them.* New York: Praeger, 1989.

West, Guida. *The National Welfare Rights Organization: The Social Protest of Poor Women.* New York: Praeger, 1981.

PREMILLA NADASEN (1996)
Updated by publisher 2005

NATION OF ISLAM

In the midsummer of 1930, a friendly but mysterious peddler appeared among rural southern immigrants in a black ghetto of Detroit called "Paradise Valley," selling raincoats, silks, and other sundries but also giving advice to the poor residents about their health and spiritual development. He told them about their "true religion," not Christianity but the "religion of the Black Men" of Asia and Africa. Using both the Bible and the Qur'an in his messages, he taught at first in the private homes of his followers, then rented a hall that was called the Temple of Islam.

This mysterious stranger often referred to himself as Mr. Farrad Mohammed, or sometimes as Mr. Wali Farrad, W. D. Fard, or Professor Ford. Master Fard, as he came to be called, taught his followers about a period of temporary domination and persecution by white "blue-eyed devils," who had achieved their power by brutality, murder, and trickery. But as a prerequisite for black liberation, he stressed the importance of attaining "knowledge of self." He told his followers that they were not Americans and therefore owed no allegiance to the American flag. He wrote two manuals for the movement—*The Secret Ritual of the Nation of Islam,* which is transmitted orally to members, and *Teaching for the Lost-Found Nation of Islam in a Mathematical Way,* which is written in symbolic language and requires special interpretation. Fard established several organizations: the University of Islam, to propagate his teachings; the Muslim Girls Training, to teach female members home economics and how to be a proper Muslim woman; and the Fruit of Islam, consisting of selected male members, to provide security for Muslim leaders and to enforce the disciplinary rules.

One of the earliest officers of the movement and Fard's most trusted lieutenant was Robert Poole, alias Elijah Poole, who was given the Muslim name Elijah Muhammad (Perry, 1991, p. 143). The son of a rural Baptist minister and sharecropper from Sandersville, Georgia, Poole had immigrated with his family to Detroit in 1923; he and several of his brothers joined the Nation of Islam in 1931. Although he had only a third-grade education,

During a Nation of Islam convention, a Black Muslim displays a newspaper featuring a picture of Elijah Muhammad. *The newspaper's headline, "A Savior is Born," refers to the anniversary of the birth of the group's founder, Wallace Fard Muhammad.* BETTMANN/CORBIS

Elijah Muhammad's shrewd native intelligence and hard work enabled him to rise through the ranks rapidly, and he was chosen by Fard as the chief minister of Islam to preside over the daily affairs of the organization. Fard's mysterious disappearance in 1934 led to an internal struggle for the leadership of the Nation of Islam. As a result of this strife, Muhammad eventually moved his family and close followers, settling on the south side of Chicago in 1936. There they established Temple of Islam No. 2, which eventually became the national headquarters of the movement.

Throughout the 1940s, Muhammad reshaped the Nation and gave it his own imprimatur. He firmly established the doctrine that Master Fard was "Allah," and that God is a black man, proclaiming that he, the "Honorable" Elijah Muhammad, knew Allah personally and was anointed his "Messenger." Prior to 1961, members of the Nation of Islam were called "Voodoo People" or "People of the Temple"; Professor C. Eric Lincoln's study *The Black Muslims in America* (1961) established the usage of the phrase "Black Muslims" in referring to the Nation of Islam. Under Muhammad's guidance, the Nation developed a two-pronged attack on the problems of the black masses: the development of economic independence and the recovery of an acceptable identity. "Do for Self" became the rallying cry of the movement, which encouraged economic self-reliance for individuals and the black community. The economic ethic of the Black Muslims was a kind of black Puritanism—hard work, frugality, and the avoidance of debt, self-improvement, and a conservative lifestyle.

During the forty-one-year period of his leadership, Muhammad and his followers established more than one hundred temples nationwide and innumerable grocery stores, restaurants, bakeries, and other small businesses. The Nation of Islam also became famous for the foods—bean pies and whiting—it peddled in black communities to improve the nutrition and physical health of African Americans. It strictly forbade alcohol, drugs, pork, and an unhealthy diet. Elijah Muhammad was prescient in his advice on nutrition: "You are what you eat," he often said. In his *Message to the Black Man in America* (1965), Muhammad diagnosed the vulnerabilities of the black psyche as stemming from a confusion of identity and self-hatred caused by white racism; the cure he prescribed was radical surgery, the formation of a separate black nation.

Muhammad's 120 "degrees," or lessons, and the major doctrines and beliefs of the Nation of Islam elaborated on aspects of this central message. The white man is a "devil by nature," unable to respect anyone who is not white and the historical and persistent source of harm and injury to black people. The central theological myth of the Nation tells of Yakub, a black mad scientist who rebelled against Allah by creating the white race, a weak hybrid people who were permitted temporary dominance of the world. But according to the apocalyptic beliefs of the Black Muslims, there will be a clash between the forces of good (blacks) and the forces of evil (whites) in the not-too-distant future, an Armageddon from which black people will emerge victorious and re-create their original hegemony under Allah throughout the world.

All these myths and doctrines have functioned as a theodicy for the Black Muslims, as an explanation and rationalization for the pain and suffering inflicted on black people in America. For example, Malcolm Little described the powerful, jarring impact that the revelation of religious truth had on him in the Norfolk State Prison in Massachusetts after his brother Reginald told him, "The white man

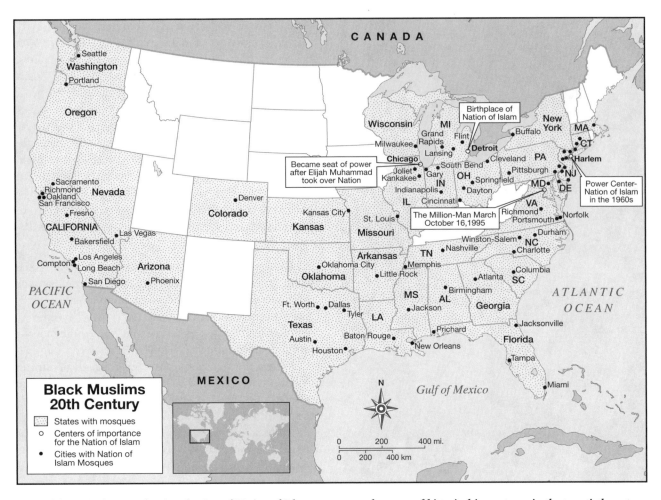

Map of the United States showing the sites of Nation of Islam mosques and centers of historical importance in the twentieth century. The Black Muslims were founded by W. D. Fard in Detroit c. 1930. Elijah (Poole) Muhammad led the organization for more than four decades, using many of the methods of Marcus Garvey to blend Islam with black nationalism, attracting large numbers of followers. MAP BY XNR PRODUCTIONS. THE GALE GROUP.

is the Devil." The doctrines of the Nation transformed the chaos of the world behind prison bars into a cosmos, an ordered reality. Malcolm finally had an explanation for the extreme poverty and tragedies his family suffered, and for all the years he had spent hustling and pimping on the streets of Roxbury and Harlem as "Detroit Red." The conversion and total transformation of Malcolm Little into Malcolm X in prison in 1947 is a story of the effectiveness of Elijah Muhammad's message, one that was repeated thousands of times during the period of Muhammad's leadership. Dropping one's surname and taking on an X, standard practice in the movement, was an outward symbol of inward changes: it meant ex-Christian, ex-Negro, ex-slave.

The years between Malcolm's release from prison and his assassination, 1952 to 1965, mark the period of the greatest growth and influence of the Nation of Islam. After

meeting Elijah Muhammad in 1952, Malcolm began organizing Muslim temples in New York, Philadelphia, and Boston, and in the South and on the West Coast as well. He founded the Nation's newspaper, *Muhammad Speaks,* in the basement of his home and initiated the practice of requiring every male Muslim to sell an assigned quota of newspapers on the street as a recruiting and fund-raising device. He rose rapidly through the ranks to become minister of Boston Temple No. 11 and was later rewarded with the post of minister of Temple No. 7 in Harlem, the largest and most prestigious of the temples after the Chicago headquarters. The Honorable Elijah Muhammad recognized his organizational talents, enormous charismatic appeal, and forensic abilities by naming Malcolm national representative of the Nation of Islam, second in rank to the Messenger himself. Under his lieutenancy, the Nation achieved a membership estimated at 500,000. But as in

Nation of Islam mosque, Chicago, Illinois. © DANIEL LAINÉ/CORBIS

other movements of this kind, the numbers involved were quite fluid and the Nation's influence, refracted through the public charisma of Malcolm X, greatly exceeded its actual numbers.

Malcolm's keen intellect, incisive wit, and ardent radicalism made him a formidable critic of American society, including the civil rights movement. As a favorite media personality, he challenged the Rev. Dr. Martin Luther King Jr.'s central notions of "integration" and "nonviolence." Malcolm felt that what was at stake, at a deeper level than the civil right to sit in a restaurant or even to vote, was the integrity of black selfhood and its independence. His biting critique of the "so-called Negro" and his emphasis on the recovery of black self-identity and independence provided the intellectual foundations for the American Black Power movement and black-consciousness movement of the late 1960s and 1970s. In contrast to King's nonviolence, Malcolm urged his followers to defend themselves "by any means necessary." He articulated the pent-up frustration, bitterness, and rage felt by the dispossessed black masses, the "grass roots."

As the result of a dispute on political philosophy and morality with Elijah Muhammad, Malcolm left the Nation of Islam in March 1964 in order to form his own organizations, the Muslim Mosque Inc. and the Organization for Afro-American Unity. He took the Muslim name el-Hajj Malik el-Shabazz after converting to orthodox Sunni Islam and participating in the hajj, the annual pilgrimage to Mecca. Malcolm was assassinated on February 21, 1965, while he was delivering a lecture at the Audubon Ballroom in Harlem.

From 1965 until Elijah Muhammad's death in February 1975, the Nation of Islam prospered economically, but its membership never surged again. Minister Louis X of Boston, also called Louis Abdul Farrakhan, replaced Malcolm as the national representative and the head minister of Temple No. 7 in New York. During this period, the Nation acquired an ultramodern printing press, cattle farms in Georgia and Alabama, and a bank in Chicago. After a bout of illness, Muhammad died in Chicago, and one of his six sons, Wallace Deen Muhammad (later Imam Warith Deen Mohammed), was named supreme minister of the Nation of Islam. However, two months later Wallace shocked his followers and the world by declaring that whites were no longer viewed as devils and they could join the movement. He began to make radical changes in the doctrines and the structure of the Nation, moving it in the direction of orthodox Sunni Islam.

The changes introduced by Imam Warith Deen Mohammed led to a splintering of the movement, especially among the hard-core black-nationalist followers. In 1978, Louis Farrakhan led a schismatic group that succeeded in resurrecting the old Nation of Islam. Farrakhan's Nation, which is also based in Chicago, retains the black-nationalist and separatist beliefs and doctrines that were central to the teachings of Elijah Muhammad. Farrakhan displays much of the charisma and forensic candor of Malcolm X, and his message of black nationalism is again directed to those mired in the underclass, as well as to disillusioned intellectuals, via the Nation's *Final Call* newspaper and popular rap-music groups such as Public Enemy. During the mid-1990s, Minister Farrakhan sought to broaden the appeal of the Nation of Islam and improve the organization's shaky finances. In 1995, Farrakhan organized the Million Man March. Farrakhan's leadership and his keynote address at the March brought him new legitimacy as a black leader. Shortly afterward, he was forced to discipline and later dismiss a chief assistant, Minister Khallid Muhammad, after Muhammad gave a series of excessive nationalist and anti-Semitic speeches at Howard University. In 1996, Farrakhan announced that the Nation of Islam would receive a one million dollar contribution from Libyan president Moammar Khaddafi. During this period, the Nation of Islam gained some notable new members, including boxer Mike Tyson and ousted NAACP leader Rev. Benjamin Chavis (who officially converted to Islam in 1997).

During his struggle with prostate cancer in the late 1990s, Farrakhan claimed that he had a "near death experience," which led him to draw closer spiritually to orthodox Sunni Islam. He directed that members of the Nation should learn how to do the formal prostration and ritual prayers in Arabic. He also instituted the traditional Islamic Friday afternoon Ju'mah prayer service in all of the Nation's mosques. Members of the Nation were also instructed to follow the lunar calendar for their Ramadan fasting period instead of performing the fast during the month of December as a counter to the Christmas celebration in the wider society as taught by Elijah Muhammad. At the Savior's Day meetings in Chicago in 2000 and 2001, Minister Farrakhan and Imam Warith Deen Mohammed held joint Friday Ju'mah prayer services together with their followers. Imam Mohammed called Farrakhan a "true Muslim" because of the adoption of the Friday services. While both leaders have reconciled their differences from the past, they intend to keep their movements separate. To celebrate the tenth anniversary of the Million Man March, Farrakhan is inviting African-American men, women, and children to Washington, D.C., in October 2005.

However, despite the Nation of Islam's nationwide visibility and the continuing popularity of its nationalist message in inner-city communities, its membership has remained small. Through more than sixty years, the Nation of Islam in its various forms has become the longest lasting and most enduring of the black militant and separatist movements that have appeared in the history of black people in the United States. Besides its crucial role in the development of the black-consciousness movement, the Nation is important for having introduced Islam as a fourth major religious tradition in American society, alongside Protestantism, Catholicism, and Judaism.

See also Islam; Malcolm X; Muhammad, Elijah

■■ *Bibliography*

Breitman, George, ed. *Malcolm X Speaks*. New York: Pathfinder Press, 1965.

Essien-Udom, E. U. *Black Nationalism: A Search for Identity in America*. Chicago: University of Chicago Press, 1962.

Farrakhan, Louis. *Seven Speeches*. Chicago: WKU and Final Call, Inc., 1974.

Lincoln, C. Eric. *The Black Muslims in America*. Boston: Beacon Press, 1961.

Malcolm X and Alex Haley. *The Autobiography of Malcolm X*. New York: Grove Press, 1965.

Mamiya, Lawrence H. "From Black Muslim to Bilalian: The Evolution of a Movement." *Journal for the Scientific Study of Religion* 21, no. 2 (June 1982): 138–152.

Mohammad, Warith Deen. *As the Light Shineth from the East*. Chicago: WDM Publishing, 1980.

Muhammad, Elijah. *Message to the Black Man in America*. Chicago: The Final Call, 1965.

Perry, Bruce. *Malcolm: The Life of a Man Who Changed Black America*. Barrytown, N.Y.: Station Hill Press, 1991.

Waugh, Earle H., Baha Abu-Laban, and Regula B. Qureshi, eds. *The Muslim Community in North America*. Edmonton: University of Alberta Press, 1983.

LAWRENCE H. MAMIYA (1996)
CHARLES ERIC LINCOLN (1996)
Updated by Lawrence H. Mamiya 2005

NATIVE AMERICANS

See Black-Indian Relations

NAT TURNER'S REBELLION

❚❚❚

Nat Turner (October 2, 1800–November 11, 1831) led the most significant slave revolt in U.S. history. Undertaken in 1831 in Virginia, Turner's Rebellion claimed more lives than any similar uprising. It had repercussions throughout the South, redrawing the lines of the American debate over slavery in ways that led toward all-out civil war within a generation. Indeed, some suggest that it represented the first major battle of the long war to end slavery.

In 1831 Virginia's Southampton County, bordering on North Carolina, contained roughly 6,500 whites and 9,500 blacks. Almost all of the latter, whether young or old, lived in perpetual bondage, including Nat Turner, a slave of Joseph Travis. Turner had been born in Southampton on October 2, 1800, only five days before the execution of black revolutionary Gabriel Prosser in Richmond, and as a boy he must have heard stories of Prosser's intended insurrection. Tradition suggests his mother was born and raised in Africa. She told her son at an early age that, on the basis of his quick intelligence and the distinctive lumps on his head, he seemed "intended for some great purpose."

Turner learned to read as a small boy, and he built a strong and composite faith from listening to the African beliefs retained within his family and the Christian values of his first master, Benjamin Turner. Confident from childhood that he had a special role to play, Nat Turner found outward confirmations for his messianic thoughts and eventually determined that his personal calling coincided with the most pressing public issue of the day—the termination of racial enslavement.

Most of what is known about the man is drawn from his *Confessions,* a remarkable autobiographical statement taken down by a young lawyer named Thomas Ruffin Gray during the rebel's final days in jail. While one can question the validity of Turner's recollections and the motivations of the disillusioned and desperate Gray (who rapidly published his lurid transcript at a profit), the confession has an underlying ring of truth and represents one of the most extraordinary firsthand texts in American history.

According to this account, Turner experienced a powerful vision in 1825 in which he "saw white spirits and black spirits engaged in battle, and the sun was darkened—the thunder rolled in the Heavens, and blood flowed in streams." Three years later another vision told him to prepare to slay his "enemies with their own weapons." But it was not until February 1831 that a solar eclipse

THE
CONFESSIONS
OF

NAT TURNER,

THE LEADER
OF

THE LATE INSURRECTION
IN SOUTHAMPTON, VA.

AS FULLY AND VOLUNTARILY MADE TO

THOMAS R. GRAY,

In the prison where he was confined, and acknowledged by him to be such,
when read before the Court of Southampton: with the
certificate, under seal of the Court convened at
Jerusalem, Nov. 5, 1831, for his trial.

ALSO,

AN AUTHENTIC ACCOUNT
OF THE

WHOLE INSURRECTION,
WITH

Lists of the Whites who were Murdered,
AND OF THE

*Negroes brought before the Court of Southampton,
and there sentenced, &c.*

━━━

RICHMOND:
PUBLISHED BY THOMAS R. GRAY.

Cover of Nat Turner's Confessions. *After leading a slave revolt in Southampton, Virginia, in 1831, Turner explained his motivations and dictated his version of the events to the young lawyer Thomas Ruffin Gray before his execution.* THE LIBRARY OF CONGRESS

Nat Turner

"And my father and mother strengthened me…saying in my presence, I was intended for some great purpose, which they had always thought from certain marks on my head and breast."

THE CONFESSIONS OF NAT TURNER,
THE LEADER OF THE LATE INSURRECTION
IN SOUTHAMPTON, VIRGINIA.
BALTIMORE: T.R. GRAY, 1831.

signaled to Turner that he must begin. He laid plans with others to act on the holiday of July 4, but when he fell ill, the date was allowed to pass. Then, on August 13 he awoke to find the sun a dim reflection of itself, changing from one hazy color to another. Taking this as another sign, he brought together a handful of collaborators on Sunday, August 21, and told them of his plan for a terrorist attack.

His intention, Turner explained, was to move through the countryside from household to household, killing whites regardless of age or sex. He hoped that this brutal show of force would be so swift as to prevent any warning and so compelling as to convince others to join in the cause. Having rallied supporters and gathered up more horses and weapons, they could march on Jerusalem, the county seat, and take the arsenal, which would give them a substantial beachhead of resistance. From there the rebellion could spread, aided by a network of enslaved black Christians and perhaps by divine intervention as well. Turner made clear, according to the *Richmond Enquirer,* that "indiscriminate slaughter was not their intention after they obtained a foothold, and was resorted to in the first instance to strike terror and alarm. Women and children would afterwards have been spared, and men too who ceased to resist."

Shortly after midnight Turner and five others launched their violent offensive, attacking the home of Turner's master and killing the Travis household, then proceeding on to other farmsteads to wreak similar vengeance. As their ranks grew, the band became more disorderly and the element of surprise was lost, but the first militiamen who offered resistance on Monday afternoon beat a hasty retreat. By Monday night as many as sixty or seventy African Americans had joined the cause, and on Tuesday morning Turner's army set out for Jerusalem. Behind them at least fifty-seven whites of all ages had been killed in a stretch of twenty miles.

When some rebels stopped at James Parker's farm, within three miles of Jerusalem, to win recruits and refresh themselves, the pause proved fatal, for the local militia had regrouped. They managed to attack and disperse the insurgents, who were off guard and poorly armed. Although Turner attempted to rally his followers, he never regained the initiative, and on Tuesday white reinforcements launched a harsh and indiscriminate counteroffensive that took well over a hundred lives. One cavalry company slaughtered forty blacks in two days, mounting more than a dozen severed heads atop poles as public warnings. Turner, his force destroyed, eluded authorities for six weeks, during which time another black preacher known as David attempted to ignite an uprising in North Carolina, fueling white fears of widespread rebellion. After an enormous manhunt, authorities captured Turner in a swamp on October 30 and hanged him publicly twelve days later.

Turner's unprecedented insurgency had a complex impact. It forced Virginia's legislature to consider openly, if briefly, the prospect of gradual emancipation. It also at-

tracted proslavery whites to the colonization movement, since many saw African resettlement as a way to remove dangerous bondsmen and reduce the free black community. For black and white abolitionists in the North, Turner's Rebellion reinforced the idea, later espoused by John Brown, that enslaved southerners were willing and able to engage in armed revolt if only weapons and outside support could be arranged. Among churchgoing slaveholders the uprising prompted tighter restrictions on black preaching and greater caution regarding slave access to the gospel. Among African Americans Turner became and has remained both a martyr and a folk hero never to be forgotten. As recently as 1969 one black Southampton resident could recall what his mother had learned in her childhood: that Nat Turner "was a man of war, and for legal rights, and for freedom."

See also *Amistad* Mutiny; Christiana Revolt of 1851; Demerara Revolt; Gabriel Prosser Conspiracy; Stono Rebellion; Tailor's Revolt

■ ■ *Bibliography*

Aptheker, Herbert. *Nat Turner's Slave Rebellion.* New York: Humanities Press, 1966.

Morris, Charles Edward. "Panic and Reprisal: Reaction in North Carolina to the Nat Turner Insurrection, 1831." *North Carolina Historical Review* 62 (1985): 29–52.

Oates, Stephen B. *The Fires of Jubilee: Nat Turner's Fierce Rebellion.* New York: Harper, 1975.

Tragle, Henry Irving. *The Southampton Slave Revolt of 1831: A Compilation of Source Material, Including the Full Text of 'The Confessions of Nat Turner.'* Amherst: University of Massachusetts Press, 1971.

Wood, Peter H. "Nat Turner: The Unknown Slave as Visionary Leader." In *Black Leaders of the Nineteenth Century,* edited by Leon Litwack and August Meier. Urbana: University of Illinois Press, 1988.

PETER H. WOOD (1996)

NATURAL RESOURCES OF THE CARIBBEAN

■ ■ ■

The character, extent, and availability of the Caribbean's natural resources are heavily influenced by the region's social and political characteristics, which result from historical relationships of the Caribbean with other, more powerful areas of the world. Those who study resources often emphasize that a region's natural resource characteristics are usually more human-influenced or socially produced than they are God-given, and it is difficult to think of another world region where this point is more applicable than it is for the Caribbean.

GEOGRAPHY AND GEOLOGY

The Caribbean's most fundamental resources—its geographical and geophysical locations—explain much about the region. Its subtropical latitudes place it within the tradewinds that arrive continuously from the east, after traversing the Atlantic Ocean. Christopher Columbus and subsequent European seafarers rode these easterly winds to the Caribbean on sailing vessels before the advent of steam power. After the earliest European colonization, the region's aboriginal peoples, the Caribs and Arawaks, were eliminated by overwork, coercion, and disease. European sailing vessels brought African slaves, again via the trade winds, to replace the declining native labor force. In subsequent decades, slave-produced agricultural staples were transported to Europe via the westerly wind belt located farther north. Thus, the Caribbean region represented one corner of the infamous "triangle trade" of colonial days: European manufactures sent to West and West Central Africa, slaves shipped west to the Caribbean, and agricultural goods sent northeast back to Europe.

The Caribbean's location within the western hemisphere also helps in understanding much about the region. Some suggest that the Caribbean is the "Mediterranean" of the Americas because it separates two continental landmasses. In the early twenty-first century, the region's strategic position between the producing area (northwestern South America) and the principal consuming area (the United States) for much of the hemisphere's narcotics makes the Caribbean an important part of illegal drug smuggling. The Caribbean's middling geographical position in the western hemisphere—off the southeastern coast of the United States—has led others to refer to the region as an "American lake," in part because the islands have been routinely subject to gunboat diplomacy, especially since the United States became a global power at the end of the nineteenth century.

In the late twentieth century, the proximity of the United States allowed the Caribbean's island states and territories to develop two of the region's natural attributes, its warm year-round temperatures and its scenic beauty, into the region's most important economic resource. Early in the twenty-first century, especially in the northern hemisphere's winter months, Caribbean tourism overshadows all other sectors of local economies. The combination of warm temperatures and abundant sunshine, together with the Caribbean's geographic hallmark of insularity, or "islandness," helps to explain the presence of the beach resorts, cruise destinations, and vacation possibilities for which the region has become well known.

The Caribbean's white sand beaches, relentlessly portrayed in North American television commercials in the winter months, are not the only scenic attractions. Especially in the small islands of the eastern Caribbean, volcanic peaks covered with tropical foliage soar above the sea-level landscapes (to over 5,000 feet on the island of Dominica), providing breathtaking vistas. Yet the entire region's seismic instability results in frequent earthquake tremors and, worse, occasionally catastrophic volcanic eruptions, which have punctuated the region's human history. The most famous eruption in Caribbean history, the explosion of Mount Pelée on French Martinique in 1902, dominated newspaper headlines throughout the world and influenced the United States to build a canal in Panama rather than in Nicaragua, which is supposedly more volcano-prone. Nearly a century later, in 1997, tiny Montserrat in the northeastern Caribbean suffered an eruption that buried its capital town in lava and igneous sand and sent two-thirds of its human population elsewhere. Given these geophysical characteristics, the ultimate resource in the small islands of the eastern Caribbean—the land that underpins human habitats—can by no means be taken for granted.

CLIMATE, SOILS, AND EROSION

Caribbean peoples are understandably wary of the region's climatic characteristics (though the same climate provides the basis for "sun and fun" tourist brochures). This is because every late summer and autumn seasonal hurricanes enter the region from the Atlantic, following paths that are generally southeast to northwest but whose specific trajectories vary from one season to the next, adding to the uncertainty and precariousness of living in the region.

Yet hurricanes have only slightly diminished the region's agricultural importance, especially in the past. In the seventeenth and eighteenth centuries, the Caribbean dominated the world in producing cane sugar, creating massive wealth for European colonial powers. Tropical agronomists have since determined that the Caribbean's subtropical climate, especially its rainfall characteristics, is ideal for a high sucrose content in sugarcane. Accordingly, cane sugar, although it is fading from the region early in the twenty-first century, has traditionally been cultivated in a wide variety of Caribbean soils.

The Caribbean's many soil types are related in part to differing kinds of bedrock. The dark-red clays of central and western Cuba, the most fertile soils of the region, are limestone-based, as are the soils of Puerto Rico and Hispaniola (the large island with the Dominican Republic on

Cocoa beans drying in large wooden trays on the Dougaldstone Estate, Grenada. *Cocoa is one of the primary crops harvested for export in Grenada and in many other island nations of the Caribbean.* © ABBIE ENOCK. TRAVEL INK/CORBIS.

the east and Haiti on the west). Both ashen soils and clays in the eastern Caribbean are related to the volcanic material underpinning these islands. The low, coralline islands far to the east—Antigua, the eastern half of French Guadeloupe, and Barbados—are uplifted oceanic deposits.

Yet bedrock, vegetation, climate, and slopes explain only part of Caribbean soil conditions. Just as important is the history of colonial exploitation. Beginning in the 1600s, Europeans directed massive deforestation of the accessible portions of most of the islands. This clearing left the insular soils unprotected from periodic drought and pounding rainfall. The crop usually taking the place of natural forests, sugarcane (a giant type of grass) tended to anchor the soil. But as sugarcane historically gave way to clean-row crop tillage and livestock herding, especially in the late twentieth century, massive soil erosion began to occur throughout the region.

The transformation of the natural forest cover to cultivated landscapes and barren hillsides has unfolded in different ways and at different rates throughout the Caribbean. Nowhere have the results been as tragic as in Haiti. As the French colony of Saint Domingue, Haiti was perhaps the world's most valuable colonial prize because of its sugar. After its slaves threw off French rule in 1803, Haiti was denied regular contact with other countries, and its population took up mainly subsistence agriculture. Since then, the need for Haitians to feed themselves has led to massive soil exhaustion and deforestation. Early in the twenty-first century, the country's nearly seven million human inhabitants eke out malnourished existences on a mountainous, degraded habitat, the most dismal human ecological plight in the western hemisphere.

The unhappy legacy of the Caribbean's agricultural history is paralleled at the start of the twenty-first century by a tourist industry that often despoils local environments. Walls and jetties designed to preserve Puerto Rican beaches have instead caused beach erosion. Stone embankments *(pedraplenes)* in northern Cuba that lead tourists to offshore cays have ruined habitats for fish, fowl, and flamingos. The demand for more electricity in Barbados has raised ocean temperatures near the island's power plant with negative biological effects. Tourism's effects have been worst on the very small islands; between 1970 and 2000, tiny Saint Martin changed from a quiet, semiarid island getaway to a jumble of franchise signs, chain-link

Harvesting sugarcane in St. Joseph's Parish, Barbados. *The Caribbean's subtropical climate, especially its rainfall characteristics, is ideal for a high sucrose content in sugarcane.* © JONATHAN BLAIR/CORBIS

fences, and rusting automobile hulls. The giant tourist ships bringing visitors and hard currency to the region in the early twenty-first century also deposit litter and trash receptacles directly into Caribbean ocean waters. Calls for a more environmentally friendly ecotourism are heard throughout the region, yet this activity is practiced seriously only in Belize, in the far western Caribbean.

FISHING, FORESTS, AND FAUNA

The tropical waters and varying depths of the Caribbean support a variety of fish. A 1996 Puerto Rican fishing census enumerated two thousand full-time and part-time fishermen, most of whom fished at different locations at different times of the year, and who therefore used different types of equipment depending on the season. In villages near deep-water zones, fishermen commonly seek tunas, mackerel, and dolphins. Rough waters all around Puerto Rico in the late summer and fall usually limit fishing to destinations closer to shore.

Despite constraints to developing large-scale fishing industries in the Caribbean, offshore fishing on every island provides limited, although locally important, sources of food. Yet these activities are highly seasonal and cannot sustain local human populations throughout the year. Barbados's flying-fish season, which lasts from December to July, sees its highest catches in March and April and provides an important food source for locals and tourists alike. In Grenada and Saint Vincent, local fishermen often focus their activities on the blackfish or pilot whale, with their greatest successes coming in September. Yet other kinds of fishing there in the late summer months are often reduced because of the low-salinity water that comes north from the mouth of Venezuela's Orinoco River.

Similar to the region's terrestrial resources, the Caribbean's marine resources are adversely influenced by industrial pollution and a historical legacy of overdevelopment. Trinidadian fishermen, in an early twenty-first-century survey, all blamed the industrialization of western Trinidad and its associated pollution for reduced fish populations in the Gulf of Paria. A similar study of the estimated 30,000 subsistence fishermen of Haiti suggested that fishing there was hampered because of depleted and degraded marine habitats. These human-created problems are made all the worse for Caribbean fishing activities by storm destruction. Between 1979 and 1999, nine hurricanes or tropical depressions hit Dominica, damaging fishing vessels, equipment, landing sites, and shore facilities.

Hurricanes also influence the region's forests. Long-term studies of Puerto Rican woodlands have identified mountain "storm forests," floral assemblages that lack the usual species diversity, giant trees, and multiple leaf canopies found elsewhere in the tropics. In September 1989, Hurricane Hugo devastated Puerto Rico's El Yunque National Forest, the only tropical forest in the U.S. National Park system. Occasional near-total hurricane destruction of insular forests in the small islands of the eastern Caribbean occurs all the way south to Grenada.

Yet centuries of vegetation clearance and associated human devastation, not the forces of nature, have reduced the region's forests to tiny upland patches, and complete removal has occurred on some of the smallest islands. Wood products and lumber used for Caribbean building are nearly all imported, and local sawmills are practically unknown today. At the beginning of the twenty-first century, Cuba and the Dominican Republic are the only countries claiming any significant forest covers. The most dismal deforestation example is Haiti. The country's original forest cover is gone, yet 50,000 rural Haitians produce charcoal from what wood they can glean, an activity that intensified after the local pig eradication (decreed by U.S. health authorities, who feared the spread of swine disease to North America) in the early 1980s.

In attempting to establish wood sources and to protect local water supplies, the reforestation of Caribbean landscapes was recommended as early as the nineteenth century. In the middle of the twentieth century, several places, including Guadeloupe and Trinidad, attempted the planting of mahogany; insect infestation and lack of knowledge led to disappointing results in both places, however. For decades, the potential success of reforestation attempts everywhere in the region has been thwarted by the large livestock populations. Goats, sheep, and cattle browse over denuded landscapes everywhere in the region, especially in the small, drought-prone islands. In addition, local herdsmen often (stealthily) cut down the small trees in reforestation plots to feed their animals.

Except for a few birds and reptiles, the animals native to the region prior to the coming of Europeans have been extinguished. Accordingly, the Caribbean's "wild animals" actually have been imported in relatively recent times. The mongoose, introduced to Trinidad from India in 1870, menaces chickens and house pets everywhere in the eastern Caribbean. The West African vervet monkeys on Saint Kitts and Barbados are said to have come on eighteenth-century slave vessels. A few untamed horses in the moun-

tains of the Dominican Republic may descend from early Spanish stock. Limited numbers of manatees still live in the shallow waters surrounding the Greater Antilles, although they have not been sighted in the eastern Caribbean since the 1700s.

MINERALS

Dutch interest in southern Caribbean salt production began about 1600, and in the early twenty-first century the Dutch-affiliated island of Bonaire, just north of Venezuela, continues to produce table and industrial salts from saline ponds. Yet the important mineral activity for which the Netherlands Antilles were well known in the twentieth century was the processing of Venezuelan oil at the refineries of Aruba and Curaçao. Although the crude petroleum refined there is not, strictly speaking, a Caribbean resource, the refineries at these tiny islands attracted thousands of Afro-Caribbean immigrants, beginning in the 1920s, who then took home the industrial and labor organizing skills they learned in the Dutch islands.

The main oil-producing country in the Caribbean is Trinidad and Tobago, which accounted for 125,000 barrels of crude oil per day in 2001. Pitch and tar from southern Trinidad were used on local roads by the end of the nineteenth century, and local oil production began in the early twentieth century. High oil prices in the 1970s inspired Trinidad and Tobago to embark on a massive industrialization scheme in southern Trinidad, an enterprise curtailed a decade later because of falling oil prices. Cuba produced 50,000 barrels of oil per day in 2001; Barbados, 1,000 per day. Most Caribbean islands import petroleum products, usually from the several oil refineries located in the region.

Jamaica became an important producer of bauxite (aluminum ore) and its dehydrated variant, alumina, in the mid-twentieth century, after the discovery of bauxite deposits there in 1942. Prices boomed into the 1960s, and the ore was exported to North America and Europe, where it was refined into metallic aluminum. In the 1970s, however, Jamaica attempted to raise bauxite prices, and hostile reactions elsewhere led to a downturn in production. By the early 1990s, Jamaican bauxite production had dropped severely, but resuscitation efforts thereafter led to some success. In 2001, despite several work stoppages and labor problems, Jamaica was still recognized as a world leader in bauxite and alumina (3.5 million tons in 2001).

In 2002, Cuba was the world's sixth leading producer of nickel. In that year it possessed an estimated 30 percent of the world's nickel reserves and exported US$600 million worth of nickel and cobalt, more than the value of the island's sugar crop. But the U.S. trade embargo against

Cuba prohibited American imports of Cuban nickel, so nearly all the ore was marketed in Europe. Further development of Cuba's nickel mining industry has involved joint financial and planning ventures involving companies from nations such as Canada and Australia and Cuba's state-owned nickel mining company, Cubaniquel. Most other countries are wary of Cuban politics, however. Typical of Caribbean resource development for centuries, the full development of Cuba's nickel potential depends far more upon global politics than it does upon natural conditions.

See also Agricultural Policy in the Caribbean; Caribbean Community and Common Market (CARICOM); International Relations of the Anglophone Caribbean; Tourism in the Caribbean

▪▪ Bibliography

Barker, David, and Duncan F. M. McGregor, eds. *Environment and Development in the Caribbean: Geographical Perspectives.* Mona, Jamaica: The Press, University of the West Indies, 1995.

Beckford, George L. "The Social Economy of Bauxite in the Jamaican Man-Space." *Social and Economic Studies* 36 (1987): 1–55.

Bermúdez-Lugo, Omayra. "The Mineral Industries of the Islands of the Caribbean." *U.S. Geological Survey Minerals Yearbook, 2001.* Available from <http://minerals.usgs.gov/minerals/pubs/country/latin.html#ac>.

Bolay, Eberhard. *The Dominican Republic: A Country between Rain Forest and Desert.* Wekersheim, Germany: Margraf Verlag, 1997.

Bush, David M., et al. *Living with the Puerto Rican Shore.* Durham, N.C.: Duke University Press, 1995.

Creswell, R. LeRoy, ed. *Proceedings of the Fifty-Fourth Annual Gulf and Caribbean Fisheries Institute, Turks and Caicos Islands, 2001.* Fort Pierce, Fla.: GCFI, 2003.

Dallmeier, F., and J. A. Comiskey, eds. *Forest Biodiversity in North, Central, and South America, and the Caribbean: Research and Monitoring,* vol. 21: *Man and the Biosphere.* Paris: UNESCO, 1998.

Díaz-Briquets, Sergio, and Jorge Pérez-López. *Conquering Nature: The Environmental Legacy of Socialism in Cuba.* Pittsburgh, Pa.: University of Pittsburgh Press, 2000.

Murray, John A., ed. *The Islands and the Sea: Five Centuries of Nature Writing from the Caribbean.* New York: Oxford University Press, 1991.

"Nickel But No Dimes." *The Economist* (September 20, 2003): 37.

Pattullo, Polly. *Fire from the Mountain: The Tragedy of Montserrat and the Betrayal of its People.* London: Converse, 2000.

Richardson, Bonham C. *The Caribbean in the Wider World, 1492–1992: A Regional Geography.* Cambridge, UK: Cambridge University Press, 1992.

Thomas, Clive Y. *The Poor and the Powerless: Economic Policy and Change in the Caribbean.* New York: Monthly Review Press, 1988.

Woods, Charles A., and Florence E. Sergile, eds. *Biogeography of the West Indies: Patterns and Perspectives,* 2d ed. Boca Raton, Fla.: CRC Press, 2001.

BONHAM C. RICHARDSON (2005)

NAYLOR, GLORIA
JANUARY 25, 1950

▐ ▐ ▐

Gloria Naylor, a writer, was born in New York City to Roosevelt and Alberta Naylor. After traveling through New York, Florida, and North Carolina as a missionary for Jehovah's Witnesses (1968–1975), she returned to New York, where she worked as a telephone operator at various hotels while she attended Brooklyn College (B.A., 1981). She received an M.A. in Afro-American Studies from Yale University in 1983.

Naylor's first published work, *The Women of Brewster Place* (1982), won the American Book Award for best first novel in 1983. Dealing with the lives of seven black women who live on one ghetto street, the novel conveys the oppression and spiritual strength that African-American women share. At the same time, by exploring the characters' differences, it emphasizes the variety of their experience. Naylor wrote a television screenplay adaptation of the novel, which starred Oprah Winfrey and appeared on *American Playhouse* in 1984. Her next novel, *Linden Hills* (1985), is concerned with the spiritual decay of a group of black Americans who live in an affluent community, having forsaken their heritage in favor of material gain. *Mama Day,* published in 1988, tells of an elderly lady with magical powers. The best-selling *Bailey's Cafe* (1992) takes place in a 1940s American diner where neighborhood prostitutes congregate. Naylor wrote a play based on the novel, which was produced and performed by the Hartford Stage Company in 1994. She also wrote the screenplay for the PBS presentation *In Our Own Words* (1985).

Naylor has said that she writes because her perspective, that of the black American woman, has been underrepresented in American literature. Her goal is to present the diversity of the black experience. Although she reworks traditional Western sources in her novels, borrowing the structure of Dante's *Inferno* for *Linden Hills* and elements of Shakespeare's *The Tempest* for *Mama Day,* Naylor utilizes black vernacular and other aspects of her own heritage in her writing.

Naylor's 1998 novel, *The Men of Brewster Place,* returns readers to the setting of her first story, this time to relate the stories of the men in the lives of the original characters. Naylor said this fifth novel was inspired by the Million Man March in Washington, D.C., which took place in the fall of 1995, as well as by the death of her father. Both events helped the author to reassess certain ideas she held about men and their roles in the lives of African-American women.

Naylor has taught at George Washington University, New York University, Princeton, Cornell, and Boston University. She has received a National Endowment for the Arts Fellowship (1985), the Distinguished Writer Award from the Mid-Atlantic Writers Association (1983), the Candace Award from the National Coalition of 100 Black Women (1986), and a Guggenheim Fellowship (1988). She was awarded a President's Medal from Brooklyn College in 1993, and an honorary doctorate of letters from Sacred Heart University in 1994.

See also Caribbean/North American Writers, Contemporary; Literature of the United States

■ ■ *Bibliography*

Hine, Darlene Clark, ed. *Black Women in America*. Brooklyn, N.Y.: Carlson, 1993.

Montgomery, Maxine, ed. *Conversations with Gloria Naylor*. Jackson: University Press of Mississippi, 2004.

Wilson, Charles E. *Gloria Naylor: A Critical Companion*. Westport, Conn.: Greenwood Press, 2001.

LILY PHILLIPS (1996)
LYDIA MCNEILL (1996)
Updated bibliography

NEAL, LARRY

SEPTEMBER 5, 1937
JANUARY 6, 1981

⊢╋╋⊣────────

The writer Larry Neal, one of the most prominent figures of the black arts movement of the 1960s and 1970s, was born in Atlanta, graduated from Lincoln University in Pennsylvania in 1961, and received an M.A. from the University of Pennsylvania in 1963. He soon became one of the most prominent of the African-American writers that emerged in the early 1960s championing the search for a distinctive African-American aesthetic. His early articles, including "The Negro in the Theatre" (1964) and "Cultural Front" (1965), were among the earliest to assert that separate cultural forms are necessary in the development of black artists in a racist society.

Neal developed his perspective on black art in the influential anthology *Black Fire* (1968), coedited with Amiri Baraka, and the essay "The Black Arts Movement" (1968), which helped give a name and direction to the nascent artistic trend. Neal argued that the purpose of black arts was to effect a "radical reordering of the Western cultural aesthetic" in part through a purging of the external European and white American cultural influences from black artistic expression. His critical thinking was further developed in books such as *Black Boogaloo: Notes on Black Liberation* (1969), *Trippin' a Need for Change* (1969, coauthored with Amiri Baraka and journalist A. B. Spellman), and *Hoodoo Hollerin Bebop Ghosts* (1971). Neal also authored plays (*The Glorious Monster in the Bell of the Horn*, 1976), screenplays (*Holler S.O.S.*, 1971; *Moving on Up*, 1973), and television scripts (*Lenox Avenue Sunday*, 1966; *Deep River*, 1967).

Neal was an instructor at the City College of New York from 1968 to 1969, and he subsequently taught at Wesleyan University (1969–1970) and Yale University (1970–1975). By the mid-1970s he was reconsidering his view of black culture. In "The Black Contribution to American Letters" (1976), he argued that while all African-American writers and literature must in some sense be political, it was important to separate the public persona of black writers from their specific private experiences, which are often wider and more inclusive than the polemical rejection of nonblack influences that characterized the black arts movement. Neal's later works include the play *In an Upstate Motel*, which premiered in New York in 1981. He died of a heart attack in Hamilton, New York, in 1981.

See also Baraka, Amiri (Jones, LeRoi); Black Arts Movement

■ ■ *Bibliography*

Anadolu-Okur, Nilgun. *Contemporary African American Theater: Afrocentricity in the Works of Larry Neal, Amiri Baraka, and Charles Fuller*. New York: Garland, 1997.

Martin, Reginald. "Total Life Is What We Want: The Progressive Stages of the New Black Aesthetic in Literature." *South Atlantic Review* (November 1986): 46–67.

Neal, Larry. "The Black Arts Movement." *Drama Review* 12 (Summer 1968).

Neal, Larry. "The Black Contribution to American Letters: Part II, The Writer as Activist—1960 and After." In *The Black American Reference Book*, edited by Mabel M. Smythe. Englewood Cliffs, N.J.: Prentice-Hall, 1976.

Neal, Larry. "The Negro in the Theatre." *Drama Critique* 7 (Spring 1964).

Van Deburg, William L. *New Day in Babylon: The Black Power Movement and American Culture, 1965–1975.* Chicago: University of Chicago Press, 1992.

REGINALD MARTIN (1996)
Updated bibliography

NÉGRITUDE

It was in Aimé Césaire's revolutionary surrealist poem *Cahier d'un retour au pays natal* (*Notebook of a Return to the Native Land*), published in 1939, that the term *négritude* first appeared in print. It had been invented by Césaire, Senegalese poet Léopold Sédar Senghor tells us, perhaps as early as 1932. The term did not come into literary and cultural history until the publication in 1948 of Senghor's *Anthologie de la nouvelle poésie nègre et malgache* (Anthology of New Black and Malagasy Poetry), whose preface, "Orphée noir" (Black Orpheus), had been written by Jean-Paul Sartre. In addition to Senghor (future president of Senegal) and Aimé Césaire (future representative of Martinique to the French Assembly), the poets of the anthology were Léon Damas of Guyana; Gilbert Gratiant and Étienne Léro of Martinique; Guy Tirolien and Paul Niger of Guadeloupe; Léon Laleau, Jacques Roumain, Jean-François Brière, and René Belance of Haiti; Birago Diop and David Diop of Senegal; Jean-Joseph Rabéarivelo, Jacques Rabémananjara, and Flavien Ranarivo of Madagascar. Each of these poets had, in his particular fashion, "returned to the source," composed poems out of the matrix of African culture and experience.

The poems in the anthology varied greatly, from Birago Diop's "Souffles" (Breaths), a haunting tribute to African beliefs that predate the colonial era ("The dead are not dead / Hear the voice of the fire / Hear the voice of the water / Listen to the wind / To the sighing bush / It is the breathing of the ancestors. . .") to a fragment of Césaire's majestic *Cahier*, which is a meditation—confessional and epic, philosophical and historical, somber and affirming—on the modern black experiences of enslavement and domination, dispossession and alienation:

my negritude is not a stone, its deafness hurled against
  the clamor of the day
my negritude is not a leukoma of dead liquid over the
  earth's dead eye
my negritude is neither a tower nor cathedral
it takes root in the red flesh of the soil
it takes root in the ardent flesh of the sky
it breaks through the opaque prostration with its
  upright patience

(Trans. Clayton Eshleman and Annette Smith. *Notebook of a Return to the Native Land.* Wesleyan, Conn., 2001, p. 35)

Négritude gathered to itself many poems with diverse themes and varied tones: Praise poems to the beauty of the black woman imagined as symbol of Africa, a lost paradise and homeland; poems inspired by or in homage to jazz, drum, or oral traditions; poems of social and political critique focusing on assimilation and betrayal, and the alienated world of the Creole bourgeoisie; exhortations to solidarity and struggle; edenic reminiscences of the black world before slavery and colonialism, and utopic visions of the black world after racist domination.

Similar concerns and patterns were echoed in a number of West African novels, such as the nostalgic *L'Enfant noir* (*The Dark Child*, 1954) by Guinean Camara Laye and *L'Aventure ambiguë* (*Ambiguous Adventure*, 1960) by Senegalese Cheikh Hamidou Kane, in which the young hero, Samba Diallo, is trapped between the values of feudal Africa and Islam, on the one hand, and the West, on the other.

Négritude was thus diverse phenomenon, but it has been associated chiefly with Senghor, its principal promoter, who defined it as the "totality of values of black African culture." It was at once a racial essence, common to all Africans and their descendants, wherever they are found, and a conscious choice to embrace the "condition" of being black in a world of white domination. In classic Senghorian négritude, the affirmation of African identity is complemented by faith in the virtue of cultural mixing (*métissage*) and an aspiration toward a universal civilization or humanism:

Let us answer "present" at the rebirth of the World
As white flour cannot rise without the leaven.
Who else will teach *rhythm* to the world
Deadened by machines and cannons?
Who will sound the *shout of joy* at daybreak to wake
  orphans and the dead?
Tell me, who will give back the *memory of life* to the
  man of gutted hopes?
They call us men of cotton, coffee, oil.
They call us men of death.
But we are men of *dance*, whose feet get stronger
As we pound upon firm ground.

(From "Prayer to the Masks." In *Léopold Sédar Senghor: The Collected Poetry,* trans. Melvin Dixon, 1991, p. 13.)

It was in Paris in the 1930s, in a climate of modernism, jazz, African primitivism, and surrealism that the idea of négritude arose. West Indian and African students had come to the capital to complete their education. They had attended French colonial schools whose objective, in keeping with the values of the Enlightenment and the French

Revolution, was to make of them "black Frenchmen." The effect of this policy of "assimilation" was that these subjects or citizens of France had learned to reject their African cultures of origin and to emulate the culture of the French. Yet, these students now felt the pull of both cultures—or, as W. E. B. Du Bois had written three decades earlier, a double consciousness—and they sought the intellectual means to rehabilitate African civilization(s).

Critical to this emergent black cultural consciousness were Paulette and Jane Nardal of Martinique. The Nardal sisters were students at the Sorbonne in the 1920s, and their home became a meeting place for young black intellectuals and writers from Africa and the Americas. Among the American visitors to the Nardal home and to that of their cousin, Louis Achille Jr., were Alain Locke, the editor of *The New Negro* (1925), and Mercer Cook, a professor of French at Howard University. In 1931 and 1932, Paulette Nardal and Dr. Léo Sajous, a Haitian, published a bilingual journal, the *Revue du monde noir (Review of the Black World)*, which featured translations of Harlem Renaissance poets from the United States and which set forth forceful arguments and appeals for racial pride and solidarity across national and continental boundaries. A remarkable contribution to the *Revue* was Paulette Nardal's article, "Awakening of Race Consciousness" in which this new international racial and cultural vision is tied to a growing feminist consciousness. (See Chapter 3 of Edwards.) In its brief existence the journal exposed the African and Caribbean students in Paris to facets of black life in the United States and to the poetry of Langston Hughes and Claude McKay. Soon thereafter, Césaire and Senghor were reciting poems by these and other black American writers, among them Jean Toomer, Sterling Brown, and Countee Cullen. Senghor read articles by W. E. B. Du Bois and Carter G. Woodson in *The Crisis* and *Opportunity* respectively. The example of these black American brothers, these "new Negroes," was crucial in spurring on Senghor and Césaire, as had been the intellectual courage of René Maran (*Batouala*, 1921) and Jean Price-Mars (*Ainsi parla l'oncle* [Thus Spoke the Uncle], 1928), and the work of European anthropologists and ethnographers Maurice Delafosse, Leo Frobenius, and Robert Delavignette, who demonstrated that precolonial African civilizations were not devoid of "culture."

A flurry of attacks against négritude began after the publication of the *Anthologie*. They were directed especially against Senghor and the proposition that "emotion is Negro as reason is Greek." Above all, the idea of a "Negro soul"—collectivist, rhythmic, spiritual, one with nature—made it all too easy to ignore the intellectual acumen and achievements of black people. The assertion of a transcendent racial identity was seen likewise as an essentialist mystification that disregarded critical factors of *difference* among blacks such as nationality, modes of economic life, history, and language. The emphasis on racial and cultural identity had also overshadowed a more political anticolonialism, dating from the 1920s and 1930s. And since négritude was a response to the psychological turmoil of a French-educated elite, it was deemed irrelevant to the vast majority of people in French West Africa and to Africans governed under the British policy of "indirect rule." One French critic also observed that négritude merely corresponded to one strain of Western humanism that privileged the intuitive and the irrational. (See chapters 22 and 23 of Hymans, 1971, for a discussion of négritude's early detractors.) Sustained critiques have been made by Stanislas Adotevi in *Négritude et négrologues* (1972) and Marcien Towa in *Léopold Sédar Senghor: Négritude ou servitude?* (1971). (See also chapter 2 of Anthony Appiah, *In My Father's House*, 1992.) In fiction, Yambo Ouologuem's *Devoir de violence* (*Bound to Violence*; 1968) denounced romanticized notions of pre-colonial Africa, and Mariama Bâ's *Un chant écarlate* (*Scarlet Song*; 1981) revealed the masculinist bias of négritude. In the French-speaking Caribbean, the emphasis on racial and cultural ties to Africa of the more political Césairian négritude has given way to an assertion of a distinct Caribbean identity (*antillanité*) and creoleness (*créolité*). (See Edouard Glissant, "L'avenir antillais," *Le Discours antillais* ["Towards Caribbeanness," excerpted in *Caribbean Discourse*, 1989] and Jean Bernabé, Patrick Chamoiseau and Raphaël Confiant, *Eloge de la créolité/In Praise of Creoleness*, 1990.)

Yet African writers and intellectuals acknowledge the critical role of négritude as a cultural and aesthetic philosophy that sought to affirm the humanity of those whose humanity had been denied by Europe on the basis of race. On American shores, Samuel W. Allen published "Black Orpheus," a translation of Sartre's preface, and an anthology of African writers, illustrated by Romare Bearden. Mercer Cook also taught, published, and lectured on African and West Indian writers. Langston Hughes, too, published several anthologies of African writing. That new renaissance of cultural nationalism, the black arts movement of the 1960s, was an American version of négritude: The same themes resonated in the works of writers such as Don Lee, Larry Neal, Sonia Sanchez, and Paul Carter Harrison (*The Drama of Nommo*, 1972). Moreover, the elaboration of black or African-inspired theoretical models for African-American literature by Houston Baker (*Blues, Ideology, and Afro-American Literature: A Vernacular Theory*, 1984) and Henry Louis Gates Jr. (*The Signifying Monkey*, 1988) can be seen as another avatar of the aesthetic ideology at the heart of négritude.

See also Césaire, Aimé; Du Bois, W. E. B.; Ethnic Origins; Hughes, Langston; McKay, Claude; Neal, Larry; Sanchez, Sonia; Woodson, Carter Godwin

■ ■ *Bibliography*

Arnold, James. *Modernism and Negritude.* Cambridge, Mass.: Harvard University Press, 1981.

Cook, Mercer, and Stephen Henderson. *The Militant Black Writer in Africa and the United States.* Madison: University of Wisconsin Press, 1969.

Edwards, Brent Hayes. *The Practice of Diaspora: Literature, Translation, and the Rise of Black Nationalism.* Cambridge, Mass.: Harvard University Press, 2003.

Fabre, Michel. *From Harlem to Paris: Black American Writers in France 1840-1980.* Urbana: University of Illinois Press, 1991.

Hymans, Jacques Louis. *Léopold Sédar Senghor: An Intellectual Biography.* Edinburgh, Scotland: Edinburgh University Press, 1971.

Kesteloot, Lilyan. *Black Writers in French.* Washington, D.C.: Howard University Press, 1990.

Vaillant, Janet. *Black, French, and African: A Life of Léopold Sédar Senghor.* Cambridge, Mass.: Harvard University Press, 1990.

EILEEN JULIEN (1996)
Updated by author 2005

NEGRO AMERICAN LABOR COUNCIL

■ ■ ■

Shortly after the American Federation of Labor and Congress of Industrial Organizations (AFL-CIO) refused to adopt internal desegregation measures at its 1959 convention, seventy-five black trade union officials, led by A. Philip Randolph, president of the Brotherhood of Sleeping Car Porters, AFL-CIO, formed the Negro American Labor Council (NALC) as a vehicle through which to pressure the labor federation to act against segregated and discriminatory unions. At its founding convention in 1960, the all-black NALC called for the elimination of Jim Crow union locals, racist bars to union leadership, and discriminatory job-training programs. Randolph, who was elected president by the delegates, dominated the council for most of its brief life. By the end of its first year the NALC had enlisted ten thousand members nationally, with its largest chapter in Detroit.

In 1961 the NALC presented to the AFL-CIO Executive Council specific charges of discriminatory practices in affiliated unions along with the recommendation that such practices be rooted out and, as a final resort, unions refusing to comply be expelled from the federation. The Executive Council rejected the proposals, labeled the NALC "separatist," and officially censured Randolph, charging the longtime labor and civil rights leader as the cause of the black rank and file's discontent with AFL-CIO leadership.

The second NALC convention, held in Chicago in the fall of 1961, featured lengthy and vigorous denunciations of the AFL-CIO Executive Council for its response to the NALC's proposal in particular, and for the failure of organized labor historically to combat racist practices and extend class solidarity to black workers.

By the time of the second convention, the NALC's membership had fallen to a little more than four thousand, largely as a result of a lack of funds to wage a sustained organizing campaign. Moreover, a number of members notified the NALC that they were not allowed to organize on behalf of the council while holding official union positions. However, as a result of the pressure brought to bear by the NALC, the 1961 AFL-CIO convention adopted an unprecedented civil rights program that Randolph called the best antidiscrimination measure ever taken up by organized labor. The AFL-CIO's civil rights resolution instituted grievance procedures and called for affiliated unions to voluntarily eliminate segregated locals and discriminatory practices. The NALC criticized the resolution for its reliance on voluntary compliance yet considered the AFL-CIO's measure an important, if insufficient, victory. One of the greater tangible achievements of the NALC was the election of an African American, Nelson Edwards, to the executive board of the United Auto Workers, for which the Detroit chapter had lobbied since its founding.

Shortly after the 1961 NALC convention, Randolph renewed his call from 1941 for a massive march on Washington to demand jobs and civil rights, partly as a way to satisfy militant black nationalists in the council. The NALC became one of the primary mobilizing organizations for the 1963 March on Washington for Jobs and Freedom. Although it was unable to win the official endorsement of the AFL-CIO, it was instrumental in gaining the support of various major unions for the demonstration. The NALC continued through the early 1960s as the leading liaison between the civil rights movement and organized labor.

At its fourth annual convention in 1964 the NALC adopted a resolution calling for a national one-day general strike on August 28, the anniversary of the March on Washington, if the pending civil rights bill was not passed by that time. The resolution became moot when the Civil Rights Act of 1964 was signed into law shortly after the NALC convention.

In 1966 Randolph resigned as president of the council and Cleveland Robinson, vice president of the Distributive, Processing, and Office Workers Union (District 65) and a longtime ally of Randolph, was elected to succeed him. The name of the organization was soon thereafter changed to the National Afro-American Labor Council, which was supplanted as the leading advocate of equality within the labor movement by the more moderate A. Philip Randolph Institute, founded by Randolph in 1964. Through the 1960s the institute also recruited black workers into the civil rights movement, assisted voter-registration drives in the South, and successfully lobbied the AFL-CIO leadership to support African-American political causes.

See also Labor and Labor Unions

■ ■ *Bibliography*

Foner, Philip S. *Organized Labor and the Black Worker, 1619–1973.* New York: Praeger, 1974.

Hill, Herbert. "Racial Practices of Organized Labor." In *The Negro and the American Labor Movement,* edited by Julius Jacobson. Garden City, N.Y.: Anchor, 1968.

Pfeffer, Paula F. *A. Philip Randolph, Pioneer of the Civil Rights Movement.* Baton Rouge: Louisiana State University Press, 1990.

THADDEUS RUSSELL (1996)

Negro Digest

See Black World/Negro Digest

Negro Elections Day

Negro Elections Day, a ceremony among African-American slaves in New England, is of disputed origin. Known also as Negro Governor's Day and by several other names, Negro Elections Day is a celebration that entailed costumes, feasting, and the election of a "governor" among certain slave populations. More of a symbolic position than anything else, an elected "governor" had no real legislative or political power.

In some cases contests of cleverness and strength were designed as a means of picking a winner, who would then become governor; in other cases personal character, morality, intelligence, and wisdom were prerequisites for appointment to governor. In a few cases the appointed governor was a descendent of African royalty or had actually been a prince or king prior to capture by slave traders.

Negro Elections Day generally fell on one of the days granted to slaves for rest and recreation. On this day slave men and women dressed in fancy garb or costume, played music, and paraded through the streets on foot or on horseback, accompanying their elected governor. The governor usually wore military dress or emblems (such as a crown) of royalty. The parade was usually followed by a dinner and dance.

Some eighteenth-century writers speculate that the election of governors was a vestige of the ceremonies accompanying the election of a king or chief that had taken place in Africa. Other writers suggest that enslaved Africans, now politically powerless, were imitating the election process that they had witnessed in the company of their white masters. However, the fact that Negro Elections Day is documented as having grown less political and more ceremonial over the years (when fewer Africans with a knowledge of original customs were being imported), combined with the fact that similar celebrations took place among slave populations in the Caribbean and Latin America, seems to buttress the belief that the practice originated in Africa.

■ ■ *Bibliography*

Aimes, Hubert H. S. "African Institutions in America." *Journal of American Folk-Lore* 18 (1905): 15–32.

Shelton, Jane deForest. "The New England Negro—A Remnant." *Harper's New Monthly Magazine* 88 (1894): 533–538.

PETRA E. LEWIS (1996)

Negro History Week

See Black History Month/Negro History Week

Negro National Anthem

"Lift Ev'ry Voice and Sing," with words by James Weldon Johnson and music by J. Rosamond Johnson, became known as the "Negro National Anthem" or "Negro National Hymn." James Weldon Johnson wrote this three-stanza hymn for a celebration of Lincoln's birthday at the

Colored High School in Jacksonville, Florida. The school choir first performed the song on February 12, 1900. During the next twenty-five years, African Americans began to perform the hymn at churches, schools, and other large gatherings.

James Weldon Johnson did not write the song as an expression of African-American solidarity, but in 1926 he acknowledged that "the song not only epitomizes the history of the race, and its present condition, but voices their hope for the future." Some writers have objected to calling "Lift Ev'ry Voice and Sing" a "national" hymn; however, the song is still performed as the unofficial anthem of African Americans.

See also Johnson, James Weldon

■ ■ *Bibliography*

Johnson, James Weldon. *Along This Way: The Autobiography of James Weldon Johnson.* New York: Viking, 1933.

"Lift Ev'ry Voice and Sing." *Crisis* 32 (September 1926): 234–236.

WILLIE STRONG (1996)

NEGRO SANHEDRIN

The Negro Sanhedrin was a short-lived organization established in 1924 with the purpose, according to its founder, Kelly Miller (1863–1939), of fostering cooperation and coordination between black organizations and forming one unified voice for black America. Miller perceived that black organizations often duplicated each others' efforts or worked at cross-purposes, offering the nation neither a clear picture of the problems of African Americans nor a single agenda for action.

Actually, Miller envisioned several organizations formed along the lines of the ancient Hebrew Sanhedrins: a greater Sanhedrin, which would function nationally to coordinate black political and social policy and be composed of representatives from the leading national black organizations, and lesser Sanhedrins, operating at the local level. Miller took care to distinguish the Sanhedrin, which would concern itself with "the immediate problems of the Negro in the United States," from W. E. B. Du Bois's Pan-African Conferences, which explored the conditions of blacks worldwide, and the Universal Negro Improvement Association of Marcus Garvey, which sought the emigration of American blacks to Africa.

Miller, a leading essayist, sociologist, and dean of the College of Arts and Sciences at Howard University, used his influence among black moderates to attract representatives from sixty-three national black organizations, including the National Association for the Advancement of Colored People, the Equal Rights League, the Race Congress, the International Uplift League, and the Friends of Negro Freedom, to an initial meeting in Chicago the week of February 11, 1924. Miller also invited several leading citizens unaffiliated with black organizations. In all, 300 delegates attended. The main address was delivered by the mayor of Chicago, William E. Dever.

In the course of their week-long meeting, the delegates identified seven problems of black American life which required interracial cooperation to resolve: the need to improve public health among black Americans; the necessity for equal schools; the end of the exploitation of black labor; the protection of the black franchise; equal rights for women; strengthening the right of protest and public utterance; and the improvement of interracial relations.

The delegates also recommended several points of internal policy aimed at the internal improvement of the black community: the need to build a strong, independent business community; the creation of black fraternal and charitable organizations; the maintenance of a "less partisan" and "more dignified" black press; the establishment of relationships with blacks around the world; the encouragement and support of black youth; and the study and promotion of African and black American culture. Miller, who referred to the Negro Sanhedrin as "an influence rather than an organization," envisioned biennial meetings on the national level, but the Negro Sanhedrin never met again.

See also Du Bois, W. E. B.; Garvey, Marcus; Pan-Africanism; Universal Negro Improvement Association

■ ■ *Bibliography*

Bracey, John H., Jr., August Meier and Elliot Rudwick, eds. *Black Nationalism in America.* New York, 1970.

Miller, Kelly. *The Negro Sanhedrin: A Call to Conference.* Washington, D.C., 1923.

Wright, W. D. "The Thought and Leadership of Kelly Miller." *Phylon* 39 (June 1978): 180–192.

MICHAEL PALLER (1996)

NEGROS BRUJOS

Negros brujos, or black witches or sorcerers, refers to African-descended practitioners of a range of African-derived rituals that included healing, casting spells, and offering spiritual guidance. In early twentieth-century Cuba, "negros brujos" acquired meaning as a catch-all term for practitioners of African-derived religions that attracted both legal suppression and scientific curiosity when black "witchcraft" became associated with the murders of Cuban children.

The popular image of the *negro brujo* solidified during the nineteenth century, as the arrival of increasing numbers of slaves led colonial officials to categorize the diverse African populations. In defining the *brujo,* they attributed to some African-descended individuals a capacity to use magic, plants, and animals to heal physical and spiritual maladies. At times, their supposed abilities to withstand or deflect the violence of white superiors and others seemed to have endowed them with powers that concerned nervous social observers. Their status as practitioners frequently offered opportunities for upward mobility both within the religion and within the communities in which they lived. While *brujos* sometimes practiced their magic within the confines of *cabildos,* the social organizations comprising free and enslaved members of African nations, pressure from the colonial government in the 1880s moved many *cabildos* to distance themselves from their African origins and to embrace a new identity as government-sponsored *sociedades.* This measure had the effect of distancing *brujos,* their sorcery, and their dancing and drumming rituals from the renovated institutions.

In the early years of the Cuban republic, images of *brujería* acquired more negative associations, linking African-derived religious practices with cannibalism and the murder of white children, usually girls, to collect their blood for rituals. The government of the republic mounted an aggressive campaign against *brujería* and *ñañiguismo* (referring to a network of secret societies) beginning in 1902. While the Spanish colonial government had not legally targeted *brujería,* the 1901 Cuban constitution allowed *brujos* to be prosecuted under laws governing public health and free association. At the very moment when a newly independent Cuban nation promoted a race-transcendent version of modern citizenship, government officials and local police sought to eradicate *brujería* practices that some Cubans identified as African in origin and primitive in content. A series of murders and trials that received extensive media coverage publicized and transformed the *negro brujo* from a social curiosity into a political menace.

In 1904 a child named Celia was the victim of an attempted rape and murder, and another named Zoila was kidnapped, murdered, and had her heart removed. The murders of these two children in and around Havana received widespread press coverage and led to the arrest of fourteen African-descended Cubans for their alleged involvement in the crimes. Several executions ensued, and correlations between the murders and *brujería* proliferated, despite a lack of clear evidence. The houses of Lucumí and Palo Monte priests were subjected to police searches similar to those directed against the Abakuá-associated *ñañigo* societies. Raids and mass arrests followed a series of child murders in the 1900s and 1910s throughout the island and were sometimes accompanied by mob violence and lynching. Urban police were quick to link Afro-Cuban religious groups with black political unrest, especially during and after the 1912 government suppression of the Partido Independiente de Color.

The campaign against the *negros brujos* found its intellectual backing in the writings of Fernando Ortiz, a young lawyer steeped in the new disciplinary practices of anthropology and criminology and who would become the island's most visible intellectual in the first half of the twentieth century. In *Los negros brujos* (1906), Ortiz historicized the *brujo* as one of the many black social types that inhabited colonial Cuban cities, especially in the neighborhoods outside the city walls. The *brujo* coexisted with the *negro curro,* or street gypsy, and the *ñañigo* to create an underworld rich in complexity but prone to crime and degeneracy. Rather than executing *brujos* for their alleged (and usually unproven) responsibility for the child murders, Ortiz preferred to keep the *brujos* alive for the progressive project of social analysis, so that their African wizardry could be more clearly defined and their "born criminal" nature could be understood. Although the campaigns of the 1900s netted a relatively small number of *brujería* convictions, they had the more lasting legacy of stigmatizing African-derived religious practices for at least two decades and fixing them as the object of scientific knowledge and state surveillance.

Popular anxieties about African-derived "witchcraft" practices were not isolated to Cuba. Public campaigns mobilized in Haiti in the early twentieth century against Vodou, and the Myal movement in Jamaica, directed against practitioners of Obeah, drew criticism—but little state intervention—as a black religious movement in general and for disrupting plantation work routines specifically. The increased migration of Haitian and Jamaican laborers to Cuba between 1910 and 1920 amplified Cuban suppression of *negros brujos,* as suspicions of Vodou and Myal witchcraft followed the arrival of new African-descended migrants and blurred distinctions with Cuban *brujería.* In Brazil, just two years after the abolition of slavery, the new republican Brazilian government criminalized witchcraft in 1890. Novelists, medical professionals, and social scientists alike amalgamated African-derived magic and religious healing practices, Candomblé cults, folk medicine, and sometimes spiritist practices into a derogatory image of witchcraft in the late nineteenth and early twentieth centuries. In doing so, they bolstered the state's efforts to enforce the 1890 ordinance, although commentators reflected and perhaps encouraged popular assumptions that patron-client relations existed between elites and the sorcerers, or *feiticeiros,* who sometimes evaded persecution under the witchcraft law. Without discounting the presence of African-derived religious practice in the Americas, the *negros brujos* scare reveals more about the racial (and racist) anxieties of postemancipation societies and state preoccupations with alternate forms of popular authority than it does about witchcraft itself.

See also Abakuá; Central African Religions and Culture in the Americas; Myal; Obeah; Partido Independiente de Color

DAVID SARTORIUS (2005)

NEGRO STRING QUARTET

❚❚❚

Founded by Felix Weir and active from 1920 to 1933, the Negro String Quartet performed in the musical programs of many churches and community organizations in Harlem and at Columbia University. Its members were Weir and Arthur Boyd, first and second violins respectively; Hall Johnson, viola; and Marion Cumbo, cello. They performed both European chamber music and the music of African-American composers, including Samuel Coleridge-Taylor and Clarence Cameron White. Johnson, who later formed his own choir and arranged many African-American spirituals, also composed and arranged music for the quartet. The Negro String Quartet was the musical descendant of the American String Quartet, also founded by Weir, which included Joseph Lymos, Hall Johnson, and Leonard Jeter. Despite its brief tenure (1914–1919), its members bequeathed a distinguished reputation to the Negro String Quartet: Johnson and Jeter were members of the original pit orchestra of the Broadway musical *Shuffle Along* (together with Eubie Blake and William Grant Still). Jeter performed the Schumann Cello Concerto with the Boston Symphony Orchestra in 1914 and was one of Marion Cumbo's cello teachers.

The Negro String Quartet's most significant performance was on November 28, 1925, at Carnegie Hall, when it accompanied Roland Hayes singing spirituals arranged by Hall Johnson for tenor, piano, and string quartet. Of that performance, the *New York Times* music critic Olin Downes wrote, "The performance had the profound and mystical feeling that the slave songs possess—a spirituality and pathos given them in fact as well as in name. Thus the final group was not merely an expected item of an entertainment, but rather the contribution of musicians and artists together in the presence of a common ideal of beauty."

See also Blake, Eubie; Still, William Grant

■■ *Bibliography*

Cuney-Hare, Maude. *Negro Musicians and Their Music.* Washington, D.C.: Associated Publishers, 1936.

Downes, Olin. "Roland Hayes Sings." *New York Times,* November 28, 1925.

Waters, Ethel, with Charles Samuels. *His Eye Is on the Sparrow.* New York: Doubleday, 1951.

TIMOTHY W. HOLLEY (1996)

NEGRO WORLD

❚❚❚

The *Negro World* (1918–1933) was the organ of Marcus Garvey's Universal Negro Improvement Association (UNIA), the most massive African-American and Pan-African movement of all time. Garvey's was a black nationalist movement organized around the principles of race first, self-reliance, and nationhood. At its height in the mid-1920s, the UNIA comprised millions of members and close supporters spread over more than forty countries in the Americas, Africa, Europe, and Australia. The *Negro World* was a faithful reflexion of all the UNIA stood for. It educated African people everywhere on the need for self-determination and racial uplift. With its international reach, it became a major recruiting tool for the organization. Like the larger movement, however, the *Negro World* was viewed with hostility and suspicion by European and other governments.

The *Negro World* began publication in 1918 in Harlem, New York, about two years after Garvey arrived in the United States from his native Jamaica. Garvey had founded the UNIA in Jamaica in 1914, and he conceived the idea of a major publication before leaving for the United States. He brought considerable experience in journalism and printing to the paper. While still a teenager, he had been a foreman printer in Jamaica, and he had published papers in Costa Rica and Panama. He had worked on possibly two papers in Jamaica and for the important *Africa Times and Orient Review* in London in 1913. The earliest issues of the paper were edited by Garvey and slipped free under people's doors in Harlem. Garvey's responsibilities in building the UNIA did not permit him to do the hands-on day-to-day work of running the paper for very long. Though he remained managing editor, he quickly initiated the paper's policy of employing some of the best editorial brains in African America. Among these were Hubert H. Harrison (1883–1927), one of Harlem's most respected intellectuals; W. A. Domingo, a Socialist and sometime publisher of his own *Emancipator;* the veteran journalist John E. Bruce (known in the newspaper world as "Bruce Grit"); William H. Ferris (1874–1941), an author and graduate of Yale and Harvard; T. Thomas Fortune (1856–1928), the "dean" of African-American journalists; and the second Mrs. Garvey, Amy Jacques Garvey (1885–1973).

Among the regular columnists, contributors, and book reviewers were important personalities in Pan-African history. These included Carter G. Woodson (1875–1950), the "father of African-American history"; the popular historian J. A. Rogers (1880–1966); and Duse Mohamed Ali (1866–1945), the editor of the London-based *Africa Times and Orient Review.*

The paper was forceful in tone. "Negroes get ready," it proclaimed from the masthead of early editions. Garvey himself wrote a bold-typed, front page editorial for each issue. This formed the text for weekly meetings of the UNIA all over the world. Coverage of Pan-African and anticolonial news was very broad. Sections of the paper were for a time published in French and Spanish. Articles were well written and sober; there was none of the sensationalism and frivolity of the popular press. Garvey credited himself with having raised the quality of African-American journalism.

Despite its overwhelmingly political orientation, the paper also acted as a literary journal. Poems from contributors around the world appeared every week for several years. The paper boasted African America's first regular book review section. Short stories, plays, and literary and cultural criticism appeared regularly. Major Harlem Renaissance figures such as Zora Neale Hurston (1891–1960) and Eric Walrond (1898–1966) published in the *Negro World.*

At the same time, the paper did not neglect its role as organ of a great movement. Proceedings of public meetings and conferences filled many pages. Weekly reports of branch meetings were faithfully recorded. Among the authors of such organizational business was Louise Little, the mother of Malcolm X.

The *Negro World*'s circulation is said to have reached 200,000 in the 1920s, making it one of the largest newspapers in African America. It was undoubtedly also the most widely circulated African newspaper internationally. People coming into contact with the paper's message in places as far apart as Dominica and Nigeria were impelled to become Garveyites, sometimes founding their own local branches of the UNIA in the process. Official circulation efforts were supplemented by itinerant seamen who, sometimes acting entirely on their own, took the paper around the world.

The United States, as well as European and other governments, waged a protracted struggle to destroy the paper. Within a year of its appearance in 1919, it was already banned in some British Caribbean territories, Trinidad and British Guiana among them. An African in Southern Rhodesia was sentenced to life in prison (the sentence later rescinded after representations to the British parliament) for importing a few copies.

The *Negro World* survived Garvey's deportation from the United States in 1927 and subsequent schisms in the UNIA, and the paper remained loyal to him until its demise in 1933. Garvey published two newspapers in Jamaica, and a magazine in Jamaica and England, after his deportation from the United States. The UNIA also briefly supplemented the weekly *Negro World* with a *Daily Negro Times* in the early 1920s. However, none of Garvey's other journalistic endeavors ever matched the power and influence of the *Negro World.* With its combination of wide circulation, international outreach, excellence of editorship, and worldwide influence, the *Negro World* may have been the best African-American newspaper of all time.

See also Garvey, Marcus; Universal Negro Improvement Association

■ ■ *Bibliography*

Martin, Tony. *Race First: The Ideological and Organizational Struggles of Marcus Garvey and the Universal Negro Improvement Association.* Westport, Conn.: Greenwood Press, 1976. Reprint, Dover, Mass.: Majority Press, 1986.

Martin, Tony. *The Pan-African Connection: From Slavery to Garvey and Beyond.* Cambridge, Mass.: Schenkman, 1983. Reprint, Dover, Mass.: Majority Press, 1984.

Martin, Tony. *Literary Garveyism: Garvey, Black Arts, and the Harlem Renaissance.* Dover, Mass: Majority Press, 1983.

Martin, Tony. *Marcus Garvey, Hero: A First Biography.* Dover, Mass: Majority Press, 1983.

Martin, Tony, editor. *African Fundamentalism: A Literary and Cultural Anthology of Garvey's Harlem Renaissance.* Dover, Mass: Majority Press, 1986.

Hill, Robert A., and Carol A. Rudisell, eds. *The Marcus Garvey and UNIA Papers,* vols. 1–7, 9. Berkeley: University of California Press, 1983-95.

TONY MARTIN (2005)

NELL, WILLIAM COOPER

DECEMBER 20, 1816
MAY 25, 1874

┃┃┃

The historian and abolitionist William Cooper Nell was born in Boston and graduated with honors from the city's African school. However, despite his achievements, Nell was excluded because of color from citywide ceremonies honoring outstanding scholars. That incident inspired him to lead a campaign to integrate Boston schools during the 1840s and early 1850s. He also championed equal access to railroads, theaters, and militia service. Nell joined the rising antislavery movement in 1831 and became one of the closest and most loyal African-American associates of abolitionist William Lloyd Garrison. In later years Nell supported himself through work as a legal copyist.

In the early 1840s, Nell began a lengthy affiliation with Garrison's *Liberator,* writing articles, supervising the paper's Negro Employment Office, corresponding with other abolitionists, and representing Garrison at various antislavery functions. Nell moved to Rochester at the end of the 1840s, where he became the publisher of Frederick Douglass's newspaper, the *North Star* (1847). By 1850 he had returned to Boston, where he ran unsuccessfully for the Massachusetts Legislature on the Free Soil Party ticket He also worked on the Underground Railroad at this time. When conflict arose between Douglass and Garrison after 1851, Nell eventually sided with Garrison, although his own political posture was probably somewhere in the middle.

Nell believed that African-American history could be a useful tool in stimulating racial pride and advancing the struggle against slavery and racial prejudice. He wrote two pioneering historical works, the pamphlet *The Services of Colored Americans in the Wars of 1776 and 1812* (1851), and the book *Colored Patriots of the American Revolution*

(1855). His careful scholarship and innovative use of oral sources contributed in important ways to the developments of African-American historiography. Beginning in 1858, to protest the 1857 *Dred Scott* decision, Nell began organizing annual Crispus Attucks Day celebrations in Boston to commemorate African-American contributions to the American Revolution and to justify black claims to full citizenship. In 1861 he was appointed a postal clerk in Boston, becoming probably the first African American named to a position in a federal agency. He held this post until his death, from "paralysis of the brain," in 1874.

See also *Dred Scott v. Sandford*; *Liberator, The*; Douglass, Frederick; Underground Railroad

■ ■ *Bibliography*

Browne, Patrick T. J. "'To Defend Mr. Garrison': William Cooper Nell and the Personal Politics of Antislavery." *New England Quarterly* 70 (1997): 415–442.

Smith, Robert P. "William Cooper Nell: Crusading Black Abolitionist." *Journal of Negro History* 55 (1970): 182–199.

Wesley, Dorothy Porter. "Integration Versus Separatism: William Cooper Nell's Role in the Struggle for Equality." In *Courage and Conscience: Black and White Abolitionists in Boston,* edited by Donald M. Jacobs, pp. 207–224. Bloomington: Indiana University Press, 1993.

ROY E. FINKENBINE (1996)
Updated bibliography

NELSON, PRINCE ROGERS

See Prince (Nelson, Prince Rogers)

NETHERSOLE, NOEL NEWTON

NOVEMBER 2, 1903
MARCH 17, 1959

┃┃┃

A financial expert and political economist, Noel Newton Nethersole was minister of finance and the first full pre-independence minister of Jamaica from 1955 until his death. However, this role, while arguably his most important in Jamaica's history, occurred fairly late in his life. Prior to holding this ministerial position, Nethersole had been a Rhodes scholar (1922) and a lawyer. He was admitted as a solicitor for Jamaica's Supreme Court in 1931. Nethersole excelled at cricket and was captain of the Jamaica cricket team between 1932 and 1939. He also served on the Jamaica Cricket Board for twenty years and was a member of the West Indian Cricket board for sixteen years. In addition, Nethersole served as chairman of the Finance Committee of the Kingston and Saint Andrew Corporation. He also served as a foundation member and first vice-president of the People's National Party (PNP), one of Jamaica's two major political parties.

As minister of finance, Nethersole has been credited with modernizing the ministry and its subsidiaries. In 1957 Nethersole created the Investment Division of the ministry, which managed the movement of capital in and out of the country. Nethersole also made history by leading Jamaica in the arduous task of raising a loan of 12.5 million U.S. dollars on the New York money market. Jamaica became the first colonial country to place such a loan in the international money market. The loan resulted in more capital being made available for public services in Jamaica, and in the country becoming less dependent on Britain. It also set the stage for the meaningful economic independence of the country. As impressive as this feat was, Nethersole's major goal was to create a central bank of Jamaica, an ambition that came to fruition shortly after his death. The street on which the Bank of Jamaica is located was officially named Nethersole Place in 1975 in honor of its founding father. Nethersole also worked on the financial aspects of the short-lived Federation of the West Indies.

Aside from his ministerial responsibilities, Nethersole, along with Ken Hill, headed the National Reform Association beginning in 1937. This organization paved the way for the PNP. In addition, Nethersole served as president of the Trade Union Council and headed the Bustamante Industrial Trade Union (BITU) when its leader, Alexander Bustamante, was detained for seventeen months during World War II. Bustamante was placed in detention in 1940 for inciting three major strikes in less than one year, which was an alleged violation of the Defense of the Realm Act. Nethersole was also chosen as the first president of the National Workers Union, and he became a member of parliament after the 1949 general election, paving the way for his revolutionary accomplishments in the finance ministry.

Despite his achievements, Nethersole was often criticized in the media for handling the country's overseas economic negotiations in secret. He was also chairman of the investigating committee within the PNP that was responsible for ejecting Ken Hill, Frank Hill, Arthur Henry, and

Richard Hart from the party because of their "leftist" views. However, Nethersole's popularity in the cricket arena and as a financial genius far outweighed what were perceived as his shortcomings. His insight, foresight, and hard work not only set the stage for the development of the Bank of Jamaica but were instrumental in carving a path toward the country's economic independence.

See also People's National Party; Politics and Politicians in the Caribbean

■ ■ *Bibliography*

Carnegie, James. *Some Aspects of Jamaica's Politics, 1918–1938.* Kingston: Institute of Jamaica, 1973.

Carnegie, James. *Noel Newton Nethersole: A Short Study.* Kingston: Bank of Jamaica, 1975.

Nettleford, Rex, ed. *Manley and the New Jamaica: Selected Speeches and Writings, 1938–1968.* Port of Spain, Trinidad and Tobago, and Kingston, Jamaica: Longmans Caribbean, 1971.

DALEA M. BEAN (2005)

NETTLEFORD, REX

FEBRUARY 3, 1933

Rex Nettleford is one of the most esteemed and versatile intellectuals in the Caribbean. Born in the rural town of Falmouth, Jamaica, he attended Cornwall College in Montego Bay and gained a B.A. degree in history at the University College of the West Indies (London University). He stayed on for a year as resident tutor in the extramural department before winning a Rhodes Scholarship to Oxford University, where he was a postgraduate in politics at Oriel College in 1957 and received an M.Phil. He returned to Jamaica, holding various university posts in extramural (later continuing) studies at what became the independent University of the West Indies in 1962. He was appointed director of the School of Continuing Studies in 1971, professor of continuing studies in 1976, pro vice chancellor (Outreach and Institutional Relations) from 1988 to 1996, deputy vice chancellor from 1996 to 1998, and vice chancellor in 1998. He became editor of the *Caribbean Quarterly,* the first journal dedicated to the study of the culture of the Caribbean, in 1967. He has lectured and toured throughout the world with UNESCO, the Organization of American States (OAS), and other agencies in London and Canada.

Nettleford has had a multifaceted career not only as an academic but also as an artist. In 1962 he cofounded with Eddy Thomas the National Dance Theatre Company of Jamaica. He became the artistic director of the company the following year and principal choreographer. He has also engaged in civic activities both at home and abroad, principally in education and the arts. He founded the Trade Union Education Institute, which attempted to bridge the gulf between classes and to encourage exchanges between scholars and laborers, and he headed the National Council on Education. He has also served in Jamaica as chairman of the Workforce Development Commission, director of the National Commercial Bank, director of the Norman Manley Awards and Memorial Foundation, and cultural advisor to the Government of Jamaica.

He has participated in many capacities in international organizations: the founding governor of the Canadian-based International Development Research Council (IDRC); the international trustee of the AFS Intercultural based in the United States; chairman of the Commonwealth Arts Organization; chairman of London's Commonwealth Arts Organization; member of the executive board of UNESCO; and chairman of the International Council on the University Adult Education. He has acted as a consultant on cultural development to UNESCO and the OAS. He serves as a board member of the Gemini News Agency; rapporteur of the International Scientific Committee of UNESCO's Slave Route Project as well as regional coordinator for the Caribbean; a member of Caricom Cultural Foundation; and a founding member and trustee of Caribbean Universities and Research Institutes.

Nettleford's writings reflect the diversity of his interests. His many books include *Mirror, Mirror: Race, Identity, and Protest in Jamaica* (1970), *Manley and the New Jamaica* (1971), *Caribbean Cultural Identity* (1978), *Dance Jamaica: Cultural Definition and Artistic Discovery* (1985), and *Inward Stretch, Outward Reach: A Voice from the Caribbean* (1995). He has also coauthored, with Maria La Yacona, *Roots and Rhythms: Jamaica's National Dance Theatre* (1969), with Slim Aarons and Arnold Newman, *Rose Hall, Jamaica: Story of a People, a Legend, and a Legacy* (1973), with Philip Sherlock, *The University of the West Indies: A Caribbean Response to the Challenge of Change* (1987), and, with M. G. Smith and Roy Augier, *The Rastafarians in Kingston, Jamaica* (1960). He edited *Jamaica in Independence; The Early Years* (1988); he coedited, with Norman Manley, *Norman Washington Manley and the New Jamaica; Selected speeches and Writings, 1938-1968* (1971); he coedited, with Vera Hyatt, *Jamaica in Independence: The Early Years* (1991) and *Race, Discourse and the Origins of the Americas*, a publication for the Smithsonian (1995). He is also the author of major national reports on cultural policy, worker participation, reform of government structure in Jamaica, and national symbols and national observances.

Nettleford has received numerous honors including the Order of Merit (OM) from Jamaica in 1975; the Gold Musgrave Medal from the Institute of Jamaica; the Living Legend Award from the Black Arts Festival, Atlanta, Georgia; and the Pelican Award from the University of the West Indies Guild of Graduates. In 1991, he became one of only four people in over a hundred years to be named a fellow of the Institute of Jamaica; in 1994 he received the Zora Neale Hurston/Paul Robeson Award for Outstanding Scholarly Achievements from the National Council for Black Studies in the United States. He was received the Pinnacle Award from the National Coalition on Caribbean Affairs (NCOCA) and the Second Annual Honor Award from the Jamaican-American Chamber of Commerce in 1999. He has been awarded honorary doctorates and degrees on both sides of the Atlantic, including a D. Litt from St. John's University in 1994; an LHD from the University of Hartford and a Presidential Medal from Brooklyn College in 1995; an LHD from City University of New York and John Jay College in 1996; a D. Litt. from the University of Connecticut and an LLD from Illinois Wesleyan University in 1997; an LLD by Queens University (Canada) in 1999; an LHD by Emory University and D.Litt. from Grand Valley State University and Sheffield University (England) in 2000; an LLD from the University of Toronto (Canada) in 2001; a DCL from Oxford University (England), an honor shared by only two other West Indians, Eric Williams and Sir Shridath Ramphal, in 2003; a D.Litt. from the University of Technology (Jamaica) in 2004; and a DFA from the State University of New York, Brockport in 2005. In 2003, the Rhodes Trust of Oxford University established the Rex Nettleford Prize in Cultural Studies and the Government of Jamaica made him an ambassador-at-large in 2004. He was made an honorary fellow of Oriel College, Oxford University, in 1998; a distinguished fellow in the UWI School of Graduate Studies; and an honorary (life) fellow of the Center for Caribbean Thought. In 2004 he was made an Officer of the Ordre des Arts et Lettres by the French government and received the Pablo Neruda Centenary Medal from the Government of Chile.

The principal focus of Nettleford's wide-ranging interests and writings is the identity and culture of the peoples of the postindependence Caribbean. He anticipated the development of modern cultural studies with his interdisciplinary approach to understanding how the dynamic process of creolization melded a people who were part African, part European, part Asian, part Native American but totally Caribbean. He was a pioneer in attempting to rediscover the African elements of the Jamaican identity and to give it expression in his National Dance Theatre Company. He was sympathetic in his treatment of the Rastafarians at a time when they were often treated as pariahs in the Caribbean. However, Nettleford was never wholly Afrocentric, because he was always too committed to inclusiveness and to recognizing the rich elements that made up the Caribbean. He is essentially antiparochial in his efforts to traverse different academic disciplines, different classes, different races, and different nations.

See also Augier, Roy; Dance, Diasporic; Manley, Norman; Sherlock, Philip

■ ■ *Bibliography*

Warner, Maureen, and Albertina Jefferson. *Rex Nettleford and His Works: An Annotated Bibliography*. Jamaica: University of the West Indies Press, 1997.

ANDREW JACKSON O'SHAUGHNESSY (2005)

NEW DEAL, THE

See Great Depression and the New Deal

NEW JEWEL MOVEMENT

■ ■ ■

Early in the morning of October 25, 1983, an invasion force numbering more then six thousand U.S. infantry and marines attacked by sea and air the tiny spice island of Grenada, southernmost of the Windward Islands in the Eastern Caribbean. After five days of unexpected resistance from Grenada's People's Revolutionary Army (PRA), the United States, backed by some Caribbean states but opposed by the great majority in the United Nations, finally asserted control.

The immediate prelude to these momentous events was an extraordinary meeting in September of the Central Committee (CC) of Grenada's ruling party, the Marxist-Leninist New Jewel Movement (NJM). After four and a half years of revolutionary rule, beginning with the armed seizure of power from autocratic Prime Minister Eric Gairy in March 1979, the majority of the CC assessed that the regime was in a state of crisis. Earlier that year, on

March 10, U.S. president Ronald Reagan in a national broadcast had declared Grenada, with its close ties to Cuba, a threat to U.S. security. Following this broadcast, there were large, coordinated naval maneuvers in the Atlantic and Caribbean. An invasion of Grenada seemed imminent, and yet many CC members averred that from the perspective of military preparedness and national morale, the country was at its lowest point since 1979. The position eventually endorsed by all was that weak leadership had been the cause of the flagging support.

Divisions began to emerge, however, when suggestions as to the way out of the crisis were proposed. Liam James, member of the inner Political Bureau and chief of security, argued that while Prime Minister Maurice Bishop had the charismatic qualities to inspire people, he lacked a "Leninist level of organization and discipline," as well as great ideological clarity. The answer, James proposed, was a model of "joint leadership," merging Bishop's strengths with those of Deputy Prime Minister and Minister of Finance Bernard Coard, generally perceived as the most ideologically developed of the top leaders. After much debate, in which Bishop, among others, expressed reservations, the proposal was carried forward to a full party gathering on September 25. Here, differences seemed to have been overcome and the meeting ended in apparent unity. The following day Bishop left on a scheduled trip to Eastern Europe, returning via Cuba on October 8. By then everything had changed. He announced that he wanted the joint leadership matter reopened for debate. Battle lines were now drawn. Some party leaders began to see his request as an unacceptable volte-face on a collective decision. For his part, Bishop began to believe that there was a conspiracy afoot.

Rumors were rife. One in particular, suggesting that Coard and his Jamaican wife, Phyllis, were planning to kill the prime minister, led to a clash between a pro-Bishop militia contingent and a unit of the regular army. When an investigation into the source was held, Bishop's number two security officer said that the rumor came from the prime minister himself. Bishop, refusing to respond to the accusation, was placed, precipitously, under house arrest.

Almost immediately, popular demonstrations began, from a people who were entirely unaware of the previous secretive, inner-party decisions and who were outraged at the detention of their popular leader. On October 19 a large demonstration freed Bishop from his home, and he, along with his closest associates, marched to the main military camp at nearby Fort Rupert and overwhelmed its guards.

In the subsequent attempt by the army to recapture the fort, there was a shootout with fatalities both on the side of the encroaching military and the newly armed pro-Bishop supporters. The PRA contingent was eventually victorious; Bishop and his closest allies were held unarmed, then shortly thereafter executed.

The killing of Bishop undermined any remaining popular support for the revolutionary process. The expected U.S. invasion came six days later. There was resistance, but most of the country was still paralyzed and in shock, with many expressing great antipathy toward those in the NJM whom they held responsible for murdering Bishop.

The NJM had been formed only a decade before in 1973. A direct product of the effervescent Caribbean Black Power movement, it emerged from the unification of two trends—the Joint Endeavour for Welfare, Education, and Liberation (Jewel), headed by Unison Whiteman, and the Movement for the Assemblies of the People (MAP), headed by Maurice Bishop. MAP was one of a few Caribbean organizations inspired by the ideas of the Trinidadian Marxist C. L. R. James.

The NJM was launched during a profound political crisis. In 1972 Eric Gairy's Grenada United Labour Party (GULP) won what many considered to be a fraudulent general election. Immediately after, he declared without prior consultation that he would lead Grenada to independence from Great Britain. Many people opposed independence under Gairy, fearing that his arbitrary and often brutal rule would worsen. Large, anti-independence demonstrations escalated into a nationwide lockdown in December 1973, when Gairy's paramilitary force—the "Mongoose Gang"—beat up Bishop and other NJM leaders as they mobilized support.

Gairy managed to ride out the general strike and declared independence, effectively defeating the opposing coalition. Out of this failure, NJM leaders, influenced by Coard, decided to transform the party from a popular, if inchoate, mass movement into a vanguard party based on Leninist principles of selective membership and "democratic centralism." Vanguardism seemed at first to serve the movement well. In 1976, as part of a broad-based alliance, the NJM contested general elections. Gairy won, though many considered it another rigged exercise. The NJM, however, emerged as the largest opposition party, and Bishop became the constitutional leader of the opposition.

In early 1979, when it was alleged that Gairy was planning to arrest and massacre NJM leaders, the party had already trained a military force and was able to respond with the seizure of power on March 13. This power was consolidated when large numbers of people came out in the streets in support of the revolution.

NJM rule combined some distinct successes with a few ultimately fatal weaknesses. NJM's economic policies, predicated on Keynesian notions of infrastructural development, led to growth and significantly reduced levels of unemployment. The structural features of the economy, however, rooted in an agrarian-based, export dependent monoculture, remained largely unchanged. The political strategy showed some innovation, as in the national budget debate, which sought to creatively involve the entire populace in a discussion of the annual budget. The broader policy on political freedoms was, however, seriously flawed, including the failure to consider multiparty elections and the detention of large numbers of opposition figures on the sometimes unsubstantiated basis that they were "counterrevolutionary."

The single most important political failure, however, was the dogmatic application of vanguardism after the seizure of power. Leninism had been a useful tool for insurrection, but turned out later to be a millstone around the party's neck. The unswerving implementation of a policy of secrecy, elitism, and exclusionism served to alienate the NJM from its support base, laying the basis for the crisis of mid-1983 and the fatal joint leadership proposal, which, in turn, led to the tragedy of October.

See also Bishop, Maurice; Gairy, Eric

▪ *Bibliography*

Brizan, George. *Grenada: Island of Conflict.* London and Basingstoke, UK: Macmillan, 1998.

Cotman, John Walton. *The Gorrión Tree: Cuba and the Grenadian Revolution.* New York: Peter Lang, 1993.

Heine, Jorge. *A Revolution Aborted.* Pittsburgh, Penn.: University of Pittsburgh Press, 1990.

Lewis, Gordon K. *Grenada: The Jewel Despoiled.* Baltimore, Md.: Johns Hopkins University Press, 1987.

Mandle, Jay. *Big Revolution, Small Country: The Rise and Fall of the Grenadian Revolution.* Lanham, Md.: North South, 1985.

Marable, Manning. *African and Caribbean Politics: From Kwame Nkrumah to Maurice Bishop.* London: Verso, 1987.

Meeks, Brian. *Caribbean Revolutions and Revolutionary Theory: An Assessment of Cuba, Nicaragua and Grenada.* London and Basingstoke, UK: Macmillan, 1993.

Noguera, Pedro. *The Imperatives of Power: Regime Survival and the Basis of Political Support in Grenada from 1951–1991.* New York: Peter Lang, 1997.

Payne, Anthony, Paul Sutton, and Tony Thorndike. *Grenada: Revolution and Invasion.* London and Sydney: Croom Helm, 1984.

Pryor, Frederic. *Revolutionary Grenada: A Study in Political Economy.* Westport, Conn., New York, and London: Praeger, 1986.

Sandford, Gregory, and Richard Vigilante. *Grenada: The Untold Story.* Lanham, Md., New York, and London: Madison Books, 1984.

Seabury, Paul, and Walter A. McDougall. *The Grenada Papers.* San Francisco: ICS, 1984.

Searle, Chris, ed. *In Nobody's Backyard: Maurice Bishop's Speeches 1979–1983: A Memorial Volume.* London: Zed Books, 1984.

Smith, Courtney. *Socialist Transformation in Peripheral Economies: Lessons from Grenada.* Aldershot, UK: Avebury, 1995.

Thorndike, Tony. *Grenada: Politics, Economics and Society.* London: Frances Pinter, 1985.

BRIAN MEEKS (2005)

NEW MEDIA AND DIGITAL CULTURE

Throughout the 1990s the terms *new media* and *digital culture* were commonly used phrases to describe several technological, social, and political developments during the period. A major consumer change during this decade was the growth in technologies available to individual consumers, the personal computer being the most influential and common of them all. The popularity of the personal computer as a consumer item in households was partly a result of the growth of the Internet beginning in the early 1990s. While the Internet was praised as a technological revolution at the end of the millennium, its origins can be dated back to the Cold War era. As tensions escalated between the United States and the former USSR after World War II, the U.S. Department of Defense put a great deal of effort into creating a communications network that would outlive a possible nuclear war. In the 1960s this research became known as the Advanced Research Projects Agency. Over the next several years the developing network of linked computers became useful for educational institutions but maintained its strong connection to military explorations. Yet the growing technology did not serve the commercial function that would define it by the 1990s. Continued technological developments and the growth of the computer workstation in the 1980s provided an environment for the Internet to become more sophisticated and influential. Many date the Internet revolution, as it became known to the general public, to 1994.

Part of the impact of the Internet is its reliance on innovations in digital technology. Digital technology is different from previous analog technology in how information is processed, stored, and displayed. Digital technology processes information as binary code, that is, zeros and ones. The information can be recalled at any point and reproduced in identical replicas. With analog technology, information is carried through varying frequency to carrier waves. Reproductions through analog technology degrade with each generation of copying. This is why a second-generation videotape is of lower quality than a first-generation tape. Thus, the digital technology's breakthrough is in recording, reproducing, and disseminating identical information to limitless numbers of people.

By the late 1990s the promises of the Internet and digital technology had reached a global scale. In fact, the world was often referred to as a global village where human communication between people in the remotest parts of the planet could happen with ease. Advertisements from technology companies, such as IBM, Sun Microsystems, Compaq, and Microsoft, showed a multiracial, harmonious world brought together by advances in technology. This period is known as the *digital boom*. A large number of what were known as start-up high technologies developed in a short period of time. Many employees involved in these companies became extremely rich during the late 1990s, but a large percentage lost their wealth when the digital economy collapsed at the turn of the millennium. For the most part blacks and Latinos did not benefit financially from this economic trend, as their numbers were extremely low on the payroll of high-technology companies.

THE DIGITAL DIVIDE

The term *digital divide* became an increasingly popular way to refer to the disparity between technology haves and have-nots. The origin of the term is debated but can be traced back to journalist Amy Harmon in 1996, then writing for the *Los Angeles Times,* and to U.S. president Bill Clinton's administration's technology initiatives during the same period. *Digital divide* refers loosely to the imbalances between those who have access and know-how and those who lack technological resources, specifically people from developing nations and rural communities and lower-income blacks and Latinos in the United States. While this period saw an astronomical growth in the number of homes that had personal computers, blacks and Latinos lagged behind whites and Asians in such purchases. Often, schools in poor communities were not equipped with the new technologies used in richer school districts. In other words, many minority communities lacked access to technology and, more importantly, technological literacy. For the most part, black Americans' participation in technology consumption and Internet usage was the standard for measuring the digital divide in the United States.

Social policy and local community attempts to counter this technological imbalance included creating computer centers in low-income neighborhoods and initiatives to equip poor schools with new computers. Several Web sites by nonprofit groups and collaborations between businesses and communities addressed more sustainable approaches to bridging technological gaps.

Yet critics of the digital divide have challenged the framework of the digital divide as too simplistic by focusing on access alone. Several writers and scholars, including Anna Everett, Lisa Nakamura, and Alondra Nelson, have offered more complex analyses of race and new technology issues. Instead of just focusing on the issue of access, these scholars analyze the formation of racial communities on the Internet and how issues of race are addressed through digital practices. Scholar and curator Erika Dalya Muhammad began to write about and curate black new media artists in the late 1990s. She was one of the organizers of the first Race in Digital Space Conference sponsored by the University of Southern California and the Massachusetts Institute of Technology in 2001. These conferences brought together scholars, journalists, artists, and business professionals to consider the myriad of social implications of new technologies and race.

New Media and Digital Art

In addition to social policy and community activism, the field of art has been an important site for countering the digital divide. During the 1990s, artists, art critics, and art historians began to refer to a range of experimental art based in recent technological innovations as *new media art*. The term expressed a level of discontent with previous labels used to describe arts that relied heavily in form and content on technology, including *media art, multimedia art,* and *interactive media art*. At the same time, because technology is always evolving—that is, new technologies are always emerging—*new media* does not adequately describe the multifaceted works that challenged traditional notions of art disciplines. What it does describe is the influence of the Internet on art making, the use of modern technologies in the art-making process and for presentation, and the close relationships between art and science.

Individual artists and collectives used technology as medium for artistic production and as a tool to criticize some of the negative effects of the digital revolution, especially the reproduction of racial imbalances. Others, such as Cinque Hicks with his multimedia project *We Are All Global Nomads* (2003), use digital technology to explore the forms of human communication facilitated by new technology and to envision future possibilities in which technology is used to counter racism and other forms of discrimination. Many of these artists question how identity is formed and the uses of the social implications of technology.

Some key figures include Fatimah Tuggar, Leah Gilliam, Roshini Kempadoo, Keith Piper, Roy LaGrone, and Mendi and Keith Obadike. Tuggar, Kempadoo, and Gilliam appropriate both archival imagery and mass media to create new narratives about identity, history, and race. In Gilliam's installation *Agenda for a Landscape* (2002) at the New Museum for Contemporary Art, the media artist considers the social, technological, and representational implications of space exploration, specifically the space robot named Sojourner Truth used by NASA to explore Mars. Important online art projects by black visual and media artists include artist Fatimah Tuggar's *Changing Space* (2002) for the Art Production Fund and Charles Nelson's *Charles Nelson Project* (2001). Black British artist Keith Piper's multimedia installation, interactive Web site, and CD-ROM, *Relocating the Remains/Excavating the Site* (1997), is a sophisticated artistic exploration of the history of the black Atlantic. Artist Damali Ayo has combined art making with activism through her project, www.rent-a-negro.com, a satire on the commodification of black culture and the rampant consumerism promoted by the Internet by the turn of the millennium. Such exhibitions as *Digital Africa* (2003) at the Electronic Arts Intermix in New York offer venues for black diasporic media artists to present their works.

Important predecessors for these artists are video artists and media activists of the 1970s and 1980s. In the mid-1960s portable recording equipment became available because of the advent of the Sony Portapak. Through this first-generation portable video camera, individuals and groups previously excluded from media production gained access to the means of creating visual media. Artists, collectives, and activists began to use video technology to produce *alternative media,* that is, programs that would not be broadcast on television or in cinemas. Many of these projects challenged the large broadcast systems and mainstream American politics. Key figures in this movement include such collectives as the Downtown Community Television and the People's Communication Network in New York and the documentary work of William Greaves and St. Claire Bourne. With regard to the medium of video art, works by Adrian Piper, such as her video installation *Cornered* (1989), and photographic works by Lorna Simpson and Carrie Mae Weems influenced these practices.

Besides photography, video, and other image-based media, music and sound recording have been greatly impacted by digital technology. Digital recording devices and software make it easier for artists to have access to high-quality sound recording, and CD burners allow artists to master and copy their own music for distribution. Just as important, the Internet became a site for artists without recording contracts to build an audience by sharing their music online. Many musical artists began sharing their music free of charge or for a small fee through Internet downloads. Yet in the late 1990s large recording companies became concerned about the availability of copyrighted music on the Internet. The companies filed lawsuits against such companies as Napster that made it easy for consumers to download music despite copyright protection. On another front, digital sound art grew in popularity. Sound art is influenced by the hip-hop movement and club culture. Key black sound artists include Paul Miller (aka DJ Spooky That Subliminal Kid), Pamela Z, and artist and scholar Beth Coleman (aka DJ Singe).

BLACK DIGITAL CULTURE

The growth in black-oriented Web sites is an important development of the Internet culture. The Internet has become an essential tool for scholars and students of African-American studies. One important site, launched in 1999, is Africana.com, spearheaded by Professor Henry Louis Gates Jr. of Harvard University. Africana.com is an online encyclopedia of African-American history and culture with a wealth of articles and accessible archival materials, such as footage of speeches by Martin Luther King Jr. and Malcolm X. Other vital black online communities include blackplanet.com, with over five million members, and blackvoices.com; Web forums such as askblack.com; and black search engines such as blackwebportal.com and everythingblack.com. Groups such as the Association of African American Web Developers have been active in increasing black professional presence on the Internet. Companies and organizations such as Black Entertainment Television and the Black Women's Health Network have used their Web sites for educational and social campaigns targeted at black communities.

One of the most significant influences that digital culture and new media have had on black communities throughout the world is in the formation of *digital diasporas*. The notion of digital diaspora has emerged as the Internet gets used to form communities among people of similar heritage, geography, race, and ethnicity located throughout the world. Several active online communities have emerged among blacks from all walks of life, including a wide range of chat rooms, from those dedicated to African nationals residing in different parts of the world to those specifically for blacks interested in science fiction. One example is Afrofuturism, a site founded by scholar

Alondra Nelson, as an online community of black diasporic artists, technology experts, scholars, and individuals interested in futurist themes in black culture and the possibilities of technology to impact culture and society. In terms of social policy, a partnership of nongovernmental organizations through the United Nations called the Digital Diaspora Network-Africa promotes access to technological resources, professional skills, and education in the African diaspora. In essence, the concept of the black diaspora continues to strengthen through the notion of the digital diaspora.

See also Digital Culture

■ ■ *Bibliography*

Alkalimat, Abdul. *The African American Experience in Cyberspace: A Resource Guide to the Best Web Sites on Black Culture and History*. London: Pluto Press, 2004.

Everett, Anna, and John T. Caldwell, eds. *New Media: Theories and Practices of Digitextuality*. New York: Routledge, 2003.

Kolko, Beth E., Lisa Nakamura, and Gilbert Rodman, eds. *Race in Cyberspace*. New York: Routledge, 2000.

Muhammad, Erika. "Black High-Tech Documents." In *Struggles for Representation: African American Documentary Film and Video*, edited by. Phyllis R. Klotman and Janet K. Cutler. Indianapolis: Indiana University Press, 1999.

Nakamura, Lisa. *Cybertypes: Race, Ethnicity, and Identity on the Internet*. New York: Routledge, 2002.

Nelson, Alondra, Thuy Linh N. Tu, with Alicia Headlam Hines, eds. *Technicolor: Race, Technology, and Everyday Life*. New York: New York University Press, 2001.

Nelson, Alondra, ed. "Afrofuturism Special Issue." *Social Text* 20, no. 2 (2002).

Wardrip-Fruin, and Nick Montfort, eds. *The New Media Reader*. Cambridge, Mass.: MIT Press, 2003.

NICOLE R. FLEETWOOD (2005)

NEW NEGRO

The term *New Negro* was often used by whites in the colonial period to designate newly enslaved Africans. Ironically, that same term began to be used at the end of the nineteenth century to measure and represent the distance that African Americans had come from the institution of slavery. Throughout the first three decades of the twentieth century, articles and books discussing the New Negro were commonplace. African-American leaders, journalists, artists, and some white Americans used the phrase to refer to a general sense of racial renewal among blacks that was characterized by a spirit of racial pride, cultural and economic self-assertion, and political militancy. William Pickens, for example, proclaimed the transformation of the "patient, unquestioning devoted semi-slave" into "the self-conscious, aspiring, proud young man" (Pickens, 1916, p. 236). While the notion of a New Negro was variously defined, it typically referred to the passing of an "old Negro," the "Uncle Tom" of racial stereotypes, and the emergence of an educated, politically and culturally aware generation of blacks.

A New Negro for a New Century (1900), a volume of historical and social essays, with chapters by Booker T. Washington and other prominent blacks, was one of the earliest of several books that sought to define the new racial personality. In subsequent decades many African Americans referred to Washington's political leadership and educational philosophy as symbolic of an accommodation that marked the "old Negro"; yet Washington's chapter, "Afro-American Education," stressed the role of education, "the grand army of school children" (p. 84), in remaking African-American consciousness. Fannie B. Williams's "Club Movement Among Colored Women in America" drew attention to the role of African-American women in the development of the "womanhood of a great nation and a great civilization," and she praised their organizations as the "beginning of self-respect and the respect" for the race (p. 404).

During the 1920s the idea of the New Negro became an important symbol of racial progress, and different political groups vied with each other over who more properly represented the new racial consciousness. Most agreed that impact of black military service during World War I, the migration of blacks to the North, and the example of blacks fighting against racial violence during the race riots of 1919 provided clear evidence of a reinvigorated African-American sense of self. Political organizations such as the National Association for the Advancement of Colored People, the National Urban League, and the Universal Negro Improvement Association of Marcus Garvey each felt that it represented an unquenchable political and racial militancy. The group of socialist and political radicals including A. Philip Randolph and Chandler Owen, who were identified with the monthly journal *Messenger* and the Brotherhood of Sleeping Car Porters, consistently argued that they represented the political ideas as the ideal of the New Negro.

In 1925 Alain L. Locke, a philosophy professor at Howard University and a leading promoter of black writers and artists, published an anthology *The New Negro, An Interpretation*. That volume proposed African-American creative artists as contenders with political spokesmen for the title of New Negro. The anthology contained contributions from such leading political leaders as W. E. B. Du Bois, Jessie Fauset, James Weldon Johnson, and Walter White of the NAACP, and Charles H. Johnson of the National Urban League, yet Locke's essays, "Enter the New Negro" and "Negro Youth Speaks," focused exclusively on a group of young writers and artists: "Youth speaks and the voice of the New Negro is heard" (Locke, 1925, p. 47). Locke offered the drawings, poetry, and prose of Aaron Douglas, Countee Cullen, Langston Hughes, Zora Neale Hurston, Claude McKay, and Jean Toomer, artists who drew inspiration from the vernacular—blues, jazz, spirituals, and the folktale—as the voice of a vibrant "new psychology" (p. 3). Locke's anthology, and the subsequent work of the young artists included in it, tied the notion of the New Negro to the work of African-American artists and firmly bound the image of the New Negro to the artistic products of the Harlem Renaissance.

After the 1920s the expression New Negro passed out of fashion, largely because the spirit that it referred to was taken for granted. Subsequent generations of scholars, however, still debate which of the various political and artistic philosophies best represented the ideal of the New Negro.

See also Identity and Race in the United States

■ ■ *Bibliography*

Foley, Barbara. *Spectres of 1919: Class and Nation in the Making of the New Negro.* Urbana: University of Illinois Press, 2003.

Locke, Alain L., ed. *The New Negro, An Interpretation.* New York: A. and C. Boni, 1925.

Pickens, William. *The New Negro: His Political, Civil, and Mental Status, and Related Essays.* New York: Neale, 1916.

Washington, Booker T., et al. *A New Negro for a New Century.* Chicago: American Publishing, 1900.

GEORGE P. CUNNINGHAM (1996)
Updated bibliography

NEWTON, HUEY P.

FEBRUARY 17, 1942
AUGUST 22, 1989

Political activist Huey Newton was born in Monroe, Louisiana, the youngest of seven siblings. When he was young his family moved to Oakland, California, were he attended Merritt College and participated in the groundswell of political activity erupting on college campuses nationwide.

He joined the increasing number of blacks who questioned the ability of the civil rights movement to deal with the problems of housing, unemployment, poverty, and police brutality that plagued urban African Americans.

In college Newton and his friend Bobby Seale were active in the effort to diversify the curriculum at Merritt, as well as in lobbying for more black instructors. Newton joined the Afro-American Association but soon became a vocal critic of the organization's advocacy of capitalism. Instead, he sought inspiration from Robert Williams, a former head of the Monroe, North Carolina, NAACP, who advocated guerilla warfare, and from third-world revolutionaries such as Cuba's Fidel Castro, China's Mao Zedong, and Algeria's Frantz Fanon. Newton believed that blacks were an oppressed colony being exploited economically and disfranchised politically within U.S. borders and argued that blacks should launch a liberation movement for self-empowerment.

In 1966 Newton and Seale founded the Black Panther Party for Self-Defense (BPP). Newton took on the title of minister of defense and acted as leader of the organization. Among the points raised in their initial program was the right to bear arms to defend their community from police repression.

In November 1966 Newton and Seale, armed with shotguns—which were legal at the time as long as they were not concealed—instituted "justice patrols" to monitor the actions of the police and inform blacks of their rights when stopped by the police. The police responded with resentment and harassment. On October 28, 1967, in culmination of a year of hostile and antagonistic relations between the Panthers and the police, Newton was arrested and charged in the shooting of one police officer and the murder of another. Reports of this incident are unclear and conflicting. Newton claimed to be unconscious after being shot by one of the policemen.

Newton's arrest heightened awareness of police brutality in the black community. While in prison Newton was considered a political prisoner; rallies and speeches focused attention on his plight. His trial became a cause célèbre, and "Free Huey" became a slogan that galvanized thousands of people on the New Left. Massive rallies and demonstrations at the courthouse demanding his release were organized by BPP members.

Newton remained active in prison, issuing speeches and directives. He was convicted in September 1968 of voluntary manslaughter and sentenced to two to fifteen years in prison. His conviction was overturned by the court of appeals because of procedural errors during his first trial. Newton, after being released from prison, tried to revive the BPP. However, during the early 1970s the

Huey P. Newton, co-founder (with Bobby Seale) of the Black Panther Party for Self-Defense. AP/WIDE WORLD PHOTOS, INC. REPRODUCED BY PERMISSION.

BPP had declined due to legal problems, internal tensions, and a factional split among BPP members on the East and West Coasts. This division was fostered by the disinformation campaign launched by the FBI, which created a climate of distrust and suspicion within the BPP. Many on the East Coast believed the ideology of Eldridge Cleaver, who had become the public spokesperson for the BPP during Newton's incarceration and who advocated politically motivated armed actions. Newton articulated the feelings of many on the West Coast by arguing that the BPP, by becoming too militant, had moved onto a plane with which average blacks could no longer identify. He wanted to focus more on community programs and political education. Newton ordered a series of purges, which debilitated the organization further.

Although Newton remained publicly identified with the BPP, many people no longer looked to him as leader. Increasingly isolated, he cultivated a small band of supporters. In 1974 Newton was accused of murdering a woman. The circumstances of this incident remain unclear. Newton fled to Cuba, feeling that he would not get a fair trial in the United States. In 1977 he returned to the United States to resume leadership of the weakened and splintering party. In his absence Elaine Brown had assumed leadership of the organization and taken it in new directions. Newton's role in the organization continued to diminish. He was retried in the 1967 killing of the policeman and convicted, but that conviction was later overturned. He also faced trial for the murder of the woman, but the charge was dropped after two hung juries.

In 1980 Newton received a Ph.D. from the University of California. His thesis was "War Against the Panthers—A Study of Repression in America." While Newton remained politically active, his visibility as a public figure was waning. He was arrested in 1985 for embezzling funds from a nutritional program he headed. Three years later, he was convicted of possessing firearms. Increasingly addicted to drugs and involved in the drug trade, he was killed in a drug-related incident on the streets of Oakland in 1989.

See also Black Panther Party for Self-Defense; Civil Rights Movement, U.S.; Cleaver, Eldridge; Seale, Bobby

■■ *Bibliography*

Hilliard, Davis, and Weise, Donald, eds. *The Huey P. Newton Reader.* New York: Seven Stories Press, 2002.

Newton, Huey P. *To Die for the People: The Writings of Huey P. Newton.* 1972. Reprint, New York: Writers and Readers Publishing, 1995.

Newton, Huey P. *Revolutionary Suicide.* New York: Harcourt Brace, 1979.

Pearson, Hugh. *The Shadow of the Panther.* Boston: Addison-Wesley, 1994.

Seale, Bobby. *Seize the Time: The Story of the Black Panther Party and Huey Newton.* New York: Random House, 1970.

ROBYN SPENCER (1996)
Updated bibliography

NEWTON, JAMES

MAY 1, 1953

The flutist, composer, and bandleader James Newton Jr. was born in Los Angeles and began his musical career in high school as an electric bass guitarist performing rhythm and blues. In 1971 he switched to saxophones and flute and began to explore jazz with the saxophonists Arthur Blythe and David Murray, the clarinetist John Carter, and the trumpeter Bobby Bradford. He studied flute with Buddy Collette and earned a B.A. in music from California State University, Los Angeles, before moving to New York in early 1978. Focusing exclusively on the flute, he performed and recorded with Murray and Blythe and formed a group with the pianist and composer Anthony Davis. By 1979 Newton had achieved international critical acclaim for his performances and recordings, which featured his distinctive full-bodied tone and exploitation of timbral shadings in the flute's higher registers.

Developing flute vocalization techniques pioneered by Yusef Lateef and Rahsaan Roland Kirk and incorporating Japanese *shakuhachi* techniques into his otherwise classical vocabulary, Newton has expanded the technical and timbral possibilities of the Western orchestral flute, and he is recognized as one of the leading innovators on the instrument. He has also broken new ground as a composer, again drawing on a range of influences that includes the black Baptist church, Duke Ellington, Charles Mingus, traditional and contemporary Asian repertory, and twentieth-century French and Viennese composers. In addition to his works for large and small jazz ensembles, other compositions include *Ninety-first Psalm* (1985) for soprano, piano, and chamber orchestra; *The King's Way* (1988) for chamber orchestra; and *The Line of Immortality* (1992) for chamber ensemble and jazz quartet. Newton's achievements as flutist, composer, and arranger in the jazz idiom are heard to best advantage on the recordings *Axum* (1982), *Luella* (1984), *African Flower* (1985), and *If Love* (1989).

In 1994 Newton and the pianist and composer Jon Jang went to South Africa, where they gave workshops in Soweto. The two have collaborated on a number of works, including *When Sorrow Turns to Joy: Songlines—The Spiritual Tributary of Paul Robeson and Mei Lanfang* (2000). This ambitious stage work is scored for two voices, flute, piano, and traditional Chinese string instruments and percussion, and it has a libretto by the poet Genny Lim. In 2001 Newton collaborated on a ballet, *Cross Roads*, which was choreographed by Donald McKayle and performed by the Limón Dance Company. A Guggenheim Fellowship recipient, Newton is professor of music at California State University, Los Angeles, and music director of the Luckman Jazz Orchestra.

See also Jazz

■ ■ *Bibliography*

Birnbaum, Larry. "The Soul of the Church." *Down Beat* (November 1991): 24–25.

Kernfeld, Barry. "James Newton." In *New Grove Dictionary of Jazz*. London, 1988.

Paget-Clarke, Nic. "An Interview with Composers Jon Jang and James Newton." *In Motion Magazine* (March 20, 2000). Available from <http://www.inmotionmagazine.com/jjjnint1.html>.

ANTHONY BROWN (1996)
Updated by publisher 2005

NEW YORK AFRICAN BURIAL GROUND PROJECT

See African Burial Ground Project

NIAGARA MOVEMENT

The Niagara Movement, which was organized in 1905, was the first significant organized black protest campaign in the twentieth century. The movement represented the attempt of a small but articulate group of radicals to challenge the then-dominant accommodationist ideas of Booker T. Washington.

The Niagara Movement developed after failed attempts at reconciling the two factions in African-American political life: the accommodationists, led by Washington, and the more militant faction, led by W. E. B. Du Bois and William Monroe Trotter. A closed-door meeting of representatives of the two groups at Carnegie Hall in New York City in 1904 led to an organization, the Committee of Twelve for the Advancement of the Interests of the Negro Race, but the committee fell apart due to the belief of Du Bois and Trotter that Washington was controlling the organization.

In February 1905 Du Bois and Trotter devised a plan for a "strategy board" that would fight for civil rights and serve as a counterpoint to Washington's ideas. Since they knew Washington was most popular among whites, they resolved to form an all-black organization. Along with two allies, F. L. McGhee and C. E. Bentley, they scheduled a meeting for that summer in western New York, to which they invited fifty-nine businessmen and professionals who were known to be anti-Washingtonites.

In mid-July 1905 Du Bois went to Buffalo. He had difficulty arranging hotel reservations, so he crossed to the Canadian side of Niagara Falls. Fearing reprisals by Washington, who had sent spies to Buffalo, the radicals kept their conference secret. On July 11–14, 1905, twenty-nine men met and formed a group they called the Niagara Movement, both for the conference location and for the "mighty current" of protest they wished to unleash. Du Bois was named general secretary, and the group split into various committees, of which the most important was Trotter's Press and Public Opinion Committee. The founders agreed to divide the work among state chapters, which would "cooperate with congressmen and legislators to secure just legislation for the colored people," and pursue educational and informational programs. Movement members would meet annually.

The Niagara Movement's "Declaration of Principles," drafted by Du Bois and Trotter and adopted at the close of the conference, was a powerful and clear statement of the rights of African Americans: "We believe that this class of American citizens should protest emphatically and continually against the curtailment of their political rights." The declaration went on to urge African Americans to protest the curtailment of civil rights, the denial of equal economic opportunity, and denial of education; and the authors decried unhealthy living conditions, discrimination in the military, discrimination in the justice system, Jim Crow railroad cars, and other injustices. "Of the above grievances we do not hesitate to complain, and to complain loudly and insistently," they stated. "Persistent manly agitation is the way to liberty, and toward this goal the Niagara Movement has started."

At the end of its first year, the organization had only 170 members and was poorly funded. Nevertheless, the Niagarites pursued their activities, distributing pamphlets, lobbying against Jim Crow, and sending a circular protest letter to President Theodore Roosevelt after the Brownsville Incident in 1906. That summer the movement had its second annual conference, at Harpers Ferry, West Virginia. This was an open meeting, and the conference speeches and the tribute to John Brown aroused much publicity.

The Niagara Movement, despite its impressive start, did not enjoy a long life. There was from the start determined opposition by Booker T. Washington—he prevented sympathetic white newspapers, and even many black ones, from printing the declaration—which dissuaded many blacks from joining or contributing funds. The loose organization, with only token communication between state chapters, and the radical nature for the time of such forthright protest also contributed to the movement's decline. Not long after the Harpers Ferry conference, factional struggles broke out between Du Bois and Trotter, as well as disagreements over the role of women in the movement. By the end of the summer of 1907 Trotter had been replaced as head of the Press Committee, and his supporters grew disenchanted with the movement. Du Bois tried to keep it going, guiding the movement through annual conferences in 1908 and 1909, after which it largely ceased to exist.

Even in its decline, however, the movement left a lasting legacy. In 1908 Du Bois invited Mary White Ovington, a settlement worker and socialist, to be the movement's first white member; by 1910 he had turned to the search for white allies by joining the newly organized NAACP. Despite its predominantly white leadership and centralized structure, the NAACP was really the successor to the Niagara Movement, whose remaining members Du Bois urged to join the NAACP. (However, William Monroe Trotter and his faction of the Niagara Movement never affiliated with the new organization.) The NAACP inherited many of the goals and tactics of the Niagara Movement, including the cultivation of a black elite that would defend the rights of African Americans through protest and lobbying against oppression and the publicizing of injustice.

See also Washington, Booker T.; National Association for the Advancement of Colored People (NAACP)

■ ■ *Bibliography*

Aptheker, Herbert. *A Documentary History of the Negro People in the United States*, vol. 2. New York: Citadel Press, 1951.

Fox, Stephen R. *The Guardian of Boston: William Monroe Trotter.* New York: Atheneum, 1970.

Harlan, Louis R. *Booker T. Washington: The Wizard of Tuskegee, 1901–1915.* New York: Oxford University Press, 1983.

GREG ROBINSON (1996)

NIXON, EDGAR DANIEL

JULY 12, 1899
FEBRUARY 25, 1987

▬ ▮ ▮ ▮ ▬▬▬▬▬▬▬▬▬▬▬▬▬▬▬▬▬▬▬▬

The civil rights leader Edgar Daniel Nixon was born in Robinson Springs, near Montgomery, Alabama, the son of Wesley and Susan (Chappell) Nixon. Wesley Nixon was a tenant farmer and, in later years, a Primitive Baptist preacher. Susan Nixon died when her son was nine, and the boy was reared in Montgomery by his paternal aunt, Winnie Bates, a laundress. He received only the most rudimentary education and at thirteen began full-time work, initially in a meatpacking plant, then on construction crews, and in 1918 as a baggage handler at Montgomery's railway station. Thanks to friendships that he made in this job, he managed in 1923 to obtain employment as a Pullman car porter, a position that he held until his retirement in 1964.

Exposed by his work to the world beyond Montgomery, Nixon grew increasingly hostile to racial segregation. He became an enthusiastic proponent of A. Philip Randolph's (1889–1979) efforts in the late 1920s and early 1930s to unionize the Pullman porters, and in 1938 he accepted the presidency of the new union's Montgomery local. In 1943 he organized the Alabama Voters League to press for the registration of Montgomery's blacks as voters, and though the campaign provoked a vigorous white counterattack, Nixon himself achieved registration in 1945.

Montgomery's black community was sharply divided between the middle-class professionals who resided near the campus of Alabama State College for Negroes and the working-class blacks who lived in the city's western neighborhoods. When the Montgomery branch of the National Association for the Advancement of Colored People (NAACP), dominated by the Alabama State College professionals, failed to support Nixon's voter registration drive actively, Nixon began organizing the poorer blacks of western Montgomery in an effort to take over the branch. In a series of acrimonious campaigns, he was defeated for branch president in 1944, elected in 1945, and re-elected in 1946.

In 1947 Nixon was elected the NAACP's state president, defeating the incumbent, the Birmingham newspaper editor Emory O. Jackson. But national NAACP officials, hostile to his lack of education, arranged in 1949 for his defeat for re-election to the state post, and in 1950 he also was ousted from the leadership of the Montgomery branch. In 1952, however, he won election as president of the Montgomery chapter of the Progressive Democratic

Association, the voice of Alabama's black Democrats. And in 1954 he created a great stir in the city by becoming a candidate to represent his precinct on the county Democratic Executive Committee. Although his bid was unsuccessful, he was the first black to seek public office in Montgomery in the twentieth century.

During his years with the NAACP, Nixon had become a close friend of Rosa L. Parks (b. 1913), the branch secretary. When Parks was arrested on December 1, 1955, for a violation of the city's bus segregation ordinance, she called Nixon for assistance. After he bailed her out of jail, Nixon began calling other black leaders to suggest a boycott of the buses on the day of Parks's trial, December 5, to show support for her. The idea, which black leaders had frequently discussed in the past, was greeted enthusiastically by many. The black Women's Political Council began circulating leaflets urging the action, and black ministers supported it from their pulpits. The boycott on December 5 proved so successful that black leaders decided to extend it until the city and the bus company agreed to adopt a pattern of bus segregation that would not require the unseating of passengers who were already seated. The Montgomery Improvement Association was formed to run the boycott, and Nixon was chosen the organization's treasurer.

Nixon, however, became increasingly unhappy with the association's president, the Reverend Dr. Martin Luther King Jr. He associated King with the Alabama State College professionals, and he felt that King's growing fame was depriving the mass of poorer blacks whom Nixon represented, and Nixon himself, of the credit for the boycott's success. After King moved to Atlanta in 1960, and the Reverend Ralph D. Abernathy followed him there in 1961, Nixon engaged in a lengthy struggle with Rufus A. Lewis, the most prominent figure among his rivals in the middle-class Alabama State College community, for leadership of Montgomery's blacks. The struggle culminated in the 1968 U.S. presidential election, when Nixon and Lewis served on alternative slates of presidential electors, both of which were pledged to Democratic candidate Hubert H. Humphrey. The Lewis slate of electors defeated Nixon's slate handily in Montgomery. Nixon thereafter slipped into an embittered obscurity. He accepted a job organizing recreational activities for young people in one of the city's poorest public-housing projects, a position that he held until just before his death in 1987.

See also Abernathy, Ralph David; Brotherhood of Sleeping Car Porters; King, Martin Luther, Jr.; Montgomery Improvement Association; Montgomery, Ala., Bus Boycott; National Association for the Advancement of Colored People (NAACP); Parks, Rosa

■ ■ *Bibliography*

Garrow, David J. *Bearing the Cross: Martin Luther King, Jr., and the Southern Christian Leadership Conference.* New York: William Morrow, 1986.

Thornton, J. Mills, III. "Challenge and Response in the Montgomery Bus Boycott of 1955–1956." *Alabama Review* 33 (1980): 163–235.

J. MILLS THORNTON III (1996)

NOBLE DREW ALI

JANUARY 8, 1886
JULY 20, 1929

■ ■ ■

Religious leader Timothy Drew, more commonly known as the Noble Drew Ali, was born in Simpsonbuck County, North Carolina. It is not clear when Ali migrated north or when he came into contact with Eastern philosophy. Although he received no formal education, Ali developed an appreciation for Asian religions. Deeply moved by their racial inclusivity, particularly that of Islam, he saw an opportunity for African Americans to be influenced by its thinking. In 1913, at the age of twenty-seven, he established the first Moorish Science Temple of America in Newark, New Jersey.

Central to Ali's philosophy was the importance of racial identity. In his opinion, the lot of the blacks in America was the result of their inaccurate knowledge of themselves. Moreover, once blacks gained a proper understanding of who they were, he believed both salvation and victory over their oppressors would be obtainable. He thus urged his followers no longer to recognize the racial designations given them by Europeans and to call themselves Moors, Moorish-Americans, or Asiatics. Ali also published and distributed the Holy Koran of the Moorish Holy Temple of Science, which served as a catechism for temple members.

By the mid-1920s, the movement had spread throughout the United States and temples had been established in Detroit, Pittsburgh, Philadelphia, New York, and Chicago. Headquarters for the temple were eventually relocated to Chicago, which proved to be both Ali's crowning achievement and his dethroning miscalculation. Since the Moorish Science phenomenon had grown beyond one person's control, he decided to appoint several educated black men to leadership positions within the organization. Shortly after the appointments, however, it became clear to Ali that his understudies were situating themselves to seize control of the movement.

After learning that some of the leaders had become rich by exploiting the rank-and-file membership, Ali rebuked them and called for an end to the corruption. Nevertheless, tension within the group continued to rise until one of Ali's opponents was killed. Even though he was not in Chicago at the time of the murder, Ali was arrested for the crime upon his arrival in the city. In 1929, while waiting to be tried, he was mysteriously killed, apparently beaten to death either by members loyal to his opposition or by the police.

See also Islam

■■ *Bibliography*

Fauset, Arthur Huff. *Black Gods of the Metropolis: Negro Religious Cults in the Urban North*. Philadelphia: University of Pennsylvania Press, 1944.

Payne, Wardell J., ed. *Directory of African American Religious Bodies*, 2nd ed. Washington, D.C.: Howard University Press, 1995.

Wilson, Peter Lambron. *Sacred Drift: Essays on the Margins of Islam*. San Francisco: City Lights Books, 1993.

QUINTON H. DIXIE (1996)

NORMAN, JESSYE

SEPTEMBER 15, 1945

Born in Augusta, Georgia, opera singer Jessye Norman was a soprano of promise from an early age. At sixteen she entered the Marian Anderson competitions, and although she did not win, she auditioned at Howard University with Carolyn Grant. Her acceptance was delayed until she completed high school. She followed her undergraduate training at Howard, earning a bachelor's degree in music in 1967, with summer study at the Peabody Conservatory under Alice Duschak before enrolling at the University of Michigan for study with Elizabeth Mannion and Pierre Bernac.

A travel grant allowed Norman to enter the International Music Competition in Munich in 1968, where she won first place with performances of Dido's *Lament* (Henry Purcell) and "Voi lo sapete" from Pietro Mascagni's *Cavalleria Rusticana*. She was immediately engaged for her operatic debut as Elisabeth in Richard Wagner's *Tannhäuser* by the Deutsche Oper (1969), with which she later appeared in Giuseppe Verdi's *Aida* and *Don Carlo,* Meyerbeer's *L'africaine*, and as the Countess in Mozart's *Le Nozze di Figaro*. In 1972 she sang Aida at La Scala and Cassandre in Covent Garden's production of Berlioz' *Les Troyens,* making her recital debuts in London and New York the next year.

Norman's American stage debut came on November 22, 1982, when she appeared as both Jocasta in *Oedipus Rex* (Stravinsky) and Dido in Purcell's *Dido and Aeneas* with the Opera Company of Philadelphia. The following year, she made her debut with the Metropolitan Opera as Cassandre in Berlioz' *Les Troyens,* subsequently offering a performance as Didon in the same opera, as well as the Prima Donna and Ariadne in *Ariadne auf Naxos* (Richard Strauss).

As recitalist, guest orchestral soloist, presenter of master classes, and recording artist, Norman was acknowledged as a musician of the highest rank. She was heard in nearly every major American city by 1990 and appeared frequently in telecasts starting in 1979 when she gave a concert version of the first act of Wagner's *Die Walküre* with the Boston Symphony Orchestra conducted by Seiji Ozawa.

Norman has excelled in French and German repertories, stylistically and linguistically, while remaining faithful to her roots in the spiritual. With a voice ranging from a dark mezzo-soprano to a dramatic soprano, she has not hesitated to reintroduce works outside of the mainstream repertory (e.g., Gluck and Haydn operas), or to perform songs of the musical theater. She has appeared on numerous recordings, including Beethoven's *Fidelio,* Berlioz' *Mort de Cléopatre,* Bizet's *Carmen,* Gluck's *Alceste,* Mahler's *Das Lied von der Erde,* Offenbach's *Tales of Hoffmann,* Purcell's *Dido and Aeneas,* Schoenberg's *Gurre-Lieder,* Strauss's *Four Last Songs* and *Ariadne auf Naxos,* Verdi's *Aida,* Wagner's *Lohengrin* and *Die Walküre,* and Weber's *Euryanthe.* Other notable recordings include *Spirituals, Spirituals in Concert* (with Kathleen Battle), and *Jessye Norman at Notre-Dame.*

Norman became the youngest recipient of the United States Kennedy Center Honors in 1997. In her hometown of Augusta, the amphitheatre and plaza overlooking the Savannah River have been named after her.

See also Anderson, Marian; Opera

■■ *Bibliography*

Bernheimer, Martin. "Jessye Norman." In *The New Grove Dictionary of Music and Musicians*, vol. 13, p. 283. London: Grove, 1980.

Ewen, David. "Jessye Norman." In *Musicians Since 1900: Performers in Concert and Opera*. New York: H. W. Wilson, 1978, pp. 586–587.

Acclaimed soprano opera singer Jessye Norman in Paris, 1986. AP/WIDE WORLD PHOTOS. REPRODUCED BY PERMISSION.

Gates, Henry Louis, Jr., and Cornel West. *The African-American Century: How Black Americans Have Shaped Our Century.* New York: Simon and Schuster, 2000.

DOMINIQUE-RENÉ DE LERMA (1996)
Updated by publisher 2005

NORTH CAROLINA MUTUAL LIFE INSURANCE COMPANY

❚❚❚

Founded by seven black men who each pledged fifty dollars, the North Carolina Mutual and Provident Association (renamed the North Carolina Mutual Life Insurance Company in 1919) opened in Durham, North Carolina, on April 1, 1899, to provide insurance for black families. The Mutual sold primarily industrial insurance, which was obtained for as little as three cents a week by industrial laborers and which paid out correspondingly small amounts for sickness and death claims. In the summer of 1900 the Mutual went into debt, the income from its policies un-

able to pay for the claims on them, and all its founding members except the president, John Merrick, a successful businessman, and Aaron Moore, a physician who became secretary, withdrew. Merrick and Moore loaned personal funds to the Mutual to prevent it from going defunct and promoted Charles Clinton Spaulding to general manager.

By the end of 1902, after Merrick and Moore had loaned the Mutual an additional $600, its profits were finally greater than its losses, and by 1906 it had quadrupled its number of policyholders, its growth corresponding first to expansion within North Carolina, then expansion to South Carolina and the reinsurance of smaller black insurers who could not meet state regulations, which at that time were being strengthened. In 1913 the Mutual demonstrated its strength by raising $100,000 to meet a higher state deposit requirement. During World War I the Mutual's life insurance in force grew from $5,000,000 to $26,000,000 because a dramatic increase in cotton prices brought greater prosperity to southern blacks.

Embodying Booker T. Washington's popular philosophy that blacks would overcome prejudice with economic development, the Mutual drew attention to itself and to Durham because the growth of its assets enabled it to launch numerous subordinate institutions, such as the

Merrick-Moore-Spaulding Land Company (1907), a real estate company; Mechanics and Farmers Bank (1908, with a branch in Raleigh, 1922); Banker's Fire, a fire insurance company (1920); Mutual Building & Loan Association (1921); the National Negro Finance Corporation (1924); and the Mortgage Company of Durham (1929)—in effect bringing economic development to the black community of Durham by itself.

In 1926, after territorial expansion that followed the black migration north and that also included southwestern states, Spaulding, now president, a position he would retain until his death in 1952, realized that the income from expansion did not compensate for the operating costs and had the Mutual retrench, not to expand again until 1938. This retrenchment, along with its conservative investments in real estate, government bonds, and especially mortgage loans, protected the Mutual during the Great Depression. At $39,000,000 just before the stock market crash of 1929, the Mutual's life insurance in force never fell below $33,000,000 during the Depression.

The Mutual's prosperity during World War II, when its insurance in force increased from $51,000,000 to over $100,000,000, enabled it to offer its policyholders dividends for the first time and to compete with the mainstream companies that now insured blacks at standard rates.

The promotion of racial solidarity during the 1960s brought blacks back to the Mutual from white insurers. The urban riots of the late 1960s put pressure on white corporations to invest in black communities, and corporations such as General Motors, IBM, Chrysler, Procter and Gamble, Sun Oil, and Atlantic Richfield did so by buying more than $400,000,000 in insurance contracts between 1969 and 1971 from the Mutual, making it the first black company to pass the billion-dollar mark.

The Mutual's tenfold growth in insurance in force from the early 1970s to the early 1990s enabled it to maintain its status as the nation's largest black insurance company. To stimulate growth, the Mutual gradually began to phase out its industrial insurance and replace it with ordinary life insurance, and, through its subsidiary, NCM Capital, to enter the pension and corporate-fund management business.

See also Entrepreneurs and Entrepreneurship; Spaulding, Charles Clinton; Washington, Booker T.

■ ■ *Bibliography*

Weare, Walter B. *Black Business in the New South: A Social History of the North Carolina Mutual Life Insurance Company.* Urbana: University of Illinois Press, 1973.

SIRAJ AHMED (1996)

NORTHRUP, SOLOMON

c. 1808
1863

Solomon Northrup, the author of a slave narrative, was born free on a farm in Minerva, New York. His father was a former Rhode Island slave who had been freed in his owner's will. Northrup spent the first half of his life on the family farm, farming and working as a violinist and laborer in the Minerva area. At the age of thirty-three or so, a series of bizarre events pulled him into slavery.

In 1841 Northrup was approached by two strangers, who asked him to play in the band with their traveling circus. After catching up with the circus, Northrup was drugged, beaten, and sold to slave traders. He was then shipped to New Orleans, where he was purchased by a planter in the Red River region of Louisiana. He spent the next twelve years as a slave under several owners in the region.

In 1852 Northrup met Samuel Bass, an itinerant Canadian carpenter, and the two plotted to arrange Northrup's freedom. Bass sent a letter to two white businessmen in Saratoga who had been acquaintances of Northrup. The letter eventually reached Henry Northrup, the former owner of Northrup's father, who traveled to Louisiana and made legal arrangements to free Northrup. Northrup finally returned to his family in Glens Falls, New York, in January 1853.

Spurred on by the success of Harriet Beecher Stowe's *Uncle Tom's Cabin,* Northrup immediately set out to write the narrative of his enslavement. He enlisted the help of David Wilson, a local writer, and the two finished the book within three months. *Twelve Years a Slave: Narrative of Solomon Northrup* was published in the summer of 1853 and became an immediate success. It sold more than thirty thousand copies over the next ten years and was reprinted several times in the nineteenth century after Northrup's death.

Since its publication Northrup's narrative has served as an important resource for scholars of slavery. Like many other slave narratives, *Twelve Years a Slave* discusses in detail the ways in which slaves presented a servile facade to their owners while practicing subtle acts of subversion and resistance. In recent years Northrup's recollections have been cited as refutation of the slave's image as a passive, ingratiating figure.

The publication of *Twelve Years a Slave* resulted in yet another set of bizarre circumstances that led to the capture of Northrup's kidnappers. In 1854 the book caused one of its readers to recall meeting the two men and Northrup shortly after the abduction. Northrup met with the reader and confirmed the recollection, and shortly thereafter the two suspected kidnappers were arrested and charged by New York authorities. Although they were widely assumed to be guilty, the two suspects were released on legal technicalities.

Northrup was paid $3,000 by the original publisher of his narrative. He used that money to purchase a house in Glens Falls, where he lived in relative obscurity and practiced carpentry for the last ten years of his life. The circumstances of his death are uncertain, but the name on the deed to his house was changed to his wife's name in 1863.

See also Slave Narratives

■ ■ *Bibliography*

Blassingame, John. *The Slave Community: Plantation Life in the Antebellum South.* New York: Oxford University Press, 1972.

Northrup, Solomon. *Twelve Years a Slave: Narrative of Solomon Northrup* (1853). Baton Rouge: Louisiana State University Press, 1965.

Osofsky, Gilbert, ed. *Puttin' on Ole Massa: The Slave Narratives of Henry Bibb, William Wells Brown, and Solomon Northrup.* New York: Harper & Row, 1969.

THADDEUS RUSSELL (1996)

NORTH STAR

▮▮▮

Frederick Douglass began publication of *North Star*, a four-page weekly newspaper, in Rochester, New York, on December 3, 1847. This was the third antislavery paper at the time; the others were William Lloyd Garrison's the *Liberator* (Boston) and the *National Anti-Slavery Standard* (New York City). Douglass's paper differed from the others in that it focused not only at abolition, but also promoted women's rights and suffrage. Martin Delany was listed as coeditor until July of the following year and remained a regular contributor; other black correspondents for the paper included James McCune Smith, William J.

Wilson, Samuel Ringgold Ward, and William Wells Brown. William C. Nell worked as printer for the paper, and his name was listed on the masthead until June 23, 1848.

By the middle of 1849, *North Star* had four thousand subscribers, but finances remained a problem and depended on contributions and fund-raising projects. By 1851, Douglass had aligned himself with the Liberty Party and became an advocate of political action as the means of abolishing slavery. This led to a break with Garrison and Nell, who were steadfast in advocating moral persuasion as the only proper course of action. In 1851, Douglass merged *North Star* with *Liberty Party Paper* as *Frederick Douglass' Paper,* subsidized by Gerrit Smith, a wealthy white abolitionist. *Frederick Douglass' Paper* ceased publication in July 1860.

North Star not only furnished an outlet for the views of Frederick Douglass and other abolitionists, but its headquarters in Rochester were an important way station on the Underground Railroad, offering assistance to more than four hundred individuals.

See also Abolition; Douglass, Frederick; *Liberator, The;* Underground Railroad

■ ■ *Bibliography*

Danky, James P., and Maureen E. Hady, eds. *African-American Newspapers and Periodicals: A National Bibliography.* Cambridge, Mass.: Harvard University Press, 1998.

Ripley, C. Peter, et al, eds. *The Black Abolitionist Papers,* vol. 4. Chapel Hill: University of North Carolina Press, 1991.

ROBERT L. JOHNS (2001)

NORTON, ELEANOR HOLMES

JUNE 13, 1937

▮▮▮

Born in Washington, D.C., civil rights leader Eleanor Holmes graduated from Antioch College in 1960, received an M.A. in American history from Yale University in 1963, and received a law degree from Yale in 1965. Norton was a leader of the Student Nonviolent Coordinating Committee (SNCC) and a participant in the Mississippi Freedom Democratic Party. In 1965 she joined the American Civil Liberties Union (ACLU), where she served as a civil rights lawyer for five years. In 1967 she married Edward Norton,

Congresswoman Eleanor Holmes Norton with Joseph Lieberman during the 2000 Democratic National Covention in Los Angeles. PHOTOGRAPH BY BOB GALBRAITH. AP/WIDE WORLD PHOTOS. REPRODUCED BY PERMISSION.

also a lawyer. The couple, who were separated in 1992, had two children. In 1968 Eleanor Holmes Norton gained attention for her active defense of freedom of speech when she represented segregationist presidential candidate George Wallace in his struggle to obtain permission from the city of New York for a rally at Shea Stadium. Keenly interested in fighting both race and gender discrimination, Norton published an article on black women in the well-known anthology *Sisterhood Is Powerful* (1970). "If women were suddenly to achieve equality with men tomorrow," she wrote, "black women would continue to carry the entire array of utterly oppressive handicaps associated with race. . . . Yet black women cannot—must not—avoid the truth about their special subservice. They are women with all that that implies."

In 1970 Norton was appointed chair of the New York City Commission on Human Rights by Mayor John Lindsay. Her achievement in detailing and correcting discriminatory practices led to a position as cohost of a weekly local television program on civil rights. In 1973 Norton helped organize the National Conference of Black Feminists, and in 1975 she cowrote *Sex Discrimination and the Law: Cases and Remedies,* a law textbook dealing with legal remedies to gender inequality.

In 1977 President Jimmy Carter appointed Norton as chair of the Equal Employment Opportunity Commission, a post she held until 1981. Charged with investigating complaints of discrimination, Norton was a visible and re-

spected force within the administration. In 1982 she accepted a post as professor of labor law at Georgetown University. Throughout the 1980s she was also a regular media commentator on civil rights and affirmative action issues.

In 1990 Norton announced her candidacy for the position of District of Columbia delegate to the U.S. House of Representatives. Despite the revelation during the campaign that she owed back taxes, she was elected to Congress, beginning the first of eight consecutive terms of service through 2005. Norton soon won praise even from her opponents for her involvement in community affairs as well as for her work in assuring Washington's fiscal viability and cutting the District's budget. She also lobbied in Congress for District statehood. In 1992, Norton won attention for her offer to escort women seeking abortion information at clinics past anti-abortion picketers, and later for her denunciation of the verdict in the Rodney King trial, which she contended was as shameful as the actual beating of King. The House vote in 1993 to give delegates limited voting privileges on the floor allowed Norton to become the first District representative to vote in Congress. In recognition of her prestige, President Bill Clinton agreed that as chair of the District of Columbia Subcommittee on Judiciary and Education, Norton would be responsible for the nomination of candidates for local U.S. attorney and federal judgeships, the first elected District of Columbia official to be privileged.

Yale Law School awarded Norton its Citation of Merit as an Outstanding Alumna of Yale Law School, and Yale Graduate School has awarded her the Yale Wilbur Cross Medal as an Outstanding Alumna of the Graduate School, the highest awards conferred by each on alumnae. Norton has also received more than 50 honorary degrees.

See also Mississippi Freedom Democratic Party; Politics; Student Nonviolent Coordinating Committee (SNCC)

■ ■ *Bibliography*

Hardy, Gayle S. *American Women Civil Rights Activists: Biographies of 68 Leaders, 1825–1992.* Jefferson, N.C.: McFarland, 1993.

Haywood, Richette, "Eleanor Holmes Norton Takes D.C. Seat." *Ebony* 46 (January 1991): 105–106.

Lester, Joan Steinau. *Fire in My Soul: Joan Steinau Lester in Conversation with Eleanor Holmes Norton.* New York: Atria Books, 2003.

EVAN A. SHORE (1996)
GREG ROBINSON (1996)
Updated by publisher 2005

NUBIN, ROSETTA

See Tharpe, "Sister"

NUMBERS GAMES

Numbers games were a pervasive form of gambling in African-American urban communities from around the turn of the twentieth century until the late 1970s, when state lotteries and other forms of legalized gambling were instituted. Until that time, the local numbers runner was a familiar figure in black neighborhoods throughout the United States, especially in Harlem, and daily street life was often organized around placing bets and collecting winnings.

There are accounts of numbers games, also known as policy gambling, in New York's white and black communities well before the Civil War, but it was not until decades later that numbers games gained real popularity among African Americans. Extremely high rates of participation made policy gambling a central economic feature of African-American urban life, with small businesses such as bars, hairdressers, and candy stores serving as collection points, or "drops."

In the nineteenth century, winning numbers were chosen from a lottery or roulette wheel. By the 1920s, rather than using lotteries, the results of which could be easily manipulated, bankers drew the winning result from the last three digits of the total volume of the daily New York Stock Exchange trades. Although odds varied from place to place, even within New York City, players attempting to match the winning numbers faced odds of one thousand to one. Those odds could be enhanced by "combinating," or betting on several groupings of the same numbers. Winners stood to gain returns of five hundred to one or even greater on a bet of as little as five or ten cents, but that return represented only a small percentage of the total bettings. Winners traditionally paid ten percent of their winnings to the runner, who was responsible for taking bets and making payments. The runner was often a charismatic fixture in the neighborhood, and a prodigious mathematician. The most famous runner in the heyday of Harlem's 1920s numbers racket was "Walking Jack" (the nickname of Alec Jackson), who was capable of retaining hundreds of numerical combinations in his memory daily. A similar figure, but from a later period, was evoked by Malcolm X in his autobiography's presentation of West Indian Archie.

For approximately every one hundred runners there was one collector, who organized the day-to-day workings of the operation, and who, together with the runner, took up to twenty-five percent of total bets as a salary. The collector was also responsible for bribing police and vice squads. At the top of the organization was the "wheel" or banker, of whom there were dozens in Harlem in the 1920s. The bankers were millionaires who controlled huge sums of money and lived legendarily lavish lifestyles financed by a percentage of total winnings as high as thirty-six percent. The most famous policy banker of the 1920s was Casper Holstein (1877–1944), a West Indian-born former porter who ruled his gambling empire from Harlem's Turf Club. Holstein had a reputation as a powerful tycoon during the Harlem Renaissance. Considered one of the most important black philanthropists of the 1920s, Holstein sponsored writing prizes for *Opportunity* magazine and donated money to build Harlem's first Elks Lodge. He later became increasingly involved in West Indian nationalist movements and had all but left numbers by the time of his death in 1944. Another important banker was Madame Stephanie St. Clair, who in the 1920s and 1930s openly boasted of her status as "Harlem's Policy Queen."

New York's numbers games were traditionally the biggest such enterprise in the country (Brooklyn had its own set of winning numbers), but African-American communities in many cities—including Buffalo, New York; Milwaukee, Wisconsin; and Paterson, New Jersey—supported policy gambling. Chicago's numbers industry was started by "Policy Sam" Young before the turn of the century, and by 1930 there were 350,000 bets per day being given to "policy kings" like John "Mushmouth" Johnson and Dan Johnson. The twelve million dollar-per-year industry controlled black votes in Chicago, and contributed hundreds of thousands of dollars per year to the campaigns of Mayor William Hale "Big Bill" Thompson, who in return only minimally enforced gambling laws.

There were many ways for bettors to choose numbers, but one of the most common demonstrates how closely numbers gambling was intertwined with African-American urban culture. Numbers were often chosen with the aid of "dream books," which assigned numerical figures to powerful words or to the appearance of certain themes in a dream. When the beloved comedienne Moms Mabley died in 1975, many gamblers bet and won with 769, the dream book number for death. In addition to dream books, many gamblers used birthdays, anniversaries, or other significant dates to select numbers. In 1969, when Willie Mays hit his 599th home run, huge numbers of gamblers bet the next day on the number 600—unsuccessfully, as it turned out.

In the late 1920s and early 1930s, two forces combined to create changes in the policy gambling industry in

New York. First, the Manhattan District Attorney's office made a concerted effort to shut down the numbers racket in Harlem, a move that was only partially successful due to the police cooperation that had made widespread policy gambling possible in the first place. Second, white gangsters (Dutch Schultz in particular), who had previously concentrated on prohibition liquor activity, saw the huge profits of numbers games and started to enter the business. Although Schultz's career in numbers was brief, control of the industry did change hands. From the 1940s until well into the 1960s, numbers games were dominated by white organized crime figures.

Despite the fact that policy gambling was no longer a locally controlled business, numbers thrived in Harlem. Reliable statistics are difficult to find, but by the 1960s it was estimated that the New York numbers games employed thousands of people in a six hundred million dollar-per-year industry, representing as much as sixty percent of Harlem's total economic life. The importance of policy gambling in African-American urban life up to the present is validated by the portrayal of numbers runners and policy bankers in the works of writers such as Ralph Ellison, James Baldwin, and Malcolm X.

Although groups like the Forty Thieves, and figures such as Ellsworth Raymond "Bumpy" Johnson (the inspiration for the movie *Shaft* [1971]), had remained active in policy gambling under the domination of Jewish and Italian organized crime figures, it was only during the 1960s that blacks began to reassert their presence in the industry. This sometimes meant demonstrating their power by becoming involved in politics. In the 1964 presidential election, for example, some runners were instructed to offer a one-dollar free play to Harlemites who promised to register and vote against Barry Goldwater. By this time there had been many changes in the way numbers games ran. Average bets had increased to fifty cents or one dollar, and the corresponding payoffs were much higher. Also, the winning number was now determined not by the New York Stock Exchange volume, but by the last three digits of the total amount of money bet (the pari-mutuel "handle") at the local harness racing track.

In 1980, attempts by New York and many other states to pre-empt numbers games with institutionalized legalized lotteries led to public demonstrations in Harlem. The state prevailed, however, and these lotteries, combined with the opening of Off-Track Betting offices and the enforcement of laws that made the taking of more than five hundred numbers bets a felony, weakened the popularity of "Harlem's favorite indoor sport." Nonetheless, policy gambling continued to be a prominent feature of urban life, though increasingly run by Latinos.

Numbers games have been attacked as a means of exploiting poor blacks. Indeed, policy gambling has undoubtedly had an adverse net financial affect on African Americans and their communities, with masses of working-class or chronically unemployed people regularly wasting a significant portion of their income. However, arguments have also been made, particularly when policy gambling was being threatened by lotteries starting in the 1970s, that numbers games at least kept money in African-American neighborhoods and financed small black businesses, or even occasionally saved them from bankruptcy. These factors, as well as the traditional thrill of gambling, have kept numbers gambling alive, with law enforcement officials in New York, Atlanta, St. Louis, Detroit, and Baltimore regularly closing down operations.

See also Harlem, New York; Mabley, Jackie "Moms"; Malcolm X

■ ■ *Bibliography*

Cook, Fred J. "The Black Mafia Moves into the Numbers Racket." *New York Times Magazine* (April 4, 1971): 26–27, 107–108, 110, 112.

Drake, St. Clair. *Black Metropolis: A Study of Negro Life in a Northern City*. New York: Harcourt Brace, 1945.

Ianni, Francis A. J. *Black Mafia: Ethnic Succession in Organized Crime*. New York: Simon & Schuster, 1975.

McCall, George J. "Symbiosis: The Case of Hoodoo and the Numbers Racket." In *Mother Wit from the Laughing Barrel: Readings in the Interpretation of Afro-American Folk Culture*, edited by Alan Dundes, pp. 419–427. Jackson: University Press of Mississippi, 1990.

McKay, Claude. *Harlem, Negro Metropolis*. New York: Dutton, 1940.

JONATHAN GILL (1996)

NURSING

This entry has two unique essays on the topic of nursing, differing mainly in their geographical focus.

NURSING IN THE CARIBBEAN
  Glenn O. Phillips

NURSING IN THE UNITED STATES
  Samuel Roberts

NURSING IN THE CARIBBEAN

Centuries before the arrival of Europeans, the practice of nursing care existed in the Caribbean. Amerindians were the earliest practitioners, using a variety of primitive methods to care for their seriously ill. The arrival of Europeans in the late fifteenth century brought a wider range of nursing challenges and new methods. However, few advances were made because the causes for the growing number of mostly tropical diseases remained unknown to health-care providers. The use of rational methods to alleviate these illnesses remained unknown. Similar to other parts of the world, early nursing care in the Caribbean remained in the hands of practitioners who addressed symptoms rather than the causes of illness.

The early Caribbean nursing care providers were dedicated, but mostly untrained, females who offered mostly a small measure of personal comfort and emotional support for patients. Nursing care was provided in homes, in privately operated sick houses, and later in modest hospitals provided by slave owners and colonial governments. Beginning in the mid-nineteenth century, nursing care in the Caribbean experienced gradual and significant changes, primarily through trial and error. New and bolder approaches to treating many tropical illnesses led to modest medical care discoveries and improvements. Nurse began to be trained and registered, and they were paid a wage and placed under the supervision of a regional medical officer. This practice was adopted in most British West Indian colonies and was supported by the most progressive members of these colonies' medical professionals.

At the beginning of the twentieth century, the nursing profession in the Caribbean benefited from the introduction of effective diagnoses and treatments of tropical and other diseases. During the 1950s, nursing care in the Caribbean made significant strides, and it emerged as one of the most progressive and innovative health-care and clinical-care systems in the nonindustrial areas of the world. These nursing advancements came as the result of introducing a series of carefully planned long- and short-term health-care measures and procedures. The coordination of local, regional, and international governmental and nongovernmental healthcare planners, educators, and administrators, along with the commitment of most Caribbean governments, is responsible for the high quality of nursing care available in the region during the first decade of the twenty-first century.

CARIBBEAN NURSING DURING AND AFTER SLAVERY

Nursing-care practices in the Caribbean slowly shifted from being provided by family members in the sixteenth century to untrained providers of bed care and then to the more informed nursing care practitioners of the nineteenth century. Still, informal providers, sometimes referred to as "bush doctors" and "African healers," continued to use techniques that were practiced in Africa to care for many of the illnesses and diseases that frequently ravaged the Caribbean population, including malaria, yellow dengue, scarlet fever, smallpox, cholera, and typhoid. These conditions were frequently fatal or required long-term nursing care. Among the leading causes of these ailments were various demographic, cultural, and socioeconomic factors, with poor nutrition often playing a role.

During slavery, most slave owners provided some measure of health- and nursing- care assistance even for their slaves. Nevertheless, a number of studies have shown that broad segments of the Caribbean population experienced poor health during this period. After emancipation, most former slave owners felt no obligation to continue to provide the medical services granted during slavery. Studies show that the overall health of the majority of the Caribbean population deteriorated even further at this time because the colonial governments had no interest in providing health-care services. Privately operated sick houses were neglected and were in many cases abandoned. Additionally, little thought was given to preventive health care. Nursing in the Caribbean made little headway during this period because the conditions that led to serious illness existed throughout the society.

NINETEENTH-CENTURY CARIBBEAN NURSES

Beginning in the 1850s, some of the more progressive Caribbean communities encouraged their local governments to support the creation of public dispensaries and public hospitals that employed an increased number of nursing-care providers. The introduction of a series of quarantine procedures also helped to improve nursing care. In some Caribbean countries, the establishment of ladies associations operated by upper-class women led to the creation of public hospitals. In addition, an increasing number of well-to-do Afro-Caribbean women operated lodging houses that served as nursing homes and private hospitals.

Two of the best-known pioneering figures in Caribbean nursing worked in Jamaica. These enterprising women were Cubah Cornwallis and Mary Seacole (1805–1881). Cornwallis operated a nursing home near Port Royal, and her most famous patient was the heir to the British throne (later King William IV), who became ill when visiting Jamaica as a midshipman. Cornwallis was later rewarded for her kindness to the Prince when Queen Adelaide, wife of King William, sent her an expensive gown in appreciation for her services. Mary Seacole operated a guesthouse and a private hospital in Kingston, and she won wide recognition for the manner in which she saved the lives of many during the cholera epidemic of 1850 to 1851, which killed between 40,000 to 50,000 persons in the Caribbean. When news of the Crimean War reached her in Jamaica, Seacole sought, but was denied, permission by the British to nurse the injured troops back to health. Using private funds, she traveled to the area of the conflict and nursed wounded British, French, and Turkish soldiers. For her heroic efforts, she was awarded the Crimean Medal, the French Legion of Honor, and a Turkish medal. Seacole wrote about her nursing adventures in *The Wonderful Adventures of Mrs. Seacole in Many Lands*, published in 1857.

During the last half of the nineteenth century, many within the European-trained medical profession began to push for additional improvements in nursing care. Colonial governments around the Caribbean opened publicly operated general hospitals and sick houses, and they employed nursing-care providers to meet the needs of the seriously ill. Stricter health quarantine regulations were also introduced, and boards of health were established to oversee the early government-operated general hospitals, maternity hospitals, leper houses, and lunatic asylums. Many of the newly created hospitals in the British West Indies were initially funded from the Slave Compensation Fund, and operated on very limited budgets. (The Slave Compensation Fund had been set up by the British Parliament under the British Emancipation Act of 1833. The fund comprised a grant of twenty million pounds to be distributed to slave owners for the loss of their slave property.) The general day-to-day nursing-care operations in these early hospitals were under the direction of a European-trained nurse, called a *matron*, who supervised the nursing staff and trained them in bedside procedures and in the rudiments of nursing care.

EARLY TWENTIETH-CENTURY NURSING

By the turn of the twentieth century, the overall focus on health care in the Caribbean had led to a gradual improvement in overall health, particularly due to new medical discoveries in the treatment and prevention of various diseases. In addition, many colonial governments began to employ better-trained medical personnel. The creation of additional district hospitals and maternity hospital wards led to the increased training of nurses, including training in midwifery.

In some areas of the Caribbean, the latest American nursing techniques and methods were also introduced. An American-trained Barbadian Adventist physician, Charles J. B. Cave (1879–1939), a graduate of the American Medical Missionary College in Battle Creek, Michigan, and later of the Medical School at the University of Edinburgh, Scotland, operated a sanitarium and training school for Barbadian women in home nursing, including midwifery and first-aid classes, until his death in 1939. Cave was trained by Dr. John Harvey Kellogg, one of the foremost American advocates for improved nursing care. Many of Cave's nursing-class graduates were later employed at private and government nursing facilities in Barbados.

Across the region, Caribbean nurses worked under colonial labor policies that restricted women in the workplace. According to one scholar, "Women's labor outside the home was accepted as expedient in certain circumstances but restricted the occupations" (Reddock, 1994, p. 62). Nursing, teaching, and limited civil-service positions provided the majority of work for women outside of the home. As in other occupations where women were employed, the leading nursing positions were filled by the wives and daughters of the white upper classes and, to a lesser degree, by relatives of the colored middle class and the business class. The wages paid to nurses remained the lowest paid to government employees, as was also the case for the majority of single women employed by the governments of the Caribbean. These low wages often forced women to resign or get married. In addition, general working conditions remained substandard. Nurses worked an average of sixty-seven hours per week, and in many areas it was compulsory for nurses to reside in the hospital. One researcher observed that nurses virtually spent their lives in the hospital. While nurses received free board and lodging, most were forced to live in "open dormitories" that allowed little privacy. Meals were often badly prepared, and the nurses often went without staples such as fruits and vegetables.

Two of the most successful Caribbean nurses during the mid–twentieth century were Nita Barrow (1916–1995) and Ena Walters of Barbados. Both received their early education at St. Michael's Girls School near Bridgetown, and they completed their first nursing-care training at the Barbados General Hospital. After further overseas training, both returned to the Caribbean and became influential leaders in the nursing profession. Barrow became a nursing instructor in public health in Jamaica, a sister tutor, the first West Indian matron of the University College Hospital, and principal nursing officer in Jamaica. In 1959 she became the first Barbadian to be appointed matron of the Barbados General Hospital, and she served in that position for twenty-six years. Both nursing administrators brought revolutionary changes in nursing education, practice, and patient care to the English-speaking Caribbean. Walters would be selected as the first chairperson of the Caribbean Regional Nursing Body, and she held that position for three consecutive terms.

CARIBBEAN NURSING SINCE THE 1950S

The nursing profession in the Caribbean made significant strides during the 1950s. Specific standards for the training, certification, and registration of nurses were established throughout the region, and the first conference of nursing administrators in the Caribbean was held in Barbados in 1951. The group saw the need to continue to work together and created the Regional Nursing Body. The organization dealt with the collective nursing issues that regional members faced. These visionary nursing administrators wished to significantly elevate both the Caribbean nursing profession and the region's health-care systems. Among the most pressing issues addressed were related recruitment, training, specialization, working conditions, the exchange of staff and the interchange of technical opinion and information. The member states were part of the Commonwealth Caribbean.

The Caribbean Regional Nursing Body continues to conduct annual conferences, and in conjunction with the Caribbean Nursing Association it dedicated and promoted May 2003 to August 2004 as "The Year of the Caribbean Nurse." The coordinators collaborated with the national nursing associations in the Dutch-, French-, English- and Spanish-speaking countries of the Caribbean to broaden public awareness of the important role of the nursing profession. The groups' planning committee also organized a yearlong program of activities. Among the most outstanding achievements of this enterprise were efforts to promote the role and advancements of Caribbean nursing care to the public. The theme of the well-publicized celebration was "Nurses: Lighting the Way to Professional Excellence." These activities were meant to increase awareness among the Caribbean public of the nursing profession, and to assist with the recruitment and retention of nurses working in the Caribbean. The thirty-first annual general meeting of the Regional Nursing Body was held in late May 2004 in Paramaribo, Suriname. Over the years, the Caribbean nurses' organizations have worked closely with the Pan American Health Organization in efforts to broaden their impact on the Caribbean community.

See also Healing and the Arts in Afro-Caribbean Cultures; Mortality and Morbidity in Latin America and the Caribbean; Nursing in the United States

▪▪ *Bibliography*

Abel-Smith, B. A. *A History of the Nursing Profession.* London: Heinemann, 1960.

Carrington, Sean, et al. *A–Z of Barbados Heritage.* Oxford, UK: Macmillan Caribbean, 1985.

Horwitz, Samuel J., and Edith F. Horwitz. *Jamaica: A Historical Portrait.* London: Pall Mall Press, 1971.

Nell Hodgson Woodruff School of Nursing, Emory University. "History of the Regional Nursing Body." Available from <http://prod-nursing.emory.edu/lecin/rnb/history.html>.

Nightingale, Florence. *Notes on Nursing: What It Is and What It Is Not.* London: Harrison, 1860.

Reddock, Rhoda E. *Women, Labour, and Politics in Trinidad and Tobago.* Kingston, Jamaica: Randle, 1994.

Seacole, Mary. *The Wonderful Adventures of Mrs. Seacole in Many Lands.* Kingston, Jamaica: Nursing Association of Jamaica, 1857. Reprint, New York: Oxford University Press, 1988.

Senior, Olive. *A–Z of Jamaica Heritage.* Kingston, Jamaica: Heinemann Educational, 1987.

Walters, Ena K. *New Dimensions in Nursing.* Bridgetown, Barbados: Ministry of Health, 1974.

Walters, Ena K. *Report of the General Nursing Council of Barbados.* Bridgetown, Barbados: Ministry of Health, 1981.

Walters, Ena K. *Nursing in Barbados: A History from the Late 18th–20th Century.* Bridgetown, Barbados: Caribbean Graphic Productions, 1995.

GLENN O. PHILLIPS (2005)

NURSING IN THE UNITED STATES

This history of black professional nursing in the United States is part of the history of women's roles in black community health activism. The period from 1890 to 1910 was marked by local efforts to establish black hospitals (many of which also had schools of nursing), which collectively may be termed a social movement in that they: (1) had strong extra-professional (lay) support mobilized through already existing networks; (2) were tied to the community's other social and political concerns; and (3) exhibited similar leadership structures. With funds from John D. Rockefeller in 1886, Atlanta Baptist Seminary (later renamed Spelman College) opened the first African-American nursing school. Initially not affiliated with any hospital, it offered a two-year course of study leading to a diploma in nursing, and by the turn of the century it

African-American "Black Cross Nurses" march in Harlem at the Universal Negro Improvement Association (UNIA) parade, 1922. During the First World War, the American Red Cross refused to accept more than a handful of applications from black nurses. © UNDERWOOD AND UNDERWOOD/CORBIS

boasted a comparatively large hospital with thirty-one beds. In the main, however, local movements to establish black hospitals and nursing schools were almost entirely internal to black communities, with black male physicians heading the efforts, though much of the leadership in fund-raising, advertisement, and community awareness fell to black women members of sororities, clubs, and church boards. The notable exception was the Phillis Wheatley Sanitarium and Training School for Nurses, established in 1896 by the women of the Wheatley Club of New Orleans, Louisiana, and later renamed the Flint-Goodridge Hospital School of Nursing. Because most municipalities refused to partially fund black hospitals, as they did white hospitals, community support was a continuing need.

Aside from the few who rose to the ranks of physician, educator, or professional social worker, the overwhelming majority of black women of any educational level found their occupational choices before the Second World War largely limited to domestic service or agriculture. Unfortunately, as one historian has observed, white professional nursing in the first half of the twentieth century may be characterized as exhibiting "no sorority of consciousness across the color line" (Hine, 1989, p. 98). Black nursing schools therefore sought to produce nurses who, in their training, were distinguished from domestic workers and equal to white professionals (even while overemphasizing Victorian gender conventions by barring married women and requiring applicants to provide letters attesting to moral standing). The nation's first black hospital, Chicago's Provident Hospital and Nurses Training School (1891), emerged in response to the rejection of Emma Reynolds from all of the city's white nursing schools.

Roughly a dozen nursing programs followed in short order, including those at Dixie Hospital Training School

Emma Reynolds and Provident Hospital

In 1889 Emma Reynolds, a young woman who aspired to be a nurse, was denied admission by each of Chicago's nursing schools because she was black. Her brother Louis Reynolds, a pastor of St. Stephen's African Methodist Episcopal Church and prominent member of the black community, turned to Daniel Hale Williams for help. A respected black surgeon, Williams tried to use his influence to get Emma into the white nursing schools, but was unsuccessful. The men decided to coordinate their efforts and create a nursing school for black women.

In 1890 Williams gathered a group of black ministers, physicians, and businessmen to pitch the idea of founding an interracial hospital and nursing school in Chicago. Winning their support, he and Louis Reynolds began the project. Prominent whites in the community, acknowledging the benefit of having medical treatment available to their black employees, also contributed to the project.

The project seemed destined for success when the Armour Meat Packing Company donated the down payment for a house. The three-story brick house became Provident Hospital and Nurses Training School in 1891. The generosity of the community's residents was a critical factor in sustaining the facility as, at the time, a hospital responsive to the black community did not generate enough income to support itself. Emma Reynolds was one of the school's first three graduates in 1894.

(1891, in Hampton, Virginia); Tuskegee Institute's John A. Andrew Hospital (1892); Provident Hospital in Baltimore, Maryland (1894); Freedmen's Hospital and Nursing School in Washington, D.C. (1894, affiliated with Howard University); the Hospital and Training School for Nurses in Charleston, South Carolina (1894); New York City's Lincoln School for Nurses (1896); St. Agnes Hospital and Nurse Training School in Raleigh, North Carolina (1896); Hubbard Hospital and School of Nursing (1900, within Meharry Medical College in Nashville, Tennessee); Lin-

coln Hospital (1901, in Durham, North Carolina); and the Mercy Hospital School of Nursing (1907, in Philadelphia). By 1920 there were thirty-six nursing schools for blacks nationwide, and by 1928 the aforementioned institutions had produced more than 80 percent of the roughly 2,800 black graduate nurses in practice. Black hospitals and nursing schools were typically small and underfunded, but within medical Jim Crow they were vital as centers of treatment, health promotion (headquartering the National Negro Health Week Movement, begun in 1915 at Tuskegee Institute), education, and intellectual exchange. Their graduates certainly encountered the color line. Mary Eliza Mahoney, the first black woman in the United States to receive a nursing degree (in 1879, from Boston's New England Hospital for Women and Children), spent most of her career in private duty, perhaps illustrating the extent to which even well-qualified black nurses were barred from hospital service. As it was in the American Medical Association, the color bar in the American Nurses Association (ANA; founded in 1896 as the Nurses' Associated Alumnae of the United States and Canada; it was renamed in 1911) operated with the requirement that membership be attained through state affiliates, many of which, especially in the South, were exclusively white.

In response to Jim Crow nursing, Martha Minerva Franklin (an 1897 graduate of Philadelphia's Woman's Hospital Training School for Nurses) and others organized the National Association of Colored Graduate Nurses (NACGN) in 1908. Even at its peak, the NACGN was never able to organize all black nurses (it had only 125 members in 1912; 500 in 1920; 175 in 1933; and 947 in 1949), but the early years of organization were followed, after 1933, by ones of renewed activism. In 1934, the nursing leader Estelle Massey Riddle (1901–1981), the first black person to obtain a masters of arts degree in nursing (from Teachers College, Columbia University, in 1931), was elected president of NACGN. She hired the association's first paid executive director, Mabel Doyle Keaton Staupers (1890–1989), a 1917 graduate (with honors) of Freedman's Hospital School of Nursing in Washington, D.C., and, in 1920, of Philadelphia's preeminent tuberculosis research facility, the Henry Phipps Institute. In New York, Keaton had been instrumental in the organization of Harlem's first inpatient tuberculosis treatment facility for blacks (the Booker T. Washington Sanatorium), serving as superintendent between 1920 and 1922. Until 1934 she was the nurse-executive of the Harlem Committee of the New York Tuberculosis and Health Association.

Both Riddle and Keaton had worked in black-white cooperative circles, illustrating the role of white philanthropy in the NACGN's efforts. After the 1915 to 1920 period of social unrest (the "Red Summer" of 1919 was particularly bloody in its antiblack and antiradical state and mob violence), an era with a focus on "race relations" dawned. The new era emphasized cooperation between black professionals and their more enlightened white counterparts and wealthy white benefactors, in an effort to curtail further uprisings through moderate reforms in education, labor, social services, and health care. Nationally, the Rockefeller Foundation's General Education Board, and especially the Julius Rosenwald Fund (which, between 1929 and 1942, allocated $1.7 million for such efforts, including the support of no fewer than seventeen black hospital and nursing school projects), were among the most prominent funders of black health and educational work. On the local level, too, lesser industrialists (such as the racially paternalistic Duke family in North Carolina, or Philadelphia's Henry Phipps, who sponsored the formal training of black pioneer public health nurses and antituberculosis work among blacks and whites in Baltimore and Philadelphia) also provided support, and in many cases had laid the groundwork before World War I. The role of white philanthropy can be overstated, however. When in 1925 the Rockefeller Foundation hired English-born academic nurse Ethel Johns to conduct a survey of black nursing and nursing education in the United States, the resulting indictment of institutional racism and official neglect was so precise and unequivocal that the Rockefeller Foundation refused to release her report or implement her recommendations, fearing reprisal from the ANA and the National League of Nursing Education (NLNE). White philanthropists' gradualist strategy instead consisted of the offer to states and municipalities of matching funds for black education, and of the underwriting of numerous research and career development projects. Cumulatively, these efforts had the effect of helping to produce a cadre of black health-care and social-science leaders whose expertise would be integral to many of the New Deal's social programs as they affected blacks. Direct support proved integral to the NACGN's success in integrating the ANA in 1950.

The Depression and war years were pivotal. Excluded from better-paying jobs and most labor unions, blacks were economically the most vulnerable after 1929. Although known to blacks for decades, the health effects of racism (including intractably high rates of tuberculosis and infant and maternal mortality) were now inescapably apparent to the national government. At the same time, as Staupers and Riddle agitated for the lowering of color restriction within nursing, hardship had reduced the number of black nursing schools to twenty-seven by 1941, and to only twenty in 1944. Aside from these, fewer than thirty nursing schools accepted African Americans. The state

nursing associations of some sixteen southern states and Washington, D.C., remained color exclusive, while many of the northern associations, too, were unsupportive (prompting black registered nurses in 1932 to found the Chi Eta Phi Sorority). President Franklin Roosevelt's always shifting and often tenuous New Deal coalition, however, included many black national and local leaders who found positions from which they could influence national policy. Both Riddle and Staupers held positions in the National Nursing Council for National Defense (established in July 1940), and Staupers served in the Federal Security Agency's subcommittee on Negro health. Though born of wartime need for nurses and for black political support, such appointments would have been unimaginable during the First World War, when the American Red Cross refused to accept more than a handful of applications from black nurses. On the advent of the 1943 passage of the Bolton Bill, creating the U.S. Cadet Nurse Corps (within the U.S. Public Health Service), NACGN leaders Staupers, Riddle, and others successfully pressed Congress for an antidiscrimination amendment. Under the Bolton Act, the USPHS provided funds to 1,225 schools, including the major black institutions. Just as important, some white institutions discarded their color-exclusion policies in order to qualify for Bolton funds. By 1945, black students in nursing programs numbered roughly 2,600 (an increase of 135 percent over 1939), and the number of black or mixed-enrollment nursing schools had increased from twenty-nine in 1941 to forty-nine in 1945 (the same year in which the NACGN successfully pressed the Army and Navy to abandon color exclusion in the armed forces). The election of Riddle (then a member of the faculty of New York University) to the ANA's Board of Directors in 1948 signaled the end of the association's Jim Crow policy (in 1950). Less than a year after this occurred, the NACGN voted to disband.

THE POSTWAR ERA

"Soap operas and scholars," one historian has noted, "seem to agree that hospital workers are doctors and nurses" (Sacks, 1988, p. 2). However, due to various federal and state hospital construction initiatives, the emergence of market-oriented or hybrid health-insurance plans (Blue Cross and Blue Shield in the 1930s, then Medicare and Medicaid in the 1960s, and managed care systems in the 1970s), and the concomitant rising demand for hospital services, hospitals arose within an expanding postwar health-care network as complex institutions characterized by bureaucracies, specialized wards, intricate payment plans, large-scale research divisions, and hierarchically segmented workforces in which the role of the registered

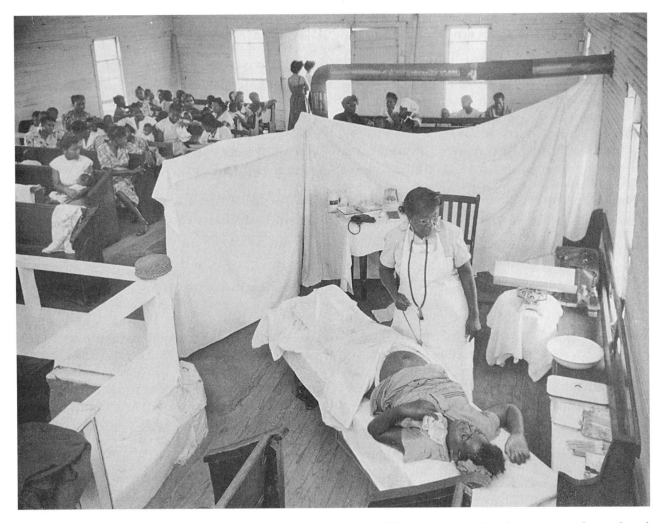

Nurse-midwife Maude Callen at work, South Carolina, 1951. *Life Magazine published a twelve-page photodocumentary on the nurse's work in the impoverished black South, generating thousands of dollars in contributions toward a clinic that Callen worked at until her retirement in 1971.* W. EUGENE SMITH/GETTY IMAGES

nurse shifted to that of supervisory position over nonprofessional nursing personnel who performed tasks once performed by nurses. By 1970, thirty-seven cents of every dollar expended on health provision went to hospitals, the largest sector of an increasingly corporatized industry.

Federal, state, and privately funded "manpower development" strategies after the late 1940s brought about a greater range of training programs designed to meet the growing need for health provision personnel. Short-duration courses and community college and baccalaureate programs in nursing gradually replaced diploma-granting schools as the greatest sources of credentialing. Hierarchies in education, prestige, and wages emerged in which blacks and Hispanics were found largely in the ranks of licensed practical nurses (LPNs), licensed vocational nurses (LVNs), and nurses assistants, while nursing's aristocracy—registered nurses (RNs)—added people

of color to their numbers, but not nearly at the same rate as did the lower grades. During the decades of professionalization, between 1900 and 1940, the proportion of registered nurses among all nursing personnel increased from 11 percent to 73 percent, but postwar segmentation left RNs as only 44 percent of all nursing workers in 1980. Meanwhile the role of the nursing assistant, the lowest grade (and with the highest nonwhite representation), had expanded the most rapidly between 1940 and 1980, from 9 percent to 41 percent of all nursing personnel.

Postwar segmentation produced a downward pressure on the income of lower-grade workers in voluntary (nonprofit) hospitals. Because of the exempting provisions of the Labor-Management Relations (Taft-Hartley) Act of 1947, these workers remained largely nonunion or only nominally organized. As a result, the disproportionately black and Hispanic staff in hospital food, janitorial, clerical, nurses aide, and vocational and practical nursing divisions—in comparison to other service sector employees—earned less, worked more, and (ironically) enjoyed fewer health benefits. Whereas the NACGN's struggle had been largely professional, black healthcare workers' struggles in the postwar decades were closely allied with the civil rights movement, whose roots could be found in the black labor struggles of A. Philip Randolph and the Brotherhood of Sleeping Car Porters, black unionists in the Congress of Industrial Organizations (CIO), and the wartime movement to support the Fair Employment Practices Commission (FEPC). In those cities where Local Hospital Workers' Union Local 1199 (based in New York City) publicly interpreted the labor struggle as a civil rights struggle, it realized the most success throughout the 1960s and 1970s. With some success, black women with grassroots experience in the civil rights movement mobilized workers at Duke Medical Center in Durham, North Carolina, in the 1970s. Inspired by the Student Nonviolent Coordinating Committee (SNCC), twenty black nurses aides in 1966 successfully struck the Lincoln Nursing Home in Baltimore, Maryland, forming (with support from the Congress of Racial Equality [CORE]) the Maryland Freedom Union. Also in Baltimore, Local 1199, CORE, and the Southern Christian Leadership Conference (SCLC) supported the demands of black workers at Johns Hopkins University Hospital for better wages, reasonable work hours, workplace respect, career development opportunities, and the integration of Hopkins Nursing School. At the same time, the civil rights movement spawned the Medical Committee on Human Rights (MCHR, the medical wing of SNCC's 1964 Mississippi Freedom Summer project), the Student Health Organization (SHO) and several other black, brown, and white New Left student health profession and community health action groups that arose to bring issues of medical neglect and health worker compensation to the fore. Finally, feeling that the desegregated ANA had remained negligent of black community health issues, in December 1971 eighteen members formed the National Black Nurses Association (NBNA), which in 2005 had 150,000 members in seventy-nine chapters (Chi Eta Phi Nursing Sorority, Incorporated, maintains 8,000 members).

At the time of the 2000 census, 93.1 percent of the more than 2 million registered nurses were women; about 12 percent (333,368) of all RNs were of ethnic minorities, including non-Hispanic African-Americans (133,041), Asians (93,415), Hispanic/Latino (54,861), and Native Americans/Alaskan Natives (13,040). Although this is nearly triple the number of nurses estimated to be of these categories in 1980 (when minorities were roughly 7 percent of RNs), much of the growth came after 1996 and may be artificial, traceable to the federal government's provision of "multiple race" categories in census data collection in the late 1990s. Black women remain underrepresented among professional nurses outside of cities with large black populations, and they remain overrepresented among LVNs, LPNs, nurses aides, and lower-grade hospital workers.

See also Black Hospitals in the U.S.; Nursing in the Caribbean

■ ■ *Bibliography*

Carnegie, Mary Elizabeth. *The Path We Tread: Blacks in Nursing, 1854–1984.* Philadelphia: Lippincott, 1986.

Fink, Leon, and Brian Greenberg. *Upheaval in the Quiet Zone: A History of Hospital Workers' Union, Local 1199.* Urbana: University of Illinois Press, 1989.

Glazer, Nona Y. *Women's Paid and Unpaid Labor: The Work Transfer in Health Care and Retailing.* Philadelphia: Temple University Press, 1993.

Hine, Darlene Clark. *Black Women in White: Racial Conflict and Cooperation in the Nursing Profession, 1890–1950.* Bloomington: Indiana University Press, 1989.

"News and Views: The State of African Americans in Nursing Education." *Journal of Blacks in Higher Education* 13 (September 1996): 52–54.

Sacks, Karen Brodkin. *Caring by the Hour: Women, Work, and Organizing at Duke Medical Center.* Urbana: University of Illinois Press, 1988.

Smith, David Barton. *Health Care Divided: Race and Healing a Nation.* Ann Arbor: University of Michigan Press, 1999.

Smith, Susan L. *Sick and Tired of Being Sick and Tired: Black Women's Health Activism in America, 1890–1950.* Philadelphia: University of Pennsylvania Press, 1995.

SAMUEL ROBERTS (2005)

OBAC Writers' Workshop

The Organization of Black American Culture (OBAC) was founded in Chicago in 1967, and its writers' workshop survived longer than any other literary group of the black arts movement. Originally conceived by a small group of intellectuals that included Hoyt Fuller, the editor of *Negro Digest,* the poet Conrad Kent Rivers, and Gerald McWorter (Abdul Alkalimat), its purpose was to nurture artists and, in keeping with the general agenda of the black arts movement, to develop close ties between artists and the black community in a collective endeavor to revolutionize black culture and black consciousness. The acronym OBAC, pronounced "oh-bah-see," echoes the Yoruba word *oba,* which refers to royalty and leadership.

Like many other black arts organizations, OBAC was predicated on a conception that artists have a special role to play as leaders of a cultural revolution. Accordingly, the original vision of OBAC was broad, comprising three separate "workshops"—writers, visual artists, and community relations—but not overlapping the work of groups such as the Association for the Advancement of Creative Musicians (AACM), founded in 1965, and nascent theater groups such as the KUUMBA Workshop, which formed shortly after OBAC. The visual arts workshop, led by Jeff Donaldson, soon evolved into an independent group, AfriCobra (1968), and the community workshop disbanded. Within a couple of years OBAC became exclusively a writers' workshop, and continued to thrive in that form until 1992.

Several of the position papers issued by OBAC during its early days have been collected in *Nommo: A Literary Legacy of Black Chicago* (1987), an anthology celebrating the first two decades of the workshop. While these manifestos stated OBAC's objectives clearly, the group's structure and activities equally revealed its fundamental values. Foremost among the tenets in OBAC's statement of purpose were:

1. the establishment of a black aesthetic;

2. the encouragement of the highest quality of literary expression;

3. the identification of critical standards for black writing; and

4. the development of black critics.

Other objectives included fostering a spirit of cooperation among writers, issuing publications, and conducting readings and forums for the public. To achieve these goals,

OBAC remained an independent, community-based organization, free of institutional affiliations. OBAC published a newsletter, *Cumbaya,* and a magazine, *Nommo*. In addition to sponsoring traditional readings and forums, OBAC conducted readings in public places such as bus stops and taverns. At weekly meetings members and visitors read their works and received criticism from members of the group.

Among its alumni OBAC boasts many well-known writers. Poets include Haki Madhubuti (Don L. Lee), Johari Amini, Carolyn Rodgers, Sterling Plumpp, and D. L. Crockett-Smith. Fiction writers include Cecil Brown and Sam Greenlee. Some, such as Angela Jackson and Sandra Jackson-Opoku, have published fine work in several genres. Regardless of individual differences, OBAC writers held in common a commitment to produce work that in some sense derived from and spoke to the black community. OBAC's emphasis on public readings reflected that commitment, producing a group of writers who are skilled and charismatic readers of their own work. The workshop embodied the vision of literary activity that at once expressed and enlivened the culture of the black community.

See also Association for the Advancement of Creative Musicians; Black Arts Movement; Madhubuti, Haki R. (Lee, Don L.); Literature of the United States; Poetry, U.S.

■ ■ *Bibliography*

Parks, Carole A., ed. *Nommo: A Literary Legacy of Black Chicago (1967–1987).* Chicago: OBAhouse, 1987.

Smith, David Lionel. "Chicago Poets, OBAC, and the Black Arts Movement." In *The Black Columbiad,* edited by Werner Sollors and Maria Diedrich. Cambridge, Mass.: Harvard University Press, 1994.

Trice, Dawn Turner. "Influential Black Writers to Gather Again." *Chicago Tribune* (February 3, 2005).

DAVID LIONEL SMITH (1996)
Updated bibliography

OBEAH

A highly charged and ambiguous term, *Obeah* (sometimes spelled *obia*) refers to various forms of spiritual power. Occurring primarily in the Anglophone Caribbean (and in Suriname, which began as an English colony), it is one of the most widespread words of African origin to be found in the region. Like *vodou* (or *voodoo*) in the Francophone Caribbean, its varying meanings, its shifting significance, and its differing valuation over time mirror unresolved tensions between colonialist and indigenist (or other anticolonialist) viewpoints. As part of this ongoing dialectic, definitions and understandings of the term continue to carry a strong moral charge, either negative or positive, depending on such variables as the ethnic background and social class of the user and the context of usage.

Attempts to find an origin for the word have themselves formed part of this dialectic. Reflecting a common bias, etymologists have generally accepted that Obeah is a kind of evil magic or witchcraft, leading them to search for phonologically similar terms with negative meanings in various African languages. The most widely accepted derivation, from Asante Twi *obayi,* referring to the antisocial use of spiritual power to harm or kill, has in turn shaped the understandings of scholars and others who have written about Obeah. On the basis of this questionable etymology, some have jumped to the conclusion that it represents the remnant of a particular form of witchcraft or sorcery brought to the Caribbean by Akan-speaking people from the Gold Coast (modern-day Ghana). However, others have argued that the term might just as easily be traced to similar sounding words from other West African languages, some of which—such as the Igbo term *abia/obia* (and its cognates in a number of neighboring languages such as Ibibio or Efik)—have entirely positive meanings revolving around healing, protection, and other socially sanctioned uses of esoteric knowledge and spiritual power (Handler and Bilby, 2001, pp. 90–92).

The earliest known occurrences of the term in writing, from Barbados, date from the early 1700s. By the late eighteenth century, the word had also begun to appear frequently in writings from Jamaica and other British Caribbean colonies. It is apparent from these early sources that during the slavery era Obeah often referred to divination, healing (frequently using herbs), and spiritual protection of various kinds, although it could also have fearful connotations, sometimes being associated with accusations of sorcery. It was not long before whites began to realize that belief in Obeah could be brought into the service of slave rebellions. One result was the rapid introduction of anti-Obeah legislation in Jamaica and a number of other colonies.

Over the course of the nineteenth century, as the influence of Christian missionaries grew, depictions of Obeah became increasingly one-sided and negative. Obeah was now often reduced by writers to a virulent form of witchcraft or sorcery with a single purpose: to harm or destroy its "victims." Such hegemonic ideas formed part of the more general denigration and stigmatization by colonial authorities (and the educational and religious institutions aligned with them) of cultural expressions identified with the black population, especially practices and beliefs understood to be of African origin. But because Obeah practitioners were in direct competition with the purveyors of hegemonic interpretations of Christianity that provided ideological support for the colonial project, they were singled out for attack and bore the brunt of a particularly fervent and sustained campaign of demonization. As a result, as Melville and Frances Herskovits state in *Rebel Destiny* (1934), "no word of African origin which has survived in the New World has taken on such grim meaning as has the word *obia* in many of the islands of the Caribbean" (p. 307).

In stark contrast to the negative characterizations of Obeah typifying the literature on the West Indies are the views of *obia* held by Maroons in Suriname and French Guiana—peoples such as the Saramaka, Ndyuka, or Aluku, whose ancestors escaped from coastal plantations during the seventeenth and eighteenth centuries and created their own autonomous societies in the interior forest. Drawing on African backgrounds, initial plantation experiences, and creolizing cultures similar to those of the enslaved in other parts of the Caribbean colonized by the English, these Maroon peoples were able to fashion and maintain alternative Afro-creole cultures beyond the reach of the European colonial powers that were attempting to establish and enforce cultural hegemony throughout the Americas. As a result, more than two centuries later, theirs remain, in a sense, the least "colonized" cultures in all of Afro-America.

All Guianese Maroons agree on the fundamental meanings of the term *obia*—meanings that are overwhelmingly positive. Among the Aluku (Boni) Maroons, for instance, the primary senses of the term are as follows:

1. medicine (herbal and other), remedy, or healing power;

2. any object, or "charm," invested with healing or protective power;

3. an instrument used for divination;

4. a god, spirit, or human ghost;

5. a positive spiritual force that pervades the universe.

Obia, in all of these senses, plays an indispensable part in everyday Aluku life, and has purely positive associations; it is readily and openly discussed and used in both private and public contexts, including major religious ceremonies, and carries no social stigma whatsoever. By the same token, the term has no connotations of witchcraft.

Thus, among the Aluku (and other Guianese Maroons), to accuse someone of employing *obia* would be absurd, for it makes no sense to accuse someone of something that is seen as having essentially benevolent uses. Interestingly enough, rather than *obia*, the word the Aluku use to refer to antisocial witchcraft or sorcery (analogous to what is denoted by the Akan term *obayi*) is *wisi*, which is derived not from an African language, but from the English word *witch* (Hurault, 1961, pp. 238–246; Bilby, 1990, pp. 200–203).

More than seventy years ago, fresh from his fieldwork among the Saramaka, Melville Herskovits noted this discrepancy between Guianese Maroon and broader West Indian notions of Obeah. In his 1930 review of Martha Beckwith's classic ethnography of rural Jamaican life, *Black Roadways* (1929), Herskovits points out that, "in the literature on the West Indies, 'obeah' is synonymous with evil magic, and Miss Beckwith tacitly accepts this interpretation. On the basis of the Suriname data, to say nothing of some of Miss Beckwith's own statements, this interpretation does not stand. If we take the case among the Bush-Negroes [Surinamese Maroons] . . . we find that obia is a healing principle" (p. 337). Although Herskovits never explored the larger implications of this insight, his assertion that the negative interpretation of Obeah widely found in West Indian literature "does not stand" when compared with Surinamese Maroon conceptions—or even when held up against the understandings of some of Beckwith's Jamaican informants—is borne out by much of what has been written on the subject both before and since, especially if one reads between the lines.

Almost all written accounts, even the most negative, hint at native understandings of Obeah considerably more complex than the stereotypical imagery that reduces it to a form of sorcery or evil magic motivated by "bad mind" and jealousy. A careful re-examination of written references to Obeah in various parts of the Caribbean, from the earliest descriptions to those of the nineteenth and twentieth centuries, reveals that most of those who have consulted Obeah practitioners have actually done so for protection and help with illness or other personal problems, or more generally to bring good fortune, rather than to wreak vengeance on enemies or inflict disease and misfortune upon innocent victims. Like fears and accusations of witchcraft in other parts of the world, anxieties regarding the working of malicious Obeah in the Caribbean likely have more to do with interpersonal tensions and mechanisms of social control in particular communities—in this case filtered through the prism of hegemonic colonial ideologies—than with the actual practice of Obeah. Those few ethnographers who have worked with self-defined

Obeah practitioners and their clients in places such as Jamaica and the Leeward Islands find little if any evidence of sorcery as a modus operandi; on the contrary, their reports tend to emphasize the therapeutic nature of the services performed by such spiritual workers for their "patients."

Over the last few decades, as part of the decolonization process in the newly independent states of the Caribbean, there has been a trend toward increasing tolerance of Obeah in at least some parts of the region. In the 1970s, Prime Minister Forbes Burnham of Guyana attempted to rehabilitate Obeah as a legitimate aspect of African religiosity that had been misrepresented and suppressed by the European colonizers. However, because it was associated with an oppressive, dictatorial regime, Burnham's recasting of Obeah in positive terms, like François Duvalier's reclamation of Vodou in Haiti, did little to further the cause of those who wished to remove the stigma long attached to African forms of spirituality in the Caribbean. In more recent years, colonial laws against Obeah have periodically been challenged elsewhere in the region, and in some cases repealed. In Barbados and Trinidad and Tobago, for instance, Obeah is no longer a legal offense; in other countries, such as Jamaica, anti-Obeah statutes remain on the books.

Whatever its legal status, Obeah everywhere (except among Guianese Maroons) continues to be widely characterized and stigmatized as a "fraudulent superstition," and it is still viewed by many as a shameful reminder of a supposedly "dark" African past, although it also has its defenders. Though in the minority, these dissenters continue to speak out against the ongoing representation of Obeah as harmful "witchcraft," seeing this negative imagery as a damaging legacy of colonialism. As a legitimate, primarily positive expression of African spirituality, they argue, Obeah deserves the same legal guarantees of protection from persecution afforded other forms of religious expression.

Without doubt, Obeah continues to play an important role in the lives of many in the Caribbean. A kind of flash point capable of bringing to the surface deep cultural contradictions bred by centuries of colonial domination, it continues to fascinate scholars and creative writers, who recognize in it an important dimension of the human condition in this part of the world.

See also Candomblé; Santería

■ ■ *Bibliography*

Bilby, Kenneth M. *The Remaking of the Aluku: Culture, Politics, and Maroon Ethnicity in French South America.* Ph.D. diss., Johns Hopkins University, Baltimore, Md., 1990.

Bilby, Kenneth M., and Jerome S. Handler. "Obeah: Healing and Protection in West Indian Slave Life." *Journal of Caribbean History* 38 (2004): 153–183.

Handler, Jerome S., and Kenneth M. Bilby. "On the Early Use and Origin of the Term 'Obeah' in Barbados and the Anglophone Caribbean." *Slavery & Abolition* 22, no. 2 (2001): 87–100.

Herskovits, Melville J. "Review of *Black Roadways*, by Martha Warren Beckwith." *Journal of American Folklore* 43 (1930): 332–338.

Herskovits, Melville J., and Frances S. Herskovits. *Rebel Destiny: Among the Bush Negroes of Dutch Guiana.* New York: McGraw-Hill, 1934. Reprint, Freeport, N.Y.: Books for Libraries Press, 1971.

Hurault, Jean. *Les Noirs Réfugiés Boni de la Guyane française.* Dakar, Senegal: IFAN, 1961.

KENNETH M. BILBY (2005)

OBLATE SISTERS OF PROVIDENCE

■ ■ ■

The Oblate Sisters of Providence, an order of black nuns, pioneered in the area of black Catholic education in America. The order was founded in Baltimore in 1828 by a group of free women of color who had fled the turmoil of slave insurrections on the French island colony of San Domingo. Elizabeth Lange, one of the order's founding members, had already been involved in educating black children in Baltimore when she was approached by a local priest with the idea of founding a "religious society of virgins and widows of color." Three other Haitian women joined Lange in the formation of the community, and the four took their vows as sisters on July 2, 1829. Lange served as the order's first mother superior. The Oblates' chapel, built in 1836, became an important center for worship among black Catholics in Baltimore. There, members of the black Catholic community could be baptized, married, confirmed, and buried.

Although tuition and boarding fees were charged at St. Frances Academy, the Oblates' school, the sisters made a regular practice of caring for and educating homeless and orphaned children. Non-Catholic children were also accepted as students. The Oblates taught both academic and trade subjects. Despite frequent difficulties, the Oblates were ever expanding. Their own numbers grew and the order drew African-American women in addition to women from San Domingo. The order of the Oblate Sisters of Providence is still in existence, and members of the order are at the forefront of leadership of black nuns in America. St. Frances Academy, the original school, continues to operate as well.

See also Catholicism in the Americas

■ ■ *Bibliography*

Gerdes, Sister M. Reginald, O.S.P. "To Educate and Evangelize: Black Catholic Schools of the Oblate Sisters of Providence (1828–1880)." *U.S. Catholic Historian* 7 (spring/summer 1988): 183–199.

Sherwood, Grace H. *Oblates' Hundred and One Years*. New York: Macmillan, 1930.

JUDITH WEISENFELD (1996)

ODETTA (GORDON, ODETTA HOLMES FELIOUS)

DECEMBER 31, 1930

╍╍╍

Born in Birmingham, Alabama, folk singer Odetta—as she is invariably known—grew up in Los Angeles, where her family moved when she was six. By the age of thirteen she was studying piano and singing. She also taught herself to play the guitar. She studied classical music and musical theater at Los Angeles City College and performed in a 1949 production of *Finian's Rainbow* in San Francisco. In the early 1950s Odetta, with her rich contralto voice, emerged as an important figure on the San Francisco and New York folk music scenes. With the encouragement of Harry Belafonte and Pete Seeger, she began performing and recording more widely, presenting an eclectic repertory of spirituals, slave songs, prison and work songs, folk ballads, Caribbean songs, and blues (*My Eyes Have Seen,* 1959; *Sometimes I Feel Like Cryin',* 1962). She also appeared in the film *Sanctuary* (1961).

In the early 1960s Odetta began to address political and social issues. She became an important advocate for civil rights and took part in the historic 1963 civil rights march in Washington, D.C. Throughout the 1960s and 1970s she continued to perform internationally and to record music (*Odetta Sings the Blues,* 1967). In 1974 she appeared in the television film *The Autobiography of Miss Jane Pittman*. A 1986 concert marking forty years of her

life as a performer was released as a live recording (*Movin' It On,* 1987).

Odetta has received acclaim throughout the world as one of the central figures of modern folk music. In 1998 she released a CD, *To Ella,* a tribute to her late friend Ella Fitzgerald. The following year, Odetta recorded *Blues Everywhere I Go*. With the release of *Looking for a Home* in 2001, Odetta returned to her roots to pay homage to a prominent influence, Leadbelly.

See also Belafonte, Harry ; Blues, The; Folk Music

■ ■ *Bibliography*

Armstrong, Don. "Odetta: A Citizen of the World." *Crisis* 90, no. 6 (June–July 1983): 51–52.

Greenberg, Mark. "Power and Beauty: The Legend of Odetta." *Sing Out* 36, no. 2 (August–October 1991): 2–8.

ROSITA M. SANDS (1996)
Updated by publisher 2005

OGBU, JOHN

1939
AUGUST 20, 2003

╍╍╍

John Uzo Ogbu, educational anthropologist, was born in the small village of Umudomi in the Onicha Government Area of Nigeria. Ogbu's scholarly career, spent entirely at the University of California at Berkeley, spanned over thirty years. He devoted most of his work to minority education and is best known for his research on black student achievement. His highly controversial work is as widely praised as it is criticized. For instance, Ogbu was the recipient of some of the most prestigious awards in education and anthropology and was named one of the four most influential figures in the history of North American education (Berube, 2000). Yet his work has frequently been criticized for downplaying the extent to which racism exists in school and society and for ignoring research that calls into question some of his basic conclusions.

Ogbu's main contribution is his application of cultural-ecological theory to explain why some minority groups are successful in school and why others are not. He is especially noted for theorizing that African Americans develop an oppositional cultural identity, or a sense of identity in opposition to white Americans, because of the injustices they encounter in society. In addition, he posits, African Americans develop an oppositional frame of reference, or a set of protective strategies to maintain their identities—and their distance from the dominant white culture. These identities, according to Ogbu, orient black students to view school success, for instance, as "acting white" and as affronts to their identities. Ogbu surmises that black children learn these attitudes and responses at an early age from their families and others in black communities with whom they form fictive kinships. For this reason, Ogbu often foreground cultural factors and gave only scant attention to system factors to explain black academic underperformance.

Ogbu conducted comparative studies in socially stratified societies in other parts of the world as well, including Israel, Japan, New Zealand, and Great Britain, and demonstrated that similar disparities existed in their schools. Other researchers have also confirmed the usefulness of Ogbu's theories in their research. Critics, however, fault several aspects of Ogbu's work, not the least significant being that he gave little attention to studies that show that black students enjoy widespread academic success, even under the most dire circumstances.

The passionate responses to Ogbu's work over the years speak both to its significance and to the scholar's own convictions. And, regardless of the merits of the praise or criticism of his work, Ogbu undeniably has left an indelible mark on the field of urban education as scholars in diverse disciplines continue to build on and critique his work.

See also Anthropology and Anthropologists; Education in the United States

■ ■ *Bibliography*

Berube, Maurice R. *Eminent Educators Studies in Intellectual Influence,* Westport, Conn.: Greenwood Press, 2000.

Ogbu, John. "Cultural-Ecological Influences on Minority Education." *Language Arts* 62, no. 8 (1985): 860–869.

Ogbu, John. "Understanding Cultural Diversity and Learning." *Educational Researcher* 21, no. 8 (1992): 5–14.

Perry, Theresa, Claude Steele, and Asa Hilliard. *Young, Gifted, and Black: Promoting High Achievement among African-American Students.* Boston: Beacon Press, 2003.

Valenzuela, Angela. *Subtractive Schooling: U.S.–Mexican Youth and the Politics of Caring.* Albany: State University of New York Press, 1999.

GARRETT ALBERT DUNCAN (2005)

O'LEARY, HAZEL ROLLINS

MAY 17, 1937

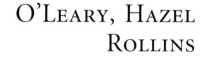

Fisk University President Hazel Rollins O'Leary, a former corporate executive and U.S. Secretary of Energy, was born and raised in the seaport city of Newport News, Virginia. She graduated from Fisk University in Nashville, Tennessee, in 1959 and earned a law degree from Rutgers in 1966. In New Jersey she began a career in law enforcement, serving as an assistant state attorney general and later as an Essex County prosecutor. In the early 1970s O'Leary moved to Washington, D.C., and became a partner at the accounting firm of Coopers and Lybrand. She later joined the Federal Energy Administration during the Ford presidency. She served in President Jimmy Carter's Energy Department as head of the Economic Regulatory Administration. While there, Rollins befriended John F. O'Leary, the deputy energy secretary. The couple married in 1980 and formed an energy consulting firm, O'Leary Associates. After John O'Leary died in 1987, Hazel O'Leary closed the consulting firm.

In 1989 O'Leary was named executive vice president for corporate affairs at the Minneapolis-based Northern States Power Company, one of the largest gas and electric utilities in the Midwest. She was in charge of environmental affairs, public relations, and lobbying. As an energy policy maker O'Leary advocated decreased dependence on oil and coal, promoted fuel conservation, and helped develop a program at Northern States Power to generate electricity with windmills. She was also a proponent of nuclear power, and her goals included the creation of safe storage methods for nuclear waste.

The policy of Northern States Power regarding the storage of nuclear waste earned O'Leary some criticism from environmental groups. In 1990 Northern States sought to build nuclear storage facilities at Prairie Island, Minnesota, next to the Mdewakanton Sioux Indian Reservation. After the Sioux protested, a judge prohibited an expansion of the nuclear waste site. O'Leary then drafted a compromise with regulators that permitted Northern States to open the storage facility on a reduced scale. Her background in energy regulation and her commitment to conservation attracted the attention of President Bill Clinton, who in 1993 offered O'Leary the post of secretary of energy. When confirmed, O'Leary became the first woman ever to hold that post.

O'Leary's tenure as energy secretary was troubled. Critics charged that she had sold access to her office by forcing companies to contribute to her favorite charity. Following her resignation on January 20, 1997, a special prosecutor was appointed to investigate the allegations. Shortly afterward, O'Leary again made headlines when she admitted in a deposition that watchdogs who made complaints in nuclear facilities were routinely harassed.

In 2000, African-American investment banking firm Blaylock & Partners of New York appointed O'Leary chief operating officer. She remained with the firm until 2002, while continuing to serve on the boards of various commercial and nonprofit organizations. O'Leary was named President of Fisk University in 2004.

See also Politics in the United States

■ ■ *Bibliography*

Haywood, Richette L. "Secretary O'Leary: Bright, Charming, Tough." *Ebony* 50, no. 4 (February 1995): 94–97.

Nixon, Will. "Bill and Al's Green Adventure." *Environmental Magazine* (May 1993).

JAMES BRADLEY (1996)
Updated by publisher 2005

OLYMPIANS

The modern Olympic Games have a history of over one hundred years. At an international sports conference held at the Sorbonne in Paris in late June 1894, a plan was advanced to reestablish in modern times a great sports festival, one that had been a major dimension of ancient Greek culture for more than a thousand years—the Olympic Games. An International Olympic Committee (IOC) was founded and two years later, in the spring of 1896, the first edition of the modern Olympics was organized in the host city of Athens, Greece. Following the plan of their *rénovateur*, the French Baron Pierre de Coubertin, the Olympics occurred every four years afterwards, except on the occasion of their interruption by the two World Wars. It was Coubertin's plan for the Olympics to be ambulatory, that is, to be hosted by major cities on all the globe's continents, those being, in somewhat peculiar European understanding, Europe, Asia, the Americas (North, Central, and South), Africa, and Australasia/Oceania. In this respect, Coubertin's goal has yet to be fully realized. An Olympic Games somewhere in Africa continues to be elusive, delaying the perspective of universal internationalism.

Though the summer Olympics have persisted since 1896, the winter Olympics date only to 1924, when their first edition was organized high in the French Alps in the village of Chamonix. The winter Olympics, too, moved around the world to various winter resort sites located largely in European countries, as well as in North America (the United States and Canada) and Asia (Japan). Climate and topography, of course, are major factors against Olympic Winter Games ever being staged in Africa, Australasia/Oceania, and most parts of Asia and South America. By 1994 both the summer and winter games had grown so astronomically in terms of the number of different sports, masses of competing athletes, an astoundingly immense cadre of judges and officials, necessary administrative functionaries, and media types from every corner of the world that organizing both games in the same year proved an almost impossible burden. Thus, the formula for presenting the winter games was changed so that they are now presented in even-numbered years between the quadrennial celebration of the summer games.

The original organizers of the modern Olympic Games envisioned a festival of sport as an expression of peace, brotherhood, and the advancement of physical culture among all peoples of the world, irrespective of ethnicity, religious attitude, or station in life. Be that as it may, the social and cultural context of many of the world's countries in the late nineteenth and early twentieth centuries ensured that the only athletes who entered the competitions were those who had the time and financial circumstance to devote toward training for achievement at a high performance level. For the most part, this situation tended to exclude blacks the world over. In other words, it became a question of opportunity.

Though opportunity for athletic achievement was devastatingly limited for Africans and African-descended peoples in the Americas, a large portion of whom lived and labored in the depths of economic distress in countries under the colonial rule of European powers, it was somewhat better for African-descended people residing in the United States. That is the major reason why the annals of black athletic achievement in early Olympic history were dominated by African Americans.

The first instances of African and African-descended people's participation in the sporting venues of the great international Olympic festival occurred in the third edition of the modern games, those celebrated for the first time outside Europe—in Saint Louis, Missouri. There, in the sweltering summer of 1904 amidst the grandeur and hoopla of the Saint Louis World's Fair, four black athletes competed: an American, a Cuban, and two South Africans. The African American was George C. Poage (1880–1962) of La Crosse, Wisconsin, who competed in four events, the 60- and 400-meter sprints, and the 200- and

Jesse Owens. *Called "the world's fastest human," Owens provided a memorable response to Adolf Hitler's racist ideology with four gold medals at the 1936 Olympics in Berlin.* UPI/CORBIS-BETTMANN. REPRODUCED BY PERMISSION.

400-meter hurdles (he placed third in both of the latter). The Cuban was Felix Carbajal, an enigmatic figure who trained for his long-distance races by running the length of Cuba and who financed his trip to Saint Louis by performing "sponsorship" exhibitions in the town squares of Cuban hamlets. Running in cut-off long trousers, he competed in the marathon, finishing a creditable fourth, which might have been a better performance had he not stopped along the route to eat green apples plucked from a tree, the results of which gave him stomach cramps. Two black South African Tswana tribesmen, masquerading as Zulu warriors in the Saint Louis Fair's Boer War battle reenactment exhibition, also competed in the Olympic marathon. Len Tua and Jan Mashiani, former Boer War dispatch runners proclaimed to be "the fleetest in the service," finished in ninth and twelfth place, respectively.

In 1908 the Olympic Games were celebrated in London, England. It was at that Olympic festival that the first black athlete to win a gold medal, in this case an American, became a matter of record. He was John Baxter Taylor (1882–1908), a University of Pennsylvania graduate. Taylor won his gold medal by running the third leg of the U.S. team's winning effort in the 1600-meter relay. African-American athletes did not compete again at the Olympics until 1924 in Paris. There, before the gaze of Pierre de Coubertin in his final appearance at the great festival that he had been primarily responsible for establishing, three black athletes competed in the colors of the United States. University of Michigan student William DeHart Hubbard became the first black athlete in Olympic history to win an individual gold medal. Hubbard won the long jump with a leap of 24.5 feet (about 7.47 meters), while African-American teammate Edward Gourdin won the silver medal. Earl Johnson, the third member of the black American contingent, won a bronze medal in the 10,000-meter cross-country race. Johnson's performance also ensured a silver medal for the Americans in the now-discontinued cross-country relay.

It would be eight years before African-American athletes once again ascended the victory podium at the Olympic Games, and the occasion began a remarkable record in Olympic history of black athletes the world over achieving gold medal results in track and field events. In 1932 at Los Angeles, Detroit's bespectacled Eddie Tolan (1908–1967) won gold in the 100 meters, earning him the distinction "world's fastest human." His teammate, Ralph Metcalfe, won the silver medal. Tolan also won the 200 meters; Metcalfe earned the bronze. After competing in the 1928 games in Amsterdam and placing seventh in the long jump, the University of Iowa's Edward Gordon won the gold medal in the long jump at Los Angeles by leaping a trifle beyond 25 feet (7.6 meters). It should not be lost to posterity that the African-Canadian Phil Edwards won bronze medals in the 800 meters in both the 1932 Los Angeles and 1936 Berlin Olympic festivals.

The most historically enduring episode of black Olympic achievement occurred in Berlin in 1936, at the so-called Nazi Olympics. They were the last Olympic Games celebrated before the outbreak of World War II. Though Jews were the chief victims of Nazi efforts to exclude "inferior races" from competing in "Hitler's Games," "negroes" came in for their share of derision. But, America's "Black Auxiliaries," a term coined by Joseph Goebbels's propaganda machine, performed so brilliantly that one of them, Jesse Owens, became the bona fide hero of the games, not only to all Americans, but to folks across the world, including many Germans of non-Nazi persuasion. Owens won four gold medals for first place finishes in the 100- and 200-meter dashes, the long jump, and the 400-meter relay. And Owens was not the entire story. Of ten American black athletes competing in track and field in Berlin, nine won medals, and their total medal count of eight gold, three silver, and two bronze outscored every national team present at the games. In fact, they outscored the medal total of their fifty-six white track and field teammates. The names John Woodruff (800 meters), Archie Williams (400 meters), Cornelius Johnson (high jump), and Ralph Metcalfe (400-meter relay), joined the name Jesse Owens etched into the Berlin stadium's gold medal victory scrolls.

Two black American women made the 1936 Olympic team and competed in Berlin. Though neither placed in their event (low hurdles), Louise Stokes and Anne Pickett became trailblazers for black women competing in future Olympic Games.

Following the conclusion of World War II, the Olympics resumed in London in 1948. These games proved to be a watershed Olympics for African-American participation and achievement. Historically black colleges, such as Tuskegee Institute and Tennessee State University, along with such organizations as the New York Mercury Club, promoted black women's competition in the 1930s. The fruits of such programs resulted in a dozen African-American women competing in track and field events in the 1948 games. Among them, Albany State College's Alice Coachman became the first female African American to win an Olympic gold medal when she won the high jump with an Olympic record of 5 feet 6 inches (about 1.68 meters). In fact, Coachman was the only woman on the American team to win a gold medal.

African-American men achieved an avalanche of gold at the London games. Baldwin-Wallace College's Harrison "Bones" Dillard, acknowledged as the world's best hurdler, failed to make the American team in the high hurdles when he inexplicably knocked over every hurdle and finished last in the qualifying event at the Olympic trials. He did, however, earn a place on the American team in the 100-meter dash and the 400-meter relay. In the 100-meter final, Dillard overtook fellow African American Barney Ewell to win in the record time of 10.3 seconds. African-Trinidadian Lloyd LaBeach finished third; Dillard, Ewell, and fellow African American Lorenzo Wright teamed with Mel Patton to win the 400-meter relay. Mal Whitfield, a black Army Air Force sergeant, won gold in the 800 meters in 1 minute 49.2 seconds, and Willie Steele leaped 25 feet 8 inches (about 7.8 meters) to win the long jump. In other sports Don Barksdale, UCLA's black basketball star, led the U.S. team to the gold medal in Olympic history's second basketball tournament, the inaugural occasion having resulted in an American gold medal in 1936. John Davis, a world-class weight lifter won the heavyweight gold medal by lifting a record total of 997.5 pounds (452.46 kilograms) in his three lifts (press, snatch, and the clean and jerk). In effect, the 1948 London games signaled to the world that African-American athletes, both men and women, would play prominent roles in Olympic achievement in the future.

For well over half a century, black athletes participating in the Olympics represented countries on the continent that Europeans refer to as "the Americas." This was particularly true, but certainly not exclusively, with reference to black athletes from the United States. Following World War II, however, from the disintegration of European colonial empires in Africa, particularly those located in sub-Saharan regions, newly independent countries arose, each embracing largely black populations filled with national pride and eagerness to join the modern world in a number of ways, including international sports. Partici-

The Jamaican bobsled team. *From left, Wayne Thomas, Nelson Stoke, Winston Watt, and pilot Dudley Stokes practice at a training facility in Riesa, Germany, prior to the 1998 winter Olympics at Nagano, Japan.* AP/WIDE WORLD PHOTOS.

pation in the Olympic Games was a natural extension of such aspirations. Starting in 1960 and continuing into the twenty-first century, African athletes have made their mark in those Olympic track events normally classified as "distance running." This history commenced with Ethiopian Abebe Bikila's marathon victories at Rome in 1960 and Tokyo in 1964, and Kenyan Kip Keino's sensational 1,500 meters upset of America's Jim Ryun at Mexico City in 1968. Keeping pace with them in the 1950s and 1960s in Olympic sprint and field events, as well as in boxing and basketball, were scores of African-American gold medalists, among the most notable of which were: boxer Floyd Patterson (Helsinki, 1952); hurdler Lee Calhoun, decathlete Milt Campbell, and basketball players Bill Russell and K. C. Jones (Melbourne, 1956); sprinter Wilma Rudolph, decathlete Rafer Johnson, and basketball player Oscar Robertson (Rome, 1960); sprinters Bob Hayes and

Wyomia Tyus, boxers Cassius Clay (Muhammad Ali) and Joe Frazier, and basketball player Walt Hazzard (Tokyo, 1964); and world-record-setting long jumper Bob Beamon, sprinters James Hines, Tommie Smith, and Lee Evans, and boxer George Foreman (Mexico City, 1968).

The post–World War II fracture of European colonial empires in Africa also played a role in the ultimate exclusion from the modern Olympic Movement of South Africa, a country that, until the 1990s, practiced apartheid. Though black South African individuals were allowed to indulge in sports in a segregated context, South Africa's Olympic teams were reserved for whites. This, of course, flew in the face of the IOC's *Olympic Charter* dictum, which maintained that no athlete be denied Olympic Games participation "on the grounds of race, religion, politics, or otherwise." There were many in the world, especially other African countries and the Soviet Union, along with marginalized racial groups in Western industrial nations, particularly African Americans in the United States, who rose to argue against South Africa remaining in the Olympic movement. African countries registered their protest by threatening to boycott the 1964 and 1968 games if South Africa was allowed to participate on the basis of its all-white team. As a result of such pressure, South Africa's 1964 Olympic Games invitation was withdrawn by its Tokyo hosts, as was its invitation to the 1968 Mexico City games. Finally, in 1970 South Africa was dismissed from its membership in the modern Olympic movement.

At the 1968 Mexico City games black athletes from the United States (Tommie Smith, Jon Carlos, Vince Matthews, Lawrence James, Ron Freeman, and Lee Evans), collectively galvanized by African-American activist Harry Edwards, registered their personal protests against the social, civil, and economic injustices experienced by blacks living in America by invoking personal demonstrations of disgust at Olympic ceremonies held commensurate with their medal awards. In that regard, one of the most enduring Olympic portraits in history is that of Tommie Smith and Jon Carlos standing on the victory podium with heads bowed and black-gloved fists held defiantly aloft.

In the face of severe global economic sanctions against South Africa for its continuance of apartheid, the Dutch-Boer political power that held it firmly in place finally crumbled in the early 1990s, leading to dissolution of the world-condemned phenomenon and an installation of Nelson Mandela as president of a new South Africa. Very rapidly, sports in growing context became "nonracial," leading to an integrated South African team in time for the Barcelona Olympics in 1992. Before that, in the 1970s and 1980s, increasing numbers of black participants in the Olympic Games occurred, reaching its all-time high in 1984, at which time the U.S. team listed twenty-one African-American female competitors, a number eclipsed almost twofold by their male counterparts. Noteworthy between 1972 and 1990 were the contributions made to American Olympic teams by African-American gold medal athletes, especially in track and field and boxing: Ray Seales for boxing and Rodney Milburn in hurdles (Munich, 1972); Edwin Moses for intermediate hurdles and "Sugar" Ray Leonard and Leon Spinks for boxing (Montreal, 1976); Carl Lewis in the 100-, 200-, and 400-meter races and the long jump and Tyrell Biggs for boxing (Los Angeles, 1984); Andrew Maynard for boxing, Florence Griffith Joyner in 100- and 200-meter races and the 400-meter relay, and Jackie Joyner Kersee in the heptathlon (Seoul, 1988).

Black athletic success during the period was not limited to U.S. citizens. Outstanding was African-Cuban Alber-

to Juantarena who won both the 400 and 800 meters in 1976 at Montreal, and African-Canadian Ben Johnson who won the 100 meters in 1988 at Seoul and set a new world record of 9.73 seconds to become the "world's fastest human," only to have his title stripped after testing positive for performance-enhancing drugs. In the 1970s and beyond, many athletes, black and white alike, questioned each other on the pharmaceutical issue. African-Canadian Donovan Bailey won the 100 meters in 1996 at Atlanta to partially vindicate old training comrade Ben Johnson, by then thoroughly disgraced. Finally, Cuban heavyweight boxing dominance, exhibited by three successive gold medals won by Teofilo Stevenson (1984, 1988, 1992), stands unparalleled in the annals of Olympic pugilism.

The first century of Olympic history closed with an indelible record of achievement by black athletes from the Americas. As the Olympics entered their second century of history, the results in 2000 at Sydney and 2004 at Athens confirmed what the second half of the twentieth century had demonstrated: black athletes from African countries, from the Americas, and expatriates from Africa residing in European countries would dominate gold medal performances in track and field events, basketball, and boxing. Evident, too, was the fact that in some Olympic events not traditionally within the province of black athletic expertise—judo, wrestling, and gymnastics, for instance, and even winter sports such as bobsledding—participation by black athletes was becoming more and more common.

See also Basketball; Boxing; Owens, Jesse; Sports

■ ■ *Bibliography*

Bunch, Lonnie G., and Louie Robinson. *The Black Olympians: 1904–1984.* Los Angeles: California Afro-American Museum, 1984.

Edwards, Harry. *The Revolt of the Black Athlete.* New York: Free Press, 1969.

Page, James A. *Black Olympian Medalists.* Englewood, Colo.: Libraries Unlimited, 1991.

Plowden, Martha Ward. *Olympic Black Women.* Gretna, La.: Pelican, 1996.

Orr, Jack. *The Black Athlete: His Story in American History.* New York: Lion Press, 1969.

Wallechinsky, David. *The Complete Book of the Olympic Games.* New York: Penguin, 2000.

ROBERT K. BARNEY (2005)

OPERA

Since its inception in early seventeenth-century Florence, Italy, opera has been the dominant form of staged musical storytelling in the European musical tradition. During the last two centuries of its evolution, African Americans and persons of African descent have played an important role in its development as an art form.

African settings and characters were often included in the plots of early opera. Indeed, the first important opera, Claudio Monteverdi's *Orfeo* (1607), included a female Moor in the finale. Cleopatra was a common role in early opera, most notably in George Frideric Handel's *Giulio Cesare* (1724), as was the Carthaginian princess Dido in Henry Purcell's *Dido and Aeneas* (1689), in numerous settings of *Didone Abbandonata* (as in Tommaso Albinoni's of 1725), and in later opera such as Hector Berlioz's *Les Troyens* (1858). Other operas from the standard repertory with an African setting or characters include Mozart's *Die Zauberflöte* (1791), Gioacchino Rossini's *L'Italiana in Algeri* (1813), Giacomo Meyerbeer's *L'africaine* (1865), and Giuseppe Verdi's *Aida* (1865) and *Otello* (1889).

African Americans have been active in opera as performers and singers since the early nineteenth century. In nineteenth-century America the boundaries between high and low musical cultures were not as rigid as they would later become. Like many of their contemporaries, black and white, trained singers often performed in minstrel and vaudeville shows, as well as in the concert hall or opera house. One of the first prominent African-American operatic singers was Elizabeth Taylor Greenfield. Born a slave in Mississippi but raised free in Philadelphia, Greenfield was known as "the Black Swan" and performed with a troupe of African-American opera singers in the United States, Canada, and England throughout the 1850s and 1860s. In 1854 Greenfield sang with tenor Thomas J. Bowes (1836–c. 1885), whom critics called "the American Mario" or "the colored Mario," after Italian opera star Conte di Candia Mario. Bowers, possibly the greatest American male singer of the period, chose "Mario" as his preferred stage name and refused to sing to segregated audiences or in concert halls from which African Americans were barred. Opera selections were also included in the program of the multitalented Luca family, a father and four sons who performed as vocalists, pianists, and violinists. After the deaths of the father, Alexander C. Luca, and one brother, tenor Simeon G. Luca, the three remaining brothers joined with the Hutchinsons, a famous abolitionist singing family, for a concert tour of the Midwest that advertised a program of "Humor, Sentiment, and Opera!" In the late 1860s and 1870s, the two Hyers sisters, Anna

Celebrated mezzo-soprano opera singer Denyce Graves as Dalila in the production of Camille Saint-Saëns's Samson et Dalila, *Metropolitan Opera House, New York City, 2005.* © JACK VARTOOGIAN/FRONTROWPHOTOS

Madah and Emma Louise, achieved renown for concerts featuring scenes from such operas as Verdi's *Il Trovatore* and *La Traviata*, and Gaetano Donizetti's *Lucia di Lammermoor*. Another prominent singer, soprano Marie Selika Smith (c. 1849–1937), who named herself Selika after the African princess in *L'africaine*, performed in the United States and Germany during the 1870s and 1880s. One of the most important performers of this period was Sissieretta Joyner Jones, known as "the Black Patti"—after the great soprano Adelina Patti—whose celebrity was established in 1892 when she was asked to give a recital at the White House for President Benjamin Harrison. In 1896 Jones formed her own troupe, the Black Patti Troubadors, which featured her in operatic excerpts.

African Americans were barred from performing in major opera houses in the United States. As a result, many well-qualified singers either pursued careers in Europe or confined their performances to recitals and the concert stage. Newspapers and magazines from the late nineteenth century stated that black artists were frequently exploited by their white managers, who garnered their financial support from both the white and black communities. Generally, African-American singers could count on two or three years of concertizing before white audiences ceased to find them novel or exotic, which forced them to turn to studio teaching as a means of making a living. There were two notable exceptions to this rule: Jones, "the Black Patti," who, in founding her own troupe, extended her singing career by fifteen years, and Nellie Brown Mitchell (1845–1924), who debuted in New York and Boston in the 1870s and, after becoming the leading soprano for James Bergen's Star Concert Company, created the Nellie Brown Mitchell Concert Company in Boston in 1886. One of Mitchell's unusual achievements was her staging of a juvenile operetta called *Laila, the Fairy Queen*, with an ensemble of fifty African-American girls ages five to fifteen, at a Boston musical festival in 1876. Mitchell's concert company lasted approximately ten years, after which Mitchell turned to private teaching in the mid-1890s.

The first known African-American opera company was the Colored American Opera Company of Philadelphia and Washington, D.C., which staged Julius Eichberg's *Doctor of Alcantara* for enthusiastic audiences in both cities in 1873 and returned in 1879 with performances of Gilbert and Sullivan's *H.M.S. Pinafore*. Twelve years later Theodore Drury (1867–c. 1943), a highly trained tenor and impresario, founded his own company. Drury began by presenting operatic selections and expanded the company's repertory to include full operas at the turn of the century. From 1900 to 1910, as well as sporadically into the 1930s, the Theodore Drury Opera Company appeared in New York, Boston, Providence, and Philadelphia. Works performed included Georges Bizet's *Carmen*, Charles Gounod's *Faust*, Verdi's *Aida*, Pietro Mascagni's *Cavalleria Rusticana*, and Ruggiero Leoncavallo's *I Pagliacci*. The productions were advertised as social affairs attended by prominent social figures and concluded with supper and dancing to Walter F. Craig's orchestra.

One unique contribution that African-American singers made to vocal literature was the development of the concert spiritual, a fusion of melodies derived from African-American religious chanting with the harmonies of the European art song. For many African-American vocalists, the first exposure to classical singing occurred in church or while listening to a recital of sacred music and

Opera Supporter

Mary Cardwell Dawson (February 14, 1894–March 19, 1962) was a teacher of voice, a pianist, and the founder and director of the National Negro Opera Company. She grew up in Pittsburgh, Pennsylvania, her family having moved there from Meridian, North Carolina, early in her life. Her musical training included study at the New England Conservatory, in Boston, and at the Chicago Musical College. She taught voice, at first in a private studio and later at the Cardwell School of Music, which she established in Pittsburgh in 1927. In the 1930s, she toured as director of the Cardwell Dawson Choir, a prize-winning organization that made appearances at the Century of Progress Exposition in Chicago and at the New York World's Fair. Dawson served as president of the National Association of Negro Musicians from 1939 to 1941.

After presenting *Aida* at a National Association of Negro Musicians convention in the summer of 1941, Dawson officially launched her National Negro Opera Company at Pittsburgh in the following October with a production of the same opera. The star was La Julia Rhea, one of many black singers who found with this company an otherwise unavailable opportunity to sing opera in the United States. Other cast members were Minto Cato, Carol Brice, Robert McFerrin, and Lillian Evanti. During its twenty-one years, the company had a difficult existence financially, but it mounted productions in Pittsburgh, Washington, D.C., New York, Chicago, and Philadelphia. The Washington production of *La Traviata* starring Lillian Evanti drew audiences totaling more than thirty thousand and was favorably reviewed. Dawson spent her final years in Washington, D.C.

DORIS EVANS MCGINTY

spirituals. Because they were not allowed on the opera stage, many classically trained African-American singers became primarily known as recitalists, and their repertories frequently included spirituals as well as European art songs and arias. One of the first recitalists to come to prominence in the twentieth century was the tenor Roland Hayes. Among those who followed in his path was contralto Marian Anderson. Initially barred from the operatic stage in the United States, Anderson became a peerless recitalist with a wide repertory of arias, songs, and spirituals. The most dramatic moment in her career occurred in 1939, when, after being barred from performing in a Washington, D.C., concert hall, Anderson gave an outdoor recital—introduced by Secretary of the Interior Harold Ickes—on the steps of the Lincoln Memorial. Nevertheless, major opera houses remained inaccessible to African Americans for another fifteen years. Other prominent African-American recitalists of the middle decades of this century included sopranos Inez Matthews (1917–1950), Ellabelle Davis (1907–1960), and Dorothy Maynor. Catherine Yarborough (1903–1986) appeared in the United States only in musical comedy but sang the role of Aida in Europe, where she was known as Caterina Jarboro. In the next generation, leading singers included Muriel Rahn (1911–1961), Carol Brice (1918–1985), and contralto Louise Parker (1926–1986), a favorite of both Leopold Stokowski and Paul Hindemith.

Outside the concert hall, African-American singers were often confined to operatic roles in works that had all-black casts such as Virgil Thomson's *Four Saints in Three Acts* (1933) and George Gershwin's *Porgy and Bess* (1935) or "ebony" versions of *Carmen* and other opera classics. Bass Paul Robeson and baritones Jules Bledsoe and William Warfield (1920–), each used the character of Joe in Jerome Kern's *Show Boat* (1927) to launch their careers. Todd Duncan and Donnie Ray Albert (1950–) also began by singing the role of Porgy in the Gershwin opera. Other singers, such as Lawrence Winters (1915–1965) and Charles Holland (1910–1987), the first black principal to sing at the Paris Opera (he debuted there in *Aida* in 1954), performed extensively in Europe.

Although some major companies, such as the New York City Opera, cast African Americans as early as the 1940s, the Metropolitan Opera in New York City did not drop its color line until 1955, when Marian Anderson sang Ulrica (traditionally a dark-skinned role) in Verdi's *Un Ballo in Maschera*. Louis Gruenberg's *Emperor Jones*, which calls for a character of African descent in the title role, had premiered at the Met in 1933; at the time, white baritone Lawrence Tibbett was cast over Paul Robeson, who was an obvious candidate for the part. Anderson's debut at the Met was soon followed by the appearances of baritone Robert McFerrin Sr., and coloratura soprano Mattiwilda Dobbs. In 1954 Dobbs, who had been signed

two years earlier by La Scala in Milan, Italy, performed in Richard Strauss's *Ariadne auf Naxos* at New York's Town Hall before making her debut at the San Francisco Opera in 1955 and at the Met in 1956, where she sang Gilda in Verdi's *Rigoletto*. In 1958 soprano Gloria Davy (1936–) became the first African American to sing the role of Aida at the Met.

The engagement of African-American operatic singers without any limitation to a select number of traditionally dark-skinned roles did not fully occur with major opera companies before the 1960s. The career of Mississippi-born Leontyne Price marks the acceptance of the African-American diva by the operatic establishment in the United States. In 1955 Price's televised performance of the title role in Giacomo Puccini's *Tosca* caused a sensation; she debuted at the Met six years later, after having established a successful career in Europe. In 1966, Price opened the new Metropolitan Opera House at New York's Lincoln Center in a role especially written for her in the world premiere of Samuel Barber's *Antony and Cleopatra*. (The production was choreographed by Alvin Ailey.) From 1955 to 1965 ten African-American singers debuted at the Met: Price, Anderson, McFerrin, Davy, Dobbs, Grace Bumbry (1937–), George Shirley (1934–), Martina Arroyo (1939–), Felicia Weathers, and Reri Grist (1932–), who had appeared in the original cast of Leonard Bernstein's *West Side Story* in 1957. Other black singers who came to prominence in the 1950s and 1960s were Margaret Tynes (1929–), Betty Allen (1930–), Hilda Harris (1936–), Gwendolyn Killebrew (1942–), Esther Hinds (1943–), Faye Robinson (1943–), and Shirley Verrett.

The 1970s and 1980s witnessed the recognition of numerous African-American divas, among them Carmen Balthrop (1948–), Barbara Hendricks (1938–), Leona Mitchell (1949–), Roberta Alexander (1949–), and Harolyn Blackwell. The two most prominent African-American women singing in opera in the 1980s and early 1990s were soprano Kathleen Battle and dramatic soprano Jessye Norman. Battle, who rose to fame after starring in a 1975 production of Scott Joplin's *Treemonisha* on Broadway, debuted at the Met as the Shepherd in Richard Wagner's *Tannhäuser* in 1978; Norman sang in the major opera houses of Europe throughout the 1970s before her first appearance at the Met in Berlioz' *Les Troyens* in 1983. In 1991 the two singers performed together in a well-received concert of spirituals at New York City's Carnegie Hall.

African American mezzo-soprano Denyce Graves (1964–) has also been hailed as one of opera's most electrifying performers. Best known for sultry stage performances including the title role in Bizet's *Carmen*, with which she established her name, and Camille Saint-Saëns'

Samson et Dalila, Graves enjoyed a meteoric rise in the 1990s.

Throughout the history of opera in the United States, male African-American singers have not enjoyed the same success as their female counterparts. Many believe that this can be attributed to a reluctance to have black male singers in mixed-race casting. Among those who have been active in opera since the 1970s are Seth McCoy (1928–), Andrew Frierson (1927–), and McHenry Boatwright (1928–1994). Musical theater has been the dominant genre for Rawn Spearman (1924–), while Thomas Carey (1931–) and Eugene Holmes (1934–) were primarily active in Europe. Bass-baritone Simon Estes, the first black male singer to star in the Wagner Festival at Bayreuth, Germany, also made his name in Europe in the 1970s before debuting at the Met in 1981. Two singers whose promising careers were cut short, respectively by cancer and AIDS, were baritones Ben Holt (1955–1989) and Bruce Hubbard (1952–1991). Among the leading singers of the current generation are Kevin Short (1960–), Antonio Green (1966–), and Vinson Cole (1950–).

By the beginning of the twentieth century, African Americans had also begun to compose opera, although the lack of financial support frequently made it impossible for their works to be staged. The first significant African-American composer was Harry Lawrence Freeman, who wrote fourteen grand-style operas including *The Octoroon* (1904), *Voodoo* (1911), and the early jazz opera *The Flapper* (1929). In addition to being one of the first African Americans to conduct a symphony orchestra in a rendering of his own work—*O Sing a New Song,* presented in Minnesota in 1907—Freeman founded the Freeman School of Music in 1911, the Freeman School of Grand Opera in 1923, and the Negro Opera Company in 1920. Among Freeman's contemporaries was Clarence Cameron White, whose opera *Ouanga,* set in Haiti in the early 1800s, was first presented in a concert version in New York City at the New School for Social Research in 1941. The opera was not staged until 1959, when it was performed at the Central High School Auditorium in South Bend, Indiana. Subsequently, it had a successful run with the Dra-Mu Opera Company in Philadelphia. Ragtime composer Scott Joplin never saw a performance of his three-act opera *Treemonisha* (1911) in his lifetime, although his first opera, *A Guest of Honor,* was staged in St. Louis in 1903 (its score is now lost). One of the most respected and prolific composers of the mid-twentieth century was William Grant Still, who collaborated with his wife, librettist Verna Arvey, and whose works include *Troubled Island* (1938)—which takes as its subject the Haitian revolt at the turn of the nineteenth century—*Blue Steel* (1935), *A Bayou Legend*

(1941), *A Southern Interlude* (1942), and *Highway No. 1, USA* (1963). Ulysses Simpson Kay (1917–) came to prominence in the late 1950s with *The Juggler of Our Lady* (1956), which was followed by such works as *The Capitoline Venus* (1971), *Jubilee* (1976), and *Frederick Douglass* (1986). In recent years two major operas have been composed by Anthony Davis, the founder of the instrumental group Episteme. Davis's *X (The Life and Times of Malcolm X)* (libretto by Thulani Davis) premiered at the New York City Opera in 1986; *Under the Double Moon,* with a libretto by Deborah Atherton, premiered at the Opera Theatre in St. Louis in 1989. In 1992 Davis's *Tania,* about the kidnapping and subsequent exploits of newspaper heiress Patricia Hearst, was premiered in Philadelphia by the American Music Theater Festival.

The development of African-American operatic talent has been furthered by the establishment of educational programs and opera companies for aspiring singers. Fisk University, Hampton University, Morgan State University, Virginia State University, and Wilberforce College, all traditionally black schools, have produced major operatic talent. By the mid-twentieth century, several African-American opera companies emerged, including the Imperial Opera Company (1930), the National Negro Opera Company (1941), the Dra-Mu Opera Company (1945), and the Harlem Opera Company (c. 1950). The 1970s witnessed a flourishing of African-American productions with the establishment of two major companies, Opera/South (1970) and the National Ebony Opera (1974), founded specifically to create professional opportunities for African-American performers, writers, conductors, and technicians. In addition to European grand opera, Opera/South has produced such works as William Grant Still's *Highway No. 1, USA* and *A Bayou Legend* (which, though written in 1941, had its world premiere in 1974), and Ulysses Kay's *Jubilee* and *The Juggler of Our Lady.*

As opera has become more accessible to African-American artists, major opera houses have produced new works and also revived lost or neglected works by African-American composers. Leroy Jenkins's *The Mother of Three Sons* premiered at the New York City Opera in 1991. In 1993, Duke Ellington's (1899–1974) unfinished opera, *Queenie Pie,* was performed for the first time at the Brooklyn Academy of Music. The Lyric Opera of Chicago and the American Music Theater Festival in Philadelphia have jointly commissioned a new opera by Anthony Davis, *Amistad,* telling the story of the 1839 capture of the eponymous slave ship and the liberation of its captors. *Amistad* was premiered during the 1997–1998 season. African-American singers are widely recognized both for their artistic excellence and popular appeal. However, male performers continue to claim that they are not cast as readily as women in European opera. African-American composers continue to encounter resistance to works about African-American subjects. "The opera world is looking for fresh blood," observed librettist Thulani Davis. "Does a black composer have the same shot? I hope the answer is yes."

Jessye Norman became the youngest recipient of the United States Kennedy Center Honors in 1997. Willie Anthony Waters became the first African American to serve as an artistic director of a major opera company when he took over the Connecticut Opera Association in 1999.

See also Anderson, Marian; Price, Mary Violet Leontyne; Robeson, Paul

■■ *Bibliography*

Duncan, John. "Negro Composers of Opera." *Negro History Bulletin* (January 1966): 79–80, 93.

Heymont, George. "Blacks in Opera." *Ebony* (November 1981): 32–36.

Kornick, Rebecca Hodell. *Recent American Opera: A Production Guide.* New York: Columbia University Press, 1991.

Ploski, Harry A., and James Williams, eds. *The Negro Almanac.* New York: Bellwether, 1989.

Rosen, Carole. *Opera.* Poole, Dorset, UK: Blandford, 1983.

Southern, Eileen. *The Music of Black Americans: A History.* New York: Norton, 1983.

Trotter, James M. *Music and Some Highly Musical People.* Boston: Lee and Shepard, 1881.

DOMINIQUE-RENÉ DE LERMA (1996)
Updated by publisher 2005

OPERATION DESERT STORM

See Military Experience, African-American

OPERATION PUSH (PEOPLE UNITED TO SERVE HUMANITY)

▪▪▪

Founded in late 1971 by the Reverend Jesse Jackson, Chicago-based Operation PUSH has always advocated a program demanding greater support of black-owned or -operated businesses and strongly encouraging corporations to hire more minority employees. With Jackson as its charismatic leader, Operation PUSH organized boycotts of companies unwilling to make agreements requiring increased minority hiring; combining his oratorical skills and national influence, Jackson was capable of effectively threatening the business of recalcitrant corporations. Originally called People United to Save Humanity, Operation PUSH grew out of, and originally had an agenda very similar to, the Southern Christian Leadership Conference's Operation Breadbasket, which Jackson headed until 1971.

One of its initiatives, PUSH for Excellence, or PUSH/EXCEL, was another plan inspired by Jackson to empower African Americans, this time through education. In the later 1970s PUSH/EXCEL received much national attention and substantial amounts of federal and private aid to establish programs to help minority schoolchildren. Several years later, auditors' reports concluded that the organization lacked concrete goals and an effective administrative structure. While it was scaled down considerably, PUSH/EXCEL continued to attempt to make schooling for black children a more enriching experience.

When Jackson left Operation PUSH in 1983 to lead his presidential campaign, the organization foundered. By the end of the 1980s it was financially insecure after a poorly supported boycott of the sporting goods company Nike left it deeply in debt. In early 1991 PUSH was forced to lay off temporarily all twelve of its salaried workers. After a plea from Jackson, prominent African Americans, black businesses, and community groups cooperated to raise the funds necessary to return Operation PUSH to a more sound financial footing.

Although he no longer held an official leadership position, Jackson remained a spokesman and adviser for Operation PUSH. In 1991 he announced a political agenda for Operation PUSH that was similar to the campaigns of the early 1980s but that incorporated pressing new concerns, such as the AIDS crisis and the problem of Haitian refugees. Operation PUSH continued to be a vocal advocate of black enterprise and entrepreneurs and continued to urge African-American youths to stay in school and not to use drugs or alcohol. In 1993 Jackson announced an Operation PUSH campaign to "save the children" of Chicago. This was part of a larger effort on the part of progressive black organizations to curb urban violence and increase opportunities for African-American children. Other initiatives forwarded by PUSH in the 1990s included cultural sensitivity training for police officers and proposals that youthful first-time criminal offenders be counseled by local ministers.

In 1996 Operation PUSH merged with the National Rainbow Coalition and is now known as the Rainbow/ PUSH Coalition. The new organization's mandate remains similar to that of the original Operation PUSH; among other things it seeks social and economic justice and empowerment, advocates increased voter registration, and attempts to influence international trade and foreign policy. The Rev. Jesse Jackson Sr. remains the group's president.

See also Jackson, Jesse; Southern Christian Leadership Conference (SCLC)

■ ■ *Bibliography*

Frady, Marshall. *Jesse: The Life and Pilgrimage of Jesse Jackson.* New York: Random House, 1996.

House, Ernest R. *Jesse Jackson and the Politics of Charisma: The Rise and Fall of the PUSH/Excel Program.* Boulder, Colo.: Westview Press, 1988.

Rainbow/PUSH Coalition home page. Available from <http://www.rainbowpush.org>.

Reynolds, Barbara. *Jesse Jackson: The Man, the Movement, the Myth.* Chicago: Nelson-Hall, 1975.

JOHN C. STONER (1996)
Updated bibliography

OPPORTUNITY: JOURNAL OF NEGRO LIFE

Opportunity was the official organ of the National Urban League; the first issue appeared in January 1923. Under the editorship of sociologist Charles Spurgeon Johnson, the journal tried to approach African-American life though a self-consciously "scientific" point of view, in contrast to the supposedly subjective emphasis of the National Association for the Advancement of Colored People journal *Crisis* and its editor, W. E. B. Du Bois.

Opportunity's circulation grew from four thousand in 1923 to eleven thousand in 1927. Despite its supposed concentration on sociology, during the 1920s the magazine played an important role in encouraging young writers and artists of the Harlem Renaissance. It sponsored yearly literary contests and award dinners at which writers such as Langston Hughes and Countee Cullen met contacts who would eventually publish their work. Among early contributors to *Opportunity* were James Weldon Johnson, Claude McKay, Angelina Weld Grimké, Gwendolyn Bennett, and Sterling Brown.

The era of optimism and creative ferment at *Opportunity* subsided somewhat with the departure of Johnson in 1929. He was succeeded by Elmer A. Carter, who published much poetry and fiction but emphasized the original vision of *Opportunity* as a sociological journal. The 1930s saw dissent on the editorial board concerning the role of the magazine. The declining circulation worried some, who argued that *Opportunity* should be a popular magazine. Others thought that it should serve mainly as the house organ of the National Urban League. The board never decided on a single policy, so *Opportunity* served a variety of purposes throughout the 1930s, printing news, economic and social criticism, poetry, short stories, and articles about the Urban League. Literary criticism flourished in regular contributions by Alain Locke and Sterling Brown. Carter even attempted in 1931 to revive the literary contests, which had ended in 1928. But the Great Depression strained *Opportunity*'s ability to publish, as private donations shriveled up and as individual subscriptions were harder to sell.

The 1940s were no easier, as wartime rationing limited paper and printing supplies. In an April 1942 editorial, Carter described the journal's dire financial straits and appealed for additional funds from its readers. Carter resigned later that year and was replaced by Madeline Aldridge. *Opportunity* began publishing on a quarterly basis in January 1943. Its content and style did not change significantly but did focus on African Americans' perceptions of the war. Despite the financial difficulties the journal faced, it remained an important forum for wartime discussions of racial equality and freedom and emerged as a champion of integration. After World War II *Opportunity* published fewer literary pieces, as the rise of periodicals dedicated to black artistic advancement provided another "proving ground" for young talent. Dutton Ferguson assumed editorship in 1947. *Opportunity*, however, had seen its best days. Its last issue appeared in 1949.

See also *Crisis, The*; Harlem Renaissance; Johnson, Charles Spurgeon; National Urban League; Sociology

■ ■ *Bibliography*

Daniel, Walter C. *Black Journals of the United States.* Westport, Conn.: Greenwood Press, 1982.

Johnson, Abby Arthur, and Ronald Mayberry Johnson. *Propaganda and Aesthetics: The Literary Politics of Afro-American Magazines in the Twentieth Century.* Amherst: University of Massachusetts Press, 1979.

ELIZABETH MUTHER (1996)

ORGANIZATION OF BLACK AMERICAN CULTURE

See OBAC Writers' Workshop

ORIGINS OF AFRICAN AMERICANS

See Ethnic Origins

ORISHA

African traditional religions became the foundation of new religions created out of the experience of Africans in the Americas. Variously called Vodou (Haiti), Santería (Cuba), Candomblé (Brazil), and Orisha (Trinidad), these religions developed in response to the physical, social, and spiritual oppression of slavery and its aftermath. They are as much systems of resistance, retention, and creative adaptation as they are religions. Their persistence and progress into the twenty-first century represent an account of the irrepressible will of the human spirit in the story of Africans in the diaspora.

The term *orisha* refers to the deities of the Yoruba pantheon. According to Bolaji Idowu (1994), the word is a composite of two ideas: *ori,* "head," and *se,* "source," suggesting the relationship between the deities and God Almighty, Olodumare, from whence they came. The strength of this Yoruba foundation/tradition among the religions of the Americas is the result in part of: (1) the numerical concentration of Yorubas in the countries mentioned; (2) their relatively late arrival (end of the eighteenth to early nineteenth centuries) to the Americas; and (3) the sophisticated and resilient structure of their religious beliefs.

Religion became the source and symbol of political resistance—as the Haitian Revolution proved—as well as cultural consolidation among Africans. They were united not only by the servitude of color but also by a common cosmology. During and after slavery, Christian churches demonized African theology, and the colonial state criminalized its practices. Throughout the Americas laws could be found banning or proscribing the use of the African drum, a central medium in Orisha worship.

What had evolved by the end of the nineteenth century, however, was an amalgam of beliefs which, though rooted in Yoruba cosmology, were uniquely adapted to the social ecology of the Americas:

1. Rather than forsake their ancestral belief system, Africans throughout the Americas used the Christian customs to which they were exposed to conceal and complement their own traditions. Through such means, Orisha integrated and reconciled what Christians would regard as conflicting theologies.

2. Unlike Africa, where shrines, even entire villages, are devoted to one *orisha,* in Trinidad any number of *orisha* are represented in a single shrine and invited to participate in the annual *ebo,* or feast held in their honor. In this way, all the ancestral deities and even new ones are recognized.

3. All shrines are in private yards in Trinidad, the majority being owned and led by women, although men continue to administer key ritual functions. Women were usually the more stable partner in the black community, with some acquiring property through their own enterprise after Emancipation.

The more recent history of the Orisha faith in Trinidad has signaled social growth and progress resulting from certain decisive events. The turning point was the Black Power movement of the early 1970s when young, educated, mainly Afro-Trinidadians demonstrated their frustration with the colonial arrangements they had inherited. Some turned—or returned—to their ancestral traditions to satisfy both spiritual and political needs. This African consciousness was given considerable boost by the 1988 state visit of the Ooni of Ife, spiritual head of the Yoruba/Orisha community. The legacy of this visit was the appointment of a head of the local Orisha community and the creation of a Council of Elders. The coming to power of the United National Congress, a Hindu-based party, in 1997 effectively challenged the Christian hegemony that had prevailed in multiethnic Trinidad since colonial days. The Orisha faith received official recognition with the legalization of Orisha marriages and a grant of lands for the development of African religious organizations.

Increasing contacts with Africa and across the diaspora have brought changes to the practice and personality of the religion as well. Prominent artists and middle-class persons have either joined or openly associated themselves with Orisha. Younger practitioners incorporate the Ifa system of divination, offer prayers in the Yoruba language, and celebrate ancestral festivals at this new threshold of the Americas where gods are shedding their masks.

See also Candomblé; Santería; Voodoo; Yoruba Religion and Culture in the Americas

■ ■ *Bibliography*

Aiyejina, Funso, and Orisa Gibbons. *Tradition in Trinidad.* Mona, Jamaica: University of the West Indies, 2000.

Idowu, E. Bolaji. *Olodumare: God in Yoruba Belief.* New York: A & B Books, 1994.

Springer, Pearl. "Orisha and Spiritual Baptist Religion in Trinidad and Tobago." In *At the Crossroads: African Caribbean Religion and Christianity,* edited by B. Sankerali. Trinidad and Tobago: Caribbean Conference of Churches, 1995.

Warner-Lewis, Maureen. *Guinea's Other Suns: The African Dynamic in Trinidad Culture.* Dove, Mass.: Majority Press, 1991.

RAWLE GIBBONS (2005)

OWEN, CHANDLER

APRIL 5, 1889
1967

■■■

Political journalist Chandler Owen was born in Warrenton, North Carolina, and graduated from Virginia Union University in Richmond in 1913. He pursued graduate work at the New York School of Philanthropy and at Columbia University as a National Urban League fellow. Owen severed ties with the league after he met A. Philip Randolph and in 1916 joined the Socialist Party. In November 1917 Owen and Randolph began publishing *The Messenger,* an independent monthly with a Socialist Party orientation; in early issues, they framed pacifist objections to World War I, supported armed defense against mob violence directed at African Americans, promoted radical industrial unionism, and voiced support for the social goals of the Russian Revolution. Owen and Randolph served brief jail sentences for their radicalism, and the authorities ransacked *The Messenger*'s offices several times in the early 1920s.

In the early 1920s Owen had become disillusioned with radical politics and was especially embittered when socialist garment workers' unions denied membership to his brother. In 1923 he left *The Messenger* to become managing editor of Anthony Overton's *Chicago Bee,* a liberal African-American newspaper, but he maintained ties with Randolph and used the *Bee* to muster support for Randolph's campaign to unionize the Pullman car porters.

During the 1930s and World War II Owen continued to move to the right and was active in the Republican Party. He served as a speechwriter and publicity chairman of the Negro division for Wendell Willkie's 1940 presidential campaign. During this period Owen also wrote about black anti-Semitism for the Anti-Defamation League of B'nai B'rith. Despite his private reservations about the Roosevelt administration, he served as a consultant on race relations for the Office of War Information (he wrote the office's pamphlet *Negroes and the War* [1942], a tabloid-size publication that praised the New Deal) and projected worse treatment for blacks if Hitler were to win.

In his later life Owen continued to serve as a speechwriter and political consultant for major Republican presidential candidates, including Thomas Dewey in 1948 and Dwight Eisenhower in 1952.

See also *Messenger, The;* Randolph, A. Philip

■ ■ *Bibliography*

Korweibel, Theodore, Jr. *No Crystal Stair: Black Life and the "Messenger," 1917–1928.* Westport, Conn.: Greenwood Press, 1975.

ELIZABETH MUTHER (1996)

OWENS, DANA ELAINE

See Queen Latifah (Owens, Dana Elaine)

OWENS, JESSE

SEPTEMBER 12, 1913
MARCH 31, 1980

■■■

Born in 1913, the tenth surviving child of sharecroppers Henry and Emma Owens, in Oakville, Alabama, James Cleveland "Jesse" Owens moved with his family to Cleveland, Ohio, for better economic and educational opportunities in the early 1920s. His athletic ability was first noticed by a junior high school teacher of physical education, Charles Riley, who coached him to break several interscholastic records and even to make a bold but futile attempt to win a place on the U.S. Olympic team. In 1933 Owens matriculated at Ohio State University on a work-study arrangement and immediately began setting Big Ten records. In Ann Arbor, Michigan, on May 25, 1935, he set new world records in the 220-yard sprint, the 220-yard hurdles, and the long jump and tied the world record in the 100-yard dash.

Jesse Owens, winnning one of the 200-meter heats at the Olympic games in Berlin. © BETTMANN/CORBIS. REPRODUCED BY PERMISSION.

In the racially segregated sports world of 1936, Owens and boxer Joe Louis (1914–1981) were the most visible African-American athletes. In late June, however, Louis lost to German boxer Max Schmeling (1905–), making Owens's Olympic feats all the more dramatic. At Berlin in early August 1936, he stole the Olympic show with gold-medal, record-setting performances in the 100 meters, 200 meters, long jump, and relays. All this occurred against a backdrop of Nazi pageantry and German dictator Adolf Hitler's (1889–1945) daily presence and in an international scene of tension and fear. Out of that dramatic moment came one of the most enduring of all sports myths: Hitler's supposed "snub" in refusing to shake Owens's hand after the victories. (Morally satisfying but untrue, the yarn was largely created by American sportswriters. The truth is that by the time Owens won his first gold medal, Hitler was no longer personally congratulating any medal winners.)

Business and entertainment offers flooded Owens's way in the wake of the Berlin games, but he quickly found most of them were bogus. Republican presidential candidate Alf Landon paid him to stump for black votes in the autumn of 1936. After that futile effort, Owens bounced from one demeaning and low-paying job to another, in-cluding races against horses. He went bankrupt in a dry-cleaning business. By 1940, with a wife and three daughters to support (he had married Ruth Solomon in 1935), Owens returned to Ohio State to complete the degree he had abandoned in 1936. However, his grades were too low and his educational background too thin for him to graduate. For most of World War II (1939–45), Owens supervised the black labor force at Ford Motor Company in Detroit.

In the era of the cold war, Owens became a fervent American patriot, hailing the United States as the land of opportunity. Working out of Chicago, he frequently addressed interracial school and civic groups, linking patriotism and athletics. In 1955 the U.S. State Department sent him to conduct athletic clinics, make speeches, and grant interviews as a means of winning friends for America in India, Malaya, and the Philippines.

In 1956 President Dwight D. Eisenhower (1890–1969; served 1953–61) sent him to the Melbourne Olympics as one of the president's personal goodwill ambassadors. Refusing to join the civil rights movement, Owens became so politically conservative that angry young blacks denounced him as an "Uncle Tom" on the occasion of the famous Black Power salutes by Olympic athletes Tommie Smith and John Carlos at Mexico City in 1968. Before he died of lung cancer in 1980, however, Owens received two of the nation's highest awards: the Medal of Freedom Award in 1976, for his "inspirational" life, and the Living Legends Award in 1979, for his "dedicated but modest" example of greatness.

See also Louis, Joe; Olympians; Sports

■ ■ *Bibliography*

Baker, William J. *Jesse Owens: An American Life.* New York: Macmillan, 1986.

Mandell, Richard D. *The Nazi Olympics.* New York: Ballantine Books, 1971.

McRae, Donald. *Heroes without a Country: America's Betrayal of Joe Louis and Jesse Owens.* New York: Harper Collins, 2003.

WILLIAM J. BAKER (1996)
Updated bibliography

PADMORE, GEORGE

C. 1902
SEPTEMBER 23, 1959

The political activist and journalist Malcolm Nurse adopted the name George Padmore in 1927. He was born in rural Arouca, Trinidad, in the British West Indies. However, his childhood and teenage years were spent in a middle-class suburb in the island's capital, Port of Spain. At the age of nineteen he briefly served as a reporter for the *Trinidad Guardian,* a daily newspaper. Due to frequent arguments with the newspaper's editor, Padmore resigned and in 1924 departed for the United States.

A desire to pursue a career in medicine and later law led him to Fisk University, New York University, and Howard University. While working among blacks in Harlem, Padmore edited a newspaper, the *Negro Champion* (later known as the *Liberator*). He joined the Communist Party in 1927 and began contributing articles to the *Daily Worker* in New York. He also worked with the Communist Party's American Negro Labor Congress.

In 1929 Padmore went to Moscow and lectured on the trade union activities of blacks in the United States. Soon he was appointed head of the International Trade Union Committee of Negro Workers (ITUC-NW), an arm of the Red International of Labour Unions, or Profintern. In June 1930 the ITUC-NW began publishing the widely read *Negro Worker,* which Padmore edited. The ITUC-NW was a vibrant group and in July 1930 organized an international conference of Negro workers in Germany.

Padmore's role as a voice for the oppressed and exploited working class was evident in numerous books and pamphlets, including *The Life and Struggles of Negro Toilers, How Britain Rules Africa,* and *Africa and World Peace.*

Padmore began to display a phenomenal organizational ability after the Italian invasion of Ethiopia in 1935. He assisted fellow Trinidadian C. L. R James in forming the International African Friends of Ethiopia. In March 1937 Padmore transformed this anti-imperialist group into the International African Service Bureau (IASB) and served as its chair.

By 1944 the IASB had been dissolved and Padmore, along with other Pan-Africanists, formed the Pan-African Federation (PAF) in England. In 1945 Padmore was the mastermind of the Fifth Pan-African Congress, held in Manchester, England.

Although Padmore was a staunch Pan-Africanist, his work incorporated other ethnic groups. By 1946 he was instrumental in establishing the London-based Asiatic African Unity Committee, comprising Indians and Africans with the intention of building a united front against imperialism. He had a close fraternal relationship with Pandit Jawaharlal Nehru of India.

In 1945 Padmore met Kwame Nkrumah (then a student from Ghana) in London. Nkrumah assisted in the Pan-African Conference in 1945 and served as the regional secretary of the PAF. Nkrumah never forgot Padmore's friendship and commitment to African unity, and in 1957, when he had become the prime minister of Ghana, he appointed Padmore his political advisor.

At the time of his death, the indefatigable Padmore had sown the seeds of anticolonialism and laid the foundation of an indestructible anti-imperialist movement that resulted in many British colonies gaining political independence.

See also Communist Party of the United States; James, C. L. R.; Journalism; Pan-Africanism; Politics in the United States

■■ *Bibliography*

Birmingham, David. *Kwame Nkrumah: The Father of African Nationalism.* Athens: Ohio University Press, 1998.

Murapa, Rukudo. "Padmore's Role in the African Liberation Movement." Ph.D. diss., Northern Illinois University, DeKalb, 1974.

Padmore, George. *The Life and Struggles of Negro Toilers,* 2d ed. Hollywood, Calif.: Sun Dance Press, 1971.

JEROME TEELUCKSINGH (2005)

PAIGE, SATCHEL

JULY 7, 1906
JUNE 8, 1982

By far the best known of those who played baseball in the relative obscurity of the Negro Leagues, pitcher and coach Satchel Paige became a legendary figure from Canada to the Caribbean basin. Born in a shotgun house (a railroad flat) in Mobile, Alabama, to John Paige, a gardener, and Lulu Paige, a washerwoman, he combined athletic prowess and exceptional durability with a flair for showmanship. In 1971 the Baseball Hall of Fame made Paige—Negro League ball incarnate—its first-ever selection from the (by then defunct) institution.

Leroy Robert Paige gained his nickname as a boy by carrying satchels from the Mobile train station. Sent to the Mount Meigs, Alabama, reform school at age twelve for stealing a few toy rings from a store, he developed as a pitcher during his five years there. After joining the semipro Mobile Tigers in 1924, he pitched for a number of Negro League, white independent, and Caribbean teams until he joined the Cleveland Indians as a forty-two-year-old rookie in 1948. The first African-American pitcher in the American League, Paige achieved a 6–1 record that helped the Indians to the league pennant. His first three starts drew over 200,000 fans.

But it was in the Negro Leagues and Caribbean winter ball that Paige attained his status as independent baseball's premier attraction. During the 1920s and 1930s he starred for the Birmingham Black Barons and the Pittsburgh Crawfords, where he teamed up with catcher Josh Gibson to form what was possibly baseball's greatest all-time battery. From 1939 to 1947 Paige anchored the strong Kansas Monarchs staff, winning three of the Monarchs' four victories over the Homestead Grays in the 1942 Negro League World Series. Developing a reputation as a contract jumper, he led Ciudad Trujillo to the 1937 summer championship of the Dominican Republic and later pitched in Mexico, Cuba, and Venezuela.

Playing before an estimated 10 million fans in the United States, Canada, and the Caribbean, the "have arm—will pitch" Paige, according to his own estimates, threw fifty-five no-hitters and won over 2,000 of the 2,500 games in which he pitched.

The six-foot, three-and-a-half-inch, 180-pound Paige dazzled fans with his overpowering fastball (called the "bee ball"—you could hear it buzz, but you couldn't see it), his hesitation pitch, and unerring control. Stories of him intentionally walking the bases full of barnstorming white all-stars, telling his fielders to sit down, and then striking out the side became part of a shared black mythology. "I just could pitch!" he said in 1981. "The Master just gave me an arm. . . . You couldn't hardly beat me. . . . I wouldn't get tired 'cause I practiced every day. I had the suit on every day, pretty near 365 days out of the year."

Probably the most widely seen player ever (in person), Paige was a regular at the East-West Classic (the Negro League all-star game), and also appeared on the 1952 American League all-star squad. His 28 wins and 31 losses, 476 innings pitched, 3.29 earned run average in the majors represented only the penultimate chapter of a professional pitching career that spanned five decades.

Paige ended his working life as he began it, on the bus of a barnstorming black club, appearing for the Indianapolis Clowns in 1967. In 1971, after the Hall of Fame belatedly began to induct Negro Leaguers, he led the way. As his Pittsburgh Crawfords teammate Jimmie Crutchfield

Leroy "Satchel" Paige. Pictured here playing for the Miami Marlins of the Negro Leagues, Paige joined major league baseball's Cleveland Indians as a 42-year-old rookie in 1948. He was inducted into the Baseball Hall of Fame in 1971. AP/WIDE WORLD PHOTOS. REPRODUCED BY PERMISSION.

put it, when Paige appeared on the field "it was like the sun coming out from behind a cloud."

See also Baseball; Gibson, Josh

■ ■ *Bibliography*

Holway, John B. *Josh and Satch: The Life and Times of Josh Gibson and Satchel Paige.* Westport, Conn.: Meckler, 1991.

Peterson, Robert W. *Only the Ball Was White: A History of Legendary Black Players and All Black Professional Teams.* New York: McGraw-Hill, 1984.

Ribowsky, Mark. *Don't Look Back: Satchel Page in the Shadows of Baseball.* New York: Da Capo Press, 2000.

Ruck, Rob. *Sandlot Seasons: Sport in Black Pittsburgh.* Urbana: University of Illinois Press, 1987.

Sterry, David, and Arielle Eckstut. *Satchel Sez: The Wit, Wisdom, and World of Leroy "Satchel" Paige.* New York: Three Rivers Press, 2001.

ROB RUCK (1996)
Updated bibliography

PAINTER, NELL IRVIN

AUGUST 2, 1942

The daughter of Frank Edward and Dona McGruder Donato Irvin, historian Nell Irvin Painter was born in Houston, Texas, but grew up in Oakland, California. She attended the University of California at Berkeley, including a year of study at the University of Bordeaux, France, where she discovered a love of history that influenced her approach to her major in anthropology. After graduation in 1964 she joined her parents in the Ghana of Kwame Nkrumah. In Ghana she taught French at the Ghana Institute of Languages and began graduate study at the University of Ghana's Institute of African Studies. Painter remained in Ghana for two years, leaving after a coup d'état deposed Nkrumah. She returned to graduate study and completed a master's degree in African history at the University of California at Los Angeles in 1967.

Painter completed her Ph.D. in U.S. history at Harvard University in 1974. Alfred A. Knopf published her dissertation under the title *Exodusters: Black Migration to Kansas After Reconstruction* in January 1977 (copyrighted 1976). She was promoted to a tenured associate professorship in history at the University of Pennsylvania in 1977. Two years later Harvard University Press published her biography of Hosea Hudson, *The Narrative of Hosea Hudson: His Life as a Negro Communist in the South.* In 1980 Painter joined the faculty of the University of North Carolina at Chapel Hill as a full professor of history. In 1986 W. W. Norton published her first general history of the United States, *Standing at Armageddon: The United States, 1877–1919.* These three books represent her writing as a social/labor historian. In 1988 Painter became a professor of history at Princeton University. She remained at Princeton until her retirement in 2005, becoming the Edwards Professor of American History in 1992 and serving as director of the Program in African-American Studies from 1997 to 2000.

In the mid-1980s Painter undertook a self-education in women's history, feminist theory, and psychology, which resulted in her essays on several women, including the plantation mistress Gertrude Thomas (1990); a biography, *Sojourner Truth: A Life, A Symbol* (1996); and Penguin Classic editions of the *Narrative of Sojourner Truth* (1998) and *Incidents in the Life of a Slave Girl* (2000). In 2002 the University of North Carolina Press published her collected essays as *Southern History Across the Color Line*.

Painter's later books represent a break from southern history. *Creating Black Americans* (2005) presents the history of African Americans from 1619 to the present, illustrated by the work of black artists. In 2005 Painter was also working on books concerning what Americans and Europeans have said about white identity, and concepts of beauty as related to sex appeal and prestige.

Throughout her academic career Painter gained several honors. As an undergraduate she was on the dean's list and in Mortar Board. As a graduate student, she received the Coretta Scott King Award of the American Association of University Women and a Ford Foundation Fellowship for the writing of a dissertation in minority studies. As an assistant professor, she was a fellow of the Charles Warren Center for Studies in American History and the Radcliffe/Bunting Institute. As an associate professor, Painter was a fellow at the National Humanities Center and a Guggenheim Fellow. As a full professor, she was a fellow of the Center for Advanced Study in the Behavioral Sciences and of the National Endowment for the Humanities. In addition to several other fellowships, she has received honorary doctorates from such institutions as Wesleyan University, Dartmouth College, the State University of New York at New Paltz, and Yale University. Radcliffe College and the University of California at Berkeley have honored her as a distinguished alumna. She has served the learned societies of the historical profession in several capacities, including as national director of the Association of Black Women Historians, president of the Southern Historical Association, and president of the Organization of American Historians.

See also Biography, U.S.; Historians/Historiography

■ ■ *Bibliography*

Painter, Nell. *Exodusters: Black Migration to Kansas after Reconstruction.* New York: Knopf, 1976.

Painter, Nell. *The Narrative of Hosea Hudson: His Life as a Negro Communist in the South.* Cambridge, Mass.: Harvard University Press, 1979.

Painter, Nell. *Standing at Armageddon: The United States, 1877–1919.* New York: Norton, 1987.

Painter, Nell. *Sojourner Truth: A Life, A Symbol.* New York: Norton, 1996.

Painter, Nell. *Southern History Across the Color Line.* Chapel Hill: University of North Carolina Press, 2002.

CRYSTAL N. FEIMSTER (2005)

PAINTING AND SCULPTURE

■ ■ ■

From the time of their first arrival in the New World, Africans were involved in a wide range of artistic endeavors. Much of the early art of African Americans was considered folk art and was connected to routines of life and work. Many Africans were highly skilled artisans who played a central role in the construction of cities and towns in early America. Their artistic expression often displayed a distinctive African sensibility that reflected traditional African practices such as the decoration of gravesites, basketry, pottery, ironwork, and quilt-making.

African-American participation in European modalities of fine artwork was slower to develop. This was due to the resistance of Europeans to the conventions of African art forms, and to the deliberate exclusion of blacks from access to the training and clients needed for successful careers as artists within the mainstream of Euro-American traditions. Despite these handicaps, the achievements of African Americans in painting and sculpture are rich and distinguished. Their history comprises determined individuals who, in addition to the usual struggles of artists to make a livelihood, had to overcome the additional burdens of discrimination and racist assumptions about the artistic abilities of persons of African descent. Black female artists had an additional burden, for they had to contend with gender bias as well.

Persons of African descent began to create Euro-American artworks at the behest of their masters or white patrons, or to prove their artistic abilities in the face of opposition to their participation in the marketplace. This process began early in America's development. By 1724 the Boston print shop of Thomas Fleet had two slave artisans, Pompey and Cesar Fleet, who made woodcuts to accompany broadside pamphlets and small books. Most of the black artisans in eighteenth-century America were anonymous. Primarily located in cities, both free blacks and slaves worked as carriage painters, silversmiths, goldsmiths, seamstresses, tailors, hairdressers, watchmakers, and makers of powderhorns, among other crafts. References to them are scarce and primarily glimpsed in newspaper advertisements for their services or in notices for runaway slaves.

Those painters whose names were recorded include Neptune Thurston, an eighteenth-century Rhode Island slave whose artistic prowess, according to a nineteenth-century tradition, was an early inspiration for the renowned artist Gilbert Stuart. Scipio Moorhead, a Boston slave, almost certainly painted a portrait of the poet Phillis

William H. Johnson (1901–1970), **Self-Portrait.** *Pictured here is one of many self-portraits painted by Johnson in his career, which was cut short by mental illness.* THE LIBRARY OF CONGRESS

Wheatley that served as the basis for the frontispiece to the 1773 London edition of her works. Wheatley returned the favor in her poem "To S. M. a Young African Painter, on Seeing his Works," the first recorded critical evaluation of an African-American artist:

> To show the lab'ring bosom's deep intent,
> And thought in living characters to paint,
> When first thy pencil did those beauties give,
> And breathing figures learnt from thee to live,
>
> How did those prospects give my soul delight,
> A new creation rushing on my sight?

NINETEENTH-CENTURY ART

Most of the work of nineteenth-century African-American artists is reflective of European and American conventions of technique and subject matter. The lack of a self-conscious "black aesthetic" in nineteenth-century African-American art has bothered some later critics, such as Alain Locke (1886–1954), who view this period as one of relatively little importance. But this perspective slights the

achievements of these artists and overlooks the efforts they made and the indignities they withstood to be accepted by their peers.

Many of these early black artists were limners—often self-taught, itinerant portrait painters. One of the first was Joshua Johnson (c. 1763–c. 1824) of Baltimore. His origins, parentage, and other pertinent information about his life are vague, given the absence of written documents.

In a December 19, 1798, advertisement in the *Baltimore Intelligencer,* Joshua Johnson posted an announcement wherein he described himself as a "self-taught genius" who had overcome "many insuperable obstacles" in his efforts to become an artist. This is a subtle reference to his African American background and the difficulties of being an artist in nineteenth-century America.

Johnson's style indicates that he came under the influence of the prominent painters Charles Wilson Peale and his nephew Charles Polk Peale. Johnson's paintings of Maryland's elite were distinguished by an individual sense of character and sharp attention to detail. Critics have described Johnson as the "brass tack artist" because of his repetitive use of the same sofa, studded with brass upholstery tacks, in many of the depictions of his subjects. Johnson painted few black subjects, though he has been identified as the painter of the matched portraits of Daniel Coker and Abner Coker, two early ministers of the African Methodist Episcopal (AME) Church.

The painter, lithographer, and daguerreotypist Jules Lion (1810–1866) was born in France and later settled in New Orleans—he was listed as a painter and lithographer in the 1838 city directory. An advertisement lists Lion as a daguerreotypist in 1840 and credits him with the introduction of this medium to New Orleans. Although there are no extant examples of his painting, he is known to have exhibited successfully at the Exposition of Paris in 1833, cofounded an art school in New Orleans in 1841, and taught drawing at the College of Louisiana. Lion typifies many early African-American artists who worked in diverse genres and media. He remained active in the New Orleans area, traveling back to France periodically until his death in 1866.

Robert Scott Duncanson (1821–1872) was hailed at the height of his career as the "best landscape painter in the West" by eastern critics. Born in Seneca County in upstate New York, Duncanson was raised in Monroe, Michigan, located at the western tip of Lake Erie, and by the early 1840s had moved to Cincinnati. His landscapes, such as *Blue Hole, Little Moon River* (1851) and *The Land of the Lotus Eaters* (c. 1861), are excellent examples of the luminous Hudson River School landscape style.

Duncanson's commissions included photographs, portraits, still lifes, and landscapes, and in the Belmont

House in Cincinnati (now the Taft Museum) he executed the first murals by a black artist. In the early 1850s he collaborated with the African-American daguerreotypist James Presley Ball in an enormous rolling panorama (over half a mile of canvas) that depicted in its unfolding the history of African Americans in the United States.

Duncanson was light-skinned, and this helped to give him access to white artistic circles, though the snubs he did receive, such as his failure to be elected to the National Academy of Design in New York, left him greatly disturbed. His physical and mental health deteriorated toward the end of his life. He made a distinctive contribution to the tradition of American landscape painting by becoming the first African-American artist to appropriate the landscape as a symbolic vehicle to express his own sense of creativity, freedom, and identity.

Boston, a major center for black cultural life in the nineteenth century, was the home of four artists of significance: William Simpson, Nelson Primus, Edward Bannister, and Edmonia Lewis. William Simpson (1818–1872) was listed in the Boston directories of 1860 and 1866. Critics of the period recall his strong talents as a portrait painter and his skill as a draftsman of exceptional ability. William Wells Brown, who escaped from slavery and became a noted writer and historian, recalled that Simpson began as a youth by "drawing instead of following his class work," and he later studied with Matthew Wilson (in 1854). Little is known about Simpson's career, and few works are extant.

Nelson Primus (1843–1916), born in Hartford, Connecticut, moved to Boston in 1864. He started out as a carriage painter in about 1858, and then began a professional career as a portrait painter. In 1859 he won a medal for drawing at the State Agricultural Society Fair. While he received high praise in Boston, his career was only partially successful in the East, and he later moved to San Francisco, where he continued to paint.

Edward Mitchell Bannister (1828–1901) was a prolific landscape painter and portraitist in late-nineteenth-century New England. Born in New Brunswick, Canada, to a father from Barbados and a local woman, he grew up with an early appreciation of the arts, encouraged by his mother. In 1850 he moved to Boston, where he worked as a hairdresser. As an artist he was largely self-taught, and by 1860 he had acquired a considerable local reputation. During the Civil War, Bannister was a leader in the effort to obtain equal pay for black soldiers, and he painted a portrait, not extant, of Colonel Robert Gould Shaw, commander of the 54th Massachusetts Regiment.

Bannister's painting *Under the Oaks* (now lost) won first place at the Centennial Exposition in Philadelphia in 1876. African-American newspapers and periodicals such as the *AME Church Review* proudly took note of Bannister's accomplishment. His work, influenced by the English landscape artist John Constable and the French Barbizon School, often featured seascapes and textured studies of clouds and trees. In 1870 Bannister moved to Providence, Rhode Island, where was accepted by his white peers (an unusual occurrence for a black professional of his era), and became a cofounder of the socially prestigious Providence Art Club. Following his death in 1901, the club hosted a memorial exhibition of more than one hundred of his works, a testament to his contribution to the American landscape tradition and to the high admiration of his fellow artists, patrons, and admirers.

The most prominent black sculptor of the nineteenth century was the remarkable Edmonia Lewis (c. 1845–1911?). The specifics of her biography remain unclear. Lewis was born in upstate New York to an African-American father and a mother of mixed Chippewa and African-American descent. Orphaned at an early age, "Wildfire" (her Indian name) was raised in Canada West (now Ontario) among the Chippewa. She attended Oberlin College, but she found herself embroiled in unseemly and unfounded accusations of poisoning two of her classmates and was obliged to leave in 1863. She moved to Boston, but the traumatic impact of the charges, which almost certainly had a racial basis, left Lewis distrustful and fostered an already strong sense of independence and self-sufficiency.

The city directory of Boston lists Lewis as a sculptor for the years of 1864 and 1865. Boston's active black and abolitionist community provided Lewis with numerous commissions to create portrait busts of leading abolitionist figures. In 1866, with the money earned from sales of a plaster bust of Colonel Robert Gould Shaw and the encouragement of the sculptor Harriet Homser, she moved to Rome. She was befriended there by a large community of American artists (including several women) and started carving in marble. *Forever Free* (1867–1868), probably her best-known work, is a commemoration of the Emancipation Proclamation. Although her work was deeply shaped by Greco-Roman neoclassical tradition, she was equally committed to portraying both African-American and Native-American heritages. After the 1880s she became less active and gradually lost contacts with America. Little is known about the last thirty years of her life, but it is believed that she was living in Rome as late as 1909.

Henry Ossawa Tanner (1859–1937) was the leading African-American painter of the late nineteenth and early twentieth centuries. Born in Pittsburgh, Pennsylvania, he was encouraged in his artistic ambitions at an early age by a supportive and relatively well-off family (his father was an AME bishop) and the intellectual community of Philadelphia. He was one of the first black artists to study at the Pennsylvania Academy of Fine Arts, studying with the artist Thomas Eakins in 1880 and 1881, but he withdrew after a racial incident. In 1891 he sailed for Europe, traveling to Italy and settling in Paris, where he experienced freedoms unknown to African Americans in the United States. He would remain in Paris for the rest of his life, making periodic trips home.

While in France, Tanner executed two genre paintings, *The Banjo Lesson* (1898) and *The Thankful Poor* (1893–1894), both displaying the influence of Eakins. These works represented Tanner's most realistic depictions of contemporary African-American life. For the remainder of his career he concentrated on visionary religious paintings, such as *Daniel in the Lion's Den* (1895) and *The Raising of Lazarus* (1896), a prizewinner at the Paris Salon of 1897. Tanner's achievements and personal encouragement would be an inspiration for several generations of African-American artists. Two painters who became pupils of Tanner were William Harper and William Edouard Scott. Harper was a landscapist in the tradition of the Barbizon painters, and he had admirable technical skill. Scott's landscapes displayed the influence of Tanner's use of light, and he later became known for his paintings of Haitian life.

The two leading black sculptors at the end of the century were Meta Vaux Warrick Fuller (1877–1968) and May Howard Jackson (1877–1931). Meta Vaux Warwick married the pioneer African-American neurologist Solomon Carter Fuller. She was born in Philadelphia, and at an early age became curious about art through her older sister, an art student. Throughout her early education, her talent and interest in art blossomed. She won a scholarship to the Pennsylvania School of Industrial Art and won a prize for Process of the Arts and Crafts (1897), a massive bas-relief composition of thirty-seven figures. After graduation, she continued her studies in 1899, attending lectures at the Colarossi Academy in Paris and later working with the renowned modernist sculptor Auguste Rodin. She was among the earliest American artists to be influenced by African sculpture and folklore, which is evident in such works as *Spirit of Emancipation* (c. 1918), *Ethiopia Awakening* (1914/1921), and *The Talking Skull* (1937). Her early works had a power and fierceness that many critics of that era found frightening. After her marriage, the birth of her sons, and a devastating fire in 1910 that destroyed much of her early work, she stopped sculpting for a period of years and created stage designs for theater groups in the community. When she resumed her career, her sculpture

was more technically and conceptually mature, largely consisting of themes centered on African-American culture, history, and identity.

May (or Mae) Howard Jackson was educated at J. Liberty Todd's Art School in Philadelphia and won a scholarship to the Pennsylvania Academy of Fine Arts in that city. Jackson was primarily a sculptor of portrait busts and portrait groups, such as *Mother and Child* (1929) and *Head of a Negro Child* (1929). In many of her works she went beyond her classical training to depict the distinct uniqueness of African-American physiognomy. Jackson had a studio in Washington, D.C., and exhibited professionally at the National Academy of Design and the Corcoran Gallery of Art. She won a prize from the Harmon Foundation in 1928. However, the general indifference of the public, despite many critical plaudits from intellectuals such as Alain Locke and W. E. B. Du Bois, filled her life with frustration, anger, and isolation.

Charles Ethan Porter (1847–1923) was a painter of still lifes and landscapes. Born in Connecticut, he attended the National Academy of Design and later traveled to Paris to study, evidently through the generosity of Mark Twain. Porter established a studio in Rockville, Connecticut, in 1884. He specialized in still lifes with elaborate floral arrangements and fruit displays, painting primarily for local white patrons. He exhibited intermittently at the National Academy of Design of New York and the American Society of Painters in Watercolor. In 1910 he became a charter member of the Connecticut Academy of Fine Arts, his only known professional association.

Laura Wheeler Waring (1887–1948), like Charles Ethan Porter, was a native of Connecticut. Born in Hartford, she studied at the Pennsylvania Academy of Fine Arts and at the Académie de la Grande Chaumière in Paris. In 1914 she won a Cresson Foreign Traveling Scholarship, which enabled her to travel to Europe and North Africa. Her interest in portraiture of African Americans of both humble and distinguished origins won high praise, and her painting *Anna Derry Washington* (c. 1930s) received the Harmon Foundation gold medal in 1927. Her portraits of women are powerful, dignified, intense images of poised strength. After she settled in Philadelphia, her paintings of leading African-American figures, including Marian Anderson, George Washington Carver, and James Weldon Johnson, were exhibited widely. Many of her paintings were commissioned by the Harmon Foundation. A memorial exhibition of these works was displayed at Howard University in 1949.

HARLEM RENAISSANCE AND THE NEW NEGRO MOVEMENT

The celebrated March 1925 issue of *Survey Graphic,* reprinted under the title *The New Negro* (1925), heralded the arrival of the movement known as the Harlem Renaissance. It established Alain Locke, a Philadelphia-born philosopher and Howard University professor, as the movement's mentor and intellectual leader. Locke became the first significant critic, curator, and historian of African-American art, and he was the author of path-breaking books, including *Negro Art: Past and Present* (1936) and *The Negro in Art* (1940). Locke urged African-American artists to look to their African ancestral legacy and incorporate the aesthetic traditions of Africa into their work to create a "racially expressive art." Locke initiated the call for African Americans to be not merely imitative of dominant European and American styles, but to develop their own self-conscious aesthetic.

The burgeoning of publications during the Harlem Renaissance provided a crucial forum for young black artists to showcase and experiment with images reflective of a cultural identity specific to African Americans. Among those active in the production of illustrations, caricatures, graphic design for book and magazine covers, and genre drawings were Aaron Douglas, Gwendolyn Bennett, Bruce Nugent, Charles Alston, Romare Bearden, E. Sims Campbell, Laura Wheeling Waring, and Lois Mailou Jones. These artists were well respected among their peers, even if at times the "new" imagery of the New Negro provoked resistance and disdain from the older, more conservative, generation of blacks.

Another crucial figure who encouraged visual arts during the Harlem Renaissance was a white real-estate developer and philanthropist, William E. Harmon (1862–1928), who founded the Harmon Foundation in 1922. The foundation, which sponsored the Harmon Awards for Distinguished Achievements among Negroes in Fine Arts, created exhibitions that toured the United States through the 1930s. These exhibitions, many supervised by his longtime assistants Mary Beattie Brady and Evelyn Brown Younger, provided an opportunity and showcase for black artists to gain national and international recognition that otherwise would not have been available to them.

Aaron Douglas (1899–1979) was probably the best-known artist to emerge from the Harlem Renaissance. Born and educated in Kansas, he is noted for his murals, paintings, book designs, and periodical illustrations. After teaching in Kansas high schools, he moved to New York in 1924, where he began studies with Winold Reiss, a German painter with an acute interest in American Indians and African Americans.

Douglas soon became a popular and prolific illustrator for periodicals such as *The Crisis, Opportunity, Theatre Arts Monthly, Sun, Boston Transcript, American Mercury, Vanity Fair, Fire!!,* and the special March 1925 issue of *Survey Graphic.* Douglas created images inspired by traditional Egyptian forms and stylized Art Deco elements. The striking mural series *Aspects of Negro Life* (1933–1934) at the Countee Cullen Branch of the New York Public Library (now the Schomburg Center for Research in Black Culture) is among his most compelling artistic achievements.

Palmer Hayden (1890–1973) was born in Widewater, Virginia, where he was educated in rural schools. Inspired by his brother, he began to draw at the age of four. He was primarily a self-taught painter, though he intermittently took courses and studied with various artists. In 1927 he entered the Harmon Foundation competition, won first prize (and $400), and traveled abroad to study and exhibit in Paris.

Hayden's early works were figurative and landscape compositions. Early narrative paintings such as *Midsummer Night in Harlem* (1936) and *The Janitor Who Paints* (1936) are stylized reflections of the stark realities faced by African Americans in general and African-American artists in particular. His most famous work is probably the John Henry series (1944–1947), twelve paintings depicting events from the folk legend.

The aesthetics and creativity of the Harlem Renaissance were not limited to New York City, but flourished in places such as Cleveland, San Francisco, Atlanta, Philadelphia, Boston, Washington, D.C., and Chicago. Many of the artists who migrated to New York came from small towns in the South. These communities provided environments that gave artists a continuously rich supply of cultural material. William Henry Johnson (1901–1970) came from such a town—Florence, South Carolina. Johnson arrived in New York in 1918 and worked at odd jobs, sending money home to his family and saving the rest to enroll in art school. In 1921 he enrolled in the National Academy of Design. With the support of his teacher and painter, Charles Hawthorne, he left for Paris in 1926. He won the Harmon Foundation gold prize for painting in 1929. He lived for most of the 1930s in Denmark, returning to the United States shortly before the outbreak of World War II. In 1939 he changed his style from one heavily influenced by postimpressionism and expressionism to flat, bright, expressively colored, essential forms that appeared "naive." Johnson felt that these works portrayed a more modernist interpretation of the African-American experience. Compositions such as *Jesus and Three Marys* (1939), *Going to Church* (1940–1941), and his Folk Family series recall his cultural roots and his quest to understand African aesthetics and symbolism. He suffered severe mental deterioration in 1945 and was institutionalized for the remainder of his life.

Archibald J. Motley (1891–1981), born in New Orleans and raised in Chicago, painted numerous portraits of family, friends, and models. In 1928 he entered the Harmon Foundation competition and won the gold medal for *Octoroon Girl* (1925); many of Motley's works display an interest in the varieties of African-American skin color. Though his best-known work is probably *Mending Socks* (1924), a sensitive depiction of his grandmother, he also created works on the blues and jazz scene in Chicago, such as *Blues* (1929) and *The Liar* (1934). Many of Motley's paintings portray the social life of blacks and reveal an urban lifestyle that was a new experience to the recently arrived blacks who migrated from the South for better opportunities.

Sargent Johnson (1887–1967) was born in Boston. His father was of Swedish ancestry; his mother was Cherokee and African American. Early in his youth, Johnson was orphaned and sent to live for a while with his maternal aunt, the sculptor May Howard Jackson. In 1915 he moved to San Francisco and set up a studio in his backyard, after studying at the A. W. Best School of Art and the California School of Fine Art. Johnson was talented in a wide range of media—worked in wood, terra cotta, plaster, copper, cast stone, mosaic, ceramic clay, and polychrome porcelain on steel. He was also adept at lithographs, etching, and drawing. Remaining in the Bay Area for the duration of his life, he exhibited regularly with the Harmon Foundation and won awards in 1927 and 1928.

Even though Johnson lived far from Harlem, he was greatly influenced by the call of the New Negro movement to employ the aesthetics of traditional African arts as well as Mexican and Native American art forms. His sculpture captured an elegant linearism and a simple and direct approach to form derived from the study of African masks and Mexican folk art. During the 1930s he became active in the Works Progress Administration (WPA; later called the Work Projects Administration) as an artist, later becoming unit supervisor in the Bay Area, the highest post in the WPA held by a black artist. Some of his most important pieces are *Sammy* (1927), his copper mask series (c. 1930–1935), and *Forever Free* (1933).

Richmond Barthé (1901–1989) was the Harmon Foundation's most celebrated and widely exhibited sculptor. His figurative style was most popular from the 1920s through the 1940s. Early in his career his work was bought by the Whitney Museum of American Art and the Metropolitan Museum of Art. Born in Bay St. Louis, Mississippi, he arrived in Chicago in 1924 and entered the School of the Art Institute of Chicago to study painting. He produced his first sculpture three years later. His early works helped him win a Julius Rosenwald Fellowship to study in New York.

Barthé worked in clay, plaster, and bronze, and his technical and conceptual skill in the execution of the figure and portrait bust was highly regarded. During the 1930s he worked for the WPA, creating bas-relief murals. Much of his inspiration, especially in his later years, came from the world of theater, dance, and sports. The power of movement and the effort to capture kinetic motion in a sculptural form greatly fascinated him. He is known for such compositions as *Ferai Benga* (1935), *The Negro Looks Ahead* (1937), and *Mother and Son* (1938).

The life of sculptor Nancy Elizabeth Prophet (1890–1960) was marked by abject poverty, remarkable skill, and a tenacious will to establish herself as an artist in spite of the harsh realities of race and gender bias. Born in Providence, Rhode Island, she was encouraged to become a teacher or a nurse, but she wanted to become an artist. She enrolled in the Rhode Island School of Design in 1918, and in 1922 she studied at the École des Beaux Arts in Paris. She continued to live, work, and exhibit in France until 1932. She had the support and admiration of W. E. B. Du Bois and Henry Tanner, who helped her exhibit with the Harmon Foundation in 1930, the same year her wood carving *Congalaise* was purchased by the Whitney Museum of American Art. Prophet worked in marble, alabaster, granite, plaster, clay, bronze, and wood. Her portrait busts were intense, powerful technical executions that abstracted the human character to reveal the psychological and physiological qualities of her subjects.

In 1932 Prophet returned to America to teach at Spelman College with Hale Woodruff. The position gave her little time to sculpt, and she left after 1945. Thereafter, she lived in poverty and obscurity in Providence, and much of her later work is either incomplete, lost, or was destroyed by her own hand.

Lois Mailou Jones (1905–1998) had an exceptional career filled with success, achievement, and productivity. She was born in Boston, educated in local schools, and supported by her parents in her decision to become an artist. She attended classes at the Boston Museum School of Fine Arts, and in 1930 she was invited to teach design and watercolor at Howard University. In 1931 she won an honorable mention at the annual Harmon Foundation exhibition for her drawing *Negro Youth* (1929). After 1937 Jones studied in Paris and Africa, and she lived for a while in Haiti. Jones's work includes portraits, landscapes, abstractions, and textile designs, all highlighting her facility

Lois Mailou Jones (1905–1998). A versatile artist, Jones worked in various media, including painting, drawing, watercolor, and stage and costume design. SCHOMBURG CENTER FOR RESEARCH IN BLACK CULTURE, NEW YORK PUBLIC LIBRARY. REPRODUCED BY PERMISSION.

with color, texture, and design, She worked in such diverse media as painting, drawing, watercolor, and stage and costume design.

James Lesesne Wells (1902–1993) was the acknowledged "dean of Negro printmakers." Born in Atlanta and educated in Jacksonville, Florida, he later studied at the National Academy of Design, and at Teachers College of Columbia University. In 1930 he won the gold medal from the Harmon Foundation for the painting *The Flight into Egypt* (1929). However, he later largely abandoned painting for printmaking, and won a Harmon Foundation award for a woodcut, *Escape of Spies from Canaan* (1932). He was proficient in a variety of techniques, including intaglio, wood, and linoleum blocks, as well as painting and drawing. His works concentrated on biblical and religious subjects and were greatly influenced by African sculptural forms, as well as the Renaissance master woodcuts of Albrecht Dürer and those of twentieth-century German expressionists. In 1926 he joined the faculty of Howard University, and he continued to produce prints of great quality and complexity for the remainder of his career.

James Porter (1905–1970), born in Baltimore, was educated at Howard University and later became head of its art department. He was a painter of traditional portraits and won prizes in the Harmon Foundation exhibitions of 1929 and 1933. He authored the first seminal history of African-American art, *Modern Negro Art* (1943). He traveled widely studying, painting, lecturing, writing, exhibiting his work, and providing a critical foundation as the first major African-American art historian.

Hale Woodruff (1900–1980) was the founder of the Atlanta School of Art. He was educated at the John Herron Art Institute in Indianapolis, the Académie Scandinave, and the Académie Moderne in Paris, where he lived for several years. He won a bronze medal in the Harmon Foundation competition of 1926. After his return from Europe in 1931, he started to teach at Atlanta University, where he established a successful art program. His first paintings were landscapes and figure studies. In 1934 he studied mural painting with the Mexican painter Diego Rivera and became increasingly interested in social realism. From 1938 to 1939, under the auspices of the WPA, he created the famed Amistad Mutiny mural series at Talladega College, Alabama, detailing the events surrounding the 1841 shipboard slave mutiny and its aftermath. He helped establish a major competition and collection of art at Atlanta University to encourage young artists, and in 1963 he was a cofounder of the artists' group Spiral. In 1946 he joined the faculty of New York University, where he remained until his retirement. In the later years of his career his canvases were greatly influenced by abstract expressionism and traditional African art.

Edwin Harleston was a portrait painter who had an uncanny ability to capture the character and personality of his subjects, imbuing them with great humanity. Born in Charleston, South Carolina, he studied at the Avery Institute, Atlanta University, the Boston Museum of Fine Arts school (from 1905–1913), and the Art Institute of Chicago (in 1925). He also assisted Aaron Douglas with the murals at Fisk University. Before his death he won Harmon Foundation awards in 1925 and 1931, the first one for a portrait of his wife.

John Wesley Hardrick (1891–1968) was a landscape and portrait painter who received minimal attention during his lifetime. Born in Indianapolis, he was educated at the John Herron Art Institute in his hometown and remained in the Indianapolis area throughout his life. He exhibited at the Harmon exhibitions and won a bronze medal in 1927. Hardrick created several murals for churches and high schools during his career.

Malvin Gray Johnson (1896–1934), born in Greensboro, North Carolina, did not live long enough to realize the full potential of the psychological intensity of his early portraits. Educated at the National Academy of Design, his work shows a great interest in African-American subject matter. He was also inspired by his interest in postimpressionism, which he expressed in a radically distinctive style. In 1929 Johnson won a first prize in the Harmon Foundation exhibition.

BLACK ART AND THE NEW DEAL

By 1934, during the Great Depression, between eleven million and fifteen million people were out of work. Approximately ten thousand of these jobless citizens were artists, both black and white, who were in desperate need of support. In 1935, President Franklin D. Roosevelt created the Works Progress Administration (WPA). Its purpose was to create all kinds of jobs at every level of the skill ladder, preserving professional and technical skills while helping individuals retain their self-respect. Artists in the program were paid $15 to $90 a month for a variety of assignments. The program was essentially terminated by 1939. In some areas, bowing to local custom, the WPA programs were segregated, though in other places they were integrated. In many places, most notably in Harlem, there were separate programs for African-American artists. The WPA gave many artists a sense of collective purpose and provided them with the resources to develop their talent for the first time in American history.

One of the leading figures in Harlem's artistic circles in the 1930s was the sculptor Augusta Savage (1892–1962). One of thirteen children, she came to New York from Cove Springs, Florida, in 1921 to study in the free art program at Cooper Union. She overcame numerous obstacles in her life, becoming an artist and an activist dedicated to the recognition of black artists. Her best work displays extraordinary power, energy, and technical prowess.

In 1929, after sculpting *Gamin,* a head of a Harlem youth, she won the first of two Rosenwald Fellowships that allowed her to study in Paris, to work at the studio of Elizabeth Prophet, and to study at the Académie de la Grande Chaumière for three years. She won citations at the Salon d'Automne and the Salon Printemps and a medallion at the Colonial Exposition of the French government. In 1932, upon her return from Europe, she opened the Savage Studio of Arts and Crafts in Harlem on 143rd Street. Many young artists, such as Norman Lewis, William Artis, Ernest Crichlow, Elba Lightfoot, Morgan and Marvin Smith, Jacob Lawrence, and Gwendolyn Knight, came to study with her. Among her many contributions to the arts was her role in establishing the Harlem Community Art Center in 1937. She created a large plaster sculpture, *Lift Every Voice and Sing* (also known as *The Harp*), for the 1939 New York World's Fair, although there were no funds to preserve the sixteen-foot-tall piece, and it was destroyed after the exhibition. After World War II she

moved to upstate New York, her active artistic involvement greatly diminished, and she drifted into obscurity.

As the WPA projects began to expand, the Harlem Artist Guild was formed in 1935 to address issues of equality and representation of black artists on WPA projects. Aaron Douglas was the first director of the guild, and Augusta Savage followed as director the next year. By 1936 Savage was an assistant supervisor for the WPA Federal Arts Project. At about this time, Charles Alston, who created important works as a muralist, realist painter, and illustrator, established a studio at 306 West 141st Street; "306" soon became the social and intellectual center of the Harlem arts community. Without the assistance of the guild, Charles Alston and Vertis Hayes may have never completed their murals for Harlem Hospital. Georgette Seabrooke Powell, a young New York artist trained at Cooper Union, contributed less controversial murals to that site, as did Elba Lightfoot. Powell also painted murals for Queens General Hospital.

The largest and most influential school to play a critical role in this area was the Harlem Community Art Center. It began as an outgrowth of the Uptown Art Laboratory, another project of Augusta Savage. In 1937 Gwendolyn Bennett replaced Savage as its director. The center served up to four thousand students a month and became a model for other WPA art centers. It is the longest-active art center still in operation from this period.

Selma Hortense Burke (1900–1995), a young sculptor who migrated from North Carolina, studied in New York, Paris, and London and later taught at the Harlem Community Art Center. Burke created works in stone, wood, and metal that were imbued with clarity of line, mass, and strength of spiritual character. Toward the end of World War II, she won a competition to execute a bronze plaque of President Franklin D. Roosevelt, and he sat for her several times. Most experts believe that, uncredited, Burke's design was used for the relief of Roosevelt on the face of the dime.

A number of African-American artists came to prominence during the 1930s. Ernest Crichlow (b. 1914), a resident of Brooklyn, became a teacher at the Harlem Community Art Center. Like Charles Alston, Crichlow created compositions influenced by social realism, often commenting on the conditions and culture of the African-American community. Gwendolyn Knight (b. 1913) was a quiet young painter who moved to New York from Barbados. She was active at "306" and the Harlem Community Art Center, and she later married the artist Jacob Lawrence. Richard Lindsey (b. 1904) was a native of North Carolina and came to New York to study at the National Academy of Design. He was active in the exhibitions of the

Harmon Foundation and at the Harlem Community Art Center, where he also worked. Lindsey was a painter and printmaker, but very little of his work has survived.

Chicago also produced a number of prominent artists during the 1930s. Rex Gorleigh (1902–1987), born in Wynne, Pennsylvania, was another painter who taught at the Harlem Community Art Center. Educated at the Art Students League and the University of Chicago, he later studied in France, worked at the WPA in Greensboro, North Carolina, and later became director of Chicago's South Side Community Art Center (SSCAC), which had opened in 1940. Despite its relatively short existence, the SSCAC had a number of distinguished artists, including Gorleigh, Charles White, Margaret Burroughs, Eldzier Corter, Gordon Parks, Archibald Motley, and Charles Sebree.

Charles White (1918–1979) established the medium of drawing in charcoal, ink, pencil, and collage as a means to depict figurative representation with intense drama. These idealized portraits and studies often had historical subjects as their focus. White continued using this style throughout his life, though he became less iconographic and more individualized in his portrayals in his later years. He was active in the WPA as well as the SSCAC.

Margaret Burroughs (b. 1917) was educated at the Art Institute of Chicago, was a versatile artist in painting, printmaking, and sculpture, and was a significant figure in Chicago area arts education. Eldzier Cortor (b. 1916) was primarily drawn to depictions of African-American women, reflecting their alienation from society and their introspection in positional studies using bedrooms and mirrors as stages. Charles Sebree (1914–1985) was a sensitive portraitist who evoked the spiritual character of the New Negro.

Another Chicago artist was Ellis Wilson (1899–1977). A Kentucky native, Wilson came to study at the Art Institute of Chicago. He was active in the Harmon Foundation exhibitions, the Savage Studio, and the Federal Arts Project. His mature style is based on strong color and flat figures that document the black working-class community.

Allan Rohan Crite (b. 1910) was born in Plainfield, New Jersey, and moved to Boston to study art. He was one of the few African-American artists to be hired for the WPA Federal Arts Project in Boston. Many of Crite's early works were paintings of street scenes and portraits. The balance of his career has been spent developing complex narratives of religious and spiritual themes.

One of the most active centers for African-American art in the 1930s and 1940s was Cleveland's Karamu Playhouse, founded in 1915. Karamu Playhouse was an interracial settlement house designed to address the cultural needs of the urban poor. By the time of the Great Depression it was recognized for its theater group. It was not until funding came from the WPA that it established a strong visual arts program.

Hughie Lee-Smith (1915–1999) studied at the Cleveland Institute of Arts and became part of the Ohio Federal Arts Project. His painted imagery is figurative and realistic, with metaphysical references to surreal or romanticized landscapes. Lee-Smith was active in numerous portrait commissions and was greatly respected for his technical skill in oil, watercolor, prints, and drawing. A significant part of his career was spent teaching at the Arts Students League in New York in addition to painting and exhibiting widely.

Elton Fax (1909–1993), born in Baltimore, moved to New York and worked with Augusta Savage and the Harlem Community Art Center. Later he became active in the Maryland Federal Arts Project. He was a versatile painter, printmaker, illustrator, and educator, and he was the author of several books on the lives of black artists. Fax played an important role in the development of regional art programs from Baltimore to New York.

SELF-TAUGHT ARTISTS

One of the most important forms of African-American artistic expression in the twentieth century has been by so-called folk, or self-taught, artists. These artists developed significant artistic styles in spite of the fact that they had no formal academic training. The work often appears naive or child-like in its artistic conventions. Many self-taught artists took up art as an avocation later in their lives, after their retirement, a religious call, or a critical change in lifestyle or career. They have made important contributions to the development of modernism from the African-American perspective.

Clementine Hunter (1886?–1988) was born on Hidden Hill Plantation in Louisiana and worked as a sharecropper. Late in life, Hunter began to paint at the encouragement of one of her guests. She had a prolific career in exhibiting and painting canvases that recalled, with deep reverence, her memories of life in Louisiana.

Horace Pippin (1888–1946), born in West Chester, Pennsylvania, began to paint later in life, despite an injury to his painting arm during World War I. He started painting by using a hot iron poker to burn the image on a piece of wood. Pippin then slowly painted in the details with numerous layers of oil paint. Many of his intensely detailed paintings deal with his haunted memories of the war. His work also includes visions of childhood experiences (including his version of southern black rural life, a reality he never experienced), landscapes, interiors, and his visions of a utopian and peaceful world. During his last years, Pippin's subtle and profoundly moving art achieved great acclaim. He was an ordinary man with an extraordinary sensibility for observing the world around him.

Minnie Evans (1892–1987), born in Pender County, North Carolina, created compositions inspired by visions and dreams after Good Friday in 1935, when a voice directed her to "draw or die." Her imagery consists of a fusion of bright colors with figurative and abstract human and plant forms. She worked in watercolor, crayon, graphite, oil, acrylic ink, collage, enamel, and tempera.

Sister Gertrude Morgan (1900–1980), who lived most of her life in New Orleans, was adept in a wide range of artistic expression. She was not only a gifted painter, but a singer and preacher as well. After she was "called" to a missionary vocation, she used her artistic abilities to spread the word of God. Believing herself to be the bride of Jesus Christ, her paintings had large areas of white—a color of holiness—which were filled with painted images of redemption, revelation, and red- and black-haired angels.

There have also been a number of important African-American self-taught sculptors. William Edmondson (c. 1882–1951), born in Davidson County, Tennessee, near Nashville, spent his working career on the railroad and later at a woman's hospital. Upon retirement he began to carve, believing he had been directed to do so by a command from God. He collected old limestone curbstone, and made grave markers for people in the community who had minimal funds to lay a headstone. As his skill increased, he produced images with great spirituality, humanity, and power. Religious figures, birds, ordinary and heroic individuals, and what he called "critters and varmits [sic]" were his favorite subjects. In 1937 he became the first African-American artist to be given a one-person show by the Museum of Modern Art in New York.

Elijah Pierce (1892–1984) was a barber, preacher, and wood carver. He was born in Baldwyn, Mississippi, and lived most of his life in Columbus, Ohio. Morality, ethics, and the stories of the Bible inspired many of the wooden panels he carved and painted, using bright colors to energize the message of his pictorial sermons.

Perhaps the most remarkable African-American sculptor was James Hampton, who migrated from Elloree, South Carolina, to Washington, D.C., where he worked as a janitor. A loner, he created *The Throne of the Third Heaven of the Nations' Millennium General Assembly* (c. 1950–1964), which was not known until it was found in a garage long after his death. It consists of more than 185 objects—mostly old furniture, light bulbs, and other household ob-

jects—covered with silver and gold foil, aluminum, and ornately decorated. The heavy use of metallic paper is a symbolic reference to heavenly or celestial light and inspired by Kongo traditions from central Africa. The work was inspired by biblical themes, notably from the *Book of Revelations,* and defines a sacred spiritual place.

POSTWAR MODERNISM

The dominant African-American aesthetic sensibility during the 1930s was social realism. One reason for this was the desire of most African-American artists to convey political themes in a realistic form that was programmatically consistent with the aesthetic that was typical for most WPA projects. Although figurative painting continued to predominate in the postwar period, African-American artistic expression became more diverse and responded to the proliferation of modernist styles, with many artists experimenting with the possibilities of abstraction and expressionism.

The African-American artist to be affected most directly by abstract expressionism was Norman Lewis (1909–1979). A native New Yorker, Lewis trained with a variety of artists, including Augusta Savage. In the 1930s he painted a number of narrative paintings in the social-realist mode, demonstrating his strong sympathies for the unemployed and homeless. In the later 1930s and 1940s, he experimented with the cubist simplification of form, and he tried to convey visually the innovations of bebop jazz, which led to an abstract style by the late 1940s. Some critics complained that he was turning his back on figurative depictions of African Americans, though his work continued to conceptually comment on the civil rights movement and other important social issues. Although Lewis was among the earliest American artists to take up the cause of pure abstraction, until recently his name had been conspicuously left out of the canon of abstract expressionist innovators.

Jacob Lawrence (1917–2000) was a painter and printmaker who began his career in the mid-1930s. He quickly established himself as an important modernist and developed a style based on expressive flat forms and direct color. He was greatly influenced by Augusta Savage, Charles Alston, and Henry Bannern during the time he spent working at the Harlem Community Art Center. His primary subject matter was African-American life and history told in a narrative format, in such works as *The Migration of the Negro* (1940–1941), a series of sixty panels representing a visual history of the Great Migration, the early-twentieth-century movement of blacks from the South to the urban North. Other important works include the Toussaint-Louverture series (1938), consisting of forty-one paintings; the thirty works in the Harlem series (1942–1943); and other connected thematic treatments of John Brown, Harriet Tubman, Frederick Douglass, African-American workers, and the theme of freedom in American history. Jacob Lawrence was the first modernist painter of critical significance to emerge from the New Negro movement and be included in the mainstream art world.

Beauford Delaney (1901–1979) came to New York in the 1920s from Knoxville, Tennessee. A sensitive portraitist, in the 1930s he experimented with brightly colored abstractions, and his subsequent portraits are highly expressionistic, dense compositions of color and form. After World War II he lived in Paris. His brother Joseph Delaney (1904–1991) was a figurative painter who was greatly influenced by the social realist painters and sought to create expressive, atmospheric compositions that reflected stresses in the life of residents in large urban areas such as New York. Thomas Sills (b. 1914), a laborer turned painter, moved to New York City from North Carolina. He is known for his "brushless" canvases with abstracted forms and bright colors, and was active from the 1950s through the early 1970s.

One of the most important African-American abstractionists was Alma Thomas (1891–1978), who studied at Howard University in the 1920s before beginning a long career teaching in the Washington, D.C., public school system. In 1943 she cofounded the first integrated gallery in Washington, D.C., the Barnett-Aden Gallery. Her own work was fairly conventional until the early 1950s, when she began to produce the colorful and lyrical abstract canvases for which she is best known.

Elizabeth Catlett (b. 1915?), a native of Washington, D.C., studied at Howard University and later with Grant Wood at the University of Iowa. She is a sculptor of immense power, versatility, and technical skill. Her media include printmaking, wood, stone, plaster, clay, and bronze. Motherhood, women, and the struggle of oppressed people have been the central themes of her compositions throughout her life. Mexican themes became important in her art after her marriage to Mexican artist Francisco Mora and her expatriation to his country.

Like Catlett and Beauford Delaney, a number of important African-American artists expatriated themselves after World War II. Ronald Joseph (1910–1992) moved to Europe in the 1940s, primarily living in Brussels. An abstractionist from the late 1930s, his restrained compositions received little recognition in the United States, and for many decades he had little contact with American artists, though he was making a comeback at the time of his sudden death in 1992.

Herbert Gentry (b. 1921) moved to Paris after World War II and studied at the Grande Chaumière. Linear movement and biomorphic form have been among his major concerns. Though primarily abstractions, a number of his canvases have featured representations of masks. In 1960 he settled in Stockholm, Sweden.

Ed Clark (b. 1926) moved to Paris in 1952; his paintings were often abstractions of the human figure. Other expatriates include Lawrence Potter (1924–1966), primarily a color field abstractionist, and Walter Williams (b. 1920), whose work often imaginatively evokes African-American childhood themes and narratives.

THE CIVIL RIGHTS MOVEMENT AND THE VISUAL ARTS

The civil rights movement of the 1960s was a turning point for black art and culture. A number of important artworks were directly inspired by the movement, such as Norman Lewis's *Processional* (1964), Jacob Lawrence's *The Ordeal of Mary* (1963), and Elizabeth Catlett's *Homage to My Young Black Sisters* (1968) and *Malcolm X Speaks for Us* (1969). In 1963, Romare Bearden contacted Norman Lewis and Hale Woodruff and formed Spiral, a group of twelve African-American artists committed to supporting the civil rights movement and furthering its connection to African-American art. They held their first group show in 1964. The group had largely disbanded by 1965, however, though their impact as a politically conscious African-American artist collective outlived the short duration of the group.

One of the central figures in Spiral, Romare Bearden (1911–1988) was in his own right one of the most significant African-American artists of the postwar period. Born in Charlotte, North Carolina, he was raised in Harlem and was a lifelong New Yorker. Spiral had a major impact on his art, which subsequently concentrated on painted, mixed-media collages that depict the African-American experience with a strong emphasis on spirituality and jazz idioms. Bearden was also an important writer on African-American art. His written works include the posthumous *History of African-American Artists* (1993), cowritten with Harry Henderson.

Benny Andrews (b. 1930) is an activist and an expressive figurative painter who has also worked in collage, using modeling paste and acrylic. Motivated by the belief that black artists should express themselves on a wide range of issues, he was active in teaching in prisons in Queens, New York, and he cofounded the Black Emergency Cultural Coalition (BECC) in 1969. John Biggers (1924–2001), who was raised in North Carolina and taught for many decades at Texas Southern University, was a figurative artist in the tradition of Charles White. He was profoundly influenced by numerous visits to Africa. His drawings, paintings, and murals were some of his most distinguished contributions to the field.

By the late 1960s, the black arts movement had evolved a more socially conscious African-American art that was community-based, militant, and African-centered in its politics. In the late 1960s and 1970s, the Chicago-based AfriCobra (African Commune of Bad Relevant Artists) started painting community murals on the walls of vacant buildings, including the *Wall of Respect* (1968) in a black Chicago neighborhood. Nelson Stevens, one of the founders of AfriCobra, painted in "Kool-Aid" colors and produced prints that contained nationalistic positive images of black males and females, as well as heroic icons such as Malcolm X.

Vincent Smith (1929–2003) was influenced by the black arts movement, avant-garde jazz and blues of the 1960s, and African art. Many of his oil paintings are mixed-media explorations of the black experience. His etchings and monoprints are eloquent narratives on the distinctive nuances of African-American life. Faith Ringgold (b. 1930), in contrast, executed huge reconfigured paintings of the American flag. She is an outspoken feminist and activist who has used her art to redefine the role of women. Over time, her paintings evolved into painted story quilts, telling complex narratives in a geometric format.

Other strategies for confronting viewers with unsettling observations on the nature of the relation between blacks and American society include those explored by Barkley Hendricks (b. 1940), who has painted larger-than-life-sized portraits of African Americans against stark ominous white backgrounds. Betye Saar (b. 1926) uses mixed media, found objects, and advertising images, as in her *The Liberation of Aunt Jemima* (1972). Mel Edwards uses found or discarded metal objects, such as parts of machines and tools, to create metaphors of the exploited classes within American society, as in his Lynch Fragment series, a lifelong, continuous series of explorations made from recycled metal machine parts.

Bob Thompson (1937-1966) worked in flat, brightly colored figures, creating compositions that echo the work of European masters, including Nicolas Poussin and the Fauves. His work has a strong symbolic component, but his development was cut short by his untimely death. Emilio Cruz (b. 1938), once a studio mate of Thompson's, has similar artistic concerns. Cruz has been concerned throughout his career with symbolism, spirituality, and the condition of humankind. The mood, tempo, and improvisational structure of jazz have been integral to his creative process.

The sculptor Selma Burke (1900–1995) in her studio, working with a model. An accomplished artist, Burke received commissions for portraits of Franklin Delano Roosevelt, Mary McLeod Bethune, Martin Luther King Jr., Duke Ellington, and a number of other luminaries. PHOTOGRAPHS AND PRINTS DIVISION, SCHOMBURG CENTER FOR RESEARCH IN BLACK CULTURE, THE NEW YORK PUBLIC LIBRARY, ASTOR, LENOX AND TILDEN FOUNDATIONS.

CONTEMPORARY AFRICAN-AMERICAN ART

The diversity in medium, style, and philosophy within African-American art has burgeoned since the 1970s. In part, this reflects better opportunities for professional education and training, more international travel—especially to the continent of Africa, the ancestral homeland. With growing public prominence and a strong sense of self-confidence, black artists have realized their role in the world at large. Thematic issues of race, sexuality, class, and gender—combined with the freedom to experiment with materials, techniques, and styles—have increased the range of possibilities of artistic expression.

Among the most important African-American abstractionists has been William T. Williams (b. 1942). He works in large-scale abstractions characterized by the use of geometry, color, and complex surface textures, creating subtle moods and atmospheres as he responds to the aesthetic impulses of his environment. Al Loving (b. 1935) also works in an abstract idiom. Spatial relationships, color, and illusion dominate his large acrylic canvases and small watercolor collages. His forms appear suspended in space, amplifying the sense of illusion.

Other abstract artists include Jack Whitten (b. 1939), who explores surface textures and organic structures that resemble intensely magnified sections of human skin or the tile mosaics of ancient floor patterns. Whitten is also interested in human efforts to decorate and ornament the skin, as in the African practice of scarification. Oliver Jackson (b. 1935), a California painter, explores the power and energy of nature. His paintings reduce humanity to a subordinate element within the grand scale of his oversized acrylics. Jackson is also a sculptor whose wood creations reveal the power, energy, and strength of his vision. Raymond Saunders (1934) has developed a very personal style in which the environment around him is reflected in large studies, articulated with iconographic symbols and markings embedded in the surface of the picture plane. Saunders uses painting as a vehicle to communicate with the community by creating a visual dialogue of ideas, images, and symbolic metaphors.

Sam Gilliam (b. 1933) exhibited unorthodox canvases in the 1972 Venice Biennale, which broke his connection to "easel" art. The huge canvases (over 100 feet long) were painted on the studio floor by pouring buckets of paint on the surface and moving the pigment across the canvas with brooms. Later he extended this process by cutting and repasting sections of these canvases, configuring them into large shaped paintings, juxtaposing bright color, texture, and form. In other commission projects he would wrap entire buildings or drape interior spaces with his creations. Gilliam has been fascinated with the properties of paint, light, colors, and texture, and their relationship to architecture and space.

Another contemporary style was exemplified in the work of the highly publicized and controversial work of Jean-Michel Basquiat (1960–1988). Although often dismissed as a mere graffiti artist, he expanded and redefined the nature of abstract expressionist painting through the use of popular heroes and symbolic metaphors in his works. Basquiat reorganized the nature of the picture plane by using popular imagery and mixed media on grand-scale surfaces to make biting commentaries on society. He was especially concerned with the politics of African-American art within the larger society. His early stardom, friendships with Pop artists Andy Warhol and Keith Haring, and the media attention he garnered (as well as his early death) have to some extent obscured his true worth. Basquiat's work was far ahead of his time and extends the range of expression for abstract American art traditions.

Robert Colescott's (b. 1925) signature style of figurative paintings is intended to place African Americans within the canons of Western art traditions. In the Knowledge Is the Key to the Past series (1970s), Colescott recreates famous historical compositions by European artists and replaces the subjects with black characters. The results are satirical indictments of Western society that disturb both white and black viewers. Bold color and complex compositions combined with the gesturally painted figures amplify the importance of the issues involved. His sociopolitical commentaries, with their deft skewering of stereotypes, have often provoked controversy, negative reactions, and great debate about the relevance of art history and the dominance of Western mainstream attitudes of inclusion and exclusion.

A number of modern artists have integrated African philosophical systems with conceptual art. Howardena Pindell (b. 1943) is a multi-talented artist and writer who works in a broad range of media, including painting, prints, video, performance art, and installations. Her works are provocative and have often been compared to those of Colescott for their political stance. David Hammons (1943), like Pindell, has embraced controversy through his creations, made from materials such as hairballs, wine bottles, greasy paper bags, bottle caps, snowballs, coal, chicken wings, and barbecued ribs. Hammons treats even the most conflicted and challenging aspects of the black experience with a sense of reverence and deep spirituality. Houston Conwill's (b. 1947) inventiveness creates sculpture, installations, and performance art that recall the time, place, and memory of African and African-American cultural rituals of the past. He has been preoccupied with defining the nature of sacred space in the African-American community and has executed numerous public commissions throughout the United States.

Richard Hunt (b. 1935) and Martin Puryear (b. 1941) are two of the most distinguished contemporary African-American sculptors. Both work in distinct styles. Hunt works in metal, usually steel, creating works that are derived from plant and animal forms. The metal is shaped to convey figuratively expressive forms of plants and insects. Puryear creates objects whose forms are inspired by architectural structures and functional objects essential to the lives of African-, Asian-, and Native-American peoples. His materials include wood, metal, fiber, stone, and wax. The expanded scale of the objects often sets up a psychological juxtaposition that challenges the notion of the function and role of the objects as art.

During the 1970s and the 1980s, sculptural traditions began to expand in the direction of environmental and installation art. One of the most important and successful artists in this stylistic genre was Fred Wilson (b. 1954). Wilson began as a mixed–media artist, using a wide variety of found objects to construct sculptural forms that had strong political commentary targeting America's inherent attitudes towards people of color. In 1994 he was commissioned to execute a unique installation at the Maryland Historical Society in Baltimore, Maryland, using the artifacts of that institution. "Mining the Museum" was a groundbreaking exhibition that redefined how museums could effectively use the objects and artifacts to educate the public about culture, history, and aesthetics. Wilson was invited to museums all over the world and throughout the United States to teach curators his theories of exhibition artistry. In 1999, he won the highly prestigious MacArthur Foundation Fellowship (often called the "genius grant").

Kerry James Marshall (b. 1955) has continued in this tradition by focusing his work on the social, civil, and popular culture of the African-American experience. Marshall's work concentrates on larger-than-life paintings, but he has expanded this type of work to include sculpture, installation art, photography, comic books, and video. In 1992, he was a recipient of a MacArthur Fellowship for his work examining and critiquing black history and identity.

Renee Stout (b. 1958), like Wilson and Marshall, works in a mixed media, installation tradition that explores the spiritual relationships within the African-American experience. Her work is very personal in the creation of boxes and spaces that reflect and use material culture to illuminate the extraordinary narrative within the lives of ordinary people of color.

Increasingly, African-American artists have become bold and confrontational in their aesthetic response to continual resistance of opportunity for all Americans. Kara Walker (b. 1969) has been most effective and intense in her approach to imaging the aesthetic issues of America. Using the eighteenth-century tradition of black cutout silhouettes, Walker creates fantastical narratives of black women, children, and men in various states of abuse, often explicit sexually, to draw direct attention to the hidden and covert practices of a culture whose history and attitudes were built on slavery. Kara Walker's work is often so startling in its detail of abuse that she forces the viewer to respond by having a conversation or reaction to the conditions of her artistic and intellectual crusade to attack racism and sexism. In 1997 she became the youngest recipient of the MacArthur Fellowship.

The proliferation of contemporary African-American art in the late twentieth and early twenty-first centuries represents the culmination of the work of many generations of creative black painters and sculptors. African-American artists first had to struggle simply to gain access to the world of fine art, and once the barriers began to open, they were faced with the equally important task of finding their own distinctive voice—and that of demanding that it be heard and given respect. Amid the turbulence of the contemporary artistic scene, few groups have been as important as African-American artists in directing the attention of artists to issues such as race, gender, identity, culture, politics, and a critical self-examination of the operations of the art world itself. At the same time, one cannot pigeonhole African-American art into one type of expression; black artists have created and are creating works in styles and forms ranging from quiet intellectual contemplation to works of militant engagement. The accomplishments of African-American art are testament to the creative expectations of black artists, as they meld the complexities of their African and multiethnic American heritages and the innovations and challenges of the electronic digital age with their personal visions. These achievements will continue to endure and lead to new forms of visual expressiveness.

See also Art in the United States, Contemporary; Bannister, Edward Mitchell; Basquiat, Jean-Michel; Black Arts Movement; Burroughs, Margaret Taylor; Catlett, Elizabeth; Delaney, Joseph; Douglas, Aaron; Fuller, Meta Vaux Warrick; Hammons, David; Harlem Renaissance; Johnson, Joshua; Lawrence, Jacob; Lewis, Edmonia; Ligon, Glenn; Locke, Alain Leroy; Marshall, Kerry James; Modernism and Primitivism; Motley, Archibald John, Jr.; Parks, Gordon; Puryear, Martin; Savage, Augusta; Stout, Reneé; Tanner, Henry Ossawa; Walker, Kara; Wheatley, Phillis; Woodruff, Hale

■ ■ *Bibliography*

Benezra, Neal. *Martin Puryear*. Chicago: Art Institute of Chicago, 1992.

Cannon, Steve, Kellie Jones, and Tom Finkelpearl. *David Hammons: Rousing the Rubble*. Cambridge, Mass.: MIT Press, 1991.

Cheekwood Museum of Art. *The Art of William Edmondson*. Jackson: University Press of Mississippi, 1999.

Columbus Museum of Art. *Elijah Pierce: Woodcarver*. Seattle: University of Washington Press, 1992.

Connecticut Gallery. *Charles Ethan Porter*. Marlborough: Connecticut Gallery, 1987.

Dallas Museum of Art. *Black Art Ancestral Legacy: The African Impulse in African-American Art*. Dallas, Tex.: Dallas Museum of Art, 1989.

Driskell, David. *Two Centuries of Black American Art*. Los Angeles, Calif.: Los Angeles County Museum of Art, 1976.

Driskell, David. *Hidden Heritage: Afro-American Art, 1800–1950*. Bellevue, Wash.: Bellevue Art Museum, 1985.

Good-Bryant, Linda, and Marcy S. Philips. *Contextures*. New York: Just Above Midtown, 1978.

Harris, Michael D., and Wyatt MacGaffey. *Astonishment and Power: Kongo Minkisi and the Art of Renee Stout*. Washington, D.C.: National Museum of African Art, 1993.

Hartigan, Lynda Roscoe. *Sharing Traditions: Five Black Artists in Nineteenth-Century America*. Washington, D.C.: Smithsonian Institution Press, 1985.

Howard University Gallery of Art. *James A. Porter: Artist and Art Historian—The Memory of the Legacy*. Washington, D.C.: Howard University Gallery of Art, 1992.

Ketner, Joseph D. *The Emergence of the African-American Artist: Robert S. Duncanson, 1821–1872*. Columbia: University of Missouri Press, 1993.

King-Hammond, Leslie. *Masks and Mirrors: African-American Art, 1700–Now*. New York: Abbeville, 1995.

King-Hammond, Leslie, and Tritobia Benjamin. *Three Generations of African American Women Sculptors: A Study in Paradox*. Philadelphia: Afro-American Historical and Cultural Museum, 1996.

LeFalle-Collins, Lizzetta, and Judith Wilson. *Sargent Johnson: African American Modernist*. San Francisco: San Francisco Museum of Modern Art, 1998.

Lewis, Samella. *African-American Art and Artists*, 3d ed. Berkeley: University of California Press, 2003.

Livingston, Jane, and John Beardsley. *Black Folk Art in America, 1930–1980*. Washington, D.C.: Corcoran Gallery of Art, 1982.

Locke, Alain. *The Negro in Art*. Washington, D.C.: Associates in Negro Folk Education, 1940.

Marshall, Kerry James, Terrie Sultan, and Arthur Jafa. *Kerry James Marshall*. New York: Harry N. Abrams, 2000.

Mosby, Dewey F. *Henry Ossawa Tanner*. Philadelphia: Philadelphia Museum of Art, 1991.

Nesbit, Peter T., and Michelle DuBois, ed. *Over the Line: The Art and Life of Jacob Lawrence*. Seattle: University of Washington Press, 2000.

Neuberger Museum of Art. *Melvin Edwards Sculpture: A Thirty-Year Retrospective, 1963–1993*. Purchase, N.Y.: Neuberger Museum of Art, 1993.

Porter, James A. *Modern Negro Art*. New York: Dryden Press, 1943. Reprint, Washington, D.C.: Howard University Press, 1992.

Powell, Richard. *Homecoming: The Life and Art of William Henry Johnson*. Washington, D.C.: Smithsonian Institution Press, 1992.

Reynolds, Gary A., and Beryl J. Wright, eds. *Against the Odds: African-American Artists and the Harmon Foundation*. Newark, N.J.: Newark Museum, 1989.

Robinson, Jontlyle Teresa, and Wendy Greenhouse. *The Art of Archibald J. Motley, Jr.* Chicago: Chicago Historical Society, 1991.

Rodgus, Kenneth. *Climbing Up the Mountain: The Modern Art of Malvin Gray Johnson*. Durham, N.C.: North Carolina Central University Art Museum, 2002.

Shaw, Gwendolyn DuBois. *Seeing the Unspeakable: The Art of Kara Walker*. Chapel Hill, N.C.: Duke University Press, 2005.

Stein, Judith E. *I Tell My Heart: The Art of Horace Pippen*. Philadelphia: Pennsylvania Academy of the Fine Arts, 1994.

Studio Museum in Harlem. *Beauford Delaney: A Retrospective*. New York: Studio Museum in Harlem, 1978.

Studio Museum in Harlem. *Tradition and Conflict: Images of a Turbulent Decade, 1963–1973*. New York: Studio Museum in Harlem, 1985.

Studio Museum in Harlem. *Harlem Renaissance: Art of Black America*. New York: Harry N. Abrams, 1987.

Taylor, William E., and Harriet G. Warkel. *A Shared Heritage: Art by Four African Americans*. Indianapolis, Ind.: Indianapolis Museum of Art, 1996.

Wilson, Fred. *Mining the Museum, an Installation*, edited by Lisa Corrin. Baltimore, Md.: Contemporary, 1995.

Wilson, James L. *Clementine Hunter: American Folk Artist*. Gretna, La.: Pelican, 1988.

LESLIE KING HAMMOND (1996)
Updated by author 2005

PALCY, EUZHAN

JANUARY 13, 1958

❙❙❙━━━━━━━━━

Born and raised in Martinique, the film director and producer Euzhan Palcy began her career as a child singer and songwriter. The commercial success of her first album led the teenager to her own weekly poetry show on television. In 1974, she wrote, directed, and performed in the first West Indian television production ever mounted in the French colony. *The Messenger* (La Messagère), released in 1975, focused on the relationship between a young girl and her grandmother. "It was the first time that the people of Martinique saw themselves on television speaking French and Creole and being themselves," recalled Palcy (Welbon, 1998).

Euzhan Palcy moved to Paris in 1975 to pursue her childhood dream of becoming a film director. She earned a master's degree in French literature, a master's degree in theater, and a D.E.A. in art and archeology from the Sorbonne. She also earned a film degree from the renowned Louis Lumière School of Cinema, where she focused on cinematography.

In 1983, with the help of her "French godfather," the director François Truffaut, and a grant from the French government, Palcy adapted the 1974 novel *La Rue Cases Nègres* by Martinique author Josef Zobel into her first feature film, *Sugar Cane Alley (Rue Cases Nègres)*. The coming-of-age story garnered over seventeen international film awards, including the Silver Lion and Best Lead Actress awards at the Venice Film Festival and the César Award for Best First Feature Film from the French Film Academy (Académie des Arts et Techniques du Cinema).

Sugar Cane Alley was an international box office success. In Martinique it even outgrossed Steven Spielberg's *E.T.: The Extra-Terrestrial*, the Hollywood blockbuster of that year.

Palcy is also the first woman of African descent to direct a feature film produced by a major Hollywood studio—her film *A Dry White Season* was released by MGM in 1989. The actor Marlon Brando felt that the anti-apartheid drama was so important that he ended a nine-year period of seclusion and volunteered to play a part in the film, for which he received an Academy Award nomination.

Palcy has directed a number of other projects, including the feature film *Siméon* (1992), the three-part documentary series *Aimé Césaire: A Voice for History* (1995), the Wonderful World of Disney television movie *The Ruby Bridges Story* (1997), and the Showtime cable television movie *The Killing Yard* (2001).

Palcy continues to be acknowledged for her contributions to media dialogues regarding social, political, and cultural issues. In 1994 Palcy was given the title Chevalier dans l'Ordre National du Mérite (Knight in the National Order of Merit) from the president of France, François Mitterand. In 1997 a movie theater in Amiens, France, was named Cinema Euzhan Palcy, and, in 2000, Martinique's first high school dedicated to the study of film was named after her. Palcy was also awarded the Sojourner Truth Award at the 2001 Cannes Film Festival. Today, she continues to develop, produce, and direct television and film projects in the United States and Europe.

See also Film; Filmmakers in the Caribbean

■ ■ *Bibliography*

Acker, Ally. *Reel Women: Pioneers of the Cinema 1896 to the Present.* New York: Continuum, 1991.

Baron, Cynthia. "Euzhan Palcy." In *The St. James Women's Filmmakers Encyclopedia,* edited by Amy L. Unterburger. Farmington Hills, Mich.: Visible Ink Press, 1999.

"Euzhan Palcy: Director, Writer, Producer." Available from <http://euzhanpalcy.com>.

Welbon, Yvonne. Interview with Euzhan Palcy at Palcy's home in Santa Monica, California, April 5, 1998.

Welbon, Yvonne, dir. and prod. *Sisters in Cinema.* Our Film Works, 2003.

YVONNE WELBON (2005)

PALENQUE SAN BASILIO

The free-black community of Palenque San Basilio is the most renowned runaway slave community in Colombian history; however, many aspects of the origins and nature of the town remain unclear. Situated in the mountains of the Sierra del María about seventy kilometers from Cartagena de Indias, in the municipality of Mahates, Palenque San Basilio stands as a testimony to the resistance of enslaved Africans and their descendants and to their insistence that they could be loyal citizens ready to contribute to the shaping of Colombia's society.

PALENQUES AND CIMARRONES

Enslaved Africans accompanied the early European conquerors in the Americas, and from the outset individuals struggled for their freedom through flight. They sought to establish themselves in inhospitable areas of northern South America whose difficulty of access offered natural protection from their persecutors. The word *palenque* is derived from the wooden palisades they built as a defensive measure around the fugitive communities. The palenques were typically agricultural communities that sought self-sufficiency; however, they were also defensive centers surrounded by high wooden palisades, defensive ditches, and sharpened wooden stakes to entrap the unwary attacker.

During the early colonial period, groups of runaways were usually led by escaped Africans. These leaders sometimes called themselves kings, referring to an African nobility or aristocracy and thus drawing legitimacy from their social standing in Africa. For example, Domingo Biohó, the self-styled *rey de arcabuco,* or king of the swamps, was also known as the king of La Matuna, the palenque he led. However, historians suggest that it was unlikely that members of royal families in Africa would have been sold into transatlantic slavery, and these references to African nobility may have been devices adopted by powerful military leaders to enhance their standing before their communities. Still, it is also recognized that many enslaved Africans were captured during military excursions and thus most of them had military experience that served them well in their attempts to defend themselves once they were able to escape their enslavement in America. As the colonial period wore on, though, the leadership of these communities changed. Later leaders were far more likely to be enslaved *criollos,* or people of African descent born in the Americas, and they typically called themselves captains or governors rather than kings.

During the sixteenth and seventeenth centuries, runaway slaves became the bane of colonial governors, especially around Cartagena de Indias, the most important port of entry for enslaved Africans arriving into Hispanic South America. These runaways escaped from mines, from haciendas, and from towns, and regrouped to form defensive communities. From their fortified camps, they sallied forth to rustle cattle, steal indigenous and other women and children, and rob travelers, terrifying the European populations of the area. The relative strength or weakness of the Spaniards and their allies shaped their response to the *cimarrones* (runaway slaves). At times the Spanish aggressively sought to destroy the palenques, whereas at other moments they were forced to negotiate uneasy truces with them. An example of this at the beginning of the seventeenth century was the community led by Benkos (Domingo) Biohó. The name *Biohó* probably comes from a region of Guinea-Bissau in West Africa. Some historians suggest that Domingo Biohó was a member of an African royal family from Guinea who in 1599, together with his wife and several other enslaved companions, escaped his Spanish owner, Juan Gómez, and eventually formed the palenque La Matuna. Successive governors of Cartagena sought to deal with the challenge of the palenque until finally in 1612 a negotiated settlement was achieved through which the fugitive slaves were recognized as free and granted privileges by the Spanish crown. The former slaves promised to return any new escapees, and they were given free passage to enter and leave the city of Cartagena; Biohó himself was granted the privilege of dressing as a Spaniard. However, in 1619 he was challenged by the guards as he sought to enter the city; violence resulted, and he was quickly tried and hung. Domingo Biohó's legacy lived on through the colonial period as the image of the rebel fugitive slave leader took hold. His name became synonymous with that of the strong African leader. Between 1600 and 1790 historical references can be found to the hanging of several individuals such as Domingo Bioo, Domingo Biho, and Dominguillo Bioho, testimony to the power of this indomitable rebel leader's legend. It was within this historical trajectory that other groups of runaways created communities such as Palenque San Basilio at various moments during the colonial period.

PALENQUE SAN BASILIO

Palenque San Basilio was created by fugitives who regrouped after escaping from the destruction of other palenques, such as Tabacal, Matudere, and Arenal, at the end of the seventeenth century. The first documentary references to San Basilio date from 1713, when a group of *cimarrones* came to an agreement with the bishop of Cartagena, Fray Antonio Mariá Casiani. Although it is tempting to associate Palenque San Basilio with Domingo Biohó's La Matuna, the historical documentation suggests only that San Basilio was created by fugitive slaves and that the Spanish were never able to reconquer them. In order to win the fugitives over to Christianity in the beginning of the eighteenth century, Casiani, with the governor's consent, granted San Basilio's residents a general pardon with the understanding that the former slaves would not harbor future runaways. Nicolás de Santa Rosa was the captain of the community and he reached an agreement with the bishop after the prelate arrived in the palenque. They built a church and a baptismal font, and the bishop said mass and christened the town San Basilio Magno, since he was a member of the order of Saint Basil. He appointed a parish priest and put the church under the care of Saint Michael the archangel. He then took a census, counting some 234 souls in the town. He read the terms of the agreement before the congregated community, and everyone accepted it and confirmed Nicolás de Santa Rosa as their leader. The town's official posts were filled and it was agreed that the community would elect its own leader and that no whites would be admitted to the palenque except for the priest. From that moment, the settlement reappeared intermittently in historical documents so that in 1772, for example, San Basilio was described as a *población de negros*, or a black community, created by runaway slaves.

The isolation of Palenque San Basilio allowed particular cultural forms to develop or to be maintained within the community. For example, the people of the town traditionally have not mixed with other populations and even today speak their own particular language, Palenquero, which is recognized as a derivative of a Bantu-based language with much vocabulary of Kikongo origin. Linguists argue that the origins of Palenquero can be traced to West Central Africa, the region from which enslaved people known as Congos and Angolas came. The existence of its own language has enabled Palenque San Basilio to preserve its social cohesion and the unique identity of its residents.

Until the end of the nineteenth century *palenqueros* (residents of Palenque San Basilio) were extremely isolated from the rest of Colombian society, with a closed agricultural economy that shaped the community's material life. They grew rice, corn, yucca, *plátano* (plantains), *ñame* (yams), and peanuts, and they raised cattle. Only with the cultivation of sugarcane in the early twentieth century did San Basilio begin to integrate into Colombian national life. Contemporary Palenque San Basilio consists of the town and the surrounding mountains, where cattle graze and the crops are grown. The women of the palenque have usually had the most contact with the outside world, since they sell their products in the city while the men take care of the cattle and prepare the ground for crops of yucca and *ñame*.

SOCIAL STRUCTURE

The basic social category in San Basilio is the *cuagro*, an age group with both male and female members. Compounds consisting of several households are divided at their fundamental level into these *cuagros*. Some anthropologists suggest that it is through this social grouping that work is organized and that rituals such as weddings and deaths are enacted. Because of the historical context in which palenques developed—a state of perpetual guerrilla warfare—the ideal of fighting and aggressive struggle has also become an integral part of San Basilio's culture and can be seen in the number of successful world-class boxers who have come from the town.

In contemporary Colombia, Palenque San Basilio stands as the symbol of the autonomy of black communities. Nonetheless, changes in the twentieth century have altered San Basilio's internal political and social structures. Community issues were traditionally discussed in meetings of the townspeople under the direction of a committee led by a respected elder through a consultative approach, but this hierarchy has been broken by the intrusion of foreign political forms. This loss of autonomy has not been purely negative. For example, Article 70, added in 1993 to the 1991 Colombian Constitution, formally recognized Afro-Colombian ethnicity and the right of black communities to claim title to land they have traditionally worked; however, in practice this continues to be a highly charged political and economic issue and has led to violence.

See also Runaway Slaves in Latin America and the Caribbean

■ ■ *Bibliography*

Arrazola Caicedo, Roberto. *Palenque: Primer pueblo libre de America.* Bogotá, Colombia: Todo Impresores, 1986.

Borrego Plá, Maria del Carmen. *Palenques de negros en Cartagena de Indias a fines del siglo XVII.* Seville, Spain: Publicaciones de la Escuela de Estudios Hispano-Americanos de Sevilla, 1973.

De Friedemann, Nina S. *Ma Ngombe: Guerreros y ganaderos en Palenque.* Bogotá, Colombia: Carlos Valencia Editores, 1987.

De Friedemann, Nina S. *La saga del negro: Presencia africana en Colombia.* Bogotá, Colombia: Instituto de Genética Humana, Facultad de Medicina Pontificia Universidad Javeriana, 1993.

Escalante, Aquiles. *El Palenque de San Basilio: Una Comunidad de descendientes de negros cimarrones.* 2d edition. Barranquilla, Colombia: Editorial Mejoras, 1979.

Navarrete, Maria Cristina. "Cimarrones y palenques en las provincias al norte del Nuevo Reino de Granada siglo XVII." *Fronteras de la Historia* 6 (2001): 87–107.

Navarrete, Maria Cristina. *Cimarrones y palenques en el siglo XVII.* Cali, Colombia: Universidad del Valle, 2003.

Schwegler, Armin. *"Chi ma Kongo": Lengua y rito ancestrales en El Palenque de San Basilio (Colombia).* 2 vols. Frankfurt and Madrid: Ibero-Americana, 1996.

Zuluaga R., Francisco U. "Cimarronismo en el suroccidente del antiguo Virreinato de Santafe de Bogota." In *De Ficciones y realidades: Perspectivas sobre literature e historia colombianas: Memorias del Quinto Congreso de Colombianistas.* Compiled by Alvaro Pineda Botero and Raymond L. Williams. Bogotá, Colombia: Tercer Mundo Editores, with Universidad de Cartagena, 1989.

RENÉE SOULODRE-LA FRANCE (2005)

PALMARES

Beginning in the middle of the seventeenth century, there were reports of the formation of communities of escaped slaves in Brazil. These communities of fugitives were known as *quilombos* or *mocambos*. In the majority of the Bantu languages of Central and West Central Africa, the word *quilombo* means "encampment." In West Central Africa during the seventeenth and eighteenth centuries, the word *kilombo* also referred to the initiation rituals of the military societies of the Imbangala people (also known as the Jagas). The Imbangala were Kimbundu-speaking people of northeastern Angola. Their expansion into the interior of Angola, the land of the Umbundu, began in the sixteenth century, and, in accordance with their political, social, and military strategy, they followed the practice of incorporating the inhabitants of the conquered regions into their group through the use of rituals.

There were other historical processes surrounding the quilombos. Whereas there has not been much systematic academic research in this area, it has been suggested that the existence of a slave culture and the re-creation of many significant elements of the kilombo ritual among the captives of Brazil served to aid the slaves in establishing quilombos. They reorganized themselves into communities of Africans from diverse regions, including Brazilian-born *crioulos*. It is possible to establish connections between the significance of kilombo in Central Africa and the establishment of quilombos in Brazil. These connections were important for their symbolic significance and for the redevelopment of certain African cultural and ritual aspects within the Brazilian slave experience.

PALMARES

The first reports of Palmares—one of the most important communities of fugitive Africans in the Americas—surfaced during the last decades of the sixteenth century. Located in Alagoas, in the old captaincy (or province) of Pernambuco, the quilombo of Palmares was established in the heart of the Portuguese colonial empire. The mountains of the area were considered an ideal location for captives to take refuge, and thousands of Africans and their descendants constructed numerous communities in this area. In fact, Palmares wasn't just one quilombo; the community was a collection of numerous, perhaps dozens, of quilombos, joined together for purposes of defense and survival. Surrounded by largely inaccessible mountains and forests, the inhabitants of Palmares could count on considerable natural protection. Because of its flora and fauna, this location also guaranteed good hunting and fishing opportunities, as well as an abundance of fruits, roots, and plants. In this way, the people of the quilombo, well hidden in the forest's interior, could guarantee their survival. This ecological environment was thus fundamental for the residents of Palmares. They had the ability to understand and manage the geography, topography, plants, and animals of these forests. In a hostile area—one not always similar to their African regions of origin—they were capable of establishing dominion over nature, transforming it from an adversary into an ally.

Even as Palmares was being born, the first inhabitants of Palmares were being reborn, for they were creating a new world—an African world reinvented in Brazil by fugitive blacks. The residents of the quilombo—Brazilian-born slaves and Africans of diverse ethnic identities—forged a world in which they could live in freedom. They re-created their cultures and organized themselves militarily in order to fight invaders, and they established economic practices in order to guarantee survival for themselves. It was the development of this original social system that concerned and frightened the landowners and Portuguese authorities.

THE ECONOMICS OF PALMARES

Palmares's economic production was not solely for the subsistence of its large population. The surpluses the Palmarinos created presented opportunities for commerce with tavern owners and the residents of nearby areas. They traded manioc (cassava) flour, palm wine, butter, and other products in exchange for firearms, gunpowder, textiles, salt, and tools. This commerce between the quilombos of Palmares, the inhabitants of small settlements, and tavern owners of the captaincy worried the authorities.

These groups had formed a clandestine mercantile network that was not just useful economically; it also created a sense of solidarity among the people of Palmares. However, many of the inhabitants of these areas were accused of giving protection to the Palmarinos. It was said that many of the expeditions against the quilombos failed due to the information passed along by their trading partners. There are even reports that many traders, peddlers, and tavern owners frequented the quilombos in Palmares, looking to establish direct commercial relations with the inhabitants.

Apart from this, constant attacks greatly frightened the populations closest to Palmares. The people of the quilombo did not do this just to obtain the products they needed, but also to intimidate and punish those who promoted punitive expeditions against them (principally the large landholders). The Palmarinos also collected tribute—in provisions, money, and arms—from the inhabitants of villages and towns. Those who would not collaborate could see their property sacked, their cane fields and plantations burnt, and their slaves kidnapped. This was the response the Palmarinos gave to those who would enslave other blacks and contribute to their destruction.

THE CULTURE OF THE QUILOMBOS

Initially, the quilombos were formed by Africans of diverse ethnicities and different languages. The culture of Palmares, then, was formed out of a combination of these various cultures. Africans from the Bantu ethnic-linguistic group, originally from the west-central areas of Africa (Congo and Angola) predominated. Despite this, the African culture of the Palmarinos was remade into something new. The religious practices forged in these quilombos had as many traces of magic and rituals of various parts of Africa as of indigenous religions and the popular Catholicism learned in the slave quarters. Indeed, some of these Africans had already come into contact with Christianity in Africa itself, dating from the beginning of the European occupation in the middle of the fifteenth century. Punitive expeditions sent by the authorities found chapels and sanctuaries in Palmares. Included within these places of worship were images of Catholic saints. This religious syncretism of the Palmarinos demonstrated the ways in which people developed their own culture in the quilombos. It was not just that their African past was re-created; the quilombo residents—not just Africans, but also Afro-Brazilians and those born free in the forests—reinvented a new Africa in Brazil. They worshiped both African gods and Catholic saints, and they created new symbols of religious significance. In a general sense—just as in Africa—they perceived their gods as harnessers of the forces of nature. Thus, plants, fire, and water could have the same spiritual power as Christian images and symbols.

By the middle of the seventeenth century, the population of Palmares had already reached more than 20,000 people. (Some chroniclers of the era, no doubt exaggerating, spoke of 30,000 residents.) Among those residing in these mountains were blacks, people of mixed heritage, and even some Indians and whites who were hiding out from the colonial authorities. Palmares was divided into numerous smaller quilombos all along the Serra da Barriga. The most important ones were named for their chiefs and commanders. The primary quilombo, known by the name Macaco (Monkey), was the political and administrative center, functioning as the capital of Palmares. It was also the most populous, with thousands of houses, and the home of Ganga Zumba, one of the principal leaders of Palmares.

The sparseness of the population distribution within this immense forest allowed for some natural protection, making it possible to devise an intelligent military defense strategy. When one quilombo was attacked, the Palmarinos would take refuge in others. That way, it was impossible to attack all of them simultaneously. Aside from the primary quilombos, there were dozens of others scattered further away. Many of these simply served as military camps or trading outposts. Other quilombos like Palmares also existed in the captaincies of Paraiba and Rio Grande do Norte. Even though this dispersion of quilombos into an extensive geographic area had occurred, there was unity and communication among them. Their economic practices proved to be complementary—while one quilombo could produce almond butter, another made palm wine. Central power remained in the hands of Ganga Zumba, even though some others had a degree of military and economic autonomy. The socioeconomic structure of Palmares was strongly oriented toward its political-military organization, particularly when attacks against the quilombos were intensified in the second half of the seventeenth century.

CONFLICTS WITH COLONIAL AUTHORITIES

The Palmarinos resisted innumerable punitive expeditions sent by the Portuguese and Dutch (during their occupation of the Northeast in the middle of the seventeenth century), as well as expeditions sent by local ranchers, who always felt a deep antipathy toward them. The Palmarinos—led by Ganga Zumba and later Zumbi—had a complex economic, military, and political organization. Portuguese colonial authorities, who encountered numerous difficulties in their attempts to destroy so many quilombos, began proposing peace treaties, looking to recog-

nize the autonomy of the quilombos under the Crown, freedom for the blacks born in Palmares, and a return of all other fugitives. While an agreement was initially accepted in 1678, it was later rejected by the quilombos and sabotaged by the ranchers and businessmen who were interested in the lands occupied by the quilombos. Nevertheless, Palmares was essentially destroyed in 1695 by a large force of *bandeirantes* (mercenary fighters), who brought in cannons to destroy the fortifications the people of the quilombos had constructed.

The colonial forces combed the mountains in search of Zumbi. More than just destroying Palmares, his capture was considered of fundamental importance for the colonial authorities. The well-protected leader of Palmares was eventually betrayed; he was found and assassinated on November 20, 1695. Despite Zumbi's death, the authorities knew that the fight against the quilombos of Palmares was not over. There still remained thousands of people within the quilombos of the Alagoas mountains, and other quilombos in nearby captaincies still existed. Thus, the attacks against Palmares continued. In 1696 the quilombo of Quissama was attacked. The gradual occupation of the Pernambucan mountains was pushing the quilombo residents into other regions.

In the early years of the eighteenth century, Palmares continued to tax the efforts of the colonial authorities. In 1703 Camoanga, the new leader of Palmares, was killed during an attack, and repressive forces remained quartered in the region until at least 1725. Even though some quilombos still populated the region, they were much more widely dispersed at this time, because they had been pushed away from the interior. Many groups from the quilombos migrated to the captaincy of Paraiba, where they established new mocambos. Thus, though they were not totally destroyed, the unity of the quilombos in the manner of Palmares would never be realized again.

Beyond Palmares and its tradition of freedom, which spanned from the end of the sixteenth century to the first quarter of the eighteenth, other traditions surfaced in different contexts within colonial Brazil that caused the metropolitan and colonial authorities a great amount of fear. Many large quilombos arose in the Captaincies of Minas Gerais and Mato Grosso in the eighteenth century, and others surfaced in diverse colonial and frontier regions into the nineteenth century.

After the abolition of slavery in Brazil, Palmares and Zumbi were transformed into symbols of political militancy. The year 1995 marked the commemoration of the 300th anniversary of the death of Zumbi. November 20, the date of his death, is a holiday in many Brazilian cities, and it is regarded as an important date in the black community. The black movements of the 1970s turned the day into the National Day of Black Consciousness. There is also a monument in homage to Zumbi in the Serra da Barriga.

In addition, many academics, social movements, and state, municipal, and federal authorities have made efforts to recognize the quilombo communities that remain in Brazil. With the right to agrarian land title officially recognized in the Brazilian Constitution of 1988, hundreds of rural black communities scattered all over Brazil are fighting for land and citizenship. They are, in essence, attempting to reclaim diverse and complex historical processes in the formation of a black rural society, encompassing the period from slavery to post-emancipation.

See also Anti-Colonial Movements; Coartación; Runaway Slaves in Latin America and the Caribbean

■ ■ *Bibliography*

Alves Filho, Ivan. *Memorial dos Palmares*. Rio de Janeiro, Brazil: Xenon, 1988.

Anderson, Robert Nelson. "The Quilombo of Palmares: A New Overview of a Maroon State in Seventeenth-Century Brazil." *Journal of Latin American Studies* 28 (1996): 545–566.

Carneiro, Edison. *O quilombo de Palmares,* 4th ed. São Paulo, Brazil: Companhia Editora Nacional, 1988.

Ennes, Ernesto. *As Guerras nos Palmares*. São Paulo, Brazil: Companhia Editora Nacional, 1938.

Freitas, Décio. *Palmares, a guerra dos escravos,* 5th ed. Porto Alegre, Brazil: Mercado Aberto, 1984.

Freitas, Mário Martins de. M. *Reino negro de Palmares*, 2nd ed. Rio de Janeiro, Brazil: Biblioteca do Exército Editora, 1988.

Funari, Pedro Paulo A. "A Arqueologia de Palmares—Sua contribuição para o conhecimento da história da cultura afro-americana." In *Liberdade por um fio: História dos quilombos no Brasil,* edited by João José Reis and Flávio dos Santos Gomes. São Paulo, Brazil: Companhia das Letras, 1996.

Kent, R. K. "Palmares: An African State in Brazil." In *Maroon Societies: Rebel Slave Communities in the Americas,* edited by Richard Price. Garden City, N.Y.: Doubleday, 1973.

Orser, Charles E, Jr., and Pedro Paulo A. Funari. "A 'República de Palmares' e a Arqueologia da Serra da Barriga." *Revista USP* 28 (1995–1996): 6–13.

Peret, Benjamim. *O Quilombo de Palmares: Cronica da "República dos Escravos," Brasil, 1640–1695*. Lisbon, Portugal: Fenda Edições, 1988.

Price, Richard. "Palmares como poderia ter sido." In *Liberdade por um fio: História dos quilombos no Brasil,* edited by João José Reis and Flávio dos Santos Gomes. São Paulo, Brazil: Companhia das Letras, 1996.

Reis, João José, and Flávio dos Santos Gomes, eds. *Liberdade por um fio: História dos quilombos no Brasil*. São Paulo, Brazil: Companhia das Letras, 1996.

Schwartz, Stuart B. "Rethinking Palmares: Slave Resistance in Colonial Brazil." In *Slaves, Peasants, and Rebels,* edited by Stuart B. Schwartz. Urbana: University of Illinois Press, 1992.

FLÁVIO GOMES (2005)

PAN-AFRICANISM

■ ■ ■

In its most general sense the term *Pan-Africanism* refers to a movement that seeks to unite and promote the welfare of all people identified with, or claiming membership in, the African or black race. Pan-Africanism is based on the idea of overcoming vast differences in language, ethnicity, religion, and geographical origin. Despite these divisions a degree of cultural unity has to some extent already been achieved among the African population of the United States because of forced interethnic mingling without regard to cultural or regional background during the slavery experience. Slavery forged African Americans into a truly Pan-African people who came to share a belief in a common destiny, deriving from the historic humiliations of slavery, colonialism, and racism. On a more positive note, Pan-Africanists also insist on recognizing the historic importance of contributions that Africa and the black race have made to civilization and human progress since the dawn of history.

Pan-Africanism assumes that the political unification of Africa will contribute to the welfare of all black people of African descent, whether or not they actually live in Africa. The African-American scholar W. E. B. Du Bois defined Pan-Africanism as "the idea of one Africa uniting the thought and ideals of all peoples of the dark continent," but observed that the idea had stemmed "naturally from the West Indies and the United States." Pan-African and black nationalist sentiments in the United States and in the Caribbean have provided much of the ideology for nationalist and decolonization movements on the African continent.

During the period 1957–1974 most of the colonial powers withdrew, at least formally, from their African colonies. Since then, political Pan-Africanism has focused on removing the vestiges of colonialism, particularly in South Africa, and on promoting economic and political unity among African nations. The institution that presently seeks to accomplish geopolitical unification of the continent is the Organization of African Unity (OAU), founded in 1963. In the United States the best-known African-American support organization is TransAfrica, founded in 1977.

Documents illustrating the history of Pan-Africanism began to appear during the late eighteenth century. Of signal importance was *The Interesting Narrative of the Life of Olaudah Equiano or Gustavus Vassa, the African, Written by Himself* (1787). Equiano's tract, published in England, has been identified by historian Imanuel Geiss (1974) as "proto-Pan-Africanism," but it lacked the militant self-assertiveness that is associated with the modern movement. Equiano, who had been enslaved as a child and traveled as a cabin boy to the New World, believed for a time that the African condition could be improved by resettling Christianized Africans from Europe and the Americas in Africa. Although he came to abandon that plan, he remained committed to the destruction of African slavery through the agencies of Christian missionary activity, free trade, and the establishment of an African nationality.

In 1787 British reformers began a campaign to resettle England's so-called black poor in the West African colony of Sierra Leone. Abolitionists saw themselves as creating a center for missionary activity and African redemption from the slave trade. Their efforts were supported by a small cadre of proto-Pan-Africanists, but Equiano eventually came to oppose African resettlement.

The diversity of the peoples who settled Sierra Leone illustrated the complexities of Pan-African identity. The first settlers were a mixed group, including African-American loyalists who had been evacuated with the British after the American Revolution and runaway slaves from the West Indies. A second group of immigrants came from Canada—ex-slaves who had fought on the British side in the American War for Independence and then temporarily settled in Nova Scotia. A third element also came from Nova Scotia but ultimately derived from a group known as Maroons, escaped slaves who had formed independent colonies in the mountains of Jamaica. These Maroons, after staging an unsuccessful revolt in 1795, were deported first to Nova Scotia and then to Sierra Leone. A fourth group were the so-called recaptives, persons of various African ethnicities deposited in Sierra Leone over the years after being recaptured from slave traders by the British fleet.

Black Americans showed an immediate interest in Sierra Leone. A group of settlers arrived from the United States in 1816, transported by Capt. Paul Cuffe, a man of mixed African and American Indian ancestry. Along with James Forten, a black sailmaker of Philadelphia, Cuffe hoped to develop Christianity, commerce, and civilization in Africa and to further thwart the slave trade while providing a homeland for African Americans. This emigrationist variety of American Pan-Africanism was undermined in 1817, however, with the formation of the American Society for Colonizing the Free People of Color in the United States, usually called the American Coloni-

zation Society (ACS). Because the ACS included a number of prominent slaveholders in its leadership and expressly denied any sympathy for abolition, the black American population was generally hostile to it. With the death of Cuffe, Forten became silent on the subjects of black nationalism and Pan-Africanism.

African Americans who supported the movement, as did Peter Williams Sr. and John Russwurm, were subjected to considerable public scorn. In the early nineteenth century, black Americans went through one of their periodic frenzies of name changing in an attempt to affirm their American loyalties. At this point even some of the more militant nationalist and Pan-Africanist organizations began to prefer the designation "Colored" over "African." Notable exceptions were the African Methodist Episcopal Church (AME) and the African Methodist Episcopal Zion Church (AMEZ).

The ideologies of black nationalism and Pan-Africanism evolved in the climate of the American and French revolutions, which gave currency to ideas of republican government and inspired certain classes of Africans to think of creating an African nation-state. One should not, however, assume that Pan-Africanism was simply an imitation of European or United States' ideology. It arose simultaneously with the European nationalisms and was a cognate rather than a derivative. C. L. R. James viewed the Haitian slave revolt (1791–1803) as the decisive event in the history of Pan-Africanism. Du Bois observed that the Haitian revolt led to the Louisiana Purchase and thus had a direct effect on white Americans' conceptions of nationalism and Manifest Destiny. It can be argued that Pan-Africanism and black nationalism in the Haitian republic were historically intertwined with the growth of the American nation and its conception of Manifest Destiny.

The Haitian revolt provided the impetus for the abortive revolution of the Jamaican Maroons in 1795. It also inspired early Pan-Africanism in the United States. Prince Hall, the Masonic lodge master from Massachusetts and sometime advocate of emigration, expressed his admiration of "our African brethren . . . in the French West Indies." There is no way of determining the extent to which Pan-Africanism touched the imaginations of the slave population of the United States, but there is some evidence that they were influenced by it. Herbert Aptheker has speculatively linked the slave conspiracy of Gabriel Prosser to the revolution in Haiti. The conspiracy of Denmark Vesey was said to have been inspired by the Haitian revolt, and Vesey was reputed to have dreamed of a black supernation uniting the southern states to the Caribbean.

Pan-African sentiments were strong among the African-American population of the early republic. The so-called Free African Societies of New York, Boston, and Rhode Island often expressed their identity with other Africans on both sides of the Atlantic. Early black newspapers revealed an interest in the history of Africa and the destiny of the African race. Overt identification with African affairs became unfashionable, however, when in 1816 the American Colonization Society was founded for the purpose of resettling the so-called free people of color in the colony of Liberia. David Walker published an incendiary *Appeal Together with a Preamble, to the Colored Citizens of the World* in 1829, in which he denounced Liberian colonization. Another early pamphleteer was Maria Stewart, who, although she referred to herself as an African, was equally hostile to the colonization movement. So too was Richard Allen, an organizer of the AME church, who believed in the unity of African peoples and a special God-given mission for them but steadfastly opposed any talk of Liberian colonization.

Peter Williams Sr., an Episcopal priest in New York, took a more tolerant view of African colonization. He eulogized Paul Cuffe, memorializing his voyages to Africa, and he remained friendly with John Russwurm, even after the latter was burned in effigy by anti-emigration activists. Classical black nationalism became practically indistinguishable from Pan-Africanism in the mid-nineteenth century. Between 1850 and 1862 the quest for a national homeland represented a desire to create, in Henry Highland Garnet's words, "a grand center of Negro Nationality." Although Martin Delany and a number of other black nationalists focused on Cuba and South America as possible sites for this "grand center," most black nationalists were inevitably drawn to Africa as the logical focus for a scheme of universal Negro improvement. Alexander Crummell, a protégé of Peter Williams, made his peace with the American Colonization Society and settled his hopes on Liberia. The entire generation of classical black nationalists, like the hero of Martin Delany's novel *Blake* (1859), believed in a commonality of interests among all African people, whether in Africa, the Caribbean, Europe, or North America.

At the time of the American Civil War, the Constitution of the African Civilization Society (1861) represented the Pan-African agenda in terms of "the civilization and Christianization of Africa, and of the descendants of African ancestors in any portion of the earth, wherever dispersed. Also the introduction of lawful commerce and trade into Africa." It also stated a commitment to "Self-Reliance and Self-Government, on the principle of an African Nationality, the African race being the ruling element of the nation, controlling and directing their own affairs."

The heavy emphasis on Christianity and civilization among nineteenth-century Pan-Africanists was among its more notable features. The cultural nationalism in the 1850s was universalist in its concepts and did not seek to promote an alternative to European or American definitions of culture. Even when celebrating the history of Africa's past attainments, nineteenth-century Pan-Africanists ironically betrayed an attachment to European definitions of progress and civilization. The early Pan-Africanists' appreciation for the African past was usually limited to a fascination with Egyptian grandeur and its Ethiopian roots.

Nonetheless, Pan-Africanism, in its attraction to Egyptian origins of civilization, initiated the movement known in the late twentieth century as Afrocentrism. William Wells Brown and other nineteenth-century African Americans celebrated the accomplishments of the ancient Egyptians and made high claims for the potential of native Africans untouched by European decadence. This fascination with Egypt appeared even in the writings of Frederick Douglass, who normally disparaged the idea of racial pride. Edward Wilmot Blyden, a West Indian migrant to Liberia who is often called the father of modern Pan-Africanism, claimed ancient Egypt as his ancestral heritage. In recent years the "Egyptocentric" approach to African history, championed by the Senegalese scholar Cheikh Anta Diop, has been immensely popular among some factions of American Pan-Africanists.

Blyden, like many later Pan-Africanists, was increasingly interested in contemporary African cultures and folklore. He was well known in the United States, where he traveled and lectured extensively. Blyden advocated the study of West African languages and cultures in the African schools and universities and insisted that pristine African societies were culturally and morally superior to those of primeval Europe. The Sierra Leone physician Africanus Horton likewise defended traditional African cultures. Toward the end of the century younger scholars, like J. E. Casely Hayford of the Gold Coast and the American W. E. B. Du Bois, also celebrated Egypt, Ethiopia, and Meroë (in the Sudan) as black sources of world civilization. At the same time, they followed in the tradition of Blyden by encouraging a respect for traditional African village life as manifested in the cultures of sub-Saharan Africa.

In 1885 Otto von Bismarck convened the so-called Berlin Conference at which the European powers partitioned the continent of Africa, and the Congo was consigned to the "protectorship" of Leopold II, King of the Belgians. While the partition awakened mixed emotions among many black Americans, Blyden, Crummell and the African-American historian George Washington Williams hoped, at first, that the Belgian model would provide a workable plan for attacking the slave trade and promoting "the three Cs." By 1890, however, Williams had denounced Leopold for his brutal exploitation of the Congo. Byden, the Pan-Africanist par excellence, continued to praise Leopold as late as 1895. Crummell supported European colonialism until his death in 1898 because of his belief that the British would hinder the spread of Islam and suppress the Arab slave trade in the Sudan. Nonetheless, Africans and black Americans were becoming increasingly disillusioned with European colonialism. Booker T. Washington, for example, spoke out against British imperialism and became active in the Congo Reform Association. Washington also encouraged African missionary activities, industrial education, and colonial reform, while his political machine contributed to a series of conferences on Africa. Washington worked behind the scenes to organize a missionary conference at the Atlanta Exhibition in 1895, where participants included Alexander Crummell and the AME bishop, Henry McNeal Turner.

Black missionary activity in Africa gave rise to a religious manifestation of Pan-Africanism called Ethiopianism. The movement derived its name from its adherents' obsession with the cryptic biblical prophecy, "Ethiopia shall soon stretch forth her hands unto God" (Psalms 68:31). Crummell, Blyden, and other Christian preachers had long employed the allusion in their sermons, but the Ethiopian movement was an independent movement of the African masses and a departure from traditional Christianity. It was what some scholars have referred to as a revitalization movement in that it revived Christian teaching by adapting it to the indigenous cultures. It often preserved elements of ancestral religions and carried with it a strong antiwhite feeling. The new militancy is often attributed to the inspiration of Bishop Turner, who visited South Africa in 1898, preaching religious independence and establishing the AME Church there. In short order, however, the zeal of South African Christians exceeded Turner's expectations, as Africans declared their independence not only from the white churches but also from the African-American-dominated AMEs. Thereafter, a much larger independent church movement came into being, revealing attitudes that were both nationalistic and Pan-Africanistic.

St. Clair Drake and George Shepperson have described the political aspect of Ethiopianism as an element of Pan-African consciousness, spreading rapidly northward and eastward and becoming more strident in its attacks on colonialism. In Nyasaland, now known as Malawi, John Chilembwe led a premature revolt in 1914, which has been attributed to the influences of Chilembwe's studies in the United States and his exposure to Ethiopian-

ism after his return to Africa. Later in the century, in Kenya in the 1950s, the Mau Mau movement had ties to the Ethiopian millennialism that Jomo Kenyatta called "The New Religion in East Africa." It was from the Ethiopian movement that the slogan "Africa for the Africans" began to take on radical political implications. Ethiopianism is important as at least one of the sources of the Rastafarian movement in Jamaica.

Edwin S. Redkey has detected grassroots Pan-Africanism in the movement that established all-black towns in Oklahoma during the 1890s. Rev. Orishatukeh Faduma, a Yoruba man from Barbados, became a missionary in Oklahoma, where he recruited for Chief Alfred C. Sam's back-to-Africa movement. J. Ayodele Langley has shown that Sam, a Twi speaker from the Gold Coast, eventually received the moral support of Casely Hayford, despite the latter's original skepticism. William H. Ferris, John E. Bruce, and Du Bois, all protégés of Alexander Crummell, had been connected with Faduma through their association with the American Negro Academy. The academy also included among its honorary members Duse Muhammad Ali, the London-based Sudanese nationalist who was editor of the *African Times* and *Orient Review*.

Ferris and Bruce, although well acquainted with the failure of Chief Sam's back-to-Africa movement, nevertheless became supporters of Marcus Garvey's similar repatriation effort after World War I. Garvey's Universal Negro Improvement Association revealed in its very name the traditional concern of Pan-Africanism. Garvey was less successful as a repatriationist than some of his predecessors, but he did a great deal to generate mass enthusiasm for African nationalism and the Pan-African movement. Garvey was an inspiration to a generation of African political leaders, and his name became a household word in small towns throughout the black world. After Garvey's death, his second wife, Amy Jacques Garvey, remained an important figure in the movement.

Garvey did much to popularize the idea of African independence, and he was unexcelled in his celebration of Africa's ancient glories. William H. Ferris, John E. Bruce, Carter G. Woodson, Arthur Schomburg, and J. A. Rogers contributed to Marcus Garvey's newspaper, *Negro World,* and did much to popularize the notion that black peoples of the upper Nile were the unrivalled progenitors of world civilization. Pan-Africanist cultural expressions in the tradition of Blyden were certainly more obvious among Garveyites than among those intellectuals who disassociated themselves from the Garvey movement.

In 1900 Henry Sylvester Williams, a Trinidad barrister, and Bishop Alexander Walters of the AME Zion Church, convened the London Conference, widely regarded as the first international meeting to apply the term Pan-African to its program. W. E. B. Du Bois, although he played an important role in the London Conference, never referred to it as the first Pan-African Congress, reserving that distinction for the meeting that he called in Paris in 1919 at the time of the Paris Peace Conference following World War I. The convention brought together fifty-seven delegates from Africa, the West Indies, and United States, but American participation was limited because of the refusal of the U.S. government to grant passports. Ida B. Wells, who was accredited as a representative of Garvey's UNIA, was thus unable to attend, and William Monroe Trotter was forced to pose as a ship's cook in order to get to Paris. Du Bois was assisted in setting up the Congress by his connections to the National Association for the Advancement of Colored People (NAACP) and the influence of the Senegalese deputy, Blaise Diagne. Du Bois insisted that the Congress had influenced the peace conference to establish a Mandates Commission for administration of the former German colonies. Du Bois worked with the Pan-African Congress at its subsequent meetings of 1921, 1923, and 1927.

During the 1920s a cultural development known as the New Negro Movement, centered in such urban centers as Harlem, Washington, D.C., and Chicago, contributed to the development of cultural Pan-Africanism. The movement found expression in the literary Garveyism of Ferris, Bruce, and Rogers, but the term came to be associated with the publication of Alain Locke's *The New Negro* (1925). The so-called Harlem Renaissance, an offshoot of this New Negro Movement, was much indebted to cultural developments in Europe and the United States after World War I, including "primitivism," cultural relativism, and the Freudian revolution in sexual values. In the view of Sterling Brown and Arthur P. Davis, this fostered a "phony exotic primitive" stereotype and "grafted primitivism on decadence." Sentimental Pan-Africanism, as expressed in the sensual imagery of Countee Cullen's poem "Heritage," appealed to wealthy whites and influential white intellectuals but avoided Pan-Africanism as a political ideology. Although Locke included an article on Pan-Africanism by Du Bois in *The New Negro,* he dismissed Garveyism. The works of Charles T. Davis, Tony Martin, and David Levering Lewis are essential correctives to the view of the Harlem Renaissance that emphasizes bohemian aestheticism to the neglect of political Pan-Africanism and the Garvey movement.

During the 1930s Pan-African cultural nationalism came to be identified with the *Négritude* movement, defined by francophone black intellectuals René Maran, Leopold Sédar Senghor, and Aimé Césaire. *Négritude* emphasized such mythic traits of the African personality as sensuality, emotional sensitivity, and the purported softness of the black man. Cheikh Anta Diop (1978) has lamented the relationship of *Négritude* to the primitive stereotype and has opined that "the Negritude movement accepted this so-called inferiority and boldly assumed it in full view of the world." Indeed, many African and African-American intellectuals did celebrate African "primitivism." Nineteenth-century black intellectuals had shown little interest in the culture of the masses, aside from the occasional militant Christianity expressed in the Negro spirituals. Twentieth-century intellectuals celebrated black American folk culture for its "pagan," pre-Christian elements and its Pan-African cultural connections.

Data collected by Leo Frobenius, the German scholar, interpreted in the light of social science, heightened the interest of Du Bois, Césaire, and Senghor in the cultures of precolonial, sub-Saharan Africa. This led black American intellectuals to a reappraisal of their folk heritage and its African roots. The development of anthropology, with its doctrine of cultural relativism and its ties to scientific relativism, made possible an increased respect for "primitive" cultures. The concepts of Franz Boas and Melville Herskovits contributed to the metaphysical foundations of a new African cultural nationalism that merged modernism with primitivism. Fashionable modern artists, such as Picasso and Modigliani, demonstrated their discontent with the conventional norms of European cultural expression by borrowing from African graphic modes. The increasing respectability of jazz, after its celebration by European and American audiences, was another factor in the transformation of Pan-African cultural nationalism.

In 1939 the Council on African Affairs was organized by Paul Robeson and Max Yergan, with Ralph Bunche and the novelist René Maran on the board of management. The council was promoted by numerous prominent black individuals and organizations throughout the 1940s but came under attack during the Red Scare of the 1950s. Meanwhile the Fifth Pan-African Congress was held in Manchester, U.K., in 1945. Du Bois was accorded a place of honor in Manchester, although Pan-African leadership by this time had passed from African-American to African leadership, represented by Kwame Nkrumah, Nnamdi Azikewe, and Jomo Kenyatta. Older West Africans, such as Ras T. Makonnen and George Padmore, continued to play significant roles. Padmore, a Trinidadian who had participated in the Manchester Conference, gained considerable influence with Nkrumah, who as president of Ghana (the former Gold Coast), hosted a conference in the Ghanaian capital of Accra in 1958. Shirley Graham, the only American officially in attendance, read an address by her husband, Du Bois, who was hospitalized in Moscow.

Since formation of the Organization of African Unity, black Americans have supported the Pan-African movement from a distance. The major emphasis in recent years has been on the struggle against apartheid in the Republic of South Africa. The efforts of African Americans in support of the South African struggle have been moderately successful. Black Americans have been unable to exert much influence over American foreign policy regarding Western and Central Africa, regions of the continent that have experienced much economic hardship and domestic unrest. The hopes of Garvey and Du Bois for an economically prosperous Africa have not yet been realized despite the attainment of political independence.

See also Abolition; African Civilization Society (AfCS); Afrocentrism; Anthropology and Anthropologists; Council on African Affairs; Du Bois, W. E. B.; Equiano, Olaudah; Gabriel Prosser Conspiracy; Garvey, Marcus; Haitian Revolution; Maroon Wars; Nationalism in the United States in the Nineteeth Century; Négritude; New Negro; Universal Negro Improvement Association

■ ■ *Bibliography*

Ajala, Adekunle. *Pan-Africanism: Evolution, Progress and Prospects*. London: A. Deutsch, 1974.

Carlisle, Rodney. *The Roots of Black Nationalism*. Port Washington, N.Y.: Kennikat Press, 1975.

Cromwell, Adelaide. *An African Victorian Feminist: The Life and Times of Adelaide Smith Casely Hayford*. Washington, D.C.: Howard University Press, 1992.

Diop, Cheikh Anta. *Black Africa: The Economic and Cultural Basis for a Federated State*. Westport, Conn.: L. Hill, 1978.

Drake, St. Clair. *The Redemption of Africa and Black Religion*. Chicago: Third World Press, 1970.

Geiss, Imanuel. *The Pan-African Movement*. New York: Africana Pub. Co., 1974.

James, C. L. R. *A History of Pan-African Revolt*. Washington, D.C.: Drum and Spear Press, 1969.

Langley, J. Ayodele. *Pan-Africanism and Nationalism in West Africa, 1900–1945*. Oxford, UK: Clarenden Press, 1973.

Martin, Tony. *The Pan-African Connection*. Cambridge, Mass.: Schenkman, 1983.

Miller, Floyd. *The Search for a Black Nationality: Black Colonization and Emigration, 1787–1863*. Urbana: University of Illinois Press, 1975.

Moses, Wilson J. *The Golden Age of Black Nationalism 1850–1925*. Hamden, Conn.: Archon Books, 1978.

Redkey, Edwin S. *Black Exodus*. New Haven, Conn.: Yale University Press, 1969.

WILSON J. MOSES (1996)

PAN-AFRICAN ORTHODOX CHURCH (THE SHRINE OF THE BLACK MADONNA)

The Pan-African Orthodox Church, which is more commonly known as the Shrine of the Black Madonna, was established in Detroit, Michigan, on March 26, 1967, by the Rev. Albert B. Cleage Jr., an ordained minister in the United Church of Christ. While this is the recognized date for its inception, the church actually began with a remnant of several earlier congregations. It has now grown from one congregation into a denomination.

A longtime resident of Detroit, Cleage returned home in 1951 after a rocky but productive pastorate in Springfield, Massachusetts, to assume ministerial duties at St. Mark's Presbyterian Mission. St. Mark's was a middle-class black congregation, and although the Cleage family had long been a part of the city's black elite, Cleage was greatly disturbed by the privilege and complacency of his parishioners. Finally, in March 1953 Cleage led "a group of dissidents" out of St. Mark's, charging that the overly pious Sunday morning Christianity at the church had become intolerable.

A week later Cleage and his followers established the Central Congregational Church. For most of the next decade he and his church enjoyed a respectful honeymoon. However, problems at Central began to surface in 1964, when Cleage was informed that several members of his parish were pleased with neither his preaching nor his politics. Over the years following the exodus from St. Mark's, Cleage became increasingly involved with radical political organizations, and shortly after his appearance in November 1963 at the National Negro Grassroots Leadership Conference, tension between black nationalist and moderate members of Central came to a head.

Although the conference was held at King Solomon Baptist Church in Detroit, many of Central's parishioners did not agree with the choice of Malcolm X (a man they saw as advocating violence as a means of change) as a keynote speaker. Moreover, they felt the integral role Cleage played in organizing the meeting would somehow taint the reputation of Central. And following a May 1964 *Illustrated News* reprint of Cleage's black nationalist platform, unhappy members of Central appealed to the Detroit Metropolitan Association of the United Church of Christ for intervention.

In a special hearing of the association's church and ministry committee, a request on behalf of the dissidents (who remained anonymous, supposedly for their protection) was made that association funds for Central Church be withdrawn until Cleage's ministry was brought in line with the mission of the United Church of Christ. Indirectly, the committee was interested in finding out two things: first, whether Cleage was indeed a black nationalist; and second, if so, whether his black nationalism was Christian. Cleage refused to cooperate on the grounds that no one in his congregation had ever approached him with a complaint, and because the names of the petitioners were withheld, suggesting that the association itself might be behind the inquiry. In any event, he believed the association had no right to interfere in the internal affairs of an autonomous congregation.

In the end Cleage and those parishioners loyal to him won both the battle and the war when those opposed to the church's black nationalist leanings withdrew their membership from Central. Three years later, on March 26, 1967, Easter Sunday, a large painting of a black Virgin Mary was unveiled at the church. Subsequently, the name of the congregation was changed to the Shrine of the Black Madonna, and in 1971 the Black Christian Nationalist Movement was officially inaugurated.

Initially, Cleage envisioned the movement as an ecumenical endeavor, with each participating congregation maintaining membership in its respective denomination. To some extent, this is the case. The "Mother Shrine" in Detroit has maintained its affiliation with the United Church of Christ. The Pan-African Orthodox Church, whose name is intentionally related to the African Orthodox Church of Bishop George Alexander McGuire, has four congregations, a farm, and a publishing house.

See also African Orthodox Church

■ ■ *Bibliography*

Cleage, Albert B., Jr. *Black Messiah*. New York: Sheed and Ward, 1968.

Cleage, Albert B., Jr. *Black Christian Nationalism: New Directions for the Black Church*. New York: Morrow, 1972.

QUINTON H. DIXIE (1996)

PANAMA CANAL

On August 15, 1914, the Panama Canal opened its doors to world commerce, significantly reducing the distance between the Atlantic and Pacific Oceans and making it possible for the United States to emerge as a regional and world power. While volumes have been written in praise of the French and the Americans who designed and financed the building of the canal, much less recognition has been awarded to the tens of thousands of West Indians who sacrificed life and limb from the 1880s through 1914 to build the Panama Canal. Neither the United States nor the Republic of Panama has built a significant monument in recognition of the importance of black West Indian labor to the building of the waterway.

However, the story of West Indians and the Panama Canal has been told by several prominent authors. The migration of West Indians to Panama between the years 1850 and 1914 is superbly narrated by Velma Newton of the University of the West Indies in *The Silver Men* (1984), while Gerstle Mack, David McCullough, George Westerman, and Michael Conniff provide, in separate volumes, valuable information and analysis on the social and economic conditions they faced. In the late 1970s, the Panamanian-born Roman Foster wrote, directed, and produced *Diggers*, a documentary that speaks eloquently of the cultural life and legacy of West Indians on the isthmus.

Who were these West Indian canal workers? What was life like for them during the construction period, which lasted from 1904 to 1914? What has been their contribution and legacy? According to George Westerman, 45,107 contract laborers were hired to work on the Panama Canal during this period, and 31,071 of these workers immigrated to Panama from the West Indies, the vast majority from Barbados. This figure does not include the many thousands that came to the isthmus during this period without a prior contract, but who nevertheless found work upon arrival. These contract workers, classified as "unskilled," were placed on the "Silver Roll," meaning they were paid in local currency. They were supervised by white Americans (far fewer in number), who were on the "Gold Roll" (they were paid in U.S. dollars). President Theodore Roosevelt sanctioned this arrangement while recognizing the centrality of black Canal workers. For example, in November 1906, on his way home from Panama aboard the *Louisiana*, he wrote in a letter to his son: "with intense energy men and machines do their task, the white men supervising matters and handling the machines, while the tens of thousands of black men do the rough manual labor where it is not worthwhile to have machines do it." (McCullough, 1977, p. 498). Hence, in what Raymond Davis calls a "split labor market," cheap black labor from the West Indies significantly lowered building costs while increasing the physical and psychological toll paid by these black workers.

Afraid of dying from malaria or yellow fever, whites abandoned the isthmus in droves. Union leaders in the

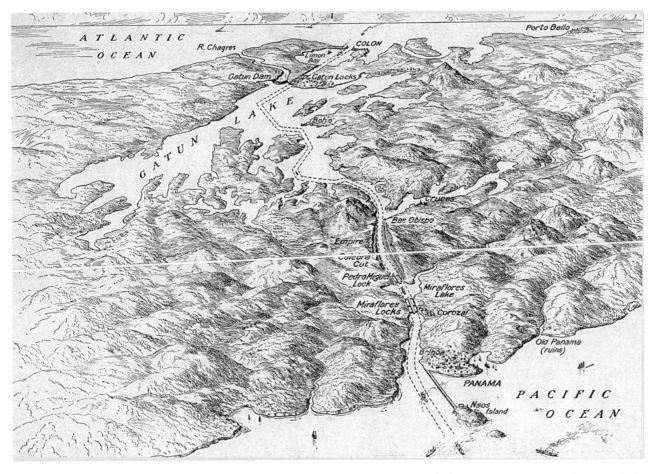

Topographical map of Panama Canal, detailing the area of Gatun Lake and the various locks along the canal, 1914. The vast majority of laborers contracted for the ambitious and very dangerous project were black immigrants from the Caribbean, who endured unhealthy conditions, unequal pay, and segregated facilities during a construction period lasting more than ten years. GETTY IMAGES

United States were "opposed (to) any wholesale shipment of men to 'that deathtrap' and particularly after an inspection team from Japan . . . reported the Isthmus was unsafe to risk the lives of their men" (McCullough, 1977, p. 473). Such work was therefore left to blacks recruited from the West Indies, who were thought to be suited by nature and habit to withstand the punishing isthmian climate.

In spite of Panama's reputation as a "pest hole," thousands of West Indian youth continued to arrive there to work under dangerous and segregated conditions. Their personal histories reveal the enormity of their sacrifices and the nature of their class exploitation and racial oppression. In 1963 the Isthmian Historical Society held an essay competition designed to elicit the personal stories of those who had worked on the Panama Canal prior to 1913. Albert Peters of the Bahamas, the winner of the competition, described the nature of life and work during the construction period.

Peters was born in the Bahamas on February 10, 1885, and like many other Caribbean youngsters affected by eco-

nomic hardship and eager for adventure, he left for Panama in 1906 at the heights of the canal construction. His parents were against the idea, for they knew of the ravages of yellow fever and malaria in Panama. Peters, like tens of thousands of Caribbean youngsters, disregarded the admonition of parents and friends and sought work and adventure as a "digger" of the Panama Canal. What Peters and the tens of thousands like him found in Panama during the first years of the 1900s, however, was drenching rain, mudslides, yellow fever, malaria, typhoid, bad food, repressive labor conditions, and low pay.

Peters "arrived in Colon 31 August 1906, at twenty-one years of age. [I] was surprised at board walks for streets. My nice clothes and shoes that I brought was not for down here in the heavy rain and mud. I sold my clothes and black derby, took the money and bought high top boots and blue dungaree suits then I started on the job. The pay was fifty cents a day or two balboas. I got malaria after a month" (Foster, 1985). His first time in the hospital, which he says was high on a hill, the man next to him

Three Jamaican men work with a compressed-air drill at Panama. *The photograph is from Willis J. Abbott's* Panama and the Canal in Picture and Prose, *1913.* GENERAL RESEARCH AND REFERENCE DIVISION, SCHOMBURG CENTER FOR RESEARCH IN BLACK CULTURE, THE NEW YORK PUBLIC LIBRARY, ASTOR, LENOX AND TILDEN FOUNDATIONS.

died. After five days on quinine, he was back to work. But, in "fifteen days I was back in there again for eight days this time. The latter part of November I left Tabernilla for Colon, got a job feeding mules. Got Malaria in Colon too and went to the hospital with a fever 104" (Foster, 1985).

The majority of the diggers who participated in the Isthmian Historical Society competition listed malaria and yellow fever as major threats to life during the construction period. Working conditions, especially during the first years, were especially hard, as the men cleared forests and fumigated against yellow fever and malaria carrying mosquitoes, built or refurbished housing for the laborers, dynamited the earth, and endured police repression (especially those who were charged with vagrancy).

Despite dangerous and unhealthy working conditions, unequal pay, no sick leave or pension, and separate and unequal facilities, West Indian canal workers were central to the building and maintenance of the Panama Canal and to the modernization of Panama. Their story deserves a more prominent part in the histories of the Panama Canal and the Republic of Panama.

See also Colón Man

■ ■ *Bibliography*

Conniff, Michael. *Black Labor on a White Canal: Panama, 1904–1981.* Pittsburgh: University of Pittsburgh Press, 1985.

Davis, R. A. "West Indian Workers on the Panama Canal: A Split Labor Market Interpretation." Ph.D. diss, Stanford University, 1981.

Foster, Roman, director and producer. *Diggers,* documentary film, 119 minutes. Roman J. Foster, 1985.

Mack, Gerstle. *The Land Divided: A History of The Panama Canal and Other Isthmian Canal Projects.* New York: Alfred A Knopf, 1944. Reprint, New York: Octagon Books, 1974.

McCullough, David. *The Path between the Seas.* New York: Touchstone, 1977.

Newton, Velma. *The Silver Men: West Indian Labour Migration to Panama, 1850-1914.* Mona, Kingston, Jamaica: Institute of Social and Economic Research, 1984.

Stuhl, Ruth C., ed. *Letters from Isthmian Canal Construction Workers.* Balboa Heights, C.Z.: Isthmian Historical Society, 1963.

Westerman, George. *Los Inmigrantes Antillanos en Panama.* Panama: Instituto Nacional de Cultura, 1980.

GEORGE PRIESTLEY (2005)

PARKER, CHARLIE

AUGUST 29, 1920
MARCH 23, 1955

Jazz alto saxophonist Charlie Parker, often known as "Bird" or "Yardbird," was the primary architect of the style of jazz called bebop, which revolutionized jazz, taking it from dance music to a black musical aesthetic and art form. He accomplished this as performer, composer, and theorist.

Charles Christopher Parker was born in Kansas City, Missouri. When he was eleven, his mother bought him an alto saxophone. By the time he was fifteen he had become a professional musician, leaving school at the same time. At first his playing was ridiculed, but after he spent some time at a retreat in the Ozark Mountains of Missouri, his technique grew immensely, and during the next couple of years he played in and around the Kansas City area. During this period he learned his craft mainly by sitting in and playing in bands, where he absorbed all he could about music.

In 1939 Parker made his first visit to New York. He stayed about a year, playing mostly in jam sessions. After that he began playing in the band of Jay McShann, touring in the Southwest, Midwest, and East. It was with this band that Parker made his first recording, in Dallas in 1941. At the end of 1942 he joined the Earl Hines orchestra, which featured trumpeter "Dizzy" Gillespie. Bird and Dizzy began an informal partnership that launched the beginning of bebop. A strike by the American Federation of Musicians made it impossible to make records for several years, and the early period of bebop's development is largely undocumented. In 1944 Parker, along with Gillespie and other modern players, joined the Billy Eckstine band. This band was one of the first to introduce the innovations being developed in the music, and it provided a platform for Parker's new improvisations.

In 1945 Parker began to record extensively with small groups that included Gillespie. His playing became more familiar to a larger audience and to other musicians, even though critics harshly criticized the new music. At the end of 1945 he took a quintet to California for what turned out to be an ill-fated trip. Audiences and musicians in the West were not familiar with bebop innovations, and Parker's addiction to heroin and alcohol finally forced him into the Camarillo State Hospital. He stayed there during the second half of 1946 and was released in January 1947. He did make several important recordings for the Dial record company before and after his stay at the hospital.

Parker returned to New York in April 1947 and formed a quintet featuring his protégé Miles Davis on trumpet, Duke Jordan on piano, Tommy Potter on bass, and Max Roach on drums. Between 1947 and 1951 Parker left a permanent imprint on jazz. With the quintet he recorded some of his most innovative compositions: "Now's the Time," "Koko," "Anthropology," "Ornithology," "Scrapple from the Apple," "Yardbird Suite," "Moose the Mooche," "Billie's Bounce," "Confirmation," and others. In addition to playing in his own quintet, Parker worked in a variety of other musical groups, including Afro-Cuban bands and a string chorus, which he led during 1950. He was featured soloist in the Jazz at the Philharmonic series, produced by Norman Granz. Parker's main venue continued to be his quintet, which changed members several times but still was vital. Within his quintet he worked in nightclubs, recording studios, and radio broadcasts, and made his first trip to Europe in 1949, returning there the next year for an extensive stay in Sweden, where he worked with Swedish musicians.

Parker's lifestyle continued to create problems for himself and his family. In 1951 he lost his cabaret card in New York because of his constant confrontations with narcotics police. This kept him from playing in New York clubs for over two years. His alcohol and drug use precipitated a downward financial spiral from which he never recovered. In 1953 he presented a landmark concert in Toronto with Gillespie, Bud Powell on piano, Charles Mingus on bass, and Max Roach on drums. The concert was at Massey Hall and featured many of the pieces Bird and Dizzy had created during the 1940s: "Night in Tunisia," "Hot House," "Wee," and others. This was Parker's last great musical statement. After the Toronto concert his physical and mental health deteriorated to the point where he attempted suicide several times, finally committing himself to Bellevue Hospital in New York. His last public performance was in early March 1955 at Birdland, the New York City club named after him. On March 23 he died of heart seizure in the New York apartment of his friend Baroness Pannonica de Koenigswarter.

Parker's contributions to jazz are extensive. He took saxophone playing to a level never reached before and in so doing led the way for others, not only saxophonists but all instrumentalists. He was able to weld prodigious skill with poetic content, and he left hours and hours of recordings of wondrous improvisations. Parker's playing struck fear in the hearts of many musicians and made some put down their instruments. John Coltrane, the gifted performer of the 1950s and 1960s, moved from alto to tenor saxophone because he felt that Parker had played all that was going to be played on the alto. Parker frequently composed using the harmonic structures of established melodies as the basis of his works. He did not invent this technique but used it more than anyone else before or since. In his improvisations he used all the intervals of the scales. In his harmonic structures he consistently used chords made up of eleventh and thirteenth intervals in order to take harmony out of the diatonic system and into chromaticism. Parker was clearly one of America's most innovative and prolific artists. In 2004, Parker was inducted into the inaugural class of Lincoln Center's Ertegun Jazz Hall of Fame.

See also Jazz

■ ■ *Bibliography*

Giddins, Gary. *Celebrating Bird: The Triumph of Charlie Parker.* New York: Beech Tree Books, 1987.

Morgenstern, Dan, Ira Gitler, and Jack Bradley. *Bird and Diz: A Bibliography.* New York: New York Jazz Museum, 1973.

Reisner, Robert G. *Bird: The Legend of Charlie Parker.* New York: Citadel Press, 1962.

Russell, Ross. *Bird Lives: The High Times and Hard Life of Charlie (Yardbird) Parker.* New York: Charterhouse, 1973.

WILLIAM S. COLE (1996)
Updated by publisher 2005

PARKS, GORDON

NOVEMBER 30, 1912

—▮▮▮——————————

A true Renaissance man, *Life* magazine photographer Gordon Parks Sr. has achieved international recognition in a wide variety of other fields including filmmaking, letters, and music. He has also pioneered as the first mainstream African-American photojournalist and as the first African American to direct a major Hollywood film.

Gordon Parks Sr. was born in Fort Scott, Kansas, the youngest in a farming family of fifteen children. His mother's death when Parks was sixteen, along with his aged father's rapidly failing ability to manage a household, led to the family's break-up, and Parks moved north to live with a married sister in Minneapolis. Unwelcome in his brother-in-law's home, the teenager was soon on his own, struggling to attend high school and support himself.

The Great Depression ended his formal education, but Parks seized every opportunity to learn by reading and attending closely to the talented individuals he encountered in his various jobs. As a teenager and later as a young husband and father, he worked as a bellhop, musician, semipro basketball player, and member of the Civilian Conservation Corps, primarily in the Midwest but also for a brief time in Harlem, New York. Relative security came with a position as a railroad dining car waiter. All the while Parks wrote, composed, and read, absorbing on his own what he had been unable to study in school.

The picture magazines of the day—*Vogue, Harper's Bazaar,* and especially the brand-new *Life* magazine (first issued in November 1936)—caught Parks's imagination. A newsreel cameraman's in-person presentation of his latest battle-action footage in a Chicago movie theater inspired Parks to take up photography himself, and in 1937 he acquired his first camera. Largely self-taught, he took his earliest photographs with only a few pointers from the camera salesman. Quickly mastering technique, he intuitively found the subjects most meaningful to him. The same local Minneapolis camera store soon gave him his first exhibition.

A successful fashion assignment for a stylish Minneapolis department store caught the attention of Marva (Mrs. Joe) Louis, who encouraged Parks to establish himself in Chicago. His fashion background served him well there (as it would later throughout his years at *Life*) photographing Gold Coast socialites. In his spare time, he documented the grim poverty of the city's South Side, the fast-growing Chicago enclave of African Americans displaced from the rural South who came north for jobs in the heavy industries surrounding the Great Lakes.

Gordon Parks's photograph of a woman and her dog looking out a Harlem window, May 1943. © CORBIS

This socially conscious camera work won for the young photographer, now responsible for a growing family of his own, the very first Julius Rosenwald Fellowship in photography. The 1942–1943 stipend enabled Parks to work with photographic mentor Roy Stryker in Washington, D.C., at the Farm Security Administration. This was the closing years of the influential New Deal agency that had undertaken a pioneering photo documentation of depression conditions in urban and rural America.

Parks continued with Stryker until 1947, first as a correspondent for the Office of War Information, and later at the Standard Oil Company of New Jersey, photographing the face of America for the company's public relations campaign. In the brief months before he began to work for *Life* magazine in 1948, Parks photographed for *Vogue* and *Glamour* and also authored two books on photographic technique: *Flash Photography* (1947) and *Camera Portraits: The Techniques and Principles of Documentary Portraiture* (1948).

Early in his more than two decades at *Life,* Parks spent two influential years assigned to the magazine's Paris office, where he covered fashion, the arts, celebrities, and political figures. The experience was seminal, providing a rich window on the diversity of contemporary creative expression as well as an opportunity for international recog-

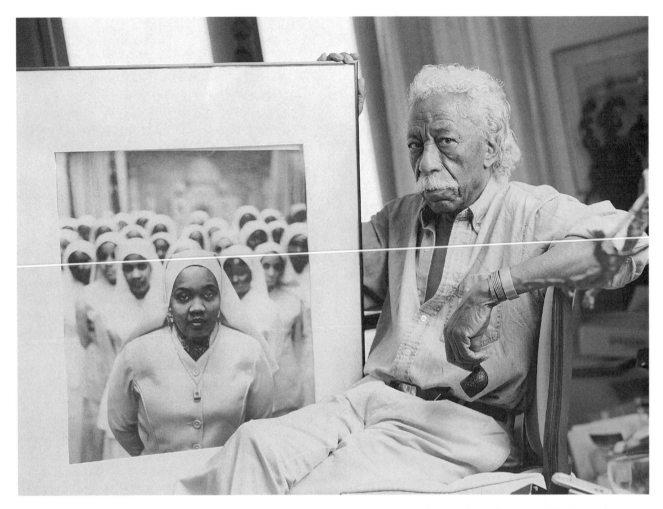

Gordon Parks with his photograph **Ethel Shariff in Chicago (1957).** *An award-winning photographer and an accomplished composer, writer, and film director, Parks was the first African American staff photographer at* Life *magazine, and was also the first African American to write, direct, and produce a film for a major motion picture company.* © DOUGLAS KIRKLAND/CORBIS

nition. Moreover, like other African Americans, he found the European experience, with its relative lack of racial barriers, especially liberating.

Back in the United States during the 1950s and early 1960s, Parks executed hundreds of photographic assignments for *Life* that reflect the magazine's far-ranging coverage: popular culture, high fashion, arts, entertainment, sports, national events, and the personalities of business, labor, and politics. Parks's direct, realistic style of photographing life in America and abroad won him international renown as the first African-American photojournalist.

Parks's longest assignment began in 1961, when he traveled to Brazil to photograph the slums of Rio de Janeiro. His story of Flavio da Silvia, a poverty-stricken Brazilian boy whom Parks found dying of asthma, attracted international attention that resulted in Flavio and his family receiving gifts, medical treatment, and, finally, a new home. At the same time, with the emerging civil rights

movement, Parks undertook a new role at *Life:* interpreting the activities and personalities of the movement, in words as well as pictures, from a personal perspective. His 1971 anthology *Born Black* is a collection of these essays and images.

A gifted storyteller, Parks began his chronological autobiographical book cycle in 1963 with *The Learning Tree,* a well-received novel that drew on the author's own childhood experiences and memories. This was followed in 1966 by *A Choice of Weapons,* a powerful first-person narrative that recounted the events and influences that enabled Parks to overcome societal prejudice and personal hardship. It is the most insightful of the series, illuminating the development of a sensitive and self-confident young man as he grows into what he will become, an artist of universal conscience and compassion.

Parks also gained distinction as a poet, composer, and filmmaker, becoming in 1969 the first African American to direct a major Hollywood film. He also produced and wrote the script for *The Learning Tree* and directed a number of other films, including the highly popular *Shaft* (1971), *Leadbelly* (1976), and *The Odyssey of Solomon Northup* (1984), about a free black sold into slavery. In addition, Parks has completed the music for a ballet about the Rev. Dr. Martin Luther King Jr. and has worked on a novel based on the life of J. M. W. Turner, the nineteenth-century English landscape painter. In 1998 he published *Half Past Autumn: A Retrospective.*

Parks is the recipient of numerous professional awards, organization citations, and honorary degrees, among them Photographer of the Year from the American Society of Magazine Photographers (1960), the Spingarn Medal from the NAACP (1972), and the National Medal of Arts from President Ronald Reagan. In 2002 he received the Jackie Robinson Foundation Lifetime Achievement Award and was inducted into the International Photography Hall of Fame and Museum. The first Gordon Parks Celebration of Culture and Diversity, a four-day event, took place in Parks's hometown of Fort Scott, Kansas, in October 2004.

Parks's greatest satisfaction and motivation is expressed in his prologue to *Moments Without Proper Names,* one of his three books of poems accompanied by his photographs:

> I hope always to feel the responsibility to communicate the plight of others less fortunate than myself, to show the abused and those who administer the abuses, to point up the pain of the underprivileged as well as the pleasures of the privileged—somehow to evoke the same response from a housewife in Harlem as I would from a seamstress in Paris or a butcher in Vladivostok.

> In helping one another we can ultimately save ourselves. We must give up silent watching and put our commitments into practice.

See also Civil Rights Movement, U.S.; Film in the United States; Photography, U.S.

■ ■ *Bibliography*

Bush, Martin H. *The Photographs of Gordon Parks.* Wichita, Kans.: Wichita State University, 1983.

Harnan, Terry. *Gordon Parks, Black Photographer.* Champaign, Ill.: Garrard, 1972.

Parks, Gordon. *Half Past Autumn: A Retrospective.* New York: Bulfinch, 1997.

Turk, Midge. *Gordon Parks.* New York: Crowel, 1971.

JULIA VAN HAAFTEN (1996)
Updated by publisher 2005

PARKS, ROSA

FEBRUARY 4, 1913

Civil rights leader Rosa Louise McCauley was born in Tuskegee, Alabama. She lived with relatives in Montgomery, where she finished high school in 1933 and attended Alabama State College. She met her husband, Raymond Parks, a barber, and they married in 1932. Rosa Parks worked as a clerk, an insurance salesperson, and a tailor's assistant at a department store. She was also employed at the time as a part-time seamstress by Virginia and Clifford Durr, two white residents of Montgomery who were staunch supporters of the black freedom struggle.

Parks had been active in civil rights work since the 1930s. She and her husband supported the Scottsboro defendants, a notorious case in which nine young black men were convicted in 1931 on questionable evidence of raping two white women. In 1943 Parks became one of the first women to join the Montgomery NAACP. She worked as a youth adviser, served as secretary for the local group from 1943 to 1956, and helped operate the joint office of the NAACP and the Brotherhood of Sleeping Car Porters. In addition, she worked with the Montgomery Voters League to increase black voter registration. During the summer of 1955, with the encouragement of the Durrs, Parks accepted a scholarship for a workshop for community leaders on school integration at the Highlander Folk School in Tennessee. It was an important experience for Parks, not only for the practical skills of organizing and mobilizing she learned but because the racial harmony she experienced there nurtured and sustained her activism.

Popularly known as the mother of the civil rights movement, Parks is best known for her refusal to give up her seat for a white man on a segregated bus in Montgomery on December 1, 1955, an incident that sparked the Montgomery bus boycott. Contrary to popular belief, Parks was not simply a tired woman who wanted to rest her feet, unaware of the chain of events she was about to trigger. As she wrote in *Rosa Parks: My Story* (1992), "the only tired I was, was tired of giving in." Parks was a veteran of civil rights activity and was aware of efforts by the Women's Political Council and the local NAACP to find an incident with which they could address segregation in Montgomery.

Parks was actively involved in sustaining the boycott and for a time served on the executive committee of the Montgomery Improvement Association, an organization created to direct the boycott. The intransigence of the city council was met by conviction and fortitude on the part of African Americans. For over a year, black people in Montgomery carpooled, took taxis, and walked to work. The result was a ruling by the U.S. Supreme Court that segregation on city buses was unconstitutional.

As a result of her involvement in the bus boycott, Parks lost her job at the department store in Montgomery. In 1957 she and her husband moved to Detroit, where she worked as a seamstress for eight years before becoming administrative assistant for Congressman John Conyers, a position she held until 1988. After she moved to Detroit, Parks continued to be active in the civil rights movement and joined the Southern Christian Leadership Conference (SCLC). She participated in numerous marches and rallies, including the 1965 march from Selma to Montgomery.

In the mid-1980s Parks supported the Free South Africa movement and walked the picket lines in Washington, D.C., with other anti-apartheid activists. She has made countless public appearances, speaking out on political issues as well as giving oral history lessons about the civil rights movement. In 1987, ten years after the death of her husband, she cofounded the Rosa and Raymond Parks Institute for Self-Development in Detroit, a center committed to career training for black youth. The institute, a dream of hers, was created to address the dropout rate of black youth.

Parks, an international symbol of African-American strength, has been given numerous awards and distinctions, including ten honorary degrees. In 1979 she was awarded the NAACP's prestigious Spingarn Medal. In 1980 she was chosen by *Ebony* readers as the living black woman who had done the most to advance the cause of black America. In the same year she was awarded the Martin Luther King Jr. Nonviolent Peace Prize by the Martin Luther King Jr. Center for Nonviolent Social Change. In addition, the SCLC has honored her by sponsoring the annual Rosa Parks Freedom award.

During the 1990s Parks assumed an increasing role as African-American elder statesperson. She wrote three books, including an autobiography and a book of letters that were written to her from children around the world. In 1996, though confined to a wheelchair, she spoke at the Million Man March. In July 1999 the U.S. Congress awarded Parks the Congressional Gold Medal of Honor, the nation's highest civilian award. Parks's legacy lives on in Troy State University in Montgomery, Alabama, where a library and museum were dedicated in her name in 2000. One year later the Rosa Parks Initiative began in Detroit, with a goal to build an $8 million monument, complete with one million roses and an interactive history of the civil rights movement, in Detroit's Belle Isle Park.

In 1999 Parks initiated a lawsuit against hip-hop duo Outkast. After first being dismissed by a federal judge, an appeals court allowed Parks to proceed with the lawsuit, in which she claimed that Outkast used her name without permission on a 1998 track. Former Detroit Mayor Dennis Archer was appointed by a federal judge to serve as a temporary, independent guardian for Parks in 2004, to ensure that Parks, suffering from dementia, was fairly represented in such matters of litigation.

See also Brotherhood of Sleeping Car Porters; Civil Rights Movement, U.S.; Montgomery Improvement Association; Montgomery, Ala., Bus Boycott; Southern Christian Leadership Conference (SCLC)

■ ■ *Bibliography*

Brown, Roxanne. "Mother of the Movement." *Ebony* (February 1988): 68–72.

Garrow, David, ed. *The Montgomery Bus Boycott and the Women Who Started It: The Memoir of Jo Ann Gibson Robinson.* Knoxville: University of Tennessee Press, 1987.

Parks, Rosa. *Rosa Parks: My Story.* New York: Dial Books, 1992.

Parks, Rosa. *Quiet Strength: The Faith, the Hope, and the Heart of a Woman Who Changed a Nation.* Grand Rapids, Mich.: Zondervan, 1994.

Parks, Rosa. *Dear Mrs. Parks: A Dialogue with Today's Youth.* New York: Lee & Low Books, 1996.

PREMILLA NADASEN (1996)
Updated by publisher 2005

PARKS, SUZAN-LORI

MAY 10, 1963

■—■—■

Playwright Suzan-Lori Parks was born in Fort Knox, Kentucky, the daughter of a U.S. Army officer. She moved around the United States with her family and completed high school in Germany. She then attended Mt. Holyoke College, graduating in 1985, and continued her education at the Drama Studio in London. There she studied acting in preparation for a career as a playwright.

Several of Parks's plays have been produced, most notably at BACA Downtown, an offshoot of the Brooklyn

Arts Council. In 1989 her *Imperceptible Mutabilities in the Third Kingdom* was produced there to favorable reviews. In 1989 BACA produced *The Death of the Last Black Man in the Whole Entire World,* which was also performed as part of the Yale Winterfest in 1992. In 1991 Parks completed a thirty-minute film, *Anemone Me,* with collaborator Bruce Hainley. The same year, her play *Devotees in the Garden of Love* was produced by the Actors Theater of Louisville, Kentucky. In 1992 she was commissioned to write two plays, *Venus,* for the Women's Project of New York, and *The America Play,* for the Theatre for a New Audience, also in New York. Parks's first Broadway play, *Topdog/Underdog,* which won a Pulitzer Prize for Drama, premiered in 2001. Two years later, Parks published her first novel, *Getting Mother's Body.* In 2005, she cowrote the screenplay for Oprah Winfrey's television film *Their Eyes Were Watching God,* an adaptation of the novel by Zora Neale Hurston.

In 1991 and 1992 Parks was a writer-in-residence at The New School in New York. She has been a guest lecturer in dramatic writing at New York University, Yale University, the University of Michigan, and the Pratt Institute. She has received numerous grants and awards, including an Obie Award in 1990 for *Imperceptible Mutabilities,* National Endowment for the Arts grants in 1990 and 1991, and a Rockefeller Foundation grant in 1990. In 1996 she won a second Obie for *Venus,* and in 2001 she won a MacArthur Foundation "Genius" grant.

In her plays and scripts Parks is concerned with poetic voice as well as with the representation of the African-American experience. Her evocative, dreamlike style has its roots in Gertrude Stein's investigations into language as well as poet Adrienne Kennedy's poetic, nonnarrative dramas.

See also Drama

■ ■ *Bibliography*

Smith, Wendy. "Words as Crossroad: Suzan-Lori Parks" (interview). *Publishers Weekly,* May 12, 2003, p. 37.

Solomon, Alisa. "To Be Young, Gifted, and African American." *Village Voice,* September 11, 1989, pp. 99–102.

ELIZABETH V. FOLEY (1996)
Updated by publisher 2005

PARSONS, LUCY

1853
MARCH 7, 1942

Little is known about the early life of the anarchist labor organizer Lucy Parsons. She claimed to have been born the daughter of a Mexican woman, Marie del Gather, and a Creek Indian, John Waller. Orphaned at age three, she said, she was then raised on a ranch in Johnson County, Texas, by her maternal uncle. However, later research has pointed to the likelihood that she was of at least partial African-American descent and born a slave in Texas. In about 1870 she met Albert Parsons, a former Confederate soldier turned Radical Republican, and she married him in 1871 or 1872.

Forced to flee Texas because of their mixed marriage, the couple settled in Chicago in 1873 and became heavily involved in the revolutionary elements of the labor movement. In 1877, Lucy Parsons took on the financial responsibility of her household by opening up a dress shop after her husband was blacklisted from the printing trade. In 1878 she began writing articles for the *Socialist* about the homeless and unemployed, Civil War veterans, and working women. She also gave birth to two children within the next few years. Known for being a powerful writer and speaker, Lucy Parsons played a crucial role in the workers' movement in Chicago. In 1883 she helped found the International Working People's Association (IWPA), an anarchist-influenced labor organization that promoted revolutionary direct action toward a stateless and cooperative society and insisted on equality for people of color and women. Parsons became a frequent contributor of the IWPA weekly newspaper, the *Alarm,* in 1884. Her most famous article was "To Tramps," which encouraged workers and the unemployed to rise up in direct acts of violence against the rich.

Although primarily a labor activist, Parsons was also a staunch advocate of the rights of African Americans. She wrote numerous articles and pamphlets condemning racist attacks and killings, one of her most significant pieces being "The Negro: Let Him Leave Politics to the Politician and Prayer to the Preacher." Published in the *Alarm* on April 3, 1886, the article was a response to the lynching of thirteen African Americans in Carrollton, Mississippi. In it, she wrote that blacks were victimized only because they were poor and that racism would inevitably disappear with the destruction of capitalism.

In 1886 Parsons and the IWPA worked with the other industrial trade unions for a general strike in Chicago in support of the eight-hour work day. The strike began on the first of May and involved almost 80,000 workers. Five days later, at a rally at Haymarket Square in support of the strike, a bomb was hurled at police officers after they attacked the demonstration. Police blamed the IWPA and began rounding up anarchist leaders, including Albert Parsons. Lucy Parsons took the lead in organizing their defense, and after they had all been convicted of murder, she traveled the country speaking on behalf of their innocence and raising money for their appeals, facing repeated arrests herself. In November of that year, her husband was hanged along with three other Haymarket defendants.

After her husband's death, Parsons continued revolutionary activism on behalf of workers, political prisoners, people of color, the homeless, and women. In 1892 she published the short-lived *Freedom's Journal*, which attacked lynchings and black peonage. In 1905, she participated in the founding of the Industrial Workers of the World, an anarcho-syndicalist trade union. Also in that year, she published a paper called the *Liberator*. In 1927, she was made a member of the National Committee of the International Labor Defense, a Communist-led organization that defended labor activists and African Americans who had been unjustly accused, such as the "Scottsboro Nine" and Angelo Herndon. After working with the Communist Party for a number of years, she finally joined the party in 1939, despairing of the advances of both capitalism and fascism on the world stage and unconvinced of the anarchists' ability to effectively confront them. After almost fifty years of continual activism, Parsons died in a fire in her Chicago home in 1942. Viewed as a threat to the political order even in death, her personal papers and books were seized by the police from the gutted house.

See also *Freedom's Journal*; Labor and Labor Unions

■ ■ *Bibliography*

Ashbaugh, Carolyn. *Lucy Parsons, American Revolutionary*. Chicago: Charles H. Kerr, 1976.

Roediger, Dave. *Haymarket Scrapbook*. Chicago: Charles H. Kerr, 1986.

JOSEPH W. LOWNDES (1996)

PARTIDO INDEPENDIENTE DE COLOR

The Cuban political party Partido Independiente de Color (PIC) was the first and, for many years, the only race-based party in Latin America and the Caribbean. Its brief and controversial existence ended in violence. Organized initially on August 7, 1908, it was banned in 1910 but resurfaced in an armed uprising in 1912, when government forces responded with swift and definitive repressive measures. Its founding members were mostly veterans of Cuba's Wars of Independence (1868–1898) and former members of the Liberal Party. Upon attaining independence in 1902, Cuba had adopted a new constitution that granted universal manhood suffrage and formal political equality to former slaves and their descendants. However, many men, especially veterans, were frustrated by exclusions from some of the state's most lucrative patronage networks. Whereas some blacks and mulattoes did experience greater political inclusion and access to jobs in the first years of the republic, progress was not fast enough for others, who made a number of demands on the state. Out of this dissatisfaction a number of groups emerged to press for greater racial equality in job distribution. One of the first was the Comité de Acción de Veteranos y Sociedades de la Raza de Color (Committee of Veterans and Associations of the Race of Color) in 1902. Although this committee dissolved shortly after its foundation, its goals would be pursued by the founders of the PIC in 1908.

The leaders of the party, Evaristo Estenoz and Pedro Ivonnet, sought to organize and mobilize Cubans of color with calls for the government to deliver on its promise of racial equality. Both were veterans of the Wars of Independence and relatively experienced politicians. Estenoz worked as a mason and was president of the masons' guild, as well as an active participant in Liberal Party politics between 1904 and 1908. Ivonnet, a descendant of Haitian immigrants who had established themselves as landowners in the eastern province of Oriente, had been active in both the Conservative and Moderate parties before founding the PIC.

Scholars disagree regarding the extent of support and the social composition of followers of the PIC. One school claims that the party appealed to blacks and mulattoes of all social classes, but an opposing school argues for a narrower constituency limited to urban inhabitants or war veterans with aspirations to jobs in the bureaucracy. The latter view holds that rural people were more concerned about wages and working conditions—concerns they shared with working-class whites—than about access to government patronage.

Whether or not it enjoyed widespread support, the party experienced difficulties soon after it was established. Participation in electoral politics proved disappointing. PIC candidates for Congress in Havana and Las Villas in the 1908 election received a very small percentage of the vote. In 1910 liberal senator Martín Morúa Delgado dealt the party a blow by calling its constitutionality into question, based as it was on racial distinctions that had been presumably eliminated by the adoption of egalitarian legislation. Party cohesion suffered a greater setback after an extensive round of arrests sent many members to jail. This provoked a split within the party as members disagreed over tactics and objectives.

On May 20, 1912, Estenoz and Ivonnet, demanding reinstatement as a legitimate party, mobilized an armed uprising in several parts of the island, principally in the provinces of Oriente and Santa Clara. Initially cautious official reaction gave way to overt repression by the middle of June. Yet repression varied from region to region. In Oriente, many died. Whereas historians disagree as to the numbers, most agree that at least three thousand alleged participants, including Estenoz and Ivonnet, were killed by government troops and vigilante groups. In regions surrounding the city of Cienfuegos, however, repression was tempered by participants' roles in patronage networks. There the police, who had achieved a delicate coexistence with some of the local leaders of the uprising, arrested and quickly released many rebels, allowing the leaders to elude capture.

This episode has a paradoxical legacy. It exacerbated divisions among Cubans of color: Whereas some defended the PIC, others defended its goals but criticized its violent strategies. If the party itself did not sustain a great deal of political support, it launched an uprising that seemed dangerous enough to justify massive repression. Appeals for racial equality that emerged soon afterward were cast in very different terms. Rather than calling for the formation of a political party, activists for racial equity in the post-1912 era sought greater inclusion in unions, formed voluntary associations, and participated in public debates about culture, citizenship, and social and economic justice.

See also Politics and Politicians in Latin America

■ ■ *Bibliography*

Bronfman, Alejandra. *Measures of Equality: Social Science, Citizenship and Race in Cuba, 1902–1940.* Chapel Hill: University of North Carolina Press, 2004.

de la Fuente, Alejandro. *A Nation for All: Race, Inequality, and Politics in Twentieth-Century Cuba.* Chapel Hill: University of North Carolina Press, 2001.

Fermoselle, Rafael. *Política y color en Cuba: La Guerrita de 1912.* Montevideo, Uruguay: Editorial Geminis, 1974.

Helg, Aline. *Our Rightful Share: The Afro-Cuban Struggle for Equality, 1886–1912.* Chapel Hill: University of North Carolina Press, 1995.

Linares, Serafín Portuondo. *Los independientes de color.* Havana, Cuba: Editorial Librería Selecta, 1950. Reprint, with prologue by Fernando Martínez Heredia. Havana, Cuba: Editorial Caminos, 2002.

Robaina, Tomás Fernández. *El negro en Cuba, 1902–1958: Apuntes para la historia de la lucha contra la discriminación.* Havana, Cuba: Editorial de Ciencias Sociales, 1990.

ALEJANDRA BRONFMAN (2005)

PASSING

The word *passing,* an Americanism not listed in the first edition of the *Oxford English Dictionary,* refers to a crossing of a line that divides social groups. Everett Stonequist cites a great variety of cases, including Jews passing as Gentiles, Polish immigrants preferring to be German, Italians pretending to be Jews, the Japanese Eta concealing their group identity to avoid discrimination, the Anglo-Indians passing as British, and the Cape Coloured as well as mixed bloods in the West Indies and Latin America moving into white groups. One could add many other cases, such as whites and blacks passing as Mexicans, or Chinese Americans passing as Japanese. There was some passing from white to black in the United States, for example, by musicians.

Passing is used most frequently, however, as if it were short for "passing for white," in the sense of crossing over the color line in the United States from the black to the white side. Louis Wirth and Herbert Goldhamer (1944) see in passing "an attempt on the parts of Negroes to enter into the white community in a fashion which would otherwise be forbidden because of racial barriers." Ratna Roy (1973) defines passing as "assimilating into white society by concealing one's antecedents."

Racial passing is a phenomenon of the nineteenth and the first half of the twentieth centuries. It thrived in a modern social system in which, as a primary condition, social and geographic mobility prevailed, especially in environments such as large cities that provided anonymity to individuals. A second constitutive feature for passing was a widely shared social-belief system, according to which certain descent characteristics, even invisible ones, were viewed as more deeply defining than physical appearance, individual volition, and self-description, or than social acceptance and economic success.

A child whose ancestors come from groups X and Y could theoretically live as an X, a Y, or an XY. In the United States, for example, the child of Irish and Italian parents may be Irish, Italian, Irish-Italian, "simply American," or become, as by marriage, a member of another ethnic group. Yet some types of ancestry (often those associated in the United States with the term "race" rather than "ethnicity") deny a descendant the legitimate possibility of choosing certain forms of identification (including even X-ness, the identity of one parent, of three grandparents, or of fifteen out of sixteen ancestors) because the identity of the remaining other part of the ancestry (Y-ness) is considered so dominant that the individual is believed to be "really" a Y. The description of Roxy in Mark Twain's *Pudd'nhead Wilson* (1894) gives full expression to this paradoxical racial identification: "To all intents and purposes Roxy was as white as anybody, but the one-sixteenth of her which was black out-voted the other fifteen parts and made her a negro. She was a slave, and salable as such." William Javier Nelson called the United States a "hypodescent" society in which children of a higher-caste and a lower-caste parent are assigned the lower-parent status, a procedure deriving from slavery. It is quite possible that the first printed instances of the expression "passing for white" appeared in runaway slave bills. In hypodescent societies X-ness is seen not as an "ethnic option" (Mary Waters's useful term; 1990) for XY, nor as a legitimate parental legacy, but only as a "disguise." Hence XY is considered a Y who is "passing for" but "not really" an X.

This "fiction of law and custom" (Twain) may seem odd in a social system that cherishes social mobility and espouses the right of individuals to make themselves anew by changing name, place, and fortune, and that has produced famous parvenus and confidence men. In Gustave de Beaumont's novel *Marie* (1835), one of the first works of fiction to thematize racial passing, the narrator Ludovic makes this point explicitly:

> A Massachusetts bankrupt can find honor and fortune in Louisiana, where there is no inquiry into the ruin he experienced elsewhere. A New Yorker, bored by the ties of a first marriage, can desert his wife on the left bank of the Hudson and go take another on the right bank, in New Jersey, where he lives in undisturbed

bigamy. . . . There is but one crime from which the guilty can nowhere escape punishment and infamy: it is that of belonging to a family reputed to be colored. The color may be blotted out; the stain remains. It seems that people find it out even when it is invisible; there is no refuge secret enough, no retreat obscure enough, to hide it.

The coexistence of the cult of the social upstart and the condemnation of the racial passer constitutes the parameters in which the phenomenon of passing took place. In the era of passing, the notion also found support that no one could "always tell" Ys by certain ineffaceable characteristics and visible signs such as their eyes or fingernails or the babies they might generate even generations later. Because this is, however, not really true, passing highlights an area of social ambiguity and insecurity. Stories of passing may appeal to modern readers' fascination with the undecidable or offer the assurance of some firmness in at least one individual identity (that based on racial ancestry) in a world of fluidity.

This makes tales of passing allegories of modernization that may appeal to people as they move toward more general identifications and experience anxieties about giving up old homes and families. In a generally mobile society, the world of passing suggests, despite its first appearance, an unchangeable hold of origin and community. One may thus say that "passing" is a misnomer because it is used only to apply to cases of people who are not presumed to be able to pass legitimately from one class to another but who are believed to remain identified by a part of their ancestry throughout their lives. Ironically, the language speaks only of those persons as passing who, it is believed, cannot really pass.

The experience of passing can be differentiated in various ways. The person who passes voluntarily may be doing it for a variety of motives that push him out of one group and pull him into another one: the possibility of economic advancement and benefits (opportunism); interracial courtship and marriage (love); escape from slavery, proscriptions, and discrimination (political reasons); and for many other motives such as for curiosity, for kicks (an "occasional thrill"), for the love of deception, for revenge, and for investigative purposes (most famously by Walter Francis White). A person may also pass inadvertently when being mistaken for white and failing to protest; and involuntarily, be it because the individual may be too young to decide for himself (as in Frank J. Webb's *The Garies and Their Friends*) or because it is arranged for him by others without his knowledge (like Tristan in Lydia Marie Child's *A Romance of the Republic*).

Walter Francis White (1893–1955). *For over twenty years, White served as secretary of the National Association for the Advancement of Colored People. His light complexion, blue eyes, and fair hair allowed him to pass for white on many occasions, a circumstance he reflects on in his autobiography* A Man Called White. THE LIBRARY OF CONGRESS

Passing may be undertaken full-time, twenty-four hours a day, or it may be "part-time" (Joel Williamson) or "segmental" (Wirth), for job purposes on a certain time segment on a daily basis or for avoiding segregation in transportation, entertainment, restaurants, and hotels. It may be permanent, at least by intention, for the duration of an individual's life; or it may be full-time but temporary or sporadic (for a shorter or longer period of a person's life, for one purpose or scheme, such as escaping from slavery, finding a job, completing a program of education, or simply while waiting for an advantageous moment to "come out"). This sporadic form of passing is sometimes associated with sexual cross-dressing and transvestitism: In William Wells Brown's *Clotel; or, The President's Daughter* (1853) or William and Ellen Craft's *Running a Thousand Miles for Freedom* (1860), for example, runaway slave women dress up as white men.

Passing may be arranged by a secretive individual alone; revealed to some confidants, friends, siblings, or family members; or it may be done in the open, forcing others to pretend that they do not know. According to Ed-

ward Byron Reuter (1931), "much 'Passing' is more a matter of acceptance or indifference than of actual and successful concealment." It may be planned by others; it may even "be unknown to the person who is passing," for example, in stories of orphans, foundlings, or switched babies (Wirth and Goldhamer, 1944). It may be done collectively by several family members (*A Romance of the Republic*), siblings (Charles Chesnutt's *The House behind the Cedars*), or friends, a couple, a whole family (Edith Pope's *Colcorton*), a town, or other large groups (George Schuyler's *Black No More*).

Passing may be experienced as a source of conflict or not. Fear and "constant anxiety," according to an anonymous author in *Century,* of discovery may so much intensify the stress, which the person who passes experiences, that giving up the subterfuge may come as a relief. "It is a great risk, and they live in almost daily fear of exposure" ("The Adventures of a Near-White").

Wirth and Goldhamer (1944) write:

For even though a person could not be identified by means of any physical marks as having Negro ancestry, there is always the possibility that someone who knew him as a Negro may discover his present mode of existence, or the possibility that he may have to account for his family and his early life. Even where the chance of such discovery is slight, there may be such constant anxiety and daily fear that the individual prefers to remain within the Negro community.

And Mary Helen Washington (1987) makes similar observations about Nella Larsen's treatment of the theme of passing:

The woman who passes is required to deny everything about her past: her girlhood, her family, places with memories, folk customs, folk rhymes, her language, the entire long line of people who have gone before her. She lives in terror of discovery—what if she has a child with a dark complexion, what if she runs into an old school friend, how does she listen placidly to racial slurs? And more, where does the woman who passes find the equanimity to live by the privileged status that is based on the oppression of her own people?

Washington also stresses that the word *passing* may "connote death—in the black community dying is often referred to as 'passing.'"

Some who pass may feel like cowards, traitors, or losers: For example, at the end of James Weldon Johnson's

The Autobiography of an Ex-Colored Man the narrator feels that he has sold his birthright for a mess of pottage. Some may also simply miss the familiar world of their pasts, their friends, and families. They may feel obliged to deny their closest relatives and friends: Thus, in the presence of her white male companion, Angela has to pretend not to recognize her own sister Virginia in Jessie Fauset's *Plum Bun* (1929); and the subject of Langston Hughes's "Passing" (1934) cannot speak to his mother in the street. An elaborate passing scenario is developed by the writer Garvin Wales in Hamilton Basso's novel *The View from Pompey's Head* (1954): To keep his racial background a secret, Wales has to hide his own mother, and his agent sends her checks for her whole life. Because of this family-disrupting aspect of passing—fully exploited by melodramatic films like *Imitation of Life*—family loyalty and race solidarity may be jointly invoked in an argument against passing.

Yet passing does not always have to be as conflictual as is often assumed. Wirth and Goldhamer stress that the people who tell their stories are more likely to be the ones who suffered from the experience: "The successful and well-adjusted person who passes is not likely to be heard from." Passing may even lead the individual who succeeds in it to a feeling of elation and exultation, an experience of succeeding as a trickster-hero who crosses a significant boundary and sees the world anew. Passing may thus lead to the higher insights of rising above and looking through the "veil" of the color line, to an experience of revelation, to seeing while not being seen—learning about the freemasonry of whiteness; surreptitiously joining an enemy camp—like a spy, a Trojan horse, a living reminder of the absurdity of racial divisions. People who cross the line in this sense, "by reason of their fair skins, are able to gain information about what white people are doing and thinking that would surprise many of them. Often have I gone into the South in my capacity of newspaper correspondent, and as a white man secured vast quantities of information on the race and other questions," writes the anonymous author of "White, but Black" in the 1924–1925 *Century* magazine. In William Henry's novel *Out of Wedlock* (1931), Mary Tanner devises a scheme for her children to pass and marry leading whites in order to undermine racial prejudice.

For reasons such as these, passing was often perceived as a threat by whites. Elmer A. Carter (1926) describes the 1924 Virginia Act to Preserve Racial Integrity as an effort "to stem the tide of pseudo Caucasians who are storming the Anglo-Saxton ramparts." The act included a provision that made it a "felony to make a willfully false statement as to color," and Walter White reports that in 1926 he was threatened by the sheriff of a southern town with an in-

dictment for passing for white. Blacks may react protectively toward the person who passes (Shiny in *The Autobiography of an Ex-Colored Man*), may be indifferent, or may be "ever the quickest to reveal the identity of those who seek to 'pass'" (*Century*).

The presence of people who are "neither black nor white and yet both" undermines the seeming certainty of the most important American racial boundary, and characters who threaten such boundaries may, like Joe Christmas in William Faulkner's *Light in August* (1932), be turned into sacrificial scapegoats. African-American writers such as Langston Hughes, George Schuyler, and Walter Francis White have explored the comic potential in passing and have used it to criticize white and black hypocrisy.

How widespread a phenomenon was passing? Since quantitative data do not exist, writers have offered dramatically heterogeneous estimates. Many African Americans have reported that they personally knew friends or relatives who were passing. In 1931 Caleb Johnson reported the Harlem assumption that more than ten thousand "have 'passed,' and are now accepted as white in their new relations, many of them married to white folks, all unsuspected." Jessie Fauset stated in an interview with the *Pittsburgh Courier* that about twenty thousand blacks were passing in New York alone. An unsigned editorial by the sociologist Charles S. Johnson in *Opportunity* (1925), titled "The Vanishing Mulatto," alerted readers to a possible interpretation of the U.S. Census statistics of 1900, 1910, and 1920. According to those figures 2,050,686 Negroes were classified as mulattoes in 1910, but only 1,660,554 in 1920. Some mulattoes, the editorial concedes, were undoubtedly recounted as blacks, but others must also have faded "into the great white multitude." Drawing on Hornell Hart, Johnson further notes a possible increase of 162,500 native whites from 1900 to 1910 and a corresponding disappearance from the black group of 355,000. E. W. Eckard (1936) assumed more modestly that there were nationally 2,600 cases per year from 1920 to 1940, but T. T. McKinney, as cited by Joseph R. Washington Jr. (1970), believed in 1937 that the figure was 10,000 per year; Walter Francis White (1947) claimed that every year "approximately twelve thousand white-skinned Negroes disappear." According to Herbert Asbury (1946), approximately thirty thousand African Americans were passing each year so that "more than 2,000,000 persons with colored blood have crossed the line since the end of the Civil War." Factoring in possible descendants of people who passed, he goes on to report the "conservative" estimate "that there are at least between 5,000,000 and 8,000,000 persons in the United States, supposed to be white, who actually possess Negro blood." About 10 percent of the

346 families Caroline Bond Day (1932) studied had members who passed, but Gunnar Myrdal (1944), drawing on a manuscript of Wirth and Goldhamer's study, pointed out that her group was not intended to be a representative sample. Edward Reuter (1931) concluded that the "actual number of persons who have left the race and been accepted as white is of course wholly impossible to determine. There is a tendency to grossly exaggerate the number." Passing was undoubtedly significant locally. The Seventh Ward in New Orleans, for example, was known as the Can't Tell Ward (Peretti, 1992), and in the 1920s a theater in Washington hired "a black doorman to spot and bounce intruders whose racial origins were undetectable to whites" (Green, 1967).

Uncertainty has not kept writers from advancing speculations not only about the general figures but also about age and sex distribution among the population of people who pass. For example, Earnest Hooton expressed his belief that it is the younger rather than the older ones who pass (Wirth and Goldhamer); and according to Charles S. Johnson's "Vanishing Mulatto" (1925), while there were "1,018 black males per 1,000 females," there were "only 886 mulatto males per 1,000 females"—permitting the conclusion that men "travel more and are not so dependent as women on family connections." This sex-ratio approach suggested that men were more likely to pass than women, an assumption shared explicitly by Edward Byron Reuter (1931). Although fictional literature often presented men as more successful at passing than women (e.g., John as opposed to Rena in Chesnutt's *The House behind the Cedars*; or Johnson's ex-colored man as opposed to the heroines of Larsen's and Fauset's novels), there exists no evidence to support the belief that men have passed at a greater rate than women. Wirth and Herbert write that "the sex ratio can give no indication of what the total amount of passing is unless one were to assume that females do not pass." Caleb Johnson (1931) assumed the opposite, with little evidence:

> While there are no statistics to support the conclusion, there is strong reason for the belief that many more women than men cross the color line from Negro to white. This is partly due to the fact that sexual attraction is stronger between the light male and the darker female than in the opposite direction. It is a matter commented on by numerous scientific observers, who agree that the male Negro almost universally prefers a woman of his own color or darker, while the primitive sex-appeal of the octoroon girl is highly potent with the average young white male. Moreover,

the social act of "passing" is easier for the girl than for the man.

Joseph Washington (1970) rightly reminds readers that "the knowledge of the sex distribution of blacks who passed was even less adequate than the knowledge of the color distribution."

Although now relegated to a footnote in cultural history, the phenomenon of passing "unleashed tremendous anxiety and fascination among whites" (Washington, 1970) and, from the 1850s to the 1930s, was "the favorite theme in Negro fiction" (Reuter, 1918). Passing was swept aside in social history by the civil rights movement and in literature by the Richard Wright school. As Nathan Huggins (1995) put it, "Passing is passé." A generation later, the time may be ripe for case studies of known individuals who passed, for example, the Trinity College–trained Theophilius John Minton Syphax, who, for forty-five years, was the white Wall Street lawyer T. John McKee until he revealed his true identity shortly before his death in 1948 (Burly, 1951); or the Columbia graduate William E. Jackson, who disclosed his racial background when he married the white woman Helen Burns in New York in 1925. At the same time, a full-fledged cultural investigation could be conducted of the period in which passing created much fascination for both black and white Americans.

See also Identity and Race in the United States; Social Psychology, Psychologists, and Race

■ ■ ■ *Bibliography*

Adams, Bruce Payton. "The White Negro: The Image of the Passable Mulatto Character in Black Novels, 1853–1954." Ph.D. diss., University of Kansas, Lawrence, 1975.

"The Adventures of a Near-White." *Independent* (1913).

Arbery, Glenn Cannon. "Victims of Likeness: Quadroons and Octoroons in Southern Fiction." *Southern Review* 25, no. 1 (winter 1989): 52–71.

Asbury, Herbert. "Who Is a Negro?" *Collier's* (August 3, 1946).

Baker, Ray Stannard. *Following the Color Line: American Negro Citizenship in the Progressive Era.* 1908. Reprint, New York: Harper & Row, 1964.

Berzon, Judith R. *Neither White nor Black: The Mulatto Character in American Fiction.* New York: New York University Press, 1978.

Brown, Sterling. *Negro Poetry and Drama and the Negro in American Fiction* (1937). Reprint, New York: Atheneum, 1969.

Bullock, Penelope. "The Mulatto in American Fiction." *Phylon* 6 (1945): 78–82.

Burly, Dan. "The Strange Will of Colonel McKee." *Negro Digest* (November 1951): 17–22.

Carter, Elmer A. "Crossing Over." *Opportunity* (December 1926): 376–378.

Davis, F. James. *Who Is Black? One Nation's Definition.* University Park: Pennsylvania State University Press, 1991.

Day, Caroline Bond. *A Study of Some Negro-White Families in the United States.* Foreword and notes by Ernest A. Hooton. Harvard African Studies no. 10. Cambridge, Mass.: Peabody Museum of Harvard University, 1932.

Devereux, George. "Ethnic Identity: Its Logical Foundation and Its Dysfunctions." In *Ethnic Identity: Cultural Continuities and Change,* edited by George DeVos and Lola Romanucci-Ross. Palo Alto, Calif.: Mayfield, 1975.

Eckard, E. W. "Burns Mantle" review of Samson Raphaelson's *White Man* (play; October 19, 1936. New York: S. French, 1935). Cited in Jacquelyn Y. McLendon's "The Myth of the Mulatto Psyche: A Study of the Works of Jessie Fauset and Nella Larsen." Ph.D. diss., Case Western Reserve University, 1986.

Ginsberg, Elaine K. *Passing and the Fictions of Identity.* Durham, N.C.: Duke University Press, 1996.

Green, Constance. *The Secret City: A History of Race Relations in the Nation's Capital.* Princeton, N.J.: Princeton University Press, 1967. Cited in Willard B. Gatewood's *Aristocrats of Color: The Black Elite, 1880–1920.* Bloomington and Indianapolis: Indiana University Press, 1990.

Holmes, Thomas Alan. "Race as Metaphor: 'Passing' in Twentieth-Century African-American Fiction." Ph.D. diss., University of Alabama, Tuscaloosa, 1990.

Huggins, Nathan Irvin. "Passing Is Passé." In *Revelations: American History, American Myths,* edited by Brenda Smith Huggins. New York and Oxford: Oxford University Press, 1995.

Jackson, Blyden. "A Golden Mean for the Negro Novel." *College Language Association Journal* 3, no. 2 (December 1959): 81–87.

Johnson, Caleb. "Crossing the Color Line." *Outlook and Independent* (August 26, 1931): 526–527.

Johnson, Charles S. "The Vanishing Mulatto." *Opportunity: Journal of Negro Life* 3, no. 34 (October 1925): 291.

Kinney, James. *Amalgamation! Race, Sex, and Rhetoric in the Nineteenth-Century American Novel.* Westport, Conn.: Greenwood Press, 1985.

Klineberg, Otto, ed. *Characteristics of the American Negro.* New York: Harper & Brothers, 1944.

Mencke, John G. *Mulattoes and Race Mixture: American Attitudes and Images. Studies in American History and Culture,* No. 4. Ann Arbor, Mich.: UMI Research Press, 1979.

Myrdal, Gunnar. *An American Dilemma: The Negro Problem and Modern Democracy.* New York & London: Harper & Brothers, 1944.

Peretti, Burton W. *The Creation of Jazz: Music, Race, and Culture in Urban America.* Urbana and Chicago: University of Illinois Press, 1992.

Reuter, Edward Byron. *The Mulatto in the United States: Including a Study of the Role of Mixed-Blood Races throughout the World* (1918). Reprint, New York: Negro Universities Press, 1969.

Reuter, Edward Byron. *Race Mixture: Studies in Intermarriage and Miscegenation* (1931). Reprint, New York: Negro Universities Press, 1969.

Rogers, J. A. *Sex and Race: Negro-Caucasian Mixing in All Ages and All Lands.* 3 vols. 1941, 1942, and 1944. Reprint, St. Petersburg, Fla.: Helga M. Rogers, 1967, 1972, and 1984.

Rogers, J. A. *Nature Knows No Color-Line* (1952). Reprint, St. Petersburg, Fla.: Helga M. Rogers, 1980.

Roy, Ratna. "The Marginal Man: A Study of the Mulatto Character in American Fiction." Ph.D. diss., University of Oregon, Eugene, 1973.

Sollors, Werner. *Neither Black nor White yet Both: Thematic Explorations of Interracial Literature.* New York: Oxford University Press, 1997.

Stonequist, Everett V. *The Marginal Man: A Study in Personality and Culture Conflict* (1937). Reprint, New York: Russell & Russell, 1961.

Stonequist, Everett V. "Race Mixture and Mulatto." In *Race Relations and the Race Problem: A Definition and an Analysis,* edited by Edgar T. Thompson. Durham, N.C.: Duke University Press, 1939.

Washington, Joseph R., Jr. *Marriage in Black and White.* Boston: Beacon Press, 1970.

Washington, Mary Helen. *Invented Lives: Narratives of Black Women 1860-1960.* New York: Doubleday, 1987.

Waters, Mary C. *Ethnic Options: Choosing Identities in America.* Berkeley: University of California Press, 1990.

"White, but Black." *Century* 109 (1924–25): 492-499.

White, Walter Francis. "Why I Remain a Negro." *Saturday Review of Literature* (October 11, 1947). Cited in Kephart, William M. "The 'Passing' Question." *Phylon* 10 (1948).

Williamson, Joel. *New People: Miscegenation and Mulattoes in the United States.* New York: Free Press, 1980.

Wirth, Louis, and Herbert Goldhamer. "The Hybrid and the Problems of Miscegenation." In *Characteristics of the American Negro,* edited by Otto Klineberg. New York: Harper and Row, 1944.

Yarborough, Richard. "The Depiction of Blacks in the Early Afro-American Novel." Ph.D. diss., Stanford University, Palo Alto, Calif., 1980.

Zack, Naomi. *Race and Mixed Race.* Philadelphia: Temple University Press, 1993.

Zanger, Jules. "The 'Tragic Octoroon' in Pre-Civil War Fiction." *American Quarterly* 18 (1966): 63–70.

WERNER SOLLORS (1996)

PATENTS AND INVENTIONS

The U.S. Constitution (article 1, section 8) empowers Congress "to promote the progress of science . . . by securing to authors and inventors the exclusive right to their respective writings and discoveries." The first U.S. Patent Act, passed in 1790, had two basic purposes: to protect inventors from unauthorized use of their work and to provide the public with increased access to information about useful inventions.

Although free blacks were legally entitled to hold patents prior to the Civil War, few actually received them. The first African American known to have received a patent was Thomas L. Jennings, for a dry-cleaning process (March 3, 1821). Following him was Henry Blair, who patented a corn-seed planter in 1834 and a cottonseed planter in 1836. In 1843 Norbert Rillieux patented a refining process that revolutionized the sugar industry.

Blacks were hindered, however, from participating fully in the system. They did not have routine access to apprenticeships in the white-dominated crafts and trades and, therefore, to the kind of training and experience that would have helped nurture their inventive skills. As a result, black inventors had to rely almost entirely on their own initiative. Furthermore, their products tended to evolve out of occupations that had been predetermined as acceptable for blacks—for example, domestic service, carpentry, and agriculture. Within these constraints, a few African Americans developed successful, important inventions. Some, such as Jennings, achieved wealth and social visibility, which they subsequently used as leverage in campaigns aimed at improving the lot of black Americans.

Slaves were not entitled to hold patents, yet some developed creative implements and techniques that enhanced the efficiency of their masters' businesses. Slave craftsmen emerged as a small, elite group distinct from field laborers and domestic servants. Because of their legal standing, the question arose as to who (if anyone) was entitled to ownership of their inventions. In 1857 one Mississippi slave owner claimed the rights to his slave's invention, a cotton scraper regarded as an innovative laborsaving device. The federal government denied this claim, reinforcing the prohibition on ownership by slaves but also declining to grant slave owners the privilege of "owning" the fruits of a slave's inventive genius. In response the Confederate Patent Act asserted the ownership rights to slave owners in such cases. It was no mere coincidence that Joseph Davis, the brother of Confederate president Jefferson Davis, had earlier been denied a patent on a steamboat propeller invented by his slave, Benjamin Montgomery.

After the Civil War no one was excluded from taking out a patent on grounds of race or legal status. The result was a dramatic increase in the number of patents awarded to blacks. On August 10, 1894, the names and inventions of ninety-two blacks were read into the *Congressional Record*. By 1900 blacks had been awarded over four hundred patents. Among them was A. P. Ashbourne for processes relating to food preparation. In 1872 Elijah McCoy received the first of many patents on automatic engine lubrication, processes critical to the railroad and shipping in-

dustries. Jan Matzeliger received a patent (March 20, 1883) for his invention of a shoe-lasting machine, followed by four others also relating to the technology of shoemaking. In the mid-1920s, after decades of innovative work in botany and agriculture at Tuskegee Institute, George Washington Carver took out patents for a cosmetic and for pigment-producing processes. Such inventions reflected the ongoing concentration of blacks in service and manual-labor occupations—a pattern influenced not just by social tradition but also by the emphasis that black leaders such as Booker T. Washington placed on industrial and technical education as the most promising path of opportunity for African Americans.

This path was consistent with the pressures of American urbanization. By the turn of the twentieth century, as blacks migrated to the cities, many had entered technical occupations in government and industry. Andrew F. Hilyer, an attorney in Washington, D.C., patented a room humidifier in 1890; Robert Pelham, a newspaper publisher in Detroit, patented a tabulating machine in 1905 and an adding machine in 1913; Garrett Morgan of Cleveland patented a gas mask in 1914 and an automatic traffic signal in 1923. Granville Woods and Lewis Latimer contributed to the emergence of electricity as an energy replacement for gas. Woods, known as the "black Edison," patented a telegraph transmitter in 1884 and, subsequently, devices to facilitate railway electrification. In 1881 Latimer patented a method for producing carbon filaments and became part of the research team of the Edison Electric Light Company.

Access to a career as an inventor became more difficult as the growing complexity of technology changed the character of innovation and discovery. In the twentieth century the solitary, self-motivated inventor was replaced by teams of salaried researchers, often with advanced degrees, working in large companies or government-sponsored laboratories. Few blacks qualified for such positions, and those who did often faced discrimination by prospective employers. This sheds light on why the participation of blacks in patenting and invention is proportionately lower today than it was a hundred years ago.

See also Inventors and Inventions

■■ *Bibliography*

Baker, Henry E. *The Colored Inventor: A Record of Fifty Years.* 1915. Reprint, New York: Arno Press, 1968.

James, Portia P. *The Real McCoy: African-American Invention and Innovation, 1619–1930.* Washington, D.C.: Smithsonian Institution Press, 1989.

Klein, Aaron. *Hidden Contributors: Black Scientists and Inventors in America.* New York: Doubleday, 1971.

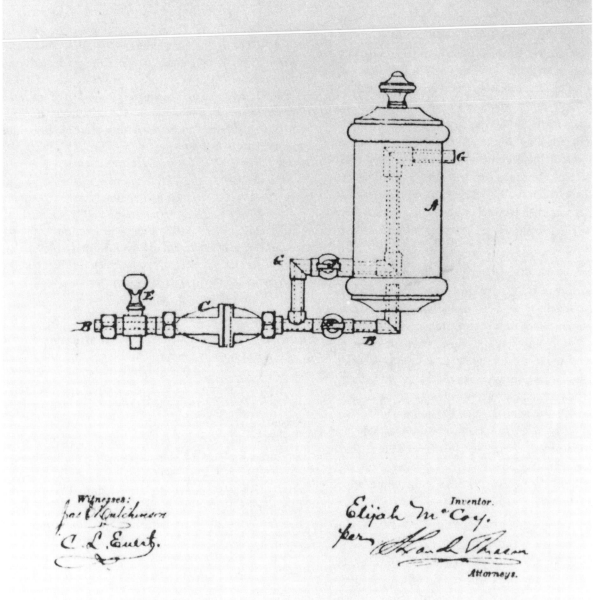

E. McCOY.

Improvement in Lubricators for Steam-Engines.

No. 130,305.　　　　　　　　Patented Aug. 6, 1872.

African American inventor Elijah McCoy's patent no. 130,305, introducing an improvement in lubricators for steam engines, 1872. PHOTOGRAPHS AND PRINTS DIVISION, SCHOMBURG CENTER FOR RESEARCH IN BLACK CULTURE, THE NEW YORK PUBLIC LIBRARY, ASTOR, LENOX AND TILDEN FOUNDATIONS.

Sluby, Patricia Carter. *The Inventive Spirit of African Americans: Patented Ingenuity.* Westport, Conn.: Praeger, 2004.

PHILIP N. ALEXANDER (1996)
Updated bibliography

PATTERSON, FLOYD

JANUARY 4, 1935

▮▮▮

The second youngest heavyweight champion in boxing history, Floyd Patterson was born in 1935 in Waco, North Carolina, one of eleven children of Thomas and Anabelle Patterson, and grew up in the slums of Brooklyn. A wayward youth, he attended Wiltwyck School, a correctional institute (1945–1947), where he learned to read and box. He was taken up by Cus D'Amato, who observed his quick hands and punching power. He twice won the Golden Gloves and took the gold medal in the middleweight division at the 1952 Olympics. He then turned pro and quickly became a contender for the heavyweight crown vacated by Rocky Marciano. On November 30, 1956, he KO'd forty-three-year-old light-heavyweight champion Archie Moore for the title.

Patterson seemed too gentle a person for his chosen career; once he helped retrieve an opponent's mouthpiece. After attaining the title, he defeated four nondescript challengers until matched with Ingemar Johansson on June 26, 1959. Patterson was knocked down seven times in the third round and lost in an upset. He went into seclusion, returning to the ring one year later to knock out Johansson in the fifth, becoming the first heavyweight titlist to regain the crown. On September 25, 1962, he fought the awesome Sonny Liston, who knocked out Patterson in the first round, a defeat that caused him to sneak out of Chicago in disguise. Their rematch in 1963 ended with the same result. Patterson retired in 1972, finishing with a record of 55–8–1.

Patterson has served as head of the New York State Athletic Commission and in 1985 was appointed director of Off-Track Betting. He was elected to the Boxing Hall of Fame in 1977 and the Olympic Hall of Fame in 1987. Patterson resigned from the New York State Athletic Commission in April 1998.

See also Boxing; Moore, Archie

■ ■ *Bibliography*
Patterson, Floyd, with Milton Gross. *Victory Over Myself.* New York: Random House, 1962.

STEVEN A. RIESS (1996)
Updated by publisher 2005

PATTERSON, PERCIVAL JAMES "P. J."

APRIL 10, 1935

▮▮▮

Percival James "P. J." Patterson, the prime minister of Jamaica, was born in Dias, Hanover, Jamaica. He was educated at Calabar High School in Kingston; graduated from the University of the West Indies, where he earned a B.A. in English, in 1958; and received his law degree from the London School of Economics in 1963. Patterson was admitted to the Jamaican bar later that year. He began his political career in 1958 when he joined the People's National Party (PNP) as a political organizer.

Between 1963 and 1972, Patterson established a private legal practice, though he remained active in national politics. In 1964 he was elected to the PNP's National Executive Committee, and in 1969 won election to the Jamaican House of Representatives. In February 1969, at age thirty-three, he was elected vice president of the PNP, the youngest person ever elected to that post.

THE TURBULENT 1970S

Patterson gained prominence as a political organizer in the 1970s. Most notably, he directed the PNP's pathbreaking 1972 electoral campaign that rallied marginalized and disenfranchised groups, particularly youths and the urban unemployed, to join a coalition with disaffected workers, peasants, and the middle class.

These alienated groups were impatient with the authoritarian politics of the incumbent Jamaica Labour Party (JLP). They were also fed up with the JLP's insensitivity to Afro-Jamaicans' desire for cultural respect and dissatisfied with the party's inability to realize the desire of ordinary people for a better life. By mobilizing these disaffected constituencies and commingling PNP populist rhetoric with radical themes in popular music and culture, the PNP swept to power in a landslide under the leadership of Michael Manley (1924–1997) in February 1972. Patterson's implementation of the party's electoral strategy identified him as an unparalleled political organizer and his success earned him a place in Manley's cabinet as minister of industry, foreign trade, and tourism.

The turbulent 1970s would test Patterson's mettle. The decade saw Jamaica turn politically leftward under the PNP's socialist banner at the very moment that the shock of the OPEC oil price hikes and the destabilizing run-up in world oil prices hit the island. As the domestic economic crisis worsened, Patterson introduced several initiatives. He shielded consumers from predatory pricing, established a consumer affairs unit to stop hoarding, spurred job growth, and encouraged import substitution by initiating agro-industrial projects for processing local produce.

Patterson was also a major actor in regional and international economic organizations. In 1974 he helped establish the Caribbean Community and Common Market (CARICOM), and he was a leading negotiator and spokesman for less-developed countries on trade issues. He was also an architect of the Lomé Convention, a special trade agreement between the European community and a group of African, Caribbean, and Pacific (ACP) countries to promote sustained development in ACP states. This agreement was signed in February 1975 as part of the North-South dialogue between rich and poor countries. In this exchange, poor countries campaigned for reforms in international trade that would benefit them. As Jamaica's minister of foreign affairs and foreign trade, ministerial chair of the Group of 77 (a United Nations coalition of developing countries), and president of the Council of Ministers of the African, Caribbean, and Pacific Group of States, Patterson was a significant contributor to the North-South dialogue.

Notwithstanding these efforts to promote a new international economic order and self-reliance at home, the PNP was defeated at the polls in 1980. Out of power, Patterson returned to practicing law. In 1981 he became a founding partner of the law firm Rattray, Patterson, Rattray, and three years later he was appointed a Queen's Counsel in recognition of excellence in the practice of the law.

THE CALL TO LEADERSHIP

With Manley at the helm, a chastened PNP was returned to power in 1989. The party's success resulted from its decision to jettison political radicalism and embrace free-market policies, and its promise to deliver economic gains for the poor. In 1992, however, an ailing Michael Manley retired from politics. Patterson, who had been deputy prime minister since 1978, was elected party president and sworn in as prime minister in March 1992.

Patterson's rise to power was a momentous event. Except for former prime minister Hugh Lawson Shearer (1923–2004), who was the first Afro-Jamaican prime minister, all previous prime ministers were of mixed racial stock. Shearer was not of mixed race, though he was brown-skinned. Patterson was Jamaica's first dark-skinned prime minister, and after Shearer only the second Afro-Jamaican to hold that office. The symbolic value of this achievement was not lost on the black-skinned Afro-Jamaican majority. More important, the 1990s had ushered in an era of great change, both domestically and internationally. This great transition—marked by the collapse of communism, the demand for democracy by restive civil societies, and the triumph of free-market capitalism—was especially challenging for poor countries and their leaders.

In Jamaica, growing poverty, economic hardship, and the triumph of market values were eroding traditional social norms and values. These were replaced by greed, selfishness, and a get-rich-quick mentality. In the absence of restraining civic norms and effective public institutions, the results were high rates of criminal violence, persistent social unrest, and government corruption.

Nonetheless, a vocal media, an invigorated public opinion, and newly emergent reform organizations countered these negative trends by demanding effective governance, insisting on probity in public life and calling for a return to democratic values. Patterson thus became prime minister at a critical juncture, when creative vision and strong leadership were called for.

How well did Patterson respond to these challenges and to the call for leadership? First, he confounded his detractors by scoring three consecutive electoral victories—in 1993, 1997, and 2002. In the country's postcolonial history, no leader had ever won three consecutive terms of office. Second, Patterson made key changes in both public policy and the political culture. In a world where national development and economic growth were increasingly dependent on new technologies of communication and on the modernization of national infrastructures, Jamaica made a quantum leap in both areas. By democratizing citizens' access to cell phones, cable broadcasts, and the Internet, the PNP satisfied their desire for leisure and luxury goods, and the party put in place new technologies that would positively influence the quantity and speed of economic transactions. The same could be said of the economic value associated with the PNP's massive expenditures on roads, bridges, highways, and electrical grids. In sum, by introducing new technologies and modernizing the island's infrastructure, the Patterson administration increased Jamaica's ability to compete in the new global environment.

Finally, by governing with a pragmatic, consultative, and nonauthoritarian style, Patterson broke with the worn-out populist style of Jamaican leaders. Though criticized by detractors for being boring and uncharismatic, Patterson's style has been viewed by many to be well-suited to the new period of ideological demobilization and pragmatic policy making.

FALLING SHORT: CRISES AND TRANSITIONAL LEADERSHIP

Despite these achievements in guiding Jamaica through a rapidly changing world and lowering the temperature of partisan politics, Patterson failed to inspire public confidence. Paradoxically, he could get the people's votes but not their enthusiasm. Moreover, though he regularly proclaimed his commitment to building civic values, scandals and disclosures of corruption in his administration only reinforced public cynicism. Thus, though Jamaicans were hungry for bold leadership and yearning for an inspired vision of a positive future, not many besides the most partisan looked to Patterson as their unerring guide.

Indeed, Patterson's inability to stem the violent crime that claimed hundreds of lives every year, his stunning ineffectiveness in reining in a security force inured to extrajudicial killing as a crime-fighting strategy, and his inability to give the inner-city poor hope have threatened to nullify his achievements.

Hence, despite innovations in infrastructural modernization and the adoption of a democratic style of political leadership, these flourishes seemed meager to a public demanding more. In fact, Patterson's seeming unwillingness to make tough decisions, his insensitivity to human-rights concerns, and his temporizing in the face of increasing crime and social discontent only encouraged critics in their view that he was not the man for the times. That assessment may not be too far from the truth, for Patterson can be viewed as the embodiment of the struggling transitional figure caught in the tide of great historical change. He is therefore likely to be judged an enigmatic, foundering figure, whose leadership proved inadequate at a major turning point in Jamaica's political history.

See also Jamaica Labour Party; Manley, Michael; People's National Party

■ ■ *Bibliography*

Bertram, Arnold. *P. J. Patterson A Mission to Perform*. Kingston, Jamaica: AB Associates, 1995.

Stone, Carl. "The Danger of Choosing Mr. Niceguy." In *The Stone Columns, the Last Year's Work: A Selection of Carl Stone's Gleaner Articles, January 1992 to February 1993*, edited by Rosemarie Stone. Kingston, Jamaica: Sangster's, 1994.

OBIKA GRAY (2005)

PATTERSON, WILLIAM
AUGUST 27, 1891
MARCH 5, 1980

Lawyer and activist William Patterson was born in San Francisco, California. When he was young, his father left the family to become a missionary while his mother worked as a domestic to raise their children. Patterson took jobs as a sea porter, a dishwasher, and an elevator operator, among other things, to help support his family and put himself through school. In 1911 he graduated from Tamalpais High School and entered the University of California at Berkeley to study engineering. He attended on and off for several years before deciding to go to the Hastings College of Law in San Francisco, where he earned his J.D. in 1919.

While in college, Patterson became politically active, combating racism and urging African Americans not to fight in World War I, which he felt was a "white man's war." After considering going to Liberia, he instead chose to move to New York City, where he opened a law firm with two friends in 1923. In New York in the midst of the Harlem Renaissance he was exposed to left-wing ideas and met such influential black activists as Paul Robeson and W. E. B. Du Bois. During this period he actively supported the International Labor Defense protests on behalf of Nicola Sacco and Bartolomeo Vanzetti, two Italian anarchists whose radical political views and status as immigrants contributed heavily to their conviction and subsequent execution in 1927 for the murder of a paymaster.

As a result of his political activity, Patterson came to the conclusion that economic exploitation and the capitalist system lay at the root of black oppression. In 1927 he joined the Communist Party, U.S.A. and went to the Soviet Union for three years to study at the University of the Toiling People of the Far East in Moscow. There he found a society he thought was free of racial, class, and religious prejudice. Patterson returned to the United States in 1930 and two years later was elected to the Central Committee of the Communist Party and ran for mayor of New York on the Communist Party ticket. From 1932 until 1946 he served as executive director of the International Labor Defense (ILD), a radical legal-action group strongly influenced by the Communist Party. As head of the ILD in the 1930s, Patterson helped coordinate the legal strategy and political protests on behalf of the Scottsboro defendants, nine young African-American men falsely accused of raping two white women. (All but the youngest were sentenced to death.)

In 1938 Patterson moved to Chicago and two years later married Louise Thompson, with whom he had three children. While there, Patterson organized Chicago's South Side and wrote for and edited various communist newspapers, including the *Daily Record* and the *Daily Worker*. From 1946 to 1956 he served as executive director of the Civil Rights Congress, an organization often aligned with the Communist Party that defended the civil rights and liberties of African Americans and radical political activists. In 1951 he and Paul Robeson presented a petition to the United Nations charging the United States with genocide by "deliberately inflicting on [African Americans] conditions of life calculated to bring about [their] physical destruction" through executions, lynchings, and systematic terrorism. In the same year he edited a book, *We Charge Genocide: The Crime of Government Against the Negro People*. Because of his involvement in the Civil Rights Congress and the Communist Party, Patterson was called before the House Committee on Un-American Activities in 1950 and found in contempt four years later for refusing to answer questions. He spent three months in prison before the decision was reversed upon appeal.

Patterson's political activity declined in the later years of his life, but he still firmly believed in a society free of racism and poverty. In 1971 he published his autobiography, *The Man Who Cried Genocide*, and in 1978 he was awarded the Paul Robeson Memorial Medal by the Academy of Arts in East Germany. Although he died in 1980 after a prolonged illness, a foundation that bears his name carries on his commitment to social justice by awarding grants to supporters of the "people's struggle."

See also Civil Rights Congress; Communist Party of the United States; Labor and Labor Unions

■ ■ *Bibliography*

Horne, Gerald. *Communist Front? The Civil Rights Congress, 1946–56*. Rutherford, N.J: Fairleigh Dickinson University Press; London and Cranbury, N.J.: Associated University Presses, 1988.

Patterson, William. *The Man Who Cried Genocide: An Autobiography*. New York: International Publishers, 1971.

PREMILLA NADASEN (1996)

PAYNE, DANIEL ALEXANDER

FEBRUARY 24, 1811
NOVEMBER 2, 1893

■ ■ ■

Daniel Alexander Payne was the principal figure in the African Methodist Episcopal (AME) Church during the second half of the nineteenth century, a period one historian termed "the era of Bishop Daniel Payne." Payne was born in Charleston, South Carolina, to free black parents who provided for his early education. He established his own school in 1828 but was forced to close it when the South Carolina legislature prohibited the teaching of blacks.

Leaving Charleston in 1835, he studied for two years at the Evangelical Lutheran Seminary in Gettysburg, Pennsylvania, but left because of failing eyesight. He obtained a license to preach and in 1839 became the first African-American clergyman ordained by the Franckean Evangelical Lutheran Synod. He opened a coeducational school in Philadelphia in 1840 and soon became involved in the antislavery movement.

Although Payne briefly served a white Presbyterian congregation in Troy, New York, he was never given charge of a Lutheran parish, so in 1841 he associated with the AME Church. He hesitated to join the denomination because many members opposed an educated clergy. Payne's preference for formal, liturgical worship and learned ministers contrasted with the emotional, spontaneous style of many of the denomination's pastors and congregations. But his untiring efforts to standardize AME worship, improve religious education, and preserve a record of the denomination's history eventually earned the respect of church leaders. Elected a bishop in 1852, he shaped the character and policies of the denomination over the next four decades. Under his leadership, the AME Church expanded its home and foreign missions, reorganized its publication program, and established hundreds of congregations among the recently emancipated slaves, a major factor in the denomination's rapid growth after the Civil War.

A noted educator, author, and theologian, Payne was named president in 1863 of Wilberforce University, the first black-controlled college in the United States. He made the institution solvent, attracted capable students and faculty, and enhanced its reputation. Although he left the presidency of Wilberforce in 1876, he remained active in its administration until his death.

Payne wrote numerous poems, essays, speeches, and sermons for the African-American press. His autobiographical *Recollections of Seventy Years* (1888) and *History of the African Methodist Episcopal Church* (1891) are important contributions to African-American literature and valuable sources for nineteenth-century African-American history. He was a conspicuous figure in the World Parliament of Religions at the World's Columbian Exposition in Chicago (1893).

See also African Methodist Episcopal Church; Autobiography, U.S.; Wilberforce University

■ ■ *Bibliography*

Coan, Josephus R. *Daniel Alexander Payne: Christian Educator.* Philadelphia: A.M.E., 1935.

ROY E. FINKENBINE (1996)

PECK, RAOUL
1953

▬▬▬

Raoul Peck was born in Port-au-Prince, Haiti, in 1953. At age eight, he and his parents fled the François Duvalier dictatorship, migrating to the Republic of the Congo in Africa. After secondary school in France, Peck studied industrial engineering in Berlin and in 1982 moved to New York City, where he worked as a taxi driver while waiting for a job at the United Nations. When this fell through, he returned to Berlin to study film at the German Film and Television Academy. While still a student, he produced a number of short films before directing his first full-length feature, *Haitian Corner* (1987). Filmed in Brooklyn for $150,000, it examines a Haitian immigrant's desire for vengeance when he thinks he recognizes one of his Tonton Macoute torturers from his time in prison in Haiti. Peck then worked as a film lecturer before directing the full-length documentary *Lumumba: La mort du prophète* in 1991. This intensely personal and poetic film focused on the life and eventual tragedy of Patrice Lumumba, the Congo's first prime minister. Peck's second feature film, *L'Homme sur les quais* (1993), is set in Haiti and is the story of a young girl who witnesses the effect of the Duvalier regime's terror on her family. Haiti is also the subject of Peck's documentaries *Désounen: Dialogue with Death* (1994) and *Haiti: Silence of the Dogs* (1994).

In 1996 Peck established the Foundation Forum Eldorado, dedicated to the promotion of cultural development in Haiti and the Caribbean. He served as minister of culture in Haiti but left after eighteen months, disillu-

sioned with the presidency of Jean-Bertrand Aristide. After writing a book on this experience, he resumed his career as a filmmaker. He directed the video documentary *Chère Catherine* (1997) and the full-length feature *Corps plongés* (1998) before returning to the story of Lumumba with his award-winning feature film *Lumumba* (2000).

Lumumba achieved significant popular and critical acclaim. Made on a modest budget of $4 million, it received wide international distribution. This success marked an important milestone in Peck's career, ensuring his recognition as a major black independent filmmaker from the African diaspora. His subsequent work focuses on social and political issues of the developing world: His documentary *Profit and Nothing But* (2001) criticizes the politics of globalization, and the feature-length HBO film *Sometimes in April* (2005) looks at genocide in Rwanda.

Peck has won numerous awards, including the 2001 Paul Robeson Prize at the Pan-African Film and Television Festival in Ouaguadougou, West Africa, and best film at the Los Angeles Pan African Film Festival (2001) for *Lumumba*. He is the president of the Caribbean Federation of Film and Video and a member of the French Association of Independent Filmmakers, Auteurs, Realisateurs, et Producteurs (ARP).

See also Documentary Film; Duvalier, François; Film in Latin America and the Caribbean

■ ■ *Bibliography*

Taylor, Clyde. "Autopsy of Terror: A Conversation with Raoul Peck." *Transition* 69 (1996): 236–246.

KEITH Q. WARNER (2005)
BRUCE PADDINGTON (2005)

PELÉ (EDSON ARANTES DO NASCIMENTO)
OCTOBER 23, 1940

▬▬▬

Pelé, born Edson Arantes do Nascimento in the town of Tres Corações in Minas Gerais, Brazil, is widely regarded as the greatest soccer player in the history of the game. Affectionately called "the black pearl" or simply "the king," Pelé rose from a life of bitter third-world poverty to become an international celebrity and one of the most committed, accomplished, and respected athletes of all time. For not only did Pelé revolutionize and popularize the

Pelé dribbles the ball during an exhibition game in Los Angeles. *The Brazilian soccer great led his national team to three World Cup championships, in 1958, 1962, and 1970.* AP/WIDEWORLD PHOTOS. REPRODUCED BY PERMISSION.

game of soccer; he also used his fame to heighten public awareness of poverty, improve the working conditions of Brazilian soccer players, and spread the message of equality through soccer.

Born to João Ramos do Nascimento, a professional soccer player, and Dona Celeste, Pelé, initially harbored dreams of becoming an aviator. Emulating his father and teammates from the Bauru Athletic Club (BAC), Pelé began playing soccer at the age of eight with neighborhood boys in his hometown of Bauru. Pelé and his friends relished in their own amateur matches played with a makeshift ball, fashioned from stuffing a large sock full of newspaper as neither Pelé nor his teammates could afford to buy a soccer ball. Like other children among Brazil's working class, Pelé sought employment. He supplemented his father's meager soccer earnings by alternately working as a shoe-shine boy and as a meat pie vendor. Although poverty informed much of Pelé's daily existence in Bauru, he was not numbed by it; rather, poverty gave Pelé keen insight into the human condition: "Poverty is a curse that depresses the mind, drains the spirit and poisons life. . . Poverty . . . is being robbed of self-respect and self reliance. Poverty is fear. Not fear of death, which though inevitable

is reasonable; it is fear of life" (Fish, pp. 14–15). It would be this realistic, yet compassionate sensibility that would form Pelé's later political and humanitarian work.

In 1955, at the age of fifteen, after winning the BAC Junior Victory Cup, Pelé was recruited by the local soccer club Santos, a testimony to his prodigious talent. In 1958, at the age of seventeen, Pelé was selected to the Brazilian national team to compete in the World Cup tournament in Sweden. Scoring a memorable goal in the final game against Sweden, Pelé's World Cup debut was stunning. Pelé had little time to revel in Brazil's victory, for the following year he began serving his one-year mandatory military duty. In 1960 he returned to Santos, and the team toured throughout Europe, playing against soccer clubs in Denmark, Italy, and Portugal.

While Brazil emerged victorious once again in the 1962 World Cup tournament, Pelé was sidelined by a nagging groin injury and forced to watch his team compete from the bench. The highly anticipated 1966 World Cup finals proved to be both disheartening and demoralizing for Pelé and the Brazilian team, as Brazil failed to emerge from the group stages.

In 1967 Pelé's Santos team went on a tour of Africa that, for Pelé, was a life-changing experience:

> It was with very strong and strange emotions that I first saw Africa. . . . It was a completely different experience from seeing the cities of Europe. . . . Everywhere I went I was looked upon and treated as a god, almost certainly because I represented to the blacks in those countries what a black man could accomplish in a country where there was little racial prejudice. (Fish, p. 203)

So greatly was Pelé revered by Africans that when he played an exhibition game in Nigeria that year, the country's civil war ground to a halt, a formerly warring nation now rapt at the sight of Pelé on the soccer field. As Pelé stated: "To these people, who had little possibility of ever escaping the crushing poverty in which they found themselves, I somehow represented a ray of hope"(Fish, p. 203).

Though Pelé generally maintained that Brazilian society was free of the kind of racism that crippled American society, in his autobiography he recalls the tragic tale of his first love, a young Portuguese girl. As school let out, then twelve-year-old Pelé watched in horror as the girl's father accosted and spanked her in front of Pelé and all of their classmates for simply sharing an innocent friendship with the young Pelé who, immobilized by humiliation, endured the man's racist verbal abuse as well (Fish, pp. 103–104). Pelé also cites the media frenzy surrounding his 1965 marriage to Rosemeri Cholbyas, evidence of Bra-

Pelé. *Considered by many the greatest soccer player of all time, Pelé greets the public at a Spanish League football match between Real Madrid and Zaragoza at Santiago Bernabeu stadium in Madrid, Spain, 2005.* AFP/GETTY IMAGES

zil's racial prejudice, for the press made much of their interracial union.

In 1969, during the Santos match against Vasco da Gama, Pelé scored his historic one-thousandth goal, which he dedicated to Brazil's young, poor street children, weeping as he entreated the public to "Remember the children, remember the poor children" (Harris, p. 75). At this point in his career, Pelé was already an international superstar, yet, his humility, compassion, and conscience enabled him to continually relate to those suffering the crushing effects of poverty.

Pelé and the Brazilian team were eager to redeem themselves in the 1970 World Cup tournament. The Brazilian team emerged victorious, going undefeated throughout the tournament, culminating in a finals victory over Italy in which Pelé scored one goal and assisted on two others. In 1970 Pelé also began planning his retirement from international football. On July 18, 1971, Pelé played his final game with the Brazilian national team in the famed Maracana stadium, against Yugoslavia. The match was an emotional one, with the crowd, over 180,000 strong, chanting: "Fica! Fica!" meaning "Stay! Stay!" Bra-

zilian fans were not the only ones to express their sadness at Pelé's impending departure; dignitaries and heads of state such as President Richard Nixon and England's Queen Elizabeth also bid Pelé farewell.

In 1972, Santos experienced several changes in management, among them the firing of Pelé's mentor, Professor Mazzei. Pelé's contract with Santos expired that same year and, as part of his renegotiations, he agreed to play one of his two remaining years for free, his salary to be donated to charity. It was also during this time that Pelé and his Santos teammates met with the Brazilian president to discuss the need for a national soccer players' union. The following year, on May 25, 1973, Pelé played his final game with Santos.

The 1970s continued with Pelé signing lucrative contracts with Pepsi to conduct soccer clinics in 150 countries, and with the New York Cosmos soccer team. While Pelé was not eager to immigrate to the United States and join a failing team, bad business investments and the threat of bankruptcy forced him to sign with the Cosmos. According to Pelé, his work in the Pepsi-Cola-sponsored clinics, which took him to countries in Asia and Africa, was a tremendously gratifying experience that strengthened his own belief in the potential for unity across racial lines:

> My trips for Pepsi-Cola . . . put me in direct contact with children of all races and colors in all countries. It constantly reminded me of a truth I had always known—there are no differences between children . . . it was our hope that the children would learn to understand the only differences between football players was in their skills, not in the color of their skin or the slope of their eyes. (Fish, p. 296)

Armed with his belief in soccer's potential to unify people of all races, Pelé stipulated that the Cosmos' parent company—Warner Communications—sponsor a soccer school for the impoverished children of Santos, Brazil. As for Pelé's contribution to the Cosmos, it was as stunning as his 1958 World Cup debut. Pelé improved the team's record and more than doubled average attendance, from eight thousand to twenty thousand a game. At the close of his career with the Cosmos, Pelé's farewell game was played against his beloved Santos; he played the first half with the Cosmos and the second with Santos, his second and final farewell to his "beautiful game."

The 1980s and 1990s found Pelé receiving several honors and translating his soccer fame into a career in public service and politics. He was named "Footballer of the Century" by the members of the Football Writers' Association of London in 1983. In 1994 he was appointed Brazil's minister of sport for four years. During his tenure with the Brazilian government, he tirelessly advocated on behalf of Brazilian soccer players, culminating in the passage of the so-called Pelé Law, which provides regulations for the sport in the interests of professional athletes. In 1998 the Queen of England bestowed an honorary knighthood upon Pelé. In 1999 he was honored at the World Sports Awards of the Century and named Footballer of the Millennium, and in 2000 The International Football Association (FIFA) honored him with the Player of the Century award.

See also Soccer

■ ■ *Bibliography*

Fish, Robert L., with Pelé. *My Life and the Beautiful Game.* Garden City, N.Y.: Doubleday, 1977.

Harris, Harry. *Pelé: His Life and Times.* New York: Welcome Rain Publishers, 2000.

Marcus, Joe. *The World of Pelé.* New York: Mason-Charter, 1976.

Mason, Tony. *Passion of the People? Football in South America.* London: Verso, 1995.

LAROSE PARRIS (2005)

PENNIMAN, RICHARD

See Little Richard (Penniman, Richard)

PENNINGTON, JAMES W. C.

JANUARY 1807
OCTOBER 22, 1870

■ ■ ■

Born James Pembroke, a slave in Queen Anne's County, Maryland, minister and abolitionist James Pennington early on became an expert blacksmith and carpenter and taught himself to read, write, and do figures. In 1827 he escaped via the Underground Railroad and was hidden by a Quaker couple in Petersburg, Pennsylvania, for whom he briefly worked. Around 1830 he traveled to the Brooklyn area (Kings County, New York), taking the name James William Charles Pennington. While there Pennington worked as a coachman and gained fame in the black community for his forthright opposition to the American Colonization Society. In the year 1831–1832 he was elected a delegate to the Negro Convention in Philadelphia. In the meantime, he began teaching, and after deciding to become a minister, he taught himself Greek and Latin. Yale College Divinity School, which barred blacks, allowed Pennington to listen to lectures. In 1840 he was hired as pastor of the Talcott Colored Congregational Church in Hartford, Connecticut. In 1848 he was hired by the First Colored (later Shiloh) Presbyterian Church in New York City. He returned to Hartford in 1856.

Pennington did not confine himself to ministerial duties. He took on the position of teacher at Hartford's Free African School. In 1841 he wrote for school use *A Textbook of the Origin and History of Colored People,* one of the earliest African-American history books. Pennington glorified blacks' African heritage and denounced negative racial stereotypes. He was also the first black member of the previously all-white Hartford Central Association of Congregational Ministers. In 1841 he formed and became leader of the Union Missionary Society, a forerunner of the American Missionary Association.

Pennington's chief fame, however, was as an abolitionist. In 1843 he attended the World's Antislavery Convention in London and subsequently toured Paris and Brussels, giving antislavery speeches and sermons. In 1849 he wrote his autobiography, *The Fugitive Black Smith*, which achieved a major success. Having revealed his identity, Pennington feared recapture, and in 1849 he accepted an invitation to England, where he attended the World Peace Conference and gave antislavery lectures under the auspices of the British and Foreign Antislavery Society. He was lionized in England and Europe and raised a great deal of money for African missions and abolitionism. In 1849, "in trust" for other black Americans, Pennington was awarded an honorary Doctor of Divinity degree from the University of Heidelberg in the German States. After the Fugitive Slave Act was passed in 1850, he visited the island of Jamaica. Despite his continuing opposition to African colonization, he recommended black settlement in Jamaica. British friends eventually bought his freedom, and he returned to America in 1853.

Pennington's later years were plagued by troubles. He was accused by opponents (mainly anticlerical Garrisonians) of misusing the funds he had raised for his freedom. In 1853 he was criticized for joining a Presbyterian association that included slaveholders. Like most black ministers, he was poorly paid and faced financial problems. His reputation was finally destroyed when his alcoholism was revealed. In 1858 Pennington left Hartford and served six different congregations in the North and postbellum South over the next twelve years. A trip abroad in 1861 was financially unsuccessful, and while in England, he was briefly imprisoned for stealing a book. Shortly after taking a teaching post in Jacksonville, Florida, in 1870 he became sick and died.

See also Abolition; Autobiography, U.S.; Slave Narratives; Underground Railroad

■ ■ *Bibliography*

Blackett, R. J. M. *Beating Against the Barriers: Biographical Essays in Nineteenth-Century Afro-American History.* Baton Rouge: Louisiana State University Press, 1986.

Grant, Callie Smith. *Free Indeed: African-American Christians and the Struggle for Equality.* Urichsville, Ohio: Barbour, 2003.

GREG ROBINSON (1996)
Updated bibliography

PENTECOSTALISM

This entry has two unique essays about the same topic, differing mainly in their geographical focus.

PENTECOSTALISM IN LATIN AMERICA AND THE CARIBBEAN
Carmelo Álvarez

PENTECOSTALISM IN NORTH AMERICA
David D. Daniels III

PENTECOSTALISM IN LATIN AMERICA AND THE CARIBBEAN

The Pentecostal movement in Latin America and the Caribbean is part of the great missionary effort that followed the missionary movement among mainline denominations in Europe, Canada, and the United States in the nineteenth century. Three models of Pentecostal missions are predominant in the region in the twentieth century: classical Pentecostalism, indigenous (Creole, *criollo*), and divine healing (Neopentecostalism).

Classical Pentecostalism came from the United States and Europe and brought its own missionary methods. It is economically and structurally dependent on foreign mission boards, and although the pastorate is indigenous, its education and training are clearly based on foreign models.

Indigenous Pentecostalism grew out of the local mainline Protestant churches. With strong roots in popular Catholic culture, it is economically and structurally independent of all foreign missions and has an indigenous pastorate.

Divine healing (Neopentecostal) churches, emphasizing exorcism and prosperity, are the offspring of dissident movements within the churches. Modeled on messianic patterns, they have an entrepreneurial structure, dependent on the charismatic hero-impresario leader.

CLASSICAL PENTECOSTALISM

The major missionary efforts of Pentecostalism in Latin America and the Caribbean have been sponsored by four North American churches: the Assemblies of God, the Church of God (Anderson, Indiana), the Church of God (Cleveland, Tennessee), and the Foursquare Gospel Church.

Founded in the United States as a fraternity of churches in 1914 at the Old Grand Opera House in Hot Springs, Arkansas, the Assemblies of God from the very beginning tended toward a Presbyterian form of government, with a general council as a governing board. The emphasis on the restoration principle of apostolic faith and practice, missionary zeal, and a cooperative effort in the missionary field gave the Assemblies of God its initial impulse and worldwide strategy. As these churches became more centralized and structured, they made Springfield, Missouri, the venue for their headquarters.

Assemblies of God churches were established in each one of the Latin American and Caribbean countries. The Assemblies of God came to Jamaica in 1937 and made an impact on this country, but it was the Canadian branch of the Assemblies of God, the Pentecostal Assemblies of Canada, that spread over the Caribbean region, planting churches in many countries and receiving many influences from the spiritual and revival forces coming from the nineteenth-century revivals in Jamaica. Today, the Assemblies of God is the largest Pentecostal denomination in Latin America and the Caribbean.

The extensive presence of the Assemblies of God has been supported by the programs and publications of the Gospel Publishing House, the major publishing house for Pentecostal literature in Latin America and the Caribbean to this day, and by the *Pentecostal Evangel*, a missionary magazine. Besides Bible institutes, private elementary and high schools, and some universities, the Assemblies of God churches also sponsor radio programs, magazines in Spanish and Portuguese, and social services such as day-care centers for the elderly and children.

The Church of God (Anderson, Indiana) was initially part of the Holiness movement of the nineteenth century. In 1907 this church began missionary work in the English-speaking Caribbean (Jamaica, Trinidad and Tobago). By 1910 missionaries had started work in Panama and afterwards in other countries: Costa Rica (1935), Mexico (1946), Peru (1962), Puerto Rico (1966), and Brazil (1970).

Founded as the "Christian Union," another offspring of the Holiness movement, the Church of God (Cleveland, Tennessee), embraced the Pentecostal movement with intense missionary fervor. The first missionaries left the United States in 1910 for the Bahamas. Later, they established themselves from Mexico (1932) through all Central American and South American countries over the next three decades. Today, the Church of God (Cleveland, Tennessee), is recognized as a Pentecostal church that combines an evangelistic fervor with a solid intellectual commitment. There are several seminaries and colleges in South America and the Caribbean that offer university-level education in theology and other fields.

The Foursquare Gospel Church originated in Oakland, California, in 1921, sparked by a fiery and charismatic leader. This church derives its name form the four-faced figures from the Bible (*Ezekiel* 1) that its founder, Aimee Semple McPherson, interpreted as Christological figures:

Christ saves, baptizes, heals, and will return. The missionary work of this church began in Panama (1928) and is established in most South American countries, including Jamaica and Haiti in the Caribbean. The Foursquare Gospel Church has active women's and youth organizations, including the ordination of women. It places particular emphasis on theological education.

INDIGENOUS PENTECOSTALISM

The better-known revivals in the region include the Valparaiso movement in Chile (1907–1910) led by Willis C. Hoover, a Methodist missionary from the United States. All-night vigils, Bible studies, and prayer groups energized a movement that would soon reach to the capital city of Santiago. Soon the movement provoked a schism, as congregations in Valparaiso and Santiago left the denomination to form the Methodist Pentecostal Church. In the following decades the Pentecostal movement in Chile sustained growth, suffered schisms, and formed new Pentecostal churches.

With Hoover at the helm, the revival spread throughout Chile at a dizzying pace. Hoover mobilized believers for street evangelism, organizing them into squads of militants who shared songs, Bible readings, open-air preaching, and personal testimony. The purpose of these efforts was to animate the poor and marginalized with a simple but demanding faith.

A similar movement, which began in Brazil in 1909, became known as the Great Revival. Three foreigners were the protagonists. Luigi Francescon, an Italian immigrant to the United States, received the baptism of the Holy Spirit at the mission of William D. Durham, Pentecostal pastor in Chicago. Wanting to preach to his own people about his new experience in the spirit, Francescon founded churches among Italian immigrants in Pennsylvania, Missouri, and California. In 1909 Francescon felt a call from the Holy Spirit to work among Italian immigrants in South America. He started work in Argentina first among Italian immigrants and later moved to São Paulo, Brazil.

Francescon organized congregations of Italian immigrants in Buenos Aires and São Paulo, where he fostered social work between the immigrants and established the Christian Congregation of Brazil. He adapted Presbyterian ecclesial structures and developed a national church in Brazil that today is one of the largest Pentecostal churches in the country. The church continues to emphasize both the spiritual and social dimensions of the gospel, developing self-support programs for their members, including cooperatives.

The other foreigners were Gunnar Vingren and Daniel Berg, Swedish immigrants with a Baptist background, who met Charles Durham in Chicago, received the baptism of the Holy Spirit, and went to the northern part of Brazil. They initially made contacts with Baptist churches in that region and finally established their own movement that later became affiliated with the Assemblies of God in Brazil. Despite the foreign roots of their founders, these Pentecostal churches became autonomous and autochthonous, in a self-support, self-governing model of mission.

Two Caribbean churches are good examples of indigenous Pentecostal churches. The first is the Pentecostal Church of God of Puerto Rico, founded by Juan L. Lugo. He was an immigrant worker in Hawaii and received the baptism of the Holy Spirit. He returned to Puerto Rico in 1916 to establish the Pentecostal Church of God of Puerto Rico, the second largest Pentecostal church in the island. This church has established missionary work and organized churches in more than forty-seven countries in the world, including Latin America and the Caribbean. Lugo also emphasized the self-support, self-governing principle. Lugo founded congregations among Hispanics in California and New York.

Another important church in the Caribbean is the Evangelical Pentecostal Church of Cuba, founded by Francisco Rodríguez from Puerto Rico, Ana Sanders from Canada, and Harriet May Kelty of the United States in 1933. These missionaries were sent by the Assemblies of God to establish the Evangelical Pentecostal Church of Cuba. In 1956 a group of Evangelical Pentecostal Church members formed the Pentecostal Christian Church of Cuba. Two Afro-Cuban pastors, Avelino González and Francisco Martínez, became the leaders of this church and led the denomination during the initial years of the Cuban Revolution, transforming its ministry and presence into an ecumenical and preferential option for the poor. Today, the Pentecostal Christian Church of Cuba participates actively in the Cuban Council of Churches, Caribbean Conference of Churches, and Latin American Council of Churches, and has had an ecumenical partnership with the Christian Church (Disciples of Christ) in the United States and Canada since 1976. It is the second largest Pentecostal Church in Cuba and it continues to grow primarily among the Afro-Cuban population in the eastern part of Cuba.

DIVINE HEALING (NEOPENTECOSTALISM)

A new offshoot of Pentecostalism concerned with divine healing has more recently emerged in the religious supermarket. This kind of Pentecostalism has become an alternative to indigenous Pentecostal churches. Exorcism and prosperity are its central elements. Energetic, charismatic leaders exhort huge gatherings and provide continuous worship services in old cinemas and auditoriums, open buildings in which the public meetings are conceived more as public spectacles than as community life and traditional worship. The hymns, sermons, and exhortations are a kind of therapy for the suffering masses. When the leader comes onstage, enough enthusiasm has already been created to generate an almost hysterical explosion of emotion in the congregation. Observers have noted that the flexible bond that results from these shared emotions demands little personal commitment and is a welcome alternative to the pain, needs, and conflicts that participants must confront daily. Faced with daily crises, people prefer a moment of ecstasy with this vibrant and untamed Jesus to the silence and existential vacuum of daily life.

From a doctrinal point of view, prosperity Pentecostals use the Bible as a fetish and a source of magical phrases as they perform exorcisms and divine healings. Rarely is the Bible actually studied, since the central acts of faith are healing and liberation. It is a Pentecostalism that emphasizes exorcism; the pastor becomes a moral agent who brings prosperity and stability. These pastors enjoy messianic authority that extends to the economic realm. This kind of Pentecostalism offers economic benefits to the pastors, incorporating them into the religious marketplace and converting the church into a commercial venture. Evangelists of this kind in Brazil, Puerto Rico, and Venezuela are known to own large properties in England, the United States, and Europe.

The Pentecostal movement that started as the outpouring of the Holy Spirit in Topeka (1901) and Azusa Street in Los Angeles (1906) became a global missionary movement that spread to all continents. The movement in Latin America and the Caribbean began as a foreign missionary enterprise, but it soon transformed into an indigenous, autonomous movement of independent and national churches. Today the movement is also expressed by divine healing churches led by a messianic-hero figure in which exorcism and prosperity theology dominate. These Neopentecostal churches, like the Universal Church of the Kingdom of God in Brazil, are organized as religious transnational enterprises.

All three predominant models of Pentecostal mission in Latin America and the Caribbean have tried to respond to the cry of the oppressed and the poor sectors of society. In their attempts they also accompanied immigrants from Europe to Latin America (Italians in South America) and displaced persons in a diaspora that spanned from the Caribbean to other countries in Latin America and Hawaii. Today, new waves of migrants from the Caribbean, primarily Afro-Caribbean persons to Great Britain, are establishing a new kind of Pentecostal movement in the European diaspora.

See also Christian Denominations, Independent; Holiness Movement; Protestantism in the Americas; Religion

■ ■ *Bibliography*

Álvarez, Carmelo E., ed. *Pentecostalismo y liberación: Una experiencia latinoamericana.* San José, Costa Rica: DEI-CEPLA, 1992.

Austin-Broos, Diane J. *Jamaica Genesis: Religion and the Politics of Moral Orders.* Chicago and London: University of Chicago Press, 1997.

Dayfoot, Arthur Charles. *The Shaping of the West Indian Church, 1492–1962.* Kingston, Jamaica: The Press, University of the West Indies, 1999.

Gutiérrez, Benjamin, and Dennis Smith, eds. *In the Power of the Spirit: The Pentecostal Challenge to Historic Churches in Latin America.* Louisville, Ky.: CELEP-AIPRAL-PC (USA) WMD, 1996.

CARMELO ÁLVAREZ (2005)

PENTECOSTALISM IN NORTH AMERICA

Among scholars of Pentecostalism there are two schools of thought as to the emergence of this religious phenomenon. The first school, identified with Vinson Synan, William Menzies, and James Goff, argues that Charles Parham (1873–1929) was the founder of the Pentecostal movement and that it began in Kansas in 1901. The competing school, which includes Walter Hollenweger, James Tinney, J. Douglas Nelson, Cecil R. Robeck, and Edith Blumhofer, argues that the Azusa Street Revival in Los Angeles from 1906 to 1913 was the true beginning and William J. Seymour the pivotal person.

The second school focuses on Azusa Street and Seymour because they were the originating center of Pentecostalism throughout the United States and in Scandinavia, Great Britain, Brazil, Egypt, and India, where it spread. The revival defined Pentecostalism, shaped its interracial relations, and gave it its multicultural character. The first school designates Parham because he was the first proponent to link glossolalia with the biblical Pentecost event recounted in several chapters in the biblical book Acts of the Apostles and to define this experience as the baptism of the Holy Spirit.

In 1901 Charles Parham operated the Bethel Bible School in Topeka, Kansas. A major religious experience for him was the baptism of the Holy Spirit as described in Acts of the Apostles, chapter 2. The Holiness Movement during the 1800s identified this experience as sanctification. The Wesleyan wing of the Holiness Movement defined the experience in terms of cleansing, while the Calvinist or Reformed wing saw it as empowerment for Christian living. Both positions understood the experience as subsequent to justification. The Reformed advocates described sanctification as a progressive process, while the Wesleyan advocates described it as an instantaneous event.

In the late 1890s Parham joined those who sought to categorize discrete experience beyond justification and sanctification. In January 1901 Parham identified glossolalia with the third experience and linked this experience instead of sanctification with Acts 2. He began preaching this new doctrine within Holiness circles in the Midwest.

In 1905 William J. Seymour, who was black, enrolled in Parham's school in Houston despite the white man Parham's enforcement of segregation laws that prevented Seymour from sitting with the white students. While Seymour adopted the new doctrine, he failed at the time to have the actual experience himself. In 1906 he carried the new doctrine to California in response to an invitation to become pastor of a small black Holiness congregation in Los Angeles headed by Julia Hutchins. Hutchins and the other members established a congregation of Evening Light Saints after withdrawing from the Second Baptist Church, which had refused to embrace their Holiness message. Hutchins, however, rejected Seymour's addition to Holiness teaching and barred him from the pulpit. Edward Lee and, later, Richard Asberry invited Seymour to resume preaching at their homes.

After Seymour and others began speaking in tongues, they outgrew the "house church," and Seymour secured larger facilities at 312 Azusa Street, the former sanctuary of First African Methodist Episcopal Church (AME). Seymour's revival on Azusa Street attracted the attention first of local whites and blacks, especially those involved in the Holiness community. But soon participants from the Holiness Movement across the United States converged by the thousands on Azusa Street to observe events, examine the new doctrine, and experience glossolalia. Within twelve months the Azusa Street Mission spawned an international movement and began a journal, *Apostolic Faith.* From 1906 to 1908, *Apostolic Faith,* the Azusa Street Mission, and Seymour held the loosely bound movement together and provided it with a center and leadership.

Like its Holiness counterpart, Pentecostalism was basically local and regional and headed by both blacks and whites, as well as both women and men. In many places local and regional movements took over entire Holiness congregations and institutions. African-American Holiness leaders who embraced Pentecostalism along with all or some of their associated congregations included W. H. Fulford (d. 1916), William Fuller (1875–1958), Charles Harrison Mason (1866–1961), and Magdalena Tate (1871–1930).

Early Pentecostalism emerged as a strongly interracial movement and struggled with its interracial identity at a time when American society was segregated. Frank Bartleman, a white Azusa Street participant and reporter, stated that at the revival "the color line was washed away in the blood [of Jesus Christ]." While Baptist, Methodist, Presbyterian, and Holiness people lived in racially segregated congregations, associations, and denominational structures, the black and white Pentecostals pastored and preached to and fellowshipped and worshipped with each other between 1906 and 1914, and many joined the predominantly black Pentecostal-Holiness group, the Church of God in Christ. The Pentecostal leadership was strongly anti–Ku Klux Klan and was often the target of Klan terrorism because of their interracial sympathies.

But racism came to counter the interracial nature of early Pentecostalism. Parham exhibited racist behavior and a patronizing attitude toward his black counterparts, especially Seymour; in 1908 blacks withdrew from the Fire-Baptized Holiness Church (later called Pentecostal Holiness Church); in 1913 another black group withdrew from the Pentecostal Holiness Church; in 1914 a white group withdrew from the Church of God in Christ; and in 1924 a white group withdrew from the half-black Pentecostal Assemblies of the World, which was led by a black minister, Garfield Thomas Haywood.

While segregation among Pentecostals came to follow the pattern of American Christianity after the Civil War, there were exceptions. Blacks and whites continued to struggle together to structure their interracial relationships during the height of segregation in the United States. In 1924 the Church of God in Christ adopted the Methodist model of establishing a minority transgeographical conference, specifically a white conference to unite the white congregations across the United States that belonged to the predominantly black denomination. In 1907 and 1931 several different groups of blacks and whites entered and withdrew from the Pentecostal Assemblies of the World.

Theologically, Pentecostalism split early into two camps over the doctrine of God: Trinitarian and Oneness. The Oneness doctrine, as opposed to the classic Christian doctrine of the Trinity, claimed that Jesus was the name of God and that God expressed Godself in the form of the Father, Son, and Holy Spirit but was not three persons in one. The Trinitarians confessed the traditional Christian doctrine of the Trinity and rejected the Oneness interpre-

tation. While the existing black Pentecostal denominations, such as the Church of God in Christ, United Holy Church, and Church of the Living God, remained Trinitarian, many independent black Pentecostal congregations in the Midwest, especially those associated with Haywood, rejected Trinitarianism. Oneness denominations identified themselves as Apostolic churches.

Haywood and the Pentecostal Assemblies of the World are the parents of most black Apostolic denominations in the United States. Significant leaders of the movement included Robert C. Lawson (1881–1961), who organized the Church of Our Lord Jesus Christ of the Apostolic Faith in 1919; Sherrod C. Johnson (1897–1961), who organized the Church of the Lord Jesus Christ of the Apostolic Faith in 1930; and Smallwood Williams, who organized Bible Way Churches of Our Lord Jesus Christ Worldwide in 1957.

While Pentecostal denominations opened more forms of ministry to women than other Protestant denominations, only a few granted women equality with men. Among black Pentecostals, full male-female equality existed only in denominations founded by black women. Magdalena Tate's denomination, the oldest Pentecostal denomination founded by a black woman, was among the Holiness groups that joined Pentecostalism after their establishment. During 1903 she founded in Tennessee the Church of Living God, Pillar and Ground of the Truth. The other major grouping of Pentecostal denominations founded by black women withdrew from the United Holy Church of America, which ordained women to the ministry but denied them the bishopric. In 1924 Ida Robinson founded the Mt. Sinai Holy Church to rectify this inequality. In 1944 Beulah Counts (d. 1968), an associate of Robinson, organized the Greater Mt. Zion Pentecostal Church of America.

Crossing Trinitarian and Apostolic divisions is a stream within Pentecostalism called the deliverance movement. The deliverance movement grew out of the white healing movement of the 1940s associated with William Branham that produced Oral Roberts, Gordon Lindsay, and A. A. Allen. The deliverance movement among black Pentecostals is related to Arturo Skinner (1924–1975), who expanded the traditional black Pentecostal emphasis on healing to include exorcisms and heightened the accent on the miraculous. In 1956 he established the Deliverance Evangelistic Centers, with headquarters in Newark, New Jersey. Deliverance ministries emerged in traditional Pentecostal congregations such as Faith Temple Church of God in Christ under Harry Willis Goldsberry (1895–1986) in Chicago. In urban centers there emerged new independent congregations that competed with traditional black

Pentecostals; Benjamin Smith (b. 1926), who founded the Deliverance Evangelistic Center in Philadelphia in 1960, and Richard Hinton, who founded Monument of Faith Evangelistic Center in Chicago in 1963, were two of the best-known leaders of these congregations.

Although Pentecostals are stereotyped as otherworldly, studies have shown a social activist stream within black Pentecostalism. A number of black Pentecostal denominations and leaders joined the Fraternal Council of Negro Churches and participated in the marches for black employment during the 1930s. Robert C. Lawson cooperated with Adam Clayton Powell Jr. and other leading Harlem ministers in campaigns for black employment. J. O. Patterson (1912–1990) of the Church of God in Christ and other ministers participated in local civil rights campaigns in Memphis, Tennessee, and other southern cities and towns in the late 1950s. Smallwood Williams led the legal battle against segregated public schools during the 1950s in Washington, D.C. Arthur Brazier (b. 1921), Louis Henry Ford (b. 1914), and other Pentecostal clergy were active in the civil rights movement in Chicago and other northern cities in the 1960s.

Studies of the black Pentecostal leadership note the occurrence of a cadre of black Pentecostals who identify with twentieth-century theological liberalism. Relations between liberal Protestantism and black Pentecostalism occur on a number of levels. A significant number of Pentecostals are graduates of liberal seminaries, some as early as the 1940s. They are graduates of schools such as Temple University, Oberlin, Union Theological Seminary (New York City), Duke, Emory, and McCormick. And the first accredited Pentecostal—and only African-American—seminary, Charles Harrison Mason Theological Seminary, is a member of Interdenominational Theological Center (ITC), a consortium of African-American seminaries affiliated with mainline denominations. The Church of God in Christ, the sponsor of Mason Seminary at ITC, embraces theological liberalism from a black perspective in the preparation of an educated clergy. A number of black Pentecostal leaders are also involved in the ecumenical movement that liberal Protestantism embraces: Herbert Daughtry (b. 1931) participates in some World Council of Churches programs, and Ithiel Clemmons (b. 1921) participates in regional and local ecumenical councils.

Black Pentecostalism also includes leaders who identify with evangelicalism. Black Pentecostals associated with the evangelical movement are often graduates of evangelical seminaries such as Fuller, Gordon-Conwell, and Trinity Evangelical Divinity School. Leaders such as William Bentley (b. 1926) and George McKinney (b. 1932) are active members of the National Association of Evangelicals along with the National Black Association of Evangelicals.

During the 1970s black Pentecostalism intersected with the "Word of Faith" movement spurred by Kenneth Hagin and his message of healing, prosperity, and positive confession. Fredrick Price (b. 1932) emerged as the Word of Faith leader among black Christians after establishing Crenshaw Christian Center of Los Angeles in 1973.

During the 1970s Pentecostalism influenced the historic black denominations, especially the AME Church. Neo-Pentecostal ministers occupied some major AME pulpits. The focal point for the movement during the early 1970s was St. Paul AME Church in Cambridge, Massachusetts, under the pastorate of John Bryant (b. 1948). During the period, college campuses became centers for the growth of Pentecostalism among black students, particularly through the college gospel choir movement.

Black Pentecostals have been leaders within the black religious music movement since the early 1900s. Black Pentecostalism became the carrier of black religious folk music, noted for its call-and-response, improvisation, polyrhythms, and diatonic harmonies. By the 1920s Arizona Juanita Dranes (b. 1905) and Sallie Sanders were popular gospel singers. Dranes and Sanders began the tradition of the Baptist and Pentecostal leadership of the gospel music movement. By the 1980s black Pentecostals such as Andraé Crouch, Edwin Hawkins, Walter Hawkins, Shirley Caesar, the Clark Sisters, and the Wynans dominated the gospel music movement.

From its beginning at the Azusa Street Revival in 1906, black Pentecostalism has grown to become the second-largest religious movement among African Americans and one of the fastest-growing religious movements in the United States and around the globe, especially in the Third World.

See also Christian Denominations, Independent; Holiness Movement; Protestantism in the Americas; Religion

■ ■ *Bibliography*

Burgess, Stanley M., and Gary B. McGee. *Dictionary of Pentecostal and Charismatic Movements.* Grand Rapids, Mich.: Regency Reference Library, 1988.

Dupree, Sherry S., ed. *Biographical Dictionary of African-American Holiness-Pentecostals, 1880–1990.* Washington, D.C.: Middle Atlantic Regional Press, 1989.

Jones, Charles Edwin. *A Guide to the Study of Black Participation in Wesleyan Perfectionist and Glossolalic Pentecostal Movements.* Metuchen, N.J.: Rowman & Littlefield, 1987.

Sernett, Milton C. *Bound for the Promised Land: African American Religion and the Great Migration.* Durham, N.C.: Duke University Press, 1997.

DAVID D. DANIELS III (1996)
Updated bibliography

PEOPLE'S NATIONAL CONGRESS

▪ ▪ ▪

The origins of the People's National Congress (PNC), the political party founded in October 1957 by Linden Forbes Sampson Burnham, the first executive president of the Co-operative Republic of Guyana, was the 1955 fracture of the People's Progressive Party (PPP), of which Burnham had been a founding leader with Dr. Cheddi B. Jagan. Among the founding members of the PNC were such African-Guyanese women as Winifred Gaskin. Gaskin had been a founding member and one-time president of the first women's political organization in the country, the Women's Political and Economic Organisation (WPEO), formed in 1946. Other women who participated included Jane Phillips-Gay, Jessica (Jesse) Burnham, and Margaret Ackman, and men included Claude Merriman, Andrew Jackson, H. M. E. Cholmondeley, Albert Ogle, Hamilton Green, Dr. J. P. Latchmansingh, Jai Narine Singh, Flavio Da Silva, Eugene Correia, Stanley Hugh, and Clinton Wong. Although the PNC became known as the political party of the African Guyanese because of the mass support of members of that group, effort was always made to include all racial groups in its rank and file.

The first annual congress of the party was held in Georgetown on October 5–7, 1957. At the congress the name of the party was changed from the PPP (the party of the Burnhamites) to the People's National Congress. The *New Nation* was adopted as the official name of the party's organ, changing it from the *PPP Thunder*. The three sessions of the congress focused on problems facing the colony's youth, women's role in politics, and the party's business affairs with the PNC's Young Socialist Movement (YSM) and the Women's Revolutionary Socialist Movement (WRSM) as important participants. To distinguish the ideologies, political philosophies, and direction of the PNC from the Marxist-Leninist leanings of the Jagan-led PPP, the new party defined itself as socialist and embraced the struggle for independence, nationalism, and racial integration. Socialism meant a society organized to produce for use rather than profit. Nationalism signified the struggle for independence from Great Britain and the power to control the country's affairs. Initially, the party operated in Georgetown out of the legal chambers of its leader, Burnham, but the first official headquarters of the PNC, Congress Place, was located on King Street. Next, it moved to Carmichael and Newmarket Streets, then to 227 Camp Street. The current headquarters of the PNC is in Sophia, Greater Georgetown.

In 1958 John P. Carter's United Democratic Party (UDP) joined the PNC, with Carter becoming the first vice chair, the number three position after Burnham, and J. P. Latchmansingh becoming chair. The executive committee of the PNC comprised eighteen members, nine each from the PNC itself and the former UDP. A general council of thirty members was established. At its annual delegates conference in 1961 the party was reorganized to include an executive committee of ten member and a general council of twenty-four. Burnham remained the leader of a party committed to all the people of the country under the slogan "One People, One Nation, One Destiny." This slogan became the national motto of independent Guyana.

The PNC was the main opposition party in the legislature until the general elections of December 1964. Following that election, the PNC won enough seats to lead a coalition government with Peter D'Aguiar's United Force (UF). The PNC-UF coalition gained 53 percent electoral votes, which translated into twenty-nine seats in the fifty-three-seat House of Assembly. The PPP became the opposition in the legislature with twenty-four seats. The forming of the coalition government ended the riots, killings, and destruction of property that had occurred during the previous three years.

The policies and programs of the PNC-UF-led government included the attainment of independence from Great Britain, the pursuit of racial harmony, and the equality of all citizens. Steps were taken to include Amerindian or indigenous citizens into full national participation to enable them to share in the benefits and responsibilities of the country. Soon after taking office and for some time thereafter, the coalition government discussed the possibility of a consultative democracy in Guyana with various groups, including the Maha Sabha (Hindu), the United Sadir Islamic Anjuman, the African Society of Cultural Relations with Independent Africa, and the Chinese Association, as well as with the Anglican archbishop of the West Indies, the Roman Catholic bishop of Georgetown, the Ethiopian Orthodox Church, the Methodist Body, the Congregational Conference, and other religious and cultural organizations. The coalition government envisioned that engaging diverse groups would promote harmony and that these groups would advise the government when matters likely to affect any section of the population arose.

Under the PNC-UF coalition government from 1965 to 1967, initiatives to launch a three-state Caribbean Free Trade Association (CARIFTA) with Antigua and Barbados developed into the Caribbean Community and Common Market (CARICOM), with most Caribbean countries as members. With independence in 1966, Guyana became a member of the United Nations and subsequently the first

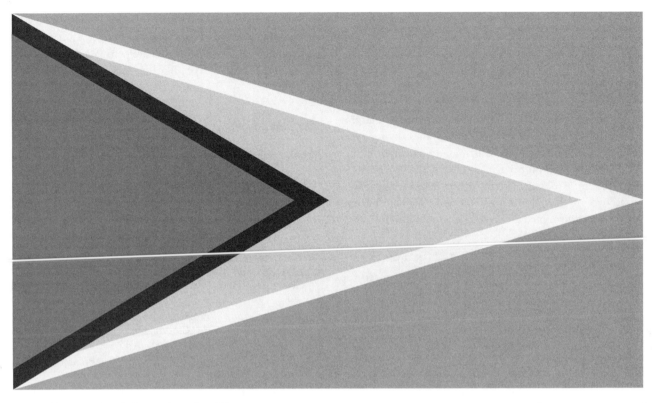

The Golden Arrowhead, Guyana's national flag. ILLUSTRATION BY THE FLAG INSTITUTE. FLAG IMAGES © EPSFLAG.COM 1998

Caribbean state to be elected to the Security Council. After the PNC won an outright victory in the general election in December 1968 and became the sole party in power, it pursued its commitment to regional integration and unity. By August 1973, when CARICOM became fully operational, its headquarters was located in Georgetown. In 1972 Guyana hosted the first Festival of Arts (CARIFESTA), and seventeen countries participated. Regional integration remained a key feature of the PNC-led government's external policy. The government also played a significant role in promoting economic self-reliance for developing countries. Guyana initiated the meeting of economists from those countries in August 1972 in Georgetown to draft a program for economic cooperation among developing countries.

The country's government, led by the PNC, believed in territorial integrity and national sovereignty. The neighboring countries Suriname and Venezuela had long claimed significant portions of Guyana, and their illegal incursions into the country began to be met with resistance. In December 1967 Suriname invaded and occupied an area of Guyana called the New River Triangle. On August 19, 1969, the Guyana Defense Force, established by the PNC regime, routed the invaders and secured the entire disputed area as Guyana's sovereign territory.

By the 1970s, the PNC adopted the doctrine of Paramountcy of the Party, or the Declaration of Sophia, which enunciated that all organs of the state were agencies of the PNC and subject to its control. During that same decade PNC politicians supported a policy of nationalizing resources for the benefit of the Guyanese people. The National Development Program focused on promoting an economic revolution, national reconstruction, and encouraging a cooperative way of life. The Guyana National Service Secretariat (GNS) was established in 1973. It combined paramilitary, educational, and development activities for youths and students. Although the GNS aimed at interior settlement, development of the country, and national unity, the agenda also served to reduce criminal activities of Guyanese youths. In 1976 the PNC government took over all the schools in the country and promised free education from kindergarten to university.

In Guyana, the first half of the 1970s was relatively prosperous economically, with prices of the country's main exports increasing on the international market. The PNC-led government took control of foreign trade with the establishment of the External Trade Bureau. Important government bureaucracies like the National Insurance Scheme provided pensions and other benefits for many. Political and administrative plans included a "feed, clothe, and house the nation" program (FCH), aiming to satisfy the basic needs of the people, to create employment opportunities, to generate self-reliance, to reorient consumption patterns in favor of locally produced products, and to reorganize foreign trade. Remarkable developments of the infrastructure of the country, including improvements to the pure water supply and health care services, were obvious. National development included a remigration scheme that encouraged skilled Guyanese living overseas to return home and to contribute to nation building. By 1976, however, oil price increases by the Organization of Petroleum Exporting Countries and decreased revenues from two of the country's major exports, bauxite and sugar, adversely affected Guyana's national development.

As the 1970s drew to a close, the challenges that the PNC-led government faced increased, partly due to a policy of nationalizing foreign companies that produced the major export earners of the country, bauxite (1971, 1974, and 1975) and sugar (1976). In November 1978 the Jonestown tragedy, when an American group in Guyana's interior committed mass suicide, added fuel to the fires of opposition forces. As the 1980s unfolded, the untimely and still unsolved tragic death of historian and political activist Dr. Walter A. Rodney, along with pressing economic issues, presaged the demise of the PNC-led government of Guyana. Unwittingly, this government, in its haste to dismantle economic relations with traditional trading partners and to initiate new relations with Cuba, the Soviet Union, North Korea, and other Soviet-bloc countries, found itself needing to govern with excessive authoritarianism.

In the 1980s the PNC-led government addressed the deteriorating social and economic situation by establishing the Social Impact Amelioration Programme (SIMAP), following the Economic Recovery Programme (ERP). SIMAP was meant to assist those most affected by the economic downturn. The World Bank, the Inter-American Development Bank, the European Union, the United Nations Development Program, and other donors provided SIMAP with financial assistance.

Following President Burnham's death in 1985, the new PNC leader, Hugh Desmond Hoyte, Queen's (Senior) Counsel (1929–2002), became the country's second executive president, a position he held until the PNC lost the elections held on October 5, 1992, to a coalition of the PPP and other political parties. On assuming office President Hoyte embarked on a course of privatization. From 1986 the government sought foreign investment in the country's economy. Hoyte marketed Guyana abroad, endeavoring to normalize and to improve relations with Western nations. As head of the PNC-led government, he promoted economic growth and prosperity in the country. Inter-

estingly, Hoyte, a lawyer like Burnham, also died in office, paving the way for the third leader of the PNC, now called the People's National Congress Reform (PNCR), in 2003: Robert Corbin, a lawyer like his forerunners, Burnham and Hoyte.

See also Burnham, Forbes

■ ■ *Bibliography*

Country Profile: Guyana, Barbados, Winward and Leeward Islands, 1987–1988. London: Economist Intelligence Unit, 1988.

Foreign Service Despatch, American Consulate, Georgetown, The Department of State, Washington, Decimal File (1910–1963), Numeric File (1963–1973), 741D, 841D, 844B, Record Group 59, National Archives at College Park (Archives 11), Md.

Guyana: A Decade of Progress. 10th Anniversary of the People's National Congress in Government. Georgetown, Guyana: Government Information Services, 1974.

Guyana in Brief. Georgetown, Guyana: Government Information Services, 1973.

Guyana Needs Progress Not Conflict: The People's National Congress, The New Road. LaPenitance: British Guiana Lithographic Company Limited, n.d.

Hoyte, Hugh Desmond. *Guyana Economic Recovery: Leadership, Will and Vision, Selected Speeches of Hugh Desmond Hoyte.* Georgetown, Guyana: Free Press, 1997.

Nascimento, Christopher A., and Reynold A. Burrowes, eds. *Forbes Burnham: A Destiny to Mold, Selected Speeches by the Prime Minister of Guyana.* New York: Africana Publishing Company, 1970.

New Nation (official organ of the People's National Congress), 1957–1980s.

Sancho, T. Anson. *The Green Way: A Biography of Hamilton Green.* Georgetown, Guyana, 1996.

Woolford, Hazel M. "The Origins of the Labour Movement" and "Women in Guyanese Politics, 1812–1964." In *Themes in African-Guyanese History,* edited by Winston F. McGowan, James G. Rose, and David A. Granger, pp. 277–295, 327–350. Georgetown, Guyana: Free Press, 1998.

BARBARA P. JOSIAH (2005)

PEOPLES NATIONAL MOVEMENT
■ ■ ■

The Peoples National Movement (PNM) was launched as a political party on January 26, 1956. Nine months after its formation, the party won the general elections and formed the government of Trinidad and Tobago. In con-

Dr. Eric Williams (1911–1981). *The founder of the socialist Peoples National Movement (PNM), Williams became the first prime minister of the independent Trinidad and Tobago in 1962. Also a respected historian, he taught at Howard University in Washington, D.C. and published several highly regarded studies on the history of the Caribbean before returning to his native Trinidad in 1955.* HULTON ARCHIVE/GETTY IMAGES. REPRODUCED BY PERMISSION.

sequence, its founder and leader, Dr. Eric Eustace Williams, an Oxford scholar and former professor of political science at Howard University who had relinquished his position as deputy chair of the Caribbean Research Council of the Caribbean Commission, became the first chief minister of Trinidad and Tobago.

From its formation the PNM demonstrated a preoccupation with policies reflecting its background and the intellectual orientation of its political leader. The party had emerged out of the Teachers' Educational and Cultural Association (TECA), formed during the 1940s and made up largely of educated, middle-class, Afro-descended professionals in search of political power. Inspired by the scholarly writings and incisive discourses of Williams, TECA members gravitated toward him and by 1955 had established the People's Education Group (PEG) and the

People's Education Movement (PEM) as platforms for his lectures and political agitation.

Williams had been very critical of the nature of colonial education in the British West Indies. Once in office, the PNM preoccupied itself with the political education of its membership and, at the national level, with policies for the development of primary, secondary and vocational, and later tertiary education of the masses.

The party also addressed issues of constitutional reform, taking to the colonial authorities a fight begun by members of the TECA/PEG for the introduction of a bicameral legislature. The PNM viewed the crown colony government in Trinidad and Tobago as unacceptable, for the governor continued to preside over the legislature, and the chief minister was limited in his power over the executive. By 1959 the party was able to persuade the colonial authorities to put in place a system that replaced the office of chief minister with that of premier, and the executive council with a cabinet under his control. Strenuous agitation by the party in the colonial legislature kept constitutional issues in constant focus. This, together with skilful diplomatic relations with the colonial office and, later, tactfully soliciting the collaboration of the main opposition party, enabled the PNM to secure full internal self-government for Trinidad and Tobago with the attainment of independence in 1962. Thereafter, the PNM pursued full sovereignty, taking the country to republican status in 1976.

Another early policy orientation was aimed at the development of the country through proper economic planning. The PNM introduced three five-year development programs, the first two of which saw the implementation between 1958 and 1968 of initiatives to promote development of the infrastructure, municipalities and communities, fisheries, forestry, tourism, public utilities, and the service sector. An important aspect involved policies for expansion and diversification of the agricultural sector, including the sugar industry, which many scholars viewed, notwithstanding, as the dominant factor in the development of the Caribbean political economy and the many ills it had inherited. The emphasis was on increasing productivity in all areas, with the object of protecting jobs and improving working conditions and the lot of small farmers.

Other development initiatives were intended to incorporate heavy and modern industrialization in the petroleum sector to maximize exploration of the country's hydrocarbon reserves. Efforts were also made to develop non-oil manufactures. Williams was deeply inspired by Arthur Lewis's model of "industrialization by invitation," and from early on the PNM administration sought to attract investment by offering generous tax concessions to foreign concerns for the creation of pioneer industries and the development of existing ones. From the late 1970s development initiatives were dominated by efforts to diversify the energy sector by developing downstream industries, including natural gas, urea, methanol, and iron and steel, but with a much greater degree of national ownership. These initiatives laid the foundation for development of the modern industrial economy of Trinidad and Tobago.

Economic development was always perceived in terms of the redistribution of income with adequate concern for the common person. Such a policy was articulated in the People's Charter of 1956, which, presented at the party's first annual convention, enunciated the fundamental principles and ideals that were to guide the development of the party and nation. The charter committed the party to a comprehensive social security program for the general welfare of all the people of Trinidad and Tobago, setting the basis for the development of greater equity in the society.

On the eve of independence, Williams advised the nation that division of the races was a policy of colonialism and that integration of the races must be the policy of independence. In consequence, the government pursued a policy of multiracial solidarity, and policies were designed for increasing access for all in the society. The full realization of these ideals remained a challenge, however, because of the deep-seated polarization and division that had resulted from the plural nature of the society.

From inception, and despite the breakup of the Federation of the West Indies in 1961, the PNM pursued regional unity as critical to the individual and collective development of countries in the English-speaking Caribbean and to the progressive use of the broad cultural heritage and indigenous art forms of its population.

The PNM was the first of the political organizations to preoccupy itself with the development of party politics in the colony and present a national and international perspective that sought to embrace the myriad classes, races, and interest groups in Trinidad and Tobago. It remains that country's longest surviving political party and, by virtue of the policies pursued from its inception regarding education, political reforms, economic development, race relations, and regional cooperation, can be considered as the architect of independent Trinidad and Tobago.

See also International Relations of the Anglophone Caribbean; Williams, Eric

■ ■ *Bibliography*

Brereton, Bridget. *A History of Modern Trinidad, 1783–1962.* London: Heinemann, 1981.

Ghany, Hamid. *Kamal: A Lifetime of Politics Religion and Culture.* San Juan, Puerto Rico: Author, 1996.

Hackshaw, John M. *Party Politics and Public Policy.* Diego Martin, Trinidad and Tobago: Author, 1997.

Sutton, Paul. *Forged from the Love of Liberty.* Port of Spain, Trinidad and Tobago: Longman Caribbean, 1981.

MICHEAL F. TOUSSAINT (2005)

PEOPLE'S NATIONAL PARTY

■ ■ ■

The People's National Party (PNP) is one of the two leading political parties in Jamaica and one of the most important in the African diaspora. It was founded on September 18, 1938, one year before the beginning of World War II, and first came to political power in 1955 while Jamaica was still a British colony.

The PNP was one of the many political parties that arose in the first half of the twentieth century in those nations struggling for independence from British colonial rule. It was strongly influenced by the earlier ideological struggles of Marcus Garvey (1887–1940), the anticolonial struggles in Africa, and the struggles of the Indian National Congress. More than any other political party in Jamaica's history, the PNP championed the goal of democratic elections under universal adult suffrage and political independence for Jamaica as the basic preconditions for the emancipation of the people, who are overwhelmingly of African descent.

The PNP was formed primarily by leaders of the black and brown Jamaican middle classes; lawyers, doctors, teachers, and journalists were heavily represented at its launching. Chief among these was Norman Washington Manley (1893–1969), the leading lawyer in the country at that time and the party president from its inception in 1938 until his death in 1969. He was succeeded as president of the PNP by his son, Michael Norman Manley (1924–1997).

In May 1938 the Jamaican people spontaneously rose up in revolt against the harsh economic conditions of the Great Depression. The mass of people could not vote, and their dissatisfaction had been expressed through anticolonial pressure groups and organizations. The 1938 upheaval transformed the political environment, however, and the same groups who had been involved in earlier civic efforts moved into the political arena and launched the People's National Party.

The Bustamante Industrial Trade Union (BITU) was formed out of the general strike, the burning of sugar estates, and spontaneous island-wide demonstrations that took place in the 1938 revolt. Initially, it was loosely affiliated with the PNP, which provided its mass base and played the leading political role. As a political party based in the urban and rural middle classes, the PNP began with weak popular support. Nonetheless, the radical intelligentsia in the PNP developed a strongly anticolonial political program.

By 1943 it was clear that the British, weakened by the fight against the Nazis, would concede universal adult suffrage to the Jamaican people and hold general elections. In anticipation of this, the BITU, which had been in a loose relationship with the PNP, broke with that party and formed the Jamaica Labour Party (JLP). As a result, the PNP lost a substantial part of its mass base. In 1944 the first general elections under British rule were held, and the PNP was soundly defeated by the JLP.

After this defeat, the PNP developed into a mass party with its own affiliated trade union—first the Trades Union Congress, and later its successor, the National Workers Union. Unlike the BITU, these organizations primarily unionized workers in manufacturing, mining, tourism, and public sectors. This combination of the middle classes, businesspeople, the working class, and poor people has been a characteristic feature of the PNP (and of many other nationalist parties formed during the colonial period). The result has been that the PNP contains ideological tendencies ranging from the moderate right to the far left. This has sometimes led to sharp interparty disputes and divisions.

The most tumultuous of these disputes occurred in 1952, when the "Four Hs"—Ken Hill, Frank Hill, Richard Hart, and Arthur Henry—were expelled from the party on the grounds that they represented a communist tendency. After this split the PNP leaned more to the moderate right in its political platform. It won the general elections for the first time in 1955, and Norman Manley became the chief minister, as distinct from prime minister—a title reserved for the chief executive of politically independent countries. The PNP then began to implement a vigorous program of reform.

Reforms implemented between 1955 and 1962 in education, housing, land distribution, industrialization, social development, and public-policy management were fundamental in shaping modern Jamaican society. Access to high school and university education was expanded, a strong civil service developed, and a sense of national cultural identity was encouraged. In addition, efforts at regional political unity with other English-speaking Caribbean countries were pursued in the form of a political federation. These reforms benefited primarily the Jamaican middle and business classes, which expanded and consolidated themselves during this period. The mass of the people remained in poverty, with income distribution becoming worse. An important debate, led by leading members of the JLP, about the growing gap between the "haves and the have-nots" began to take place. Additionally, political federation with other Caribbean countries was unpopular with the mass of people. The result was that the PNP was defeated in national elections in 1962. Thus, Jamaica was led into political independence in 1962 not by the party that had championed it, but by the more conservative Jamaica Labour Party.

In 1969 Norman Manley died and was succeeded as president of the PNP by his son, Michael Manley. In general elections in 1972 the PNP was returned to power. Mi-

Children gather around Norman W. Manley (1893–1969), founder of the People's National Party, as he makes his way to the cathedral for Jamaica's Independence Day celebrations, August 6, 1962. GETTY IMAGES

chael Manley became the first prime minister from the PNP. The Jamaican people, although experiencing substantial economic growth under the preceding Jamaica Labour Party government, felt that inequalities in society had been intensified and that black Jamaicans and black Jamaican culture were insufficiently recognized and respected. This was a period of global radicalization, including the Cuban revolution in 1959 and other revolutionary struggles in Latin America, a further round of struggles for independence in Africa, and the civil rights, Black Power, and antiwar movements in the United States. The radical tendencies in the PNP were also revived, and the period of democratic socialism (1972–1980), led by Michael Manley, developed.

The democratic socialist period was marked by reforms in the field of education and housing. As a result of the policy of free education, many people from the poorer strata of Jamaican society gained access to secondary edu-

cation for the first time. Large working-class housing programs were begun, and legislation improving the status of women and children was enacted (the status of illegitimacy, which established legal disabilities in inheritance and other family rights for children born out of wedlock, and which had greatly disadvantaged the overwhelming majority of children, was abolished). Black Jamaican culture was promoted and Jamaica became a strong voice in the international arena supporting African liberation movements and a new international economic order that would benefit developing countries.

The PNP government under Michael Manley was less successful in its economic reforms, however. The measures instituted to tax the transnational corporations that controlled bauxite mining in Jamaica led to disinvestment and an eventual fall in revenue. The huge expenditure on social welfare programs created large budget deficits, devaluations, and, eventually, structural adjustments recommended by the International Monetary Fund. Manley's radical international stance—including close relations with Cuba and the Non-Aligned Movement—alienated the government of the United States. The upshot of the economic and political crisis at the end of 1980 was that the PNP under Michael Manley was defeated in a national election characterized by violence.

In 1989 the PNP, still under the leadership of Michael Manley, was returned to power. By then it had shifted from its far-left position to a platform consistent with neoliberal globalization. Following this policy line, a period of rapid deregulation of the economy ensued. This led to unprecedented inflation (90 percent in 1991) and frequent devaluations. In March 1992 Michael Manley resigned because of poor health and was succeeded as prime minister by an eminent black lawyer, P. J. Patterson (b. 1935).

Patterson, who remained prime minister of Jamaica in 2005, continued this same policy line. Because of the weak competitive base of Jamaica, the rapid opening to the global economy was accompanied by a regime of high interest rates as a means of curbing inflation, raising funds to finance the budget, and stabilizing the currency. A long recession (1991–2002) ensued, which led to a major banking crisis from which the country began to recover only in 2005.

These austerity programs have meant a huge increase in both domestic and foreign debt, significant reductions in social expenditures, and an intensification of income inequalities. This has substantially reduced the political support of the Jamaican people for the PNP. Nevertheless, because of its deep social roots, especially in the black middle and working classes (as well as the divisions in the opposition Jamaican Labour Party), the PNP won an unprecedented four consecutive terms in the general elections held during this period of serious hardship—the longest continuous period in Jamaican political history that one party has been in power. It will remain in power at least until the next general elections are held in 2007.

See also Manley, Michael; Manley, Norman; Patterson, Percival James "P. J."; International Relations of the Anglophone Caribbean

■ ■ *Bibliography*

Gray, Obika. *Radicalism and Social Change in Jamaica, 1960–1972.* Knoxville: University of Tennessee Press, 1991.

Munroe, Trevor. *The Politics of Constitutional Decolonization: Jamaica 1944–62.* Kingston, Jamaica: Institute of Social and Economic Research, University of the West Indies, 1972.

Post, Ken. *Arise Ye Starvelings: The Jamaican Labour Rebellion of 1938 and its Aftermath.* The Hague, Netherlands: Martinus Nijhoff, 1978.

Stephens, Evelyne Huber, and John D. Stephens. *Democratic Socialism in Jamaica: The Political Movement and Social Transformation in Dependent Capitalism.* New York: Macmillan, 1986.

DON ROBOTHAM (2005)

PEOPLE UNITED TO SERVE HUMANITY

See Operation PUSH (People United to Serve Humanity)

PERFORMANCE ART
■ ■ ■

Performance Art is a quintessential catch-all phrase. With definitions as simplistic as that offered by W. W. Norton's *Glossary Online*—"Multimedia art form involving visual as well as dramatic and musical elements"—to the slightly more nuanced, if not infuriating, "live art by artists. [S]ince each performer makes his or her own definition in the very process and manner of execution" (1988, p. 9) provided by art historian RoseLee Goldberg, that which definitively separates performance art from either theater, or dance, or even body performance, for video recording remains deliciously elusive. Such is the nature of a "form" that struggles against formula, launches tirades against discipline, and hurls insult at tradition.

In the twenty-first century, when one hears the term *performance art,* it is usually in reference to modes of performance that evolved in lower Manhattan and industrial Los Angeles during the 1970s, known at the time as the highly controversial "conceptual art." Art colleges such as the California Institute of the Arts (CalArts) near Los Angeles and Cooper Union in Manhattan had begun to engage the political and social movements of the time in their course offerings. They sought to invest art and the practice of art with the timeliness of its moment of production. An example of this is the Feminist Arts program founded in part by Judy Chicago at CalArts, as well as the happenings launched in the loft district of lower Manhattan by art students like Adrian Piper.

In addition to the urgency of progressive social movements and anti–Vietnam War activism, the major urban centers of the United States were beginning to experience industrial flight, leaving behind entire manufacturing districts of architectural promise. Empty factories, sometimes still retaining the mechanized detritus of their former occupants, offered artists a cheap and communal place to live and work and show their work outside of the traditional gallery system of exhibition. Squatting itself became an art practice, as well as a political statement; an instance of disturbing the "naturalness" of art-making as always genteel, sophisticated, and most importantly, buffered and bracketed from the struggles of everyday living through an exclusive (and therefore highly limited) system of patronage and consumption. These were patronless artists, for a time, courtless jesters, clanless tribes, turning out their living spaces for communal experiences of the absurd, the sublime, the disturbing, the disjointed, which was always already the everyday experience of the object of capital: the worker, the citizen. These spaces were never located in "safe" areas of the city, and the circle of participants seemed limited to fellow rebellious students and radicals. Something had to be done—in a more visible space. What is an artist without an audience?

In this climate, conceptual artists took to the street, like their activist comrades and foes, bringing art to the people, taking the scale of art objects from the grand and elusive into the common and banal. Showing up was half the point of the "piece." Doing dances in metered parking places (Susan Rose), or giving calling cards to white racists who assumed themselves to be in the company of other white people of like mind (Adrian Piper), unmarked the boundary between make-believe, where it was thought that art with a capital *A* resided, and the public sphere, a highly contested site of negotiations and exchanges among people of differing ancestry, cultural practices, religious beliefs, and social classes. No longer solely relegated to the gallery, nor charged with only showing the audience beauty, the urban art (graffiti should also be considered part of this movement, albeit the "street" coming into the "gallery," or rendering the sidewalk experience as a gallery) movements of conceptual art, happenings, and ritual/puppet theater, in collapsing production with existing, experience with consumption, created a confrontational climate with the shadow side of everyday social interactions, considered at the time by dominant white structures of power as mere "decorum."

Deemed too political, too disturbing, too ugly, too pedestrian, or too pornographic, conceptual art was anti-art; it was an experience rather than an object that the art lover would take home at the end of the evening. Yet, performance art has become acceptable. Perhaps Andy Warhol and his art of the commercial icon (like the rows and rows of Marilyn Monroe's face or Campbell's Soup® cans)

marked the shift of "uptown coming downtown," as they would say in New York. There arrived the moment when the trace of performance—the objects created to facilitate the activity, whatever it was—began to accumulate value, much as any piece in a gallery or museum. The collectors called themselves *hipsters*. The archivists in the group became authoritarians as well as historians on the fragments (as did RoseLee Goldberg with her book, *Performance Art* [1988]). The patrons returned. Definitions (much like this one) began to proliferate, artists began to mature or die trying not to, the ephemeral quality of the work became its own undoing—there needed to be a record in order to prove one's presence as an artist.

Performance art returned to the gallery, and one could argue that the 1980s real-estate boom in urban centers helped to push artists back into the arms of the patrons. It was safer to reside in the bosom of the patron than risk the demolition crews and eviction notices. Stability of the live/work environment took precedence, and was codified in numerous city building codes. Codification is another word for relegation, especially when spatial usage agreements are involved. For those female and colored bodies who were not as enticing an investment, public art funds and private small philanthropic institutions once again institutionalized the nonwhite male body, creating funding sources and opportunities for performance in the public sector. Zoning laws, application forms, performance permits, and tax codes made the production of performance art just another public object, sufficiently contained and controlled, though such laws ostensibly provided for its continued existence, its institutionalization. Finally back in the schools, in the galleries, and in the museums, performance art is now understood by audiences of art, again with a capital *A*, as an art form, just not one that can be pinned down. Arguably, this is why those who regularly attend "manifestations," "interventions," "installations," "showings," "happenings," "gatherings," "incidents," "ciphers," "jams," and "performances" go in the first place.

FALSE STARTS

This amorphous form is typically traced back through time to beginnings in high European art. Interestingly, artists performing as opposed to creating art objects was a revolt against high-bourgeois norms and ideals. The Parisian futurism of 1903 to 1912 (the movements' "Manifesto" was published in *Le Figaro* on February 20, 1909) set up a template that subsequent "styles" of antiestablishment art were to utilize and rework over the span of the twentieth century. Initially a group of artists producing art events together, futurism spread throughout European art salons. Plastic, visual, and literary artists thrust themselves into performance as a way to have a more immediate connection with their audience, to enjoy their work, and to make of life an artwork, thereby guaranteeing that living itself was artistry. Moreover, the futurist artists believed that art, like life, should have no logical, determined pattern, nor should its objects speak beyond their users.

Similar in structure to so-called "primitive" cultural practices at the time, a succession of early twentieth-century performance art collectives—futurism, cubism, dadaism, and surrealism—were in deep conversation with the shifting world around them, especially the rapid colonization of the continent of Africa by European powers (German chancellor Otto von Bismarck's now infamous meeting to partition the continent of Africa began in November 1884). With that in mind, the reader of this entry may step into an "othered" history and definition of *performance art*, one that does not always trace itself through Paris, nor even call itself "performance art" most of the time.

SCULPTURES, COLONIALISM, AND INTERRUPTED RITES

It should not come as a surprise, though it still shocks, that cubism (1907–1914), dadaism (1916 in Germany, 1920–1924 in Paris), and surrealism (1925–1938) had their birthing through Parisian contacts with *objets d'art* of conquered African city-states and colonial subjects seeking education in the metropole (centers of imperial power). Gold amulets and exquisitely carved wooden furniture from the Ghanaian Federation, bronze castings with jeweled inlays and ivory sculptures from the Yoruba sixteen-state federation, wood sculptures and otherworldly instruments from the Songhai empire labeled as *fétiches* (or in English, *fetishes*) and deemed naive, these *objets d'arts* flooded into Europe as war booty between roughly 1870 and 1914 (though the flow is still a major problem in contemporary developing Africa). These objects were not "art objects" in a hard and fast sense; they were spirit houses divorced from their performative moment. But their effects were not entirely lost in translation. European artists saw and experienced in the sculptures, dance wands, cloth, and power amulets a presence of the flesh and an adoration of the *concept* that they felt had become foreign to a rapidly industrializing Europe.

They moved their art back to the streets, the parlors, the night clubs, the dance halls, the parks, the stairwells of subways and waterways—art in Europe returned to the scale of the human, to following footprints along the sidewalk, meandering to no particular point at no particular rate, in marked contrast to the insistence of an ever-industrializing cityscape for synchronization and amelioration of difference, space, and memory. These pieces were confrontations meant to provoke the audience, to challenge their sense of self and social order. Frequently very elaborate productions that used minimal, common, street-gutter language, these precursors to late twentieth-century performance art strove for disarray, an anarchy without a subsequent new order. This art had political yet antirepublican ideals and goals. Eventually surrealism would connect in meaningful ways with actual Africans and other black French colonial subjects between 1932 and 1936 through the poetry and manifestations of Aimé Césaire (the Martinican poet, playwright, and politician), Léopold Senghor (the first president of liberated Senegal), and Léon Gontran Damas (the French Guyanese poet and member of the National Assembly). These three men, surrounded by a bevy of black thinkers, writers, poets, dancers, actors, and singers from around the African diaspora, birthed the cultural and political movement known as *Négritude*, which, though Parisian, sought to create a Pan-Africanism through artistic and cultural practices.

One must now reconsider the famous picture of futurist Guillaume Apollinaire's studio filled with African "art."

HOW DID IT GET BLACK? OR, ENTER THE MOOR

Throughout the transatlantic slave trade, performance practices mobilized specific types of tools for both Africans and Europeans seeking a way to comprehend this monumental human tragedy. Dances, songs, street/spontaneous theater set pieces, masquerades, costumes, and even specific types of culinary events that are now lumped under the category of "traditional folk expressions" (or if not so sophisticated, "that ole timey Negro stuff") had their beginnings as "artful performance," back in their day. Such festivals as John Canoe, Bumba Meu boi (The master's bull is mine), and Crop Over, all "folk manifestations" from the nineteenth century, had elements that could be identified as constituting a performance art practice.

Body-based, these performance styles use the flesh of the performer as stage, device, backdrop, setting, time period, and "soundtrack." Multi- or crossmodal techniques as varied as music, dance, sculpture, live painting (on any surface, with any colorant), theater, ritual and/or spell casting are employed freely, without regard to training or discipline. The story line is disjunctive, if there is one at all, jumping through time, stopping time flow for emphasis of the idea over the continued, unbroken narrative arc. The time it takes to execute the piece, its duration, also becomes a performer and is manipulated, usually against the narrative arc; this is known as time-based art. Such works are participatory, engaging the audience as source material or requiring the audience to "complete" the piece as they see fit either mentally or by becoming a player/maker in the piece. By its very construction, the piece is unstable, incomplete, a deconstructive act, and therefore productive of discourse/dialogue/new clarity about old, murky ideas. The piece is repeatable but not reproducible, uniquely performed every time but still recognized as itself, though sometimes confused for real life activity rather than a performance as it blurs social domains. It dissimulates in order to draw out "truths," utilizing trickster characters, set pieces, and phrases.

Invoking godspace through creating a physicalized reality, the act denies any truths other than the physical body's functions, which can be inferred by witnesses as proof for the need for divine intervention; or proof of the absence of a divine spirit, hence the futility or absurdity of human social networks; or conversely, proof of the inherent divinity of humanity itself. So the question for this definition that wants to remain undefined is: When is a black person not in the midst of a performance art piece?

This, though rather flippant, can be distilled as the baseline concept with which most artists of African descent who work in time-based mediums delight in destabilizing, shouting out loud, writing about, reading random lists to passersby, leaving trails and clues on canvases, marking up otherwise excellent records to make one listen more carefully to the distortion. Black performance art is a slave narrative that requires no witness: it finds the audience, flat on its feet, and forces them to recognize their participation in the event—staged or otherwise.

GENRES AND MODES

From a more traditional vantage point, performance art can be broken into genres, reflecting the artist's original training, if any. Adrian Piper, William Pope.L, and Robbie McCauley could be characterized as conceptual artists, since they all use "classic" modes of performance art engagement. Yet, Piper is trained as a visual artist, Pope.L as a visual artist who performs, and McCauley as a theater artist who specializes in the monologue. Bill T. Jones, Rhodessa Jones, Joanna Haigood, Bebe Miller, Blondell Cummings, Alonzo King, and Jawole Willa Jo Zollar were all trained as dancers in "high Western Art Aesthetic" traditions, but broke with or metamorphosed their training by taking strategic positions with regard to their art. Haigood and King could be said to perform only as dancers, since text is often missing from their work, yet they restructure dance technique itself—Haigood brought in aerialism and site-specific work, while King layers tradi-

tional African diaspora body positions over *toes en pointe*. Bill T. Jones, Rhodessa Jones, Zollar, Cummings, and Miller continue to work between dance theater with large companies or as solo performers in work that registers as performance art.

Anna Deavere Smith's work is often categorized as performance art, but others argue that she is a thespian, a very gifted one who can hold upwards of thirty-five characters per performance. The work of Damali Ayo, Navin June Norling, and Kara Walker, though based in the plastic and visual arts, also seeps out into performance and digital realms, especially the work of Ayo. Using literature, musical composition, dance, and classic conceptual art modes, Keith + Mendi Obadike have mutated into "net artists," using the World Wide Web as staging device, tool, and technique. Philip Mallory Jones's multichannel video installations are based in his training as a film student but also his contact with conceptual artists and traditional "folk" performers of the African diaspora.

What coheres these artists is perhaps merely approach and the audience's perception of their skin color as a resonator or amplifier of the performance. They manipulate stereotypes as a character and utilize humor in their text or scenario and set it against bathos in gesture, frequently through the use of their own personal narratives, somewhat analogous to slave narratives. Their subject matter and presentational format uses political and confrontational material, especially around race and gender, with an almost deathly serious approach to texts that seem hyperreal, speculative, or ridiculous.

Categorizing artist by genre distorts the true quality of their work, which is a multimodal approach to a series of questions or assumptions. Moreover, when viewed through the lens of genre, there are very few performance artists of African descent, yet a great deal of African diaspora performance exists in forms that defy westernized classification systems. Even those artists that seem to fit neatly into the flow of art history, frequently fall out or suffer extreme professional consequences because of the blackness of their skin or their art's content. By working through periods, perhaps one can establish the particularities of performance art by tracing social forces and political change in black American life.

TIME SIGNATURES

Since performance art is itself concerned with "what happens when," more so than "who did what," suppose that, following art texts like Robert Hughes' *The Shock of the New* and Goldberg's *Performance Art*, among others, a series of periods were created to name chunks of time that have performances comprised of similar components, ad-

Artist and educator William Pope.L crawls as part of an exhibit at the Maine College of Art's Institute of Contemporary Art in 2002. The museum's retrospective eRacism *highlighted 25 years of Pope.L's performance and visual artistry.* AP/WIDE WORLD PHOTOS. REPRODUCED BY PERMISSION.

dressing similar issues, in recognizable ways, by clusters of people, many of whom would have worked together literally, or at least been aware of one another's body of work.

For example, it has been argued in the edited volume *Black Theatre* (2002) that the experience and response to enslavement should be considered types of theater, if not performance art. Saidiya Hartman, in *Scenes of Subjection* (1997), eloquently argues for the ways in which both European enslavers and African slaves created nuanced meanings and justifications for the brutal exchanges and reductions of human beings into monetized objects. Thus, one could start the timeline on the sea, *Trans-Atlantic Trials and Tribulations* (roughly 1500–1865), where slaves partook in "dancing" for exercise aboard slave ships, singing songs for sustenance, or "choosing" the life of a slaving sailor in order to escape chattel slavery itself.

Once on land, where Hartman's book does the bulk of its exquisite analysis, one enters the era of *Plantation Puttin Ons* (1575–1880), which includes pretending to dance while practicing to fight, as well as pretending to worship baby Jesus while keeping various *lwa*, orishas, *nkisi*, and even Qur'anic phrases up and ready so as not to pretend to be free. The performances from this era cannot actually be labeled "African American," because the

system of slavery was a global one, with Africans often landing in various ports in the Caribbean first, where they were trained, or at least put through a dehumanizing and rigorous tests of wills and work in the hopes of increasing the value of their labor, or cutting the loss of their voyage-weakened body. The dates, therefore, include all plantation societies in the New World.

Once in the new land, primarily West Africans had to negotiate the new languages of the Europeans, as well as account for their new status as "nigger," no longer beholden to ethnic and socioreligious groups. A new social ordering was forged, often through interpolating the myths and rituals of each groups' deities and ancestors. The nineteenth century witnessed the height of these new social formations, many of which birthed new performance practices cherished by whites and noninitiated blacks alike. *Conjurations* (1745–1935) encompasses such practices as John Canoe, the lantern dance, second line Carnival groups, roots working (a combination of biochemical knowledge with esoteric text, utterances, gestures, and chants meant to heal or do harm to another individual), Moko Jumbi (stilt-walking), spirituals/blues, just-so tales, Brer Rabbit and Aunt Nancy, and pretending to only read so as to serve God better, though actually using the Bible as a divination device. It is important to note that many of the spiritual aspects of these performances were not necessarily documented, so that the practices themselves became part of the folklore of slavery, rather than the active performance of "slipping the yoke."

Shifting more to the British territories that came to call themselves the United States, the liberation of Africans after the attempted eradication of Native Americans, and the splitting of the Union, one could talk about the era of *Emancipation* (1865–1877), which includes Reconstruction and land grant schooling meant to train free blacks, primarily to be laboring, agrarian "citizens." Emancipation Day parades, black family reunions, founder's days, and Juneteenth all began in this moment, even under the specter of the white supremacist performance art known as Jim Crow. This was literally a caricature of a black dandy popular in black face presentations that ridiculed the rapid successes of the free black population while waxing rhapsodic and nostalgic about the subjugated, agrarian black body and its "folk" practices. *Minstrelsy*, as this form was called, which began around 1825 and became an international sensation, ironically had very little room for actual black performers.

The minstrelsy form included usually no less than four male performers who sang, danced, and acted as though a "nigger." Jim Crow, which was also a popular dance-based set piece, was first documented on stage in

1828, performed by the comedian Thomas D. Rice. Interestingly, when blacks began to enter vaudeville, then silent films, they were required to "blacken up" and act like a "nigger," Bert Williams being one of the more famous black thespians who attempted to bring a bit of humanity to these performances. Mammy, Sambo, Coon, and Pickaninny are standard characters of this format, each with its own specific repertoire of set pieces, gestures, dances, and songs. As minstrelsy was widely performed as late as 1950 in the United States, and those characters continue to ghost through filmic representations of black people produced by Hollywood in particular, and finally, since they turn up as sites of investigation in contemporary black performance art, the age of the minstrel is still ongoing.

Seeking to document, perform, and archive actual black performance practice, the age of the *Harlem Renaissance/WPA Project* (1920–1935) includes such gifted writers-researchers-performers as Zora Neale Hurston, Katherine Dunham, Pearl Primus, Langston Hughes, and Josephine Baker, though they all worked under white patronage or federal funding. As lynching became a common performance practice of white supremacy, as the urgency to establish black autonomous practices grew, and as artists could no longer expect patronage for potentially racially explosive art, the era of *Un-hand Me* (1943–1964) took shape through the work of performers like Paul Robeson, Nina Simone, and Dick Gregory, and the New Negro Theater Troupe. In the everyday practices of black people, campaigns like the "Double V" project launched in Pittsburgh included signifying through hairstyle and clothing the desire for a United States win in World War II and then an end of racial segregation at home upon the return of the victorious black soldiers. This was not to be.

The civil rights movement focused the energies of several local campaigns to end segregation and what had become known as Jim Crow laws. Eventually, the nonviolent protests of the Student Nonviolent Coordinating Committee (SNCC), the Southern Christian Leadership Conference (SCLC), and other groups came to a shocking halt upon the assassination of Martin Luther King Jr., one of the leaders of the movement, in 1968. In response, a new style of protest erupted, one that did not consider violence to be out of the question, but one that needed to stir the new Negro into a black consciousness. The *Black Arts Movement* (1965–1975) created performances based on the essential differences of black people versus white people, whatever those happened to have been at the time. Artists and organizations like Amiri Baraka, the Association for the Advancement of Creative Musicians (AACM), Sun Ra, the African Commune of Bad Revolutionary Artists (Afri-COBRA), and La MaMa (Ellen Stewart) took the

maligned minstrel characters and began to give them voices that spoke of things other than watermelon, shoe shines, alligators, and corn pone.

Characterized by Marxist analysis of the black condition, performances of the Black Arts Movement were also in conversation with worldwide liberation struggles in African colonies. Marred by repressive, violent, and extreme state response, especially by the FBI's COINTELPRO (counterintelligence program), the Black Arts Movement appeared to dissipate, but it could be argued that it shifted focus from the materialist to the spiritualist analysis of the black condition.

The *Rootswork and Motherships* period (1977–1988) includes artists who continued to labor under the idea of an art for and by the people, but who also found themselves dealing with black cultural productions that seemed to penetrate white culture through market practices, known as concerts. Ed Bullins (playwright), Jayne Cortez (poet), George Clinton and Funkadelic (musicians), the LA Rebellion (filmmakers), Bucket Dance Theater, Dance Theater of Harlem, Hattie Gossett (poet), Ntozake Shange (playwright, poet, and dancer), Jawole Willa Jo Zollar (dancer), Robbie McCauley (monologist), and Carroll Parrott Blue (filmmaker) all labored in this era to create a decidedly black aesthetic. They sought an aesthetic that did not cleave to artistic divisions like dance, music, film, theater, or literature, for though they have been identified above by their primary modality, since they worked through their themes in ritualistic style, their shows included various techniques of performance, what is often called "spectacle" by dominant society, not necessarily art.

In a similar vein, when what later became known as hip-hop hit the cultural scene, the artists working in the *Rap and Rhetoric* era (1978–1993), made use of multimodal performance practices, interpolating one type of artistic production with another, including machinists techniques for bending equipment to new uses. Afrika Bambaataa, DJ Kool Herc, Jean-Michel Basquiat, Fab 5 Freddy, Marley Mal, Salt-n-Pepa, Queen Latifah, X-Clan, Public Enemy, Rennie Harris Pure Movement, Jungle Brothers, and Boogie Down Productions all produced work that was marketed primarily as sound recordings (or evidence of its existence as in Rennie Harris), but the recordings are actually archival moments of a vast, site-specific work. Rap also "played" with the concept of distribution as performance, using techniques that today would be considered viral, to promote not the recording label (since they were self-produced), but rather the artist or "crew" responsible for the work, and hence, specific locales. Often considered the "CNN of the 'hood," rap began "reporting" on the myriad failings of civil society with regard to primarily race and class, telling stories of addiction and epidemics, to name a few.

Afflictions, Epidemics, Endgames (1982–1997) was a period characterized by the influx and traffic of crack cocaine, the surge of AIDS, the proliferation of restrictive local ordinances and laws about public space and drug trafficking, yuppies, savings and loan scandals, and degenerative discourse about "decorum." Artists and organizations working to expand the boundaries of blackness beyond masculinist discourses of nation included Bill T. Jones, Blondell Cummings, Rhodessa Jones, Whoopi Goldberg, the Poetry for the People project at the University of California–Berkeley under June Jordan, Pomo Afro Homos, Alonzo King's Lines Ballet, Anna Deveare Smith, Grace Jones, Junebug Theater, the Urban Bush Women, and Portia Cobb. These artists struggled to interrogate the social moment and its salience for black people, albeit from a far more complicated stance.

These complications—of gender identity, of class and caste, of urbanism or ruralism—have always been part and parcel of the articulation of a unified blackness, but frequently to the disregard of those people who did not easily conform to a blackness defined by black male coolness and radical separatism from other cultures. Drawn into a seeming battle with itself, blackness has been revealed as a particularly fractured, even fictitious creation. Identity politics in the *Postblack and Digital Frontierism* era (1998 to the early twenty-first century) manifests a profound shift in discourse as some artists began to articulate their identity as multiple and hybrid, and not necessarily in struggle with whiteness at all. Interpolated or implicated in the terrain of market capitalism in the twenty-first century, postblack artists work in off-limit terrains, questioning the relegation of blackness to specific iterations like the documentary, the realist novel, the modern jazz dance concert, or collectible music recordings. Afrofuturists, including DJ Spooky, and artists like Kara Walker, Damali Ayo, Joanna Haigood, Susan Smith-Pinelo, Carroll Parrott Blue, Kalamu ya Salaam, Keith + Mendi Obadike, Tara Hargest, and William Pope.L, can be located in this site of performance making, though it would be erroneous to assume that they consider themselves no longer black.

OUT OF BOUNDS AND TEMPORAL LOBES

This approach does not necessarily give greater clarity, since one period does not relinquish control so easily over the next, as is frequently the case with neat timelines. Many players in one era resurface in another, making their mark through reworked material and new foci of performance. The suggested periods, indeed the entire thrust of this definition, is further thwarted by the existence of a number of black artists who did and still do ascribe to the norms and strategies of the European aesthetic. In particular, Adrian Piper was at the forefront of the conceptual art scene in 1970s New York and considers herself, first and foremost, an artist. That her work is primarily about being a black woman who does not appear like one is irrelevant to the process of her work, but central to its success as art. Her blackness is not definitive for her; rather, it is a moment of confrontation with the racist subconscious of the white patrons at the happenings, interventions, and installations that she has produced from 1971 to 2003.

A few of the suggested time periods are grouped to show a rerouting of historical trajectories, to superimpose African art-making practices as the progenitors of a black art aesthetic, displacing Europe altogether. The black arts movement, particularly the Association for the Advancement of Creative Musicians, sought out African rituals, but in its waning period, which could be called *Rootsworks and Motherships*, indigenous forms of African-descended cultural practices began to take precedence over "pure" African ones. Instead of "happenings," a passerby may have enjoyed a "ritual" or "conjuration." They would have needed to "vibe" with the multidimensionalists (a term used by AACM member Maia to describe her ability to work across several artistic disciplines at once) rather than "participate." By the late 1980s, it was clear that purity or authenticity could not be the focus of a truly vibrant art form and actually served as breaking points for many flourishing groups. But this is to be expected of body-based temporal art endeavors: beyond the written word, keeping the story straight past five years or more is a gargantuan task when one considers that most of these performers have yet to be adequately documented. Who was where, with whom, and when are the questions that practitioners, critics, aficionados, and scholars alike face as they attempt to describe that which was created to exist beyond description, to defy commoditization, and to destroy spatial constructs called "boundaries," "territories," and "states."

A strictly "African-American" performance art is in the end an improbable proposition, because perhaps more so than in any other field, performance art, conjurations, and multidimensionalism are distinctively black productions that are transcultural, Pan-African, and global in scope.

See also Dance, Diasporic; Drama; Experimental Theater; Jones, Bill T.; Minstrels/Minstrelsy; Piper, Adrian; Smith, Anna Deavere

■ ■ *Bibliography*

Bean, Annemarie, ed. *A Sourcebook of African-American Performance: Plays, People, Movements.* New York and London: Routledge, 1999.

Bessire, Mark H. C. *William Pope.L: The Friendliest Black Artist in America.* Cambridge, Mass.: MIT Press, 2002.

Chang, Jeff. *Can't Stop, Won't Stop: A History of the Hip-Hop Generation.* New York: St. Martin's Press, 2005.

Flowers, Arthur. *Mojo Rising: Confessions of a 21st Century Conjureman.* New York: Wanganegresse Press, 2001.

Goldberg, RoseLee. *Performance Art: From Futurism to the Present.* New York: Harry N. Abrams, 1988.

Goler, Veta. "Living with the Doors Open: An Interview with Blondell Cummings." In *The Citizen Artist: 20 Years of Art in the Public Arena, an Anthology from High Performance Magazine, 1978–1998,* edited by Linda Frye Burnham and Steven Durland. Gardiner, N.Y.: Critical, 1998.

Harrison, Peter C., Victor L. Walker, and Gus Edwards, eds. *Black Theatre: Ritual Performance in the African Diaspora.* Philadelphia: Temple University Press, 2002.

Hartman, Saidiya V. *Scenes of Subjection: Terror, Slavery, and Self-Making in Nineteenth-Century American Culture.* New York: Oxford University Press, 1997.

Hughes, Robert. *The Shock of the New.* 1981. Revised ed. New York: Knopf, 1991.

jess, tyehimba. *African American Pride: Celebrating Our Achievements, Contributions, and Enduring Legacy.* New York: Citadel, 2003.

Keith + Mendi Obadike. Available at <http://obadike.tripod.com>.

"Performance Art." A definition provided by *Glossary Online.* Norton Sony Classical Essentials of Music. Available at <http://www.wwnorton.com/classical/glossary/p.htm>.

Piper, Adrian. Adrian Piper Research Archive. Available at <http://www.adrianpiper.com>.

Schneider, Rebecca. *The Explicit Body in Performance.* London: Routledge, 1997.

ANNA BEATRICE SCOTT (2005)

PERRY, LINCOLN

See Stepin Fetchit (Perry, Lincoln)

PHILANTHROPY AND FOUNDATIONS

■ ■ ■ ────────

The beginnings of organized African-American philanthropy can be traced to the early black churches, mutual aid societies, and fraternal organizations among free blacks in the late eighteenth century. The introduction of black self-help organizations resulted from the social and economic inequalities faced by free blacks in northern cities when the state provided little or no social welfare assistance. This spontaneous social organization reflected African-Americans' distinctive culture. Robert Harris (1979), a scholar of early black self-help organizations, stated, "The benevolent societies combined African heritage with American conditions to transform an amorphous free black population into a distinct free black community. . . . In the final analysis, the early black benevolent society functioned as the wellspring for Afro-American institutional life."

The first known black American mutual aid organization was the African Union Society of Newport, Rhode Island, founded in 1780. The society was primarily concerned with the moral rectitude of free blacks and provided material assistance by recording births, deaths, and marriages and by seeking to apprentice black youths in useful trades. Another of the earliest mutual aid organizations, African Lodge No. 459 (later renamed the Prince Hall Grand Masons), was founded in Boston in 1787 in Prince Hall and was the first black Freemasonic society. The lodge provided members with protection against reenslavement due to delinquent debts and provided the poor with food and other provisions. The Free African Society of Philadelphia was founded in 1787 to provide material aid to free blacks and support to religious institutions.

In the first half of the nineteenth century black churches and mutual aid organizations were active in the abolitionist movement, including the Underground Railroad, by raising money, donating goods and services, and volunteering their time on behalf of escaping slaves. Through collective action, groups such as the International Order of Twelve Knights, the Daughters of Tabor, and the Knights of Liberty, all founded in the 1850s, were responsible for liberating and sheltering thousands of slaves through the Underground Railroad. Collectively, these organizations used the financial and volunteer contributions of black Americans to provide other black Americans with social services that they could not obtain through government or from most white charitable organizations, though some white philanthropies, such as the various state abolition societies, were important sources of financial and moral support for African Americans. Further, since the leaders of these organizations, in particular black ministers, received financial support directly from the black community, they could speak freely about the community's aspirations for equal rights without fear of financial repercussions from those who disagreed with their positions.

In most of the South before Emancipation there existed a de facto ban on black mutual aid societies, and Virginia, Maryland, and North Carolina legally prohibited such organizations. Despite the hostility, southern free blacks successfully maintained benevolent societies. Among such groups were the Resolute Beneficial Society of Washington, D.C., established in 1818; the Burying Ground Society and the Beneficial Society of Richmond, Virginia, both formed in 1815; and the Brown Fellowship Society (1790), Christian Benevolent Society (1839), Humane Brotherhood (1843), and Unity and Friendship Society (1844), all of Charleston, South Carolina.

Before the Civil War most black philanthropy was concentrated at the local level. In 1835 there were forty black mutual aid organizations in Baltimore and eighty in Philadelphia. In the latter city in 1848 almost half of the adult free black population was affiliated with African-American philanthropic societies.

Some of the early black benevolent societies included both men and women in the same organization. The African Benevolent Society of Newport, Rhode Island, founded in 1808, accepted free blacks without regard to gender, as did the African Marine Fund of New York City. In general, women belonged only to organizations that stressed education, but were not ordinarily members of other types of benevolent societies. There were, however, female auxiliaries for most of the groups, and black women played a key role in literary associations.

Notwithstanding the separate and unequal living conditions that characterized the lives of black and white Americans during the eighteenth and nineteenth centuries, it is important to note that many black organizations also provided the larger white society with services and other assistance during times of emergency. For example, during the great plague that struck Philadelphia in 1793, the Free African Society provided the entire city with extensive nursing and burial services.

Following the Civil War, there was a national concern to establish programs that would enable the freed slaves, many of whom could not read or write, to become self-sufficient. The Freedmen's Bureau, officially known as the Bureau of Refugees, Freedmen, and Abandoned Lands, was formed by Congress in 1865, and along with nearly a hundred independent volunteer freedmen's aid societies, sought to provide assistance to both ex-slaves and impoverished whites. During the bureau's seven-year tenure, it established more than four thousand schools and forty hospitals, as well as distributed free food.

In the late nineteenth and early twentieth centuries, philanthropists from the North played a crucial role in disbursing aid to African Americans in the South. Notwithstanding the combined efforts of the bureau and the freedmen societies, when Julius Rosenwald started his eponymous fund in 1917, there was not a single standard public eighth grade or high school in the South for black children. From 1913 to 1932 Rosenwald helped establish 5,357 public schools in fifteen southern states. A key feature of this effort was that in each case, the local black community contributed to the building of the schools by donating both money and labor. In later years the Rosenwald Fund would support fellowships for black schoolteachers, black hospitals, and efforts to improve black-white relations.

By far the most influential foundation in shaping black educational opportunities was the General Education Board (GEB), founded by John D. Rockefeller in 1902. The GEB was involved in all aspects of black education during the early to mid-1900s, including encouraging consolidation of one-room schools, training teachers, and providing transportation for students in rural areas. From 1902 to 1960 the GEB distributed $62.5 million in support of black education. In addition to the Rosenwald Fund and the General Education Board, other, smaller philanthropic institutions that were active in promoting educational opportunities for black Americans include the Peabody Fund, the Slater Fund, and the Phelps-Stokes Fund.

The Peabody Fund, established in 1867, was intended to popularize the idea of universal education as a means of integrating ex-slaves and poor whites into the emerging bourgeois southern order. The organizers of the fund were concerned about the dangers of an unruly, uneducated class of paupers in a society lacking a significant public welfare structure. The Peabody Fund gave considerable material aid to southern schools until 1910, when it was merged into the Slater Fund, which had pursued a similar program of educational promotion since its founding in 1882.

The Slater Fund particularly applauded and assisted the work of black educators such as Booker T. Washington, who accepted the racial status quo in the South and insisted that the primary means of black advancement was through the acquisition of industrial skills. From 1891 to 1911 the Slater Fund supported a few model industrial schools such as Hampton Institute (now Hampton University) and Washington's Tuskegee Institute (now Tuskegee University), eventually giving these two schools half of its annual appropriations. After 1911 the fund pursued its interest in manual training by preparing black teachers in county training schools; it helped build 384 such schools in the South over the next two decades. In 1937 the Slater Fund merged with the Jeanes Fund and the Virginia Randolph Fund to form the Atlanta-based Southern Education Fund, which still exists.

Another important source of philanthropy for black education, the Phelps-Stokes Fund, was founded in 1911 to administer a bequest from Caroline Phelps Stokes to increase educational opportunities for black Americans, Native Americans, and poor whites. The fund made several small grants to black educational institutions from its founding until the 1940s, when its emphasis shifted to supporting historically black colleges through the Cooperative College Development Program. Through this program the fund dispensed more than $6 million to black colleges and helped establish the United Negro College Fund in 1943, a joint fund-raising effort by over thirty historically black colleges and universities.

As the role of foundations in African-American education grew, at least two issues arose. First, what was the appropriate type of education for black Americans? Most foundations began their efforts by supporting industrial education to provide training for specific, often rural, trade skills rather than a liberal arts education in the humanities or sciences. With these interests in mind, foundations provided support for Tuskegee Institute and Hampton Institute, among others. (The Rosenwald Fund was largely an exception to this.) Second, throughout the Jim Crow era, foundations generally accepted the idea of separate schools for black Americans. To be sure, funding for integrated education in the early twentieth-century South was a near impossibility. As a result, foundations sought to develop and strengthen separate black educational institutions rather than encourage integrated institutions. An additional problem was the attempt of the foundations to placate the white South, and the conviction of many foundation leaders that academic education for African Americans was pointless. For example, in 1899, a trustee of the GEB was quoted as stating, "The Negro should not be educated out of his environment. Industrial work is his salvation. . . . Except in the rarest of instances, I am bitterly opposed to the so-called higher education of Negroes." Many foundations relied on their experiences in helping to shape black education in the United States as a guide for developing similar educational programs in Africa.

By the 1930s many of the remaining foundations were paying greater attention to academic instruction. In addition, several foundations supported comprehensive studies of the adverse socioeconomic conditions and legal barriers confronting African Americans. For example, the Laura Spelman Rockefeller Memorial Fund financed *The Negro in American Civilization* (1930), the Phelps-Stokes Fund supported a never-completed encyclopedia project on black Americans (1930s and 1940s), and the Julius Rosenwald Fund provided support for *Alien Americans: A Study of Race Relations* (1936). The most influential study

of black America in the middle decades of the century, *An American Dilemma* (1944), by the Swedish-born scholar Gunnar Myrdal, was supported by the Carnegie Corporation of New York. The report concluded that the American dilemma was the inconsistency between the stated belief in equality and social justice for all and the documented legal barriers that prevented black Americans from fully participating in American society.

The strategies employed by foundations to promote black-white relations have changed markedly over time. Concerned that black Americans be sufficiently moral and upstanding, foundations in the early twentieth century supported the Negro Boy Scouts, the National Negro Business League, and, later, the National Urban League. However, beginning at the end of World War I, as foundations began to recognize black Americans' long-standing desire for equality and began to fear that continued denial of their aspirations might encourage them to become communists, foundations became more interested in supporting black and white cooperation. In 1919 the Rosenwald Fund helped to create the Commission on Interracial Cooperation (CIC) to bring together black and white community leaders throughout the South. The fund also provided support for the American Council on Race Relations and the Southern Regional Council, the successor to the CIC.

Notwithstanding the agendas of white philanthropic institutions, African Americans established and supported their own evolving needs and aspirations. Black fraternal orders that emerged close to the turn of the twentieth century have over time adapted to modern needs. One such organization, the Ancient Egyptian Arabic Order Nobles Mystic Shrine, Inc., was founded in 1893. With 47,000 members in the 1990s, this organization runs programs to address delinquency and drug abuse, and supports medical research on health problems of special concern to blacks. Another, the Improved Benevolent Protective Order of Elks of the World, was founded in 1898, and claimed 450,000 members. It supports a variety of causes, including scholarships, for which it raises a million dollars annually. Despite such activities, however, many fraternal orders have experienced dramatic declines in membership. Since the end of World War II, one alternative source of black philanthropy has been the growing ranks of collegiate associations. The eight largest black fraternities and sororities have a combined membership of well over 650,000. In terms of direct material aid, the black church has been the most enduring source of black self-help. Perhaps the best-known example of church welfare was the "Peace Mission" in New York's Harlem, operated during the Great Depression, by Father Divine. Father Divine operated grocery stores nationwide, fed the hungry full meals for ten cents apiece at his own restaurants, and published and distributed newspapers and magazines for which his followers often volunteered to work. He was also known for the free meals he provided the hungry on Sundays.

As the civil rights movement came of age in the 1950s and 1960s, black Americans mobilized their collective financial and volunteer resources, along with those of their supporters, to challenge and eventually overturn laws that sanctioned keeping black and white Americans separate but equal. The black church, with its independent leaders, as exemplified by the Rev. Dr. Martin Luther King Jr. and T. J. Jemison, harnessed and directed a national effort involving several hundred thousand children, women, and men to volunteer in marches, sit ins, and demonstrations. Moreover, the nonprofit civil rights organizations that gained new prominence during this time, for example, the National Association for the Advancement of Colored People (NAACP), the NAACP Legal Defense and Educational Fund, the Congress of Racial Equality (CORE), and the Southern Christian Leadership Conference (SCLC), have been replicated by other groups concerned with ensuring equality for women and Asians, Latinos, and Native Americans, as well as gays and lesbians.

White foundations not only provided some support for many of the civil rights organizations but also began to fund projects aimed at directly promoting black socioeconomic advancement through education and redistributive social programs. In particular, the Rockefeller and Ford foundations were at the forefront of these efforts. The Rockefeller Foundation launched its equal opportunity program, which primarily focused on supporting integrated higher education. From the mid-1960s to the mid-1970s, grants were awarded to predominantly white colleges located throughout the United States to recruit minority students.

Stating that full equality for black Americans was the most urgent concern challenging the country, the Ford Foundation launched an unprecedented effort to improve the socioeconomic and political conditions of the urban poor, among whom black Americans were disproportionately represented. From 1960 to 1970 the Ford Foundation awarded more than $25 million for its Great Cities School Improvement project, which focused on assisting major urban school districts to become more responsive to the needs of black children with rural backgrounds, and the Gray Areas project, which focused on the health, housing, welfare, and employment needs of residents in urban cities. The Gray Areas project served as the model for several of the education and training provisions that were later authorized in the Economic Opportunity Act of 1964.

Ford also established major programs to support civil rights organizations, voter education, black colleges, and community economic development.

The Ford Foundation's activism was not without repercussions. For example, in 1967 a Ford-supported demonstration project in New York to encourage local community control of public school districts led to school strikes as the local councils, teachers' unions, and school board struggled for control of the public school system. Similarly, when Carl Stokes was elected as the first black mayor of Cleveland, many charged that the election outcome had been influenced by Ford-sponsored voter education programs. The concern that foundations had undue influence in public matters led in part to the Tax Reform Act of 1969, which placed new restrictions on foundation activities in several areas, including voter registration.

Before the 1970s few black Americans were on the boards or professional staffs of foundations. However, as a consequence of the civil rights movement, black Americans are now represented, albeit in small numbers, at every level within foundations and are key decision makers in determining how limited philanthropic resources will be allocated to address unlimited needs. For example, Franklin A. Thomas, a black American, was named president of the Ford Foundation, the largest foundation in the United States, in 1979. As a result of these developments, the black community has both a continuing tradition of philanthropy and self-help within its own community and has started a new chapter as individual black Americans begin to help shape the funding priorities of older philanthropic institutions in helping everyone.

In the 1970s black Americans began to develop new types of charitable organizations to confront both old and new problems. Despite significant socioeconomic progress among black Americans, a significant proportion continued to require a broad range of social services. In addition, the increased support of black charitable organizations by government agencies and foundations led some to question whether these organizations could be as independent to advocate on behalf of black Americans' interests as the black church had in the past.

Recognizing the need to develop new ways to provide an independent, black-controlled funding source to support black-run social protest and social service organizations, a number of black fund-raising organizations emerged in various cities across the United States to raise money from African Americans to support black organizations. In 1972 a number of these groups formed the National Black United Fund (NBUF). NBUF's mission was to develop a fund-raising mechanism that would allow them to raise money primarily from African Americans throughout a particular city and distribute that money to black organizations.

For many years, one national charitable organization, the United Way, had sole access to the federal government's work-site charitable payroll deduction campaigns. Through these campaigns, federal workers agreed to contribute a given amount of money from each paycheck to charity. In the early 1980s NBUF won a series of Supreme Court cases that challenged United Way's monopoly to access the federal government's work-site charitable payroll deduction campaigns and was allowed to participate in these campaigns. Later, NBUF began to gain access to the campaigns of private employers.

NBUF's success has enabled a wide range of women, minorities, and special interest groups to develop identical organizations to raise money for their causes. Further, the development of black charitable organizations has resulted in greater responsiveness to the black community from all charitable organizations seeking contributions from black Americans.

Established in 1999, the National Center for Black Philanthropy's goal is to promote and strengthen the participation of African Americans in all aspects of philanthropy, educate the public about black philanthropy, and document the contributions of black philanthropy to American society. The organization holds national and regional conferences involving philanthropists, scholars, foundation executives, and fund-raisers.

Perhaps the most interesting new development is the establishment of foundations by African Americans. For example, the Jackie Robinson Foundation, named after the man who broke the color barrier of organized baseball in 1947, focuses on supporting educational programs for youth. More than two hundred years after blacks had to rely on pooling their modest contributions to develop a different form of philanthropy, a growing number of black Americans have amassed enough wealth to create their own foundations and to underwrite major charitable activities. For example, businessman Reginald Lewis made a contribution of $2 million to Howard University and $3 million to Harvard University, among many other contributions. Entertainer Bill Cosby and his wife Camille made a historic gift of $20 million to Spelman College as one of their many charitable contributions.

Two other extraordinary gifts suggest that black philanthropy is on the cusp of a new renaissance. In 1995, at the age of eighty-seven, Oseola McCarty donated $150,000 to the University of Southern Mississippi for a scholarship program with a preference for deserving African-American students. What made this gift so remarkable is that McCarty saved the money from her lifelong job washing and ironing clothes. Alphonse Fletcher, Jr., a thirty-eight-year-old Wall Street money manager, made headlines when he pledged $50 million in recognition of the fiftieth anniversary of *Brown v. Board of Education*. At age twenty-eight, he previously made a gift of $4.5 million to Harvard University, his alma mater.

The efforts of African Americans to help themselves have been advanced or hindered by the funding priorities of wealthy white philanthropists and foundations. Of the thousands of foundations that have been created in the United States, only a few have had a sustained interest in social justice and equality for black Americans. Like the evolution of black philanthropy, white foundations have awarded or declined support for projects based, in part, on the social norms and values that were accepted at a given time.

A new development has been the interest of some foundations—Charles Stewart Mott, Ford, Rockefeller Brothers Fund, Carnegie Mellon, and W. K. Kellogg—in championing the importance of supporting ethnic- and gender-based philanthropy, including black philanthropy.

The diverse mix of approaches that African Americans have developed indicates that black philanthropy will remain an important vehicle through which the community will continue to help itself and others. America's changing demographics and unprecedented intergenerational wealth transfer, conservatively estimated at $41 trillion, will only magnify black philanthropy's importance.

See also Bureau of Refugees, Freedmen, and Abandoned Lands; Father Divine; Hall, Prince; Hampton Institute; Mutual Aid Societies; Tuskegee University; Underground Railroad; United Negro College Fund

■ ■ *Bibliography*

Carson, Emmett D. "The Evolution of Black Philanthropy: Patterns of Giving and Voluntarism." In *Philanthropic Giving: Studies in Varieties and Goals*, pp. 92–102. New York: Oxford University Press, 1989.

Carson, Emmett D. "Patterns of Giving in Black Churches." In *Faith and Philanthropy in America*, pp. 232–252. San Francisco: Jossey Bass, 1990.

Carson, Emmett D. *A Hand Up: Black Philanthropy and Self-Help in America*. Washington, D.C.: Joint Center for Political Studies, 1993.

Dillard, Jems Hardy, et al. *Twenty Year Report of the Phelps-Stokes Fund, 1911–1931*. New York: Phelps-Stokes Fund, 1932.

Embree, Edwin R., and Julia Waxman. *Investment in People: The Story of the Julius Rosenwald Fund*. New York: Harper & Row, 1949.

Harris, Robert L., Jr. "Early Black Benevolent Societies, 1780–1830." *Massachusetts Review* (autumn 1979): 603–625.

Jones, Thomas Jesse. *Educational Adaptations: Report of Ten Years' Work of the Phelps-Stokes Fund, 1910–1920.* New York: Phelps-Stokes Fund, 1920.

Magat, Richard. *The Ford Foundation at Work: Philanthropic Choices, Methods, and Styles.* New York: Plenum Press, 1979.

Nielsen, Waldemar A. *The Big Foundations.* New York: Columbia University Press, 1972.

Rhind, Flora M., and Barry Bingham. "Philanthropic Foundations and the Problem of Race." In *U.S. Philanthropic Foundations: Their History, Structure, Management, and Record.* New York: Harper & Row, 1967.

Rimer, Sara. "$50 Million Gift Aims to Build on Legacy of Brown v. Board." *New York Times* (May 18, 2004): A23.

Stanfield, John H. *Philanthropy and Jim Crow in American Social Science.* Westport, Conn.: Greenwood Press, 1985.

Willie, Charles V. "Philanthropic and Foundation Support for Blacks: A Case Study from the 1960s." *Journal of Negro Education* 50 (1981): 270–284.

EMMETT D. CARSON (1996)
Updated by author 2005

PHILLIPS, CARYL

MARCH 13, 1958

▌▌▌────────────────────

A cursory glance at Caryl Phillips's biography suffices to understand why such notions as "home," belonging, and unbelonging are central to his writing. Phillips was born in St. Kitts, in the eastern Caribbean, to parents with roots in Africa but also in Madeira and India. When he was only twelve weeks old, his family moved to Leeds, in northern England, and his childhood was spent in mostly white, working-class areas, where he and his three younger brothers were often the only black children. In 1979 Phillips graduated from Oxford—yet another facet to an already complex background—and almost immediately afterwards he started on a successful, peripatetic writing and academic career that has taken him all over the world, including a position as a professor of English at Yale University. Though based in New York City, he still frequently goes to St. Kitts and to England—particularly London—two islands that remain essential pieces in his identity puzzle.

Phillips's work is, like his life, marked by complexity and plurality. If Phillips is now mainly known for his wide-ranging essays and above all for his award-winning novels, it is worth noting that his first published books were plays, *Strange Fruit* (1981), *Where There Is Darkness* (1982), and *The Shelter* (1984), which concentrate on issues of race, class, and gender, and, like all dramatic writing, give pride of place to individual experiences and voices. These indeed remain major preoccupations in Phillips's novels, though always set against a well-researched historical and social background that has been either neglected or misrepresented in traditional historiography. Whereas his first novel, *The Final Passage* (1985), focuses on individuals who were part of the Caribbean exodus to Britain in the 1950s, his second work of fiction, *A State of Independence* (1986), explores the plight of a returnee who decides to go back to his native West Indies after living in England for some twenty years.

Slavery is another major historical episode that Phillips revisits almost obsessively in his next three works of fiction because he regards "the peculiar institution" as a founding event of modern societies both in Europe and the New World, explaining at once their heterogeneous population but also their inherent racism and their exclusion of the other, whether black, female, or Jewish. This is perhaps best suggested in *Higher Ground* (1989), his third novel, which puts side by side the story of an eighteenth-century African interpreter who assists the slave traders in their gruesome transactions, the prison narrative of a young African American in the 1960s, and the sad tale of a young Jewish woman whose exile in postwar London leaves her mentally vulnerable. His fourth work of fiction, *Cambridge* (1991), mostly set in the nineteenth-century Caribbean, takes a closer look at the ironies of plantation societies from the contrasted yet intertwined points of view of a white female planter and a black male slave, while his next novel, *Crossing the River* (1993), explores the history of the African diaspora through the stories of three African children sold into slavery by their father in the eighteenth century. While dispersed in time and space, Nash, Martha, and Travis are nonetheless bound by the love of their guilty father, who eventually regards Travis's wife, a white Englishwoman, as one of his own diasporic children.

A similar gesture of inclusion can be found in *The Nature of Blood* (1997), a novel in which Phillips brings together the African and Jewish diasporas, juxtaposing the exclusion suffered by Jews in fifteenth-century Venice and during the Holocaust with the narratives of an Othello-like figure and a black Jew in contemporary Israel. Clearly, Phillips's repeated and formally daring exploration of an often forgotten past is not gratuitous. Not only is it meant to trigger reflection on human nature, on man's divisive instinct as well as on his need for company, but it also compellingly demonstrates the crucial role played by the past in shaping the present, which is likewise the message of *A Distant Shore* (2003), in spite of its contemporary setting. This subtle novel, which earned Phillips many awards, follows Dorothy, a newly retired English teacher, and Solomon, an African refugee, whose paths cross in an England refusing to come to terms with its changing humanscape. Phillips's novel *Dancing in the Dark* (2005) focuses on an actual figure of the African diaspora, Caribbean-born Broadway entertainer Bert Williams, who lived at the turn of the twentieth century. Though not a slave himself, Bert is victim of "performative bondage." Like many other Phillipsian characters, he bears the burden of the slavery past.

Many of the issues tackled in Phillips's fiction are present in his nonfiction, which can be regarded as a political blueprint for his creative imagination. Phillips is the author of three book-length essays, often with an autobiographical slant: *The European Tribe* (1987), *The Atlantic Sound* (2000), and *A New World Order* (2001). While the first one views Europe through the eyes of the young writer who is both of and not of the Old Continent, the other two dwell, like his novels, on the suffering but also the human richness that goes into the making of the transatlantic identity.

See also Literature of the English-Speaking Caribbean

■ ■ *Bibliography*

Clingman, Stephen. "Forms of History and Identity in *The Nature of Blood*." *Salmagundi* 143 (summer 2004): 141–165.

Ledent, Bénédicte. *Caryl Phillips*. Manchester and New York: Manchester University Press, 2002.

Yelin, Louise. "Caryl Phillips." In *British Writers*, edited by George Stade and Sarah Hannah Goldstein, pp. 379–394. New York: Scribner's, 1999.

BÉNÉDICTE LEDENT (2005)

PHILLIPS-GAY, JANE

NOVEMBER 2, 1913
FEBRUARY 21, 1994

▬▮▬▮▬▮▬▬▬▬▬▬

Jane Phillips-Gay, Order of Roraima (OR), was one of the first African-Guyanese women to enter the British Guiana legislature. Phillips-Gay was also a trade unionist and an ordained Baptist minister. She attended Georgetown's St. Ambrose Primary, Brickdam Roman Catholic, Christ Church Anglican, and the Collegiate School from 1918 to 1930. She married Ivan Gay on December 30, 1942.

Phillips-Gay became involved in trade union activities in the 1940s and was closely associated with Dr. Joseph Prayag Lachmansingh, a champion of sugar workers in their struggles against colonial planters and officials. In 1946 the Guiana Industrial Workers Union (GIWU) was formed, and two years later, in 1948, Phillips-Gay became the assistant general secretary. She was actively involved in the strike of 1948, now commemorated as Enmore Martyrs' Day for the sugar workers who were killed for their protest actions. One year later, in 1949, she rose to the rank of secretary of the union. Trade union activism enabled her to become popular among sugar workers and proved valuable to her career as a politician.

Phillips-Gay was a member of the first women's political organization in British Guiana, the Women's Political and Economic Organization (WPEO), formed in 1946. The organization was active in the struggle for equal opportunities for women and for their employment. As a member of the People's Progressive Party (PPP), formed in 1947 by Forbes Burnham and Dr. Cheddi B. Jagan, she contested the colony's 1953 general elections. Although along with two other women, Jessica Burnham and Janet Jagan, Phillips-Gay was successful in her electoral bid, the PPP did not appoint any of the women to ministerial positions. By the time of the general elections in 1957, the PPP had split, and Phillips-Gay, as a member of what became known as the People's National Congress (PNC), founded by Burnham, unsuccessfully contested the East Demerara electoral seat. On October 5, 1957, Phillips-Gay became a founding member of the Women's Auxiliary of the PNC. In both the 1961 and 1964 general elections, she was an unsuccessful candidate for the legislature.

In addition to her involvement with the struggles of sugar workers and women, Phillips-Gay was also concerned with the conditions of children and worked on behalf of the unemployed and the underpaid. In her capacity as chairperson of the Women's Auxiliary, her contributions to public service included organizing social and cultural events for inmates of the Palms, a government-run home for aged and indigent persons. She was awarded the national honor, Order of Roraima.

See also People's National Congress; Politics: Women and Politics in Latin America and the Caribbean

■ ■ *Bibliography*

Chase, Ashton. *A History of Trade Unionism in Guyana, 1900–1961*. Georgetown, Guyana: New Guyana Company, 1966.

George, Keith George. "Jane Phillips-Gay, Activist." In *The African-Guyanese Achievement 1: 18. 155th Anniversary of African Slave Emancipation*. Georgetown, Guyana: Free Press, 1993.

"Outstanding African Guyanese, Jane Phillips-Gay, OR." In *Emancipation: The African-Guyanese Magazine* 1, no. 18 (2000–2001).

Who Is Who in British Guiana, 1945–1948. Georgetown, British Guiana: *Daily Chronicle*, 1948.

Woolford, Hazel M. "Women in Guyanese Politics, 1812–1964." In *Themes in African-Guyanese History*, edited by Winston F. McGowan, James G. Rose, and David A. Granger. Georgetown, Guyana: Free Press, 1998.

BARBARA P. JOSIAH (2005)

PHOTOGRAPHY

▪▪▪

This entry has two unique essays about the same topic, differing mainly in their geographical focus.

DIASPORIC PHOTOGRAPHY
Isolde Brielmaier

PHOTOGRAPHY, U.S.
Deborah Willis

DIASPORIC PHOTOGRAPHY

Not long after its invention in 1840, photography was taken up by practitioners throughout the African diaspora. From Africa to Cuba, in Europe and the United States, photographers of African backgrounds used the camera to document their surroundings both for official purposes and to create personalized portraits and artistic works. African diasporic photography, therefore, has an extensive history and forms an important and rich tradition within the practice of photography in general.

AFRICAN PHOTOGRAPHY IN THE NINETEENTH CENTURY

One of the first photographers in West Africa was actually an African-American. Augustus Washington (1820/21–1875) was said to have worked in both the United States and Liberia. In 1857, the *New Era*, a newspaper in Sierra Leone, announced his arrival as a daguerreotypist new to Freetown, the capital. By the 1880s the Freetown newspapers were filled with advertisements for studio equipment and photographic supplies and services, as well as requests for photographers.

Alphonso Lisk-Carew (1887–1969) was another early photographer of the African Diaspora. Lisk-Carew was a Creole man who began his work in Sierra Leone in 1905. He established one of the most successful studios in Free-town and, together with the assistance of his younger brother Arthur, tailored his services to both the city's Creole and European communities. Lisk-Carew created a range of images in Freetown, including portraits of the city's established and more notable members of society. These images were often reminiscent of Victorian portraits from Europe, with their subjects appearing in stiff, frontal poses and pictured neatly positioned and seated in outdoor settings such as porches and gardens. Lisk-Carew also took photographs at ceremonies and events and during his travels into the interior of Sierra Leone and Liberia. Many of these photographs were featured in picture postcards that were created for colonial markets and the tourist trade in Africa. Other early photographers of African backgrounds who worked in Africa include Gerhardt L. Lutterodt, who worked in Ghana; N. Walwin Holm (b. 1865), who founded a studio in Accra, Ghana in 1882; and George S.A. da Costa, who was born in Lagos, Nigeria, in 1853 and became a well-known professional photographers in that city in 1895.

TWENTIETH-CENTURY AFRICAN PHOTOGRAPHERS

By the early 1900s, many African photographers had established studios in cities throughout the continent. Unlike the early practitioners who preceded them, these photographers catered almost exclusively to local African customers. Meïssa Gaye (1892–1982) was a Guinean portrait photographer active in Dakar and St. Louis, Senegal. In 1945, Gaye opened and operated the Tropical Photo Studio in St. Louis. Salla Casset (1910–1974) was also a popular portrait photographer in Dakar during the 1940s and 1950s.

In Bamako, Mali, Seydou Keïta (1923–2001) operated a highly successful photography studio from approximately 1949 up until he retired in 1977. Keïta won renown for his elaborate portraits, which featured his fashionable patrons seated before richly patterned textiles that framed the images and toned down the sense of three-dimensional space behind the sitter. Patrons worked together with Keïta to create portraits that best reflected how they saw themselves. Accordingly, they often appeared holding or leaning on props—such as a car, a musical instrument, or a sewing machine—alluding to a certain profession or signaling a desire to attain a specific status. Keïta's portraits were often viewed and appreciated by his patrons within their homes. The Malian photographer Malick Sidibé (b. 1936) established Studio Malick in 1962. Many of his photographs focus on the young people of Bamako. Throughout his career, Sidibé attended social gatherings such as parties, weddings, and dances, taking photographs of peo-

Malian Men with Musical Instruments. *Photograph by Seydou Keïta.* © CONTEMPORARY AFRICAN ART COLLECTION LIMITED/CORBIS

ple participating in a variety of leisure activities in public spaces.

In the eastern region of the African continent, photographers of South Asian descent—who were by this time second- and third-generation Kenyans and Tanzanians—had also established studios. One of these photographers, Narayandas Vithaldas Parekh, operated the popular Parekh Studio in Mombasa, Kenya, from the late 1940s up until 1982. Parekh worked with African clients from a range of ethnic and social backgrounds to create portraits that incorporate elements of Hinduism, international fashion, European photo manual techniques, and the lighting and poses of Indian film.

During the 1950s and 1960s, photography also played a critical role in journalism in Africa. Both before and after many countries had attained independence, staff writers and photographers at various newspapers in cities such as Nairobi, Lagos, and particularly Johannesburg, began to use photography as a way of documenting rapidly changing cultural and political situations. In the 1950s, black photojournalists in South Africa such as Robert "Bob" Gosani (1934–1972) and Peter Magubane (b. 1932) gained greater access to photography. These photographers were integral in documenting daily life and events in South Africa for local newspapers and popular publications such as the black urban magazine, *Drum*. They produced exten-

sive visual accounts of South Africa's changing political climate and the country's long fight against apartheid.

PHOTOGRAPHY THROUGHOUT THE AFRICAN DIASPORA

Across the Atlantic Ocean in Brazil and Cuba—countries with sizeable African populations—the practice of photography developed along its own trajectory. In late-nineteenth-century Brazil, most of the early photographers (and the viewers of photography) were of European origin. Individual and group portraits of wealthy European residents were common at this time. However, by the early 1900s, with growing urbanization and a developing middle class in Brazilian cities such as São Paulo, the audience for photography broadened. A range of illustrated magazines, such as *Revista da Semana* (1900) and *Illustração Brasileira* (1901), began to feature photographs. Over a decade later, in the 1920s, the photo club movement began in Rio with a growing and largely middle-class membership of amateur photographers. By the 1940s this movement had spread to São Paulo. In the early 1950s, Brazil also saw the rise of photojournalism, particularly as the photography magazine *O Cruzeiro* (launched in 1928) experienced tremendous growth, reaching a circulation of over 700,000 by the end of the decade. Over the next several decades, from the 1960s to the 1980s, the profile of photography and photographers became more visible with the emergence of several additional publications and public exhibitions. The interest of art museums, scholars, and critics also turned to photography, including the first inclusion of Brazilian photography in the International Biennale of São Paulo.

While many of the recognized practitioners of Brazilian photography were still of European origin and middle-class backgrounds, by the 1970s the subject matter of photographic images began to diversify. In 1978, in Bahia (a northern state of Brazil with the country's largest population of African descent), a photographer named Artistides Alves presented the exhibition *Fotobahia,* which eventually led to the informal establishment of Grupo de Fotógrafos da Bahia. This organization was established to present the work of contemporary photographers and provide opportunities for emerging photographers in the region. One of their strategies was to mount exhibitions on the beaches and streets. After gaining official recognition from the Cultural Foundation of the State of Bahia, the group elected Maria Sampaio and Célia Aguiar as its coordinators and changed its name to Nucleus of Photography in 1987. Working to train young photographers and provide technical support and exhibition venues, Nucleus of Photography tried to open up the arena of photography for wider participation by diverse peoples by gaining access to what had previously been more elite and widely inaccessible institutions.

Since the 1990s, greater attention has been allotted to Brazilian photographers from African backgrounds. One such important photographer is Bauer Sá (b. 1950) who has explored the relationship of black people in his native Salvador, Brazil, to African-based religions of the region. Other Afro-Brazilian photographers receiving international attention include Walter Firmo (b. 1937); Denise Camargo (b. 1964), editor-in-chief of the photography magazine *Iris,* and Carla Osório (b. 1972), whose exhibition *Black People in Espirito Santo* garnered critical acclaim during the first National Black Arts Festival in 1995.

Photographers of the African diaspora in Europe, the Caribbean, and the United States continue to use traditional photographic conventions while also experimenting with other approaches in order to produce more artistic works. Many of these photographers have found themselves uprooted. They have migrated, been displaced, were born overseas, or have chosen to train and work outside of their native countries, and they have often looked to photography as a creative means to address, question, and explore issues of identity, self-definition, and memory. David Damoison (b. 1963), whose mother is French and whose father is from Martinique, has focused his photographic work on documenting black life throughout the Caribbean. The Afro-Cuban photographer René Peña Gonzales (b. 1957) has spent his career creating surrealistic images of daily scenes in his native Cuba. The Jamaican photographer Rose-Ann Marie Bailey (b. 1971) has drawn upon her intense interest in light and texture to create photographs that explore the culture and history of her people.

From the 1990s onward, photography of the African diaspora has received widespread attention within both institutional and commercial contexts in the United States and Europe. Since the first image by Seydou Keïta was displayed in 1990 at New York's Museum for African Art (attributed to an "unknown photographer"), interest in photography by African peoples and people of African descent has increased steadily. In 1995 and 1996, the Nigerian curator Okwui Enwezor mounted *In/Sight: African Photographers, 1940 to the Present* at the Solomon R. Guggenheim Museum in New York City—the first exhibition ever of African photographers in the United States. Several related exhibitions followed, including a solo show of portrait photographs by Seydou Keïta at the National Museum of African Art in Washington D.C. In 1991 the Paris-based organization Éditions Revue Noire began producing literature on African and African diasporic photography. The

organization continues to serve as an invaluable archive and resource of images, original documents, and other important information on the topic. University scholars and museum curators have also begun to generate more indepth research on individual photographers.

CONTEMPORARY PHOTOGRAPHERS

Since the mid-1990s, galleries throughout Europe and the United States have also displayed the work of African photographers within a commercial context. Gallery exhibitions include the presentation of works by Keïta and Sidibé of Mali, Zwelethu Mthethwa (b. 1965) of South Africa, and Samuel Fosso (b. 1962) of the Central African Republic. Prominent photographers of the diaspora who have received critical attention since 1990 also include the Nigerian Rotimi Fani-Kayodé (1955–1989) who worked in London and was one of the founding members of Autograph, the Association of Black English Photographers, as well as several Brazilian photographers, including Charles Silva Duarte (b. 1965) and Eustáquio Neves (b. 1955). The public attention received by these artists has been central in bringing about a greater awareness of the important and varied tradition of photography as it is practiced throughout the African diaspora.

See also African Diaspora; Photography, U.S.

■ ■ *Bibliography*

Bell, Clare, Okwui Enwezor, et al. *In/Sight: African Photographers, 1940 to the Present.* Exhibition Catalogue. New York: Solomon R. Guggenheim Museum, 1995.

Carvalho, Maria Luiza Melo, comp. *Novas Travessias: Contemporary Brazilian Photography.* New York: Verso, 1996.

Éditions Revue Noire. *Anthology of African and Indian Ocean Photography.* Paris: Éditions Revue Noire, 1999.

Jenkins, Gareth, ed. *Havana in My Heart: 75 Years of Cuban Photography.* Chicago: Chicago Review Press, 2002.

Lumanière, Michelle. *You Look Beautiful Like That: The Portrait Photographs of Seydou Keïta and Malick Sidibé.* New Haven, Conn.: Yale University Press, 2001.

Magnin, André. *Seydou Keïta.* Zurich and New York: Scalo, 1997.

Magnin, André. *Malick Sidibé.* Zurich and New York: Scalo, 1998.

Miessgang, Thomas, and Barbara Schroder. *Flash Afrique: Photography from West Africa.* Vienna: Kunsthalle, 2002.

Ward, Viditz Vera. "Alfonso Lisk-Carew: Creole Photographer." *African Arts* 19, no. 1 (November 1985): 46–51, 88.

Wride, Tim B. *Shifting Tides: Cuban Photography after the Revolution.* Los Angeles: Los Angeles County Museum of Art and Merrell Publishers, 2001.

ISOLDE BRIELMAIER (2005)

PHOTOGRAPHY, U.S.

African Americans shaped the practice of photography from its origin in 1840 and have participated in its history as practitioners and subjects. The larger American public was fascinated with the daguerreotype as soon as Louis-Jacques-Mandé Daguerre (1787–1851) publicized the process in France in 1839. The French inventor Nicéphore Niépce (1765–1833) produced the earliest extant photographic image made by a camera obscura in 1827. After the death of Niépce, Daguerre successfully fixed an image and in January 1839 announced to the Paris press his discovery, which he named the *daguerreotype*. Six months after the public announcement of the process in Paris, Jules Lion, a free man of color, a lithographer, and portrait painter, exhibited the first successful daguerreotypes in New Orleans.

The African-American public was enthusiastic about Daguerre's process of making likenesses (which we now call photographs). These were numerous free black men and women who established themselves as daguerreans, photographers, inventors, artists, and artisans who had gained local and national recognition in their respective cities. Portraits of prominent and lesser-known African Americans were produced regularly in galleries and studios throughout the country. The portraits of well-known African Americans soon became popular, and the practice of private photography—the photographing of individuals for personal collections and albums—became more and more the artistic method for creating a likeness. Most of the photographs taken at this time were not intended for publication or public presentation, but noted citizens and other families from all walks of life thought it important to have their likenesses preserved for posterity.

During most of photography's early history, images produced by African-American photographers presented idealized glimpses of family members in romanticized or dramatic settings. Photographers such as C. M. Battey and James VanDerZee sought to integrate elements of romanticism and classicism, as did the painters of the previous centuries. Most photographs taken in the early years were made to commemorate a special occasion in the sitter's life—such as marriage, birth, graduation, confirmation, and anniversaries—or the achievement of a particular social or political success.

One of the earliest known photographical studies in America of African-American physiognomy was conducted in 1850 by Harvard scientist Louis Agassiz and J. T. Zealy, a white daguerreotypist in Columbia, South Carolina. The latter was hired to take a series of portraits of African-born slaves on nearby plantations. The daguerreo-types were anatomical studies of the faces and the nude upper bodies of African men and women. The photographs were to give visual evidence of the "natural difference in size of limbs, heads, and configurations of muscles," thereby establishing a theory that blacks were different and inferior. Much of the work of nineteenth-century black photographers was in sharp contrast to these scientific and stereotypical images.

The first publicized exhibition of a work by a black photographer was held on March 15, 1840, in the Hall of the St. Charles Museum in the city of New Orleans. The exhibition, reported to have drawn a large crowd, was organized and sponsored by the artist Jules Lion. In 1854 Glenalvin Goodridge, a black photographer from York, Pennsylvania, won the prize for "best ambrotypes" (a process using a wet plate) at the York County fair. Other black photographers who won distinction in the nineteenth century at exhibitions and expositions include James Presley Ball, who exhibited his daguerreotypes in 1855 at the Ohio Mechanics Annual Exhibition, and Harry Shepherd, who won the first prize at the 1891 Minnesota State fair and later exhibited photographs of the Tuskegee Institute (now University) at the Paris Exposition in 1900. In 1895 Daniel Freeman, known as the first black photographer in Washington, D.C., exhibited his works in the Negro Building at the 1895 Atlanta Exposition.

Between the end of the Civil War and the turn of the twentieth century, numerous itinerant photographers flourished in the North. But even earlier several African-American photographers were able to open their own studios. In the 1840s and 1850s James Ball and Augustus Washington (1820–?) operated galleries in Cincinnati, Ohio, and Hartford, Connecticut; Jules Lion had his own studio in New Orleans. (Ball and Washington were active abolitionists who often used their photographic skills to expose the inhumane institution of slavery and promote the abolitionist movement.) Harry Shepherd opened his first portrait gallery in St. Paul, Minnesota, in 1887, where he employed eight attendants. He advertised that "his patrons are among all classes—from the millionaires to day wage workers." Shepherd was one of the few African-American members of the National Photographers Association of America.

Fanny J. Thompson, a musician and composer living in Memphis, Tennessee, in the 1880s, studied photography and was one of the first to record African-American women working in the field. The Goodridge brothers—Glenalvin, Wallace, and William—began their careers in York, Pennsylvania, in the 1850s before settling in East Saginaw, Michigan, in 1866. They opened their first studio the following year. In 1884 they were commissioned by the

U.S. Department of Forestry to photograph views of the Saginaw Valley woodlands.

At the turn of the century photography expanded in a variety of ways. Newspapers, journals, and books published photographic images. Courses in photography were offered in schools and colleges, and correspondence courses were also available. C. M. Battey, an accomplished portraitist and fine-art photographer, was a noted educator in photography. Battey founded the Photography Division at Tuskegee Institute in Alabama in 1916. In 1917 *Crisis* magazine highlighted Battey in the "Men of the Month" column as "one of the few colored photographers who has gained real artistic success." Battey did the most extensive portrait series of African-American leaders produced in the nineteenth century and early twentieth centuries. His photographic portraits of John Mercer Langston, Frederick Douglass, W. E. B. Du Bois, Booker T. Washington, and Paul Laurence Dunbar were sold nationally and were reproduced on postcards and posters.

From 1900 to 1919 African-American photographers flourished in larger cities, producing images of both rural and urban experiences. They included Arthur Bedou (1882–1966) of New Orleans; King Daniel Ganaway (1883–?) of Chicago, who in 1918 received first prize in the John Wanamaker Annual Exhibition of photographers; and Arthur Laidler Macbeth (1864–?) of Charlestown, South Carolina, Baltimore, and Norfolk. Macbeth won many awards and citations for his photographs and was among the pioneers in motion pictures. He invented "Macbeth's Daylight Projecting Screen" for showing stereopticon and moving pictures in the daytime.

In 1911 Addison Scurlock, who was Howard University's official photographer, opened a studio in Washington, D.C., which he operated with his wife and sons, Robert and George, until 1964; after that time his sons continued to operate the studio. In New York City James VanDerZee, undoubtedly the best known of black studio photographers, began capturing the spirit and life of New York's Harlem in the 1920s and continued to do so for more than fifty years.

During the period of the Harlem Renaissance through the Great Depression and the New Deal, photographers began to exhibit their work widely in their communities. In the 1920s young black photographers who viewed themselves as artists moved to the larger cities in search of education, patronage, and support for their art. Harlem was a cultural mecca for many of these photographers. In 1921 the New York Public Library's 135th Street branch in Manhattan (now known as the Schomburg Center for Research in Black Culture) organized its first exhibition of work by black artists, titled "The Negro Artists." Two pho-

African American Photographers Guild

Designed to celebrate those contributions made by African Americans in the field of photography, the African American Photographers Guild (AAPG) is also devoted to providing an environment for African Americans wishing to learn about photography. Levels of expertise of the members vary; some are established professionals, while others are intrigued by, or just discovering, the craft. The program is mainly committed to fostering excellence in photography and documenting the culture and experience of African Americans. Work by professional African-American photographers and photo hobbyists are promoted through sponsored exhibitions and publications.

AAPG also helps emphasize the historical significance of African Americans in the field of photography and informs the public of how valuable and creative a medium of expression it can be. On its Web site (www.aapguild.org) are listings of African-American photographers from the 1840s to the present, an instructional site for the amateur and professional photographer, discussion and mailing lists, and chat rooms. The AAPG is open to all commercial, freelance, and newspaper photographers.

tographers, C. M. Battey and Lucy Calloway of New York, displayed six photographs in this exhibition of over sixty-five works of art. The Harmon Foundation was one of the first philanthropic organizations to give attention, cash awards, and exhibition opportunities to black photographers. These awards came to be known as the William E. Harmon Awards for Distinguished Achievement Among Negroes. In 1930 a special prize of $50 for photographic work was added in the name of the Commission on Race Relations.

A year earlier, James Latimer Allen (1907–1977) exhibited his portraits of African-American men, women, and children in a Harmon Foundation exhibition. Allen also photographed such writers of the period as Alain Locke, Langston Hughes, Countee Cullen, and Claude

McKay. Other photographers active between 1920 and 1940 included several students of C. M. Battey, among them Elise Forrest Harleston (1891–1970) of Charleston, South Carolina, and P. H. Polk (1898–1985) of Tuskegee, Alabama. Harleston opened a photography studio with her painter husband, Edwin Harleston, after studying with Battey in 1922. Polk opened his first studio at Tuskegee in 1927. The following year he was appointed to the faculty of Tuskegee Institute's photography department, photographed prominent visitors such as Mary McLeod Bethune and Paul Robeson, and made extensive portraits of scientist-inventor George Washington Carver. Richard S. Roberts (1881–1936) of Columbia, South Carolina, began studying photography through correspondence courses and specialist journals, and opened his studio in the early 1920s. According to Roberts's advertisements, his studio took superior photographs by day or night. Twin brothers Morgan (1910–1993) and Marvin Smith (1910–) were prolific photographers in Harlem in the 1930s and early 1940s. They photographed members of the community, as well as political rallies, bread lines during the Great Depression, families, and "Lindy Hoppers" in the Savoy Ballroom.

During the Depression, numerous images were taken of the lives of African Americans. The Resettlement Administration, later known as the Farm Security Administration (FSA), was created in 1935 as an independent coordinating agency; it inherited rural relief activities and land-use administration from the Department of the Interior, the Federal Emergency Relief Administration, and the Agricultural Adjustment Administration. From 1935 to 1943 the FSA photography project generated 270,000 images of rural, urban, and industrial America. Many of the heavily documented activities of the FSA were of black migrant workers in the South. In 1937 Gordon Parks Sr. decided that he wanted to be a photographer after viewing the work of the Farm Security Administration photographers. He was hired by the FSA in 1941, and during World War II he worked as an Office of War Information correspondent. After the war he was a photographer for Standard Oil Company. In 1949 he became the first African-American photographer to work on the staff of *Life* magazine.

Roy DeCarava is the forerunner of contemporary urban photography. He studied art at Cooper Union in New York City, the Works Progress Administration's Harlem Art Center, and the George Washington Carver Art School. In 1955 DeCarava collaborated with Langston Hughes in producing a book titled *The Sweet Flypaper of Life,* which depicted the life of a black family in Harlem. In 1952 DeCarava became one of the first black photogra-

phers to receive a Guggenheim Fellowship. In 1954 he founded a photography gallery that became one of the first galleries in the United States devoted to the exhibition and sale of photography as a fine art. DeCarava founded the Kamoinge Workshop for black photographers in 1963.

From the 1930s through the 1960s photographers began working as photojournalists for local newspapers and national magazines marketed to African-American audiences, including *Our World, Ebony, Jet, Sepia,* and *Flash,* among others. Only a few African-American photojournalists, most notably Gordon Parks Sr., Richard Saunders, Bert Miles, and Roy DeCarava, were employed for the larger picture magazines such as *Life, Look, Time, Newsweek,* and *Sports Illustrated.* Most of them learned photography while in the military and studied photography in schools of journalism.

This period also encompassed the beginning of reportage and the documentation of public pageantry and events. In the 1930s smaller handheld cameras and faster films aided photographers in expressing their frustration and discontent with social and political conditions within their communities. The civil rights movement was well documented by photographers such as Moneta Sleet Jr. (New York and Chicago), Jack T. Franklin (Philadelphia), Charles "Teenie" Harris (Pittsburgh), Howard Morehead (Los Angeles), Bertrand Miles (New York), Austin Hansen (New York), and U.S. Information Service Agency photographers Richard Saunders and Griffith Davis.

From 1935 to the early 1990s musical pioneers were the frequent subjects of Chuck Stewart (1927–), Milt Hinton, Roy DeCarava, and Bert Andrews (1931–1993), who photographed performing artists in the studio, onstage, and in nightclubs. Hinton received his first camera in 1935 while he was playing in Cab Calloway's band. As a jazz bassist and photographer, Hinton photographed his musician friends and colleagues. In 1950 Chuck Stewart, who studied photography at Ohio University, began photographing jazz musicians and vocalists onstage and in his studio in New York City. His photographs were used for album covers, publicity stills, and illustrations for books and articles of jazz. Stewart photographed virtually every well-known musician and vocalist from 1950 to 1990; his coverage includes blues, bebop, fusion, salsa, and popular music. Bert Andrews photographed black theatrical productions on and off Broadway from the early 1960s through the early 1990s. Among the production companies whose plays he photographed are the Negro Ensemble Company, the New Federal Theatre, and the Frank Silvera Writers' Workshop.

During the active years of the civil rights and Black Power movements—the early 1960s through the 1970s—a significant number of socially committed men and women became photographers, documenting the struggles, achievements, and tragedies of the freedom movement. Student Non-Violent Coordinating Committee (SNCC) photographers Doug Harris, Elaine Tomlin, and Bob Fletcher were in the forefront in documenting the voter registration drives in the South; Robert Sengstacke, Howard Bingham, Jeffrey Scales, and Brent Jones photographed the activities of the Black Panther Party and desegregation rallies in the North and on the West Coast. From 1969 to 1986 six African-American photographers received the coveted Pulitzer Prize in photography. The first was Moneta Sleet Jr. in 1969 for his photograph of Coretta Scott King and her daughter at the funeral of Rev. Dr. Martin Luther King Jr. Following in subsequent years were Ovie Carter (1975) for international reporting for his photographs of famine in Africa and India; Matthew Lewis (1975) for his portrait studies of Washingtonians; John White (1982) for work published in the *Chicago Sun-Times*; Michel Du Cille (1985) for the photographs of the Colombian earthquake; and Ozier Muhammad (1985) for international reporting for the photographic essay "Africa: The Desperate Continent."

In the 1970s universities and art colleges began to offer undergraduate and graduate degrees in photography, and African-American photographers began studying photography and creating works for exhibition purposes. Others studied in community centers and workshops. The symbolic and expressive images of the works produced in the 1980s and 1990s offer sociological and psychological insights into the past, as well as examinations of contemporary social themes, such as racism, unemployment, child and sexual abuse, and death and dying. Most of these works are informed by personal experiences. Significant contributors to the development of this genre are Albert Chong, Hank Sloane Thomas, Roland Freeman, Todd Gray, Chester Higgins, Lynn Marshall-Linnemeier, Deborah Jack, Jeffrey Scales, Coreen Simpson, Lorna Simpson, Elisabeth Sunday, Christian Walker, Carrie Mae Weems, Carla Williams, and Pat Ward Williams.

Many of the photographers working in the early twenty-first century explore social issues that reflect or respond to politics, culture, family, and collective history. The issues addressed in contemporary photography create a revised interpretation of the visual experience through digital technology, using genres including portraiture, landscape, and documentary photography.

See also Harlem Renaissance; Parks, Gordon; Photography, Diasporic; VanDerZee, James

■ ■ *Bibliography*

Coar, Valencia Hollins. *A Century of Black Photographers: 1840–1960*. Providence: Rhode Island School of Design, 1983.

Crawford, Joe. *The Black Photographers Annual*, 4 vols. New York: Author, 1972–1980.

DeCarava, Roy, and Langston Hughes. *The Sweet Flypaper of Life* (1955). Reprint, Washington, D.C.: Howard University Press, 1984.

Parks, Gordon. *A Choice of Weapons*. New York: Harper, 1966.

Parks, Gordon. *Born Black*. Philadelphia: Lippincott, 1971.

Parks, Gordon. *Moments Without Proper Names*. New York: Viking, 1975.

Willis-Thomas, Deborah. *Black Photographers, 1840–1940: An Illustrated Bio-Bibliography*. New York: Garland, 1985.

Willis-Thomas, Deborah. *Black Photographers, 1940–1988: An Illustrated Bio-Bibliography*. New York and London: Garland, 1989.

Willis, Deborah, *Reflections in Black: A History of Black Photographers, 1840 to the Present*. New York: Norton, 2000.

DEBORAH WILLIS (1996)
Updated by publisher 2005

PHYLON

■ ■ ■

Phylon was a quarterly journal founded by W. E. B. Du-Bois, edited by him from 1940 to 1944, and published under the auspices of Atlanta University. The journal was designed to replace the school's earlier publications, which had initiated a more scientific approach to the study of race. Even though other institutions had used this approach and some scholars were adapting their works to it, it was still necessary to revisit and revise what had and was taking place relative to race in academia. The focus was to be cultural and historical rather than biological and psychological. The original editorial board and contributing editors included Ira DeAugustine Reid, William Stanley Braithwaite, Mercer Cook, Horace M. Bond, and Rayford W. Logan. While the articles were to be devoted to the social sciences, there were works by and about individuals and topics germane to the humanities. Literary issues were addressed by such critics as Arthur P. Davis, Nick Aaron Ford, and Hugh Gloster, and original poetry and fiction also were published, including work by authors such as Langston Hughes and Countee Cullen. The journal ceased publication in 1988.

Freedom's Odyssey: African American History Essays from Phylon (1999), edited by Alexa B. Henderson and Janis Sumler-Edmond, contains twenty-nine scholarly essays on African-American history that appeared in the journal. The topics include slave revolts, abolitionism, desegregation, and the civil rights movement.

See also Journalism; Literary Magazines; Quarles, Benjamin

■■ *Bibliography*

"Apology." *Phylon* 1 (1940): 3–5.

DeSantis, Christopher C. "Phylon." In *Oxford Companion to African American Literature,* edited by William L. Andrews, Francis Smith Foster, and Trudier Harris. New York: Oxford University Press, 1997.

Henderson, Alexa B., and Janis Sumler-Edmond, eds. *Freedom's Odyssey: African American History Essays from* Phylon. Atlanta, Ga.: Clark Atlanta University Press, 1999.

HELEN R. HOUSTON (2001)

PINCHBACK, P. B. S.

MAY 10, 1837
DECEMBER 21, 1921

Born free in Macon, Georgia, Pinckney Benton Stewart Pinchback, a politician, was the son of William Pinchback, a white planter, and Eliza Steward, his emancipated slave, who was of mixed blood. Along with his brothers and sisters, Pinchback was taken to Cincinnati to escape enslavement by his white relatives at his father's death. Denied any share of his father's estate, Pinchback went to work as a steward on a Mississippi riverboat. In 1862, during the early stages of the Civil War, he volunteered for the Union army in New Orleans and was assigned to recruit for the Corps d'Afrique and a cavalry company, where he protested the unequal treatment of African-American troops.

Pinchback played an important role in establishing the Republican Party in Louisiana following the war and was elected to the state's 1867 Constitutional Convention. He was president of the state senate in 1871 and served as lieutenant governor at the death of Oscar J. Dunn. He became acting governor during the impeachment of Governor Henry Clay Warmoth. Pinchback was an advocate of universal suffrage, civil rights, the legal suppression of discrimination, and tax-supported education. He moved away from the Radical Republicans in 1871 and supported the reelection of Ulysses S. Grant.

There was backing for Pinchback's own nomination for governor in 1872, but he withdrew in favor of W. P. Kellogg. Elected congressman-at-large, he also served as governor again and was then elected to the U.S. Senate. He was unseated when the election was contested, however. Under Governor F. T. Nicholls, Pinchback was ap-

pointed to the State Board of Education, where he was instrumental in founding Southern University. He became surveyor of customs at the port of New Orleans. Pinchback was a keen businessman, dealing in cotton, and a founder of the Mississippi River Packet Company. He was admitted to the bar in 1886.

Pinchback moved to New York City, then to Washington, D.C., in 1897, where he resumed his political career, supporting Booker T. Washington, and became a leader of the city's light-skinned social elite. He married Nina Hawthorne; they were the parents of six children. One grandson was Jean Toomer, the Harlem Renaissance novelist. Pinchback died in 1921 and was buried in New Orleans.

See also Politics in the United States

■■ *Bibliography*

Haskins, James. *Pinckney Benton Stewart Pinchback.* New York: Macmillan, 1973.

MICHEL FABRE (1996)

PINDLING, LYNDEN OSCAR

MARCH 22, 1930
AUGUST 26, 2000

Sir Lynden Oscar Pindling was hailed as a national hero in his native Bahamas and called the "Father of the Nation" by the former prime minister (1992–2002) Hubert Ingraham. Pindling was a "consummate politician" and leader, and he did more than anyone else to shape Bahamian society in the late twentieth century. He led the fight for black majority rule, served as the country's first prime minister, and was the "architect of Independence for the Commonwealth of The Bahamas" (Craton, 2002).

Pindling was in born in Over-The-Hill (the black section of the city), Nassau, the only child of Arnold F. Pindling, a former police officer and businessman who migrated from Jamaica to the Bahamas in 1923, and Viola Pindling (née Bain), who hailed from Acklins Island in the southern Bahamas. Lynden Pindling obtained his degree at the University of London and attended Inns of Courts at Middle Temple, where he successfully qualified as a lawyer, completing the LL.B. in August 1952. He was called to the bar of the Middle Temple in February 1953.

Pindling then returned to Nassau. He was called to the Bahamas bar in late 1953, and then he joined the recently established Progressive Liberal Party (PLP). Pindling and five other successful PLP candidates were elected to the House of Assembly in June 1956. H. M. Taylor, the chairman of the PLP, failed to retain his seat, however, and Pindling was elected as parliamentary leader of the PLP. This was the beginning of the PLP's eleven-year struggle for majority rule, and the first step in Pindling's rise to leadership of the party. By 1963 he was both the party's leader in Parliament and chairman of the PLP.

Pindling and the PLP supported the January 1958 general strike led by Randol Fawkes, the Bahamas Federation of Labour, Clifford Darling, and the Bahamas Taxi Cab Union. In fact, Pindling and the PLP pushed for constitutional reform. Although no structural changes were made in the constitution immediately following the strike, important electoral changes were instituted, including the widening of the franchise, abolition of the company vote (which had allowed persons holding companies to vote on every company), and reduction of the plural vote (which had allowed one person to vote in every constituency where he held land), all of which helped to democratize the election process. The Bay Street politicians, comprised of merchant-class whites, including Roland Symonette and Stafford Sands, were still firmly in control, however, and won a resounding victory in 1962.

April 27, 1965, became known as "Black Tuesday" in the Bahamas. On that day, Pindling threw the speaker's mace, the symbol of parliamentary power, out of the House of Assembly as a protest against the Constituencies Commission report and a *Wall Street Journal* article of October 5, 1966, that was unfavorable to the Bahamian government. The Commission's report allocated the constituencies (seats) in New Providence and the Out Islands to the advantage of the governing party, the United Bahamian Party (UBP), and Pindling opposed what he saw as an unfair advantage for the UBP. The general election that followed in 1967 ended in a tie, but Labour Party leader Randol Fawkes sided with the PLP, and independent Alvin Braynen agreed to become speaker. Pindling thus formed the first PLP government bringing majority rule. He became *premier* of the Bahamas, a designation changed to *prime minister* following constitutional reform in 1969. He then led the PLP to victory in six successive general elections (1967, 1968, 1972, 1977, 1982, and 1987) and went on to serve as a member of Parliament for forty-one years and as prime minister for twenty-five years. When the PLP was defeated in the election of 1992, he was the longest-serving elected head of government in the British Commonwealth.

The Bahamas under Pindling and the PLP was transformed peacefully from a racially and economically oppressive colony into a modern, prosperous, independent, and stable nation. Under his administration, the Bahamas gained its independence on July 10, 1973, in what Dame Doris Johnson (1972) deemed "The Quiet Revolution." The government extended educational opportunities to all Bahamians through the building of primary and secondary schools, the provision of thousands of scholarships for education, both at home and abroad, and the establishment of the College of The Bahamas, thus laying the foundation for the rise of a newly educated and professional class inclusive of black Bahamians, who had previously been mostly deprived of the right to vote and the right to education and economic opportunities taken for granted by the white elite. The PLP government also established the Industrial Training Centre (now called the Bahamas Technical and Vocational Institute) and The Bahamas Tourism Centre. Low-cost housing was expanded and numerous new subdivisions were developed to accommodate the new middle class. Electrification was provided to most islands of the Bahamas, as were telecommunications. For example, the use of radio was expanded and national television introduced. The financial services industries also grew tremendously during this period.

In addition, public health measures were introduced. The supply of potable water and sewage waste disposal was greatly improved. Health care was improved and extended through the establishment of new clinics in many islands, and doctors were posted to the major population centers. National insurance to assist the unemployed, ill, and disabled was introduced in 1974. In addition, security was enhanced through the formation of the Royal Bahamas Defence Force and the strengthening of the Royal Bahamas Police Force. The islands of the Bahamas were more closely linked through the establishment of Bahamasair, and the tourism industry expanded to welcome more than three million visitors a year.

Shortly after independence, Pindling and the PLP sought and obtained membership in the United Nations, the Organization of American States, the Caribbean Community, and the Commonwealth of Nations. The Bahamas later joined other international organizations, including the United Nations Educational, Scientific, and Cultural Organization (UNESCO).

Pindling will be remembered internationally as the chairman of the biennial Commonwealth Heads of Government meeting in Nassau in 1985, and as the chairman of the Commonwealth Conference on South Africa. In the latter capacity, he was instrumental in "setting the stage for the release of Nelson Mandela from his long captivity" (*Official Programme*, 2000).

Despite being diagnosed with prostate cancer in 1996, Pindling led the PLP into the 1997 general election, which the governing Free National Movement (FNM) won by a landslide. After a forty-one-year career in the House of Assembly, Sir Lynden Pindling (he was knighted by Queen Elizabeth in 1983) resigned on July 7, 1997, after giving an eloquent speech in which he stated, "I am done now . . . I have reached the end of my political journey. I have run my course. I did my best." Upon his death, Pindling was survived by four children, five grandchildren, and Marguerite, his wife of forty years.

See also International Relations of the Anglophone Caribbean; Urban Poverty in the Caribbean

■ ■ *Bibliography*

Craton, Michael. *Pindling: The Life of Times of Lynden Oscar Pindling, First Prime Minister of the Bahamas, 1930–2000.* Oxford, UK: Macmillan Caribbean, 2002.

Craton, Michael, and Gail Saunders. *Islanders in the Stream: A History of the Bahamian People; Vol. 2: From the Ending of Slavery to the Twenty-First Century.* Athens: University of Georgia Press, 1998.

Fawkes, Randol F. *The Faith that Moved the Mountain: A Memoir of a Life and the Times.* Nassau, Bahamas: 1988/1997.

Johnson, Doris. *The Quiet Revolution in the Bahamas.* Nassau, Bahamas: Family Island Press, 1972.

Official Programme for the State Funeral. Nassau, Bahamas: Government Printing Department, September 4, 2000.

Roker, Patricia B., ed. *The Vision of Sir Lynden Pindling: In his Own Words, Letters, and Speeches, 1948–1997.* Nassau, Bahamas: Media Publishing, 2000.

D. GAIL SAUNDERS (2005)

PIPER, ADRIAN

SEPTEMBER 20, 1948

▮▮▮

Adrian Margaret Smith Piper was born the only child of Daniel Robert Piper and Olive Xavier Smith Piper in Harlem, New York. She trained at the School of Visual Arts in New York and earned a doctorate from Harvard in 1967. Through work as a philosopher and conceptual artist, Piper creates provocative works of art that challenge stereotypes of racial and gender identity. Piper began making conceptual art in the mid-1960s while completing her graduate studies in philosophy and intensely studying Immanuel Kant's *Critique of Pure Reason.* Kant's writings inspired Piper to investigate her own experiences of racial discrimination. For a conceptual artist such as Piper, the act of thinking about a preferred set of questions can constitute a large portion of the creative work. Conceptual art may take the form of writing, performance, collage, installation, or other objects. It might also be objectless, existing as a performance or conversation taking place solely inside the head of the artist. Piper's artwork takes many forms, including journal writing, drawings, collage, video art, photography, and performance.

While Piper's artwork is indebted to her studies in philosophy, it is also deeply informed by her own experiences. As a light-skinned African-American woman with access to cultural institutions of white privilege, Piper often is mistaken for a white person without intending to "pass" herself off that way. This experience of being misread, primarily by white people, has afforded her the opportunity to witness racism from an "inside" perspective. On several occasions she has found herself privy to comments that evidence fears or biases toward African Americans by educated and politically savvy whites who would not express such ideas in mixed company. When Piper announces, or "outs," her identity as black, she is both confronting these expressions of racism and revealing that such biases persist, even in the most enlightened communities. Her perceived cultural ambiguity has invited hostility from a number of people who feel deceived because of their inability to perceive the variances and nuances of African-American female identity. Piper's artwork exposes the illogic inherent in distinct racial categories, where one's color is used as an objective signifier of status or culture.

Piper's style of confrontation, whether in her artwork or critical writings, is sharply courteous. By using this tactic of extreme politeness, Piper has said that she hopes to force those who refuse to acknowledge their own racism to note the "wrongness" of their own behavior. She has also said her artwork helps her to use her own negative experiences constructively and to avoid feeling trapped and powerless in the wake of other people's professed expectations.

Piper's artwork observes, questions, and reveals the phenomenon of racial inequality as a way to seek further enlightenment about the nature of humanity. It attempts to reveal that one's bias against, discrimination toward, and fear of African Americans is a result of an illogical and emotional weakness of character by subjecting it to interrogations of critical thinking and logic.

See also Performance Art

The Chicago offices of the **Pittsburgh Courier** *in 1941. Founded in 1910, the newspaper had a national circulation and a wide readership throughout black America.* THE LIBRARY OF CONGRESS

■ ■ *Bibliography*

Piper, Adrian. *Out of Order, Out of Sight: Selected Writings in Art Criticism 1967–1992,* vols. 1 and 2. Cambridge, Mass.: MIT Press, 1996.

WENDY S. WALTERS (2005)

PITTSBURGH COURIER

The *Pittsburgh Courier* was for several decades among the most influential African-American newspapers in the United States. Founded in January 1910 by Edwin Nathaniel Harleston, a security guard with an interest in literary endeavors, the weekly publication was nurtured into prominence under the guidance of Robert L. Vann. An attorney and acquaintance of Harleston's, Vann was asked to handle the fledgling newspaper's incorporation procedures and to solicit financial investors. By the autumn of 1910, however, Harleston had resigned from the ownership group and Vann was named editor. Vann accepted $100 a year in *Courier* stock shares as compensation, and by 1926 he was the majority stockholder.

When the *Courier*'s first issue was published, the black population in Pittsburgh was approximately twenty-five thousand, but only one of the city's six newspapers carried any news concerning the African-American community. That paper, the *Pittsburgh Press,* carried black-oriented items in a segregated section titled "Afro-American News," but its content was generally of sensational crime and other lurid aspects of black life. Under Vann's leadership the *Courier* flourished, reaching a circulation of fifty-five thousand in the early 1920s. This was accomplished by a number of adept strategies that included hiring well-known journalist George Schuyler in 1925 to write his "View and Reviews" column.

That same year Vann sponsored Schuyler on a nine-month tour of the South to write a series of on-the-road observations. This strategy allowed the *Courier* to build a national circulation among African-American readers, particularly in southern cities with large black populations. At the same time, Vann was increasing the paper's national advertising, hiring additional professional staff, and focusing on national stories.

As the *Courier* broadened its national coverage, its attention to local events weakened. Still, by the end of the 1920s H. L. Mencken observed that the *Courier* was the "best colored newspaper published." A significant operational decision was the construction of the *Courier*'s own printing and production plant in 1929. During the Great Depression the *Courier* was able to keep and conserve its revenues because it maintained its own production facility.

It was also during the 1930s that the *Courier* undertook one of its first major campaigns as a national opinion leader for African Americans. At issue was the enormously popular radio program "Amos 'n' Andy." The *Courier* attacked the racial stereotypes presented in the program and in 1930 and 1931 launched a drive to obtain one million signatures on a petition to remove it from the air. Although the effort fell some 400,000 signatures short of its goal, the *Courier* firmly established its place as a national forum for African-American expression.

During the 1930s *Courier* readers could faithfully follow the exploits of heavyweight champion Joe Louis, and the paper's increase in circulation coincided with Louis's reign. Journalists such as P. L. Prattis, William G. Nunn, and sportswriter Chester Washington joined the staff, and the paper launched various crusades against Jim Crow discrimination and for civil rights.

Vann died in 1940, and his wife Jessie Ellen (Matthews) Vann succeeded him as publisher. By May 1947 the *Courier* attained a circulation high of 357,212 readers nationally. It championed the causes of racial equality in the U.S. armed forces and covered black military achievements in World War II. Although it also covered the black baseball circuit, emphasizing the Homestead Grays over the major league locals, the Pittsburgh Pirates, the *Courier* fought vigorously for the integration of major league baseball.

During the 1950s and 1960s the *Courier* experienced steady declines in circulation, and in 1966 it was purchased by the Sengstacke Group, which continued the weekly as the *New Pittsburgh Courier*.

See also *Baltimore Afro-American; Black World/Negro Digest; Chicago Defender; Guardian, The; Liberator, The; North Star;* Journalism; Schuyler, George S.

■ ■ *Bibliography*

Buni, Andrew. *Robert L. Vann of the* Pittsburgh Courier: *Politics and Black Journalism*. Pittsburgh: University of Pittsburgh Press, 1974.

Wolseley, Roland E. *The Black Press, USA*. Ames: Iowa State University Press, 1990.

CLINT C. WILSON II (1996)

PLESSY V. FERGUSON

In *Plessy v. Ferguson,* 163 U.S. 537 (1896), the Supreme Court upheld an 1890 Louisiana statute that required railroads to provide separate but equal accommodations for blacks and whites and forbade persons from riding in cars not assigned to their race. It gave constitutional sanction to virtually all forms of racial segregation in the United States until after World War II.

Plessy arose as part of a careful strategy to test the legality of the new Louisiana law. In September 1891, elite "persons of color" in New Orleans formed the Citizens Committee to Test the Constitutionality of the Separate Car Law. They raised three thousand dollars for the costs of a test case. Albion Tourgee, the nation's leading white advocate of black rights, agreed to take the case without fee. Tourgee, a former judge, was a nationally prominent writer most noted for his novel about Reconstruction, *A Fool's Errand.*

In June 1892, Homer A. Plessy purchased a first-class ticket on the East Louisiana Railroad, sat in the "white" car, and was promptly arrested and arraigned before Judge John H. Ferguson. Plessy then sued to prevent Ferguson from conducting any further proceedings against him. Eventually his challenge reached the United States Supreme Court.

Before the Supreme Court, Tourgee argued that segregation violated the Thirteenth Amendment's prohibition of involuntary servitude and denied blacks equal protection of the law, which was guaranteed by the Fourteenth Amendment. These amendments, along with the Declaration of Independence, Tourgee asserted, gave Americans affirmative rights against invidious discrimination. He asserted that the Fourteenth Amendment gave constitutional life to the Declaration of Independence, "which is not a fable as some of our modern theorists would have us believe, but [is] the all-embracing formula of personal rights on which our government is based." Joining Tourgee in these arguments was Samuel F. Phillips, a former solicitor general of the United States, who in 1883 had unsuccessfully argued the civil rights cases.

The Court rejected Tourgee's arguments by a vote of seven to one. In his majority opinion, Justice Henry Billings Brown conceded that the Fourteenth Amendment was adopted "to enforce the absolute equality of the two races before the law," but asserted that the amendment "could not have been intended to abolish distinctions based upon color, or to enforce social, as distinguished from political, equality, or a commingling of the two races." Ignoring the reality of the emerging Jim Crow South, the Court denied that "the enforced separation of the two races stamps the colored race with a badge of inferiority." Brown believed that segregation was not discriminatory because whites were also segregated from blacks. Thus, if segregation created a perception of inferiority "it is not by reason of anything found in the act, but solely because the colored race chooses to put that construction upon it." Reflecting the accepted social science and popular prejudices of his age, Brown argued:

> Legislation is powerless to eradicate racial instincts or to abolish distinctions based upon physical differences, and the attempt to do so can only result in accentuating the difficulties of the present situation. If the civil and political rights of both races be equal, one cannot be inferior to the other civilly or politically. If one race be inferior to the other socially, the Constitution of the United States cannot put them upon the same plane.

Thus, as long as segregated facilities were "equal," they were permissible. Segregation had now received the sanction and blessing of the Supreme Court.

In a bitter, lone dissent, Justice John Marshall Harlan, a former slave owner, acknowledged that the "white race" was "the dominant race in this country." But, as Harlan read the Constitution, there was in the eye of the law no superior, dominant, ruling class of citizens and no caste. The Constitution was color-blind, and neither knew nor tolerated classes among citizens. In respect of civil rights, all citizens were equal before the law and the humblest the peer of the most powerful. The law regarded "man as man" and took no account of surroundings or color when civil rights as guaranteed by the supreme law of the land were involved. Harlan protested that the Court's decision would "stimulate aggressions, more or less brutal and irritating, upon the admitted rights of colored citizens" and "encourage the belief that it is possible, by means of state enactments, to defeat the beneficent purposes which the people of the United States had in view when they adopted the recent amendments to the Constitution." In prophetic language, he asserted, "The thin disguise of 'equal' accommodations for passengers in railroad coaches will not mislead any one, nor atone for the wrong this day done." Harlan argued that the Louisiana law was "inconsistent with the personal liberty of citizens, white and black" and "hos-

tile to both the spirit and letter of the Constitution of the United States."

More than five decades would pass before the Supreme Court recognized the fundamental truth of Harlan's dissent. Meanwhile, the South built a social and legal system rooted in racial segregation. In January 1897, Homer Plessy pled guilty to attempting to board a "white" railroad car and paid a twenty-five-dollar fine.

See also Fourteenth Amendment; Jim Crow; Thirteenth Amendment

■ ■ *Bibliography*

Finkelman, Paul, ed. *Race, Law, and American History*. Vol. 4, *The Age of Jim Crow: Segregation from the End of Reconstruction to the Great Depression*. New York: Garland, 1992.

Kull, Andrew. *The Color Blind Constitution*. Cambridge, Mass.: Harvard University Press, 1992.

Lofgren, Charles A. *The Plessy Case: A Legal-Historical Interpretation*. New York: Oxford University Press, 1987.

Logan, Rayford W. *The Betrayal of the Negro: From Rutherford B. Hayes to Woodrow Wilson* (1954; originally published as *The Negro in American Life and Thought: The Nadir, 1877–1901*). New York: Collier, 1965.

Medley, Keith Wheldon. *We as Freemen: Plessy v. Ferguson*. New York: Pelican, 2003.

Woodward, C. Vann. *The Origins of the New South, 1877–1913*. Baton Rouge: Louisiana State University Press, 1951.

Woodward, C. Vann. *The Strange Career of Jim Crow*. New York: Oxford University Press, 1955.

PAUL FINKELMAN (1996)
Updated bibliography

POETRY, U.S.

African-American poetry is the first formal literature created by Africans and their descendants in the New World. It is a body of literature that emerged out of the largest forced migration in human history, the subsequent enslavement of those migrants, and the racial circumscription encountered by their descendants. Black verse has therefore embodied and emphasized concerns at once aesthetic, spiritual, and, necessarily, political. Gwendolyn Brooks's striking metaphor, which imagines the poetry of the oppressed as "pretty flowers under blood," makes this point explicit. Many poets posit America as a location of exile and alienation, yet it is the only home most black Americans have ever known. Contemporary African-American verse echoes the more than two hundred years of black poetry that preceded it, finding its animating principle in the exploration of what the critic George Kent termed "exile rhythms," as they continue to reverberate in black life. Consequently, the quests for home and freedom—in all of their philosophical, spiritual, and physical dimensions—are a continuing preoccupation for black poets.

Some of the primary responses to this predicament of exile and lingering discrimination can been found in black vernacular, or oral folk culture—that is, in the lyrics and music of ring shouts, field hollers, work songs, spirituals, blues, and jazz. With their emphases on transcendence, perseverance, improvisation, and humor, these forms provide the aesthetic, philosophical, and epistemological foundations on which much black poetry rests. Black folk poets of the eighteenth and nineteenth centuries combined African polyrhythmic structures, West African-based African-American "call and response" patterns, and European forms and language to create a New World literature. While the lyrics and structures of these forms constitute one line of development, the eighteenth century also witnessed the birth of a written African-American poetry. This poetry, primarily modeled on European and Euro-American source material, developed under the gaze of white slave masters, editors, and publishers. Not surprisingly, these poetries are very different. Yet, despite the surface differences between the oral and written black traditions in poetry, especially prior to the twentieth century, there is a sameness in the desires they articulate. In the later nineteenth century, some poets working in the more formal literary tradition attempted to infuse their work with African-American oral culture—a practice that was increasingly employed during the Harlem Renaissance, and that continues today.

A "DIFFICULT MIRACLE": BLACK POETRY OF THE EIGHTEENTH AND NINETEENTH CENTURIES

The dynamic tension between the ideal of freedom and the reality of enslavement or oppression has informed African-American poetry from its inception. The written tradition of black poetry emerged in the second half of the eighteenth century, in an Anglo-American world wrestling with the potent ideas of liberty and self-determination—an intellectual set of concerns bequeathed by the European Enlightenment but given political import in the context of British colonial rule and the revolutionary responses it spawned. The evangelical Great Awakening, an influential eighteenth-century Methodist revivalist movement noted for its emotional fervor, emphasized human equality through Christian salvation. This emphasis on equality "at

the foot of the Cross" resonated with African Americans and had a profound influence on early African-American verse.

The prelude to the written tradition of African-American verse occurred in 1746, the year of one of the first documented lynchings, in Deerfield, Massachusetts. Lucy Terry (1730–1821), then an enslaved African sixteen-year-old, wrote "Bars Fight," inaugurating the African-American literary tradition with the composition of a ballad of twenty-six lines that commemorated a Native American ambush of white settlers. Acknowledging the literary and extraliterary challenges confronting the creation of black verse, the poet June Jordon (b. 1936) has labeled African-American poetry, especially its beginnings, nothing short of a "difficult miracle."

It was indeed miraculous that Africans, despite the fierce assaults on their humanity and identity during the Middle Passage and slavery, would enter the continuum that is Western poetic discourse while still in bondage. It may have been especially difficult for African-American poets contemplating an almost 3,000-year-old tradition in poetry that marked, for Europeans and Euro-Americans, the highest level of human artistic achievement. Jupiter Hammon (1711–1806), a slave to three generations of a wealthy New York family and the first published African-American writer, produced an eighty-eight line broadside titled *An Evening Thought, Salvation, by Christ, with Penetential* (sic) *Cries* in 1760. This poem's significance rests not in its aesthetic qualities, but in its use of the weight and authority of Christian discourse to make an argument for black (spiritual) equality and (transhistorical) liberation, a rhetorical method that would be repeated throughout the African-American verse tradition.

The African-American written tradition truly begins with the Gambian-born Phillis Wheatley (c. 1753–1784), who was the first black person—and the second woman—to publish a book in British North America. Wheatley wrote in daring and direct opposition to the racial hierarchy of eighteenth-century Europe and America, which associated blackness with mental and cultural inferiority. Her *Poems on Miscellaneous Subjects, Religious and Moral* (1773) reveals a poet politically engaged, spiritually devoted, and artistically ambitious. Wheatley's neoclassicism, her expressed desire to write a song in the "bolder notes" of Homer, Virgil, and Ovid, and her incorporation of a capacious and radically inclusive Christianity were all marshaled to articulate her central concern, the theme of liberation.

During the nineteenth century, over one hundred and thirty black poets would respond to Wheatley's call for a poetry at once political and beautiful. George Moses Horton (1797?–1883?) was the first black southerner to publish a book. This iconoclast published three volumes of poetry: *The Hope of Liberty* (1829), *The Poetical Works of George M. Horton, the Colored Bard of North Carolina* (1845), and *Naked Genius* (1865), published shortly after his emancipation. Horton's poetry stands alone in the nineteenth century in its unique examination of the slave's psyche, love, marriage, financial hardship, and death. His life spanned most of the tumultuous nineteenth century, an era that encompassed slavery, Emancipation, Reconstruction, and the post-Reconstruction period (or "nadir"), a period of extreme political, social, and economic subjugation, and systematic violence. Ann Plato, most likely a free black citizen of Hartford, Connecticut, wrote *Essays: Including Biographies and Miscellaneous Pieces of Prose and Poetry* (1841), which included twenty poems in the neoclassical style favored by Wheatley. James Monroe Whitfield (1822–1871) wrote "America" (1853), declaring, "America, it is to thee, / Thou boasted land of liberty,— / It is to thee I raise my song, / Thou land of blood and crime and wrong."

A year later, the writer-activist Frances Ellen Watkins Harper (1825–1911) published *Poems on Miscellaneous Subjects* (1854), a book of poems and essays with a title revealing a recursion to Wheatley, a clear indication that black writers were fully aware of their own burgeoning literary tradition. Harper—born free like Whitfield, but in the slave South—published other collections, including *Moses, a Story of the Nile* (1869), an almost 700-line blank-verse epic retelling of the *Book of Exodus,* and *Sketches of a Southern Life* (1872), a significant contribution to American and black poetry due to the realistic manner in which it rendered the dignity, knowledge, humor, and speech of African Americans in the South. Alberry Allson Whitman (1851–1901), born a slave in Kentucky, wrote technically complex, heroic, and romantic poetry in order to contribute to racial advancement and to challenge himself artistically. He authored the expansive *Leelah Mislead* (1873), *Not a Man Yet a Man* (1877), and *The Rape of Florida* (1884), among other epics. In addition to Whitman and Harper, some other extended verse writers were Elymas Payson Rogers, George Boyer Vashon, James Madison Bell, and Francis A. Boyd. Although many black writers crafted historical, weighty poems, others, especially after the Civil War, turned inward to explore more emotional, subjective concerns. These poems were transgressive in that they made black speaking, thinking, and feeling their primary focus. Ann Plato, George Moses Horton, and later, T. Thomas Fortune, Eloise Bibb Thompson, and Henrietta Cordelia Ray were among those who adopted this style.

Paul Laurence Dunbar (1872–1906), the northern-born son of southern slaves, was the most significant poet of the nineteenth century. In his eleven volumes of poetry, starting with *Oak and Ivy* (1893), *Majors and Minors* (1895), and *Lyrics of a Lowly Life* (1896), Dunbar's formal versatility was as evident as his cross-racial popularity was immense. Dunbar wrote in both standard English and in black vernacular, or dialect, a dichotomy that would influence his popularity and critical reception. Some critics and many readers praised the authenticity and artistry of his dialect verse, noticing Dunbar's ability to mask the exile rhythms, communal healing, and thematics of liberation in his poems. Daniel Webster Davis and James Edwin Campbell also wrote dialect poems. Fenton Johnson was a transitional figure who fashioned poetry reminiscent of Dunbar in its lyricism and use of black speech. The tone of despair in his last volume, *Songs of the Soil* (1916), encapsulated the mood of the nadir period and the tone of Euro-American modernism.

THE HARLEM RENAISSANCE: 1919–1940

The Harlem Renaissance, sometimes called the New Negro Renaissance or New Negro movement, was an artistic flowering that peaked in the 1920s but began to wane during the Great Depression. The Great Migration (the movement of blacks from the American South to the North during the early twentieth century), the smaller migration to New York City from the Caribbean, the return of black soldiers from World War I, and the rise of a new, more militant black leadership who responded to the brutality of the post-Reconstruction nadir were some of the factors contributing to its emergence. With these changes came a corresponding shift in African-American racial pride and self-assertion, as well as a surge in artistic energy. Alain Locke (1886–1954), a professor of philosophy at Howard University, captured this new, more assertive and defiant attitude in *The New Negro* (1925), an anthology of essays, fiction, poetry, and artwork. Poetry was one of the more prominent means of literary expression in the period, and poets were given monetary awards and the chance to publish by the journals *The Crisis* and *Opportunity,* sponsored by the NAACP and the National Urban League, respectively. The black poetry anthologies that appeared between 1922 and 1941, such as James Weldon Johnson's *The Book of American Negro Poetry* (1922) and Countee Cullen's *Caroling Dusk* (1927), were also important publishing venues.

During this era, artists and critics continued grappling with black representation in art, artistic freedom, art as propaganda, white patronage, and the proper use of folk material. Claude McKay (1890–1948), a pioneer of the

Harlem Renaissance, foregrounded the contributions of Anglo-Caribbean immigrants who helped nourish the literary, cultural, and political environment of the Harlem Renaissance. McKay's *Harlem Shadows* (1922), which included the still popular "If We Must Die," yoked traditional poetic forms, especially the sonnet, to a critique of racial and economic oppression and exploitation. Jean Toomer's (1894–1967) modernist-inspired *Cane* (1923), a generically restless long poem that was a swan song for the South left in the wake of the Great Migration, was also influential to black poets. In *Color* (1925), which includes the poem "Heritage," the erudite Countee Cullen (1903–1946) asked the question that many African-American artists in the Harlem Renaissance and after would repeatedly consider: "What is Africa to me?" Langston Hughes (1902–1967), the prolific Afro-modernist and self-proclaimed folk poet, embraced vernacular material with his wedding of jazz and blues forms to traditional verse. Hughes published his signature poem, "The Negro Speaks of Rivers" (1921), in *The Crisis,* and later authored the collections *The Weary Blues* (1926) and *Fine Clothes to the Jew* (1927). James Weldon Johnson's free-verse *God's Trombones, Seven Negro Sermons in Verse* (1927) is a masterwork of the era; with its poetic articulation of black sermonic tradition it complements the strand of religiously influenced poetry from the eighteenth century to the present. In *Southern Road* (1932), Sterling Brown (1901–1989) used language that foreshadowed the subtitle of Stephen Henderson's important *Understanding the New Black Poetry: Black Speech and Music as Poetic References* (1972), creating poems that explore the rhythms of black American life. One of Brown's most enduring legacies is in his uniting of the blues and ballad forms, as in "Ma Rainy," which portrays its eponymous subject.

The blues not only served as a structuring form and verse referent for poets of the Harlem Renaissance, but, as critic Hazel Carby has suggested, the blues lyrics performed by Ma Rainy (1886–1939) and Bessie Smith (1895?–1937), to cite just two examples, were a significant oral poetry. For many women poets in the literary arena, however, black female representation and voice was a complex undertaking within the confines of the "Cult of True Womanhood," the ubiquitous ideology that venerated female domesticity, piety, and sexual purity. Often living outside of Harlem and saddled with traditional domestic responsibilities and gender discrimination—within and outside of the publishing world—women poets experienced specific challenges. The writer and poet Akasha Gloria Hull and others have pointed out that many women established informal and formal multigenerational networks in their cities and expressed political and romantic desire within the more conventional lyric genre, as was the

case with Alice Dunbar-Nelson (1975–1935), Angelina Weld Grimké (1880–1958), and Georgia Douglas Johnson (1880–1966). Johnson authored four books of verse, including *The Heart of a Woman* (1918) and *Bronze* (1922). Other poets, such as Anne Spencer, Gwendolyn Bennett, Mae Cowdery, Helene Johnson, Gladys Mae Casely Hayford (Aquah Laluah), and the Ethel Trew Dunlap, offered the Renaissance a dazzling array of unique poetry ranging from lesbian and Pan-African verse to poetry that explored gender and racial equality.

POETRY OF THE MID-TWENTIETH-CENTURY FREEDOM MOVEMENT: 1940–1960

The 1940s and 1950s were decades of economic expansion, cultural conformity, and ideological consensus resulting from World War II and its aftermath, which served as a unifying force and manufacturing juggernaut. African Americans might also characterize this era as a moment of increased political rebellion and agitation with its sit-ins, boycotts, and mass demonstrations against injustice. Many black poets during this period embraced the new formalism (a return to more traditional European forms and metrics) and the dense and highly allusive high modernism of the academy. Others opted for a more radical experimentation with language, as a reading of the magazines *Free Lance* and *Yugen* will attest. The writer Aldon L. Nielsen calls the tradition of experimental black poetry a "continuum within a tradition of fracture," with black poets locating this experimental impulse in black vernacular forms as well as Euro-American innovation. Russell Atkins, Amiri Baraka (Leroi Jones), Bob Kaufman, Oliver Pitcher, Harold Carrington, Stephen Jonas, Ted Joans, and Tom Postell were just a few of the writers pushing the boundaries of referential language. Some of these poets made use of unique typography and oral performance in an attempt to approach the sublimity of jazz.

During the World War II period, Gwendolyn Brooks (1917–2000), Melvin B. Tolson (1898–1966), Robert Hayden (1913–1980), and Margaret Walker (1915–1998) became prominent literary figures, wining prestigious academic, national, and international recognition for their work, while Langston Hughes continued to write poetry. His bebop-influenced *Montage of a Dream Deferred* (1951) is a long poetic exploration of the desire for home and equality in America—the exile rhythms—that would serve as a primary concern for the major black poets of the era. Margaret Walker's collection *For My People* (1942), written in free verse, folk ballad, and sonnet form, has been compared to a sermon because of its imaginative interweaving of history, biblical imagery, and African-

American folk elements. Black history and folklore also serve as source material for some of the multitextured and technically masterful poems of Robert Hayden. His "Middle Passage" (1945) remains an extraordinary testament to a prolific forty-year writing career that produced many fine volumes, *The Lion and the Archer* (1948) and *A Ballad of Remembrance* (1962) among them.

American modernism was also energized through the dense, compressed, and allusive poetry of Melvin B. Tolson, who first gained national recognition for his frequently anthologized "Dark Symphony" (1939). Tolson's *Libretto for the Republic of Liberia* (1953) is a sweeping, dense, long poem written to celebrate Liberia's centennial. His epic *Harlem Gallery: Book I, The Curator* (1965) is a singular achievement in black poetry in its importation of high modernist technique and black vernacular forms. One of the most significant, influential, and gifted voices of this era (and beyond) belonged to Gwendolyn Brooks, who wrote more than twenty poetry volumes. The first African American to win a Pulitzer Prize—for *Annie Allen* (1949)—Brooks's poetry wrests the ordinary lives of black folk from its moorings in transparent language and vivifies its everyday heroism through a brilliant use of polished technique and explosive metaphor. Samuel W. Allen (Paul Vesey), Owen Dodson, Margaret Esse Danner, Raymond Patterson, and Ray Durem were also important poets of the era.

The Black Arts Movement: Early 1960s–Early 1970s

The 1960s witnessed a proliferation of black art. Mirroring the late nineteenth century and the 1920s, energized writers responded to social and economic injustice, and the seemingly endless attacks on African-American humanity, most recently evidenced in the brutal assaults on freedom-movement participants and the assassinations of Malcolm X, Medgar Evers, and Martin Luther King. The black arts movement, the cultural arm of the Black Power political movement, called for a politically engaged, revolutionary art. Its precursor texts came from poets as diverse as A. B. Spellman, Dasein poets such as Percy Johnston, and poets from the Umbra Workshop (established in New York in 1962) such as Lorenzo Thomas, Askia M. Touré, and Norman H. Pritchard, as well as from Hughes, Brooks, Tolson, and Sterling Brown. Black arts poetry, then, reflected its roots in the continuum of black avant-garde experimentalism, vernacular expression, and the enduring legacy of socially committed verse inaugurated during the eighteenth century. Baraka and Larry Neal's *Black Fire* (1968), Clarence Major's *The New Black Poetry* (1969), Addison Gayle's essay collection *The Black Aesthetic* (1971), and

Stephen Henderson's *Understanding the New Black Poetry*, were some of the anthologies that established a canon of black arts verse. These texts disseminated an ideological and aesthetic framework for understanding this new black "collective" art. Amiri Baraka (b. 1934), the most prominent poet of this era, produced *Black Magic: Collected Poetry 1961–1967* (1969), among other works.

The verse in these collections are frequently didactic, ritualistic, irreverent, and, like the black experimental culture from which it was in dialogue, many of these poems attempt to approximate jazz improvisation. Baraka's programmatic "Black Art" demands a poetry as palpable as "teeth or trees or lemons." His transformation to black cultural nationalist from Beat writer was at least as stunning as the shift of his fellow poet Gwendolyn Brooks, whose black arts–inspired long poem *In the Mecca* (1968) explored the dynamics of gender, race, and poverty in Chicago. Nikki Giovanni's *Black Feeling, Black Talk* (1968) and *Black Judgement* (1969) presented a bifurcated lyric and political voice; Sonia Sanchez became the blues woman of the movement with her frank discussions of black female sexuality and interpersonal relations in *Homecoming* (1969); while Haki Madhubuti's *Don't Cry, Scream* (1969) called for political action instead of the resignation he found in the blues. Quincy Troupe, Etheridge Knight, Carolyn M. Rogers, Jayne Cortez, and Mari Evans represent the diversity of voices that contributed to this movement.

The formal and thematic range of the poetic voices during the black arts movement, along with government attacks on Black Power, ultimately contributed to its rupture. Important volumes such as Jay Wright's *The Homecoming Singer* (1971), Audre Lorde's *The First Cities* (1968), and Lucille Clifton's *Good Times* (1969) are just a few of the texts that benefited from the new black aesthetic even as they pointed in new directions. These works and others illustrate how black arts engendered, above all else, an explosion of black poetries with radically different approaches to language, genre, history, and the representation of blackness. The title poem of Audre Lorde's magnificent volume *Coal* (1976) foregrounded these myriad possibilities of expression, including the articulation of feminist and lesbian identity, when it pondered "Is the total black, being spoke / From the earth's inside / There are many kinds of open."

Poetry Since 1970

It is impossible to name all of the poets who made significant contributions to black poetry during the previously discussed periods of literary history. The contemporary era only expands this difficulty, for there has been such a

Cover of Rita Dove's **Thomas and Beulah,** *winner of the 1987 Pulitzer Prize for Poetry.* CARNEGIE-MELON UNIVERSITY PRESS, 1986. REPRODUCED BY PERMISSION.

proliferation of black verse since the 1970s that only a small sample of poets can be recognized here. Contemporary African-American poetry can best be characterized by its embrace of the full weight of its literary tradition, including its origins in African forms and Euro-American verse traditions. Its formal and thematic range has produced many poets of distinction, from the experimentalist poetics of Harryette Mullen, Will Alexander, Ed Roberson, and Erica Hunt to the dramatic monologues of Ai. Rita Dove's (b. 1952) traditional sonnet sequences and "elliptical" narrative verse, as seen in her Pulitzer Prize–winning *Thomas and Beulah* (1986), stands firmly on terrain established by Gwendolyn Brooks and Melvin Tolson. The expansive desires of Wheatley have found contemporary ex-

pression in significant long poems by Jay Wright, N. J. Loftis, Derek Walcott, Amiri Baraka, Gayle Jones, Brenda Marie Osbey, and Julia Fields among many others. For other poets, the lyric impulse continues, as illustrated in the work of June Jordon, Audre Lorde, Toi Derricotte, and Essex Hemphill, and in the incomparable poetry of Yusef Komunyakaa (b. 1947), whose jazz-and-blues saturated *Neon Vernacular: New & Selected Poems 1977–1989* (1994) also received a Pulitzer Prize. The influence of black music is also evident in the poetry of Michael S. Harper, Al Young, Sherley Ann Williams, Nathaniel Mackey, and Paul Beatty, to cite only a small number of poets who highlight the blues, jazz, or hip-hop in their work. Contemporary African-American poetry, grounded in black vernacular and American poetry traditions, continues to produce remarkable poems that explore the exile rhythms in black life, while also contributing some of the most exciting, challenging, and engaging texts in American poetry.

See also Autobiography, U.S.; Baraka, Amiri (Jones, LeRoi); Biography, U.S.; Black Arts Movement; Brooks, Gwendolyn Elizabeth; Cullen, Countee; Drama; Dunbar, Paul Laurence; Hammon, Jupiter; Horton, George Moses; Hughes, Langston; Literary Criticism, U.S.; Literary Magazines, U.S.; Literature; Locke, Alain Leroy; Lorde, Audre Geraldine; McKay, Claude; Novels, U.S.; Toomer, Jean; Wheatley, Phillis

■■ *Bibliography*

Bruce, Dickson D. *Black American Writing from the Nadir: The Evolution of a Literary Tradition, 1877–1915.* Baton Rouge: Louisiana State University Press, 1989.

Carby, Hazel. "It Just Be's Dat Way Sometime: The Sexual Politics of Women's Blues." In *Unequal Sisters: A Multicultural Reader in U.S. Women's History,* edited by E. C. Du Bois and Vicki L. Ruiz. New York: Routledge, 1990.

Cook, William W. "The Black Arts Poets." In *The Columbia History of American Poetry,* edited by J. Parini and B. Miller. New York: Columbia University Press, 1993.

Herron, Carolivia. "Early African American Poetry." In *The Columbia History of American Poetry,* edited by J. Parini and B. Miller. New York: Columbia University Press, 1993.

Hull, Gloria T. *Color, Sex, and Poetry: Three Women Writers of the Harlem Renaissance.* Bloomington: Indiana University Press, 1987.

Jackson, Blyden. *A History of Afro-American Literature.* Vol. 1, *The Long Beginning, 1746–1895.* Baton Rouge: Louisiana State University Press, 1989.

Keller, Lynn. *Forms of Expansion: Recent Long Poems by Women.* Chicago: University of Chicago Press, 1997.

Miller, R. Baxter. *Black American Poets Between Worlds, 1940–1960.* Knoxville: University of Tennessee Press. 1986.

Nielsen, Aldon Lynn. *Black Chant: Languages of African-American Postmodernism*. New York: Cambridge University Press, 1997.

Sherman, Joan. *Invisible Poets: Afro-Americans in the Nineteenth Century*, 2d ed. Urbana: University of Illinois Press, 1989.

Thomas, Lorenzo. "'Communicating by Horns': Jazz and Redemption in the Poetry of the Beats and the Black Arts Movement." *African American Review* 26 (1992): 291–298.

Werner, Craig. "Harlem Renaissance." In *The Oxford Companion to Women's Writing in the United States,* edited by C. N. Davidson and L. Wagner-Martin. New York: Oxford University Press, 1995.

KEISHA BOWMAN (2005)

POITIER, SIDNEY

FEBRUARY 20, 1927

Sidney Poitier with Lilia Skala in a scene from the 1963 film Lilies of the Field. *For his performance, Poitier became the first African American to win an Academy Award in the category of best actor.* AP/WIDE WORLD PHOTOS, INC. REPRODUCED BY PERMISSION

The actor, director, and filmmaker Sidney Poitier was born in Miami and reared on Cat Island in the Bahamas. The youngest of eight children, he was forced to leave school at fifteen in order to work on his parents' tomato farm. He then moved to Miami to live with his married brother Cyril. Shortly thereafter, Poitier left for New York City, enlisted in the U.S. Army, and served as a physiotherapist until World War II ended in 1945. Upon his return to New York, he supported himself with a series of menial jobs while studying to become an actor. After an unsuccessful audition, he spent six months trying to rid himself of his West Indian accent and eventually became a member of the American Negro Theatre, for which he often played leading roles. He also won minor parts in the Broadway productions of *Lysistrata* (1946) and *Anna Lucasta* (1948), before trying his hand at film. In 1950 he married Juanita Hardy, a dancer, with whom he had three children; Poitier and Hardy were eventually divorced.

Poitier's big break came when he was cast as a young doctor in Twentieth Century Fox's "racial problem" film *No Way Out* (1950). Leading roles followed in such films as *Cry, the Beloved Country* (1951), *Go Man Go* (1954), *Blackboard Jungle* (1955), *Band of Angels, Edge of the City,* and *Something of Value* (the last three all released in 1957). With his performance as an escaped convict in *The Defiant Ones* (1958), Poitier became the first African American to be nominated for an Oscar in the best actor category; he also won the New York Film Critics and Berlin Film Festival awards for best actor. The next year, Poitier took on the title role in Otto Preminger's motion picture version of *Porgy and Bess* (1959), for which he also won critical acclaim.

As an actor, Poitier became known for sensitive, versatile, and eloquent interpretations and powerful on-camera presence, as well as for his good looks. He was one of the first African Americans to become a major Hollywood star, and during the 1960s he played leading roles in many influential and controversial films. After originating the role of Walter Lee Younger on Broadway in Lorraine Hansberry's *A Raisin in the Sun* (1959), Poitier was featured in such diverse films as *Paris Blue* (1960), *Pressure Point* (1961), *A Patch of Blue* (1965), *The Bedford Incident* (1965), *Duel at Diablo* (1966), *Guess Who's Coming to Dinner?* (1967), *In the Heat of the Night* (1967), and *To Sir, with Love* (1967). In 1963 he became the first African American to win an Academy Award for best actor (for his performance in *Lilies of the Field*).

The late 1960s proved a transitional period for Poitier, who was accused of portraying unrealistic "noble Negro" or "ebony saint" characters by the militant black community. He confessed to feeling himself caught between the demands of white and black audiences. He attempted to diversify his roles by taking on such films as *They Call Me Mr. Tibbs!* (1970), *A Warm December* (1973), and *The Wilby Conspiracy* (1975), and by applying his talents to directing. In 1968, Poitier joined with Paul Newman, Steve McQueen, Dustin Hoffman, and Barbra Streisand to form First Artists, an independent production company. The popular Western *Buck and the Preacher* (1972) marked his debut as both director and star; *A Warm December* (1974), the hit comedy *Uptown Saturday Night* (1974), *Let's Do It Again* (1975), and *A Piece of the Action* (1977) all featured him in this dual role. In 1975 he was elected to the Black Filmmakers Hall of Fame, and his film *Let's Do It Again* earned him the NAACP Image Award in 1976. That year, Poitier married the actress Joanna Shimkus, with whom he had two children.

His first autobiography, *This Life,* was published in 1980. Twenty years after this memoir, Poitier reopened the door on his life with *The Measure of a Man: A Spiritual Autobiography* (2000), a book describing his early childhood in the Bahamas and exploring the history of some of his greatest roles.

Over the next decade, Poitier concentrated on directing such works as *Stir Crazy* (1980), *Hanky Panky* (1982), *Fast Forward* (1985), and *Ghost Dad* (1990). In 1982 he became the recipient of the Cecil B. DeMille Golden Globe Award and the Los Angeles Urban League Whitney M. Young Award. Poitier returned to acting in 1988 for starring roles in *Shoot to Kill* and *Little Nikita,* both of which were released that year. He has continued to act in films and a number of made-for-television movies since then, appearing in *Separate but Equal* (1991), *Sneakers* (1992), *Children of the Dust* (1995), *The Jackal* (1997), and other films.

In addition to creative filmmaking, Poitier has produced a record album called *Sidney Poitier Reads the Poetry of the Black Man,* and he has narrated two documentaries on Paul Robeson: *A Tribute to the Artist* (1979) and *Man of Conscience* (1986). In recognition of his artistic and humanitarian accomplishments, he was knighted by Queen Elizabeth II, and the NAACP honored him with its first Thurgood Marshall Lifetime Achievement Award in 1993. In 2000, Sidney Poitier won the NAACP Image Award for outstanding actor in a television movie for *The Simple Life of Noah Dearborn,* as well as a Life Achievement Award from the Screen Actors Guild. At the 2002 Academy Awards, Poitier won the Honorary Lifetime Achievement Award.

See also American Negro Theatre; Film

■ ■ *Bibliography*

Ewers, Carolyn H. *The Long Journey: A Biography of Sidney Poitier*. New York: New American Library, 1969.

Goudsouzian, Aram. *Sidney Poitier: Man, Actor, Icon*. Chapel Hill: University of North Carolina Press, 2004.

Marill, Alvin H. *The Films of Sidney Poitier*. Secaucus, N.J.: Citadel Press, 1978.

Poitier, Sidney. *This Life*. New York: Knopf, 1980.

Poitier, Sidney. *The Measure of a Man: A Spiritual Autobiography*. San Francisco: HarperSanFrancisco, 2000.

ED GUERRERO (1996)
Updated by publisher 2005

POLITICAL IDEOLOGIES

■ ■ ■

Black political ideologies are sets of beliefs, values, and ideas that assist people in understanding the complicated world of politics. These ideologies work as shortcuts that help individuals determine what it means to be black in the American political system; identify the relative political significance of race compared to such other personal characteristics as gender and class; determine the extent to which blacks should solve their own problems or look to the system for assistance; and determine the required degree of tactical separation from whites necessary for successful advancement of group interests. Ideology lets black people answer the political questions of who or what is the enemy, who are friends, what is America like, what is the nature of whites, and what strategies with regard to whites are necessary or desirable. Among the most important political ideologies in African-American intellectual history are black nationalism, liberal integrationism, feminism, and conservatism. These ideologies motivate social movements, inspire academic works, and structure individual beliefs.

BLACK NATIONALISM

Black nationalism is a political worldview that insists on some form of cultural, social, economic, and political autonomy for African Americans. Some nationalist thinkers articulate an international agenda and press for the goal of a separate black state. Other nationalists look toward racial self-determination within America. Scholars have identified at least five manifestations of black nationalism: cultural nationalism, educational nationalism, religious nationalism, community nationalism, and revolutionary nationalism. Each of these nationalisms emphasizes the immutable and unique relevance of race, perceives whites as actively resistant to black equality, articulates a language of self-determination and racial pride, and insists on African-American self-reliance through the creation of separate institutions such as schools, churches, political parties, and businesses.

Modern black nationalism is rooted in the social and political movements of Marcus Garvey in the early twentieth century and in the Black Power movement of the mid-twentieth century. Marcus Garvey promoted nationalism through the Universal Negro Improvement Association (UNIA), which was the largest mass-based movement of African Americans in the twentieth century. Garveyism identified the international and historical bases of black subjugation and declared the right and necessity of black separation from oppressive polities by developing separate political representation, cultural icons, and economic institutions. In the 1960s black nationalists from organizations such as the Black Panthers advocated the development of distinct and black-controlled centers of politics, economics, and culture as the central strategy for addressing black inequality. Some scholars suggest that black nationalism is the most prevalent political ideology among masses of African Americans today. Nationalism is apparent in the artistic, religious, and political choices of many ordinary African Americans that reflect a preference for supporting autonomous black institutions.

LIBERAL INTEGRATIONISM

Liberal integrationism is the most widely recognizable alternative to nationalism. Liberal integrationists want a society in which African Americans enjoy the political, economic, and social freedoms and rights of other citizens. Integrationist thought accepts that liberal democratic tenets of representative democracy, liberalism, and capitalism are the most appropriate ways to order society, but they argue that the current American system only works for privileged members of society. Integrationism is an ideology that seeks to access that privilege for African Americans by pursuing a strategy that effectively argues that the interests of the larger society are intimately bound up with the destinies of African Americans.

Liberal integrationism is closely aligned with the liberal tradition in American political thought, but has a greater emphasis on equality, collective rather than individual rights, and a reliance on a strong central government. This ideology emphasizes not only equality of opportunity but also equality of outcome. Electoral participation, federal litigation, pressure for government-based economic redevelopment, and support for race-targeted government programs are the hallmarks of liberal integrationist strategy. These policies and strategies seek to bring people together across racial lines to jointly pursue common political goals.

The contemporary civil rights movement was largely initiated within a liberal integrationist framework. This movement cited the historic, categorical exclusion of blacks, and therefore argued that redress could only come through similarly collective-oriented strategies and policies. Liberal integrationism is an ideological tradition that encompasses aspects of the political philosophy of Frederick Douglass, Martin Luther King Jr., Ralph Bunche, and W. E. B. Du Bois. Today, many black elected officials from the Democratic Party and leaders of civil rights organizations such as Jesse Jackson, Maxine Waters, and Kweisi Mfume continue to work for black equality within the liberal integrationist tradition.

BLACK CONSERVATISM

Black conservatism locates the source of black inequality in the behavioral or attitudinal pathologies of African Americans and stresses the significance of moral and personal rather than racial characteristics to explain unequal life circumstances. Conservatives stress self-reliance, hope for a colorless society, and shun government assistance. Core concepts of black conservatism include an appeal to self-help, an attack on the state as an overly intrusive institution, and a belief that the free market is nondiscriminatory. It stresses that political strategies are inferior to strategies of economic development and rejects policy strategies that diminish the honor of African Americans by allowing a perception of undeserved benefits for blacks. Black conservatism is rooted in a history of racial uplift, a belief that African Americans must fortify their moral and economic strength in order to compete in the American meritocracy.

Twentieth-century black conservatism is grounded in the work of Booker T. Washington. His accomodationist philosophy found institutional expression in the Tuskegee method of industrial education designed to instill a work ethic and manual skills in post-Reconstruction blacks with the promise of making African Americans profitable and pliable members of society. His work planted the ideological roots of the emphases on thrift, industriousness, and moral character. Many conservatives are willing to acknowledge that there is a history of racial discrimination in the United States, but most argue that the external factors of black inequality have been largely addressed and that in contemporary America, black pathology is the true perpetrator of inequality. Because of this they are often maligned as "Uncle Toms," but like adherents to other black ideologies, not all conservatives agree with one another. Some point to the continuing legacy of racism operating in the lives of African Americans, while others argue that even historical racism is not a significant explanatory variable in black life chances. In the contemporary era such black Republicans and conservative media personalities as Clarence Thomas, Armstrong Williams, Alan Keyes, and Colin Powell continue the black conservative tradition.

BLACK FEMINISM

Black feminism focuses on the intersection between race, gender, class, and sexuality and seeks gender equality within the African-American community as well as racial equality within the American state. Feminism both stakes out a new intellectual ground and maps a unique political strategy through a diverse set of ideas that are variously attentive to issues of class, religion, private/public dichotomies, interracial alliances, and sexual identity. Many black feminists prefer to use the term *Womanism* to distinguish that black feminism is not simply an articulation of white feminist thought by black women. Womanism emphasizes that black women make unique contributions to the understanding of relations of power, domination, and resistance. Central tenets of this ideology include a blurring of identity politics, an unwillingness to ignore either race or sex in pursuit of political goals, an insistence on insurgent political action aimed at liberation of broad categories of people, and a centering of often-ignored persons within political movements.

Black feminism emerges from the experiences of African-American women in the middle of the twentieth century who were engaged in social and political action. These black women confronted patriarchal domination by men in the black liberation movement and the paternalist racism in the women's movement. These black women activists often found that their political agenda was sacrificed on the altar of unity, so they articulated a new agenda that made the issues of black women equally important as the issues of black men. This ideology derives from an attempt to address real material circumstances and to create a way to understand how race, gender, class, and sexuality intersect in black people's lives to create unique forms of political, economic, and social oppression.

Writers like Michelle Wallace, bell hooks, and Alice Walker are among the best known black feminists. Their work tells the stories of black women, which often include the challenges that black women face within African-American communities. Their work also analyzes how those experiences reveal the failures of the American democratic promise. Black feminism has also had an important influence on legal theory through such authors as Kimberle Crenshaw and on black religious thought through such scholars as Katie Cannon and Jacquelyn Grant. These writers have shaped new directions in their fields of inquiry by showing how black women's experiences do not fit neatly within existing frameworks of knowledge.

CONCLUSION

These traditions within black thought are common ways that African Americans organize political ideas. Most individuals have worldviews that are some combination of elements from multiple political perspectives. These ideologies allow African Americans to understand persistent social and economic inequality, to identify the significance of race in that inequality, to determine the role of whites in perpetuating or eliminating that inequality, and to devise strategies for overcoming that inequality.

See also Politics; Universal Negro Improvement Association

■ ■ *Bibliography*

Carmichael, Stokely, and Charles Hamilton. *Black Power: The Politics of Liberation*. New York: Random House, 1967.

Collins, Patricia Hill. *Black Feminist Thought: Knowledge, Consciousness, and the Politics of Empowerment*. New York: Routledge, 1991.

Dawson, Michael C. *Black Visions: The Roots of Contemporary African-American Political Ideologies*. Chicago: University of Chicago Press, 2001.

Faryna, Stan, Brad Stetson, and Joseph G. Conti, eds. *Black and Right: The Bold New Voice of Black Conservatives in America*. Westport, Conn.: Praeger, 1997.

Gaines, Kevin. *Uplifting the Race: Black Leadership, Politics, and Culture in the Twentieth Century*. Chapel Hill: University of North Carolina Press, 1996.

Harris-Lacewell, Melissa V. *Barbershops, Bibles, and BET: Everyday Talk and Black Political Thought*. Princeton, N.J.: Princeton University Press, 2004.

Pinkney, Alphonso. *Red, Black, and Green: Black Nationalism in the United States.* Cambridge, U.K., and New York: Cambridge University Press, 1976.

MELISSA V. HARRIS-LACEWELL (2005)

POLITICS

◄─■┃■──

This entry consists of two distinct articles examining African-American political experience in Latin America and in the United States.

POLITICS AND POLITICIANS IN LATIN AMERICA
Ollie A. Johnson III

POLITICS IN THE UNITED STATES
Hanes Walton Jr.
Mervyn Dymally

WOMEN AND POLITICS IN LATIN AMERICA AND THE CARIBBEAN
Dessima M. Williams

POLITICS AND POLITICIANS IN LATIN AMERICA

The black political experience is complex and diverse. The Spanish, Portuguese, and French colonial rulers and their descendants enslaved and exploited Africans and their descendants for four centuries. The exact nature of the black experience varied greatly according to numerous factors, including colonial power, political system, economy, culture, leadership, and the size and concentration of the black population. In general, Afro–Latin Americans have struggled to resist, survive, and overcome the brutal conditions into which they were placed.

Some blacks have created majority or all-black associations, organizations, and political parties to articulate their demands and defend their interests. Other blacks have worked across racial lines through armed groups, social movements, labor unions, professional associations, and political parties to achieve their goals. Africans and their descendants in the Americas have had diverse opinions on the relative importance of racial identity and on the best strategies to improve black living conditions. These inevitable differences remain vivid given the large number of Afro–Latin Americans and the negative consequences of centuries of white dominance.

SLAVERY

Most of the Africans captured in West and Central Africa for shipment to the Americas never completed the journey. Many Africans died before arrival in the New World as a result of the horrific conditions of the African slave trade. At the same time, about ten to twelve million Africans survived the deadly transatlantic Middle Passage.

Blacks have been involved in politics in Latin America since they arrived in significant numbers as servants and slaves in the 1500s. The early African presence was concentrated in the Caribbean and Mexico. Eventually, Brazil received the largest number of Africans. Wherever they were, the black masses were enslaved from the 1500s to the 1800s. Slavery in agriculture, mining, and domestic service comprised Africans' brutal reality in the Spanish and Portuguese colonies in the Americas. From the 1500s to the 1700s, Africans outnumbered Spanish and Portuguese immigrants and represented the largest demographic group. During this period, indigenous people experienced a dramatic population decline throughout the Americas because of colonial European violence and diseases.

Today there are black people in every country in Latin America. Although they represent one third of Latin America's population, they are not distributed evenly throughout the region. In the Caribbean, African descendants are the largest percentage of the national populations. The South American countries of Argentina, Chile, Paraguay, Bolivia, and Uruguay have very small black populations. In Central America and Mexico, the African-descendant communities are small and concentrated on the Atlantic and Pacific coasts. There are some majority black communities on the Pacific coast of Colombia and Ecuador. In absolute numbers, Brazil and Colombia have the largest black populations in South America.

The 1500s, 1600s, and 1700s represented a holocaust of death, enslavement, and subordination of the African and indigenous populations by the Spanish and Portuguese colonial forces. Some Africans escaped their oppression and created maroon societies or runaway communities called *quilombos* in Brazil and palenques in areas colonized by the Spanish. The earliest black political leaders in the Americas were the rulers of these communities such as Gaspar Yanga in Mexico, Benkos Bioho in Colombia, and Zumbi dos Palmares in Brazil. However, most Africans lived and died under slavery. Black women were often raped and abused sexually by their white masters and overseers, thereby creating the initial and ultimately large mulatto population.

Developments during the 1800s brought opportunities for change, and the African-descendant population took advantage. Blacks in Haiti defeated French colonialism and abolished racial slavery with a revolution (1791–1804) that provoked fear among white elites in the United States, Spanish America, and Brazil. Independence struggles against Spain also created opportunities for Afro–Latin Americans to not only take up arms for national sovereignty but also against slavery. In Mexico, Vicente Guerrero, of African and indigenous ancestry, helped lead the military struggle for independence and became Mexico's president in 1829. Generals Simón Bolívar and José de San Martín led the independence struggle in South America and included mulattos and blacks among their followers and supporters. Independence and abolitionist movements, as well as ongoing slave escapes and revolts, led to the abolition of slavery during the course of the century.

POSTSLAVERY TRENDS

Slavery ended last in Puerto Rico (1873), Cuba (1886), and Brazil (1888). In these countries and others, blacks did not enjoy the full benefits of freedom because the ruling white authorities were not committed to assisting the newly freed population with better education, housing, and employment options. The late 1800s and early 1900s were years of extreme white racism throughout the Americas. Afro–Latin Americans often lived in slavelike conditions for decades after formal abolition. Many white elites were ashamed of their dark multiracial societies and actively recruited and subsidized European immigration. This whitening signaled a percentage decline of Latin America's black population.

By 1900 sovereignty in Cuba and Puerto Rico was thwarted by U.S. occupation. Cuba witnessed the efforts of independence leaders José Martí and Afro-Cuban Antonio Maceo distorted by various U.S. interventions and support for corrupt national leaders. Despite formal independence in 1902, some Afro-Cuban independence fighters such as Evaristo Estenoz and Pedro Ivonet remained unsatisfied with low Afro-Cuban political representation, jobs, and veterans benefits. Estenoz and others formed the Independent Party of Color (Partido Independiente de Color, or PIC) in 1907, the first black political party in the Americas. Frustrated with their marginalization and the eventual banning of their party, PIC leaders mobilized their supporters and called for armed rebellion. The Cuban government's response was unexpected. In 1912 the government killed the PIC's leadership and led a massacre of thousands of blacks. The killings had a chilling effect on independent Afro-Cuban political organizing for decades.

Under even greater repressive occupation than Cuba, Puerto Rico's independence movement declined because of external and internal forces. Pedro Albizu Campos, a Puerto Rican of African ancestry, was one of the most articulate and dynamic leaders for independence from the 1920s until his death in 1965. A graduate of Harvard Law School, Albizu Campos was familiar with American culture and politics. He returned to Puerto Rico in the 1920s, joined the Puerto Rican Nationalist Party, and dedicated his life to working for independence from the United States. Because of his effectiveness, Albizu Campos was imprisoned by U.S. authorities in 1936 and spent more than twenty years incarcerated in the United States and Puerto Rico.

In the 1930s there were two attempts to organize black political parties as a way to mobilize the black population and maximize its influence within the political arena. In Brazil, the Brazilian Black Front (Frente Negra Brasileira) was founded in the city of São Paulo in 1931. The Front's leaders such as Jose Correa Leite, Gervasio de Morães, Raul Amaral, and Arlindo and Isaltino Veiga dos Santos, protested desperate living conditions and racial discrimination and encouraged Afro-Brazilians to participate in politics. Expanding to different states throughout the country and enjoying increased popularity, the leadership transformed the Front into a political party. The "New State" dictatorship of President Getulio Vargas banned all political parties from 1937 to 1945. The Front never recovered.

In 1936 in Uruguay, black activists founded the Black Autochthonous Party (Partido Autoctono Negro, or PAN) to improve educational opportunities, fight racial discrimination, and support Afro-Uruguayan political participation. The party's founders were Elemo Cabral, Ventura Barrios, Pilar Barrios, and Salvador Betervide. Like the Brazilian Black Front, the PAN promoted black unity rather than racial separation. Both groups wanted to racially integrate their country's government by increasing black political representation. Although unsuccessful in getting blacks elected to public office, the Front and PAN expressed deep concerns about the political, social, and economic situation of blacks in their respective countries. The PAN fragmented and declined by the early 1940s.

One of the first successful black Latin American politicians of the twentieth century was Colombia's Diego Luis Córdoba. First elected to Congress in 1933, Córdoba held a series of distinguished elected and appointed positions until his death in 1964. A member of the left wing of the Liberal Party, Córdoba defended the poor and working classes and denounced racial discrimination against blacks. He successfully supported the legislation that passed in 1947 creating the new department (equivalent to a U.S. state) of Choco, a majority black area on Colombia's North Pacific coast. Initially elected to Congress as a deputy from the department of Antioquia, Córdoba later represented Choco as a senator from 1947 until 1964.

CONTEMPORARY BLACK POLITICS: 1960S–PRESENT

In the 1960s and 1970s most Latin American countries experienced some type of authoritarian rule. The dictatorships routinely violated the rights and liberties of the people and often cancelled or manipulated elections. Many governments were actively hostile to explicit political organizing by blacks. Governments generally accused black activists of being racist, threatening to divide the country, and creating problems where they did not exist. However, because of poverty, racial inequality, racial discrimination against blacks, inspiring examples of black activism in the United States, African nations, and the English-speaking Caribbean, and their own traditions of political struggle, Afro–Latin Americans continued probing for ways to exert political power. Since the 1980s most Latin American countries have made the transition to civilian rule, and this process has increased black opportunities for partisan electoral competition and popular participation.

BRAZIL. Brazil has the largest population of African ancestry in the Western Hemisphere. Afro-Brazilian politics were reinvigorated with the emergence of new black movement organizations in the late 1970s. These groups protested racial discrimination and violence against blacks and criticized the Brazilian military dictatorship (1964–

1985). Since 1970, black activists and intellectuals have been fighting to improve the oppressive conditions under which the vast majority of Afro-Brazilians live. Groups such as the Unified Black Movement (Movimento Negro Unificado, or MNU), the Black Cultures Research Institute (Instituto de Pesquisas das Culturas Negras, or IPCN), and Geledes—the Black Women's Institute (Instituto da Mulher Negra, Geledes) have been leaders in challenging the racial status quo in Brazil.

Many black politicians have also worked to change government inaction against racism and racial inequality. Activists-turned-politicians such as Abdias do Nascimento and Benedita da Silva took the arguments of the black movement into the Brazilian Congress. During the 1980s and 1990s black elected officials worked within the national Chamber of Deputies and Federal Senate to condemn the Brazilian "myth of racial democracy" as a smoke screen preventing government recognition of pervasive racial discrimination against blacks. One of the problems Nascimento and da Silva faced was the underrepresentation of blacks in Congress. In a country in which Afro-Brazilians officially represent almost fifty percent of the population, they made up less than five percent of Congress. Overcoming great obstacles, Nascimento, da Silva, and other progressive politicians and black movement activists persuaded political parties and the government to address the issue of race.

In Latin America, Brazil has experienced the most extensive range of state action. Nationally, the Brazilian government in 1988 created the Palmares Foundation (Fundação Cultural Palmares) whose purpose is to work with educational, governmental, and private institutions and the public to increase awareness of Afro-Brazilian contributions to Brazilian society and culture. The foundation publishes materials by and about Afro-Brazilians and sponsors educational forums. Moreover, President Fernando Henrique Cardoso's administration (1995–2003) welcomed and encouraged political debate and discussion regarding public policies to improve the situation of blacks.

By the end of the Cardoso administration, the national government and some state governments began passing controversial affirmative action legislation. Several states, including the large state of Rio de Janeiro, have adopted racial quotas for public university admissions. At the state and local levels in São Paulo, Rio de Janeiro, Minas Gerais, and Rio Grande do Sul, government agencies such as the Council for Participation and Development of the Black Community (Conselho de Participação e Desenvolvimento da Comunidade Negra) and the Special Office for Afro-Brazilian Affairs (Secretária pela Promoção e Defesa Afro-Brasileira) were created to assist blacks.

The administration of President Luiz Inácio Lula da Silva (2003–2007) has also addressed racial issues in innovative ways. Strongly influenced by the Workers Party's black activists and elected officials, the government created the Special Office for the Promotion of Racial Equality (Secretária Especial de Políticas de Promoção da Igualdade Racial, or SEPPIR) on March 21, 2003. The head of the Special Office is Matilde Ribeiro, a black activist who has been given cabinet minister status to recognize the government's commitment to pursuing pro-racial equality policies. Her efforts are based on "Brasil Sem Racismo" (Brazil Without Racism), a twenty-page document outlining the Lula presidential campaign's pledge to work toward eliminating discrimination, prejudice, and racism. The Lula administration has given greater visibility to its pro-black initiatives than any previous presidential administration. In a related and unprecedented move, President Lula appointed three additional Afro-Brazilians, Marina Silva (Environment), Gilberto Gil (Culture), and Benedita da Silva (Social Welfare), to cabinet minister positions.

ECUADOR. In contrast to Brazil, Latin America's largest and most populous nation with 180 million citizens, Ecuador is geographically small and has a population of thirteen million. Afro-Ecuadorians are often neglected when national governments develop their policy priorities. During the 1980s and 1990s, leftist lawyer Jaime Hurtado Gonzalez, leader of the Democratic Popular Movement (Movimiento Popular Democratico, or MPD), was the most visible Afro-Ecuadorian politician. Hurtado served as national representative in Congress from 1979 to 1984 and was later a presidential candidate. He and an aide were assassinated on February 17, 1999, in the capital of Quito near the national Congress. Hurtado did not attempt to organize the Afro-Ecuadorian community around issues of racial empowerment or political advancement. He consistently emphasized exclusion and exploitation based on class. Hurtado's political party is influential in the majority black province of Esmeraldas. Rafael Erazo, an activist and member of the MPD from Esmeraldas, is a first term member (2003–2007) of Congress and Ecuador's only black provincial deputy.

CUBA. Cuba is a unique case for examining the role of blacks in Latin American politics. The Cuban Revolution of 1959 brought Fidel Castro to power, where he remains more than four decades later. This Caribbean socialist revolution succeeded in transforming the country's political institutions and culture. Cubans worked hard to create an egalitarian society with an emphasis on free education and health care. The revolution has survived despite the sustained hostility of the U.S. government and the Cuban exile community concentrated in southern Florida. As the poorest segment of the country, blacks participated in and benefited from the revolutionary government's policies.

Under the revolution, Afro-Cubans have improved their levels of educational attainment and health care access while expanding political participation with increased government positions. Afro-Cubans have been government ministers, ambassadors, and members of parliament. The Cuban government is ruled by one political party, the Communist Party. Some blacks such as Esteban Lazo Hernandez and Pedro Saez Montejo have risen to positions of national leadership within the Communist Party.

At the same time, the official ban on political opposition outlaws independent black political organizing. Afro-Cubans cannot create groups to protest racial discrimination and pursue their race-specific political interests. This prohibition became a volatile issue in the 1990s during the Cuban economic crisis. The disappearance of Eastern European socialist regimes and the Soviet Union devastated the Cuban economy. The Cuban government responded by opening the economy to foreign investment, promoting tourism, and allowing Cubans to open small businesses. Afro-Cubans experienced a new racism as they were denied equal opportunities to work in the revitalized tourist industry. They protested their treatment and forced President Castro to acknowledge their concerns. As the economic situation remains difficult, resulting in increased prostitution and other crimes, racial inequality has reemerged as a significant issue.

DOMINICAN REPUBLIC. Sharing the island of Hispaniola with Haiti, the Dominican Republic has developed a strong racist ideology, *antihaitianismo* (anti-Haitianism). Rooted in the white supremacy of Spanish colonialism and the Haitian occupation of the country from 1822 to 1844, the ideology holds that Dominicans are different from and better than Haitians. By exaggerating and idealizing the Hispanic and Catholic heritage of Dominicans and demonizing the African and vodou characteristics of Haitian culture, this ideology has penetrated significant sectors of Dominican culture, society, and politics. Reinforced through various political and military conflicts between Haiti and the Dominican Republic over the years, *antihaitianismo* has evolved into an elite control mechanism that allows Dominican leaders to divert attention away from serious domestic problems by blaming them fully or partially on Haitians. Thus, Dominican poverty, political instability, economic crises, corruption, and other major issues have been frequently blamed on Haitians.

One of the glaring ironies of the popularity and usefulness of *antihaitianismo* is that many Dominicans are

Peña Gomez, leader of the leftist Dominican Revolutionary Party (Partido Revolucionario Dominicano, or PRD), campaigning during presidential elections in 1996. Gomez, formerly mayor of the capital city Santo Domingo, ran unsuccessfully for president three times. © C. DOUCE/E. ALONSO/CORBIS SYGMA.

black and some proponents of *antihaitianismo* are black Dominicans who de-emphasize their African heritage and lighten themselves culturally by claiming nonblack ancestors and describing themselves as Indian. Blas Jiménez, the Afro-Dominican scholar, writer, and poet, has led the fight against this ideology and called on Dominicans to embrace their black identity and respect their Haitian brothers and sisters. The most successful Afro-Dominican politician was Peña Gomez, former mayor of the capital, Santo Domingo, and leader of the leftist Dominican Revolutionary Party (Partido Revolucionario Dominicano, or PRD). A strong opponent of American intervention in the country, Gomez ran unsuccessfully three times for president. He likely was denied election in 1994 through electoral fraud. Throughout his career and especially during his presidential campaigns, Peña Gomez was subjected to racist, anti-Haitian advertising that criticized his dark complexion, religious beliefs, humble origins, and even accused him of being Haitian. Throughout his political career, Pena Gomez refused to publicly confront and denounce the white racism of *antihaitianismo*. Following in the footsteps of Peña Gomez, Afro-Dominican entertainer Johnny Ventura was elected mayor of Santo Domingo, the country's largest city. Many Dominican politicians are mulattos, but few celebrate the country's African heritage and criticize the widespread white racist stereotypes of Haitians and Afro-Dominicans.

COLOMBIA. Since the 1960s, armed insurgents have been active in Colombia. This ongoing state of civil war as well as the country's central role in the international drug trade has contributed to widespread violence. A majority of Afro-Colombians are poor and especially vulnerable to the armed conflict in various parts of the country. Although traditional black communities are located on the Pacific and Atlantic coastal regions, blacks have migrated to other regions, including the capital of Bogotá, to seek better employment opportunities and to avoid the violence.

The national government has rarely conducted a racial census. As a result, there is uncertainty regarding the most accurate figure for the black population. Many Afro-Colombian scholars and activists argue that minimally between twenty-five and thirty-five percent of the national population is Afro-Colombian. There are black mayors and local elected officials in the historic Afro-Colombian regions, but blacks remain underrepresented politically at the national level. In the 1990s and in more recent years, Juan de Dios Mosquera, leader of the black human rights group Cimarron, has been one of the most visible and articulate activists demanding greater black representation in Congress and public policies to improve Afro-Colombian educational, employment, housing, and health care opportunities. High-profile black activists and politicians include Senator Piedad de Córdoba, former Choco senator Daniel Palacios, and former representatives Augustin Valencia and Zulia Mena.

The Colombian constitution of 1991 defined the nation as pluri-ethnic and multicultural in recognition of the important, but neglected, roles of indigenous and black groups in the country's development. Two years later, Law 70 was passed recognizing the Afro-Colombian population as an ethnic group with certain territorial, economic, political, and cultural rights. In 1994 the Office of Black Community Affairs (Dirección de Asuntos para las Comunidades Negras) was formed within the Interior Ministry to develop public policies to assist black communities in attaining their full constitutional rights. Despite these achievements, black community leaders like Carlos Rosero of the Black Communities Process (Proceso de Comuni-

dades Negras, or PCN) argue that the government has not done enough to implement Law 70 and other policies to improve Afro-Colombian living standards.

LATIN AMERICA. Black political leaders and organizations are gaining visibility in Latin America. They are being elected to office in greater numbers, rising in the ranks of political parties and labor unions, and participating more in public debates. Nonetheless, they have fewer resources than other groups and are thus at a distinct disadvantage in their political struggles. This resource deficit and ongoing political struggles have prompted some Afro-Latin American activists to internationalize their struggle by establishing relationships with each other and taking their concerns to major international financial and governmental institutions around the world.

Many Afro-Latin Americans are protesting, organizing, and fighting. Although these efforts are rarely front-page news, they illustrate that important segments of the black population refuse to be ignored and refuse to be quiet. Afro–Costa Rican leader Epsy Campbell, in her capacity as an elected official (deputy) and as a leader of the Afro-Caribbean and Afro-Latin American Women's Network (La Red de Mujeres Afrocaribeñas y Afrolatinoamericanas), has emphasized that the issue of gender and sexism must be raised by black politicians and political organizations. The network has worked since the early 1990s to give black women a mechanism to organize against racism, sexism, and other forms of oppression. The ongoing activities of Epsy Campbell and black women activists throughout Latin America demonstrate that they are challenging male chauvinism in black communities.

Blacks are underrepresented in national legislatures as well as state assemblies and city councils. As a result, some black politicians and activists who have supported race-specific government initiatives have built alliances and coalitions with nonblacks to achieve their goals. Black leaders have attempted to convince nonblack members of political parties, legislatures, and government bureaucracies of the necessity for state action to combat racial discrimination, poverty, and racial inequality.

Black legislators from Latin America organized two unprecedented meetings creating the foundation for new Afro-Latin American activism. On November 21–23, 2003, in Brasília, Brazil, and May 19–21, 2004, in Bogotá, Colombia, black elected officials from Brazil, Colombia, Costa Rica, Uruguay, Peru, Ecuador, Panama, and Honduras met to examine the situation of Afro-descendants in the Americas. The deputies, representatives, and senators agreed that black people in different Latin American countries often face similar hardships. These leaders have decided to meet again and discuss how they as elected officials can best work to improve the living conditions of their people.

See also Albizu Campos, Pedro; Anti-Colonial Movements; Anti-Haitianism; Coartación; da Silva, Benedita; Emancipation in Latin America and the Caribbean; Frente Negra Brasileira; Maroon Societies in the Caribbean; Movimento Negro Unificado; Nascimento, Abdias do; Palmares; Racial Democracy in Brazil

■ ■ *Bibliography*

Andrews, George Reid. *Afro-Latin America, 1800–2000.* New York: Oxford University Press, 2004.

Davis, Darien J., ed. *Slavery and Beyond: The African Impact on Latin America and the Caribbean.* Wilmington, Del.: Scholarly Resources, 1995.

Conniff, Michael L., and Thomas J. Davis. *Africans in the Americas: A History of the Black Diaspora.* New York: St. Martin's Press, 1994.

De la Fuente, Alejandro. *A Nation for All: Race, Inequality, and Politics in Twentieth-Century Cuba.* Chapel Hill: University of North Carolina Press, 2001.

Fontaine, Pierre Michel, ed. *Race, Class, and Power in Brazil.* Los Angeles: Center for Afro-American Studies, UCLA, 1985.

Hanchard, Michael George. *Orpheus and Power: The Movimento Negro of Rio de Janeiro and São Paulo, Brazil, 1945-1988.* Princeton, N.J.: Princeton University Press, 1994.

Hanchard, Michael, ed. *Racial Politics in Contemporary Brazil.* Durham, N.C.: Duke University Press, 1999.

Minority Rights Group, ed. *No Longer Invisible: Afro-Latin Americans Today.* London: Minority Rights Publications, 1995.

Moore, Carlos. *Castro, the Blacks and Africa.* Los Angeles: CAAS/UCLA, 1989.

Moore, Carlos, Tanya R. Sanders, and Shawna Moore, eds. *African Presence in the Americas.* Trenton, N.J.: African World Press, 1995.

Nascimento, Abdias do, and Elisa Nascimento. *Africans in Brazil.* Trenton, N.J.: African World Press, 1994.

Rout Jr., Leslie B. *The African Experience in Spanish America: 1502 to the Present Day.* Cambridge: Cambridge University Press, 1976.

Sagas, Ernesto. *Race and Politics in the Dominican Republic.* Gainesville: University Press of Florida, 2000.

Silva, Benedita da, Medea Benjamín, and Maisa Mendonca. *Benedita da Silva: An Afro-Brazilian Woman's Story of Politics and Love.* Oakland, Calif.: Institute for Food and Development Policy, 1997.

Wade, Peter. *Blackness and Race Mixture: The Dynamics of Racial Identity in Colombia.* Baltimore, Md.: Johns Hopkins University Press, 1993.

Walker, Sheila, ed. *African Roots/American Cultures: Africa in the Creation of the Americas.* Lanham, Md.: Rowman & Littlefield, 2001.

OLLIE A. JOHNSON III (2005)

POLITICS IN THE UNITED STATES

African-American politics has a long, complex, and frequently painful history in the United States. By definition slaves were noncitizens, outside of the political process. Yet slaves contrived in various ways to fashion a political role for themselves. In New England African Americans elected black governors and kings during Negro Election Day festivals that combined voting with parades, food, and entertainment. During the colonial period, free blacks tried to enter the political process whenever possible, but were unable to exercise significant influence on the political system. In the half century following the end of the American Revolution, free black voting was largely restricted, but through petitions, community organizations, emigrationist activities, newspapers, and eventually the Antebellum Convention Movement, free blacks expressed themselves politically.

Beginning in the 1830s, at the same time that the Abolition movement offered blacks a voice within a national reform movement, blacks themselves set up numerous committees and organizations to struggle for suffrage, civil rights, and education. Nevertheless, the political status of African Americans remained uncertain, and it eroded during the late 1840s and 1850s as a result of growing white racism, immigrant labor competition, Fugitive Slave Laws, and other factors. Many African Americans became convinced that freedom in the United States was unattainable, and turned their attention to colonization schemes in Africa, Canada, Haiti, and other places.

The outbreak of the Civil War galvanized blacks, who saw the war as a struggle for their liberation. Throughout the first two years of the war, African-American leaders such as Frederick Douglass campaigned for blacks to be armed and devoted their attention to securing aid for freemen who escaped behind Union lines, as well as civil rights and suffrage for the free black community. By 1862 blacks were permitted to enlist in the Union army. Thousands joined, recognizing the importance of the struggle, and black leaders served as recruiting agents.

For a brief period during Reconstruction, fortified by constitutional amendments guaranteeing equal citizenship and suffrage and white northern efforts to ensure southern compliance, black males for the first time participated fully in the electoral system. Black elected officials, sponsored by southern Republican parties in exchange for black voting support, appeared on the national scene, and black state legislators and convention delegates made decisive contributions to the political culture of their states. Meanwhile, there was widespread black involvement in municipal politics in the South's few cities of importance. Richmond, Virginia, had thirty-three black city council members between 1871 and 1896, while in the deep South, leaders such as William Finch of Atlanta and Holland Thompson of Montgomery, Alabama, were elected to positions on city councils. In 1873 Mifflin Gibbs was elected a municipal judge in Little Rock, Arkansas. Many smaller towns elected black mayors. Between 1870 and 1900 twenty African Americans were elected to the House of Representatives, and two served in the Senate.

White Southerners never really accepted blacks as equal members of the body politic, however, and following the withdrawal of northern pressure—both military and political—from the South during the mid-1870s, the scope of black public participation narrowed. Black officeholding all but disappeared, and black voting power was vitiated by voting fraud, intimidation of voters, and electoral devices such as redistricting. As early as 1878 the city of Atlanta changed from ward elections to at-large voting to dilute the black vote. Other cities soon followed suit. Even where black suffrage was unfettered, the dissolution of southern Republicanism left blacks no effective weapon against Democratic regimes other than through alliance with third parties such as the Populists, who were ambivalent about black support.

In the upper South, black Republicans continued to be elected in small numbers. George White, an African American, represented North Carolina in Congress from 1897 to 1901, while blacks such as Richmond's John Mitchell Jr. served on city councils in Virginia during the 1890s. Violence and legislative action against black voting during the 1890s cut off even these avenues of influence.

Meanwhile, the political influence of blacks in the urban North also diminished. In the immediate postbellum period, some blacks were elected to office. In 1866, with the aid of white voters, state representatives Charles L. Mitchell and Edward G. Walker of Boston became the first blacks elected to office from a large urban area. In 1876 George L. Ruffin was elected to Boston's Common Council, and in 1883 he became the first African American appointed to the Massachusetts judiciary. In most cities, however, the percentage of African Americans in the population remained too small for blacks to play a significant role, and as immigrant-backed machines hostile to blacks took control of city governments, black voting power diminished. Moreover, city governments were often dependent on state legislatures, which controlled budgets and selected police chiefs and other officials. These outside bodies could act to curtail or eliminate black voting strength. (Similarly, in 1871 the U.S. Congress stripped Washington, D.C., whose population was one-third black, of its elected government.) Even after many cities obtained "home rule" at the end of the century, Progressive elites instituted at-large voting and granted power to unelected city commissions and civil service workers to curb the power of blacks and ethnic whites.

Through most of the late nineteenth century, the Republican Party maintained its alliance with both southern and northern black populations through government appointments and support for education. Many black voters and party leaders measured party support not through its defense of civil rights but by the amount of political patronage granted the black community. Still, as early as the 1870s many blacks grew dissatisfied with shrinking party patronage and the party's inaction over violations of black rights, and distanced themselves from the Republicans. Beginning in the 1880s some blacks flirted with joining the Democrats. However, neither party was willing to risk alienating white voters or grant more than token assistance in exchange for the black vote. Others joined third parties or attempted to build up separate black institutions but were unable to mount effective challenges to prevailing political trends.

By 1900 virtually all southern blacks were disfranchised, while their counterparts in the North were unable to exert significant influence. A few political clubs, such as New York's United Colored Democracy, were formed, but they were merely satellite party groups, given minor patronage positions in exchange for promoting white candidates. Black political power remained largely dormant for a generation, except for the influence black strongmen such as Charles Anderson in New York City, Robert Church Jr., in Memphis, and, above all, Booker T. Washington wielded over Republican Party patronage. The ratification in 1920 of the Nineteenth Amendment, which gave women of all races the right to vote, had little discernible impact on black political strength. In the first years after the turn of the century, former border states such as Maryland were the only places with significant African-American influence on municipal government. For example, in 1890 Harry Sythe Cummings became the first of several blacks over the following years to sit on the Baltimore City Council.

The Great Migration of southern blacks to northern and Midwestern cities during the late 1910s and 1920s brought in its wake large numbers of new voters. The voting power of the increased population was strengthened by the increasing ghettoization and residential concentration of African Americans. Their votes were organized in exchange for patronage by ward leaders selected by urban machines, such as New York's J. Raymond Jones and Chicago's William Dawson. In many places, city council and other municipal elected offices remained largely powerless, and ward committee positions were the most powerful city jobs most blacks held. In a few areas, blacks became a large enough segment of the population to elect black officials. In 1915, after the creation of a largely black district in Chicago, Republican Oscar DePriest won election to the city's Board of Alderman. In 1919 Charles Roberts was elected to New York City's Aldermanic Board. Similarly, Frank Hall was elected to the Cincinnati City Council in 1931. The growing strength of black organizations was evidenced by DePriest's election in 1928 as the first northern black congressman. As important, the migration and the Great Depression helped foster increasing black community militancy, and civil rights joined patronage as a primary concern of African-American voters.

During the 1930s, as a result of aid from New Deal social programs, urban machine involvement, and labor union activism, the majority of black voters were drawn into the Democratic Party coalition. Meanwhile, black Democratic elected officials, beginning with Arthur Mitchell in 1934, entered Congress as well as state legislatures and municipal bodies. While the Democrats did not commit to civil rights action or provide aid proportionate to the level of black support, they made symbolic gestures toward the black community and instituted several relatively race-neutral government programs. While blacks backed Democratic candidates, many remained registered Republicans. A small number of blacks supported minor parties, notably the Communist Party, whose advocacy of civil rights and interracialism won it the support or approval of many African Americans.

In the years after World War II, black political activity increased. The war brought renewed migration to the North of southern blacks, who swelled urban voting blocs. The migration made possible the election of larger numbers of black officials such as Harlem, New York, minister Adam Clayton Powell Jr., who in 1941 became the first African-American member of the New York City Council, and who three years later was elected to Congress.

At the same time, civil rights became a national issue. In 1948 the adoption of a strong civil rights platform at the Democratic National Convention prompted a walkout by some white Southerners. Democratic presidential candidate Harry Truman was elected nevertheless, and his victory helped demonstrate the electoral clout of urban African Americans. Gradually, over the following years, northern Democrats championed that party's transition to a strongly pro-black position.

Postwar black population growth in the urban North continued to be heavy, and its effects were heightened by declining white populations, as whites migrated to nearby suburbs. In 1953 New York State assemblyman Hulan Jack was elected to the powerful position of Manhattan borough president. Soon after, Newark and Detroit, two cities with heavy concentrations of black residents, gained their first black city councilmen.

In 1944 the U.S. Supreme Court struck down the "white primary," a leading method by which southern blacks were deprived of the ballot. The decision increased both southern black voter registration and pressure for suffrage rights. Beginning with the South Carolina Progressive Democratic Party in 1944, blacks formed satellite political organizations to encourage voter registration and unity. The migration of rural blacks to southern industrial centers also accelerated during the 1950s, and all the deep South states had majority urban populations by 1960. The large potential vote the migrants made up was partially unleashed by registration efforts and the reduction of barriers to registration. A few blacks even won election to office. In 1948 Oliver Hill became Richmond's first black city councilman in a half century, and in 1957 Hattie Mae White was elected to Houston's school board.

To neutralize the power of the black vote, both white Southerners and their northern counterparts adopted various electoral stratagems: At-large elections were instituted for political offices; runoff elections assured a solid white bloc vote against black candidates; cities annexed adjacent white suburbs to dilute the percentage of blacks in the city; black areas were divided or merged with nearby white areas to prevent the formation of black majority districts (Tuskegee, Alabama, gerrymandered its black voters out of the city, a move struck down by the U.S. Supreme Court in 1960 in *Gomillion v. Lightfoot*).

The civil rights movement of the 1960s made possible the return of blacks as full-fledged actors on the national political scene. Not only did the movement's demonstrations bring black concerns temporarily to the top of the American political agenda, but also grassroots lobbying and voter registration efforts, through such organizations as the Mississippi Freedom Democratic Party, and the National Democratic Party of Alabama gave masses of previously disfranchised southern blacks a channel for political self-expression. The culmination of the nonviolent movement's triumphs was the Voting Rights Act of 1965, which banned most of the measures used to curb black voting. The black vote unleashed by the act, and its subsequent extensions and amendments, completely transformed the southern political landscape and made possible the election of large numbers of black officials. By 1970 black city councilmen and state representatives had been elected in several southern states, and in 1972 Andrew Young of Georgia and Barbara Jordan of Texas became the first southern blacks elected to Congress in the twentieth century. Meanwhile, throughout the country, the conjunction of white urban depopulation and the growing power of black political organizations brought about an explosion of black mayors in large cities (beginning with Carl Stokes of Cleveland, Ohio, and Richard Hatcher of Gary, Indiana, in 1967), members of Congress (including Edward Brooke, who in 1966 became the first African American elected to the U.S. Senate by popular vote). However, legal challenges to existing electoral districts and systems were unavailing, and many states, both in and outside of the South, continued to practice both "massive resistance" and more subtle forms of subterfuge to thwart black electoral progress. As a result, change was continually retarded.

Despite the unprecedented political and electoral strides made by African Americans, the future of black politics remained uncertain. An African-American political class, made up of elected officials and black political leaders such as Jesse Jackson, has grown up during the years since 1965. Through such forums and networks as the Congressional Black Caucus, formed in 1971, its members have succeeded in articulating black concerns within mainstream political channels and in obtaining a certain share of national political influence (in part a result of the disproportionately high seniority rate of blacks in Congress). However, entrenched racism and the poor socioeconomic status of African Americans remain obstacles to full integration of the community into the nation's body politic. Even as blacks such as former governor L. Douglas Wilder of Virginia demonstrate crossover electoral appeal, black frustration with mainstream party policies that appear to downplay their needs has resulted in chronic low voter turnout and has led some frustrated activists to turn from mainstream political parties toward independent black institutions.

ANTEBELLUM POLITICS

African-American involvement in American politics began in the period from 1619 through 1865. During much of that time, the historical record of African-American political involvement is thin. Nevertheless, there is much to indicate that African-American political activity, both as part of the larger American body politic and as African Americans' organizing institutions that mirrored and challenged their white counterparts, often was an offshoot of African values and customs.

COLONIAL ERA. African-American politics began in the seventeenth century, and political participation grew during the eighteenth. The most direct actors were free African Americans. Two categories of political participation were available to them during this era: pressure and electoral politics. As an example of the former category, in New Netherlands (later New York) in 1661, free blacks petitioned the director-general and lords councilor of the colony to mandate that their adopted children be recognized as free. The petition was granted. In 1726 a free black petitioned the chief justice of the General Court in North Carolina, asking the colonial judiciary to uphold his free status and voluntary choice of association. The court denied this request. In 1769 a group of free blacks in Virginia successfully petitioned the House of Burgesses to have their families exempted from taxation.

As for electoral participation, the small free black population was allowed to participate in certain places. In the thirteen colonies, prior to the Revolution, there was sporadic voting by free blacks. Only four southern colonies explicitly denied free blacks the vote, and even in these colonies it is not improbable that here and there people willingly acquiesced in the casting of an occasional ballot by a black man or a mulatto. The earliest record of such black voting came from South Carolina, where the 1701 and 1703 gubernatorial elections were marked by widespread complaints over free black votes.

The legal flexibility that made free black voting possible resulted from the fact that there were free blacks at that time, and their existence went all but unnoticed. The vast majority of African Americans during the colonial era were slaves, who could not legally vote or engage in formal political activities. Some slaves may have been allowed to vote in close elections by their plantation masters. Historical research has uncovered such practices in Rapide Parish—dubbed "the ten-mile district"—in Louisiana, and these practices continued from the early nineteenth century until the eve of the Civil War. Manipulated as this voting was, it did develop a group of individuals who were at least socialized into the evolving political process.

The slaves' exclusion from electoral participation did not mean that they were entirely cut off from political expression. Such expression can, of course, be found—indirectly—in the acts of slaves who resisted punishments, escaped, purchased their freedom, or revolted, or who destroyed the property of the masters. This behavior, motivated by ingrained concepts of freedom and liberty fueled by memories of one's own or one's forebears' liberty in an African past, as well as responding to an immediate situation of oppression, contained a clear political message.

Moreover, slaves played an active role in the political culture in some areas of Colonial and early national New England through the celebration of Negro Election Day as part of the Colonial election day festivities. The ceremonial election of black "governors" and "kings" began in the mid-eighteenth century in ports and administrative centers with large slave populations. The earliest evidence of the ceremony is from Salem, Massachusetts, in 1741; Newport, Rhode Island, in 1756, and Hartford Connecticut, from sometime before 1766. It quickly spread throughout New England and adjacent areas such as Albany, New York, with black leaders' "jurisdictions" shrinking to the county or town level as more towns participated. Although this was only ceremonial voting, it was an exercise that probably helped to develop black political leadership and promoted the organization of the slave community. At least it represented the demand by African Americans to participate in the public life of the larger society, as filtered through their own appreciation of African political traditions. In some areas, such as New Hampshire, black community members even formed "slave courts" that regulated the conduct of slaves and punished offenses.

The Colonial political system did shape the fledgling efforts of African Americans to participate in the political process. For example, whether the election was for "governor" or "king" seems to have depended on the type of colony in which the election was held: Blacks in charter colonies, which elected their own governors, had black "governors," while those in royal colonies, whose governors were appointed by the king of England, selected "kings." Similarly, there were rude party divisions of blacks into "Tories" and "Whigs" (based on masters' political leanings). The institutions African Americans built covertly expressed their struggle against political powerlessness and satirized the white institutions that surrounded and excluded them.

The immediate context of the white election day ritual, however, was not the only operative variable in the establishment of Negro Election Day. There was also the influence of African background and heritage. The religious-political Adae ceremony of the Ashanti provides an illustration of a similar custom. Other customs—the coronation ritual of the Maradi, and the harvest festival of the Jukun-speaking peoples—similarly illustrate those ceremonial traditions. Indeed, peoples of African heritage in Brazil, Martinique, Cuba, and other areas of the New World engaged in similar election proceedings. Descriptions of the ritual in Newport clearly indicate African features such as songs, dances, drums, and games. Also, the ritual took place, as in Africa, in a large open space under a tree. After the 1820s, with the emancipation of most northern blacks, Negro Election Day ceremonies declined, and were largely replaced with carefully staged parades that commemorated the end of local slavery. Unlike the election day ceremonies, the emancipation parades often had an explicitly oppositional political component.

REVOLUTIONARY AMERICA. When the First Continental Congress met in September 1774, African Americans' political participation, save for events such as slave revolts, had not really arrived at the stage of coherent collective action. The rare political actions of blacks were still individual, and they lacked a strong sense of community and racial consciousness. However, by the time that revolutionary America had transformed itself into an independent nation and developed a federal system, African-American politics had begun to evolve beyond the strictly individual stage, to achieve some collective bases of action.

The revolutionary struggle that led to the creation of the United States of America had a profound effect on African-American ideology and political activities. Blacks, conscious of the irony of white colonists campaigning for "liberty" while denying it to their slaves, made use of revolutionary rhetoric and the wartime needs of the country to carve out a political space for themselves. Between 1773 and 1774 African Americans in Massachusetts presented five collective antislavery petitions to the General Court, Massachusetts's governing body. One of the early petitioners, from 1773, challenged the legislators, "We expect great things from men who have made such a noble stand against the designs of their fellow-men to enslave them." Scores of other petitions protesting slavery and discrimination were presented to the legislatures of the newly independent states in the following years.

When war broke out, many free African Americans joined the fledgling American army, recognizing that military service was a traditional mark of citizenship. Partly for the same reason, white authorities soon attempted to bar blacks from military service. Once white opposition to arming slaves, at least in the northern states, melted away under pressure of military necessity, blacks enlisted in disproportionate numbers in the Continental Army. Meanwhile, slaves in Virginia, promised freedom by royal governor Lord Dunmore if they fought on the side of England, rushed in large numbers to his offshore base.

Revolution in America did little to improve the political participation of African Americans. Four of the new state constitutions denied free blacks the right to vote; five more states would eventually deny it, and only four would never deny it. Thus only four of the thirteen original colonies—plus Vermont, admitted to the Union in 1791—permitted African Americans to vote. In all of these four states—Massachusetts, New Hampshire, Rhode Island, and New York—the Negro Election Day celebrations continued to be observed regularly, though New York imposed a discriminatory property requirement for black voters in 1821. In Connecticut, which denied African-

American suffrage in 1818, the blacks' last "governor" held office shortly before the Civil War.

Nevertheless, the petitions and military service did exert an influence on the new governments in the years after the war's end. State legislatures in the North passed gradual abolition statutes, and even southern states passed laws simplifying manumission. Many veterans were freed, and some were franchised. Wentworth Cheswell of New Hampshire, probably the first person of African descent elected to office in North America, served as a justice of the peace as early as 1768, and was town selectman for New Market, New Hampshire, several times after 1780. In 1806 he was an unsuccessful candidate for the state senate. In 1831 Alexander Twilight of Vermont became the first African American elected to a state legislature.

Most of the states abolished the slave trade within their borders, although the U.S. Constitution delayed federal action until 1808. Meanwhile, African Americans and white antislavery allies appealed to the judiciary, bringing a handful of test cases challenging slavery in state courts. In 1783 Quock Walker brought a freedom suit in Massachusetts. Judge Richard Cushing ruled slavery incompatible with the state's constitution, resulting in the effective end of slavery in Massachusetts. By 1800 a number of northern states had passed emancipation statutes.

The development of two opposing national political parties, the Federalists and the Democratic-Republicans (later the Democratic Party), increased black political involvement. To the extent that blacks participated in campaign and electoral politics, they overwhelmingly supported the Federalists, led in part by such antislavery figures as Alexander Hamilton and John Jay, over Thomas Jefferson and the Democrats, who were identified with slavery and southern interests. The Federalist Party sought the support of black leaders such as New York City's Joseph Sidney and Philadelphia's Absalom Jones, and in 1809 established a black political club, the Washington Benevolent Society, which maintained active branches in Boston and New York City. Black voting played a notable role in the Federalists' narrow victory in New York in 1813.

With the changing structure of government and electoral context came a change in political protest behavior. Not only did African Americans send their petitions and memorials to various state executives and legislatures, but by 1797 they were also sending petitions to the Congress of the United States. On January 23, 1797, four African Americans living in Philadelphia petitioned Congress though Representative John Swanwick of Pennsylvania for a redress of their grievances, which were related to a North Carolina law of 1788 that provided for the capture and re-

selling of illegally manumitted slaves. Seven days after the petition arrived, Congress debated whether to accept or reject "a petition from fugitive slaves." By a vote of 50–33, Congress rejected the petition. This initial petition was soon followed by another, which arrived in "the second day of the new century," in 1800. Absalom Jones had his representative, Robert Waln of Pennsylvania, present a petition to Congress to demand the banning of the slave trade and the 1793 Fugitive Slave Act. However, Congress voted 85–1 not to consider the petition.

Thus, in this early national period, when African-American political participation was still closely circumscribed by denials of the right to vote, to serve on juries, to hold office, and to bring a legal suit against a white person, black political participation showed signs of expanding and extending itself into new directions. Not only did African Americans show increasing inclination to exert pressure and redirect their focus, they now began to take on a collective impulse. The influence of the African heritage and background was a strong spur to organization, in the form of mutual aid and fraternal organizations, educational societies, and black religious organizations, which grew up in African-American communities and served as the centers of collective effort and activism. For example, in Rhode Island, on November 10, 1780, free blacks established the African Union Society; in Massachusetts they formed The Sons of Africans Society in 1808. New York saw an African Society in 1809; Pittsburgh, an African Education Society in 1832; Boston, an African Lodge in 1787; and New York City, an African Marine Foundation in 1810. That these groups bore African names was no mere accident of simple naming. In the extant constitutions, preambles, laws, minutes, proceedings, resolutions, and reports of these African organizations, a budding "race consciousness" and sense of racial solidarity is openly expressed. Out of this sense of race-based community came the collective action that marked antebellum black pressure politics.

"Africa" did not simply provide the internal cohesion for these interest/pressure groups; it would also become a symbol of freedom and liberty. With the beginning of the emigration and colonization efforts, the influence of Africa directly reentered the contextual political realities of African Americans. The initial pioneering effort of Paul Cuffe, who personally returned thirty-eight free Negroes to Sierra Leone in 1815, was institutionalized (though substantially changed) in December 1816, when the American Colonization Society (ACS) was formed. Five years later, the society established the colony of Liberia. Although the two efforts had outwardly similar objectives, Cuffe sought Africa as a place of freedom and liberty. On the other hand, the motives of the society were at best mixed and questionable, since the society wished to send free blacks to Africa in part to eliminate what they saw as the anomalous position of the free black in the North. The implication that free blacks have no role to play in American society soon came under attack by African Americans, who saw the ACS as racist, and this served to catalyze their subsequent organizing efforts.

Finally, the late 1820s saw the beginning of African-American newspapers, which provided a forum for spokespersons who would take up the struggle on behalf of their "colored fellow citizens." (Freedom's Journal, founded in New York City in 1827, was the earliest.) The numerous efforts of such individuals and papers heralded not only a rising sense of solidarity and community but also vindicated the acts of pressure and protest in the revolutionary and the early national period that seemed, at first blush, so futile.

Thus elements of the African background provided the underpinning for fledgling African-American pressure group activity in the new nation by 1830. The first Negro convention was held on September 20, 1830, in Philadelphia, with delegates from seven states. Another convention met the next year, and black conventions subsequently were organized four times during the 1830s, three times in the 1840s, and twice in the 1850s. At the 1864 national convention in Syracuse, New York, the movement reorganized itself into the National Equal Rights League. The national convention movement directed, albeit in a rather unstable way, a mass self-help movement of the churches, mutual aid societies, and fraternal organizations, and took these efforts into the political area. With the emergence of such mass political action in both the electoral and protest areas, African-American politics had come of age.

The national organization, where possible, set up state and local affiliates. Some state and local auxiliaries pursued policies and directions independent of those of the national organization. When they were meeting and functioning properly, the national, state, and local bodies issued resolutions, petitions, prayers, and memorials addressed to state legislatures and to Congress. While their chief interest was the antislavery struggle, the conventions acted on other issues as well. Political rights such as suffrage, jury service, and repeal of discriminatory legislation were major concerns. Despite their support of abolitionist groups, the convention members also chided the American Anti-Slavery Society, founded in 1833, for its unwillingness to champion "social equality."

Temperance, education, and moral reform stood high on the agenda of many Negro conventions and allied groups throughout the era. Equally important was the fight for women's equality and voting rights. As early as Maria Stewart in the 1830s, African-American women played prominent roles in black politics. Just as many white feminists became politically committed through abolitionist activities, so black leaders from Sojourner Truth to Frederick Douglass attended feminist conferences and pressed for the end of gender discrimination.

The convention movement was supplemented by countless local political committees and pressure groups that campaigned for civil rights and educational opportunity. Black groups formed in the early 1830s, such as the Phoenix Society in New York City and the American Moral Reform Society, based in Philadelphia, added civil rights petitioning to their temperance and educational efforts. Meanwhile, African Americans in New York City and Philadelphia organized committees to protest denials of equal suffrage and to stimulate black political involvement. African Americans in Boston successfully lobbied to overturn a state law forbidding racial intermarriage, and organized protests that desegregated most of the state's railroads. In 1855 the Legal Rights Association sued in a New York City court protesting segregated streetcars and won a judgment. In 1849 Benjamin Roberts pursued a test case challenging segregated schools in Boston to the Massachusetts Supreme Court. Although he lost, the state legislature integrated the schools in 1855.

ABOLITIONIST AMERICA. In December 1833 the American Anti-Slavery Society, the first national abolitionist organization, was founded in Philadelphia. This marked the awakening of abolition as a full-fledged sociopolitical movement, and it catapulted blacks into the center of the political system. The electoral efforts of most free blacks in this era were focused on their work for and participation in a host of antislavery third parties. They attended their conventions and served as low-level officers at the conventions, especially as secretaries. They succeeded in having resolutions and platforms adopted that called for equality. They campaigned for the standard-bearers of these parties. Where they could, they voted for these candidates. And in several states in the expanding new nation, these antislavery parties sought to have the state extend suffrage to free blacks, but to no avail.

When the first antislavery party, the Liberty Party, was formed on April 1, 1840, at Albany, New York, it announced that its goal was "the absolute and unqualified divorce of the General Government from Slavery, and also the restoration of equality of rights, among men, in every state where the party exists or may exist." The Liberty Party's leaders reached out to free blacks, and shortly after the founding of the party, influential black leaders began to associate with it, attending party conventions and providing what limited electoral support they could muster. In return, the Liberty Party welcomed black supporters into party councils and leadership positions.

The brightest spot in the party's history was the election of John M. Langston on the party's ticket to a township clerk position in Ohio in 1855. Langston's nomination for office was the first ever given an African American by a political party. Despite this achievement, the Liberty Party was unable to compete with subsequent abolitionist parties. Its numbers declined through the 1850s, and it dissolved in 1860.

African Americans also became involved in the Free Soil Party. At its founding convention in Buffalo, New York, on August 9, 1848, the party adopted a platform calling for the exclusion of slavery from the District of Columbia and the territories of the United States, though it conceded the legality of slavery in existing states. While the party called for jury trials for captured fugitive slaves, it made no commitment to expanding black equality, and many of its leaders opposed black suffrage. Free blacks participated in the convention, and later in the campaign, despite the party's limited positions on equality and the liberation of slaves. Although unsuccessful in its initial presidential bid, the party tried again in 1852. This time the national nominating convention adopted a resolution favoring black suffrage, and elected Frederick Douglass secretary of the convention. Despite the work of Douglass and other free blacks, the party polled fewer votes than it had in 1848, and dissolved after the election.

There were other antislavery parties in which African Americans participated. Frederick Douglass attended the convention of the new National Liberty Party in Buffalo, New York, on June 14–15, 1848. The party's poor performance in the 1848 presidential election—which may have been the consequence of its stiff competition from the Liberty Party and the Free Soil Party—led to its collapse soon afterward. Another party, the Political Abolition Party, took up the struggle in 1856. It had an even more dismal showing than expected; it collected only 484 votes for its presidential candidate. It did not again contest a presidential election.

The antislavery parties were never large organizations, although they helped swing the balance in several elections. Their failure during the 1850s was largely the result of the entry of the Republican Party into the political fray. The Republicans captured the political imagination of many free blacks, and a significant degree of their support. In 1860 the Republican candidate, Abraham Lincoln, won the presidency, with the overwhelming support of free blacks and attentive slaves.

EMIGRATIONIST POLITICS Beginning in the 1840s, the African heritage began to influence African-American political participation and action in a new and more direct way, through the doctrine of African-American political nationalism. The historians John Bracey Jr., August Meier, and Elliott Rudwick describe the dynamics of this era:

> In the 1840s a number of converging developments turned Negro ideologies in more nationalist directions: the essential failure of the antislavery movement to liberate the slaves; the evidences of racism among many white abolitionists . . . increasing trends toward disfranchisement and segregation in public accommodations in many of the northeastern states, combined with the continuing pattern of discrimination in the Old Northwest that made the black man's condition there similar to that in the South; and the growing hopelessness of the economic situation. . . .

One result of the growing estrangement of African Americans from the mainstream of American politics was the national convention movement's increasing withdrawal from interracial groups and endorsement of independent black political organizations. Of course, this trend did not contradict its members' goal of equality in the United States. While blacks were nationalistic about their color, and were determined to build separate black institutions, their nationalism did not preempt their demands for inclusion as Americans. Black institutions were created as a halfway measure, as a means to the end of integration.

The events of the 1850s aggravated the obstacles confronting African Americans. The Fugitive Slave Act of 1850 made life unsafe and dangerous for large numbers of free blacks, and the Kansas-Nebraska Act threatened to extend slavery into new territories. Finally, the U.S. Supreme Court's decision in the 1857 Dred Scott Decision, that blacks had no rights as United States citizens and that a state could not forbid slavery, was responsible for convincing large numbers of black activists of the necessity for radical action. A few supported the idea of a violent overturning of the slave system, and threw their support to the white abolitionist John Brown, who planned a slave insurrection. At the same time, a number of African Americans mounted emigration and colonization efforts. Some emigrationists favored mass emigration to Africa. For them, Africa would be the place to create a great nation, a place where freedom and liberty would prevail and a place where an African nation might arise that would eventually rival that of America. Larger numbers moved to the relatively safe haven of Canada. Others favored Haiti, Central

America, or other places. National emigration conventions were held in 1854, 1856, and 1858.

On the eve of the Civil War, the essential features of African-American political culture had taken form and had started to mature. The dual influences of America and Africa had converged in the era of abolitionism and black nationalism to shape a political culture that had one message: In a society where racism is a permanent feature, equality and liberty for African Americans could not be left solely to the efforts of whites; instead, in a time of political and democratic restriction, a special role had to be played by African Americans themselves.

RECONSTRUCTION TO THE PRESENT

During the Reconstruction era, stretching from 1865 through 1877, the nature of African-American politics was radically transformed. The Fifteenth Amendment, ratified in 1870, gave African-American men the right to vote. Before the Civil War only a segment of the African-American community in the North was allowed to participate in politics; during the Reconstruction era, the entire community was permitted to participate. The results were striking, electing twenty African-American congressmen, two senators, a governor, six lieutenant governors, numerous local officials, state legislators, and delegates to state constitutional conventions. In addition to the figures who served in official positions, Reconstruction also energized large elements of the African-American community in political struggles. However, the gains achieved during Reconstruction were largely overturned in the years after the political compromise of 1877, when federal troops were withdrawn from the southern states, where most African Americans lived.

By the turn of the century, most southern states had adopted poll taxes, literacy tests, and other measures that disfranchised the vast majority of their black populations. Segregation was rigidly imposed on African Americans, whose hard-won citizenship rights were largely ignored. Even in the northern states, where African Americans retained voting rights, de facto housing and employment discrimination eroded the dream of equality. From the 57th until the 70th congresses there were no African Americans in the House or the Senate, and few local or state officials. In the face of such burdens, blacks organized what political protests they could.

The political struggle of African Americans from the end of Reconstruction to at least the 1960s, and in many ways to the present, has been focused on one goal: to reshape the political landscape so that the political and economic liberties of African Americans would be restored. When this goal was unworkable through major party politics, some blacks turned in independent, and sometimes separatist, directions. As early as the 1880s, many blacks, particularly in the North, grew dissatisfied with the Republican Party, which refused to act effectively against deteriorating race relations or to offer the black electorate patronage commensurate with its voting support. Black activists such as T. Thomas Fortune and Peter H. Clark urged African Americans to be politically independent and either explore the possibility of supporting the Democratic Party or establish an independent political party. Neither party was generally prepared to offer significant rewards. The resulting frustration led some African Americans to eschew major party politics altogether.

THIRD-PARTY POLITICS. Beginning in the 1870s, many black voters supported factions and splinter groups of the Republicans such as the National Republicans and the Greenback Party, as well as statewide organizations such as Virginia's Readjusters. These groups generally opposed the tight-money, probusiness slant of the mainstream Republicans. While they supported racially liberal platforms and welcomed black electoral support, most of these groups were not interested in campaigning for black interests or soliciting black participation in party activities.

The first national third party that blacks supported was the Prohibition Party, whose presidential campaigns attracted a solid core of black voters through the mid-twentieth century. The Prohibition Party did not target civil rights issues, but their radical reform message encompassed black interests. Temperance had long been a concern of black leaders in an attempt to raise the moral image and economic standing of African Americans. The elite nature of the party, particularly in the South, offered blacks with middle-class aspirations a measure of status, and the movement's strong Christian ideology contributed to general ideals of racial harmony and fairness. During the 1884 and 1888 campaigns, Prohibitionists realized that blacks represented swing votes on temperance measures, so the party reached out to them, sponsoring interracial rallies with black speakers and inviting African Americans to join organizing committees and convention delegations. For example, the African Methodist Episcopal bishop Henry McNeal Turner spoke for Prohibition Party candidates and was a delegate to the party's 1888 national convention. Philadelphia had a strong black Prohibitionist party in the late nineteenth century, at times supported by such stalwarts of black Philadelphia life as AME bishop Benjamin Tanner and physician Nathan Mossell. Also, the Prohibition Party generally opposed urban Democratic machines dominated by white ethnics, who were traditional antagonists of the black community. During the twentieth century, as the party grew more racially restrictive and black elites found other political channels, support for the Prohibitionists waned.

The Populist Party, the political arm of an agrarian movement of the 1890s, revolved around a platform of democratic reform, debt relief, and monetary expansion that appealed to southern and Midwestern black farmers who supported party candidates for president and for state offices. Prominent southern blacks such as former Georgia state legislator Anthony Wilson supported the party. Many Populists, such as Tom Watson of Georgia, called for interracial economic unity and took radical positions in support of the legal rights of African Americans. Populists helped elect black officials, such as North Carolina congressman George White in 1896. Populist representatives often voted funds for black education. However many white Populists were ambivalent about black participation and voting support, fearing white racist backlash, and were cautious about challenging discrimination. With the help of voting fraud and manipulation in Black Belt areas, southern Democrats beat back Populist challenges during the 1890s. Some Populist leaders, such as the South Carolina senator "Pitchfork" Ben Tillman, had rarely disguised their racial demagoguery. Others, such as Georgia's Tom Walton, underwent a notorious transformation, from supporting interracial cooperation during the heyday of the Populist era to becoming a virulent racist and defender of lynching. Black populists also despaired of joint black-white efforts. John B. Payner, a Texas Populist who was one of the party's leading orators, became an embittered supporter of separate black institutions, acknowledging that the price for their survival was a subservient relation to white authorities.

As a result of their own entrenched racism, many Populists responded by supporting black disfranchisement campaigns. Despite the reversal of southern Populist leaders on black issues, small numbers of blacks continued to support the declining party during its presidential campaigns of 1900, 1904, and 1908.

During most of the twentieth century, when the vast majority of blacks in the South were unable to vote, the center of black voting strength and political influence shifted to the urban North. The record of black activity in third parties during the first half of the twentieth century reveals a strong tie between black political participation and the politics of economic protest. A few blacks offered support for candidates running on economic reform platforms, including the Progressive (Bull Moose) Party in 1912 and the Progressive Party in 1924, despite the refusal of party leaders to seat black delegates or to reach out to black voters. However, in 1948 Henry Wallace, running for president on the Progressive Party ticket, campaigned strongly for black votes. Wallace made civil rights a centerpiece of his platform and organized integrated tours of the South. However, while he was supported by such black leaders as Paul Robeson and W. E. B. Du Bois, a strong Democratic Party platform on civil rights sharply reduced Wallace's appeal.

Throughout this period, the Communist, Socialist, and other workers' parties repeatedly sought and gained black support for their ideologies and platforms. In the late nineteenth century a number of African-American leaders, such as Peter H. Clark of Cincinnati and T. Thomas Fortune, expressed sympathy with socialist ideas. The Socialist Party, founded in 1901, gained few black converts in its first two decades, though W. E. B. Du Bois expressed strong sympathy with socialism as early as 1907 and briefly joined the party in 1912. It vigorously denounced the exploitation of workers, but subordinated race to class in its policies, refusing to recognize the special problems facing African Americans. Many of its leaders held racist views, and while the party platform opposed disfranchisement and leaders such as Eugene V. Debs publicly opposed racial discrimination, the Socialists offered no special support for black interests. After World War I, the party's platform became more inclusive. Larger numbers of blacks, inspired by African-American Socialist orators such as A. Philip Randolph, H. H. Harrison, Cyril V. Briggs, Richard Moore, Chandler Owen, and Frank Crosswaith, moved to support party candidates.

The Communist Party of the U.S.A., formed in 1921, shared the class-based approach of the Socialists. By the end of the 1920s, in accordance with Moscow's ideological support of non-Western nationalism, the party developed a platform calling for worker unity in the North and African-American "self-determination" in the southern Black Belt. While black party membership was always low, the Communists attempted to exert a disproportionate influence on black life. Unlike the Socialists, the Communists'—especially in the South—actively shifting position on the Nazi-Soviet alliance destroyed its southern base. The decline of the Communist and Socialist parties after 1950 was accompanied by the formation of several minor Marxist political parties, notably the Trotskyist-influenced Socialist Workers' Party, beginning in the 1950s. Probably the most influential African-American Trotskyist was the West Indian historian and theorist C. L. R. James, who lived in the United States from 1938 until his expulsion in 1953. Tiny parties such as the Workers' World Party drew black support during the 1980s. These parties actively sought a black constituency through powerful denunciations of racism and integrated leadership but were unable, due in part to lack of money for broad-based campaigns, to draw more than a small percentage of the black vote.

Beginning in the 1960s, various New Left and other radical parties without large black constituencies sponsored black candidates for political office. For example, in 1968 during the height of the antiwar movement, Dick Gregory, an African American, ran for president on the Freedom and Peace Party's ticket. In 1992 Leonora B. Fulani, running as the presidential candidate of the New Alliance Party, became the first black minor party presidential candidate to qualify for federal matching campaign funds.

SEPARATIST PARTIES. The antimainstream impulse developed largely as a consequence of the political discrimination that the white majority in various states has used to block the entrance of blacks into mainstream political parties. An equally significant development, however, is the appearance and growth of independent black political parties and factions throughout the twentieth century. The southern states, particularly Mississippi, provided the most promising conditions for these independent parties. Yet the appearance of national black separatist parties in 1904, 1963, and 1992 indicates that the impulse was not limited to the South.

The first black party was the Negro Protective Party, formed in Ohio in 1897, but this was not a truly independent organization. Taking advantage of black discontent over Republican inattention to black needs, the Ohio Democratic Party financed a small group of black Democrats and independents, who formed a party and ran a slate of candidates for governor and other state offices on a platform of civil rights and control of white mobs. Many "party" candidates were paid off by Republicans to withdraw their candidacies so as not to cut into the black Republican vote. The party's gubernatorial candidate, Sam J. Lewis, received only 477 votes, and the few remaining candidates for other posts did even worse.

The first nationally based black political party was the National Liberty Party, which grew out of local Civil and Personal Liberty leagues. On July 5, 1904, a convention of the leagues was organized in St. Louis, Missouri, and was attended by delegations from thirty-six states. Iowa editor George Edwin Taylor was chosen as the party's presidential candidate. The party gained only a few votes, and it disappeared after the election.

Although two independent black presidential candidates ran in Alabama on the ticket of the Afro-American Party in 1960, the next serious attempt to build a nationwide black party came with the formation of the Freedom Now Party. Organized by African-American lawyer Conrad Lynn as a national party at a convention in Washing-

ton, D.C., during the famous March for Jobs and Freedom in 1963, it ran candidates in elections in New York, California, and Connecticut. When these candidates did poorly in November elections, it switched strategy to concentrate its efforts exclusively on Michigan. In 1964 the party ran a slate of thirty-nine candidates for statewide offices in that state, hoping to demonstrate its electoral strength and to educate black voters. All the candidates were overwhelmingly defeated, however, and the party dissolved soon after the election.

In the years after 1964, black activists tried on numerous occasions to establish national black parties, but without success. In 1968 the Peace and Freedom Party (not to be confused with the aforementioned Freedom and Peace Party) was created. Run by an alliance of white leftists and members of the Black Panther Party, the party selected Eldridge Cleaver as its presidential candidate. It was on the ballot in some five states, and Cleaver received almost 37,000 votes. However, the alliance disintegrated soon after the election, although some candidates ran on the Peace and Freedom ticket in California elections in 1970. In 1976 the National Black Political Assembly, an outgrowth of the 1972 National Black Convention, formed the National Black Independent Political Party. Plagued by poor funding and bad management, it succeeded neither in persuading well-known black elected officials to run for president, nor in gaining sufficient signatures to place the party slate on the ballot in any state. In 1980 the National Black Independent Political Party held a founding convention to form a nucleus of support for a 1984 campaign but was unable to overcome internal debate, and its platform was overshadowed by Jesse Jackson's independent candidacy for the presidential nomination of the Democratic Party. In 1992, after Jackson declined to seek the Democratic Party nomination, Ron Daniels, former chair of the National Black Political Assembly, ran for president on the Campaign for a New Tomorrow ticket, but had difficulty getting his name on the ballot in many states and finished poorly.

Satellite political organizations have proven more successful in achieving African-American political aims. While black-supported and -run, these groups have organized themselves within existing party structures. During the end of the nineteenth century and the first part of the twentieth century, this independent spirit expressed itself in the form of numerous "Black and Tan" factions in Republican parties of southern states such as Texas, Louisiana, and Tennessee. Black delegates to state conventions, opposed by "lily-white" delegations, would try to gain their groups a fair share of patronage and political influence. If defeated at the state level, they would form their

Booker T. Washington with Theodore Roosevelt. *Roosevelt was among the party presidential candidates of his era who would recognize black delegates at conventions, but once nominated refused to award them their share of the political spoil.* © CORBIS

own slate of delegates and candidates for local office, and appeal to the national conventions for recognition. Often, deals would be struck. Occasionally, as in Louisiana and Mississippi in the 1920s, the Black and Tan faction would win clear control of patronage.

Most factions dissolved by the turn of the twentieth century, however, as increasing numbers of blacks were disfranchised or left the Republicans and as the party courted white southern support. Sometimes party presidential candidates such as Theodore Roosevelt would recognize the black delegates, but once nominated refuse to award them a share of the spoils. In 1920 the Texas Black and Tans, tired of this strategy, ran their own candidates for the position of Republican presidential electors, receiving some 27,000 votes. In Virginia during the early 1920s a "lily-black" party ran newspaper editor John R. Mitchell

for governor. The Tennessee and Texas Black and Tans disappeared in the early 1930s, as patronage and national party support was withdrawn.

During the 1930s southern blacks turned to the Democratic Party. However, excluded by white-dominated state parties, they began building shadow parties. The first example of this was the South Carolina Progressive Democratic Party. Formed at a convention in Columbia in May 1944, the party worked in support of Franklin D. Roosevelt's Democratic candidacy while evading the state's white primary. Its representatives attended the national convention in an unsuccessful attempt to unseat the regular state delegation, and sponsored a black candidate for U.S. senator, who won some 4,500 votes in the election. While the party continued after the election, it reformed as a political caucus, working in voter registration and unsuccessfully challenging the regular state delegation at the 1948 and 1956 conventions before being absorbed completely into the state party. (In 1970 South Carolina blacks, dissatisfied with the fused party, formed the short-lived United Citizens' Party.)

Two notable examples of satellite parties are the Mississippi Freedom Democratic Party (MFDP) and the National Democratic Party of Alabama (NDPA). The MFDP, created in 1964, was formed as part of an effort by the Student Nonviolent Coordinating Committee and other civil rights groups to dramatize the state's denial of voting rights to blacks and involve long-disfranchised Mississippi African Americans in the political process. The MFDP sponsored candidates for office in the Mississippi Democratic Party primary and sent a delegation to the 1964 Democratic national convention, urging without success that their delegation be seated in place of the white-only regular state delegation. In 1968, however, the MFDP (reorganized as the Loyal Democratic Party of Mississippi) succeeded in unseating the Mississippi delegation. While the party continued to operate into the 1970s, it was unable to elect large numbers of candidates to state or local office and eventually became part of the state Democratic Party, without a distinct status. The NDPA, one of a number of black political organizations in Alabama during the 1960s, was organized in 1968 to remedy the failure of the Alabama Democratic Party to open its organization to African Americans. In that year, the NDPA, inspired by the success of the MFDP, successfully fought to obtain recognition as the official state delegation at the Democratic national convention. While its platform and activity pushed the regular party into a more progressive racial posture, the NDPA was also unable to survive the 1970s as an independent black political organization.

The push to form separatist and independent parties suggests that African Americans had never completely forgotten or abandoned their African heritage. Although African Americans often supported the major parties, they shared the frustration that drove others to form separatist groups in search of access to political power. Even if it remained a minor channel of blacks' political activity, the independent impulse showed a stubborn ability to survive. Despite the failure of third-party and independent candidates to win election to state and national offices, their campaigns provided an opportunity for black candidates to be included in the political process during a time when African Americans were underrepresented in the mainstream political parties.

THE DUAL IMPULSES IN AFRICAN-AMERICAN POLITICS. The impulses motivating African-American politics may be illuminated by the remarks of Samuel DuBois Cook, who wrote, "Black political parties are, after all, expressions of radically abnormal conditions and consequences—basic defects in the political system. They have had a special mission—correction of those fundamental differences" (Cook 1972). He continued, "Black political parties fostered the notion and ideal of self-help, self-propulsion, group consciousness and solidarity, and political sensitivity, awareness and appreciation."

Harold Cruse offered these thoughts on African-American political parties as a means to achieve liberation:

The politics of ethnicity is more exactly the "politics of plurality." The demise of the civil rights era, beginning with 1980, points to political organization as the only alternative. Political organization also permits a renewed opportunity to make up for longstanding organizational deficiencies that have hampered black progress in economic, cultural, educational, and other social fields.

Cruse asserted that the "only option left" is to "organize an independent black party." Moreover, he argued, the ultimate aim of this black party would not be solely for the "expedient purposes of electoral politics." As he sees it, the African-American political party should not simply be an electoral political entity, but among other things a cultural political entity—that is, concerned with preserving those crucial values emanating from what we have here called the background impulses, such as self-help, self-propulsion, group consciousness, self-determination, and self-liberation.

Which of the two motors driving African-American politics—the mainstream or the separatist independent—will come to dominate the political lives of America's black men and black women remains to be seen. Clearly, the second impulse will continue as long as there is political discrimination and racism in the American political system. The separatist impulse, moreover, gives African-American politics much of its unique flavor and may prove to be the most enduring cultural legacy of African-American political activism.

BLACK CANDIDATES IN NATIONAL AND STATE ELECTIONS. African-American activists in both major parties have run for their party's nomination for president. Candidates such as Shirley Chisholm in 1972, Jesse Jackson in 1984 and 1988, Carol Moseley-Braun in 2004, and Reverend Al Sharpton in 2004 for the Democrats and Alan Keyes for the Republicans in 1996 and 2000, hoped to influence their parties on issues significant to the African-

Jesse Jackson announcing his candidacy for president of the United States, 1987. UPI/CORBIS-BETTMANN. REPRODUCED BY PERMISSION.

American community. Below the presidential level, particularly at the senatorial and gubernatorial levels, this same phenomenon has signaled that community leaders and activists have changed their tactics and strategies in order to advance their agenda among party elites and leading candidates.

During the twentieth century, independent black political movements provided African Americans with their best opportunities to compete in the general election for seats in the U.S. Senate. Of the twenty African-American candidates for the U.S. Senate in general elections between 1920 and 1990, seventeen ran on third-party or African-American party tickets. Republican Edward Brooke of Massachusetts, who served in the Senate from 1967 to 1979, was the first African-American senator elected by popular vote. Since 1990, however, more African-American candidates for the U.S. Senate have been Democrats, including Carol Moseley-Braun of Illinois, who in 1992 became the first female African American elected to the U.S. Senate. Among unsuccessful African-American

candidates for the U.S. Senate in the early twenty-first century were Ronald Kirk (Democrat of Texas) in 2002 and Denise Majette (Democrat of Georgia) in 2004. As of 2005, Barack Obama (Democrat of Illinois) was the only African American serving in the U.S. Senate.

Historically, the vast majority of African-American gubernatorial candidates were sponsored on either third-party or African-American party tickets, mostly the latter. The first such African-American gubernatorial candidate was Sam J. Lewis in Ohio in the 1897 state election; he ran as the candidate of the Negro Protective Party. Through 1990, L. Douglas Wilder, Mervyn Dymally, and George Brown were the only African Americans to have received a major party nomination for governor or lieutenant governor and survive until the general election. In 1989 Wilder, a Democrat of Virginia, became the first African American to be elected governor of a U.S. state. By the early 2000s, although no African Americans held gubernatorial offices, several had been elected as lieutenant governors, including Joe Rogers of Colorado, Michael Steele of Maryland, and Jennette Bradley of Ohio, all Republicans.

At the local level, African-American mayoral candidates prior to the Voting Rights Act of 1965 ran on small African-American or third-party tickets. As the black percentage of the population of major cities increased, more black mayors were elected. Similarly, in legislative districts with predominantly black populations it became relatively easy to elect black candidates. For example, seventy-one African Americans were elected to the U.S. House of Representatives between 1865 and 1992, all on major party tickets.

CHANGING STRATEGIES IN AFRICAN-AMERICAN POLITICS. In the past, the efforts of African-American activists were primarily centered on increasing the number of African-American elected officials at the city, county, and congressional levels in the major parties. They also made challenges at the national party conventions, particularly at the Democratic conventions to further effect change. In addition, symbolic protest efforts have taken place via third and minor parties as well as with black parties and several notable independent candidacies. Initiated with the Voting Rights Act of 1965 and reinforced by subsequent renewals, there has been a steady progression of new faces, new firsts, and new levels of achievement. Many of these activists have been motivated by conservative efforts to undermine the civil rights achievements of the 1960s and 1970s.

In the mid twentieth century this activism was directed toward creating a political majority in one of the mainstream parties and then forcing the parties to take a leading role in ending segregation and white supremacy. With Democratic leadership and Republican cooperation these efforts were directly responsible for the three major civil rights acts of the 1960s. Following these achievements, activists turned their attention to the implementation, support, and protection of these acts. However, the conservative revolution that began in the 1980s attacked affirmative action, one of the tools of the civil rights movement. In addition, African-American conservatives and their allies in the Republican Party sought rollbacks to entitlement programs, economic assistance packages, and federal aid to cities. In this way many individual and group gains were lost.

In the forty years since the adoption of the Voting Rights Act of 1965, community activists and civil rights leaders have recognized that achieving equal rights was only the beginning. Community economic needs and employment opportunities still required additional efforts. The civil rights revolution had occurred during a period

of deindustrialization in the United States, when many low-wage jobs were being automated or exported, and labor unions were losing their bargaining power. Increasing the number of elected officials alone could not reverse the economic decline of many urban areas. At the same time the Democratic Party was shifting its emphasis from a platform focused on the needs of low-income Americans to improving conditions for the middle class. The impact of these shifts was felt and seen everywhere. As the Democratic Party moved to a centrist position, some activists focused their efforts on gaining more powerful national offices, and many community leaders and local officials sought higher offices to effect change in their communities. These efforts have proven difficult given the candidate-centered nature of the political process and the loss of political parties' control over candidate selection. In the late twentieth and early twenty-first centuries, the national media have provided opportunities for high-profile activists to initiate campaigns outside traditional party channels. Because of this, ambitious African-American leaders have put themselves forward as candidates for national offices.

At the presidential level, African-American politicians have focused more on bringing issues to the forefront of debate and less on capturing the nomination. One way of doing this is to make a significant showing in the party's presidential primaries and then bargaining with the final party nominee to secure personal power and priority for crucial issues. In this way Jackson was able to advance his campaign manager, Ron Brown, toward the chairmanship of the DNC after his 1988 showing, and Sharpton achieved similar influence in 2004.

With its emphasis on small government, fiscal conservatism, and traditional social values, the Republican Party attracted few African-American partisans during the mid-to-late twentieth century. During the 1990s and 2000s, African-American senatorial and presidential candidates within the Republican Party sought to attract African-American voters as well as to build a base among the white conservative electorate in the country. Alan Keyes in presidential and senate campaigns proved only a minor success in this area. The highest-ranking African American in the party, Representative J. C. Watts of Oklahoma, was the lone African-American Republican in Congress when he retired in 2002, amid rumors that he was frustrated by his inability to achieve a meaningful leadership position within the party despite his accomplishments in Congress and his national publicity efforts supporting Republican policy positions. A few Republican Party activists, however, like Ward Connerly have been quite successful in assisting conservative Republicans at the state level to roll back af-

U.S. Secretary of State Colin Powell at a conference with President George W. Bush and U.S. National Security Adviser Condoleezza Rice. *Rice was appointed Secretary of State when Powell resigned in 2005, becoming the first black woman to hold the post of America's top diplomat.* PHOTOGRAPH BY J. SCOTT APPLEWHITE. AP/WIDEWORLD PHOTOS. REPRODUCED BY PERMISSION.

firmative action programs. Others like Armstrong Williams have supported Republican media elites in reducing government intervention and federal assistance. They have also acted as a counterweight to the protests and criticisms of civil rights community activists. This is where these activists have given the party its most success.

Overall, African-American voters in 2005 continued to support the Democratic Party in large numbers, and the majority of African-American politicians were Democrats. With the departure of Watts from Congress, the Republican Party had no African-American representatives and few in top party leadership positions, although both Colin Powell and Condoleezza Rice were recognized as potential candidates for the presidency. During the 2004 elections African-American Republican candidates for state and national offices attempted to build a base in the community and to recruit more members to the party. In addition, the Republican National Committee was anticipating several high-profile campaigns in 2006, including the candidacy

of Reverend Keith Butler for Senate in Michigan and former professional football star Lynn Swann's run for the governor's office in Pennsylvania. In response to such challenges, Democratic leaders recognized that the loyalty of black voters could not be taken for granted and that greater efforts were needed to sustain the party's dominance among African Americans.

Among the biggest items on the political agenda for 2005 and the following year's mid-term elections is the campaign to renew the Voting Rights Act, key elements of which are due to expire in 2007. The politics of renewal is in full swing, even as the African-American community and its allies celebrate the 40th anniversary of the Act.

See also Abolition; Affirmative Action; Chisholm, Shirley; Civil Rights Movement, U.S.; Civil War; Communist Party of the United States; Congressional Black Caucus; Fifteenth Amendment; Free Blacks; Jackson, Jesse;

James, C. L. R.; Mayors; Reconstruction; Turner, Henry McNeal

▪ ▪ Bibliography

Amer, Mildred L. *Black Members of the United States Congress, 1789–2001*. New York: Novinka Books, 2002.

Aptheker, Herbert. "Slave Guerrilla Warfare" and "Buying Freedom." In Herbert Aptheker, ed. *To Be Free: Studies in American Negro History*, pp. 11–30. New York: International Publishers, 1948.

Aptheker, Herbert, ed. *A Documentary History of the Negro People in the United States*. New York: Citadel Press, 1951.

Bell, Howard Holman. *A Survey of the Negro Convention Movement, 1830–1861*. New York: Arno Press, 1969.

Berlin, Ira. *Slaves without Masters: The Free Negro in the Antebellum South*. New York: Pantheon Books, 1974. Reprint, New York: New Press, 1992.

Bracey, John H., Jr., August Meier, and Elliott Rudwick, eds. *Black Nationalism in America*. Indianapolis: Bobbs-Merrill, 1970.

Brooke, Edward. *The Challenge of Change: Crisis in Our Two-Party System*. Boston: Little, Brown, 1966.

Cook, Samuel DuBois. *Black Political Parties: An Historical and Political Analysis*. New York: Free Press, 1972.

Cruse, Harold. *Plural but Equal: A Critical Study of Blacks and Minorities and America's Plural Society*. New York: William Morrow, 1987.

Draper, Theodore. *The Rediscovery of Black Nationalism*. New York: Viking Press, 1970.

Field, Phyllis F. *The Politics of Race in New York: The Struggle for Black Suffrage in the Civil War Era*. Ithaca, N.Y.: Cornell University Press, 1982.

Fleming, George James. *An All-Negro Ticket in Baltimore*. New York: Holt, Rinehart and Winston, 1960.

Hamilton, Charles V. *The Black Experience in American Politics*. New York: Putnam, 1973.

Henry, Charles P. *Culture and African American Politics*. Bloomington: Indiana University Press, 1990.

Link, Arthur S. "The Negro as a Factor in the Campaign of 1912." *Journal of Negro History* 32 (1947): 81–89.

Logan, Rayford W., and Irving S. Cohen. *The American Negro: Old World Background and New World Experience*. Boston: Houghton Mifflin, 1970.

Merritt, Richard L. *Symbols of American Community, 1735–1775*. New Haven, Conn.: Yale University Press, 1966. Reprint, Westport, Conn.: Greenwood Press, 1976.

Olbrich, Emil. *The Development of Sentiment on Negro Suffrage to 1860*. Madison, Wis., 1912. Reprint, New York: Negro Universities Press, 1969.

Porter, Dorothy, ed. *Early Negro Writing, 1760–1837*. Boston: Beacon Press, 1971. Reprint, Baltimore, Md.: Black Classic Press, 1994.

Porter, Dorothy, ed. *Negro Protest Pamphlets: A Compendium*. New York: Arno Press, 1969.

Porter, Kirk, and Donald Johnson, eds. *National Party Platforms, 1840–1972*. Urbana: University of Illinois Press, 1973.

Reidy, Joseph. "Negro Election Day and Black Community Life in New England, 1750–1860." In Kenneth L. Kusmer, ed. *Black Communities and Urban Development in America 1720–1990: Vol. 1, The Colonial and Early National Period*, p. 234. New York: Garland, 1991.

Scott, James C. *Domination and the Acts of Resistance: Hidden Transcripts*. New Haven, Conn.: Yale University Press, 1990.

Smith, Robert C. *Encyclopedia of African American Politics*. New York: Facts On File, 2003.

Smith, Robert S. "The Black Congressional Delegation." *Western Political Quarterly* 34 (1981): 203–221.

Sweet, Leonard I. *Black Images of America, 1784–1870*. New York: Norton, 1976.

Thomas, Lamont D. *Rise to Be a People: A Biography of Paul Cuffe*. Urbana: University of Illinois Press, 1986.

Walton, Hanes, Jr. *The Negro in Third Party Politics*. Philadelphia: Dorrance, 1969.

Walton, Hanes, Jr. *Black Politics: A Theoretical and Structural Analysis*. Philadelphia: Lippincott, 1972.

Walton, Hanes, Jr. "Black Presidential Participation and the Critical Election Theory." In Lorenzo Morris, ed. *The Social and Political Implications of the 1984 Jesse Jackson Presidential Campaign*, pp. 49–64. New York: Praeger, 1990.

Walton, Hanes, Jr., and Robert C. Smith. *American Politics and the African American Quest for Universal Freedom*, 3d ed. New York: Pearson, Longman, 2005.

Wesley, Charles. *Neglected History*. Wilberforce, Ohio: Central State College Press, 1965. Reprint, Washington, D.C.: Association for the Study of Negro Life and History, 1969.

White, John. *Black Leadership in America, 1895–1968*. New York: Longman, 1985.

White, Shane. "'It Was a Proud Day': African Americans, Festivals, and Parades in the North, 1741–1831." *Journal of American History* 81 (1994): 13–50.

HANES WALTON JR. (1996)
MERVYN DYMALLY (1996)
Updated by Walton 2005

WOMEN AND POLITICS IN LATIN AMERICA AND THE CARIBBEAN

Politics in the Latin American and Caribbean region owes as much to women, whether they are revolutionary or reform-minded, as it does to their male counterparts. Women have been successful in a range of political activities: rebellion against slavery, attainment of voting rights, and national independence. The growth of trade unionism and party politics, including Communist Party formation and development, has also relied on women's political participation and overall leadership. Street protests, public education, and advocacy as responses to the injustices of late twentieth- and early twenty-first-century globalization have often been advanced by working-class women and female policy analysts in Latin America and the Caribbean. Importantly, where governments have engaged with liberalization and the Washington consensus, women have also helped to clarify, amplify, and modify policy choices.

Women's many contributions to Caribbean and Latin American politics date back at least to the eighteenth century, when brown women and black women dared to do as much as men so they could be participant-subjects and not mere observers in a public sphere controlled by the legitimacy of Europeans, whiteness, male dominance, and upper-class status. All across the Americas, the early and continuing advent of women in the political arena would change the presumption that public political intercourse was and remains bounded by gender exclusions of female actors and the values associated with them.

Seen from the point of view of all who contest and hold office, it appears that politics are a man's world. Though attitudes are changing, studies show, for example, that both women and men believe that men are emotionally better suited for politics than women. Other studies show that women are generally more likely to vote for a man than for a woman. Gender biases against women have contributed to women's limited public-sphere roles, and such exclusions have added to their political invisibility. More, for example, is recorded about male Carib or Kalinago warriors than about females who played equally pivotal roles in the development of today's Caribbean. This is not to deny that women themselves have shied away from politics for a variety of reasons, including the fact that in its public culture and representation, politics carries an unhealthy masculinist identity, largely anathema to the values of cooperation and justice which themselves are ascribed more to women than to men.

Undeniably, if societies are to be democratic and progress, women's equitable and meaningful participation is mandatory. Only a few women served as parliamentarians in the West Indies Federation (1958–1962), a political and administrative grouping of English-speaking colonies. In 1995 the United Nations recommended that at least 30 percent of all decision-making bodies be female, especially parliaments, cabinets, and other political and policy-level structures. According to a survey conducted by the Inter-Parliamentary Union in early 2005, parliaments across the Latin American and Caribbean region were about 19 percent female; the upper houses included only about 19.5 percent women and lower houses about 18.8 percent. These figures represent improvements from 1997. Moreover, the 2005 ratio of women to men in Caribbean and Latin American parliaments is better than in many other parts of the developing world: Sub-Saharan African parliaments, for example, are only about 10 to 15 percent female, while the governments of Arab states are only about 3 to 8 percent female. Worldwide, woman made up about 12 to 16 percent of parliamentarians in 2005. All, however, are still far from the fifty/fifty democratic ideal.

FORBEARS

Women's participation in Latin American and Caribbean politics included running away to become maroons or bush-based freedom fighters before emancipation. Cubah, a Jamaican slave revered as an African Queen Mother, is recorded as committed to fighting the white slavery establishment in the 1680s (Mathurin, 1975, p. 21). Nanny, a celebrated and "remarkable Ashanti chieftainess," is perhaps the best known of the eighteenth-century figures. For a half century until her death in the 1750s, Nanny combined the private role of wife with the public roles of priestess, community organizer, military strategist, guerilla leader, wartime negotiator, and peacetime political leader (Mathurin, pp. 35–37). She was so politically successful that a village for free people was named Nanny Town in her honor. Nanny laid a foundation for the role of black women's resistance to injustice, and it is said that "of all the black resistance leaders of her time Nanny was foremost among those who resolved never to come to terms with the English [colonial presence in Jamaica]" (Mathurin, p. 37).

Nanny was not the only woman who dared to confront the militarism and injustice of colonialism. Gammay of Grenada was as fierce a freedom fighter against slavery in the 1790s as was her better-known male contemporary, Julien Fedon. Their joint leadership gave birth to the first successful rebellion against British slavery in Grenada (1795–1796). So strategic was Gammay's political-military advisory role to Fedon that it is said he was unable to launch his revolt until Gammay, his principal field lieutenant, operating as a vendor in the only market allowed at the time in Grenville, had canvassed supporters and gathered enough intelligence to guide the operations. Gammay's invisibility in recorded history may well be explained by her gender and social status: as a slave woman, she would be seen only as a market vendor and not as a complex political analyst shielded by a vendor's identity; as a full-blooded African female, she would not be recognized in the way that the schooled, French-mulatto Fedon was. This would have been true for innumerable women, accounting in part for their absence in recorded history.

Where Nanny would lay the foundation for the model of the daring, lone woman leader, Gammay set the stage for the more traditional, gendered division of labor between women and men in today's political life: women perform the behind-the-scenes analysis and mobilization, and men undertake the role of public leader—commander, spokesperson, and titleholder. That partnership has become the model for how women and men share political leadership. However, by the end of the twentieth century, unequal and stereotypical male-female power sharing would begin to unravel as women ascended, on their own, to significant places in government and other leadership positions. Both models of women's engagement in politics continue today.

ROOTS FROM THE NINETEENTH CENTURY

The participation of the region's women in contemporary public political life evolved from diverse historical backgrounds. For the majority of political women, activism arose from more traditional roles of mothering and caregiving in household, village, and community. Cleaning the church, washing and ironing the robes of the priests and the ceremonial clothes of male religious leaders, taking care of the sick, elderly, and homebound in the community—these activities were a continuation of what women did in their homes. Thus, one model of the political engagement of women was politics as the art of mothering (caregiving, nurturing, negotiating difference). For some observers this also explains the agenda that many women bring to political leadership in national government—motherhood in and as policy formulation, and thus a focus on issues such as child welfare, health care, and social security protections for the vulnerable. The politics of mothering took radical form in the 1970s in such groups as the Argentinean Mothers of the Plaza de Mayo, mothers and grandmothers mobilized to petition the state for answers to the disappearances of their children and grandchildren. In Catholic Latin America, the model is Mary, the mother of Jesus, who is held up as an icon of humility, submission, and sacrifice for others. Thus *marianismo* (subservient female culture and behavior) characterizes the political culture of many ordinary Latin American women.

For others, such as Haitian women, experiences as resistance leaders in the fight against slavery and for independence in the late 1970s inform current struggles for survival and justice. Such Haitian groups as Kay Fanm (Women Stand Strong) are made up of activist feminists who are engaging in antidictatorship and anti-imperialist organizing among women. These groups draw inspiration from the lives of such Haitian women as Poto Mitans, that is, women as the main supporting beams of home, church, and community going as far back as the slavery period.

For still others, experiences as subjugated black females continue to inform political engagement and non-

engagement. In the post-emancipation Anglophone Caribbean, women's early public roles were very much in the social sphere. They formed mothers' unions in Christian churches, friendship groups in secular society, and savings or *susu* collectives for financial viability in the economic sector. They were also leaders in such organizations as the Young Women's Christian Association (YWCA), the Soroptimists, and other women's clubs. Women who come into politics from social work and social activism seem to carry with them experiences of being negotiators and bridge builders, and they are attentive to people's needs. Coming into the political sphere from these civil society groups, they also seem to have gained, prior to coming into office, self-confidence that allows them to be flexible, risk-taking, and politically generous. Finally, they often have developed the formal and informal support networks that are so useful when they enter politics.

Large numbers of women have also entered politics directly, through the struggle for political rights and freedoms and the attainment of power through electoral office. Mary Eugenia Charles, who served as prime minister of Dominica from 1980 to 1995, began her political career fighting for the right to political expression. Janet Jagan, president of Guyana from 1997 to 1999, was a founding member and political activist in the People's Progressive Party, one of Guyana's foremost socialist parties. Thus, women in Latin America and the Caribbean have taken various paths into national political life.

TWENTIETH CENTURY

Cuban women became the first women in the region to gain the right to vote in 1934. Today adult suffrage is enjoyed by almost all in the region, with the important exception of indigenous women in many countries. Women have gone further and played their role in the revolutionary seizure of power. Celia Sánchez fought Cuban dictatorship from the mountains to bring about the 1959 Cuban revolution. Grenada's Jacqueline Creft, Scotilda Noel, Claudette Pitt, and Murie François joined the revolutionary New Jewel Movement and helped support both women and revolutionary Grenada. For three decades, Guatemala's Rigoberta Menchú, the 1992 Noble Peace Prize laureate, followed the political tradition of resistance to the injustice of dictatorship and championed human rights, especially those of indigenous Central Americans.

Caribbean women have also filled the ambassadorship ranks. A leading pioneer was the Dominican Republic's Minerva Bernardino, representative to the United Nations for twenty-one years (1950–1971); she later represented her country in various European capitals. Chile's Ana Figuero Gajardo was a delegate to the UN Security Council in 1952, a very rare achievement for a woman, even today. Jamaican scholar Lucille Mathurin Mair became one of the Caribbean's most accomplished diplomats, serving as Jamaica's ambassador to Cuba, the United States, and Canada. She also served as assistant secretary-general for the United Nations Decade for Women (1976–1985). Nora Astorga Gadia was revolutionary Nicaragua's UN ambassador in the 1980s, and she went on to become her country's deputy minister of foreign affairs before her untimely death in 1988. Mexico's Rosario Green served for a short period as UN deputy assistant secretary-general.

Ruth Nita Barrow, who served as governor-general of Barbados, was that country's representative to the United Nations from 1986 to 1990, emerging from leadership posts in the World Council of Churches, the YWCA, and the global anti-apartheid movement. This route through the social-service and social-justice sector remains typical of the women who reach top political posts. Nita is held up as one of the region's most successful women in politics—in the nongovernmental world, as well as with the state. Nita followed Nanny's model of standing largely on her own power base and not that of others, even though her brother, Errol Barrow, was prime minister of Barbados and would have contributed to her political ascendancy. Former dean of the Faculty of Arts and Sciences of the University of the West Indies, Marjorie R. Thorpe served as Trinidad and Tobago's permanent representative to the United Nations from 1988 until 1992. Female diplomats from Belize, Jamaica, and the Bahamas have followed at the United Nations, including Grenada's Ruth Rouse, who began serving as her country's UN ambassador in 2004.

WOMEN AS NATIONAL POLITICAL LEADERS

Among the first women to hold high public office in Latin America in the early twentieth century was Eva Duarte de Perón, second wife of Juan Perón, president of Argentina from 1946 to 1955 and 1973 to 1974; both were left-wing populist leaders with a large working-class following. Never elected to office and reviled by Argentinean elites, Eva Perón was adored by poor and ordinary people who saw her exercise of political citizenry to be a great achievement for the excluded, the poor, the rural poor, and of course, women. Evita, as she was affectionately referred to by the Argentinean masses, made her mark in politics by taking up the needs of the social class from which she emerged, the poor and downtrodden. As the wife of a powerful president, the female Perón's vantage point in the public arena was that of proximity to power, if not elected power itself. She performed as a politician with un-

paralleled success for a decade before her premature death at age thirty-three.

Eva Perón was among the first of "first ladies" to transform that office into an active political staging post to benefit her husband and herself. This is yet another way in which women have been political actors. In the Anglophone Caribbean, political strategist, journalist, and effective social activist Beverly Anderson Manley occupied the post of first lady from 1972 until her divorce in the 1980s. She helped her husband, Jamaican prime minister Michael Manley, raise the profile of Jamaica in regional, third world, and global politics. Beverly Manley also raised the visibility of Jamaican women as political players by being an active spokesperson rather than a demure wife and first lady. In Costa Rica, Margarita, and in Peru, Fujimura both attempted runs as president while being first ladies.

Argentina gave the world the first elected female president: Maria Estella Martínez Cartas de Perón, who was elected in July 1974 and was removed in a coup in March 1976. (The first woman elected to the office of head of government was Prime Minister Sirimavo Bandaranaike of Ceylon [Sri Lanka] in 1960. She was followed by Prime Minister Indira Gandhi of India in January of 1966.) Maria Perón's electoral achievement was followed by that of the interim executive president of Bolivia, Lydia Gueiler Tejada, who served for nine months between November 1979 and July 1980. Haiti's Ertha Pascal Trouillot, a supreme court judge, served as president from March 1990 to February 1991, a postdictatorship period in Haiti.

Latin America's longest-serving female president was Nicaragua's Violeta Barrios de Chamorro, a devout Catholic, *marianismo*, and political centrist who served as president from 1990 to 1997. Widow to a newspaper publisher with presidential ambitions, Chamorro was recruited to head a warring political opposition to a revolutionary government. In December 1997 Guyana, an Afro-Indian country, elected its first woman president: Janet Rosenberg Jagan, a United States–born white Jewish activist whose husband, Cheddi Jagan, had also been president. She served two years before an early resignation for health reasons in July 1999. Mireya Moscoso Rodríguez was elected and served as executive president of Panama in September 1999. She served until September 2004. Like Chamorro and Jagan, Rodríguez was a widow of a former president. Though few in number, and often criticized by feminists, these women have helped to erase female invisibility in Caribbean and Latin American politics.

One of the first women in the region to serve as head of state, and the first woman governor in the British Commonwealth, was Hilda Louisa Gibbs Bynoe, a Grenadian medical doctor appointed to be governor of nonindependent Grenada, Carriacou, and Petite Martinique in 1968. She resigned during a popular uprising over dictatorship and independence in 1974. As a powerful and accomplished black woman, Bynoe captured the attention of women across the region. In 2005, women are governor generals in the Bahamas, St. Lucia and Canada.

Jamaica's Portia Simpson, who grew up in her country's lower socioeconomic strata, is one of Jamaica's most admired national politicians. Simpson's career has been a long ascendancy within the party system, amid debates about whether or not a woman can lead a dynamic—some would say turbulent—Jamaica.

In trade union activism, from Bolivia to Trinidad, from Mexico to Barbados, women have made their mark—one example from the mid-twentieth century is Elma François of Trinidad and Tobago. In addition, Guatemala's Rigoberta Menchú has helped women across the region in the politics of human rights and peace.

In the diaspora, black Caribbean women have been political pioneers. United States congresswoman Shirley Chisholm, daughter of a Barbadian mother and a Guyanese father, became the first black woman elected to the U.S. House of Representatives. She was also the first black person to make a serious run for the presidency of the United States. Representative Chisholm was tireless in her efforts to promote racial justice via the political rights of ordinary black men and women in inner-city New York. Audre Lorde, a feminist activist born of Grenadian parents in Brooklyn, would mirror Shirley Chisholm's influence within nongovernmental, academic, and lesbian organizing circles.

TRANSFORMATIONAL WOMEN LEADERS

Grenadian-born scholar Peggy Antrobus has both written about and at times exemplified what a transformational woman leader is and can achieve. Typically, she has argued, such women leaders arise from the nongovernmental sector, where there is more room for creativity in the use of power as something more than the exercise of control by and for small and often elite groups. For example, in Guyana, Viola Burnham, Andaiye, Jocelyn Dow, and many other women working in nongovernmental organizations have been effective in spearheading sustainable development, as well as promoting the rights of racial groups and indigenous people. Thus, for every woman or cluster of women in high office of state politics, there are comparable groups of highly skilled and dedicated women who are building the politics of transformation, most often in nongovernmental women's groups.

CONCLUSION

If women in Latin America and the Caribbean are to make a mark on and in politics, it will not be because of mere access to high office. That has already been achieved. Evidence suggests that effectiveness in carrying out a given political agenda requires political access in large numbers—a critical mass—and that has been in development for some time. The important mark is for women in the Caribbean, Latin America, and worldwide to be able to change the public agenda of civil society and of the state in relation to contemporary critical issues, such as ending poverty, addressing environmental dangers, and eliminating moral and ethical injustices caused in no small measure by the global, preponderantly masculinist culture in which women actively participate. Exercising leadership within that environment has all too often meant conforming, which has further meant ignoring the real needs of women, men, and society in the interest of a stifling agenda.

The challenge now for women in Latin America and the Caribbean is to transform the sphere of politics into a more user-friendly and empowering arena for those occupying that space, as well as for those who depend on politics—that is, the global citizenry. It is the politics of transformation, and not just entry and accommodation, to which women must now address themselves. In a postcolonial Latin America and Caribbean, politics must become an ethical, connective tool for management and change. The question is whether women can effect such a shift while working inside the arena of traditional party politics that lead to the holding of office. Perhaps they can work more effectively outside traditional political structures to help create an alternative system to deal with the agenda of people-centered development and democracy.

Much depends on the commitment of the state to change, which would include promoting gender justice and encouraging the appropriate culture to support it. Black women and brown women in the postcolonial American hemisphere are actively pursuing both paths to effective participation in politics—as lone heroines and as behind-the-scenes supporters of other political women and men. Altogether, the presumption of politics as the work of men crumbles even as women resocialize and empower themselves.

See also Barrow, Nita; Charles, Eugenia; Chisholm, Shirley; Da Silva, Benedita; Lorde, Audre; Politics and Politicians in Latin America; Politics in the United States; Simpson-Miller, Portia

Bibliography

Antrobus, Peggy. *The Global Women's Movement: Origins, Issues, and Strategies.* London and New York: Zed, 2004.

Barriteau, Eudine. *The Political Economy of Gender in the Twentieth-Century Caribbean.* London: Palgrave Macmillan, 2001.

Inter-Parliamentary Union. "Women in National Parliaments: Statistical Archive." Available from <http://www.ipu.org/wmn-e/world-arc.htm>.

Mathurin, Lucille. *The Rebel Woman in the British West Indies During Slavery.* Kingston: Institute of Jamaica, 1975.

Waring, Marilyn, Gaye Greenwood, and Christine Pintat. "Inter-Parliamentary Union Presents—Politics: Women's Insight, Survey at Headquarters, March 6." Released March 2000. Available from the United Nations Information Service: <http://www.unis.unvienna.org/unis/pressrels/2000/wom475.html>.

DESSIMA M. WILLIAMS (2005)

Battle of White Plains and retreating to the winter camp at Valley Forge. Nothing is known of his later life. African-American historians have often pointed to Poor's heroism as an example of the African-American contribution to the nation's founding. Poor appeared on a U.S. commemorative postage stamp in 1975.

See also Free Blacks, 1619–1860; Military Experience, African-American

Bibliography

Quarles, Benjamin. *The Negro in the American Revolution.* Williamsburg, Va.: Institute of Early American History and Culture, 1961.

GREG ROBINSON (1996)

POOR, SALEM

C. 1758
?

Revolutionary War soldier Salem Poor was born free in Massachusetts, probably in 1758. We know little about his early life, except that he married young. In 1775 he left his wife to enlist in the Massachusetts Militia. Following the outbreak of war at Lexington and Concord, he joined the Patriot forces in Boston. On June 17, 1775, Poor served at the Battle of Bunker Hill (actually fought on Breed's Hill), helping to repulse several British charges. Some later accounts have credited him with the killing of British Lt. Col. James Abercrombie.

So exceptional was Poor's bravery that on December 5, 1775, fourteen Massachusetts officers signed a petition to the General Court, the colony's legislature, which stated, "A Negro Man Called Salem Poor . . . in the late Battle of Charleston, behaved like an Experienced Officer, as Well as an Excellent Soldier, to Set Forth Particulars of his Conduct Would Be tedious, Wee Would Only begg leave to say in the person of this Sd. Negro Centers a Brave & gallant Soldier." The petition suggested the Continental Congress offer Poor "The Reward due to so great and Distinguisht a Caracter." There is no record of any reward actually given to Poor.

In June 1775 Gen. George Washington barred black soldiers from military service but permitted those already serving, such as Poor, to finish their tours of duty. At the end of 1775 Washington reversed his order. Poor reenlisted and served at least through 1776, seeing action at the

POOR PEOPLE'S CAMPAIGN

The Poor People's Campaign, also known as the Poor People's Washington Campaign, was conceived in 1967 by the Rev. Dr. Martin Luther King Jr. and other Southern Christian Leadership Conference (SCLC) activists as a means of extending the civil rights agenda to include broad-based demands for economic justice. In the context of massive unrest in urban black communities, King and his colleagues felt that constitutional rights were inadequate to alleviate the crushing poverty and exploitation still faced by the majority of African Americans. At the same time, with the strategy of peaceful protest fast losing ground among the urban poor, they were eager to conduct a campaign that would reassert the legitimacy of a nonviolent approach to social change. In a mood of deep pessimism, the Poor People's Campaign was born.

Initially, the campaign's primary goal was to achieve federal legislation that would ensure full employment, establish a guaranteed income, and promote construction of low-income housing. To that end, organizers intended to bring thousands of poor people from a variety of racial and ethnic backgrounds to Washington, D.C., where they would conduct massive civil disobedience demonstrations and disrupt the city until the government acceded to their demands. The campaign would dramatize the urgency of poor people's plight through mass demonstrations and the erection of a tent city within plain sight of the federal government. The campaign, declared King, would highlight the need for a "new turn toward greater economic justice" in a society more concerned with property and profits than with people.

The campaign was set to begin on April 22, 1968. Although the planning stage had been marked by sharp dissension within SCLC's ranks about the wisdom and feasibility of such an effort, King had insisted on pushing ahead with the project, but he interrupted final preparations in order to travel to Memphis, Tennessee, to support striking sanitation workers. After his assassination there on April 4, the SCLC, now under the untested leadership of the Rev. Ralph Abernathy, decided to press forward with the campaign as a fitting tribute to King's memory.

The first group of travelers to Washington, D.C., arrived on April 28; they were later joined by caravans from Tennessee, New Mexico, Chicago, the Mississippi Delta, and elsewhere. With a permit to house 3,000 people on a fifteen-acre strip of land in West Potomac Park, the construction of Resurrection City began on May 13; its population peaked at 2,500 in late May. From there, organizers led daily sojourns to federal agencies, presenting demands that outlined a predominantly economic agenda.

The highlight of the campaign was Solidarity Day, which drew a crowd of between 50,000 and 100,000 (according to press and police estimates) to the Lincoln Memorial on June 19 for music and speakers, including Coretta Scott King. Rev. Abernathy, in his speech, underscored the need for economic justice and an end to racism. Although he acknowledged that his effort did not match King's, Abernathy believed he had solidified his own position at SCLC's helm and that the campaign had successfully brought together the nation's poor and galvanized grassroots efforts to eradicate poverty.

From the start, however, the campaign was plagued by crises—timing problems, lack of coordination, inadequate resources, poor leadership, the absence of a clearly focused program, and interethnic frictions. Demonstrations at government agencies were spottily attended, and they failed to produce the mass arrests organizers had hoped would mobilize the community and lead to nationwide boycotts. Resurrection City was afflicted by heavy rains that lasted throughout most of the campaign, and it was not the model of nonviolence and interracial harmony that King had envisioned; by June 6 only three hundred residents remained. In addition, internal disputes over direction and goals divided action-oriented militants from more cautious figures such as Bayard Rustin, who opposed the use of civil disobedience.

At the same time, campaigners faced growing hostility from local and national government leaders. Before the Poor People's Campaign had even begun, it had been roundly criticized by President Lyndon B. Johnson and by moderate civil rights leaders such as NAACP Executive Secretary Roy Wilkins. Southern congressional leaders had sought to prevent the mass mobilization from taking place, and local media had stirred fears of insurrection if large numbers of poor descended on the city. Black mayor Walter Washington arranged for police training in riot control before the marchers arrived. As the campaign continued through June, the patience of those in power wore increasingly thin; the Justice Department refused a second extension of Resurrection City's permit, and police not only began to respond violently to demonstrators, they launched an unprovoked tear-gas attack on the encampment itself.

On June 19, Rev. Abernathy declared, "Today, Solidarity Day, is not the end of the Poor People's Campaign. In fact, today is really only our beginning." But just five days later, as hundreds of protestors were being arrested at the Capitol grounds, the tent city was surrounded by more than fifteen hundred police, who evacuated and sealed off the camp. Organizers and participants straggled home to continue the struggle. The campaign had not achieved its goals, and its failure helped bring to a close the civil rights era in which Martin Luther King Jr. had been so instrumental.

See also King, Martin Luther, Jr.; National Association for the Advancement of Colored People (NAACP); Rustin, Bayard; Southern Christian Leadership Conference; Wilkins, Roy

■ ■ *Bibliography*

Fager, Charles. *Uncertain Resurrection: The Poor People's Washington Campaign.* Grand Rapids, Mich.: Eerdmans, 1969.

Garrow, David. *Bearing the Cross: Martin Luther King, Jr., and the Southern Christian Leadership Conference.* New York: Morrow, 1986.

Gilbert, Ben W., et al. *Ten Blocks from the White House: Anatomy of the Washington Riots of 1968.* New York: Praeger, 1968.

King, Martin Luther, Jr. *Where Do We Go from Here? Chaos or Community.* Boston: Harper & Row, 1967.

McKnight, Gerald. The *Last Crusade: Martin Luther King, Jr., the FBI, and the Poor People's Campaign.* Boulder, Colo.: Westview, 1998.

MARSHALL HYATT (1996)
Updated bibliography

POPULAR CULTURE

■■■

Black popular culture is the individual and collective expression of identity that reflects the social, historical, and cultural politics surrounding the black presence in the Americas. The black body is a site for modern consumer culture industries such as fashion, music, film, and advertising. Within a media-driven contemporary society, blacks use the body, self-adornment, movement, language, and music to construct and locate themselves socially and culturally in society (Gray, 1995). Black cultural production occurs in a myriad of institutions and spaces including churches, urban and rural neighborhoods, colleges and universities, and social and civic organizations. One of the spaces in which black cultural production is exercised is aggrieved communities that exist on the margins of society because of racist social, economic, and legislative policies that are the result of dominant and pervasive ideologies articulated by the ruling class. Colonial and imperialist encounters such as the transatlantic slave trade, Jim Crow, apartheid, and racist and sexist policies imposed by government institutions created deplorable socioeconomic conditions for people of African descent worldwide. Within these highly contested spaces emerges the cultural production of blackness through cultural signifiers, practices, and consciousness.

By recognizing the convergence of history, culture, and power, blacks divert power away from mainstream culture toward a culture in touch with their present conditions tied to common traditions in an effort to build an uncommon and distinctive future. Blacks have used organic and technological means to present their experiences and aspirations to the larger world (Lipsitz, 1990). They merge the oldest African-American oral and folk traditions with new technology in order to create a visual and aural presence in society. The struggle that ensues over power and meaning establishes a space for black cultural expression. An example of this occurrence is black youth style.

The representation of black youth styles, expressed through the body, language, hair, music, and fashion, occurs in relation to African-American cultural traditions. In *The Black Atlantic,* Paul Gilroy (1994) discusses blackness as a socially situated production that is constantly invented and reinvented from tradition. Black cultural expressive forms are not fixed, essential, or unchanging. Traditions are structured differently, appropriated, modified, and transformed within specific historical, social, and cultural conditions. This is the condition of the "changing same," a condition that must be constantly situated and theorized and not assumed in the manner of either essentialism or radical social construction (Gray, 1995). As is the case with black youth culture, the construction and reorganization of black youth style is imbued with struggles over power and access.

When located within institutionally structured settings like visual media, black popular culture is largely represented as fear and menace by dominant media institutions invested in the circulation of pop cultural iconography and images that are palatable to the ruling class. A broader representation of black cultural production can be found in alternative and independent media spaces and reflect social and historical movements. For example, in the 1970s, the Los Angeles School of Black Filmmakers (1974–1978) contributed a variety of films that offered critical perspectives on black life and a myriad of representations of black figures and characters. Founders of this movement included Julie Dash, Haile Gerima, Charles Burnett, Billy Woodberry, Ben Caldwell, and Jamaa Fanaka. The Los Angeles School of Black Filmmakers consisted of African-American and African students studying at the University of California at Los Angeles whose films were the direct result of the cultural expression of the civil rights, Black Power, and black arts movements of the 1960s and 1970s. In the many media representations of success and achievement, blacks appeared as objects rather than as the subjects of their own construction. Black cultural producers like the members of the Los Angeles School of Black Filmmakers created alternative images that reaffirmed black cultural expression and challenged dominant constructions of blackness found in black popular culture, like those found in blaxploitation films which were at their peak during this time. Black youth cultural production is also a space where blacks create identities and cultural expressions.

Symbols of black youth culture travel to the commercial mainstream through advertising, film, and television. They labor discursively in several directions at the same time. As consumers and producers of media images, black youth, in the manner of organic intellectuals, seem to understand implicitly and negotiate effectively the dual nature of representations. W. E. B. Du Bois's theory of double consciousness resonates with contemporary blacks because of the need to exist in two worlds that are largely separate and unequal for survival. Black youth culture and style collide with American and European commercial culture (magazines, music videos, television, advertising), transporting them into a "media hyperspace where they are magnified into a spectacle of hyperblackness" (Gray, 1995). Marketing professionals actively shape the meanings of the category of "the black consumer" for the public at large; promote powerful normative models of collective identity that equate social membership with conspicuous consumption; and believe that African Americans use consumption to defy racism and share collective identities most valued in American society. Black cultural production can typify and resist this assumption simultaneously.

A contemporary example of this can be found in hip-hop culture.

Hip-hop culture arose out of the malaise of a postwar society destroyed largely by the effects of racist and sexist socioeconomic policies. An example of this is the systematic use of highways and freeways to literally destroy once thriving communities, resulting in the loss of a solid financial base because of white flight. The demarcation of deteriorating tenements as "affordable" housing, colloquially known as the "slums" or "projects," and the introduction and infiltration of crack cocaine into black and brown communities created the socioeconomic conditions out of which hip-hop culture was born in large urban centers. Hip-hop culture was a blend of African-American, West Indian, African, and Latino cultural expressions.

It emerged not only to offer a different sense of blackness but also to alter many of the ways that society understands the function of blackness, especially as it exists in contemporary popular culture (Boyd, 1997, p. xxi). Hip-hop culture did not come about in a vacuum. It is reflective of the cultural production of blackness that has occurred continuously in a postwar society and falls squarely into a long history of black popular cultural production.

There are many traditional and contemporary examples of black popular culture, including blues, jazz, reggae, Gandy dancers, rap, turntablism, break dancing, art, fashion, advertising, stepping, sports, cheers, double-dutch, poetry, and literature. However, the unifying principle of black pop cultural production is the coalescence of African peoples in the global struggle for equality and freedom through expression.

See also Blaxploitation Films; Filmmakers, Los Angeles School of; Hip Hop

■ ■ *Bibliography*

Bobo, Jacqueline. *Black Women as Cultural Readers*. New York: Columbia University Press, 1995.

Boyd, Todd. *Am I Black Enough for You?: Popular Culture from the 'Hood and Beyond*. Bloomington: University of Indiana Press, 1997.

Collins, Patricia Hill. *Black Feminist Thought*. New York: Routledge, 1991.

Dates, Janette L. and William Barlow, eds. *Split Image: African Americans in the Mass Media*. Washington, D.C.: Howard University Press, 1993.

Davis, Angela Y. *Blues Legacies and Black Feminism*. New York: Pantheon, 1998.

Dent, Gina, ed. *Black Popular Culture: A Project by Michele Wallace*. New York: Dia Center for the Arts, 1992.

DuBois, W. E. B. *The Souls of Black Folk*. New York: Fawcett, 1961.

Gayle, Addison, Jr., ed. *The Black Aesthetic*. Garden City, N.Y.: Doubleday, 1971.

George, Nelson. *The Death of Rhythm and Blues*. New York: Pantheon Books, 1988.

Gilroy, Paul. *The Black Atlantic: Modernity and Double Consciousness*. London: Verso, 1994.

Gray, Herman. *Watching Race: Television and The Struggle for "Blackness."* Minneapolis: University of Minnesota Press, 1995.

Guerrero, Ed. *Framing Blackness: The African American Image in Film*. Philadelphia: Temple University Press, 1993.

Hall, Stuart, ed. *Representation: Cultural Representations and Signifying Practices*. London: Sage, 2000.

hooks, bell. *Outlaw Culture: Resisting Representations*. New York: Routledge, 1994.

Lipsitz, George. *Time Passages: Collective Memory and American Popular Culture*. Minneapolis: University of Minnesota Press, 1990.

Rose, Tricia. *Black Noise*. Hanover, N.H.: Wesleyan University Press, 1994.

NSENGA K. BURTON (2005)

PORT ROYAL EXPERIMENT

■ ■ ■

The Port Royal Experiment has often been called a rehearsal for Reconstruction. It was designed to discover whether African Americans liberated from their slavemasters could work as free laborers. On November 7, 1861, planters on the South Carolina Sea Islands fled the Union's naval forces, leaving their enslaved laborers on the land. Military forces led by Lieut. Gen. William W. Reynolds occupied and looted the islands. William W. Pierce, a civilian attorney from Boston, was assigned to scout the land and direct efforts on behalf of the "contrabands" of war now under their control. He went north and in Boston and New York joined with abolitionists and reformers such as Edward Philbrick to form an educational association named Gideon's Band. Shortly thereafter, missionary teachers arrived to assist the newly independent blacks.

Missionaries from Gideon's Band, later assisted by the American Missionary Association, opened schools in the face of military hostility and racism. Within a short time, conflict emerged over the use of the land. Northern officials wanted to grow cotton to ease the wartime shortage. The former slaves, however, were used to laboring for others and interpreted "free labor" to mean independence. Like many whites, they preferred subsistence farming to wage labor on cash crops as part of large work groups. Eventually, the military coerced many blacks into growing cotton on abandoned plantations. Pierce, a free labor advocate, ordered blacks to grow cotton on the abandoned plantations. The federal government provided supplies and meager salaries for the freed people. At the same time, cotton agents and soldiers lined their pockets with commissions and profits on the cotton.

On July 7, 1862, Congress passed a bill that effectively displaced the absentee white landowners, and in March 1863 their abandoned properties were divided into lots and sold. Although 2,000 acres were bought by groups of blacks, who pooled their wages, most of the lands were bought by military officers and speculators. A consortium of abolitionists headed by Philbrick and Edward Atkinson, a Boston textile manufacturer, bought eleven plantations. They wished not only to profit, but to prove the superiority of black wage work. Philbrick opened plantation stores and stocked fine goods, hoping to create a desire for cash among African-American farmers.

In January 1865, Gen. William T. Sherman awarded all unclaimed land to the freedmen. Several months later, however, President Andrew Johnson allowed planters to reclaim land not already sold to investors. In early 1866 freedmen who refused to sign lease agreements with white owners were forced off the land by the military. Some left; others contracted to work for planters. A few did manage to retain title to lands.

Despite the small and isolated nature of Port Royal, the experiment aroused great attention in antislavery circles. The failure of the experiment, as far as black uplift was concerned, presaged the later collapse of Reconstruction. Differences between northern free labor ideology and black desire for autonomy would again appear, and the fragility of black independence in the face of white opposition would once again be demonstrated.

■■ *Bibliography*

Foner, Eric. *Reconstruction: America's Unfinished Revolution, 1863–1877*. New York: Harper and Row, 1988.

Rose, Willie Lee. *Rehearsal for Reconstruction: The Port Royal Experiment*. Indianapolis, Ind.: Bobbs-Merrill, 1964.

ELIZABETH FORTSON ARROYO (1996)

POWELL, COLIN

APRIL 5, 1937

Born and raised in New York City, army officer, chair of the Joint Chiefs of Staff, and Secretary of State Colin Lu-

ther Powell grew up in a close-knit family of Jamaican immigrants in the Hunts Point section of the Bronx. After attending public schools, Powell graduated from the City College of New York (CCNY) in 1958. Although his grades were mediocre, he discovered an affinity for the military. Participating in CCNY's Reserve Officer Training Corps (ROTC) program, he finished as a cadet colonel, the highest rank attainable. He received his commission as a second lieutenant in the U.S. Army after completing college.

Powell served for two years in West Germany and two years in Massachusetts, where he met his wife, Alma. In 1962, already a captain, Powell received orders to report to Vietnam. He was one of the second wave of more than 15,000 military advisors sent by the United States to Vietnam, and he served with a South Vietnamese Army unit for most of his tenure. During his first tour of duty, from 1962 to 1963, Powell won the Purple Heart after being wounded by a Vietcong booby trap near the Laotian border.

After returning to the United States, Powell spent almost four years at Fort Benning in Georgia, serving as, among other things, an instructor at Fort Benning's Army Infantry School. In 1967, now a major, he attended an officers' training course at the United States Army Command and General Staff College at Fort Leavenworth, Kansas, finishing second in a class of more than twelve hundred. In the summer of 1968 the army sent Powell back to Vietnam. On his second tour, Powell served primarily as a liaison to Gen. Charles Gettys of the Americal Division and received the Soldier's Medal for his role in rescuing injured soldiers, including General Gettys, from a downed helicopter.

Powell returned to the United States in mid-1969 and began moving between military field postings and political appointments, a process that would become characteristic of his career. In 1971, after working in the Pentagon for the assistant vice chief of the army, he earned an M.B.A. from George Washington University in Washington, D.C. Shortly thereafter, the Nixon administration accepted Powell as a White House Fellow; he worked at the Office of Management and Budget (OMB), then headed by Caspar Weinberger. In 1973, after a year at OMB, Powell received command of an infantry battalion in South Korea; his mission was to raise morale and restore order in a unit plagued by drug abuse and racial problems. He then attended a nine-month course at the National War College and received a promotion to full colonel in February 1976, taking command of the 2nd Brigade, 101st Airborne Division, located at Fort Campbell, Kentucky.

In 1979 Powell was an aide to Secretary of Energy Charles Duncan during the crisis of the nuclear accident

Colin Powell. PHOTOGRAPH BY GREG GIBSON. AP/WIDE WORLD PHOTOS. REPRODUCED BY PERMISSION.

at Three Mile Island in Pennsylvania and the oil shortage caused by the overthrow of the shah of Iran. In June of that year, while working at the Department of Energy (DOE), he became a brigadier general. Powell returned to the field from 1981 until 1983, serving as assistant division commander of the Fourth Infantry (mechanized) in Colorado and then as the deputy commanding general of an army research facility at Fort Leavenworth. In mid-1983, he became military assistant to Secretary of Defense Caspar Weinberger. In 1986 Powell, by then a lieutenant general, returned to the field as the commander of V Corps, a unit of 75,000 troops in West Germany. The following year, in the wake of the Iran-Contra scandal, he returned to serve as President Ronald Reagan's national security advisor. During the Intermediate Nuclear Forces (INF) arms-control negotiations with the Soviet Union, Powell was heralded as being a major factor in their success.

In July 1989 President George H. Bush nominated Powell, a newly promoted four-star general, to be the first black chair of the Joint Chiefs of Staff, the highest military position in the armed forces. As chair, Powell was responsible for overseeing Operation Desert Storm, the 1991 in-

ternational response to the 1990 Iraqi invasion of Kuwait. Through his commanding and reassuring television presence during the successful Persian Gulf War, Powell became one of the most popular figures in the Bush administration. Reappointed chair in 1991, he was the recipient of various military decorations as well as a Presidential Medal of Freedom from Bush. In the same year the NAACP gave Powell the Spingarn Medal, its highest award for African-American achievement.

When Bill Clinton was elected president in 1992, he and Powell had differences over Clinton's plan to substantially reduce the defense budget. Powell also disagreed with Clinton's proposal to end the ban on homosexuals in the military and was instrumental in limiting the scope of that change to a controversial "Don't Ask Don't Tell" policy. Powell retired from the army in September 1993 at the end of his second term as chair of the Joint Chiefs. Upon his departure, President Clinton awarded Powell his second Presidential Medal of Freedom. After leaving government, Powell, by now one of the most admired Americans, continued his public activities. In October 1994 he traveled to Haiti as part of an American diplomatic mission, and he succeeded in brokering a deal with members of the ruling junta that enabled the country to return to constitutional rule without bloodshed.

Powell's reputation for honesty and moderation led to a widespread Powell-for-president boom. By mid-1995, national polls showed Powell leading all candidates in a presidential campaign, although he had not expressed views on domestic issues or even identified which political party he favored. His celebrity increased following publication of his best-selling memoir, *My American Journey* (1995). For several months Powell weighed a presidential run; he announced publicly that he was a Republican, but that he favored affirmative action. However, in December 1995 he stated that he did not have the "fire in his belly" to become president, and he withdrew from consideration. He remained in touch with Republicans leaders, and he made a popular speech at the Republican convention. In later years he toured the country as a much-sought-after inspirational speaker and advisor. In April 1997 Powell founded America's Promise, a private foundation to aid disadvantaged youth.

In 2001 Powell reentered government, this time as a diplomat rather than a soldier. As President George W. Bush's secretary of state, Powell immediately faced an array of challenges. Despite the administration's campaign promises to limit foreign entanglements, it soon proved impossible in the wake of nuclear controversy in North Korea, the ongoing Palestinian/Israeli conflict in the Middle East, the attacks of September 11, 2001, and the subsequent response of the United States, especially in Afghanistan and Iraq. Powell became the government official who most often had to explain American foreign policy, both to the United Nations and to other governments, in the wake of the September 11, 2001, terrorist attacks on the United States.

Powell's role as spokesperson for the administration became more difficult as official policy seemed to diverge from that suggested by his own experience and opinions; he felt that a military campaign against Iraq required not only victory but also a lengthy commitment to the reconstruction and maintenance of Iraq. Many analysts suggested that Powell's influence on foreign policy matters in the Bush administration paled in comparison to that of Vice President Dick Cheney, National Security Advisor Condoleezza Rice, and Secretary of Defense Donald Rumsfeld.

Despite speculations about internal dissention, Powell continued to faithfully advance the administration's policy agenda. In early February 2003 he presented the United Nations Security Council with the case for military action against Iraq. Presenting supposed evidence based on U.S. and other intelligence sources, Powell diagrammed what he called "a deliberate campaign" by Iraq to mislead UN weapons inspectors and to hide existing stockpiles of chemical and biological weapons as well as the means to produce more of both. This assertion has been one of the most questionable claims made by the Bush administration. American military forces in Iraq in 2003 and 2004 failed to discover most of the weapons that Saddam Hussein's government allegedly possessed. The absence of credible ties between Saddam Hussein's regime and the Al Qaeda operatives linked to September 11 damaged the legitimacy and approval ratings of both Powell and the administration more broadly. Despite that, throughout much of 2003, Powell consistently maintained higher approval ratings than any of the other major administration officials, including the president.

Shortly after the beginning of Operation Iraqi Freedom, conservative former speaker of the house Newt Gingrich blasted the State Department for its handling of the effort to create the desired international coalition for the military offensive against Iraq. Calling the State Department a "broken instrument," Gingrich recommended congressional hearings as well as White House initiatives to overhaul Powell's domain. While the administration offered a defense of the department's record, Powell's aides defended the secretary more passionately, saying that he stood "in the way of reckless foreign policy." That defense ironically used phrasing reminiscent of Bush's Democratic opponents, who often later accused the administration of having a "reckless" foreign policy. Somewhat confounding those who anticipated that Powell would wilt in the face of internal divisions within the administration as well as pressure from those who opposed the war in Iraq, he continued to serve the Bush administration as secretary of state with grace, loyalty, and resolve until his resignation in January 2005.

See also Military Experience, African-American; Politics in the United States

■ ■ *Bibliography*

Harari, Oren. *The Leadership Secrets of Colin Powell*. New York: McGraw-Hill, 2002.

Means, Howard. *Colin Powell: Soldier/Statesman—Statesman/ Soldier*. New York: D. I. Fine, 1992.

Powell, Colin, with Joseph E. Persico. *My American Journey*. New York: Random House, 1995.

Steins, Richard. *Colin Powell: A Biography*. Westport, Conn.: Greenwood Press, 2003.

JOHN C. STONER (1996)
Updated by author 2005

POWERS, HARRIET

OCTOBER 29, 1847
JANUARY 1, 1910

Harriet Powers was born in slavery in Georgia. Powers's husband, Armstead, was also enslaved. After the Civil War, they farmed land around the town of Athens in the northeastern section of the state, while Powers also managed the household. Historians believe that they had eight children, from their oldest daughter Amanda to their youngest son Marshall. By the mid-1890s they had fallen upon hard financial times, and Powers sustained their farm after Armstead left her and the children had grown and moved away. Powers never learned to read and write, but she survived by taking in sewing, selling quilts, and mortgaging property to acquire equipment and personal possessions and to liquidate debts.

Only two of Powers's story quilts are known to have been preserved. One is owned by the Smithsonian Institution's National Museum of American History in Washington, D.C., and the other by Boston's Museum of Fine Arts. They are unique and distinctive examples of both the African continuities and American influences that informed the culture of southern slaves and their descendants. In the tradition of other West and Central African household objects, such as stools, doors, and bowls, for example, the quilts are meant for daily use as well as the soul's contemplation. (According to Maude Southwell Wahlman, Powers alternatively may have intended them to serve as "adult baptismal robes" [1993, p. 73].) Scholars have suggested that Powers's appliquéd figures, which were very popular among black women seamstresses from the Revolutionary War era through Reconstruction, originated across the Atlantic in the appliquéd flags, banners, and other textiles crafted by guilds of Fon men from Dahomey (present-day Benin). Appliqué is the technique of sewing shapes onto cloth surfaces, and while many of Powers's designs, which were applied with the assistance of a sewing machine, reference biblical stories, they also appear in the work of Fon craftsmen to symbolize individual West African gods.

Powers combines Christian motifs such as the cross, the all-seeing, all-knowing eye of God, and the dove (representing the Holy Spirit) with images that researchers have traced to a Kongo cosmogram known as the four moments or stations of the sun, which symbolizes creation and the continuity of life: birth, life, death, and rebirth. The only known surviving photograph of Powers depicts the quilter wearing an apron appliquéd with such trademark symbols.

Powers's quilts are visual equivalents of the West African griot, who memorized historical events and myths and recited them for entertainment and illumination at community gatherings. They relay stories of secular legends and figures, or occurrences from oral tradition and personal experience, in addition to parables and tales from the "Good Book" featuring familiar characters: Adam, Eve, Job, Jonah, Satan, and Jesus, for example. One of Powers's pictorial quilts, containing eleven scenes, was displayed at the 1886 Cotton Fair in Athens, Georgia. It merged African, Christian, and Masonic symbols to tell such biblical stories as the temptation of Adam and Eve by Satan in the garden of Eden, the expulsion of Adam and Eve from paradise, Abraham and Isaac, Noah and the ark, Jacob's dream of angels ascending a ladder to heavenly glory, John's baptism of Jesus, and Jesus' crucifixion and resurrection. Powers did not intend to sell this quilt and rebuffed offers to purchase it when approached by a white art teacher from Athens named "Jennie" (Oneita Virginia) Smith. Several years later, however, desperate for money, Powers reestablished contact with Smith and reluctantly sold her creation for five dollars. However, Smith recorded and preserved an invaluable commentary on the quilt's sources and symbolism, as told to her by Powers. Even after the quilt had changed ownership, Powers lovingly revisited it several times.

In the post-Reconstruction South, annual fairs flaunted the agricultural might of the state, attested to the region's gradual postwar recovery, memorialized the Confederate dead and surviving widows and veterans, and became standard-bearers of the economic and cultural attractions of individual cities and counties. They included exhibits of black Americans' domestic and manual accomplishments, often offering them—food, sewing, carvings, for instance—for sale. By the late nineteenth century, southern black communities were organizing separate buildings or pavilions at these fairs to house their cultural and material productions. With the collapse of the Reconstruction in 1877, the commitment of the southern black leadership to "uplift" the race educationally, economically, domestically, and politically intensified. Anticipating the rise in lynching and racial and sexual violence that would mount as the century drew to a close, African Americans seized upon expositions to demonstrate their people's ethos of hard work, religious piety, and creativity to those white southerners threatened by the economic competition and social parity that might follow the former slaves' hard-won liberation.

These demonstrations of mechanical, artistic, and intellectual achievements proved globally effective. For example, the scholar W. E. B. Du Bois traveled to Paris to launch an exhibit of books, photographs, and other objects produced by southern blacks at the 1900 World's

Fair. Similarly, Smith had intended to display Powers's quilt in the Negro Building of the 1895 Cotton States and International Exposition in Atlanta, where Booker T. Washington famously admonished his fellow descendants of slaves to "cast down your bucket where you are."

Perhaps because of Smith's patronage, Atlanta University acquired a second story quilt from Powers for presentation to Reverend Charles Cuthbert Hall, a longtime trustee. Containing fifteen sections, it was exhibited in the Negro Pavilion of the 1897 Tennessee Centennial Exposition in Nashville. It combines Powers's Bible scenes, intermingling African and Christian motifs, with panels commemorating meteorological and astronomical events that she had heard from old-timers. These include Black Friday (May 19, 1780), when serial forest fires darkened skies on the eastern seaboard; and Georgia's infamous cold snap of February 10, 1895, during which beasts, fowl, and human beings froze and died in the uncommonly frigid weather and extremely heavy snow. Two meteor showers—the Leonid meteor storm that occurred from November 12 to 14, 1833, and several consecutive nights of fireballs and falling stars during mid-August 1846—are additional events "recorded" by Powers's quilt and corroborated by scientific accounts. By referencing temporal events alongside stories of the sacred and ineffable, Powers affirms the cornerstone religious ideas, cherished by blacks since enslavement, underscoring that God mediates in humanity's worldly affairs, and that possessing faith in a higher power means demonstrating it through earthly deeds, rather than dedicating one's energies merely to anticipating a pleasant heavenly reward.

Powers spent the latter years of life in penury, surviving by selling land and animals to meet debts. County records indicate that she died possessing a mere seventy dollars. Yet, according to quilter Kyra E. Hicks, Powers has earned posthumous recognition as the symbolic foremother of African-American women quilters (2003, pp. 217, 228). Twentieth-century black women artists such as Faith Ringgold and Deborah Willis can trace their penchant for telling stories derived from personal and oral sources to Powers, and to those anonymous slave seamstresses who informed Powers's art. Although the Georgia-born Alice Walker's short story "Everyday Use" (1973) and essay "In Search of Our Mothers' Gardens" (1983) do not specifically focus on Powers, they offer a compelling theory of the former slave woman's quilt-making. In both pieces, Walker's themes are that women's everyday work—quilting, cooking, gardening, sewing—knits together and inspires black families and communities, and that the speech, culture, and folkways of rural black American women who quilt, cook, garden, and sew merit serious consideration as art. Like the photographer and former slave Robert E. Williams (1833?–1917), who lived in nearby Augusta, Powers produced a body of work that documents the imagination and creativity of those considered most marginal and inconsequential in postbellum American society.

Powers's quilts are central to the study of African-American vernacular art. They confirm the conclusions of researchers, including Robert Farris Thompson and Michael A. Gomez, that the slaves retained a significant amount of cultural memory through the Middle Passage and subsequent centuries of servitude. Like the *sankofa* of Ghana, a symbolic bird whose head has turned to scrutinize what is behind it, while its feet face forward, Powers's quilts look backward to an African past and forward to a future where African and American religion and design commingle to create a new art.

See also Folk Arts and Crafts; Folk Religion; Textiles, Diasporic

■ ■ *Bibliography*

Frye, Gladys-Marie. *Stitched from the Soul: Slave Quilts from the Antebellum South.* New York: Dutton Studio, 1990; New ed., Chapel Hill: University of North Carolina Press, 2002.

Frye, Gladys-Marie. "'A Sermon in Patchwork': New Light on Harriet Powers." In *Singular Women: Writing the Artist*, edited by Kristen Frederickson and Sarah E. Webb. Berkeley: University of California Press, 2003.

Hicks, Kyra E. *Black Threads: An African American Quilting Sourcebook.* London and Jefferson, N.C.: McFarland, 2003.

Lyons, Mary E. *Stitching Stars: The Story Quilts of Harriet Powers.* New York: Scribner's, 1993.

Perry, Reginia A. *Harriet Powers's Bible Quilts.* New York: Rizzoli and St. Martin's Press, 1994.

Wahlman, Maude Southwell. *Signs and Symbols: African Images in African-American Quilts.* New York: Studio Books, 1993.

BARBARA MCCASKILL (2005)

PRESBYTERIANS

The African-American constituency of the Presbyterian Church dates from the 1730s, when the Reverend Samuel Davies began to evangelize slaves of Scotch-Irish Presbyterian immigrants in the Valley of Virginia. Davies reported instructing and baptizing 150 slaves in 1757. Unlike the Baptists and Methodists, American Presbyterians failed to attract large numbers of blacks in either the South or the North. At the end of the nineteenth century there were fewer than 30,000 African Americans in the northern and southern Presbyterian churches combined. These two major branches of Presbyterianism had split in 1861 over the Civil War, but they finally closed ranks in 1983. The black minority has grown slowly. By 1990 it was reported that only 2.47 percent, or 64,841 of the almost three-million-member reunited Presbyterian Church in the U.S.A. (PCUSA) were African Americans.

Reputedly, Presbyterian slaves were well instructed in the rudiments of Christianity. Many were taught to read and recite the creed and passages of the Bible by their owners. The emphasis of Puritan Presbyterians on a trained clergy and a literate laity had the effect of exposing black Presbyterians to pious learning as indispensable for Christian discipleship. The Presbyterians, however, were slow to oppose slavery. The issue was first raised in 1774 at a meeting of the Synod of New York and Philadelphia, but no action was taken. In 1787 the synod approved the ultimate goal of abolition; however, successive deliverances of the General Assembly induced the practice of Presbyterians to condemn slavery in principle while warning local judicatories not to interfere with the civil order.

The first black Presbyterian preacher was John Chavis, who was born in Granville County, North Carolina, in 1763. From 1801 to 1808 he served as a missionary to slaves in Virginia and opened a school that was patronized by many leading white families. The first African-American pastor was John Gloucester, who was manumitted by Gideon Blackburn, a Tennessee missionary, to preach the gospel. In 1807 Gloucester was permitted by the Presbytery of Philadelphia to organize the First African Presbyterian Church, which competed with Richard Allen's Bethel African Methodist Episcopal Church for members from the burgeoning black community of South Philadelphia. Gloucester's three sons entered the Presbyterian ministry. Jeremiah organized the Second African Presbyterian Church of Philadelphia in 1824, James organized Siloam Presbyterian Church in Brooklyn in 1847, and Stephen served the Lombard Central Presbyterian Church of Philadelphia. Among the earliest black congregations in the North were Shiloh Presbyterian Church in New York City (organized in 1822 as First Colored Presbyterian Church) and Washington Street in Reading, Pennsylvania (1823). The first black Presbyterian congregation in the South was Beaufort-Salem Presbyterian Church, organized in Sheldon, North Carolina in 1828. The Ladson Presbyterian Church of Columbia, South Carolina (1828), was first governed by white elders and named after the white minister who was its first pastor. The slaves of the members of the First Presbyterian Church of Macon, Georgia, organized the Washington Avenue Church of that city in 1838.

After the Civil War, blacks spurned the southern branch of the church, the Presbyterian Church in the United States (PCUS), and rallied to the northern PCUSA missionaries following the Union armies. Many became members of the northern church. Fewer than 4,000 blacks remained in the southern church, which tried to organize them into an independent Afro-American Presbyterian Church in 1874. That effort was abandoned in 1916 because of poor support from whites. During Reconstruction the northern church launched a mission to attract and minister to the recently freed people. By 1882 its Board of Missions for Freedmen sponsored two universities, Lincoln University, near Oxford, Pennsylvania, and Biddle University (later Johnson C. Smith) in Charlotte, North Carolina, as well as two colleges, five boarding schools, and 138 parochial schools. Following the Presbyterian tradition of educational excellence, these institutions made a signal contribution far beyond the ranks of the black constituency. Until the church's Board of National Missions phased it out in the twentieth century, this remarkable educational system enrolled 19,166 students and 494 teachers. At its peak the board supervised 438 churches and missions, 388 schools, 272 ministers, and 27,916 communicants.

Black Presbyterians caucused for greater recognition and freedom as early as 1859, when their ministers began meeting with black Congregational clergy in Philadelphia. Prior to the Civil War, Samuel Cornish, Theodore Wright, Henry Highland Garnet, and J. W. C. Pennington, all Presbyterian clergy, were leading black abolitionists. Lucy Craft Laney, the daughter of a Presbyterian minister and born a slave, founded the Haines Normal Institute in Augusta, Georgia, in 1867. In 1891 Daniel J. Sanders became the first black president of J. C. Smith University. Blacks in the northern church became more assertive, establishing the Afro-American Presbyterian Council in 1894. The purpose was to create more fellowship among themselves in an overwhelming white church, and to gain greater influence in the boards and agencies of the denomination. At the turn of the century, outspoken black pastors like Francis J. Grimké of the Fifteenth Street Presbyterian Church in Washington, D.C., and Matthew Anderson of Berean in Philadelphia consistently fought racism in the church and the proposed mergers of the northern church with the PCUS and the Cumberland Presbyterian Church, both with lingering Confederate allegiances.

Pressure from the African-American constituency moved the northern church to begin elevating blacks to key positions. In 1938 Albert B. McCoy became the first black executive of the Unit of Work for Colored People. Charles W. Talley was appointed field representative of the

Atlantic Synod in 1945. During this period, George Lake Imes became the field representative for Negro Work in the North and West. He was followed by Robert Pierre Johnson, who served as associate stated clerk of the General Assembly in 1972. Jesse Belmont Barber, Frank T. Wilson, Emily V. Gibbes, Elo Henderson, Mildred Atris, Rachel Adams, and Bryant George were among the black men and women who served in prominent executive positions after World War II.

Lawrence W. Bottoms was an executive of the PCUS prior to his election in 1974 as its first black moderator. The PCUS began to respond to civil rights agitation after 1969. Under Bottoms's leadership in new church development in black communities, and with the rising militancy of a newly formed Black Leadership Caucus, African-American membership in the southern church doubled to about 8,000 before the 1983 merger with the United Presbyterian Church (which was formed by the union of PCUSA and the United Presbyterian Church of North America in 1958).

Northern black Presbyterians figured prominently in the civil rights program of the National Council of Churches during the 1960s. The Afro-American Presbyterian Council of 1894 went through several reincarnations and finally developed into the Concerned Presbyterians in 1963 and Black Presbyterians United in 1968. The former caucus, with white allies, enabled the election of the controversial pastor of St. Augustine Presbyterian Church in the Bronx, Edler G. Hawkins, as the first black moderator of the United Presbyterian Church in 1964. This group was also a major factor in the creation of the Commission on Religion and Race, which steered the church through the 1960s and played a leading role in the Black Manifesto call for slavery reparations in 1969 and the Angela Davis crisis of 1971. Gayraud S. Wilmore, a professor at the Pittsburgh Theological Seminary, J. Metz Rollins, a pastor and civil rights activist in Tallahassee, and Robert Stone, a New York City pastor, were chosen to head this unprecedented commitment of the church to the struggle led by the Southern Christian Leadership Conference. Since the union, Asian, Hispanic, and Native-American minorities have played a larger role in the church's program in racial and intercultural affairs. African Americans, however, came together across regional lines in 1983 to form a National Black Presbyterian Caucus, which continues to monitor church policy and practice in the field of racial and ethnic relations.

See also Allen, Richard; Baptists; Cornish, Samuel E.; Garnet, Henry Highland; Pennington, James W. C.; Protestantism in the Americas; Religion; Wright, Theodore Sedgwick

■ ■ *Bibliography*

Brown, Karen V., and Phyllis M. Felton, eds. *African American Presbyterian Clergywomen: The First Twenty-Five Years.* Louisville, Ky.: Witherspoon Press, 2001.

Murray, Andrew W. *Presbyterians and the Negro: A History.* Philadelphia: Presbyterian Historical Society, 1966.

Swift, David E. *Black Prophets of Justice: Activist Clergy Before the Civil War.* Baton Rouge: Louisiana State University Press, 1989.

Wilmore, Gayraud S. *Black and Presbyterian: The Heritage and the Hope.* Philadelphia: Geneva Press, 1983.

GAYRAUD S. WILMORE (1996)
Updated bibliography

PRICE, GEORGE

JANUARY 15, 1919

George Cadle Price, a politician, was born in Belize of mixed African, European, and Mayan ancestry. He was educated at St. John's College, Belize's most prestigious secondary school, and at St. Augustine Seminary in Mississippi. Deciding against taking holy orders, he returned to Belize and in 1942 became the secretary of a wealthy merchant-politician. Price was a member of the Christian Social Action Group, formed by graduates of St. John's College, which from 1945 promoted Catholic ideals of social justice. He topped the polls in the Belize City Council election in 1947, and he rapidly became Belize's most distinguished politician.

When the British government devalued the colony's currency in 1949, Price helped form a protest committee. This group became the core of the People's United Party (PUP), which worked with the General Workers' Union to develop an anticolonial movement. On April 28, 1954, when the first election was held with universal adult suffrage, the PUP won two thirds of the vote and eight of the nine elected seats in the new Legislative Assembly. Price consolidated his leadership of the party in 1956 and, on the basis of its opposition to colonialism and with support from all the ethnic groups in the country, it won all the seats in 1957.

The British government distrusted Price, but in the 1961 elections the PUP won all eighteen seats, and after a new constitution granted internal self-government in 1964, Price became premier. The state, under Price's leadership, assumed an active role in developing the economy, and a new capital, Belmopan, was built inland. The PUP won every national election in 1965, 1969, 1974, and 1979, but because Guatemala claimed the territory, independence was delayed until September 21, 1981, when Price became the prime minister.

In 1984, after an economic crisis, the PUP was defeated by the United Democratic Party (UDP), but Price remained his party's leader. After the 1989 election, when the PUP won 50.3 percent of the vote and fifteen of the twenty-eight seats in the House of Representatives, Price again became prime minister. Guatemala's government recognized Belize's independence in 1991, but in 1993 the Guatemalan president was overthrown. Growing anxieties about Belize's security and the presence of thousands of Central American immigrants resulted in the closest of general elections on June 30, 1993. The PUP won more votes, but the UDP, which won sixteen of the twenty-nine seats, formed a new government. In October 1996 Price resigned as his party's leader but he retained his seat in his Belize City constituency in the 1998 and 2003 elections, which were won decisively by the PUP.

Price was awarded the Order of CARICOM by that Caribbean organization in 2001, and on September 19, 2004, when he was still a member of the government as senior minister with responsibility for disaster preparedness and management, he received Belize's highest honor, the Order of National Hero. This distinguished and long-serving statesman was honored for his dedication to his country, his integrity and modesty, and his unpretentious lifestyle.

See also Anti-Colonial Movements; Caribbean Community and Common Market (CARICOM); International Relations in the Anglophone Caribbean

■ ■ *Bibliography*

Greene, Edward. *George Price: Father of the Nation Belize.* Belize: ION Media, 2000.

Shoman, Assad. "Party Politics in Belize." In *Political Parties and Democracy in Central America,* edited by Louis W. Goodman, William M. LeoGrande, and Johanna Mendelson Forman. Boulder, Colo.: Westview Press, 1992.

O. NIGEL BOLLAND (2005)

PRICE, MARY VIOLET LEONTYNE

FEBRUARY 10, 1927

▶ ▮ ▮ ▮ ◀

Born in Laurel, Mississippi, the soprano Leontyne Price came to be regarded as a prima donna *assoluta* during her exceptionally long operatic career (1952–1985).

Leontyne Price, in costume for Antony and Cleopatra *at the* **Metropolitan Opera House in New York City, 1966.** THE LIBRARY OF CONGRESS

Price's parents had been involved in the musical life of Laurel and provided her with piano lessons from the age of four. Soon thereafter she joined her mother in the church choir and, after attending a recital by Marian Anderson in Jackson, Mississippi, in 1936, she resolved on a career in music. At that time African-American women could aspire in music only for roles in education, and it was with that major in mind that Price enrolled at Central State College in Ohio. Before she graduated in 1949, however, her vocal talent was manifest and she was encouraged to enter the Juilliard School of Music, where she studied with Florence Kimball. As Mistress Ford in a school production of Verdi's *Falstaff,* she attracted the attention of American composer Virgil Thomson, who enlisted her for the role of Cecilia in a 1952 revival of his *Four Saints in Three Acts* (1934), a work calling for an all-black cast, thus initiating her professional career and terminating her formal study.

Following this production in New York and performances at the Paris International Arts Festival, Price was engaged for the role of Bess in George Gershwin's *Porgy and Bess,* with which she toured in Berlin, Paris, and Vienna into 1954. In November of that year, she made her New York debut at Town Hall. The following February she appeared in the title role of Puccini's *Tosca* on television, later adding Mozart's *Die Zauberflöte* and *Don Giovanni,* and Poulenc's *Dialogues des Carmélites* to her NBC telecasts. In 1956 she sang the role of Cleopatra in Handel's *Giulio Cesare.*

It was in the Poulenc opera as Madame Lidoine that Price made her debut with the San Francisco Opera in

1957, following this with the leading soprano roles with that company in Verdi's *Il Trovatore* and Puccini's *Madama Butterfly* and debuts that year at the Arena di Verona, Covent Garden, and the Vienna Staatsoper (*Aida*). Her debut with the Lyric Opera of Chicago was as Liù in Puccini's *Turandot* (1959).

The Metropolitan Opera had only begun adding black singers to its roster in 1955 with Marian Anderson and Robert McFerrin, followed by the debuts of African-American artists Mattiwilda Dobbs (1956), Gloria Davy (1958), and Martina Arroyo (1959). Actually, Price had already appeared in the Metropolitan Opera Jamboree, a fund-raising broadcast from the Manhattan Ritz Theater, April 6, 1953, when she performed "Summertime" from *Porgy and Bess,* but her formal debut was as Leonora in Verdi's *Il Trovatore* on January 27, 1961, when she won an unprecedented forty-two-minute ovation, fully justifying her selection as the leading lady to open the next Met season (as Puccini's Minnie in *La Fanciulla del West*) and that of the next year (repeating her 1957 Vienna role of Aida, in which she was heard each season for the following five years). During the last six years of the "old Met," she particularly excelled in the Italian repertory (as Liù in Puccini's *Turandot,* Cio-Cio-San in Puccini's *Madama Butterfly,* and Elvira in Verdi's *Ernani,* which she had sung for Herbert von Karajan at the 1962 Salzburg Festival).

The new home of the Metropolitan Opera at Lincoln Center was inaugurated in 1966 with a new opera by Samuel Barber, *Antony and Cleopatra,* written specifically for Price. When she concluded her career in opera performances on January 3, 1985, with *Aida* at the Metropolitan Opera, she had proved her interpretive leadership in the Italian repertories of Verdi and Puccini, but she had expanded the previously practiced limits to move far past any stereotypes, excelling in German, Spanish, French, and Slavic works, as well as in spirituals and other American literature. Her principal opera roles, in addition to those mentioned, were the Prima Donna and Ariadne (*Ariadne auf Naxos*), Amelia (*Un Ballo in Maschera*), Fiordiligi (*Così fan tutte*), Donna Anna (*Don Giovanni*), Tatiana (*Eugene Onegin*), Minnie (*La Fanciulla del West*), Leonora (*La Forza del Destino*), Manon (*Manon Lescaut*), and the title role in *Tosca.*

Price's recorded legacy is extensive. In addition to many of the operatic roles in which she appeared onstage—Bizet's *Carmen,* Mozart's *Don Giovanni* and *Così fan tutte,* Puccini's *Madama Butterfly* and *Tosca,* Verdi's *Aida, Un Ballo in Maschera, Ernani, La Forza del Destino,* and *Il Trovatore*—she has recorded Samuel Barber's *Hermit Songs* and music of Fauré, Poulenc, Wolf, and R. Strauss, as well as Verdi's *Requiem* and Beethoven's Ninth

Symphony. She has also recorded excerpts from *Porgy and Bess* (with her then-husband William Warfield), an album of popular songs with André Previn (*Right as Rain*), and *Swing Low, Sweet Chariot,* a collection of fourteen spirituals. In 1992 RCA reissued on compact disc forty-seven arias by Price under the title *Leontyne Price: The Prima Donna Collection,* arias that had been recorded from 1965 to 1979.

See also Anderson, Marian

■ ■ *Bibliography*

Blyth, Alan. "Mary Violet Leontyne Price." In *The New Grove Dictionary of Music and Musicians,* vol. 15. London: Grove, 1980, pp. 225–226.

"Leontyne Price." In *Baker's Biographical Dictionary of Musicians,* 7th ed., edited by Nicholas Slonimsky, p. 1363. New York: Schirmer, 1992.

Lyon, Hugh Lee. *Leontyne Price: Highlights of a Prima Donna.* New York: Vantage Press, 1973.

Sargeant, Winthrop. *Divas.* New York: Coward, McCann & Geoghegan, 1973, pp. 134–167.

DOMINIQUE-RENÉ DE LERMA (1996)

PRIDE, CHARLEY FRANK

MARCH 18, 1938

The country singer and guitarist Charley Pride was born in Sledge, Mississippi. Though he grew up steeped in the African-American Mississippi Delta blues culture he encountered on his parents' sharecropper farm, as a child he gravitated toward the country music that was largely favored by whites. He taught himself guitar by the age of fourteen, but by his late teens he was concentrating on becoming a professional baseball player. Aside from a two-year stint in the U.S. Army, Pride played for Negro American League teams in Detroit, Memphis, and Birmingham from 1955 to 1959. Starting in 1960 he worked off-season as a tin smelter in Great Falls, Montana, and during the season played for the Class C Pioneer League team there, occasionally singing for the fans between innings. He also sang occasionally in nightclubs, where country music producers from Nashville heard him. After a brief time in the major leagues with the Los Angeles Angels in 1961, he returned to Montana. A final, unsuccessful tryout for the New York Mets in 1963 convinced Pride to give up baseball. On the trip back to Montana, he stopped off in Nashville, where his velvety baritone quickly earned him a reputation in the local country music scene.

From the mid-1960s on, Pride's love songs, starting with "Atlantic Coastal Line" (1965) and "Snakes Crawl at Night" (1965), were among the most popular recordings in country music, and Pride quickly became the first African-American star in country music since DeFord Bailey (1899–1982) more than three decades earlier. However, the all-white country music industry at first proved wary of an African-American star and took advantage of Pride's "white" sound, hiding the fact of his race. His first recordings were released without the usual publicity photos, while some country disc jockeys who knew Pride's race boycotted his music. Nonetheless, country music fans embraced Pride from the start, and he had numerous hit singles, including the Grammy Award–nominated "Just Between You and Me" (1966), "All I Have to Offer You Is Me" (1969), "Is Anybody Going to San Antone?" (1970), "Kiss an Angel Good Morning" (1973), "My Eyes Can Only See as Far as You" (1976), and "You're My Jamaica" (1979). Pride won the Country Music Association's Entertainer of the Year award in 1971, and that year he also won two Grammy Awards, for best sacred album (*Did You Think to Pray?*) and best gospel performance ("Let Me Live"). During this time he also toured extensively and became one of the few African Americans to perform at Nashville's Grand Ole Opry.

Pride's success continued unabated through the 1980s, with hit recordings including "Honky Tonk Blues" (1980), "I'm Missin' Mississippi" (1984), and "Amy's Eyes" (1989). Since then, he has also pursued a career in business; he owns three radio stations and a cattle ranch in Dallas and is a majority shareholder of First Texas Bank in Dallas, where he lives. Pride was married in 1956; he and his wife, Rozene, have three children.

In 1999 Pride was honored with a star on the Hollywood Walk of Fame, and in 2000 he was inducted into the Country Music Hall of Fame.

See also Music in the United States

■ ■ *Bibliography*

Burton, Charlie. "Charley Pride." *Rolling Stone* (May 27, 1971): 52–53.

Millard, B. "Alone in the Spotlight." *Journal of Country Music* 14, no. 2 (1992): 18–22.

Pride, Charley, and Jim Henderson. *Pride: The Charley Pride Story*. New York: William Morrow, 1994.

JONATHAN GILL (1996)
Updated by publisher 2005

PRIMITIVE BAPTISTS

■ ■ ■

The "Primitive" or "Antimission" Baptists (also known as "Old School," "Old Line," "Hardshell," "Square Toed," or "Old" Baptists) separated from mainstream Baptists in the early nineteenth century, in opposition to Baptist participation in the emerging evangelical Protestant culture. Primitive Baptists, who considered themselves descended from the original "primitive" Church, objected to missionary activities they believed were inconsistent with a Calvinist belief in predestination. They also opposed national organizations that threatened local church autonomy, as well as a centralized, paid "hireling" clergy. They denounced ministerial education, Bible and tract societies, and Sunday schools as innovations and "human institutions" contrary to the Bible and historic Baptist principles. Their opponents charged them with retreat from Christian responsibility in the world, and with a morbid inward-turning faith.

The split among Baptists involved African Americans as well, although few joined the Primitive party. For example, the Huntsville (Alabama) African Baptist Church (today the St. Bartley Primitive Baptist Church), the historic center for black Primitive Baptists, was established with seventy-six members in 1820. Following its pastor, the Reverend William Harris, a free black, it entered the white Flint River Baptist Association the following year. When division came in the late 1820s, the church joined the Primitive faction. Forced out of the white association after the Civil War, the Huntsville church joined with other black Primitive Baptists to form the Indian Creek Primitive Baptist Association in northern Alabama. In 1895, this association had some two thousand members.

Around 1906 there was a movement among black Primitive Baptists for a national convention. This led to an organizational meeting in Huntsville, Alabama, the following year called by Elders Clarence Francis Sams of Florida, James H. Carey of North Carolina, and George S. Crawford of Florida. Eighty-eight elders from seven southern states attended and organized the National Primitive Baptist Convention of the United States of America, headquartered in Tallahassee, Florida. The convention, still the major Primitive Baptist body, had some six hundred churches and 250,000 members in the early 1990s. Evident by the existence of a national organization—albeit a loose organization without centralized authority—National Primitive Baptists tend to be less theologically rigid than their white counterparts. They remain committed to sixteen articles of faith, including the doctrine of divine election and visible sainthood, baptism by immersion, and foot washing as a form of religious observance.

However, the National Primitive Baptists do not impose a common confession on associations and individual congregations, resulting in some variation in belief, especially concerning social action. Despite their ideological opposition to political action and other "worldly activities," the churches do serve as community centers, and churches do supply funds to needy members. In 1967 the convention even considered a proposal to establish foreign missions, though it ultimately rejected the idea.

See also Baptists

■ ■ *Bibliography*

Mathis, James R. *The Making of the Primitive Baptists: A Cultural and Intellectual History of the Antimission Movement, 1800–1840.* New York: Routledge, 2004.

Piepkorn, Arthur Carl. "The Primitive Baptists of North America." *Concordia Theological Monthly* 42, no. 5 (May 1971): 297–313.

Sutton, Joel Brett. "Spirit and Polity in a Black Primitive Baptist Church." Ph.D. diss., University of North Carolina, 1983.

TIMOTHY E. FULOP (1996)
Updated by publisher 2005

PRINCE, LUCY TERRY

C. 1730
AUGUST 21, 1821

—I-I-I—

The history of African-American poetry begins in 1746 with Lucy Terry Prince, who at the age of sixteen wrote a vivid poem in rhyming couplets describing a victorious Native American raid in Deerfield, Massachusetts. Prince's poem is the most complete contemporary account of the murder of two white families who resided in a section of town called the Bars. "Bars Fight, August 28, 1746" became part of Deerfield's oral tradition, remaining unpublished until 1855, when it appeared in a volume of local history. The poem may also have been sung as a ballad.

Prince was known in her community as a storyteller, and her home became a meeting place where people came to hear her orations. Prince's New England community also remembered her for two outstanding uses of oratorical skills. In one, she spoke for three hours before the Board of Trustees of Williams College in an ultimately unsuccessful plea for one of her sons to gain admission to the school. In the other, she defended herself before the U.S. Supreme Court in a land-claims case against a neighbor. Prince won the case and earned high praise from Supreme Court Justice Samuel Chase.

Lucy Terry was born in Africa and brought to New England as an infant slave. In 1756 she married Abijah Prince, a manumitted slave who then purchased his wife's freedom. The couple moved to Vermont, where Abijah had been given land, and their son, Cesar (one of six children), served in the American Revolution.

See also Poetry, U.S.

■ ■ *Bibliography*

Kaplan, Sidney, and Emma Nogrady Kaplan. *The Black Presence in the Era of the American Revolution.* Amherst: University of Massachusetts Press, 1989.

MARTHA E. HODES (1996)

PRINCE, MARY

C.1788
?

—I-I-I—

Born a slave in Brackish Pond, Bermuda, Mary Prince wrote the first full-length narrative by a female slave, *The History of Mary Prince, a West Indian Slave, Related by Herself,* which was published in England in 1831. In this often harrowing narrative, Prince documents her experiences under slavery, offering a glimpse of the diversity of slave experience within the "Black Atlantic." Detailing the physical and often psychological abuse she was forced to suffer at the hands of a series of cruel slave owners, Prince describes the trauma of being sold at a slave market, flogged while naked, raking salt for ten years in the harsh marshes of the Turks Islands, and being forced to bathe her slave master.

In 1828 Prince's owners, the Woods, agreed to take her with them to England. This was a potentially risky enterprise, as slavery had been considered abolished in England since 1772 when Lord Mansfield passed judgment in the habeas corpus trial of *James Somerset the Black vs. Charles Stewart.* Mansfield found not only that slaves who came to England on their own or with their masters could not be forced to return to slavery but also that since slavery did not exist as a legal institution within the borders of Great Britain, "slaves" there were to be considered free people. While in London, the Woods' continued and increased abuse of Mary culminated in her decision to walk away from the enslaved life. Because her husband was still in Antigua, Prince desired to return to him there but wanted to do so as a freewoman. With the aid of the Anti-

Slavery Society, she sued the Woods, claiming that since they had violated the Amelioration Act of 1823, which legally prohibited excessive cruelty by slave owners, she should be completely manumitted. As a means to document evidence of their cruelty, Prince dictated the details of her life, which were transcribed by Susanna Strickland, an aspiring poet, and edited by Thomas Pringle, a writer and the secretary of the Anti-Slavery Society. Because the narrative provided a female slave's perspective, it became immensely popular and went through three editions in quick succession. Hoping to hinder public acceptance of the narrative, writer James MacQueen, in an article for *Blackwood's Magazine,* accused Pringle and Prince of fabricating the narrative to spread lies and abolitionist propaganda. Pringle sued MacQueen for libel, and although judgment was found in his and Prince's favor, the damages MacQueen paid were a paltry three pounds sterling. This ideological triumph would be short-lived, however, because the court decided against Prince in her suit for freedom, claiming she had exaggerated her abuse by the Woods.

Other than the trial summaries in *The Times* and attendance at Susanna Strickland's wedding to Captain Moody, further written documentation of Prince is limited to a brief mention in Strickland's 1851 short story, "Rachel Wilde, or, Trifles from the Burthen of Life," in which the main character, loosely based on Strickland, admits that she knows that "Mary P.'s" narrative is not false because she took it down herself.

Prince's narrative is different from the traditional model of U.S. slave narratives in a number of ways. In addition to providing crucial evidence for understanding the diversity of global slavery, as well as the specifics of slavery in the British West Indies, the narrative documents the victimization of slave women by male and female slave owners, slave participation in the British West Indian judicial system and in the local economy as entrepreneurs, and the influence of the nonconformist religions in providing a venue to assert slave subjectivity. Her narrative and life offer testimony to her courage and determination to be seen and treated as a human being.

See also Women Writers of the Caribbean

■ ■ *Bibliography*

Haynes, Roberta R. "Voice, Body and Collaboration: Constructions of Authority in *The History of Mary Prince.*" *The Literary Griot* 11, no. 1 (1999): 18–32.

Paquet, Sandra Pouchet. "The Heartbeat of a West Indian Slave: *The History of Mary Prince.*" *African American Review* 26, no. 1 (1992): 131–146.

Rauwerda, A. M. "Naming Agency and 'A Tissue of Falsehoods' in *The History of Mary Prince.*" *Victorian Literature and Culture* 29, no. 2 (2001): 397–411.

Salih, Sarah. "Introduction." In *The History of Mary Prince.* London: Penguin Books, 2000.

Sharpe, Jenny. "'Something Akin to Freedom': The Case of Mary Prince." *Differences* 8 no. 1 (1996): 31–55.

Whitlock, Gillian. "The Silent Scribe: Susanna and 'Black Mary.'" *International Journal of Canadian Studies* 11 (1995): 249–260.

NICOLE N. ALJOE (2005)

PRINCE (NELSON, PRINCE ROGERS)

C. JUNE 7, 1958

■ ■ ■

Singer and composer Prince Rogers Nelson, who goes by the name Prince, is reluctant to divulge information about his early years. He was born to two jazz musicians in an interracial marriage and raised in Minneapolis, Minnesota. He began playing music at a very young age, alternating among piano, keyboards, guitar, and drums. He formed his own band, Grand Central, while still in junior high school. Prince made his first demonstration record in 1976, playing all the parts himself. In 1978, after his manager subtracted several years from Prince's age and heralded him as "a new Stevie Wonder," Prince signed a contract with Warner Brothers and made *For You.* That album combined several African-American musical styles, taking the heavy bass of funk and mixing it with the dance beat of disco, while providing an overall feeling of rock in both arrangement and content. His second album, *Prince* (1979), was a great commercial success, producing the hit single "I Wanna Be Your Lover."

Prince, who adopted a visually androgynous persona in photos, public appearances, and performances, first received notoriety for sexually explicit lyrics on his third album, *Dirty Mind* (1980), which included songs about incest, oral sex, and a ménage-à-trois. His breakthrough album, *1999* (1982), included the hit songs "1999" and "Little Red Corvette," both of which featured a vocal style ranging from reedy falsetto to muscular baritone.

In 1984 Prince produced, wrote, scored, and starred in the film *Purple Rain,* whose soundtrack sold more than seventeen million copies and won an Oscar for best original music score, in addition to three Grammy Awards and three American Music Awards. After this, Prince continued to pursue film projects. His film *Under the Cherry*

Moon (1987) failed to achieve wide popularity, but his soundtrack for *Batman* reached the top of the popular album charts in 1989. His film *Graffiti Bridge* (1992) achieved only moderate success.

Since 1987 Prince has recorded his own albums and produced music by others in his Paisley Park Studios, a Minneapolis production facility built with the assistance of Warner Brothers. In 1987 he also released *Sign o' the Times,* which combined the rhythms of funk with gospel and pop styles, but it failed to muster significant appeal. In 1992 he released an album whose title was a symbolic visual representation that he thereafter officially adopted as his unpronounceable name. The Artist Formerly Known as Prince, as he came to be called, spent several years in a contract dispute with Warner Brothers. His last album with them, *Chaos and Disorder,* was released in 1996. Sales of his albums dwindled during the 1990s. In 1997 he released a triple CD, *Emancipation,* the first in his new deal with EMI. He reassumed the name Prince in 2000.

During the 1980s and 1990s, Prince worked with many prominent figures in popular music, including Chaka Khan, Sheena Easton, Stephanie Mills, the Bangles, Stevie Nicks, Sheila E., Patti LaBelle, and M. C. Hammer. He also collaborated with the gospel singer Mavis Staples, and worked several times with the jazz trumpeter Miles Davis.

In 2004 Prince was inducted in the Rock and Roll Hall of Fame. That same year, his album *Musicology* was released by Columbia Records, and the artist embarked on a sold-out musical tour. Prince was awarded Grammy Awards in 2005 for best male R&B vocal performance for "Call My Name," and best traditional R&B vocal performance for "Musicology." In addition, the NAACP honored Prince with its Vanguard Award for work that "increases understanding and awareness of racial and social issues," and an Image Award for best album for *Musicology.*

See also Music in the United States

■■ *Bibliography*

Hahn, Alex. *Possessed: The Rise and Fall of Prince.* New York: Billboard Books, 2003.

Norment, Lynn. "Prince Reclaims His Throne." Interview. *Ebony* 59, no. 11 (September 2004): 196–200.

DAVID HENDERSON (1996)
Updated by publisher 2005

PRINTMAKING

Historically, printmaking has fallen into the category of graphic arts, and includes relief printing, engraving, etching, aquatint, silkscreen printing, and lithography. Although the African forebears of African Americans had their own traditions of printed and/or multiple arts (as seen in the relief and resist textile-printing techniques of numerous West African peoples), there is no evidence that these printing traditions survived in the Americas. Therefore, a discussion of African Americans in the graphic arts rightfully belongs within the larger historical picture of printmaking in America.

Occasional African-American graphic artists emerged from the late eighteenth century to the end of the nineteenth century. Possibly the earliest known black American printmaker—and the most obscure—was Scipio Moorhead. Moorhead's talents were praised by a fellow black Bostonian, the famous Senegalese-born poet Phillis Wheatley, in her poem "To S.M., a Young African Painter, on Seeing His Work." A copperplate engraving of the poet, which appeared as the frontispiece to the 1773 London edition of her volume of poetry, has been attributed to Moorhead.

Moorhead, like many of the African-American artists who came after him, learned to paint and/or make prints through an apprenticeship with a sympathetic white artisan. Numerous black artists during the antebellum period, such as Robert M. Douglass Jr. and Patrick Reason, trained with artisans and cultivated clients from the growing ranks of northern white abolitionists. Reason's skillfully realized 1848 copper engraving of the runaway slave and antislavery lecturer Henry Bibb demonstrates that these black artists were capable of both mastering the intricacies of the various graphic arts techniques and making their work a part of the abolitionist movement.

In contrast to those antebellum black artists whose careers were linked with the struggle for black emancipation, many nineteenth-century artists of color avoided social issues altogether, choosing instead to do common portraiture, picturesque landscapes, and other forms of nonracial art. For example, Jules Lion in New Orleans and James P. Ball in Cincinnati both headed thriving lithography businesses that catered to largely white clienteles. After the Civil War and continuing into the first decade of the twentieth century, African-American lithographer Grafton Tyler Brown produced numerous stock certificates, street maps, and landscapes, mostly of California, the Pacific Northwest, and the Nevada territories.

Henry Ossawa Tanner and his student William Edouard Scott, although known primarily as painters, were the first African-American graphic artists to move beyond commercial work and create fine art prints. Working through the first two decades of the twentieth century, Tanner and Scott borrowed art techniques learned from the French impressionists and applied these to their respective etchings and lithographs of landscapes, marine settings, and occasional portraits and genre scenes. Etchers William McKnight Farrow, Allan Randall Freelon, and Albert Alexander Smith, though active at the height of the Harlem Renaissance and the Great Depression, also subscribed to this belated/modified form of visual modernism.

Two graphic artists who, during the period of the Harlem Renaissance, broke away from European-American artistic conventions and embraced more avant-garde, African design sensibilities were Aaron Douglas and James Lesesne Wells. Douglas's bold, angular renderings of African Americans, as seen in his series of relief prints illustrating the Eugene O'Neill play *The Emperor Jones* (1926), recalled the highly stylized and distorted representations of human anatomy found in traditional African sculpture. Similar approaches to the human figure and to two-dimensional design appeared in Wells's graphic works, such as his relief print *African Fantasy* (1929).

With the onset of the Great Depression, Douglas and Wells continued their experiments in design and form, but their innovations were tempered by the social and economic realities of the times. Consequently, these graphic artists and others turned toward an art of social realism, an approach that placed humanity, social concerns, and the environment at the center of artistic matters.

A more socially engaged art scene in America, with the graphic arts playing a major role in this ideological shift, was further encouraged by the creation of the Works Progress Administration/Federal Arts Projects, or the WPA/FAP, in 1935. This government program, apart from helping to put Americans back to work, provided support for the creation of art in public places, the implementation of scholarly inventories of American design, the development of community art centers, and the establishment of artists' workshops. Significant numbers of African-American artists participated in WPA/FAP graphic workshops in Atlanta, Chicago, Cleveland, Philadelphia, New York, and Washington, D.C. A few of these black printmakers—such as the Philadelphia-based Dox Thrash, who helped develop a new printmaking process—were considered major figures in their respective art communities, regardless of race.

From the end of World War II to the historic signing of the Civil Rights Act of 1968, African-American art and culture underwent numerous shifts and emphases, which are reflected in the graphic arts of those transitional years. Toward the end of the 1940s, visual commentaries on the racial inequities in America were present in the prints of several black artists, most notably Elizabeth Catlett in works such as her relief print *I Have Special Reservations* (1946). Concurrent with these images of black protest were the more idealistic and uplifting representations of an artist such as Charles White, whose relief print *Exodus #1* (1949) focuses on black aspirations and Afro-America's sense of racial pride.

By the 1950s and early 1960s many African-American graphic artists worked with themes and stylistic approaches that differed radically from the political and/or culture-specific works of Catlett and White. Etcher/engraver Norma Morgan and relief printmaker Walter Williams, though two very different artists, developed essentially nonracial formulas for their work. Williams subscribed to a figurative expressionist sensibility, as seen in his relief print *Fighting Cock* (1957), while Morgan's copper engraving *David in the Wilderness* (1956) illustrates her adherence to a romantic realist agenda.

Beginning in the late 1960s the rumblings of the civil rights movement and the strong identification with an African heritage propelled many African-American artists to revisit social themes and ethnic styles that had been pioneered by Catlett and Wells. The results were works that spoke to the issue of black solidarity, such as the silkscreen *Unite* (1970) by Chicago artist Barbara Jones-Hogu, and works that recalled African colors and imagery, such as the relief print *Jungle Rhythms #2* (1968) by New York artist Ademola Olugebefola.

This atmosphere of a heightened racial consciousness ushered in an abundance of work from about 1968 to 1976 that reflected African-American sensibilities, most often in the form of a race-specific figurative art. This new black imagery among artists, coinciding with a newfound enthusiasm within the greater art world for the art of the print, resulted in many different examples of African-American graphic art. Among the many artists who produced important graphic works during this period were Samella Lewis, Ruth Waddy, Lev Mills, and Leon Hicks. *Injustice Case* (1970), a relief "body" print by David Hammons, and *The Get-A-Way* (1976), a lithograph by Margo Humphrey (b. 1942), show the wide range of approaches to the figure, as well as to issues of culture, that African-American graphic artists grappled with during the 1970s. Nonfigurative art was explored in depth during this period as well, as seen in the abstract prints of etcher and lithographer John E. Dowell Jr.

The 1970s and 1980s, like the Depression years, were a period in which graphic workshops among black artists proliferated. Apart from the important printmakers and printmaking activities based within college and university art departments (such as the printmaking department at Howard University, headed by etcher Winston Kennedy [b. 1944]), several African-American-managed graphic arts workshops produced major works. These include Workshop, Inc., in Washington, D.C., founded by silkscreen artist Lou Stovall; WD Graphic Workshop, also in Washington, founded by etcher Percy Martin; Brandywine Graphic Workshop in Philadelphia, founded by lithographer Allan Edmunds Jr.; and the Printmaking Workshop in New York, founded by master printmaker Robert Blackburn. Major African-American artists known primarily as painters and sculptors, such as Romare Bearden, Jacob Lawrence, Betye Saar, Sam Gilliam, Richard Hunt, and Mel Edwards, have all produced prints under the supervision of these workshop founder/directors. Since the 1980s these workshops and others have provided many African-American artists with the opportunity to explore new graphic-arts techniques, as well as traditional printmaking media, in service to contemporary issues and ideas in the visual arts.

See also Art in the United States, Contemporary; Folk Arts and Crafts; Harlem Renaissance

■ ■ *Bibliography*

Porter, James A. *Exhibition of Graphic Arts and Drawings by Negro Artists*. Washington, D.C., 1947.

Porter, James A. *Modern Negro Art* (1943). New York: Arno, 1969.

Powell, Richard J. *Impressions/Expression: Black American Graphics*. New York, 1980.

Powell, Richard J. "The Afro-American Printmaking Tradition." *PrintNews* 3, no. 1 (February/March 1981): 3–7.

Powell, Richard J. "Current Expressions in Afro-American Printmaking." *PrintNews* 3, no. 2 (April/May 1981): 7–11.

Wye, Deborah. *Committed to Print: Social and Political Themes in Recent American Printed Art*. New York: Museum of Modern Art, 1988.

RICHARD J. POWELL (1996)

PROCTOR, HENRY HUGH

DECEMBER 8, 1868
MAY 12, 1933

❙❙❙

The clergyman and civil rights activist Henry Hugh Proctor was born near Fayetteville, Tennessee, to former slaves Richard and Hannah (Murray) Proctor. After attending public school in Fayetteville, he became a teacher in Pea Ridge, Tennessee, and then teacher and principal of the Fayetteville public school. He attended Central Tennessee College in Nashville from 1884 to 1885 and then studied at Fisk University, where he became friendly with W. E. B. Du Bois (1869–1963), a fellow student, and finally received his B.A. in 1891. In 1894 Proctor graduated from Yale Divinity School and was ordained a Congregational minister. He became pastor of the elite First Congregational Church in Atlanta, Georgia, a black church built and funded by the American Missionary Association (AMA), whose congregation formed, in one commentator's words, the "black Atlantan social register." He served there until 1920.

In 1903 Proctor cofounded and became first president of the National Convention of Congregational Workers Among Colored People, which was designed to make Southern black Congregational churches self-sufficient, as well as to improve theology departments and promote black hiring in AMA colleges. In 1904 the National Council of Churches named him to the largely symbolic post of assistant moderator. That same year, he obtained his Doctor of Divinity Degree from Atlanta's Clark University.

In 1906, in the aftermath of the notorious riot in Atlanta, Proctor joined with white attorney Charles T. Hopkins to form the Interracial Committee of Atlanta, which was mildly successful in reducing racial tension. The two men recruited forty blacks and whites to draw up plans for reducing racial tensions. Proctor decried the lack of recreational facilities for black youth, and he made the First Congregational Church into an institutional church, providing sports, schools, and employment counseling, as well as a kindergarten, library, girl's home, and model kitchen. Proctor designed an auditorium that seated one thousand, and in 1910 he organized the Atlanta Colored Music Festival. He regarded the spiritual as a powerful weapon of black pride. His pastoral service and musical work were so popular that the membership of the First Congregational rose from one hundred in 1900 to one thousand when he left in 1920.

Proctor was an expert orator, best known for his speech "The Burden of the Negro," which he delivered hundreds of times. In it, Proctor preached self-help and discipline. He counseled elite blacks to devote themselves to aiding the black masses while retaining their "social reserve" against interclass mixing. Proctor was influenced by Du Bois and Booker T. Washington (1856–1915), both of whom were his personal friends. Although conservative on many political issues, he fought black disenfranchisement and supported civil rights efforts. He also wrote religious articles and two books, *Sermons in Melody* (1916) and *Between Black and White* (1925).

In 1919 Proctor spoke to African-American troops in Europe. When he returned to the United States the following year, he assumed the pastorate of the Nazarene Congregational Church in Brooklyn, and in 1926 he became moderator of the New York City Congregational Church Association, an organization of black clergymen. Proctor died in New York.

See also Atlanta Riot of 1906; Civil Rights Movement, U.S.; Du Bois, W. E. B.; Washington, Booker T.

■ ■ *Bibliography*

Grant, Donald L. *The Way It Was in the South: The Black Experience in Georgia.* Secaucus, N.J.: Carol Publishing Group, 1993.

Lewis, David Levering. *W. E. B. Du Bois: Biography of a Race, 1868-1919.* New York: H. Holt, 1993–2005.

Proctor, Henry Hugh. *Between Black and White: Autobiographical Sketches.* Boston: The Pilgrim Press, 1925.

SABRINA FUCHS (1996)

PROFESSIONAL ORGANIZATIONS

▪▪▪

Professional associations regulate entry into their respective professions, set standards for their practice, provide training and forums for the exchange of information among members, and serve as formal and informal networks through which members advance their careers. Until the middle of the twentieth century, most major American professional associations excluded African Americans from membership. Blacks responded by organizing their own societies. Even after they achieved equality in the general associations, African-American professionals maintained separate organizations to address their special needs in the often overwhelmingly white professions.

The first African-American professional associations were established on a local level in the late nineteenth century. Excluded from the Medical Society of the District of Columbia, black doctors founded the National Medical Society in 1870. Physicians in other cities and states organized similar societies in the next two decades. In 1895 African-American physicians formed the National Medical Association (NMA), the first national black professional society. (The American Medical Association [AMA], the country's largest and most prestigious medical society, officially adopted a color bar in 1872.) At first, the NMA included related medical professions in addition to physicians, but these soon began to establish their own organizations. The National Dental Association arose in 1897, the National Association of Colored Graduate Nurses in 1908, and the National Pharmaceutical Association in 1933.

The National Negro Business League (NNBL) was founded in 1900 by Booker T. Washington. While primarily an organization of businesspeople, it also included special sections for lawyers, pharmacists, morticians, real-estate brokers, and bankers. In 1909, the lawyers' section became the National Negro Bar Association and remained affiliated with the NNBL until 1925. Reconstituted as an independent organization in that year, the National Bar Association (NBA) also forged links among the many local black legal societies, the first of which, the Colored Bar Association of Mississippi, was founded in 1891. The NBA regularly took a strong stand on civil rights issues and emphasized the need for African-American lawyers especially in light of the important role they could play in the struggle for equal rights.

By the late 1940s color barriers in the larger American professional associations were beginning to fall. In 1943 the American Bar Association adopted a resolution stating that membership was "not dependent upon race, creed, or color." Others followed suit. When blacks were admitted to the American Nurses Association in 1948, the National Association of Colored Graduate Nurses dissolved. In 1948 E. Franklin Frazier became the first African American to head a predominantly white professional association when he was elected president of the American Sociological Association. Only in the 1970s did several others achieve similar positions. A major milestone was reached in 1994, when Lonnie Bristow was elected to the presidency of the venerable, powerful AMA.

Nevertheless, progress in integrating the mainstream professional associations was slow. Many local societies remained segregated through the 1960s, and because some of the national organizations required members to belong to the local groups, this remained an effective bar to participation by blacks, especially in the South. Moreover, many black professionals in the late 1960s and early 1970s believed that the general organizations did not serve them adequately. Members of some professions formed caucuses within the general professional associations to press them to take stronger stands against discrimination and white cultural biases, recruit more minority practitioners, and find ways to better serve the African-American community as a whole. In many cases, these caucuses evolved into independent national organizations, joining the older associations such as the NBA and the NMA in serving the growing number of African-American professionals in the 1980s and 1990s.

See also Frazier, Edward Franklin

■ ■ *Bibliography*

Mjagkij, Nina, ed. *Organizing Black America: An Encyclopedia of African American Associations.* New York: Routledge, 2001.

Shaw, Stephanie J. *What a Woman Ought to Be and to Do: Black Professional Women Workers during the Jim Crow Era.* Chicago: University of Chicago Press, 1996.

DANIEL SOYER (1996)
Updated bibliography

PROTESTANTISM IN THE AMERICAS
▬ ▬ ▬

European Protestants had continuous contact with Africans in the Americas from at least the docking of the first slave-trading ship in Virginia in 1619. In the seventeenth century, English and Dutch Protestants settled most of the eastern seaboard of North America. During the same period, they and Danish Protestants established their rule or cultural influence over Jamaica, Barbados, the Virgin Islands, and other smaller islands in the West Indies, Suriname and Guiana in South America, and Belize and the Caribbean coast of Nicaragua in Central America. African slaves were brought to all of these locations.

However, sustained religious interactions had to wait for nearly a century after 1619. There was substantial resistance among the European Protestants to proselytizing the slaves for a variety of reasons, including fear of both lost productivity and the encouragement of a pride that would make slaves "ungovernable." Many English feared that Christianizing the slaves would make them automatically eligible for freedom, a notion that had vague precedents in medieval law, with some court cases in its favor in the seventeenth century. However, from the 1660s onward, the combined actions of several English colonial legislatures and instructions by the Bishop of London made it clearer that a slave's religious affiliation would not necessitate manumission.

One of the first advocates for proselytizing the slaves was George Fox, the founder of the Religious Society of Friends (Quakers), who visited Barbados, Jamaica, and England's North American colonies between 1671 and 1673. Fox advocated inclusion of slaves in religious services (or "meetings for worship," as the Quakers termed them), and strongly denied allegations that Quakers were encouraging slaves to rebel. One of his traveling companions, William Edmondson, was one of the first Europeans to denounce slavery, calling it "an aggravation, and an oppression upon the mind" in a subsequent visit to Barbados in 1676. However, the exhortations of Fox and Edmundson had little immediate effect, inasmuch as Quakers were then being sporadically but severely repressed in both Barbados and England.

The first organized missionary efforts by the Anglican Church toward Africans in the Americas were the work of the Society for the Propagation of the Gospel in Foreign Parts (SPG). In Barbados, the SPG became the owner of two sugar-growing estates as a result of Christopher Codrington's will in 1710, and the society appointed a series of chaplains and catechists to the slaves on those plantations, though little was achieved over the next century. In the first two decades of the eighteenth century, the SPG also appointed ministers to African slaves in such far-flung locations as New York, South Carolina, and Saint Kitts. Their proselytizing work was slow going, however, in part because the SPG ministers insisted on slaves learning an extensive catechism before being baptized. SPG missionaries worked for humane treatment of the slaves, but they did not openly advocate manumissions.

The revivals of the mid-eighteenth century led to the first large-scale conversions of blacks in the western hemisphere. The first of the evangelical groups to be active in this endeavor was the Moravian Brethren, a church that amalgamated pietist and Anabaptist influences. The Brethren's missionary work among slaves began in 1732 in the Danish Virgin Islands, and was then extended to Berbice (later British Guiana), Jamaica, Antigua, Barbados, and North Carolina. Methodists began their evangelism in North America and the West Indies in the 1760s, establishing biracial congregations that were, in places such as South Carolina and Antigua, overwhelmingly composed of blacks. Baptist evangelical work commenced at about the same time, with Separate Baptists (seceding from Congregationalists) bearing the brunt of the work during the First Great Awakening (c.1730–c.1770). The evangelicals' emphasis on religion of the heart, rather than mastery of a catechism, and their openness to emotional expression in worship facilitated the participation of blacks.

Also in the mid-eighteenth century, the Quakers in North America became the first Christian group to adopt a strong antislavery stance. In part, they grounded their opposition in the Golden Rule, but, as pacifists, they also noted that many slaves were taken captive during wars, and they felt that they could not be complicit with the ill-gotten fruits of warfare. Anthony Benezet, a Quaker schoolteacher in Philadelphia, corresponded widely and converted others such as the Methodist John Wesley to the antislavery cause. Many evangelicals, especially Moravians and Methodists, were affected by the Quaker position against slavery. In general, while evangelical Protestantism was attractive to many blacks because of its strong egalitarian tendencies, economic necessity and the racism of their white American converts eventually forced each of the evangelical sects to abandon or to curtail their antislavery message in the late eighteenth and early nineteenth centuries.

Independent black churches developed in the late eighteenth and early nineteenth century in both North America and the Caribbean, due to the pressures of their white racist co-religionists, and also because of the desire of many black Christians for cultural autonomy—in Daniel Coker's echo of a verse from Isaiah, to be able to "sit down under our own vine to worship and none shall make us afraid." The tiny Silver Bluff Baptist Church, an independent black Baptist church founded in Silver Bluff, South Carolina, on the eve of the American Revolution, had a worldwide effect on black Protestantism. One of its members, David George, went on to found black Baptist churches in Nova Scotia and Sierra Leone. George Liele, who had founded the Silver Bluff Baptist Church, evacuated with British loyalists at the end of the Revolution, and moved to Jamaica, where he founded a Baptist Church in Kingston. There he met and converted Moses Baker, another American émigré, who proceeded to found a Baptist church in the parish of Saint James in western Jamaica, sponsored by a Quaker planter, Isaac Lascelles Winn. Another convert of Liele's, Andrew Bryan, pastored the First African Baptist Church in Savannah, Georgia. Among Methodists, Peter Spencer's African Union Church in Wilmington, Delaware, provided the core for a new black denomination in 1813, and Richard Allen's Bethel African Methodist Church was instrumental in forming the African Methodist Episcopal (AME) Church in 1816. Other independent black denominations followed in North America, including the African Methodist Episcopal Zion (AMEZ) Church (1822), the Colored Methodist Episcopal (CME) Church (1870), and the National Baptist Convention (1895).

In the early nineteenth century, black church leaders throughout the hemisphere took a variety of stances on slavery. Many, like Richard Allen, openly opposed slavery, as Allen showed in a 1795 tract, while others soft-pedaled any opposition—as did Andrew Bryan, who owned slaves himself and counseled slaves in his congregation to obey their masters. George Liele assured Jamaican planters that slaves attending his church would not be permitted to plan revolts there, but an 1807 Jamaican law still shut down independent black Baptist congregations such as Liele's. Differences in the political climate between Allen's Pennsylvania, with its heavy Quaker influence, and Bryan's Georgia undoubtedly affected the two men's stances.

In most areas where slavery was legal, a clandestine black church grew up entirely outside of any white control, an "invisible institution" little understood by otherwise well-informed contemporaries. African spiritual practices, including such traditions as vodou and myalism (a spiritual healing practice), blended strongly with Christianity in these clandestine churches. In the southern United States, this was often referred to as "brush arbor" religion; in Jamaica, the Native Baptists fit this description well, and they grew substantially after the repressive 1807 law.

Advocacy of antislavery in Georgia and other slave territories undoubtedly meant rebellion, a reality grasped by the African Methodist Denmark Vesey, who staged an abortive revolt in Charleston, South Carolina, in 1822, and the Baptist lay preacher Nat Turner, who led a revolt in 1831 in Southampton, Virginia. One of the most massive slave revolts in the hemisphere took place in Jamaica over a two-week period beginning in Christmas, 1831. As many as twenty thousand slaves were involved and massive property damage was inflicted on white planters. Jamaicans were not unfamiliar with slave revolts—they recalled a revolt of similar size, for example, coordinated by a spiritual leader recently imported from the Gold Coast in 1760—but one distinguishing feature of the 1831 revolt was the prominent leadership of black Christians, most notably Sam Sharpe, a lay leader in the Missionary Baptist Church and a "Daddy" among the Native Baptists. Sharpe conceded that, as a slave, he had been relatively well treated, but he defiantly stated that he would rather die than remain a slave. The revolt was so permeated by Baptist influence that it has often been called the "Baptist War." It coincided with a concerted campaign by evangelical Christians in Great Britain to abolish slavery in the West Indies, as black Jamaicans were immensely frustrated with the various maneuvers undertaken by Jamaican planters to stave off emancipation. The Jamaican planters were ultimately unsuccessful, as the British Parliament enacted a law abolishing slavery in the West Indies to take partial effect on August 1, 1834, and full effect four years later.

Some black North American clergy played prominent roles in the abolitionist movement in the United States.

Jermain Loguen, an AMEZ minister in Syracuse, New York, was an activist who opposed the Fugitive Slave Law of 1850, and he played a key role in the 1851 rescue of Jerry Henry, a fugitive slave who had been jailed by federal marshals who intended to return him to slavery. Loguen and his associates spirited Henry to freedom in Canada across Lake Ontario. Thomas Henry, an AME minister, was a correspondent of John Brown and may well have known of his plans for the ill-fated insurrection at Harper's Ferry, Virginia, in 1859. Many black clergy chose not to play leading roles in the abolitionist movement, favoring community-building work instead. AME minister Richard Robinson articulated this position when he asserted that it was useless for black ministers to flaunt outspokenly radical antislavery stands, because it would only make them more of a target: "Every colored man is an abolitionist, and slaveholders know it." When the Emancipation Proclamation permitted the enlistment of black soldiers in 1863, however, black ministers such as Henry McNeal Turner played an active role in obtaining recruits for the United States colored regiments. At least twelve black ministers, including Turner, also served as military chaplains during the Civil War.

After Emancipation (Canada and British West Indies, 1834; Danish West Indies, 1848; United States, 1865), it was unclear throughout the hemisphere how much the dominant political forces would permit freedom to be combined with empowerment of the freed persons. In both the United States and the Caribbean, the immediate post-Emancipation period was one of intense educational efforts among the freed men and women, with such efforts slackening off within a decade or two, as philanthropic zeal lessened among those whites who had adopted education of blacks as a cause. The American Missionary Association in the United States, funded mainly by Congregationalists, was responsible for the founding of such schools as Atlanta, Dillard, Hampton, Fisk, and Howard Universities. With little resources, predominantly black denominations in the United States were responsible for the founding of their own colleges and universities, including Wilberforce (AME), Morris Brown (AME), Livingstone (AMEZ), Lane (CME), and Paine (CME). Most of these institutions of higher education were located in the southern states, the main exception being Wilberforce in southwestern Ohio.

Throughout the hemisphere, the freedom delivered by Emancipation often did not include meaningful economic options, with landlessness, racist coercion, and unjust legal systems trapping many former slaves in sharecropping or peonage arrangements that were almost indistinguishable from slavery. In Jamaica, such conditions helped to bring about the Morant Bay Rebellion of October 1865. Similar to the Baptist War of 1831, the leader, Paul Bogle, and many other of the rebels were Native Baptists, and the conspirators met in Native Baptist chapels. Hundreds of blacks were hanged in the aftermath of the revolt, including Bogle and his co-conspirator, George William Gordon. The 1865 rebellion and its draconian suppression resulted in the dismissal of Jamaica's governor, Edward J. Eyre, and the imposition of Crown Colony government.

After Emancipation, there was often an informal merging of the black churches founded by the missionaries and those black churches that could be characterized as "Independent" or "Native" in origin. This resulted in a large increase in membership in these denominations, but also in an increase of social-class and regional tensions within those same denominations. The AME Church, for example, had about 20,000 members in 1858, growing to 452,725 in 1896, an increase of over twenty times. A significant transformation in the American black churches occurred after 1915, when, in response to significant continuing human rights abuses, greater economic opportunities, and boosterism by African-American newspapers in northern states, many African Americans left the South to make their homes in northern cities. Black denominations struggled to meet the new demand by the often poorer migrants. The AME Church also opened missions in the West Indies and British Guiana, although their failure to supply consistent episcopal oversight stymied their growth in that region, at least until 1972, when Frederick Talbot, a native of Guyana (formerly British Guiana), assumed the episcopal duties in that region.

The Universal Negro Improvement Association (UNIA) and African Communities League, founded by Marcus Garvey, an immigrant from Jamaica to Harlem, New York, in 1914, stimulated pride in blackness and in Africa. Garvey promoted a black nationalism that would encompass the mother continent and the entire black diaspora, and he formed the Black Star steamship line in order to further these aims. In doing so, he built upon the black nationalism of several notable nineteenth-century black clergy, such as Alexander Crummell (Episcopal), Edward Blyden (Presbyterian), and Henry McNeal Turner (AME). Problems with the seaworthiness of the vessels and with Garvey's economic management prevented the UNIA from any sizeable involvement in trade or emigration, and, in any event, the administration of President Calvin Coolidge obtained the conviction of Garvey on mail fraud and deported him to Jamaica in 1927, after he had served two years in the Atlanta Penitentiary. But the black nationalism of Garvey was an enduring legacy to African Americans in this hemisphere, including black Protestants. Some of the new religious movements that claimed inspiration from Garvey, including the Black Jews, the Moorish Science Temple, the Nation of Islam, and Rastafarianism, had an authentic claim to the rebellious traditions of the Native and Independent Churches while their connections to Protestantism per se was tenuous or idiosyncratic at best.

The Los Angeles revival of 1906, presided over by a Louisiana-born African American minister, William Joseph Seymour (1870–1922), inaugurated the era of Pentecostalism, a brand of Protestantism that advertised its adherence to the "full gospel," which included a Spirit Baptism manifested by speaking in tongues, and also in faith healing. In the remainder of the twentieth century, this interracial religious movement spread far and wide, reaching parts of the Americas that had previously been primarily Catholic. Other Protestant new religious movements also proselytized aggressively and successfully in the Caribbean and Latin America. Seventh-day Adventists had notable successes in the Caribbean. A 1978 revelation by the patriarch of the Church of Jesus Christ of Latter Day Saints (Mormons) that black men could at last be admitted to the priesthood was reportedly facilitated by the dawning realization on the church hierarchy that the prospects for its missions in predominantly black and racially mixed Brazil was dependent on its ridding itself of obvious signs of any antiblack bigotry.

In the eighteenth century, the established church (the Anglican Church through much of the Protestant Americas) was the church of the wealthy and powerful, while the churches that derived from the dissenting churches in England, such as the Baptists and Methodists, were often composed mostly of "plain folk" and slaves. Among the predominantly white churches, there has been much social mobility in the membership of this latter class of churches, as Methodists and Baptists have made substantial inroads into the middle and upper classes. Among black Protestants, there have always been some congregations that have heavily represented the black middle class, and there have always been the aspiration and accompanying practices to enable social mobility through economic mutual aid, teaching middle-class life habits, and engaging in social action to oppose white racism. Since Emancipation, some black laity and clergy have criticized the financial demands of churches for high-ticket items—such as building programs and (sometimes) ministers' salaries—as imposing an excessive drag on the economic advancement of members of their congregations. While black clergy have often strongly asserted the effectiveness of their church work in this regard, it must also be conceded that there have been times and places in the Americas (such as the late-nineteenth-century United States) where racist opposition was strong enough to retard much social mobility among black Protestants.

ROLE OF GENDER IN CONGREGATIONS AND LEADERSHIP

African women often served in positions of religious leadership, filling such roles as diviners and mediums. This tradition of female religious leadership survived the Middle Passage. In the western hemisphere, the strong support given by Quakers, and later more equivocal support by Methodists, for women's ministry did not go unnoticed by black women. One such female minister, "Old Elizabeth" (c.1765–1866), clearly influenced by both Quakers and Methodists, carried her ministry from Michigan to Virginia in the early to mid-nineteenth century. She, Jarena Lee, and Zilpha Elaw recorded narratives of their ministry or dictated them to others. None of the preaching women in the early nineteenth century were ordained. All of these women experienced great opposition from men who were against women's ministry on various grounds, including citing scriptural injunctions. Elizabeth's reply was typical: She had not been ordained by men, but "if the Lord had ordained me, I needed nothing better."

Some black women have started their own religious communities or denominations as a result of the resistance they have experienced from men, from nonblacks, or from both. One example is Rebecca Cox Jackson, a Philadelphia woman who grew up in the AME Church and had a call to the ministry and to celibacy. Leaving her husband, she traveled to Albany to join the Shakers, eventually returning to Philadelphia and founding a Shaker religious community composed mostly of black women.

In most Protestant congregations, women have composed a substantial majority, and predominantly black denominations were no exception. In virtually all of these congregations, there has been substantial female leadership. One role that has been particularly significant in many black congregations is that of "church mother." These are often elderly and spiritually mature women, who frequently have an important if informal role in church governance. A church mother might be a wife or widow of a preacher or bishop, but this is not always the case. Many church mothers are also exhorters, who traditionally delivered their spiritual messages from the floor of the church, not from the pulpit (which was understood to be man's space).

Eventually, many Protestant denominations began to ordain women. Antoinette Brown Blackwell, a white female Congregationalist, was the first woman to be ordained in 1853. Sarah Ann Hughes was ordained as a deacon in the AME Church in 1885, but her ordination was removed two years later. However, the AMEZ Church ordained two women, Julia A. J. Foote and Mary J. Small— in 1894 and 1895, respectively—, and these ordinations stood. During the early twentieth century, many women served as pastors in black denominations, although generally without formal ordination. In 1948, the AME Church ordained Rebecca Glover as an assistant pastor, and eight years later, the same denomination gave full ordination rights to women. The first African-American woman elected to the episcopacy was Leontine T. C. Kelly, in the Methodist Church, in 1984. Four years later, Barbara Harris, an African American woman, became the first female bishop in the Episcopal Church, and in 2000, Vashti McKenzie, became the first female bishop in the AME Church.

Black Baptist churches do not have denomination-wide policies on women's ordination. However, women have often served in very powerful leadership roles in the black Baptist churches. One example is Nannie Helen Burroughs, a notable educator and church leader in the National Baptist Convention. In 1900, she helped to organize the Woman's Auxiliary Convention of the National Baptist Convention, and she served as either secretary or president of the Women's Convention until her death in 1961.

PROTESTANTISM AND THE STATE

While each of the British colonies inherited the Anglican establishment, the Anglican Church was rendered weak and ineffectual by the remote supervision of its branches in the colonies through the Bishop of London. In the colonies that became the United States, the fear of imposition of a bishop in the western hemisphere helped to fuel rebellion and, ultimately, the disestablishment of all of the colonial church establishments, whether Anglican, Congregationalist, or Dutch Reformed. Instead of "church" and "sect," the United States pioneered the formal equality in the eyes of the law of all religious bodies as "denominations." The principle enshrined in the First Amendment of religious liberty, however, was not automatically seen to apply to African Americans. Rather, they won their religious liberty piecemeal. One landmark decision was rendered by the Pennsylvania Supreme Court in 1816, a decision which supported Richard Allen and the African Methodists in Philadelphia in their resistance to attempts by white Methodists to rule them against their will. This decision enabled Allen to call the first General Conference of the AME Church. In the wake of this decision, a tenuous religious freedom for African Americans spread throughout most of the northern states and, even more tenuously, through parts of the Upper South. Meanwhile,

any antislavery religious sentiment in the South was ruthlessly suppressed, and independent black churches were often regarded as deeply suspect, especially in the wake of the 1822 Vesey plot and Turner's 1831 revolt.

The Thirteenth (1865) and Fourteenth (1868) Amendments more solidly cemented religious liberty for African Americans throughout the United States. In effect, the right of African Americans to form not only congregations but also denominations became universally conceded. Despite some church burnings, the black churches proved to be a bulwark for the defense of African Americans throughout the long nadir of Jim Crow, disfranchisement, and lynchings. Black churches assumed a variety of political and social functions in addition to their spiritual activities, so much so that they were sometimes called a "nation within a nation." In contemporary times, many American politicians, even presidential candidates, have sought African-American votes by attending black churches, and the economic liberalism and social conservatism of many African Americans has often created a perception of a "swing vote" to which politicians from both the Democratic and Republican parties can successfully appeal.

In Canada and the British West Indies, the delineation between the "Church" (i.e., Anglicanism) and the dissenting sects was more pervasive and long standing. Still, the remoteness of the Anglican establishment was not remedied in the West Indies until 1824, when the first resident bishop was appointed to the Caribbean. In the first third of the nineteenth century, the Anglican ministers were widely seen as promoting the interests of the planter class, while the dissenters (especially the Baptists), through their fearless use of social critique, were seen as encouraging change and rebellion, implicitly if not explicitly. This bifurcation began to break down somewhat in the later nineteenth century. The Anglican Church in the West Indies was disestablished and disendowed around 1870, and indigenous leadership of that church was especially encouraged after that date. In the predominantly Catholic areas of the Americas, Protestants have always been seen as a dissenting force, although, evangelical Protestants have sometimes ascended to the leadership roles in government, sometimes with the complicity of the American military (General Efrain Rios Montt served as president of Guatemala from 1982 to 1983, for example, though his rule was, in fact, more of a dictatorship).

PROTESTANTISM, HUMAN RIGHTS, AND LIBERATION THEOLOGY

White and black Protestants have often disagreed, within and across racial lines, on human rights issues. In the late nineteenth and early twentieth centuries, many white Protestants retreated in their commitment to human rights for African Americans. For example, the Congregationalist minister Henry Ward Beecher preached strong antislavery sermons in the 1850s, though he roundly disparaged as worthless anyone or anything deriving from Africa in the 1880s. By the 1920s the Ku Klux Klan had made substantial inroads among white Protestants, even in some northern states, such as Indiana. At this time, there were some black conservatives, such as Booker T. Washington, who, in public if not in private, defended the view that African Americans should concern themselves mainly with economic progress, which would cause white Americans to respect their human rights.

On the other hand, many black Protestants, and a small minority of white Protestants, were strongly committed to the support of human rights for African Americans throughout this period. Some, such as AMEZ bishop Alexander Walters and AME minister (later bishop) Reverdy Ransom, were strong supporters of the founding of the National Association for the Advancement of Colored People (NAACP) in 1909. Although the NAACP was avowedly secular, it developed strong connections with black churches throughout the United States. Ransom and the Baptist minister George Woodbey were outspoken advocates of socialism, with its view of collective ownership of the means of production. When a newly formed ecumenical organization, the Federal Council of Churches (ancestor of the National Council of Churches), refused to advocate for antilynching laws in the U.S. Congress, Ransom and other black clergy formed the Fraternal Council of Negro Churches in 1934. The Washington, D.C.–based FCNC was dedicated mostly to lobbying Congress, but it prepared the way for other organizations of black clergy and laity who were prepared to mobilize in a more extensive way. The most notable of these later organizations was the Southern Christian Leadership Conference, founded in 1957 by the Baptist minister Martin Luther King Jr. and others.

The FCNC and SCLC were increasingly dedicated toward racial integration as the preferred alternative to the degradation of Jim Crow and racial bigotry. In so doing, they were joined during the 1950s and 1960s by the National Council of Churches, an ecumenical organization of mostly white Protestants. The National Council of Churches and SCLC, together with the NAACP and some labor unions, were the major forces behind the passage of the Civil Rights Act of 1964. But some black Protestants, influenced by the advocacy of Black Muslim minister Malcolm X and others, as well as the memory of Marcus Garvey, preferred a more racially separatist, or black national-

ist, approach toward building an American community that more fully respected human rights. The Black Power movement, as this tendency became known, was also a major force behind a fuller recovery and celebration of African-American culture and history, which in the early 1960s was still being almost entirely overlooked in mainstream American culture.

The black liberation theology and Caribbean liberation theology movements that emerged in the aftermath of the 1960s were influenced strongly both by the civil rights and Black Power movements, the thought of Martin Luther King Jr., and Malcolm X. Many of the black nationalist elements of these new theologies were of Caribbean origin, especially the influence of the Rastafarians, who saw the Ethiopian emperor Haile Selassie as the second coming of Christ, and who developed a sophisticated critique of African-American Christian culture and Biblical interpretation in favor of a more Afrocentric approach. These liberation theology movements, led by James H. Cone and others, posited that God was on the side of the oppressed. Jesus was celebrated as the "Black Messiah,"or at least as nonwhite, and hence an implicit source of critique of the European and white American varieties of oppression over the previous centuries. Like both King and Malcolm X, black liberation theologians called for a form of black Christianity that was fully engaged in combating social and economic problems in the black community, and while unsparing in their critique of white racism, these theologians also drew on the black nationalist exhortation to self-reliance. Later versions of liberation theology by William R. Jones, Anthony Pinn, and others have highlighted issues of theodicy, as well as advocating more humanist versions of liberation theology, as compared to the more orthodox Christian versions that prevailed in the early 1970s. While black churches have made effective and selective use of some of these forms of liberation theology, this form of theological discourse has flourished far more on college and university campuses than in many local grassroots Protestant congregations.

See also African Methodist Episcopal Church; African Methodist Episcopal Zion Church; African Union Methodism; Allen, Richard; Baptists; Black Power Movement; Blyden, Edward Wilmot; Burroughs, Nannie Helen; Coker, Daniel; Crummell, Alexander; Garvey, Marcus; Harris, Barbara Clementine; King, Martin Luther, Jr.; Liberation Theology; Liele, George; Malcolm X; Morant Bay Rebellion; Moravian Church; Nat Turner's Rebellion; Nation of Islam; Rastafarianism; Sharpe, Samuel; Social Gospel; Theology, Black; Turner, Henry McNeal

▪ ▪ Bibliography

Angell, Stephen Ward. *Bishop Henry McNeal Turner and African-American Religion in the South.* Knoxville: University of Tennessee Press, 1992.

Collier-Thomas, Bettye. *Daughters of Thunder: Black Women Preachers and their Sermons, 1850-1979.* San Francisco: Jossey-Bass Publishers, 1998.

Cone, James H. *Martin and Malcolm and America: A Dream or a Nightmare.* Maryknoll, N.Y.: Orbis Books, 1991.

Dayfoot, Arthur Charles. *The Shaping of the West Indian Church, 1492–1962.* Barbados: Press of the University of the West Indies, 1999.

Frey, Sylvia R., and Betty Wood. *Come Shouting to Zion: African American Protestantism in the American South and British Caribbean to 1830.* Chapel Hill: University of North Carolina Press, 1998.

Higginbotham, Evelyn Brooks. *Righteous Discontent: The Women's Movement in the Black Baptist Church, 1880-1920.* Cambridge, Mass: Harvard University Press, 1993.

Hood, Robert E. *Must God Remain Greek? Afro Cultures and God-Talk.* Minneapolis, Minn.: Fortress Press, 1990.

Johnson, Paul E. *African-American Christianity: Essays in History.* Berkeley: University of California Press, 1994.

Lincoln, C. Eric, and Lawrence H. Mamiya, *The Black Church in the African American Experience.* Durham, N.C.: Duke University Press, 1990.

Raboteau, Albert J. *Slave Religion: The "Invisible Institution" in the Antebellum South,* updated ed. Oxford, U.K.: Oxford University Press, 2004.

Sawyer, Mary R. *Black Ecumenism: Implementing the Demands of Justice.* Valley Forge, Penn.: Trinity Press International, 1994.

Sernett, Milton C., ed. *African American Religious History: A Documentary Witness.* 2d ed. Durham, N.C.: Duke University Press, 1999.

Turner, Mary, *Slaves and Missionaries: The Disintegration of Jamaican Slave Society, 1787–1834.* Urbana: University of Illinois Press, 1982.

STEPHEN W. ANGELL (2005)

PRYOR, RICHARD

DECEMBER 1, 1940

▌▌▌

Born in Peoria, Illinois, comedian Richard Franklin Lenox Thomas Pryor overcame a troubled life in an extended family headed by his grandmother, Marie Carter, to become a preeminent comedian, film star, screenwriter, producer, and director, beginning in the early 1960s.

During Pryor's boyhood, Peoria was like the Deep South. Segregation and discrimination in housing, employment, and places of public accommodation were deeply embedded in southern Illinois. Forty percent of the

Richard Pryor performing stand-up comedy, 1982. AP/WIDE WORLD PHOTOS. REPRODUCED BY PERMISSION.

black population of Peoria was unemployed, while 32 percent worked for the Works Project Administration (WPA). Odd jobs supported the rest, including the Pryor family, which ran small carting firms, pool halls, and, Pryor claimed, houses of prostitution. Peoria remained segregated for a time even after the 1954 Supreme Court decision that forbade it.

At age eleven, Pryor, the son of Gertrude Thomas and Leroy "Buck" Carter Pryor, and, he once said, the seventh of twelve "Pryor kids," began acting at the Carver Community Center under the guidance of the drama teacher, Juliette Whittaker. Over the years she became the recipient of some of Pryor's performing awards; he also contributed to the private school she later founded, the Learning Tree.

After dropping out of school, Pryor joined the army in 1958, where his life was no less troublesome. After military service, he worked for his father's carting firm and the Caterpillar factory in Peoria. He also haunted the local clubs and watched television for the appearances of African-American entertainers such as Sammy Davis Jr. and Bill Cosby, personalities he wanted to emulate and eventually replace.

Within a few years Pryor was playing small clubs in East St. Louis, Chicago, Windsor (Canada), Buffalo, Youngstown, and Cleveland. Much of his comic material was drawn from his army service and the early Cosby comedy routines. By 1964 he had attracted enough attention to be booked for his first national television appearance, on Rudy Vallee's *Broadway Tonight* show. Three years later, after stops on the Ed Sullivan, Merv Griffin, and Johnny Carson shows, Pryor appeared in the film *The Busy Body* with Sid Caesar and other comedians—the first of more than forty films he acted in, wrote, produced, and/or directed into the early 1990s. His first major role was in *Lady Sings the Blues* (1972), with Diana Ross, in which Pryor played a character called Piano Man.

The Richard Pryor Show ran briefly on NBC-TV for part of 1977. It was innovative and conveyed a wide range of both comedy and tenderness, but it was too daring for the executives of NBC. Amid legal wrangling, the show went off the air and, typically, Pryor laid the blame on NBC. In 1984 he played himself as a boy in *Pryor's Place,* a children's show that aired on Saturday mornings. It too was short-lived, this time without recrimination.

From 1970 through 1979, Pryor starred or costarred in twenty-one films. He contributed to the script of *Blazing Saddles* (1973), and in the same year wrote for and appeared on *The Flip Wilson Show* and was a cowriter for Lily Tomlin's television specials, for which he won Emmy Awards in 1973 and 1974. He continued to perform in clubs and theaters around the country; these performances provided material for his two *Richard Pryor Live in Concert* films (both in 1979). The recordings of his performances earned him three Grammy Awards: *That Nigger's Crazy,* 1974; *Is It Something I Said?,* 1975; and *Bicentennial Nigger,* 1976. *That Nigger's Crazy* also became a certified gold and platinum album.

In 1980 he produced his first film, *Bustin' Loose,* starring himself and Cicely Tyson. Two years later he produced and wrote *Richard Pryor: Live on the Sunset Strip.* *Jo Jo Dancer, Your Life Is Calling,* which Pryor produced, directed, and helped write, was based upon his near-fatal self-immolation that occurred when he was freebasing cocaine in 1980. In 1986 Pryor, who had also survived two heart attacks, discovered that he had multiple sclerosis, but he continued to perform onstage.

Pryor was known as a "crossover" star, one who appealed to both black and white moviegoers. This label resulted from the "buddy" films he made with Gene Wilder—*Silver Streak* (1976), *Stir Crazy* (1980), and *See No Evil, Hear No Evil* (1989)—although he had starred with white actors in sixteen other movies. Few of Pryor's films during the 1980s were memorable, not even the concert film *Richard Pryor: Here and Now* (1983), although *Brewster's Millions* (1985) and *Harlem Nights* (1989) attracted loyal audiences. But *Richard Pryor: Live on the Sunset Strip* most typified his pungent, raunchy comedy that echoed the African-American man in the street, which was precisely what made Pryor the great comedian he was.

When he was at his peak, few comedians could match Pryor's popularity. Most contemporary comedy is said to be "post-Pryor" because of the standards he set. His life was his act, but he shaped his personal experiences into rollicking comedy. His major themes were racism in its several forms and the battle of the sexes. Usually, the women bested the men. His topics were current and to the point, and his favorite character was an old, foul-mouthed, wise black man named Mudbone from Mississippi.

Richard Pryor became the first recipient of the Kennedy Center's Mark Twain prize for humor on October 20, 1998. Because of ill health, Pryor was not able to get out of his chair, but in his official response he wrote, "It is nice to be regarded on a par with a great white man— now that's funny! Seriously though, two things people throughout history have had in common are hatred and humor. I am proud that, like Mark Twain, I have been able to use humor to lessen people's hatred."

In August 2004 the first Richard Pryor Ethnic Comedy Award was given at the Edinburgh Fringe Festival in Scotland.

See also Comedians; Cosby, Bill; Davis, Sammy, Jr.

■■ *Bibliography*

Haskins, Jim. *Richard Pryor, a Man and His Madness: A Biography.* New York: Beaufort Books, 1984.

"Richard Pryor." *Contemporary Black Biography,* Volume 24. Edited by Shirelle Phelps. Detroit: Gale Group, 2000.

Williams, John A., and Dennis A. Williams. *If I Stop I'll Die: The Comedy and Tragedy of Richard Pryor.* New York: Thunder's Mouth Press, 1991.

JOHN A. WILLIAMS (1996)
Updated by publisher 2005

PURVIS, ROBERT

AUGUST 4, 1810
APRIL 19, 1898

▪▪▪

Abolitionist and political leader Robert Purvis was born in Charleston, South Carolina, the second of three sons of William Purvis, a British cotton merchant, and Harriet Judah, a free woman of color. Although both his parents owned slaves, Robert credited his father with instilling in him a deep hatred of the "peculiar institution."

In 1819 William Purvis sent his family to Philadelphia, intending eventually to settle with them in England.

The children were enrolled in the Pennsylvania Abolition Society's Clarkson School, and Robert later attended Amherst Academy in Massachusetts, a preparatory school affiliated with nearby Amherst College. In 1826 William Purvis died, leaving the bulk of his fortune—some $200,000—to his sons. When the eldest son died without issue, his brothers received his share. A shrewd businessman, Robert Purvis put his legacy to good use, investing in bank stock and real estate.

Light-skinned and wealthy, Purvis rejected suggestions that he relocate and "pass." In 1831 he married Harriet Forten, the daughter of African-American businessman and abolitionist James Forten. With his Forten in-laws he threw himself into the antislavery struggle. A tireless member of the Philadelphia Vigilance Committee, he sheltered runaways and conveyed them to the next "safe house" in his carriage. With William Lloyd Garrison, he was a founding member of the American Anti-Slavery Society in 1833, and in 1834 he crossed the Atlantic to meet leaders of the British antislavery movement. With his father-in-law, he helped steer white abolitionists, among them Garrison and Arthur Tappan, away from African colonization and toward a sweeping program designed to achieve racial equality. Purvis also had a profound influence on his young niece, educator and social reformer Charlotte Forten, who spent much of her early life in the Purvis household.

For two decades the Purvises lived in an elegant home in Philadelphia, where they entertained abolitionists from the United States and Europe. In 1842, with racial violence escalating, they moved to an estate in Byberry, some twelve miles outside Philadelphia.

Purvis welcomed the outbreak of the Civil War, demanding that President Abraham Lincoln make emancipation his goal. With the end of the war came an invitation to head the Freedmen's Bureau. However, Purvis declined the offer, fearing that this was a ploy by President Andrew Johnson to keep the support of African-American voters even as he set about destroying the bureau.

Initially a staunch Republican, Purvis became disheartened as the party retreated from the principles it espoused during Reconstruction. In the Philadelphia mayoral race of 1874, his endorsement of the Democratic candidate was denounced by other African-American leaders. He was also criticized for his stance on the Fifteenth Amendment, which was ratified in 1870. A lifelong champion of women's rights, Purvis contended that African-American men should not be enfranchised unless women received the vote.

In the last two decades of his life Purvis assumed the role of an elder statesman. Never afraid to speak up, he took both major parties to task for, as he saw it, abandoning the struggle for racial justice. Robert Purvis died in Philadelphia at the age of eighty-seven, survived by his second wife and four of his eight children.

See also Abolition; Bureau of Refugees, Freedmen, and Abandoned Lands

■ ■ *Bibliography*

Boromé, Joseph A. "Robert Purvis and His Early Challenge to American Racism." *Negro History Bulletin* 30 (1967): 8–10.

Winch, Julie. *A Gentleman of Color: The Life of James Forten.* New York: Oxford University Press, 2002.

JULIE WINCH (1996)
Updated by author 2005

PURYEAR, MARTIN
MAY 23, 1941

The oldest of seven children, sculptor Martin Puryear attended both elementary and secondary school in Washington, D.C. His father, Reginald, worked as a postal service employee, and his mother, Martina, taught elementary school. He developed strong interests in biology and art and aspired to be a wildlife illustrator. Always interested in working with his hands, Puryear as a young man made numerous objects, including guitars, chairs, and canoes.

Puryear entered Catholic University in Washington in 1959. Although initially a biology major, he shifted in his junior year to the study of painting and sculpture. Following graduation in 1963, Puryear entered the Peace Corps and served for two years in Sierra Leone, where he taught English, French, art, and biology. In addition to his teaching, he studied the craftsmen of West Africa, particularly the carpenters, from whom he learned a wide variety of traditional techniques. In 1966 he moved to Stockholm, where he enrolled at the Swedish Royal Academy. In addition to his formal studies in printmaking, Puryear pursued an interest in Scandinavian woodworking and began to work independently, making wood sculptures in the studios of the academy. He traveled widely during his two years in Stockholm, visiting the Soviet Union and Western Europe, as well as the region of Lapland in northern Scandinavia.

In 1968 Puryear returned to the United States, and the following year he entered Yale University to study sculpture at the graduate level. In addition to his exposure to the part- and full-time faculty (including James Rosati, Robert Morris, Richard Serra, and Salvatore Scarpitta) at Yale, Puryear visited New York often, familiarizing himself with recent developments in contemporary art. Following receipt of his master of fine arts degree in 1971, he taught at Fisk University in Nashville for two years. His first important sculptures were made in the early 1970s, and these were shown in a solo exhibition held in 1973 at the Henri Gallery in Washington and at Fisk.

In 1973 Puryear left Fisk and established a studio in Brooklyn. The following year he accepted a teaching position at the University of Maryland, and he commuted between New York and College Park, Maryland, from 1974 to 1978. It was during this period that his work became known to a larger audience. In 1977 the Corcoran Gallery of Art in Washington, D.C., organized the first museum exhibition of his work; this show included *Cedar Lodge* (1977), a large, quasi-architectural sculpture, as well as *Some Tales* (1977), a wall-mounted sculpture consisting of six linear wooden elements. In the same year, Puryear created *Box and Pole for Art Park* in Lewiston, New York. For this first outdoor commission, the sculptor constructed a wooden box made of milled wood with dovetailed corners, and a hundred-foot-tall pole, thereby contrasting the concentrated strength of the former with the upward, seemingly infinite reach of the latter.

If 1977 found Puryear being accorded increasing attention in the art world, it was also a time of great loss. On February 1, 1977, his apartment and studio—including virtually all of the sculptor's work to date—were lost in a fire. The following year he left the East Coast to accept a teaching position at the University of Illinois, Chicago; he lived in Chicago until 1991. During this period, Puryear achieved ever-increasing recognition and was included in numerous important group exhibitions (including the Whitney Biennial in 1979, 1981, and 1989; the Museum of Modern Art's International Survey of Recent Painting and Sculpture in 1984; and the Walker Art Center's Sculpture Inside Outside in 1988). In 1989 he was selected as the sole American representative to exhibit in the twentieth São Paulo Bienal in Brazil, and he received the grand prize for his installation of eight works. The same year, he received a John D. and Catherine T. MacArthur Foundation Fellowship. In the fall of 1991 a large retrospective of Puryear's work opened at the Art Institute of Chicago. This exhibition of some forty sculptures toured to the Hirshhorn Museum and Sculpture Garden, Washington, D.C.; the Museum of Contemporary Art, Los Angeles; and the Philadelphia Museum of Art.

During the 1980s Puryear's work grew to full maturity. He pursued a number of different sculptural directions

Alien Huddle, *a red cedar and pine sculpture by Martin Puryear.*
REPRODUCED BY PERMISSION OF MARTIN PURYEAR

simultaneously, including approximately forty wall-mounted sculptures, many in the form of nearly circular "rings"; increasingly large-scale, three-dimensional sculptures, most made principally of wood but often incorporating new materials such as wire mesh and tar; and, finally, several outdoor commissions, some of which were sited permanently.

Puryear concentrated on the "ring" sculptures between 1978 and 1985. Constructed primarily of thin wood strips laminated in place and often painted, the "rings" were the sculptor's most refined work to date. Around 1984 they evolved into larger, more imposing wall-mounted works that grew increasingly independent of the supporting wall. A sculpture such as *Greed's Trophy* (1984), in the collection of New York's Museum of Modern Art, suggests an enormous hunting trap, its wire-mesh shape projecting nearly five feet from the wall. At this time Puryear also began to apply tar to his wire-mesh surfaces—in a work such as *Sanctum* (1985), in the collection of the Whitney Museum of American Art. This new element grants the undulating surface of the sculpture a sense of spatial enclosure as well as a tremendous physical presence. Since the mid-1980s, Puryear's sculpture has grown in new directions, as the artist has pressed the boundaries of abstraction to include allusions to living forms as well as objects. Puryear worked with distinction and great range in public, completing *Bodark Arc* (1982), commissioned for the Nathan Manilow Sculpture Park, south of Chicago, and *Ampersand* (1987–1988), commissioned for the Minneapolis Sculpture Garden. Throughout his work, Puryear has demonstrated a remarkable ability to create sculpture with multiple references, in which viewers discover images, memories, and allusions through their experience of the works.

In the first years of the twenty-first century, Puryear branched out into new projects, including a set of woodblock illustrations for a new edition of the classic Jean Toomer novel *Cane* (2000) and a growing series of commissions for large pieces of public art.

See also Art in the United States, Contemporary; Painting and Sculpture

■ ■ *Bibliography*

Benezra, Neal. *Martin Puryear.* Chicago: Art Institute of Chicago, 1991.

Crutchfield, Margo A. *Martin Puryear.* Richmond: Virginia Museum of Fine Arts, 2001.

Davies, Hugh M., and Helaine Posner. *Martin Puryear.* Amherst: University Gallery, University of Massachusetts at Amherst, 1984.

Hughes, Robert. "Martin Puryear: A Master of Both Modernism and Traditional Crafts, He Creates Sculptures that are a Synthesis of Beauty but Free of Cliche." *Time* 158, no. 1 (July 9, 2001): 78.

NEAL BENEZRA (1996)
Updated by publisher 2005